McGill's Life Insurance

Huebner School Series   *Gary K. Stone, Editor*

Fundamentals of Financial Planning
Robert M. Crowe and Charles E. Hughes (eds.)

Readings in Income Taxation
James F. Ivers III (ed.)

McGill's Life Insurance
Edward E. Graves (ed.)

Group Benefits: Basic Concepts and Alternatives
Burton T. Beam, Jr.

Planning for Retirement Needs
Kenn Beam Tacchino and David A. Littell

Readings in Wealth Accumulation Planning
James F. Ivers III and Eric T. Johnson (eds.)

Readings in Estate Planning I
Constance J. Fontaine (ed.)

Readings in Estate Planning II
Ted Kurlowicz (ed.)

Planning for Business Owners and Professionals
Ted Kurlowicz, James F. Ivers III, and John J. McFadden

Financial Planning Applications
W.J. Ruckstuhl, J.B. Kelvin, D.M. Cordell, and D.A. Littell

Retirement Planning Handbook
David A. Littell and M. Donald Wright (eds.)

Tax Planning for Business Operations
Jeffrey B. Kelvin (ed.)

Huebner School Series

McGill's Life Insurance

Edward E. Graves, Editor
Lynn Hayes, Managing Editor

The American College/*Bryn Mawr, Pennsylvania*

This publication is designed to provide accurate and authoritative information about the subject covered. The American College is not engaged in rendering legal, accounting, or other professional advice. If legal or other expert advice is required, the services of an appropriate professional should be sought.

Library of Congress Catalog Card Number 93-74339
ISBN 0-943590-55-8

Printed in the United States of America

To Dr. Dan McGill, who has kept Dr. Solomon S. Huebner's dream alive

Contents

Preface xiii

About the Editor xvii

1   *Economic Bases of Life Insurance* 1
Dan M. McGill
Revised by Edward E. Graves

2   *Basic Principles* 19
Dan M. McGill
Revised by Edward E. Graves

3   *Term Insurance* 32
Dan M. McGill
Revised by Edward E. Graves

4   *Whole Life Insurance* 44
Dan M. McGill
Revised by Edward E. Graves

5   *Variations of Whole Life Insurance* 54
Edward E. Graves

6   *Annuities* 109
Dan M. McGill
Revised by Edward E. Graves and Joseph W. Huver

7   *Individual Disability Income Insurance* 138
Edward E. Graves

8   *Long-Term Care Insurance* 171
Burton T. Beam, Jr.

9   *Family Uses of Life Insurance* 189
                                  Edward E. Graves

10   *Needs Analysis, Surrender Options,* 202
                              and Policy Illustrations
                                      Dan M. McGill
                              Revised by Edward E. Graves

11   *Tax Treatment of* 237
                        Life Insurance and Annuities
                      Ted Kurlowicz and James F. Ivers III

12   *Business Uses of Life Insurance* 265
                    Ted Kurlowicz and John J. McFadden

13   *Basis of Risk Measurement* 302
                                      Dan M. McGill
                    Revised by Norma Nielson and Donald Jones

14   *Time Value of Money* 322
                                      Dan M. McGill
                    Revised by Norma Nielson and Donald Jones

15   *Net Premiums* 340
                                      Dan M. McGill
                    Revised by Norma Nielson and Donald Jones

16   *The Reserve* 360
                                      Dan M. McGill
                              Revised by Edward E. Graves

17   *Gross Premiums* 383
                                      Dan M. McGill
                    Revised by Norma Nielson and Donald Jones

18   *Modified Reserve Systems* 401
                                      Dan M. McGill
                    Revised by Norma Nielson and Donald Jones

19   *Surrender Values* 409
                                      Dan M. McGill
                    Revised by Norma Nielson and Donald Jones

20   *Surplus—An Insurance Company's Capital* 420
Norma Nielson and Donald Jones

21   *Selection and Classification of Risks (Part 1)* 435
Dan M. McGill
Revised by Jeremy S. Holmes and James F. Winberg
Representing the Home Office Life
Underwriters Association

22   *Selection and Classification of Risks (Part 2)* 452
Dan M. McGill
Revised by Jeremy S. Holmes and James F. Winberg
Representing the Home Office Life
Underwriters Association

23   *Insurance of Substandard Risks* 468
Dan M. McGill
Revised by Jeremy S. Holmes and James F. Winberg
Representing the Home Office Life
Underwriters Association

24   *Reinsurance* 476
Dan M. McGill
Revised by Jeremy S. Holmes and James F. Winberg
Representing the Home Office Life
Underwriters Association

25   *Settlement Agreements* 491
Dan M. McGill
Revised by Edward E. Graves

26   *The Regulation of Life Insurance (Part 1)* 520
Jon S. Hanson

27   *The Regulation of Life Insurance (Part 2)* 555
Jon S. Hanson

28   *Types of Life Insurance Carriers* 588
Jon S. Hanson

29   *Life Insurance Marketing* 617
Michael B. Petersen, Walter H. Zultowski,
Archer L. Edgar, and Ram S. Gopalan

30   *Financial Statements and Ratings (Part 1)* 631
                                              Harry D. Garber

31   *Financial Statements and Ratings (Part 2)* 652
                                              Harry D. Garber

32   *Life Insurance Company Investments* 666
                                              Francis H. Schott

33   *Group Life Insurance* 687
                                              Burton T. Beam, Jr.

34   *Fundamental Legal Concepts* 734
                                                Dan M. McGill
                                      Revised by Burke A. Christensen

35   *Basic Principles of Contract Law* 747
                                                Dan M. McGill
                                      Revised by Burke A. Christensen

36   *Formation of a Life Insurance Contract (Part 1)* 753
                                                Dan M. McGill
                                      Revised by Burke A. Christensen

37   *Formation of a Life Insurance Contract (Part 2)* 771
                                                Dan M. McGill
                                      Revised by Burke A. Christensen

38   *Avoidance of the Contract by the Insurer* 787
                                                Dan M. McGill
                                      Revised by Burke A. Christensen

39   *Waiver, Estoppel, and Election by the Insurer* 803
                                                Dan M. McGill
                                      Revised by Burke A. Christensen

40   *The Incontestable Clause* 817
                                                Dan. M. McGill
                                      Revised By Burke A. Christensen

41   *The Beneficiary (Part 1)* 830
                                                Dan M. McGill
                                      Revised By Burke A. Christensen

42   *The Beneficiary (Part 2)* *844*
                                              Dan M. McGill
                                   Revised by Burke A. Christensen

43   *Assignment of Life Insurance Contracts* *850*
                                              Dan M. McGill
                                   Revised by Burke A. Christensen

44   *Protection against Creditors* *863*
                                              Dan M. McGill
                                   Revised by Burke A. Christensen

                    Appendix: How Much Life Insurance Is Enough? *873*
                                              Thomas J. Wolff

                                               About the Authors *895*

                                                         Index *899*

Preface

This is a basic text on life insurance. It presupposes no prior knowledge of the subject, and it covers all the topics that constitute the foundation for the study of more specialized aspects of life insurance. Although emphasis is placed on the primary principles, the underlying reasons for contract provisions, actuarial computations, underwriting practices, and legal doctrines are also stressed. Technical terms are carefully defined and employed, and visual demonstrations of complex concepts are interspersed throughout the more technical sections of the book.

This book is a major revision of *Life Insurance* by Dan M. McGill, PhD, CLU. It was first published in 1959 with a revised edition published in 1967. The copyright was originally held by Richard D. Irwin, Inc., Homewood, Illinois, but was subsequently transferred to Dr. McGill, who graciously donated the copyright to The American College so that his book could be revised for use in the CLU/ChFC curriculum.

Special thanks are in order to Samuel H. Weese, PhD, CLU, CPCU, President and CEO of The American College, and Gary K. Stone, PhD, CLU, Vice President of Academics at The American College, for their tireless efforts in bringing this project to fruition. Both Dr. Weese and Dr. Stone were instrumental in convincing Dr. McGill that his classic text should be the foundation upon which all CLU/ChFC students build. Without their leadership, this revision would never have been started, much less completed.

This revision is the collective effort of 18 experts from insurance companies, colleges and universities, professional insurance associations and societies, actuarial societies, and insurance marketing agencies. This first edition of *McGill's Life Insurance* contains 15 completely new chapters that are not based on the original McGill text. Burton T. Beam, Jr., CLU, CPCU, wrote chapters 8, "Long-Term Care Insurance," and 33, "Group Life Insurance." Archer Edgar, Ram Gopalan, Michael Petersen, and Walter Zultowski, all from the Life Insurance Marketing Research Association (LIMRA), wrote chapter 29, "Life Insurance Marketing." Harry Garber, FSA, wrote chapters 30 and 31, "Financial Statements and Ratings." Jon Hanson, JD, authored chapters 26 and 27, titled "The Regulation of Life Insurance," and chapter 28, "Types of Life Insurance Carriers." Joseph Huver, CLU, ChFC, MSFS, wrote the material on structured settlements in chapter 6 on annuities. James F. Ivers III, JD, LLM, ChFC, wrote the material on income taxation of life insurance in chapter 11. Donald Jones, FSA, and Norma Nielson, PhD, wrote chapter 20, "Surplus—An Insurance Company's Capital." Ted Kurlowicz, JD, LLM, CLU, ChFC, authored the estate tax material in chapter 11 and the business uses of life insurance portion of chapter 12. John McFadden, JD, wrote the qualified plan material in chapter 12. Francis Schott, PhD, wrote chapter 32, "Life Insurance Company Investments." The author of the appendix ("How Much Life Insurance Is Enough?") is Thomas J. Wolff, CLU, ChFC.

Chapter revisions required extensive research and significant rewriting in many cases. All the authors revising chapters contributed significantly to this book and should be recognized for their accomplishments; their contributions are no less important than those of the authors of the new text materials just mentioned. Burke Christensen, JD, CLU, Vice President of Educational Services and General Counsel of the American Society of CLU & ChFC, revised the 11 chapters (34–44) devoted to legal concepts applicable to life insurance. He had to complete an enormous amount of research and double-checking before he could even decide whether the McGill version had to be rewritten. Donald Jones and Norma Nielson, the authors of chapter 20, revised the chapters dealing with life insurance mathematics, reserves, asset shares, and nonforfeiture values (13–15 and 17–19). James Winberg, CLU, ChFC, FLMI, FALU, worked with Jeremy Holmes on behalf of the Home Office Life Underwriters Association to revise the chapters on home office underwriting and on reinsurance (21–24).

The manuscript benefited from the constructive criticism and helpful suggestions of many reviewers. Special acknowledgment is appropriate for the assistance of Larry Brown, LLB; Dr. Robert M. Crowe, PhD, CLU, ChFC, CFP; Dr. Gary Stone PhD, CLU; and C. Bruce Worsham, JD, LLM, CLU, each of whom read several chapters, except Dr. Stone, who read the entire manuscript. Helpful suggestions were provided by my colleagues on the faculty at The American College, especially Stephan R. Leimberg, JD, CLU, and William J. Ruckstuhl, CLU, ChFC, as well as by Robert J. Doyle, Jr., CLU, ChFC, a former colleague.

I want to express thanks and appreciation to those employees at The American College who have made this book a reality through extraordinary effort and tolerance for frustration. Although many will remain unnamed, special mention is necessary for Wendy Cox, Keith de Pinho, Elizabeth Fahrig, Sally Kennedy, Barbara Keyser, Maria Marlowe, Rosemary Pagano, Suzanne Rettew, and Emily Sims of Editorial Services; Jane Dawson, Judith Hill, Deborah Ann Jenkins, and Monica Peta of the Vane B. Lucas Memorial Library; Patricia G. Berenson, Susan Doherty, Jane Hassinger, Christina Liberace, and Evelyn Rice of Production Services; and Jill Schoeniger, Manager of Publications. Special thanks go to Margaret Terrell-Reeves for her diligent and conscientious typing and tracking of numerous drafts of the manuscript. Finally, I extend my gratitude to Lynn Hayes, the managing editor, whose outstanding editing skills and unwavering commitment to excellence have made an unmistakable imprint on this book.

Many individuals have supplied information and other support that permitted this manuscript to culminate in the first edition of *McGill's Life Insurance*. Especially noteworthy are John Angle, FSA; Ben Baldwin, CLU, ChFC; Joseph Belth, PhD, CLU, CPCU; Kenneth Black, Jr., PhD, CLU; Richard Breen, JD, LLM, CLU, ChFC; William Broundie, CLU, ChFC; Patrick Collins, CLU; James

Douds, JD; Joseph Higgins, FSA; Walter Miller, FSA; Alan Press, CLU; James Reiskytl, FSA; George Rejda, PhD, CLU; Gordon K. Rose, CLU; Harold D. Skipper, Jr., PhD, CLU; Fred Stitt, CLU; Edward Stoeber, JD, CLU; and Richard Weber, CLU.

Without the pioneering work of Dr. Solomon Stephen Huebner, none of this would have been possible.

Every attempt has been made to ensure that this volume is accurate and up-to-date. Since I have full confidence in Murphy's law and expect you will find some errors or shortcomings, I would appreciate your critical reactions and suggestions for improvement. With your help we can make future editions of this classic text even better.

Edward E. Graves

About the Editor

Edward E. Graves, CLU, ChFC, associate professor of insurance at The American College, has served on the College's faculty since 1976. He is responsible for the courses in the Chartered Life Underwriter (CLU) and Chartered Financial Consultant (ChFC) designation programs that deal with individual life insurance products and life insurance law. Mr. Graves has published articles on these subjects in industry journals and is the coauthor of a number of textbooks for both The American College and the American Institute for Chartered Property and Casualty Underwriters. He is consulting editor on life insurance products for the Journal of the American Society of CLU & ChFC, and he served on the Insurance Task Force of the Financial Products Standards Board from 1987 to 1989. More recently Mr. Graves was a member of the task force that created the Life Insurance Illustration Questionnaire (IQ) for the American Society of CLU & ChFC. His professional memberships include the American Risk and Insurance Association, the American Society of CLU & ChFC, and the International Association for Financial Planning. He earned his BS degree from California State University at Los Angeles. He holds a master's degree from the University of Pennsylvania.

McGill's Life Insurance

Economic Bases of Life Insurance

Dan M. McGill
Revised by Edward E. Graves

A human life possesses many values, most of them irreplaceable and not conducive to measurement. These values are founded on religious, moral, and social relationships. From a religious standpoint, for example, the human life is regarded as immortal and endowed with a value beyond the comprehension of mortal man. In a person's relationship with other human beings, a set of emotional and sentimental attachments is created that cannot be measured in monetary terms or supplanted by material things. A human life may be capable of artistic achievements that contribute in a unique way to the culture of a society.

Such values, however, are not the foundation of life insurance. Although not oblivious to these values—in fact, the life insurance transaction has strong moral and social overtones—life insurance is concerned with the *economic* value of a human life, which is derived from its earning capacity and the financial dependence of other lives on that earning capacity. Since the economic value may arise out of either a family or a business relationship, it seems advisable to discuss the functions of life insurance under two headings: family purposes and business purposes.

FAMILY PURPOSES

Source of the Economic Value of the Human Life

In terms of its physical composition, the human body is worth only a few dollars. In terms of earning capacity, however, it may be worth millions of dollars. Yet earning power alone does not create an economic value that can logically serve as the basis of life insurance. A human life has an economic value only if some other person or organization can expect to derive a pecuniary advantage through its existence. If an individual is without dependents and no other person or organization stands to profit through his or her living either now or in the future, then that life, for all practical purposes, has no monetary value that needs to be perpetuated. Such an individual is rare. Most income producers either have dependents or can expect to acquire them in the normal course of events. Even those income earners with no family dependents often provide financial support to charitable organizations. In either case, a basis exists for insurance.

Preservation of Family's Economic Security

In many cases an income producer's family is completely dependent on his or her personal earnings for subsistence and the amenities of life. In other words, the "potential" estate is far more substantial than the existing estate—the savings that the family has been able to accumulate. The family's economic security lies in the earning capacity of each income earner, which is represented by his or her "character and health, training and experience, personality and power of industry, judgment and power of initiative, and driving force to put across in tangible form the economic images of his mind."[1] Over a period of time, these economic forces are gradually converted into income, a portion of which is devoted to self-maintenance, a portion to support of dependents, and if the income is large enough, a portion to savings to meet future needs and contingencies. If the individual lives and stays in good health, the total income potential will eventually be realized, all to the benefit of the family and others who derive financial gain from his or her efforts. If an income earner dies or becomes permanently and totally disabled, the unrealized portion of his or her total earnings potential will be lost, and in the absence of other measures, the family will soon find itself destitute or reduced to a lower income than it previously enjoyed.

This need not happen, however, since there are contracts that can create a fund at death at least to partially and possibly to fully offset the lost income of the insured. Those contracts, of course, are life insurance. By means of life insurance, an individual can assure that the family will receive the monetary value of those income-producing qualities that lie within his or her physical being, regardless of when death occurs. By capitalizing this life value, an income earner can leave the family in the same economic position that they would have enjoyed had he or she lived.[2]

The Moral Obligation to Provide Protection

Most people assume major responsibility for the support and maintenance of their dependent children during their lifetime. In fact, they consider it one of the rewarding experiences of life. In any case the law attaches a legal obligation to the support of a spouse and children. Thus if there is a divorce or a legal separation, the court will normally decree support payments for dependent children and possibly alimony for the dependent spouse. In some cases such payments, including alimony, are to continue beyond the provider's death, if the children are still dependent or if the alimony recipient has not remarried.[3] Nevertheless, it takes a high order of responsibility for a parent to voluntarily provide for continuation of income to dependents after his or her own death. It virtually always involves a reduction in the individual's own standard of living. Yet few would deny that any person with a dependent spouse, children, or parents has a moral obligation to provide them with the protection afforded by life insurance, as far as his or her financial means permit.

Dr. S. S. Huebner had the following to say concerning the obligation to insure:

> From the family standpoint, life insurance is a necessary business proposition which may be expected of every person with dependents as a matter of course, just like any other necessary business transaction which ordinary decency requires him to meet. The care of his family is man's first and most important business. The family should be established and run on a sound business basis.

It should be protected against needless bankruptcy. The death or disability of the head of this business should not involve its impairment or dissolution any more than the death of the head of a bank, railroad, or store. Every corporation and firm represents capitalized earning capacity and goodwill. Why then, when men and women are about to organize the business called a family should there not be a capitalization in the form of a life insurance policy of the only real value and goodwill behind that business? Why is it not fully as reasonable to have a life insurance policy accompany a marriage certificate as it is to have a marine insurance certificate invariably attached to a foreign bill of exchange? The voyage in the first instance is, on the average, much longer, subject to much greater risk, and in case of wreck, the loss is of infinitely greater consequence.

The growth of life insurance implies an increasing development of the sense of responsibility. The idea of providing only for the present must give way to recognition of the fact that a person's responsibility to his family is not limited to the years of survival. Emphasis should be laid on the "crime of not insuring," and the finger of scorn should be pointed at any man who, although he has provided well while he was alive, has not seen fit to discount the uncertain future for the benefit of a dependent household . . . Life insurance is a sure means of changing uncertainty into certainty and is the opposite of gambling. He who does not insure gambles with the greatest of all chances and, if he loses, makes those dearest to him pay the forfeit.[4]

Measurement of Monetary Value

It seems agreed that an individual should protect his or her earning capacity for the benefit of dependents by carrying life insurance in an appropriate amount. The question logically arises at this point as to how much is an "appropriate" amount.

Some have suggested that a person should capitalize this economic value at an amount large enough to yield, at a reasonable rate of interest, an income equal to the family's share of those earnings. In an attempt to obtain the same general result, others have recommended that a person capitalize this value at a figure large enough to yield an annual income equal to a specified percentage, such as 50 percent, of those personal earnings at the time of the provider's death. In response to the significant inflation in recent decades, some suggest capitalizing the worker's full income (or more) so that the income portion that would otherwise have gone to income taxes and the insured's self-maintenance can be used to offset general price inflation. All of these approaches are based on the assumption that the income from personal efforts is a perpetuity. All would preserve the capitalized value of a portion of those earnings into perpetuity. Such an assumption is theoretically invalid. Personal earnings are subject to termination at any time by the producer's death or disability and, in any case, will generally not continue beyond the date of retirement. Therefore in capitalizing the earnings of an individual, their terminable nature can be taken into account.

The technically accurate method of computing the monetary value of a person is too complex for general use.[5] It involves an estimate of the individual's personal earnings for each year from his or her present age to the date of retirement, taking into account the normal trend of earnings and inflation. From each year's income the cost of self-maintenance, life insurance premiums, and personal income taxes is deducted. The residual income for each year is then discounted at an assumed rate of interest and against the possibility of its not being earned. In the latter calculation, the three contingencies of death, disability, and unemployment have to be considered. The sum of the discounted values for each year of potential income is the present value of future earnings or the monetary value of the life in question.[6]

In determining the economic value of a human life for purposes of insuring this value against loss by death, one should not discount the projected flow of income to the family for the probability of the provider's death. The objective is to determine the present value of the income flow to the family if the family provider survives to the end of his or her income-producing period since ideally insurance will be sufficient to permit the family to enjoy the same standard of living that it would have enjoyed had the provider(s) not died.

Five-step Procedure for Estimating Economic Value

A reasonably accurate estimate of a person's economic value for purposes of life insurance can be derived by a simple-to-understand method that can be used by anyone with access to a computer, a financial calculator, or compound-interest discount tables. There are five steps in this procedure:

1) Estimate the individual's *average* annual earnings from personal efforts over the remaining years of his or her income-producing lifetime.
2) Deduct federal and state income taxes, life insurance premiums, and the cost of self-maintenance.
3) Determine the number of years between the individual's present age and the contemplated age of retirement.
4) Select a reasonable rate of interest at which future earnings will be discounted.
5) Multiply (1) minus (2) by the present value of $1 per annum for the period determined in (3), discounted at the rate of interest selected in (4).

In the first step an effort should be made to anticipate the pattern of future earnings. In the majority of cases, particularly among semiskilled and clerical workers, earnings will reach their maximum at a fairly early age, perhaps around 40, and will remain at that level (except for inflation adjustments) until retirement. The earnings of professional people continue to increase until about age 55, after which they level off or decline somewhat unless they are adjusted for inflation. The earnings of still other groups may continue to rise until shortly before retirement. It is difficult to estimate accurately the average annual income that can be expected. Inflation, technological change, and increased global competition are accelerating the rate of change and our society's economic volatility.

The costs in the second step are also difficult to estimate, but income taxes and the cost of self-maintenance can be approximated within a reasonably close margin of error unless Congress makes a drastic change in the future tax rates. The purpose of step (2), of course, is to arrive at the family's share of personal earnings. If the individual can directly estimate what portion of those earnings go to the support of the family, the determination of the income tax liability, life insurance premiums, and the cost of self-maintenance can be dispensed with. In the typical case it is probably relatively accurate to assume that less than half of the provider's gross personal earnings is devoted to the support of the family. In the low-income brackets, the percentage is undoubtedly a little higher but in no event more than two-thirds; in the higher-income brackets, the percentage might be lower than one-half.

The purpose of step (3) is to determine how long the family can expect to receive the income projected in step (2), ignoring, for reasons indicated above, the probability that the individual may die before reaching normal retirement age.

The rate of interest selected in step (4) should be in line with the rate generally payable on proceeds left with the insurance company since it is usually a conservative estimate of conditions over the relevant future period. Another acceptable interest rate estimate is the rate used by the Pension Benefit Guaranty Corporation (PBGC is a federal agency located in Washington, DC) for valuing defined benefit pension liabilities.

Calculating Present Value

The present value of $1 per annum, the only new element involved in step (5), is obtained directly from a financial calculator or a computer using financial software. Alternatively it can be derived from a compound-discount table that shows the present value of a series of future income payments—specifically, $1 per annum—for various periods of time and at various rates of interest. The present value of a series of annual end of the year payments of $1 per annum for 40 years at 5 percent interest, for example, is $17.16. If a 4.5 percent interest rate is assumed, the present value is $18.40. Such a computation recognizes that a dollar due some years hence is not worth a dollar in the pocket now. A dollar due 40 years from now is worth only 14 cents today if a discount rate of 5 percent is assumed. This is equivalent to saying that 14 cents (actually $0.142045682) invested at 5 percent compound interest will amount to $1 at the end of 40 years.

The entire process of computing the monetary value of a human life can be illustrated with the example of a married man aged 35, with gross annual earnings of $40,000, whose income is expected to remain at that level until retirement. It can probably be assumed that $20,000 per year will be devoted to the family. If the person plans to retire at age 65, the income can be expected to flow in for the next 30 years. At 5 percent interest, $1 per year for 30 years is worth $15.37 today. Therefore an income flow of $20,000 per year for 30 years is worth $20,000 x $15.37, or $307,400 ($307,449 without rounding). A person aged 35 who can be expected to devote an average of $45,000 per year to his or her family over the next 30 years is worth $691,650 (when $15.37 is the rounded-off version of $15.37245103; $691,760 without rounding) to the family today if the income is discounted at 5 percent. If possible, that income should be capitalized in the form of a life insurance policy on the producer of the income.

Diminishing Nature of the Economic Value

It must be apparent that, from any given point, the economic value of a producer tends to diminish with the passage of time. His or her earning level may continue to increase for a certain period or indefinitely, but with each passing year, the remaining period of productivity becomes shorter. Each year of income that is realized means that there is less that remains to be earned. Since an individual's economic value is nothing more than the unrealized earning capacity represented by native ability and acquired skills, his or her value must diminish as potential income is converted into actual income. This principle is illustrated by the diagram in figure 1-1.

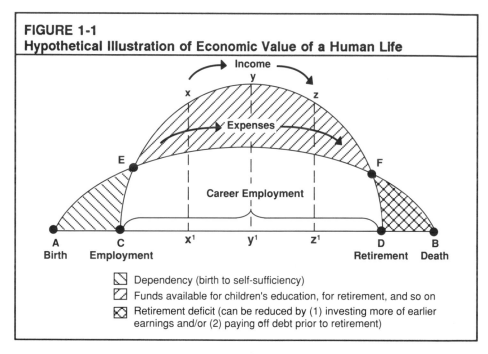

FIGURE 1-1
Hypothetical Illustration of Economic Value of a Human Life

The chord *AB* represents the lifetime of an individual born at point *A* and dying at point *B*. The arc *AB* represents the cost of maintenance and, during his or her productive years, the individual's income tax liability. The arc *CD* represents earning capacity. During the period *A to* C, there are no earnings, but there are costs of maintenance represented by the triangle *AEC*. Earnings commence at *C* and may represent part-time work or sums earned for running errands. The area of arc *CD* that extends above arc *AB* represents earnings in excess of taxes and the cost of self-maintenance. Point *D* marks the age of retirement, and the area *DFB* symbolizes the second major period in the individual's life, during which the cost of self-maintenance exceeds his or her income.

In figure 1-2 the monetary value of the individual is at its peak at point *E* since net earnings are just commencing. At the point where xx^1 intersects the arcs, the earnings rate has increased, but potential future earnings have declined.

The earnings potential shows further decreases at yy^1 and zz^1; at point F, it has shrunk to zero.

Figure 1-1 is diagrammatic and obviously unrealistic. Neither earnings nor maintenance expenses follow a symmetrical curve. For example, the childhood period starts with a highly unsymmetrical outlay for maternity costs. Income is also likely to commence earlier than at point C, particularly among lower-income groups, and under no circumstances is it likely to decline so gradually to the age of retirement. In most occupations people reach their maximum earnings in their 40s, and earnings decline only slightly to retirement, when they terminate abruptly. Figure 1-2 shows a fairly typical pattern of earnings among clerical and professional groups.

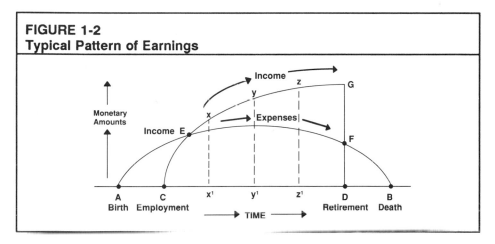

FIGURE 1-2
Typical Pattern of Earnings

Bases for Insurance

These diagrams roughly illustrate the economic foundation of three broad categories of life insurance. The first is represented by the area *AEC*. During this period the individual's needs are met by the parents or other persons responsible for the child's welfare. If the child dies before becoming a producer, the investment in nurturing, maintenance, and education is sacrificed. This can be a sizable sum, especially if the child has been educated at private schools. Various studies have shown that the cost of rearing a child to age 18 ranges from 1.5 times to 3.25 times the parents' annual income. At today's prices the cost may be even higher. While most parents regard these expenditures as one of the duties and privileges of parenthood and justifiably shrink from labeling them as an investment to be recovered in the event of the child's death, such costs do create a substantial insurable value. This value can logically serve as one of the bases for juvenile insurance—a strong segment of the life insurance business.

The second category of insurance is portrayed by the area in arc *CD* lying above arc *AB*. The surplus earnings represented by this area are the source of support for the individual's dependents and a broad measure of the economic loss to the family if the producer(s) should die. A portion of these earnings will go toward insurance premiums, and another portion should be set aside for both spouses' old-age needs, but the share that is destined for the care and maintenance of the family should be capitalized and preserved for the family through the medium of life insurance. This is family insurance in the purest sense.

Finally, the individual's retirement needs, are represented by the area *DFB.* Although the income vacuum may be partially filled by federal OASDI (Old Age, Survivors, and Disability Income)—social security—benefits, pension plans and other tax-qualified plans (such as profit sharing, income deferral, and thrift or savings), and individual investments, the most realistic source of funds to cover any income shortage is through investment income life insurance and annuities. This remaining need can be satisfied with group life insurance through employment and/or a personal insurance program. For long-term planning purposes, however, individuals should not rely on group life insurance for any more than the funds that can and will be kept in force after an unforeseen job loss. Individuals should check their employer's plan to find out how much of the group life insurance they can convert to individual insurance after termination.

Analysis of Needs

The foregoing approach to the problem of determining how much life insurance a person should carry has been termed the *human life value* approach. It is based on the proposition that a person should carry life insurance in an amount equal to the capitalized value of his or her net earnings. Another approach is to analyze the various needs that the family would experience if the income producer dies. The presumption is that these needs will have to be met through life insurance, although other resources, particularly federal OASDI benefits, are taken into account in the ultimate determination of the amount of insurance needed. This technique is identified as the *needs approach,* and purely from a sales standpoint, is regarded as more realistic than the human life value approach.

It would be difficult, if not impossible, to prepare a list of all needs that might possibly arise after the death of the income producer. Family circumstances differ, and a list of needs that would be appropriate for one family might be quite unsuitable for another. Moreover, within any particular family, the needs picture changes from time to time. The most that can be attempted in this section is to outline the general categories of needs that are likely to be found in any family situation. These categories are discussed in the order in which they arise, which in most cases is also the order of importance.

Cleanup Fund

The first need is a fund to meet the expenses resulting from the insured's death and to liquidate all current outstanding obligations. There are many types of obligations to be met, and ready cash should be available for that purpose. Such a fund is usually referred to as a *cleanup fund,* although some planners prefer to substitute the terms *probate fund* or *estate clearance fund.*

The principal items of expense to consider include the following:

- hospital, doctors', and nurses' bills incident to the insured's last illness that are not covered by insurance
- burial expenses, including funeral costs, cemetery lot, and marker

- personal obligations, including unpaid notes, household bills, installment payments, personal loans, and unsatisfied judgments, if any
- unpaid pledges, whether or not they are legally binding obligations
- the cost of estate administration, including executor's or administrator's fee, appraisers' fees, legal fees, and court costs
- estate, inheritance, income, and property taxes

Mortgages might well be included in the list, but in view of their size and the special problems frequently encountered in their connection, they are usually treated as a separate need.

It is difficult to estimate precisely the size of the fund that will be needed since an individual's obligations vary from year to year. Moreover, last-illness expenses can be estimated only within a broad range since the person may die suddenly or may linger for months or years. The needs will also vary with the size of the estate. In the typical estate, for example, estate and inheritance taxes will be insignificant items, if present at all; in a sizable estate, they may constitute the largest item of expense, running into hundreds of thousands or even millions of dollars. Executors' or administrators' fees and legal expenses are based on the size of the estate, the former normally being a fixed percentage of the probate estate. In the typical estate, however, a cleanup fund equal to half the annual family income should suffice, although individual circumstances may justify a larger cleanup fund.

Readjustment Income

Few individuals are able to leave an estate, including life insurance, substantial enough to provide their dependents with an income as large as they enjoyed while the income earner was alive. This means that an adjustment will generally have to be made in the family's standard of living. To cushion the economic and emotional shock, however, it is desirable to postpone that adjustment for a period following the income producer's death. The length of the period depends largely on the magnitude of the change that the family will have to make in living standards. If the adjustment is slight, a year should suffice. If the adjustment is drastic, 2 years or more should be allowed. If the surviving spouse must refresh or acquire skills to gain employment, an even longer period may be needed. Whatever the duration, the income during this readjustment period should be approximately equivalent to the family's share of the producer's earnings at the time of his or her death.

Income during Dependency Period

After the expiration of the readjustment period, income should be provided in a reduced amount until the children, if any, are able to support themselves. This is sometimes called the *critical period* income. Two concepts are involved: how much income should be provided and for how long.

Obviously, as much income as is consistent with the family's other needs should be provided. As a minimum, there should be enough income that the family can remain intact and the surviving spouse can devote adequate time to the care and guidance of the children during their formative years. Although the children may have to engage in part-time employment, it should not be so extensive that it impairs their health or interferes with their education. The needs of this period constitute a large portion of the total demand for individual life insurance policies.

The most important determinants of the income's duration are the present ages of the insured's children and the type of education they will receive. In any case, income should continue until the youngest child is 18. If there are several children, the income can be reduced somewhat as each reaches the age of self-sufficiency. If the children are to receive a college education, income will have to continue for a longer period. In that event, the income during the period the children are in college may be provided by special educational insurance policies. For planning purposes, the immediate death of the income producer is assumed. The projected income is then presumed to be needed for a period equal to the difference between the present age of the youngest child and the age at which the child is expected to become self-supporting.

Life Income for Surviving Dependent Spouse

The needs that exist during the readjustment and dependency periods are primarily family needs. It is presumed that the family unit will be preserved under the guidance of the surviving parent and that the resources of the various members of the family will be pooled to meet the needs of the group. After the children have become self-supporting, however, the widow(er) will still have needs as an individual and will require an income from some source.

If the surviving spouse is a full-time homemaker until the children finish at least part of their education, he or she may subsequently be able to obtain employment, but the earning power for people entering the workforce at that age will have declined substantially. After the birth of children, for example, a wife sometimes gives up her job or the opportunity to become self-supporting. As the years pass, whatever occupational skills she may have possessed are either obsolete or have atrophied and she will most likely have to return to the labor market as a middle-aged woman with deficient skills. Under such circumstances, employment opportunities are limited. Many individuals feel a moral obligation therefore to provide their spouses with incomes that will continue throughout the remaining years of their lives. The income may be modest, but it can be the difference between complete dependency on welfare services and reasonable self-sufficiency.

Special Needs

There are certain needs that are not found in every family situation and, even when they are found, are not likely to enjoy as high a priority as those previously discussed. Three of the most prominent of these are mortgage redemption, educational, and emergency needs.

Mortgage Redemption Needs.   Home ownership is very prevalent among American families today, but most of the homes are burdened with a mortgage, frequently financed by a life insurance company. These mortgages are usually amortized over a period of 15 or 30 years, but it is highly probable that an

unliquidated balance will still be outstanding upon the death of a person with dependent children.

In some cases, of course, the widow(er) may want to sell the house and move into a smaller one or into an apartment, and it would not be essential to provide funds for the liquidation of the mortgage. In fact, it may actually be easier to dispose of a home if it has an assumable mortgage (becoming rare) with favorable terms than if it is clear of debt. In many—if not most—cases, however, it is contemplated that the survivors will continue to occupy the family residence, and funds to pay off the mortgage may be needed. If the family can occupy the home rent free, it will greatly reduce the amount of income that they would otherwise require.

Educational Needs. The income provided for a surviving spouse during the period when the children are dependent should normally be adequate for secondary school expenses, as well as for general maintenance. If a college education for one or more of the children is envisioned, however, additional income will be needed. Under present conditions, college expenses range from about $4,000 to $25,000 per year. The cost might be less if the family happens to live in the vicinity of a college or university and the college student resides at home; it might be considerably higher if the institution has a high tuition schedule. In any event, there is no question that a college or professional education is beyond the means of many children who lose an income-earning parent in childhood. Life insurance companies have a variety of policies that will meet this need in a very convenient manner. In many cases, however, the limited funds available for life insurance premiums must be devoted to higher-priority needs.

Emergency Needs. From time to time in the life of a family, unforeseen needs for money arise because of illness, surgery, major dental work, home repairs, or many other reasons. It is unrealistic for the family income providers to leave enough income for the family to subsist on only if everything goes well and no unusual expenditures are incurred. Therefore a liquid fund should be set up from which additional income can be provided if and when it is needed. Some financial planners suggest that the emergency fund often warrants a higher priority than income for dependents. The actual setting of priorities is properly the responsibility of the income earner(s).

Retirement Needs

Retirement needs do not fall within the categories previously described. On the contrary, the need arises only if the others do not. Yet retirement planning is a contingency that the financial planner and estate planner must anticipate and one that must be considered in arriving at the amount of insurance a family head should carry. To be more precise, this contingency determines the *type* of insurance the family provider(s) should purchase since if the family needs are met with the right kind of insurance (assuming adequate funds for premiums), the cash values under this insurance will usually be sufficient to take care of the postretirement needs of the insured and the spouse, if still living.

Monetary Evaluation of the Foregoing Needs

It is interesting to compare the monetary value of the above needs with the economic value of the human life, computed earlier. For purposes of comparison, assume—as in the earlier illustration—that the family head is a male aged 35, has gross annual earnings of $40,000, and devotes $20,000 per year to his family. Assume further that he has a wife aged 30 and two children, ages 2 and 5, and that an income of $1,700 per month is to be provided during the first 2 years, $1,460 per month during the next 14 years, and $971 per month thereafter for the life of the surviving spouse.

In computing the present value of the foregoing series of income payments, it is advisable to treat them as a life income of $971 per month payable from the surviving spouse's age 30 with an additional income of $240 per month for 16 years and another $50 per month for 2 years. On the basis of the 1983 Individual Annuity Table and 4 percent interest, a life income of $971 per month for a female aged 30, with payments guaranteed for 20 years, has a present value of approximately $220,000. Provision must be made for guaranteed payments during the children's dependency, since in the event of the widow's early death, the income to the children will be reduced by $971 per month to $489 ($729 per month during the first 2 years). Guaranteed installments are available only in multiples of 5 five years (up to 20 years), and at age 30, a 20-year guarantee can be obtained at a sacrifice of only 1 cent per $1,000 of principal sum, compared to the cost of a 15-year guarantee that would be one year short of the 16-year dependency period. The present value on a 4 percent interest basis of $489 per month for 16 years is $69,263, and the present value of $240 per month for 2 years is $5,526. The present value of the family's income needs when the figures are rounded to the nearest hundred dollars is $294,800.

The total increases when the lump-sum needs (cleanup fund and mortgage redemption fund), educational needs, and emergency needs are added. Even if no provision is made for the children's college education, a cleanup fund of $20,000, a mortgage redemption fund of $80,000, and an emergency fund of $30,000 will increase the total to $424,800. If $80,000 is provided to each of the children for a college education, the total income requirements reach $584,800.

It is not likely that these needs will have to be met entirely through personal life insurance. If the individual in the example is covered under the federal OASDI program with benefits approaching the maximum—which, in view of his earnings, is very probable—nearly two-thirds of the income needed until the youngest child is 18 will be provided by the federal government.[7] This would reduce the personal insurance requirements by approximately $170,000. If the husband had attained "fully" insured status for social security at the time of his death—also a reasonable assumption—the widow at age 62 would become entitled to a life income of $800 per month, which would reduce the personal insurance requirements by another $29,600. The individual may also be covered by group life insurance, with benefits of possibly $150,000 or more. Therefore it is not beyond the realm of possibility that all the needs, including those requiring lump-sum payments, may be met in full with the purchase of $235,000 of additional life insurance.

The retirement needs of the husband do not impose additional *quantitative* requirements. If the husband purchases $300,000 of life insurance (roughly the

equivalent of the income needs computed earlier) on the ordinary life plan (the lowest premium type of permanent insurance) before age 35, it will have accumulated at least $125,000 in cash values by age 65. This will provide him with a life income, with payments guaranteed for 10 years, of more than $1,012 per month. If his wife is also alive and in need of old-age protection, the accumulated sum could be converted into a joint-and-last-survivor annuity,[8] which would provide a lower (a 7.5 percent to 14 percent reduction) income per month as long as either the husband or the wife survives. Such an income, supplemented by federal OASDI benefits and possibly retirement benefits from an employer pension plan, should meet their old-age needs with ample margins. (If the insured keeps premium outlays down through a liberal use of term insurance, the cash values available at age 65 will be reduced accordingly.)

Amount of Insurance Needed

Ideally, the life of each productive member of society should be insured for an amount equal to his or her full economic value, as measured by contributions to those who depend on that income. Upon the death of the income producer, the insured sum should then be liquidated in a manner consistent with the purposes for which it was created, meeting the various needs in the order of their importance. If the insured lives to retirement, the sums accumulated through premium payments should, with the exception of amounts required for cleanup and other necessary purposes, be used to satisfy the postretirement needs of the insured and his or her spouse.

As a practical matter, attaining this ideal is difficult, even when death benefits available under the federal OASDI program and employer benefit plans are taken into account. The basic obstacle is that when both the economic value and the needs are at their maximum — at younger ages — the funds available for premium payments are at their minimum. In the lower income groups, the bulk of the family income is spent on the necessities of life; very little is saved. As the family income rises, aggregate expenditures for consumer goods increase, but they constitute a smaller percentage of total income. Thus more money is available for insurance premiums and other forms of savings. By that time, however, the need for insurance may have declined somewhat.

Various formulas have been developed in an attempt to establish the proper relationship between family income and the amount of insurance to carry. A rule of thumb that has gained some acceptance is that 10 percent of gross family income should be devoted to life insurance premiums. Although this ratio is probably unrealistic at lower income levels, as the income level increases, it becomes attainable. Another rule states that the typical wage earner should carry insurance equal to some specified multiple of annual gross income, while persons in the higher income brackets should capitalize a higher multiple of annual earnings. Such rules of thumb are too simplistic because they do not take into consideration either (1) accumulated assets or (2) family composition and objectives.

Note that in the early 1990s approximately 1.88 percent of American families' disposable personal income[9] went into life insurance premiums.[10] This reflects a long slow decline from the high of 5.5 percent back in 1935 and is approximately the same percentage that prevailed during the last decade.

The average American family in the early 1990s owned enough life insurance of all types to replace approximately 27 months of its disposable income after federal income taxes. This reflects a slight increase from the characteristic 21 months of disposable income coverage prior to 1985.

For a discussion of how to ascertain the amount of life insurance an individual should purchase, see chapter 10 and the appendix, "How Much Life Insurance Is Enough?"

BUSINESS PURPOSES

Life insurance serves a wide variety of purposes in the business world, but most of the services can be grouped under these four headings:

- key person indemnification
- credit enhancement
- business continuation
- employee benefit plans

Key Person Indemnification

Perhaps the most direct application of the principles of family insurance to the business world is key person insurance. Its purpose is to indemnify a business concern for the loss of earnings caused by the death of a key officer or employee. In many business concerns, there is one person whose capital, technical knowledge, experience, or business connections make him or her the most valuable asset of the organization and a necessity to its successful operation. This is more likely to be true of a small organization, but innumerable examples can also be found in large organizations. A manufacturing or mining enterprise may depend on one or a few individuals whose engineering talents are vital to the concern. An employee with unusual administrative ability or the ability to develop and motivate a superior sales organization may also be a key person. An educational institution or other organization that depends partly on charitable giving may regard a highly successful fund raiser as a key person.

It is difficult to estimate the economic loss that the organization would suffer in the event of the key person's death. In most cases the loss is measured in terms of earnings, but occasionally it is based on the additional compensation that would have to be paid to replace the key employee. In some cases, the reduction in earnings is assumed to be temporary (5 years, for example), while in other cases, a permanent impairment of earning power is envisioned. The basis for indemnity can usually be established rather accurately when the key person protection is required in connection with a specific research project or other undertaking of temporary duration.

Insurance is purchased on the life of the key employee by the business and is made payable to the business as beneficiary. In most cases, some form of permanent insurance, usually ordinary life, is purchased, and the accumulating cash values are reflected as an asset on the business's books. If key person protection is needed for only a temporary period, term insurance is normally used. Premiums paid for key person insurance are not deductible as a business expense, but in the event of death, the proceeds are received free of federal income tax.

Credit Enhancement

Life insurance can enhance a business concern's credit in two general ways: by improving its general credit rating and by making collateral available.

The first credit function of life insurance is closely allied to (if not identical with) key person insurance. Anything that stabilizes a business concern's financial position improves its credit rating. Insuring the lives of key personnel not only assures banks and other prospective lenders that the business will have a financial cushion if a key person dies but also improves the firm's liquidity through the accumulation of cash values that are available at all times. As a result, the firm is able to command more credit and is able to obtain it on better terms.

A more specific use of life insurance for credit purposes is pledging it for collateral. It is important to note, however, that the collateral can serve two different purposes. It can protect the lender only against loss arising out of the death of a key person or the borrower, or it can provide protection against the borrower's unwillingness or inability to repay the loan.

An example of the first situation is a firm that has borrowed as much as is justified on the basis of conventional operating ratios but would like to borrow additional sums to take advantage of an unusual business opportunity. If the bank has confidence in the business and feels that the only contingency to fear is the death of the business head or other key person, it can safely extend the additional credit upon assigning to the bank a life insurance policy in an appropriate amount on the life of the proper official. The policy need not have cash values; therefore term insurance is frequently used. The basic security behind the loan is the earning capacity of the business and the integrity of its officials. The policy provides protection only against the death of the person whose business acumen assures the loan's repayment. Such loans, secured only by the assignment of a term insurance policy on the borrower's life, are common in personal or nonbusiness transactions—for example, an aspiring doctor who borrows money from a benefactor for medical school, repaying the funds after establishing a practice. In the interim, the benefactor is protected by a term insurance policy on the budding physician's life. This is a character loan, pure and simple; the only hazard to repayment is premature death.

A loan based on cash values is in a different category. The basic security lies in the policy values; the amount of the loan therefore is always less than the cash value under the policy assigned to the lender. If the borrower dies before the loan is repaid, the lender recovers funds from the death proceeds, with the difference paid to the insured's designated beneficiary. If the borrower lives but the loan is not paid at maturity, the lender can recover the funds by surrendering the policy for cash or by exercising the policy loan privilege. If the loan is repaid at maturity, the policy is reassigned to the borrower. Life insurance policies are widely used for this purpose in both business and personal situations. Policy-owners frequently borrow from an insurance company through the policy loan privilege, rather than through assignment to a bank or other lender.

Business Continuation

One of the important forms of business organization in this country is the general partnership, which is subject to the rule of law that any change in the membership of the partnership causes its dissolution. In accordance with this rule, the death of a general partner dissolves the partnership, and the surviving partners become liquidating trustees, charged with the responsibility of paying over the deceased's fair share of the business's liquidated value to his or her estate. Liquidation of a business, however, almost invariably results in severe shrinkages among the assets. Accounts receivable yield only a fraction of their book value, inventory is disposed of at sacrifice prices, furniture and fixtures are sold as secondhand merchandise, and goodwill is lost completely. Moreover, liquidation deprives the surviving partners of their means of livelihood.

In the absence of a prior agreement among the partners, any attempt to avoid liquidation is beset with legal and practical complications. Even if the surviving partners can raise the cash to purchase the deceased's interest — an unrealistic assumption in most cases — they have to prove, as liquidating trustees, that the price paid for the interest is fair. In some states, their fiduciary status prevents their purchasing the deceased's interest at any price since it is virtually tantamount to trustees purchasing trust property. Furthermore, it is seldom practical for the widow(er) or other heir to become a member of the reorganized partnership or to purchase the surviving partner's interests.

In order to avoid this impasse, it is becoming increasingly common for the members of a partnership to enter into a buy-sell agreement. Such an agreement binds the surviving partners to purchase the partnership interest of the first partner to die at a price set forth in the agreement and obligates the deceased partner's estate to sell his or her interest to the surviving partners. The various interests are valued at the time the agreement is drawn up and revised from time to time thereafter. Each partner is insured for the amount of his or her interest, and either the partnership or the other partners own the insurance. Upon the first death among the partners, the life insurance proceeds are used by the partnership or the partners, as the case may be, to purchase the deceased's interest. Thus the business continues in operation for the benefit of the surviving partners, and the deceased's heirs receive the going value of his or her business interest in cash.

All parties benefit by the arrangement. After the first death, the surviving partners can enter into a new buy-sell agreement, or they can continue under the original agreement with the necessary valuation and insurance adjustments. Life insurance is uniquely suited to financing such agreements since the very event that creates the need for cash also provides the cash.

The same sort of agreement is desirable for the stockholders in a closely held corporation. Closely held corporations are so similar in basic characteristics to partnerships that they have been described as "incorporated partnerships." Although the death of a stockholder does not legally dissolve the corporation, the same practical difficulties may be encountered in any attempt to continue the business. These difficulties arise because stockholders of a closely held corporation are also its officers, earnings are distributed primarily in the form of salaries, and no ready market exists for the stock.

Upon the death of a principal stockholder in a close corporation, the surviving stockholders are faced with three choices (apart from liquidation), all of which may prove undesirable: (1) to accept the widow(er) or other adult heir of the deceased into the active management of the corporation, (2) to pay dividends, approximately equivalent to the salary of the deceased stockholder, to the widow(er) or other heir without any participation in management on the heir's part, or (3) to admit outside interests to whom the deceased's stock may have been sold into active management of the company. The surviving spouse faces the possibility of having to dispose of the deceased's stock at a sacrifice price, either to the surviving stockholders or to outsiders, neither of whom would normally be inclined to offer a fair price, or of retaining the stock and receiving no dividends. These difficulties can be avoided by a binding buy-sell agreement financed by life insurance. Under such an agreement, the surviving stockholders will get the corporation's stock, and the widow(er) will receive cash for a speculative business interest.

Similar agreements can be arranged between a sole proprietor and one or more key employees. Life insurance can provide at least a portion of the purchase price, and the remainder can be financed by interest-bearing notes to be paid off from the business's earnings after the proprietor's death.

Employee Benefit Plans

Employee benefit plans provide three broad types of benefits that can be financed through insurance:

- disability benefits, including income replacement and indemnification of medical, surgical, and hospital costs
- death benefits
- old-age benefits

The plans that provide such benefits are usually referred to, respectively, as group health insurance, group life insurance, and pensions, including group annuity plans. While *accidental* death benefits may be and usually are provided under a group health plan, life insurance contracts, *per se,* are used only in connection with group life insurance and certain forms of pensions. Suffice it to say that death benefits under a group life insurance contract may be provided in the form of yearly renewable term insurance, permanent types of contracts, or a combination of the two. The employer always bears a portion of the cost, and some may pay it all. The benefits payable on behalf of any particular employee are determined by a formula that minimizes selection against the insurer. In other words, the employees are not permitted to choose the amount of coverage since those in poor health could be expected to apply for the largest amounts of insurance.

For a complete discussion of the business purposes of life insurance, see chapter 12.

NOTES

1. S. S. Huebner, *Life Insurance,* 4th ed. (New York: Appleton-Century-Crofts, Inc., 1950), p. 14.
2. Capitalization is the creation of a fund large enough to generate ongoing investment income approximating the salary or wages of the individual.
3. In such event, the parent and ex-spouse are required to provide life insurance or to set funds aside in trust.

4. Huebner, *Life Insurance,* p. 23.
5. See Louis J. Dublin and Alfred J. Lotka, *The Money Value of a Man,* rev. ed. (New York: Ronald Press Co., 1946), for a comprehensive discussion of the subject.
6. *Ibid.,* p. 195.
7. This assumes that the widow will not remarry during the period and that both children survive the period.
8. See chapter 6 for a description of the joint-and-last-survivor annuity.
9. Disposal personal income is gross income minus federal income taxes.
10. *Life Insurance Fact Book 1992,* American Council of Life Insurance, p. 73.

2

Basic Principles

Dan M. McGill
Revised by Edward E. Graves

Insurance has been defined in many different ways. Willett, for example, has defined it as "that social device for making accumulations to meet uncertain losses of capital which is carried out through the transfer of the risks of many individuals to one person or to a group of persons."[1] Kulp states that "insurance is a formal social device for the substitution of certainty for uncertainty through the pooling of hazards."[2] In the same vein, Riegel and Miller say that from a functional standpoint, "insurance is a social device whereby the uncertain risks of individuals may be combined in a group and thus made more certain, small periodic contributions by the individuals providing a fund out of which those who suffer loss may be reimbursed."[3] Finally, Pfeffer, in his search for a generic definition, concludes that "insurance is a device for the reduction of the uncertainty of one party, called the insured, through the transfer of particular risks to another party, called the insurer, who offers a restoration, at least in part, of economic losses suffered by the insured."[4]

CONCEPT OF RISK POOLING

Underlying all these definitions is the concept of risk pooling or group sharing of losses. That is, persons exposed to loss from a particular source combine their risks and agree to share losses on some equitable basis. The risks may be combined under an arrangement whereby the participants mutually insure each other, a plan that is appropriately designated "mutual insurance," or they may be transferred to an organization that, for a consideration, called the "premium," is willing to assume the risks and pay the resulting losses. In life insurance, such an organization is a stock life insurance company. While several elements must be present in any sound insurance plan, the essence of the arrangement is the pooling of risks and losses.

Illustration of the Insurance Principle

The basic principle involved in insurance can best be illustrated in terms of a simple form of insurance such as fire insurance. Suppose that in a certain community, there are 1,000 houses, each worth $100,000 and each exposed to approximately the same probability of destruction by fire. The probability that any one of these houses will be destroyed by fire in any particular year is extremely remote, possibly no more than one out of 1,000. Yet if that contingency should occur, the loss to the owner would be staggering—$100,000. If it could be assumed, however, that only one of the 1,000 houses would be destroyed by fire in a particular year, a contribution of only $100 by each home owner would provide a fund large enough to reimburse in full the unfortunate person whose home was lost. If each home owner were willing to assume a certain loss of $100, he could rid himself of the risk of a $100,000 loss. Over the years, only a relatively small percentage of the homes would be destroyed; and through their willingness to contribute a series of small annual sums to a mutual indemnity fund, the property owners would eliminate the possibility of a catastrophic loss to any of their group. The aggregate premium payments over 60 years of home ownership for any one person would still be very small, relative to the potential loss being protected against.

Application to Life Insurance

The principle of loss sharing can be applied in identical fashion to the peril of death. The simplest illustration involves insurance for one year, with all members of the group the same age and possessing roughly similar prospects for longevity. The members of this group might mutually agree that a specified sum, such as $100,000, will be paid to the designated beneficiaries of those members who die during the year, the cost of the payments being borne equally by the members of the group. In its simplest form, this arrangement might envision an assessment upon each member in the appropriate amount as each death occurs. In a group of 1,000 persons, each death would produce an assessment of $100 per member. Among a group of 10,000 males aged 35, 21 of them could be expected to die within a year, according to the Commissioners 1980 Standard Ordinary Mortality Table (1980 CSO Table); if expenses of operation are ignored, cumulative assessments of $210.00 per person would provide the funds for payment of $100,000 to the beneficiary of each of the 21 deceased persons. Larger death payments would produce proportionately larger assessments based on the rate of $2.10 per $1,000 of benefit.

The 1980 CSO mortality table is sex distinct and therefore has different rates at each age for men and women. The rate per $1,000 of benefit for women aged 35 is $1.65, according to the 1980 CSO table. It is very important to note that most large insurance companies base their rates on their own statistics rather than 1980 CSO. The companies that issue policies only to the healthiest applicants will have rates significantly lower than those of the CSO tables used for reserving purposes by the regulators. Even insurance companies issuing policies to applicants in just average health usually experience a rate lower than CSO rates.

Assessment Insurance

Over a century ago, plans based on the assessment technique were widely used in the United States, although confined to fraternal societies and so-called "business assessment associations."[5] Assessments were levied to cover future claims rather than to pay claims that had already been incurred. For example, the Ancient Order of United Workmen, organized in 1868 and the first society to provide death benefits—$2,000 each—levied an assessment of $1 against each member after the payment of each death claim, in order that funds would be available for the prompt settlement of the next claim. Later plans adopted the practice of levying assessments at regular intervals — usually, once a year — rather than after each death.

Flat Assessments

The early societies generally levied the same assessment on all members, regardless of age. This "flat assessment" plan was based on the theory that there would be a continual flow of new members at the younger ages, with little variation from year to year in the average age of those in the group. Hence the total death rate would not increase, and the annual assessments would remain relatively constant over the years.

Unfortunately, this assumption was invalid. It is not true that the total death rate will not increase so long as the average age of the group does not rise. Suppose, for example, that a fraternal society was organized with 2,000 members, all 40 years of age, and that after several years, its membership was composed of 1,000 persons aged 30 and 1,000 aged 50 — an admittedly unrealistic assumption. The average age would still be 40, as it was at the society's inception. However, since the death rate increases more rapidly from ages 40 to 50 than it decreases from ages 40 to 30, the number of deaths in the group will be greater under the later distribution of ages than under the original. The 1980 CSO Table shows a male death rate of 3.02 per 1,000 at age 40, 1.73 per 1,000 at age 30, and 6.71 per 1,000 at age 50. With 2,000 members aged 40, the society could expect 6.04 deaths in one year, whereas with 1,000 members aged 30 and 1,000 aged 50, it could expect 8.44 deaths. The disparity would have been even larger if a higher average age had been assumed.

Moreover, the average age was virtually certain to increase. Newly organized societies consisted predominantly of young and middle-aged members. Older aged applicants were not solicited, since their admission to the group would have increased the assessments and placed the younger members at a greater financial disadvantage. As the society grew older, however, there was a tendency for the average age to climb because of the difficulty of offsetting the increase in the age of the current membership by the flow of new entrants.

This difficulty can be explained by a simple example. If a society commenced operations with five members aged 20, 21, 22, 23, and 24, the average age of the group would be 22. Assume that during the first year of operation the youngest member, aged 20, dies and is replaced by a new member. If the new member is also 20, the average age of the group will be 22.8, since each of the surviving members is now one year older. If any one except the oldest of the original five members dies and is replaced by a member 20 years of age or more, the average age will increase. The practical effect of this phenomenon is that deceased and withdrawing members of a fraternal society have to be replaced by more than an equivalent number of younger members if the average age of the group is not to increase.

As assessments increased in magnitude and frequency, young and healthy members tended to withdraw from the society, frequently to join a younger society where protection could be obtained at a lower cost, while the old and infirm members remained. This had the obvious effect of increasing the average age even more rapidly, thus further accelerating the withdrawal of the young and healthy members. Under such circumstances it soon became impossible to attract new members. The increase in the proportion of aged and infirm members was accompanied by a corresponding increase in death rates. The inevitable result was an abnormally high rate of assessment and, not infrequently, a collapse of the organization. The attendant loss to those aged members who had all their lives contributed to the benefits of others was disheartening and often tragic.

Graded Assessments

Once the weakness of the flat assessment plan became apparent, many societies began to grade the assessment according to the age at entry, a typical scale ranging from $0.60 at age 20 to $2.50 at age 60. However, the rate for any given member remained fixed and did not increase as the member grew older and constituted a heavier mortality risk. While not as crude as the flat assessment plan, the graded assessment arrangement proved unsatisfactory and, like the former, worked a hardship upon the younger members.

A third plan called for assessments that would increase as the member grew older. If based on valid mortality data, such increasing premiums were theoretically sound, but from a practical standpoint, the arrangement was defective because it required low premiums in the younger productive years and high premiums in the older years of lessening productive capacity. More serious, it prompted healthy members to withdraw from the plan as premiums increased, lowering the health level of the residual group and producing an abnormal increase in mortality rates. This process is called either *antiselection* or *adverse selection* and, while present in many aspects of life insurance and in many different forms, is particularly identified with an insurance plan that has premiums that increase with age.

Finally, some plans provided for a reduction in benefits with advancing age, the assessment rate remaining level. This technique is defensible and is found today in many plans of group life insurance.

As a result of the weaknesses explained above, the assessment plan no longer occupies an important place in the field of life insurance. The plans that had been established on that basis have either become insolvent or have been reorganized in accordance with more commonly accepted principles of life insurance management.

YEARLY RENEWABLE TERM INSURANCE

Similar in many respects to assessment insurance is yearly renewable term insurance, a plan widely used in connection with group insurance[6] and reinsurance[7] but having only a limited appeal for individuals needing insurance in the later stages of life. An understanding of its nature and limitations is essential for an appreciation of the more complex forms of insurance.

Yearly renewable term insurance is the simplest form of insurance offered by regular life insurance companies. It provides insurance for a period of one year only but permits the policyowner to renew the policy for successive periods of one year each without the necessity of furnishing evidence of insurability. In other words, the policyowner can renew the policy without submitting to a medical examination or providing other evidence of good health. For reasons that will be apparent later, the right to renew is often limited to a specified period or to specified ages. If the insured dies while the policy is in force, the face amount is paid to the designated beneficiaries. If the insured does not die during the period of protection, no benefits are payable at the expiration of the policy or upon the insured's subsequent death. Instead, the premiums paid to the insurance company are used to pay the claims of those who die during the period of protection. It should not be inferred, however, that the surviving policyowner did not receive any return on the contributions to the company. The protection enjoyed while the insurance was in force had a definite monetary value that was reflected in the premium charged by the insurance company. It will be demonstrated later that the cost of insurance protection for those who do not die is a most important element in the financial operations of a life insurance company.

Determining the Premium

The premium for yearly renewable term insurance is determined by the death rate for the attained age of the individual involved.[8] This is attributable to the fact that each premium purchases only one year of insurance protection. Moreover, each group of policyowners of a given age is considered to be a separate class for premium purposes; each group must pay its own death claims, the burden borne pro rata by the members of the group. Since the death rate increases with age, the premium for yearly renewable term insurance increases each year.

To illustrate, the female death rate at age 25, according to the 1980 CSO Table, is 1.16 per 1,000. If an insurance company should insure a group of 100,000 women aged 25 for $1,000 for one year, it could expect 116 death claims, aggregating $116,000. Inasmuch as premiums are paid to the life insurance company in advance, the cost of the anticipated death claims would be distributed pro rata over the 100,000 policyowners, and a premium of $1.16 would be exacted from each policyowner. It should be noted that (1) the premium is precisely the same as the death rate applicable to those insured, and (2) those policyowners who, according to the mortality projection, will die during the year contribute on the same basis as those who will survive. The implication of the latter is that each policyowner pays a share of his or her own death claim, a principle that underlies all life insurance contracts. The proportion, however, varies with the type of contract, age at issue, and duration of the protection. The implications of the former are made clear in the following paragraphs.

If the 99,884 survivors of the original group of 100,000 policyowners should be insured for another year, they would be exposed to the death rate for persons aged 26, or 1.19 per 1,000, which would theoretically produce 119 deaths and claims totaling $119,000. That sum divided equally among the 99,884 participants would yield a share, or premium, of $1.19 per person. If the 99,765 survivors should desire insurance for another year, provision would have to be made for $122,000 in death claims, necessitating a premium of $1.22.

For the first several years, the premium would continue to increase slowly, being only $1.35 at age 30, $1.65 at age 35, and $2.42 at age 40. Thereafter, however, the premium would rise sharply, reaching $3.56 at age 45, $4.96 at 50, $7.09 at 55, $9.47 at 60, and $14.59 at 65. If the insurance should be continued beyond age 65, the cost would soon become prohibitive, soaring to $22.11 per $1,000 at age 70, $38.24 at 75, $65.99 at 80, and $116.10 at 85. The premium at

90 would be $190.75 per $1,000; at 95, $317.32. Finally, if a woman aged 99 should want $1,000 of insurance on the yearly renewable term basis, she would have to pay a premium of $1,000, since the 1980 CSO Table assumes that the limit of life is 100 years and that a person aged 99 will die within the year.

Limiting the Period of Renewability

If the surviving members of the aforementioned group should continue to renew their insurance year after year, the steadily increasing premiums would cause many to question the advisability of continuing the insurance. After a point, there would be a tendency for the healthy individuals to give up their protection, while those in poor health would continue to renew their policies, regardless of cost. This is the adverse selection to which reference has previously been made. The withdrawal of the healthy members would accelerate the increase in the death rate among the continuing members and, unless ample margins were provided in the insurance company's premium rates, could produce death claims in excess of premium income. In this event, the loss would be borne by the company, since the rates at which the policy can be renewed are guaranteed for the entire period of renewability. It is for this reason that companies offering yearly renewable term insurance on an individual basis often place a limit on the period during which the insurance can be renewed.

Even without restrictions on the period during which the insurance can be renewed, yearly renewable term insurance is not usually feasible for long-term protection. Dissatisfaction with increasing premiums causes many policyowners to discontinue their insurance, often at a time when, because of physical condition or other circumstances, they cannot obtain other insurance. They are also likely to resent that after years of premium payments at increasing financial sacrifice, the insurance protection is lost, with no tangible benefits for the sacrifice involved.

More important, however, is the fact that few, if any, individuals are able and willing to continue their insurance into the advanced ages where death is most likely to occur. Yet the great majority of individuals need insurance that can be continued until death, at whatever age it might occur. This need led to the development of *level premium* insurance.

LEVEL PREMIUM PLAN

Level premium insurance is just what the name implies—a plan of insurance under which premiums do not increase from year to year but, instead, remain constant throughout the premium-paying period. It does not imply that the insured must pay premiums as long as he or she has insurance protection, only that all premiums required will be of equal size.[9]

It must be apparent that if premiums that have a natural tendency to increase with each passing year are leveled out, the premiums paid in the early years of the contract will be more than sufficient to meet current death claims, while those paid in the later years will be less than adequate to meet incurred claims. This is a simple concept, but it has manifold ramifications and far-reaching significance.

With the level premium technique the redundant premiums in the early years of the contract create a fund that is held "in trust"[10] by the insurance company for the benefit and to the credit of the policyowners. This fund is called a *reserve,* which is not merely a restriction on surplus as in the ordinary accounting sense, but a fund that must be accumulated and maintained by the insurance company in order to meet definite future obligations. Since the manner in which the fund is to be accumulated and invested is strictly regulated by law, it is usually referred to in official literature as the *legal reserve.* Technically the reserve is a composite liability account of the insurance company, not susceptible of allocation to individual policies, but for present purposes it may be viewed as an aggregate of individual accounts established to the credit of the various policyowners.[11]

Term Policies

From the standpoint of an individual policy, the excess portions of the premiums paid in the early years of the contract are accumulated at compound interest and subsequently used to supplement the inadequate premiums of the later years. This process can be explained most simply in connection with a contract that provides protection for only a temporary period, as opposed to one that provides insurance for the policyowner's whole of life. Figure 2-1, therefore, shows the level premium mechanism in connection with a term policy issued at age 25, to run to age 65. The level premiums to age 65 are based on the 1980 CSO Female Table and an interest assumption of 4.5 percent. In other words, it is assumed, with respect to the level premium calculations, that the reserves are invested at 4.5 percent, and with respect to the yearly renewable term premiums, that each premium earns 4.5 percent for one year before being disbursed in the form of death benefits.

In this example no allowance is made for expenses, which makes it easier to understand. It also conforms to the legislative and regulatory approach of setting reserves strictly on the basis of interest and mortality without consideration of other operating costs.

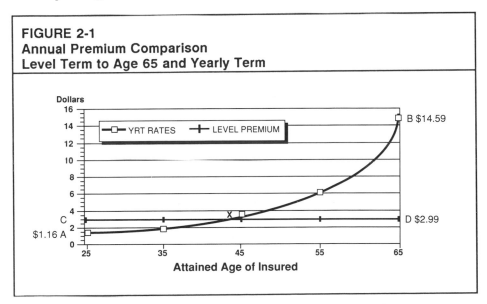

FIGURE 2-1
Annual Premium Comparison
Level Term to Age 65 and Yearly Term

In figure 2-1 the curve *AB* represents the premiums at successive ages that would be required to provide $1,000 of insurance from age 25 to age 65 on the yearly renewable term basis. The premium ranges from $1.16 at age 25 to $14.59 at age 65. The line *CD* represents the level premium that would be required to provide $1,000 of insurance from age 25 to age 65 on the level term basis. The amount of this level premium that would be paid each year through age 64 is $2.99. This exceeds the premiums that would be payable on the yearly renewable term basis prior to age 44 but is smaller than those payable thereafter.

The triangle *AXC* represents the excess portions of the level premiums paid prior to age 43; the triangle *BXD* represents the deficiency in premiums after that age. It is apparent that the second triangle is much larger than the first. The disparity in the size of the two areas is attributable to the fact that the sums represented by the triangle *AXC*, which constitute the reserve under the contract, are invested at compound interest, and the interest earnings are subsequently used along with the principal sum to supplement the inadequate premiums of the later years. The reserve is completely exhausted at age 65 (the expiration of coverage), having been used to pay the policy's share of death claims submitted under other policies, which is another way of saying that the reserve, including the investment earnings derived therefrom, is gradually used up after age 44 in the process of supplementing the then deficient level premium. The reserve under this particular contract—term to 65, issued at age 25—reaches its maximum size at age 53, diminishing thereafter at an accelerating rate until exhausted at the expiration of the policy.

Ordinary Life Policies

The functioning of the level premium plan is even more striking—though more difficult to grasp—when applied to a policy providing insurance for the whole of life. A comparison of the level premium required under an ordinary life policy with that required on the yearly renewable term basis is presented in figure 2-2. As in the case of figure 2-1, the age of issue is 25, and the premiums are based on the 1980 CSO Female Table and 4.5 percent interest, with no allowance for expenses.

In this case, an annual level premium of $6.09 per $1,000 paid as long as the insured lives would be the mathematical equivalent of a series of premiums on the yearly renewable term basis, ranging from $1.16 per $1,000 at age 25 to $956.94 at age 99.

The 1980 CSO Female Table assumes that everyone who survives to age 99 will die during the year, producing a net premium on the yearly renewable term basis equal to the face of the policy, less the interest that will be earned on the premium during the year. In figure 2-2 line *CD* bisects the curve *AB* between the ages of 53 and 54.

The disparity between the areas bounded by *AXC* and *BXD* is very much greater in this case than in figure 2-1. Even more amazing, however, is the fact that the excess premiums (area *AXC)* in the early years of an ordinary life contract (or, for that matter, any type of insurance contract except term) will not only offset the deficiency in the premiums of the later years when the term premium is in the hundreds of dollars, but with the aid of compound interest will also accumulate a reserve equal to the face of the policy by the time the insured

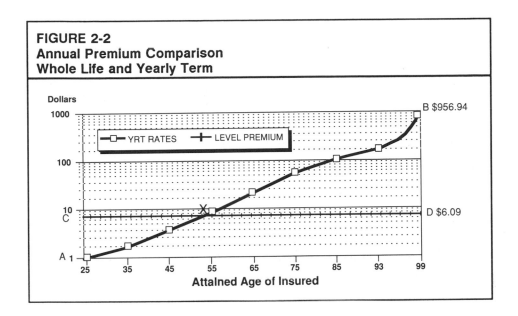

FIGURE 2-2
Annual Premium Comparison
Whole Life and Yearly Term

reaches the terminal age in the mortality table. This is in contrast to the level premium term contract, under which the reserve is completely used up at the expiration of the contract. The difference is because the risk (probability of occurrence) under a contract providing protection for the whole of life is one "converging into a certainty," while the risk under a term policy is a mere contingency—one that may or may not occur. Under a whole life contract, provision must be made for a death claim that is certain to occur, the only uncertainty being the time it will occur.

By the time an insured has reached 99, the reserve under his or her policy must have accumulated to an amount that, supplemented by the final annual premium and interest on the combined sums for the last 12 months of the contract, will equal the face amount of the policy. This must be the case if each class of policyowners is to be self-supporting, since there are no other funds for the payment of the claims of the last members to die. In effect, such policyowners pay off their own death claims, in addition to paying their share of the death claims of all other members of the group. It should not be surprising therefore that the aggregate premiums paid by long-lived persons can exceed the face amount of the policy.

The manner in which the level premium arrangement makes provision for a risk converging into a certainty is explained more thoroughly in the next section.

Effect of Level Premium Technique on Cost of Insurance

Under a level premium type of contract, the accumulated reserve becomes a part of the face amount payable upon the death of the insured. From the standpoint of the insurance company, the effective amount of insurance is the difference between the face amount of the policy and the reserve. Technically speaking, this is the *amount at risk*. As the reserve increases, the amount at risk decreases. The significance of this relationship under discussion is that as the death rate increases, the amount at risk (the effective amount of insurance) decreases, producing a *cost of insurance*[12] within practicable limits. This process is illustrated in table 2-1.

TABLE 2-1
Influence of the Reserve on Cost of Insurance, Ordinary Life Contract for $1,000 Issued at Age 25; 1980 CSO Female Table and 4.5 Percent Interest

Year	Attained Age at Beginning of Year	Reserve End of Year Even Dollars	Net Amount at Risk	Death Rate per 1,000	Cost of Insurance
1	25	$ 5	$995	$ 1.16	$ 1.15
5	29	22	978	1.30	1.27
10	34	55	945	1.58	1.49
20	44	139	861	3.32	2.86
30	54	252	748	6.61	4.94
40	64	397	603	13.25	7.99

As stated earlier, the net level premium for an ordinary life contract on a female issued at age 25, calculated on the basis of the 1980 CSO Table and 4.5 percent interest, is $6.09. Since the death rate at age 25 is 1.16 per 1,000, about $5 of the first premium is excess and goes into the policy reserve. If the policyowner should die during the first year, the company would use the $5 in settling the claim and would have to draw only $995 from the premiums contributed by the other policyowners in the age and policy classification of the deceased. This would mean that each member's pro rata share of death claims in the first year would be only $1.15 (1.16 x 0.995), instead of $1.16, the yearly renewable term premium for $1,000 of insurance at age 25 (with no allowance for interest). By the end of the 5th year, the reserve, or accumulation of excess payments, will have increased to $22 per $1,000, which sum would be available for settlement of a death claim under the policy. The net amount at risk would have decreased to $978, which would necessitate a contribution from the other policyowners (and the deceased) of only $1.27, instead of the yearly renewable term premium of $1.30. The reserve will have grown to $139 per $1,000 by the end of the 20th year, which would reduce the cost per $1,000 from $3.32 to $2.86. By the time the insured has reached 65, the reserve under the policy will have accumulated to $397, and the actual amount of protection will have shrunk to $603. A death claim in the 40th year of the contract would be settled by payment of the $397 in the reserve and $603 from the current year's premium payments (of all the policyowners). The pro rata share of each policyowner for all death claims during the year would be only $7.99, as compared to $13.25 if no reserve had been available. The influence of the reserve on the cost of insurance is even more striking at the advanced ages.

The true nature of level premium insurance should now be apparent. Under the level premium plan, a $1,000 policy does not provide $1,000 of insurance.

The company is never at risk for the face amount of the policy—even in the first year. The amount of actual insurance is always the face amount, less the policyowner's own accumulated excess payments. Since the excess payments may be withdrawn by the policyowner at any time through the cash surrender or loan privilege,[13] they may be regarded as a savings or accumulation account. Thus a level premium policy does not provide pure insurance but a combination of

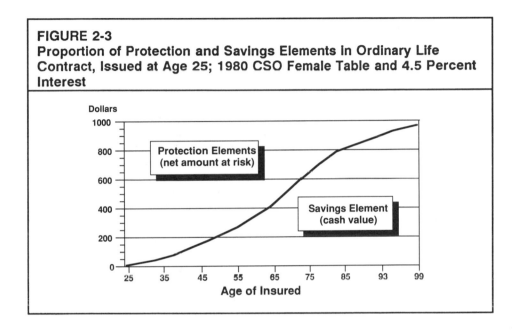

FIGURE 2-3
Proportion of Protection and Savings Elements In Ordinary Life Contract, Issued at Age 25; 1980 CSO Female Table and 4.5 Percent Interest

decreasing insurance and increasing cash values, the two amounts computed so that in any year their sum is equal to the face amount of the policy. This is illustrated in figure 2-3 for an ordinary life policy of $1,000 issued at age 25, the calculations are based on the 1980 CSO Female Table and 4.5 percent interest.

The area below the curve represents the reserve under the contract or, as mentioned above, the policyowner's equity in the contract. The area above the curve represents the company's net amount at risk and the policyowner's amount of protection. As the reserve increases, the amount of protection decreases. At any given age, however, the two combined will equal the face amount of the policy. By age 95 the protection element of the contract has become relatively minor, and by age 100—the end of the contract—it has completely disappeared. At age 100, the policyowner will receive $1,000, composed entirely of the cash value element.

This combination of protection and accumulated cash values is characteristic of all level premium plans, with the exception of most term contracts, and fundamentally, one contract differs from another only in the proportion in which the two elements are combined. This basic truth should be kept in mind as the study of contract forms is undertaken.

Yearly term insurance is all protection and has no cash value, while single premium life insurance is at the other end of the spectrum with the highest cash values and lowest proportion at risk. Accumulated cash values should be thought of as some degree of prefunding. Single premium policies are fully prefunded, and lower premium policies that develop cash values are only partially prefunded. The shorter the premium-paying period, the higher the relative proportion of cash value to death benefit.

Further Significance of Level Premium Plan

The impact of the level premium plan is felt throughout nearly all operations of a life insurance company. It accounts for a major portion of the composite assets of the United States life insurance companies that exceed $1.69 trillion and are increasing at more than $100 billion per year. The other main contributor to this asset growth is the reserve component for annuities and pension plans. The investment of these funds has presented the life insurance institution with one of its most challenging problems but, at the same time, has enabled the institution to contribute in a most material way to the dynamic expansion of the American economy. The level premium plan underlies the system of cash values and other surrender options that has made the life insurance contract one of the most flexible and valuable contracts in existence. It has caused the life insurance contract to be regarded as one of the most acceptable forms of collateral for credit purposes. Despite these positive contributions—and the complications introduced into company operations—the greatest significance of the plan lies in the fact that it is the only arrangement under which it is possible to provide insurance protection to the uppermost limits of the human life span without the possibility that the cost will become prohibitive.

NOTES

1. Allan H. Willett, *The Economic Theory of Risk and Insurance* (Philadelphia: University of Pennsylvania Press, 1951), p. 72.
2. C. A. Kulp, *Casualty Insurance*, 3d ed. (New York: Ronald Press Co., 1956), p. 9.
3. Robert Riegel and Jerome S. Miller, *Insurance Principles and Practices* (New York: Prentice-Hall, Inc., 1947), p. 19.
4. Irving Pfeffer, *Insurance and Economic Theory* (Homewood, Ill.: Richard D. Irwin, Inc., 1956), p. 53.
5. Business assessment associations were local societies organized for the sole purpose of offering insurance at rates much lower than those charged by regular or old-line life insurance companies. They were neither fraternal in character nor organized on the lodge system.
6. See chapter 31.
7. See chapter 24.
8. This ignores expenses of operation and interest earned on invested prepaid premiums, but the principle involved is still valid.
9. As a matter of fact, arrangements are sometimes found under which the premium for the first few years of the contract is lower than that required for the remainder of the premium-paying period. See discussion of modified life policies in chapter 5. There are also policies with increasing premiums over a period up to 20 years that are followed by

level premiums thereafter. See discussion of graded premium whole life policies in chapter 5.

10. This is not a trust fund in the legal sense, which would require the insurance company to establish separate investment accounts for each policyowner and render periodic accountings.

11. In practice each policy is credited with a cash value or surrender value, which is not the same as the reserve but has its basis in the redundant premiums of the early years.

12. The cost of insurance is an actuarial term referring to the sum obtained by multiplying the death rate at the insured's attained age by the net amount at risk. Its derivation and significance are described in chapter 16.

13. Cash surrender and other surrender options are discussed in chapter 25.

3

Term Insurance

Dan M. McGill
Revised by Edward E. Graves

There are five basic types of life insurance contracts: term, whole life, universal life, endowment, and annuity. The function of the first four is to create a principal sum or estate, either through the death of the insured or through the accumulation of funds set aside for investment purposes. The function of the annuity, on the other hand, is to liquidate a principal sum in a scientific manner, regardless of how that sum was created. This dissimilarity in the basic functions of life insurance and annuities has caused some to question the propriety of classifying annuities as a type of life insurance contract, but there appear to be enough similarities to justify the practice. This chapter discusses term insurance contracts.

Note: Endowment life insurance policies are still viable and popular in other countries, but United States tax law changes have nearly eliminated endowment sales in this country.

NATURE OF TERM INSURANCE

Term insurance provides life insurance protection for a limited period only: The face amount of the policy is payable if the insured dies during the specified period, and nothing is paid if the insured survives. The period may be as short as one year, or it may run to age 65 or above. The customary terms are one, 5, 10, 15, and 20 years. Such policies may insure for the agreed term only, or they may give the insured the option of renewing the protection for successive terms without evidence of insurability. Applications for term insurance are carefully underwritten; various restrictions may be imposed on the amount of insurance, the age before which it must be obtained, the age beyond which it cannot be renewed, and the like.

Term insurance may be regarded as temporary insurance and, in principle, is more nearly comparable to property and casualty insurance contracts than any of the other life insurance contracts in use. If a person insures his or her life under a 5-year term contract, no obligation is incurred by the insurance company unless the death of the insured occurs within the term. All premiums paid for the term protection are considered to be fully earned by the company by the end of the term, whether or not a loss has occurred, and the policy has no further value. This is similar to auto and homeowners insurance.

The premium for term insurance is initially relatively low, despite the fact that it contains a relatively high expense loading and an allowance for adverse selection. The reason premiums can be low is that most term contracts do not cover the period of old age when death is most likely to occur and when the cost of insurance is high. In other words, a term policy insures against a contingency only and not a certainty, as do other kinds of policies.

Renewability

Many term insurance contracts contain an option to renew for a limited number of additional periods of term insurance, usually of the same length. The simplest policy of this type is the yearly renewable term policy, which is a one-year term contract renewable for successive periods of one year each. Longer term contracts, such as the 10-year term, may also be renewable. The following is a typical renewal provision:

> *Renewal Privilege.* The insured may renew this policy for further periods of 10 years each without medical examination, provided there has been no lapse in the payment of premiums, by written notice to the company at its home office before the expiration of any period of the insurance hereunder and by the payment in each year, on the dates above specified, of the premium for the age attained by the insured at the beginning of any such renewal period in accordance with the table of rates contained herein.

The key to the renewable feature is the right to renew the contract without a medical examination or other evidence of insurability. Where the term policy contains no renewal privilege, or where it can be renewed only upon evidence of insurability satisfactory to the company, the insured may find that coverage cannot be continued as long as needed. Because of poor health, a hazardous occupation, or some other reason, the insured might be unable to secure a renewal of the contract or to obtain any other form of life insurance protection. The renewal feature prevents this situation. Its chief function is to protect the insurability of the named insured.

Under a term insurance the premium increases with each renewal, based on the attained age of the insured at the time of the renewal. The term insurance premium for a person aged 50 or above, for example, is higher than the premium for a whole life contract acquired before age 35. Within the contract period, however, the premium is level. Over a long period of time, punctuated by several renewals, the premium will consist of a series of level premiums, each series higher than the previous one. Moreover, the rate will continue to increase with each renewal. The scale of rates at which the insurance can be renewed is published in the original contract and cannot be changed by the company as long as the contract remains in force. Evidence of renewal is usually provided in the form of a certificate to be attached to the original contract, although some insurance companies issue a new contract with each renewal.

Insurers have mixed feelings about renewable term insurance. There is no question that, properly used, it fills a real need. However, it presents certain problems to the company that writes it. Whether the policy is on the yearly renewable term plan or a longer term basis, there is likely to be strong selection against the company at time of renewal, and this adverse selection will become greater as the age of the insured—and hence, the renewal premium—increases. Resistance to increasing premiums will cause many of those who remain in good health to fail to renew each time a premium increase takes effect, while those in poor health will tend to take advantage of the right of renewal. As time goes on, the mortality experience among the surviving policyowners will become increasingly unfavorable. While dividend adjustment can provide for adverse mortality experience, it requires substantial margins in the premium rates. As a result, each dollar of protection on the term basis tends to cost middle-aged or older policyowners more than under any other type of contract.

As a further safeguard against adverse selection, companies generally do not permit renewals to carry the coverage beyond a specified age such as 65, 70, or 75 (although some insurers guarantee renewability to age 95 or 99). In addition, limitations on yearly renewable term are usually more stringent; coverage is frequently restricted to 10 or 15 years or, occasionally, 15 years or to age 65, whichever is earlier. Renewable term insurance therefore is satisfactory for individual coverage to both the policyowner and the company when coverage does not extend into the higher ages.

Convertibility

In addition to the renewable privilege, a term policy may contain a provision that permits the policyowner to exchange the term contract for a contract on a permanent plan, likewise without evidence of insurability.[1] In other words, a term insurance policy may be both renewable and convertible. The convertible feature serves the needs of those who want permanent insurance but are temporarily unable to afford the higher premiums required for whole life and other types of cash value life insurance. Convertibility is also useful when the policyowner desires to postpone the final decision as to the type of permanent insurance to be purchased until a later date when, for some reason, it may be possible to make a wiser choice. Thus convertible term insurance provides a way to obtain temporary insurance and an option on permanent insurance in the same policy.

Insurability is protected by the convertible feature in an even more valuable manner than under the renewable feature since convertibility guarantees access to permanent insurance — not just continuation of temporary protection. The two features together afford complete protection against loss of insurability.

The conversion may be effective as of the date of the exchange or as of the original date of the term policy. If the term policy is converted as of the current date, conversion is usually referred to as the *attained age* method since the current age determines the premium level. A conversion using the original date of the term policy for the conversion is referred to as the *original age* method or a *retroactive conversion.*

Retroactive Conversion

Some insurers allow a policy to be converted retroactively within the first few years after issue. When the conversion is effective as of the original date, the premium rate for the permanent contract is that which would have been paid had the new contract been taken out originally, and the policy form is that which would have been issued originally. It is these two features that motivate the insured to convert retroactively in most instances. The advantage of the lower premium is obvious, but in many cases, the contract being issued at the original date contains actuarial assumptions or other features more favorable than those being incorporated in current policies.

Offsetting these advantages, however, is the fact that a financial adjustment—involving a payment by the insured to the company—is required, which may be quite substantial if the term policy has been in force for several years. This adjustment may be computed on a variety of bases, but a great number of companies specify that the payment will be the larger of (1) the difference in the reserves (in some companies, the cash surrender values) under the policies being exchanged or (2) the difference in the premiums paid on the term policy and those that would have been paid on the permanent plan, with interest on the difference at a stipulated rate. Under the second type of financial adjustment, an allowance is frequently made for any larger dividends that would have been payable under the permanent form. Some companies require a payment equal to the difference in reserves, plus a charge of up to 8 percent to provide the previously forgone investment return.

The purpose of the financial adjustment, regardless of how it is computed, is to place the insurance company in the same financial position it would have enjoyed had the permanent contract been issued in the first place. Therefore, apart from the possibility of obtaining more favorable actuarial assumptions, there does not seem to be any financial advantage to the insured to convert retroactively. The insured will admittedly pay a smaller premium but—by making up the deficiency in the term premium—will, in effect, pay it over a longer period of time; actuarially, the two sets of premiums are equivalent. Some people are under the mistaken impression that by making the financial adjustment required for conversion as of the original date, they are investing money retroactively and being credited with retroactive interest. The fact is, however, that the insured pays the company the interest it would have earned had the larger premium been paid from the beginning.

The insured should consider many factors in making a choice between the two bases of conversion, one of the most important being the state of his or her health. The insured would be ill advised to convert retroactively—and pay a substantial sum of money to the insurance company—if his or her health were impaired. The sum the insured pays would immediately become a part of the reserve under the contract and would not increase the amount of death benefits in the event of the insured's early demise—or ever, for that matter. The payment would simply reduce the effective amount of insurance.

In most cases, if the insured has surplus funds to invest in insurance, he or she should consider purchasing additional insurance or perhaps prepaying premiums on existing policies, including the newly converted one. Subject to certain limitation, most companies permit the insured to prepay fixed premiums, either in the form of so-called premium deposits or through discounting of future premiums. The two procedures are very similar. The principal difference is that under the discount method, credit is taken in advance for the interest to be earned on the funds deposited. Under both arrangements, the funds deposited with the company are credited with interest at a stipulated rate and, in some instances, are credited with the interest earned by the company in excess of the stipulated rate. In the event of the insured's death, the balance of any such deposits is returned to the insured's estate or designated beneficiaries in addition to the death benefit of the policy. Some companies permit withdrawal of premium deposits at any time, in which case a lower rate of interest may be credited, while others limit withdrawals to anniversary or premium due dates. A few companies permit withdrawals only in case of surrender or death. Some companies credit no interest or otherwise penalize the insured if the funds are withdrawn.

Time Limit for Conversion

As previously noted, a retroactive conversion must take place within a specified number of years after issue. If the term of the policy is no longer than 10 years, a conversion as of a current date can usually be accomplished throughout the full term. If the term is longer than 10 years, the policy may stipulate that the conversion privilege must be exercised, if at all, before the expiration of a period shorter than the term of the policy. For example, a 15-year term policy must usually be converted, if at all, within 12 years from date of issue, a 20-year term policy within 15 years.

The purpose of a time limit is to minimize adverse selection. There is always a substantial degree of adverse selection in the conversion process. Those policyowners in poor health as the time for conversion approaches are more likely to convert and pay the higher premiums than those who believe themselves to be in good health. If the decision to convert must be made some years before the expiration of the term policy, a higher percentage of healthy policyowners, uncertain of their health some years hence, will elect to convert. Even so, experience has shown that the death rate among those who convert is higher than normal. This accounts for the fact that premium rates for convertible term insurance are somewhat higher than those for term policies not containing the conversion privilege.

If the policy is renewable, the only time limitation may be that it is converted before age 60 or 65. In other cases, the contract will state that the policy must be converted within a certain period before the expiration of the last term for which it can be renewed. In all cases, conversion may be permitted beyond the time limit, but within the policy term, upon evidence of insurability.

Some companies issue term policies that are automatically converted at the expiration of the term to a specified plan of permanent insurance. It is doubtful that this procedure is effective in reducing adverse selection since healthy individuals may fail to continue the permanent insurance.

Select and Ultimate Term Insurance (Re-entry Term)

The life insurance industry has developed a term insurance policy intended to charge higher premiums to those in poorer health when they renew their term insurance, thereby reducing the degree of adverse selection. The product is commonly called re-entry term insurance. It is really a policy subject to two different premium schedules. The lower premium rate is based on select mortality (that applicable to an insured who has recently given evidence that he or she is in good health). The select rates are available as long as the insured is able to provide new evidence of insurability at each renewal date and at other dates specified by the insurer.

The higher premium schedule is based on ultimate mortality rates (that applicable to insureds at least 15 or 20 years after they last provided evidence of insurability). The insureds who cannot provide evidence of insurability acceptable to the insurance company when requested or required must pay the higher premium schedule rates to renew their coverage. They are known to be in poorer health and have to pay for the increased risk right away and probably for each subsequent renewal (unless they experience an improvement in their health).

It is hard to argue with the logic or concept of equity in this approach. In order to get the lower premiums while healthy the individual should be willing to pay the higher premium when his or her health deteriorates. However, it is questionable whether the policyowner knows or realizes the full import of a decision to buy re-entry term insurance. Young people in good health believe they are immortal and will never have to pay the higher rates. Few of them stop to consider that they may actually end up paying the ultimate rates and that when that happens they will usually be precluded from buying coverage from another insurer. The single premium schedule term insurance they could have bought instead of re-entry term might have been a significant bargain. Unfortunately, when that realization sinks in, it is too late to select that option.

Re-entry term is economical for those who remain healthy into their retirement years, but it may end up being very costly for anyone whose health deteriorates at about the same rate as the general population's. On average, people start to experience declining health between the ages of 45 and 55. If they reach their life expectancy (at least 50 percent should), they can live 40 to 50 years in an impaired physical condition—paying the higher term rates for many more years than they enjoyed the lower term rates.

It is suggested that the decision to purchase re-entry term insurance should involve comparison of the high rates of competing insurers for similar coverage. Once the insured cannot provide satisfactory evidence of insurability, the lower premium schedule is irrelevant. Pro forma cash flow simulations of the premiums (both high and low rates) for each policy being considered at a range of premium increase dates are helpful in making such comparisons. Another important point for evaluation is whether the insurer considers the policy a new contract with a new contestable period after the insured fails a re-entry test. Some insurers treat the new premium as an adjustment on continuing coverage, but others impose a new contestable period.

Guarding against Contestability

In general it is a good idea to keep existing coverage in force until after the intended replacement coverage has actually been issued and the policy delivered. It is important for the policyowner to realize that new policies remain contestable for at least one year (and often for 2 years). If the insured dies while the policy remains contestable, the claim will be investigated much more thoroughly and take longer to settle than one for a policy that is already incontestable.

Long-Term Contracts

While most term contracts provide protection for a relatively short period, subject to renewal for successive periods of the same duration, some term contracts are designed to provide long-period protection in the first instance. These policies often give prospective policyowners the option to purchase waiver-of-premium and accidental death benefits.

A term to 65 contract, for example, provides protection on a level premium basis from the age of issue to age 65. It is not to be confused with yearly renewable or other forms of term insurance that can be renewed until the insured reaches age 65. The period covered by this contract is normally somewhat shorter than the life expectancy, but its termination date coincides with the age generally regarded as the normal retirement age. Hence it probably comes closest to limiting its protection to the years when the insured's income is derived from personal efforts. Since the term is shorter than that of whole life contracts, the premium will be smaller. It is customary to provide for cash and other surrender values. A conversion privilege may be offered, but if so, it must usually be exercised some time before the expiration of the policy. A typical form requires conversion prior to age 60.

Nonlevel Term Insurance

The preceding discussion has presumed that the amount of insurance is level or uniform throughout the term of the policy. This is not necessarily the case since the amount of insurance may increase or decrease throughout the term. As a matter of fact, a substantial—if not predominant—portion of term insurance provides systematic decreases in the amount of insurance from year to year. This type of term insurance, appropriately called *decreasing term insurance,* may be written in the form of a separate contract, a rider to a new or existing contract, or as an integral part of a combination contract. Mortgage redemption insurance is probably the most familiar form of decreasing term insurance.

Increasing term insurance in the form of a return-of-premium provision has been around for a long time, but in recent years the concept has enjoyed a much wider application in connection with various arrangements, specifically split-dollar plans, which may contemplate borrowing or encumbering the cash value of an underlying policy. In order to provide a uniform death benefit to the insured's personal beneficiaries, contracts developed for these uses frequently make provision for the automatic purchase of an additional amount of term insurance each year in the exact or approximate amount that the cash value increases. Increasing term insurance may be provided on a year-to-year basis through the operation of the so-called fifth dividend option (which is described at a later point).

CRITIQUE OF TERM INSURANCE

Term insurance has long been a controversial type of insurance. Many people, not familiar with or perhaps not sympathetic to the principle of level premium insurance, advocate the use of term insurance in all situations to the virtual exclusion of permanent insurance. There are certain insurance "consultants" who, when they find permanent plans in an insurance program, will advise their surrender for cash and replacement with term insurance. On the other hand, the insurance companies, mindful of the limitations of term insurance and fearful of possible adverse public reaction, tend to discourage its indiscriminate use. This has given rise to a widespread impression that insurance companies are opposed to term insurance, preferring the higher-premium forms that add more to income and assets. It might be helpful therefore to point out the areas that can legitimately be served by term insurance and to analyze briefly some of the fallacious arguments that have been advanced in favor of term insurance.

Areas of Usefulness

Term insurance is suitable when either (1) the need for protection is purely temporary or (2) the need for protection is permanent, but the insured temporarily cannot afford the premiums for permanent insurance. In the first case, term insurance is the complete answer, but it should be renewable in the event that the temporary need should extend over a longer period than was originally anticipated. Theoretically the policy need not be convertible, but since relatively few people carry an adequate amount of permanent insurance and since the loss of insurability is a constant threat, it is advisable to obtain a policy with the conversion privilege.

The second broad use of term insurance requires that the policy be convertible. The conversion privilege is the bridge that spans the gap between the need for permanent insurance and the financial ability to meet the need. In this case, since the insured's financial situation might persist longer than anticipated, the policy should be renewable as well as convertible. Thus the renewable and convertible features serve quite different functions and, ideally, should be incorporated in all term policies.

Temporary Need for Protection

Examples of temporary needs that can and should be met through term insurance are encountered daily. One of the most obvious is the need to hedge a loan. A term policy in the amount of the loan payable to the lender not only protects the lender against possible loss of principal but also relieves the insured's estate of the burden of repaying the loan if the insured dies. A mortgage redemption policy serves the same purpose. An individual who has invested heavily in a speculative business venture should protect his or her estate and family by obtaining term insurance in the amount of the investment. If a business firm is spending a considerable sum in an experimental project, the success of which depends on the talents and abilities of one individual or a few individuals, term insurance on the appropriate person or persons will protect the investment. A parent with young children is likely to need more insurance while the children are dependent than he or she will need when they have grown up and become self-sufficient. The additional insurance during the child-raising period can be—and usually is—provided through term insurance. Frequently decreasing term insurance is superimposed on a plan of permanent insurance.

Lack of Finances for Permanent Insurance

The second function of term insurance is particularly important to young people who expect substantial improvement in their financial situation as the years go by. Young professionals who have made a considerable investment in their education and training but whose practices must be built up gradually are likely prospects for term insurance. Young business executives are also good prospects.

Danger of Relying Solely on Group Term Insurance

In these times of fierce competition and corporate downsizing it can be precarious to rely heavily on employer-provided group life insurance to satisfy all or most of a family's death benefit needs. Individuals should find out how much of the employer group coverage can be converted after an involuntary termination of employment — for example, mandatory early retirement, workforce reduction, plant closing, reorganization after a merger or acquisition, employer bankruptcy, statutory banning of a product (freon, for instance), or chronic health impairment resulting from accident or decease. Individual term insurance may be appropriate to cover the potential net reduction in coverage after postemployment conversion of the existing coverage. The safest way for the individual to cover this risk is to purchase an individual policy while he or she is still employed. The cost of such risk aversion is the amount spent on premiums for coverage in excess of the individual's current needs between policy formation and a premature employment termination.

Fallacious Arguments in Favor of Term Insurance

Some of the fallacious arguments in favor of term insurance can just as aptly be described as criticisms of level premium insurance. Upon analysis, most of the arguments can be merged into two sweeping allegations: (1) Level premium insurance overcharges the policyowner, and (2) the accumulation and protection elements should be separated.

The basis for the first allegation is the indisputable fact that if a policyowner dies in the early years of the contract, premium outlay under the level premium plan is considerably larger than it would have been under a term plan. It follows, then, according to the term advocates, that the policyowner paid a larger premium than was necessary. Term advocates question whether it is wise for the insured to pay in advance for something he or she may never need or live to enjoy. They argue that it is better "to pay as you go and get what you pay for."

There is no question that insureds would be far better off financially with term insurance if they could be sure that they would die within a relatively short time. On the other hand, they would be far worse off if they guessed wrong and lived to a ripe old age. Although no one knows whether he or she will die young or live to an excessively old age, the chances of living to an age where the total term premiums exceed the total premiums paid under a level premium plan are relatively high.

The level premium plan protects the insured against the consequences of living too long and having to pay prohibitive premiums for insurance protection. In effect, it shifts a portion of the premium burden of those who live beyond their life expectancy to those who die young and produce an exceedingly large return on their premium outlay. Since at the outset no one can know which group he or she will be in, payment of the level premium by all is an eminently fair and satisfactory arrangement.

Those who argue that level premium insurance overcharges policyowners sometimes assert that the reserve under permanent forms of insurance is forfeited to the company in the event of the insured's death. To correct this "inequity," they contend, the normal death benefit should be increased by the amount of the reserve.

This argument, it should be apparent, strikes at the very heart of the level premium plan. As stated before, the essence of this plan is a gradual reduction in the net amount at risk as the reserve increases. If the reserve is to be paid in addition to the face amount of the policy, this reduction in the amount at risk does not occur, and premiums that were calculated on the assumption that the risk is to be a decreasing one will clearly be inadequate. Some companies offer a contract that promises to return the reserve in addition to the face amount of the policy, but the premium is increased accordingly.

The second allegation—that the savings and protection elements of the contract should be separated—is based on the proposition that an individual can invest his or her surplus funds more wisely and with a greater return than the life insurance company can. Those who believe this recommend that individuals buy term insurance and then place the difference between the term premium and the premium they would have paid for level premium insurance in a separate investment program. Some suggest investing this difference in premiums in government bonds, others recommend investment trusts or mutual funds, while others advocate an individual investment program in common stocks. This argument needs to be analyzed in terms of the objectives of any investment program.

Investment Program Objectives

The principal investment program objectives are safety of principal, yield, and liquidity.

Regarding safety of principal, the life insurance industry has compiled a solvency record over the years that is unmatched by any other type of business organization. It has survived wars, depressions, and inflations; composite losses to policyowners have been relatively rare. Even the few companies seized by the regulators in recent years have been able to rescue most of their policyowners' contracts. This exemplary record has been achieved through quality investments and concentration on government bonds—federal, state, and local—high-grade corporate bonds, and real estate mortgages, and through emphasis on diversification. Investments are diversified as to type of industry, geographical distribution, maturity, and size. Many of the larger companies have from 100,000 to 200,000 different units of investment. The individual policyowner's reserve or investment is commingled with all other policyowners' reserves. The insurance company has invested in assets to offset these liabilities (reserves). In effect therefore each policyowner owns a pro rata share of each investment unit in the company's portfolio. The insured may have as little as one cent invested in some units. Such diversification—which is the keystone of safety—is obviously beyond the reach of the individual investor. Only by investing exclusively in federal and state government bonds, with the consequent interest rate risk and sacrifice of yield, could the individual investor hope to match the safety of principal that his or her funds would enjoy with a reputable life insurance company.

Life insurance companies unquestionably obtain the highest possible yield commensurate with the standard of safety that they have set for themselves. As a group life insurance companies in the United States earned over 9.0 percent of their mean ledger assets during most of the past decade, reaching 9.87 percent in 1985. This figure, which represents the net investment income (but does not reflect capital gains and losses) after deducting all expenses allocable to investment operations but before deducting federal income taxes, is the highest during the 20th century for the United States life insurance industry. Net rates have been declining since 1985 as general investment returns have sagged for all sectors of the economy. Many individuals therefore may be able to secure a higher yield than that provided by a life insurance company by investing in common stocks or other equity investments, especially if unrealized capital appreciation is taken into account, and some exceptional investors will be able to do it under virtually any circumstances. It is highly questionable, however, that the *typical* life insurance policyowner can, over a long period, earn a consistently higher yield than a life insurance company, regardless of the type of investment program he or she pursues. Moreover, it should be noted that the annual increases in cash values are not subject to federal income taxes as they accrue,[2] while the earnings from a separate investment program would be taxed as ordinary income.

With respect to the third objective of an investment program, the liquidity of a life insurance contract is unsurpassed. The policyowner's investment can be withdrawn at any time with no loss of principal. This can be accomplished through surrender for cash or through policy loans. The insured never faces the possibility of liquidating his or her assets in an unfavorable market; nor can the insured's policy loans be called because of inadequate collateral. Certain types of investments approach the liquidity of life insurance cash values, but no investment whose value depends on the market can match the liquidity of the demand obligation represented by the life insurance contract.

More important perhaps than any of the preceding factors is the question of whether savings under a separate investment program would have been accomplished in the first place. Life insurance that develops cash values is a form of "forced" saving. Not only do its periodic premiums provide a simple and systematic mechanism for saving, but when the savings feature is combined with the protection feature, there is also far more incentive for the insured to save than there would otherwise be. An individual who is voluntarily purchasing a bond a month or setting aside a certain amount per month in some other type of savings account may skip a month or two if some other disposition of money is more appealing. If, however, failure to set aside the predetermined contribution to a savings account would result in loss of highly prized insurance protection that might be irreplaceable, he or she will be far more likely to make the savings effort. The insured saves because it is the only way of preserving his or her protection.

The foregoing is not to disparage other forms of investment. All have their place in an individual's financial program. Level premium life insurance, however, should be the foundation of any lifelong financial program.

NOTES

1. *Permanent plan* or *permanent insurance* refers to whole life, universal life, and other cash value types of insurance, as distinguished from the temporary protection afforded by term insurance.
2. Except in the case of death, most of the earnings on the reserve of a life insurance contract are eventually taxed to the insured but usually at a time when he or she is in a much lower tax bracket.

4

Whole Life Insurance

Dan M. McGill
Revised by Edward E. Graves

In contrast with term insurance, which pays benefits only if the insured dies during a specified period of years, whole life insurance provides for the payment of the policy's face amount upon the death of the insured, regardless of when death occurs. It is this characteristic—protection for the whole of life—that gives the insurance its name. The expression has no reference to the manner in which the premiums are paid, only to the duration of the protection. If the premiums are to be paid throughout the insured's lifetime, the insurance is known as *ordinary life;* if premiums are to be paid only during a specified period, the insurance is designated *limited-payment life.* Hence there are two principal types of whole life contracts:

- ordinary life insurance
- limited-payment life insurance

PRINCIPAL TYPES OF WHOLE LIFE INSURANCE

Ordinary Life Insurance

Ordinary life insurance (also called continuous premium whole life) is a type of whole life insurance for which premiums are based on the assumption that they will be paid until the insured's death. It is desirable to define ordinary life insurance this way since in an increasing number of cases, life insurance is purchased with no intention on the policyowner's part to pay premiums as long as the insured lives. In many cases the insurance is purchased as part of a program that contemplates the use of dividends to pay up the insurance by the end of a period shorter than the life expectancy of the insured. In other cases the plan may be to eventually surrender insurance for an annuity or for a reduced amount of insurance. The point is that ordinary life should not be envisioned as a type of insurance on which the policyowner is irrevocably committed to pay premiums as long as the insured lives or even into the insured's extreme old age. Rather, it should be viewed as a type of policy that provides permanent protection for the lowest total premium outlay and some degree of flexibility to meet changing needs and circumstances for both long-lived persons and those with average-duration lifetimes. It is the most basic lifelong policy offered by any life insurance company, and it enjoys the widest sale. Ordinary life insurance is an appropriate foundation for any insurance program, and in an adequate amount it could well serve as the entire program. Its distinctive features are discussed below.

Permanent Protection

The protection afforded by the ordinary life contract is permanent—the term never expires, and the policy never has to be renewed or converted. If insureds continue to pay premiums or pay up their policy, they have protection for as long as they live, regardless of their health; eventually, the face amount of the policy will be paid. This is a valuable right because virtually all people need some insurance as long as they live, if for nothing more than to pay last-illness and funeral expenses. In most cases the need is much greater than that.

In one sense ordinary life can be regarded as an endowment. As discussed in chapter 5 an endowment insurance contract pays the face amount of the policy, whether the insured dies prior to the endowment maturity date or survives to the end of the period. If age 100 is considered to be the end of the endowment period—as well as the end of the mortality table—then an ordinary life policy is equivalent to an endowment contract that pays the face amount as a death claim if the insured dies before age 100 or as a matured endowment if he or she survives to age 100.

During the years when the American Experience Table of Mortality (which has a terminal age of 96) was being used for new insurance, many insurers labeled their ordinary life contract as an "endowment at 96." For that matter, many companies today offer an "endowment at 95" in lieu of an ordinary life contract. Ironically, many prospects will buy an "endowment at 95" when they will not buy an ordinary life policy. Of course, the ordinary life policy could just as aptly be described as a "level premium term to 100" if it were to be assumed that all individuals who survive to age 99 die before their 100th birthday.

Lowest Premium Outlay

Inasmuch as the premium rate for an ordinary life contract is calculated on the assumption that premiums will be payable throughout the whole of life, the lowest rate is produced. As will be noted later, the net single premium for a whole life policy is computed without reference to the manner in which the periodic premiums will be paid and at any particular age is the same for ordinary life insurance and any form of limited-payment life insurance. Naturally, the longer the period over which the single-sum payment is spread, the lower each periodic payment will be.

Thus the *net* annual level premium per $1,000 of ordinary life insurance, issued at age 25 and calculated on the basis of the 1980 CSO Male Table and 4.5 percent interest is only $7.49, while the comparable *net* annual level premium for a 20-payment life policy is $11.07. The *gross* annual premiums[1] per $1,000 charged by two life insurance companies for the same two contracts at ages 25 and 35 are shown in table 4-1.

Limited-payment insurance contracts provide benefits that justify the higher premium rates. If, however, the insured's objective is to secure the maximum amount of permanent insurance protection per dollar of premium outlay, then his or her purposes will be best served by the ordinary life contract. Its moderate cost brings the policy within reach of all people except those in the older age brackets.

TABLE 4-1				
Sample Gross Annual Premiums per $1,000				
	Ordinary Whole Life		20-Pay Whole Life	
Issue Age	Company A	Company B	Company A	Company B
25	$9.28	$11.90	$13.28	$17.70
35	$13.21	$16.90	$19.26	$22.50

Cash Value or Accumulation Element

As level premium permanent insurance, ordinary life accumulates a reserve that gradually reaches a substantial level and eventually equals the face amount of the policy. As is to be expected, however, the reserve at all durations is lower than that of the other forms of permanent insurance. In other words, the protection element tends to be relatively high. Nevertheless, it is the opinion of many that the ordinary life contract offers the optimal combination of protection and savings. The contract emphasizes protection, but it also accumulates a cash value that can be used to accomplish a variety of purposes.

The cash values that accumulate under an ordinary life contract can be utilized as surrender values, paid-up insurance, or extended term insurance, whose significance will be explained in the next section of this chapter. Cash values are not generally available during the first year or two of the insurance because of the cost to the company of putting the business on the books. Common exceptions are single premium policies and some durations of limited-payment whole life policies whose the first-year premiums are large enough to exceed all first-year expenses incurred to create the policy and maintain policy reserves. (The interdependence of expenses and cash values is described in chapter 19.)

Flexibility

Ordinary life, in common with other forms of whole life insurance, provides a limited degree of flexibility. This flexibility is derived from several different contract provisions, but one of the most significant is the set of provisions referred to as *nonforfeiture* or *surrender* options. Designed originally to preserve the policyowner's equity in the policy reserve, surrender provisions are increasingly being used to adapt policy coverage to changing circumstances and needs. Most policies stipulate that the surrender value may be taken in one of three forms: cash, a reduced amount of paid-up whole life insurance, or paid-up term insurance.

Cash Value. The policy may be surrendered at any time for its cash value; in that event the protection terminates, and the company has no further obligation under the policy. While this privilege provides a ready source of cash to meet a financial emergency or to take advantage of a business opportunity, it should be exercised with restraint since it diminishes the further usefulness of the policy.

A policy that has been surrendered for cash cannot be reinstated except by special permission of the company, which is usually withheld unless the insured can provide evidence of insurability that would satisfy the criteria for issuing a new policy to a first-time applicant.

Reduced Amount of Paid-up Whole Life. The second option permits the insured to take a reduced amount of paid-up whole life insurance, payable upon the same conditions as the original policy. The amount of the paid-up insurance is the amount that can be purchased at the insured's attained age by the net cash value (cash value, less any policy indebtedness [policyowner loans plus accrued interest], plus any dividend accumulations) applied as a net single premium. Note that the paid-up insurance is purchased at *net* rates, which constitutes a sizable saving to the purchaser. According to the 1980 CSO Table and a 4.5 percent interest assumption, the cash value at the end of 20 years on an ordinary life contract issued at age 30 is $220, which is sufficient, as a net single premium, to purchase $615 of paid-up whole life insurance. The protection continues in the reduced amount until the insured's death unless the reduced policy is surrendered for cash, and no further premiums are called for under this plan.

Paid-up Term. The third option provides paid-up term insurance in an amount equal to the original face amount of the policy, increased by any dividend additions or deposits and decreased by any policy indebtedness. The length of the term is that which can be purchased at the insured's attained age with the net cash value applied as a net single premium. At age 50 the aforementioned cash value of $220 would purchase $1,000 of term insurance for about 16.5 years. If the insured fails to elect an option within a specified period after default of premiums, this option automatically goes into effect.

If the financial status of the policyowner makes it impracticable to continue premium payments, or if the need for insurance protection undergoes a change, the policyowner may wish to elect one of the surrender options. After his or her dependents have become self-supporting, for example, the policyowner may elect to discontinue premium payments and continue the protection on a reduced scale for the remainder of the insured's life. If, on the other hand, the need for insurance continues, he or she may elect to eliminate premium payments but continue the full amount of protection for a definite period of time. The elimination of fixed payments may be particularly attractive as the insured approaches retirement and anticipates a reduction in income.

Annuity or Retirement Income. Another use of surrender values that is growing in popularity is applying them to the purchase of an annuity or retirement income. If the life insurance policy does not specifically give the insured the right to take the cash value in the form of a life income (purchased at net rates), the insurer will grant the privilege upon request. More and more insureds are purchasing ordinary life insurance to protect their families during the child-raising period with the specific objective of eventually using the cash values for their own retirement. The cash value of an ordinary life policy purchased at age 25 will usually be in the range of 50 percent to 60 percent of the face amount at age 65. The comparable percentage range for an ordinary life policy purchased at age 35 is 40 percent to 55 percent, and even a policy issued as late as age 40 will accumulate a cash value at age 65 only slightly less than one-half of the face amount (35 percent to 50 percent). Therefore if an individual procures $50,000 of ordinary life insurance at age 35, for example, he or she would have approximately $24,000 in cash value at 65, which at net rates would provide a life income somewhere in the range of $140 to $165 per month. Supplemented by federal OASDI (Old-Age, Survivors, and Disability Insurance) benefits, private retirement plan benefits, and income from other savings, this could provide the insured with an adequate retirement income.

Some people might feel that the interruption of premium payments on an ordinary life policy would in some way amount to failure to complete the program. There are, of course, situations where this might be the case. However, if the ordinary life plan is deliberately selected with the idea of discontinuing premiums at an advanced age, there can be no suggestion of failure to complete the undertaking. Neither should an insured be reluctant to convert ordinary life insurance to reduced paid-up insurance if a change of circumstance makes the reduced amount adequate for his or her needs, particularly if retirement status makes paying life insurance premiums an unjustified burden. Life insurance is designed to provide protection where the need exists. If it becomes a burden and represents a very real sacrifice on the part of the insured, the burden can be lightened when the need for protection ceases. This is an advantage of the ordinary life contract that should be recognized at the outset and utilized as the occasion arises.

Disposition of Dividends. Another source of flexibility is in the latitude provided the insured in the disposition of policyowner dividends. The insured has various options (which are analyzed in chapter 25) but two of particular interest permit the insured to use the dividends to pay up the policy or to mature it as an endowment. Either option makes it possible for the insured to discontinue premium payments within the foreseeable future, which may be a prime consideration.

Conversion. A final source of flexibility is the right to convert to other forms of insurance. It is customary to include a provision in all whole life policies giving the insured the right to exchange the policy for another type of contract, sometimes subject to certain conditions. Whether this privilege is specifically granted or not, an exchange can usually be negotiated. Virtually all companies will permit any form of permanent insurance to be converted to another form without evidence of insurability, as long as the new contract calls for a larger premium.

Most companies, however, will not permit a higher-premium contract to be exchanged for a lower-premium contract without evidence of insurability. Such an exchange not only reduces future premiums but also requires the company to return a portion of the reserve to the insured, thereby increasing the actual amount at risk. Moreover, insurers always suspect an impairment of health under such circumstances.[2] If the insured is converting to a higher-premium form, however, the net amount at risk will be reduced more rapidly, and the company does not have to fear adverse selection.

The ordinary life contract has a unique advantage in this regard because it is the lowest-premium form of fixed-premium permanent insurance and hence can be converted to any other form of permanent insurance without evidence of insurability. Therefore the insured, whose savings objective may entail substantial amounts of limited-payment insurance but whose current financial situation limits the funds available for insurance might well inaugurate his or her insurance program with ordinary life, with the idea of converting it later to higher-premium forms. If feasible, ordinary life is preferable to term insurance under such circumstances since if the more ambitious program is never realized, the insured will still have permanent protection and a modest cash surrender value. Moreover, if conversion is ultimately effected, the financial adjustment involved—whether it be the lump-sum payment of the difference in reserves or merely a shift to the higher-premium basis—will not be so drastic.

Limited-Payment Life Insurance

Limited-payment life insurance is a type of whole life insurance for which premiums are limited by contract to a specified number of years. The extreme end of the limited-payment policies spectrum is the single-premium whole life policy. However, few people can afford the premium or are willing to pay that much in advance.

The limitation in limited-payment policies may be expressed in terms of the *number* of annual premiums or of the *age* beyond which premiums will not be required. Policies whose premiums are limited by number usually stipulate 1, 5, 7, 10, 15, 20, 25, or 30 annual payments, although some companies are willing to issue policies calling for any desired number of premiums. The greater the number of premiums payable, naturally, the more closely the contract approaches the ordinary life design. For those who prefer to limit their premium payments to a period measured by a terminal age, companies make policies available that are paid up at a specified age—typically, 60, 65, or 70. The objective is to enable the insured to pay for the policy during his or her working lifetime. Many companies issue contracts for which premiums are payable to an advanced age, such as 85, but for all practical purposes, these contracts can be regarded as the equivalent of ordinary life contracts.

Since the value of a limited-payment whole life contract at the date of issue is precisely the same as that of a contract purchased on the ordinary life basis, and since it is presumed that there will be fewer premium payments under the limited-payment policy, it follows that each premium must be larger than the comparable premium under an ordinary life contract. Moreover, the fewer the guaranteed premiums specified or the shorter the premium-paying period, the higher each premium will be. However, the higher premiums are offset by greater cash and other surrender values. Thus the limited-payment policy will provide a larger fund for use in an emergency and will accumulate a larger fund for retirement purposes than will an ordinary life contract issued at the same age. On the other hand, if death takes place within the first several years after issue of the contract, the total premiums paid under the limited-payment policy will exceed those payable under an ordinary life policy. The comparatively long-lived policyowner, however, will pay considerably less in premiums under the limited-payment plan than on the ordinary life basis.

There is no presumptive financial advantage between forms. The choice depends on circumstances and personal preference. The limited-payment policy offers the *assurance* that premium payments will be confined to the insured's productive years, while the ordinary life contract provides maximum permanent protection for any given annual outlay. The limited-payment policy contains the same surrender options, dividend options, settlement options, and other features that make for significant flexibility.

An extreme form of limited-payment contract is the single-premium life insurance policy. Under this plan the number of premiums is limited to one. The effective amount of insurance protection is, of course, substantially less than the face amount of the policy, and the investment element is correspondingly greater. Such contracts therefore are purchased largely for accumulation purposes. They offer a high degree of security, a satisfactory interest yield, and ready convertibility into cash on a basis guaranteed by the insurer for the entire duration of the contract. Since the single premium represents a substantial amount of money and since it is computed on the basis that there will be no return of any part of it in the event of the insured's early death, it has only limited appeal for protection purposes.

The limited-payment principle is applicable to any type of contract and is frequently used in connection with endowment contracts. However, it is important to differentiate between a limited-payment policy (in which paid-up status is guaranteed at the end of the premium-paying period) and a vanishing-premium approach (which uses policyowner dividends to pay all of the premiums after they are adequate to do so). Vanishing-premium approaches have been sold much more frequently than limited-payment policies over the last decade. The notable difference between the two is that under the vanishing-premium approach dividends are not guaranteed and may decline in the future. If dividends turn out to be inadequate to pay the premiums, the policyowner will have to resume actual premium payments out of pocket or let the policy lapse. There is no guarantee that so-called vanishing premiums will actually vanish or that if they do vanish, they will never reappear.

JOINT-LIFE INSURANCE

The typical life insurance contract is written on the life of one person and is technically known as *single-life insurance*. A contract can be written on more than one life, however, in which event it is known as a joint-life contract, also called a first-to-die joint-life policy. Strictly speaking, a joint-life contract is one written on the lives of two or more persons and payable upon the death of the *first* person to die. If the face amount is payable upon the death of the *last* of two or more lives insured under a single contract, it is called either a survivorship policy or a second-to-die policy. Such policies have become quite popular as a means of funding federal estate taxes of wealthy couples whose wills make maximum use of tax deferral at the first death. Joint-life policies are fairly common for funding business buy-sell agreements.

The joint-life policy may cover from two to 12 lives, but because of expense and other practical obstacles, most companies limit the number to three or four lives. (Theoretically there is no limit on the number of lives that can be insured under a joint contract. A few insurers will issue policies on more than 12 lives if they all have related business interests.) The contract is most often written on the whole life plan, either ordinary life, limited-payment or universal life. It is seldom written on the term plan since separate term policies on each life for the same amount would cost little more than a joint policy and would offer the advantage of continued protection to the survivor or survivors.

The premium for a joint-life policy is somewhat greater than the combined premiums on separate policies providing an equivalent amount of insurance. In other words, the premium for a $200,000 joint-life policy covering two lives is larger than the sum of the premiums on two separate contracts providing $100,000 each. This is because only $100,000 is payable upon the death of the first of the two insureds to die with separate policies, while $200,000 is payable under a joint-life policy. Moreover, since two lives are covered, the cost of insurance is relatively high, and cash values are relatively low. However, a joint-life policy costs less than two separate policies providing $200,000 each.

The provisions of the joint-life contract closely follow those of the single-life contract. The clause allowing conversion to other policy forms differs in that it allows conversion policies on separate lives as follows: (1) conversion to single-life policies on the same plan as that of the joint policies upon divorce or dissolution of business, (2) division of the amount of insurance among the insured lives either equally or unequally, and (3) dating of the new policies as of the original date of issue of the joint policy.

Business partners sometimes take out a joint policy covering the lives of all partners and written for an amount equal to the largest interest involved. Upon the death of the first partner, the surviving partners receive funds with which to purchase the deceased's partnership interest. Stockholders in a closely held corporation may follow the same practice. Since the insurance usually terminates upon the first death of the partners or stockholders, the remaining members of the firm will not only be without insurance but—of greater consequence—may also be uninsurable.

Some life insurers have introduced joint-life policies that are designed specifically for business buy-sell funding. Some of them offer a short period of extended coverage for the surviving partners or shareholders and guarantee their insurability under a new joint-life policy similar to the previous one. A few insurers have even introduced joint-life policies that allow allocations of unequal amounts of death proceeds to match actual unequal ownership interests.

A joint-life policy may be suitable for a husband and wife when the death of either will create a need for funds, as would be true if death taxes were involved. Even here, dissatisfaction sometimes arises when the survivor faces the fact that he or she no longer has any coverage under the contract.

"SPECIAL" WHOLE LIFE POLICIES

One of the most controversial recent developments in the life insurance industry is the widespread introduction and vigorous promotion of "special" policies. Usually on the ordinary life plan, these policies carry a premium rate lower than those of the regular forms. Such policies have long been offered by many companies, but in recent years many more companies have begun to offer them to meet the growing price competition.

A company may justify a special low rate on a particular policy—which, in all other respects, is identical to the regular policy—by limiting the face to a specified *minimum amount* or by limiting its issue to *preferred risks*—that is, to groups that should experience a lower rate of mortality than that among insured lives generally because of more rigorous underwriting requirements. In some cases, both practices are factors.

The purpose of the minimum amount is to reduce the expense rate per $1,000 of insurance. Many items of expense reflected in a policy's gross premium are not affected by the policy's face amount—for example, the medical examiner's fee, inspection fee, accounting costs, and general overhead. If the average size of the policy can be increased, therefore, the expense rate per $1,000 will be lower. A class of policies in which the minimum face amount is $50,000 can be expected to develop an *average* face amount double that of the regular classes in which the minimum is $10,000. Some companies do not offer their special policy in less than a specified amount ($50,000, $100,000, $250,000, $500,000, or $1 million, for example). The savings in the expense rate alone can be quite substantial. Then, because the gross premium is lower, expenses that vary directly with the size of the premium—notably, commissions and premium taxes—will also be less per $1,000 of insurance. In fact, in many companies the commission rate on special policies is lower than that on other whole life policies.

The savings realized by superior selection depend on the nature of the standards imposed, the test of which is actual mortality experience. The potential savings are fairly large since selection standards have a significant impact on mortality rates. Furthermore, preferred-risk policies are almost always issued on a minimum-amount basis and thus reap the expense savings described above. At most ages and in most companies the difference in premiums between a special whole life policy and a regular ordinary life policy ranges from $2 to $3 per $1,000. On a multimillion-dollar policy, the savings can be very attractive.

The case for special policies is based largely on the grounds of equity. If a policyowner takes out a policy of such size that its expense rate is lower than average, or if he or she is a better risk than average, the policyowner should be given the benefit of the savings in the form of a lower premium.

The principal argument against bargain policies is the arbitrary nature of the underlying classification. For example, the reasons that justify a lower expense loading per $1,000 for a policy of $200,000 than for one of $50,000 argue just as forcefully for an even lower rate for a $1 million policy, a $2 million policy, and so on. In fact, the logical conclusion is that premium rates per $1,000 should decrease as the size of the policy increases. However desirable such a practice might be from the standpoint of equity, it would tremendously complicate the operation of the business and might, in fact, be impractical. Furthermore, limiting the expense discount to policies of $50,000 or over, or limiting it to any other arbitrary amount, is only partial recognition of the relatively lower expenses on large policies.

By the same token, if the principle of granting a lower rate to superior risks is sound, it should be extended to all other kinds of policies and not be limited to the whole life variety.[3] The soundness of the principle has been questioned in some quarters, however, on the grounds that it is contrary to the basic insurance principle of averaging. It is argued that to get average results, coverage of large groups is essential—which, from a practical standpoint, requires including people with widely varying prospects of longevity in the same group. Some insureds must bear more than their theoretically accurate share of mortality costs, while others will contribute less than their true share.

While not a part of the argument for or against special policies, it should be observed that placing larger policies or superior risks in a separate class with a lower premium rate inevitably results in a higher cost of insurance for smaller policies and insureds who cannot qualify as preferred risks.

FUNCTIONS OF WHOLE LIFE INSURANCE

At this point, the purposes served by whole life insurance should be clear. In summary, the whole life policy

- provides protection against long-range or permanent needs
- accumulates a savings fund that can be used for general purposes or to meet specific objectives

The protection function is particularly applicable to a surviving spouse's need for a life income, last-illness and funeral expenses, expenses of estate administration, death taxes, philanthropic bequests, and the needs of dependent relatives other than the surviving spouse. The general savings feature of the whole life policy is useful in a financial emergency or as a source of funds to take advantage of an unusual business or investment opportunity. The policyowner may use the policy for the specific purpose of accumulating funds for his or her children's college education, to set a child up in business, to pay for a child's wedding, or to supplement the insured's retirement income.

NOTES

1. The gross premium is the premium actually paid by the policyowner. It is the net premium increased by an allowance for the insurer's expenses and contingencies.
2. Some companies are willing to issue a policy on a lower-premium plan without evidence of insurability if the amount of insurance is increased to such an extent that the company is relieved of the obligation to refund a portion of the reserve and suffers no reduction in premium income.
3. As a matter of fact, this is now being done on an increasingly broader basis through a system of graded premiums.

5

Variations of Whole Life Insurance

Edward E. Graves

ENDOWMENT POLICIES

As mentioned previously, level premium term insurance to age 100 is identical to whole life insurance. There is also another type of life insurance that is identical to whole life insurance—endowment at age 100. However, the majority of endowment contracts mature at ages less than 100. At earlier maturity dates they are not identical to whole life policies.

Endowment life insurance policies are a variation of whole life insurance. They not only provide death benefits and cash values that increase with duration so that a policy's cash value equals its death benefit at maturity but they also allow the purchaser to specify the policy's maturity date.

A whole life contract provides a survivorship benefit at age 100 that is equal to the death benefit that would have been payable prior to the insured's age 100. Endowment contracts merely make the same full survivorship benefit payable at younger ages. Among the wide variety of endowments available are 10-, 15-, 20-, 25-, 30-, 35-, and 40-year endowments (or longer), or the maturity date can be a specific age of the insured, such as 55, 65, 70, or older.

The endowment contract was designed to provide a death benefit during an accumulation period that is equal to the target accumulation amount. Purchasing an endowment policy with a face amount equal to the desired accumulation amount assures that the funds will be available regardless of whether the insured survives the target date. The policy was popular with purchasers who were beyond the chronological midpoint of their careers and sought accumulation for retirement or other objectives. As Dr. Solomon S. Huebner often pointed out, young people prefer term life insurance; with more experience and age purchasers prefer whole life because of its level premiums; the mature market prefers endowments with the earlier cash value accumulations that they can use during their own lifetimes.

With the advent of double-digit inflation rates during the late 1970s and early 1980s, most consumers were moving away from long-term fixed-dollar contracts including nearly all forms of life insurance and particularly endowment policies. This happened in an economy where tax-sheltered investment in real estate had taken on a frenzied pitch as consumers turned to much shorter maturity contracts and investments. This was a reasonable reaction to runaway inflationary expectations.

Although endowment contracts were readily available, sales were declining in the United States even before the federal income tax law was changed in 1984 to take away the tax-free buildup of flexible-premium endowment policies' cash value. Congress was concerned that life insurance policies (especially endowment and universal life) with high cash values relative to their death benefit amounts were being used as a tax-advantaged accumulation vehicle by the wealthy. Congress had, by then, developed a dislike for any form of real or perceived tax shelter. The legislators therefore developed a test for flexible-premium life insurance. This so-called corridor test—Sec. 101(f) of the Internal Revenue Code—took away the tax preference that flexible premium endowments previously enjoyed, although it retained the preference for policies in force before 1985. Subsequently adding Sec. 7702 to the Internal Revenue Code extended the corridor test to all life insurance policies, including fixed-premium endowments, entered into after October 22, 1986. (See table 5-1.)

Since 1984, sales of new endowment contracts have been very limited. While contracts are still available from a few insurers, most new sales are for policies used in tax-qualified plans where the tax treatment is controlled by other factors.

Outside of the United States, especially in countries with high savings rates, however, the endowment policy is still quite successful and widely purchased to accumulate funds for a variety of purposes. It is frequently purchased to fund retirement and sometimes to fund children's higher education.

It is interesting to note that endowment policies purchased in other countries are usually bought for the same reasons permanent life insurance policies are purchased in the United States. Regardless of the society or its tax laws, the primary factor motivating life insurance sales is an individual's concern about financial security for his or her children, spouse, parents, and/or business partners. The individual's particular needs tend to change in predictable ways over a normal life cycle.

ADJUSTABLE LIFE INSURANCE

Families' changing needs for life insurance over long durations prompted some insurers to introduce whole life insurance that can be adjusted when needed to accommodate life cycle shifts. The adjustable life policy—a typical whole life policy at any time it is in force—gives the policyowner the right to request and obtain a reconfiguration of the policy at specified intervals. It appeals to purchasers who want the ability to restructure their coverage without assuming any of the investment or mortality risks. Adjustable life insurance policies offer all of the same guarantees regarding cash values, mortality, and expenses as traditional whole life policies do. The elements subject to change are the premium, face amount, and cash value. Most changes can be made without evidence of insurability, but the insurer can require such evidence if the proposed change increases the amount at risk.

Events that frequently prompt policy adjustments include dependent children's starting private school or entering college, the self-sufficiency of the youngest child(ren), loss of employment, the start of a new business venture, failure of a business, change of career, or retirement. As you might surmise, a large proportion of adjustments involve lowering the premium level to lessen the cash flow burden during prolonged reductions in income, increases in expenses, or both. Empty nesters, on the other hand, may request a change that increases premiums because they can often redirect their income after their children are grown.

TABLE 5-1
Corridor Test for Cash Value Life Insurance

Age	Death Benefit Must Exceed Cash Value by This Multiple	Cash Value May Not Exceed This % of Death Benefit
0 to 40	2.50	0.40
41	2.43	0.41
42	2.36	0.42
43	2.29	0.44
44	2.22	0.45
45	2.15	0.47
46	2.09	0.48
47	2.03	0.49
48	1.97	0.51
49	1.91	0.52
50	1.85	0.54
51	1.78	0.56
52	1.71	0.58
53	1.64	0.61
54	1.57	0.64
55	1.50	0.67
56	1.46	0.68
57	1.42	0.70
58	1.38	0.72
59	1.34	0.75
60	1.30	0.77
61	1.28	0.78
62	1.26	0.79
63	1.24	0.81
64	1.22	0.82
65	1.20	0.83
66	1.19	0.84
67	1.18	0.85
68	1.17	0.85
69	1.16	0.86
70	1.15	0.87
71	1.13	0.88
72	1.11	0.90
73	1.09	0.92
74	1.07	0.93
75 to 90	1.05	0.95
91	1.04	0.96
92	1.03	0.97
93	1.02	0.98
94	1.01	0.99
95	1.00	1.00

Source: IRC Sec. 7702(d)(2)

POLICY DIAGRAMS

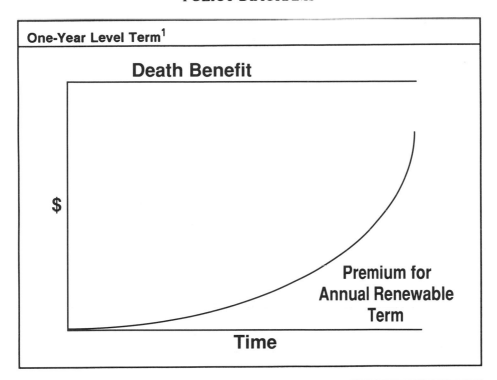

One-Year Level Term[1]

Death Benefit

$

Premium for
Annual Renewable
Term

Time

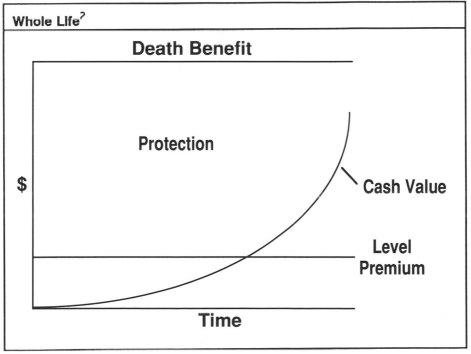

Whole Life[2]

Death Benefit

$

Protection

Cash Value

Level
Premium

Time

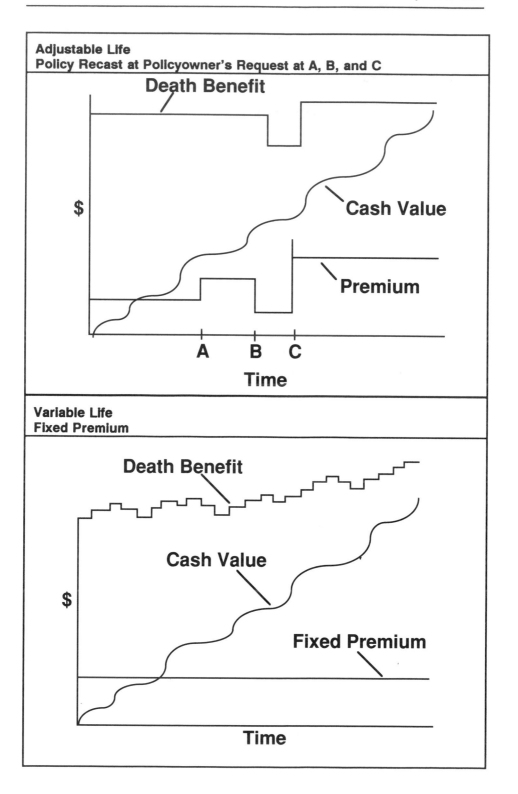

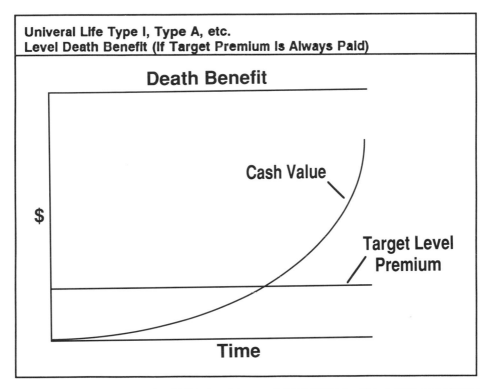

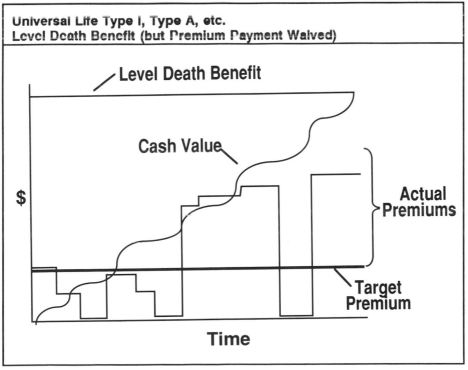

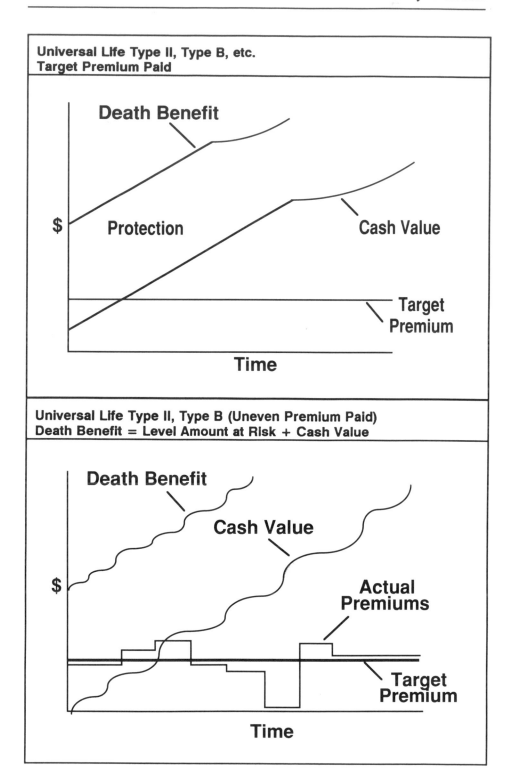

Universal Life Type II, Type B, etc.
Target Premium Paid

Death Benefit

Protection

$

Cash Value

Target
Premium

Time

Universal Life Type II, Type B (Uneven Premium Paid)
Death Benefit = Level Amount at Risk + Cash Value

Death Benefit

Cash Value

$

Actual
Premiums

Target
Premium

Time

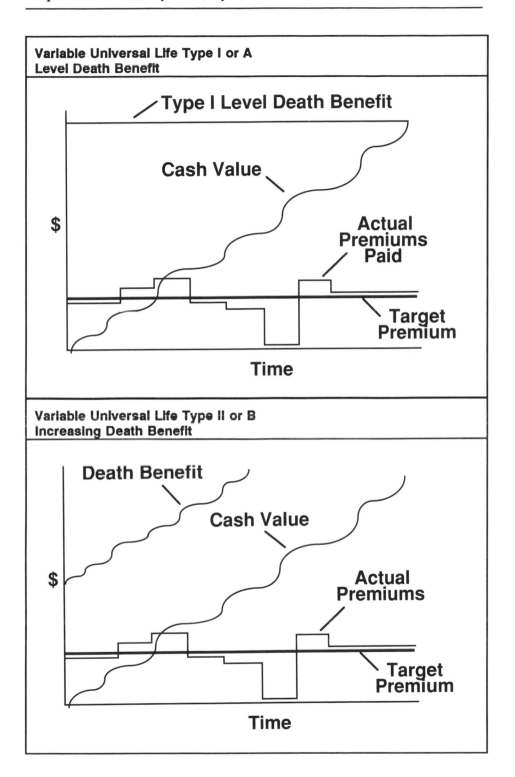

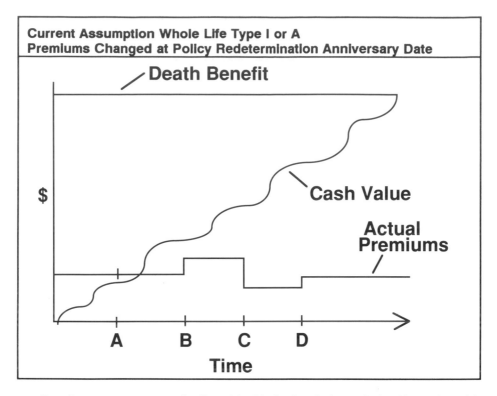

Current Assumption Whole Life Type I or A
Premiums Changed at Policy Redetermination Anniversary Date

Death Benefit

$

Cash Value

Actual
Premiums

A   B   C   D

Time

One important aspect of adjustable life is that it is a whole life policy with fixed premiums. Although premiums can be changed, such a change requires a formal adjustment agreed to by both insurer and policyowner before it can be made. The premium remains fixed and inflexible between formal adjustments.

This policy was introduced in the mid-1970s and had gained modest success with a few insurers before the advent of universal life policies. Interest in adjustable life waned after the runaway success of universal life in the 1980s. Some of the insurers that maintained adjustable life as part of their product line, however, found that it had renewed acceptability after universal life lost its predominant share of new product sales in the low-interest environment of the early 1990s.

Unfortunately the terminology that has developed to describe adjustable life and universal life has been confusing. Many insurers have used the word adjustable in the title or name for their universal life policies. Consequently many agents have come to regard adjustable life as simply an alternate name for universal life. Many of them are unaware that generic adjustable life policies predate universal life.

VARIABLE LIFE INSURANCE

Adjustable life insurance was one of two major life insurance variations introduced in the decade before universal life insurance. The other, which was introduced in 1976, is variable life insurance, the first life insurance policy designed to shift the investment risk to policyowners. This product had a long and expensive gestation period. It not only had to run the gauntlet of state insurance department approvals but it also needed (and finally acquired after many years of negotiations) approval by the Securities and Exchange Commission (SEC).

A variable life insurance policy provides no guarantees of either interest rate or minimum cash value. Theoretically the cash value can go down to zero, and if so, the policy will terminate. As the SEC pointed out, in order for policyowners to gain the additional benefit of better-than-expected investment returns, they also have to assume all of the downside investment risk. Consequently, the SEC required variable life policies to be registered with the SEC and all sales to be subject to the requirements applicable to other registered securities. In other words, policy sales can be made only after the prospective purchaser has a chance to read the policy prospectus. The SEC also requires that the insurance company be registered as an investment company and that all sales agents be registered with the SEC for the specific purpose of variable life insurance policy sales. Agents who sell variable life insurance policies must be licensed as both life insurance agents and securities agents.

SEC Objections to Variable Life

There were two main stumbling blocks in gaining SEC approval of variable life products. The first one was the maximum compensation to agents for the sale of this product. The SEC wanted the sales load not to exceed 8 percent of the sale price. Keeping in mind that most securities are sold on a cash-sale basis rather than on an installment-sale basis, this presented some serious drawbacks from the insurance companies' standpoint. The insurance companies and the SEC finally compromised on a 20 percent load on the first year's premiums. This was argued to be the equivalent of an 8 percent load over the lifetime of the policy.

The other major stumbling block had to do with whether or not insurance companies would be permitted to allow flexible-premium payments under these policies. Initially the SEC did not relent on this issue. Therefore the first generation of variable life insurance products were fixed-premium products, and the only real innovation was the variable investment aspect—that is, the policyowner was permitted to select among a limited number of investment portfolio choices, with the death benefit amount varying as a function of the portfolio's investment performance.

Investment Choices

Generally the first generation of variable life insurance policies gave the purchaser three investment options into which the funds could be directed. The policyowner was free to put all of the funds into one of these choices or to distribute the funds in whatever proportions he or she desired among the three options. There was usually a minimum requirement of at least 5 or 10 percent of incoming funds that had to be allocated to any investment option the policyowner selected. The purpose of this minimum requirement was to eliminate administrative costs that exceeded the amount of money being directed into a particular option.

Very often the options were a stock fund, a bond fund, and either a treasury fund or a money market fund. The funds were essentially mutual funds run by the insurance company and set aside as separate accounts (required by the SEC) that do not constitute part of the insurance company's general investment fund and put such assets beyond the claims of its general creditors. These separate funds have to be reported as separate items on the insurance company financial statements for both statutory purposes and generally accepted accounting purposes. (Stock insurance companies must issue both types of reports; mutual companies are only required to issue statutory reports. See chapters 30 and 31 for a discussion of life insurance company financial statements.)

By allowing the policyowner to direct the funds backing the policy, the policyowner becomes the portfolio director, within limits. Obviously the policyowner has no control over what assets are purchased and sold by the individual funds that can be selected. That portion of the investment decision process is still within the hands of the insurance company's portfolio management team. The important thing is that the policyowner plays a participative role in portfolio management and consequently can benefit directly from better-than-expected results or bear the full brunt of poor investment performance. The results of the investment performance are credited directly to the policy cash values.

Ability to Tolerate Risk

Individuals who are already experienced in equity investments are quite comfortable with the variable life insurance policy. However, this policy is subject to daily portfolio fluctuations and can provoke great anxiety in individuals who are not used to or comfortable with such market value fluctuations.

Part of the challenge of marketing variable life policies is this volatility. Many life insurance agents are reluctant to try to sell any policy whose success depends on the investment decisions of the policyowner. They are afraid that some purchasers will expect the life insurance agent to give them investment advice.

A variable life policy is a market-driven phenomenon, and to some extent its popularity is influenced by general investment market conditions. The policy becomes more acceptable to consumers after a long period of market increases and falls out of favor when the market experiences a general decline in prices. In the early 1990s when interest rates dropped to very low levels, people used to higher yields on bonds and other investment instruments turned to variable life insurance contracts as one alternative to reinvesting in certificates of deposit.

Insurance Charges

Assuming the right investment choices are made, variable life insurance allows the policyowner's money to work harder for him or her. But variable life insurance contracts are not exclusively investments. They are in fact life insurance contracts, and they sustain mortality charges for the death benefits they provide. Consequently, the return on the invested funds within a variable life insurance contract will never equal that of a separate investment fund that does not provide death benefits but invests in assets of a similar type and quality.

Variable life insurance should not be purchased as a short-term investment vehicle. The combination of sales load, mortality charges, and surrender charges will significantly reduce any potential gains in the policy's early years.

Linkage of Death Benefits with Investment Performance

Since the primary reason for life insurance is to provide death benefits, it makes sense to link superior investment performance with increases in the death benefit level. Theoretically this is a way of keeping up with inflation. In fact, studies indicate that such a linkage would more than keep pace with inflation. However, there is an important caveat. Although investment performance in equities tends to equal or exceed inflation in the economy over the long term, the correlation is not perfect in the short term. In other words, it is possible for inflation to exceed increases in the investment performance for short durations of time (possibly 2 or 3 years). This is another reason why life insurance should be looked at as a long-term financial security purchase and not a short-term investment.

There is more than one way to link the policy's death benefit to the associated portfolio's investment performance. In the early generation of fixed-premium variable life insurance contracts insurance companies settled on two different approaches — the level additions method or the constant ratio method.

Regardless of which linkage design was chosen, all of the early contracts had the purchaser select a target level of investment performance as a benchmark against which actual investment performance would be measured. Performance in excess of the target level would be used to fund incremental increases in the death benefit; performance below the target amount would require downward adjustments in the death benefits to make up for the deficit.

Level Additions Model

The level additions model uses excess investment returns (return in excess of the target rate) to purchase a level single-premium addition to the base policy. The face amount or death benefit will rise as long as investment performance equals or exceeds the target rate. This model does not cause as rapid an increase or decrease as the constant ratio method of linking the policy's death benefit to investment performance. The strength of the level addition design is that it does not require an ever-increasing investment return to support incremental increases in death benefits. Additional coverage is added more slowly, but it is more easily supported once it is added. Similarly, downward adjustments in death benefits are less rapid, and they are less likely to accelerate in future years. Furthermore, policies using the level additions design provide a minimum base value guarantee equal to the amount of coverage when the policy was first purchased.

Constant Ratio Method

The constant ratio method also uses the excess investment earnings as a net single premium to purchase a paid-up additional amount of coverage. The difference is that under this method the paid-up additional coverage is not a level benefit amount but a decreasing benefit amount because it is designed to maintain a ratio between the death benefit and the policy reserve that satisfies the corridor test. Under this policy design more volatile increments are added to or subtracted from the contract as investment performance differs from the target amount.

Like the level addition model, this design has a minimum death benefit guarantee equal to the initial face amount of the policy. Consequently, if the initial stage of the contract has lower returns than the target level, the policy reserves will drop below the level necessary to sustain the guaranteed death benefit amount. The policy will have to remain in force for the investment returns to exceed the target rate for a long enough period to bring the reserve back up to a level capable of supporting incremental increases in coverage before the policyowner will see increases in the death benefit.

Usually variable life policies have positive excess investment earnings in the early years of the contract and do provide incremental increases in the death benefit before the investment earnings drop below the target rate. Looking at variable life insurance policies since 1976, most policies have experienced investment earnings over the target rate more frequently and for longer durations than they have experienced investment earnings below the target rate. There is no guarantee that this will always be true, but the expectation is that overall investment earnings will exceed the target amount over the bulk of the policy duration. Many variable life policyowners have been pleasantly surprised at how well their policies have done over two decades.

In the long run, regardless of the policy design, the excess investment earnings over the target level must support any incremental additions to the policy. If investment earnings are negative (the actual earnings are lower than the target rate), then the adjustments will have to be downward from any previously attained levels above the policy's initial face value. If investment earnings are positive (the actual earnings are above the target rate), the adjustments will be upward.

Increased Number of Investment Fund Options

Variable life insurance designs have not been static since their introduction in the mid-1970s. Life insurance companies are now offering many more investment fund options than they made available in the early stages of this product's development. Some insurance companies have more than a dozen funds to choose from in their current product offering. There are usually a variety of stock funds, including growth stock funds, income stock funds, balanced stock funds, and international stock funds. Bond fund offerings are likewise more robust and include different durations and different types of issuers (large corporations, small corporations, state governments, and federal government) as well as Government National Mortgage Association (GNMAs) funds and collateralized mortgage obligations (CMOs).

In addition, many insurance companies offer a managed fund as one of the portfolio choices. The policyowner can put all of the policy funds in a managed portfolio fund and have the investment allocation decisions made by a professional money manager working for the insurance company. This appeals to policyowners who do not want to spend a lot of time studying the market and making investment decisions. With a managed portfolio policyowners can reap all of the long-term advantages of a variable insurance contract without having to perform the investment allocation function themselves.

Some insurance companies have even formed alliances with large mutual fund groups that make their entire range of mutual funds available. Such alliances make it possible for smaller life insurance companies to gain access to the administrative services already in place in these large mutual fund family groups.

Policy Cash Values

Policy premiums paid under variable life insurance contracts are often subject to an administrative charge; the balance of the premium payment goes into the cash value account. The actual value of the cash component is determined by the net asset value of the separate account funds that make up the policy portfolio. The cash value of a variable life policy fluctuates daily. Each day's net asset value is based on the closing price for the issues in the portfolio on that trading day. Cash value accounts are further diminished by mortality charges to support the death benefits.

As with traditional life insurance contracts, the policyowner has access to the cash value via policy loans. Variable life insurance policies usually limit maximum policy loans to a slightly smaller percentage of the total cash value than is traditionally available in whole life policies.

The earnings on the cash value are obviously affected by any outstanding policy loans. The policyowner accrues indebtedness at the applicable policy loan interest rate, and that is the yield applicable to the assets associated with the portion of the cash value offset by the outstanding loan. Whenever the policy loan interest rate is lower than the portfolio investment earnings rate, the insurance company experiences a lower effective investment return. The only time the insurance company experiences a financial gain from policy loans is when the policy loan interest rate exceeds that earned by the portfolio backing the policies.

Policy loans can be repaid at any time in part or in full, but there is no requirement that policy loans be repaid in cash at any time during the existence of the life insurance contract. For any portion of the loan not repaid interest accrues on a compound basis. Just as in any other form of whole life policy, outstanding policy loans under a variable life insurance policy reduce the death benefit payable. The policy loan is always fully secured by the remaining cash value in the policy. Whenever the outstanding loans plus accrued interest equal the remaining cash value, the net cash value becomes zero and the policy terminates.

The net cash value in the contract is also closely related to the nonforfeiture options available under the policy. Variable life insurance contracts provide the same range of nonforfeiture options as do traditional whole life policies. The net cash surrender value can be obtained by surrendering the contract to the insurance company, or the net cash value can be applied as a single premium to purchase either a reduced amount of paid-up insurance or the same amount of extended term insurance. The duration of the extended term insurance will be the longest period of coverage for the same death benefit amount that can be obtained from the insurance company for the policy's net cash value.

Variable life insurance policies also contain the usual form of reinstatement provisions, including a specific prohibition on reinstatements if the policy has been surrendered for its cash value. Contracts also have the standard waiver-of-premium option since premiums are fixed and the policy will lapse if they are not paid.

The Prospectus

Variable life insurance policies cannot be sold without an accompanying prospectus. The prospectus mandated by the SEC is similar in many respects to the prospectus required of new stock issues. It is a full disclosure of all of the provisions of the contract, including expenses, investment options, benefit provisions, and policyowner rights under the contract. It is a lengthy and detailed document. Most purchasers are reluctant to read the entire document, but it is an important source of information that is not available anywhere else. In fact, one of the authors of this book has observed that the prospectus for a variable life insurance contract offers more information to prospective purchasers than even very aggressive information seekers can obtain for traditional life insurance contracts.

As always, the SEC focus is on providing thorough and accurate information. The prospectus for a new stock issue from a stock life insurance company therefore provides more information about the company to potential investors than would ever be available to purchasers of life insurance products (except for SEC registered variable and variable universal life).

Expense Information

The prospectus has very thorough information about all of the expense charges levied by the insurance company against variable life insurance contracts. This includes commissions paid to soliciting agents, state premium taxes, administrative charges, collection charges, and possibly fees for specific future transactions.

Administrative charges usually differ between the first year of the contract and all renewal years. It is common for first-year administrative charges to run in the neighborhood of $15 to $50 per month. The same administrative charges in the second policy year and thereafter drop to a lower level, perhaps $5 to $10 per month. The prospectus also indicates whether or not there is any maximum guarantee on those administrative fees over the duration of the contract.

In addition, the prospectus sets forth the manner in which charges are made against the asset account to cover the cost of insurance under the contract. This is usually referred to in the prospectus as the *cost-of-insurance charge*. The prospectus specifies exactly what rate will be used to determine cost-of-insurance charges and explicitly specifies if there is any maximum rate above the intended rate. It also explains the manner in which charges are levied against the separate account itself—essentially the fees associated with managing the various mutual fund type of accounts from which the policyowner can choose. Part of that charge is always some specified percentage (usually less than one full percent) of the assets in the separate accounts themselves. There also may be specific charges to establish and maintain trusts necessary in managing those assets. These charges are very similar to the charges levied by mutual fund administrators on investors in the fund.

Surrender Charges

One very important item that is clearly spelled out in the prospectus and should always be considered important information when considering the purchase of any life insurance policy—variable or traditional—is the surrender charge applicable to policy surrenders. In most cases this information is set forth in a tabular form, giving the policy year and the applicable percentage for the surrender charge in that year. Under some contract designs the surrender charge is specified in terms of percentage of premiums; under other contracts it is specified in terms of the aggregate account balance in the separate funds. Surrender charges are applicable only if the policy is surrendered for its cash value, allowed to lapse, or under some contracts if the policy is adjusted to provide a lower death benefit. Surrender charges are commonly levied during the first 10 to 15 years of the contract. The actual number of years and specific rates are always set forth in the prospectus.

The maximum duration of surrender charges is usually a good indicator of how long the insurer intends to amortize excess first-year acquisition costs. The surrender charge is applicable only to policies surrendered before the insurance company's front-end expenses have been recovered. Sometimes these surrender charges are called contingent deferred sales charges.

Investment Portfolio Information

The prospectus sets forth the investment objectives of each of the available investment funds and a record of their historical performance. There is detailed information on the current holdings of each of the available portfolios, usually supplemented by information about purchases and sales of individual equities or debt instruments by the fund over the previous 12 months. Further information is given about earnings during that same period of time and usually for longer intervals of prior performance if those portfolio funds have been in existence long enough to give investment results for trades over 5 or 10 years. Any investment restrictions applicable to these portfolios as indicated in the trust instruments themselves are fully disclosed.

There are also projections of future performance under the contract if portfolio funds generate a fixed level of investment earnings over the projected interval. Under SEC regulations the permissible rates of return that can be projected are the gross annual rates after tax charges but before any other deductions at 0, 4, 6, 8, 10, or 12 percent. The insurance company can decide which of those permissible rates it chooses to project.

Much of the detailed information in the prospectus concerns ownership and voting rights regarding procedures to change any of the trust documents or restrictions. These elements are very similar to those found in self-standing mutual funds not associated or affiliated with life insurance policies or protection.

Risks the Policyowner Assumes

As mentioned earlier, fixed-premium variable life insurance contracts are very similar to whole life insurance contracts; the main difference is that the policyowner assumes the investment risk and therefore can participate in favorable investment returns. The fixed-premium provision does not allow the policyowner to increase or decrease the death benefit by negotiated adjustment; favorable results automatically translate into increased death benefit amounts.

One unique benefit is that the policy does guarantee a minimum death benefit level equal to the original face amount of the contract, regardless of how badly the investment performance turns out to be. In other words, if all of the required premiums are paid, the insurance company guarantees that the death benefit equal to the original face amount of the policy will be paid even if the investment funds are otherwise inadequate to support the policy. Therefore the variable feature of this contract can provide additional coverage if investment experience warrants, but the policyowner will never be required to pay more or permitted to pay less than the guaranteed premium.

A fixed-premium variable life insurance policy provides more guarantees to the policyowner than its more recently developed cousins with truly flexible provisions, such as universal life and variable universal life.

VARIABLE ADJUSTABLE LIFE INSURANCE

The same companies that developed adjustable life contracts subsequently developed a variation on that contract—variable adjustable life. As its name suggests, this coverage is an adjustable life policy that can be negotiated to change the death benefit level up or down, increase or decrease premium amounts to a new fixed level, and/or shorten or lengthen the premium-paying period. The new feature is, of course, the policyowner's ability to choose the investment portfolio, within limits. This contract actually overcomes one of the shortcomings of the fixed-premium variable life contract by allowing the policyowner to negotiate with the insurance company a changed policy configuration that more closely fits the policyowner's changed circumstances.

The policyowner does not have the unilateral right to skip premium payments or vary the amount of any one premium payment at will without prior negotiation with the insurance company. As with the first generation of variable life insurance contracts, the death benefit is tied to investment performance but guaranteed never to be less than the original amount of coverage under the policy.

Most of the insurance companies offering variable adjustable life coverage chose not to enter the universal life market. In fact, they introduced variable adjustable life insurance as a defensive move to enhance their competitiveness after the marketing success of universal life with its flexible-premium design.

UNIVERSAL LIFE INSURANCE

Universal life insurance was introduced in 1979 as a revolutionary new product. It was the first variation of whole life insurance to offer truly flexible premiums. It also included adjustment provisions similar to those contained in the adjustable life contract. These policies shifted some of the investment risk to the policyowner, but they did not give the policyowner any option to direct the investment portfolio. Two other features initiated with universal life policies: (1) the policyowner's ability to withdraw part of the cash value without having the withdrawal treated as a policy loan and (2) the choice of either a level death benefit design or an increasing death benefit design.

The economic conditions of the early 1980s were a perfect incubator for the universal life variation of whole life. The economy was experiencing extremely high inflation rates and very high nominal rates of investment return. The real rate of return, however (nominal rate of return minus inflation rate), was quite low. Inflationary expectations were so rampant that investors were avoiding long-term investments, and the demand for short-term investments was outstripping the supply of funds, leading to what is known as a *reverse yield curve* (the cost of borrowing short-term funds is actually higher than the cost of borrowing for long-term mortgages). During more normal economic conditions, higher rates for borrowing are associated with longer-term investments, and lower rates are associated with the shortest investment durations.

Both short-term investment returns and inflation were hovering near 20 percent annual rates. This prompted many policyowners with traditional life insurance contracts to pull the cash value out of their existing life insurance contracts via policy loans or policy surrenders and invest the funds directly in these new high-yield investments. This process is commonly referred to as *disintermediation.*

Life insurance companies were looking for a way to stem this outflow of funds that was forcing many of them to liquidate some of their long-term investments at a loss to honor policyowner requests. In such an inflationary environment the traditional fixed-dollar life insurance contract lost much of its appeal.

Stock insurance companies were the first ones to introduce universal life policies. Mutual insurance companies were concerned that federal income tax law precluded them from offering universal life insurance policies; mutual insurance companies that introduced universal life insurance usually formed a downstream subsidiary stock insurance company with the parent mutual insurance company controlling the subsidiary. (See chapter 28 for a discussion of holding companies.)

The real advantage was that nearly every insurance company introducing a universal life policy did so through a brand-new company that invested all of its assets into a new money portfolio and earned very high short-term investment yields. These yields seemed astronomical when compared with the yields being earned by traditional life insurance companies with long-term investment portfolios. Although the tremendous immediate advantage of higher yields could not persist over the entire duration of the life insurance contract, it was successfully exploited in the marketplace for the few years it lasted.

After normal investment conditions returned and yields dropped to lower levels, the universal life policies decreased in popularity. Insurers selling universal life insurance started investing in longer-term assets to increase their returns, and the total portfolios associated with universal life policies became very similar to those of seasoned insurance companies with large blocks of traditional whole life policies in force.

Flexible Premiums

The true innovation of universal life insurance was the introduction of completely flexible premiums after the first policy year, the only time a minimum level of premium payments for a universal life policy is rigidly required. As usual, the first year's premium can be arranged on a monthly, quarterly, semiannual, or annual basis. The insurance company requires only that a minimum specified level of first-year premium payments be equaled or exceeded. After the first policy year, it is completely up to the policyowner as to how much premium to pay and even whether or not to pay premiums.

Of course this sounds too good to be true. If only one year's premium needs to be paid and the policyowner can skip all other premium payments, life insurance would be free for all years after the first. To the contrary, the aggregate premiums paid, regardless of their timing, must be adequate to cover the costs of maintaining the policy. Consider the analogy of an automobile's gas tank, where premium payments are synonymous with filling the tank. Premium payments (tank refills) can be made frequently to keep the tank nearly full at all times. With that approach the automobile is never likely to run out of gas. The same automobile, however, can operate on a just-in-time philosophy, where premium payments of minimal amounts are made only as frequently as necessary to keep the car from running out of gas. The vehicle operator has full discretion in deciding how to maintain an adequate amount of gasoline in the car. If the operator fails to keep enough gas in the tank, the vehicle may run out of gas and be inoperable until the tank can be refilled. Likewise, under a universal life insurance policy, if the policy cash value is allowed to drop too low (the cash value is inadequate to cover the next 60 days of expense and mortality charges), the policy will lapse. If an additional premium payment is made soon enough, the policy may be restarted without a formal reinstatement process. However, if an injection of additional funds comes after the end of the grace period, the insurance company may force the policyowner to request a formal reinstatement before accepting any further premium payments.

Prefunding

With the advent of universal life insurance the insurance company shifted the investment risk to the policyowner by asking the policyowner to determine the amount, if any, of prefunding. The policyowner can pay maximum premiums and maintain a very high cash value (keeping the automobile gas tank full at all times). On the other hand, the policyowner can pay minimal premiums and just barely cover the mortality and expense charges because there is little or no prefunding (constantly run near empty).

The higher the amount or proportion of prefunding, the more investment earnings will be utilized to cover policy expenses. This gets down to the basic adage that there are two sources of money: people at work and money at work. By putting money into the policy early, the money starts earning money and therefore reduces the amount of premium payments needed from people at work at later policy durations. The ultimate extreme of prefunding is the single-premium approach, where an adequate fund is created at the inception of the policy to cover all future costs. The more common approach is a level premium structure in which partial prefunding creates an ever-increasing cash value that in turn generates increasing investment returns to offset mortality and administrative costs.

At the other end of the spectrum is the minimum-premium approach, which is virtually synonymous with annual renewal term insurance. There is minimal, if any, prefunding, and premium payments barely cover the current mortality and expense charges. Under this approach the premiums must increase as the insured ages since mortality rates increase with the age of the insured. Premiums increase rapidly at advanced ages because there is still a maximum amount at risk (the cash value is very low, and the mortality rate must be applied to nearly the full death benefit amount). Under the partial prefunding approach, however, cash value increases make the amount at risk decrease (amount at risk equals the policy's face amount minus its cash value) as the insured ages, and the increasing mortality rate is applied to a smaller at risk amount.

Under traditional whole life insurance policies insurance companies designed a wide range of level premium contracts, each with a different level of fixed premiums. Contracts with a higher level premium tended to develop larger cash values at earlier policy durations. Once the policy cash value was adequate to prefund the policy totally, the policy could be converted to a guaranteed paid-up status. Under participating designs, dividends could exceed the premiums once the policy had developed a large enough cash value to prefund all future policy elements.

A lot of the misunderstanding of life insurance stems from the investment component of policy prefunding. A one-half percent increase in investment earnings at each policy duration is sufficient to justify a discernible lower gross premium. The difficulty comes in trying to predict what level of investment earnings will actually be developed. It is highly unlikely that investment earnings rates will always increase. The only safe thing to predict is that future investment earnings rates will change. Some of those changes will be downward, and no one knows for sure what the actual pattern will be.

As noted earlier, in the past policies have generally done much better than the guaranteed amounts. However, because few policyowners discuss life insurance with their friends, the general public is not aware of how much actual performance has exceeded guaranteed or expected levels. In a recent article about the 50th policy year of a whole life policy issued by a company that charges high premiums and generates high early cash values, a policyowner observed that his policy now provides more than five times the original death benefit. The cash value in the policy is more than four times the value of all premiums paid over the 50 years. This particular policy is a participating policy, and the policyowner dividends are now greater than 13 times the annual premium.

It is unlikely that the positive deviations from the guarantees over the next 50 years will be as strong as those mentioned here for the last 50 years. The intense competition and resulting premium reductions have drastically decreased the cash value build-up in the early policy years.

Prudent insurance management requires insurers to seek maximum prefunding before granting any sort of premium reduction or elimination. This is necessary to ensure that the insurance company has adequate funds on hand to honor the promises under the contract even in the worst possible economic conditions in the future. Otherwise, the insurance company will not have enough funds in case that worst-case scenario actually occurs.

Insurance companies are no better than economists (or any other group) at predicting future interest rates and investment returns. But the insurance contract is highly dependent on those returns. If they are high enough, the insurance company can return part of the premiums. If they are not, the insurer may need all of the investment returns and still have difficulty meeting the promises in the contract. Philosophically and economically it is justifiable to have more premium money collected up front rather than delaying the collection of funds in the hope that rosy economic conditions will prevail in the future.

Under the traditional contracts the only mechanism for returning any policy overfunding in the early years was policyowner dividends. With universal life policies, however, the accumulations from prefunding are credited to the policy's cash value and are quite visible to the policyowner. The earnings rates applied to those accumulations are also clearly visible as they fluctuate with current economic conditions. This open disclosure for universal life policies eliminates some of the doubts about fair treatment often directed at whole life insurance.

Withdrawal Feature

As noted above, another new feature introduced with universal life policies is the policyowner's ability to make partial withdrawals from the policy's cash value without incurring any indebtedness. In other words, money can be taken out of the policy cash value just like a withdrawal from a savings bank, and there is no obligation to repay those funds; nor is there any incurring interest on the amount withdrawn. Withdrawals do affect the policy's future earnings because the fund still intact to earn interest for future crediting periods is reduced by the amount of the withdrawal. Its effect on the death benefit depends on the type of death benefit in force. (This will be discussed later in the chapter.)

Target Premium Amount

Nearly every universal life policy is issued with a target premium amount. The target amount is the suggested premium to be paid on a level basis throughout the contract's duration or for a shorter period of time if a limited-pay approach was originally intended to fund the policy. The target premium amount is merely a suggestion and carries no liability if it is inadequate to maintain the contract to any duration, much less to the end of life.

In some insurance companies that target premium is actually sufficient to keep the policy in force (under relatively conservative investment return assumptions) through age 95 or 100 and to pay the cash value equivalent to the death benefit amount if the insured survives either age 95 or 100. On the other hand, some companies with a more aggressive marketing stance have chosen lower target premiums, which are not adequate to carry the policy in force to advanced ages even under more generous (and of questionable validity) assumptions of higher investment returns over future policy years. If in fact the investment return credited to the policy cash value falls short of the amounts assumed in deriving the target premium, the policy may essentially run out of gas before age 95 or 100.

In cases where the policy does run out of gas, the policyowner will be faced with two options: (1) to increase the premium level or (2) to reduce the death benefit amount. Neither one of these options is necessarily desirable, but they are the only acceptable ways under the contract's provisions to correct for unfulfilled optimistic assumptions about investment returns in the contract's early years.

Some insurance companies have introduced a secondary guarantee associated with their target premium. These companies have pledged contractually to keep the policy in force for, say, 15 or 20 years and to pay the full death benefit as long as the target premium has been paid in an amount equal to or greater than the target premium amount at each suggested premium-payment interval. Even these guarantees do not extend to age 95 or 100, but they are at least a guarantee that the premium suggested as a target will be adequate to provide the coverage at least as long as the guarantee period. Probably the best indication of whether or not the target premium is adequate to keep the policy in force up through age 95 or 100 is to compare it with premiums for a traditional whole life policy of a similar face amount and issue age. Universal life policy target premiums less than premiums for a comparable whole life policy should be suspect; they may be intentionally low by design because the insurance company does not expect the policy to remain in force until the very end of life in the majority of cases. The only people who will ever really find out whether or not their policy target premiums are adequate are those who pay the premiums religiously throughout the duration of the contract and live to be an age that is old enough to test the target premium.

Additional Premium Payments

The flexible features of universal life premiums allow policyowners to make additional premium payments above any target premium amount at any time the policyowner desires without prior negotiation or agreement with the insurance company. (The only limitation on paying excess premiums is associated with the income tax definition of life insurance.) However, the insurance company reserves the right to refuse additional premium payments under a universal life policy if the policy's cash value is large enough to encroach upon the upper limit for cash values relative to the level of death benefit granted in the policy.

Skipped Payments or Payments Lower than Target Premium

The premium flexibility also allows the policyowner to skip premium payments, again without any prior negotiation or notification, or to pay premium amounts lower than the target premium suggested at the time of purchase. The lower limitations on premium payments have two constraints. The first is that nearly every company specifies a minimum acceptable amount for any single payment. This is easy to understand in that a check for $.50 is likely to generate $5 to $10 (or more) in processing costs. Insurance companies usually set this minimum amount per transaction at a level above their estimated cost of processing such a transaction.

The other constraint for minimum premium payments has to do with whether or not there is enough cash value in the contract to meet the mortality and administrative charges for the next 60 days. In other words, if the tank is running on empty, more premium is required. This constraint is also easily justified.

Death Benefit Type

As mentioned earlier, universal life insurance gives policyowners a choice between level death benefits and increasing death benefits. The level death benefit design is much like the traditional whole life design. When the death benefit stays constant and the cash value increases over the duration of the contract, the amount at risk or the protection element decreases. The one new aspect of a level death benefit designed under universal life policies is not really a function of universal life itself but a function of a tax law definition of life insurance that was added to the Code shortly after the introduction of universal life insurance policies, requiring that a specified proportion of the death benefit is derived from the amount at risk. Whenever the cash value in the contract gets high enough that this proportion is no longer satisfied, the universal life policy starts increasing the death benefit even though the contract is called a level death benefit contract. This phenomenon does not occur until ages beyond normal retirement, and it is not a significant aspect of this design.

The increasing death benefit is a modification that was introduced with universal life policies. Put quite simply, under this approach there is always a constant amount at risk that is superimposed over the policy's cash value, whatever it may be. As the cash value increases, so does the total death benefit payable under the contract. This design pays both the policy's stated face amount and its cash value as benefits at the insured's death. Policies with an increasing death benefit design overcome the criticism of whole life policies that the death benefit is partially made up of the contract's cash value portion. By selecting the increasing death benefit option under a universal life policy the policyowner is ensuring that the death benefit will be composed of the cash value and an at-risk portion equal to the original face value of the contract.

There is nothing magical about this larger death benefit amount. As is said often, there is no free lunch. The policyowner pays a higher premium for the larger amount at risk under this design.

There are similarities between the increasing death benefit design for universal life and the paid-up additions option under a participating whole life policy. Under a whole life policy dividends are used to purchase single-premium additions to the base policy. In both types of policies the excess investment earnings are used to increase the cash value and the death benefit.

Because the mechanics of the two death benefit designs and the universal life policies are slightly different, the effect of partial withdrawals on the death benefit amount differs. Partial withdrawals do not reduce the death benefit amount under the level death benefit design. They do, however, decrease the amount of the policy's cash value and correspondingly increase the amount at risk. As a result, the mortality charge will increase after the partial withdrawal to pay the mortality risk applicable to the greater amount at risk.

Partial withdrawals under the increasing death benefit design will in fact reduce the death benefit payable because the withdrawal decreases the cash value that constitutes part of the death benefit amount. However, such withdrawals will not reduce the mortality charges for the amount at risk because that at-risk amount remains constant. Reducing the cash value by the amount of the partial withdrawal does, however, have a negative impact on the amount of investment earnings credited to the cash value.

Effect of Policy Loans

Another aspect of policy design ushered in with universal life policies is the differential crediting rate on the cash value, depending on whether there are policy loans outstanding. Most universal life policies credit current interest rates on the cash value as long as there are no outstanding policy loans. Once the policyowner borrows funds from the cash value, the insurance company usually credits a lower interest rate or earnings rate to the portion of the cash value associated with the policy loan. This is another effort to curb disintermediation.

Some of the earliest universal life policy designs had several different bands with different crediting rates. In other words, the first $500 or $1,000 of policy loan interest rate may have been credited with one interest rate and each successively larger band would have carried a higher policy loan interest rate. This structure still exists in a few universal life policies offered in the marketplace today, but by and large, many insurance companies have dropped the multiple-rate, banded approach to premium loan interest charges. It had such a complex structure that it was hard to explain to policyowners, and tracking it required much more complex computer software. Many universal life policies sold today credit the cash value with the current rate for nonborrowed funds and a lower rate, which is often 2 percent of or 200 basis points lower than the current rate, for borrowed funds.

Internal Funds Flow

Although universal life insurance policies are still relatively young in the overall realm of life insurance products, some policies are already in their fifth or sixth generation of policy series from the company that introduced them. As with all products, the individual policy designs constantly evolve in response to the economy, competitive pressures, and innovative zeal. As previously noted, most of the first generation of universal life policies were heavily front-end-loaded products. They took a significant proportion of each premium dollar as administrative expenses, and the remaining portion was then credited to the policy cash value account.

After the funds had reached the policy cash value account, they were subject to charges for current death benefits in the form of a mortality charge based on the amount at risk. In most insurance companies the mortality rate actually charged was often in the neighborhood of 50 percent of the guaranteed maximum mortality rate set forth in the policy contract for each attained age of the insured. The difference in the mortality rate actually being charged and the maximum permitted mortality rate published in the policy represents the safety margin the life insurance company is holding in reserve. If the future mortality costs for the block of policies turn out to be more expensive than initially assumed, the insurance company can increase the mortality rate as long as it does not exceed guaranteed maximum rates specified in the contract itself.

After deductions for expenses and mortality, the universal life cash value account is then increased at the current crediting rate to reflect investment earnings on that cash value. These are the dollars at work for the policyowner to help reduce his or her current and future out-of-pocket premium expenses. The actual rate credited is a discretionary decision on the part of the insurance company, and it tends to fluctuate freely, reflecting current economic conditions. There have been times when some insurers were reluctant to credit the current interest rate to the policy's cash value. As interest rates were dropping gradually and steadily over the last decade, many insurance companies were hesitant to allow their current interest crediting rate to drop below 10 percent, and interest crediting rates seemed to stick around that point. Eventually the economic folly of crediting interest rates in excess of actual earnings on the invested assets became apparent, and single-digit interest rates replaced double-digit rates in the crediting formula.

Interest crediting rates have been the focal point of most of the competition among companies selling universal life policies. There has been very little emphasis on the mortality rates charged or the expense charges levied against incoming premiums. In reality all three concepts constitute the total cost of insurance. Interest rates can be (and have been) intentionally elevated to a level above what the investment portfolio actually supported but they are still viable because of compensating higher levels of mortality charges and expense deductions. When consumers choose to focus only on one of the three elements, it is not surprising that the marketing efforts zero in on that element. The assessment of overall policy efficiency requires that all factors be considered in concert.

As the universal life insurance policies evolved, more of them moved to a back-end loading design. In other words, they lowered or eliminated the up-front charge levied against incoming premium amounts and instead imposed new or increased surrender charges applicable during the contract's first 7 to 15 years. Surrender charges are usually highest during the first policy year and decrease on a straight-line basis over the remaining years until the year in which the insurance company expects to have amortized all excess first-year expenses. At that point the surrender charge is reduced to zero and will not be applicable at later policy durations. The actual surrender charge itself can be levied on either the cash value amount or on the target premium level. Some insurers have developed a hybrid that depends on both approaches to generate the full surrender charge. The surrender charge usually decreases by the same percentage on each policy anniversary until the applicable charge reaches zero.

Companies with the highest surrender charges tend to have little or no front-end expenses charged against premiums. Some companies have policies that combine moderate front-end loading and moderate surrender charges. There seems to be a discernible trend toward higher surrender charges and little or no front-end loading in most universal life policies being marketed today.

The actual component of the front-end loading can be a flat annual charge per policy plus a small percentage of premium dollars actually received, and a charge of a few cents per each $1,000 of coverage in force under the policy. The charges applicable to the premiums and the amount of coverage are usually deducted monthly from the policy cash value account. Similarly, the current interest crediting rate is also usually applied monthly. These are the deposits and withdrawals from our "gas tank."

Some companies have actually eliminated charges based on the amount of coverage in force. Competitive pressures have also caused many insurance companies to minimize front-end loading in order to emphasize that nearly all premium dollars go directly into the cash value account. The actual expenses are still being exacted internally, but the manner in which they are handled is not easily discernible by the consuming public. For example, expenses can be embedded in the spread between actual mortality costs and actual mortality charges or in the spread between investment earnings and the interest rate credited to the cash value accounts.

It is important to realize that no insurance company is able to operate without generating legitimate costs of operations above the amount needed to pay death benefits only. These expenses must be covered somehow, and the method of allocating them is nothing more or less than a cost-accounting approach. The exact allocation formula is always arbitrary and to some extent guided by the philosophy of the insurance company management team. It must address such issues as equity among short-term and long-term policyowners, the appropriate duration for amortizing excess first-year expenses, and how much investment and operations gains to retain for company growth and safety margins and how much to distribute to policyowners.

Flexibility to Last a Lifetime

The astonishing flexibility of premiums under universal life policies and the ability to adjust death benefits upward and downward have created life insurance policies that can literally keep pace with the policyowner's needs. The policy can be aggressively funded when the premium dollars are available, and premium payments can be intentionally suspended during tight budget periods, such as the formation of a new business or while children are attending college. The policy death benefit can be increased (sometimes requiring evidence of insurability) if the need exists, and once any temporary needs have expired, the policy can be adjusted downward to provide lower death benefits if that is what the policyowner wants. The ability of a universal life contract to fit constantly changing policyowner needs and conditions has led some companies to label this coverage irreplaceable life insurance. Some see it as the only policy ever needed because its versatility will allow it to compensate for any necessary changes.

Probably the most serious drawback to universal life policies is the competitive forces insurance marketers use to try to convince the prospect that their own version of universal life is better than anyone else's. In reality all universal life policies are similar, and only future investment performance will really determine which one turns out to be slightly more efficient than its competitors. Consumers will be better off seeking a policy that does well over the long haul than looking for a policy that wins every short-term contest because no policy can be best in all facets at every duration. Sometimes focusing on a single competitive advantage prompts insurance companies to make short-term adjustments that are not necessarily in their own or the policyowner's best interest in the long-term scenario.

CURRENT ASSUMPTION WHOLE LIFE

Current assumption whole life is a variation of traditional whole life that lies somewhere between adjustable life and universal life. Its cash value development is more like that of universal life than any other policy. It has a redetermination feature that essentially recasts the premium amount, and in some instances the death benefit, in reaction to the most recent interval of experience. That interval varies from one company to another but is frequently 5 years, although it can be as short as 2 years or as long as 7 years. The main feature that differentiates current assumption whole life from universal life is the absence of total premium flexibility in the renewal years.

Current assumption whole life is sometimes described as universal life with fixed premiums. This is an oversimplification since premiums can and will be restructured at specified policy anniversary dates. However, the analogy is probably useful in getting a mental image of this type of policy and how it differs from the traditional whole life policy, the adjustable life policy, and the universal life policy. It is just another example of refinements in policy design that fill in some of the missing points along a continuum of possibilities between both extremes—all fixed components and guarantees at one end and all flexible and nonguaranteed components at the other.

There are still quite a few guaranteed elements in current assumption whole life policies. There is a guaranteed death benefit and a minimum guaranteed interest rate to be credited on policy cash values. Some companies guarantee the mortality charge and the expense charges. When mortality and expense charges are guaranteed, the policy is often referred to as an *interest-sensitive whole life policy* because interest credited to the cash value becomes the only nonguaranteed element in the contract. However, the bulk of the current assumption whole life policy has some degree of flexibility in the expense elements. Because many of these designs periodically recast the premium amount based on recognition of the most recent interval of experience, some of these policies are referred to as *indeterminate premium whole life policies*. The idea is that there is a guaranteed maximum possible premium that could be charged, but the actual mortality interest and expenses give rise to lower premium amounts actually being assessed as a result of favorable experience under the policy.

Current assumption whole life policies are nonparticipating policies that have some after-the-fact adjustment mechanisms without actually creating explicit policyowner cash dividends. These adjustment mechanisms allow the insurer to constantly fine-tune its policy and keep it competitive in the marketplace, based on actual company experience underlying the particular blocks of policies. From a company standpoint one of the big advantages of this policy design is its ability to eliminate the need for any deficiency reserve for the block of policies. Policy reserves can be calculated on the basis of the maximum chargeable premium and the minimum interest rate guarantee. Reserves will always be based on these factors even though the premiums actually collected are lower than the premium assumption underlying the reserve and, more important, are less than the guideline premium for reserve valuation.

For competitive purposes in the marketplace, current assumption whole life gives the insurance company a product with a mechanism for sharing favorable investment returns with policyowners. These policies take away the advantage that participating whole life policies had over nonparticipating whole life policies. They are not so rigid that a change in market conditions automatically renders them obsolete, as was the unfortunate case with nonparticipating whole life policies before 1980. Most of the insurance companies offering current assumption whole life policies are stock insurance companies that sold mainly nonparticipating whole life contracts prior to 1980.

Most current assumption whole life policies base their maximum possible mortality rate on 1980 Commissioners Standard Ordinary (CSO) Table rates. Since most insurance companies experience mortality significantly less costly than indicated by the CSO rates, the differential provides a very large safety margin for the insurer if it is later necessary to increase mortality rates and possibly even increase premiums on policy anniversaries when redetermination occurs.

Cash Value Illustrations

There are some variations in the way insurance companies approach the illustration of current assumption whole life policies. As with every other type of illustration, an insurance company tries to have its illustration be enough different from any other company's that the illustrations are not directly comparable. Nevertheless, it is possible to classify these variations into two basic categories.

The first category has a guaranteed cash value column and a separate column for excess accumulations (or some other descriptive title indicating that these values supplement the guaranteed cash value amounts). The total cash value for the policy is the sum of the guaranteed cash value and the accumulation supplements. The most complete representation tends to have three different columns for cash values—one for the guaranteed amount, one for the excess accumulations, and one representing the total of the two components. Any insurance company has wide discretion in how it depicts this approach in its illustrations. For example, illustrations often depict only the total cash value column and may or may not explicitly indicate that the cash value depends on projections of nonguaranteed amounts.

The second basic category merely has a single column titled "Enhanced Cash Value" (or an equivalent thereof). There is rarely any inclusion of the guaranteed cash value amount. This approach makes the policy look more like the cash value accumulation account reported under most universal life policies: Premiums are shown as an incoming item that is reduced by expense charges before being added to the cash value account. Interest on the account balance is usually credited before any mortality charges are deducted. After mortality charges are deducted, the end-of-year fund balance is derived. The significant difference between the accumulation accounts in current assumption whole life and universal life is that universal life policies tend to charge off both expenses and mortality before crediting investment earnings. Current assumption whole life policies tend to deduct expenses from premiums but then credit that amount to the cash value and reflect a credit for investment earnings before deducting a mortality charge.

This approach has led many people to describe current assumption whole life as a hybrid of universal life and traditional whole life because it has cash value accumulations of excess interest crediting but still maintains a rigid level premium structure that can be changed on redetermination anniversaries.

Low Premium/High Premium Designs

The proportion of excess accumulations under these policy designs is highly dependent on the premium level in the base design.

Some insurance companies use a relatively low-premium current assumption whole life design. Adjustments on redetermination dates are more likely to involve an adjustment of the death benefit to make the policy compatible with the premium level being paid. At the other end of the spectrum some insurers utilize a high-premium design of current assumption whole life, where the premium paid is usually more than adequate and normally does not ever require an upward adjustment on a redetermination date. The high-premium design is more likely to involve projections of how long premiums may be needed until the policy is expected to be self-supporting without further contributions from the policyowner. It is a form of *vanishing premium* design. The caution, however, is that excess accumulations are not guaranteed; nor is the projected period of premium payments guaranteed to make the policy fully paid up at the end of that period. The policy will be paid up only if the future experience under the policy from that date forward is such that the interest credited and the accumulated account generate enough funds to meet all mortality charges and expenses over the entire remainder of the contract. There are no guarantees that this accumulation account might not have to be supplemented at some point if mortality charges and expenses cost more than the accumulation account can provide.

On the optimistic side, the policy could continue to exceed expectations even after it reaches paid-up status. If the investment returns on the accumulated fund keep the balance in that account more than adequate to pay all mortality charges and expenses, the policy could continue to enhance the benefits on each redetermination date. This would most likely involve an increase in death benefits since there are no further premiums to reduce at that point.

Redetermination

The level of premiums influences the frequency of redetermination. The longer the premium design, the more frequent the policy's redetermination dates. In some of the more recent policy designs redetermination can be every year; more often the redetermination frequency is every 2 years or every 5 years. On policy anniversaries when redetermination is applicable, the insurance company looks at its actual experience for the block of policies since the previous redetermination date and decides what adjustments, if any, are necessary, based on the assumption that past experiences are indicative of what to expect in the period before the next redetermination.

Policyowner Options

The policyowner generally selects the method he or she prefers to adjust the policy from an available group of options when redetermination occurs. For example, if the redetermination results in a potentially lower premium, the policyowner usually has the option of continuing the past level of premiums and having the favorable results applied to enhance the policy's cash value or increase the death benefit (assuming the insured can provide satisfactory evidence of insurability), or the policyowner may choose to pay the lower policy premium amount.

When past experience is less favorable than expectations, the policyowner again has a range of options, including lowering the death benefit, increasing the premium amount, or maintaining the status quo and allowing the policy accumulation account to decrease as the mortality and expense charges exceed the investment earnings on the accumulated fund. This last choice, if available, may have restrictions on its use.

Uses of Current Assumption Whole Life

In a current assumption whole life policy current interest rates are used to enhance the accumulation account, but the policy does not provide the premium flexibility of a universal life policy. Current assumption whole life is an appropriate policy choice for individuals who need the discipline imposed by its fixed-premium design but want to participate at least in part in the positive investment returns beyond the guaranteed interest rate in the policy. Under this type of policy the policyowner assumes some of the investment risk and a limited portion of the mortality risk. If actual experience turns out to be poor, the policy may be periodically downgraded on each redetermination date. If actual experience is positive, the policyowner participates in the upside as the quid pro quo for assuming those risks or a portion thereof. Costs in the long run may turn out to be much less than the original projections if experience is favorable enough over the duration of the contract. The real challenge with this and many other life insurance products in which policyowners assume some of the risk is to make sure policyowners understand the nature and extent of the risk being assumed.

VARIABLE UNIVERSAL LIFE

Variable universal life insurance is one of the most recently developed variations of whole life. This policy incorporates all of the premium flexibility and policy adjustment features of the universal life policy with the policyowner-directed investment aspects of variable life insurance. Obviously this design discards the fixed-premium features of the variable life insurance contract.

One of the most interesting aspects of variable universal life insurance is that it eliminates the direct connection between investment performance above or below some stated target level and the corresponding formula-directed adjustment in death benefits. Instead variable universal life insurance adopts the death benefit designs applicable to universal life policies, namely, either a level death benefit or an increasing death benefit design where a constant amount of risk is paid in addition to the cash accumulation account. Under the first of those options the death benefit doesn't change, regardless of how positive or negative the investment performance under the contract turns out to be. If the policyowner wants to have the death benefit vary with the performance of the investments under the contract, he or she must choose the increasing death benefit design. All of the increase or decrease is a direct result of the accumulation account balance, rather than the result of purchasing paid-up additions (or some form of modified premium addition) as is the case under fixed-premium life insurance.

Variable universal life policies offer the policyowner a choice among a specified group of mutual fund types of separate accounts that are usually created and maintained by the insurance company itself. Some insurance companies have made arrangements with other investment companies to utilize separate account portfolios created and maintained by those investment management firms.

Like variable life insurance, variable universal life insurance policies are technically classified as securities and are subject to regulation by the SEC. The SEC requires registration of agents marketing the product, the separate accounts supporting the contracts, and the contracts themselves. In addition, policies must conform with the SEC requirements that the investment funds be separate accounts that are segregated from the insurance company's general investment portfolio and therefore not subject to creditors' claims applicable to the insurer's general portfolio in times of financial difficulty. Variable universal life contracts are also subject to regulation by the state insurance commissioners. Nearly 80 percent of the states have adopted the National Association of Insurance Commissioners (NAIC) model variable life insurance regulation in its modified form (which is less restrictive than the original model regulation). (See chapters 26 and 27 for a thorough discussion of life insurance regulation.)

Because variable universal life is a registered investment product, policies must be accompanied by a prospectus, which is governed by the same rules applicable to prospectuses for variable life policies. The prospectus provides the necessary information for a meaningful evaluation and comparison of policies.

Ultimate Flexibility

Probably the easiest way to describe variable universal life insurance is to say that it is a universal life insurance policy with the added feature that the policyowner gets to choose the investments, as under fixed-premium variable life insurance contracts. Variable universal life offers the ultimate in both the flexibility afforded to the policyowner and the amount of risk shifted to the policyowner. There are no interest rate or cash value guarantees and very limited guarantees on the maximum mortality rates applicable. Policyowners have wide-open premium flexibility under this contract and can choose to fund it at whatever level they desire as long as it is at least high enough to create coverage similar to yearly renewal term and not in excess of the amount that would drive the cash accumulation account above the maximum threshold set forth in I.R.C. Sec. 7702. Policyowners do not need to negotiate with the insurance company or inform the insurer in advance of any premium modification or cessation.

These contracts permit partial withdrawals that work just like those under universal life policies. Early partial withdrawals may be subject to surrender charges, and surrender charges are applicable to total surrenders in the policy's early years when the insurance company is still recovering excess first-year acquisition costs. The surrender charges vanish at a specified policy duration.

Variable universal life can be aggressively prefunded so that the policy can completely support itself from its cash value. If adequate premiums are contributed to the contract, this can be accomplished in a relatively short number of years. As with universal life and current assumption whole life, variable universal life policies have no guarantee that once the cash value is large enough to carry the policy it will always be able to do so. The policyowner assumes the risk of investment return and to a limited extent some of the risk of mortality rate charges. Consequently the policyowner has to make adjustments and either pay more premiums or reduce the death benefit at some future time if in fact the cash value subsequently dips below the level needed to totally prefund the remaining contract years.

By choosing the increasing death benefit option under this contract policyowners are afforded an automatic hedge against inflation. This inflation protection is general in nature and subject to a timing mismatch in that investment experience may not keep pace with short-term bursts of inflation.

Over the long haul, however, the investment-induced increases in coverage should equal, if not exceed, general increases in price levels.

Many variable universal life policies offer an additional cost-of-living adjustment rider to further assure timely death benefit increases associated with increases in the consumer price index. These riders trigger death benefit increases paid for by term charges against the policy's cash value.

As with variable life, the policyowner is able to switch investment funds from one of the available choices to any other single fund or combination thereof whenever desired. Some insurance companies put a limit on how many fund changes can be made without incurring explicit costs for those changes. Some companies allow one change of funds per year at no cost, others allow one change per open fund per year with no explicit charges, and others specify in the prospectus a given number of fund changes that can be accomplished during any given time interval (usually annually but sometimes other intervals such as quarterly or monthly) without incurring additional charges. Within some companies there is a banding of charges, depending on the number of fund reallocations or redirections during the specified period of time. The cost per transaction goes up as the number of transactions increases in the time interval. Theoretically policyowners could redirect funds on a daily basis, but such aggressive reallocation could generate significant internal expenses and would probably be a strong indication that the policyowner is attempting to be more aggressive than warranted for this type of contract.

Switching investment funds is accomplished without any internal or external taxation of inherent gains in the funds. The internal buildup of the cash value is tax deferred at least as long as the policy stays in force and will be tax free if the policy matures as a death claim.

Variable universal life insurance policies are still primarily life insurance contracts that generate cash value as part of the prefunding level premium mechanism. They are not strictly investment contracts and should not be viewed as such. Philosophically there seems to be a conflict when policyowners manage variable life or variable universal life policies for maximum aggressive growth when in fact the reason for the contracts is to provide a financial safety net for beneficiaries. If the primary coverage is for its death benefits, it seems more appropriate that the investment allocations not pursue the most aggressive growth objectives. A more conservative growth approach is suggested.

On the other hand, if the primary objective for acquiring the contract is for its cash value and the policyowner intends to use the policy's cash values prior to the insured's death, perhaps the more aggressive growth stance is acceptable. In this case the policyowner is likely to be the beneficiary and the risk bearer.

Income Tax Burdens for Early Depletion

Variable universal life policies should not be utilized as short-term investment vehicles. There are two potential traps for policyowners who significantly deplete the policy's cash values at various intervals during the first 15 policy years. These income tax burdens are in addition to any surrender charges that may be applicable within the policy itself.

One potential trap is the modified endowment contract provisions of the Tax Code, which treat all cash value distributions as taxable income until all investment returns have been taxed before the remainder of the distribution is treated as recovery of capital. Such treatment is possible whenever material policy changes are made and the policy fails the seven-pay test (reaching the cash value amount for a policy paid up after 7 years). If the policy fails the seven-pay test, not only will the distributed amounts be subject to income tax (up to the extent of the gain) but there may also be a 10 percent penalty tax applicable to those taxable gains if the policyowner is younger than 59 1/2 years of age. High cash value/high premium configuration variable universal life policies are the most likely candidates for this tax trap. Making sure that the cash value before and after any material change is lower than what it would be if the policy were fully paid up after 7 years will in most cases avoid this potential problem.

The other potential trap again deals with high levels of cash value approaching the upper limits permitted under the Tax Code. If a reduction in the death benefit level forces a distribution of the cash value in order to retain life insurance status under the Code, those distributions may be taxable income to the extent that they represent gain in the policy. The most stringent constraints apply to such "forced out" withdrawals during the first 5 years of the policy's existence. Slightly less binding constraints are applicable for policy years 6 through 15. Any policyowner contemplating a switch from the increasing death benefit design to the level benefit design during the policy's first 15 years should consider these rules before making the switch. As long as there is no forced distribution or concurrent request by the policyowner for a discretionary distribution of cash value funds, there will be no problem. Conversely, if the increasing death benefit form of the contract is already prefunded near the maximum limitations, there is the possibility that some cash value will be forced out to maintain compliance with the Tax Code limitations on life insurance policies.

Neither of these tax traps has any consequence if there are no gains in the contract (premiums paid exceed cash value) when distributions are made. Also under Modified Endowment Contract (MEC) provisions the taxation will be applicable only if there are distributions of the cash value. If the funds are left in the contract and allowed to remain part of the cash value, there will be no taxation even though the potential still exists for any distribution once the policy has become classified as a MEC.

Variable universal life contracts are not desirable for policyowners who do not wish to assume the investment risk under the contract. Potential policyowners who say they want to assume the investment risk but become extremely anxious over any short-term fall in the value of the selected investment portfolio funds should also be cautioned. A successful life insurance agent once facetiously suggested that anyone purchasing variable life or variable universal life insurance should cancel his or her subscription to the *Wall Street Journal* to minimize the likelihood of daily assessments of the investment fund performance. Realistically, maybe the best prospects for variable life contracts and variable universal life contracts are those who do in fact have a subscription to the *Wall Street Journal* and are more attuned to the daily fluctuations in fund values. Policyowners are not likely to find asset value information regarding the specific funds backing their policies in the *Wall Street Journal* anyway. The separate account requirements imposed by the SEC have prompted most insurance companies to use funds that are not available to the general public. These funds are very rarely publicly traded and therefore not included in the *Wall Street Journal's* daily listing of funds.

Variable universal life insurance has become a viable contract for corporate-owned life insurance. Its flexibility is compatible with the constantly changing needs of the corporation owning the policy. Corporate management is usually fairly sophisticated in understanding the investment process and the short-term upward and downward fluctuations in portfolio holdings.

METHODS OF COMPARING LIFE INSURANCE POLICY COSTS

Net Cost Method

There are as many different methodologies of comparing life insurance policies as there are generic types of coverage. Historically the traditional net cost method was widely utilized. Its methodology is quite simple, easy to understand, and even easy to calculate. The starting point is a specification of the duration of coverage to be evaluated. Often this was for either 10 years or 20 years of coverage. The actual mechanics of the evaluation involve taking all of the net premiums paid under the policy and adding them together, then subtracting the cash surrender value for the interim being considered and all dividends paid over that interval. One of the reasons this method is so easy to understand is that it does not take into account the time value of money. In other words, it ignores interest.

The final cost derived under net cost method can be considered the amount the insurance company retains. The main criticism of this methodology is that after 20 years the net cost is usually negative. That is, the cash value amounts at the end of the interval plus dividends paid over the interval exceed the aggregate of premiums paid. The implication is that the policyowner has received insurance free of charge. The serious shortcoming of using this methodology is that it gives equal weight to payment amounts that may be separated by 10 or 20 years. By doing so, it totally ignores the opportunity costs of earnings forgone because the funds were not invested in an investment account. (See table 5-2.)

The net cost method is not appropriate for comparing policies, whether they are the same type or different types. It is totally unacceptable under the state statutes and regulations for purposes of making replacement evaluations. In fact, under some state statutes insurance agents are prohibited from using the net cost method.

Interest-adjusted Indexes

The logic of using interest-adjusted indexes is similar to that of the traditional net cost approach with the exception that interest-adjusted indexes explicitly take into account the time value of money. The National Association of Insurance Commissioners developed the interest-adjusted cost indexes and also derived model laws requiring their use. These statutes were drafted and adopted during the 1970s prior to the high interest and inflation rates experienced in the late 1970s and early 1980s. Almost every one of the statutes mandates that the rate of interest to be used is 5 percent annually.

Essentially the interest-adjusted method takes all payments for premiums and treats them as if they had been put into interest-bearing accounts to accumulate

TABLE 5-2
Traditional Net Cost

10-Year Traditional Net Cost		20-Year Traditional Net Cost	
Dividends	$ 2,178	Dividends	$10,487
Cash value	14,820	Cash value	35,900
Total	16,998	Total	46,387
Less		Less	
Premiums paid	21,870	Premiums paid	43,740
Cost	4,872	Cost	−2,647
Divide by $1,000's face	48.72	Per $1,000	−26.47
Divide by number of years	4.872	Per $1,000 per year	−1.3235

$100,000 Whole Life Policy
Issue Age 48 Male Participating

Policy Year	Age	Premium	Cash Value	Dividend	Accum. Dividend	Accum. Premium
1	48	$2,187	$ 0	$ 0	$ 0	$ 2,296
2	49	2,187	1,456	76	76	4,708
3	50	2,187	2,963	120	200	7,239
4	51	2,187	4,516	170	380	9,898
5	52	2,187	6,119	185	584	12,689
6	53	2,187	7,775	217	830	15,620
7	54	2,187	9,470	280	1,151	18,697
8	55	2,187	11,210	325	1,534	21,928
9	56	2,187	12,992	390	2,001	25,321
10	57	2,187	14,820	415	2,516	28,883
11	58	2,187	16,698	455	3,097	32,624
12	59	2,187	18,625	550	3,801	36,551
13	60	2,187	20,605	615	4,606	40,675
14	61	2,187	22,638	707	5,544	45,005
15	62	2,187	24,720	775	6,596	49,552
16	63	2,187	26,857	845	7,771	54,326
17	64	2,187	29,042	952	9,111	59,339
18	65	2,187	31,276	1,020	10,587	64,602
19	66	2,187	33,559	1,140	12,256	70,128
20	67	2,187	35,900	1,250	14,119	75,931

interest until the end of the interval for evaluation. In a like manner, all dividend payments are carried as if they are deposited in an interest-bearing account, and that account balance is calculated for the end of the interim of evaluation. After all premium payments and all dividend payments have been adjusted to the end of the comparison interval, the policy cash value and accumulation dividends are subtracted from the accumulated value of all the premiums paid. This resulting amount is then time adjusted to the end of the evaluation interval.

The next step is to take that future net cost and divide it by the future value of an annuity due, based on the specified interest rate and the period of time being evaluated. At 5 percent interest the factor to use for a 10-year evaluation is 13.2068. Likewise the factor to divide into the future value amount over a 20-year interval, again assuming a 5 percent interest rate, is 34.7193. The result represents the level annual cost for the policy. This will still be an aggregate amount that must be converted to a per-thousand amount, which is accomplished by dividing the level annual cost amount by the number of thousands of dollars in the policy death benefit. (For example, the aggregate level annual cost for a $50,000 policy is 50 times greater than it would be for a $1,000 policy. We would therefore divide the level annual policy cost by 50 to determine the level annual cost per thousand dollars of coverage.)

These future values appear on most sales presentation materials utilized by insurance agents. For that reason there is usually no need to calculate them independently. The numbers presented will be based on the 5 percent mandated interest rate and the methodology described in the statutes. The same methodology works for any other interest rate the evaluating party thinks is appropriate.

The future value factor for an annuity due can easily be derived on a financial calculator. Merely specify the number of periods in the evaluation interval (such as 10 or 20) on the N key, and enter the interest rate on the I key and the payment amount of $1.00 on the PMT key. Press the FV key to solve for the future value. The resulting factor is then divided into the net future value of the accumulated premium amounts in excess of the accumulated dividends and end-of-period cash value. If there are terminal dividends available at the end of the interval, they are subtracted from the accumulated premiums *before* dividing by the annuity due factor to determine the surrender cost index. (See table 5-3.)

Determining the payment cost index is similar to calculating the surrender cost index except that there is no recognition of the end-of-period cash value. Under this index calculation, dividends over the internal and terminable dividends at the end of the interval are the only items subtracted from the accumulated premium amounts. This gives a future value of net premiums that is then divided by the annuity due factor for the appropriate period and appropriate interest rate. Future values contained in agents' sales materials are usually based on either a 10- or 20-year interval and a 5 percent annual interest rate. (See table 5-4.)

Sample Comparison

A simple example of a fictitious policy is presented in table 5-5. In the example there are $15 premiums per year over a 10-year interval and dividends of $0.00 the first year and $1.00 the second year, increasing by $1.00 each year until they reach $9.00 in the 10th policy year. The accumulation at 5 percent of all premiums paid is $198.10; the accumulation of all dividends is $54.14. Subtracting the accumulated value of dividends from the accumulated value of premiums yields a future value of net premiums equal to $143.97. Subtracting the cash value at the end of 10 years ($120) from that amount yields a future value of net cost equal to $23.97. This future net cost is then divided by the future value of an annuity due for 10 years, or 13.2068, which yields a surrender cost index of $1.814676. In the same table we can see that by ignoring the cash value, the payment cost index becomes $10.90.

TABLE 5-3
Interest-adjusted Net Surrender Cost Index

10-Year Surrender Cost Index		20-Year Surrender Cost Index	
Dividends	$ 2,515.779	Dividends	$14,119.04
Cash value	14,820.00	Cash value	35,900.00
Total	17,335.78	Total	50,019.04
Less		Less	
Premiums paid	28,883.24	Premiums paid	75,931.00
Cost	11,547.46	Cost	25,911.97
Divide by $1,000's face	115.4746	Per $1,000	259.1197
Divide by annuity factor	8.743575	Per $1,000 per year	7.463274
		(34.7193)	

$100,000 Whole Life Policy
Issue Age 48 Male Participating

Policy Year	Age	Premium	Cash Value	Dividend	Accum. Dividend	Accum. Premium
1	48	$2,187	$　0	$　0	$　0	$ 2,296
2	49	2,187	1,456	76	76	4,708
3	50	2,187	2,963	120	200	7,239
4	51	2,187	4,516	170	380	9,898
5	52	2,187	6,119	185	584	12,689
6	53	2,187	7,775	217	830	15,620
7	54	2,187	9,470	280	1,151	18,697
8	55	2,187	11,210	325	1,534	21,928
9	56	2,187	12,992	390	2,001	25,321
10	57	2,187	14,820	415	2,516	28,883
11	58	2,187	16,698	455	3,097	32,624
12	59	2,187	18,625	550	3,801	36,551
13	60	2,187	20,605	615	4,606	40,675
14	61	2,187	22,638	707	5,544	45,005
15	62	2,187	24,720	775	6,596	49,552
16	63	2,187	26,857	845	7,771	54,326
17	64	2,187	29,042	952	9,111	59,339
18	65	2,187	31,276	1,020	10,587	64,602
19	66	2,187	33,559	1,140	12,256	70,128
20	67	2,187	35,900	1,250	14,119	75,931

Calculations under interest-adjusted indexes can be done by hand, but they are easier and quicker when done on a computer or financial calculator. Index values are sensitive to the interval being evaluated and the insured's age of issue for the policies being compared.

These cost indexes are an acceptable means of comparing similar policies. Usually the policy with the smaller numerical values for surrender cost and payment cost indexes is preferable to policies with higher index values. The method is not acceptable, however, for comparing dissimilar policies—for example, a term policy with a whole life policy. It is also not well suited for evaluating policy replacements.

TABLE 5-4
Interest-adjusted Net Payment Cost Index

10-Year Payment Index		20-Year Payment Index	
Accum. dividends	$2,515.779	Accum. dividends	$14,119.04
Accum. premiums	28,883.24	Accum. premiums	75,931.00
Future value of		Future value of	
net premiums	26,367.46	net premiums	61,811.97
Convert to per $1,000	263.6746	Per $1,000	618.1197
Divide by factor		Per $1,000 per year	17.80334
13.2068	19.96507		
Payment Index	19.96507	Payment Index	17.80334

$100,000 Whole Life Policy
Issue Age 48 Male Participating

Policy Year	Age	Premium	Cash Value	Dividend	Accum. Dividend	Accum. Premium
1	48	$2,187	$ 0	$ 0	$ 0	$ 2,296
2	49	2,187	1,456	76	76	4,708
3	50	2,187	2,963	120	200	7,239
4	51	2,187	4,516	170	380	9,898
5	52	2,187	6,119	185	584	12,689
6	53	2,187	7,775	217	830	15,620
7	54	2,187	9,470	280	1,151	18,097
8	55	2,187	11,210	325	1,534	21,928
9	56	2,187	12,992	390	2,001	25,321
10	57	2,187	14,820	415	2,516	28,883
11	58	2,187	16,698	455	3,097	32,624
12	59	2,187	18,625	550	3,801	36,551
13	60	2,187	20,605	615	4,606	40,675
14	61	2,187	22,638	707	5,544	45,005
15	62	2,187	24,720	775	6,596	49,552
16	63	2,187	26,857	845	7,771	54,326
17	64	2,187	29,042	952	9,111	59,339
18	65	2,187	31,276	1,020	10,587	64,602
19	66	2,187	33,559	1,140	12,256	70,128
20	67	2,187	35,900	1,250	14,119	75,931

Cash Accumulation Method of Comparison

The cash accumulation comparison method is much more complex than the net cost method and requires a computer to make the calculations. A significant amount of data must be entered into the computer program in order to calculate the results accurately. One of the strengths of this method is that it is acceptable to compare permanent insurance policies with term policies. It can also be used for evaluation of replacement proposals.

TABLE 5-5
Interest-adjusted Cost Method
(Amounts are per $1,000 of coverage)

	Premiums		Dividends		
Year	Per Year	Accum. @ 5%	Per Year	Accum @ 5%	Cash Value
1	$ 15	$ 15.75	0	$ 0	$ 0
2	15	32.29	1	1.05	0
3	15	49.65	2	3.20	23
4	15	67.89	3	6.51	34
5	15	87.03	4	11.04	43
6	15	107.13	5	16.84	56
7	15	128.24	6	23.99	75
8	15	150.40	7	32.54	100
9	15	173.67	8	42.56	115
10	15	198.10	9	54.14	120
TOTALS	150	198.10	45	54.14	120

Surrender Cost Index		Payment Cost Index	
Future value of premiums	$198.1018	Accum. premiums	$198.1018
		Less accum.	
Minus FV of dividends	−54.13574	dividends	−54.13574
FV of net premiums	$143.9661	FV of net premiums	$143.9661
Less net cash value	−120		
FV of net cost	$ 23.96606		
Divide by annuity factor	13.2068	Divide by annuity factor	13.2068
Surrender Cost Index	1.814676	Payment Cost Index	10.9009

The technique is simply to accumulate the premium differences between the policies being compared, while holding the death benefits of both policies constant and equal. For example, to compare a cash value contract with a term contract, set the death benefits equal at the beginning of the period, and use the premium amount for the whole life policy to determine the amount to deposit into a side fund to accumulate at interest. The calculation is basically a buy-term-and-invest-the-difference approach to comparing the policies. At the end of the interval being evaluated the side fund accumulation amount can be compared to the cash value in the whole life or other form of cash value insurance policy. The policy with the greater accumulation at the end of the comparison interval is considered the preferable of the two contracts. (See tables 5-6 to 5-10.)

TABLE 5-6
Cash Accumulation Comparison Method

Male Aged 48—$100,000 Whole Life
Dividends Buy Paid-up Additions
Annual Renewable Term (ART) Decreased to Equalize Death Benefits
Interest Rate 3% (on accumulations)

Policy Year	WL Premium	ART Premium	Prem Diff.	Accum. Diff. @ 3%	WL Cash Values	Term Plus Side Fund	WL + Paid-up Adds.	ART Face Amount
1	$2,187	$ 365	$1,822	$ 1,877	$ 0	$100,000	$100,000	$ 98,123
2	2,187	386	1,801	3,788	1,456	100,075	100,075	96,287
3	2,187	409	1,778	5,733	2,963	100,203	100,203	94,470
4	2,187	434	1,753	7,710	4,516	100,527	100,527	92,817
5	2,187	460	1,727	9,720	6,119	100,972	100,972	91,252
6	2,187	491	1,696	11,759	7,775	102,321	102,321	90,562
7	2,187	528	1,659	13,820	9,470	104,408	104,408	90,588
8	2,187	574	1,613	15,896	11,210	107,549	107,549	91,653
9	2,187	628	1,559	17,979	12,992	111,463	111,463	93,484
10	2,187	685	1,502	20,066	14,820	114,876	114,876	94,810
11	2,187	753	1,434	22,145	16,698	119,071	119,071	96,926
12	2,187	838	1,349	24,199	18,625	124,156	124,156	99,957
13	2,187	946	1,241	26,203	20,605	130,507	130,507	104,304
14	2,187	1,071	1,116	28,138	22,638	136,789	136,789	108,651
15	2,187	1,226	961	29,972	24,720	143,896	143,896	113,924
16	2,187	1,427	760	31,654	26,857	152,719	152,719	121,065
17	2,187	1,679	508	33,127	29,042	162,745	162,745	129,618
18	2,187	1,942	245	34,374	31,276	170,345	170,345	135,971
19	2,187	2,483	−236	35,100	33,559	183,682	183,682	148,582
20	2,187	3,127	−940	35,185	35,900	196,132	196,132	160,947

TABLE 5-7
Cash Accumulation Comparison Method

Male Aged 48—$100,000 Whole Life
Dividends Buy Paid-up Additions
Annual Renewable Term (ART) Decreased to Equalize Death Benefits
Interest Rate 5% (on accumulations)

Policy Year	WL Premium	ART Premium	Prem Diff.	Accum. Diff. @ 5%	WL Cash Values	Term Plus Side Fund	WL + Paid-up Adds.	ART Face Amount
1	$2,187	$ 365	$1,822	$ 1,913	$ 0	$100,000	$100,000	$ 98,087
2	2,187	386	1,801	3,900	1,456	100,075	100,075	96,175
3	2,187	408	1,779	5,963	2,963	100,203	100,203	94,240
4	2,187	433	1,754	8,104	4,516	100,527	100,527	92,423
5	2,187	457	1,730	10,325	6,119	100,972	100,972	90,647
6	2,187	486	1,701	12,628	7,775	102,321	102,321	89,693
7	2,187	521	1,666	15,008	9,470	104,408	104,408	89,400
8	2,187	564	1,623	17,463	11,210	107,549	107,549	90,086
9	2,187	615	1,572	19,987	12,992	111,463	111,463	91,476
10	2,187	666	1,521	22,583	14,820	114,876	114,876	92,293
11	2,187	729	1,458	25,243	16,698	119,071	119,071	93,828
12	2,187	806	1,381	27,955	18,625	124,156	124,156	96,201
13	2,187	905	1,282	30,698	20,605	130,507	130,507	99,809
14	2,187	1,019	1,168	33,460	22,638	136,789	136,789	103,329
15	2,187	1,159	1,028	36,212	24,720	143,896	143,896	107,684
16	2,187	1,342	845	38,910	26,857	152,719	152,719	113,809
17	2,187	1,570	617	41,504	29,042	162,745	162,745	121,241
18	2,187	1,804	383	43,981	31,276	170,345	170,345	126,364
19	2,187	2,300	-113	46,061	33,559	183,682	183,682	137,621
20	2,187	2,885	-698	47,631	35,900	196,132	196,132	148,501

TABLE 5-8
Cash Accumulation Comparison Method

Male Aged 48—$100,000 Whole Life
Dividends Buy Paid-up Additions
Annual Renewable Term (ART) Decreased to Equalize Death Benefits
Interest Rate 7% (on accumulations)

Policy Year	WL Premium	ART Premium	Prem Diff.	Accum. Diff. @ 7%	WL Cash Values	Term Plus Side Fund	WL + Paid-up Adds.	ART Face Amount
1	$2,187	$ 365	$1,822	$ 1,950	$ 0	$100,000	$100,000	$ 98,050
2	2,187	385	1,802	4,014	1,456	100,075	100,075	96,061
3	2,187	407	1,780	6,200	2,963	100,203	100,203	94,003
4	2,187	431	1,756	8,513	4,516	100,527	100,527	92,014
5	2,187	454	1,733	10,964	6,119	100,972	100,972	90,008
6	2,187	481	1,706	13,556	7,775	102,321	102,321	88,765
7	2,187	514	1,673	16,296	9,470	104,408	104,408	88,112
8	2,187	553	1,634	19,185	11,210	107,549	107,549	88,364
9	2,187	600	1,587	22,226	12,992	111,463	111,463	89,237
10	2,187	646	1,541	25,431	14,820	114,876	114,876	89,445
11	2,187	701	1,486	28,801	16,698	119,071	119,071	90,270
12	2,187	769	1,418	32,334	18,625	124,156	124,156	91,822
13	2,187	857	1,330	36,020	20,605	130,507	130,507	94,487
14	2,187	956	1,231	39,859	22,638	136,789	136,789	96,930
15	2,187	1,077	1,110	43,837	24,720	143,896	143,896	100,059
16	2,187	1,236	951	47,924	26,857	152,719	152,719	104,795
17	2,187	1,433	754	52,085	29,042	162,745	162,745	110,660
18	2,187	1,628	559	56,329	31,276	170,345	170,345	114,016
19	2,187	2,060	127	60,408	33,559	183,682	183,682	123,274
20	2,187	2,563	-376	64,235	35,900	196,132	196,132	131,897

TABLE 5-9
Cash Accumulation Comparison Method

Male Aged 48—$100,000 Whole Life
Dividends Buy Paid-up Additions
Annual Renewable Term (ART) Decreased to Equalize Death Benefits
Interest Rate 10% (on accumulations)

Policy Year	WL Premium	ART Premium	Prem Diff.	Accum. Diff. @ 10%	WL Cash Values	Term Plus Side Fund	WL + Paid-up Adds.	ART Face Amount
1	$2,187	$ 365	$1,822	$ 2,005	$ 0	$100,000	$100,000	$ 97,995
2	2,187	385	1,802	4,188	1,456	100,075	100,075	95,887
3	2,187	405	1,782	6,566	2,963	100,203	100,203	93,637
4	2,187	428	1,759	9,158	4,516	100,527	100,527	91,369
5	2,187	448	1,739	11,987	6,119	100,972	100,972	88,985
6	2,187	473	1,714	15,071	7,775	102,321	102,321	87,250
7	2,187	501	1,686	18,432	9,470	104,408	104,408	85,976
8	2,187	535	1,652	22,093	11,210	107,549	107,549	85,456
9	2,187	574	1,613	26,076	12,992	111,463	111,463	85,387
10	2,187	610	1,577	30,419	14,820	114,876	114,876	84,457
11	2,187	652	1,535	35,149	16,698	119,071	119,071	83,922
12	2,187	703	1,484	40,297	18,625	124,156	124,156	83,859
13	2,187	767	1,420	45,888	20,605	130,507	130,507	84,619
14	2,187	836	1,351	51,963	22,638	136,789	136,789	84,826
15	2,187	918	1,269	58,554	24,720	143,896	143,896	85,342
16	2,187	1,026	1,161	65,687	26,857	152,719	152,719	87,032
17	2,187	1,157	1,030	73,388	29,042	162,745	162,745	89,357
18	2,187	1,265	922	81,741	31,276	170,345	170,345	88,604
19	2,187	1,555	632	90,610	33,559	183,682	183,682	93,072
20	2,187	1,867	320	100,023	35,900	196,132	196,132	96,109

TABLE 5-10
Cash Accumulation Comparison Method

Male Aged 48—$100,000 Whole Life
Dividends Buy Paid-up Additions
Annual Renewable Term (ART) Decreased to Equalize Death Benefits
Interest Rate 12% (on accumulations)

Policy Year	WL Premium	ART Premium	Prem Diff.	Accum. Diff. @ 12%	WL Cash Values	Term Plus Side Fund	WL + Paid-up Adds.	ART Face Amount
1	$2,187	$ 364	$1,823	$ 2,041	$ 0	$100,000	$100,000	$ 97,959
2	2,187	384	1,803	4,306	1,456	100,075	100,075	95,769
3	2,187	404	1,783	6,819	2,963	100,203	100,203	93,384
4	2,187	425	1,762	9,610	4,516	100,527	100,527	90,917
5	2,187	445	1,742	12,714	6,119	100,972	100,972	88,258
6	2,187	467	1,720	16,167	7,775	102,321	102,321	86,154
7	2,187	492	1,695	20,005	9,470	104,408	104,408	84,403
8	2,187	521	1,666	24,271	11,210	107,549	107,549	83,278
9	2,187	554	1,633	29,012	12,992	111,463	111,463	82,451
10	2,187	582	1,605	34,292	14,820	114,876	114,876	80,584
11	2,187	613	1,574	40,170	16,698	119,071	119,071	78,901
12	2,187	649	1,538	46,712	18,625	124,156	124,156	77,444
13	2,187	694	1,493	53,990	20,605	130,507	130,507	76,517
14	2,187	736	1,451	62,094	22,638	136,789	136,789	74,695
15	2,187	783	1,404	71,117	24,720	143,896	143,896	72,779
16	2,187	844	1,343	81,156	26,857	152,719	152,719	71,563
17	2,187	912	1,275	92,322	29,042	162,745	162,745	70,423
18	2,187	936	1,251	104,802	31,276	170,345	170,345	65,543
19	2,187	1,087	1,130	118,610	33,559	183,682	183,682	65,072
20	2,187	1,208	979	133,939	35,900	196,132	196,132	62,193

As noted before, this comparison method really requires a computer in order to be efficient. Not only does the difference in premium have to be allocated to a side fund and accumulated interest but there is also a necessary adjustment of the amount at risk. The side fund accumulated with the term policy acts much like the cash value in the whole life policy, and the amount of term coverage being purchased has to be adjusted so that when it is added to the side fund it will exactly equal the death benefit under the permanent policy to which it is being compared. Using a computer, once a spreadsheet has been built with all of the logic to make the necessary comparisons, it is just a matter of plugging in new values for premiums, cash values, and accumulation account amounts.

Equal Outlay Method

The equal outlay method is somewhat similar to the cash accumulation method. Again, the same amount of premium dollars is expended, on the one hand for a cash value contract and on the other for a term policy. The amount by which the cash value contract premiums exceed the term premiums is deposited into a side fund, and the difference in premium amounts is accumulated at specified interest rates. Then the death benefit of the term insurance plus the accumulated side fund amounts are compared with the death benefit under the cash value contract in which dividends, if any, have been used to purchase paid-up additions and the death benefit amount reflects both the base policy death benefit amount and the value of those paid-up additions. Under this type of comparison the policy producing the greater death benefit is considered the preferable contract. (See tables 5-11 to 5-15.)

Both this method and the cash accumulation method are very sensitive to the interest rate chosen for purposes of the side fund accumulation. Manipulating the interest rate can skew the comparison results. The higher the interest rate used, the more the equal outlay method will tend to favor the lower-premium policy with the side fund combination.

Comparisons That Isolate Interest Rates

There are three other comparison methods that all utilize an assumed cost of coverage to isolate an interest rate for comparison purposes. One of the problems of comparing any life insurance policies is that there are degrees of freedom in the parameters involved. We cannot make a single-factor comparison without choosing assumptions for the other factors and doing so in a way that those factors are also comparable. In other words, if we want to calculate a policy's internal cost of insurance, we have to make some assumptions about interest rates; if we want to calculate interest rates, we have to make some assumptions about the cost of insurance.

Comparative Interest Rate Method

The comparative interest rate method is really a modification of the cash accumulation method, whereby we are calculating the interest rate that would make a term insurance policy side fund exactly equal to the difference between the

TABLE 5-11
Equal Outlay Comparison Method

Male Aged 48—$100,000 Whole Life
Dividends Purchase Paid-up Additions
Interest Rate 3%

Policy Year	WL Premium	ART Premium	Prem Diff.	Accum. Diff. @ 3%	WL Cash Values	Term Plus Side Fund	WL + Paid-up Adds.
1	$2,187	$ 372	$1,815	$ 1,869	$ 0	$101,869	$100,000
2	2,187	401	1,786	3,765	1,456	103,765	100,075
3	2,187	433	1,754	5,685	2,963	105,685	100,203
4	2,187	468	1,719	7,626	4,516	107,626	100,527
5	2,187	504	1,683	9,588	6,119	109,588	100,972
6	2,187	542	1,645	11,570	7,775	111,570	102,321
7	2,187	583	1,604	13,569	9,470	113,569	104,408
8	2,187	626	1,561	15,584	11,210	115,584	107,549
9	2,187	672	1,515	17,612	12,992	117,612	111,463
10	2,187	722	1,465	19,649	14,820	119,649	114,876
11	2,187	777	1,410	21,691	16,698	121,691	119,071
12	2,187	838	1,349	23,731	18,625	123,731	124,156
13	2,187	907	1,280	25,762	20,605	125,762	130,507
14	2,187	986	1,201	27,772	22,638	127,772	136,789
15	2,187	1,076	1,111	29,749	24,720	129,749	143,896
16	2,187	1,179	1,008	31,680	26,857	131,680	152,719
17	2,187	1,295	892	33,549	29,042	133,549	162,745
18	2,187	1,428	759	35,337	31,276	135,337	170,345
19	2,187	1,671	516	36,929	33,559	136,929	183,682
20	2,187	1,943	244	38,288	35,900	138,288	196,132

TABLE 5-12
Equal Outlay Comparison Method

Male Aged 48—$100,000 Whole Life
Dividends Purchase Paid-up Additions
Interest Rate 5%

Policy Year	WL Premium	ART Premium	Prem Diff.	Accum. Diff. @ 5%	WL Cash Values	Term Plus Side Fund	WL + Paid-up Adds.
1	$2,187	$ 372	$1,815	$ 1,906	$ 0	$101,906	$100,000
2	2,187	401	1,786	3,876	1,456	103,876	100,075
3	2,187	433	1,754	5,912	2,963	105,912	100,203
4	2,187	468	1,719	8,012	4,516	108,012	100,527
5	2,187	504	1,683	10,180	6,119	110,180	100,972
6	2,187	542	1,645	12,416	7,775	112,416	102,321
7	2,187	583	1,604	14,721	9,470	114,721	104,408
8	2,187	626	1,561	17,097	11,210	117,097	107,549
9	2,187	672	1,515	19,542	12,992	119,542	111,463
10	2,187	722	1,465	22,058	14,820	122,058	114,876
11	2,187	777	1,410	24,641	16,698	124,641	119,071
12	2,187	838	1,349	27,289	18,625	127,289	124,156
13	2,187	907	1,280	29,998	20,605	129,998	130,507
14	2,187	986	1,201	32,759	22,638	132,759	136,789
15	2,187	1,076	1,111	35,563	24,720	135,563	143,896
16	2,187	1,179	1,008	38,400	26,857	138,400	152,719
17	2,187	1,295	892	41,256	29,042	141,256	162,745
18	2,187	1,428	759	44,116	31,276	144,116	170,345
19	2,187	1,671	516	46,864	33,559	146,864	183,682
20	2,187	1,943	244	49,463	35,900	149,463	196,132

TABLE 5-13
Equal Outlay Comparison Method

Male Aged 48—$100,000 Whole Life
Dividends Purchase Paid-up Additions
Interest Rate 7%

Policy Year	WL Premium	ART Premium	Prem Diff.	Accum. Diff. @ 7%	WL Cash Values	Term Plus Side Fund	WL + Paid-up Adds.
1	$2,187	$ 372	$1,815	$ 1,942	$ 0	$101,942	$100,000
2	2,187	401	1,786	3,989	1,456	103,989	100,075
3	2,187	433	1,754	6,145	2,963	106,145	100,203
4	2,187	468	1,719	8,415	4,516	108,415	100,527
5	2,187	504	1,683	10,804	6,119	110,804	100,972
6	2,187	542	1,645	13,321	7,775	113,321	102,321
7	2,187	583	1,604	15,970	9,470	115,970	104,408
8	2,187	626	1,561	18,758	11,210	118,758	107,549
9	2,187	672	1,515	21,692	12,992	121,692	111,463
10	2,187	722	1,465	24,778	14,820	124,778	114,876
11	2,187	777	1,410	28,021	16,698	128,021	119,071
12	2,187	838	1,349	31,426	18,625	131,426	124,156
13	2,187	907	1,280	34,995	20,605	134,995	130,507
14	2,187	986	1,201	38,730	22,638	138,730	136,789
15	2,187	1,076	1,111	42,630	24,720	142,630	143,896
16	2,187	1,179	1,008	46,692	26,857	146,692	152,719
17	2,187	1,295	892	50,915	29,042	150,915	162,745
18	2,187	1,428	759	55,291	31,276	155,291	170,345
19	2,187	1,671	516	59,714	33,559	159,714	183,682
20	2,187	1,943	244	64,155	35,900	164,155	196,132

TABLE 5-14
Equal Outlay Comparison Method

Male Aged 48—$100,000 Whole Life
Dividends Purchase Paid-up Additions
Interest Rate 10%

Policy Year	WL Premium	ART Premium	Prem Diff.	Accum. Diff. @ 10%	WL Cash Values	Term Plus Side Fund	WL + Paid-up Adds.
1	$2,187	$ 372	$1,815	$ 1,997	$ 0	$101,997	$100,000
2	2,187	401	1,786	4,161	1,456	104,161	100,075
3	2,187	433	1,754	6,506	2,963	106,506	100,203
4	2,187	468	1,719	9,048	4,516	109,048	100,527
5	2,187	504	1,683	11,804	6,119	111,804	100,972
6	2,187	542	1,645	14,794	7,775	114,794	102,321
7	2,187	583	1,604	18,037	9,470	118,037	104,408
8	2,187	626	1,561	21,558	11,210	121,558	107,549
9	2,187	672	1,515	25,381	12,992	125,381	111,463
10	2,187	722	1,465	29,530	14,820	129,530	114,876
11	2,187	777	1,410	34,034	16,698	134,034	119,071
12	2,187	838	1,349	38,922	18,625	138,922	124,156
13	2,187	907	1,280	44,222	20,605	144,222	130,507
14	2,187	986	1,201	49,965	22,638	149,965	136,789
15	2,187	1,076	1,111	56,184	24,720	156,184	143,896
16	2,187	1,179	1,008	62,911	26,857	162,911	152,719
17	2,187	1,295	892	70,183	29,042	170,183	162,745
18	2,187	1,428	759	78,036	31,276	178,036	170,345
19	2,187	1,671	516	86,407	33,559	186,407	183,682
20	2,187	1,943	244	95,317	35,900	195,317	196,132

TABLE 5-15
Equal Outlay Comparison Method

Male Aged 48—$100,000 Whole Life
Dividends Purchase Paid-up Additions
Interest Rate 12%

Policy Year	WL Premium	ART Premium	Prem. Diff.	Accum. Diff. @ 12%	WL Cash Values	Term Plus Side Fund	WL + Paid-up Adds.
1	$2,187	$ 372	$1,815	$ 2,033	$ 0	$102,033	$100,000
2	2,187	401	1,786	4,277	1,456	104,277	100,075
3	2,187	433	1,754	6,755	2,963	106,755	100,203
4	2,187	468	1,719	9,491	4,516	109,491	100,527
5	2,187	504	1,683	12,514	6,119	112,514	100,972
6	2,187	542	1,645	15,859	7,775	115,859	102,321
7	2,187	583	1,604	19,558	9,470	119,558	104,408
8	2,187	626	1,561	23,653	11,210	123,653	107,549
9	2,187	672	1,515	28,189	12,992	128,189	111,463
10	2,187	722	1,465	33,212	14,820	133,212	114,876
11	2,187	777	1,410	38,777	16,698	138,777	119,071
12	2,187	838	1,349	44,941	18,625	144,941	124,156
13	2,187	907	1,280	51,767	20,605	151,767	130,507
14	2,187	986	1,201	59,324	22,638	159,324	136,789
15	2,187	1,076	1,111	67,688	24,720	167,688	143,896
16	2,187	1,179	1,008	76,939	26,857	176,939	152,719
17	2,187	1,295	892	87,171	29,042	187,171	162,745
18	2,187	1,428	759	98,482	31,276	198,482	170,345
19	2,187	1,671	516	110,877	33,559	210,877	183,682
20	2,187	1,943	244	124,456	35,900	224,456	196,132

available cash value policy death benefit and the term insurance death benefit. The comparative interest rate method looks for the interest rate that would make the buy-term-and-invest-the-difference comparison exactly equivalent in the death benefits provided. To make that calculation both the outlays for premiums and side funds and the death benefit levels must be held equal. This method is often referred to as the *Linton yield method,* named for actuary Albert Linton, who first published the approach in the early 1900s. (See table 5-16.) Its primary drawback is the complexity of the calculation, which requires not only a computer program to accurately calculate the interest rate desired but also a large amount of policy information that must be entered into the program before it can be run.

Another caution with using software for this type of comparison is that each comparison should use the same assumed term premium rates to derive the interest rate. Otherwise there will have been manipulation (intentional or unintentional) of the interest rates derived by the calculations. The policy generating the highest comparative interest rate is assumed to be the preferable policy when making comparisons by this method.

Belth Yearly Rate of Return Method

Joseph Belth, a retired professor of insurance and publisher of the *Insurance Forum* newsletter, has developed more cost comparison approaches than any other scholar known to this author. This chapter presents two of his many different policy comparison approaches. (See table 5-17.) He is quick to point out that there is no perfect comparison method because the wide range of objectives that insurance policies address requires that different levels of priority be placed on the death benefits and cash values in different situations. Each methodology puts its primary emphasis on the elements considered to be the highest priorities for that particular approach.

Under the Belth yearly rate of return approach only one year of the policy is considered in making an individual calculation. Such a calculation can be made for each and every year of coverage over the given interval. The objective is to identify the benefits provided by the policy during that year — the end-of-year cash value plus the dividends paid during the year and the net death benefit for the policy year — and the investments in the policy necessary to derive those benefits — a combination of the beginning-of-the-year cash value and the premium paid for that year of the policy. The yearly rate of return formula divides the sum of the benefits by the sum of the investments and then subtracts the number 1 from that amount. This process is repeated for each year over the comparison interval. The policy with the highest rates of yearly return in the largest number of years over the observation interval is considered the preferable policy.

The calculation under the Belth yearly rate of return method depends on a realistic assumed term rate, not a manipulated rate that is intentionally much too high or low that it skews the results. This method does not necessarily make it easy to identify a predominant policy. The highest yearly rate of return may change back and forth among the policies being compared.

TABLE 5-16
Linton Yield Method—20 Year

Male Aged 48—$100,000 Whole Life
Dividends Buy Paid-up Additions
Annual Renewable Term (ART) Decreased to Equalize Death Benefits
Interest Rate 3.132% (on accumulations)

Policy Year	WL Premium	ART Premium	Prem Diff.	Accum. Diff. @ 3.132%	WL Cash Values	Term Plus Side Fund	WL + Paid-up Adds.	ART Face Amount
1	$2,187	$ 365	$1,822	$ 1,879	$ 0	$100,000	$100,000	$ 98,121
2	2,187	386	1,801	3,795	1,456	100,075	100,075	96,280
3	2,187	409	1,778	5,748	2,963	100,203	100,203	94,455
4	2,187	434	1,753	7,735	4,516	100,527	100,527	92,792
5	2,187	460	1,727	9,759	6,119	100,972	100,972	91,213
6	2,187	491	1,696	11,814	7,775	102,321	102,321	90,507
7	2,187	528	1,659	13,896	9,470	104,408	104,408	90,512
8	2,187	573	1,614	15,995	11,210	107,549	107,549	91,554
9	2,187	627	1,560	18,105	12,992	111,463	111,463	93,358
10	2,187	683	1,504	20,222	14,820	114,876	114,876	94,654
11	2,187	752	1,435	22,336	16,698	119,071	119,071	96,735
12	2,187	836	1,351	24,429	18,625	124,156	124,156	99,727
13	2,187	944	1,243	26,477	20,605	130,507	130,507	104,030
14	2,187	1,068	1,119	28,460	22,638	136,789	136,789	108,329
15	2,187	1,222	965	30,347	24,720	143,896	143,896	113,549
16	2,187	1,422	765	32,086	26,857	152,719	152,719	120,633
17	2,187	1,672	515	33,622	29,042	162,745	162,745	129,123
18	2,187	1,934	253	34,936	31,276	170,345	170,345	135,409
19	2,187	2,472	-285	35,736	33,559	183,682	183,682	147,946
20	2,187	3,113	-926	35,900	35,900	196,132	196,132	160,232

TABLE 5-17
Belth Yearly Cost and Yearly Return Methods

Male Aged 48—$100,000 Whole Life
Dividends Buy Paid-up Additions
Annual Renewable Term (ART) Decreased to Equalize Death Benefits
Interest Rate 3.132% (on accumulations)

Policy Year	WL Premium	ART Rate	Divi-dends	WL Cash Values	Yearly Benefit	Yearly Invest-ment	Yearly Return %	Yearly Cost
1	$2,187	3.72	$ 0	$ 0	$ 372	$ 2,187	-82.99	$22.96
2	2,187	4.01	76	1,456	1,927	2,187	-11.88	7.76
3	2,187	4.33	120	2,963	3,503	3,643	-3.84	7.65
4	2,187	4.68	170	4,516	5,133	5,150	-0.33	7.56
5	2,187	5.04	185	6,119	6,777	6,703	1.11	7.82
6	2,187	5.42	217	7,775	8,492	8,306	2.24	7.91
7	2,187	5.83	280	9,470	10,278	9,962	3.17	7.84
8	2,187	6.26	325	11,210	12,091	11,657	3.72	7.94
9	2,187	6.72	390	12,992	13,967	13,397	4.25	7.87
10	2,187	7.22	415	14,820	15,850	15,179	4.42	8.25
11	2,187	7.77	455	16,698	17,800	17,007	4.66	8.46
12	2,187	8.38	550	18,625	19,857	18,885	5.15	8.04
13	2,187	9.07	615	20,605	21,940	20,812	5.42	7.97
14	2,187	9.86	707	22,638	24,108	22,792	5.77	7.58
15	2,187	10.76	775	24,720	26,305	24,825	5.96	7.59
16	2,187	11.79	845	26,857	28,564	26,907	6.16	7.52
17	2,187	12.95	952	29,042	30,913	29,044	6.43	7.08
18	2,187	14.28	1,020	31,276	33,277	31,229	6.56	7.19
19	2,187	16.71	1,140	33,559	35,809	33,463	7.01	6.58
20	2,187	19.43	1,250	35,900	38,395	35,746	7.41	5.98

Belth Yearly Price Method of Protection

Under the Belth year price approach we must assume an investment or interest rate and thereby calculate the cost of protection. Again, the calculations are made one year at a time for each of the years in the comparison interval (usually 10 or 20 years as in most other comparison methods). Using this methodology the beginning cash value plus the current premium are accumulated at the assumed rate of interest to derive a year-end surrender value. After computing the theoretical end-of-year value from the beginning cash value and the premium plus interest, we subtract the actual end-of-year cash value plus dividends paid during the year. This is the difference assumed to have been available to pay mortality charges.

The next step is to divide the difference between theoretical year-end values and actual year-end values plus dividends by the amount at risk per $1,000 of coverage. The actual formula looks quite formidable, but when its terms are defined, it is really quite simple and straightforward.

$$\text{Cost per } \$1,000 = \frac{(P + CVP) \times (1 + i) - (CSV + D)}{(F - CSV) \times (0.001)}$$

P	=	Premium
CVP	=	Cash surrender value previous year
i	=	Net aftertax interest rate
CSV	=	Cash surrender value current year
D	=	Dividend current year
F	=	Face amount of coverage

After making a yearly price-of-protection calculation for each policy being compared for each year in the comparison interval, it is then a matter of identifying the policy with the lowest cost of protection for the largest number of years over that interval. In most cases that policy would be the preferable one of those under consideration.[3] The benchmark prices derived by Professor Belth (see table 5-18) are based on United States population data, rather than on insured lives data, and represent a relatively high cost of providing death benefits only; there is no allowance for company overhead or operations.

In most cases term rates for standard-issue policies to people in good health will be below these benchmark prices, which are only a crude yardstick and should not be used as the criterion for automatically rejecting a policy. These benchmark prices would have no validity at all for evaluating rates on policies issued or proposed to persons in poor health who are charged associated higher premiums. Such premiums might legitimately be multiples of the benchmark prices.

Both Belth methods of policy comparison are appropriately used for comparing similar and dissimilar policies. With some modification these methods are even appropriate for comparing replacement evaluations. Part of their attractiveness is their simplicity and their ability to be calculated without the need of a computer. Calculations are actually simple enough they can be done by hand; nevertheless, the process can be expedited with a good calculator or a computer.

TABLE 5-18
Joseph Belth's Benchmark Prices of Insurance

Age	Price
Under Age 30	$ 1.50
30-34	2.00
35-39	3.00
40-44	4.00
45-49	6.50
50-54	10.00
55-59	15.00
60-64	25.00
65-69	35.00
70-74	50.00
75-79	80.00
80-84	125.00

NOTES

1. See chapter 3 for a discussion of term insurance.
2. See chapter 4 for a discussion of whole life insurance.
3. *Insurance Forum*, June 1982, p. 168.

6

Annuities

Dan M. McGill
Revised by Edward E. Graves and Joseph W. Huver

The term *annuity* is derived from the Latin word *annus,* meaning year, and hence connotes an annual payment. A broader and more contemporary definition, however, is that an annuity is a periodic payment to commence at a specified or contingent date and to continue throughout a fixed period or for the duration of a designated life or lives. The person whose life governs the duration of the payments is called the *annuitant.* The annuitant may or may not be the person who receives the periodic payments, although he or she usually is. The income under the annuity contract may be paid annually, semiannually, quarterly, or monthly, depending on the conditions of the agreement. Normally the income is paid monthly.

If the payments are to be made for a definite period of time without being linked to the duration of a specified human life, the agreement is known as an annuity *certain* (exemplified by mortgages and bank loans). If the payments are to be made for the duration of a designated life, the agreement is called a *life annuity* or, more accurately, a *single life* annuity. It is also referred to as a *whole life* annuity to distinguish it from a *temporary life* annuity, under which payments are to be made during a specified period of time but only for as long as a designated person is alive. In other words, a temporary life annuity terminates with the death of the designated individual or at the expiration of the specified period of time, whichever occurs earlier. The word *life* in the title of an annuity indicates that the payments are based on life contingencies or continue only as long as a designated person is alive. This chapter is concerned primarily with life annuities created by insurance companies.

NATURE OF ANNUITIES

Comparison with Life Insurance

The primary function of life insurance is to *create* an estate or principal sum; the primary function of an annuity is to *liquidate* a principal sum, regardless of how it was created. Despite this basic dissimilarity in function, life insurance and annuities are based on the same fundamental pooling, mortality and investment principles.

In the first place, both life insurance and annuities protect against loss of income. Life insurance furnishes protection against loss of income arising out of premature death; an annuity provides protection against loss of income arising out of excessive longevity. It might be said that life insurance provides a financial hedge against dying too soon, while an annuity provides a hedge against living too long. From an economic standpoint, both contingencies are undesirable. A second common feature is the utilization of the pooling technique. Insurance is a pooling arrangement whereby all make contributions so that the dependents of those who die prematurely are partially compensated for loss of income; an annuity is a pooling arrangement whereby those who die prematurely make a contribution on behalf of those who live beyond their life expectancy and would otherwise outlive their income. A third common feature is that the contributions in each case are based on probabilities of death and survival as reflected in a mortality table. For reasons that will be apparent later, the same mortality table is not used for both sets of calculations. Finally, under both arrangements, contributions are discounted for the compound interest that the insurance company will earn on them.

The Annuity Principle

The annuity concept is founded on the unpredictability of human life. A person may have accumulated a principal sum for his or her old-age support that, assuming that the sum is to be liquidated over his or her remaining years, should be adequate for the purpose. Such a result, however, requires estimating the length of the individual's lifetime. He or she might have average health and vitality for his or her age and could expect to live exactly the calculated life expectancy (derived from a mortality table). But because the individual could not be sure of not surviving beyond this predicted life expectancy, to be on the safe side, he or she would have to plan to spread the accumulated principal over a much longer period than he or she is likely to live. Even then there would be some danger of surviving the period and finding the assets and income totally consumed prior to death. On the other hand, the individual might die after only a few years, leaving funds to his or her estate that could have and should have been used to provide the person with more comforts during his or her lifetime.

If the individual were willing to pool savings with those of other people in the same predicament, the administering agency, relying on the laws of probability and large numbers, could provide each of the participants with an income of a specified amount as long as he or she lives—regardless of longevity. No one could outlive his or her income. Such an arrangement, however, implies a willingness on each participant's part to have all or a portion of his or her unliquidated principal at the time of death used to supplement the exhausted principal of those who live beyond their life expectancy.

Each payment under an annuity is composed partly of principal and partly of the income on the unliquidated principal. For each year that goes by, a larger proportion of the payment is composed of principal. If a person exactly lives out his or her life expectancy, as computed at the time the individual enters on the annuity, the principal will be completely exhausted with the last payment prior to death. If the person lives beyond his or her life expectancy, each payment will be derived from funds forfeited by those who die before attaining their life expectancy. It is an equitable arrangement since at the outset no one can know into what category he or she will fall. There is no other arrangement under which a principal sum can—with certainty—be completely liquidated in equal installments over the duration of a human life.

Classifications of Annuities

Annuities may be classified in many different ways, depending on the point of emphasis. For most purposes, they can be classified by the following:

- number of lives covered
- time when payments commence
- method of premium payment
- nature of the insurer's obligation

Number of Lives Covered

This is a simple dichotomy and refers only to whether the annuity covers a single life or more than one life. The conventional form is a single-life annuity. If the contract covers two or more lives, it may be a *joint* annuity or a *joint-and-survivor* annuity. A joint annuity provides that the income will cease upon the first death among the lives involved; it is seldom issued. A joint-and-survivor annuity, on the other hand, provides that the income will cease only upon the last death among the lives covered. In other words, payments under a joint-and-survivor annuity continue for as long as either of two or more specified persons live. This is a very useful contract, and it enjoys a wide market. Annuity contracts involving more than two lives are rarely sold.

Time When Payments Commence

Annuities may also be classified as *immediate* or *deferred*. An immediate annuity is one in which the first payment is due one payment interval after the date of purchase. If the contract provides for monthly payments, the first payment is due one month after the date of purchase; if annual payments are called for, the first payment is due one year after the date of purchase. However, in all these cases the annuity is "entered on" immediately. The first payment begins to accrue immediately after purchase. An immediate annuity is always purchased with a single premium; the annuitant exchanges a principal sum for the promise of an income for life or for a term of years, as the case might be.

The immediate annuity has been supplanted in importance by the deferred annuity, under which a period longer than one payment interval must elapse after purchase before the first benefit payment is due. As a matter of fact, there is normally a spread of several years between the date of purchase and the time when payments commence. This contract is usually, but not always, purchased with periodic premiums payable over a number of years, up to the date income benefits commence. It is suitable for many people, including a person of ordinary means who wants to accumulate a sum for his or her old age.

Method of Premium Payment

Deferred annuities may be purchased with either single premiums or periodic premiums. Originally an annuity was envisioned as a type of contract one would buy with a lump sum, accumulated perhaps from a successful business venture or possibly inherited, in exchange for an immediate income of a stipulated amount.

Immediate annuities are still purchased with a lump sum, but most annuities today are purchased on an installment basis. High income taxes and estate taxes as well as inflation have made it difficult for most people to accumulate the purchase price (consideration) for a single-premium annuity. The deferred annuity provides an attractive and convenient method of accumulating the necessary funds for an adequate old-age income.

Nature of the Insurer's Obligation

The dichotomy here is *pure* versus *refund* annuities. A pure annuity, frequently referred to as a *straight life annuity,* provides periodic—usually monthly—income payments that continue as long as the annuitant lives but terminate at that person's death. The annuity is considered fully liquidated upon the death of the annuitant, no matter how soon that may occur after purchase, and no refund is payable to the deceased annuitant's estate. Moreover, no guarantee is given that any particular number of monthly payments will be paid. This nonrefund feature may be applied to either an immediate or a deferred annuity. In other words, it is possible to obtain a contract under which no part of the purchase price will be refunded even if the annuitant dies before the income commences. On the other hand, the contract could call for a refund of all premiums paid, with or without interest, in the event of the insured's death before commencement of the annuity income, with no refund feature after the annuitant enters on the annuity. In the description of a deferred annuity therefore it is necessary to distinguish between the accumulation and liquidation periods in labeling the contract as pure or refund.

A refund annuity is any type that promises to return (in one manner or another) a portion or all of the purchase price of the annuity. These contracts take several forms, the most important of which are discussed in the next section. As might be expected, refund annuities are far more popular than pure annuities.

SINGLE-LIFE ANNUITIES

Immediate Annuities

The discussion in this section is not limited to immediate annuities in the technical sense but also includes the liquidation phase of deferred annuities. In other words, it is a description of the various arrangements under which a principal sum can be liquidated on the basis of life contingencies. The principles involved are equally applicable to the life-income options of life insurance contracts where the death benefit funds the lifelong payments.

Pure Annuities

As stated above, a pure annuity is one that provides periodic benefit payments of a stipulated amount as long as the annuitant lives, with the payments ceasing upon the death of the annuitant. The consideration paid for the annuity is regarded as fully earned by the insurance company by the time the benefit payments begin. The payments may be made monthly, quarterly, semiannually, or annually. The more frequent the periodic payments, the more costly the annuity is in terms of annual income. That is, 12 monthly payments of $100 each, the first due one month hence, are more costly than one annual payment of $1,200 due one year hence. This is due to the greater expense of drawing 12 checks, loss of interest by the insurance company, and the greater probability that the annuitant will live to receive the payments. If the annuitant should die 6 months and one day after purchasing the annuity, he or she would receive six monthly payments of $100 each in one case and nothing in the other. The principle would hold true regardless of the year in which the annuitant dies. Occasionally, annuities are made apportionable—that is, they provide for a pro rata fractional payment covering the period from the date of the last regular payment to the date of death. This feature necessitates an increase in the purchase price since premiums for the usual type of annuity are calculated on the assumption that there will be no such pro rata payment.

The pure annuity provides the maximum income per dollar of outlay and for that reason is perhaps most suitable for people with only a limited amount of capital. According to typical actuarial assumptions, $1,000 of capital will provide monthly income between $7 and $10 for males and between $6 and $9 for females under a straight life annuity to those aged 65 (see table 6-1 later in this chapter). If payments are guaranteed for 10 years, whether the annuitant lives or dies, the monthly income will be reduced approximately $.50 for each $1,000 increment.[1] On an investment of $100,000, the difference in monthly income will be $50, which might be the difference between dependency and self-sufficiency for an elderly person. For a person aged 70 the difference in monthly income from $100,000 will be $100, and at 75 the difference will be $175—too large to ignore.

At younger ages, however, because of the high probability of survival, the difference in income between an annuity without a refund feature and one with a refund feature is extremely small. A person aged 35 can obtain an annuity with a 5-year guarantee for the same cost as a pure annuity and an annuity with a 10-year guarantee at the sacrifice of only a few cents of monthly income per $1,000 of outlay. Even someone aged 55 can obtain a 10-year guarantee at a reduction in monthly income of less than 50 cents. In general therefore males under 60 and females under 65 should not purchase a pure annuity unless the limited amount of capital makes it imperative. Below those ages, annuitants' chances of surviving the typical periods of guaranteed payments are so good that they gain little in monthly income by giving up the refund feature.

Refund Annuities

Most people have strong objections to placing a substantial sum of money into a contract that promises little or no return if they should die at an early age. Therefore to make annuities salable insurance companies have found it necessary to add a refund feature. The refund feature may take two general forms: a promise to provide a certain number of annuity payments whether the annuitant lives or dies or a promise to refund all or a portion of the purchase price in the event of the annuitant's early death.

Life Annuity Certain. The first type of contract goes under various names, including *life annuity certain, life annuity certain and continuous, life annuity with installments certain, life annuity with a period certain guarantee,* and *life annuity with minimum guaranteed return.* The essence of the agreement is that a stipulated number of monthly payments will be made whether the annuitant lives or dies, and payments will continue for the whole of the annuitant's life if he or she lives beyond the guaranteed period. Contracts may be written with payments guaranteed for 5, 10, 15, or 20 years, although not all insurers offer such a wide range of choices. A few companies will even guarantee payments for 25 years.

This type of refund annuity is composed of two elements: an annuity certain and a pure deferred life annuity. The annuity certain covers the period of guaranteed payments and, true to its characteristics, provides the payments whether the annuitant is alive or not. The deferred life annuity becomes effective at the end of the period of guaranteed payments and provides benefits only if the annuitant survives the term of the annuity certain. The benefits are deferred and are contingent upon the annuitant's being alive to receive them. Therefore the second portion of the company's promise can properly be described as a *pure deferred* life annuity. If the annuitant does not survive the period of guaranteed payments, no payments are made under the deferred life annuity, and no refund is forthcoming. If the annuitant does survive the term of the annuity certain, the deferred life annuity provides benefits for the remainder of the annuitant's life.

An annuity with a period certain is always more expensive per dollar of income than a straight life annuity since it is not based solely on life contingencies. Some of the payments are a certainty; the only cost-reducing factor is the compound interest earned on the unliquidated portion of the purchase price. Therefore the longer the term of the period certain—or to put it more specifically, the longer the period of guaranteed payments—the more costly this type of refund annuity will be or the lower the yield on the purchase price. Since it is not based solely on life contingencies, the cost of an annuity certain does not depend on the age of the annuitant; it varies directly with the length of the term. At any particular age, however, the longer the period of guaranteed payments, the less expensive the deferred life annuity will be since the higher the age at which the deferred life annuity commences, the smaller the probability that the annuitant will survive to that age. This means that the larger the number of guaranteed payments, the smaller the portion of the purchase price going into the deferred life annuity.

Installment Refund Annuity. There are two important types of contracts that promise to return all or a portion of the purchase price. The first is called the *installment refund annuity.* This contract promises that if the annuitant dies before receiving monthly payments equal to the purchase price of the annuity, the payments will be continued to a contingent beneficiary or beneficiaries until the full cost has been recovered. According to the rates of a sample of insurers, $100,000 will provide a monthly life income between $650 and $950 on the installment refund basis to a male annuitant aged 65 at the time of purchase. If the annuitant dies after receiving 100 payments ($65,000 to $95,000), the payments will be continued to a contingent beneficiary until an additional $35,000 to $5,000 is paid out, making an aggregate of $100,000. If he dies after 13 years, there will be no further payments since the entire purchase price will already have been recovered. It is understood, of course, that payments to the annuitant continue as long as he lives even though the purchase price may long since have been recovered in full.

Cash Refund Annuity. The contract may promise, upon the death of the annuitant, to pay to the annuitant's estate or a contingent beneficiary a lump sum that is the difference, if any, between the purchase price of the annuity and the sum of the monthly payments, in which case the contract is called a *cash refund annuity.* The only difference between the cash refund and installment refund annuities is that in the former, the unrecovered portion of the purchase price is refunded in a lump sum at the time of the annuitant's death; in the latter, the monthly installments are continued until the purchase price has been completely recovered. The cash refund annuity is naturally somewhat more expensive because the insurance company loses the interest it would have earned while liquidating the remaining portion of the purchase price on an installment basis.

A frequently asked question is how a life insurance company can afford to promise to return the annuitant's investment in full whether he or she lives or dies and yet continue monthly payments to annuitants who have already recovered their investment. It would seem that every dollar paid to an annuitant in excess of his or her investment would have to be offset by the forfeiture of a dollar by an annuitant who died before recovering the purchase price. The answer lies in compound interest. Note that the insurance company does not promise to pay out benefits equal to the purchase price *plus interest.* Under this type of refund annuity the interest earnings on the unliquidated portion of the premiums of all annuitants receiving benefits provide the funds for payments in excess of any particular annuitant's purchase price (investment).

Fifty Percent Refund Annuity. An annuity contract that guarantees a minimum return of one-half of the purchase price is a compromise between the straight life annuity and the 100 percent refund annuity. Logically enough, such a contract is called a *50 percent refund annuity.* Under its terms, if the annuitant dies before receiving benefits equal to half of the cost of the annuity, monthly installments are continued until the combined payments to both the annuitant and a contingent beneficiary equal half of the cost of the annuity. If the beneficiary so elects, it is customary to provide that he or she can receive the present value of the remaining payments in a lump sum. Since the guarantee under this contract is smaller than that under the 100 percent refund annuity, the cost is lower. Conversely, the income per dollar of purchase price is larger.

A form of annuity sometimes written provides that, regardless of the number of payments received prior to the annuitant's death, 50 percent of the cost of the contract will be returned in the form of a death benefit. This contract is not a refund annuity in the strict sense. Instead, one-half of the premium is used by the company to provide a straight life annuity, and the other half is held on deposit. Earnings from the half held on deposit are used to supplement the annuity benefits provided by the other half of the premium. At the annuitant's death the premium deposit is returned to the annuitant's estate or to a designated beneficiary in the form of a death benefit.

Modified Cash Refund Annuity. Finally, another variation of the refund annuity is found among contributory pension plans. Called a modified cash refund annuity, it promises that if the employee dies before receiving retirement benefits equal to the accumulated value of *his or her* contributions with or without interest, the difference between the employee's benefits and contributions will be refunded in a lump sum to the employee's estate or a designated beneficiary. In other words, the refund feature is based on the employee's contributions and not on the portion of the total cost of the annuity paid by the employer.

The range of monthly income amounts provided under various forms of annuities per $1,000 of premium accumulations are shown in table 6-1. The principal sum of $1,000 does not refer to a single premium of that amount paid at the various ages but to a sum accumulated through periodic premiums that contain an allowance for expenses or through the maturity by death of an insurance contract purchased with gross premiums. In other words, these benefits, which may be augmented by dividends, are based on premiums without policy fees and could not be purchased with a lump-sum payment on quite so favorable a cost basis, but they do illustrate the variations in yield among the various annuity forms.

TABLE 6-1
Range of Monthly Annuity Benefits Available per $1,000
of Purchase Price (Immediate Annuities)

Type	Range	Male Age				
		60	65	70	75	80
Life	Low	$6.42	$ 7.00	$ 8.33	$ 9.60	$12.18
Life	High	9.32	10.00	11.26	12.82	15.12
10-Year Certain + Life	Low	5.60	6.50	7.32	8.26	9.00
10-Year Certain + Life	High	9.03	9.50	10.26	10.94	11.60
Refund	Low	5.89	6.50	7.46	8.27	9.61
Refund	High	9.06	9.50	10.50	11.55	12.87
Type	Range	Female Age				
		60	65	70	75	80
Life	Low	$5.20	$6.00	$ 7.12	$ 8.38	$ 9.90
Life	High	8.66	9.00	10.11	12.60	10.00
10-Year Certain + Life	Low	5.07	5.75	6.52	7.51	8.37
10-Year Certain + Life	High	8.52	9.00	9.67	10.46	11.08
Refund	Low	5.44	5.75	6.18	7.58	8.27
Refund	High	8.52	9.00	9.85	11.00	11.74

Source: Best's Flitcraft Compend 1993

Table 6-1 illustrates the inconsequential cost of a refund feature at younger ages and its high cost at advanced ages. It is interesting to note that at the higher ages, both the installment refund and the cash refund forms are less expensive—or, conversely, yield more—than a life annuity with a 10-year guarantee.

At the advanced ages they cost less than even a 15-year guarantee. Remember, however, that the benefits under each of the forms are the actuarial equivalent of those under all the other forms, and the annuitant must choose the form that is most appropriate to his or her financial and family circumstances.

With the computing power available today it is possible for insurance companies to design annuity contracts with any length of period certain or with a refund guarantee for any specified portion from none to all of the purchase price. In practice, however, each insurer is likely to offer only a few options regarding period certain choices and refund potions. The costs of getting regulatory approval are probably the single most important impediment to offering a full spectrum of choices.

Deferred Annuities

It is helpful in considering deferred annuities to distinguish between the accumulation period and the liquidation period. The preceding discussion of immediate annuities related entirely to the liquidation phase of annuities. It was assumed that the funds needed to provide the various income payments were on hand, and no consideration was given to the manner in which the funds had been accumulated.

Accumulation Period

With deferred annuities, however, there is always a period during which funds are accumulated with the insurance company to reach the amount necessary to provide the benefits promised at a specified future date. The sum may be accumulated through a lump sum premium to which compound interest is added during the intervening years, or it may be accumulated through a series of periodic premiums. If the premiums are made periodically, they can range almost anywhere between a rigid schedule of level payments and (at the other extreme) flexible payments where the timing and amount of each payment is at the discretion of the purchaser.

Because it is impossible to predict the amount available to fund benefits, annuity contracts that allow flexibility in premium payments during the accumulation phase cannot specify in advance the level of benefit payments that will be paid during the liquidation phase. Instead, they specify the amount of benefit per each $1,000 of fund balance when the annuity switches over to the liquidation phase. The fund itself is merely an accumulation device similar to a defined-contribution pension plan prior to retirement.

Regardless of how the contributions are made to the fund, there is a question about of the company's obligation in the event the purchaser dies prior to the date the income is scheduled to commence. The agreement might provide that there is to be no refund of premiums if the annuitant dies before receiving any payments. If so, the annuity could be described as a "pure" annuity with respect to the period of accumulation. Such a contract has little popular appeal. Under private pension plans, however, employer contributions are almost invariably applied to the purchase of pure deferred annuities. If the employee terminates employment before retirement, the employer recovers the employer's contributions, plus interest, but if the employee dies, employer contributions on his or her behalf remain with the insurance company to provide benefits to employees who remain with the employer to retirement. Such an annuity can be purchased at a much lower premium than one that promises to return contributions to the date of death, with the result that the employer can either finance the pension plan at the lowest possible outlay or can provide larger retirement benefits than he or she could otherwise afford.

Almost without exception deferred annuities sold to individuals promise to return all premiums with or without interest in the event of the annuitant's death before "entering on" the annuity. The usual contract provides for a return of either gross premiums without interest or the cash value (whichever is larger). Such a contract therefore is a type of refund annuity with respect to the period of accumulation.

Liquidation Period

Everything about immediate annuities discussed earlier applies with equal force to the liquidation phase of deferred annuities. Once the necessary funds have been accumulated and the annuitant is ready to enter on the annuity, he or she usually has the option of taking the income under any of the benefit plans described. Thus annuitants might choose a straight life annuity, a life annuity with guaranteed installments, an installment refund annuity, or a cash refund annuity. As a matter of fact, they may be given the choice of taking cash in lieu of a life income. It is not inconsistent for annuitants to choose a pure or straight life annuity for the liquidation phase of an annuity that was a refund type of annuity during the accumulation phase. Conceivably some individuals might purchase an annuity that provides for no refund during the period of accumulation and elect to liquidate it on a refund basis. Most annuitants, however, prefer the refund basis during both the accumulation and the liquidation phases.

A deferred annuity that had fixed level premiums, known as a *retirement annuity,* is an annuity form that was widely available in the past. It was popular back when nearly all annuity contracts had heavy front-end expense loadings. A wide range of options permitted the annuitant to adjust the contract during the deferral period to changes of circumstances not anticipated when the contract was purchased. The retirement annuity was an early step in the development of increased annuity contract flexibility. The more flexible and lower-cost annuities available today have nearly eliminated the fixed-premium retirement annuity from the market.

Structuring the Contract

The premiums for an annuity contract may be quoted in units of $100 annual premium or in terms of the annual premium needed to provide a monthly life income of $10 at a designated age. In the first case, the premium will be an even amount, and the income will vary with the age of issue and the age at which the income will commence. In the second case, the income will be a fixed even amount, and the premium will vary.

The structure of the deferred-annuity contract can best be understood by the following example. In accordance with the rate basis of several leading companies, for each $10 unit of monthly life income to be paid to a male annuitant at age 65 with payments guaranteed for 10 years, between $1,052 and $1,538 must be accumulated by age 65, regardless of the age at which the annuitant purchases the annuity.[2] Obviously, the younger the age at which the annuitant begins to contribute toward the accumulation objective, the smaller each annual contribution or deposit can be. To accumulate $15,380—the amount needed to provide $100 per month at age 65 with payments guaranteed for 120 months—a man aged 25 will have to contribute only $112 per year to age 65, while a man aged 45 will have to deposit $441 per year.[3] A man aged 55 will have to deposit $1,195 per year for 10 years.

The level premiums or deposits, as they are usually called, are accumulated at a rate of compound interest equal to or greater than the specified long-term rate guaranteed in the contract—usually between 3 percent and 5 percent. Some deferred annuity contracts also include a short-term (such as one, 2, 3, or 5 years) interest rate guarantee that is competitive with current investment yields and higher than the guaranteed long-term rate. These short-term interest rate guarantees are often combined with a bail-out provision allowing the contract to be terminated without a surrender charge if the interest rate actually being credited falls below a stipulated rate (often 2 percentage points [200 basis points] below the short-term guaranteed rate). The bail-out provision may seem much more attractive than it really is for two reasons: (1) It is highly unlikely that competitors will be able to pay higher rates if and when the release is triggered, and (2) a cash-out will be subject to income taxes and possibly a 10 percent penalty tax (see chapter 11).

In the event of the annuitant's death before age 65 (or whatever the maturity date) the company will return the accumulated gross premiums without interest or the cash value, whichever is larger. The cash value is equal to the gross premiums improved at a guaranteed rate of interest after deducting a charge for expenses. After about 10 years, the cash value exceeds the accumulated value of premiums paid (without interest) and thus becomes the effective death benefit. (It is of interest to note that, while this is an annuity contract, there is an insurance element during the accumulation period in that the death benefit exceeds the cash value.)

The annuitant may withdraw the full cash value at any time during the deferral period, whereupon the contract terminates and the company has no further obligation. Under some contracts the annuitant may borrow against the cash value, which would not bring about a termination of the contract.

Liquidation Options

At the maturity date the annuitant may elect to have the accumulated sum—$15,380 in the example—applied under any of the annuity forms offered by the company, even though the premium deposits were predicated on the assumption that the income would be provided under a life annuity with 120 guaranteed installments. The actual monthly income might be more or less than the amount originally anticipated, depending on the option elected. Moreover, the annuitant is usually given the privilege of taking cash in lieu of an annuity. This is known as the *cash option,* and it exposes the company to serious adverse selection. Persons in poor health tend to withdraw their accumulations in cash, while those in excellent health usually choose an annuity. To offset this selection some companies provide a retroactive reduction in the investment earnings rate applied to accumulations under a deferred annuity if the annuitant selects the cash option. The resultant penalty can be a substantial dollar amount, and it usually applies also to exchanges of annuity contracts.

Under most contracts the annuitant may choose to have the benefit payments commence at an earlier or a later date than the one originally specified in the contract with an appropriate adjustment in the amount of monthly benefits. The privilege of having the income begin at an earlier age than the age that was specified in the contract is, it should be recognized, an option to convert the cash value to an *immediate* annuity. There is usually no age limit below which the benefit payments cannot begin, although the option is subject to the general requirement that the periodic income payments equal or exceed a stipulated minimum amount.

On the other hand, there is usually an upper age limit, sometimes as high as age 80 or as low as age 70, beyond which commencement of the income benefits cannot be postponed. The option to postpone the commencement of benefit payments may be particularly attractive if the annuitant is still in good health at the original maturity date and plans to work for a few more years. The life income payable at any particular age, whether the maturity date is moved ahead or set back, is the same amount that would have been provided had the substituted maturity date been the one originally selected and funded with the actual amount accumulated.

JOINT ANNUITIES

There are basically two types of joint annuities. One provides income benefits only until the first of two or more annuitants' death. The other continues benefit payments until the last of the named annuitants dies.

Joint-Life Annuity

A joint-life annuity is a contract that provides an income of a specified amount as long as the two or more persons named in the contract live. In other words, the income ceases at the first death among the covered lives. As a result, the coverage is relatively inexpensive.

This contract has a very limited market. It might be appropriate for two persons, elderly sisters, for example, who have an income from a stable source large enough to support one but not both of the sisters. If they can purchase a joint-life annuity in an amount adequate to support one sister without disturbing the other income, the combined income will be adequate for their needs while both sisters are alive. Upon the death of one of the sisters, the income from the original source will meet the survivor's needs. Such a contract is always sold as a single-premium immediate annuity.

Another use of joint-life annuities is to provide income while a spouse or other caregiver must give custodial care to one of the annuitants. In a few cases parents may dislike their children's spouses so strongly that they establish a trust payable to the natural child only if he or she survives the resented in-law. A joint-life annuity could provide support until the trust funds become available to the beneficiary.

Joint-and-Last-Survivor Annuity

A joint-and-last-survivor annuity is a far more appealing contract than the joint-life annuity because the income under this form of annuity continues as long as any of two or more persons live. It is ideal for a husband and wife or for families in which there is a permanently disabled dependent child, for example.

For most combinations of ages, the joint-and-last-survivor annuity is the most expensive of all annuity forms. To provide an income of $100 per month on the joint-and-survivor basis to a man and woman both aged 65, for example, requires an accumulation of $18,350. If the man is 65 and the woman 60, a sum of $19,827 is needed to provide $100 per month on the joint-and-survivor basis. Compare those figures to the $14,285 required to provide a life income of $100 per month with no refund feature to only a man aged 65.

The joint-and-survivor annuity can be purchased as a single-premium immediate annuity, in which event the cost will be somewhat higher than the accumulation figures quoted above, or it may be one of the optional forms made available under an annual-premium deferred annuity. A joint-and-survivor annuity may also be made available for the settlement of life insurance and endowment proceeds.

Although a typical contract does not contain a refund feature, most insurance companies offer a contract under which 120 monthly installments are guaranteed, and a few offer 240 guaranteed installments. When so written, if the last survivor dies before the minimum number of payments has been made, the remaining installments will be continued to a contingent beneficiary. As under single-life annuities, the contingent beneficiary may be permitted to take the present value of the remaining installments. When both husband and wife are 65, a life income of $100 per month with 120 guaranteed installments requires an accumulation of $18,560—only $120 more than such an annuity without a refund feature.

In its conventional form the joint-and-survivor annuity continues the same income to the survivor as is payable while both annuitants are alive. A common modification, which reduces the cost, provides that the income to the survivor will be decreased to two-thirds of the original amount on the theory that the survivor does not require as much income as the two annuitants do. This contract or option, as the case may be, is called a *joint-and-two-thirds annuity*. Such a contract written in an original amount of $100 on the lives of a husband and wife, both aged 65, requires an accumulation of slightly more than $15,960. The benefits can be duplicated by placing a single-life immediate annuity in the appropriate amount on each annuitant and a conventional joint-and-survivor annuity on both lives. Thus an immediate annuity on each life for $100 per month and a joint-and-survivor annuity in the amount of $100 per month will provide $300 per month as long as both annuitants live and $200 per month to the survivor.

In a *joint-and-one-half annuity* the income to the survivor is reduced to one-half the original amount. This form has not had the popular appeal of the joint-and-two-thirds annuity. The computing capacity at insurance companies makes it possible to design the survivor benefit to be any specified proportion of the predeath benefit. Consequently many insurers have introduced more than the one-half and two-thirds options.

The joint-and-last-survivor form is widely used by private pension plans to pay the retirement benefits to married plan participants. It is common to provide that where the joint-and-two-thirds annuity has been elected by the employee, the income is to be reduced only if the employee dies first. If the wife or other dependent dies first, the employee continues to receive the full income. Federal law now requires written consent of the nonemployee spouse in order to drop the survivorship benefit.

VARIABLE ANNUITIES

The conventional concept is that an annuity provides payments of a fixed amount over a specified period or throughout the lifetime of one or more persons. The persistent inflation over recent decades, however, has focused attention on the need for protecting the purchasing power of annuity benefits. This has given rise to a type of contract that attempts to achieve that objective by providing benefits that vary with changes in the insurer's investment performance, which in turn often coincide approximately to changes in the purchasing power of the dollar. Such a contract has appropriately been named a *variable annuity.*

If a contract is to provide benefits with stable purchasing power, it must provide more dollars when prices rise and fewer dollars when prices decline. Theoretically this could be achieved by adjusting the benefits to changes in an appropriate price index, such as the Consumer Price Index published by the Bureau of Labor Statistics. This is not practical from the standpoint of the insurance companies, however, since there is no mechanism by which the value of the assets backing the annuity can be adjusted automatically, or otherwise, to changes in the dollar value of the annuity promises. As a practical solution, contracts have been developed that provide benefits adjusted to changes in the market value of the assets—typically, common stocks—in which the annuity reserves are invested. The theory is that over a long period of time, the market value of a representative group of common stocks tends to conform rather faithfully to changes in the consumer price level. Moreover, inasmuch as the insurance company's liabilities to its annuitants are expressed in terms of the market value of the assets offsetting the liabilities, funds for the payment of annuity benefits will be available in the proper proportions at all times.

Supporters of the variable annuity feel that annuitants need some kind of protection against inflation, and they believe that a common stock investment program administered by a life insurance company is the best approach yet developed. Critics of the variable annuity approach question whether continuing inflation is inevitable, and even if it is, whether common stock investments provide an effective hedge against rising prices.

Accumulation Units

At present variable annuities are most often issued on a deferred basis. During the accumulation period, premium payments—or deposits, as they are frequently called—are applied to the purchase of accumulation units. The accumulation unit is assigned an arbitrary value, such as $10, at the inception of the plan, and the initial premiums purchase accumulation units at that price. Thereafter the units are revalued each month to reflect changes in the market value of the common stock that makes up the company's variable annuity portfolio. On any valuation date, the value of each accumulation unit is determined by dividing the market value of the common stock underlying the accumulation units by the aggregate number of units. Dividends are usually allocated periodically to the participants and applied to the purchase of additional accumulation units, although they may simply be reinvested without allocation and permitted to increase the value of each existing accumulation unit. Capital appreciation or depreciation is always reflected in the value of the accumulation units, rather than in the number of units. (In other words, both realized and unrealized gains and losses are reflected for individual participants through an increase or decrease in the value of their accumulation units.) A portion of each premium payment is deducted for expenses, and the remainder is invested in accumulation units at their current market value.

A hypothetical accumulation is shown in table 6-2. In this example the initial purchase is made at age 35 with a gross consideration (premium) high enough to cover a $200 acquisition each month after paying insurer expenses. The assumptions behind the table 6-2 numbers are that the accumulation units change value once each year and that a full $200 is available each month to acquire more units. The units in this example grow at approximately 7.5 percent most years but fluctuate more or less than that in some years as stock prices are prone to do over short intervals. In this case there is an accumulation of $258,459.62 at the end of the 30th year (end of age 64 or beginning of age 65) consisting of 31,751.8 accumulation units.

Annuity Units

At the beginning of the liquidation period, the accumulation units are exchanged for annuity units. The number of annuity units that will be acquired by the annuitant depends on the company's assumptions as to mortality, dividend rates, and expenses, and upon the market value of the assets underlying the annuity units. In essence, the number of annuity units is determined by dividing the dollar value of the accumulation units ($258,459.62 in our example) by the present value of a life annuity at the participant's attained age in an amount equal to the current value of one annuity unit (assumed to be $35 in this case) adjusted for monthly payments. Although the number of accumulation units of a particular person increases with each premium payment and each allocation of dividends, the number of annuity units remains constant throughout the liquidation period (7,384.6 annuity units in this case). The units are revalued each year, however, reflecting the current market price of the common stock and the mortality, investment, and expense experience for the preceding year.[4] The dollar income payable to the annuitant each month is determined by multiplying the number of annuity units by the current value of each unit. During the annuity—or liquidation—period, the higher the market price of the stock and the greater the dividends, the greater the dollar income of the annuitant will be. During the accumulation stage, however, it is to the annuitant's advantage for stock prices to be relatively low since he or she will thus be able to acquire a larger number of accumulation units for each premium payment.

Some of the more recent variable annuity contracts differ from the above by using only one unit rather than two, by discounting for mortality before as well as after retirement, and by limiting variations in the unit value to investment experience only.

TABLE 6-2
Variable Annuity Accumulation Units
Deferred Annuity Purchased at Age 35 at $200 per Month

Year	Age	Unit Value	New Units	Total Units	Total Value
1	35	$1.00	2,400.00	2,400.00	$ 2,400.00
2	36	1.08	2,232.56	4,632.56	4,980.00
3	37	1.16	2,076.80	6,709.36	7,753.50
4	38	1.24	1,931.91	8,641.26	10,735.01
5	39	1.34	1,797.12	10,438.38	13,940.14
6	40	1.07	2,242.99	12,681.37	13,569.07
7	41	1.15	2,086.50	14,767.88	16,986.75
8	42	1.24	1,940.93	16,708.81	20,660.76
9	43	1.88	1,276.60	17,985.41	33,812.56
10	44	2.12	1,132.08	19,117.48	40,529.06
11	45	2.28	1,053.09	20,170.57	45,968.74
12	46	2.45	979.62	21,150.20	51,816.39
13	47	2.63	911.28	22,061.47	58,102.62
14	48	2.83	847.70	22,909.17	64,860.32
15	49	3.04	788.56	23,697.73	72,124.84
16	50	3.27	733.54	24,431.27	79,934.21
17	51	3.52	682.36	25,113.63	88,329.27
18	52	3.78	634.76	25,748.39	97,353.97
19	53	3.50	685.71	26,434.10	92,519.37
20	54	3.25	738.46	27,172.57	88,310.84
21	55	3.00	800.00	27,972.57	83,917.70
22	56	3.60	666.67	28,639.23	103,101.24
23	57	4.01	598.50	29,237.74	117,243.32
24	58	4.97	482.90	29,720.63	147,711.55
25	59	5.76	416.67	30,137.30	173,590.85
26	60	6.25	384.00	30,521.30	190,758.13
27	61	7.16	335.20	30,856.50	220,932.51
28	62	7.90	303.80	31,160.29	246,166.32
29	63	8.09	296.66	31,456.96	254,486.78
30	64	8.14	294.84	31,751.80	258,459.62

Surrender Provisions

A participant in a variable annuity plan should not normally be permitted to surrender his or her accumulation units for cash or to take other action that might involve temptations to play the stock market. When the variable annuity is used as part of a pension plan, surrender values are not generally made available. When the variable annuity is sold as an individual contract, surrender privileges are made available but on a much more restricted basis than in connection with ordinary annuities. Under all plans the current value of the accumulation units is payable, usually as a continuing income, upon the death of the participant during the accumulation period.

In a landmark decision,[5] the United States Supreme Court held that an individual variable annuity contract is a security within the meaning of the Securities Act of 1933 and that any organization that offers such a contract is an investment company and subject to the Investment Company Act of 1940. Hence any company that offers individual variable annuity contracts is subject to dual supervision by the Securities and Exchange Commission and the various state insurance departments. Persons selling variable annuities must pass the series 6 licensing exam of the National Association of Securities Dealers (NASD).

ACTUARIAL CONSIDERATIONS

The insurance company's cost of providing annuity benefits is based on the probability of survival rather than the probability of death. In itself this fact would seem to have no greater significance than that the insurance company actuaries, in computing premiums for annuities, have to refer to the actuarial probabilities of survival rather than probabilities of death. As a matter of fact, however, writing annuities poses a unique set of actuarial problems.

In the first place, insurance companies have found that the mortality among persons who purchase annuities tends to be lower age for age than that of people who purchase life insurance. There may be several reasons for this, including the peace of mind that comes with an assured income for life, but certainly one of the most important is the selection practiced against the company. Individuals who know that they have serious health impairments rarely, if ever, purchase annuities. In fact, many persons contemplating purchasing immediate annuities subject themselves to a thorough medical examination to make sure that they have no serious impairments before committing their capital to annuities. On the other hand, people who know or suspect that they have an impairment usually seek life insurance. Whatever its origin, the mortality difference between life insurance insureds and annuitants is so substantial that special annuity mortality tables must be used for the calculation of annuity premiums.[6]

Second, the trend toward lower mortality that has been such a favorable development with respect to life insurance has been very unfavorable with respect to annuities. Many annuity contracts run for 60 to 75 years, counting the accumulation period, and rates that were adequate at the time the contract was issued may, with the continued increase in longevity, prove inadequate over the years. All mortality tables, of course, contain a safety margin—which, for life insurance mortality tables, means higher death rates than those likely to be experienced, and for annuity mortality tables, lower rates of mortality than anticipated. While a long-run decline in mortality rates increases the safety margin in life insurance mortality tables, it shrinks the margin in annuity mortality tables, sometimes to the point of extinction. Therefore an annuity mortality table that accurately reflects the mortality among annuitants at the time it was compiled gradually becomes obsolete and eventually overstates the expected mortality.

Finally, a high percentage of annuitants are women, who as a group enjoy greater longevity than men, which has intensified the first two factors mentioned above. It also forced companies to introduce a rate differential between male and female annuitants long before a rate differential based on sex was applied to the sale of life insurance policies. However, court decisions have required insurers to base some group annuity contracts on unisex mortality rates.

Revised Mortality Tables

Life insurance companies cope with these problems or complications in various ways. In the first place, they compute annuity considerations on the basis of mortality tables that reflect the annuitants' lower mortality. A number of annuity tables have been constructed and used since the 1937 Standard Annuity Table that was in common use until the 1950s. First, the Annuity Table for 1949 or some modification thereof was widely used for writing individual annuities, but it has been supplanted by three newer tables: the 1955 American Annuity Table, then the 1971 Individual Annuity Table, and currently the 1983 Individual Annuity Table on which all annuity calculations in this book are based.

For many years companies dealt with the specific problem associated with the continuing decline in mortality rates among annuitants by using age *setbacks*. In other words, a person was assumed to be one, 2, or 3 years younger than his or her actual age. Thus a person who was actually 65 and had a life expectancy of an individual that age was presumed for the purpose of premium calculations to have the life expectancy of a person aged 64, 63, or even 62, thereby increasing the premium for a given amount of income. Ages for females were usually set back 4 or 5 five years in addition to the setback for males in recognition of the sex differential in mortality. Thus if male ages were set back one year, female ages were set back as much as 6 years. If the reduction in mortality had been reflected equally at all ages, the setback technique could have been utilized indefinitely without serious distortion of the equities among annuitants at different ages. However, the reduction is not at a uniform rate at various ages, which has definitely limited the efficacy of the setback technique.

Ironically the 1983 Individual Annuity Table was derived from separate male and female experience and has gender-distinct probabilities even though legal and social events have prompted many insurers to base their annuity products on unisex mortality. Comparison of the male and female mortality rates indicates that the practice of deriving female tables using an age setback of male tables as the only adjustment was a very crude approach to a very complex relationship. The practice should have entailed varying setbacks at each age to accurately adjust male mortality rates to represent longer-lived females.

The most recent approach to the "problem" of declining mortality is an annuity table that, by means of projection factors, attempts to forecast and make suitable adjustments for future reductions in mortality rates. For example, the Annuity Tables for 1949, 1955, 1971, and 1983 all contain a set of projection factors that can be used to adjust the mortality assumptions for all ages from year to year or, in lieu of that, to project the basic rates of mortality to some future date. The projections make allowances for anticipated future reductions in mortality.

Higher Interest Assumptions

Historically insurance companies attempted to hedge future improvement in annuitant mortality by using an unrealistically low interest assumption in the premium formula. The rates were substantially lower than those used in the calculation of life insurance premiums. The effectiveness of this technique can be judged by the fact that an interest margin of .25 percentage point (25 basis points) is capable of absorbing a general reduction in mortality of 6 percent or 7 percent. Intensified competition among insurance companies and between insurance companies and investment media, however, has caused companies to adopt interest assumptions much closer to the level of their actual investment earnings. Considerations for individual deferred annuities are generally being computed today on the basis of interest assumptions running from 2.5 to 5.5 percent, while immediate annuities may be priced on the basis of slightly higher interest assumptions.

Computing Premiums on a Participating Basis

A final approach to adjusting annuity mortality for anticipated future increases in life expectancy is to compute the premiums (or considerations) on a participating basis, which permits conservative assumptions (safety margins) with respect to all factors entering into the computations. Annual-premium annuities issued by mutual companies are almost invariably participating during the accumulation period and may be participating on some basis during the liquidation period. Some stock companies also issue annuities that are participating during the accumulation period. Single-premium immediate annuities, whether written by mutual or stock companies, are usually not participating.

USES OF THE ANNUITY

Because it is the single-premium life annuity that most frequently comes to mind when annuities are mentioned and since this form requires the deposit of a substantial sum of money, most people have the impression that annuities appeal only to the wealthy. This is not at all the case. The range of the annuity's usefulness is nearly as wide as that of the life insurance contract, and forms have been devised to fit virtually every conceivable need or circumstance.

The market for annuities is composed of two broad classes of individuals: those who have already accumulated an estate either through inheritance or by their own personal efforts and those who are seeking to accumulate an estate. The first class may be subdivided into the wealthy and those with only moderate resources.

Wealthy individuals purchase annuities as a hedge against adverse financial developments. Large estates can be wrecked through business reverses, unwise investments, and reckless spending. Insurance company records abound with cases of individuals who at one time were wealthy but whose fortunes melted away, leaving payments from annuities purchased in their more affluent days as their sole source of income. There are also numerous cases of individuals who are dependent on relatives for whom they had purchased annuities during a more solvent period. Wealthy people, then, purchase annuities in a search for security. To them yield is a secondary consideration.

Yield, on the other hand, is a primary consideration for those persons, mostly middle-aged and elderly, who have accumulated a modest estate and hope that it will be the source of financial security during the remaining years of their lives. The life annuity, perhaps in the joint-and-survivor form, is the answer to the problem of this group, since it maximizes income by including a portion of the principal in each monthly payment and promises a continuation of the benefit payments and some deferral of income taxes as long as the annuitant or annuitants live. Although some people in these circumstances are reluctant to invest their capital in an annuity because they want to leave an estate to their children or other close relatives, many parents feel that, having reared and educated their children, their greatest responsibility is providing for their own old-age maintenance, thus relieving the children of that burden. The annuity is an ideal instrument for accomplishing this objective.

Furthermore, there are situations in which the entire capital accumulation may not be needed to provide for the parents' old-age support. In such cases, a portion of the estate can be used to purchase an annuity of suitable form and size, making it possible for the remainder of the estate to be distributed to the children during the parents' lifetime, when it may be of the greatest use to the children. Most young people would probably prefer to receive a smaller share of their parents' estate when their need for capital is the greatest than to wait for a larger share when the need may be less urgent. Moreover, many parents, if they could safely do so, would prefer to distribute a portion of their estate to their children during the parents' lifetime so that they can witness the enjoyment it brings. Annuities can be used in a similar manner to provide living bequests to charitable, educational, and religious organizations.

The annuity is also an attractive savings medium for the person who has not yet accumulated an estate but wants to achieve financial independence in old age. Professional people find annuities especially attractive for that purpose. The same is true of athletes, entertainers, and others who enjoy a very large income but for a limited period of time. Annuities are an appropriate investment because they can be purchased through flexible periodic premiums or through single-premium deposits as the annuitant comes into possession of large sums.

STRUCTURED SETTLEMENTS

Over the past decade the courts have handed down guilty verdicts in at least 5,000 cases involving personal injury or wrongful death in which the negligent party was found liable for at least $1 million in damages. More than 95 percent of these cases were settled before they ever went to trial although the settlement is still enforceable by the court. Most such cases were settled on a lump-sum basis.

Quite frequently the courts are seeking lifetime financial support for the injured party or throughout the minority of dependent heirs. Consequently it is usually acceptable to the court to have the liability paid in the form of periodic payments instead of as a single lump-sum payment. Insurance companies can and do issue immediate annuity contracts that will guarantee the payments over the required lifetime or over the mandated support period. These contracts are specifically tailored to the needs of the injured or wronged parties (claimants).

While the concept of paying periodic payments over time for claimant damages can be traced to the 1950s, independent full-time structured settlement specialists were not common until the 1970s. Since then the number of cases using structured settlement contracts to satisfy the plaintiffs' claims has grown substantially. The most frequent cases in which a structured settlement may be appropriate usually involve general liability, medical malpractice, defective products, automobile accidents, or worker's compensation injuries.

Personal injury claim adjusters and/or defense attorneys work together with a structured settlement specialist to form a defense team. Their goal is to arrange settlements that will be appropriate and help to offset any damages suffered by the claimant, consistent with the issues of liability and the claimant's future needs (both known and unanticipated).

Suitable structured settlements will provide an adequate amount of immediate cash for liquidity needs, reimbursement for past expenses, legal fees, and other cash needs. If the recipient is unable to work, an income stream can be designed to fund normal living expenses, custodial and medical services, rehabilitation costs, and where appropriate, tuition for educational programs.

Annuities Utilized in Structured Settlements

The usual structured settlement provides for annuities to pay out periodic payments that meet the recipient's financial needs as much as possible. One of the primary advantages of structured settlements is that the periodic payments of income are received tax free by the claimant during his or her life and by the claimant's beneficiaries thereafter for the balance of any guarantee period. Two of the requirements for the claimant's income-tax-free treatment are the absence of any evidence of ownership by the annuitant of the annuities funding the structured settlement and the absence of constructive receipt or economic benefit in the annuity itself. Therefore all timing decisions, as well as the exact amount of money, are predetermined by the defendant or its insurer, who are the legal owners of the annuity.

If the claimant has no reduction in life expectancy from the injuries that caused the claim, standard rates are applied on life annuities. Likewise, if there is no life contingency, standard rates are used for fixed-period annuities. (An example of a fixed-period annuity is payments of $1,000 a month for 5 years and $2,000 a month during years 6 through 10. This is also referred to as a step-rate annuity.) Annuity benefit payments can generally be increased on a compound annual rate, ranging from 3 percent to 6 percent. In addition to life income guarantees, period-certain and joint-life guarantees can be used, depending on the circumstances involved.

One of the most significant innovations that benefits both the claimant and the defendant is the rated age, or substandard life annuity (see figure 6-1). In a catastrophic injury case, the structured settlement broker submits the medical data to different insurance companies for evaluation. Each company makes its own judgment as to the claimant's life expectancy and bases its annuity quotes on that opinion. Because this is largely subjective, life expectancy estimates vary from one company to another, just as rated-up life insurance varies from one life insurance company to another. Then the broker presents the bids to the defendant and his or her legal counsel to make an informed selection. The life insurance company underwrites the proposed annuitant's current condition, including any preexisting health impairments.

The cost of a substandard annuity bears an inverse relationship to the cost of substandard life insurance. The lower the life expectancy, the lower the annuity cost and the higher the life insurance cost. A difference of 20 years in life expectancy could result in a 50 percent cost differential. Generally, this kind of annuity may be purchased only by defendants or their insurers in personal injury and wrongful death cases, and the number of insurers issuing such contracts is rather small. The claimant or plaintiff needs to cooperate in good-faith bargaining to achieve a fair settlement.

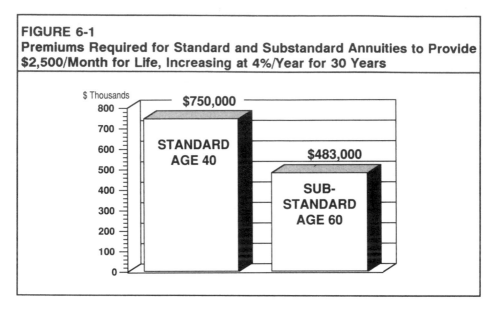

FIGURE 6-1
Premiums Required for Standard and Substandard Annuities to Provide $2,500/Month for Life, Increasing at 4%/Year for 30 Years

The substandard annuity provides the defense team with an extremely valuable financial vehicle. Less than one percent of the life insurance companies offer this discounted underwriting specialty.

Advantages of Structured Settlements

The advantages of a structured settlement for each of the individuals entities involved are explained below.

For the Injured Party

Financial Security. The major advantage of a structured settlement for the injured party is financial security. A lifetime income is especially practical and desirable when a minor or someone acknowledged to be incompetent is involved. The approach is attractive, particularly to the court, whenever there is reason to be concerned about protecting the injured party's future finances. In cases of wrongful death, a structured settlement may be used to provide replacement earnings to the claimant's spouse and children.

Benefits that Match Needs. An injured party needs regular income to meet living expenses and medical care costs. On occasion, when future medical costs are estimated to be substantial but the timing of these costs is unknown, a medical trust, similar to an emergency fund recommended by financial planners, can be used. Typically, the medical trust is created with the defendant as grantor under a trust agreement that is part of the settlement agreement.

Management of Benefits. Claimants and their families or guardians are usually not trained to manage large sums of money. Dissipation of funds through mismanagement, imprudent investment, unwise expenditures, misuse, or even neglect is a high risk. This risk is significantly reduced through the use of periodic payments in a structured settlement.

Guaranteed Payment. Because the income payments are guaranteed for life or for a fixed period, the settlement can never be prematurely exhausted. There could be some reduction and delay in getting benefits if the insurer issuing the settlement agreement fails. Executive Life Insurance Co. is an example where the state guarantee funds are paying reduced benefits after a delay.

Income-Tax-Free Payments. Whether payments are in a lump sum or periodic, they represent personal injury damages, which are excluded from income tax under IRC Sec. 104(a)(2). (See figure 6-2.) (Further clarification of the tax-free nature of structured settlements is given in Rev. Ruls. 79-220, 79-313, and 77-230.)

FIGURE 6-2
Capital Needed to Produce $2,500 Net Monthly,
Increasing at 4%/Year for 30 Years

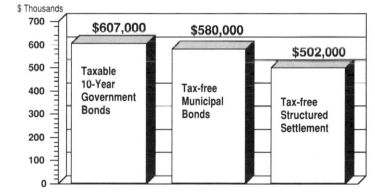

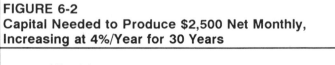

According to data from the Economic Report of the President, 1992, the 25-year average yield (1967–1990) of 10-year government bonds is 8.27 percent. This rate is assumed to apply to the settlement annuity tax-free and to the government bond fund. The income tax rate used on the government bond fund is 28 percent. The long-term Standard & Poor's municipal bonds averaged a yield of 7.02 percent over the period 1967–1990; this rate was used to calculate the municipal bond fund above. If the actual investment returns in future years are lower than these past yields the amount of capital needed will increase.

The Periodic Payments Settlement Act of 1982 codified the above revenue rulings and clarified that the interest as well as the principal portion of periodic payments is income tax free. This same act not only amended IRC Sec. 104(a)(2) but also created IRC Sec. 130, which allowed for continuation of the tax-free treatment of qualified assignments. A qualified assignment allows the defendant or his or her insurer to assign the obligation to make the future payments to a third-party assignee. Usually, the assignee is an affiliate of the life insurance company providing the annuity payments and as assignee assumes the ultimate obligation from the defendant as assignor to make future payments guaranteed under the settlement agreement. The assignee typically is the parent of the life insurance company providing the annuity, an affiliate life insurance company, or an affiliate shell company incorporated to hold the assignments. With the assignment, the defendant or the insurer receives an absolute release and closes the file. The annuity is purchased by the assignee, and the claimant or plaintiff is perceived to receive an enhancement of security (even though it is the status of a general creditor) because life insurance companies and their affiliates are regarded as being more stable than property and casualty companies in terms of solvency.

For the Plaintiff Attorney

Attorneys are assured that their client's settlement is guaranteed and will not be subject to dissipation as is a lump-sum settlement. Some attorneys even believe that recommending a structured settlement insulates them from exposure to legal malpractice since they are not taking a sizable portion of the total value of the entire benefit payable as a lump sum right in the beginning.

For the Defendant

A properly designed periodic payment program may result in less outlay than a lump-sum payment. More important, this approach to a settlement may expedite agreement among the parties, thus freeing up the insurer's or self-insured's reserves more quickly. A structured settlement almost always saves defense costs.

For the Judge

Lump-sum settlements have an obvious disadvantage. The judge or jury must determine how much money the plaintiff will need for the rest of his or her life. If the plaintiff lives longer than expected, the lump sum is exhausted; if the plaintiff dies sooner than expected, his or her heirs could receive a windfall unintended in the settlement. Guaranteed periodic payments for life, however, assure the plaintiff of financial security regardless of when he or she dies and are therefore easier for a judge or jury to award.

For the Public

The public benefits from the structured settlement because the injured party will not become a ward of the state and will be assured of a guaranteed income and proper care. In addition, the delay of prolonged litigation is avoided, thereby reducing court costs and placing more burden on the already overloaded judicial system.

Disadvantages of Structured Settlements

If a life insurance company becomes insolvent, the insured may have to absorb all of the losses in excess of any Guarantor Association limitations. However, with the proviso that the insured is still insurable, he or she may replace life insurance coverage with another viable carrier. In the case of structured settlements, however, the income reduction from choosing a minimum benefit guarantee is not easily replaced. There may be insufficient funds from the insured's other assets to offset the benefit reduction.

Besides the structured settlement specialist's due diligence, the availability of a qualified assignment and compliance with the Uniform Periodic Payment of Judgments Act will mitigate any financial risks arising from a life insurer's insolvency. For obvious reasons, therefore, structured settlement specialists should select only the most secure and well-managed insurance companies.

Because there is no right to accelerate or decelerate future payments, problems can occur if more immediate cash is needed than the stream of payments will provide. This may be due to an unprecedented financial reversal, a medical necessity, an educational need, or inflation over and above expectations. The unfortunate fact is that the periodic payment schedule may not be changed. The original design of the structured settlement should therefore anticipate increasing payments annually, or at least periodically, building in periodic deferred lump sums, or including a medical trust for future medical and custodial needs. In addition to providing an adequate amount of immediate cash for the benefit of the injured party, a well-designed structured settlement will carefully consider the needs of the claimant's dependents.

Sample Structured Settlement Case

The following illustration involves a claimant, John Doe, aged 40, who is totally and permanently disabled due to an accident and will require substantial future medical and custodial care. In addition, his 3-year-old child, Annemarie, will require college funds since John Doe is no longer able to provide any income to save for this goal. As 50 percent of the total settlement, up-front cash of $1.125 million should be sufficient to pay the plaintiff attorney's legal fees and to establish an emergency fund for John Doe. In addition, the income from a medical trust and a $1,000-a-month annuity should be adequate, according to the interpretation of the life care plan that was used as a guide to ascertain John Doe's capital needs for the future. Independent living income of $30,000 a year, increasing at 3 percent compounded interest annually, should provide enough funds to maintain the Doe family's routine cost of living and to help offset future inflation.

The average costs for room, board, and tuition at public and private universities were used to ascertain college fund requirements for Annemarie. These costs were then projected at the average inflation rate. Because many students take 5 years to complete their undergraduate college education, payments are forecast for a 5-year period. The proposed structured settlement is presented in figure 6-3.

FIGURE 6-3
Proposed Structured Settlement

Claimant: John Doe	Age: 40	Life Expectancy: 35 Years	
	Guaranteed Total Payments	Estimated Total Payments	Cost
Immediate Cash, Including Legal Fees	$1,125,000	$1,125,000	$1,125,000
Medical Trust Fund Cash Seed	200,000	200,000	200,000
Annuity Seed (Payments of $1,000 monthly, compounding at 4% each year, starting in one month and continuing for the claimant's life, with the first 20 years guaranteed)	357,337	883,827	263,677
Independent Living Income (Payments of $2,500 monthly, compounding at 3% each year, starting in one month and continuing for the claimant's life with the first 20 years guaranteed	806,111	1,813,862	583,707
College Funds for Daughter, Aged 3			
Payment at age 18	25,000	25,000	15,094
Payment at age 19	38,000	38,000	15,467
Payment at age 20	41,000	41,000	15,623
Payment at age 21	44,000	44,000	15,818
Payment at age 22	47,000	47,000	15,940
Totals	**$2,683,448**	**$4,217,689**	**$2,250,326**

Structured Settlement Services

Prior to designing a structured settlement proposal tailored specifically to the claimant, the structured settlement specialist receives the pertinent data from the claims adjuster and/or the defense attorney. The more data available for this purpose, the more appropriate the design is to the injured party's needs. The structured settlement specialist then provides proposals and present-value estimates of streams of income to the defense team, adopting the design to incorporate any variables they suggest. After a verbal settlement is reached, the structured settlement specialist usually provides the defense attorney with sample closing documents for reviews, such as a settlement agreement and release, a qualified assignment, and a medical trust agreement.

Very often the party purchasing a structured settlement is a property/casualty insurer providing liability coverage to the defendant. Structured settlement specialists devote a fair amount of effort and resources to informing possible purchasers of the potential savings available.

Profile of a Structured Settlement Specialist

Many structured settlement specialists have been claims representatives or claims adjusters. This is good experience for becoming a structured settlement specialist because so many aspects of structured settlements involve the resolution of personal injury claims. Many specialists also have backgrounds in finance, law, investments, or life insurance, through which they have become familiar with the claims process and personal injury law.

The structured settlement company generally has a limited general agency relationship with approximately 12 life insurance companies who provide over 80 percent of the structured settlement annuities. Those 12 life insurers typically require a minimum production of structured settlement contracts each year from a specialist in order to continue representing the insurer and selling their contracts. They are highly selective about the companies to which they extend the general agency, probably because of the highly technical nature of the business. None of the companies that have major life insurance sales forces allow their regular life and annuity field sales force to participate in structured settlements. Generally, these same life companies do not allow structured settlement companies to sell their regular life and annuity products.

National Structured Settlement Trade Association

The National Structured Settlement Trade Association was created in 1986, primarily by independent structured settlement broker companies. Its goals are to advance the expansion of structured settlement concepts, promote favorable legislation and regulations, provide continuing education, develop guidelines for operational procedures, and establish a code of ethics for its members.

The year 1994 marks the first conferment of the association's certified structured settlement specialists. They completed studies in the following categories:

- structured settlements and periodic payment judgments
- casualty claim practices
- medical trusts
- evaluation of claims
- negotiation methods
- alternative investments
- macroeconomics
- business ethics

Uniform Periodic Payment of Judgments Act/(Sec. 18)

To promote the widespread use of structured settlements, the Uniform Periodic Payment of Judgments Act was approved in 1990 by the National Conference of Commissioners of Uniform State Laws. Sec. 18 of that act limits the number of life insurance companies that may qualify as structured settlement annuity providers as follows:

- The (Commissioner) shall publish a list of insurers designated by the (Commissioner) as qualified to participate in the funding of periodic payment judgments under Sec. 11. The list must be updated as often as necessary to keep current.
- In order for an insurer to be designated by the (Commissioner) as a qualified insurer, it must
  (1) request the designation
  (2) be an admitted insurer
  (3) have a minimum of $100 million of capital and surplus, exclusive of any mandatory security valuation reserve
  (4) have one of the following ratings from two or more of the following rating organizations:
    - A.M. Best Company (A+, A+g, A+p, A+r, or A+s)
    - Moody's Investors Service Claims Paying Rating (Aa3, Aa2, Aa1, or Aaa)
    - Standard & Poor's Corporation Insurer Claims-Paying Ability Rating (AA−, AA, AA+ or AAA)
    - Duff & Phelps Credit Rating Company Insurance Company Claims Payable Ability Rating (AA−, AA, AA+ or AAA)

Even though many of the states have not adopted the Periodic Payment of Judgments statute, structured settlement specialists tend to use the most financially secure, highly rated life insurance companies (those most likely to be approved under the act should it later be adopted). Any changes in the rating system itself, such as A++ of A.M. Best, will be phased in by the states who adopt the Uniform Act.

Postsettlement Opportunities for Other Advisers

Life insurance and financial advisers can certainly provide additional services for recipients of lump-sum settlements as well as structured settlements. The injured party is usually represented by an attorney who specializes only in personal injury cases. Frequently, the attorney refers his or her client to the local bank but in most cases does not get involved in any planning after the settlement. Life insurance and financial advisers can provide valuable postsettlement services.

While planning is even more critical if the injured party receives all of the proceeds in a lump sum, financial planning services are still necessary for those who receive a structured settlement of some up-front cash and the balance in periodic income. Keep in mind that most large settlements involve an injured party who is no longer able to work. Therefore financial planning is crucial not only to preserve capital but also to ensure an adequate income currently and in the future. Can you imagine an injured person who has no education or training in finance or investments trying to do it alone? Can you imagine an employer giving a check for $500,000 to an employee with the following words, "This represents the present value of all your future benefits toward your long-term disability plan. Even though you are only 45 we hope that you will make the right decisions on current and future investments because this is the last check you'll ever see from us."

Obviously, financial and estate planning are essential. In addition, the establishment of wills and trusts (and their periodic reevaluation) is also a vital service needed by accident victims whose income productivity has been impaired. Furthermore, with the creation of new insurance products (such as survivor life), a qualified life insurance adviser can help create the necessary liquidity for estate taxes and clearance costs for individuals who may be disabled but still insurable.

NOTES

1. The income figures in this chapter reflect the amounts of monthly life income payable per $1,000 of capital accumulated with an insurance company through periodic premiums. Because of expense allowances, the same income cannot be obtained from a lump-sum payment of $1,000 to an insurance company at the ages mentioned.
2. Rate basis: 1983 Individual Annuity Mortality Table.
3. These deposits, or level premiums, include a charge for insurance company expenses and vary among companies whose policies have the same maturity value. The deposits illustrated are for a contract on which dividends are paid prior to maturity.
4. More precisely, the value of an annuity unit at the end of each fiscal year is obtained by dividing the current market value of the funds supporting the annuity units by the present value of the total number of annuity units expected to be paid over the future lifetimes of all participants then receiving annuity payments, in accordance with the assumptions as to mortality, investment earnings, and expense rates for the future.
5. *Securities and Exchange Commission v. Valic,* 359 U.S. 65 (1959).
6. Selection against the company is present in the use of settlement options under life insurance contracts. Some companies are so concerned about adverse selection under settlement options that a smaller monthly income is provided under the life-income option when the beneficiary elects the option than when the insured elects it for the beneficiary.

7

Individual Disability
Income Insurance

Edward E. Graves

The ability to work and earn an income is the most valuable economic asset most people possess. Their involvement in the work force provides their livelihood after they emerge from the dependency of childhood. Only a very small percentage of people have inherited or accumulated so much wealth that their unearned income is large enough to allow them the luxury of not participating in the work force. The majority of the population must work for a living, and those persons unable to work often suffer severe economic hardship.

In the United States it is usually taken for granted that people will enjoy a healthy life and an ability to participate in the work force from the end of their teens or early twenties until age 65 or even later. For the bulk of the population this is an accurate assumption. However, health impairments can limit or preclude an individual from participating in the work force either temporarily or permanently. Accidents, illnesses, and congenital defects take their toll on individual lives. Within the working-age population (people between the ages of 18 and 65) susceptibility to injury and illness increases with age.

It is important to note, however, that we live in an ever-changing environment and threats to good health change over time. Tuberculosis and polio are examples of once widely spread communicable diseases that devastated millions of lives. Nearly all cases of tuberculosis were fatal before the development of effective medical treatment, and those who survived polio were usually disabled for life. Vaccinations have nearly eradicated polio and rendered tuberculosis medically controllable in the United States and most of the world. More recently there has been a significant reduction in deaths from heart disease, which can be mainly attributed to improved diet (especially reduced ingestion of saturated fats) and increased exercise. Other indications of improvement are statistics showing a per capita decrease in the consumption of cigarettes and distilled spirits such as whiskey and other so-called hard liquors. However, the information is not all good. For example, the air we breath has been deteriorating in quality. As buildings have been made more energy efficient through increased insulation, they trap more of the fumes from cleaning fluids and other toxic substances used within the buildings. We don't know yet what effect these changes will have on long-term health and mortality statistics.

In the last decade we have also seen the emergence of a frightening and devastating disease called AIDS. It is communicable both sexually and by intravenous blood contamination, and it can be spread from a mother to a fetus or newborn child. AIDS impairs the ability of infected individuals to recover from illnesses because the body's immune system has been destroyed. The disease is not fully understood, but we do know that it can have long latency periods (up to

12 years documented so far and suspected to be longer when we have had an opportunity to observe longer periods) followed by an immune-system breakdown that makes the body susceptible to deterioration from diseases that otherwise would pose no serious threat to healthy individuals. Victims of AIDS often die from communicable diseases that are rarely, if ever, fatal to persons without AIDS. There is no cure for the disease, and within a few short years it has spread to all nations of the world. As the above examples indicate, we are subjected to a bevy of constantly changing threats to our continued good health.

The changing environmental and health risks are not confined strictly to illnesses. For example, in recent years many Americans have embarked on rigorous fitness programs to improve their health. However, large numbers of minor and major disabling accidents have resulted from jogging, high-impact aerobics, and other activities. An example of changing risk is reflected in the automobile accident statistics after the federal government imposed a maximum speed limit of 55 miles per hour during the late 1970s and early 1980s. The lower speed limit resulted in a decreased number of automobile accidents and in fewer injuries and associated disability claims. Since some states have raised the maximum speed limit above 55 miles per hour, insurance claims data indicate that injuries, disabilities, and deaths from automobile accidents are again increasing.

LIKELIHOOD OF BECOMING DISABLED

As indicated above, the risk factors affecting disability are constantly changing. The disability risk is quite different from life insurance risk because of the possibility of multiple disability claims. It is common for an individual to sustain as many as 12 work loss disabilities prior to retirement. Also there can be a wide variation in the duration of any single disability claim. The history of American disability income insurance demonstrates that economic conditions can also influence the disability risk. Disability claims soared during the Depression because many unemployed insureds injured themselves to collect disability benefits. In fact, the disability insurance claims during the Depression threatened the financial solvency of some major insurance companies. As a result, many insurance companies abandoned the disability insurance market during the Depression. Consequently this type of coverage is written predominately by fewer than 20 companies today. There is a much higher concentration of coverage in a few specialty insurance companies for disability insurance than there is for life insurance. It has been difficult for other insurance companies to successfully reenter the disability insurance market because there is a scarcity of data on disability claims outside of that complied by the specialty disability insurance companies, which are not interested in sharing that data with their competitors.

Disability Probabilities

A new table of disability probabilities has been developed by the Society of Actuaries and has been adopted by the National Association of Insurance Commissioners for reserve purposes. This table, referred to as the 1985 Individual Disability Table, is based on experience from the 1970s. The 1985 Commissioners Disability Table is the counterpart to the 1980 Commissioners Standard Ordinary (CSO) Mortality Table used for life insurance purposes.

It is interesting to note that the probability of becoming disabled for at least 90 days before age 65 is higher than the probability of dying before age 65 for persons between the ages of 20 and 55. As can be seen in tables 7-1 and 7-2, a person has a 54 percent likelihood of becoming disabled for at least 90 days between the ages of 25 and 65. This percentage is more than twice the 24 percent probability that a person aged 25 will die prior to attaining age 65. These comparisons are based on the 1980 CSO Mortality Table for death and the 1985 Commissioners Disability Table for morbidity.

These mortality and morbidity tables are based on joint probabilities and are applicable for families or small businesses with up to six key persons. The individual probabilities are found in the column under 1. In the morbidity table the joint-life columns indicate the probability that at least one person out of the number indicated at the top of the column will become disabled for at least 90 days prior to reaching age 65. For the mortality table, the column represents the probability of at least one person out of the number of persons indicated at the top of the column dying before attaining the age of 65. The numbers in these joint tables are based on all individuals in the joint calculation being the same age. In other words, if there were three business owners all aged 40, there is an 86 percent probability that at least one of those three individuals will sustain a disability that will last for at least 90 days prior to attaining age 65. In a like manner, from the probability of death table, we can see that there is a 52 percent probability that at least one of the three owners aged 40 will die prior to attaining age 65. As can be seen from the table, increasing the number of lives increases the probability of sustaining at least one 90-day disability period out of that group of individuals.

TABLE 7-1 Probability of at Least One Person Dying before Age 65						
	Number of Persons					
Age	1	2	3	4	5	6
20	25%	44%	58%	68%	76%	82%
25	24	42	56	67	75	81
30	23	41	55	66	74	80
35	22	40	54	64	73	79
40	21	39	52	63	71	77
45	20	37	50	60	68	75
50	18	33	45	55	63	70
55	15	28	38	48	55	62
60	9	18	25	32	39	44
Based on 1980 CSO Mortality Table						

Unfortunately most individuals, business owners, and managers are not aware of the high likelihood that their management team will sustain a disability lasting more than 90 days. However, most of them are quite aware that a 90-day absence on the part of any one of their key managers or owners would have a very negative effect on the business. Most businesses and families have trouble living within their income when all resources are fully utilized. The loss of a productive person in the work force usually results in a loss of income and makes it even more difficult to get by on the reduced cash flow. Disability income insurance can usually provide protection from such cash-flow crunches.

From the standpoint of the individual, a prolonged disability not only means loss of income because of an inability to work but also entails additional costs, such as a wheelchair, rehabilitative therapy, and/or a specially equipped automobile, to cope with the new limitations. The individual sees an increase in the cost of living at the same time he or she suffers a loss of income. Disability is often referred to as a living death. People live beyond the termination of their income but still sustain the costs of everyday living for themselves and for dependents. The resulting economic pressure often pushes individuals near or past the breaking point. Even in cases where insurance relieves the economic pressure, disabled persons suffer psychologically as they become dependent on the very people they previously supported.

TABLE 7-2
Probability of at Least One Person Becoming Disabled for 90 Days before Age 65

	Number of Persons					
Age	1	2	3	4	5	6
25	54%	79%	90%	95%	98%	99%
30	52	77	89	95	98	99
35	50	75	88	94	97	99
40	48	73	86	93	96	98
45	44	69	83	90	95	97
50	39	63	78	87	92	95
55	32	54	69	79	86	90
60	9	18	25	32	39	44

Based on 1985 Commissioners Disability Table

Probabilities of Extended Disability

Although table 7-2 presents the probability of being disabled for 90 days or more, there is obviously the probability of becoming disabled for different durations of time. Further, there are probabilities for different severities of disabling conditions such as total and partial disability. These probabilities are extremely important for partial-disability benefits and residual-disability benefits. Unfortunately this type of information is not readily available because, as mentioned earlier, the companies that possess such information are not eager to share it with their competitors and did not supply data for the 1985 table. The Commissioners Disability Table, which deals with total disability, indicates that persons who have sustained a total disability of one year have a greater than 50 percent probability that disability will continue for an additional 2 years and, in fact, that there is at least a 32 percent probability that the disability will last an additional 5 years beyond the already completed one-year period. (See tables 7-3 and 7-4.) The longer a disability continues, the less likely the individual is to recover. Individuals who have sustained 2 years of total disability have at least a 62 percent probability that the disability will last an additional 2 years and a greater than 41 percent probability that it will last for an additional 5 years. These percentages also increase with age. The numbers above are for individuals in their early 20s, whereas persons in their mid-50s have a 78 percent chance that the disability will continue for at least 2 years after they have sustained 2 years of total disability and a 60 percent probability that they will remain disabled for an additional 5 years. (See table 7-5 for the average duration of disabilities sustained at various ages.)

Disabilities that last for fewer than 90 days are much more likely to result in total recovery. In fact, insurers providing rehabilitation benefits have determined that the earlier a disabled person starts therapy, the higher the likelihood of recovery. There seems to be a psychological element involved in recovery. Persons who are at the beginning of a disability expect to recover and will work eagerly to aid the recovery process. However, persons who have been disabled for longer periods of time gradually lose confidence in their ability to recover. To be successful, rehabilitation therapy should start as soon as possible after disability occurs.

TABLE 7-3 Likelihood a Disabled Person Will Remain Disabled 2 More Years		
Age When Disabled	Already Disabled 1 Year	Already Disabled 2 Years
22	52%	63%
27	54	64
32	56	68
37	59	70
42	62	72
47	65	74
52	69	77
57	73	78
Based on 1985 Commissioners Disability Table		

SOURCES OF FUNDS FOR DISABLED PERSONS

People become disabled in many different ways, and what causes the disability may affect the type of protection, if any, that is available. For example, injuries in the workplace will be covered under workers' compensation, which provides medical expenses, and persons losing their jobs as a result of such injuries will usually be eligible for unemployment compensation benefits. Such benefits are usually limited to 26 weeks and therefore do not provide long-term protection against disability. If the worker was "disability insured" prior to the injury, disability benefits under social security will be payable after 6 months of disability.

The very strict requirements for disability benefits under social security include the individual's inability to perform the duties of any gainful employment. Even with this restrictive definition for benefits, the social security system paid disability benefits to 3.19 million persons in 1991. The Social Security Administration dispensed nearly $30 billion in 1991 to pay disability benefits.

TABLE 7-4 Likelihood a Person Will Remain Disabled at Least 5 More Years		
Age When Disabled	Already Disabled 1 Year	Already Disabled 2 Years
22	32%	41%
27	35	46
32	39	49
37	42	54
42	45	57
47	49	58
52	52	60
57	55	60
Based on 1985 Commissioners Disability Table		

TABLE 7-5 Average Duration of Disabilities That Last at Least 90 Days for Various Onset Ages	
Age at Inception of Disability	Length of Disability (in Years)
30	4.7
35	5.1
40	5.5
45	5.8
50	6.2
55	6.6
Based on 1985 Commissioners Disability Table (excludes disabilities less than 90 days)	

There are five states that provide nonoccupational disability funds: California, Hawaii, New Jersey, New York, and Rhode Island. These programs vary from one state to another; California's program is the most generous. Benefits in all five of these states are usually linked to the worker's income level and number of dependents. The elimination period tends to be anywhere from one day to 7 days, and the limit on the benefit period tends to be anywhere from 26 weeks to one year. Private disability insurers in these states try to coordinate elimination periods of private coverage with the maximum benefits available under the state disability benefit program. Without coordination there is a possibility of overinsurance, which may provide a temptation for some individuals to malinger rather than expedite the recovery process.

Automobile accidents are a leading cause of injury and disability in the United States. In those states having no-fault auto insurance coverage, disability payments are usually provided in the mandatory no-fault coverage. However, most states do not have no-fault disability benefits.

The federal government has extensive disability income provisions for military personnel and civil servants. These programs provide very generous benefits, and individuals covered by these programs would not be candidates for private disability insurance coverage.

Many employers in the private sector provide some sort of sickness pay or salary continuation covering short-term disabilities. Benefits are often limited to a period of 2 weeks to a maximum of 26 weeks. If the employer offers disability benefits beyond 26 weeks, they are typically through disability income coverage provided by the employer as an employee benefit. Disability income coverage is usually classified as either short-term or long-term disability coverage. Short-term disability coverage is generally defined to be that with a benefit-period limitation of fewer than 5 years. Short-term disability policies have a much lower premium than long-term policies and are therefore much more popular among employers providing disability coverage. It is estimated that less than 50 percent of the work force enjoys short-term disability coverage and that less than 20 percent is insured for long-term disability. The cost of providing short-term disability coverage is usually 2 percent to 4 percent of payroll, while long-term disability coverage runs 2.5 percent to 6 percent of payroll for most private-sector employers. The lower end of the premium range is associated with longer waiting periods, and the higher premiums are associated with the shortest waiting periods.

The majority of the work force has no long-term disability protection unless their disability is so severe that they qualify for social security benefits. Individual disability income policies are available generally to those persons in middle-income or high-income occupations with low-risk classifications. There are many high-risk occupations for which disability income coverage is either hard to obtain or nonexistent. Very little disability income coverage is in force for low-income individuals because their low discretionary income usually puts disability income premiums beyond their reach. Disability income coverages are generally designed for people with incomes in excess of $20,000 per year. The coverage is based on occupation, and premiums vary from one occupation to another. Physicians, surgeons, dentists, lawyers, architects, accountants, and business executives without personal health problems find it easy to obtain disability income coverage. Agents specializing in disability income coverages often target self-employed individuals as a preferred market. This is probably in recognition of the fact that more than one-half of United States businesses employ fewer than 20 persons. These businesses are less likely to have disability income coverage in place than large employers with more than 1,000 workers.

DISABILITY INCOME INSURANCE POLICIES

There is a wide variation of disability income coverages and related disability policies. Many of these variations involve the definition of disability itself, the duration of benefits available, the elimination period, whether and how partial-disability benefits are provided, the waiver-of-premium protection, how recurring disability is handled, and how, if at all, cost-of-living adjustments are made to disability benefits.

Situations Warranting Coverage

Insurance companies that offer disability income policies are very concerned about overinsurance and consequently limit the amount of benefits relative to the individual's income. As a result, many individuals with in-force coverage through their employers or other sources are ineligible for additional disability income protection.

Anyone who earns at least $20,000 per year from gainful employment and is not already covered by private disability insurance has a significant need for disability income protection. Obviously this includes the self-employed, business owners and partners, individual workers, and anyone who would have an inadequate income if he or she were to become disabled and be unable to continue working for compensation.

Unfortunately premier-quality disability insurance is not available for many occupations. Agents marketing disability income insurance must become familiar with the occupational classifications and direct their prospecting toward individuals engaged in insurable occupations. If their agency contract allows it, agents may direct a prospect to another insurer that would issue some coverage on a nonoccupational basis. As with life insurance, insurance companies differ widely in how they classify occupations for disability insurance. Some companies will not insure plumbers for disability income; other insurers will offer a special disability policy for plumbers; still other insurers will offer their regular policy to plumbers at higher than standard premium rates.

Further, many corporate events can alter employer-provided disability income protection and therefore increase the need for individual protection. First, corporate mergers or acquisitions may result in a change in management and management philosophy, which may result in the termination of previously provided benefits. Second, bankruptcy or severe financial problems may prompt management to cut back on employee benefits such as disability income insurance. Third, the insurance company that provides disability income protection through the employer could terminate the policy. In this case, if the employer is unable to find another insurance company willing to write the coverage, there will be no replacement disability protection. Even if coverage could be obtained from another insurer, management may decide not to seek replacement coverage.

Since most employers do not provide disability income insurance, it is quite possible that an employee who leaves a job in which he or she had disability income protection may not be provided with that protection by a new employer. Such job changes create a definite need for individual disability income protection. One advantage of relying on individual protection rather than on employer-provided group protection is that the individual is not subject to termination at the whim of corporate decision makers. Also individual coverage is portable and can go with the insured to new geographic locations and new career paths. Changes in occupation may require the insured to inform the insurance company of such changes, and the premium may be adjusted if there is a significant change in the risk classification for the occupation.

Disability income coverages are also important for partnerships and closely held corporations. Such coverages can provide the financial means for healthy partners or stockholders to purchase the ownership interest of the disabled partner or stockholder. Disability income policies can also be used by the business enterprise to replace lost income or revenue that results from a key person's disability.

Policy Provisions

The primary objective of disability income policies is to replace lost income when an individual is no longer able to continue earning that income because of injury or illness. The concept is simple, but the variations of both risk and coverage provisions make disability income insurance very complex. As mentioned earlier, there can be multiple claims, and in most cases separate claims are mutually exclusive. However, it is possible to have multiple disabilities affecting an individual concurrently. One way that insurance companies differentiate between risks is by the definition of disability that they use in their contracts. For social security purposes, disability is defined as "the inability to engage in any substantial gainful activity by reason of any medically determinable physical or mental impairment which can be expected to result in death or which has lasted or can be expected to last for a continuous period of not less than 12 months." This is one of the most restrictive definitions in use. Essentially, if a person is able to do anything for pay, he or she is not disabled. Only a few private insurance company contracts use similarly restrictive definitions, but these products should not be considered quality disability income products. They are commonly referred to in the insurance industry as "any occupation" definitions, which means that benefits are payable only if the individual is disabled severely enough that he or she cannot engage in any occupation.

Much more common in private insurance is a definition stating that disability is "the inability to perform the duties of any occupation for which the individual is reasonably suited by reason of education, training, or experience." This type of coverage will not provide benefits if the insured is able to enter a new career that is reasonably comparable to the one in which he or she was engaged prior to the disability.

The most generous benefits are available under disability income policies utilizing an "own-occupation" definition of disability. These policies define disability as "the inability to perform the material and substantial duties of the individual's regular occupation." For example, these policies will even provide benefits for a surgeon who becomes disabled while insured and after recovery is no longer able to perform surgery but can still practice medicine. Many specialists within the professions will often insist on such definitions when they are seeking disability income coverage. (Some insurers have ceased issuing own-occupation coverages to health care providers in recent years.)

Many disability policies provide a two-stage definition of disability. They provide protection for the insured's own occupation for a period such as 2, 3, or 5 years and then continue to provide benefits only if the individual is unable to perform the duties of any occupation for which he or she is reasonably suited by reason of education, training, or experience. Obviously this is less generous than a policy that would provide benefits for the inability to perform one's own occupation to age 65 or for lifetime. However, the insurance company anticipates that the individual can use the benefits during the first-stage definition to prepare for an occupation that he or she will be able to perform when the second stage of the definition becomes effective.

To this point the definitions discussed have dealt with total disability. Currently many disability policies also provide benefits for either partial disability or residual disability. Both types of benefits (partial and residual) are intended to encourage insureds to return to the work force prior to total recovery. Some experts argue that the absence of these benefits encourages disabled insureds to malinger so that they can collect total-disability benefits. It should be emphasized that partial-disability benefits and in many policies residual-disability benefits are payable only following a period for which total-disability benefits have been paid.

Partial-Disability Benefits

Partial disability is usually defined as the inability to perform some stated percentage of the duties of the insured's occupation or to perform at such a speed that completion of those duties takes a longer-than-normal amount of time. The more severe the limitations, the higher the benefit that will be paid. Theoretically, under such a contract, an individual could return to work on a full-time basis at full salary and still be eligible for partial-disability benefits.

Residual-Disability Benefits

Residual disability benefits, on the other hand, provide for a replacement of lost earnings due to less than total disability. Here the focus is on how much income reduction has been sustained as a result of the disability rather than on the physical dimensions of the disability itself. Residual benefits are particularly well suited for self-employed professionals such as accountants, attorneys, and physicians whose caseload often determines their income. A disability that reduces their capacity for work would automatically lead to a reduction in income.

Policies providing residual-disability benefits usually specify a fraction (representing the proportion of lost income) that will be multiplied by the stated monthly benefit for total disability to derive the residual benefit payable. The numerator of that fraction is usually income prior to disability minus earned income during disability; the denominator of the fraction is income prior to disability. The contract will specify a definition of each form of income. The definitions differ from one insurance company to another, and these differences become extremely important for individuals whose income fluctuates widely. Some contracts may specify predisability income as the average monthly income during the 6 months immediately preceding the onset of disability; others may specify predisability income as the greater of the average monthly income during the 12 months preceding the onset of disability or the highest 12 months of consecutive earnings during the 3 years preceding the onset of disability. There are many variations, but the important concept here is that persons subject to income fluctuation should insist on a definition allowing the *greater* of two different base periods so that they will not be unduly penalized as a result of a single base period applied during a slump in income. Most of the definitions either explicitly or implicitly include not only income earned from work activities but also pension or profit-sharing contributions made on behalf of the individual. Thus an individual with a $60,000 nonfluctuating salary and a 10 percent pension plan contribution would be considered to have a predisability income of $66,000.

The income received during residual disability that is used to calculate the income loss is usually defined to include all money received during the period being evaluated even if the money represents payment for services rendered prior to the disability. A few insurance company definitions exclude payments made on services rendered prior to the disability from residual income.

Let's consider an example. An individual with a $66,000 annual predisability income has a policy providing $3,500 per month for total disability. This individual has been able to return to work following a total disability and is earning $2,500 per month during the current period of residual disability. Subtracting $2,500 in residual earnings from the predisability income of $5,500 per month results in a lost income of $3,000 per month. The lost-income ratio ($3,000 ÷ $5,500) is then multiplied by the stated monthly benefit for total disability ($3,500) to determine a residual-disability benefit of $1,909 (rounded to the nearest dollar). Most residual-disability benefits cease whenever the income loss drops below 20 percent of the predisability income. In this example, residual benefits would cease when the monthly income exceeds $4,400.

It is also common to find a clause within residual-disability-benefit provisions that specifies that the minimum benefit payable for residual-disability periods is at least 50 percent of the benefit payable for total disability. At least one insurance company will provide 100 percent of the total-disability benefit during residual disability if the lost income exceeds 75 percent of the predisability income. Under most policies residual-disability benefits are payable to the end of the benefit period. For long-term disability contracts this would be age 65 or later. Some policies impose an 18- or 24-month limitation on residual benefits for partial disabilities beginning after a specified age, such as 54.

Another aspect of residual-disability coverages is whether or not they require a prior period of total disability for residual benefits to be payable. The more generous policies pay residual-disability benefits for partial disabilities not preceded by a period of total disability. Obviously this generosity increases the premium for the benefits. Policies that do require a prior period of total disability, often called a qualification period, vary as to the period's duration; the most common qualification periods are 30, 60, 90, or 120 days.

Ability to Keep the Coverage in Force

Disability income contracts generally include some provision on renewability. Top-quality contracts will be at least guaranteed renewable to some specified age such as 65 or even lifetime, or better still they will be noncancelable. Guaranteed renewable means that the policyowner has the right to continue the coverage in force by paying the premium due. The premium itself may be increased on a class basis for all guaranteed-renewable policies in a classification, but the premium cannot be increased on an individual basis. The important point is that the insurance company does not have the option to refuse renewal of these contracts before the end of the guaranteed-renewal period. Noncancelable disability contracts guarantee not only that the individual can keep the policy in force by paying the premium but also that the premium will not increase.

Some disability insurance contracts have less generous renewability provisions than guaranteed renewability or noncancelability. These policies offer very questionable protection for the insured because the insurance company is allowed to refuse renewal of the contract in some circumstances. Some policies are optionally renewable, which gives the insurance company the option to refuse renewal at any anniversary date. Others are conditionally renewable and set forth specific conditions upon which the insurance company has the right to refuse renewal of the contract on the next policy anniversary. Sometimes the conditions refer only to items controlled by the insured, such as a change in occupation, but more often they refer to factors beyond the insured's control, such as the performance factors of the insurance company itself. The real problem with any renewability provisions that are less generous than guaranteed renewability is that a policy may be terminated when an insurance company refuses to review the policy of an individual who has become uninsurable and can no longer obtain coverage from other sources.

Policies containing restrictive renewability provisions are often issued by companies that are not committed to the long-term disability market. Many life insurance companies move into and out of the disability income market on a relatively short-term basis. They often enter the disability segment of the business in the years following record profits reported by the disability income specialty companies. A few years later they are dissatisfied with the profitability of their disability coverages and decide to exit the market or to increase their premium structure to a point at which they are no longer competitive with market leaders. They handle the in-force coverage issued during their active years in different ways. Some companies reinsure all the coverage with another company that is committed to the disability market. Others choose to retain the coverage and work off that particular block of policies until they all expire as a result of nonrenewal, expiration date, or death of the insured. Some companies apply both techniques by setting a relatively low reinsurance threshold, maintaining the policies and servicing claims as they come due.

The insured is best protected under guaranteed renewable or noncancelable disability insurance policies from an insurance company that has a good track record and commitment to the disability income market. Some major life insurance companies have entered into agreements to have their own life insurance field force sell the top-quality disability products of a specialty company. This is explicit recognition of the specialty carrier's success and the life insurance company's inability to match its performance with the resources available to the specialty company. In many cases these agreement allow the field force to earn production credits in their own company for the disability coverages placed with the other insurance company. Some disability insurance companies even allow the marketing insurer to sell the coverage under its own name much like other private-able products.

Long-term-care Insurance

Long-term-care (LTC) insurance, a related coverage, provides benefits to persons needing nursing home care or home health care. Some disability insurance policies make an optional rider available that provides extra benefits if the insured needs and receives nursing home care. These riders explicitly cover

Alzheimer's disease and do not require prior hospitalization as a condition for benefit eligibility.

Some disability insurers include a long-term-care insurance conversion privilege in long-term disability policies. This is essentially a form of guaranteed LTC insurability. It can be very valuable because the underwriting criteria for LTC issued at age 65 or later are often very stringent. LTC insurance is the closest thing to disability income insurance that can be purchased at age 65 or older but only if the person is in very good health.

Another related coverage is now available from a few insurers in the form of HIV riders to disability income policies for health care workers. The riders pay benefits for up to 10 years to insureds who become HIV positive and sustain at least a 20 percent reduction of income. Such policy riders are generally restricted to physicians, dentists, medical technicians, residents, interns, paramedics, ambulance drivers, and registered nurses.

When Benefits Start

Disability income policies generally have an elimination period before benefit payments begin. Most insurance companies give the purchaser an option to select the duration of this period. The elimination period is the time between the onset of the disability and the beginning of eligibility for disability payments. Since benefits are paid on a monthly basis at the end of the month, the first benefit payment will be 30 days after the end of the elimination period. Common elimination periods are 30, 60, 90, or 120 days. A few policies are available with a zero-day elimination period but only for disability due to accident; the premium increase to get rid of the elimination period is significant because it includes benefits for many more very short-term disabilities.

Obviously the longer the elimination period, the more severe a disability must be before benefits will be payable. Even a 30-day elimination period will preclude benefit payments for minor injuries and illnesses when full recovery takes place within the 30-day period. Premium levels are affected by the length of the elimination period, and longer elimination periods are associated with lower premium levels. However, selection of a particular elimination period should not be based solely on the premium differential.

Many factors should be considered when selecting the elimination period for a disability income policy. The ability of the insured to pay living costs and other expenses during the elimination period is of utmost importance. Another pertinent factor is whether or not the insured has other sources of funds available for short-term disabilities. For example, he or she may be employed by a firm that provides salary continuation or sick pay. In this case the elimination period chosen might equal or exceed the maximum salary continuation period from the employer. Individuals purchasing coverage in states that have nonoccupational disability coverages should choose elimination periods that equal or exceed the maximum benefit period under the state plan. The individual may have an adequate accumulation of emergency funds to sustain a relatively long elimination period without alternative sources of income during that elimination period. Insureds should not select an elimination period that is longer than they are able to financially sustain themselves, given the available sources of funds subsequent to the onset of a disability.

Insurance companies differ as to whether they require the elimination period to be satisfied with consecutive days or whether they allow the accumulation of nonconsecutive disability days to satisfy the elimination period. In some policies it is spelled out explicitly in the contract that the elimination period can be satisfied with nonconsecutive days. In other policies the language of the contract is silent on this point, and the company's claims-handling philosophy must be ascertained to determine the answer. Policies requiring consecutive days of disability to satisfy the elimination period provide a less generous benefit than those allowing accumulation of nonconsecutive days to satisfy the elimination period.

Residual-disability benefits provided in many policies specify what is commonly known as a qualification period, which specifies the number of days of total disability that must be sustained before residual-disability benefits are payable. The most generous residual-disability policies have a zero-day qualification period and therefore require no total-disability period prior to eligibility for residual or partial benefit payments. Under that type of contract, residual benefits could begin at the end of the elimination period to replace lost income, such as the income lost by a surgeon suffering from severe arthritis. A policy that has residual benefits with a qualifying period equal to the elimination period could also start paying residual benefits at the end of the elimination period if the individual had been totally disabled for the entire elimination period and recovered enough to return to work with a reduced income immediately after the end of the elimination period. It is quite common for the qualification period associated with residual benefits to actually exceed the elimination period, but there is not necessarily a connection between the elimination period and the qualification period. In fact, many insurance companies do not offer a choice relative to the qualification period for residual benefits.

Recurring Disability

Most disability policies have provisions setting forth a specified period of recovery (usually measured by return to work) that automatically separates one disability from another. For example, suppose an individual became disabled as a result of an automobile accident and was totally disabled for 6 months. The individual then returned to work for 8 months before having a relapse and becoming totally disabled again from causes associated with the automobile accident. The new disability will be treated as a separate disability because the recovery and return to work exceeded 6 months, which is the specified period separating recurring disabilities in most disability income policies. If the return to work lasted fewer than 6 months, the second period of disability would be treated as a continuation of the initial disability, and no new elimination period would be applicable. However, because the individual had returned to work for 8 months, the second period of disability is treated as a new disability, and a new elimination period will be applicable before benefits are again payable.

For disability policies with a limited benefit period, it can be advantageous to have each relapse classified as a new disability. The advantage is that any new disability starts with a full benefit period. Consider a policy with a 2-year maximum benefit period in our example above. Six months of that benefit period were used up before the employee returned to work. When the relapse occurs with less than 6 months of recovery, the second period of disability will be eligible for only 18 months of benefit payments. In the case of an 8-month recovery, the insured will have to sustain a new elimination period but will then be entitled to the full 24 months of benefit payments if the disability lasts that long. The issue of qualifying for a new benefit period can be extremely important for short-term disability policies, but it is not a significant issue for policies providing long-term benefit periods running to age 65.

Duration of Benefit Period

Just as disability income policies differ according to definitions of disability and length of elimination period, they also differ according to the duration of benefits that they will provide once the individual becomes disabled. Benefit periods are one of the most important factors in determining the level of disability income premiums. Most insurance companies offer choices for the benefit duration and charge the appropriate premium for the duration selected. Short-term disability contracts often provide choices such as 2 years, 3 years, or 5 years for the maximum benefit period. In the long-term category the maximum benefit period may often go to age 65 or even for lifetime. Some long-term disability coverages are automatically renewable to age 65 and conditionally renewable to age 70 or 75 if the individual continues to work at his or her occupation. Obviously the longer the potential benefit period, the higher the premium necessary to support such benefits.

Some companies differentiate between disabilities caused by injury and disabilities caused by illness. It is not uncommon for policies that use that type of classification to provide lifetime benefits if the disability results from injury but to limit benefits to age 65 if the disability stems from illness. Other companies offer a total range of options or the selection of the maximum benefit period for both injury and illness. For example, an individual could select injury to age 65 and illness to age 65, injury to lifetime and illness to 65, or the maximum of lifetime for both injury and illness. Companies that differentiate between injury and illness as a source of disability will not usually allow the maximum benefit period for illness to exceed the maximum benefit period for injury. In other words, you cannot choose the lifetime duration period for disability resulting from illness if you purchase coverage for disability from injury only to age 65.

The disability definition in concert with the maximum benefit period is the real essence of coverage. Coverage for a surgeon in his or her own occupation to age 65 is quite different from coverage to age 65 that provides own-occupation coverage only for the first 2 years and then provides coverage for any occupation for which the insured is reasonably qualified by reason of education, training, or experience to age 65. Comprehensive protection requires a combination of a generous definition of benefits and a maximum benefit period of age 65 or lifetime.

Short-term Disability

Short-term disability policies do not provide comprehensive protection against disability, but their main appeal is the premium savings associated with the relatively short maximum benefit period. The premium for a 2-year benefit period can be as low as 40 percent of the premium required to extend benefits to age 65. That percentage differential is for individuals aged 18 through 40. The percentage of premium reduction for short-term benefit periods reduces with age. At age 55 an individual is likely to pay nearly 50 percent of the long-term premium to obtain 2-year benefit coverage. As would be expected, 5-year benefit periods require higher premiums than 2-year benefit periods and range from 55 percent of the long-term premium for the ages between 18 and 25 to over 70 percent of the long-term premium by age 55.

Premiums for disability income policies are similar to life insurance policy premiums in that they are based on the policyholder's age at the time of policy issuance and remain level for the duration of the coverage. Consequently an individual can lock in the greater percentage differential by buying the policy at a younger age and keeping it in force.

Short-term disability policies are sufficient to cover most disabilities since, by frequency of occurrence, well over one-half of all disabilities have durations of less than 2 years. The real shortcoming of these policies is that they do not provide adequate protection for the severe disability that lasts longer than the 2-year or 5-year benefit period. Consider a policy that provides $3,000 per month. If the individual is disabled, he or she receives $36,000 per year in benefits. For a 2-year benefit period the individual is limited to benefits of $72,000 per disability; for a 5-year benefit period he or she is limited to $180,000 per disability (paid out on a monthly basis for the duration of the benefit period if the disability lasts that long). A long-term disability policy to age 65 providing $3,000 per month in benefits could provide up to $1.7 million in benefits for an individual disabled at age 18.

In a short-term disability policy, the full benefit period is available for each separate disability the insured sustains, and an insured who sustains many separate disabilities could theoretically collect almost as much under short-term disability contracts as the maximum benefits payable under a long-term disability contract. The problem in selecting coverage is that no one knows in advance who is going to sustain a long, uninterrupted disability. Because individuals cannot control when and how they will be disabled, there is always the possibility that an individual could be disabled for longer than the benefit period available under short-term disability contracts. A short-term disability contract is clearly inadequate for a person who does sustain a catastrophic disability loss.

Long-term Disability

Some companies provide disability income coverages with benefit periods of 10 years, which are invariably classified as long-term disability contracts. The benefit period provides more protection than short-term disability contracts but is still less than lifetime coverage. In recent years the predominant maximum benefit period for long-term disability policies is to age 65. Such coverage ensures that the individual will have a source of replacement income until the normal retirement age for most individuals. The availability of medicare, social security, pensions, and other benefits beyond the age of 65 makes it less important to rely on disability income benefits beyond age 65.

Even those policies purporting to provide lifetime benefits for disability include limitations on disabilities occurring after specified ages such as 50, 55, or

60. Disabilities with their first onset after the specified age will often be limited to benefit periods of 2 or 5 years or may terminate at a specified age such as 65, 68, or 70. In other words, lifetime benefit payments are only available for disabilities that initially occurred before the specified age limitation and that remained continuous and uninterrupted for the remainder of the insured's life.

Long-term disability policies are being issued to high-income individuals for significant amounts of coverage, such as $10,000 to $50,000 in benefits per month. Such policies present a potential liability of millions of dollars to the insurance company. For example, an insurance company could pay out $12 million between the ages of 45 and 65 for an individual insured for $50,000 in benefits per month. Even short-term disabilities under such policies result in benefit payments of $600,000 per year.

With such amounts at risk it is understandable that insurance companies are more restrictive in writing long-term disability policies than they are in writing short-term policies. Fewer occupations qualify for long-term disability coverage than for short-term disability policies. Long-term disability policies are rarely available to any occupation that involves physical labor or direct involvement in dangerous processes. For example, funeral directors are insurable for long-term disability as long as they do not participate in the embalming process. Pressmen who work in lithography are often eligible for long-term disability policies, but pressmen who work in printing plants are generally ineligible.

Long-term disability benefits continue for as long as the insured individual is disabled according to the contract provisions. Insurance companies often require repeated verification that the disability still satisfies the qualifications for benefit eligibility. Benefits for total disability will cease when the individual has recovered enough that the disability no longer satisfies the criteria of total disability. In long-term disability policies providing residual benefits, benefit payments may continue at a reduced amount when the individual has recovered enough to return to work but still sustains more than a 20 percent reduction in income. Total recovery of the insured will terminate any benefit payments under disability income policies. Short-term recovery with relapses often triggers a resumption of disability income benefits. Recovery is generally measured by a return to work. If the intervening work period is less than 6 months, the disability will be considered a continuation of the prior disability and the benefits will resume without having to satisfy a new elimination period. If the recovery and return to work last more than 6 months, most policies require that the recurrent disability be treated as a new disability rather than a continuation of the old one, and consequently, it must satisfy a new elimination period.

Obviously no benefits are payable under lapsed or terminated disability income policies. It is relatively unusual for such policies to lapse or to be terminated while an individual is disabled since most policies provide waiver-of-premium protection. Lapses and terminations usually occur before the onset of a disability and preclude the payment of benefits for subsequent disabilities. There is limited protection from lapses in the grace period that allows continuation of coverage by payment of premiums within 31 days after their due date. Most insurance companies will allow lapsed policies to be reinstated automatically if the premium is paid within 15 days after the end of the grace period. Lapsed policies will often be reinstated within 30 or 60 days of the end of the grace period without evidence of insurability if the insured applies for reinstatement.

However, the insurance company has the right to impose evidence-of-insurability requirements in any case.

Residual Benefits

Residual benefits in disability income policies are designed to provide less than full benefits at the time during the recovery period when the insured is no longer totally disabled and is able to return to work but with a reduction in earnings. As mentioned earlier, this type of benefit is aimed more at measuring and offsetting the loss of income than at ascertaining the degree of physical incapacity. Obviously the loss of income must be due to the limitations resulting from the insured's disability. Under some policies the total monthly benefit may be payable as a residual benefit if the lost income equals or exceeds 80 percent of the predisability income.

The basic philosophy behind providing residual-disability benefits or partial-disability benefits is to encourage an insured's rehabilitation so that he or she can return to work as soon as possible. In the absence of residual benefits or partial benefits, the insured is often motivated to continue to meet the total-disability definition and not to risk a reduction in benefits by attempting to return to work.

Residual benefits may be payable for a relatively long period of time if the insured plateaus at some level of partial recovery. However, residual benefits are subject to the maximum benefit period provisions in the contract. For example, in a short-term disability contract providing the maximum of 5-year benefits, the combination of total-disability and residual-disability benefits is not permitted to exceed 5 years in aggregate for any one disability. Since residual benefits can and sometimes do exceed one year in duration, the residual-benefit provisions must deal with cost-of-living adjustments in policies that contain inflation protection. For residual benefits this means that the predisability income amount must be adjusted annually for continuous periods of disability. Without such adjustments the percentage of lost income would be underrepresented in the benefit calculation during periods of inflationary wage and price increases.

Each insurance company tends to have its own variation as to adjustment mechanisms for the predisability income amount during prolonged disability benefit periods. In general, the predisability income amounts are adjusted in much the same manner as the total-disability amount is adjusted under the cost-of-living adjustment provisions. This provision may be a flat stated percentage on a simple interest calculation basis, a compound interest escalation, or in some way tied to a consumer price index for items in general or for specific health care cost increases. Sometimes the provision is even a hybrid of a stated amount that can be increased more rapidly when consumer index prices exceed a threshold amount during any given one-year period. Another variation will have no increases at all unless there has been an inflationary index exceeding a stated threshold amount, such as 3 percent or 5 percent during the previous 12-month period.

Level of Benefits Payable

Disability income policies specify the amount of monthly benefits to be payable during periods of total disability after the elimination period has been satisfied. At the time of policy issuance the stated monthly benefit amount will be in line with the insured's income and should provide fairly complete protection. However, over time the stated benefit amount is likely to become inadequate as the insured's income increases because of both inflation and job promotions. Disability income policies are available with provisions to counteract such erosion in benefit levels. These provisions fall into two different categories. First, there are provisions that provide increases in the benefit payments during periods of disability when benefits are being distributed. Second, there are provisions that are aimed at increasing the stated benefit level at various time intervals while the coverage is in force but the insured is not disabled.

COLA Riders

Provisions dealing with increasing benefits during periods of disability are often referred to as either cost-of-living adjustments (COLAs) or inflation-protection provisions. They tend to provide either a fixed-percentage increase per year or a floating-percentage increase where the floating amount is determined by some external index such as a consumer price index. These benefits are almost always provided as an optional rider for an additional premium over and above the base policy. Many companies that do provide COLA riders offer purchasers a choice about the percentage increase ceilings on the rider. In other words, a COLA with a 3 percent annual increase will have one premium whereas a COLA with a 4 percent annual increase will have an appropriately higher premium. Some companies allow the purchaser to choose any rate between zero and 7 percent for annual increases.

In addition to these annual increase limitations, COLA riders usually contain an aggregate limit on benefit increases such as two times the original monthly benefit amount. For example, an insured may purchase a 5 percent flat benefit increase rider to a policy originally providing $2,000 per month in benefits and may subsequently become disabled for a continuous period of 20 years. After the individual has been disabled for one year, the benefit amount will increase to $2,100 per month, reflecting the 5 percent increase. After 2 years the benefit will increase to $2,205 if the increases are based on a compound interest adjustment or to $2,200 if the increases are based on a simple interest adjustment. If the COLA rider contains an aggregate limit of twice the original benefit amount, the policy will reach that upper limit of $4,000 per month after about 14 1/2 years of continuous disability if the adjustments are made on a compound basis. It will reach the $4,000 limit after 20 years of continuous disability if the adjustments are made on a simple basis.

COLA riders are extremely important in protecting the purchasing power of disability income benefits because insurance companies will not allow purchasers to obtain coverage for benefit levels in excess of their current discretionary income. Insurance companies are very concerned (with good reason) about overinsurance with disability coverages. Consequently they will not allow individuals to insure for excess amounts in anticipation of future inflation. The only way for insureds to keep future benefit payments in line with inflationary requirements is to obtain COLA riders with their base policies. However, purchasing COLA riders will not keep the initial benefit level in line with inflation prior to the onset of a disability. Many disability policies are in force for years before a disability occurs. Income and expense levels may have increased three-fold over that interval, but the level of disability benefits payable will not have changed unless additional coverage has been purchased in the interim.

There are basically three approaches to keeping disability income benefits in step with increased income for insured individuals who are not disabled. First, the oldest and least attractive method is to purchase new policies to supplement the in-force policies incrementally as income increases. The drawback to this approach is that it requires evidence of insurability every time incremental amounts of coverage are obtained. If the individual's health deteriorates, additional coverage may not be available at any price.

Guaranteeing the Right to Purchase Additional Insurance

The second approach to adjusting disability benefit levels is through a rider that guarantees the right to purchase additional coverage at specified future intervals up to some specified maximum age, such as 45, 50, or 55. This approach is similar to the first one in that additional coverage must be purchased every time an adjustment is needed. However, it differs in that additional amounts can be acquired at the specified intervals regardless of the health of the insured. These incremental purchases are subject to underwriting requirements regarding the individual's current income. In other words, the insurance company will not issue new coverage if the incremental addition would increase aggregate disability income benefits above the underwriting guidelines for that individual's current income on the option date. This is another way for insurance companies to prevent overinsurance and to minimize adverse selection.

Increasing the Base Benefit Amount

Third, the most attractive way to adjust benefits upward for inflation while the insured is not disabled is to use riders that automatically increase the base benefit amount on a formula basis, such as a stated flat-percentage amount at each policy anniversary. Even this approach requires purchasing additional coverage, and the premium will be increased appropriately. As with the second approach, the additional increment of coverage will be purchased at premium rates based on the insured's attained age at the time it is added to the policy. The real advantage to this approach is that the changes are automatic unless they are refused by the policyowner.

Insurance companies are not required to provide any inflation adjustments, and some insurance companies selling disability income policies choose not to make such riders available. Insurance companies that offer both options—purchasing additional coverage in the future and automatic percentage increases in benefits—will limit future incremental additions and make sure that they are in line with the earnings of the insured. Such companies will often refuse to issue the options if the insured has another policy that already contains such riders or if the base policy was issued on an extra premium basis because of health problems.

Insurance companies offering both automatic benefit adjustments and future purchase options as separate riders on the same base policy often suggest that the automatic increases be tied to inflationary expectations and that future purchase options be used to cover income increases due to career promotions. One problem with the latter suggestion is that many career promotions may come at ages beyond the guaranteed future purchase dates. In those cases the only way to increase coverage will be to purchase a new policy for which the individual must show acceptable evidence of insurability.

Premium Payments

Premiums can be paid on an annual, quarterly, or monthly basis for these policies with premiums paid on a quarterly basis showing the lowest persistency. All the forms of automatic payment available for life insurance policies are also available for disability income policies. They can be set up on a payroll-deduction basis or an automatic bank draft plan. Premiums must be paid on a timely basis to keep the coverage in force, but the policies do contain a 31-day grace period for late premium payments.

In an attempt to make disability income insurance less costly, a few companies have introduced low-load policies. By reducing agent commissions and other expenses, the savings in premiums can be passed on to purchasers. It is not clear that this will result in more policy sales because it also reduces the incentive to the agent on a product that is already difficult to convince clients to purchase.

Most disability income policies automatically include the waiver-of-premium provision. For long-term disability policies some companies will waive premiums after 90 days of disability, while other companies will waive premiums after 60 days of disability. Some short-term disability policies may contain options as to what elimination period is applicable to the waiver-of-premium provision. Obviously the premium will vary according to the length of the elimination period. The shorter the elimination period, the higher the premium for the waiver-of-premium provision if it is charged separately. Disability policies differ as to whether the waiver of premium requires consecutive days or allows aggregate nonconsecutive days from short disability periods to satisfy the elimination period.

Some policies waive only future premiums after the waiver-of-premium elimination period has been satisfied; other policies will retroactively waive prior premium payments made after the onset of disability but before the waiver-of-premium eligibility requirements have been met. Once the insured individual recovers and no additional disability benefits are payable, premiums will no longer be waived and premium payments must be resumed.

Insurance companies do differ as to what mode of premium payments is assumed during a premium waiver. For example, if premiums are being waived on a monthly basis, the insured may recover shortly after a premium has been waived and would have to resume premium payments the following month. However, if premiums are being waived on an annual basis, recovery after 3 months or 6 months would result in an additional 9 months or 6 months of coverage without cost to the individual while he or she is not disabled unless other adjustments are made. Some insurance companies provide that policies on an annual premium-paying mode will switch to a monthly mode for purposes of waiver of premium during periods of disability. At least one company will actually change the mode from monthly to annually for waiver purposes after the insured is disabled continuously for a period of at least 12 months.

Sometimes policies differ as to whether or not the waiver includes the cost of riders under the policy. The higher-quality policies generally include all riders as part of the waiver, but other policies waive premiums only for the base policies, and thus premiums for supplemental riders will have to be paid even during periods of benefit eligibility. Premium waivers generally do not continue beyond age 65 even in policies providing lifetime benefits.

Return-of-Premium Option

Some insurance companies offer on an optional basis a policy provision that will return some portion of premiums at specified intervals, such as 5 years or 10 years. For example, one company has an option that will return 60 percent of premiums paid at the end of each 5-year interval if no claims have been made during that 5-year period. This particular option can increase premiums by more than 40 percent over the base premium level. Other companies offer variations in the percentage of premium to be returned, such as 70 percent or 80 percent of the premiums paid, and in the duration of the interval over which the coverage must be without claims in order to collect the return of premium. The interval may be as long as 10 years under some company policy provisions.

The return-of-premium option is not available from some of the companies providing the highest-quality coverage for disability income policies. This type of option is definitely not an essential element of disability protection. Individuals who do suffer a disability and collect substantial benefits under the policy will find that the return-of-premium option merely increases the cost of coverage without increasing the benefit payable during disability.

The return-of-premium option has the strongest appeal to individuals who are convinced they will not become disabled. In fact, it may be the inducement necessary to convince these people to purchase disability income insurance.

There is one important negative aspect to return-of-premium options. The significant cost of this option may prompt individuals to limit the size of benefits they purchase to something less than the 60 percent or 70 percent of income generally available under most insurance company underwriting guidelines. The insured should have an adequate amount of disability income protection before considering the inclusion of a return-of-premium option. Protection levels should not be compromised in order to include an option that is not basic protection.

Rehabilitation Benefits

The higher-quality disability income policies may include some type of rehabilitation benefits, although many insurance policies do not include any such benefits. The policies that do include rehabilitation benefits tend to require the insurance company's prior approval of the rehabilitative program in writing. Some companies limit the amount of rehabilitation benefits to 24 or 36 times the monthly total-disability benefit payable. Receiving rehabilitation benefits generally does not disqualify the individual from collecting total-disability benefits. In other words, the better policies will pay the full total-disability benefit and at the same time pay additional rehabilitation expenses over and above the monthly benefit payments. Policy provisions often require that rehabilitation programs be provided at accredited educational institutions, state or local governments, or otherwise licensed and recognized providers of sanctioned rehabilitation training. The objective of these programs is either full recovery from a disability or retraining the individual to accommodate a long-term or permanent limitation stemming from a disability.

In most cases it is extremely important that rehabilitative therapy be initiated as soon as possible after the onset of the disability. Unfortunately the insured is often the one who must initiate negotiations with the insurance company regarding rehabilitation benefits. The insured should inquire about viable rehabilitation treatment as soon as possible and then negotiate with the insurance company to determine which, if any, of the suggested treatments are covered under the rehabilitation benefits of the policy. Many policies require that the insurance company and insured agree to a written rehabilitation plan before therapy begins in order to qualify for reimbursement.

Pursuit of rehabilitative therapy without prior consent of the insurance company may negate rehabilitation benefits. It is extremely important for the insured to keep the insurance company informed of his or her status and treatment. Sometimes the insured will have to make a choice between different types of rehabilitative therapy that may or may not be acceptable to the insurance company. This situation forces the insured to choose between covered therapy or noncovered therapy and to absorb the cost of noncovered therapy.

Presumptive Disability

Many disability income policies include provisions setting forth specific losses that will qualify for permanent total-disability status. They are referred to as presumptive-disability provisions because the individual is presumed to be totally disabled even if he or she is able to return to work or gain employment in a new occupation.

Presumptive-disability provisions generally include loss of sight, loss of speech, loss of hearing, or the total loss of use of or the severance of both hands, both feet, or one hand and one foot. As with other disability coverages, the presumptive-disability benefits will cease if the insured individual recovers to an extent that he or she no longer qualifies for the presumptive disability. For example, an individual may lose the use of both hands because of paralysis from a stroke or other causes. If the individual gradually recovers use of one or both of the hands, he or she no longer qualifies for presumptive disability benefits.

Presumptive-disability provisions differ as to whether or not the benefits will be paid as of the first day presumptive-disability requirements have been met or if the regular elimination period will still be applicable. Obviously the policies that provide presumptive-disability benefits from the first day of disability onset are more generous in terms of benefits.

Some disability income policies do not include presumptive-disability provisions. Policies that do provide for presumptive-disability benefits rarely charge a separate premium for the coverage and usually include it automatically as a part of the base policy.

Incontestability

The laws of all states require that disability income policies contain incontestability provisions. These provisions give the insurance company a specified period during which it can contest the validity of the contract on the basis of fraud, concealment, or material misrepresentation in the application. If the insurance company has not canceled, rescinded, or otherwise terminated the coverage before the end of the contestable period, the insurance company will not be able to deny claims after the policy becomes incontestable even for reasons of fraud, concealment, or material misrepresentation in the application.

Generally the incontestable clause specifies that the policy will remain contestable for 2 years after the date of issue during the lifetime of the individual insured. Some insurance companies, however, include a provision that extends the contestable period for any disabilities occurring during the first 2 years of coverage. Under such a policy, if an individual were disabled for 13 months out of the first 2 years of the policy, the policy would remain contestable for 37 months (24 + 13). This type of extension provision is not found in the better disability income policies available in the marketplace.

Treatment of Organ Donations

Disability income policies differ as to how they treat disabilities intentionally induced by the insured for the purpose of donating vital organs or tissue to other human beings. The most generous policies provide the same disability benefits for such operations as for any other covered disability. The normal elimination period will be applicable, and then the appropriate level of benefits will be provided. Policies containing this coverage usually require that the policy be in force for a minimum of 6 or 12 months before benefits will be payable for such purposes. This is done to prevent people from purchasing disability policies with the express intention of making tissue donations.

If this protection is provided in a disability income policy, it is usually part of the base policy and covered in the base premium. Therefore this provision is rarely an option with a separate premium payable. Many insurance companies do not provide benefits at all for elective or voluntary surgery, which may be spelled out in the exclusion section of the policy or other sections setting forth limitations and coverage. If there is any question about whether the policy provides such protection, the question should be forwarded to the insurance company's home office. Many companies that intend to provide benefits for voluntary surgery often make it an explicit part of their promotional materials for the coverage.

Social Security Rider

Many insurance companies make an optional provision available that requires a separate, extra premium to cover additional benefits payable when the individual is disabled under the base policy but does not qualify for social security disability benefits. The supplemental benefit is paid over and above the base disability benefit of the underlying policy. When claiming benefits under this option, the insured is generally required to apply for the social security or other social insurance benefits and then supply the insurance company with evidence that the benefits have been denied by the Social Security Administration or other governmental agency. Some policies further require that the insured must appeal the government's benefit denial before benefits will be paid under this rider. Under most of these riders, the benefit payments are not retroactive and the first benefit payment will not be dispensed until the insurance company has accepted the denial of government benefits. In most cases the first benefit payment will be 13 or more months after the onset of disability. The delay occurs because it usually takes social security 5 or 6 months to process the claim denial after the 5-month elimination period. The insurance company then generally requires at least one month to process the claim to verify the denial.

The reason for this type of rider is that underwriting guidelines limit the amount of coverage that an individual can purchase to avoid overinsurance. In setting these guidelines the insurance companies often take into consideration the level of benefits that might be payable under social security for disability purposes. The maximum benefit available in the base policy can be supplemented under this rider so that the total benefits collected from the insurance company are essentially the same as would have been collected if the individual qualified for social security disability benefits.

It is quite common for an insured individual to satisfy the eligibility requirements of a disability income policy and be eligible to collect total-disability benefits from the insurance company while at the same time be *denied* disability benefits from the Social Security Administration. This occurs because the insurance companies generally use a much more liberal definition of disability than that used by the Social Security Administration.

Benefits under the social security rider will terminate for any period that the insured does receive benefits from social security or other specified governmental units in the contract. Provisions differ as to whether or not the social security rider benefits will continue during periods of residual disability. Some policies have the rider benefits terminate once the insured is no longer totally disabled. Benefits under social security riders terminate at age 65 even if the individual continues to be totally disabled. Election to take early retirement benefits under social security will also terminate benefits under a social security rider.

Under some policies the insurance company can require the insured to reapply for social security benefits periodically. Such requirements are reasonable and are merely used to ensure that the insured collects the maximum amount available under the governmental benefit provisions.

A few insurance policies will actually apply cost-of-living adjustments to benefits paid under the social security rider. Under such a policy both the benefits payable under the rider and the base benefit will be adjusted to reflect changes in the cost of living. These adjustments will be applicable after the individual has been receiving benefits for 12 consecutive months.

Hospitalization Benefits

For an additional premium, some disability income policies provide the option of adding supplemental income benefits for periods of hospitalization. The intent of the additional benefits is to recognize that during a period of hospitalization, the insured's need for income may rise because of deductibles, coinsurance provisions, exclusions, and other benefit limitations in his or her medical expense coverage. The benefit payable will be for a stated dollar amount, which under some policies begins with the first day of hospitalization and under other policies is subject to an elimination period that may or may not be the same as that for total-disability benefits. These riders generally contain a limitation on the duration of benefits for any single hospitalization.

Some contracts provide no elimination period at all, and hospitalization benefits are payable from the first day of hospitalization regardless of the length of the elimination period for total-disability benefits. Other contracts have a specified elimination period applicable to the hospitalization rider, which is often the same duration as the elimination period applicable to total-disability benefits although it may sometimes differ.

Dividends

Many insurance companies issuing disability income policies provide participating contracts that pay policyowner dividends. In most cases little or no dividends are paid during the first 2 years of coverage, while under some policies no dividends are paid during the first 3 years of coverage. The level of dividends payable is a function of the company's profitability on its disability income policies and thus subject to fluctuation. In general, dividends do increase with policy duration. As with dividends in life insurance policies, however, dividends cannot be guaranteed. Any dividend illustration is merely an extrapolation of past experience adjusted for expectations of future results.

Many disability income policies are issued on a nonparticipating basis and pay no policyowner dividends. Purchasers of these policies know the full cost in advance since there is no future reduction in cost through dividends.

INSURANCE COMPANY LIMITATIONS ON THE AMOUNT OF COVERAGE

Insurance company statistics have shown that the higher the percentage of a person's predisability income that is replaced by disability income benefits, the higher the likelihood that claims experience will exceed claims expected. In other words, high levels of disability benefits tend to stimulate higher aggregate claims. This is especially true if the benefits exceed the cash income available prior to disability. There have been a surprising number of fraudulent claims in disability income insurance where the insured intentionally maimed himself or herself with the express intent of ceasing work and collecting disability income benefits. Some of the more notorious cases have involved medical practitioners who injected painkillers before severing fingers or other extremities of the body. In cases where fraud was detected, the individuals were unable to collect disability income benefits even though they were permanently disabled.

Minimizing Fraudulent Claims

In order to minimize the motivation for fraudulent claims or even padding of legitimate claims by malingering, insurance companies limit the amount of coverage they will issue to any individual in relation to that individual's income. Generally speaking, disability income coverage is not available for benefit amounts that exceed 60 or 70 percent of the individual's income. In fact, as the level of income increases, the percentage of income replacement that insurance companies will issue decreases. High-income professionals are often limited to less than 50 percent of their income level in setting the maximum benefit level for their disability policies.

Some experts advise that, for individuals providing full disclosure to the insurance company, the appropriate amount of disability income protection to purchase is the maximum amount available from an insurance company that provides quality coverage. Insurance companies will want to know about existing sources of disability protection, such as group policies through the employer, group policies through professional associations or other affinity groups, and salary continuation or sick pay programs. The financial underwriting aspect of disability income policy issuance is just as important as the medical evaluation.

Business owners having financial difficulties and facing bankruptcy present a high risk of adverse selection. A high stress level increases the likelihood of a stroke, heart attack, or other stress-related disability. Stressed individuals with a history of high blood pressure or heart problems present an even higher risk.

The underwriting process for disability income insurance is much more complex than that for life insurance. Although the underwriting for life insurance and for disability insurance coverages has many similarities, disability coverages entail more refined classifications and therefore a more involved evaluation process. The evaluation process is more complicated because disability can be, and often is, a recurrent condition throughout an individual's lifetime. For example, an individual with a bad back may require repeated hospitalization and rehabilitation therapy even though he or she may have a long life. Joint problems associated with knees and elbows often start with injuries at a young age and get progressively worse with wear and the onset of arthritis. Such problems can greatly increase the medical expenses for maintaining good health. The job of underwriting for disability insurance is to correctly classify individuals as to how costly their medical maintenance will be over their lifetime. The individual is to be classified appropriately on the basis of existing information so that the price charged in the premium for that individual and similar individuals will adequately cover the cost of claims for that group over the duration of their coverage.

In some ways it is similar to logistical planning for an ongoing business operation where different functions utilize resources at different rates. For example, telephone bills for telemarketing employees will greatly exceed those for secretarial support staff. Managers must anticipate and plan for needed resources at the applicable cost when they are needed. The insurance companies must do the same with claims. They have to anticipate the frequency of claims and the severity of each claim based on benefit levels that will be paid. Misclassifying an individual into a lower risk classification and charging too low a premium will result in inadequate resource allocation for that insured's future needs. If the misclassification is widespread in all rate categories, the insurance company will be charging inadequate premium levels and may be forced to delay and limit claims settlement unless it can increase premiums for the group of policies. In cases where the insurance company is able to increase premiums on a class basis, it may both increase premiums and cut back as much as possible on claims. By properly classifying insureds in the first place, the company minimizes the need to adjust for past misclassifications at the time of claims settlement.

Modifying the Standard Issue

There are many more ways to adjust for anticipated claims differences in disability coverages than there are in life insurance coverages. Depending on the company, 40 percent to 60 percent of issued policies may require some sort of modification or adjustment from the "standard issue." This varies significantly from life insurance coverages, of which over 80 percent is issued as standard. As in life insurance, disability premiums can be increased for individuals presenting a higher level of risk to the insurance company. Another modification in disability insurance is to insist on a longer elimination period for some high-risk insureds, which eliminates more of the short-term problems and disabilities. In some cases a longer elimination period may be applicable to specified causes or conditions, or the insurance company may insist on a relatively long elimination period that applies to all causes of disability. Such an approach does not preclude coverage for a particular condition, but it limits application to bouts with the problem of longer durations. Another less frequently used method of adjusting for higher risk is to insist on a shorter benefit period for specified problems or conditions, which puts a predictable upper limit on the potential claims payments. The most limiting modification is an outright exclusion of any benefits associated with disabilities stemming from specified causes or conditions. Although this approach may seem drastic, it at least allows individuals to obtain disability coverage for causes other than the major problem that is preventing them from getting full disability protection.

Proper disability underwriting demands a sophisticated knowledge of medical problems and medical treatment. The home office underwriters often require much more information and supporting documents than are necessary to satisfy life insurance underwriters. The home office disability underwriter must get an accurate picture of the individual and the applicable risk without ever meeting that individual. The entire image must be created by the information supplied from the field agent to the home office staff. Very rarely will the home office underwriter even talk to the applicant by telephone. The documents presented with the application must bring the applicant to life and make him or her real to the home office underwriter.

The disability underwriting process commonly includes one or more requests from the home office for additional information. Although this does delay the issuance of coverage, it does not necessarily indicate that the coverage will not be issued. Disability insurers use many resources in an attempt to accept and insure all applicants who fall within their acceptable risk classifications. Obviously some risks will not meet the minimum company standards and will be rejected outright. Individual applicants who are rejected by one company may not necessarily be uninsurable; another company may classify risks in a different manner and apply different cutoff standards. Individuals who experience difficulty in obtaining disability insurance should shop for coverage from other insurance companies on a sequential basis and should not apply for coverage with many insurance companies concurrently. There are brokers who specialize in substandard insurance who can be helpful in obtaining disability coverage for individuals with serious health problems.

Policy Exclusions

There are a few exclusions typically found in disability income policies. Disabilities resulting from war or any sort of military service are nearly always excluded from coverage by a specific policy exclusion provision. This provision often defines war to include declared wars, undeclared wars, and any acts of war. Exclusions also preclude benefit payments for any sickness or injury sustained during military service since they will usually be covered by military hospitals or veterans administration hospitals. It is also fairly common for these policies to exclude benefits for disabilities resulting from a normal pregnancy and disabilities resulting from travel in aircraft if the insured has duties relating to the plane's flight or maintenance.

The total exclusion provision in disability policies is usually rather short. Longer exclusion clauses often indicate that the coverage may be less generous than that provided by premier-quality policies.

BUSINESS USES OF DISABILITY INSURANCE

The disability of business owners or key employees poses a serious risk to a business's financial health. Just as a family suffers from the loss of the income of its breadwinners, a business suffers from the loss of its productive resources. The problems are particularly acute for small enterprises in which the work force may not be large enough to have a backup for critical skills that could be interrupted because of disabilities. Good examples of business owners in need of disability insurance are self-employed attorneys, accountants, physicians, and dentists who operate solo practices and employ a support staff of one or more persons. When these business owners become totally disabled, the primary business activities are often halted. However, it is necessary to maintain the business premises and at least a skeletal support staff so that business can be resumed when the business owner recovers from the disability. For example, accounts receivable must still be collected and ongoing expenses must still be paid.

Business Overhead Insurance

Overhead expense policies are available to cover many of the ongoing costs of operating a business while the business owner is totally disabled. These policies tend to be limited to benefit durations of one or 2 years and have relatively short elimination periods. The intent is to keep the necessary staff and premises available for the resumption of business if the business owner recovers from the disability. However, if the disabled business owner has not recovered within the one- or 2-year benefit period, it is expected that the business will either be sold or terminated. There is a relatively low probability that an individual who has been disabled for 2 years will recover from the disability. For example, if the original onset of the individual's disability was at age 35, the probability of recovery is 23 percent, based on 1964 Commissioners Disability Table figures. Likewise, if the onset of the disability was at age 45 and continues for 24 months, there is only a 15 percent likelihood of recovery. For individuals aged 55 sustaining 2 years of disability, only 8 percent are likely to recover. Consequently it is not unreasonable that business overhead expense policies limit benefit periods to a maximum of 24 months. Preliminary estimates based on the 1985 Individual Disability Table indicate that the probability of recovering has slipped even lower.

Insurance companies are extremely cautious in writing this coverage and in keeping the benefit amount in line with established stable costs for previous periods. Consequently the application for such coverage must be accompanied by supporting financial statements to verify the stability of the business and to establish the appropriate level of insurable expenses. These expenses include such things as salaries for secretaries, nurses, and other staff necessary to resume business upon the business owner's recovery as well as the ongoing expenses for rent, utilities, taxes, accounting services, and so forth.

In most cases it would be impossible for the disabled individual to cover these ongoing business expenses through disability benefits payable under an ordinary disability income policy. Continuing the business through a disability of up to 2 years often depends on the existence of a business overhead policy. In the absence of such coverage the business owner must expend accumulated assets, such as savings and investments, to keep the business entity operational. Business overhead expense coverage provides a less painful method of meeting these ongoing business expenses. A business overhead policy greatly increases the likelihood of a business's continuing after the business owner recovers from a serious disability. The business owner is best protected by a combination of appropriate business overhead expense coverage and a disability income policy for the replacement of lost personal income.

Disability Income Coverage for Key Persons

Business entities are dependent on their personnel to carry out their activities and generate revenues and profits. Very often there are a few key individuals whose unique talents and experiences are crucial to the success of the business entity. The loss of an individual's contributions by reason of disability or death could deal a devastating blow to the financial well-being of the enterprise. In fact, sometimes the dependence is so critical that losing the individual's participation could lead to the bankruptcy or termination of the business itself. This is particularly true of professionals operating as sole practitioners.

Many business enterprises have recognized the importance of key individuals who make the most critical contributions and have obtained disability income insurance covering these key individuals. The justification for such coverage is very similar to that for key person life insurance policies. Proceeds from key person disability policies can be used to replace lost revenue directly attributable to the key person's disability, to fund the search for individuals to replace the insured person, to fund the extra cost of hiring specialized individuals to replace the multiple talents of the insured, and to fund training costs that may be incurred to prepare replacements to carry out the duties the insured performed. Some or all of these considerations may prompt enterprises to obtain key person disability policies. The motivation itself may help the business managers determine the appropriate amount of coverage to obtain. The costs of training, hiring, and compensating are usually rather easy to ascertain, while estimating lost revenue is a very difficult and complex task.

Even though a business entity may determine a desired amount of disability income protection for each key individual, it may not be able to obtain that amount of coverage. The underwriting processes of insurance companies limit the maximum amount of coverage available on any one individual. A wide range of guidelines is utilized for setting these limitations, and it is usually difficult to get an insurer to waive any of these limitations. Sometimes a business entity is able to make a strong enough argument on both financial and economic grounds to justify an exception and obtain the desired amount even though it exceeds underwriting guideline limitations.

Benefits from key employee disability policies are payable to the business entity when the insured key employee is disabled. The policies used for these purposes are usually the same as the group or individual disability income policies available to the general populace. They are subject to the same range of policy provisions already discussed with respect to definitions of disability, benefit periods, elimination periods, waiver of premium, renewal period, and other considerations.

Disability policies owned by the corporation or business entity with benefits payable to that entity are not deductible business expenses for federal income tax purposes. Payment of those premiums does not create a taxable income to the insured employee. Consequently the receipt of insurance proceeds under the policy by the business entity is not considered taxable income to the business.

Salary Continuation Plans

Disability income policies can be purchased by the business entity to fund formal corporate salary continuation plans. Formal plans can be set up in two different ways. The corporation can own the policy and be the beneficiary under the policy, or the corporation can pay the premiums on a policy owned by the employee to whom benefits will be paid. When the corporation is the owner of the policy and the beneficiary, premium payments are nondeductible by the corporation and the corporation will receive the insurance proceeds free of any federal income tax liability. Premium payments for such coverage will not be considered taxable income to the employee.

When the corporation merely pays the premiums on a policy owned by the employee, the premiums are deductible expenses of the corporation as long as they meet reasonable expense criteria. The premium payments are not considered taxable income to the employee; however, benefits paid under the policy will be taxable income to the employee.

Sometimes informal salary continuation plans are set up where the corporation pays a large enough bonus to the employee for the employee to buy an individual disability income policy. If the bonus payments are reasonable compensation, they are deductible by the corporation. The bonus is taxable income to the employee. The premium payments made by the employee are not deductible. Any benefit payments received by the employee will have no effect on the corporation and will be received free of any federal income tax liability by the employee.

Disability Buy-Sell Funding

A business owner's disability often threatens the viability of that enterprise. In order to preserve the value of the business it is often necessary to shift the business owner's ownership interest to one or more other individuals who can continue conducting the affairs of the business. In cases in which there is multiple ownership of the business prior to the disability, the most likely parties to purchase the ownership interest of the disabled owner are the nondisabled co-owners. Unfortunately few business owners have adequate amounts of liquid assets to make an outright purchase of the ownership interest from the disabled co-owner.

Just as buy-sell agreements triggered by the death of an owner can be funded with life insurance, buy-sell agreements triggered by the disability of an owner can be funded with disability policies. Special disability policies have been designed specifically for the purpose of funding buy-sell agreements. These policies can fund either an installment purchase or a lump-sum buyout. It is now possible to obtain lump-sum coverage for amounts as high as $50 million for a single disability policy if the underwriting criteria are met. This is a relatively recent development within the disability insurance market.

The disability risk for business owners is just as real as the disability risk for other individuals. The same probabilities of occurrence apply. Any attorney drafting the necessary documents to establish a new business entity, whether it is a partnership or a corporation, would be considered negligent if he or she did not at least recommend buy-sell agreements covering both death and disability of the respective owners. These buy-sell agreements stipulate how the business ownership interests are to be transferred to the surviving or continuing owners upon the death or disability of one of them. In the case of a disability buyout, the agreement must stipulate what definition of disability is to be used and how long after the onset of the disability the ownership is to be sold to the nondisabled partners or co-owners. The agreement must further stipulate how and when the ownership interest is to be valued and on what conditions any salary continuation will be provided prior to the actual buyout.

If disability policies are to be used for the purpose of funding such buyouts, the definition used in the disability policy should be the same definition as that specified in the buy-sell agreement. In a similar manner the elimination period for the disability policy should exactly dovetail with the elimination period specified in the buy-sell agreement. Sometimes buy-sell agreements contain a reversal clause to deal with a shareholder's potential recovery after the buyout starts but before the full purchase price has been paid.

Funding the buy-sell agreement can be accomplished by either an entity plan where the corporation buys the stock from the disabled individual or by a cross-purchase plan where each of the nondisabled co-owners purchases a portion of the ownership interest from the disabled owner. Under an entity arrangement the corporation purchases policies on each of the owners and has the benefits payable to the corporation for purposes of purchasing the stock from the disabled owner. The arrangements must be set up very carefully with the advice of tax counsel. (These transactions are subject to the attribution rules and other tax considerations that are beyond the scope of this course. More thorough treatment of these tax issues is provided in The American College course HS 331 Planning for Business Owners and Professionals.)

Under the cross-purchase arrangement each one of the business owners purchases policies insuring the other co-owners and paying benefits to the purchaser-owner of the policy. This arrangement provides benefits to each of the nondisabled owners after the insured becomes disabled, and the proceeds can be used to purchase the ownership interest from the disabled individual.

The tax treatment of a cross-purchase buy-sell occurring as a result of a disability is relatively simple. Premiums paid by the individual shareholders are nondeductible. The disability benefits they receive under these policies are tax free with respect to federal income taxes. The sale proceeds for the ownership interest of the disabled individual are capital gains to the seller by the amount that the proceeds exceed his or her basis. Since the transaction is not by reason of death, there is no basis step-up available for the ownership transfer.

For the entity-type buy-sell agreement (stock redemption) the premiums paid by the corporation for the disability policies are nondeductible. However, the disability benefits received by the corporation are tax free with respect to federal income taxes. The redemption amounts paid to the disabled owner for the ownership interest will most likely be a combination of capital gain and ordinary income. Full consideration of these tax issues is beyond the scope of this course. Further information is available in other American College courses, such as HS 321 Income Taxation and HS 331 Planning for Business Owners and Professionals.

8

Long-Term Care Insurance

Burton T. Beam, Jr.

Since the beginning of the 1980s, long-term care insurance has evolved from being virtually nonexistent to being an important form of insurance product carried by an estimated 2 to 3 million persons. The number of insurance companies with individual long-term care products has gradually increased to about 100, and the major providers of employee benefits are now making group products available.

During its relatively short life, long-term care products have been hailed as a major source of financial security and criticized as a coverage that fails to meet consumers' real long-term care needs. In this environment long-term care products have continued to evolve, with newer and more comprehensive products being introduced on an almost weekly basis. Long-term care coverage can probably best be described as having grown from infancy to somewhere between the childhood and teenage years. Coverage will change to meet consumer demands and expectations, and the largely untapped market for coverage will continue to grow as the American population ages.

The first portion of this chapter looks at the need for long-term care. This is followed by a brief description of sources of long-term care other than insurance. The chapter continues with a discussion of how and why insurance policies have evolved into the products now being offered. It then contains an analysis of the more common products in the marketplace today—both individual and group. The chapter concludes with a checklist for comparing policies.

NEED FOR LONG-TERM CARE

An Aging Population

Long-term care has traditionally been thought of as a problem primarily for the older population. The population aged 65 or over is the fastest-growing age group; today it represents about 11 percent of the population, a figure that is expected to increase to between 20 percent and 25 percent over the next 50 years. The segment of the population aged 85 and over is growing at an even faster rate. While less than 10 percent of the over-65 group is over 85 today, this percentage is expected to double over the next two generations.

An aging society presents changing problems. Those who needed long-term care in the past were most likely to have suffered from strokes or other acute diseases. With longer life spans today and in the future, a larger portion of the elderly will be incapacitated by chronic conditions, such as Alzheimer's disease, arthritis, osteoporosis, and lung and heart disease—conditions that often require continuing assistance with day-to-day needs. The likelihood that a person will need to enter a nursing home increases dramatically with age. One percent of persons between the ages of 65 and 74 reside in nursing homes, and the percentage increases to 6 percent between the ages of 75 and 84. At age 85 and over, the figure rises to approximately 25 percent. Statistics of the Department of Health and Human Services indicate that persons aged 65 or older face a 40 percent chance of entering a nursing home at some time during the remainder of their lives.

It should be noted that the elderly are not the only group of persons who need long-term care. Many younger persons are unable to care for themselves because of handicaps resulting from birth defects, mental conditions, illnesses, or accidents.

Increasing Costs

Nearly $50 billion is spent each year on nursing home care. This cost is increasing faster than inflation because of the growing demand for nursing home beds and the shortage of skilled medical personnel. The cost of complete long-term care for an individual can be astronomical, with annual nursing home costs of $30,000 to $50,000 not unusual. Costs of $1,000 to $2,000 per month can easily be incurred in part-time home health care.

Inability of Families to Provide Full Care

Traditionally long-term care has been provided by family members, often at considerable personal sacrifices and great personal stress. However, it is becoming more difficult for families to provide long-term care for the following reasons:

- the geographic dispersion of family members
- increased participation in the paid work force by women and children
- fewer children in the family
- more childless families
- higher divorce rates
- the inability of family members to provide care because they, too, are growing old

Inadequacy of Insurance Protection

Private medical expense insurance policies (both group and individual) almost always have an exclusion for convalescent, custodial, or rest care. Some policies, particularly group policies, do provide coverage for extended-care facilities and for home health care. In both cases the purpose is to provide care in a manner that is less expensive than care in a hospital. However, coverage is provided only if a person also needs medical care; benefits are not provided if a person is merely "old" and needs someone to care for him or her.

Medicare is also inadequate because it does not cover custodial care unless this care is needed along with the medical or rehabilitative treatment provided in skilled nursing facilities or under home health care benefits.

One factor that may have an effect on the need for long-term care protection is the extent to which any future national health insurance program covers long-term care. Because of the cost, coverage will probably be modest if it exists at all. However, the Clinton proposal at the time this chapter is being written does contain some limited home health care benefits for persons who need convalescent care.

SOURCES OF LONG-TERM CARE

There are several sources other than insurance that are available for providing long-term care. However, there are drawbacks associated with each source.

One source is to rely on personal savings. Unless a person has substantial resources, however, this approach may force an individual and his or her dependents into poverty. It may also mean that the person will not meet the financial objective of leaving assets to heirs.

A second source is to rely on welfare. The medicaid program in most states will provide benefits, which usually include nursing home care, to the "medically needy." However, a person is not eligible unless he or she is either poor or has a low income and has exhausted most other assets (including those of a spouse). There is also often a social stigma associated with accepting welfare. One strategy that is sometimes used is to give a person's assets away at the time nursing home care is needed and ultimately rely on medicaid. (This will work only if income, including pensions and social security, is below specified limits). However, medicaid benefits are reduced (or their onset postponed) if assets were disposed of at less than their fair market value within a specific time period (called the look-back period) prior to medicaid eligibility. One approach is to purchase long-term care insurance in an amount sufficient to provide protection for the length of the look-back period. If care is needed, a person can rely on the insurance coverage and transfer assets to heirs. When the insurance coverage runs out and the look-back period is over, the person can apply for medicaid. Because of recent tax law changes that extend the medicaid look-back period, anyone using this strategy should reevaluate its viability.

Several states have attempted to encourage better coverage for long-term care, often with grants provided by The Robert Wood Johnson Foundation. One aspect of these experiments has been to waive or modify certain medicaid requirements if a person carries a state-approved long-term care policy. For example, in Connecticut a person can apply for and receive medicaid benefits without having to exhaust current assets if the individual had maintained an approved long-term care policy and its benefits have run out. In essence, these programs increase the assets that a person can retain and still collect medicaid benefits, with the increase in the allowable asset threshold related to the amount of long-term care coverage carried and exhausted.

Life-care facilities are growing in popularity as a source of meeting long-term care needs. Residents in a life-care facility pay an "entrance fee" that allows them to occupy a dwelling unit but usually does not give them actual ownership rights. The entrance fee is typically not refundable if the resident leaves the facility voluntarily or dies. (There may be some partial refund if a person leaves within a specified time period.) Residents pay a monthly fee that includes meals, some housecleaning services, and varying degrees of health care. If a person needs long-term care, he or she must give up the independent living unit and move to the nursing home portion of the facility, but the monthly fee normally remains the same. The disadvantages of this option are that the cost of a life-care facility is beyond the reach of many persons, and a resident must be in reasonably good health and able to live independently at the time he or she enters the facility. Therefore the decision to use a life-care facility must be made in advance of the need for long-term care. Once such care is needed or is imminent, this approach is no longer viable.

A few insurers now include long-term care benefits in some cash value life insurance policies. Essentially an insured can begin to use these accelerated benefits while he or she is still living. For example, if the insured is in a nursing home, he or she might be able to elect a benefit equal to 25 percent or 50 percent of the policy face amount. However, any benefits received reduce the future death benefit payable to heirs. One potential problem with this approach is that the acceleration of benefits may result in the reduction of the death benefit to a level that is inadequate to accomplish the purpose of life insurance—the protection of family members after a wage earner's death. If benefits are accelerated, there is less left for the surviving family. In addition, the availability of an accelerated benefit may give the insured a false sense of security that long-term care needs are being met when in fact the potential benefit may be inadequate to cover extended nursing home stays.

DEVELOPMENT OF INSURANCE COVERAGE

It is common for insurance coverages to evolve over time. However, the evolution of long-term care products has been dramatic with respect to the magnitude of the changes and the speed with which they have occurred.

Early Policies

Coverage

The long-term care policies in existence in the early 1980s were primarily designed to provide care during the recovery period following an acute illness. They seldom met the needs of persons who needed long-term care for chronic conditions. The following provisions were characteristic of many of these policies:

- benefit periods of less than one year
- a prerequisite for benefits in a skilled nursing facility, often a prior hospitalization of 3 to 5 days
- a prerequisite of a higher level of out-of-hospital care before benefits could be received for a lower level of care. For example, home health care might be covered, but only if a person had spent 3 to 5 days in a skilled nursing facility.
- benefits limited to only the highest level of care, such as care in a skilled nursing facility
- the exclusion of benefits for care needed as a result of Alzheimer's disease or other organic brain diseases
- no inflation protection to meet higher long-term care costs in the future

● the lack of guaranteed renewability provisions. This meant that many insurance companies had the right to cancel their policies if they so desired.

Cost

The earliest long-term care policies were very expensive for the coverage provided. To some extent this was to be expected. Anytime a new coverage is written, considerable uncertainty exists about future costs. There simply is little or no actuarial data on which to base rates. As a result, pricing is subjective and conservative.

Improper Sales Practices

Unfortunately the sale of early long-term care policies was often accompanied by improper sales practices. Consumers were led to believe that policies were much more comprehensive than they actually were. In effect, consumers felt that they were purchasing "nursing home" insurance that would cover them anytime nursing home care was needed. Only when such care was needed did many of these consumers realize that their coverage was very limited. Even if they realized the policy's limitations soon after purchase, few of these early policies contained a free-look provision that allowed the return of the initial premium within the first 10 to 30 days of the policy.

Evolution of Coverage

Criticism of the early long-term care policies created considerable pressure for change. Consumer groups argued for more government regulation. The federal government conducted studies and held hearings, with the results painting a less than flattering picture of long-term care policies. Change itself, however, resulted primarily from the actions of insurance companies themselves and from the state regulators of insurance. But the threat of federal regulation was always present.

The negative publicity about early policies had a dampening effect on the public's perception of long-term care insurance. This led many insurance companies to modify their policies and companies entering the business to offer more comprehensive policies. At the same time the National Association of Insurance Commissioners (NAIC) began to take a very active interest in long-term care insurance. This culminated in the adoption of the Long-term Care Insurance Model Act in 1987. In 1988 model regulations were issued to enable the states to implement the model act. The act and the regulations have been amended every year since. Sometimes these amendments changed previous act provisions; at other times, new issues were addressed. The model act, which is discussed in more detail later, has been adopted by the majority of states. However, the version in force in a given state is not always the latest NAIC version. A few states still have little regulation of long-term care policies, and other states have adopted legislation different from the model act, although it may be similar to that recommended by the NAIC.

The long-term care policies of many insurance companies are now in their third and fourth generations, and one company issued its seventh generation of policies in late 1993. While coverage is still not always complete, there is little comparison between the early policies and most of what is marketed today. Not only have policies become more comprehensive over the last few years, but premiums have also tended to drop as more credible statistics about long-term claims have become available. However, many of the latest enhancements to policies are accompanied by an increased charge.

Effect of Changes on Existing Policyowners

As policies have evolved, insurance companies have been faced with the decision of how to treat existing policyowners. Until recently many long-term care policy upgrades were accompanied by reduced premiums. At one extreme, companies made no effort to let existing policyowners know of these changes. If the policyowner found out, he or she might be allowed to exchange an old policy for the newer form. However, the premium may or may not be based on the original age of issue. If the conversion was based on the current attained-age rates, a higher premium might result. In some cases, the policyowner could get the new policy only if current underwriting rules were satisfied. Finally, for some insurers the policy provisions of the new policy, such as any preexisting-conditions provisions, were again applicable for conversions.

At the other extreme, many insurance companies took a more consumer-oriented approach. Existing policyowners were automatically given the enhanced coverage at the original-age cost and without any policy restrictions.

Current enhancements to long-term care products usually result in an increased premium. Again, insurance company practices vary. Some companies allow the policyowner to add the enhanced benefits by paying the new premium based on the policyowner's original age of issue. Other companies may require evidence of insurability and use attained-age rates.

NAIC MODEL LEGISLATION

Because of its widespread adoption by the states, it is appropriate to discuss the NAIC model legislation regarding long-term care. The legislation consists of a model act that is designed to be incorporated into a state's insurance law and model regulations that are designed to be adopted for use in implementing the law. This discussion is based on the latest version of the model legislation, which, as mentioned earlier, seems to be amended annually. Even though most states have adopted the NAIC legislation, some states may not have adopted the latest version. However, the importance of the model legislation should not be overlooked. With most insurers writing coverage in more than one state, it is likely that the latest provisions have been adopted by one or more states where an insurer's coverage is sold. Because most insurance companies sell essentially the same long-term care product everywhere they do business, the NAIC guidelines are often, in effect, being adhered to in states that have not adopted the legislation.

Before proceeding with a summary of the major provisions of the NAIC model legislation, it is important to make two points. First, the model legislation establishes guidelines. Insurance companies still have significant latitude in many aspects of product design. Second, many older policies are still in existence that were written prior to the adoption of the model legislation or under one of its earlier versions.

The model legislation applies to any insurance policy or rider that is advertised, marketed, offered, or designed to provide coverage for not less than 12 consecutive months for each covered person in a setting other than an acute care unit of a hospital for one or more of the following: necessary or medically necessary diagnostic, preventive, therapeutic, rehabilitative, maintenance, or personal services. The 12-month period has been the source of considerable controversy because it, in effect, allows policies to provide benefits for periods as short as one year. Many critics of long-term care insurance argue that coverage should not be allowed unless benefits are provided for at least 2 or 3 years. Statistics would seem to support their views. Approximately 40 percent of all persons who enter nursing homes after age 65 have stays in excess of one year. This figure drops to about 15 percent for stays of 3 years or longer.

The model legislation focuses on two major areas—policy provisions and marketing. Highlights of the criteria for policy provisions include the following:

- Many words or terms cannot be used in a policy unless they are specifically defined in accordance with the legislation. Examples include adult day care, home health care services, personal care, skilled nursing care, and usual and customary.
- No policy can contain renewal provisions other than guaranteed renewable or noncancelable. Under neither type of provision can the insurance company make any unilateral changes in any coverage provision. Under a noncancelable provision, premiums are established in advance and cannot be changed. Under a guaranteed renewable provision, the insurance company is allowed to revise premiums on a class basis.
- Limitations and exclusions are prohibited except in the following cases:
  - preexisting conditions
  - mental or nervous disorders (but this does not permit the exclusion of Alzheimer's disease)
  - alcoholism and drug addiction
  - illness, treatment, or medical condition arising out of war, participation in a felony, service in the armed forces, suicide, and aviation if a person is a non-fare-paying passenger
  - treatment in a government facility and services available under medicare and other social insurance programs
- No policy can provide coverage for skilled nursing home care only or provide significantly more coverage for skilled care in a facility than for lower levels of care.
- The definition of preexisting condition can be no more restrictive than to exclude a condition for which treatment was recommended or received within 6 months prior to the effective date of coverage. In addition, coverage can be excluded for a confinement for this condition only if it begins within 6 months of the effective date of coverage.
- Eligibility for benefits cannot be based on a prior hospital requirement or higher level of care.
- Insurance companies must offer the policyowner the right to purchase coverage that allows for an increase in the amount of benefits based on

reasonable anticipated increases in the cost of services covered by the policy. The policyowner must specifically reject this inflation protection if he or she does not want it.

- A policy must contain a provision that makes a policy incontestable after 2 years on the grounds of misrepresentation alone. The policy can still be contested on the basis that the applicant knowingly and intentionally misrepresented relevant facts pertaining to the insured's health.

Provisions of the model legislation that pertain to marketing include the following:

- An outline of coverage must be delivered to a prospective applicant at the time of initial solicitation. This outline must contain (1) a description of the coverage, (2) a statement of the principal exclusions, reductions, and limitations in the policy, (3) a statement of the terms under which the policy can be continued in force or terminated, (4) a description of the terms under which the policy may be returned and the premium refunded, and (5) a brief description of the relationship of cost of care and benefits.
- A shopper's guide must be delivered to all prospective applicants.
- The policy must allow policyowners to have a free 30-day look.
- An insurance company must establish procedures to assure that any comparisons of policies by its agents or other producers will be fair and accurate and to assure that excessive insurance is not sold or issued.
- The expected loss ratio under the policy must be at least 60 percent.
- Applications for insurance must be clear and unambiguous so that an applicant's health condition can be properly ascertained. The application must also contain a conspicuous statement near the place for the applicant's signature that says the following: "If your answers to this application are incorrect or untrue, the company has the right to deny benefits or rescind your policy." The purpose of these requirements is to control postclaim underwriting.
- No policy can be issued until the applicant has been given the option of electing a third party to be notified of any pending policy lapse because of nonpayment of premium. The purpose of this provision is to eliminate the problem of policy lapse because a senile or otherwise mentally impaired person fails to pay the premium.
- If one long-term policy replaces another, the new insurer must waive any time periods pertaining to preexisting conditions and probationary periods for comparable benefits to the extent that similar exclusions were satisfied in the original policy.

The NAIC continues to discuss additional changes to the model legislation. Probably the most significant proposal is to require long-term care policies to have nonforfeiture values. However, the proposal would have these values in the form of extended benefits rather than cash. To prevent unnecessary policy replacement, there are also proposals to limit first-year commissions to no more than twice the amount of one year's renewal commission. One additional proposal would, if adopted, mandate the upgrading of old policies when newly improved policies are introduced.

CHARACTERISTICS OF INDIVIDUAL POLICIES

For many types of insurance, policies are relatively standardized. For long-term care insurance the opposite is true. Significant variations (and therefore differences in cost) exist from one insurance company to another. A policyowner also has numerous options with respect to policy provisions.

The discussion in this section of the chapter focuses on issue age, benefits, renewability, and cost. The provisions and practices described represent the norm in that most policies fit within the extremes that are described. However, the norm covers a wide spectrum.

Issue Age

Significant variations exist among insurance companies with respect to the age at which they will issue policies. At a minimum, a healthy person between the ages of 55 and 75 will be eligible for coverage from most insurance companies. Most companies also have an upper age of 80 or 85, beyond which coverage will not be issued. Coverage written at age 85 or older, if available, is often accompanied by restrictive policy provisions and very high premiums.

Considerably more variation exists with respect to the youngest age at which coverage will be written. Some companies have no minimum age. Other companies sell policies to persons as young as age 20. Still other companies have minimum ages in the 40-to-50 age range. One reason for not issuing policies to persons under age 40 is the fear of the high number of potential claims resulting from AIDS.

Benefits

Benefits under long-term care policies can be categorized by type, amounts, duration, the ability to restore benefits, and the degree of inflation protection.

Types

There are several levels of care that are frequently provided by long-term care policies:

- *skilled nursing care*, which consists of daily nursing and rehabilitative care that can be performed only by, or under the supervision of, skilled medical personnel and must be based on a doctor's orders
- *intermediate care*, which involves occasional nursing and rehabilitative care that must be based on a doctor's orders and can be performed only by, or under the supervision of, skilled medical personnel
- *custodial care*, which is primarily to handle personal needs, such as walking, bathing, dressing, eating, or taking medicine, and can usually be provided by someone without professional medical skills or training
- *home health care*, which is received at home and includes part-time skilled nursing care, speech therapy, physical or occupational therapy, part-time services from home health aides, and help from homemakers or chore-workers

- *adult day care*, which is received at centers specifically designed for the elderly who live at home but whose spouses or families cannot be available to stay home during the day. The level of care received is similar to that provided for home health care. Most adult day-care centers also provide transportation to and from the center.

Most policies cover at least the first three levels of care, and many cover all five. Some policies also provide benefits for respite care, which allows occasional full-time care at home for a person who is receiving home health care. Respite-care benefits enable family members who are providing much of the home care to take a needed break.

It is becoming increasingly common for policies to contain a bed reservation benefit. This benefit continues payments to a long-term care facility for a limited time (such as 20 days) if a patient must temporarily leave because of hospitalization. Without a continuation of payments, the bed may be rented to someone else and unavailable upon the patient's release from the hospital.

Some newer policies provide assisted-living benefits. These benefits are for facilities that provide care for the frail elderly who are no longer able to care for themselves but do not need the level of care provided in a nursing home.

Amounts

Benefits are usually limited to a specified amount per day that is independent of the actual charge for long-term care. The insured purchases the level of benefit he or she desires up to the maximum level the insurance company will provide. Benefits are often sold in increments of $10 per day up to frequently found limits of $100 or $150 or in a few cases as much as $300. Most insurance companies will not offer a daily benefit below $30 or $50.

The same level of benefits is usually provided for all levels of institutional care. A high proportion of policies that provide home health care limit the benefit to one-half the benefit amount payable for institutional stays. However, some insurers have introduced home health care limits that are as high as 80 percent to 100 percent of the benefit for nursing homes.

Some policies are written on an indemnity basis and pay the cost of covered services up to a maximum dollar amount. For example, a policy may pay 80 percent to 100 percent of charges up to a maximum dollar amount per day.

Duration

Long-term care policies contain both an elimination (waiting) period and a maximum benefit period. Under an elimination period, benefit payments do not begin until a specified time period after long-term care has begun. While a few insurance companies have a set period (such as 60 days), most allow the policyowner to select from three or four optional elimination periods. For example, one insurance company allows the choice of 30, 90, or 180 days. Choices may occasionally be as low as 30 days or as high as 365 days.

The policyowner is also usually given a choice regarding the maximum period for which benefits will be paid. For example, one insurer offers durations of 2, 3, or 4 years; another makes 3, 6, and 12-year coverage available. At the extremes, options of one year or lifetime may be available. However, a policy with a lifetime benefit will be more expensive than one with a shorter maximum benefit limit. In some cases, the duration applies to all benefits; in other cases, the duration specified is for nursing home benefits, with home health care benefits covered for a shorter time.

A few insurers extend the maximum period (if it is less than a lifetime limit) by a specified number of days (such as 30 days) for each year the insured does not collect any benefit payments. Such an extension is usually subject to an aggregate limit, such as one or 2 years.

A few policies (usually written on an indemnity basis) specify the maximum benefit as a stated dollar amount, such as $50,000 or $100,000.

Restoration

A few policies provide for restoration of full benefits if the insured has been out of a nursing home for a certain time period, often 180 days. However, most policies do not have this provision, and maximum benefits for a subsequent claim will be reduced by the benefits previously paid.

Inflation Protection

Most long-term care policies offer some type of inflation protection that the policyowner can purchase. In some cases, the inflation protection is elected (for a higher premium) at the time of purchase; future increases in benefits are automatic. In other cases, the policyowner is allowed to purchase additional benefits each year without evidence of insurability.

Inflation protection is generally in the form of a specified annual increase, often 5 percent. This percentage may be on a simple interest basis, which means that each annual increase is a percentage of the original benefit. In other cases, the increase is on a compound interest basis, which means that each increase is based on the existing benefit at the time the additional coverage is purchased. Some policies limit aggregate increases to a specified multiple of the original policy, such as two times. Other policies allow increases only to a maximum age, such as 85.

There are two approaches to pricing any additional coverage purchased. Some insurers base premiums on the insured's attained age when the original policy was issued; other insurers use the insured's age at the time each additional increment of coverage is purchased.

Inflation protection is usually less than adequate to offset actual inflation. The maximum annual increase in benefits is usually 5 percent. This is significantly below recent annual increases in the cost of long-term care, which has been in the double digits over the last decade.

Eligibility for Benefits

Almost all insurance companies now use a criterion for benefit eligibility that is related to several so-called activities of daily living. While variations exist, these activities often include eating, bathing, dressing, transferring from bed to chair, using the toilet, and maintaining continence. In order to receive benefits, there must be independent certification that a person is totally dependent on others to perform a certain number of these activities. For example, one insurer lists seven activities and requires total dependence for any three of them; another insurer requires dependence for two out of a list of six.

Newer policies contain a second criterion that, if satisfied, will result in the payment of benefits even if the activities of daily living can be performed. This criterion is based on cognitive impairment, which can be caused by Alzheimer's disease, strokes, or other brain damage. Cognitive impairment is generally measured through tests performed by trained medical personnel. Because eligibility for benefits often depends on subjective evaluations, most insurance companies use some form of case management. Case management may be mandatory, with the case manager determining eligibility, working with the physician and family to decide on an appropriate type of care, and periodically reassessing the case. Case management may also be voluntary, with the case manager making recommendations about the type of care needed and providing information about the sources for care.

Preexisting Conditions

The most common preexisting conditions provision specifies that benefits will not be paid for a long-term care need within the first 6 months of a policy for a condition for which treatment was recommended or received within 6 months prior to policy purchase. Less restrictive provisions, and perhaps no such provision, are sometimes found but usually only in policies that are very strictly underwritten.

Exclusions

Most long-term care policies contain the exclusions permitted under the NAIC model act. One source of controversy is the exclusion for mental and nervous disorders. This is an area that insurers frequently avoid because of the possibility of fraudulent claims and the controversies that often arise over claim settlements. The usual exclusion is stated as follows: "This policy does not provide benefits for the care or treatment of mental illness or emotional disorders without a demonstrable organic cause." Many policies also specifically specify that Alzheimer's disease and senile dementia, as diagnosed by a physician, are considered as having demonstrable organic cause, even though state law frequently requires these disorders to be covered.

Underwriting

The underwriting of long-term care policies, like the underwriting of medical expense policies, is based on the health of the insured. However, underwriting for the long-term care risk focuses on situations that will cause claims far into the future. Most underwriting is done on the basis of questionnaires rather than on the use of actual physical examinations. Numerous questions are asked about the health of relatives. For example, if a parent or grandparent had Alzheimer's disease, there is an increased likelihood that the applicant will get this disease in the future. In addition, the insurance company is very interested in medical events, such as temporary amnesia or fainting spells, that might be an indication of future incapacities.

Underwriting tends to become more restrictive as the age of an applicant increases. Not only is a future claim more likely to occur much sooner, but adverse selection can also be more severe.

Most insurers have a single classification for all acceptable applicants for long-term care insurance, but it is becoming more common to have three or four categories of insurable classifications, each with a different rate structure.

In the past, insurance companies were accused of "underwriting at the time of claims" by denying benefits because of restrictive policy provisions and supposed (or actual) misstatements in the distant past. The regulations of many states regarding preexisting conditions and the mandatory inclusion of an incontestability provision have caused this problem to become less severe over time. This, however, puts many insurance companies in the position of having to underwrite more accurately prior to policy issuance.

Renewability

Long-term care policies currently being sold are guaranteed renewable, which means that an individual's coverage cannot be canceled except for nonpayment of premiums. While premiums cannot be raised on the basis of a particular applicant's claim, they can (and often are) raised by class.

Premiums

Premium Payment Period

The vast majority of long-term care policies have premiums that are payable for life and determined by the age of the insured at the time of issue. For example, a policy may have an annual cost of $800 at the time of purchase. Assuming the policy is guaranteed renewable, this premium will not change unless it is raised on a class basis. Long-term care policies of this nature are often advertised as being "level premium." This is misleading because premiums may be (and in a few cases have been) increased by class. As a result, the current NAIC model act prohibits the use of this term unless a policy is noncancelable, which means that rates cannot increase.

A few companies have guaranteed renewable policies with scheduled premium increases. These increases may occur as frequently as annually or as infrequently as every 5 years.

While most premiums are paid annually for the insured's lifetime, a few insurers offer other modes of payment. Lifetime coverage can sometimes be purchased with a single premium. Some insurers are now also beginning to offer policies that have premium payment periods of 10 or 20 years, after which time the premium is paid up.

Factors Affecting Premiums

Numerous factors affect the premium that a policyowner will pay for a long-term care policy. Even if the provisions of several policies are virtually identical, premiums will vary among companies. For example, the premiums for three similar policies from three different companies are shown in table 8-1. Each policy has a daily benefit of $100 per day, a waiting period of 20 days or less, a lifetime benefit period, and coverage for home health care.

TABLE 8-1
Comparison of Long-Term Care Premiums for Similar Policies

Age	Company A	Company B	Company C
40	$ 680	$ 1,670	$ 1,220
45	850	2,000	1,370
50	1,090	2,450	1,440
55	1,440	3,060	1,830
60	2,010	4,200	2,370
65	2,900	5,750	3,250
70	4,300	7,660	4,650
75	6,290	11,300	6,630
79	9,530	14,710	10,180

Age. Age plays a significant role in the cost of long-term care coverage, as shown by the rates in the table. These figures demonstrate that long-term care coverage can be obtained at a reasonable cost if it is purchased at a young age.

Types of Benefits. The benefits provided under a policy have a significant bearing on the cost. Most policies cover care in a nursing home. However, many policies also cover home health care and other benefits provided to persons who are still able to reside in their own homes. This broader coverage increases premiums by 30 percent to 50 percent.

Duration of Benefits. The longer the maximum benefit period, the higher the premium. The longer the waiting period, the lower the premium. With many insurers a policy with an unlimited benefit period and no waiting period will have a premium about double that of a policy with a 2-year benefit period and a 90-day waiting period.

Inflation Protection. Policies may be written with or without automatic benefit increases for inflation. All other factors being equal, the addition of a 5 percent compound annual increase in benefits will usually raise premiums by about 50 percent.

Waiver-of-Premium. Most long-term care policies have a provision that waives premiums if the insured has been receiving benefits under the policy for a specified period of time, often 60 or 90 days. The inclusion of this benefit usually increases premiums by about 5 percent.

Spousal Coverage. Most insurance companies offer a discount of 10 percent to 15 percent if both spouses purchase long-term care policies from the company.

Nonsmoker Discount. A few insurers offer a discount, such as 10 percent, if the insured is a nonsmoker.

GROUP COVERAGE

Success in the individual marketplace led to interest in group long-term care insurance as an employee benefit. The first group long-term plan was written in 1987, and a small but growing number of employers, mostly large ones, now make coverage available. The number of insurance companies writing coverage has also grown, but it still remains relatively small and is primarily limited to the largest group insurance carriers.

At best the growth of group long-term care insurance can be described as slow and cautious for several reasons. First, the individual long-term care insurance market is still in an early evolving state. The situation is not unlike the early days of disability income insurance. Second, the tax status of group long-term coverage is uncertain. It appears that employer-provided benefits, unlike medical expense benefits, may result in taxation to employees, although some tax experts argue that benefits should be tax-free under existing Internal Revenue Code provisions. To the extent that employers want to spend additional benefit dollars, they want to spend them on benefits for which employees receive definite and unquestionably favorable tax benefits. As a result almost all group long-term care plans are financed solely by employee contributions. Third, there is uncertainty about whether long-term care can be included in a cafeteria plan on a tax-favored basis. Finally, participation in group plans has been modest among older employees, often because they find it too expensive. A surprise with many of the early plans, however, has been the higher-than-expected participation by employees in the 40-to-50 age bracket.

For the most part, group long-term care policies are comparable to the better policies being sold in the individual marketplace. However, there are a few differences, mostly because of the characteristics of group coverage:

- Eligibility for coverage generally requires that an employee be full-time and actively at work. At a minimum, coverage can be purchased for an active employee and/or the spouse. Some policies also make coverage available to retirees and to other family members of eligible persons, such as minor children, parents, parents-in-law, and possibly adult children. There may be a maximum age for eligibility, but it is often age 80 or 85.
- The cost of group coverage is usually slightly less that the cost of individual coverage. To some extent this is a result of the administrative services, such as payroll deduction, being performed by the employer.
- An employee typically has less choice in benefit levels and the duration of benefits under a group policy. The amounts and duration of benefits are selected by the employer and normally apply to all employees. However, some policies do allow choice but to a lesser extent than is allowed under individual policies.
- If a participant leaves employment, the group coverage can usually be continued on a direct-payment basis, under either the group contract or an individual contract.

CHECKLIST FOR COMPARING LONG-TERM CARE POLICIES

With the numerous variations in long-term care policies, it is very difficult for consumers, life insurance agents, and financial planners to compare policies. In the final analysis, two policies may have the same cost even though one policy may clearly be superior in some areas while the other has some other provisions that are preferable. In such cases a final selection decision is difficult and highly subjective. To make an informed decision, many factors must be compared as objectively as possible.

To facilitate such comparisons several states have prepared consumer guides that are usually available for the asking. *The Consumer's Guide to Long-Term Care Insurance* prepared by the Health Insurance Association of America is also available. This guide contains the following checklist for policy comparisons:

Long-Term Care Policy Checklist

	Policy A	Policy B
1. What services are covered? Skilled care Intermediate care Custodial care Home health care Adult day care Other		
2. How much does the policy pay per day for: Skilled care? Intermediate care? Custodial care? Home health care? Adult day care?		

3. How long will benefits last?
 	
In a nursing home, for
    Skilled nursing care?
    Intermediate nursing care?
    Custodial care?
At home?		

Long-Term Care Policy Checklist (Continued)

	Policy A	Policy B
4. Does the policy have a maximum lifetime benefit? If so, what is it? For nursing home care? For home health care?		
5. Does the policy have a maximum length of coverage for each period of confinement? If so, what is it? For nursing home care? For home health care?		
6. How long must I wait before preexisting conditions are covered?		
7. How many days must I wait before benefits begin? For nursing home care? For home health care?		
8. Are Alzheimer's disease and other organic mental and nervous disorders covered?		

9. Does this policy require:
 	
Physician certification of need?
An assessment of activities of daily living?
A prior hospital stay for:
  Nursing home care?
  Home health care?
A prior nursing home stay for home health care coverage?
Other?		

10. Is the policy guaranteed renewable?		
11. What is the age range for enrollment?		

Long-Term Care Policy Checklist (Continued)

	Policy A	Policy B
12. Is there a waiver-of-premium provision? For nursing home care? For home health care?		
13. How long must I be confined before premiums are waived?		
14. Does the policy offer an inflation adjustment feature? If so: What is the rate of increase? How often is it applied? For how long? Is there an additional cost?		

15. What does the policy cost?
 	
Per year?   With inflation feature
              Without inflation feature
Per month? With inflation feature
              Without inflation feature		

16. Is there a 30-day free look?		

9

Family Uses of Life Insurance

Edward E. Graves

This chapter addresses the various family situations that give rise to a need for funds that life insurance can supply. Some of the situations apply to almost all families, while others may be relatively complicated and apply only to special circumstances. Nevertheless there are many planned and unplanned needs for funds that can be satisfied with life insurance policies. Policies with cash values can provide funds during the insured's lifetime and benefits after the insured's death. Death benefits can be paid within a few days of the claim filing and are therefore an excellent source of immediate cash to the surviving family members. Life insurance makes the funds available upon death to meet any of the beneficiary's subsequent needs unless the contract intentionally directs the funds to a restricted use or availability.

SOURCES OF IMMEDIATE FUNDS

The death of an insured family member usually terminates an income stream that the family has relied upon. The costs of daily living for survivors, final expenses for the deceased insured, and emergency repairs and replacement associated with events surrounding the family member's death create an immediate need for funds. Families having an adequate source of emergency funds in liquid holdings, such as money market funds, bank balances, cash management accounts, life insurance cash values, and so forth, may easily meet any need for immediate cash following the death. However, the need for additional funds becomes urgent if the family does not have an emergency fund or has depleted it immediately prior to the death.

One of the goals of proper planning is to make sure the emergency fund is adequate to meet the survivors' needs until life insurance proceeds and other potential sources of funds become available. Life insurance proceeds often provide a significant portion of the emergency fund itself. (This reliance on the immediate availability of death benefits should not be associated with policies that are still contestable—in force less than 2 years. There could be some delay in settling claims of contestable life insurance polices. After a policy becomes incontestable, however, it is reasonable to count on quick availability of death benefits.)

Cash to Meet Daily Living Needs

Surviving family members will be faced with financial demands of maintaining the household and meeting the needs of household members. There will be continuing costs for food, transportation, and utilities. Mortgage payments may have to be continued and, even if they are insured, will have to be paid temporarily. It will take a while for the survivors to ascertain whether or not there is current life insurance on the mortgage and to file a claim if coverage exists. In the absence of coverage, the surviving family members will have to continue making mortgage or rent payments.

The surviving family members often, at least temporarily, continue their established lifestyle and generate the same level of expense that they encountered before the death. This means a continuation of bills for cable TV services, magazine subscriptions, newspapers, club memberships, entertainment, and miscellaneous costs. If the surviving family members are aware of their financial situation and they have planned for the death contingency, they will know whether or not they can afford to maintain the same standard of living or if cost cutting will be necessary. Even if the household budget does have to be trimmed, it is unrealistic to expect the survivors to cut back on their expenses immediately after the death. Changes in a family's living standard are usually accomplished through a certain amount of trial-and-error adjusting over a period that often exceeds one year.

Private school tuition for the children is a good example of a cost that cannot necessarily be trimmed immediately. The children are often kept in the same school if at all possible to complete the year in progress. This is much easier if the tuition has been paid in advance, but in the case of ongoing monthly tuition bills, the family may be forced to curtail other expenses in order to finance the school costs. At the end of the school year family members will have to decide what level of school costs they can afford to over a longer period. This may mean a move to less expensive private schools or enrollment in public schools. In some cases, the transition may require many years as the students gradually move to less expensive forms of schooling each year.

Another aspect of the time required to change the family unit's standard of living is the difficulty of getting individuals to change their habits. Children who are used to unrestricted use of air conditioning, heating, and local transportation will have to break old habits and learn new ones in order to cut costs further if that becomes necessary. Some adults require even longer transition periods than children.

The emotional turmoil following the death of a close family member usually lasts about one year. As survivors cope with the emotions of anger, denial, depression, bargaining, and finally acceptance of the death, the grieving process often distracts them from concentrating on financial issues. They may forget to pay important bills, such as premiums on homeowner's and auto insurance, that could worsen their financial position. Creditors insisting that they be paid immediately can be an additional source of emotional stress at this time. Survivors who are able to convince these creditors that adequate life insurance will be available are usually not pressed for collection until proceeds have been received.

So far the focus has been on routine living expenses. Quite frequently a family death sets off a chain of events that generate additional costs, such as transportation for children, parents, and other family members to the funeral. These expenses can be significant if the family members live far away. Feeding and housing these temporary guests can also be expensive.

Cash to Pay Expenses Associated with Death

Burial or cremation expenses are by no means the only expenses associated with death. The final expenses depend very heavily on the individual circumstances of each death. Some people undergo a lengthy period of hospital treatment and incur large medical bills. Their deductible and copay portion of medical care costs and the full cost of any care or treatment not covered by insurance could accumulate to a big debt. Home care or convalescent care is rarely covered by private insurance and has limited coverage under medicare for those over 65. Prolonged medical care and rehabilitative treatment will often leave the family's finances devastated even before death occurs. Following death there are usually funeral expenses (and sometimes transportation expenses to get the body back to hometown funeral directors); cemetery or mausoleum charges are also usually incurred. The expenses for the final disposition of the body, although they can be rather modest, are subject to a wide variation in services provided and generally end up being a significant expense.

Many of the final expenses associated with a death are often incurred after the funeral. There are the costs of settling financial and property matters in closing the deceased's estate. Included are court fees related to the appointment of an executor or administrator to manage and settle the estate. There may be fees charged by the executor or administrator and attorneys' fees in addition to the court costs for probate if there is a will.

Managing the estate prior to final property disposition may be extremely complex. This may require the services of specialized investment managers and/or real estate managers to safeguard the property until it can be sold or distributed. The provisions of the will and the nature of the property involved may necessitate a long period of estate management before the estate can be closed. Some assets may be hard to sell in the economic conditions following death. The terms of the will may require the establishment of trusts and other legal work that is also very time consuming. Even the task of locating heirs or other beneficiaries of the estate may require a lengthy search to cut through the bureaucratic red tape to obtain death certificates for all potential recipients who predeceased the insured. The longer this process takes and the more complex it is, the more it will cost.

The administrator or executor has responsibility for settling all the outstanding debts and closing out all the financial affairs of the deceased. This includes filing tax returns and paying tax liabilities. This process is much more easily addressed when there is adequate cash available through life insurance policy proceeds. It is usually not advisable to have such proceeds payable directly to the estate. Rather, they should be paid to a trust or to an individual with an interest in the estate. Cash can then be made available to the estate by cash purchases of assets from the estate or loans to the estate.

The size of the estate and the nature of the assets it contains heavily influence the optimal planning strategies for minimizing taxes and accomplishing individual objectives. Paying policy proceeds directly to the estate is less of a problem for small estates with no federal estate or gift tax liability than it is for large estates. The most important point is that any planning must be done in the appropriate manner prior to death to achieve best results. For sizable estates where there have been transfers of life insurance policy ownership, it would be even better if the planning is done at least 3 years prior to the death. Policy ownership and beneficiary designations in effect, as well as trusts previously in effect at the time of death, will govern tax treatment. The estate may be subject to much higher taxes than would have been payable if there had been appropriate preparation before death. Even if an administrator or executor knows how to minimize taxes, his or her hands will be tied unless assets have been properly positioned and the necessary documentation, trusts, and other instruments are in place before the insured's death.

Funds for Emergencies, Repairs, or Replacements

Although accidents and natural disasters are a relatively minor cause of death (5 percent of United States deaths), people who die from accidents may leave survivors with serious property damage that needs to be corrected immediately. Surviving family members may have to deal with salvaging, repairing, or replacing such damaged property. Just about any personal or real property can be damaged or destroyed by the same events that cause death—autos involved in traffic accidents, homes and their contents destroyed by a wind storm or other natural disaster, utility lines damaged by an earthquake or lightning strike, water wells polluted by flooding, and any number of other potential losses.

The important point is that surviving family members may be faced with an immediate need for cash in order to cope with the property damage coincident with the death. For example, they may have to purchase a replacement auto or rent alternative temporary housing. Even if the property loss is insured, the family may have to spend a significant amount of cash before a property insurance settlement is available. A homeowners policy, for example, requires that damaged structures be temporarily repaired or protected in order to prevent additional damage from water, wind, theft, and many other sources. Failure to take such measures could drastically reduce the amount of the eventual property insurance claim settlement.

Some property damage is not insurable at all, such as flood damage to a residence. The family auto may not be covered for the physical damage to the vehicle caused by the fatal collision. Death benefits from the life insurance policy, however, are usually available very quickly. If the death and the property destruction occur at the same time and the claims are filed for each on the same day, the claim for the death benefit will probably be settled much sooner than the claim for the property damage. Consequently it is more likely that the life insurance proceeds will provide an immediate source of emergency funds following a death associated with property damage than will the property insurance. Moreover, the cash value of a life insurance policy can provide emergency funds for property loss in cases where there is no death in conjunction with the damage. For example, a policy loan may be the quickest way to obtain the cash needed to buy plywood and tarps to seal up a damaged house after a storm or fire.

The urgency of caring for surviving family members may necessitate extra expense while damaged property is being repaired. For example, in a rural area the family might have to rent or buy a mobile home that they can move to the site so that they can care for livestock. The duration of such arrangements will depend on how long it takes to repair the damaged property. After a severe storm, materials and craftsmen may be in short supply and thus delay any attempt to rebuild. Such delays can cause drastic increases in the amount of funds necessary to recover from the property damage. Ideally families will have an emergency fund that is adequate to cover the worst possible situation. The sad reality is that too few families have adequate emergency funds, if any, available.

INCOME TO FAMILY SURVIVORS

Dependents

The financial needs of family survivors do not terminate at the closing of the deceased's estate. Minor children and other dependents may need support for a lifetime or at least for many years until they become self-supporting. Life insurance and other accumulated assets can provide that necessary financial support. With proper planning, a surviving spouse should be supported during this dependency period as well, rather than being forced to enter the labor market. In some cases whether or not the spouse works is not a discretionary planning option because the spouse may be disabled or may otherwise be unable to enter the work force. In fact, there is a possibility (although it is relatively infrequent) that the surviving spouse could have become disabled at the time the insured spouse died.

When planning the income needs of family survivors it is important to include all persons who depend on the income of the person to be insured. Such planning is important for each member providing income to the family unit. This often includes both husband and wife, and it could include children living at home who contribute income to support the family.

Children

In today's world of frequent marriages and divorces it is common to have more than one group of minor children to be supported. The husband and wife may have children from previous marriages in addition to the children of the current marriage. This situation could involve the finances of three or more separate households, or all the children could live together with the husband and wife. The other sources of support available to children of previous marriages obviously affect the children's financial needs. The income needs of the youngest children — usually the children of the current marriage and those with the longest period of dependency — should usually be given top priority.

Other children who may need lifelong financial support are children with physical disabilities or mental impairments that will prevent them from ever becoming self-supporting. Their dependency can continue many years beyond the death of both parents. Planning for the financial support of these children can be very complex. Severely handicapped children may require institutional care, which can be extremely expensive in private facilities and is available through public institutions only if the family withdraws financial support so the child can qualify for welfare programs. Any asset or trust established for these children's support must be very carefully structured. The rendering of public institutional support often gives the government the right to take possession of assets that are for the benefit of the child receiving the institutional care. In some cases the government has even been able to invade trusts.

Parents caring for permanently dependent children have to consider the long-term need for finances to support themselves and the impaired child. Some degenerative diseases shorten life expectancy predictably, and parents can plan for their financial dependents with the knowledge that their impaired child is less likely to survive them. But other permanently dependent children have normal or unknown life expectancies. Planning for such a child's support may have to extend beyond the parents' lives.

Parents and Other Dependents

Another group of family dependents who may have a relatively short and predictable period of dependency are the husband's and wife's parents. The financial demands of providing parental support can be minimal—providing room and board in the home for example. At the other end of the spectrum, support of a parent in an institution can be very expensive. Care for an elderly parent in an upscale institution often costs more than two times the median family income.

The voluntary assumption of financial support for another individual often implies a willingness to provide that support as long as it is needed. That need may extend beyond the death of the supporter. Careful planning and adequate amounts of life insurance can assure extended parental support even if the supporting child predeceases that parent. Otherwise the supporting child's death may force the parent to drastically change living arrangements and lower his or her standard of life.

Financial dependence is not restricted to children, spouses, and parents. In some cases distant relatives and current or ex-in-laws may have to be supported for one reason or another. For example, some families assume the responsibility for refugees from war-torn or storm-ravaged areas. Some take in foster children and develop emotional bonds that are as strong as those between natural parents and children. Many of these foster parents extend financial support above and beyond that required by the foster parent program.

Another potential group of financial dependents is illegitimate children. Sometimes the parents assume financial responsibility voluntarily; in other cases there are court-imposed obligations to provide support. These types of dependencies are much less frequent than court-ordered support of legitimate children stemming from divorce suits, but in either case the legal requirements for parental support of minor children are geared to mere sustenance. Most parents strive to provide much more to dependent minor children than they are obligated to give under the law. With careful planning and financing, this parental largesse can be continued after the parent's death.

Nondependents

Many people make a regular discretionary payment to their adult children to enhance their standard of living although there is clearly no parental obligation to make these gifts, and the children are not dependent on the payments for necessities. Nevertheless, many parents in these circumstances have a strong desire to continue such enhancement payments at least until the grandchildren become self-supporting, even if the period of payments extends beyond the grandparent's life.

Payments to enhance someone's lifestyle, however, are not necessarily restricted to children or other family members. Payments are sometimes extended to lifelong domestic helpers and care givers as an informal pension, perhaps for the recipient's remaining lifetime. Life insurance can fund these payments if the benefactor dies first.

Level of Support

Any sort of plan to provide ongoing income payments to dependents or others after death requires the provider to make decisions about the amount of the payments and their duration. A starting point is to decide whether the income payments constitute partial support, full support, or full support plus an enhancement element. Another factor to consider is whether the payments are intended to be level or to change over time. In some cases there may be an intent to phase out these income payments by decreasing them over a given interval in the expectation that the recipient will achieve financial independence. Conversely, when the intent is to provide full support, income payments may have to be increased to compensate for the effects of inflation.

The duration of support payments can vary widely, depending on the provider's objectives. Payments may go to a very specific and predictable date, such as age 21 of the grandchild, age 35 of a child, age 90 of a spouse or other dependent, or to a specified calendar year. Alternatively, payments may be designed to continue for an unknown length of time, such as the remaining lifetime of the recipient, until the recipient remarries, or until the birth of a child. Income payments can even be designed to be perpetual so that the capital sum supporting the income payments is not reduced or depleted. By using a perpetual-funding approach for lifetime incomes, the capital sum is a transferrable asset after the income objectives are satisfied. A common application is the qualified terminal interests property trust (QTIP) used for estate planning purposes. In such a trust a lifetime income is paid to the surviving spouse, and the trust corpus is then distributed to children (or others) after the spouse dies.

FUNDS TO REPAY DEBT

Many personal debt agreements have a clause specifying that the full remaining balance will become due and payable upon the death of the debtor. This separate clause may be present whether or not there is any credit life insurance covering the loan agreement. Although lending institutions regularly offer credit life insurance at the time the loan is initially created, such coverage is not mandatory and is often refused by the borrower. When credit life insurance is in force, the remaining loan balance will be repaid to the lender by the credit life insurance company as long as a death claim is filed so that the insurer can extinguish the debt. However, there is always the possibility that credit life insurance benefits will not be collected if the survivors or the executor or administrator is not aware of the insurance. Credit insurance information, therefore, should always be noted in files pertaining to the insured's debt.

Credit life insurance is not the only way of repaying debts that become due and payable at death. All types of life insurance policies provide death benefits that are suitable for repayment of debts. A single large policy can provide enough funds to extinguish many or all outstanding debts. Moreover, the standard types of individual life insurance policies may be lower in costs than credit life policies.

There are some debts that do not become due and payable at the death of the borrower. This is more likely to be the case when both husband and wife are liable for the debt. Adequate amounts of individual life insurance will give the survivor the option of either paying off the debt or continuing to repay it according to schedule. That option is not available under credit life insurance because benefits automatically extinguish the debt once a claim has been filed.

FUNDS TO PAY DEATH TAXES

Individuals who acquire a sizable net worth during their lifetime may be subjected to taxes on that net worth at their death. There is a federal estate tax applicable to estates in excess of $600,000. The tax is progressive in nature with a lower rate (such as 38 percent) applicable to smaller estates, increasing to 55 percent for large estates. Federal taxes must usually be paid within 9 months of the owner's death. This presents a real problem for individuals or families whose most important and largest assets are illiquid forms of investment, such as family-owned businesses and investment real estate. These assets cannot be quickly converted to cash without a significant decrease in value. In most cases the family would prefer to retain the asset and its future income-generating potential. Life insurance proceeds can provide the necessary cash to pay the tax liability and to preserve the assets being taxed for the benefit of family survivors.

Federal gift taxes can also be a sizable tax liability at death. The rates are the same as those for federal estate taxes. They apply to all nonexempt gifts on a cumulative basis. In other words, the aggregate amount of gifts made since 1932 is taken into consideration in determining the applicable gift tax rate for the gifts currently being taxed. For donors in the highest tax brackets the gift tax can equal 55 percent of the value of the gift itself.

The gift tax triggered by the donor's often involves gifts that were completed by reason of the death. Examples include jointly owned property after one of the joint owners dies and life insurance proceeds under some policy ownership and beneficiary designation situations. Settlement of the estate may also result in gift taxes due on gifts made shortly before death.

Some states impose estate taxes in addition to the federal estate taxes. These taxes, like the federal taxes, are due within a relatively short period of time and must be paid with liquid funds. Careful planning is required to provide for these state and federal taxes, especially if life insurance is to be the funding mechanism. The policies themselves may in fact be subject to the tax and increase the tax liability being funded by the policy. Good tax counseling can save unnecessary taxes and provide the optimal tax-saving strategy for the family whose objectives and considerations preclude the usual steps to minimize taxes.

FUNDS FOR DEPENDENTS' EDUCATION

Minor children need uninterrupted support for their education—from their first day in the classroom to the realization of their educational objective. The funding requirements for educating children vary widely from one family to another. A public school education that terminates at high school has relatively modest costs compared to the costs of a private school education including preschool, prep school, private university, and professional school. The disparity in costs is a function of both each school's tuition and the duration of the schooling itself. The factors influencing parents' educational goals and decisions often involve a complex mixture of family history, family philosophy toward education, family income, and the abilities and personality of the child. Children are often encouraged to attain at least the same level of education as their parents. But planning on an ivy league education, for example, will be for naught if the child does not have adequate financial support to enable him or her to attend a school of that caliber.

For very young children the planning horizon for education may exceed 20 years. Although primary school costs in the next few years may remain relatively similar to those today, adjustments for inflation must be made for educational costs to be incurred more than a decade into the future. Choosing the appropriate inflation factor involves some guessing, but it is safe to assume that the inflation rate will be greater than zero. Some authorities on the subject recommend a planning assumption of 7 percent to 8 percent annual inflation in taxation costs.

Permanently disabled children have special educational needs. Sometimes these children require lifelong training and education. Each family situation is likely to have its own unique set of needs and challenges, and each involves long-term planning.

Educational needs of the family are not restricted to the children. A surviving spouse may need further education to increase future income potential to help support the family. The spouse may need a modest refresher course or training to return to a prior occupation. On the other hand, the spouse's need may be extensive, such as preparing to enter the job market for the first time or trying to upgrade to a higher-paying career. There is even the possibility that a surviving spouse may need training for a less demanding career if he or she has become permanently disabled in some manner.

One very important consideration in providing education or training to the surviving spouse is whether the survivor will be able to earn any income while pursuing his or her education or training. Funding spousal education on a full-time basis usually requires prefunding family support while the spouse is a full-time student and prefunding the educational or training costs themselves.

In some cases the surviving spouse may be able to pursue the education on a part-time basis while he or she is employed in the workforce. This is a heavy emotional burden and a physically challenging avenue for a surviving spouse who becomes a single parent. Pursuing education on a part-time basis may greatly lengthen the period of time needed to complete the educational program. This will delay any significant increases in earned income for the surviving spouse and family members. If the potential increase in income because of further education is large enough, it may actually be less costly to prefund a full-time educational program. Obviously each situation must be evaluated on an individual basis.

FUNDING TRUSTS AT DEATH

Trusts are contractual arrangements for the ownership and management of assets by a trustee according to the trust agreement. The trustee manages trust assets on behalf of and for the benefit of the trust beneficiaries. There are many different motivations for the establishment of a trust. One is to get professional management from a corporate entity, such as a trust company or a bank trust department, so that the trustee will not predecease any of the trust beneficiaries. Tax considerations sometimes justify the creation of a trust.

Life insurance is often an integral part of the trust funding. The trust itself often owns life insurance on the grantor, who names the trust as beneficiary of that insurance. Trusts can also be beneficiaries of insurance policies not owned by the trust. Those insurance proceeds provide the funds necessary for the trust to carry out its objectives. Some trusts are set up specifically for the purpose of funding life insurance premiums and receiving proceeds. If estate tax minimization is the objective of the trust, the trust is subject to more stringent requirements that can change many times during the existence of the trust.

Trusts have always been an important means of extending family financial management by the parents beyond the parents' lifetime. In these arrangements the trust is often used to distribute funds periodically rather than in a lump sum. The objective is usually to protect a child from a propensity to spend funds frivolously. By spreading out the distribution, the child is unable to get access to and squander the entire sum immediately after the parents' death. Final distribution from such trusts is often predicated on the beneficiary's attainment of a specified age and is usually the parents' best guess as to when the child will be mature enough to handle the funds responsibly.

Trusts can also be set up for the benefit of children with mental impairments or other problems that would preclude them from ever becoming capable of managing their own finances. The nature of the trust depends very heavily on the type of care being provided to such children, especially on whether the care is private or public.

Trusts can also be an important tool for sequestering assets from a spouse to prevent the assets from being directed to a stepchild or to an unforeseen family member if the surviving spouse were to remarry after the insured's death.

Life insurance and trusts are often combined in creative ways to fund charitable gifts. Sometimes the entire arrangement is for the exclusive benefit of the charity. In other arrangements the trust is set up for a combination of family objectives and gifts to charitable institutions. Such arrangements usually involve a stream of income payments and subsequent distribution of the trust corpus. The charity or the family member can be the recipient of either the income payments, the corpus, or both.

CHARITABLE DONATIONS

Life insurance policies are often used to increase the value of gifts to charities. This can be accomplished either by giving the policy itself to the charitable organization or by naming the charity as the beneficiary on the existing life insurance policies. Where federal estate tax considerations are important, a new life insurance policy may be purchased by the charity itself at the request of the donor, who would give the necessary permission and information to complete the policy application and would provide the funds for premium payments.

Most states have enacted specific statutes expressly stating that charitable organizations have an insurable interest in the life of the donor. The statutes were prompted by an IRS decision claiming that a charity lacked an insurable interest in the donor. In part that decision was based on a New York statute that has since been modified to recognize such insurable interest.

Life insurance can also be used for charitable giving even if the charity is not a beneficiary of the insurance policy. The donor can use adequate amounts of life insurance to fund all of the needs of surviving family members and thereby free up personal property and other assets for lifetime gifts to the charities.

Gift tax and estate tax considerations are often strong motives for making charitable gifts. Because tax laws can — and probably will — change, tax planning should be carefully coordinated by a knowledgeable tax adviser.

FUNDING FOR GIFTS TO INDIVIDUALS

The use of life insurance is not limited only to benefitting family members and related trusts and charities. Life insurance can easily be used to benefit anyone the donor specifies. The motivation could be friendship, long-term loyalty, respect for another's accomplishments, support of a common endeavor, or any other commitment about which the individual feels strongly. The intended recipient can be made beneficiary of a life insurance policy or a beneficiary of a trust funded by life insurance proceeds.

One of the strong factors favoring life insurance policies is that the proceeds do not generally go through probate and are not a matter of public record. The proceeds are payable quickly and directly to the beneficiary. Complications of settling or managing the estate have no bearing on nor do they delay the payment of proceeds under a life insurance policy unless the proceeds are payable directly to the insured's estate. In estates large enough to have a federal estate tax liability, therefore, it is generally not a good idea to have life insurance proceeds payable to the insured's estate.

SUPPLEMENTING RETIREMENT INCOME

Life insurance policies can be an important source of supplemental retirement income funds. The policy proceeds can obviously be an important source of funds for the surviving spouse. These funds can supplement any other source of retirement income available from corporate pensions, IRAs, other qualified plans, investments, and social security.

Life insurance can even provide supplemental retirement funds to the insured individual. This can be accomplished by utilizing the cash value of the life insurance prior to the insured's death. Some policies, such as universal life policies, allow partial withdrawals of cash value amounts without terminating the policy itself. Under any life insurance policy having a cash value, the policyowner can always gain access to the funds by either taking out a policy loan or surrendering the policy for the entire cash surrender value. (Surrendering the policy, of course, terminates any death benefit protection.)

FINDING HOME HEALTH CARE OR NURSING HOME CARE

The prematurity values of life insurance policies can be used for home health care or nursing home care if that is deemed desirable or necessary. Access to the cash value is available through policy loans, partial withdrawals of the cash value, or outright surrender of the policy.

Long-term-care riders are available with some life insurance policies to provide for home health care or nursing home care needs. In some cases the rider is available without any additional charge; in other cases there is a nominal charge. In essence these riders make a portion of the death benefit, usually one or 2 percent of the face value of the policy, available each month that the insured qualifies for the benefit. The subsequent death benefit payable is reduced dollar-for-dollar for each accelerated benefit payment made under these riders. Their pre-death-benefit payments are usually subject to an aggregate limitation of 50 percent of the face value of the policy, although a few insurance companies have increased the aggregate limitation to 70 or 80 percent of the policy face value.

Long-term-care riders allow life insurance policies to do double duty. They make benefits available for both the insured's lifetime objectives and the survivors' objectives. This can create a complication, however, in that lifetime uses directly reduce the residual benefit payable upon death. It is important to recognize and evaluate the potential conflicts when planning for these needs.

TRANSFERRING ASSETS TO YOUNGER GENERATION

Life insurance is often used as a way of leveraging assets when transferring property to younger generations. Children, grandchildren, and great-grandchildren can all be recipients of life insurance proceeds. They can also be recipients of life insurance policies. Members of the younger generation may own life insurance policies and also be beneficiaries of the same policies. Parents or grandparents often pay the premiums on policies owned by their children or grandchildren with gifts that are small enough to qualify for the annual gift tax exclusion.

Intergenerational transfers, however, may be subject to generation-skipping taxes as well as to gift and estate taxes. Such asset transfers therefore often involve very sophisticated arrangements to deal with the many complex constraints of both federal and state laws. Improper planning can increase the potential tax liabilities significantly. In many cases the costs of poor planning could be many times the cost of expert tax advice.

DISCREETLY PROVIDING FOR CONFIDENTIAL NEEDS

Because life insurance is a contract and can be situated so that it is not property of the estate, it can escape public disclosure. This makes it a very desirable vehicle for accomplishing discreet postdeath funding, such as private business agreements in which life insurance proceeds are used to retire an outstanding personal debt. Life insurance and disability insurance are sometimes utilized to guarantee future payments under secret liability settlements. The insurance will continue the periodic payments if the liable person dies or is disabled.

Through proper arrangements life insurance proceeds can even be arranged to provide anonymous gifts to the intended recipients. This requires a third party who knows of the arrangement and can file the claim for death benefits.

Life insurance has long been used as a funding device for partners in nontraditional living arrangements or those in amorous involvements outside of wedlock. Insurance companies are not eager to issue policies for some of these purposes and may decline the application if the purpose is openly set forth. However, the insurance company is unable to stop a policyowner from changing beneficiary designations on an existing policy. This contractual flexibility allows policyowners to accomplish their objectives indirectly if they cannot do so directly at the time they apply for the policy.

10

Needs Analysis, Surrender Options, and Policy Illustrations

Dan M. McGill
Revised by Edward E. Graves

NEEDS ANALYSIS

There are many different approaches to determining the amount of life insurance appropriate for any given client. Just trying to sort through them can itself be very time consuming and confusing. Financial journalists tend to prefer simplistic rules of thumb, such as some multiple of annual income, because it's short and easy to explain. However, there is a trap in this seductive simplicity.

An attempt to determine life insurance needs that does not rely upon a fair amount of client information is of questionable worth. The rule-of-thumb approach ignores information about how much the client has already accumulated and any existing external sources of finance such as trusts and inheritances. The simplistic rule-of-thumb approach can err in either direction; that is, it can either overinsure or underinsure the client.

Simplistic rules of thumb may perform a positive function if they are the only approach or logic that motivates the client to purchase needed insurance. Sometimes clients do resist providing the information necessary for an appropriate and thorough analysis of their needs.

In this chapter it is assumed that clients are serious about their financial future and that the financial services professional has established enough trust for the information-gathering and analysis process to proceed. Problem solving in this arena requires complete and accurate information about current income, potential future income, accumulated assets, investments, pensions, and other qualified plan holdings. In addition, it is important to develop a profile of the client's priorities and goals or objectives. A fair amount of time and energy is often spent in gathering the necessary information before any steps can even be taken toward analysis and recommendation.

The conceptual approach to determining needs is very easily explained. The client's desires must be translated into estimated costs, and then those costs must be evaluated to determine how much of the funding is already in place. Any deficit between the intended goals and objectives and current financial sources is usually a candidate for life insurance. Life insurance provides a means of completing the financing of family goals and objectives that individuals work toward during their lifetime. In essence, life insurance can be a personally arranged and collectively financed means of replacing lost income, and in some ways it is analogous to trusts and inheritances in wealthy families.

Deriving Components of Need

Lump-Sum Needs at Death

Postdeath financial needs are conveniently separated into two main categories: (1) lump-sum needs at death and (2) ongoing income. The cash needs at death include such items as final costs not covered by insurance; repayment of outstanding debt that becomes due and payable upon death; estate taxes, if applicable; the expenses of the funeral, burial, and cremation, if applicable; the costs of probate court to prove the validity of the will; attorneys' fees; and operational expenses to cover the ongoing costs of the survivors' household. The surviving family members need funds to pay for the mortgage or rent, utility bills, property insurance premiums, property taxes, food, clothing, transportation costs, and costs of child care and/or education. The amounts associated with each of these categories vary widely from one individual to another and from one family to another. Each case must be evaluated individually. Reliance on general guidelines rather than on individual evaluation increases the likelihood that important and potentially costly needs may be overlooked or ignored.

The lump-sum needs at death should also include an emergency fund. This is a form of safety net or shock absorber to help the survivors cope with unexpected emergencies that could otherwise devastate an already strained cash-flow budget. This kind of planning can prevent the necessity of trading off essential expenditures against funding for emergencies.

There is no general consensus on the appropriate amount for an emergency fund. Estimating the needs for this purpose should be based on a realistic assessment of the survivors' finances. The need for an emergency fund may be even greater in families where the finances are already stretched even before death than in families where disposable income is high enough to spend a significant proportion on relatively frivolous discretionary items. A household where nearly all the major appliances and automobiles are operating on borrowed time can look forward to more failures and earlier expenditures on these items than households where these items are relatively new and well maintained.

Another important factor in setting the level of the emergency fund is whether the family has other liquid or near-liquid assets that could easily be used to cover such emergencies. Money market accounts and listed security holdings may be acceptable sources of funds to cover all or part of any potential emergency, thus reducing or eliminating the amount of funds from life insurance death proceeds needed to cover emergencies.

Many financial planners suggest that prefunding of children's educational needs be classified under the lump-sum category rather than being provided for out of income. Obviously the amount needed to prefund children's education is a function of the current ages of those children, the costs associated with the intended educational institutions, the number of years for which educational support is intended to be provided, and the proportion of financing for education that the parents intend to prefund. For some families the intent will be to provide nothing more than a public school education through high school, while at the other end of the spectrum a family may provide full funding for private preparatory schools and an Ivy League education up to the completion of a professional degree such as a JD or MD or even a PhD program. Each family will have its own target somewhere along that continuum of possibilities.

Ongoing Income Needs

The ongoing income needs of the surviving dependent family members already exist at the instant of death. These needs for income will continue until those dependents can become self-supporting. In some families that can be a relatively short time and in others it may take decades. In some families the dependent spouse will never become self-sufficient, and there is no intent that he or she attempt to do so. At the other end of the spectrum is the family where all family members are expected to become self-sufficient shortly after the head of the household dies. In some cases such an extreme expectation may be unrealistic and even constitute neglect on the part of the deceased. In most families there is both a desire and the financial ability to prefund the survivors' income needs at least until the youngest child becomes self-sufficient, often when he or she completes formal education. This type of evaluation becomes more difficult when there are children with special needs that will keep them from ever becoming self-sufficient. Such special children may actually have ongoing income needs many years beyond the death of the surviving parent.

It is common to classify the survivors' ongoing income needs in four categories:

- income for readjustment period immediately after death
- adjusted income starting after the initial transition period and continuing until the youngest child becomes self-sufficient
- income, if any, for the surviving spouse after the children have become self-sufficient (the blackout period)
- the surviving spouse's income after eligibility for social security benefits and private pension benefits

Since the purpose of life insurance is to fund the unfunded portion of these objectives, it is important to consider any and all existing funds that can provide part or all of these needs. For simplicity and efficiency, most planners suggest using some target percentage of the insured's current income as the target income level rather than calculating a composite of each individual anticipated need component. It is often suggested that the survivors will need about 70 percent of the predeath income to carry on after death.

Once the desired income goal has been set, the deficits in each future period can be estimated by deducting the existing sources at their anticipated benefit or income levels.

The most commonly available source of income is social security benefits. The surviving parent and each child will be eligible for benefits as long as the children are under 16 and living with the surviving spouse. The children's benefits will actually continue until they are 18, but the surviving spouse's benefit will stop when the youngest child reaches 16. Other potential sources of income include employer-provided plan benefits such as deferred compensation, death-benefit-only plans, and any qualified plan participation funds that are not forfeited or terminated upon the employee's death.

Projecting future cash flow and deducting the existing sources of income are the first steps in determining the income deficit. The next step is to find the present value of all those future income needs. This calculation can be done in many different ways and with many different levels of specificity. Often it is broken up into component segments so that the income deficit will be the same throughout that particular component period. If the calculation is done that way, the final calculation of the total income need is the sum of the present values of each of the separate, individually calculated segments.

Most financial advisers suggest that these components be kept at a minimum and that simplifying assumptions be made whenever possible or appropriate in order to keep this estimation process from becoming too cumbersome and time consuming. It is important to remember that this is still an estimation process intended to simulate unknown future occurrences. The estimates are made without the benefit of knowing what future inflation rates and investment returns will be. Financial advisers and insurance agents are no more omniscient than economists when it comes to estimating future investment income and inflation rates.

In fact, some advisers suggest that all values should be done in current dollar amounts and no discounting applied to future income periods. They maintain that such discounting merely complicates an imprecise estimation process and that ignoring inflation as well will probably make the estimates somewhere near what will ultimately happen. There is much merit in these suggestions. An inordinate amount of time and resources can be spent trying to estimate to the penny future income flows. Computers make it possible to estimate every last detail in fractions of a cent. However, just because a computer spits out numbers with four-decimal-place accuracy or more does not mean that those numbers will really be anywhere near the numbers that will actually unfold in the future.

After future income needs have been estimated and combined into a total, there is another important step that must be completed to translate this need into a stated funding objective. Future income payments can be comprised solely of investment earnings on a capital sum, or they can be a combination of investment earnings and liquidation of part of the capital sum. The advantage of using investment earnings only to supply such income streams is that the capital sum is not being depleted, and consequently a termination date on the income stream is not necessary. This means that individuals relying upon the income will not outlive their income stream. The disadvantage of this strategy is that it takes more money in the capital fund to fully fund this approach than it takes to fund a program that relies on liquidation of part of the principal.

A serious shortcoming of the liquidating approach is that the fund will eventually be totally dissipated. The strategy requires estimating the insured's likely maximum age at death and planning liquidation for that date or later. Any liquidation planning predicated on the beneficiary's death at an early age runs a high risk of liquidating the proceeds while the beneficiary is still dependent on them. As one famous agent likes to put it, they run out of money before they run out of time. Financial advisers are well advised to plan for a liquidation in such a way that the beneficiary is likely to run out of time before he or she runs out of money.

There are essentially two ways of eliminating this potential problem associated with liquidating the principal sum over the beneficiary's lifetime. One approach is to use policy proceeds at death to provide a life income through policy settlement options or separate annuity contracts. These arrangements guarantee lifelong income payments regardless of how long the recipient lives. The other approach (nonliquidating) is the previously mentioned capitalization at a high enough level that all the income benefits can be provided from the investment income only.

Within the life insurance industry the liquidating approach is often referred to as the financial needs analysis, and a nonliquidating approach is often referred to as the capital needs analysis.

Another advantage of the nonliquidating approach is the simplicity of calculating the needed capital fund. The desired income level is easily capitalized by dividing that income amount by the applicable interest rate representing the aftertax investment return anticipated on the capital sum. For example, if $100,000 per year is desired, and the capital sum generating those income payments can realistically expect to generate a 5 percent return after taxes, a $2 million fund is sufficient. This is determined by taking the desired income amount and dividing into that the realistic estimate of the aftertax investment return rate. In our example it was .05, or 5 percent. That division yields the $2 million capital fund amount needed. Obviously the lower the aftertax investment return rate, the higher the capital fund needed to throw off the same amount of income. Similarly higher marginal tax rates will lower the aftertax return rate and increase the size of the fund needed to generate the income.

To see how one successful, well-known agent and American College trustee approaches needs analysis, see the appendix, "How Much Life Insurance Is Enough?"

SURRENDER OPTIONS

The surrender values provided under the Standard Nonforfeiture Law can be taken by the policyowner in one of three forms:

- cash
- paid-up cash value life insurance
- extended or (paid-up) term insurance

These forms are properly referred to as *surrender benefits,* but since the policyowner has the option or privilege of choosing the form under which the surrender value is to be paid, the benefits are usually referred to as *surrender options.*

The Standard Nonforfeiture Law requires that a surrender benefit be granted whenever a value appears under the formula. This may be as early as the end of the first year under some policies and later than 3 years under other policies. Under most plans and at most ages of issue, a surrender value will appear in the second policy year. Formerly no cash or other surrender benefits were required in the case of term insurance policies of 20 years or less. Under the current law a level-premium term policy for more than 15 years[1]—or one that expires after age 65, regardless of its duration—must provide surrender benefits if the mandated formula indicates that one exists.

The nature and significance of the various standard forms of surrender benefits will be discussed in the following sections.

Cash

The simplest form in which the surrender value may be taken is cash. After the policy has been in force long enough to have no surrender charges, there is an exact equivalence between the surrender value of a policy and the cash that can be obtained upon its surrender, leading many persons to refer to the surrender value generically as the *cash* surrender value. The new law requires that the surrender value of a policy be made available in the form of cash, but it does not compel a company to grant cash values until the end of 3 years in the case of ordinary insurance. This limitation on cash values was provided in order to relieve the companies of the expense of drawing checks for the relatively small values that might have developed during the first and second policy years. It does not, however, relieve the company of the obligation to make available in some noncash form of benefit any surrender value that might accumulate during the first 2 years. Most companies waive this statutory provision and provide a cash value as soon as any value develops under the policy.

The law permits a company to postpone payment of the cash surrender value for a period of 6 months after demand thereof and surrender of the policy. This *delay clause* was given statutory sanction in order to protect companies against any losses that might otherwise arise from excessive demands for cash during an extreme financial emergency. The law has made the inclusion of a delay clause mandatory and has made the delay period of 6 months uniform. It is contemplated that the clause would be invoked only under the most unusual circumstances. Mutual Benefit Life Insurance Company was already experiencing a run on its assets from demand for policy surrenders and maximum policy loans *before* it sought both the protection of the delay clause and intervention by the state insurance commissioner. Even though the company was in poor financial shape, it was reluctant to impose the delay clause until loss of confidence was so widespread that it had no other choice.

As might be expected, provision is made for deduction of any policy indebtedness (policy loans plus accrued interest) from the cash value that would otherwise be available.

Impact of Electing Surrender Benefits

The impact of the election of each surrender benefit on the structure of the underlying insurance contract is illustrated in figures 10-1 through 10-4. In each case the underlying contract will be assumed to be a whole life policy, but the principle involved is applicable to any type of contract with some modification.

Figure 10-1 shows the change produced in cash value life insurance contracts by the exercise of the cash surrender option. The figure indicates that up to the point of surrender, the contract is a combination of protection and cash value. By surrendering the policy for cash, however, the policyowner takes the cash value element of the contract and, in so doing, terminates the protection element as well. Subject only to any reinstatement privilege, if any, that might exist, the company has no further obligations under the contract. Generally the reinstatement rights are available only to policies that have terminated for reasons other than a cash surrender.

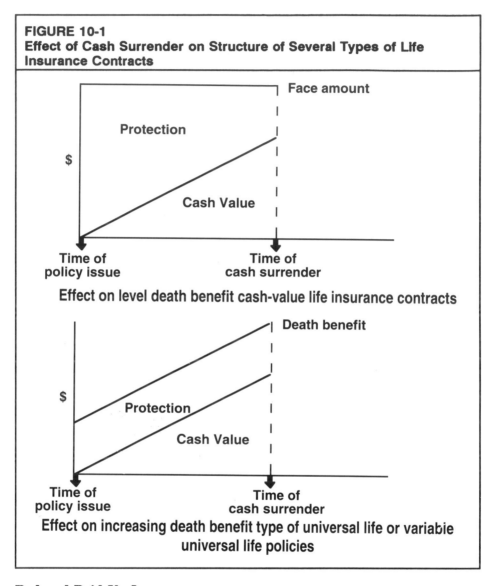

FIGURE 10-1
Effect of Cash Surrender on Structure of Several Types of Life Insurance Contracts

Effect on level death benefit cash-value life insurance contracts

Effect on increasing death benefit type of universal life or variable universal life policies

Reduced Paid-Up Insurance

This form of surrender benefit is referred to as *reduced paid-up insurance,* in recognition of the fact that under this option, the withdrawing policyowner receives a reduced amount of paid-up cash value insurance, payable upon the same conditions as the original policy. If the original policy was either an ordinary life or a limited-payment life policy, the insurance under this option will be paid-up whole life insurance. If the original policy was an endowment contract, this option will provide an endowment with the same maturity date but in a reduced amount. Some companies make this option available under a term policy, in which case an appropriately reduced amount of term insurance is paid up to the expiry date of the original term policy.

The amount of paid-up insurance provided under this option is the sum that can be purchased at the insured's attained age by the net surrender value (cash value, less any policy indebtedness, plus the cash value of any dividend additions or deposits) applied as a net single premium computed on the mortality and interest bases specified in the policy for the calculation of the surrender value. The amount of paid-up insurance available at various durations under an ordinary life and under a 20-payment life policy, issued at age 35, is shown in table 10-1.

TABLE 10-1
Example of Surrender Benefits at Selected Durations for Ordinary Life and 20-Payment Life (Issue Age 35, Male 1980 CSO Mortality, 4.5 Percent Interest)

	Ordinary Life				20-Payment Whole Life			
Policy Year	Cash Value	Reduced Paid-up Insurance	Extended Term Insurance		Cash Value	Reduced Paid-up Insurance	Extended Term Insurance	
			Yrs.	Days			Yrs.	Days
3	6	28	1	297	7	29	2	42
5	28	122	6	261	40	157	9	216
10	92	331	13	211	142	468	20	318
15	168	498	16	15	266	743	25	145
20	250	630	16	170	420	1,000	27	242
25	336	721	15	186	487	1,000	22	175
30	429	794	14	9	558	1,000	18	88
35	523	850	12	119	629	1,000	14	300

All values are per $1,000 of insurance.

Paid-up insurance is provided under this option at net premium rates, despite the fact that maintenance and surrender or settlement expenses will be incurred on the policies.[2] The law made no specific allowance for expenses on the theory that the margins in the mortality and interest assumptions underlying the net rates are sufficient to absorb any expenses that will be involved. In the case of participating insurance, however, any margins available for this purpose are reduced by the payment of dividends on the paid-up insurance.

It is interesting to note that there is a surrender privilege under reduced paid-up whole life and endowment policies. The law states that such policies can be surrendered for cash within 30 days after any policy anniversary, provided the original policy was in force long enough to grant a cash value. In other words, the cash surrender privilege of the paid-up policy cannot be used to subvert the provision in the law that cash values need not be granted until the end of 3 years.

The effect of the reduced paid-up insurance option on the structure of the whole life policy is illustrated in figure 10-2. It is readily apparent that the most important impact is on the protection element of the contract. In the example, the cash value before surrender had accumulated to a sum half the face of the policy, which at age 60, for instance, would purchase a paid-up whole life policy in an amount approximately 75 percent of the original face. The entire shrinkage comes out of the protection element, however, since the investment element continues to increase until it equals the reduced face at the end of the mortality table. The same phenomenon occurs with a surrender at any duration. As was pointed out above, this cash value element of a reduced paid-up policy can be converted into cash by surrendering the policy pursuant to its terms.

Universal life insurance and variable universal life policies provide a nonguaranteed form of reduced paid-up option. The policyowner can reduce the death benefit so that the existing cash value is sufficient to cover all future charges, helped by the future earnings credited to the cash value. The nonguaranteed element is the fact that the policyowner bears the investment risk, and if the earnings on the cash value drop below the level anticipated when the policy benefit was reduced, further adjustment(s) may be needed.

The policyowner has to explicitly request a death benefit reduction to create the equivalent of a reduced paid-up surrender option for a universal or variable universal life policy.

Extended Term Insurance

The extended term insurance option provides paid-up term insurance in an amount equal to the original face of the policy, increased by any dividend additions or deposits and decreased by any policy indebtedness. The length of the term is such that it can be purchased at the insured's attained age by the application of the net surrender value as a net single premium. This gives effect to the statutory requirement that the present value at the time of surrender of any paid-up surrender benefit must be at least the equivalent of the surrender value. The period for which term insurance is provided for various durations under an ordinary life policy, and under a 20-payment life policy, issued at age 35, is shown in table 10-1.

Universal and variable universal life insurance policies do not have a *guaranteed* extended term surrender option. However, they are automatically configured to work similarly to extended term insurance. These policies have no fixed or required premiums, and the viability of the contract depends on the account balance of the policy's cash value. The policy will remain in force as long as the cash value is sufficient to cover the next 60 days of charges for mortality (term charges) and administration and until these charges consume the cash value.

The law provides that if there is any indebtedness against the policy at the time of its surrender, *both* the amount of term insurance and the surrender value used as a net single premium shall be reduced by the amount of the loan. By the same token, if there are any dividend additions standing to the credit of the policy, the *amount* of the additions will be added to the face amount of the extended insurance, and the *cash value* of the additions will be added to the sum applied as a net single premium.[3]

This may be illustrated by a $1,000 policy that at the time of surrender has a surrender value of $500, dividend additions of $100 that have a cash value of $75, and a policy loan of $250. Under such circumstances the face of the extended policy is $850 ($1,000 + $100 − $250), and the net single premium is $325 ($500 + $75 − $250).

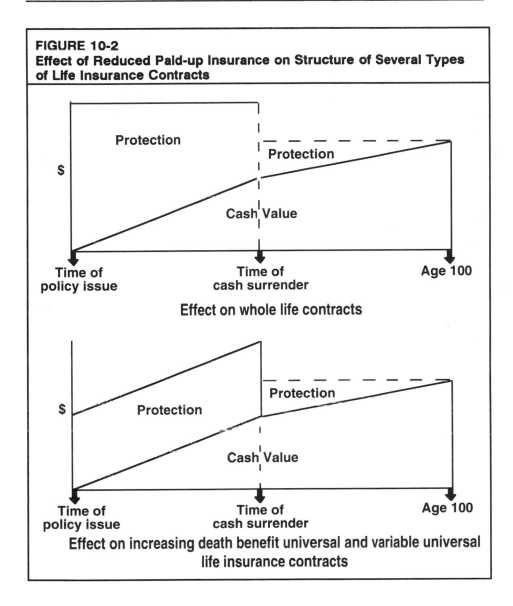

FIGURE 10-2
Effect of Reduced Paid-up Insurance on Structure of Several Types of Life Insurance Contracts

Effect on whole life contracts

Effect on increasing death benefit universal and variable universal life insurance contracts

It is readily apparent that the policy loan should be deducted from the surrender value to determine the net single premium, since it is only the *net* value that is available for the purchase of extended insurance, but many persons do not understand why it is also necessary to deduct the policy loan from the face of the policy. The requirement is founded on underwriting considerations. If the policy indebtedness is not deducted from the face of the extended policy, the companies will be exposed to a virulent form of antiselection.

Consider the case of a person suffering from an incurable illness who has a $200,000 life insurance policy with a $100,000 cash value. If, to meet the cost of medical treatment or for any other reason, he or she borrows the maximum amount against the cash value, say $95,000, and then dies shortly thereafter, the company will be obligated to pay only $105,000, since the policy loan is an encumbrance against both the cash value and the death proceeds. The total return will thus equal the face of the policy, or $200,000. If, on the other hand, he or she borrows $90,000, for example, surrenders the policy, and applies the remaining equity, $10,000, to the purchase at net rates of $200,000 of extended term insurance, death within the next few years will result in a total pay-ment — the face plus the loan — of $290,000. Under present practice as required by law, the ill policyowner can extend only $110,000, thus limiting the total obligation of the company to $200,000, as was the original intent.

The theory on which the deduction of policy loans is based is that the cancellation of an unliquidated policy loan constitutes a prepayment of a portion of the face amount. To ignore policy indebtedness in determining the face amount of extended insurance would be to make available, without medical or other evidence of insurability, additional term insurance equivalent to the policy indebtedness. This strategy would violate all the tenets of sound underwriting.

The effect of deducting the policy loan from *both* the surrender value and the amount of extended insurance is to produce a shorter period of term insurance than would be available if no loan existed. This is a natural consequence of the fact that the deduction is a much greater proportion of the cash value than it is of the face amount of the policy. Theoretically the amount of term insurance should not be the face amount less the loan, as required by law, but should be the face amount less the portion thereof having a cash value equal to the loan; in other words, a proportionate part of the *policy* would be *surrendered* to pay the loan, and only the remainder would be continued as term insurance. If this method were used, a lower amount of coverage would be extended and the *period* of term insurance would not be affected by policy indebtedness. The rule laid down by law in effect *increases* the total insurance extended and thus reduces the term, since the net cash value remains the same.

Thus if a policy of $1,000 has a cash value of $500 and policy indebtedness of $200, the net cash value of $300 (*one-half* of the death benefit it will support) will support a $600 benefit. Seen from the loan perspective, a $400 reduction in coverage will be required to offset $200 of loan forgiveness. The proper amount of extended insurance is $600, instead of $800, as presently provided. In other words, the *amount* of the term insurance is reduced by 20 percent, whereas the *cash value* available to purchase it is reduced by 40 percent. The *period* of insurance, therefore, must be less than it would be if no indebtedness existed.

From the standpoint of the companies, paid-up term insurance is a more attractive surrender benefit than paid-up whole life or endowment insurance. The companies consider the favorable features of extended term insurance to be (1) the relatively large amount of insurance involved, with the correspondingly low expense *rate;* (2) the definite date of expiry, which limits the maintenance expenses and minimizes the problem of tracing policyowners; (3) the uninter-rupted continuation of the original amount of coverage, as modified by dividend additions and policy loans, for those persons who contemplate eventual reinstatement; and (4) its adaptability to liberal reinstatement requirements, which stems from the fact that the amount at risk is normally decreased by reinstate-ment, in contrast to the increase in the amount at risk that occurs on the reinstatement of reduced paid-up insurance.

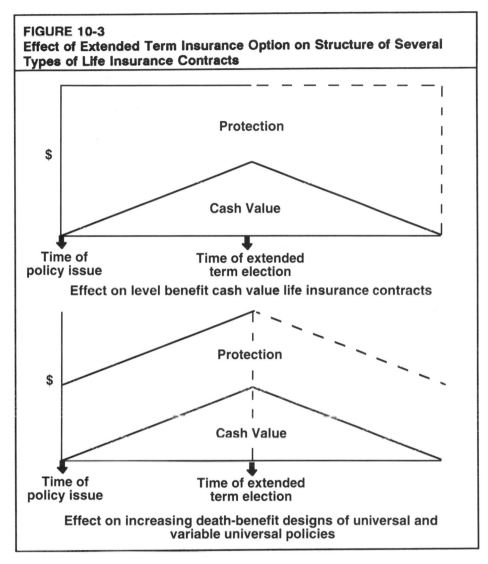

FIGURE 10-3
Effect of Extended Term Insurance Option on Structure of Several Types of Life Insurance Contracts

Effect on level benefit cash value life insurance contracts

Effect on increasing death-benefit designs of universal and variable universal policies

The only real disadvantage of extended term insurance from the insurer's standpoint is the adverse mortality selection encountered, and this can be hedged through the use of the higher mortality assumptions authorized by law or minimized through making the extended term option the *automatic* paid-up benefit. All things considered, the extended term option is so attractive that most companies designate it as the option to go into effect automatically if the insured does not elect another available option within 60 days after the due date of the premium in default.

The change produced in the structure of a whole life insurance policy by its surrender for extended term insurance is plotted in figure 10-3. This diagram reveals that, in direct contrast to the situation under reduced paid-up insurance, the protection element grows progressively larger, and the investment element progressively smaller, until the policy finally expires. The investment element is at a peak at the time of surrender but is gradually used up in the payment of term insurance premiums, being completely exhausted at the point of expiry. Because of the complementary nature of the protection and investment elements in any insurance contract, the protection element becomes constantly larger, eventually equaling the face of the extended insurance. This explains why the amount at risk is *reduced* through the reinstatement of a policy that has been running under the extended term option.

The investment element of a paid-up term insurance policy can be obtained by surrendering the insurance for cash, subject to the same conditions governing the surrender of reduced paid-up insurance. Extended term insurance is normally nonparticipating with respect to dividends.

AUTOMATIC PREMIUM LOANS

A policy provision found in some—but not all—policies that bears a close resemblance to the paid-up term insurance option but is technically not a surrender option (since the policy is not surrendered) is the automatic premium loan feature. It grew out of the conventional premium loan clause, which states that at the request of the policyowner any premium may be paid by means of a loan against the surrender value, provided that a surrender value is then available and large enough to cover the loan. Such a loan usually bears interest at the rate applicable to all policy loans.

The automatic premium loan clause provides that any defaulted premium will be automatically paid and charged against the cash value without request from the policyowner unless he or she elects to surrender the policy for cash or one of the paid-up insurance options.

The effect of the premium loan clause is to extend the original plan of insurance for the original face amount decreased by the amount of premiums loaned with interest. Such extension will continue as long as the cash value at each premium due date is sufficient to cover another premium. It should be noted that each premium loan increases the cash value, lengthening the period during which the process can be continued. At the same time, however, the indebtedness against the cash value is growing, not only by the granting of additional premium loans but also by the accrual of interest. Eventually a premium due date will be reached when the unencumbered cash value is no longer large enough to cover another full premium.

The principal advantage to the policyowner of an automatic premium loan provision is that in the event of inadvertent nonpayment of the premium or temporary inability to pay the premium, the policy is kept in full force. Several collateral advantages flow from this basic fact. First, premium payments can be resumed at any time (as long as the equity in the policy remains sufficient to pay premiums as they become due) without furnishing evidence of insurability. This is in contrast to the reinstatement of policies surrendered for paid-up insurance, in which case evidence of insurability is almost invariably required. Second, special benefits—such as waiver of premium, disability income, and accidental death or double indemnity—remain in full force, contrary to the situation under the paid-up insurance options. Finally, if the policy is participating, the policyowner continues to receive dividends, which is usually not true of paid-up term insurance and might not be true under reduced paid-up insurance.

On the other hand, unless the provision is used only as a temporary convenience, as intended, it may prove disadvantageous to the policyowner. If premium payments are not resumed, not only will the *period* during which the policy is kept in force usually be less than under extended insurance, but the *amount* payable in the event of death will be less, and the disparity will become greater with each passing year.

In the event of the insured's death during the period covered, the insurer is better off financially under the automatic premium loan arrangement than under extended term insurance, since the former receives additional premiums by way of deduction from the policy proceeds, but offsetting this advantage to some extent are the additional outlays for commissions, premium taxes, and dividends (if participating).

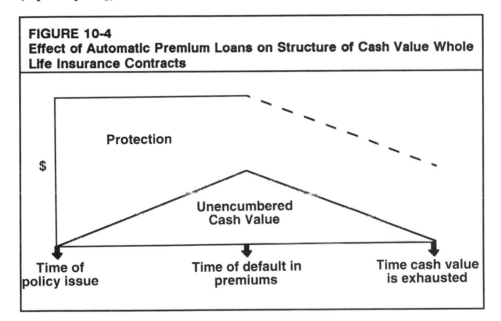

FIGURE 10-4
Effect of Automatic Premium Loans on Structure of Cash Value Whole Life Insurance Contracts

Protection

$

Unencumbered Cash Value

Time of policy issue   Time of default in premiums   Time cash value is exhausted

The effect of the automatic premium loan feature on the structure of a whole life policy is shown in figure 10-4. Upon default of the first premium the effective amount of protection is reduced by the amount of the *gross* premium. Each year thereafter that the feature is permitted to operate, the amount of protection is reduced by the gross premium due that year, plus interest on that premium and all unpaid premiums of previous years. Hence the protection element will decline at a constantly increasing rate. The surrender value will be exhausted, however, before the protection element is reduced to zero.

The effective or unencumbered investment element also turns downward, but not immediately, and it never declines at the same rate as the protection element, so the solid and broken lines are not parallel. The nominal investment element—cash value—increases with the payment of each gross premium (regardless of the source of the funds) by the amount of the net premium, plus interest at the contractual rate and benefit of survivorship, less the cost of insurance.

POLICY ILLUSTRATIONS

Life insurance sales nearly always rely on multiple-year policy illustration sheets. There are some basic similarities among policy illustrations, such as a listing of the annual premium and the policy's cash value for each policy duration up to 20 years after policy issuance. However, despite the similarities, there are no uniform standards applicable to policy illustrations. The organization of illustrative information within a single report varies drastically from one insurance company to another even if the same information is contained in the report.

Policy illustrations or ledger sheets usually cover at least 10 years of data and often cover 15 or 20 years. The years are usually presented in a single column of such an illustration with the figures in this column referring to the number of years after the date of policy issuance. Some illustrations present both the years column and an attained-age column in order to show the age of the insured at each displayed policy duration. There are, however, some illustrations that present only the attained-age information and do not present the years of duration since policy issuance. Presentation of only one of these columns is not a serious omission because the omitted column can be derived from the column that *is* included in the illustration.

The one convention that is very frequently followed is to represent separate years on separate rows of the policy illustration. Each column generally represents a separate category of data such as age, premium, cash value, loan, and so forth.

Participating Policy Premiums

The following is an example of one of the simpler illustrations showing only policy year, gross annual premium, dividends, and net premium after dividends. Policy illustration 1 in table 10-2 does not even present the cash values for the policy.

There are some shortcomings with even this simple type of illustration. The summation of premium payments from the different years is inappropriate unless the values are adjusted by an interest factor to make them comparable. In fact, it is inappropriate to combine any dollar amounts from different time periods unless they are adjusted for interest.

It is appropriate to add or subtract values from the same time period. In the example, the dividends are deducted from the gross premium due in the same period in order to correctly determine the net premium due. These net-premium-due values can all be adjusted for interest to determine what beginning balance would be needed in an interest-bearing account to pay all of the net-premium-due amounts as they become payable. This adjusted amount is the present value of all 20 net-premium payments. When a 5 percent interest rate is used, the present value of these net premiums due is $2,273. In other words, an account with a present balance of $2,273, which is earning 5 percent interest, would be sufficient to pay all 20 premiums because the interest earnings of $1,484 plus the starting fund balance would cover the aggregate payments of $3,757.

TABLE 10-2
Policy Illustration 1

$50,000 Graded Premium Paid-Up at Age 95 Policy
Insured: Female, Aged 32   Initial Annual Premium: $170

Year	Gross Annual Premium	Dividend Used to Reduce Premiums	Premium Due
1	$ 170	$ 0	$ 170
2	170	50	120
3	175	52	123
4	180	53	127
5	185	53	132
	880	208	672
6	190	54	136
7	195	55	140
8	200	56	144
9	205	57	148
10	215	58	157
	1,885	488	1,397
11	230	59	171
12	245	60	185
13	260	61	199
14	275	65	210
15	295	70	225
	3,190	803	2,387
16	315	75	240
17	340	80	260
18	360	90	270
19	390	100	290
20	420	110	310
	$5,015	$1,258	$3,757

Dividends shown are not guarantees of future dividends. They are merely based on the current level of dividends, which may change in the future.

Another way of adjusting payments from different time periods is to calculate the accumulated values. This calculation merely adjusts all payments to the end of the selected time period. The same result is obtained by depositing each net premium due into an interest-bearing account and letting the interest accumulate in the account. The balance in the account at the end of the period is the accumulated value for the specified interest rate, time period, and payments. This accumulated value for the example in illustration 1, based on 5 percent interest for the full 20 years, is $6,032. This value may be thought of as an opportunity cost of the premium payments. The policyowner is giving up the equivalent of the accumulated value that could have been invested had it not been allocated to life insurance premiums.

Obviously the particular interest rate used has a strong influence on the adjusted present values and accumulated values. There is an inverse relationship between the interest rate and the resultant present values. That is, higher interest rates result in lower present values, and lower interest rates produce higher present-value amounts. To illustrate this point, reconsider the present value given above. The value was $2,273 when based on 5 percent interest. The calculated present value of the same premiums was $1,524 based on 10 percent interest. Similarly the accumulated value of those 20 net premiums was $6,032 when based on 5 percent interest, but would have had an accumulated value of $10,252 if it had been based on 10 percent interest. This demonstrates the direct relationship between interest rates and accumulated values. Higher interest rates produce higher accumulated values and lower interest rates produce lower accumulated values.

The choice of the proper interest rate is both important and difficult. The difficulty arises from the fact that the rate chosen should represent actual aftertax investment rates of return for the particular policyowner over the selected future period. Any attempt to represent unknown future interest rates is necessarily an estimate or a guess. It is important to select an interest rate that is a relatively accurate representation of actual rates over the period because slight changes in the interest rate result in significant changes of the present values and accumulated values being calculated and compared.

The interest-adjusted indexes required by law in nearly every state specify an interest rate of 5 percent. The concern of these state statutes or regulations is not the accuracy of the interest rate in representing the actual future interest but rather a need for comparability of indexes for different policies. Indexes based on different interest rates are not directly comparable. Thus the prescribing of one interest rate results in comparison indexes that can be used without needing any further adjustments.

Ledger statements and policy illustrations that do not include interest adjustments are really based on an implicit assumption that the interest rate is zero and the inflation rate is zero. Dollar amounts from different time periods are comparable without adjustment if, and only if, funds can be borrowed without paying interest and if prices remain stable or unchanged over the time interval. The subtotals in the first illustration after every 5 years are examples of unadjusted values from different years that have been added together. Similar illustrations that include policy cash values often imply that the coverage is free because the cash value eventually exceeds the aggregate premiums paid unless the premiums are adjusted for interest. Many policy illustrations are intended to preserve the traditional net-cost policy comparisons that ignore interest. Illustrations that present interest-adjusted figures are preferable because of their enhanced accuracy over unadjusted values.

There are many types of policy illustrations. The simplest types, which are similar to the illustration already discussed, merely show how much will have to be paid out-of-pocket to keep the policy in force. Many illustrations omit the suggested dividends but contain cash value and death-benefit values. It is very common for policy illustrations to show increasing death benefits based on the application of policy dividends to purchase paid-up additional insurance. The use of dividends to purchase one-year term insurance is another method of increasing the policy death benefit without altering the policy.

The more complex policy illustrations can be separated into the following five categories: minimum-deposit policies, split-dollar policies, comparisons of two policies, policies with side investment funds or annuity contracts, and universal life policy illustrations. Many of these illustrations are dependent on the policyowner's marginal tax rate for federal income taxes.

Policy illustrations that have more than four columns of values often derive some of their data from information that is not provided in the illustration. The relationship between columns is sometimes defined in the footnotes to the policy illustration, but often the relationships between columns are only partially described, if at all.

Combination Coverage

Illustration 2 (see table 10-3) is an example showing where policy dividends are used to purchase additional coverage. The basic policy is for $18,000 of whole life insurance, supplemented with additional paid-up coverage purchased with dividends. There are no figures in the illustration to indicate the level of the policy dividends, but there is a footnote indicating that the dividend levels assumed for the calculation are not guaranteed. The first column merely lists the policy year or duration. The second column shows the gross annual premium that is constant for this policy. The illustration does not show that any funds were borrowed from the policy cash value.

The third column of illustration 2 is labeled "total paid-up value." This label is ambiguous because it does not indicate whether the paid-up value is for the dividend additions only or for both coverages as a result of applying the cash values of both coverages. Study of the illustration reveals that a paid-up value occurs in the second policy year before there is any cash value associated with the coverage purchased with dividends. Thus it can be deduced that the total paid-up value is the amount of fully paid-up coverage the policyowner is eligible for if the total cash value is applied to the purchase. This illustration is based on the assumption that the policyowner will not exercise any policy loans during the 20 years displayed.

The column titled "guaranteed cash value end of year" is relatively easy to interpret. The word *guaranteed* indicates that this is the scheduled cash value for the base whole life policy. Values for the supplemental coverage cannot be guaranteed because the dividends used to purchase the additional coverage are not guaranteed.

The "enhancement reserve fund" column essentially shows the cash value for the paid-up supplemental policies purchased with policy dividends. The "total cash value end of year" column merely lists the sum of the guaranteed cash value and the enhancement reserve fund.

The last two columns in illustration 2 show the relationship between the premium paid and the annual increase in the policy cash value. During the first through eighth policy years the policy premium exceeds the incremental increase in the cash value. The cash value increases exceed the policy premium in the ninth and all subsequent policy years. Although this comparison may lead some

TABLE 10-3
Policy Illustration 2

Combination of Whole Life
and Additional Coverage Purchased with Policy Dividends

$18,000   Whole Life   Insured: Female, Aged 40
  7,000   Additional Coverage   Annual Premium: $320
$25,000   Death Benefit

Year	Gross Annual Premium	Total Paid-Up Value	Guaranteed Cash Value End of Year	Enhancement Reserve Fund	Total Cash Value End of Year	Total Cash Value Increase End of Year	CV Increase Less Net Payment
1	$ 320	$ 0	$ 0	$ 0	$ 0	$ 0	$ −320
2	320	285	101	0	101	101	−219
3	320	1,098	402	0	402	301	−19
4	320	1,863	704	0	704	302	−18
5	320	2,577	1,005	0	1,005	301	−19
6	320	3,291	1,324	0	1,324	319	−1
7	320	3,958	1,642	0	1,642	318	−2
8	320	4,583	1,960	0	1,960	318	−2
9	320	5,226	2,296	7	2,303	343	23
10	320	5,926	2,647	44	2,691	388	68
11	320	6,570	2,983	90	3,073	382	62
12	320	7,228	3,334	146	3,480	407	87
13	320	7,907	3,703	215	3,918	438	118
14	320	8,569	4,072	296	4,368	450	130
15	320	9,214	4,440	391	4,831	463	143
16	320	9,846	4,809	498	5,307	476	156
17	320	10,494	5,194	619	5,813	506	186
18	320	11,131	5,580	755	6,335	522	202
19	320	11,755	5,965	905	6,870	535	215
20	320	12,398	6,367	1,072	7,439	569	249
	$6,400					$7,439	$1,039

The current dividend scale is expected to continue, and it is now adequate to provide
the needed $7,000 of benefits as term insurance for the first 8 policy years, then as
whole life additions. The dividends are not guaranteed.

consumers to think they are getting their coverage free after the ninth policy year, such an interpretation is incorrect because the cash value is not made available to the policyowner other than as policy loans that are subject to compound interest charges.

The three column totals in illustration 2 have the same flaw as those in the previous illustration: They are only appropriate if both interest rates and inflation rates are zero. The accumulated value of the $320 annual premium after 20 years is $11,110 based on 5 percent interest, or $20,161 if it is based on a 10 percent interest rate. The accumulated value of the last column in illustration 2 is only $557 if based on a 5 percent interest rate. This is less than the column sum of $1,038 because of the negative quantities in the first 8 years, which accrued larger negative balances until they were counterbalanced in subsequent years with positive values. The accumulated value is $1,076 for a 10 percent interest rate.

The only important concept to be discerned from this illustration is that the premium is sufficient to create an internal buildup of funds in the policy, which also earns investment income. These internal funds are essential for the level-policy mechanism to work.

Split Dollar

Policy illustrations can get very complex. It is important to use a marginal tax rate in the policy illustration that is the same as the marginal tax rate for the prospective policyowner. Minor variations in the tax rate can result in significant changes in the aftertax costs to the policyowner and other involved participants. Illustrations based on tax rates that are significantly different from those of the prospect are misleading and could be considered deceptive sales practices. The size limitations of standard office stationery tend to limit the amount of information that can be displayed on a single sheet. Consequently many related items are not included in policy illustrations.

It is essential to show both the corporate information and the individual insured information for this type of illustration.

Universal Life

The final illustration presents an early version of a universal life policy. This particular policy provides a death benefit of $100,000 until the policy cash value exceeds $95,000. Thereafter a death benefit will be $5,000 higher than the policy cash value. In illustration 3 (table 10-4) the annual premium of $1,300 is paid for 25 years. The illustrations for universal life policies may include (as this one does) a column for partial withdrawals. These are policyowner withdrawals of funds from the policy cash value that are not policy loans and do not accrue interest, nor are they expected to be returned to the policy. Because universal life policies can have both policy loans and partial withdrawals, it is likely that some illustrations will have columns for both. If the total of all partial withdrawals ever exceeds the total premiums paid for the policy, the excess will be subject to federal income tax.

The premium less withdrawals column in illustration 3 is a non-interest-adjusted column indicating the cumulative amount of past premiums paid after reductions for any partial withdrawals of funds. The present value of these premiums over 25 years and of withdrawals in the subsequent 5 years is $10,512 based on 5 percent interest. If the premiums had been deposited in a 5 percent interest-bearing account, that account would still have a balance of $45,432 after the five annual withdrawals of $6,500 each. Based on 10 percent interest, the same calculations indicate a present value of $10,478 and an accumulated value of $182,835. These adjusted figures negate the impression that the policyowner will have no investment in the policy at the end of the 30 years, as the unadjusted numbers might imply.

This illustration is quite different from a traditional policy illustration in that it has three separate cash value columns, each calculated for a different assumed rate of interest earnings for the cash value. The "guaranteed cash value" column is comparable to the traditional examples because it is based on the interest rate guaranteed in the policy. However, even the "guaranteed cash value" column has its own properties for universal life policies because the premium level is usually inadequate if the cash value interest earnings do not exceed the guaranteed rate. That is why the cash values peak at $11,449 in the 19th policy year and decline to zero by the 26th policy year.

The column showing the assumed cash value is calculated using the assumption that the cash value will earn 9 percent interest every year. At that level of investment earnings or higher, the $1,300 premium for 25 years is clearly adequate to keep the policy in force. This scenario would develop ever-increasing cash values for the policy. There are no guarantees or suggestions that the investment earnings will always equal or exceed 9 percent. This is merely an example of how the cash value would grow if the actual earnings turn out to be exactly 9 percent each policy year.

The "current cash value" column is another example of how the cash value will increase at an even higher interest rate if that rate is earned every policy year. The interest rate used in illustration 3 for the current cash value is 11 percent each year. These columns are just demonstrations of what compound interest can do at sustained high levels. During the 1981–82 high-interest-rate period, there were companies using rates as high as 14 percent in their illustrations. There were many arbitrary predictions during that time, one being that interest rates would never again drop below 12 percent. These predictions have already proven to be erroneous. It is unrealistic to expect interest rates to stay at historically high levels over any protracted period of time. There is a very low probability that the cash value of the policy in illustration 3 will reach $134,000 in the 30th policy year. It is questionable whether even a 9 percent rate of return is achievable over such an extended period. The assumed cash value of $74,000 after 30 years may turn out to be overly optimistic.

As previously stated, this policy is of the earlier design and would not be offered with such a narrow final amount of at-risk death protection. The policies issued after the tax law change in October 1986 would provide a larger spread between the cash value and the death benefit. The cash value in the illustrated policy is too high for the $100,000 death benefit in the 24th policy year if the amounts in the "current cash value" column are actually attained. If the cash value of the policy attains the amounts in the "assumed cash value" column, there will be no problem of satisfying the test for life insurance in Sec. 101(f) of the Internal Revenue Code.

TABLE 10-4
Policy Illustration 3

Universal Life

Death Benefit: $100,000 Insured: Female, Aged 40, nonsmoker
Planned Annual Premium: $1,300

				End of Year			
Policy Year	Annual Premium	Partial With-drawal	Premi-ums Less With-drawals	Guar. Cash Value	As-sumed Cash Value*	Current Cash Value**	Current Death Benefit
1	$1,300	$ 0	$ 1,300	$ 114	$ 153	$ 166	$100,000
2	1,300	0	2,600	943	1,175	1,212	100,000
3	1,300	0	3,900	1,773	2,275	2,357	100,000
4	1,300	0	5,200	2,604	3,473	3,627	100,000
5	1,300	0	6,500	3,438	4,769	5,025	100,000
6	1,300	0	7,800	4,262	6,161	6,555	100,000
7	1,300	0	9,100	5,077	7,659	8,233	100,000
8	1,300	0	10,400	5,873	9,287	10,091	100,000
9	1,300	0	11,700	6,649	11,048	12,140	100,000
10	1,300	0	13,000	7,393	12,956	14,405	100,000
11	1,300	0	14,300	8,107	15,040	16,924	100,000
12	1,300	0	15,600	8,777	17,308	19,719	100,000
13	1,300	0	16,900	9,392	19,781	22,827	100,000
14	1,300	0	18,200	9,951	22,482	26,288	100,000
15	1,300	0	19,500	10,439	25,427	30,138	100,000
16	1,300	0	20,800	10,845	28,645	34,431	100,000
17	1,300	0	22,100	11,164	32,159	39,218	100,000
18	1,300	0	23,400	11,371	36,006	44,566	100,000
19	1,300	0	24,700	11,449	40,218	50,546	100,000
20	1,300	0	26,000	11,380	44,847	57,252	100,000
21	1,300	0	27,300	11,133	49,933	64,777	100,000
22	1,300	0	28,600	10,685	55,533	73,238	100,000
23	1,300	0	29,900	10,011	61,704	82,766	100,000
24	1,300	0	31,200	9,058	68,524	93,521	100,000
25	1,300	0	32,500	7,792	76,075	105,617	110,617
26	0	6,500	26,000	0	75,659	110,198	115,198
27	0	6,500 .	19,500	0	75,284	115,288	120,288
28	0	6,500	13,000	0	74,973	120,945	125,945
29	0	6,500	6,500	0	74,704	127,229	132,229
30	0	6,500	0	0	74,400	134,213	139,213

The guaranteed cash value is based on a 4% interest rate.

*Interest rate used for assumed cash value is 9%.
**Interest rate used for current cash value is 11%.

There are many other possibilities that could be illustrated for universal life policies and traditional policies. Universal life policies can be used in any type of situation in which whole life policies can be used. Whether they would be the preferred policy can only be determined after analysis and realistic estimation of future interest earnings in the policy. The required space for further illustrations puts them beyond the scope of this chapter.

The most important thing to remember about illustrations is that the values in the columns should be adjusted for interest before adding column values. When the illustration does not include interest-adjusted values, it is advisable to provide present values and accumulated values—at representative values—for the aftertax cash outlay columns. Another element of extreme importance is the use of appropriate marginal tax rates in illustrations that match the applicable tax rate to the prospective policyowner.

The proliferation of illustrations in recent years has prompted calls for standards or guidelines. The American Society of CLU & ChFC has taken the initiative and adopted a *Professional Practice Guideline*, which is a checklist of guidelines for sales material and presentations. Although these guidelines are not intended to be minimum standards, they do give explicit guidance on many issues concerning illustrations. This document was adopted by the membership of the American Society of CLU & ChFC at its 1988 annual meeting and is presented on the following pages.

The principal items addressed in the checklist are interest rates, mortality expenses, dividends, benefit changes, surrender charges, waiver-of-premium benefit base, policy comparisons, and issues of replacement. This document can be used to ensure that all relevant questions have been explained to a prospect. Obviously, not every item will always be applicable. For example, dividends might not be involved in a proposal because of the type of coverage under consideration.

One suggestion is to make customized copies of the guidelines that are tailored to specific policies and situations. These checklists could even be shared with prospects to see if they feel that all their questions have been answered and that they understand all the answers. There could be separate guidelines for a nonparticipating policy, a participating policy, a universal life, each type of policy replacement, and any other anticipated situation. Making separate guidelines would eliminate any questions that are not appropriate for an individual situation.

The practitioner should frequently review the full checklist as a reminder of all the relevant issues. It is important to include a discussion of each applicable factor in presentations. Some additional items that fit each practitioner's special needs might be added to the checklist. The guidelines should be reviewed and a copy should be kept handy for frequent use.

Policy Illustration Factors and Issues

What Was the Situation Before?

Life insurance policy illustrations became an integral part of the selling process after the arrival of universal life and interest-sensitive whole life policies. Prior to that a schedule of guaranteed cash values was sufficient to describe traditional policies.

EXHIBIT 10-1
A Professional Practice Guideline*
The American Society of CLU & ChFC

Disclosure Checklist for Life Insurance Sales Material and Presentations

This Professional Practice Guideline is intended to serve as a checklist of information for members of the American Society of CLU & ChFC to be evaluated before a prospect or client is asked to make a buying decision. The Guideline is not intended to set minimum levels of required performance, but rather to provide ideals to which one may aspire. It has been developed primarily for non-SEC-regulated products and addresses sales presentations that rely on future benefit and/or cost illustrations or projections.

Most life insurance products sold today are adjustable either as a traditional "participating" product or as one of the family of products referred to as "interest sensitive." While adjustable products incorporate guarantees, the sales illustrations and projections are usually designed to convey to the prospect what benefits and/or costs may be under a set of assumptions more optimistic than the guarantees. Since the insurance company generally limits its responsibility to the guarantees, risks associated with the development of a higher benefit or lower cost than generated by the guarantees are borne by the policyowner.

To be consistent with this Guideline, "a sales communication package" (consisting of both written and verbal explanations) should not be finalized until all elements of the Guideline checklist have been evaluated. The question of which elements of the following checklist constitute relevant information in a particular situation is a matter of professional judgment.

I. Mortality

    A. The mortality expense used in an illustration may reflect

        1. the company's actual current or recent mortality experience
        2. actual current or recent mortality experience modified at an assumed rate of increase or decrease
        3. a combination of mortality and other expenses
        4. zero mortality

    B. Which of the above is used in the illustration?

II. Interest Rate

    A. The interest assumption used in an illustration may be based upon

        1. interest rates earned by the company on

---

*Reprinted with permission from the June 1988 issue of *Society Page*, a publication of the American Society of CLU & ChFC.

EXHIBIT 10-1 (Continued)
A Professional Practice Guideline
The American Society of CLU & ChFC

        a. all investments now held
        b. new investments
        c. new investments over a certain number of past years
        d. other combinations of actual investments

    2. an independent index such as

        a. Treasury bills
        b. Moody's long-term bond index
        c. other indexes

    3. another basis not tied to company results or an index

  B. Interest rates may be the gross interest rate resulting from investments, indexes or other measures, or the gross interest rate reduced by

    1. investment expenses
    2. investment expenses and other expenses
    3. expenses and profit
    4. a fixed amount or percentage

  C. Are interest assumptions constant or may they change over future years? Which of the above is used in the illustration?

III. NAIC Requirements

  A. Items B and C below are largely based on interrogatories that companies are required to answer as part of their annual statement filing. Members should therefore expect that companies should be able to provide the information needed to complete these items with respect to the policy(ies) illustrated.

  B. Basis of illustration

    1. Is the policy of the traditional participating variety, or does it contain nonguaranteed pricing elements using a means other than dividends?
    2. If the policy is not participating, describe the nonguaranteed elements involved (such as nonguaranteed interest crediting rates, mortality charges, loadings, etc.)

EXHIBIT 10-1 (Continued)
A Professional Practice Guideline
The American Society of CLU & ChFC

3. If the policy is participating, does the company state that the contribution principle* is being followed in the illustrative dividend scale? If it is not, how does it differ?

4. If the policy is not participating, what is the company's policy with respect to determination and redetermination of nonguaranteed pricing elements, with particular reference to (a) the degree of discretion reserved by the company and (b) whether any of the elements are guaranteed to follow an outside index?

C. Basis of dividends or nonguaranteed factors

1. Are any of the underlying experience factors different from current experience? If so, describe how and for what factor(s).

2. If the policy is participating, is there a substantial probability that the current illustrative dividend scale cannot be continued if current experience continues?

3. If the policy is not participating, is there a substantial probability that current illustrations cannot be supported by currently anticipated experience?

IV. Special Considerations

A. Some contracts provide for future benefit increases. Are such increases subject to evidence of insurability?

B. Some Disability Premium Waiver provisions waive a term cost of insurance and some waive a level (permanent) cost. Specifically what is waived?

C. Are any surrender charges illustrated? Are surrender charges fixed or determined at company discretion?

D. Comparisons for replacement transactions can call for special disclosure(s) such as the following:

1. Is the current experience of the product to be replaced being used and have all available amendments which might improve the performance of the product been taken into consideration?

---

*The contribution principle states that aggregate divisible surplus should be distributed in the same proportion as the policies are considered to have contributed to the divisible surplus.

EXHIBIT 10-1 (Concluded)
A Professional Practice Guideline
The American Society of CLU & ChFC

2. Will suicide and incontestable provisions be extended by the replacement?
3. Are there any differences in assumptions of the old and new product that will affect the comparison?
4. Will the replacement produce a short-term loss? How long will it take any superior performance of the replacing product to offset any short-term loss?
5. Are any assumptions of either product contradicted by either carrier's past experience?
6. Is the replacement clearly to the advantage of the policyowner?

The American Society of CLU & ChFC recognizes that some insurance companies may not be prepared to furnish all information needed to enable a member to evaluate all the elements of this Professional Practice Guideline. The Guideline was developed by the Ethical Guidance and Professional Practice Standards Committee of the Society as a recommended checklist of information that should be evaluated before a consumer is asked to make a buying decision. Members are encouraged to help the companies with which they place business become more sensitive to offering disclosure information that exceeds the mere threshold requirements of the law.

The availability of personal computers to the field underwriting force made such illustrations possible. The software used to generate policy illustrations usually enabled the agent or broker to set and change the interest rate assumption. Some policy illustration software allows control of additional factors such as expenses or mortality.

In most software the interest assumption rate is the same for every year illustrated. Few illustration programs allow for changing interest rates at different policy durations. Thus most policy illustrations are based on a selected interest rate projected for the entire period being illustrated. During the early 1980s when prime interest rates and inflation rates were both in double-digit ranges, it was common to see policy illustrations projecting interest rates of 12 to 15 percent for more than 30 years. In some cases illustrations used interest rates near 20 percent.

Such presentations created an unrealistic expectation on the part of many buyers. Even though the illustrations cautioned that the future projections presented were not guaranteed, most policyowners incorrectly assumed that lower interest rates would only change the results slightly. Many of these consumers have become irate over the magnitude of the shortfall when comparing actual cash values with the optimistic projections made back at the time of policy purchase.

Related optimistic illustrations that have created ill will are those depicting so-called vanishing premiums. The premiums are really continuous for the full duration of the coverage, but future policyowner dividends are used to pay premiums. If and when future dividends plus increments of prior accumulations exceed the premium, the owner will not have to pay the premiums out-of-pocket. Many illustrations based on overly optimistic assumptions indicated that buyers would only have to pay cash premiums for a few years (5–9 years being rather common). Now that actual performance is unfolding, it is clear that premium payments in cash will be required for significantly more years than expected in most cases.

As investment returns drop and life insurer investment earnings dwindle, policy dividends are being reduced. These dividend reductions not only increase the amount of premium payments but also create the potential for vanished premiums to reappear. This happens when the dividend equals or exceeds the premium prior to the dividend cut but is less than the premium after the cut.

Neither the field force nor the buyers of policies anticipated the rapid decline in investment returns experienced in recent years. Even more important, they were not aware of policy sensitivity to such changes because most transactions were based on a single illustration showing only a guaranteed interest rate and a current rate. Very few presentations utilized multiple illustrations based on a sufficient range of rates to demonstrate policy sensitivity.

What Is the Nature of the Change?

There have been complaints about life insurance policy illustration abuses from both outside and inside the insurance industry. Outspoken critics include financial writer Jane Bryant Quinn and Senator Metzenbaum from Ohio. Even within the insurance industry ranks, agents, brokers, actuaries, and others have called for more disclosure about illustrations and urged the use of conservative interest assumptions and other controllable factors. In 1988 the American Society of CLU & ChFC created its Professional Practice Guideline (PPG) shown above.

Responding to criticism of the PPG, the American Society of CLU & ChFC has created a life insurance Illustration Questionnaire (IQ), hereafter referred to as IQ. This document poses much more detailed questions about all aspects of the factors making up the illustration. There are no suggested answers; instead, the questionnaire is to be completed by insurance company home office staff. Agents and brokers can use it as a tool to educate themselves about policy illustrations. The IQ was introduced in April 1992 and is being provided to members of the Society; nonmembers can request a copy by contacting The American Society of CLU & ChFC at (610) 526-2500. The IQ appears on the following pages.

As you can see, the primary focus of these questions is to obtain detailed information about the *nonguaranteed* elements of policy illustrations. Although the questions stop short of proprietary pricing information, they should elicit enough information to determine that illustrations from another insurer are probably not directly comparable because of differences in the underlying assumptions.

Policy illustrations are projections of what could happen under a policy if actual experience serendipitously mirrored all the assumed factors used to calculate the illustration. However, it is almost a certainty that actual experience will deviate from the illustration on multiple factors. The actual future numbers for each—cash values, premiums, and death benefits—can vary drastically from those shown in an illustration.

A study of policy illustrations by a task force of the Society of Actuaries, released in 1992, showed the following major findings:

- Policy illustrations work well to educate clients in the mechanics of how policies work.
- Policy illustrations are not an adequate tool for comparing costs of policies from different insurance companies. Illustrations do not create accurate projections of future performance because of differences in assumptions and the problems of estimating future parameters.

Another opinion was provided in the October 26, 1992, edition of *Probe* by John C. Angle, FSA. He proposed that rather than trying to educate producers and consumers about interpreting illustrations, it is advisable to issue a prospectus for the policy that would disclose in minute detail how the insurance company determines each aspect of the policy and reveal any subsidization being provided. Such disclosure is already being provided for variable life insurance policies. Angle thinks that there is a strong possibility that illustrations will be subjected to stringent regulation by insurance commissioners if more voluntary disclosure is not forthcoming.

Mel Todd, an actuary, suggested to the 1992 Million Dollar Round Table (MDRT) meeting that illustrations should be overseen by the state insurance regulators; this would ensure uniformity and comparability. Unofficial communications from the NAIC and the offices of the California insurance commissioner indicate that both are considering such regulations.

This information prompted both the American Counsel of Life Insurance and the National Association of Life Underwriters to create task forces in late 1992 to address the problems of policy illustrations. Both organizations may positively influence subsequent steps by legislators and regulators to set illustration standards.

How Does This Change Affect Clients?

The criticism and cautions about policy illustrations are prompting some consumers to be even more skeptical of insurance sales materials. To some extent this is a positive development because it reduces their expectation or reliance on the fact that actual future performance will match illustrated values. However, it also erodes confidence in the industry and its contracts.

The realization that illustrations are not a good device for selecting an insurance company increases the anxiety level of both purchasers and producers. This may encourage consumers to focus more heavily on financial strength and company ratings as selection criteria rather than policy illustrations.

Those consumers who still believe policy illustrations are a fairly accurate depiction of actual future performance need to be enlightened about the potential fluctuation in the nonguaranteed policy elements. Otherwise they will build their expectations on the most optimistic numbers presented in the illustration and may be tempted to initiate litigation against the insurer for deceptive sales practices. Such ill will does not help the insurance industry or its field marketing force.

⊡☺ American Society of CLU & ChFC

Introduction to the Life Insurance Illustration Questionnaire (IQ)

The Life Insurance Illustration Questionnaire (IQ) is an educational tool; its use by companies or agents is entirely voluntary. Some insurance companies may be unable to provide some information or unwilling to do so if they view that information as proprietary.

The purpose of the IQ is to help the student of life insurance understand the different non-guaranteed performance assumptions which insurance companies use to design and create sales illustrations. It has been developed primarily for non-SEC regulated products. Students should understand that sales illustrations are useful in developing the best combination of policy specifications to achieve the buyer's objective. However, illustrations have little value in predicting actual performance or in comparing products and companies.

Most life insurance products sold today have adjustable pricing. This can be accomplished either as a traditional "participating" product or as a product with "non-guaranteed pricing elements" such as changeable interest crediting rates, mortality charges, expense charges, etc. All adjustable pricing products incorporate some guarantees. However, the sales illustrations are usually designed to present potential benefits and costs under a set of non-guaranteed assumptions more optimistic than the guarantees. The insurance company generally limits its responsibility to the guarantees. So the risks associated with the inability of a product to achieve the higher illustrated benefits, or lower illustrated costs, than those generated by the guarantees are borne by the policyholder. A study of the responses to the IQ should help the student better understand those risks.

Life Insurance Illustration Questionnaire

Educational Information about current company illustration practices should be provided separately where company practices differ. For example, company practices may differ for traditional participating plans, universal life, indeterminate premium term plans and joint life.

This educational information covers the following plan(s):
(Ed. note. At this point, the responding company identifies the products covered by this IQ response.)

I. General

Basic Information

1. Are one or more of the policies participating? Specify:

   If so, does the company employ the contribution principle* with respect to these policies? If not how does it differ?

   * The contribution principle calls for the aggregate divisible surplus to be distributed in the same proportion as the policies are considered to have contributed to the divisible surplus.

---

2. Are one or more of the policies non-participating? Specify. Describe the non-guaranteed elements.

   If so, what is the company's policy and discretion with respect to the determination and redetermination of non-guaranteed pricing elements? Are there any guaranteed pricing elements?

3. Whether participating or non-participating, do the underlying experience factor(s) for any non-guaranteed factor(s) used in the illustration differ from current experience? If so, describe.

4. Whether participating or non-participating, is there a substantial probability that the current illustrative values will change if current experience continues unchanged?

5. Whether participating or non-participating, is it company policy to treat new and existing policyholders of the same class the same or consistently with respect to the underlying factors used in pricing? If not, describe.

II. Mortality

Basic Information

1. Are the mortality rates underlying the illustration lower than actual recent company experience? Define actual recent experience (e.g., company experience for the last 5 years).

2. Does the illustration assume mortality improvements in the future?
   If so, describe.

3. Do the mortality rates or cost of insurance charges include some expense charge?
   If so, describe.

Additional Information

1. Do the underlying mortality rates vary by product (e.g., whole life vs. universal life vs. survivorship life) or policy size? If so, specify. (Provide general description of differences - not the actual rates used).

2. Indicate approximate duration when all mortality rates are the same by attained age.

III. Interest or Crediting Rates

Basic Information

1. Describe the basis of the interest rate used in the dividend scale or credited in the illustration. Include in description whether the rate is gross or net of expenses and/or margins.

   Do the interest rate(s) reflect the earnings on all invested assets? A portion of the assets? New investments over certain number of years? (If so, specify number of years). An index? (If so, specify).

2. Do the company investment earnings rates required to support the interest rate used in the dividend scale or credited in the illustration at any policy duration exceed the company's actual current earnings rate on the investment segment backing that block of policies?

3. Does the interest rate used in the dividend scale or credited in the illustration vary between new and existing policies?

4. Do the interest rates used in the dividend scale or credited in the illustration vary by policy duration?

Additional Information

1. Do the illustrative interest rates vary by product, class or otherwise? If so, specify including general description of variations.

2. Do the illustrative interest rates include capital gains? If so, include general description of capital gain recognition.

IV. Expenses

Basic Information

1. Do the expense charges used in the dividend scale or charged in the illustration reflect actual recent company experience? If so, what is the experience period? If not, describe basis.

2. How are investment expenses and taxes assessed?

3. Are expense charges used in the dividend scale or charged in the illustration consistently determined for new and existing policies?

Additional Information

1. Do the illustrative expense charges vary by product, class or otherwise? If so, specify, including general description of variations.

2. Do the expense charges used in the dividend scale or charged in the illustration vary by duration after the initial expenses are amortized? If so, describe.

3. Are the expense charges used in the dividend scale or charged in the illustration adequate to cover the expenses incurred in sale and administration? If not, how are remaining expenses covered (e.g. charges against interest rate, increased mortality charges)?

V. Persistency

Basic Information

1. If the actual persistency is better than that assumed, would that negatively impact illustrated values?

2. Non-guaranteed persistency bonuses are amounts illustrated as being paid or credited to all policyholders who pay premiums (sometimes of a minimum specified amount or more) for a specified number of years. Does the illustration involve such a bonus?

   a. If so, what is its form (e.g. cash amount, additional interest credit, refund of mortality or loading charges)?

   b. What conditions must be met to pay or credit the bonus?

   c. Is there any limitation on company discretion in deciding whether to pay or credit the bonus?

   d. Does the company set aside any reserve or other liability earmarked for future bonuses?

3. Does the illustration include a guaranteed bonus?

   a. If so, what is its form (e.g. cash amount, additional interest credit, refund of mortality or loading charges)?

   b. What conditions must be met to pay or credit the bonus?

   c. Is there any limitation on company discretion in deciding whether to pay or credit the bonus?

   d. Does the company set aside any reserve or other liability earmarked for future bonuses?

What Should Be Done?

The insurance field force should learn more about the illustrations they use. Agents can ask the insurance company to supply them with answers to the IQ, as 47 companies with 53 percent of industry assets have done. These answers will help explain differences in how illustrations are calculated. It is important to realize that illustrations from different insurers will probably be based on unlike assumptions. These variations are often significant enough to render direct comparison of policy illustrations from separate insurance companies meaningless.

Agents and brokers should present illustrations based on a conservative range of the assumptions that can be varied. This will demonstrate that future performance is subject to change and should also indicate how sensitive the policy values are to changes in interest rates and other assumptions in the illustration software. Emphasizing the possible fluctuation in future policy performance should minimize the buyers' expectation that the policy will exactly match any one set of illustrated values.

Anyone using policy illustrations to sell life insurance should remind prospects that it is difficult to accurately estimate future rates of investment earnings and increasing expenses due to inflation, even though insurance companies are forced to estimate these future rates and other variable factors when designing policies. Policy illustrations also necessitate estimates of future investment returns; however, estimated rates should be conservative in order to minimize the likelihood of overstating future policy values. Most illustrations use one estimated interest rate for each and every year illustrated. The actual policy performance will reflect the constantly changing interest rates of investments in the economy. It is fairly safe to say that the actual policy will not produce the illustrated values.

It should also be emphasized that the policy illustration depicts a combination of guaranteed and nonguaranteed elements. The nonguaranteed elements should be explicitly identified and explained to prospective purchasers. These elements usually include interest in excess of a guaranteed minimum rate, mortality rates lower than the guaranteed maximum rates, and favorable deviations from assumed insurer operating expenses. The nonguaranteed elements, whose exact level will never be known in advance, can be depicted as policy dividends or as separate factors in the policy simulation (as is usually the case with universal life illustrations). The insurer must have the ability to vary these factors when necessary to survive during periods of worse-than-expected conditions; there is also the potential for positive variations when better-than-expected conditions prevail. Policyowners should be cautioned to expect actual policy performance to fall somewhere between an illustration based strictly on guaranteed values and an illustration based on conservatively optimistic factor levels.

Where Can I Find Out More?

- "Report of the Task Force for Research on Life Insurance Sales Illustrations." Committee for Research on Social Concerns, Society of Actuaries, 475 N. Martingale Road, Suite 800, Schaumburg, IL 60173-2226. Phone (708) 706-3500.

- John C. Angle. "Looking a Gift Horse in the Mouth." *Probe,* October 26, 1992. Probe Inc., Route 1, Box 88A, Nanjemoy, MD 20662.
- John C. Angle. "Those Pesky Dividend Illustrations." *Probe,* August 10, 1992. Probe Inc., Route 1, Box 88A, Nanjemoy, MD 20662.
- Classes on Illustration Questionnaire from the American Society of CLU & ChFC, 270 S. Bryn Mawr Avenue, Bryn Mawr, PA 19010. Phone (610) 526-2500.

NOTES

1. Twenty years in some states.
2. It should be noted that certain other types of expenses—for example, commissions, premium taxes, underwriting expenses, and service fees—are not incurred.
3. Dividend *deposits* will also be added to the sum applied as a net single premium and *may* be added to the face amount of the extended insurance.

11

Tax Treatment of Life Insurance and Annuities

Ted Kurlowicz and James F. Ivers III

This chapter is intended as an overview of the federal tax treatment of life insurance and annuity contracts. It is based on the law in effect at the publication date. Any legislation passed subsequently could, of course, affect the rules described. This overview is not intended to be a detailed treatment of the subjects covered. When financial services professionals are confronted with a tax issue, they must utilize more in-depth reference sources. Nevertheless, this chapter should serve as a helpful guide to the tax rules and issues that surround life insurance products.

INCOME TAXATION OF DEATH PROCEEDS OF LIFE INSURANCE

In general, proceeds paid under a life insurance contract by reason of the insured's death are excludible from gross income for federal income tax purposes.[1] Although there are exceptions to this general rule, the income tax treatment of life insurance death proceeds is generally favorable to taxpayers. On the other hand, the estate and gift tax treatment of policy proceeds is more troublesome and generally requires careful planning to minimize tax liability.

The basic requirement for the income tax exclusion for life insurance proceeds is that they be paid by reason of the death of the insured. Currently proposed Treasury regulations also extend the exclusion to certain "qualified accelerated death benefits" made on behalf of an insured who is terminally ill and expected to die within one year.

Transfer-for-Value Rule

The most important exception to the general rule of exclusion for life insurance death proceeds is the "transfer-for-value" rule.[2] Essentially, this rule provides that if a policy is transferred from one owner to another for valuable consideration, the income tax exclusion is lost. Upon the death of the insured in such cases, only the amount the transferee owner paid for the policy plus any premiums subsequently paid (that is, the transferee's total consideration) will be recovered income tax free by the policy beneficiary. The transfer-for-value rule is not limited to situations involving an outright sale of a policy; it may also apply where noncash consideration for a policy transfer can be inferred.

The transfer-for-value rule is an exception to the general rule of exclusion for policy proceeds. There are also exceptions to the exception (strangely enough, a common phenomenon in the tax law). Policy transfers that will not be jeopardized by the transfer-for-value rule are as follows:

- transfers in which the transferee owner is the insured
- transfers to a partner of the insured
- transfers to a partnership in which the insured is a partner
- transfers to a corporation of which the insured is a shareholder or an officer
- transfers in general in which the tax basis of the policy in the hands of the transferee is determined by reference to its basis to the transferor. A bona fide gift is a common example of such a transfer.

It is worth noting that if a policy becomes subject to the transfer-for-value trap, the transfer-for-value "taint" can be removed by another transfer of the policy that falls within one of the exceptions just described.

> *Example:* Leo is a shareholder in the Freedom Corporation and a partner in the Lincoln Partnership. He sells a policy on his life to Anne, who is also a shareholder in Freedom. This transfer will subject the policy to the transfer-for-value rule because it falls outside the exceptions to the rule. However, if Anne later sells the policy to Jane, a partner in the Lincoln Partnership, the transfer-for-value taint will be removed because the subsequent transfer is to a partner (Jane) of the insured (Leo).

Income Tax Definition of Life Insurance

The full exclusion for life insurance death proceeds depends in part on whether the policy itself meets the definition of life insurance under Sec. 7702 of the IRC. There are two alternative tests under this definition. A policy will qualify as life insurance for income tax purposes if it meets either of these two tests.

The first test is called the cash value accumulation test. This test will generally apply to more traditional cash value policies such as whole life policies. Under this test the cash value is generally limited to the "net single premium" that would be needed to fund the policy's death benefit. The net single premium is calculated by the insurance company using an assumed interest rate and certain mortality charges.

The second test is two-pronged. Policies that are designed to pass the second test must qualify under both a "guideline premium" requirement and a death benefit requirement. The guideline premium requirement limits the total premium that can be paid into the policy at any given time. The death benefit requirement (the second prong of the test) is met if the contract's death benefit exceeds a specified multiple of its cash value at all times. This multiple varies according to the insured's attained age. Generally, universal life and other similar types of policies will be tested under this second two-pronged test.

Other Considerations

The income tax exclusion for death proceeds can also be jeopardized by other factors. These include the issue of whether the policyowner has an insurable interest in the insured at policy inception, creditor-debtor relationships that involve life insurance, and various situations involving corporate-owned life insurance. These topics are not covered in detail in this chapter.

Settlement Options

Death proceeds of life insurance may be paid in a lump sum or in a series of payments under a settlement option. Payments under a settlement option generally include an element of interest earned, which is taxable, on the death benefit. However, the principal portion of a settlement option payment still qualifies for the income tax exclusion if a lump-sum payment under the same contract would have so qualified. Common settlement options include the installment option, the life-income option, the fixed-amount option, and the interest-only option. The amount of each payment under a settlement option that is attributable to the face amount of the policy is received tax free. The portion that represents interest on the policy proceeds is generally taxable. The portion representing the death benefit is calculated by prorating the face amount over the option's payment period. This is the excludible portion. Any excess amount of each payment represents interest. If the interest-only option is used, all interest paid or accrued will be taxable. If the fixed-amount option is used, the payment period is calculated by determining the number of fixed payments needed to exhaust the policy's face amount at its guaranteed interest rate. If the life-income option is used, the present value of any refund or period-certain feature is subtracted from the excludible amount to be prorated.

As previously stated, the interest element of a payment under a settlement option is generally taxable. However, with respect to policies covering insureds whose date of death is prior to October 23, 1986, an annual exclusion for the first $1,000 of interest received annually is still available. The exclusion is available only to surviving spouse beneficiaries and only for settlement options whose payments represent a combination of interest and principal. Therefore no interest exclusion would be allowable under the interest-only option. It is important to remember that no interest exclusion is available with respect to policies covering insureds whose date of death is after October 22, 1986.

INCOME TAXATION OF LIVING PROCEEDS OF LIFE INSURANCE POLICIES

Amounts paid under a life insurance contract while the insured is still living may take one of several forms. The most common of these are policy dividends, withdrawals from the policy's cash value or investment fund, policy loans, and proceeds from the cash surrender of a policy.

To properly determine the income tax effects of a financial transaction with a policy, the policyowner's tax basis in the policy must first be known. A policyowner's basis is initially determined by adding the total premiums paid into the policy and subtracting the dividends, if any, that have been paid by the insurer. If nontaxable withdrawals have previously been made from the policy, such amounts would also reduce the policyowner's basis. Policy loans generally have no direct effect on basis unless the policy is a modified endowment contract (MEC), discussed later in this chapter. However, it is important to remember that if a policy is surrendered, the principal amount of any loan outstanding against the policy is includible in the surrender value of the policy for tax purposes.

Policy dividends are treated as a nontaxable return of premium and will reduce basis. If total dividends paid exceed total premiums, dividends will be taxable to that extent. If dividends are used to reduce premiums or otherwise paid back into the policy (for example, to buy paid-up additions), the basis reduction caused by the payment of the dividend is offset by a corresponding basis increase when the dividend is reinvested in the policy.

If a policy is surrendered for cash, the taxable amount is the total surrender value minus the policyowner's current basis in the policy. Dividends left with the insurer to accumulate at interest are not included in the surrender value for tax purposes because they have already reduced the policyowner's basis in the contract.

> *Example:* Mark Sellers, aged 40, owns a level premium whole life policy. Mark has paid $24,000 in premium and has received $4,000 in dividends from the policy. The face amount of the policy is $100,000. The total cash value of the policy is $28,000. The policy is also subject to an outstanding loan of $15,000. Mark decides to surrender his policy for cash. The tax effects of Mark's surrender of his policy are as follows:

> Surrender Value

> | | |
> |---|---|
> | Policy loan | $15,000 |
> | Net cash value ($28,000 total value less $15,000 policy loan) | 13,000 |
> | Total surrender value | $28,000 |

> Basis

> | | |
> |---|---|
> | Premium paid | $24,000 |
> | Minus dividends | 4,000 |
> | Total basis | $20,000 |

> Taxable Gain

> | | |
> |---|---|
> | Surrender value | $28,000 |
> | Minus basis | 20,000 |
> | Taxable gain | $ 8,000 |

The so-called inside buildup (cash value or investment fund) of a permanent life insurance policy is not subject to taxation as long as it is left inside the policy. Loans from a policy are not taxable unless the policy is a modified endowment contract. If a policyowner withdraws funds from a policy's cash value, the general rule is that the withdrawal is first treated as a nontaxable return of basis. The excess, if any, of the amount of the withdrawal over the policyowner's current basis is taxable in the year of withdrawal. However, there are important exceptions to this general rule. These exceptions include certain withdrawals from universal life policies and withdrawals from policies classified as modified endowment contracts.

If a withdrawal is made from a policy that results in a reduction in the policy's death benefit during the first 15 years of the policy, the withdrawal may first be taxed as income to the extent of income earned within the contract.[3] A death benefit reduction resulting from a cash value withdrawal typically occurs in a universal life contract. This "income first" or LIFO (last in, first out) method of taxation is the reverse of the general rule of "basis first" or FIFO (first in, first out) taxation that life insurance typically enjoys. In addition, unfavorable LIFO tax treatment is the rule with respect to withdrawals and loans from policies that are classified as modified endowment contracts.

Modified Endowment Contracts (MECs)

Any life insurance policy that falls under the definition of a MEC is subject to an income first or LIFO tax treatment with respect to loans and most distributions from the policy. A 10 percent penalty tax also generally applies to the taxable portion of any loan or withdrawal from a MEC unless the taxpayer has reached age 59 1/2.[4] With respect to loans (not withdrawals) from a MEC, the policyowner does receive an increase in basis in the policy equal to the amount of the loan that is taxable. However, as shown in the example below, the nontaxable portion of a loan from a MEC will not affect the policyowner's basis. A nontaxable portion of a withdrawal, on the other hand, will reduce basis.

> *Example:* Assume that Mark Sellers' policy in the previous example is a MEC and that the $15,000 loan from the policy is taken out this year. Mark has a total of $8,000 in untaxed gain in the policy. The loan will first be treated as a distribution of that untaxed gain to the extent of $8,000. The remaining $7,000 of the loan is not taxable to Mark. The $8,000 taxable portion of the loan will also be subject to the 10 percent penalty tax because Mark is under age 59 1/2. Mark's basis in the policy will be increased by $8,000 (the taxable portion of the loan). Therefore Mark's basis is now $28,000 ($20,000 + $8,000).

A policy will be treated as a MEC if it fails a test called the "7-pay test."[5] This test is applied at the inception of the policy and again if the policy experiences a "material change." A material change generally includes most increases and certain decreases in future benefits under a policy. A common example of a material change is an increase in death benefits under the policy resulting from a flexible premium payment.

The 7-pay test is designed to impose MEC status on policies that take in too much premium during the first 7 policy years, or in the 7 years after a material change. For each policy a "net level premium" is calculated. If the total premium actually paid into the policy at any time during the 7-year testing period is more than the sum of the net level premiums that would be needed to result in a paid-up policy after 7 years, the policy will be a MEC. Stated simply, the 7-pay test is designed to discourage a premium schedule that would result in a paid-up policy before the end of a 7-year period.

There are many specific rules regarding MECs, including effective date and grandfathering provisions, rules designed to prevent certain tax avoidance techniques, and modest relief provisions for certain situations. These rules are quite involved and are beyond the scope of this chapter.

Nontaxable Policy Exchanges

In cases where a policyowner is merely continuing his or her investment in a life insurance or annuity contract by exchanging one contract for another, the tax law provides that the exchange will not result in a taxable event for income tax purposes. This "nonrecognition" provision under IRC Sec. 1035 applies to exchanges of a life insurance contract for another life insurance contract or an annuity contract and to exchanges of one annuity contract for another annuity. Exchanges of annuity contracts for life contracts are not protected by this nonrecognition provision.

If a policyowner takes advantage of the nontaxable exchange provision, his or her basis in the new policy is generally the same as his or her basis in the old policy. If the policyowner receives cash as part of the exchange, the exchange will be partially taxable. The taxable amount is the lesser of the cash received or the untaxed gain in the old policy.

In order for the favorable nonrecognition treatment to apply, both the old and the new contracts must relate to the same insured. Note that losses from the sale, exchange, or surrender of life insurance policies are not deductible in any event.

DEDUCTIBILITY OF PREMIUM PAYMENTS

The general rule is that premium payments for life insurance policies are not deductible for federal income tax purposes. This rule generally applies regardless of who owns the policy or whether it is used for personal or for business purposes. However, in certain situations life insurance premiums may be deductible. In these situations, the premiums are deductible because they also fit the definition of some other type of deductible expense, not because they are premium payments. For example, a premium payment for a policy owned by a charitable organization is deductible by the payor if the charity owns the policy outright. The premium is deductible because it is treated as a charitable contribution, not because it is a life insurance premium. Similarly, in cases where a corporation pays the premium on a policy covering an employee and the death benefit is payable to the employee's beneficiary, the premium may be deductible as compensation paid to the employee. Note, however, that the Internal Revenue Code specifically disallows deductions for premium payments whenever the corporation is directly or indirectly a beneficiary under the policy, regardless of any other rule that might otherwise permit a deduction.[6]

Other situations in which premium payments may fit the definition of a particular deductible expense include premium payments made on behalf of an ex-spouse (alimony) and certain premiums paid by a lender pursuant to a loan arrangement.

In summary, there are two important concepts to remember when determining the deductibility of a life insurance premium payment. The first is the general rule that premium payments are nondeductible. The second is that a deduction can sometimes be obtained for a premium if the premium can be properly characterized as some other specific type of deductible expense under the Internal Revenue Code. This determination will usually require a substantial knowledge of tax law, and the advice of a competent tax professional should be sought.

INCOME TAXATION OF ANNUITY CONTRACTS

Although the income tax rules regarding annuity contracts[7] have been tightened over the past several years, annuities still enjoy a significant tax advantage as vehicles for long-term investment planning and retirement planning. The primary tax advantage is that the amount invested in the annuity contract accumulates on a tax-deferred basis. That means that the income earned on the contract is not taxable until it is received by the contract beneficiary. However, if the annuity contract is held by a taxpayer other than a natural person (such as a trust or corporation) the tax deferral feature will be lost unless the entity holds the contract as an agent for a natural person.

The income taxation of amounts received under an annuity contract involves the taxation of the contract at two separate stages: first, during the accumulation period before the annuity benefit starting date, and second, during the period of actual annuity benefit payments under the contract.

Payments before the Annuity Starting Date

The general rule for taxation of amounts received as loans and withdrawals before the annuity starting date is that such amounts will be taxable to the extent of income earned on the contract. This treatment represents a LIFO type of tax treatment similar to that applied to life insurance policies that are classified as modified endowment contracts. In addition, a 10 percent penalty will generally apply to the taxable portion of such payments, unless the payments are made after the taxpayer reaches the age of 59 1/2 or are made by reason of the taxpayer's death or disability.

It is important to note that if the taxpayer's entire investment in the annuity was made prior to August 14, 1982, he or she may receive amounts before the annuity starting date and treat those amounts as a nontaxable return of his or her investment until the amount received exceeds the taxpayer's basis in the contract. This FIFO method of taxation was the general rule until 1982 tax legislation changed it. Existing contracts were grandfathered by that legislation.

For annuity contracts in which the taxpayer made investments both before August 14, 1982, and after August 13, 1982, income in the contract must be allocated to the appropriate investment period. All income attributable to pre-August 14, 1982, investments receives FIFO tax treatment, and income attributable to post-August 13, 1982, investments receives LIFO tax treatment.[8] These rules generally apply to loans from the contract as well as withdrawals.

Taxation of Amounts Received As an Annuity

To determine the taxation of annuity payments during the actual period when the contract is annuitized, the so-called exclusion ratio applicable to the specific contract must be calculated. The exclusion ratio is the ratio of the amount invested in the contract to the total amount expected to be received under the contract. This fraction is then multiplied by the amount of each annuity payment to determine the amount that represents a nontaxable return of the taxpayer's investment (the excludible amount). The balance of the annuity payment is includible in the taxpayer's gross income.

> *Example:* Lynda Komav purchased a deferred annuity many years ago. The annuity benefit payments are scheduled to begin this year. The annual payment to Lynda is $10,000. Lynda's investment in the annuity is $80,000. The total amount expected to be received under the contract is $200,000. Her exclusion ratio is 40 percent ($80,000 + $200,000). Therefore $4,000 of each $10,000 payment is excludible from Lynda's gross income ($10,000 x .40).

The amount invested in the contract is generally the premium paid minus previous nontaxable distributions, if any. If the annuity provides a period certain or other guarantee feature, the actuarial value of that feature must be subtracted from the amount invested to determine the exclusion ratio.

The amount expected to be received (expected return) under the annuity must also be calculated. If the annuity payments are to be made for the life of an individual, the life expectancy tables in the Treasury regulations must be used to calculate the expected return.[9] If the annuity is for a fixed period of time, the total annuity payments to be received represent the expected return. Special rules apply to the calculation of the exclusion ratio for equity-based (variable) annuity contracts.

Current tax law provides that the full amount of the annuity payment will be includible in the recipient's gross income once the total of the excludible portion of each payment received equals the taxpayer's investment in the contract. At that point, basis has been fully recovered. If the taxpayer dies before basis is fully recovered, a deduction is available for the unrecovered basis on the taxpayer's final return. However, if the annuity benefit starting date was before January 1, 1987, a life beneficiary is permitted to use his or her exclusion ratio for life, regardless of whether the total tax-free amounts received are more or less than the taxpayer's investment in the contract. Correspondingly, no deduction is allowable in such cases if the beneficiary dies before basis is fully recovered.

LIFE INSURANCE IN ESTATE PLANNING

Life insurance planning is an essential component of the estate planning process for wealthy individuals. For individuals of modest wealth, life insurance coverage often represents the most significant asset left to beloved heirs. Because of the relative importance of life insurance in an individual's estate plan, it is critical that life insurance planning be performed appropriately.

In this chapter, we first discussed the income tax treatment of life insurance products. Our discussion now focuses on the uses of life insurance for transfer tax planning purposes. First, we will provide a brief overview of the transfer tax system. Second, we will explain the general transfer tax treatment of life insurance products. This includes the federal transfer taxes and death taxes imposed by the various states. Third, we will discuss the basic purposes of life insurance in an individual's estate plan. Finally, we will review some practical planning applications for life insurance in the estate planning process.

THE FEDERAL TRANSFER TAX SYSTEM

The federal tax system consists of three components — gift taxes, estate taxes, and generation-skipping-taxes. The federal estate and gift taxes are separate tax systems imposed on different types of transfers, but the systems are unified with respect to tax brackets and tax base (see table 11-1). The generation-skipping transfer taxes are separate taxes applied under different rules in addition to any applicable estate or gift taxes.

TABLE 11-1
Marginal Federal Tax Rates for Estate Taxes and Gift Taxes

Amount Subject to Tax	Tax Rate	Amount Subject to Tax	Tax Rate
$10,000	18%	>$500,000 – <$750,000	37%
>$10,000 – <$20,000	20%	>$750,000 – <$1,000,000	39%
>$20,000 – <$40,000	22%	>$1,000,000 – <$1,250,000	41%
>$40,000 – <$60,000	24%	>$1,250,000 – <$1,500,000	43%
>$60,000 – <$80,000	26%	>$1,500,000 – <$2,000,000	45%
>$80,000 – <$100,000	28%	>$2,000,000 – <$2,500,000	49%
>$100,000 – <$150,000	30%	>$2,500,000 – <$3,000,000	53%
>$150,000 – <$250,000	32%	>$3,000,000	55%
>$250,000 – <$500,000	34%	>$10,000,000 – <$21,040,000	add 5%

Source: Sec. 2001 of Internal Revenue Code

Federal Gift Taxes

Federal gift taxes will apply only if both of the following two elements are present:

- There is a completed transfer and acceptance of *property*.
- The transfer was for less than full and adequate consideration.

The essential elements of a taxable gift reveal some noteworthy facts. First, only property transfers are subject to gift taxation. Thus, the transfer of services by an individual is not a taxable gift. Second, the taxation of a transfer does not require an element of donative intent; simply a transfer must be made for less than full consideration.

Exempt Transfers

Certain transfers are exempt from the gift tax base by statute. First, a transfer of property pursuant to a divorce or property settlement agreement is deemed to be for a full and adequate consideration under some circumstances. Second, transfers directly to the provider of education or medical services on behalf of an individual are not taxable gifts to the recipient of the services. Finally, gifts that are disclaimed by the donee in a qualified disclaimer are not treated as taxable gifts.

The Annual Exclusion

Much of the planning and complexity associated with gift planning involves the annual exclusion. Qualifying gifts of $10,000 or less may be made annually by a donor to any number of donees without gift tax. The exempt amount can be increased to $20,000 if the donor is married and the donor's spouse elects to split gifts on a timely filed gift tax return.

To qualify for an annual exclusion, the gift must provide the donee with a present interest. Outright interests or current income interests in a trust will provide the beneficiary with a present interest. Trust provisions providing the beneficiaries with current withdrawal powers can be used to qualify gifts to a trust for an annual exclusion even if the trusts provide for deferred benefits. Use of the annual exclusion in the transfer of life insurance products is discussed below.

Deductions from the Gift Tax Base

Two types of gifts are fully deductible from the transfer tax base. First, the *marital deduction* provides that unlimited qualifying transfers made by a donor to his or her spouse are fully deductible from the gift tax base. The marital deduction will prove quite useful if it is necessary to rearrange ownership of marital assets in the implementation of the estate plan. This deduction is similar to the marital deduction against federal estate taxes discussed later.

The *charitable deduction* provides that qualifying transfers to a legitimate charity will be deductible against the gift tax base. Thus, all qualifying donations will avoid gift tax.

The Unified Credit

A cumulative credit of $192,800 is currently available against federal gift tax due on taxable transfers. Under the unified nature of the federal estate and gift taxes, this credit provides a dollar-for-dollar reduction of transfer tax otherwise payable against taxable transfers either during lifetime or at death or both. The credit of $192,800 can be used against each dollar of transfer tax until it is exhausted. The tax credit of $192,800 is equivalent to an exemption of $600,000 of taxable transfers from the federal estate or gift tax. Thus, the credit is often casually referred to as the $600,000 unified credit. Since no taxes are due on transfers until aggregate transfers by the donor have exceeded $600,000, the first tax rate bracket applicable to a transfer actually subject to tax is 37 percent. The unified credit is discussed further below.

The Federal Estate Tax

The most difficult task in calculating the estate tax is often determining the assets that are included in the decedent's estate tax base. Some of the included assets are obvious, such as individually owned property. But the estate tax rules often cause the inclusion of property in surprising circumstances. For example, property previously transferred by a decedent can be brought back to the estate tax base by provisions of the statute.

The Gross Estate

The starting point in the federal estate tax calculation is determining the property included in the decedent's gross estate.[10] It includes the property included in the probate estate, which is all property that passes under the deceased's will or, in the absence of a valid will, under the state intestacy law, but it also includes property transferable by the decedent at death by other means. The gross estate of the decedent includes the following:

- property individually owned by the decedent at the time of death
- (some portion of) property held jointly by the decedent at the time of death
- insurance on the decedent's life if either (1) incidents of ownership were held by the decedent or transferred by gift within 3 years of death or (2) the proceeds are deemed payable to the estate
- pension or IRA payments left to survivors
- property subject to general powers of appointment held by the decedent at the time of death
- property transferred by the decedent during his or her lifetime if the decedent retained (1) a life interest in the property, (2) a reversionary interest valued greater than 5 percent of the property at the time of death, or (3) rights to revoke or amend the transfer at the time of death

As the list above indicates, the gross estate of the decedent is defined much more broadly than the probate estate, and the reduction of just the probate estate will often have very little effect on the size of the federal estate tax paid.

Items Deductible from the Gross Estate

Certain items are deductible from the gross estate for estate tax calculation purposes. First, legitimate debts of the decedent are deductible from the gross estate if these debts are obligations of the gross estate. Second, reasonable funeral and other death costs of the decedent are deductible from the gross estate. Third, the costs of estate settlement such as the executor's commission and attorney fees are deductible to the extent such fees are reasonable.

Marital Deduction. As with the gift tax, qualifying transfers to a surviving spouse are deductible under the marital-deduction rules. Since the marital deduction is unlimited, the usual dispositive scheme (100 percent to the surviving spouse) for married individuals will result in no federal death taxes for a married couple until the death of the survivor of the two spouses. As a client's wealth increases, sophisticated planning is needed to make optimal use of the marital deduction. Planning for the marital deduction for life insurance proceeds will be discussed later in this chapter.

Charitable Deduction. As discussed earlier, the federal estate tax charitable deduction provides that transfers at death to qualifying charities will be fully deductible from the estate tax base. The charitable deduction is an excellent device to reduce the gross estate of a wealthy individual.

Credits against the Estate Tax

The unified credit discussed above with respect to gift taxes is similarly applicable to transfers occurring at death. If the unified credit has not been exhausted to shelter lifetime gifts, it is available against transfers made at the death of a decedent.

The state death tax credit provides a dollar-for-dollar reduction (with certain limits) against federal estate tax due for any state death taxes paid by the estate. The state death tax credit is limited, and the maximum state death tax credit available to a particular estate is provided for by a progressive rate schedule in the federal tax code. The size of the credit against the federal estate tax is equal to the lesser of the state death tax actually paid or the maximum state death tax allowable under the progressive credit schedule. State death taxes are usually equal to at least the maximum state death tax allowable under the federal estate tax rules.

Generation-Skipping Transfer Tax (GSTT)

The GSTT was created by the Tax Reform Act of 1986. Its purpose is to prevent the federal government from losing transfer tax if a transferor attempts to skip one generation's level of transfer tax by transferring property to a generation more than one generation below the level of the transferor (for example, a grandparent makes a gift of property to a grandchild). Although the GSTT is designed to prevent a transferor from finding a transfer tax loophole in the federal estate and gift tax systems, it is different from the unified estate and gift tax system in many ways. The GSTT is applied at a flat rate equal to the highest current estate or gift tax bracket on every taxable generation-skipping transfer. Thus any taxable transfers will be currently subject to a 55 percent rate if the GSTT applies. This GSTT is applicable in addition to any estate or gift tax that might otherwise be applicable to the transfer. Thus if the GSTT applies, a transfer could easily be subject to a tax rate in excess of 100 percent of the value of the asset transfer.

The GSTT applies to three different types of transfers. First, the GSTT applies to a *direct skip* that is an outright transfer during life or at death to an individual who is more than one generation below the transferor. The direct skip gift tax applies only if the parents of the skip beneficiary are alive at the time of the direct skip.

The GSTT is also applicable to a *taxable distribution*. A taxable distribution is a distribution of either income or principal from a trust to a person more than one generation below the level of the trust grantor. The recipient of the taxable distribution is a skip beneficiary of the trust. Thus, a taxable distribution can occur when a trustee makes a distribution to a skip beneficiary even if a nonskip beneficiary still holds a current beneficial interest in the trust.

Finally, a *taxable termination* is also subject to a GSTT. A taxable termination occurs when there is a termination of a property interest held in trust by death, lapse of time, or otherwise, and a skip beneficiary receives the remainder interest outright in the trust.

There is a cumulative $1 million exemption against GSTT for all generation-skipping transfers of an individual. The exemption can be applied against transfers during life or at death. A married individual can split gifts and make up to $2 million total of generation-skipping transfers without GSTT. The exemption should be affirmatively allocated to specific transfers in the gift or estate tax return of the transferor. Otherwise, the GSTT rules provide a default mechanism for allocating the exemption to transfers at an individual's death, which will often result in less than optimal use of the exemption.

TRANSFER TAX IMPLICATIONS OF LIFE INSURANCE

The financial services professional involved in life insurance planning must thoroughly understand the estate, gift, and generation-skipping transfer tax implications of life insurance. Often life insurance planning is specifically driven by the need to provide solutions to the client's estate planning problems. As we discussed earlier in this chapter, unique tax advantages usually exempt life insurance policy cash value build-up and death benefits from income taxes. Thus the potential *transfer* taxes applicable to life insurance proceeds become the most significant tax costs facing the insured and his or her family.

FEDERAL GIFT TAXATION OF LIFE INSURANCE TRANSFERS

Gifts of life insurance are treated in the same manner as gifts of any other asset as far as the $10,000 annual exclusion or the gift tax provisions. That is, the outright gift of a policy is a transfer of property that provides a present interest and is subject to gift taxes when the transfer is made.

Valuation of Life Insurance Policies

To thoroughly understand all the ramifications of federal gift taxation triggered by transferring a life insurance policy for "insufficient consideration in money or money's worth," it is useful to review the principles of life insurance policy valuation. The value of the policy at the time of the gift becomes the tax base of the transfer for gift tax purposes.

The value of a life policy that has been gifted depends on the type of policy and the timing of the transfer. Gift and estate tax regulations provide a method for determining the value of a policy.

If the policy is paid up at the time it is transferred (or is a single-premium policy), the gift tax value of the policy is the amount of premium the issuing insurer would charge as a single premium for the same type of policy of equal face amount on the insured's life, based on the insured's age at the transfer date. An insured's impaired health is not addressed by the Treasury regulations, but the IRS has argued that the insured's adverse health at the time of the policy gift increases its valuation.

If the policy is in a premium-paying state at the time it is transferred, the gift tax value of the gift is generally equal to the sum of (1) the interpolated terminal reserve and (2) the unearned premium on the date of the gift.

> *Example:* Mr. Smythe owns a policy with a face amount of $1 million on his life. He gives the policy to his daughter on July 1st of this year. The policy reserve was $50,000 on December 31st of last year. The policy reserve will grow to $70,000 at the end of this year.
>
> If Mr. Smythe made a timely premium payment of $15,000 on January 1 of this year, the value of the policy at the time of the gift is determined as follows:
>
> | | |
> |---|---:|
> | The terminal reserve at the end of the current year | $70,000 |
> | The terminal reserve at the end of last year | −50,000 |
> | The increase in the terminal reserve over the current year | $20,000 |
>
> •   •   •   •   •
>
> | | |
> |---|---:|
> | One-half of the increase in the terminal reserve (the increase in terminal reserve at the time of the gift halfway through the year) | $10,000 |
> | The terminal reserve at the end of last year | +50,000 |
> | Interpolated terminal reserve | $60,000 |
>
> •   •   •   •   •
>
> | | |
> |---|---:|
> | The interpolated terminal reserve | $60,000 |
> | One-half annual premium (amount unearned at the time of gift) | +7,500 |
> | Value of policy at the time of gift | $67,500 |

Often a donor will continue to pay annual premiums, even after an absolute transfer of the insurance has been made. Each premium paid subsequent to the policy's transfer is considered a gift. As long as the transfer is outright to a donee, the gift of the policy is one of a "present interest." Therefore, the $10,000 annual gift tax exclusion will be applicable, not only to the gift of the policy itself but also to the gift of each premium payment as it is made. However, when gifts of life insurance policies are made in trust, the exclusion is forfeited unless the donee has at least a temporary unrestricted power of withdrawal over the property transferred to the trust.

The Problem of Inadvertent Gifts

Sometimes there is an inadvertent gift of life insurance policy proceeds. This can happen when a policy that is owned by one individual on another's life matures by reason of the insured's death and a person other than the policyowner has been named as beneficiary. For example, if a wife purchases a policy on her husband's life and names her children as beneficiaries, the proceeds that otherwise would have been payable to her are payable instead to her children at her husband's death. The transaction is treated as if the policyowner (the wife) had received the proceeds and made a gift in that amount to her children. Moreover, gift splitting is not allowed, since there is no longer a spouse with whom to split the gift.

FEDERAL ESTATE TAXATION OF LIFE INSURANCE

The most fundamental issue associated with estate planning with life insurance products is whether the death benefits will be subject to federal estate taxation. Estate taxes are payable on property included in a decedent's gross estate if the decedent's estate exceeds the available deductions and credits. Frequently, life insurance is the single largest asset or group of assets in the gross estate. Including life insurance can often mean the difference between a federal estate tax liability and no tax liability. For this reason, we should look at the factors that determine when life insurance is included in the decedent-insured's gross estate for federal estate tax purposes:

- Life insurance proceeds payable to the executor (that is, to or for the benefit of an insured's estate) are includible in the estate, regardless of who owned the contract or who paid the premiums.
- A policy is included in the estate of an insured if he or she possessed an incident of ownership in the policy at the time of his or her death.
- Because of the unique rules of Sec. 2035, life insurance is included in the gross estate of an insured who transferred incidents of ownership in the policy by *gift* within 3 years of his or her death.

Life Insurance Payable to an Estate

In general, life insurance should not be payable to a decedent's estate. There are many reasons in addition to avoiding federal estate taxation why estate planners seldom recommend such a beneficiary designation. These reasons include the following:

- Insurance payable to a decedent's estate subjects the proceeds to the claims of creditors.
- Insurance payable to a decedent's estate subjects the proceeds to costs of probate administration such as executor's fees but provides no corresponding advantages.
- In some states, life insurance proceeds, otherwise exempt from state death taxes (either fully or partially) if payable to a named beneficiary, become subject to such taxes if they are payable to the decedent-insured's estate.

In some instances, death benefits payable to named beneficiaries are included in an insured's gross estate if the proceeds can or must be used to pay settlement costs. Proceeds payable to a named beneficiary (such as a trustee) are includible in the insured's gross estate if the beneficiary has a legal obligation to use the proceeds to pay the settlement costs for the estate. For example, life insurance used as collateral for a loan is payable to the estate to the extent that the loan is a debt of the estate.

Failure to make an effective beneficiary designation could also cause the proceeds to be payable to the estate.

> *Example:* Mr. Jones is the designated beneficiary of his wife's life insurance policy. Mr. Jones murders his wife and because of the "slayer's statute" under state law, he cannot collect the proceeds. If no contingent beneficiary is named, the proceeds are returned to the estate, and they are subject to probate expenses and inclusion in Mrs. Jones's gross estate for federal estate tax purposes.

It should be noted that life insurance is includible in the gross estate, as discussed below, if the insured held any incidents of ownership at the time of death whether or not such policy is payable to the estate. Thus it may not cause any additional harm from an estate tax standpoint if the policy is paid to the estate. However, in instances where the insured did *not* own incidents of ownership, it is critical to avoid having the proceeds deemed payable to the insured's estate.

Possession of Incidents of Ownership

When insurance proceeds are paid to a named beneficiary other than the insured's estate, incidents of ownership in the policy at the time of death are the key criteria for determining inclusion. If the insured held an incident of ownership at the time of his or her death, the policy will be included in his or her gross estate. An incident of ownership is broadly defined for this purpose as any right to the economic benefits of the policy. The regulations provide that incidents of ownership include (but are not limited to) the power to

- change the beneficiary
- assign the policy
- borrow on the policy
- surrender the policy
- exercise any of the other essential contract rights or privileges

Like any other property, the insurance policy is an asset that may be freely assigned by a policyowner in a gift or sale. Thus, it is possible for the policyowner to transfer all right, title, and interest to any other individual or entity. It is also possible to transfer limited interests to others while retaining some of the privileges and rights in the policy. But to remove the proceeds from the scope of the federal estate tax, the insured must divest himself or herself of all significant rights and privileges under the contract.

The issue of incidents of ownership has been involved in a great deal of litigation over the years. This is because the facts and circumstances of a particular situation are often unusual and cannot be easily categorized into one of the traditional ownership rights. In many cases, inclusion will occur even if the insured is unaware that such incidents are held or is incapable of exercising the incidents.

The discussion below is not intended to be an exhaustive survey of all possible scenarios, but it will offer some guidance in using life insurance in many estate and business planning situations. The scenarios that follow examine some hidden incidents of ownership after the client has effectively transferred all *traditional* ownership rights to a life insurance policy.

Incidents Held by the Insured in a Fiduciary Capacity

The IRS's position is that an incident of ownership that can be exercised by the insured as trustee will cause the policy to be included in the insured's gross estate. This rule applies even if the insured is *not* a beneficiary of the trust. This is a unique treatment of life insurance as an asset of the estate. In many other circumstances, the trustee is not deemed to control an asset (other than life insurance) personally if ownership rights can be exercised only in favor of the beneficiaries.

It seems clear, therefore, that the insured should not gift a policy on his or her life to a trust in which the insured will be trustee even if the trust is irrevocable and the insured cannot benefit. The mere participation of the insured as fiduciary is enough to cause inclusion of the death proceeds in such insured's gross estate for tax purposes.

Power of the Insured to Replace the Trustee of a Life Insurance Trust. One recurring problem is whether the ability of the grantor (creator) of the irrevocable life insurance trust to substitute trustees is an incident of ownership.[11] The IRS has made its position clear on this issue. The IRS has held that a grantor's unqualified power to remove and replace the trustee of a life insurance trust was a retention of the powers of the trustee (including the exercise of incidents of ownership) and has compelled inclusion of the policy proceeds if the insured merely possesses the right to replace one independent trustee with another.

Right or Option to Repurchase Policy

Several recent rulings have addressed the issue of whether the retention of the right or option to repurchase a policy will cause its inclusion in the insured's gross estate. The cases have involved different facts and circumstances. In one, the insured retained the right to repurchase the policy after making a gift of the policy to a third party. In others, business life insurance used to fund buy-sell agreements was subject to contingent repurchase options.

The IRS's position in these rulings is that an unrestricted right or option to repurchase the policy is an incident of ownership. However, an option to repurchase the policy subject to a contingency beyond the insured's control does not create an incident of ownership unless the contingency has occurred and the option is available at the time of the insured's death.

Incidents Attributed to Business Owner

The regulations provide that incidents of ownership held by a corporation will, in some circumstances, be attributed to a majority shareholder. Thus, corporate-owned life insurance may cause estate tax problems for an insured shareholder. The incidents are attributed if (1) the corporation owns life insurance on the life of a controlling (greater than 50 percent voting power) shareholder, and (2) the benefits are *not* payable to, or for the benefit of, the corporation. The IRS has published an analogous ruling for general partnerships causing inclusion in a partner's estate if a partnership-owned policy on the partner's life is not payable to the partnership.

The regulations offer some guidance as to what is meant by "payable to or for the benefit of the corporation." Life insurance payable to the corporation to fund a corporate need will *not* cause incidents to be attributed to the insured. Examples of corporate-owned life insurance used to meet corporate needs include the following:

- key person coverage
- funding for stock-redemption agreements
- funding for deferred-compensation plans

Life insurance is also deemed payable for the benefit of the corporation, in some instances, even if it is payable to a third party. For example, life insurance payable to satisfy a business debt will not cause corporate incidents to be attributed to the insured-shareholder. It is not unusual for a creditor to require insurance on a key person when loaning funds to a corporation. Insurance purchased by the corporation on a majority shareholder's life for this purpose will not cause inclusion in the shareholder's estate. However, the value of the stock held by the decedent *will* increase for estate tax purposes to the extent that the corporation's debt is satisfied.

Transfers of Policies within 3 Years of Death

Policies are often transferred to others so that they will not be in the decedent-insured's gross estate. Inclusion will still result, however, if the insured dies within 3 years of a gratuitous transfer.[12] Under this 3-year rule, life insurance transferred to a third party for less than full consideration within 3 years of an insured's death is automatically includible in the insured's gross estate. Transfers made more than 3 years before the insured's death are not normally includible in the insured's estate if the insured has retained no incidents of ownership. In addition, *sales* to a third party for the full fair market value of the policy will not be included even if the sale occurs within 3 years of the insured's death.

Most of the disputes and litigation between the taxpayer and the IRS on this issue have involved the question of whether a transfer of the policy has occurred. Usually, these have been cases in which a third party, such as a family member or life insurance trust, has applied for and owned the policy covering the decedent's life. Generally, the IRS has attempted to treat the third-party owner as an agent of the insured for the purpose of acquiring the life insurance by applying the "constructive transfer" theory to the transaction. That is, the IRS has treated the insured as the original owner who is deemed to have transferred the policy to the third-party owner at the time application is made for the policy by the third party.

The IRS has been largely unsuccessful in litigating these cases because the courts have given the term "transfer" its traditional meaning. Following its loss in a recent circuit court case, the IRS announced that it will no longer litigate life insurance cases where the policy covering the decedent's life was owned and applied for by a third party.[13] Thus, inclusion of a life insurance policy in the decedent's estate will be avoided if a third party applies for and owns the policy covering the decedent's life, even if the decedent makes premium payments within 3 years of his or her death. (Of course, such premium payments are gifts by the insured and may be taxable under the gift tax rules.)

Life Insurance and the Federal Estate Tax Marital Deduction

Life insurance proceeds payable at the insured's death to the insured's surviving spouse can qualify for the federal estate tax marital deduction. Since the marital deduction is unlimited, the full value of life insurance proceeds payable in a qualifying manner to the surviving spouse will be deductible from the insured's gross estate.

The federal estate tax marital deduction is available only under the following circumstances:

- The property in question must be included in the decedent's gross estate.
- The property in question must pass or have passed from the decedent to the surviving spouse.
- The surviving spouse must be a citizen of the United States. (Property left to a resident alien will qualify for the marital deduction only if the property is payable or assigned in a timely fashion to a qualified domestic trust.)
- The property in question left to the surviving spouse must not provide a nondeductible terminable interest. A life interest in property left to a surviving spouse will qualify only if (1) the remainder following the life interest is payable to the surviving spouse's estate, (2) the surviving spouse has a general power of appointment over the property subject to the life interest at the time of his or her death, or (3) the executor of the deceased spouse's estate makes the qualifying terminal interest property (QTIP) election.[14]

Under these rules, life insurance proceeds payable outright to a citizen surviving spouse as named beneficiary will qualify for the marital deduction. If the proceeds are payable to the insured's estate, the proceeds will qualify for the marital deduction if the surviving spouse receives the proceeds under the terms of the decedent's will or the state intestacy statute.

Qualification for the marital deduction becomes more complicated if the surviving spouse does not receive the proceeds outright. For example, life insurance proceeds payable to a surviving spouse under available settlement options may or may not qualify for the marital deduction. Some settlement options terminate payment at the surviving spouse's death. If the remaining payments are not payable to the surviving spouse's estate or subject to the surviving spouse's control, the marital deduction will not be available unless the estate is eligible to make the qualified terminable interest property (QTIP) election.

If the proceeds of a life insurance policy are payable to a trust benefiting the surviving spouse, qualification will depend on whether the trust otherwise qualifies for the federal estate tax marital deduction. Thus, the marital deduction depends on whether the trust provides all income to the surviving spouse and the remainder interest is payable to the surviving spouse's estate or subject to the surviving spouse's general power of appointment. Absent such provisions, the trust can qualify only if the deceased spouse's executor makes the QTIP election.

Value of the Policy Includible in the Gross Estate

Policies on the Life of the Decedent

If a life insurance policy must be included in the decedent-insured's gross estate for federal estate tax purposes, the amount that is included is the *face amount* of the policy. The face amount is the death benefit adjusted by (1) deducting any policy loan or other encumbrance and (2) adding any accrued or terminal dividends.

Policies Owned by a Decedent on the Lives of Others

Under third-party ownership of life insurance, which has become extremely popular for estate planning, it is quite possible that a policyowner will die before the actual insured. When this happens, a life insurance policy is treated the same way as any other property the decedent owned at the time of death. That is, the policy is included in the decedent's gross estate at its fair market value determined in the same manner as discussed above with respect to determining the gift tax value of the policy.

Responsibility for Payment of Federal Estate Taxes by Life Insurance Beneficiaries

Federal estate taxes attributable to life insurance proceeds included in the decedent's gross estate will be recoverable by the executor from the beneficiary of the life insurance policy unless the decedent's will provides a contrary provision for tax apportionment.[15] This rule ensures that an executor will be able to collect estate taxes caused by life insurance even though the life insurance is paid to a named beneficiary and is not subject to the executor's control.

FEDERAL GENERATION-SKIPPING TRANSFER TAXATION OF LIFE INSURANCE PRODUCTS

Life insurance is subject to the federal generation-skipping transfer tax (GSTT) in some circumstances. As explain earlier, the GSTT is a particularly burdensome tax since it is applied (1) in addition to the federal estate or gift tax applicable to a transfer and (2) at the highest marginal transfer tax rate. Life insurance proceeds that are payable directly to, or may someday benefit, skip persons might be subject to the GSTT.

Direct-Skip Transfers

A direct-skip transfer, as previously discussed, involves a gift or bequest of property directly to a skip person, such as a gift from a grandparent to a grandchild. With life insurance, a direct-skip transfer could involve the payment of policy proceeds on a grandparent's life to a grandchild as the named beneficiary. The GSTT could also be applied to a gift of the policy to a grandchild while the insured grandparent is still alive. The direct-skip rules exempt the skip beneficiary from the GSTT if his or her parent is deceased at the time of the transfer.

Taxable Distributions and Terminations

The GSTT implications of life insurance trusts are more common and, in all probability, more difficult to avoid. Since all individuals have a $1 million exemption from the GSTT, only sizable estates are generally affected. It is critical to avoid inadvertent problems that may result in the GSTT when employing life insurance trusts that *may* benefit skip persons.

The GSTT applies to trusts in two circumstances—taxable distributions and taxable terminations. A taxable distribution occurs if a distribution of trust income or principal is made to a skip (with respect to the grantor of the trust) beneficiary.

> *Example:* Mrs. Reece creates an irrevocable life insurance trust for the benefit of her children and grandchildren. At Mrs. Reece's death, the trustee is directed to hold the proceeds and to distribute as much income and principal to the various beneficiaries (a general sprinkle power) as the trustee determines in its sole discretion. If the trustee makes a distribution to any of Mrs. Reece's grandchildren, a taxable distribution has occurred for GSTT purposes.

A taxable termination occurs when either

- a trust terminates and all remainder persons are skip persons or
- all interests in the trust held by nonskip persons terminate

> *Example:* Assume the facts from the example above. Suppose Mrs. Reece had instead provided that the insurance proceeds would be held in trust for her children with all income payable annually to her children in equal shares. At the death of Mrs. Reece's last child, the trust will terminate, and the remainder will be distributed to her surviving grandchildren in equal shares. When Mrs. Reece's last child dies and the trust terminates, a taxable termination occurs.

PRACTICAL USES FOR LIFE INSURANCE IN THE ESTATE PLANNING CONTEXT

The goal of life insurance in the estate plan depends on many factors specific to the client. However, the goals for life insurance in general can be divided into two categories: Life insurance can serve either as an estate enhancement or as an estate liquidity/wealth replacement device. The goals of a specific client for his or her life insurance planning depend on his or her age, family circumstances, and financial status.

Estate Enhancement Purposes

A vast majority of individuals have the perception that their accumulated estate will not be as substantial as they would like at the time of their death. In many cases, a decedent's estate will not be sufficient to provide for the basic needs of his or her heirs. This is particularly true for (1) young clients, (2) clients with family members dependent on their income, and/or (3) clients with small to moderate-sized estates. These clients generally have estate enhancement as the primary goal for their life insurance coverage since they are either too young or have otherwise failed to accumulate sufficient wealth to provide for their heirs. Furthermore, these clients might have their peak earning years in front of them. The basic support needs of their family, such as educational, medical, and retirement savings programs, depend on this income. It is essential for these clients to investigate their life insurance coverage needs and secure sufficient insurance to enhance their estates to a size that is, at the very least, adequate to handle their dependent family members' basic needs. Since their death will cause the loss of income otherwise available to meet those basic needs, life insurance is the perfect estate enhancement device to replace the financial loss created by premature death.

Estate Liquidity/Wealth Replacement Purposes

For older clients or clients with large estates, estate liquidity/wealth replacement planning is the primary goal of life insurance coverage. Their children's support and educational expense needs are usually a thing of the past. In addition, these older clients are nearing the end of their income-producing years and should, presumably, have less income to replace. If they have accumulated enough wealth or have an adequate retirement plan, their needs for estate enhancement from life insurance should have diminished in importance relative to their estate liquidity/wealth replacement needs.

A prospective insured may need coverage for estate liquidity/wealth replacement for the following purposes:

- *Probate expenses.* Although clients with substantial accumulated wealth should have sufficient assets in their estate to provide for the basic needs of their heirs, life insurance planning for such individuals remains critical. Estate settlement costs usually increase with the size of the estate. The cost for professionals, such as executors, attorneys, accountants, and appraisers, to settle an estate is often based on a percentage of the total size of the probate estate. Generally, the larger the estate, the greater the complexity and need for costly professional help. One advantage of life insurance is that it avoids probate if paid to a named beneficiary.

- *Death taxes.* As discussed above, federal estate taxes, generation-skipping taxes, and state death taxes also increase with the size of the estate. The federal estate tax and state death taxes in many states are based on a progressive rate schedule. Larger estates are subject to higher transfer-tax brackets. Thus, wealthy individuals often desire life insurance to replace the wealth lost to death taxes.

- *Liquidity needs.* Wealthy clients often face an additional problem. Frequently, their accumulated wealth contains assets that are not liquid. For example, wealthy individuals often own closely held businesses that may be unmarketable to outsiders. Death taxes and other estate settlement costs are based on the full value of such assets owned by the estate and must be paid in cash. The liquidity problems faced by an estate often result in the forced sale of estate assets on undesirable terms.

The problems faced by wealthy individuals' estates and heirs can often be mitigated by life insurance. For these individuals, the goal of life insurance is estate liquidity or wealth replacement. The wealthy client can purchase life insurance to provide death proceeds equal to the size of the anticipated shrinkage of the estate for death taxes and other settlement costs. In addition, because the life insurance benefits are paid in cash, the estate can be settled immediately. Thus, the nonliquid assets can either be retained by the estate to distribute to family heirs or sold later when an appropriate buyer can be found.

Estate Planning Techniques with Life Insurance

Much of the discussion that follows concerns the appropriate design of life insurance for estate liquidity purposes. It is important to arrange life insurance coverage appropriately to solve individuals' estate liquidity problems. An inappropriate life insurance plan can lead to the inefficient use of life insurance as an asset in the estate plan. Improperly designed, life insurance will *add* to the estate's settlement costs.

There are many practical uses for life insurance in the estate planning context. We will now discuss the following:

- gifts of policies to family members
- gifts of policies to trusts
- providing estate liquidity
- providing equal shares to all heirs
- the second-to-die policy

Outright Gifts of Life Insurance Policies

Although the 3-year rule causes estate tax inclusion if the insured transfers incidents of ownership within 3 years of his or her death, transferring or assigning the policy to family members might still be an appropriate planning step. The insured simply has to live more than 3 years following the transfer to avoid inclusion of the proceeds in his or her gross estate. And even if the insured dies within 3 years, he or she will be no worse off from an estate tax standpoint since the policy would have been included in any event had the transfer or assignment not occurred.

There are many reasons why estate planners recommend a life insurance policy gifting program. Some of the reasons include the following:

- The donee feels no richer after receiving the life insurance policy and will seldom dispose of it foolishly.
- The donor-insured's financial position is not markedly affected by making a gift of life insurance.
- The gift tax cost to transfer a policy is usually nominal compared to the potential estate tax savings. Through efficient use of the donor-insured's annual exclusion, the gift of a policy and subsequent premiums may actually avoid gift taxes entirely.
- The gift of a life insurance policy is particularly advantageous for older donors whose estate planning concerns have risen in priority in relation to their other financial planning goals. Usually older insureds can select appropriate beneficiaries with more certainty, and they are less concerned about a policy's cash surrender value. If a life insurance policy is gifted more than 3 years before the donor's death, the transfer tax savings will be substantial.
- The gift of a new policy is perhaps the best estate planning gift available. The most appropriate method to design this gift is to permit a third party, such as the donor's child or an irrevocable trust, to apply for and own the insurance policy. The design and benefits of the life insurance trust will be covered later in this chapter.

Gifts of Policies to Trusts

Revocable Trusts

One useful estate planning device involves gifting a life insurance policy to a revocable trust. Although there are no tax benefits in using the revocable trust approach, the trust is advantageous because it provides asset management and dispositive flexibility. It should be noted, however, that revocable life insurance trusts do not offer protection from estate taxes, do not shift the burden of income taxes, and generally do not affect state death taxes.

The revocable trust works extremely well in cases where estate tax planning is not the life insurance plan's primary concern. For example, a young couple with minor children might find a revocable trust to be helpful in their plan. If the total family wealth (including policy death benefits) is less than the unified credit equivalent ($600,000), federal estate tax will be avoided, regardless of the life insurance plan design. Even if the couple's wealth exceeds $600,000, the unlimited marital deduction could shield the deceased spouse's estate from immediate taxes. Estate taxes will probably be deferred for many years unless *both* spouses die prematurely, an unlikely event. Under these circumstances, because the primary need for life insurance is estate enhancement, a revocable trust could be created to receive policy proceeds. At the death of the grantor-insured, the trust would become irrevocable. The trustee would then manage the proceeds for the surviving spouse, if necessary, and the minor children.

Irrevocable Life Insurance Trusts

If the insured is older and wealthier, and if larger policies are involved, setting up an irrevocable trust to serve as the owner and beneficiary of a life insurance policy is often recommended. Irrevocable life insurance trusts holding policies on the life of the grantor or his or her spouse offer attractive estate-tax-saving opportunities (even though trust income used to pay policy premiums may be taxed to the grantor for income tax purposes).

> *Example:* Jim Arena has a gross estate of $4.2 million. His estate planner estimates a total of $2 million in expenses and taxes to settle his estate. Jim sets up an irrevocable trust to purchase the insurance coverage of $2 million. The trust beneficiaries are Jim's five children and 10 grandchildren. Jim provides the trust with a gift of $75,000 annually to pay the policy premium. At the time each gift is made, each beneficiary is provided with the right to withdraw his or her share of the gift ($5,000). This withdrawal right lapses in 30 days. By providing such withdrawal rights (a so-called Crummey power), Jim is assured that the gifts qualify for the $10,000 annual gift tax exclusion. At the time of Jim's death, the proceeds payable to the trust will avoid estate taxes.

Providing Estate Liquidity

An irrevocable life insurance trust is often the best solution to an estate owner's liquidity problems.

Unless the executor of an estate wishes to go through a series of complex and burdensome requests for an extension, the tax due by an estate must be paid within 9 months of the date of death. If the gross estate is composed of liquid assets, the executor or administrator faces no problem in meeting the 9-month deadline successfully. For example, if the estate is composed of sufficient cash, marketable securities, or life insurance proceeds, there will be ample liquidity to ensure that the tax can be paid within the required time. Conversely, if the federal estate tax liability exceeds the amount of liquid assets available, there will be an estate liquidity deficit. To meet the 9-month deadline, a forced liquidation of assets—possibly at a loss—will be necessary.

Estate liquidity deficits frequently occur when a decedent owns a closely held business interest at the time of death. The fair market value of this asset must be included as part of the decedent's gross estate, which results in a higher federal estate tax liability.

Life insurance is the most effective way to supply needed dollars to meet federal estate tax obligations. First, the dollars, in the form of death proceeds, are free of federal income taxation. Second, if the life insurance is owned by someone (or some entity) other than the insured, the policy's face amount will not be included as part of the decedent's gross estate. Finally, the sizable death benefit may be purchased for pennies on the dollar in the form of premium payments.

Few situations are more tragic than a forced liquidation of a family business and other personal assets to pay federal estate taxes when the surviving family members depend on the income that is derived from the business. Life insurance is a viable way to assure a family that a forced liquidation for this purpose will never be necessary.

Providing Equal Shares to All Heirs

There are many estate planning situations in which it is the estate owner's wish to equalize inheritances among children.

A prime example is when an estate owner has brought some of his or her children into a family business and intends to provide these children with an ownership interest in the enterprise. The plan may be to pass the interest to these children either during the estate owner's lifetime or after his or her death. However, if there are other children in the family who have no contact with the business, the estate owner may wish to provide other assets for those children so that there is equality among all of his or her children. Life insurance in this context is appropriate.

> *Example:* Mr. Limberger is president and sole shareholder of Cutnslash, Inc., a highly successful retail discount store. He has four adult children, two sons and two daughters. The two daughters have expressed an interest in taking over the business when Mr. Limberger reaches age 59 1/2. The two sons have no interest in the business since they are both practicing physicians. He arranges for the two daughters to receive the business at his retirement or death. To equalize the inheritances of his children, Mr. Limberger acquires life insurance on his life in an amount equal to the anticipated fair market value of Cutnslash, Inc. He pays the premiums, and the sons are designated equal beneficiaries. Mr. Limberger's goal of equal shares for all heirs has been achieved.

The Second-to-Die Policy

The use of a survivorship (second-to-die) policy should be considered in estate planning for a married couple. The federal estate tax marital deduction is now unlimited in nature and scope. With the advent of the unlimited federal estate tax marital deduction, however, came an increased potential for overqualification for the marital deduction. There is a greater propensity by estate owners to leave their entire estates to their surviving spouses, which assures no estate tax liability at the first death.

There is, unfortunately, a serious flaw in this approach. The concept of the federal estate tax marital deduction is based on a deferral of estate tax liability—it is *never* to be thought of as a complete avoidance of the estate tax. Although the deduction is unlimited, to use the deduction to its fullest extent creates a stacking of estate taxes at the second death. The estate tax liability from the estate of the first to die is added to the estate of the second to die. The result is a higher estate tax liability overall.

The unlimited marital deduction has created a need for greater planning for the death of the second spouse. That is why the second-to-die policy was instituted. Many life insurers offer a second-to-die policy that jointly insures a husband and wife. At the death of the first spouse, no death benefit is paid; at the death of the second spouse, the policy proceeds are paid to the named beneficiary. (The second-to-die product is discussed fully in chapter 5.)

Second-to-die coverage is often a perfect fit in a married couple's estate plan. The most common use of second-to-die coverage is in an estate plan in which taking the unlimited marital deduction after the death of the first spouse will result in more substantial death taxes at the death of the second spouse. With second-to-die coverage, policy benefits will be paid when the insured married unit incurs these more substantial taxes—at the second death of the spouses.

> *Example:* Reginald Carney, aged 62, and his wife, Alice, aged 60, have a substantial estate. They have two children, Dave and Doris. They currently have the following total assets:
>
> | | |
> |---|---|
> | Reginald | $2,200,000 |
> | Alice | 850,000 |
> | Jointly held | 1,050,000 |
>
> The couple has an optimal marital-formula estate plan. That is, each spouse's will creates a unified credit bypass trust funded with the $600,000 unified credit equivalent; the remainder of their estate is sheltered by the marital deduction. Under this scenario, no federal estate tax will be due at the first death of Reginald and Alice; however, a substantial estate taxes will be due at the death of the survivor. With their current wealth, and if there is no growth, $1,565,800 in federal estate tax will be incurred at the second death. If their estate grows substantially, the taxes will increase.
>
> Suppose Reginald and Alice are, not all that surprisingly, unhappy with the potential shrinkage of their family wealth due to death taxes. To minimize the devastating effect of the death taxes, the couple has their children purchase a second-to-die policy on their lives with a face amount of $1.5 million. Alice will gift the $20,000 annual premium to the children.
>
> This plan serves the following three purposes:
>
> - The second-to-die proceeds will replace the family wealth lost to death taxes.
> - The annual gifts will keep the taxable estate from growing as fast as it otherwise would.
> - The life insurance proceeds will escape estate taxes since the children, not the insureds, own the policy.

Second-to-die life insurance works particularly well with the current estate tax system. However, the financial services professional should never ignore the first death coverage needs when assisting in the estate planning process.

CONCLUSION

Life insurance is extremely effective for use in the estate planning process. The ability to remove the proceeds from the gross estate through gifts of policies and third-party ownership should be part of the estate plan of wealthy individuals who face estate liquidity problems. The ability to pay estate taxes with discounted dollars makes the life insurance product a unique planning tool.

NOTES

1. IRC Sec. 101(a)(1).
2. IRC Sec. 101(a)(2).
3. IRC Sec. 7702(f)(7)(B).
4. IRC Sec. 72(v).
5. IRC Sec. 7702A.
6. IRC Sec. 264(a)(1).
7. IRC Sec. 72.
8. IRC Sec. 72(e)(5).
9. Treas. Reg. Sec. 1.72-9.
10. IRC Secs. 2033–2042 define which property interests must be included as part of the decedent's gross estate for purposes of imposing the federal estate tax.
11. Rev. Rul. 79-353, 1979-2, C.B. 325. See also *Estate of Wall*, 101 T.C. No. 21, for a case where the tax court disagreed with the IRS's reasoning in Rev. Rul. 79-353.
12. See IRC Sec. 2035.
13. Action on Decision (AOD) 1991-012 *(Estate of Headrick v. Comm'r)*.
14. See IRC Sec. 2056.
15. See IRC Sec. 2206.

Business Uses of Life Insurance

Ted Kurlowicz and John J. McFadden

Designing the appropriate compensation package for the owners and employees of a business is a critical step in the business planning process. In small closely held businesses, the business owner's needs will often dictate both the size and form of compensation provided to the employees. In addition, nonowner key employees of closely held businesses must be compensated appropriately or the businesses could lose their services to competitors. Finally, larger publicly held corporations must compete for the services of valued executives, and employee benefit packages represent a significant portion of the total compensation expense.

LIFE INSURANCE IN EMPLOYEE BENEFIT PLANNING

The compensation package provided by an employer is usually divided into two portions—cash compensation and fringe benefits. The establishment of a small business's fringe benefit plans is usually dictated more by the specific needs of the business owners than by tax considerations. For example, the need for life or health insurance depends on the owners' age, marital status, and number of dependents. Nevertheless, the tax treatment of various types of compensation arrangements is extremely important. The tax benefits of certain types of compensation include one or more of the following:

- the deductibility of such compensation as a business expense of the corporation
- the receipt of such compensation income tax free by the employee
- the deferral of taxation of the fringe benefit into a later tax year

The purpose of compensation planning is to design the compensation package to meet the needs of the owners and of the business. Some components of the compensation package will be dictated by the specific needs of the business owners. In other cases, the tax costs or benefits of providing such compensation will be balanced to maximize the overall compensation available to the owners.

The shareholder-employees of a closely held corporation have an advantage for the purposes of fringe benefit plans such as health insurance and group term life insurance. The corporation is permitted to fully deduct reasonable contributions for these benefit plans, including contributions made on behalf of owner-employees. In addition, the employer contribution for benefits under such plans are not taxable to employees unless the death benefits under group term life coverage exceed $50,000.

In many instances business owners and key employees desire permanent life insurance coverage as an employee benefit. Permanent life insurance has the benefit of portability and predictable level premium costs. Life insurance needs for most business owners and executives will continue beyond the employment years for estate planning purposes.

GROUP TERM LIFE INSURANCE (SEC. 79) PLANS

Group term life insurance is a benefit plan provided by an employer to a group of participating employees. Such plans, also known as Sec. 79 plans, allow the employer a tax deduction for premium payments on behalf of a participant unless the premium amounts cause the reasonable compensation limit to be exceeded (an unlikely event).

If the coverage provided by the plan is nondiscriminatory, the first $50,000 of coverage is provided tax free to all plan participants. If the plan discriminates in favor of key employees with respect to coverage or benefits, the actual premiums paid on behalf of such key employees are taxable as ordinary income. A key employee, as defined under the qualified plan rules, generally includes the shareholder-employees and officers of a closely held corporation. Thus it is important that the plan qualify as nondiscriminatory under Sec. 79 to avoid the adverse tax treatment of shareholders-employees. Otherwise, it is usually better for the employer to adopt an informal bonus plan (discussed below) and permit the shareholder-employees to purchase individual coverage (assuming all selected employees can be underwritten on an individual basis), while permissibly discriminating against other classes of employees.

The taxable amounts of coverage (that is, amounts above $50,000) are taxed according to a rate schedule — the so-called Table I — provided by IRS regulations. Recent tax law changes directed the IRS to develop regulations that increase the Table I cost for coverage over age 64 to appropriate actuarial costs in 5-year age brackets. Previously, the rates were level at age 60 and beyond. The Table I cost for ages above 64 are now determined in 5-year brackets based on the same mortality assumptions used in determining the lower age brackets. Table I rates in 5-year age brackets for ages under 65 remain the same as in the old table. A comparison of the old Table I rates with the new Table I rates is presented in table 12-1.

The effect of these rate changes is to increase the taxable costs of Sec. 79 coverage in excess of $50,000 (or the full amount for key employees if the plan is discriminatory), particularly for the older participants.

> *Example:* Suppose a retired executive has $150,000 of postretirement group term life coverage. Since $100,000 of this coverage is subject to tax, the executive would have to include $1,404 (12 x $1.17 x 100) in income annually at age 64. Under the old Table I rates this annual taxable income would remain constant for the rest of the tax years this coverage remained in force. Under the new rates the annual taxable income incurred by the executive jumps to $2,520 at age 65, and $4,512 at age 70.

TABLE 12-1		
Cost per Month per $1,000		
TABLE I RATES		
5-Year Age Bracket	Old Table	New Table
Under 30	$0.08	$0.08
30 to 34	0.09	0.09
35 to 39	0.11	0.11
40 to 44	0.17	0.17
45 to 49	0.29	0.29
50 to 54	0.48	0.48
55 to 59	0.75	0.75
60 to 64	1.17	1.17
65 to 69	1.17	2.10
70 and above	1.17	3.76

Requirements under Sec. 79

Through a contract held directly or indirectly by the employer coverage under a Sec. 79 plan must provide the following:

- general death benefits excludible from income tax under Sec. 101(a). Thus travel and accident and health (including double-indemnity) policies do not qualify under the group term life rules of Sec. 79.
- coverage to a group of *employees*. Employees must generally be common law employees. Thus a shareholder can be covered only if he or she is an actual employee of the corporation. A group is either all employees of the employer or less than all employees if the group is determined by reference to factors such as age, marital status, length of employment, employment classification, and/or membership in a union subject to collective bargaining. Such a plan can cover fewer than all employees, which will hold down the plan's overall cost, as long as the plan complies with the nondiscrimination rules discussed below. A group must also generally include at least 10 employees. Special rules discussed below, however, provide an exception for smaller groups.
- insurance protection that precludes individual selection of the amount of coverage. The coverage can be based on formulas related to age, service, job classification, and compensation. For example, a plan that provides a death benefit five times the participant's annual salary precludes individual selection.

Nondiscrimination Rules Applicable to Sec. 79 Plans

Groups with 10 or More Members

The nondiscrimination requirements focus on both the coverage and benefits provided by the plan. Under the *coverage* test the plan must meet one of the following requirements:

- cover at least 70 percent of all employees
- have no more than 15 percent of the participants from the key employee group
- benefit a reasonable classification of participants

For the purpose of this test, the corporation can exclude (1) employees with less than 3 years of service, (2) part-time or seasonal employees, and (3) employees subject to collective bargaining. Generally speaking, it will be difficult for a closely held corporation to exclude any nonkey employees if shareholder-employees and other key employees participate in the plan.

The *benefits* test requires that the benefits be either a flat amount or a uniform percentage of compensation (for example, 2.5 times current salary). The benefit restrictions permit voluntary purchase of additional coverage by the participant.

Groups with Fewer than 10 Members

The IRS regulations provide more stringent requirements for groups with fewer than 10 members. These groups must meet the following requirements or the favorable tax treatment will be lost:

- All full-time employees must be covered (a 6-month waiting period is permissible).
- Evidence of insurability may be tested only on the basis of a medical questionnaire.
- The benefits must be provided (1) on a uniform percentage of compensation or (2) in brackets where no bracket can be more than 2.5 times the next lowest bracket and the lowest bracket must be at least 10 percent of the highest.

Postretirement Coverage

Although not technically a nondiscrimination rule, the welfare benefit plan rules apply to postretirement group term provided through retired lives reserves (RLR) plans. These rules make it generally infeasible to fund postretirement group term life coverage to retired shareholder-employees in excess of $50,000. This is unfortunate since most of these individuals have substantial estates and desire permanent postretirement coverage of higher face amounts.

EXECUTIVE BONUS (SEC. 162) LIFE INSURANCE PLANS

One type of employee compensation arrangement that is currently advantageous for shareholder-employees is the Sec. 162 life insurance plan. The primary advantage is the ability to avoid the nondiscrimination rules applicable to other fringe benefits.

Sec. 162 plans have the additional advantage of simplicity, which holds down their administrative costs. Because of tax and labor law compliance rules, compensation and fringe benefits planning has become increasingly complex, but the executive bonus plan is refreshingly simple. Shareholder-employees and executives who participate in the plan apply for, own, and name the beneficiary on permanent life insurance policies covering their lives. The personally owned nature of the policy offers them maximum flexibility. The premiums for such policies are provided through a bonus payment by the employer-corporation. The corporation either pays the premium directly to the insurer or gives the amount necessary to pay the premium as a bonus to the employee, who is then billed directly by the insurance company.

The income taxation of the plan is also easy to illustrate to clients. The premium amount paid directly to the insurer (or bonus to the employee) is treated as gross compensation income to the employee under Sec. 61(a)(1). This compensation is treated as ordinary income subject to the employee's normal individual income tax rate. If the bonus along with the employee's other compensation represents reasonable compensation, the corporation deducts the amount of the bonus as an ordinary business expense under Sec. 162(a)(1)—thus the origin of the name *Sec. 162 plans*. Although the tax burden of the plan is immediate to the executive, the bonus can be designed as a zero-tax bonus (making it large enough to pay the tax on the bonus) to reduce the executive's out-of-pocket costs. Moreover, the executive, as the owner of the policy, can use policy dividends to reduce future premiums (and the need for future taxable bonuses).

The primary advantage of a closely held corporation's adoption of a Sec. 162 plan is its exemption from the federal nondiscrimination and administrative reporting rules applicable to most other types of fringe benefit plans. The board of directors of a closely held business or professional corporation can pick and choose the participants who will be included and limit the plan to those shareholder employees who want individual life insurance coverage. In addition, there are no discrimination rules with respect to benefit limits. Theoretically, the plan could provide any amount of life insurance premium to purchase coverage on the life of a shareholder-employee who desires substantial coverage.

However, the corporation should use caution in providing unlimited coverage since the corporate deduction for bonus payments to the plan is limited by the reasonable compensation rules. If the limit is exceeded, the corporate income tax deduction will be lost with respect to amount of any bonuses to shareholder-employees that are deemed unreasonable, and the excess bonus will be treated as a dividend payment rather than as compensation. It is prudent for the corporation to adopt the Sec. 162 plan by board of directors' resolution and to provide evidence in the minutes to the corporate purpose for establishing the plan (for example, by indicating the need to retain or attract key executives by offering the Sec. 162 plan as a benefit).

Coordination of the Sec. 162 Plan with the Corporation's Group Term Life Insurance Plan—the Group Term Carve-out

Do the substantial individual insurance benefits available under a Sec. 162 plan render the Sec. 79 plan obsolete? The answer to this question depends on many factors. Does the corporation already have a Sec. 79 plan in place that benefits employees? Does the current plan meet the burden of the nondiscrimination rules? Does the corporation wish to continue to provide group term life insurance coverage to nonowner, nonhighly compensated employees? Generally speaking, the group term life insurance plan concept should not be dropped simply because of the popularity of the Sec. 162 bonus plan. If they meet the nondiscrimination requirements, Sec. 79 plans still offer favorable tax treatment. The corporation gets an ordinary business expense deduction for contributions to the plan. The first $50,000 of coverage per employee can be provided tax free to the employee—including shareholder-employees and other key employees. And the corporation may want to avoid lowering employee morale by terminating a popular fringe benefit arrangement covering a broad cross-section of employees and replacing it with a highly discriminatory executive bonus plan limited to a few key employees.

What is generally recommended is that shareholders and other key employees who require (and for whom the corporation wishes to provide) more substantial life insurance coverage participate in a Sec. 162 bonus life insurance plan to supplement a Sec. 79 plan. From the executive's standpoint, the Sec. 79 plan could still provide each key employee with the $50,000 of tax-free coverage. Additional group term coverage for these key employees would be taxable to the participants and could be deemed discriminatory, which would result in all benefits becoming taxable as income. This excess coverage could instead be "carved out" of the group term life insurance plan through a Sec. 162 bonus arrangement. Thus the executive bonus plan is also commonly referred to as a Sec. 79 executive carve-out bonus plan. The carved-out portion of coverage is actually superior to what could be provided under a Sec. 79 plan even if no nondiscrimination rules were applicable to group term coverage (see table 12-2). Key shareholder-employees participating in the plan receive permanent individual life insurance policies providing them with a tax-free cash surrender value (CSV) build-up and other flexibilities associated with owning individual permanent life insurance.

The executive bonus arrangement is also more favorable to shareholder-employees in their postretirement years. The nondiscrimination rules generally limit the funding of retired lives reserves plans to $50,000 of postretirement coverage per participant. Executive bonus plans provide participating employees with permanent coverage without the $50,000 limitations, and since the plan is held individually by the employee, it is available during his or her retirement years.

Reporting and Disclosure Requirements

It is unclear whether Sec. 162 bonus life insurance plans will be deemed welfare benefit plans under the provisions of ERISA. Since the plan provides taxable benefits to a select group of highly compensated executives, most of the reporting and disclosure requirements would not apply in any case. However, if the plan is deemed a welfare benefit plan, a written plan document should be made available to the Department of Labor on request. As a precaution, the plan should be adopted through a formal corporate resolution to satisfy the writing requirement. Written notice of the plan in a claims procedure manual or booklet should also be given to every plan participant. Finally, a corporate officer should be appointed as "named fiduciary" of the plan to comply with any potential applicability of ERISA provisions.

TABLE 12-2		
Comparison of Sec. 79 Plan and Carve-out Plan		
	Sec. 79	Sec. 79 Carve-out
Coverage	Must meet the nondiscrimination test	Carve-out excess coverage on a discriminatory basis
Benefits	Flat amount or uniform percentage of compensation	Any amount of bonus for carve-out portion that can be justified as reasonable
Income Tax to Executive	Amounts above $50,000 taxed at Table I costs (all taxable to key employee if discriminatory) and cost rises with age	Amount of bonus taxable
Premium Deductibility	Fully deductible	Fully deductible

Estate and Gift Tax Planning Considerations

The Sec. 162 bonus life insurance plan involves ownership of an individual life insurance policy by an insured-employee. As such, the life insurance proceeds will be included in the insured-employee's gross estate for federal estate tax purposes under the provisions of Sec. 2042. This may not be a desirable result, particularly since the highly compensated plan participants are probably accumulating substantial estates irrespective of the bonus life insurance plan. If the gross estate inclusion is a concern to the participating executive(s), the plan can be designed with third-party ownership of the individual life insurance policy. For example, the life insurance can be owned by the insured-employee's spouse or by an irrevocable trust created by the insured-employee. If the third party is the initial applicant and owner of the policy, the proceeds should be excludible from the insured's gross estate even if the insured dies immediately after the coverage becomes effective. If estate tax problems become a concern at a later date, a plan participant could gift an existing policy to a third-party owner. In this event, the insured must survive the 3-year period following the policy transfer to get the insurance proceeds out of his or her gross estate for federal estate tax purposes (Sec. 2035).

The gift tax consequences of such a transfer depend on the circumstances of the transfer. If an individual third-party owner, such as a spouse, is selected as the donee of the life insurance policy, the original transfer of the policy plus any premiums paid by the employer will be treated as a gift from the insured-employee to the third party. The gift, in this case, will qualify for the $10,000 annual gift tax exclusion as a gift of a present interest. Of course, any premiums paid by the employer will still be treated as taxable income to the insured-employee and as gifts from the insured employee to the policyowner. If the policy is transferred instead to an irrevocable trust created by the insured, the transfer of the policy and any premiums paid subsequently by the employer will be treated as a gift from the insured-employee to the beneficiaries of the trust. However, the gifts under these circumstances will qualify for the annual exclusion only if the beneficiaries are provided with current withdrawal rights to premiums added to the trust.

SPLIT-DOLLAR LIFE INSURANCE PLANS

Split-dollar life insurance is perhaps the most frequently used form of permanent life insurance as an executive compensation benefit. Although split-dollar arrangements are not limited to the employer-employee relationship, they are almost always formed in this way. Split-dollar life insurance plans have a long and varied history. The first IRS rulings on such arrangements were issued in the 1950s, but many new types of split-dollar arrangements have been developed since then to adapt to changing tax laws and the needs of the insured executives. The following discussion summarizes several forms of split-dollar arrangements. However, it is important to note that there are numerous variations within each arrangement and that the general rule is almost the exception in actual practice.

Basic Concepts

Split-dollar life insurance plans split a life insurance policy's premium obligations and policy benefits between two individuals or entities. The parties to a split-dollar agreement are normally an employer and employee. The two parties share the premium costs while the policy is in effect, pursuant to a prearranged agreement. At the death of the insured or the termination of the agreement, the parties split the policy benefits or proceeds in accordance with their agreement. Plans must meet minimal reporting and disclosure compliance requirements. Most of the administration is handled by the insurer.

Split-dollar plans are an excellent fringe benefit option for a closely held corporation since the plans can be limited to a select group of shareholder-employees and other key personnel. Depending on the employer's and employee's tax brackets, split-dollar plans in a group term carve-out might be a viable alternative to a Sec. 162 plan. Since the corporation's tax bracket and the amount of compensation provided to shareholder-employees are largely in the control of the shareholder-employees, selecting the appropriate executive life insurance arrangement can be made optimally at their discretion.

Policy Ownership

The owner of the underlying policy in a split-dollar plan can either be the employer or the insured-employee. Under the *endorsement* method the employer owns the policy and has primary responsibility for premium payment. The employer's share of the benefits is secured through its ownership of the policy. The insured designates the beneficiary for his or her share of the death proceeds, and an endorsement is filed with the insurer stipulating that the beneficiary designation cannot be changed without the insured's consent.

Under the *collateral assignment* method the insured is the policyowner and has premium payment responsibility. The corporation loans the employee the corporation's share of the annual premium, and the corporate amounts are secured by the assignment of the policy to the corporation. The corporation receives its benefits as assignee of the policy at the earlier of the employee's death or the termination of the split-dollar plan.

Taxation of the Split-Dollar Plan

Since a split-dollar plan is most often provided as a fringe benefit, the taxation of split-dollar life insurance varies depending on the type of split-dollar plan, but it is based on the general premise that the employee is taxed on the economic benefit that he or she receives annually from the plan.

TABLE 12-3 PS 58 Rates One-Year Term Premiums for $1,000 of Life Insurance Protection						
Age	Premium	Age	Premium	Age	Premium
15	$1.27	37	$ 3.63	59	$ 19.08
16	1.38	38	3.87	60	20.73
17	1.48	39	4.14	61	22.53
18	1.52	40	4.42	62	24.50
19	1.56	41	4.73	63	26.63
20	1.61	42	5.07	64	28.98
21	1.67	43	5.44	65	31.51
22	1.73	44	5.85	66	34.28
23	1.79	45	6.30	67	37.31
24	1.86	46	6.78	68	40.59
25	1.93	47	7.32	69	44.17
20	2.02	40	7.09	70	40.00
27	2.11	49	8.53	71	52.29
28	2.20	50	9.22	72	56.89
29	2.31	51	9.97	73	61.89
30	2.43	52	10.79	74	67.33
31	2.57	53	11.69	75	73.23
32	2.70	54	12.67	76	79.63
33	2.86	55	13.74	77	86.57
34	3.02	56	14.91	78	94.09
35	3.21	57	16.18	79	102.23
36	3.41	58	17.56	80	111.04
				81	120.57

These rates are used in computing the cost of pure life insurance protection that is taxable to the employee under qualified pension and profit-sharing plans.

The rate at the insured's attained age is applied to the excess of the amount payable at death over the cash value of the policy at the end of the year.

In Rev. Rul. 64-328, C.B. 1964-2, the IRS ruled that the tax consequences of the basic split-dollar plan are the same regardless of whether the plan is designed under the endorsement or collateral assignment method. The economic benefit is the pure insurance element, measured by the cost of one-year term life insurance conferred on the insured during the year. The term cost is the employee's share of the amount of protection in a given year multiplied by the term rate for the employee's attained age. In Rev. Rul. 66-110, C. B. 1966-1, the IRS has also ruled that the term cost is the lesser of the PS 58 rates (see table 12-3) or the insurance company's standard rates for a one-year term policy. Any contributions made by the employee to the split-dollar plan can be applied against the economic benefit to reduce the taxable cost of the plan.

> *Example:* Suppose the XYZ Corporation offers a split-dollar plan to its sole shareholder and company president, Mr. Joffe, aged 45. If the policy has a $100,000 face amount death benefit and the corporation has the rights to the cash surrender value of $40,000, Mr. Joffe's share, which is the pure amount at risk, is $60,000. For the tax year Mr. Joffe received an economic benefit of $378 (60 multiplied by the PS 58 cost per $1,000 of $6.30). If Mr. Joffe makes no contributions to the plan, the taxable benefit to him for the year is $378.

Of course, the many variations of split-dollar life insurance may cause other taxable benefits to be conferred on the employee. For example, the employer might pay all or part of the employee's share of the premium. In addition, policy dividends that benefit the employee by providing cash, additional insurance, or reduction of the employee's premium will be taxable to the employee.

Reporting and Disclosure Requirements

Even though split-dollar plans are included in the category of welfare benefit plans, most of the ERISA requirements are not applicable. Split-dollar plans are definitely exempt from the ERISA vesting, funding, and participation rules generally applicable to qualified plans. It is possible that the requirements of establishing an ERISA claims procedure and appointing a plan fiduciary can also be avoided. To qualify for such an exemption, the split-dollar plan must provide benefits paid exclusively from insurance contracts and either be (1) a plan for a select group of management and highly compensated employees or (2) a small welfare benefit plan having fewer than 100 participants at the start of the year. Since split-dollar plans are generally established by closely held corporations to limit participation to shareholder-employees and key executives, the plans will generally qualify for these exemptions. At a minimum the employer must provide plan documents to the Department of Labor on request.

Traditional Split-Dollar Plans

In traditional split-dollar plans a corporation and an employee split a life insurance policy covering the life of the employee. The corporation contributes an amount equal to the annual increase in the cash surrender value, while the executive pays the remainder of the annual premium. The death benefit is split between the participating executive and the corporation as follows:

- The corporation receives a return of its contributions (which equal the cash surrender value).
- The beneficiary named by the insured receives a death benefit equal to the pure amount at risk.

The traditional split-dollar arrangement provides the following advantages:

- Discrimination in favor of shareholder-employees and other key executives is permissible.
- The employer can provide a life insurance benefit to selected employees with minimal charge to corporate earnings and with predictable tax cost to the employee.
- The employer's share is secured at all times by its distributive portion of the policy.
- The plan is preferable to a Sec. 162 bonus plan since the corporation is generally in a lower tax bracket than a highly compensated executive.
- The corporation can use the plan to help the participating shareholder-employees purchase insurance to fund a buy-sell agreement.

The split-dollar plan will not provide the corporation with a current income tax deduction even if the employee incurs taxable compensation. Thus the corporation has to use taxable income to contribute its share of the premium.

This traditional arrangement makes sense under the current tax setting only in certain circumstances. It should generally not be used for shareholder-employees of a closely held corporation unless the executive's marginal income tax rate exceeds the corporation's marginal rate. Otherwise, the taxable corporate income contributed to the plan will be subject to higher rates. If the participating shareholder-employees are in a lower bracket, it makes sense to use a Sec. 162 bonus arrangement. A Sec. 162 plan will provide a corporate tax deduction for the full amount of the bonus and meet the objective of providing the shareholder-employee with an individually owned unencumbered life insurance policy. From a tax standpoint, the bonus amount could have the effect of reducing the corporation's taxable income to zero if all corporate income is paid out as compensation. In any instance, the earnings required to pay the bonus payments to the shareholder-professionals will be taxed at a lower bracket in the hands of the shareholder-employee than they would in the corporation's.

For business corporations, the traditional split-dollar arrangement continues to make sense in most instances. The corporate tax structure permits corporations to retain income at favorable rates. The corporate income tax rates will be generally lower than individual rates. In addition, the new 36 percent and 39.6 percent marginal brackets applicable to individuals makes the corporate tax rate lower at higher levels of income. Since the retained income of a closely held corporation is, within limits, subject to the control of the shareholder-employees, the corporation's taxable income may be reduced to this favorable level through payment of deductible salaries and bonuses to the shareholder-employees and other key executives (if the "reasonable compensation" tests can be satisfied). The retained amounts of income taxable at lower corporate brackets can then be used for corporate contributions to a split-dollar plan covering a few shareholder-employees. Thus the use of corporate taxable income for a nondeductible split-dollar expenditure will be less costly from a tax standpoint than paying fully taxable bonuses to shareholder-employees that will incur 36 percent or 39.6 percent income taxes.

The class of employees to be covered by the split-dollar plan is another important consideration. If coverage under the plan will extend beyond the shareholder group, the split-dollar plan may be more favorable from the corporation's standpoint than an executive bonus plan. This is particularly true if younger executives covered by the plan do not stay with the current employer for their entire working careers. Under these circumstances, the corporation may not want to permanently lose its contributions, as occurs in an executive bonus plan. The split-dollar plan will provide the corporation with a return of its actual contributions (possibly also including a return on the invested funds), reducing its charge to earnings for providing the plan. Of course, it may be possible to design a dual plan with an executive bonus plan for shareholder-employees and split-dollar coverage for junior executives. Generally speaking, split-dollar plans are more favorable when a lower corporate cost is indicated by such factors as the desire to cover a group larger than the shareholder-employees.

Equity Split-Dollar Plans

Equity split dollar is an arrangement that is often used to provide a valuable fringe benefit for shareholder-employees. It is particularly popular from the employee's perspective since excess cash surrender value builds up for his or her benefit during the split period. The equity split-dollar arrangement works as follows:

- The employee's premium share is equal to the PS 58 cost. The employee might pay the actual term insurance cost in the alternative.
- The employer pays the remainder of the premium.
- The employer's share is equal to the lesser of its premium contributions or the CSV.
- The employee receives a death benefit equal to the excess over the employer's share. During his or her lifetime, the employee also builds up an interest in the excess of the policy CSV over the employer's share.

As with other split-dollar variations, the equity method involves careful consideration of all corporate goals, including tax planning. One obvious advantage of this arrangement is that the corporation receives its contributions back exactly. It is important for a closely held corporation where the actual corporate outlay must be minimized. This is certainly an important goal if executives outside the shareholder group will be covered by the plan. In addition, the corporation will not show a profit on its interest in the plan and will be providing, in effect, a pure interest-free loan to the participant.

There are some federal income tax implications with equity split-dollar arrangements that cannot be ignored. First, the employee must provide the annual term cost (or PS 58 cost) with aftertax dollars. Again, the corporation receives no federal income tax deduction for its contribution to the plan. One method of reducing the employee's outlay and coincidentally providing the corporation with a valuable tax deduction is to give the employee a bonus equal to his or her annual contribution to the plan. If reasonable compensation tests are met, these bonus amounts will be deductible against corporate income, and they will reduce the employee's out-of-pocket costs of participating in the plan. The bonus arrangement is particularly valuable when (1) corporate tax rates are relatively high, and (2) the plan is limited to shareholder-employees.

A more significant issue is the tax at the time the equity split-dollar plan terminates at the employee's retirement and the employer is repaid. The taxation of the policy transfer to the employee is a disputed question at this time. Since excess CSV has accrued to the employee's benefit, will the transfer of the policy result in current income taxation to the employee under Sec. 83? The tax code provides that transfers of property in exchange for services rendered represent gross income in the year the property is transferred. Private letter rulings on this issue involve the use of an endorsement method split-dollar plan. In these rulings the IRS determined that the transfer of excess cash surrender value to the employee at the rollout date was a transfer of property under Sec. 83. If this design is used, therefore, the transfer of the policy at retirement will result in an immediate and substantial income tax liability to the employee for this excess CSV. Depending on the circumstances, this may be both an unacceptable and an unexpected result.

A reasonable interpretation of authority seems to indicate that the employee should get a basis in the contract equal to the employee's cumulative contributions to offset his or her gain at transfer. This is the rationale behind having the employee provide PS 58 costs (which are generally higher than actual term costs) since the employee's additional accumulation of basis will be important at the time the policy is rolled out.

Will the transfer be subject to income taxes if the collateral assignment method is selected? The answer to this question is not clear. In the collateral assignment method, the corporation theoretically has contractual rights limited to its return of premium and does not actually transfer property at the rollout date. However, the IRS has stated in its rulings on split-dollar that the arrangement will be taxed as to the substance of the arrangement regardless of the actual technical design of the split-dollar plan. The conservative thinking is that the excess CSV will probably be treated as a taxable transfer regardless of the form of the split-dollar plan.

Reverse Split-Dollar Plans

As an alternative to equity arrangements for providing substantial retirement benefits to executives through the split-dollar medium, reverse split-dollar (RSD) plans have achieved recent popularity. In the RSD variation, the corporation and executive roles are reversed. The basic form of RSD involves the payment of the pure insurance portion of the premium by the corporation. The measure of the corporation's premium share depends on the variation of RSD selected. The executive pays the balance of the premium. The corporation's share at the employee's death is the pure insurance proceeds. The plan is designed for individual ownership of the policy by the executive (or a third party), and the executive retains all rights in the policy other than the corporation's death benefit. At some point in the future, usually the executive's retirement, the plan is terminated and the executive receives the policy unburdened by the employer's right to the death benefit.

The RSD plan is designed to meet some specific goals and should be used only when circumstances indicate. First, there should be a corporate need for the pure insurance on the executive's life. For example, the corporation may use the death proceeds as key person indemnification, to fund a stock redemption or to fund a death-benefit-only (DBO) plan. Since the corporate need ceases when the executive retires, the temporary nature of the RSD plan is appropriate. Of course, the split-funding nature of the policy helps hold the cost down for the executive who receives a substantial CSV benefit at retirement when the corporation's interest terminates. The RSD plan is a good alternative to a traditional rollout or equity split dollar when these client objectives must be met.

The RSD plan appears to illustrate quite favorably. However, there are a couple of major tax problems with the plan as it is often illustrated. One critical decision that must be made is the amount that the corporation will be required to pay for its right to the death benefit. Initially, many such illustrations showed the corporation paying the actual PS 58 cost (or some variation of PS 58 cost funding) for the amount of its death benefit coverage each year. The variations on the PS 58 funding involved a level premium averaging of the PS 58 cost over the term of the split period. The use of averaged PS 58 cost funding was favorable to the executive since it involved substantial prefunding of the plan by the corporation. First, as discussed earlier, PS 58 costs are usually significantly higher than the actual term insurance cost charged by the insurer. Second, because of the leveling effect, contributions by the corporation in the early years were higher than required. This prepayment and compound interest resulted in the corporation's contribution to fund some, if not all, of the executive's CSV build-up. In some illustrations of RSD, the executive pays nothing (or nearly nothing depending on the type of life insurance policy) for his or her interest in the ordinary life contract.

These optimistic illustrations were relying upon earlier IRS split-dollar rulings using PS 58 costs to value the economic benefit to the employee for ordinary income tax purposes. The theory behind these illustrations was that the employer was paying a "fair price" (as defined by the IRS) for its share of the death proceeds. In addition, since the executive was the owner of the policy, the thinking was that the termination of the plan at the executive's retirement did not result in a taxable transfer since the corporation did not own the policy and thus had nothing to transfer.

The actual taxation of this arrangement is unclear at this point, but it appears that leveled PS 58 (or even actual PS 58 funding) might be a dangerous approach for federal income tax purposes. Although there are no rulings on the subject, several commentators have observed that the IRS could treat the annual increase in CSV caused by any employer overfunding of the plan as ordinary income to the employee under Sec. 61. Of course, this may not be a terrible result since the corporation should get a corresponding tax deduction for any amounts included in the executive's income. This tax benefit may outweigh the tax burden to the executive under the new rate structure applicable to corporations and individuals. Nevertheless, to avoid this controversy, many illustrations currently show the employer paying no more than the actual term insurance costs for the pure death benefit coverage.

To avoid a taxable transfer, the executive should maintain current individual rights in the life insurance policy so that no substantial restrictions exist that will terminate at the executive's retirement. The executive should also have a basis in the policy that is equal to any contributions he or she actually makes. Recall that the IRS has stated in previous rulings that it will treat a split-dollar arrangement according to its substance rather than its form. Therefore even though the executive is the owner of the policy in the RSD plan, a taxable transfer could be deemed to occur if (1) restrictions lapse at some point in the future, and (2) the corporation has somehow enhanced the executive's interest in the policy above the executive's basis.

RSD is a useful arrangement in some circumstances if the income and estate tax problems can be avoided. There are many circumstances in which the corporation needs temporary life insurance coverage on a shareholder-employee or key executive. In addition, the ordinary life insurance policy received unencumbered at retirement is a valuable and popular asset to the employee. Recall from previous discussions that RLR plans are limited generally to $50,000 of postretirement coverage. In an RSD plan postretirement coverage is unlimited and, what's more, the executive has current access to a substantial growing CSV.

Split Dollar as an Executive Carve-out

As with executive bonus plans, a split-dollar carve-out arrangement can be designed to meet the corporation's objective of providing substantial levels of life insurance coverage for key executives in addition to coverage under the company's group term life insurance plan. Split-dollar plans are exempt from the Sec. 79 nondiscrimination requirements, along with most of the reporting and disclosure compliance applicable to many other types of fringe benefit arrangements. Furthermore, split-dollar arrangements allow corporate employers to discriminate freely in the class of employees participating (and in the level of benefits provided). The discrimination can eliminate all but shareholder-employees and other key executives from coverage. In addition, a split-dollar plan will provide an individual permanent life policy that offers postretirement coverage greater than the $50,000 maximum in qualified plans. It has the dual advantages of giving select executives low-cost permanent life insurance coverage and giving the employee an incentive to continue with the corporation.

Nondiscriminatory group term life coverage should still be adopted (or continued) if this coverage is otherwise desirable for the employer. Remember, Sec. 79 provides significant tax advantages to both the employer and employee. The split-dollar carve-out alternative is simply one method of providing excess (discriminatory) life insurance coverage to shareholder-employees and other key executives without running afoul of nondiscrimination rules. The individuals participating in the split-dollar carve-out should still be covered under the group term life insurance plan, but their coverage should be limited to $50,000, or permissible nondiscriminatory level of death benefits, if greater. If cost is a concern and the corporation does not need to provide life insurance to a broad class of employees, it should avoid the Sec. 79 plan.

Estate Tax Considerations of Split Dollar

Traditional Split Dollar

The estate tax implications of traditional split-dollar life insurance plans are well established. If estate liquidity will be a concern for the executive participating in a split-dollar plan, some kind of third party ownership—the executive's spouse or an irrevocable trust—should, in lieu of the insured, enter into the split-dollar arrangement with the employer at its inception.

The majority shareholder in a split-dollar arrangement faces a more difficult problem. It is imperative for the majority shareholder to avoid corporate incidents of ownership in the split-dollar policy since these will be attributed to him or her if the proceeds are not deemed payable to the corporation. IRS rulings have made it clear that corporate incidents, such as the ability to borrow from the policy, should be avoided in a traditional split-dollar arrangement between the corporation and a majority shareholder. If corporate incidents of ownership are attributed to the majority shareholder, the death proceeds will be includible in the insured's gross estate, regardless of whether or not a third party actually held the insured's interest in the split-dollar agreement. Practitioners therefore generally recommend collateral assignment of the policy if a majority shareholder is involved.

One solution to avoid inclusion in the majority shareholder's estate is for the participant to create an irrevocable trust to enter into the split-dollar agreement with the corporation. The trust would collaterally assign the policy to the corporation to secure the corporation's share of the death benefit (limiting the corporation's rights to merely being repaid by the trust). It is unclear at this point, however, whether this design will avoid inclusion in the majority shareholder's estate under the attributed-incidents rule of the tax code. The safest solution is to effect a rollout of the policy to the trust as soon as practical.

Reverse Split Dollar

Estate tax concerns about RSD plans—designed for the insured-executive to own the policy from its inception—have been alleviated somewhat by a recent private letter ruling. The existing law requires the entire proceeds to be includible in the insured's estate at his or her death including the death proceeds payable to the corporation. Thus RSD has the potential for creating a huge estate liquidity problem for a participant. However, the IRS has ruled that the amount payable to the corporation is a deductible debt of the estate and will not create additional estate tax. That is, the corporation's death proceeds share will be included in the insured's gross estate for tax purposes, but the estate will receive a deduction for the amounts payable to the corporation.

LIFE INSURANCE IN DEFERRED-COMPENSATION PLANS

Deferred-compensation plans are an important part of the employee compensation package. Under a deferred-compensation plan, part of the employee's compensation over the employee's service-providing years is deferred until a later period, such as the employee's retirement. This deferral meets two goals. First, the deferred compensation will provide income for the employee during his or her retirement. Second, the deferred-compensation plan can realize a tax-planning objective since taxation of properly designed deferred compensation is deferred until the income is received.

Deferred-compensation plans can be categorized as either *qualified* or *nonqualified*. Qualified plans must meet a plethora of federal nondiscrimination and administrative compliance standards. These standards, of course, increase the cost of such plans since a broad base of employees must be included and significant administrative fees must be paid. However, the corporation gets an immediate income tax deduction for contributions to the plan while the employee's tax on plan benefits is deferred until the benefits are received. For the purpose of this discussion, qualified plans will include pension plans, IRAs, profit-sharing plans, and Sec. 403(b) plans.

Nonqualified plans provide a similar deferral of the employee's receipt of ordinary income. However, nonqualified plans also cause a deferral of the employer's tax deduction until such benefits are paid. Because closely held corporations often want to maximize the benefits for shareholder-employees, the goal of their retirement plans is to discriminate in favor of shareholder-employees and key executives to the fullest extent of the nondiscrimination rules. Since discrimination is permitted in nonqualified arrangements, these plans are often more favorable to the closely held corporation.

LIFE INSURANCE IN QUALIFIED PLANS, IRAs, AND 403(b) PLANS

A qualified plan may provide a death benefit over and above the survivorship benefits required by law, even without using life insurance. In a defined-contribution plan, probably the most common form of death benefit is a provision that the participant's vested account balance will be paid to the participant's designated beneficiary if the participant dies before retirement or termination of employment. Defined-benefit plans, unless they use insurance as discussed below, usually do not provide an incidental death benefit; in such cases, the survivors receive no death benefit other than whatever survivor annuity provision the plan provides.

However, a qualified plan must generally purchase life insurance in order to provide any substantial preretirement death benefit. This gives the plan significant funds at a participant's death, which is particularly important in the early years of his or her employment when the amount contributed on the participant's behalf is still relatively small.

An insured preretirement death benefit can be provided in either a defined-benefit or defined-contribution plan. Contributions to the plan by the employer may be used to pay life insurance premiums as long as the amount qualifies under the tests for *incidental benefits*.

In general the IRS considers that nonretirement benefits—life, medical, or disability insurance, for example—in a qualified plan will be incidental and therefore permissible as long as the cost of providing these benefits is less than 25 percent of the cost of providing all the benefits under the plan. In applying this approach to life insurance benefits, the 25 percent rule is applied to the portion of any life insurance premium that is used to provide current life insurance protection. Any portion of the premium that is used to increase the cash value of the policy is considered to be a contribution to the plan fund that is available to pay retirement benefits, and it is not considered in the 25 percent limitation.

The IRS has ruled, using its general 25 percent test, that if a qualified plan provides death benefits using ordinary life insurance (life insurance with a cash value), the death benefit will be considered incidental if either (1) less than 50 percent of the total cumulative employer contributions credited to each participant's account has been used to purchase ordinary life insurance, or (2) the face amount of the policy does not exceed 100 times the anticipated monthly normal retirement benefit or the accumulated reserve under the life insurance policy, whichever is greater. In practice defined-benefit plans using ordinary life insurance are usually designed to take advantage of the 100-times rule, while defined-contribution plans, including profit-sharing plans, that use ordinary life contracts generally make use of the 50 percent test.

If term insurance contracts are used to provide the death benefit, then, because the 25 percent test will be applied to the entire premium, the aggregate premiums paid for insurance on each participant should be less than 25 percent of aggregate additions to the employee's account. Term insurance is sometimes used to fund death benefits in defined-contribution plans but rarely in defined-benefit plans.

The IRS has not yet ruled on the use of universal life insurance and similar products in qualified plans, but it informally takes the position that the total premiums for such products must meet the same 25 percent limit as that for term insurance. This is almost certainly incorrect, however, since a substantial part of the premium for a universal life policy, as for an ordinary life policy, goes toward increasing the cash value. The limit in theory therefore should be higher than 25 percent.

The discussion so far is somewhat simplified because insurance can be used in qualified plans in many ways, and the IRS has issued numerous rulings, both revenue rulings and private letter rulings, applying the basic 25 percent test to a variety of different fact situations. Thus there is considerable room for creative design of life-insurance-funded death benefits within qualified plans.

If life insurance is provided for a participant through a qualified plan (that is, by using employer contributions to the plan to pay insurance premiums), part or all of the cost of the insurance is currently taxable to the participant. Life insurance provided by the plan is not considered part of a Sec. 79 group term plan, and consequently the $50,000 exclusion under Sec. 79 does not apply.

If life insurance with a cash value is used, and if all the death proceeds are payable to the participant's estate or beneficiary, the term cost or cost of the "pure amount at risk" is taxable to the employee. The term cost is the difference between the face amount of insurance and the cash surrender value of the policy at the end of the policy year. In other words, the cost of the policy's cash value is not currently taxable to the employee because the cash value is considered part of the plan fund to be used to provide the retirement benefit. As discussed earlier, the term cost is calculated using either the PS 58 table of rates provided by the Internal Revenue Service (see table 12-3) or the insurance company's rates for individual one-year term policies at standard rates, if these are lower and if the insurance company actually offers such policies.

If the plan uses term rather than cash value insurance to provide an insured death benefit, the cost of the entire face amount of insurance is taxable to the employee.

If the plan allows employee contributions, the nondeductible employee contributions can be used to offset taxable income resulting from the inclusion of any form of insurance in the plan. Unless the plan provides otherwise, however, insurance will be considered to have been paid first from employer contributions and plan fund earnings, so this offset is not available unless the plan makes specific provision for it.

> *Example:* Participant Al, aged 45, is covered under a defined-benefit plan that provides an insured death benefit in addition to retirement benefits. The death benefit is provided under a whole life policy with a face amount of $100,000. At the end of this year the policy's cash value is $40,000. The plan is noncontributory (that is, Al does not contribute to the plan).
>
> For this year Al must report an additional $378 of taxable income on his tax return (60 times the PS 58 rate of $6.30 per thousand for a participant aged 45, which reflects the amount of pure insurance coverage in effect his year). The employer is required to report the insurance coverage on Al's Form W-2 for the year.

Taxation of Beneficiaries

Taxation of an insured death benefit received by a beneficiary can be summarized in the following points:

- The pure insurance element of an insured plan death benefit (the death benefit less any cash value) is income tax free to a participant's beneficiary.
- An additional $5,000 may qualify for the employer death benefit exclusion of Code Sec. 101(b).
- The total of all PS 58 costs paid by the participant can be recovered tax free from the plan death benefit (if it is paid from the same insurance contracts that gave rise to the PS 58 costs.)
- The remainder of the distribution is taxed as a qualified plan distribution. This taxable portion of the distribution may be eligible for 5- or 10-year averaging if the plan participant was over 59 1/2 at death. If the decedent participated in the plan before 1987, there are also some favorable "grandfather" tax provisions that may apply.

Compared with the tax treatment of life insurance personally owned or provided by the employer outside the plan, there is usually an economic advantage to insurance in a qualified plan, all other things being equal. Insurance outside the plan is paid for entirely with aftertax dollars, so there is no tax deferral. Although the death benefit of nonplan insurance may be entirely tax free instead of partially tax free, the deferral of tax with plan-provided insurance can result in a measurable net tax benefit.

Furthermore, the pure insurance amount of a qualified plan death benefit is not subject to the 15 percent excess accumulation tax of Code Sec. 4980A. PS 58 costs can also be recovered free of the excess accumulation tax. Finally, although qualified plan death benefits are, in general, included in a decedent's estate for federal estate tax purposes, it may be possible to exclude the insured portion of the death benefit if the decedent had no incidents of ownership in the policy.

Fully Insured Pension Plans

A fully insured pension plan is one that is funded exclusively by life insurance or annuity contracts. There is no trusteed (uninsured) side fund. A plan is considered fully insured for the plan year if it meets the following requirements:

- The plan is funded exclusively by the purchase of individual insurance contracts. Under the regulations, such contracts can be either individual or group and can be life insurance or annuity contracts or a combination of both.
- The contracts provide for level annual (or more frequent) premiums extending to retirement age for each individual. However, the employer's cost need not be level since the regulations permit the employer to experience gains and to use dividends to reduce premiums.
- Plan benefits are equal to the contract benefits and are guaranteed by a licensed insurance company.
- Premiums have been paid without lapse (or the policy has been reinstated after a lapse).
- No rights under the contracts have been subject to a security interest during the plan year.
- No policy loans are outstanding at any time during the plan year.

Fully insured pension plans were once common, but the high investment returns of the late 1970s lured many pension investors away from traditional insured pension products. Today, however, fully insured plans are coming into their own, and life insurance agents and pension sponsors should take another look at these products. The immediate reason is that recent changes in the pension law's minimum funding rules have made many noninsured plans "overfunded," and fully insured plans may offer a solution to this widespread problem. But even when overfunding problem is not a factor, fully insured plans may offer advantages.

Fully insured plans have always been exempt from ERISA's minimum funding rules for pension plans, and the impact of recent unfavorable changes in the rules makes this exemption even more advantageous.

In addition, fully insured plans are eligible for a simplification of the ERISA reporting requirements (Form 5500 series). An insured plan need not file Schedule B, Actuarial Information with its Form 5500 (or 5500–C/R) and thus does not need a certification by an enrolled actuary. This reduces the cost and complexity of plan administration to some degree. Finally, a fully insured plan is exempt from the requirement of quarterly pension deposits since that is also tied to the minimum funding requirements. Fully insured plans are, however, subject to Pension Benefit Guaranty Corporation (PBGC) coverage and annual premium requirements.

Fully insured funding can be used either with a new plan or an existing plan. The employer can be a corporation or an unincorporated business. Typically, a group type of contract is used, with individual accounts for each participant. All benefits are guaranteed by the insurance company. The premium is based on the guaranteed interest and annuity rates, which are typically conservative, resulting in larger initial annual deposits than in a typical uninsured plan. Excess earnings beyond the guaranteed level are used to reduce future premiums.

Using excess earnings to reduce future premiums results in a funding pattern that is the opposite of that found in a trusteed plan. In the insured plan for a given group of plan participants, the funding level is higher at the beginning of the plan and drops as participants move toward retirement. This maximizes the overall tax deduction by allowing more of it to be taken earlier. It also often permits deductions for an existing plan that has reached the full funding limitation with uninsured funding. By comparison, a traditional trusteed plan starts with a relatively low level of funding, which increases as each participant nears retirement.

Coordination of Death Benefits

A lump-sum insured death benefit is often provided in a fully insured plan in addition to the preretirement survivor annuity required by law in most plans. If so, the total death benefit must not exceed the incidental limits. For example, if the lump-sum benefit is at the maximum limit, it can be reduced by the actuarial present value of the preretirement survivor annuity.

Survivorship Benefits

In addition to cash death benefits, insured or otherwise, death benefits can be provided in the form of annuity options with survivorship features—that is, annuities that continue partial or full payment to a beneficiary after the death of the participant. Survivorship annuities for the participant's spouse are required in certain cases. However, survivorship annuities for the spouse in a form somewhat different from the qualified joint-and-survivor annuity or survivorship annuities for beneficiaries other than the spouse can be included as benefit options in a qualified plan. These options must not exceed the plan's incidental limits for death benefits.

Designing Incidental Death Benefits

It is relatively uncommon for a qualified plan to provide term life insurance to participants because the tax treatment provides no advantage to the employee. It is more common, however, to use cash value life insurance as funding for the plan because the PS 58 rates or the insurance company's term rates may prove to be a relatively favorable way to provide life insurance.

The decision whether to include life insurance in a qualified plan depends on the plan's objective. The employer must first decide whether and to what extent it will provide death benefits to employees—under a group term or other plan or as an incidental benefit in a qualified plan. The death benefit should be so designed to produce the lowest employer and employee cost for the benefit level desired. A death benefit should be included in the qualified plan only to the extent it is consistent with this objective.

Other Plans

A Keogh plan is a qualified plan available to a proprietor or one or more partners of an unincorporated business. Life insurance can be used to provide a death benefit for regular employees covered under the plan, and the rules discussed in this chapter apply. Life insurance can also be provided under the plan for a proprietor or partners, but the tax treatment for proprietors and partners is slightly less favorable.

Life insurance can also be used to provide an incidental benefit under a tax-deferred annuity plan on much the same basis as in a qualified profit-sharing plan. Covered employees will have PS 58 costs to report as taxable income, as in a regular qualified plan.

Life insurance contracts are not permissible investments for an individual retirement plan (IRA). In effect, this means that an IRA cannot provide an insured death benefit. Similarly, a SEP (simplified employee pension) plan cannot purchase life insurance since SEPs are funded with individual IRA contracts.

LIFE INSURANCE IN NONQUALIFIED DEFERRED-COMPENSATION PLANS

Advantages of Nonqualified Plans

A nonqualified deferred-compensation plan is an employer-provided retirement plan that does not meet the qualified plan rules. The nonqualified approach may be advantageous for a closely held corporation if it has the following objectives:

- to exceed the maximum benefit and contribution levels applicable to qualified plans for selected employees
- to provide a retirement plan for owners and other key employees without including rank-and-file employees in the plan
- to avoid the administrative compliance standards applicable to qualified plans
- to permit shareholder-employees or other key executives to temporarily defer taxes on income into a later tax year

Types of Nonqualified Deferred-Compensation Plans and Salary Reduction Arrangements

A salary reduction plan, also called an *in lieu of* plan, is an agreement between the employer and the participating employee either to reduce the employee's salary or to defer an anticipated bonus and provide that such amounts be received in future tax years. These plans defer compensation that the employee would otherwise receive in cash, and they generally provide an investment return on the amounts deferred. One type of salary reduction plan, the *top-hat plan,* is a deferred-compensation plan for a select group of management or highly compensated employees in which the participant elects to defer current salary amounts to provide benefits at his or her retirement.

As discussed later, the taxation for such compensation will be deferred only if specific requirements are met. Salary reduction arrangements have decreased in popularity with the reduction of individual income tax rates.

Salary Continuation Plans

Most nonqualified plans fit into the broad category of salary continuation plans. Salary continuation plans can be designed to provide deferred-compensation benefits at the participant's death, disability, and/or retirement. These arrangements have no current cash option available to the employee. The death or disability benefits are a percentage of the employee's compensation and are provided to the employee or his or her designated beneficiary. (Disability salary continuation plans are covered in more detail in chapter 7.)

Salary continuation plans designed to provide retirement benefits can be categorized as *excess-benefit plans* or *supplemental executive retirement plans (SERPs).* An excess-benefit plan is a retirement plan in which selected participants, generally shareholder-employees and key executives, will receive retirement benefits in excess of those possible under the qualified plan limitations. That is, these plans provide (1) benefits in excess of the 100-percent-of-salary or $115,641 (for 1993) limitation in defined-benefit plans or (2) contributions in excess of the 25-percent-of-salary or $30,000 limitation in defined-contribution plans.

A SERP generally complements the qualified plan benefits for a selected group of participants. SERPs provide benefits for a corporation's key executives and, unlike excess-benefit plans, supplement the retirement benefits at levels both above and below the qualified plan limitations. These plans will meet the goal of providing discriminatory benefits to shareholder-employees and other key executives. A closely held business can use a salary continuation plan to provide a substantial retirement, disability, and death benefit to the owners without necessitating the costly inclusion of rank-and-file employees.

Death-Benefit-Only (DBO) Plans

DBO plans are nonqualified plans designed to provide death benefits to a participant's heirs. While DBO plans can provide a lump sum to the participant's survivors, they generally pay installment benefits at the participant's death. Since a DBO is a nonqualified plan, participation can be based on discriminatory factors. Survivor benefits are taxable as ordinary income to the recipient-survivor and are deductible by the corporation when paid to the survivors. The DBO plan benefits will be included in the participant's estate unless (1) the decedent participated in no other nonqualified deferred-compensation plan with the employer that provided living benefits, and (2) the participant did not reserve the right to change the beneficiary initially designated. If estate inclusion is a problem, the employer and employee should consider a Sec. 162 bonus plan or a split-dollar agreement (both discussed earlier) with the use of an irrevocable life insurance trust (ILIT).

Requirements for Income Tax Deferral in Nonqualified Deferred-Compensation Plans

The taxation of nonqualified deferred-compensation benefits links the timing of the corporation's deduction to the participant's receipt of benefits. The key to success is deferring the income tax liability until the receipt of the benefit. To avoid current taxation on the deferred benefit, the employee cannot (1) be in *constructive receipt* of the income or (2) receive a current *economic benefit* from the deferred amounts.

To avoid constructive receipt the employee's receipt of the income must be

- subject to *substantial limitation or restriction*. This requirement is met if the employee simply has to wait a certain time period (for example, until retirement) for the benefits.
- deferred by binding agreement prior to the time when the employee earns the compensation. The employee cannot have the choice of taking cash when the income is earned. In the salary reduction agreement the employee and employer make an agreement to defer the receipt of the salary or bonus before the related services are performed.

Any economic benefit currently received from the nonqualified plan is immediately taxable to the participant even if the benefit is not constructively received. The participant receives an economic benefit if funds are vested or set aside for the employee outside the claims of general corporate creditors. Under such circumstances the economic benefit exists because the employee has a cash equivalency in the form of a secured and funded promise.

An economic benefit also exists if the funds are placed in an irrevocable trust on behalf of the participant. The corpus of the trust will be a cash equivalent because the employer has given up control of the assets in the plan. To avoid an economic benefit, the plan assets must be subject to substantial risk of forfeiture. The assets can be set aside in (1) a reserve account held by the employer, (2) a revocable trust, or (3) a rabbi trust.[1] Under a reserve account or revocable trust there is no economic benefit because all plan funds are subject to the employer's control. In a rabbi trust, because the assets are available to the general creditors of the corporation by the terms of the trust, no economic benefit exists.

Financing the Employer's Obligation in Nonqualified Deferred-Compensation Plan with Life Insurance

The employer can finance its obligation in a nonqualified plan through corporate-owned life insurance. This type of financing is attractive since life insurance as a corporate asset is a good match for the type of liabilities created by the various nonqualified arrangements. The accumulation in an ordinary life insurance policy or the benefits of an annuity policy can be useful in the participant's retirement years to provide for any salary continuation benefits offered by the plan. Of course, the primary benefit of the life insurance financing is its ability to meet the employer's death benefit obligation should the participant die prematurely. The life insurance financing is particularly appropriate to provide benefits in a DBO plan.

Nonqualified plan policies are owned by and payable to the employer. As such, they avoid the constructive-receipt or economic-benefit problems because the general creditors have access to the funding policies. The premiums are, of course, nondeductible; however, the cash surrender value builds up tax free, and the proceeds will be nontaxable when received (the corporate alternative minimum tax [AMT], discussed later in this chapter, may create an alternative tax liability under these circumstances). The corporation receives a deduction when the benefits are actually paid to the participant.

For quick reference table 12-4 shows the applications of the various types of executive life insurance plans discussed in this chapter.

KEY PERSON PROTECTION

The success of a closely held business often depends on the personal services of key owner-employees and key non-owner-employees. The loss of a key employee's services due to death or disability will probably result in a loss of income, at least temporarily, to the closely held business. In addition, the business could incur increased expenses if a replacement employee has to be recruited at a higher salary and requires extensive training. This key employee exposure should be considered to protect the income of the business.

The first step in handling this risk is to identify the key employees. Key employees have several characteristics distinguishing them from other employees, including the following:

- A key employee might have a specialized skill critical to the success of the particular closely held business. Potential replacements may possess this skill, but replacement employees might have to be recruited at higher salary levels.
- The employee has a significant customer or client base and is responsible for attracting significant amounts of business.
- The key employee might be a source of capital if his or her loss would damage the closely held business's credit rating.

Identifying the key employee might be more difficult than it seems. The owners of a closely hold business are generally material participants in the business and can be classified as key employees. But beyond the owners the key employee risk is often overlooked. The business owners might uncover this risk by considering the damage to the business that would occur if a specific managerial employee was absent for longer than the normal vacation period.

Valuing the Key Employee

Determining the key employee's value to the closely held business is even more speculative than the valuation of the business itself. The actual valuation method employed depends on the characteristic of the employee that creates the key employee status. Determining the value of the key employee who attracts

TABLE 12-4
Comparison of Methods for Inclusion of Life Insurance in the Compensation Plan

	Qualified Plans	Nonqualified Plan Benefits	DBOs	Sec. 79 Plans	Sec. 162 Bonus Plans	Split-Dollar Plans	Reverse Split Dollar Plans
Corporate Income Tax Deduction	Up to incidental limits	Benefits deductible when paid	Benefits deductible when paid	Yes, if reasonable compensation	Yes, if reasonable compensation	No deduction	No deduction
Current Income Taxation to Employee	PS 58 costs less employee contribution	No	No	Table 1 costs for coverage above $50,000	Full amount of bonus	PS 58 cost less employee contribution	Uncertain
Employee's Share of Death Benefit	Full proceeds	Full deferred-compensation benefit	Full proceeds	Full proceeds	Full proceeds	Amount at risk (traditional plan)	Cash surrender value (full proceeds after RSD plan terminates
Income Taxation of Benefits Received by Heirs	Tax free to extent of amount at risk	Yes	Yes	No	No	No	No
Proceeds in Employee's Estate for Estate Tax Purposes	Yes	Yes	No, unless the decedent possessed living nonqualified benefits	Yes, unless assigned to third-party owner more than 3 years prior to death	Yes, unless assigned to third-party owner more than 3 years prior to death	Yes, unless assigned to third-party owner more than 3 years prior to death	Yes, unless assigned to third-party owner more than 3 years prior to death (estate gets a deduction for amount of death benefit payable to corporation)
Employee Access to Cash Surrender Value	No, unless profit-sharing plan (indirect access through plan loan provisions in other qualified plans)	No	No	N/A	Yes	No, unless a rollout occurs	Yes, unless restricted by plan agreement

substantial business might be relatively easy. The net income resulting from the business he or she produces in excess of the amount of net income that could be expected from a similarly situated but less effective employee could be capitalized in some manner. Or if business goodwill is attributed to one key employee, the income level above the amount expected for a similar business can be attributed to that employee. This income attributed to goodwill can be capitalized to arrive at a current value for the employee.

> *Example:* A business currently has $500,000 of tangible assets and generates $100,000 a year in net income. Similarly situated businesses have a rate of return on tangible assets of 10 percent. In this case $50,000 of income can be attributed to capital, and $50,000 can be attributed to goodwill and the management skill of the key employee. Using business valuation capitalization methods, we can capitalize the $50,000 of earnings at the 10 percent expected return rate and reach a value for the key employee. The capitalization factor in this case is 10 (100 ÷ 10).

Net income attributed to goodwill   x   Capitalization factor   =   Value of goodwill resulting from employee

$$\$50,000 \text{ x } 10 = \$500,000$$

In this case the key employee's value to the business is $500,000.

The value of a key employee, particularly when more than one key employee is present, is usually more difficult to determine than in the example above. The firm may have to consider various subjective factors to arrive at a proxy for the key employee's value. For example, the firm should consider replacement salaries and the training required for a replacement employee to become effective. A simple approach might be to take the key employee and pick some multiple of current salary as a proxy for his or her value.

Key Employee Life Insurance

A business can purchase life insurance on the life of the key employee to cover the risk of an income loss and/or increase in expenses resulting from the key employee's death. Term insurance can be purchased if the primary concern is the key employee's dollar value to the business. Decreasing term might be appropriate because the key employee exposure decreases as the insured approaches retirement since the business can expect to have his or her services for a fewer number of years.

Key employee insurance, however, is usually coupled with some other purpose such as providing a retirement benefit for the key employee. Permanent life insurance is typically purchased to meet this objective. The life insurance death benefit will be received by the business as indemnification for the income loss and/or increase in expenses resulting from the key employee's death. If the insured survives to retirement, the corporation can use the cash surrender value to fund a deferred-compensation retirement benefit. Another approach is for the business to transfer the policy to the employee at retirement.

The business should be the owner and beneficiary of key employee life insurance. This should pose no insurable interest problems since the business will suffer a pecuniary loss at the death of the key employee. The premiums for key employee insurance will be nondeductible, while death benefits will be received tax free. An additional benefit of key employee insurance is that no accumulated-earnings tax problems should result since the accumulation of earnings to insure the key employee death risk will meet the reasonable-business-needs test. For incorporated businesses key employee life insurance may, however, increase exposure to the alternative minimum corporate tax discussed later.

FUNDING BUY-SELL AGREEMENTS WITH LIFE INSURANCE

The death of an owner of a closely held business is typically disruptive for the business and often leads to its failure. When a business owner dies, the executor of his or her estate has the role of collecting, preserving, and distributing the decedent's assets. Of course, such assets include both the business and personal assets owned by the decedent at the time of his or her death. The closely held business presents many difficulties for the executor unless the decedent's estate was appropriately planned for business continuation.

A properly designed buy-sell agreement will assure that the estate will be able to sell its interest in the closely held business for a reasonable price. The purchasers of the business interest, perhaps the surviving co-owners of the business, will obtain the business interest and avoid the difficulties associated with passing the business interest through probate. Without an appropriate continuation plan, the executor may be compelled to sell the business interest to pay the estate's settlement costs and federal estate taxes and/or state inheritance taxes. The settlement costs must be paid in cash promptly after the business owner's death. For example, the federal estate taxes are due 9 months after death. Some state death taxes have earlier deadlines. Under these circumstances, the executor will have a tenuous bargaining position, and a forced sale of the business interest may yield far less than full fair market value. Without a buy-sell agreement therefore the surviving co-owners face a great deal of uncertainty. The survivors may be pressured to provide distributions of business income for the decedent's heirs. They may also face the prospect that the executor or the heirs may choose to sell the business interest to outsiders. In any event, the failure to plan for business continuation increases the probability that the business will ultimately fail.

Benefits of the Buy-Sell Agreement

Although contemplating death is not pleasant for anyone, proper estate planning employing a buy-sell agreement offers several advantages. The benefits of such an agreement can be summarized as follows:

- It guarantees a market for the business interest.
- It provides liquidity for the payment of death taxes and other estate settlement costs.

- It helps establish the estate tax value of the decedent's business interest making the estate planning process more reliable for the owner.
- It provides that the business will continue in the hands of the surviving owners and/or employees.
- It makes the business a better credit risk since its probability of continuation is enhanced.

Basic Structure of a Buy-Sell Agreement

A properly designed buy-sell agreement has several provisions that will generally be included regardless of the type of agreement. The parties to a buy-sell agreement should be aware that the agreement is an important legal contract that carries out a critical purpose. The parties are advised to obtain competent legal counsel to assist in forming the agreement. Provisions of the typical buy-sell agreement include the following:

- *parties to the agreement.* All buy-sell agreements contain a provision that clearly identifies the various parties.
- *purpose of the agreement.* A buy-sell agreement should contain a statement indicating its purpose. One advantage of incorporating a statement of purpose is to document the intent of the agreement should a dispute arise later.
- *commitment of the parties.* The obligation of all parties to the agreement should be clearly stated. For example, it should be clear that the estate of the deceased business owner will sell the business interest to the parties who become purchasers under the terms of the agreement.
- *description of the business interest.* The agreement should clearly describe the business interest that is actually to be bought and sold.
- *lifetime transfer restrictions.* Most buy-sell agreements contain a first-offer provision preventing the parties to the agreement from disposing of the business interest to outsiders while the parties are living.
- *purchase price.* The buy-sell agreement should specify a purchase price or, in the alternative, a method for determining the purchase price at which the business interest will be bought and sold.
- *funding provisions.* The terms of the agreement should specify how the purchase price will be funded. For example, if the agreement is funded with life insurance, the agreement should indicate how such life insurance will be structured and funded.
- *details of the transfer.* The actual specifics of the transfer of the business should be described. For example, when and where settlement will occur are important terms of the agreement.
- *modification or termination of the agreement.* The agreement should provide for its modification or termination should all parties decide that the agreement in its current form no longer meets their goals.

Sole Proprietorship Continuation Agreements

The sole proprietorship is by far the most common form of business ownership. It is distinct from other forms of business ownership in many ways.

Most important, there is no legal distinction between the business and personal assets of the owner. Only one individual can be the owner of a sole proprietorship. As such, when the sole proprietor dies or loses legal capacity to transact business, the sole proprietorship must terminate. Planning for this contingency is essential if the sole proprietor's family can expect to get full value for the business interest.

Since there is only one owner of a sole proprietorship, its buy-sell agreement necessarily has a definite buyer and a definite seller. The buy-sell agreement will bind the proprietor's estate to sell and the purchaser to buy the proprietorship assets. There is no question as to who will be the purchaser and the seller since there is only one owner with a business interest to sell.

Choosing a Purchaser

A critical step for a proprietorship buy-sell agreement is to find the appropriate purchaser. A natural successor to the sole proprietor may not exist. That is, there are no co-owners of the sole proprietorship waiting to take over. Quite often, the sole proprietor has no family successors who are capable and/or willing to step in at the sole proprietor's death. Choosing the appropriate buyer requires careful planning. Often a key employee or group of employees will be selected as purchaser. Such individuals, if available, are logical choices for two reasons. First, the key employee or employees of the sole proprietorship are familiar with the business interest. This is particularly important if the business requires unique skills to perform its function. Second, the key employees may be willing to enter into a buy-sell agreement to protect their own future employment. Without a buy-sell agreement, the sole proprietorship will often be liquidated or sold to outsiders at the death of the proprietor. This could leave the key employees unemployed and without a future in the proprietorship.

If there are no key employees or natural successors to the sole proprietor, a careful search will have to be made. It is often recommended that the sole proprietor hire and provide a training program for an employee who has the potential to take over the business. Or the sole proprietor could seek a buyer from competitors who may desire to take over the proprietor's business at some point in the future. This is particularly appropriate for a professional practitioner who has developed substantial goodwill and a large patient/client list. The death of the sole practitioner will result in the loss of that goodwill unless a purchaser can be found for a buy-sell agreement.

Life Insurance Funding

The life insurance arrangements for a sole proprietorship buy-sell agreement are relatively simple. The purchasing party is obligated to provide sale proceeds to the deceased proprietor's estate. Accordingly, the applicant, owner, and premium payer for such life insurance should be the purchasing party. The purchaser should obtain sufficient coverage on the life of the sole proprietorship to make the required payments to the estate. Insurable interest exists for such a policy since the purchaser has a financial obligation created by the death of the sole proprietor-insured. The insurance funding the agreement should be reviewed periodically, and the purchaser should obtain additional coverage necessitated by an increase in the value of the proprietorship.

Buy-Sell Agreements for Partnerships

A general partnership terminates by operation of law at the death of the partner unless the partnership agreement provides for continuation. Without lifetime planning a deceased partner's interest in the partnership will have to be liquidated by the surviving partner(s). The surviving partners are required to provide a fair liquidation price to a deceased partner's estate. However, it is often difficult for the surviving partners to provide these payments without a tremendous burden on the future partnership income.

The goal of the surviving partners is to continue the business of the partnership without interruption. Certainly, they would like to keep liquidation payments to a minimum. Therefore the surviving partners' goals are, obviously, incongruent with those of the deceased partner's estate. Without a prearranged agreement, a dispute between the heirs and the surviving partners is nearly inevitable. The estate may be compelled to settle for far less than the fair market value of the business. If the surviving partners cannot make the required payments, the partnership may have to be sold or terminated—a result that generally benefits neither the heirs nor the surviving partners. The solution is a binding partnership buy-sell agreement.

A partnership buy-sell agreement is different from that of a sole proprietorship. Since there is more than one owner, the partnership buy-sell agreement must address the possibility that any of the partners will be the next to die. Therefore the partnership buy-sell agreement contains mutual promises between the partners that provide for different purchasers and sellers depending on the circumstances. That is, each partner will bind his or her estate to sell if he or she is the first to die. Each partner will also agree to purchase the partnership interest held by the deceased partner's estate if he or she is among the surviving partners.

Types of Partnership Buy-Sell Agreements

Entity Approach. Under the entity approach, it is the partnership that becomes the purchaser in the buy-sell agreement. Technically, the partnership *liquidates* the interest held by the deceased partner's estate. That is, the partnership makes payments to the estate that liquidate the interest the estate holds. Liquidation payments are divided into two components. The first component is a payment in exchange for the decedent's partnership interest. These payments are subject to capital-gain tax treatment. The remaining payments are ordinary income items that are taxable on the estate's income tax return, such as the deceased partner's share of partnership income and unrealized receivables. Under an entity buy-sell agreement both the partners and partnership are parties to the agreement. The partnership agreement provides for continuation of the partnership's business by the survivors.

Cross-Purchase Approach. In a cross-purchase agreement the individual partners are the sellers and purchasers. The partners each make mutual promises to be a buyer or seller depending on the circumstances. Each partner agrees to purchase a share of any deceased partner's interest. Each partner also binds his or her estate to sell its partnership interest to the surviving partners. Although the surviving partners purchase the interest from a deceased partner's estate, the tax treatment of the purchase and sale is similar, but not identical to, the entity approach. That is, some portion of the purchase price will be treated as the exchange of a capital asset—the partnership interest. The remaining portion of the purchase payments will be treated as distributions of income to the deceased partner's estate.

The choice between the entity or cross-purchase approach is a complex one. Details such as the number of partners, the differences in income tax treatment, the cost basis of the different partners, and the financial considerations of the partnership will dictate the appropriate choice. A partnership should not enter into a buy-sell agreement without careful consideration and planning with respect to the form of the agreement.

Insurance Arrangements for Partnership Buy-Sell Agreements

Entity (Liquidation) Agreements. The entity buy-sell approach provides that the partnership will liquidate the interest of a deceased partner at his or her death. If life insurance is used to fund the agreement, the partnership is a logical choice for applicant, owner, and beneficiary of the policies. After all, the partnership will have the obligation to pay the deceased partner's estate. The partnership should acquire life insurance on the life of each partner who becomes a party to the agreement. To the extent possible, the partnership should maintain face amounts of coverage that equal its obligations under the buy-sell agreement.

Generally the partnership should adopt the entity approach if it is in a better financial position to make the premium payments than the individual partners. This will be particularly true if some partners are younger and/or own smaller partnership interests. The partnership ownership of life insurance creates a pooling approach to funding the buy-sell agreement. The business might also adopt the entity approach if there are a large number of partners entering into the agreement. Fewer individual life insurance policies are usually required if the partnership has more than two partners.

Cross-Purchase Agreements. The cross-purchase agreement provides that the surviving partners are obligated to buy a prearranged share of a deceased partner's interest from his or her estate. The agreement is generally funded by life insurance policies owned by the individual partners. Each partner should purchase life insurance policies on the life of the other partners whose deaths will obligate the policyowner to purchase the decedent's partnership interest. Thus the individual partners become owners, beneficiaries, and premium payers for life insurance policies covering the lives of the other partners. At the death of a partner, the surviving partners receive the death proceeds from the policies, which will be transferred to the deceased partner's estate in exchange for the partnership interest. Each partner should secure a policy with a death benefit equal to his or her share of the purchase price of a deceased partner's interest.

Corporate Buy-Sell Agreements

Many closely held enterprises are incorporated by their owners. A corporation is a separate legal entity apart from its shareholders. As such, it provides limited liability to its investors and is a separate taxpayer with entirely different tax rates and rules than those applicable to individual taxpayers. Although the corporation as a separate entity has, potentially, a perpetual life, the continuation problems that plague other forms of closely held enterprises are often applicable to closely held corporations as well. From a practical standpoint, a closely held business, regardless of its form, cannot continue without the services of at least one key individual. In a closely held corporation, the key individual or individuals usually include the shareholders. The death, retirement, or disability of these key individuals threatens the future of the corporation. For this reason, the closely held corporation and its shareholders should consider adopting a buy-sell agreement.

Types of Corporate Buy-Sell Agreements

Entity (Stock Redemption) Buy-Sell Agreement. Under a stock-redemption agreement the corporation is the "purchaser" of the stock at the death of a shareholder. Each shareholder subject to the agreement binds his or her estate to transfer the stock to the corporation in exchange for the required purchase price. Thus both the shareholders and corporation are parties to the stock redemption agreement. The actual form of transaction is that the corporation redeems a deceased shareholder's stock in exchange for a redemption distribution. The corporation either retires the stock or holds it as treasury stock. This reduces the number of shares of stock outstanding in the corporation. From the surviving shareholder's standpoint, the practical effect of a stock redemption is that the percentage ownership held by each surviving shareholder increases proportionately when a deceased shareholder's stock is redeemed.

The tax treatment of a stock redemption is extremely complex and beyond the scope of this discussion. However, a stock redemption is treated as a distribution of cash or property from the corporation to a shareholder. Under many circumstances, the redemption distribution is treated as a taxable dividend to the redeemed shareholder. Under certain exceptions, a redemption is treated as a sale or exchange subject to capital gains. The reader should be aware that it is essential to qualify the stock redemption as a sale or exchange to avoid disastrous tax consequences to the redeemed shareholder's estate. Generally speaking, a stock-redemption plan will not qualify for the desired sale-or-exchange treatment if family members of the decedent own stock in the corporation and plan to be the decedent's successors in the corporation.

Another tax problem associated with the stock-redemption agreement is the loss of income tax cost basis for the surviving shareholders. Since the corporation is the purchaser in the stock-redemption agreement, the surviving shareholders will not be treated as contributors to the purchase. Thus the surviving shareholders will not receive an increase in their income tax basis in their stock since the corporation, not the shareholders, provides the purchase price.

Corporate Cross-Purchase Buy-Sell Agreements. The corporate cross-purchase agreement is analogous to the partnership cross-purchase agreement discussed earlier. That is, each shareholder agrees to purchase a specified percentage of the shares of stock held by a deceased shareholder at the time of death. Each shareholder must also agree to bind his or her estate to sell the stock owned at his or her death. The corporation is not a direct party to the buy-sell agreement. The corporation should, however, issue stock certificates endorsed with a statement that the stock is subject to the terms of the buy-sell agreement.

If few shareholders are involved, the cross-purchase agreement is advantageous from a tax standpoint in two respects. First, the sale of stock by a deceased shareholder's estate will always be treated as a sale or exchange. Thus the estate gets favorable capital-gains tax treatment. This makes the cross-purchase agreement the preferable form of buy-sell agreement for a family corporation where a stock redemption would often result in taxable dividends to the estate. Second, the surviving shareholders are direct purchasers, and each receives income tax cost basis in his or her stock equal to the amount of the purchase price paid.

Insurance Arrangements for Corporate Buy-Sell Agreement

Stock-Redemption Agreements. The stock redemption buy-sell agreement requires that the corporation redeem a deceased shareholder's shares of stock at his or her death. If life insurance is chosen as the agreement's funding mechanism, the corporation should be the applicant, owner, and beneficiary of the policies. Ownership of the policies is particularly important for a corporation that does not have an abundance of retained earnings. Under most state corporate laws, a corporation cannot make a distribution of any kind to a shareholder, including a stock redemption, unless the corporation has adequate surplus. The receipt of life insurance proceeds at a shareholder's death provides the necessary surplus to redeem the deceased shareholder's stock. Therefore the corporation should acquire life insurance on the life of each shareholder who becomes a party to the agreement. To ensure that the death proceeds will be adequate to meet the corporation's obligation, the stock-redemption agreement should be updated periodically to prevent the face amounts of life insurance coverage from becoming inadequate as the value of the corporation rises.

Cross-Purchase Agreements. The cross-purchase agreement provides that the surviving shareholders are obligated to buy a prearranged share of a deceased shareholder's stock from the deceased's estate. If life insurance is the chosen funding mechanism for the agreement, each shareholder should purchase adequate life insurance on the life of the other shareholders. Each individual shareholder then becomes owner, beneficiary, premium payer, and beneficiary for the life insurance policies covering the lives of the other shareholders. At a shareholder's death the surviving shareholders will receive the death benefits from the policies and will transfer the death benefit proceeds to the deceased shareholder's estate in exchange for the appropriate amount of his or her stock. Since individual shareholders must be relied upon to maintain the funding for agreement, there is often the concern that some parties will not live up to the terms of the contract. To ensure that the cross-purchase agreement is carried out, a trustee is often used as an overseer to hold the policies and consummate the purchase and sale of stock at a shareholder's death.

Tax Implications of Corporate-Owned Life Insurance (COLI)

A regular corporation, often referred to as a C corporation, is a separate taxpayer with different tax rules from those applicable for individual income tax purposes. One distinct tax rule is the corporate alternative minimum tax. The corporate AMT has a particular negative impact on COLI. The life insurance product generally is exempt from income taxes. That is, the cash surrender value build-up in a policy is usually not subject to current income taxes. In addition, the death proceeds are received by the named beneficiary tax free. However, the corporate AMT may result in additional taxes for a stock-redemption plan funded with life insurance.

The AMT is a tax equal to 20 percent of the corporate alternative minimum taxable income (AMTI). AMTI is determined by adding a list of tax-preference items to the corporation's regular taxable income. The corporation pays the AMT if it exceeds the corporation's regular income tax liability for the year. Among the preferences added to AMTI is 75 percent of current adjusted earnings. COLI creates an increase in current adjusted earnings to the extent that the policy provides income not counted in the regular income tax base. COLI increases current adjusted earnings in the following manner:

- by the excess of the annual increase in cash surrender value over the annual premium paid for the policy (with adjustments for policy distributions)
- by the amount of death proceeds received by the corporation over the policy's AMT tax basis in the policy at the time of death

Thus the current adjusted earnings preference will affect an insured stock-redemption agreement funded with COLI, and the AMT liability could have a significant impact on the agreement in the year of a shareholder's death. The tax imposed as a result of the AMT could cause the stock-redemption agreement to be underfunded by the amount of such tax. A reasonable ballpark estimate is that the corporate AMT will result in the need to overfund the death benefit in policies funding corporate stock redemptions by an amount from 15 to 17 percent.

The corporate AMT also has a significant impact on the complexity of a corporation's tax reporting. If COLI is owned by and payable to the corporation, a separate set of books must be maintained to track the AMT basis over the insurance policies' holding period. The normal federal income tax basis will apply if the policies are cash surrendered or exchanged in a manner that creates normal income taxes. The AMT basis, which will often be different from regular income tax basis, will apply solely to determine the AMT liability resulting from the corporation's ownership of such policies.

Buy-Sell Agreements for S Corporations

For federal income tax reasons, many corporations make a special election to receive S corporation status. This election is particularly favorable for shareholders who desire a direct pass-through of tax items (that is, taxable income, deductions, and so forth) directly to the individual shareholders. The S corporation generally pays no tax at the corporate level, and shareholders are taxed similarly to, although certainly not identically to, partners of a partnership. The reader should be aware of the growing importance of S corporations and the special factors that need to be considered for continuation planning for such entities.

Preserving the S Election through Buy-Sell Agreements

Shareholders make the S corporation election for important tax reasons. It is imperative that they preserve this election to avoid adverse tax consequences. For this reason, continuation planning is particularly important for an S corporation. Actions that cause the S corporation to fail to meet the requirements for S status will cause termination of the S election. Unless the termination is deemed inadvertent by the IRS, a future S election will be unavailable for 5 years.

Only certain corporations are eligible for S elections. A corporation is ineligible for S status if it has

- more than 35 shareholders
- shareholders who are corporations, partnerships, nonresident aliens, or ineligible trusts
- more than one class of stock
- ownership in a subsidiary corporation

A mandatory buy-sell agreement operative on the death of an S corporation shareholder can prevent the transfer of such stock to ineligible shareholders. Either the standard stock-redemption or cross-purchase agreement will cause the deceased S corporation shareholder's stock to be held by the entity or individuals who already qualify for the S election. Thus an effective buy-sell agreement for an S corporation prevents the termination of the S election by transfer to an ineligible shareholder. As with other buy-sell agreements, the provisions of the S corporation buy-sell agreement should be binding and enforceable on all parties.

Tax Treatment of the S Corporation Buy-Sell Agreement

Generally speaking, the cross-purchase arrangement will not change the tax implications of an S corporation buy-sell agreement. Since the entity is not involved in the agreement, the unusual tax characteristics of S corporations will not apply. Should a stock redemption agreement be adopted by the S corporation, the tax implications are distinctly different from those applicable to normal corporate stock-redemption agreements. The S corporation has its own unique tax accounting system for determining the reporting of tax items affecting the corporation. Generally, all income received by the S corporation will be reported proportionally by the shareholders of the S corporation on their individual income-tax returns. A stock-redemption agreement for the S corporation will normally be funded by policies owned by and payable to the corporation. Since such life insurance is an aftertax expense, the policies funding this stock redemption agreement will be paid for by dollars taxable to the individual shareholders. Thus, similar to a partnership entity buy-sell agreement, the S corporation shareholders pay for the funding of a stock redemption agreement in proportion to their ownership in the corporation. Finally, accounting rules that record the retained earnings of the S corporation are particularly complex. These accounting rules affect every aspect of the S corporation's participation in a stock-redemption plan.

NOTE

1. A rabbi trust is a trust, usually irrevocable, established by a corporate employer to finance payment of deferred-compensation benefits for an employee. The corporation places cash and other assets into the rabbi trust to finance its promise to pay benefits at the employee's retirement. The trust contains a provision, however, that trust assets are available to the corporation's creditors. A rabbi trust is so named because the first trust of this kind ruled on by the IRS was established for a rabbi.

13

Basis of Risk Measurement

Dan M. McGill
Revised by Norma Nielson and Donald Jones

As stated in an earlier chapter, insurance is a mechanism through which certainty replaces uncertainty. This occurs when many people exposed to loss from a particular hazard contribute to a common fund so those who suffer a loss from that cause can be compensated. The certainty of losing the premium replaces the uncertainty of a larger loss. For a plan of insurance to function, the pricing method needs to measure the risk of loss and determine the amount to be contributed by each participant. The theory of probability provides such scientific measurement.

THEORY OF PROBABILITY

The theory of probability develops mathematical representations of uncertainty. A fraction between zero and one, called the *probability*, describes the chance of each possible outcome or collection of outcomes. A set of possible outcomes is called an *event*. One interpretation of the probability fraction is that its numerator is the number of times we expect an event to happen; the denominator is the number of times the event could possibly happen. The probability associated with the combination of all possible outcomes must be one. The probability that a particular event will *not* happen is one minus the probability that it will happen. These principles can be clarified by a few simple illustrations.

For example, consider the probability associated with tossing a coin. The coin will fall either heads up or tails up when tossed. Two possible outcomes exist, and only one is the outcome of tossing a head. Therefore the probability of tossing a head is ½. The probability that the coin will fall *either* heads or tails is ½+½ or one.

Another example is drawing a card at random from a deck of 52 playing cards. The chance that the ace of spades will be drawn from the deck is 1/52. Of the 52 cards, only one is the ace of spades. Of the 52 cards, four are aces. Thus the probability of drawing an ace of any suit is 4/52. The probability that a card drawn randomly will *not* be an ace is one minus the probability of drawing an ace, or 48/52.

Sometimes we need to know the probability of a particular combination of events. If the occurrence of one event does not change the probabilities associated with another event, the events are *independent*. We find the probability that two independent events will happen by multiplying together the separate probabilities that each event will happen. Consider the independent tossing of a nickel and a dime. The probability that both will fall heads up is ½ x ½, or ¼, since the chance is ½ that each separate coin will fall heads up. The probability that at least one of the two coins will fall tails up is 3/4 (1 − 1/4). Confirm these results by looking at table 13-1 showing the different ways in which the coins may fall.

TABLE 13-1 Combinations of Tossing Two Coins	
Nickel	Dime
Heads up	Heads up
Heads up	Tails up
Tails up	Heads up
Tails up	Tails up

Only these four combinations can be made with the two coins. The first combination is the only one of the four that meets the condition that both coins land heads up. Conversely, the last three of the four meet the condition that at least one of the coins will fall tails up. The probability that three coins tossed simultaneously all fall heads up is found to be ½ x ½ x ½ or 1/8 in this same manner. This same pattern is followed for any number of coins tossed

APPLICATION TO LIFE INSURANCE

Probabilities for life insurance are represented in a *mortality table*. Conceptually it is much like drawing cards from a deck. Table 13-2 shows portions of the 1979−81 U.S. Life Table that we can use to illustrate these ideas.

Column (2) in table 13-2 shows the number of survivors on each birthday out of 100,000 newborns. We call the number at the youngest age, here 100,000, the *radix* of the table. The number surviving at age one is 98,740. As with a deck of cards, if we draw at random one of the 100,000 members at age zero, the probability is 98,740/100,000 that the newborn will be a survivor at age one. Then the probability of *not* being a survivor at age one is

$$1 - \frac{98,740}{100,000}$$

This equals 1,260/100,000, or 0.01260, the probability of dying between age zero and age one. With the probability of dying denoted as q_x in general where the subscript x represents the age of those dying, q_1 denotes that probability for age one. For the convenience of the user, an alternate method can be used to find q_1 in the mortality tables. Look up the number of lives at age zero who die before attaining age one—1,260 in column (3)—and divide that number by the number of lives at age zero.

TABLE 13-2 U.S. Life Table				
Age Interval	Of 100,000 Born Alive		Proportion Dying	Average Remaining Lifetime
(1) Period of Life between Two Ages x to x + 1	(2) Number Living at Beginning of Age Interval l_x	(3) Number Dying during Age Interval d_x	(4) Proportion of Persons Alive at Beginning of Age Interval Dying during Interval q_x	(5) Life Expectancy (Average Years of Life Remaining) at Beginning of Age Interval e_x
0–1	100,000	1,260	0.01260	73.88
1–2	98,740	92	0.00093	73.82
2–3	98,648	64	0.00065	72.89
3–4	98,584	49	0.00050	71.93
4–5	98,535	40	0.00040	70.97
.	.	.	.	.
.	.	.	.	.
.	.	.	.	.
45–46	93,599	343	0.00366	32.27
46–47	93,256	374	0.00401	31.39
47–48	92,882	410	0.00442	30.51
48–49	92,472	451	0.00488	29.65
49–50	92,021	495	0.00538	28.79
.	.	.	.	.
.	.	.	.	.
.	.	.	.	.
80–81	43,180	2,972	0.06882	7.98
81–82	40,208	3,036	0.07552	7.53
82–83	37,172	3,077	0.08278	7.11
83–84	34,095	3,083	0.09041	6.70
84–85	31,012	3,052	0.09842	6.32

The mortality table is very versatile. It provides enough information to develop probabilities over any age span. For example, the probability that a newborn life will live to age 80 is 43,180/100,000 = 0.43180. Likewise, the probability that a newborn life will die between ages 49 and 50 is 495/100,000 = 0.00495.

To find probabilities for anyone older than a newborn, the denominator changes. Consider, for example, the probability of someone aged 45 surviving to age 49 in a population with characteristics similar to those from which table 13-2 was derived. Again refer to column (2) to find 93,599 lives at age 45. Of these,

92,021 are still living at age 49. The probability of a person aged 45 surviving to age 49 is, therefore, 92,021/93,599, or 0.98314. Then the probability that a person aged 45 will die before age 49 is $1 - 0.98314 = 0.01686$. Again, this probability can be found using other numbers from the table. It is the ratio of the number who die between ages 45 and 49 divided by the number alive at age 45. The number of people dying between ages 45 and 49 is the sum of the numbers for four individual ages as found in column (3): $343 + 374 + 410 + 451 = 1,578$.

Sometimes a different question can have the same answer. For example, What is the probability that someone aged 45 will die after age 80?" Following the pattern above, we might first think of adding the numbers from column (3) of those dying at ages greater than 80. This sum would equal exactly the number of lives at age 80 because each life must be in one of the groups dying at a later age. So the answer to the question is $43,180/93,599 = 0.46133$. A different way to ask —and solve—the same question is, What is the probability that a person aged 45 will live until age 80?" Using the number from column (2) of people still living at age 80 (43,180) the answer is the same—0.46133.

Let's summarize the pattern of the reasoning in the symbols shown at the top of the columns of table 13-2.

- The probability that a life aged x will survive n years to age x+n is

$$\frac{1_{x+n}}{1_x}$$

- The probability that a life aged x will survive n years and die between ages x+n and x+n+1 is

$$\frac{1_{x+n} - 1_{x+n+1}}{1_x}$$

- The *mortality rate* for the interval x to x+1 is the probability that a life aged x will die within a year. This rate is denoted by the special symbol q_x and is computed as $(1_x - 1_{x+1})/1_x$ or, using a simpler notation, $d_x/1_x$. The mortality rates are in column (4) of table 13-2:

$$\frac{1_{x+n} - 1_{x+n+1}}{1_x} = \frac{d_{x+n}}{1_x}$$

Life Expectancy

An additional column in a mortality table may show the *expectation of life* or *life expectancy* at each age. Column (5) in table 13-2 shows this value. The life expectancy at any age is the average number of years remaining once a person has attained that same age. Life expectancy is an average future lifetime for a representative group of persons at the same age. The probable future lifetime of any individual, of course, depends on his or her state of health, among other things, and may be much longer or much shorter than the average.

For most mortality tables, life expectancy is greatest at age one. It is usually less at age zero due to the high mortality rate in the first year of life. On the

other hand, the average age at death, which is the sum of the life expectancy and
the *attained age* (or number of years already lived), increases with age.   The
excerpt in table 13-3 from the 1979—81 U.S. Life Table illustrates this.

TABLE 13-3 Life Expectancy		
Attained Age	Life Expectancy	Average Age at Death
0	73.88	73.88
1	73.82	74.82
45	32.27	77.27
80	7.98	87.98

In table 13-3 the life expectancy at age zero is slightly larger than it is at age one,
but they are very close. Contrary to the general impression, actuaries do not use
the insured's life expectancy in the calculation of premium rates. Rates computed
in this way would be too low for life insurance because half of the insureds will
die before their life expectancy and some deaths will occur at each attained age.

The Law of Large Numbers

Probabilities for coin tossing, card drawing, and mortality tables all depend on
the *law of large numbers*, known more formally as Bernoulli's Law. This law
asserts that in a series of trials, the ratio of the number of occurrences of an event
to the number of trials approaches the actual underlying probability of the event
as the number of trials increases. In other words, in n tosses of a coin, the
number of heads observed divided by n, will be closer to ½ more often when n is
large than when n is small. In the extreme, for only one toss, the result will be
either zero or one—both of which are far from ½. When n is 2, the ratio will
be 0, ½, or one, and it will be zero or one only half the time. Table 13-4
illustrates the idea by showing the pattern for just a few tosses.

The law of large numbers asserts that the probability of the number of heads
being *near* one-half increases to one as the number of tosses increases. In the
table you can see that the probability increases from zero to nearly 1.000 as the
number of tosses increases from one to 256. This mathematical law forms the
basis of the actuarial application of probability to insurance.

Construction of Mortality Tables

While the application of mortality tables is similar to applications of
probabilities in coin tossing and card drawing, the building of the probabilities in
mortality tables has a different basis than does the determination of probabilities
for coins and cards. For cards and coins we can theorize the probability by
physically counting the number of favorable outcomes compared to the number
of total outcomes. In the simple world of coins and cards this is possible.

TABLE 13-4 Probabilities			
Number of Tosses	Probability that Proportion of Heads Will Be More than .25 and Less than .75	Probability that Proportion of Heads Will Be More than .40 and Less than .60	Probability that Proportion of Heads Will Be More than .45 and Less than .55
1	0.000	0.000	0.000
2	0.500	0.500	0.500
4	0.375	0.375	0.375
8	0.711	0.273	0.273
16	0.960	0.196	0.196
32	0.993	0.403	0.403
64	1.000	0.618	0.618
128	1.000	0.750	0.750
256	1.000	0.882	0.882

In the complex and changing world of life and death, actuaries use statistical methods to estimate the probabilities. The first step is to select a sample population representative of the population where the resulting probabilities are to be used. In life insurance this means that both populations should have the same smoking habits and gender, should be buying the same type of contract (insurance or annuity, individual or group, permanent insurance versus term insurance), and that similar underwriting information is available—that is, that medically examined applicants are grouped separate from nonmedical applicants.

TABLE 13-5 Number of Deaths in Sample Population		
Age	Number under Observation	Number Dying during the Year
1	10,000	60
2	30,000	120
3	80,000	240
4	60,000	180
Etc.	Etc.	Etc.

The next step is to observe the mortality experience of the representative population for a period of time. The observation period should be as recent as possible, sufficiently long to give adequate data, and free of nonrepresentative events such as war and epidemics.

After following the sample population during the observation period, the data are processed into the number of life-years and the number of deaths observed in each age interval. We will use a one-year interval for our examples here, although in practice the age intervals can be different from one year. Suppose analysis has produced the values in table 13-5.

From these figures, death rates may be computed for the respective ages as shown in table 13-6. Death rates at the other ages to be included in the table are obtained in like manner.

TABLE 13-6 Death Rates at Respective Ages		
Age	Rate of Death Expressed as a Fraction	Rate of Death Expressed as a Decimal
1	$\dfrac{60}{10,000}$	0.006
2	$\dfrac{120}{30,000}$	0.004
3	$\dfrac{240}{80,000}$	0.003
4	$\dfrac{180}{60,000}$	0.003

This illustration assumes the observation of many lives at each age. In practice, such a large "exposure" is not likely to be obtained during any one year. The results of the investigation, if limited to a single year, even in a very large life insurance company, will be subject to considerable distortion because of the small number of lives involved. Therefore actuaries usually study the experience of several years in deriving the rates to be incorporated in a mortality table. Rates derived for a 5-year period are the ratios for the number of deaths that occur at each age during the 5 years to the total exposure at that age. Each person who survived the 5-year period would have contributed five years' exposure—one year in each of the 5 one-year intervals. Most mortality tables in use today include the combined experience of several large companies over a period of years. The 1980 CSO (Commissioners Standard Ordinary) Table is based on the experience of *several* life insurers during the period of 1970 to 1975.

Adjustments to Mortality Data

Adjustments of several types occur in converting raw mortality rates into a usable mortality table. Among the most important of these adjustments are smoothing, projections, and safety margins.

Smoothing

For theoretical and practical reasons actuaries want the schedule of mortality rates to be smooth with respect to age. First, resistance to disease declines and the degeneration of the body system increases in continuous and minute gradations. Thus sharp changes in the death rates by age should not occur. Second, if the mortality rates are irregular by age, then the premiums and reserves based on them also will be irregular. Such a pattern is not desirable.

In most mortality studies a smooth set of mortality rates cannot be obtained by the simple procedure described above because sufficient data are not available. Actuaries have developed methods that produce smooth sets of rates from the initial nonsmooth sets. These methods, called graduation techniques, are based on mathematics and statistics and their use requires a high degree of specialized training.

Projections

Projections reflect changes that have occurred in mortality since the observation period. At least 5 years usually pass between the observation period and the publication of a public mortality table. For the table's users, who want current rates for pricing, mortality rates published with projections fill this need. A table of projection factors may be provided as well so that users can adjust the published rates for future use.

Safety Margins

Another adjustment provides a margin of safety. The appropriate adjustment depends on the purpose of the table. In a life insurance mortality table, including a safety margin means increasing the mortality rates above those anticipated. In an annuity table, including a safety margin means lowering the rates of mortality below those expected.

In early life insurance tables, safety margins occurred implicitly through the use of data from an earlier period known to have had rates of mortality higher than those currently being experienced. In some mortality tables, the margins are provided explicitly. For example, the observed rates for the 1941 CSO Table were increased by use of a mathematical formula. While the adjustment may appear arbitrary, it had a definite objective. Insurance commissioners use this table to monitor solvency of life insurance companies. The adjustment was made in such a way that the table would be appropriate for at least 95 percent of the ordinary insurance business under regulation. On the other hand, the rates entering the GA 1951 Table, an annuity table described in table 13-10, were reduced by 10 percent at all ages for males and 12.5 percent for females. All subsequent Group Annuity Tables including the GA 1983 are sex distinct.

The security behind insurance contracts depends on the existence of safety margins in the contract premiums. Savings developed by the use of conservative actuarial assumptions can be returned as dividends to owners of participating policies. For nonparticipating policies, the safety margins must be smaller in order for premium rates to be competitive.

Completing the Table

The previous section describes statistical procedures that transform observations into a smooth series of mortality rates with the needed margins. From that point it is an arithmetic procedure to prepare the other columns of the mortality tables. The first step is a choice of radix for the number of lives at the first age shown. This number is arbitrary and usually is chosen so the number dying at the end of the life span will not be less than a whole number.

To illustrate we reproduce the construction of table 13-2. We have derived the q_x column values by the statistical procedures and chosen arbitrarily to set l_0 = 100,000. Having determined the radix and the rates of death, the partially complete table appears as table 13.7.

TABLE 13-7			
Constructing a Mortality Table			
Age Interval	Of 100,000 Born Alive		Proportion Dying
(1) Period of Life between Two Ages x to x + 1	(2) Number Living at Beginning of Age Interval l_x	(3) Number Dying during Age Interval d_x	(4) Proportion of Persons Alive at Beginning of Age Interval Dying during Interval q_x
0–1	100,000	1,260	0.01260
1–2	98,740	92	0.00093
2–3	98,648	64	0.00065
3–4	98,584	49	0.00050
4–5	98,535	40	0.00040

Now $d_0 = l_0 \times q_0$ = 100,000 x (0.01260) = 1,260 and $l_1 = l_0 - d_0$ = 100,000 − 1,260 = 98,740. With these two values entered in the proper places in the table, we repeat the process at each age. That is, $d_1 = l_1 \times q_1$ = 98,740 x (0.00093) = 92 and $l_2 = l_1 - d_1$ = 98,740−92= 98,648.

Reflecting Differences in Mortality from Published Tables

Despite the amount of work involved in developing a mortality table, it still falls far short of fitting every situation where mortality rates are needed. As explained below, variations in the published rates are needed to reflect mortality for a group of individuals who are more or less healthy than average, to adjust for the amount of time that has passed since a group of life insurance policies was issued, and to make it easier to consider what events short of death may trigger a policy benefit or other important change.

Nonstandard Mortality

Mortality varies among different types of lives. A life insurance company uses the mortality table that seems most appropriate for its business. For example, a company may use one table for annuitants and another for lives insured, one for men and another for women, and one for smokers and another for nonsmokers. Different tables or adjustments to standard tables are used to estimate the lower mortality of *preferred* risks, those whose personal characteristics suggest better-than-average mortality. Similarly developed tables or adjustments that reflect higher mortality are used for *substandard* risks, those whose personal characteristics suggest worse-than-average mortality.

Select, Ultimate, and Aggregate Mortality

Studies show that the rate of mortality among recently insured lives is lower, age for age, than that among those insured for some years. For example, the mortality rate for a group of 35-year-olds insured 5 years ago will be higher than the mortality rate for a group of newly insured 35-year-olds. Sometimes underwriting—the process of deciding whether to issue a policy and on what terms—includes extensive medical screening. Underwriting screens out applicants suffering from a disease or physical condition likely to prove fatal in the near future. This disparity in death rates is greatest during the first year of insurance, and it diminishes gradually after that but never completely disappears. The difference is measurable for at least 15 years, but for practical purposes actuaries generally assume that the effect of selection "wears off" after approximately 5 years.

To illustrate, the death rate of policyowners insured at age 25 will be substantially lower than that of policyowners now 25 who were insured at age 20. One year later, when these policyowners are age 26, the difference in the death rates will be somewhat smaller. At age 30, death rates for the two groups will be almost the same.

Issue Age	Deaths per 1,000 Lives Insured						Attained Age
	Policy Year						
	(1)	(2)	(3)	(4)	(5)	(6)	
36	1.42	1.64	1.76	1.86	1.94	2.02	41
37	1.56	1.77	1.92	2.07	2.16	2.29	42
38	1.67	1.90	2.10	2.26	2.40	2.56	43
39	1.76	1.99	2.21	2.44	2.63	2.87	44
40	1.79	2.03	2.34	2.61	2.90	3.19	45
41	1.82	2.12	2.51	2.86	3.23	3.55	46

TABLE 13-8
Select Mortality Table

One way to recognize the reduced mortality in the early years of insurance is by a mortality table that shows the rate of mortality not only by age but also by duration of insurance. This recognizes the time passed since an applicant was approved to receive a policy. The result is called a *select* mortality table. While in theory actuaries could create an entire series of mortality tables (one for each age of issue), such extensive effort is not usually necessary. Since the effect of selection is negligible after 5 years, different rates are needed only for durations below 6 years. Select mortality tables usually are presented in the form shown in table 13-8.

Table 13-8 gives insight into the mortality reduction due to selection. Column (1) shows the death rate at the various ages during the first year of insurance when the effect of selection is greatest. Column (6) shows the rate after the effect of selection has worn off. Contrast the various death rates for attained age 41 by comparing the six values. All six of these rates apply to a life aged 41; however, the rates apply to six different periods since issue of insurance.

Companies use select tables in developing gross premiums for both participating and nonparticipating insurance and for testing, through asset share calculations, described later in this book, the appropriateness of existing or proposed schedules of dividends and surrender values. Companies also base profit projections for new blocks of nonparticipating business on select tables. Another important use is for tabulating mortality experience for analysis and comparison. Comparisons among companies, or of the experience of different periods within the same company, would be far less valuable unless the comparisons considered the relative proportion of new business and the lower rates of mortality experienced on those recent issues.

If the construction of a mortality table excludes the effects of selection, the table is called an *ultimate* mortality table. That is, it reflects only the rates of mortality that can be expected after the influence of selection has worn off. Standing alone, column (6) of table 13-8 is an ultimate mortality table. Using an ultimate table during the early years of a life insurance contract provides companies with a source of extra mortality savings. This in turn helps to offset the heavy expenses incurred in placing the business on the books.

A mortality table may be constructed from the experience of insured lives, without regard to the duration of insurance. Such a table is an *aggregate* mortality table. An aggregate table blends in the experience of recently selected lives without segregating it by duration.

Additional Decrements

In the construction process discussed above for mortality tables, death is the only factor that decreases the number of persons living at each age. Actuaries call such downward reductions *decrements*. For calculation of statutory reserves — those required by state laws or statutes — and cash values, companies use mortality tables that recognize one decrement only. However, operating an insurance company requires more than the basic information required to comply with state laws. Often the actuary combines this additional information with death rates to produce a table that considers more than one decrement.

Several important decrements other than death can be included. For example, the table used to calculate gross premium needs to recognize that policies will lapse before maturity. Calculating the cost of a pension plan needs to include projections for both the number of employees who will die and the number who will leave employment before reaching retirement. If disability benefits are to be provided, accurate projections are needed for the number of covered lives who will become disabled as defined in the policy and the length of time they will remain so disabled. Some pension plans, including the federal Old Age, Survivors, and Disability Insurance (OASDI) program, need to include the probabilities of remarriage in the estimates of the cost of surviving spouse benefits.

Tables that include rates for more than one decrement are called *multiple-decrement tables*. The construction of multiple decrement rates is complicated and is beyond the scope of this book. However, once the rates are available the construction of the multiple-decrement table is very similar to the procedure described above for the single-decrement mortality table.

COMMON CHARACTERISTICS OF PUBLIC TABLES

The methods discussed in this chapter for applying the laws of probability to life insurance have produced a multitude of mortality tables for a variety of purposes. Generally, proprietary company tables are used for premium and dividend calculations. Different tables are used for solvency accounting and reporting to regulators. In the remainder of this chapter we describe important and interesting characteristics of some public tables. Table 13-10 provides a summary of these and other tables developed over the past century.

Two principal kinds of public mortality tables exist. First is the set of United States Life Tables published as a by-product of the decennial census. Census data are used to construct a table for the total population and for each of several sub-populations. The purpose of these tables is to display the public health of the country and to provide a general model for the uncertainty of length of life.

The other principal kind of public table is required by statute in the various states for use by insurance companies for specific purposes. Sections of these codes, which usually follow model laws developed by the National Association of Insurance Commissioners (NAIC), specify how the assets and liabilities on the annual statements of the insurance companies will be calculated. Insurance and annuity contracts in force create liabilities for life insurers. Valuing these liabilities requires reasonable assumptions about several factors, including mortality. The statute specifies a reasonable assumption for the mortality rates of insureds by naming a specific mortality table—the *statutory table*.

Until 1941 the statutes required tables that were selected from among those in existence in the actuarial profession. The 1941 CSO Table was the first constructed at the request of the NAIC for calculating minimum reserves and surrender values. In keeping with this purpose it was also the first to have an explicit *margin* added to the mortality rates.

Of the mortality tables listed in table 13-10, those described in rows 3 through 9 are descendants of the 1941 CSO. The 1958 and 1980 CSOs are updated tables used for ordinary life insurance. The 1980 CSO (see table 13-9) differs from its predecessors in several ways. It was the first time actuaries developed and published separate rates for men and women. Another difference was in the treatment of the "hump" in the mortality rates for males around age 20. The raw data in most mortality studies show rates for males reaching a low near age 10, then rising to a maximum near age 21, and falling again to a minimum near age 29. After this, they start a long continuous rise to the end of life. In previous mortality tables, the smoothing process eliminated this hump in the initial rates. In the 1980 CSO, however, because the hump in the male data was more pronounced than ever (due to auto accidents, homicides, drug overdoses, and suicides) it was not eliminated. An examination of table 13-9 shows a hump of 1.91 per 1,000 at age 21, then a reduction to the low of 1.70 at age 28, and then a rise back to 1.91 at age 33. The slight hump apparent in the female data was lost in the smoothing process.

The 1980 CSO also was the first to include selection factors in a table developed for regulatory purposes.

The 1958 and 1980 CET Tables, intended for use with extended term insurance, illustrate the need for mortality tables appropriate to their intended use. There were insufficient data to derive mortality rates for extended term coverage at all ages, so the general level of the mortality was determined and then applied to the pattern of mortality for ordinary life insurance. The resulting tables are based on multiples of the ordinary mortality tables rather than being derived directly from the mortality of lives with extended term coverage.

Further illustrations of tables constructed to be appropriate for the relevant population are the 1961 CSG, CSI, and CIET Tables. These are tables constructed at the request of the NAIC for group, industrial, and industrial extended term policies.

The 1983 Smoker-Nonsmoker tables also were constructed at the request of the NAIC. At the time, companies did not possess sufficient experience on insured lives to construct a table in the usual way. The committee that developed there tables estimated the proportion of smokers at each age of the 1980 CSO population and the relative mortality of smokers versus nonsmokers. Combining this information, the committee estimated mortality rates of the smoking and nonsmoking components of the 1980 CSO populations that were consistent with the overall mortality rates.

The UP-1984 Table was constructed by actuaries to value pension benefits. The Pension Benefit Guarantee Corporation (PBGC) adopted this table to fulfill its mission of protecting defined-benefit pension plan participants with federal guarantees. The PBGC uses this table to value the obligations of pension plans that employers wish to terminate. The table is a unisex table and includes suggestions for complying with laws governing sex discrimination in the distribution of benefits.

Rows 10 through 15 of table 13-10 are tables used for annuity contracts. Only the 1971 and 1983 tables were constructed at the request of the NAIC. The mortality experience of lives covered under group annuities and pensions is different from that for lives covered under individually purchased annuities. These differences indicate a need for separate individual annuitant mortality (IAM) tables and group annuitant mortality (GAM) tables.

All public tables, like those described in this chapter, are intended to provide a minimum basis for valuation. Company solvency is the prime concern. For setting premiums and dividend scales, most major life insurance companies rely on their own recent experience.

TABLE 13-9
Commissioners 1980 Standard Ordinary (CSO) Table of Mortality
Male Lives

Age (x) at Beginning of Year	Number Living at Beginning of Designated Year (l_x)	Number Dying during Designated Year (d_x)	Yearly Probability of Dying (q_x)
0	10,000,000	41,800	0.004180
1	9,958,200	10,655	0.001070
2	9,947,545	9,848	0.000990
3	9,937,697	9,739	0.000980
4	9,927,958	9,432	0.000950
5	9,918,526	8,927	0.000900
6	9,909,599	8,522	0.000860
7	9,901,077	7,921	0.000800
8	9,893,156	7,519	0.000760
9	9,885,637	7,315	0.000740
10	9,878,322	7,211	0.000730
11	9,871,111	7,601	0.000770
12	9,863,510	8,384	0.000850
13	9,855,126	9,757	0.000990
14	9,845,369	11,322	0.001150
15	9,834,047	13,079	0.001330
16	9,820,968	14,830	0.001510
17	9,806,138	16,376	0.001670
18	9,789,762	17,426	0.001780
19	9,772,336	18,177	0.001860
20	9,754,159	18,533	0.001900
21	9,735,626	18,595	0.001910
22	9,717,031	18,365	0.001890
23	9,698,666	18,040	0.001860
24	9,680,626	17,619	0.001820
25	9,663,007	17,104	0.001770
26	9,645,903	16,687	0.001730
27	9,629,216	16,466	0.001710
28	9,612,750	16,342	0.001700
29	9,596,408	16,410	0.001710
30	9,579,998	16,573	0.001730
31	9,563,425	17,023	0.001780
32	9,546,402	17,470	0.001830
33	9,528,932	18,200	0.001910
34	9,510,732	19,021	0.002000
35	9,491,711	20,028	0.002110

TABLE 13-9 (Continued)
Commissioners 1980 Standard Ordinary (CSO) Table of Mortality
Male Lives

Age (x) at Beginning of Year	Number Living at Beginning of Designated Year (l_x)	Number Dying during Designated Year (d_x)	Yearly Probability of Dying (q_x)
36	9,471,683	21,217	0.002240
37	9,450,466	22,681	0.002400
38	9,427,785	24,324	0.002580
39	9,403,461	26,236	0.002790
40	9,377,225	28,319	0.003020
41	9,348,906	30,758	0.003290
42	9,318,148	33,173	0.003560
43	9,284,975	35,933	0.003870
44	9,249,042	38,753	0.004190
45	9,210,289	41,907	0.004550
46	9,168,382	45,108	0.004920
47	9,123,274	48,536	0.005320
48	9,074,738	52,089	0.005740
49	9,022,649	56,031	0.006210
50	8,966,618	60,166	0.006710
51	8,906,452	65,017	0.007300
52	8,841,435	70,378	0.007960
53	8,771,057	76,396	0.008710
54	8,694,661	83,121	0.009560
55	8,611,540	90,163	0.010470
56	8,521,377	97,655	0.011460
57	8,423,722	105,212	0.012490
58	8,318,510	113,049	0.013590
59	8,205,461	121,195	0.014770
60	8,084,266	129,995	0.016080
61	7,954,271	139,518	0.017540
62	7,814,753	149,965	0.019190
63	7,664,788	161,420	0.021060
64	7,503,368	173,628	0.023140
65	7,329,740	186,322	0.025420
66	7,143,418	198,944	0.027850
67	6,944,474	211,390	0.030440
68	6,773,084	223,471	0.033190
69	6,509,613	235,453	0.036170
70	6,274,160	247,892	0.039510

TABLE 13-9 (Concluded)
Commissioners 1980 Standard Ordinary (CSO) Table of Mortality
Male Lives

Age (x) at Beginning of Year	Number Living at Beginning of Designated Year (l_x)	Number Dying during Designated Year (d_x)	Yearly Probability of Dying (q_x)
71	6,026,268	260,937	0.043300
72	5,765,331	274,718	0.047650
73	5,490,613	289,026	0.052640
74	5,201,587	302,680	0.058190
75	4,898,907	314,461	0.064190
76	4,584,446	323,341	0.070530
77	4,261,105	328,616	0.077120
78	3,932,489	329,936	0.083900
79	3,602,553	328,012	0.091050
80	3,274,541	323,656	0.098840
81	2,950,885	317,161	0.107480
82	2,633,724	308,804	0.117250
83	2,324,920	298,194	0.128260
84	2,026,726	284,248	0.140250
85	1,742,478	266,512	0.152950
86	1,475,966	245,143	0.166090
87	1,230,823	220,994	0.179550
88	1,009,829	195,170	0.193270
89	814,659	168,871	0.207290
90	645,788	143,216	0.221770
91	502,572	119,100	0.236980
92	383,472	97,191	0.253450
93	286,281	77,900	0.272110
94	208,381	61,660	0.295900
95	146,721	48,412	0.329960
96	98,309	37,805	0.384550
97	60,504	29,054	0.480200
98	31,450	20,693	0.657980
99	10,757	10,757	1.000000

TABLE 13-10
U.S. Mortality Tables

	Name	Purpose	Database
1	79–81 US Life Table	US mortality; general purpose	1979–81
2	1941 CSO	Company solvency and minimum nonforfeiture for ordinary insurance	Insurance company experience, 1930–40
3	1958 CSO	Company solvency and minimum nonforfeiture for ordinary insurance	Insurance company experience, 1950–54
4	1958 CET	Company solvency and minimum nonforfeiture for ordinary extended term	58 CSO plus the greater of .00075 or 30% of mortality rate
5	1961 CSG	Company solvency and minimum premiums for group insurance	Insurance company experience, 1950–58
6	1961 CSI	Company solvency and minimum nonforfeiture for industrial insurance	Insurance company experience on white insureds, 1954–58; US life table for ages > 75
7	1961 CIET	Company solvency and minimum nonforfeiture for industrial extended term	61 CSI plus loading
8	80 CSO	Company solvency and minimum nonforfeiture for ordinary insurance	Insurance company experience, 1970–75
9	80 CET	Company solvency and minimum nonforfeiture for ordinary extended term	80 CSO plus the greater of .00075 or 30% of mortality rate

Gender	Type	Margins	Comments
Combined and sex distinct	Aggregate	None	For two centuries, life tables for U.S. population, with subpopulations by sex, race, and geographic region prepared as part of decennial census
Male	Ultimate	Explicit by formula	First table commissioned by the NAIC; first with explicit margins
Combined; female equal to male with 3-year setback	Ultimate	Explicit; sufficient to cover experience of 33 small companies	
Combined	Ultimate	Proportional to 58 CSO	First special table for extended term insurance
Combined	Aggregate	Explicit	
Combined	Aggregate	Explicit and substantial	
Combined	Aggregate	Proportional to 61 CET	
Sex distinct	Aggregate, pol years 6 and up	Math formula using the life expectancy based on the basic table	10-year selection factors were provided making this the first CSO Table available on a select basis
Combined	Ultimate	Proportional to 80 CSO	

TABLE 13-10 (Concluded)
U.S. Mortality Tables

	Name	Purpose	Database
10	49A	General use for annuities	Group and industrial experience for several years about 1943
11	51 GA	For employee annuitants	49A rates for ages < 65; company experience 1946−50 for ages > 65
12	71 GAM	For minimum reserves on employee annuitants	Insurance company experience, 1964−68
13	71 IAM	For minimum reserves on individual annuitants	Insurance company experience, 1960−67
14	83 GAM	For minimum reserves on employee annuitants	Insurance company experience, 1964−68, with projections to 1983
15	83 IAM	For minimum reserves on individual annuitants	Insurance company experience, 1971−76 for ages > 50; 71 IAM for ages < 50
16	84-UP	Used by PBGC in pension termination cases and general pension work	1965−69 noninsured pension plans and group life
17	83 Smoker-Nonsmoker	Company solvency and minimum nonforfeiture for ordinary insurance	Various

Gender	Type	Margins	Comments
Combined	Aggregate	Only to bring it to 1949	First table with projection factors provided to update the table
Male	Aggregate	Margin to make it safe for all occupations	First table for employee annuitants; has projection factors as 49a
Sex distinct	Aggregate	8% for males and 10% for females	Had new projection factors
Sex distinct	Aggregate	10% reduction	
Sex distinct	Aggregate	10% reduction	83 IAM proj factors up age 82; lower reduction factors above
Sex distinct	Aggregate	10% reduction	Had new projection factors
Combined 80% male	Aggregate	Developed by consul. to manage unisex regulations in the 70s	
Sex distinct	Aggregate, policy years 6 and up	80 CSO margins	Mortality rates for smokers and nonsmokers consistent with 80 CSO rates were found for each age

14

Time Value of Money

Dan M. McGill
Revised by Norma Nielson and Donald Jones

Money held today is worth more than money promised in the future. The premiums, products, and financial operations of life insurance companies not only reflect life contingencies but also depend heavily on this time value of money. Particularly when a company collects level premiums over the life of a policy, it accumulates sums of money that it manages for many years before that money is disbursed. Companies invest these funds in income-producing assets with the earnings credited on a compound interest basis to benefit policyowners. Three different examples of interest rate crediting are as follows:

- internal policy accumulations
- policy dividend accumulation
- policy proceeds left at interest

Each of them may differ from the other and all of them will fluctuate with economic conditions. To illustrate the concept this chapter deals only with level interest assumptions, but insurance companies must accommodate nonlevel interest patterns. Premiums, surrender values, reserves, and dividends all reflect the differing value of money over extended periods.

Because interest earnings play such a vital role in the pricing practices and operations of a life insurance company, it is essential to consider the concept further. In order to explain their products to customers and assure that policy illustrations are appropriate, agents need a clear understanding of the relationship between interest rates and the financial features of life insurance. Today's financial calculators and computer spreadsheets make these computations readily accessible to everyone in the financial community.

DEFINITION OF TERMS

Interest represents the difference between the *principal*—the value of the original capital invested—and the amount that must be repaid by the borrower after a specified term. To an investor interest is the income from invested capital. To a borrower it is the price paid for the use of money.

Interest income is usually expressed as a *percentage rate* of the principal *per year*. Thus if an invested principal of $100 earns $5.50 during a 12-month period, the rate of return is 5.5 percent. The rate of interest may be expressed in various forms, but in this chapter we will express it as either a percentage—for example, 5.5 percent—or as its equivalent decimal fraction—0.055. To obtain the interest earnings on any given principal sum for a specified period, multiply the appropriate decimal fraction by the principal sum. For example, the interest earnings on $1 invested for one year at 5.5 percent is $1 x 0.055 = $0.055, or 5½ cents. The equation $S = P (1 + i)$ represents the amount to which any given principal sum will accumulate in one year when invested at a specified rate of interest. In the equation, S represents the *future value* or sum at the end of the year; P represents the *principal* at the beginning of the year or present value; i is the *rate of interest*. If the principal is $1, the equation can be simplified to $S = 1 + i$. Once the amount to which $1 will accumulate in one year is known, the future value of any principal sum can be determined by multiplying it by that factor. Figure 14-1 shows the accumulation of interest on a principal amount of $100.

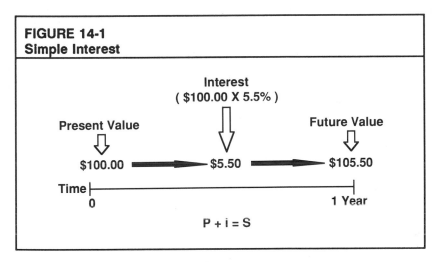

FIGURE 14-1
Simple Interest

Interest
($100.00 X 5.5%)

Present Value   Future Value

$100.00 ➞ $5.50 ➞ $105.50

Time |————————————————| 1 Year
0

P + i = S

The same reasoning applies to the death benefit payable under a life insurance policy. A payment deferred for one year by the beneficiary would earn interest under the policy's interest-only option. With 5.5 percent interest the payment received on a $100,000 policy would be that original face amount plus interest at 5.5 percent for the one-year delay period. The eventual payment amount would be computed as $100,000 x 1.055 = $105,500.

The term *simple interest* is used if interest is paid on only the original principal invested. If interest earnings are not distributed but are added to the original principal and reinvested at the same interest rate or a different rate of interest, the result is *compound interest*. Compound interest is simply interest on interest. While interest may be compounded annually, semiannually, monthly, daily, or at other agreed-upon intervals, only annual compounding is illustrated in this chapter.

COMPOUND INTEREST FUNCTIONS

Life insurance calculations use compound interest. Premium and reserve computations assume that companies keep funds continuously invested until those funds are paid out in settlement of claims. The company's computations further assume that interest earnings are added to the original principal and reinvested.

To understand the relationships, it will be helpful to examine four basic compound interest series.

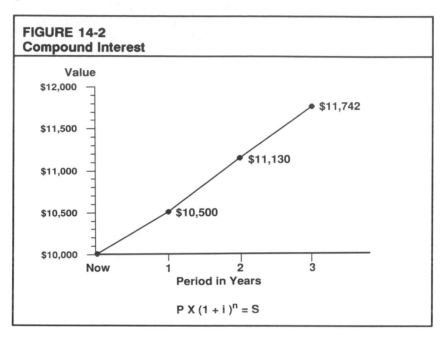

FIGURE 14-2
Compound Interest

$$P \times (1 + i)^n = S$$

Future Values

The first series shows the amount to which a principal sum of $10,000 invested for a number of years (or other units of time) will increase over time. This applies compound interest to accumulate interest earnings. Figure 14-2 illustrates this concept. If you invest $10,000 at 5.5 percent for one year, the combined amount of principal and interest at the end of the year, according to the simple formula previously stated, will be $10,000 x 1.055, or $10,550. If the $10,550 is then invested for another year at 5.5 percent, the combined amount of principal and interest at the end of the second year will be $10,550 x 1.055, or $11,130. This is equivalent to multiplying $10,000 by 1.055^2 where the expo- nent—indicated in this example by the superscript "2"—denotes the number of times the base—in this case 1.055—is multiplied by itself. If the sum of $11,130 is again invested for another year at 5.5 percent, the principal and interest at the end of the third year will be $11,130 x 1.055, or $11,742, which is the equivalent of multiplying $10,000 by 1.055^3. If this process continues, the accumulated principal and interest will always equal the sum obtained by multiplying $10,000 by 1.055 raised to an exponent equal to the number of years of compound interest earned.

The future value of any principal sum invested for any period of time at any rate of interest can be computed by the same process. If S represents the future value, or sum, at the end of the period, i the rate of interest, P the principal invested, and n the number of years, the general formula becomes $S = P(1 + i)^n$. If the principal is $1, as is shown in most compound interest tables, the formula is $S = (1 + i)^n$. Table 14-1 shows the accumulated amount of 1 at the end of each of 30 years at various rates of compound interest. A student who wants to compute the future value of $500, for example, at the end of 23 years with interest at 5.5 percent compounded annually looks up the factor (the number in the table opposite 23 years in the column headed 5.5 percent), 3.4262, and multiplies that factor by 500. This produces the answer of $1,713.10.

TABLE 14-1
Future Value of 1 at Various Rates of Compound Interest

$$(1+i)^n$$

Year	3.5%	4.0%	4.5%	5.0%	5.5%
1	1.0350	1.0400	1.0450	1.0500	1.0550
2	1.0712	1.0816	1.0920	1.1025	1.1130
3	1.1087	1.1249	1.1412	1.1576	1.1742
4	1.1475	1.1699	1.1925	1.2155	1.2388
5	1.1877	1.2167	1.2462	1.2763	1.3070
6	1.2293	1.2653	1.3023	1.3401	1.3788
7	1.2723	1.3159	1.3609	1.4071	1.4547
8	1.3168	1.3686	1.4221	1.4775	1.5347
9	1.3629	1.4233	1.4861	1.5513	1.6191
10	1.4106	1.4802	1.5530	1.6289	1.7081
11	1.4600	1.5395	1.6229	1.7103	1.8021
12	1.5111	1.6010	1.6959	1.7959	1.9012
13	1.5640	1.6651	1.7722	1.8856	2.0058
14	1.6187	1.7317	1.8519	1.9799	2.1161
15	1.6753	1.8009	1.9353	2.0789	2.2325
16	1.7340	1.8730	2.0224	2.1829	2.3553
17	1.7947	1.9479	2.1134	2.2920	2.4848
18	1.8575	2.0258	2.2085	2.4066	2.6215
19	1.9225	2.1068	2.3079	2.5270	2.7656
20	1.9898	2.1911	2.4117	2.6533	2.9178
21	2.0594	2.2788	2.5202	2.7860	3.0782
22	2.1315	2.3699	2.6337	2.9253	3.2475
23	2.2061	2.4647	2.7522	3.0715	3.4262
24	2.2833	2.5633	2.8760	3.2251	3.6146
25	2.3632	2.6658	3.0054	3.3864	3.8134
26	2.4460	2.7725	3.1407	3.5557	4.0231
27	2.5316	2.8834	3.2820	3.7335	4.2444
28	2.6202	2.9987	3.4297	3.9201	4.4778
29	2.7119	3.1187	3.5840	4.1161	4.7241
30	2.8068	3.2434	3.7453	4.3219	4.9840

Instead of reading 3.4262 from a compound interest table, the y^x function of a calculator could be used. To solve the same problem, a calculator that uses so-called algebraic notation, such as the TI BA-II Plus, would require the following set of key strokes:

Pressing the '=' key then produces the answer, the factor 3.4262. For calculators like the HP 12-C, using so-called 'reverse Polish' notation, the future value factor is found with the following series of key strokes:

Those with ready access to a computer spreadsheet, such as Lotus 1-2-3, would enter the formula $(1.055)^{\wedge}23$ into a spreadsheet cell and press ENTER to obtain the needed solution.

Likewise, future value problems can be solved using a financial calculator. For most calculators with financial function keys, the future value of an initial $500 principal at the end of 23 years with interest at 5.5 percent compounded annually requires the following key strokes to produce the $1,713.10 answer:

Despite the fact that different strokes are needed to solve mathematical formulas, the key strokes for financial functions are similar for algebraic notation and reverse Polish calculators (although the former may require that a CPT (computer) key be pressed before the FV key). If you do not obtain the correct answer, check your calculator to be certain it is set for beginning-of-year computations.

The spreadsheet solution with an initial $500 principal amount is a simple extension of the formula $(1.055)^{\wedge}23$. Enter the formula $(1.055)^{\wedge}23*500$ to verify the $1,713.10 answer.

Relationship Between Interest Rate and Accumulation Period to Future Values

If a higher rate of interest is used in the compounding process, or if a longer period of accumulation is used, a higher future value results. While this is a somewhat obvious statement in the context of future value, it is important to make this explicit statement here because similar relationships that the student will encounter later in this chapter are less obvious.

Present Values or Discounted Values

The second series, called *present values*, calculates the value today that is equivalent to a given sum due at a designated time in the future. This process is called *discounting*. The process of discounting is particularly vital to life insurance company operations since the companies deal heavily in future promises. Their contracts provide for benefits to be paid in the future. Companies finance these benefits through premium income and future interest earnings. Their very solvency depends on establishing an equivalence between future benefit payments and receipts from premiums and investments. This equivalence is established through the discounting process whereby all values are reduced to a common basis. That common basis is present value.

The discounting process implicitly recognizes that a dollar due one year from now is worth less than a dollar due now. And a dollar due 5 years from now is worth less than a dollar due in one year. Money in hand can be invested to produce more money or capital. The difference in value between money in hand and money due in the future depends on the rate of return that can be obtained from invested capital. Also the longer the period before the future money will be received, the greater the expected interest earnings and the greater the difference between the value of the present and future capital.

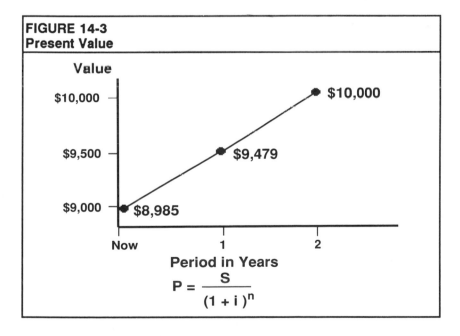

FIGURE 14-3
Present Value

$$P = \frac{S}{(1 + i)^n}$$

The present value of an amount due at a specified date in the future is that principal sum that, if invested now at an assumed rate of interest, would accumulate to the required amount by the due date. For example, $1 invested at 5.5 percent compound interest will accumulate in 10 years to $1.71. This is the meaning of the statement that $1 is the present value at 5.5 percent compound interest of $1.71 due in 10 years. This suggests how easily the present value of a sum due in the future can be obtained by reversing the accumulation process described above. The higher the rate of return available on invested capital, the greater the difference between the value of present and future money, and vice versa.

Derivation of Present Values

As explained earlier, the amount to which a given sum will accumulate is found by multiplying the principal by 1 plus the rate of interest raised to an exponent equal to the number of interest-compounding time units in the period (years in our example). If, instead, the amount at the end of the period is given, the beginning principal may be found by dividing the future amount by 1 plus the rate of interest raised to the proper exponent. For example, $1 invested for one year at 5.5 percent interest will accumulate to $1.055 by the end of the year. If the process is to be reversed, the principal is found by dividing $1 by 1.055. If the amount due 2 years from now is $11,130, the present value of the amount at 5.5 percent compounded annually is $11,130 ÷ $(1.055)^2$ = $11,130 ÷ 1.1130 = $10,000. Similarly, if $10,000 is due one year from now, it is worth only $10,000 ÷ 1.055, or $9,479, today, based on an interest rate of 5.5 percent.

If $10,000 is to be paid 2 years from now, its value now is only $10,000 ÷ $(1.055)^2$ = $10,000 ÷ 1.1130 = $8,985. Figure 14-3 illustrates this derivation. Conversely, $8,985 invested at 5.5 percent compound interest will, at the end of 2 years, amount to $10,000.

The present value of 1 at 5.5 percent compound interest can be derived for any number of years and arranged in tabular form for convenient use by use of this general formula,

$$P = \frac{S}{(1+i)^n}$$

In standard actuarial notation the present value of 1 due n years from now is represented by the symbol v^n where $v = 1/(1+i)$ and n = number of years:

$$v^n = \left[\frac{1}{(1+i)}\right]^n$$

These values are shown for 30 years in table 14-2 or can be computed easily using a financial calculator or computer spreadsheet.

Once you have a table of values for v^n, the present value of any amount due at the end of any number of years is determined by multiplying the future amount by the appropriate value of v^n. Thus the present value of $1,000 due 15 years from now is, at 5.5 percent compound interest, $1,000 x 0.4479, or $447.90.

Once again, the financial calculator can produce the same answer. For the present value of $1,000 to be received at the end of 15 years with interest at 5.5 percent compounded annually requires the following key strokes:

1000 FV 15 N 5.5 I 0 PMT

Pressing the PV key, or the CPT and PV keys, yields an answer of $447.93 (the 3 cents difference between table value and the calculation value is due to the rounding in the table values). The spreadsheet user would enter the formula $(1/1.055)\wedge 15*1000$ to obtain this solution.

One final note about present values is important for anyone working or investing in the financial marketplace. Sometimes banks and other commercial organizations use approximation methods that produce results slightly different from those obtained by the precise determination of present values described here. For example, interest may be deducted in advance. For small amounts and short terms the differences produced by the alternate methods of discounting are inconsequential.

TABLE 14-2
Present Value of 1 at Various Rates of Compound Interest

$$V^n = \frac{1}{(1 + i)^n}$$

Year	3.5%	4.0%	4.5%	5.0%	5.5%
1	0.9662	0.9615	0.9569	0.9524	0.9479
2	0.9335	0.9246	0.9157	0.9070	0.8985
3	0.9019	0.8890	0.8763	0.8638	0.8516
4	0.8714	0.8548	0.8386	0.8227	0.8072
5	0.8420	0.8219	0.8025	0.7835	0.7651
6	0.8135	0.7903	0.7679	0.7462	0.7252
7	0.7860	0.7599	0.7348	0.7107	0.6874
8	0.7594	0.7307	0.7032	0.6768	0.6516
9	0.7337	0.7026	0.6729	0.6446	0.6176
10	0.7089	0.6756	0.6439	0.6139	0.5854
11	0.6849	0.6496	0.6162	0.5847	0.5549
12	0.6618	0.6246	0.5897	0.5568	0.5260
13	0.6394	0.6006	0.5643	0.5303	0.4986
14	0.6178	0.5775	0.5400	0.5051	0.4726
15	0.5969	0.5553	0.5167	0.4810	0.4479
16	0.5767	0.5339	0.4945	0.4581	0.4246
17	0.5572	0.5134	0.4732	0.4363	0.4024
18	0.5384	0.4936	0.4528	0.4155	0.3815
19	0.5202	0.4746	0.4333	0.3957	0.3616
20	0.5026	0.4564	0.4146	0.3769	0.3427
21	0.4856	0.4388	0.3968	0.3589	0.3249
22	0.4692	0.4220	0.3797	0.3418	0.3079
23	0.4533	0.4057	0.3634	0.3256	0.2919
24	0.4380	0.3901	0.3477	0.3101	0.2767
25	0.4231	0.3751	0.3327	0.2953	0.2622
26	0.4088	0.3607	0.3184	0.2812	0.2486
27	0.3950	0.3468	0.3047	0.2678	0.2356
28	0.3817	0.3335	0.2916	0.2551	0.2233
29	0.3687	0.3207	0.2790	0.2429	0.2117
30	0.3563	0.3083	0.2670	0.2314	0.2006

Relationship between Interest Rate and Discounting Period to Present Values

The relationship between interest rates and discounting period to present value is an inverse one. The magnitude of the difference between present and future values depends on the interest rate that is used for discounting. Assuming a higher rate of interest means that more interest is made or lost over time. That means the present values of future amounts are smaller for higher interest rates. For example, the present value of $100 to be paid 20 years from now based on 3 percent interest is $100 x .5537, or $55.37. The present value assuming 5.5 percent interest is $100 x .3427, or $34.27. *A higher rate of interest means a lower present value of a specific future value.* Similarly, the longer the discounting period, the lower the present value. For example, the present value of $100 to be paid 30 years from now based on 3 percent interest is $100 x .4120, or $41.20, compared to $55.37 for a 20-year discounting period.

Future Value of Annual Payments

The third compound interest series deals with the future value of periodic equal annual payments. This stream of annual payments is called an *annuity*.

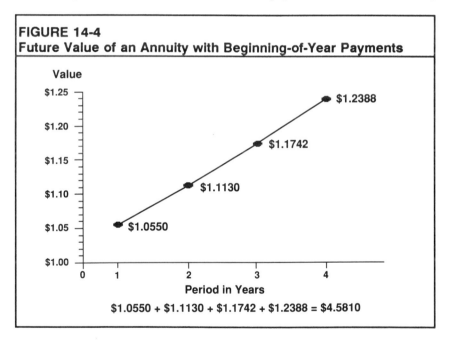

FIGURE 14-4
Future Value of an Annuity with Beginning-of-Year Payments

$1.0550 + $1.1130 + $1.1742 + $1.2388 = $4.5810

Beginning-of-Year Future Values

An annuity with payments at the beginning of the period is called an *annuity due*. Premium payments on most life insurance policies, although they include a mortality factor as well as interest, are one common example of beginning-of-period payments. Figure 14-4 shows the future values based on a 5.5 percent interest rate of four $1 payments made at the beginning of the year. Adding together the future values of the four payments—$1.055 + $1.113 + $1.1742 + $1.2388 gives us the $4.5810 future value of all four payments.

This process can be continued for any number of years to produce a table of annuity values. The elements of table 14-3 are created by simply adding the elements of table 14-1. To illustrate, the first five figures in the 5.5 percent column of table 14-1 are reproduced in table 14-1 extract.

TABLE 14-1 EXTRACT		
Year	5.5%	$(1.055)^n$
1	1.0550	$(1.055)^1$
2	1.1130	$(1.055)^2$
3	1.1742	$(1.055)^3$
4	1.2388	$(1.055)^4$
5	1.3070	$(1.055)^5$

The first number in the table 14-1 extract is the same as the first figure in the 5.5 percent column of table 14-3. To obtain the second number in table 14-3—2.168 —add the first two numbers above. The third number in the table 14-1 extract, 1.1742, is added to 2.1680 to produce 3.3423, the third number in table 14-3 in the 5.5 percent column except for a difference due to rounding. Add 1.2388 to this to yield 4.5811, the fourth number in the 5.5 percent column in table 14-3, and so on. To repeat, the values in table 14-3 assume payments of $1 occur *at the beginning* of each year.

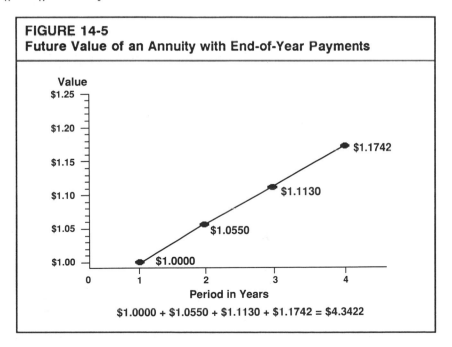

FIGURE 14-5
Future Value of an Annuity with End-of-Year Payments

$1.0000 + $1.0550 + $1.1130 + $1.1742 = $4.3422

TABLE 14-3
Future Value of 1 per Year at Various Rates of Compound Interest
Annuity Due—Payments Made at the Beginning of Year

$$S_n = (1+i) + (1+i)^2 + \ldots + (1+i)^n$$

Year	3.5%	4.0%	4.5%	5.0%	5.5%
1	1.0350	1.0400	1.0450	1.0500	1.0550
2	2.1062	2.1216	2.1370	2.1525	2.1680
3	3.2149	3.2465	3.2782	3.3101	3.3423
4	4.3625	4.4163	4.4707	4.5256	4.5811
5	5.5502	5.6330	5.7169	5.8019	5.8881
6	6.7794	6.8983	7.0192	7.1420	7.2669
7	8.0517	8.2142	8.3800	8.5491	8.7216
8	9.3685	9.5828	9.8021	10.0266	10.2563
9	10.7314	11.0061	11.2882	11.5779	11.8754
10	12.1420	12.4864	12.8412	13.2068	13.5835
11	13.6020	14.0258	14.4640	14.9171	15.3856
12	15.1130	15.6268	16.1599	16.7130	17.2868
13	16.6770	17.2919	17.9321	18.5986	19.2926
14	18.2957	19.0236	19.7841	20.5786	21.4087
15	19.9710	20.8245	21.7193	22.6575	23.6411
16	21.7050	22.6975	23.7417	24.8404	25.9964
17	23.4997	24.6454	25.8551	27.1324	28.4812
18	25.3572	26.6712	28.0636	29.5390	31.1027
19	27.2797	28.7781	30.3714	32.0660	33.8683
20	29.2695	30.9692	32.7831	34.7193	36.7861
21	31.3289	33.2480	35.3034	37.5052	39.8643
22	33.4604	35.6179	37.9370	40.4305	43.1118
23	35.6665	38.0826	40.6892	43.5020	46.5380
24	37.9499	40.6459	43.5652	46.7271	50.1526
25	40.3131	43.3117	46.5706	50.1135	53.9660
26	42.7591	46.0842	49.7113	53.6691	57.9891
27	45.2906	48.9676	52.9933	57.4026	62.2335
28	47.9108	51.9663	56.4230	61.3227	66.7114
29	50.6227	55.0849	60.0071	65.4388	71.4355
30	53.4295	58.3283	63.7524	69.7608	76.4194

End-of-Year Future Values

An annuity with payments *at the end* of each period is called an *ordinary annuity*. A homeowner's mortgage with its payment due at the end of the first month is a common example of an ordinary annuity. Figure 14-5 illustrates a 4-year ordinary annuity. Figure 14-5 can be compared with figure 14-4 to better understand the difference between this and a 4-year annuity due. Three of the four payments align perfectly, with a payment of $1 at the end of year 0 in table 14-5 corresponding exactly to a payment of $1 at the beginning of year 1 in table 14-4 and so on.

The correspondence between most of the payments, illustrated in figure 14-6, eliminates the need for a separate table. Table 14-3 with its beginning-of-year values can also be used to find the future value of a series of annual payments made *at the end* of each year. An adjustment is made to reflect the difference in timing of the first and last payments. An example follows to clarify the method.

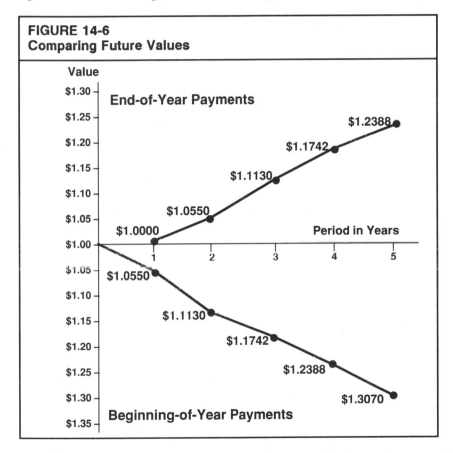

FIGURE 14-6
Comparing Future Values

To derive ordinary-annuity future values from annuity due values, use the factor from the annuity due table for one period less than the actual number of payments and add 1.0000 to that factor. The result will be the present value factor for an ordinary annuity. For example, to find the factor for a 5-year ordinary annuity, add 1.0000 to the future value factor for a 4-year annuity due of $1 per year.

Suppose you need to find the amount to which $1,000 per year, payable for 5 years at the end of each year, will accumulate by the end of the last period at 5.5 percent interest. Since the first payment is not due until one year from now, interest will be earned for only 4 years. From table 14-3, the amount of $1 per annum in advance at 5.5 percent interest for 4 years is $4.5811. The last of the five payments, however, will be made at the end of the period and will not earn any interest. This last payment of $1 added to $4.5811 yields $5.5811, the amount of $1 per annum payable at the end of each year over a 5-year period at 5.5 percent interest. Since $1 payments made in this manner will amount to $5.5811, then $1,000 payments made in the same manner will, obviously, amount to $1,000 x 5.5811, or $5,581.10.

Calculator and Spreadsheet Functions

Most financial calculators can be set directly to do either beginning-of-year or end-of-year calculations of the future value of an annuity. The end-of-year calculator solution to finding the future value of $1 per year for 5 years and annual compounding of interest entails the following keystrokes:

When the user presses the FV (or CPT and FV) button, the calculator produces the answer of 5.5811, which is 1 plus the 4th-year value from table 14-3.

Computer spreadsheet functions usually assume end-of-year payments. The typical spreadsheet function to obtain the same answer is formatted @FV(payment, interest rate, term of years). This problem is solved with the formula @FV(1,0.055,5). Spreadsheet users enter the interest rate as a decimal rather than as a percent.

Test your spreadsheet or calculator's financial functions to be certain that you understand whether it is performing computations that assume payment at the beginning of a year or the end of a year. Enter the three factors specified above for 5 years of payments at 5.5 percent interest. If the answer is 5.5811, then the computation assumes end-of-year payments. If the answer is 5.8881, then the computation assumes beginning-of-year payments. The HP-12C calculator is easily set for beginning or end-of-period payments through the function and the BEG or END key. The BA-II Plus calculator is set by using the 2nd, BGN, and SET keys.

Another way to check your calculator or spreadsheet assumption about timing of payments is to solve for the future value of a single payment of $1 at an interest rate greater than zero. If the payments are assumed to be at the end of the period, the calculated FV will be $1. If the payment is assumed to be made at the beginning of the period, the calculated FV will be greater than $1 because of the interest earned during the period.

Also be certain you understand how interest is being compounded. Many manual calculations assume annual compounding. Some calculators, including the HP-12C and the BA-II Plus, can be set for monthly, weekly, or other compounding intervals. The interest rate must be appropriately adjusted to coincide with the length of the compounding period.

Present Value of Annual Payments

The fourth and final compound interest series determines the present value of a number of equal annual payments at various rates of interest. This series is used by life insurance companies to find amounts payable under the settlement options[1] that liquidate insurance proceeds over several years. An understanding of this series is particularly important here so that we can extend it in the next chapter to include computations that combine these values with life contingencies.

Derivation of Present Values

Table 14-4 showing the present value of annuity payments is derived from the values presented in table 14-2 in the same manner that table 14-3 was derived from the values in table 14-1. As in table 14-2, the values in this series are for annual payments of $1 due *at the end* of each year (ordinary annuity). (Adjustments similar to those described in the previous section can be made to derive the present value of payments due *at the beginning* of each year.) Remember that in table 14-2 at 5.5 percent interest, the present value of $1 payable one year from now is $0.9479. The present value of the second payment of $1 due 2 years from now is $0.8985; the payment due in 3 years is worth $0.8516 now. The present value of all three payments is, of course, the sum of the present values of each taken separately, or $2.6980, as depicted in figure 14-7.

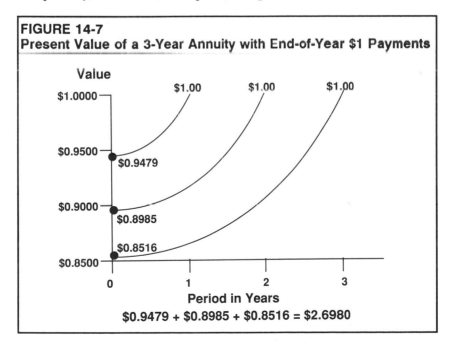

FIGURE 14-7
Present Value of a 3-Year Annuity with End-of-Year $1 Payments

$0.9479 + $0.8985 + $0.8516 = $2.6980

The present value factors in table 14-4 are based on the assumption that each $1 payment is made at the end of the period. Many life insurance calculations involve payment streams that are made at the beginning of the period, such as premium payments. When the number of payments, the interest rate, and amount of each payment are all the same, the present value of an annuity due is higher than the present value of a corresponding immediate annuity. This is purely a result of the earlier timing of the payments.

In order to convert ordinary-annuity present values factors into annuity due present value factors, first, find the ordinary-annuity factor for the appropriate interest rate and for one payment period less than the total number of payments to be made. Then add 1.000 to that factor to represent the $1 payment at the beginning of the stream. The result is a present value factor representing the specific annuity due payments of $1 per period.

Figure 14-8 depicts a 3-year annuity due of $1 per year. The first payment is not discounted because it is made now and worth the full $1 amount. The second payment is one year away and is worth $0.9479 now when discounted at 5.5 percent interest. The third payment is worth $0.8985 now. All three $1 payments have a present value equal to the sum of their individual present values ($2.8464 in this example). The difference between the present value of the 3-year annuity due and the corresponding ordinary annuity does not seem important. However, consider the amount involved if each annual payment is for $10 million instead of $1. The difference in timing amounts to $1,484 million, which is one year of additional interest earned when each payment is made one year earlier.

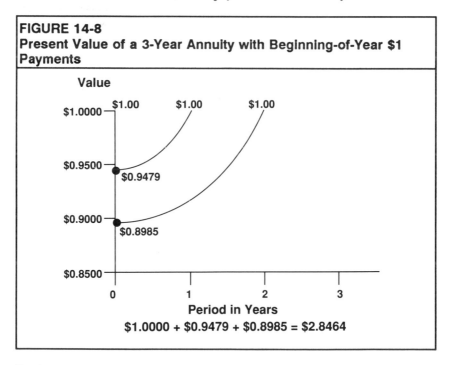

FIGURE 14-8
Present Value of a 3-Year Annuity with Beginning-of-Year $1 Payments

By the process of cumulative addition, the present value of a series of annual payments of $1 for any number of years can be found. Table 14-4 shows these values at various rates of interest for durations up to 30 years. The value for 2 years in table 14-4 is the sum of the first two values in table 14-2. The value for 3 years is the sum of the first three values in table 14-2 (2.6979, which is the same present value depicted in figure 14-7), and so on.

TABLE 14-4
Present Value of 1 per Year at Various Rates of Compound Interest
Immediate Annuity—Payment at End of Year

$$a_n = v + v^2 + \ldots + v^n$$

Year	3.5%	4.0%	4.5%	5.0%	5.5%
1	0.9662	0.9615	0.9569	0.9524	0.9479
2	1.8997	1.8861	1.8727	1.8594	1.8463
3	2.8016	2.7751	2.7490	2.7232	2.6979
4	3.6731	3.6299	3.5875	3.5460	3.5052
5	4.5151	4.4518	4.3900	4.3295	4.2703
6	5.3286	5.2421	5.1579	5.0757	4.9955
7	6.1145	6.0021	5.8927	5.7864	5.6830
8	6.8740	6.7327	6.5959	6.4632	6.3346
9	7.6077	7.4353	7.2688	7.1078	6.9522
10	8.3166	8.1109	7.9127	7.7217	7.5376
11	9.0016	8.7605	8.5289	8.3064	8.0925
12	9.6633	9.3851	9.1186	8.8633	8.6185
13	10.3027	9.9856	9.6829	9.3936	9.1171
14	10.9205	10.5631	10.2228	9.8986	9.5896
15	11.5174	11.1184	10.7395	10.3797	10.0376
16	12.0941	11.6523	11.2340	10.8378	10.4622
17	12.6513	12.1657	11.7072	11.2741	10.0046
18	13.1897	12.6593	12.1600	11.6896	11.2461
19	13.7098	13.1339	12.5933	12.0853	11.6077
20	14.2124	13.5903	13.0079	12.4622	11.9504
21	14.6980	14.0292	13.4047	12.8212	12.2752
22	15.1671	14.4511	13.7844	13.1630	12.5832
23	15.6204	14.8568	14.1478	13.4886	12.8750
24	16.0584	15.2470	14.4955	13.7986	13.1517
25	16.4815	15.6221	14.8282	14.0939	13.4139
26	16.8904	15.9828	15.1466	14.3752	13.6625
27	17.2854	16.3296	15.4513	14.6430	13.8981
28	17.6670	16.6631	15.7429	14.8981	14.1214
29	18.0358	16.9837	16.0219	15.1411	14.3331
30	18.3920	17.2920	16.2889	15.3725	14.5337

Application of the Values

Annuity values, typically based on a present value of $1, are used in several different ways by life insurance companies. For example, determining what payment amount each $1 of death benefit can buy if paid to the beneficiary in 20 annual end-of-year installments under the fixed-period settlement option earning

5.5 percent interest requires the present value of $1 per annum for 20 years, which is $11.9504. This number is then divided into $1 to yield $0.08368. Stated differently, at 5.5 percent compound interest, $1 will provide 8.4 cents at the end of each year for 20 years. Therefore, each $1,000 of death benefit would provide $1,000 x 0.08368, or $83.68 per year for 20 years.

From a different perspective, $11.95 of savings invested at 5.5 percent will provide $1 per year for 20 years. The first payment will occur one year from now; payments will continue for 19 years. At the end of 20 years none of the money will remain. Similarly $14.53 will provide $1 annual payments for 30 years.

Annuity values also can be used to determine the amount available from larger investments. If $11.95 will provide $1 per year for 20 years, then $1,000 will provide an annual payment of $1,000 ÷ 11.95 = $83.68. The rule is as follows: To find the amount of annual payments due at the end of each year that a given principal sum will provide, divide the sum by the present value of $1 per year at the applicable rate of interest for the period.

Amounts payable under life insurance settlement options are payable *at the beginning* of the year.[2] Likewise, annual premiums are due at the beginning of the year. Therefore life insurance companies must modify the values shown in table 14-4 to reflect the present value of a series of periodic payments due at the beginning of the year. The adjustment involved is simple and very similar to the adjustment made for future values.

Consider, for example, a series of annual payments of $1 due at the beginning of each year for 25 years. The first payment is due immediately and is worth $1. Twenty-four additional payments remain, the first of which is due one year from now. The present value of the entire series is obtained by adding $1 to the present value of $1 per annum (end of year from table 14-4) for one year less, in this case, 24 years. The result at an interest rate of 5.5 percent is $13.1517 + $1, or $14.1517.

Calculator and Spreadsheet Functions

Financial calculators and spreadsheets are also used to perform present value computations. The financial calculator solution to valuing a temporary annuity that pays $1 per year at the end of each of 20 years at 5.5 percent interest requires input similar to that used for future value computations:

Then press the PV (or CPT and PV) button. The present value of $1 per annum for 20 years is $11.9504 as before. If this is divided into 1, the annual payment for 20 years purchased by $1 is $0.08368. The typical computer spreadsheet function to obtain the same answer is formatted @PV(payment, interest rate, term of years). This problem is solved with the formula @PV(1,0.055,20).

CURRENT INTEREST ASSUMPTIONS

In the broad financial market the interest rate paid reflects the degree of risk associated with the future payment. The riskier the venture, the higher the interest rate paid. The more secure the principal, the lower the interest rate paid. Many of the illustrations in this chapter assume 5.5 percent interest. This rate is only representative of rates that could be used by companies in computing premiums and reserves on their various products.

The actuaries designing a permanent cash value life insurance product must select the interest rate carefully, as it will be guaranteed for the lifetime of the contract and subject to a statutory maximum. While companies tend to select a conservative rate, perhaps one percentage point less than they expect to earn on their investments over a long period, they also must offer rates that are competitive with other insurers and with other financial intermediaries. Permanent life insurance contracts in force today have been issued over a period of many years. Interest rate guarantees in those policies range from 3.5 percent to nearly 6 percent.

Flexible premium contracts like universal life also quote interest rate guarantees with this same range, but they derive most of their marketing appeal from the possibility that they will pay rates higher than those guaranteed. As demonstrated in chapter 16, reserves under such contracts are recalculated on a similar interest basis.

NOTES

1. Settlement options are discussed in chapter 25.
2. As a matter of fact, life insurance settlement options usually provide for *monthly* payments, which necessitates a further modification.

15

Net Premiums

Dan M. McGill
Revised by Norma Nielson and Donald Jones

The *premium* is the price charged by a life insurance company for an insurance or annuity contract. This term arises from the very first insurance arrangements. In the Middle Ages a lender, for an additional payment—or "premium"—over the interest charge, would waive repayment of the loan should the insured vessel or cargo be lost at sea. The expression has survived the practice and is still used to designate the monetary consideration for an insurance company's promise.

To calculate a premium the first step is to develop a number that equates to the value of benefits promised under the contract. The premium for a life insurance contract is usually expressed as a *rate* per \$1,000 of face amount. On the other hand, the premium for an annuity contract normally is expressed as a rate per specified amount of income, such as \$100 per year or \$10 per month. If the premium is paid in one sum, it is called a *single premium*. Alternatively, the premium may be paid more frequently with annual, semiannual, quarterly, or monthly frequencies occurring most often. In fact, life insurance companies often use the equivalent of daily premiums when adjusting a policy's death benefit payment either up or down. A downward adjustment reflects any unpaid fractional premiums; an increase reflects the refund of premium amounts paid to cover any period after the insured's death.

The computation of premiums requires three fundamental assumptions:

- a rate of mortality
- a rate of interest
- a rate of expense

The expense rate may provide a margin for contingencies. Only the first two factors—the rate of mortality and the rate of interest—enter the calculation of the *net premium*. The net premium is sufficient to provide all benefits owed under the contract, whether payable because of death or survival. If the actual experience conforms to the projected experience, the net premiums will be exactly equal to the total of all claims.

The amount added to the net premium to cover expenses of operation, to provide for contingencies, and to allow any profit is called *loading*. The net premium increased by the loading is called the *gross premium*, which is the premium payable by the policyowner. This chapter describes how actuaries derive net premiums. Chapter 17 extends this discussion to illustrate the development of gross premiums.

NET SINGLE PREMIUM

The first step in deriving any premium is to find the net *single* premium for that policy. Then a set of more frequent premiums that are equivalent to the single premium may be developed if needed, as is usually the case. Finally, an amount is added for expenses and contingencies. This section describes how to calculate the net single premium.

An important feature of premium calculation develops because mortality tables display annual rates. Calculations start with the assumption that premiums are paid at the beginning of each policy year and benefits are paid at the end of the policy year. Annuity contract calculations also start with payments made annually. Then premiums for contracts with benefits and payments more than once yearly are computed by assuming that deaths occur uniformly throughout the policy year.

Concept of the Net Single Premium

The objective of life insurance rate making is to assure that the company collects enough from each group of insureds to pay the benefits promised under the contract. If the contract is purchased with a single or lump sum, that sum is the present value of future benefits. Rate making, the process of valuing the promises in the contract, involves three steps.

The first step is to learn the benefits promised under the contract and the length of time that the promise remains in effect. Life insurance benefits take two basic forms: (1) a death benefit that is the company's promise to pay a specified amount—called the *face amount*—if the insured dies while he or she is covered and (2) an endowment benefit that is the company's promise to pay a specified amount if the insured should survive to the end of the covered period. Some contracts contain both promises, while others contain only the first.

The second step is to select a mortality table to use in measuring the probabilities involved. Whether the company's promise is to pay upon death, survival, or both, the rate of mortality determines the value of the promise. Unless otherwise stated, this book uses the 1980 Commissioners Standard Ordinary (CSO) Mortality Tables to illustrate premium computations. In practice, however, a company must adopt the most appropriate mortality table for the group of persons insured.

The third step is to select an interest rate to be used in adjusting for the time value of money. The fact that premiums are paid in the present while the benefits to be received from the company must be fulfilled in the future significantly reduces the cost of all forms of insurance. (See chapter 14 for discussions of the time value of money.) The rate at which expected benefits are discounted greatly influences the size of the net single premium. The lower the rate, the higher the premium, and vice versa. All calculations in this section assume 5.5 percent interest.

Two Techniques of Calculation

The net single premium is always the sum of the present values of all the expected benefits. It may be computed according to either of two techniques, however. The first uses probabilities for each insured and is called the *individual approach*. The second assumes a large group of insureds and is called the *aggregate approach*.

The individual approach incorporates the necessary three steps by finding the product of these three factors for each year of the contract:

(1) the amount (which is defined in the contract)
(2) the discount factor (as discussed in chapter 14)
(3) the probability of payment (as shown in the mortality table)

The probability of dying, factor (3), is a scientific estimate that will always contain an element of uncertainty. That uncertainty is acceptable, however, if a company sells a sufficiently large number of policies. As discussed in chapter 13, the law of large numbers assures that the average of many such payments actually made will be near the value expected—that is, (1) x (2) x (3).

The individual approaches can be illustrated with the calculation of the net single premium for a one-year term policy issued to a male at age 32. This contract pays the $1,000 face of the policy if the insured dies during the year of coverage and nothing if he survives. The three factors are as follows:

(1) the possible amount of $1,000
(2) the discount factor 1/$1.055 = $0.947867 that reflects the fact that any payment will be made at the end of one year
(3) the probability that a 32-year-old male will die within one year. According to the 1980 male CSO Table, 17,470 out of 9,546,404 males aged 32 will die within the year. Thus the probability is 17,470/9,546,404 = .001830.

The expected present value of this uncertain payment is

$$(\$1,000) \times (.94787) \times (.001830) = \$1.73$$

The aggregate approach, on the other hand, uses the large numbers shown in a mortality table directly and requires less proficiency with combining decimal numbers. The process begins by assuming that the number of persons shown in the mortality table as living at the issue age is the starting population for the insurance arrangement. The rates in the table predict how many payments are expected to occur at each subsequent age. A discount factor reduces the aggregate payments at each age to the present value. In the final step the total of these present values is divided by the number of lives at issue age.

The two methods give identical premiums. This is demonstrated by recalculating, using the aggregate method, the net single premium for the same policy as was shown earlier. To apply the 1980 male CSO Table using the aggregate approach, 9,546,404 males aged 32 are assumed to apply for a one-year term policy for $1,000. Of those, 17,470 die during the following year. Therefore the company must have $17,470,000 on hand at the end of the year to pay claims. Some of that money can come from interest earned during the policy's one-year term. The insurance company needs to collect only the present value of this amount from the policyowners at issue. Therefore, the amount that must be collected from the group is $17,470,000 divided by $1.055, or $16,559,242. Since it is not known at the beginning of the year which persons will die, each must pay the same amount into the fund. That is the total contribution divided by the 9,546,404 receiving coverage:

$$\$16,559,242 \div 9,546,404 = \$1.73$$

Since both techniques have educational value, their use will be alternated in this chapter's illustrations.

Term Insurance

Term insurance policies that provide protection on a level premium basis for several years are important in practice and for illustration. The net single premium for a 5-year term policy for $1,000 issued to a female aged 32 will be calculated by the individual approach.

The individual approach was defined earlier for one uncertain future payment. The 5-year term policy has five uncertain future payments. The present value of each expected future payment is calculated. The net single premium for the term insurance is the *sum* of these expected present values. Stated differently, the net single premium, developed using the individual approach, is the sum of the following five products:

(1) For the possible payment at the end of the first policy year, the amount is $1,000, the discount factor for one year is 1/1.055, and the probability of payment is, according to the 1980 female CSO Table, 14,037 out of 9,680,912, or 0.00145. The expected present value is the product of these factors:
$$\$1,000 \times 0.94787 \times 0.00145 = \$1.37$$

(2) For the possible payment at the end of the second policy year, the amount is $1,000, the discount factor for 2 years is $(1/1.055)^2$, and the probability of payment is, according to the 1980 female CSO Table, 14,500 out of 9,680,912, or 0.00149. The expected present value is the product of these factors:
$$\$1,000 \times 0.898452 \times 0.00149 = \$1.35$$

(3) For the possible payment at the end of the third policy year, the amount is $1,000, the discount factor for one year is $1/(1.055)^3$, and the probability of payment is, according to the 1980 female CSO Table, 15,251 out of 9,680,912 or 0.00157. The expected present value is the product of these factors:
$$\$1,000 \times 0.851614 \times 0.00157 = \$1.34$$

(4) For the possible payment at the ends of the fourth policy year, the expected present value is
$$\$1,000 \times 0.807217 \times \frac{15,901}{9,680,912} = \$1.33$$

(5) For the 5th policy year, the expected present value is

$$\$1,000 \times 0.765134 \times \frac{16,933}{9,680,912} = \$1.34$$

In summary, the net single premium for the 5 years of coverage is

$$1.37 + 1.35 + 1.34 + 1.33 + 1.34 = \$6.73.$$

The aggregate approach achieves this same result by adding the terms before dividing by the number of policyowners who are alive to share the costs at issue, 9,680,912.

Whole Life Insurance

An insurance policy that provides protection for the whole of life is called whole life insurance. The face amount of the policy is payable upon the insured's death, whatever the insured's age. Eventual payment of the face is certain. The only uncertainty is the year in which the policy will become a claim. However, because whole life also can be viewed as a term insurance policy for the remaining life span, the techniques for computing the net single premium are the same as for a term policy.

Under the individual approach, the net single premium for a whole life insurance policy issued to a male aged 32 is the sum of the expected payments at the end of his 33d year, his 34th year, and every year up to and including his "last age" according to the table being used for the calculation. Since this is age 100 in the 1980 CSO Tables, the example involves 68 separate probabilities. For the sake of brevity, table 15-1 shows only the equations for the first 5 and last 5 years.

Adding the results of these 68 computations produces a sum of $140.23. That number represents the expected present value of possible payments at the end of each year from age 32 to 99, inclusive.

One interesting and significant result arises from the fact that a whole life policy inevitably will become a claim. The net single premium at any age of issue would be $1,000 per $1,000 of insurance except for the interest earnings on the advance deposit. The entire process of calculating the probability that death will occur at each of the possible ages is important only to help find the amount of interest that will be earned on the advance premium before the death claim must be paid.

Endowment Insurance

An endowment insurance contract promises to pay a death benefit if the insured should die during the term of the contract or to pay an endowment amount (usually equal to the death benefit) if the insured should survive to the end of the term. Endowment contracts have been dropped by United States life insurers as a result of federal income tax law changes. These policies do not satisfy the tax code definition of life insurance if they endow at ages below 95. Endowment policies that were issued before 1985 and have been kept in force continue to be treated as life insurance under the transition provisions of the tax

---

TABLE 15-1
Calculating Net Single Premium for Whole Life Insurance Policy Issued to Male Aged 32

Age 32: ($1,000) x (.947867) x $\left(\dfrac{17,470}{9,546,404}\right)$ = $1.73 Cost of first year's mortality

Age 33: ($1,000) x (.898452) x $\left(\dfrac{18,200}{9,546,404}\right)$ = $1.71 Cost of 2d year's mortality

Age 34: ($1,000) x (.851614) x $\left(\dfrac{19,021}{9,546,404}\right)$ = $1.70 Cost of 3d year's mortality

Age 35: ($1,000) x (.807217) x $\left(\dfrac{20,028}{9,546,404}\right)$ = $1.69 Cost of 4th year's mortality

Age 36: ($1,000) x (.765134) x $\left(\dfrac{21,217}{9,546,404}\right)$ = $1.70 Cost of 5th year's mortality

• • •

Age 95: ($1,000) x (.032497) x $\left(\dfrac{48,412}{9,546,404}\right)$ = $0.16 Cost of 64th year's mortality

Age 96: ($1,000) x (.030803) x $\left(\dfrac{37,805}{9,546,404}\right)$ = $0.12 Cost of 65th year's mortality

Age 97: ($1,000) x (.029197) x $\left(\dfrac{24,054}{9,546,404}\right)$ = $0.07 Cost of 66th year's mortality

Age 98: ($1,000) x (.027675) x $\left(\dfrac{20,694}{9,546,404}\right)$ = $0.06 Cost of 67th year's mortality

Age 99: ($1,000) x (.026232) x $\left(\dfrac{10,757}{9,546,404}\right)$ = $0.03 Cost of 68th year's mortality

---

code.[1] Endowment policies are still available in many countries. They are even the most frequently purchased type of life insurance in some countries where high savings rates are common.

An endowment insurance contract is a combination of a pure endowment and term insurance. The former pays only if the insured survives the specified period of years, and the latter pays only if the insured does not survive the specified period. The net single premium for the endowment insurance contract is then the sum of the respective net single premiums for the pure endowment and term insurance contracts.

The net single premium for a $1,000 10-year endowment contract issued to a female at aged 45 is the sum of these same two components. Using the aggregate approach we calculate the amount that, if invested at issue in a 5.5 percent fund, would be sufficient to pay the term insurance benefits of the contract for 9,409,244 45-year-old females (9,409,244 is the number living at age 45 in the 1980 female CSO Table). The calculation is shown in table 15-2.

TABLE 15-2
Calculating Net Single Premium for 10-year Endowment Insurance Contract Issued to Female Aged 45

Policy Year	Benefit Amount	Number of Deaths	Discount Factor	Amount Required at Issue
1st	$1,000	33,497	0.947867	$31,750,700.90
2d	1,000	35,628	0.898452	32,010,047.86
3d	1,000	37,827	0.851614	32,214,002.78
4th	1,000	40,279	0.807217	32,513,893.54
5th	1,000	42,883	0.765134	32,811,241.32
6th	1,000	45,727	0.725246	33,163,323.84
7th	1,000	48,711	0.687437	33,485,743.71
8th	1,000	52,011	0.651599	33,890,315.59
9th	1,000	55,797	0.617629	34,461,845.31
10th	1,000	59,602	0.585431	34,892,858.46
TOTAL				$331,193,973.31

The total required at age 45 for the 9,409,244 lives is $331,193,973.31. The net single premium is the amount per individual:

$$\$331,193,973.31 \div 9,409,244 = \$35.20.$$

Since the pure endowment contract has only one possible payment, its net single premium can be calculated by the three-factor product that was used above. Here the factors are as follows:

(1) the amount $1,000
(2) the discount factor $1/(1.055)^{10} = 0.585431$
(3) the probability of payment—the ratio of the number surviving at age 55, 8,957,282, divided by the number at issue, 9,409,244

Thus by the individual method, the net single premium for the pure endowment is $557.31. The net single premium for the 10-year endowment insurance contract is obtained by adding the net single premiums for the 10- year term insurance and the 10-year pure endowment:

Net single premium, 10-year term policy, at age 45	$ 35.20
Net single premium, 10-year pure endowment, at age 45	557.31
Net single premium, 10-year endowment insurance contract	$592.51

It is interesting to consider the sources of funds to pay the pure endowment benefit. The net premium of $557.31 deposited with the company at the beginning of the term is available. Interest on this amount for the 10-year period will be $557.31 x $(1.055)^{10}$ − 557.31, or $394.66. At the end of the 10-year period the net premium plus interest is $951.97. Yet the policy promises $1,000 if the insured is alive on that date. From what source does the difference $1,000− $951.97, or $48.03, come?

Benefit of Survivorship

The difference is attributable to the *benefit of survivorship* — the pro rata share of each survivor in a fund created by the premiums, plus accumulated interest of those persons who failed to survive the period. According to the 1980 female CSO Table, 451,962 persons out of 9,409,244 alive at age 45 will die within the next 10 years. Each of those persons deposits $557.31 with the company at the inception of the contract. That money is not returnable in case of death. By the end of the period, each deposit has accumulated to $951.97, creating an aggregate fund of $951.97 x 451,962, or $430,254,265.10, which is forfeited by those who died and available to the survivors. Divided by the number of survivors, 8,957,282, the fund yields $48.03 per survivor. This sum added to the accumulation of $951.97 provides the $1,000 promised under the contract.

This concept underlies all contracts that provide benefits based on survival to the end of a specified period. The longer the period and the higher the rate of mortality, the greater the benefit of survivorship. For purposes of comparison recognize that the benefit of survivorship under a 20-year endowment issued at age 45 is $135.53 per survivor.

The following demonstrates how the entire premium for an endowment insurance contract can be derived by the group or aggregate approach:

Total aggregate mortality claims = 331,193,973.31 (see table 15-2)

Total pure endowment payments = number of lives at age 55 x 1000 x discount
factor

$$= 8,957,282 \times 1000 \times 0.585431 = 5,243,870,600$$

$$\text{Net single premium} = \frac{331,193,973.31 + 5,243,870,600}{9,409,244 \text{ number at issue (45)}}$$

$$= \$592.51$$

Life Annuities

The previous chapter discussed *annuitiescertain. Certain* means that payments occur unconditionally for a known term without regard to any contingencies. This chapter discusses *life annuities*. The adjective *life* defines the payments as occurring only upon survival of a designated life. The terminology used to describe life annuities is consistent with the terminology used for annuities certain. A *life annuity due* has its first payment due at issue or contract date; a *life annuity immediate* has its first payment due at the end of one payment interval; a *deferred life annuity* has its first payment due after the completion of a deferment period.

Life annuities play dual roles for any insurance company. The company can be on the paying end or on the receiving end of a life annuity. The company pays annuities to annuitants, beneficiaries, and retirees; these are usually annuities-immediate. It receives premiums from policyowners in the form of annuities; these are usually annuities due. As we calculate the net single premiums for life annuities, remember that these concepts are applied to value both benefit payments and premium receipts.

The appropriate mortality rates differ between computations for annuities and for insurance policies. This important difference occurs simply because annuitants live longer. The table must be chosen to reflect the experience of annuitants or insured lives.

Calculating Life Annuity Present Values

To compute the net single premium for a life annuity, view the annuity as a series of pure endowments. Just as the pure endowment pays only if the insured survives to the end of a specified period, a life annuity pays only if the annuitant is alive on the date the payment is due.

Calculating the present value of the life annuity requires three dates: (1) the contract or issue date, (2) the due date of the first payment, and (3) the due date of the last possible payment. Consider each payment a pure endowment payable on its due date. The net single premium of the annuity is the sum of the net single premiums on the contract date for the payments or "pure endowments" specified by the annuity.

The dates for the net single premium of a *life annuity immediate* payable to a 70-year old male are as follows: (1) The contract date is at age 70, (2) the first payment is at age 71, and (3) the last possible payment is at the end of the mortality table. When using the 1983 Individual Annuity Mortality (IAM) Table for Males, the payments could extend to age 115. While the table ends at age 115, the payments would, of course, continue after age 115 if the annuitant survives. The following discussion uses the individual method to illustrate this calculation for annual payments of $100.[2]

The probability that the first payment of $100 will be made is 7,747,886 ÷ 7,917,081 = 0.97863. The numerator is the number of persons alive at age 71; the denominator is the number alive at age 70. Since one year will elapse before the payment, if it occurs at all, the sum set aside at the time of purchase can be discounted at 5.5 percent. The present value of the first payment, therefore, is figured as follows:

$$\frac{7{,}747{,}886}{7{,}917{,}081} \text{ x } \$100 \text{ x } .947867 = \$92.76$$

The probability that the second payment occurs is the probability that a person now aged 70 will be alive at age 72. Again discount the contingent payment, this time for 2 years. The present value of the second payment is determined as shown in the following equation:

$$\frac{7{,}564{,}671}{7{,}917{,}081} \text{ x } \$100 \text{ x } .898452 = \$85.85$$

TABLE 15-3
Calculating Net Single Premium for Life Annuity Immediate Payable to Male Aged 70

Age 71: $\frac{7{,}747{,}886}{7{,}917{,}081}$ x 100 x .947867 = $92.76 Present value of first annuity payment

Age 72: $\frac{7{,}564{,}671}{7{,}917{,}081}$ x 100 x .898452 = $85.85 Present value of second annuity payment

Age 73: $\frac{7{,}366{,}999}{7{,}917{,}081}$ x 100 x .851614 = $79.24 Present value of third annuity payment

Age 74: $\frac{7{,}154{,}571}{7{,}917{,}081}$ x 100 x .807217 = $72.95 Present value of fourth annuity payment

Age 75: $\frac{6{,}927{,}099}{7{,}917{,}081}$ x 100 x .765134 = $66.95 Present value of fifth annuity payment

• • •

Age 111: $\frac{487}{7{,}917{,}081}$ x 100 x .11134 = $.000685 Present value of 41st annuity payment

Age 112: $\frac{148}{7{,}917{,}081}$ x 100 x .105535 = $.000197 Present value of 42d annuity payment

Age 113: $\frac{35}{7{,}917{,}081}$ x 100 x .100033 = $0.000044 Present value of 43d annuity payment

Age 114: $\frac{6}{7{,}917{,}081}$ x 100 x .094818 = $0.000007 Present value of 44th annuity payment

The denominator in the first term does not change in these equations or any of the other 43 separate equations. The first five and last four equations needed to compute the net single premium for the entire series of contingent payments are shown in table 15-3.

The present value of all payments is $901.82; the present value at age 70 of a payment at extreme ages, such as 111, is zero when rounded to the nearest cent. We show the figures to six decimals to emphasize that only the last computation produces an answer that is literally zero.

Thus in consideration of $901.82 paid in a single sum at the inception of the contract, an insurance company could afford to pay a 70-year-old man an income of $100 per year as long as he lives, the first payment being made at age 71. The computation of the net single premium for such an annuity also can be viewed on an aggregate basis. Either premium computation presumes that the company enters into sufficient contracts to experience average results.

The net single premium for an immediate annuity *with guaranteed payments* for a specified number of years, whether the annuitant survives or not, is similar to the immediate annuity above. Simply replace the probability of payment with 1.00 for each year during the certain period. Because no contingency is involved, the discount factor is the only cost-reducing factor during this period.

To take a simple example, consider an immediate annuity purchased at age 70 to provide an income of $100 per year with the payments guaranteed for 5 years. Using the 1983 IAM Table for Females and the aggregate method, 8,837,346 payments are assumed to be payable at the end of each of the first 5 years instead of the number of persons shown as living in the mortality table at those ages. The mortality table values are used as before beginning with the sixth payment. Determining the net single premium for the entire series of payments involves 45 separate equations. The first 10 and last five are shown in table 15-4. The sum of the present values of these 45 payments is $1,045.88.

The net single premium for a *temporary* life annuity is calculated using the same underlying principles as the calculations in table 15-4. Since the promised payment is zero after the term of the annuity, the computations end with that age. For a 10-year life annuity issued to a male at age 70, for instance, the first probability would be the chance of survival to age 71, or

$$\frac{7,747,886}{7,917,081} = 0.97863$$

and the last probability would be the chance that the annuitant would survive to age 80, or

$$\frac{5,560,108}{7,917,081} = .70229$$

Deferred Whole Life Annuity

The amount that must be on hand at age 70 to provide a life income of $100 per year, with no payments guaranteed, was shown in table 15-3 to be $901.82. This amount may be paid to the insurance company in a single sum at the purchaser's age 70. Alternatively, the present value of that amount may be

---

TABLE 15-4
Calculating Net Single Premium for Immediate Annuity with Payments Guaranteed for 5 Years for Female Aged 70

Age 71: 1 x 100 x .947867 = $94.76 Present value of first year's payment

Age 72: 1 x 100 x .898452 = $89.85 Present value of 2d year's payment

Age 73: 1 x 100 x .851614 = $85.16 Present value of 3d year's payment

Age 74: 1 x 100 x .807217 = $80.72 Present value of 4th year's payment

Age 75: 1 x 100 x .765134 = $76.51 Present value of 5th year's payment

Present value of 5-year annuity certain → $427.03

Age 76: $\dfrac{8,046,977}{8,837,346}$ x 100 x .725246 = $66.04 Present value of 6th year's payment

Age 77: $\dfrac{7,864,680}{8,837,346}$ x 100 x .6874368 = $61.18 Present value of 7th year's payment

Age 78: $\dfrac{7,664,060}{8,837,346}$ x 100 x .65159887 = $56.51 Present value of 8th year's payment

Age 79: $\dfrac{7,443,971}{8,837,346}$ x 100 x .617629 = $52.02 Present value of 9th year's payment

Age 80: $\dfrac{7,203,323}{8,837,346}$ x 100 x .585431 = $47.72 Present value of 10th year's payment

• • •

Age 111: $\dfrac{2640}{8,837,346}$ x 100 x .11134 = $0.00 Present value of 41st year's payment

Age 112: $\dfrac{922}{8,837,346}$ x 100 x .105535 = $0.00 Present value of 42d year's payment

Age 113: $\dfrac{254}{8,837,346}$ x 100 x .100033 = $0.00 Present value of 43d year's payment

Age 114: $\dfrac{49}{8,837,346}$ x 100 x .094818 = $0.00 Present value of 44th year's payment

Age 115: $\dfrac{5}{8,837,346}$ x 100 x .089875 = $0.00 Present value of 45th year's payment deposited with the company years before the time the income is to commence. More likely still, the present value may be accumulated through a series of periodic deposits before the income is to begin. If the funds are deposited with the company before annuity payments begin, a smaller premium is required.

The adjustment can be most clearly explained in terms of a nonrefund annuity purchased with a single premium some years before the annuity starting date. Assume that a male aged 30 purchases an annuity contract that will pay him an annual income of $100 for life beginning at age 70. Under the contract's terms nothing is paid or refunded in the event of his death before age 70. Note that in this example the income is to begin one year earlier than the earlier example that derived the premium for an immediate annuity.

Pure Endowment and General Annuity Approaches

The premium for this deferred annuity can be calculated in two different ways. First is the "pure endowment approach." It consists of calculating the net single premium for an *immediate* life annuity providing $100 per year, with the first payment at 70, and considering this net single premium to be the amount of a pure endowment promised at age 70. Next the net single premium at age 30 for this pure endowment due at age 70 is calculated.

To illustrate the pure endowment approach recall that $901.82 for a male at age 70 will provide a life income of $100 per year beginning at age 71. With $100 added to this sum, the $100 payments could begin at age 70, the additional $100 taking care of the payment to be made on the effective date of the contract. Since no time elapses, no interest is earned and no life contingency is involved. Therefore the net single premium at age 70 for an annuity that will provide $100 immediately and $100 per year thereafter as long as the annuitant lives is $1,001.82.

A sum less than $1,001.82 deposited with the company at age 30 will provide that same payment stream commencing at age 70. Two reasons justify a substantial reduction: First, funds deposited at age 30 will earn interest for 40 years. Second, a substantial probability exists that the purchaser will not survive to age 70 to receive payments. The sums forfeited by those who fail to survive to that age reduce, through the benefit of survivorship, the amount that each annuitant must pay at the outset. Therefore the sum that must be deposited with the company at age 30 is as follows:

$$\frac{7,917,081}{9,878,453} \text{ x } \$1,001.82 \text{ x } 0.117463 = \$94.31 \text{ (the net single premium)}$$

The second method available to determine the net single premium for an annuity is the "general annuity" method. Using the same example as above, each payment is treated as a separate pure endowment to be discounted to age 30. The first payment of $100 will be discounted for 40 years and multiplied by the probability of the annuitant's surviving to age 70. The second payment will be discounted for 41 years and multiplied by the probability of survival to 71, and so on to age 114 when the 1983 IAM Table is used. The first five and last five equations of the process are set forth in table 15-5 using the 1983 IAM for females and 5.5 percent interest.

TABLE 15-5
Calculating Net Single Premium for Deferred Whole Life
Annuity for Female Aged 30 (General Annuity Method)

1st payment: $\dfrac{8,837,346}{9,939,483}$ x 100 x .117463   = \$10.44

2d payment: $\dfrac{8,733,975}{9,939,483}$ x 100 x .111339471   = \$9.78

3d payment: $\dfrac{8,621,263}{9,939,483}$ x 100 x .105535   = \$9.15

4th payment: $\dfrac{8,497,815}{9,939,483}$ x 100 x .100033   = \$8.55

5th payment: $\dfrac{8,362,020}{9,939,483}$ x 100 x .094818   = \$7.98

• • •

41st payment: $\dfrac{2,640}{9,939,483}$ x 100 x .013078   = \$0.00347

42d payment: $\dfrac{922}{9,939,483}$ x 100 x .012396   = \$0.0001115

43d payment: $\dfrac{254}{9,939,483}$ x 100 x .011750   = \$0.000030

44th payment: $\dfrac{49}{9,939,483}$ x 100 x .011138 = \$0.0000055

45th payment: $\dfrac{5}{9,939,483}$ x 100 x .010557 = \$0.0000005

The sum of the present values of all 45 payments is \$117.96. This compares with a value or \$94.31 developed earlier for males. The difference illustrates vividly the spread between male and female mortality.

The net single premium also can be obtained by using the aggregate approach as shown in table 15-6. As usual, only the first five and last five equations appear in the table.

TABLE 15-6
Calculating Net Single Premium for Deferred Whole Life Annuity for Female Aged 30 (Aggregate Approach)

1st payment:	8,837,346	x	100	x	0.117463	=	103,806,117.30
2d payment:	8,733,975	x	100	x	0.111339	=	97,243,204.25
3d payment:	8,621,263	x	100	x	0.105535	=	90,984,499.07
4th payment:	8,497,815	x	100	x	0.100033	=	85,006,192.79
5th payment:	8,362,020	x	100	x	0.094818	=	79,287,001.24

• • •

41st payment:	2,640	x	100	x	0.013078	=	
42d payment:	922	x	100	x	0.012396	=	3,452.59
43d payment:	254	x	100	x	0.011750	=	1,142.91
44th payment:	49	x	100	x	0.011138	=	298.45
45th payment:	5	x	100	x	0.010557	=	54.58

$$\text{Present Value of payments} = \frac{5.28}{1,172,546,028.40}$$

$$\text{Net single premium} = \frac{1,172,546,028.4}{9,939,983} = \underline{\$117.96}$$

NET LEVEL PREMIUM

Few life insurance contracts are purchased with single premiums. Few persons have sufficient savings to buy adequate life insurance on a single-premium basis. This would also run counter to the prevailing practice in consumer finance, where installment purchases have become the pattern.

Apart from the trends of the times, financing life insurance on an installment basis is appropriate. Since the fundamental purpose of life insurance is to provide protection against the loss of future earnings—which by definition are received in periodic installments—paying the cost of that protection over a similar time frame is logical.

Another reason most people prefer installment financing of life insurance is the lower total cost if the insured dies early. One monthly premium purchases as much life insurance protection as a single premium—only the period of coverage is reduced. If the insured dies within a few years after the single-sum purchase of a life insurance policy, the cost will be many times greater than if annual (or more frequent) installment payments are made. On the other hand, if policyowners live beyond the period, the total amount of the annual premiums paid will exceed the single premium, and with each passing year the disparity will become greater.

Concept of the Level Annual Premium

Policyowners must be given a fair choice between paying for insurance with a single premium and with a set of level annual premiums. The prices must be determined in a manner that leaves the financial position of the company unaffected by the policyowner's decision. Such pricing is referred to as *actuarially equivalent* pricing. To be the actuarial equivalent of a policy's net single premium, its net level premiums must reflect (1) the possibility that the insured may die having made only some of the payments, and (2) the smaller amount invested that will reduce the investment earnings to the company. Expressed in positive terms the net level premium must reflect (1) the probability that the insured will survive to pay premiums and (2) the period during which the premiums will earn investment income.

Deriving the net level annual premiums integrates two computations described earlier in this chapter. No new computational skills are required. The rule for determining net level annual premiums is this: Divide the net single premium for the policy in question by the present value of a life annuity due of $1 for the premium-paying period. The process is illustrated on the following pages using net single premiums derived above.

Term Insurance

The earlier example found the net single premium for a $1,000 5-year term policy issued to a female aged 32 to be $6.73. What level annual premium paid at the beginning of the contract and on each of the next four anniversary dates, if the insured is then living, is the equivalent of $6.73? The answer to this question, following the rule stated above, requires that one know the present value of a temporary life annuity due of $1 for a term of 5 years for a female aged 32. The 1980 CSO Table is used for this calculation since that is the table used to derive the $6.73 premium. In other words, the same mortality and interest assumptions must be used to determine the present value of the annual premiums as are used to determine the present value of benefits. Since the mortality rates of the 1980 CSO Tables are greater than the mortality rates of the 1983 Individual Annuity Tables, the present value of an annuity due calculated according to the 1980 CSO Table is smaller than the present value of an annuity due based on the 1983 Individual Annuity Table. The present value is computed as shown in table 15-7.

The sum of the five payments, the present value of a 5-year temporary annuity due of $1 for a female aged 32, is $4.50. This means that a premium of $1 for each period will purchase a policy with a net single premium of $4.50. The net single premium for the 5-year term policy, however, is $6.73. Hence, to determine the size of five level annual premiums payable beginning at age 32 that are equivalent to $6.73, divide $6.73 by $4.50. The net level annual premium for a $1,000 5-year term policy issued to a female aged 32 is $6.73 ÷ $4.50 = $1.50. The maximum amount any policyowner might pay is $7.50—five annual premiums of $1.50 each. This exceeds the net single premium of $6.73. The difference reflects (1) the loss of interest and (2) the chance that the insured will die before making all the installment payments contemplated. If the net single premium is paid, the company has $6.73 on which to earn interest from the beginning. Under the net level premium arrangement, however, only $1.50 is available at the outset. The longer the period involved, the greater the disparity between the net single premium and the sum potentially payable by the insured under the annual premium arrangement.

TABLE 15-7
Calculating Net Level Premium for $1,000 5-year Term Policy Issued to Female Aged 32

Age 32: $\dfrac{9,680,912}{9,680,912}$ x 1.00 = $1.00 Present value of first annuity payment

Age 33: $\dfrac{9,666,875}{9,680,912}$ x .947867 = $0.95 Present value of 2d annuity payment

Age 34: $\dfrac{9,652,375}{9,680,912}$ x .898452 = $0.90 Present value of 3d annuity payment

Age 35: $\dfrac{9,637,124}{9,680,912}$ x .851614 = $0.85 Present value of 4th annuity payment

Age 36: $\dfrac{9,621,223}{9,680,912}$ x .807217 = $0.80 Present value of 5th annuity payment

---

Ordinary Life Insurance

Ordinary life insurance is whole life insurance for which premiums will be paid throughout the lifetime of the insured. To obtain the net level annual premium for an ordinary life policy, the net single premium for a whole life policy is divided by the present value of a *whole* life annuity due of $1. Since the whole of life is the longest premium-paying period contemplated under any whole life insurance policy, the present value per $1 per annum is greater than for any other premium-paying period. This produces the lowest level annual premium of any whole life policy because the net single premium for a whole life policy at any particular age is the same, regardless of the premium paying-period. The longer the period over which the premiums are spread, the smaller each periodic premium will be.

Earlier in this chapter, the net single premium for a whole life insurance for a 32-year-old male was determined. Here the present value of a life annuity due of $1 for the whole of life for a male aged 32 is calculated by the aggregate approach. Then the level annual premium for an ordinary life insurance policy can be determined.

The present value of the life annuity due must recognize the possibility that the insured may not be alive at age 33 (and each age thereafter to the end of the mortality table) to pay the second and subsequent premiums. The probability of survival is the probability of a payment occurring. The first five and last five computations are shown in table 15-8.

TABLE 15-8
Calculating Net Level Premium for Whole Life Policy Issued to Male Aged 32

Age 32: $\dfrac{9,546,404}{9,546,404}$ x 1 x 1.00   = $1.00

Age 33: $\dfrac{9,528,934}{9,546,404}$ x 1 x .947867 = $0.95

Age 34: $\dfrac{9,510,734}{9,546,404}$ x 1 x .898452 = $0.90

Age 35: $\dfrac{9,491,712}{9,546,404}$ x 1 x .851614 = $0.85

Age 36: $\dfrac{9,471,685}{9,546,404}$ x 1 x .807217 – $0.80

• • •

Age 95: $\dfrac{146,721}{9,546,404}$ x 1 x .034284 = $0.00053

Age 96: $\dfrac{98,309}{9,546,404}$ x 1 x .032497 = $0.00033

Age 97: $\dfrac{60,504}{9,546,404}$ x 1 x .030803 = $0.00020

Age 98: $\dfrac{31,450}{9,546,404}$ x 1 x .029197 = $0.00010

Age 99: $\dfrac{10,757}{9,546,404}$ x 1 x .027675 = $0.00003

As the last line of table 15-8 shows, the present value of the 68th payment is very slight, only $0.00003. Still, it must be taken into account. The sum of all the payments' present values is $16.49. Dividing this number into the net single premium of $140.23 for a whole life policy issued at age 32 produces a net level annual premium of $8.50. Stated differently, the $1,000 whole life policy that costs $140.23 if purchased with a single-sum payment can also be purchased with premium payments of $8.50 annually.

Limited-Payment Life Insurance

The net single premium for a whole life policy can be spread over any number of years by means of the appropriate life annuity due. Suppose a male policyowner, aged 32, wants to pay for his policy in 20 annual installments. Then the present value of a 20-year temporary life annuity due of $1 per annum is determined. This annuity's first payment is at age 32 and its last possible payment is at age 51. The present value of such an annuity is $12.35. This number is smaller than the corresponding whole life annuity due and divided into the same net single premium, $140.23, produces a larger level annual premium. The level annual premium for a 20-payment life policy issued at age 32 is

$$\$140.23 \div \$12.35 = \$11.36.$$

For a 10-payment life policy, end the computations at age 41. Following the formula previously given, this yields a present value for the temporary life annuity due of $7.88. Dividing 7.88 into $140.23 gives a 10-payment life premium of $17.80.

Finally, if the whole life policy is to be paid up at age 65, the annuity value needed for the denominator is the present value of a series of payments of $1 per year, extending from age 32 to 64 and contingent on the insured's survival.

Endowment Insurance

The net level premium for an endowment insurance policy is derived in exactly the same manner as that of any other policy. Once again, the procedure to determine the net level annual premium is to divide the net single premium by the present value of a temporary life annuity due of $1 for the premium-paying period. All endowment policies, of course, are limited-payment policies in the sense that the premium is not payable for the whole of life. Usually premiums are payable for the full term of an endowment insurance contract.

As found earlier in this chapter, the net single premium for a $1,000 10-year endowment issued to a female aged 45 is $592.51. The present value of a 10-year temporary life annuity due of $1 for a female at age 45 is $7.82. The net level annual premium, therefore, is $592.51 ÷ $7.82, or $75.77.

Deferred Annuity

Deferred annuities usually are financed with annual—rather than single—premiums. Premiums may be paid throughout the period of deferment or may be limited to a shorter period of years. The annuity contract may promise to return the annuitant's premiums with or without interest. The annual premium in this case does not involve life contingencies but rather is a sum of money that must be set aside annually to accumulate at an assumed rate of compound interest to a predetermined amount at a specified date. For example, $1,151.88 must be on hand at age 65 to provide an income of $100 per year to a male. How much would a male aged 40 have to set aside each year, including a payment on his 40th birthday, to accumulate a sum of $1,151.88 by his 65 birthday, assuming such annual payments earn compound interest at the rate of 5.5 percent? Such a program includes 25 payments, the first at age 40 and the last at age 64. The period of accumulation is 25 years. At the end of 25 years $1 per year earning 5.5 percent interest will accumulate to $53.9660. Dividing $1,151.88 by $53.9660 shows that $21.34 must be set aside during each of 25 years to accumulate the required single premium. This computation presumes that premiums are to be returned if the annuitant dies before age 65.

Alternatively, the contract may provide that the company retains all premiums paid in the event of death before the annuity income commences. If premiums will not be refunded, the net level annual premium for a deferred annuity is determined by the same methods as life insurance. Again, however, the premium annuity's present value must be computed using the same mortality rates as those used for the benefit annuity. Using the 1983 Individual Annuity Mortality Table, the net level premium for a nonrefund deferred annuity purchased by a female aged 40, with income to begin at 65, is computed as a temporary life annuity due. That annuity makes one payment immediately with 24 subsequent payments due. The net single premium for that annuity is $311.38. The net level premium is $311.38 ÷ $13.95198, or $22.32.

THE EFFECT OF GENDER-DISTINCT MORTALITY ON PREMIUMS

Lower mortality rates exist among females. Historically this has resulted in higher rates for annuities and periodic settlements under life insurance policies. The corresponding rate reductions for life insurance on females arose more recently. The differential premiums reflect the use of separate mortality rates for female lives. Such rates may be found, for example, in the 1955−60 Basic Tables or in special reports on intercompany mortality experience.[3] Despite differences in premiums, the policy reserves, surrender values, and dividend scales are usually the same as those used for males.

NOTES

1. IRC Sec. 7702(j).
2. Although the great majority of annuity contracts provide *monthly* income, the premiums derived here use the *rates* per $100 of *annual* income. In practice, this rate is derived first and then computed to a monthly equivalent.
3. These reports have separated the data for male and female lives since 1957.

16

The Reserve

Dan M. McGill
Revised by Edward E. Graves

The calculation of a net single premium involves an equation, one side of which represents the present value of the benefits promised under the contract and the other the sum of money that must be on hand to provide the benefits. At the inception of the contract, the two sides of the equation are in balance. Moreover, the net single premium can be converted into a series of net level premiums without impairing the balance of the equation. However, once the contract has run for one or more premium-paying periods, the situation changes. The present value of future benefits and the present value of future net premiums are no longer equal. As the years go by, the present value of future benefits increases since the date of death draws steadily nearer, while the present value of future premiums declines since there are fewer to be received. The benefit side of the equation increases each year until it eventually equals the face amount of the policy, whereas the side representing premium payments (yet to be collected) declines until it ultimately reaches zero.[1]

If the equation is to remain in balance, a third element must be introduced; that element is the *reserve*. Thus the reserve may be defined as the difference between the present value of future benefits and the present value of future net premiums. It is the balancing factor in the basic insurance equation.

TYPES OF RESERVES

The foregoing definition of the reserve reflects the *prospective* concept of the reserve, stemming from the emphasis on the future. Under the prospective method of valuation, no consideration is given to past experience apart from the basic mortality and interest assumptions entering into the formula. This approach works well for fixed-premium contracts. On the other hand, the reserve may be derived entirely by reference to past experience; this reserve is known appropriately as the *retrospective* reserve (the appropriate method to use to calculate reserves for flexible-premium contracts). The retrospective reserve represents the net premiums collected by the company for a particular class of policies, plus interest at an assumed rate, less the death claims paid out. Both concepts are mathematically sound and with the same set of actuarial assumptions will produce identical reserves at the end of any given period. If the actual experience is more favorable than that assumed in the reserve computations, the savings will go into surplus, to be disposed of in accordance with the company's judgment; the greater portion is normally distributed to policyowners as dividends.

In theory the reserve can be calculated on the basis of either the gross premium or the net premium. Under gross premium valuation, the loading element is taken into consideration; under net premium valuation, only mortality and interest are taken into account. Viewed prospectively, the gross premium reserve is equal to the excess of the present value of future claims and future expenses over the present value of future gross premiums. Viewed retrospectively (as is done for universal life policies), it is the excess of gross premiums collected in the past over death claims and expenses incurred, with this difference growing at an assumed rate of interest. Gross premium valuation was the accepted practice among American life insurance companies until 1858, when the state of Massachusetts enacted legislation requiring the use of the net premium basis. Other states followed Massachusetts' lead, and today net premium valuation is prescribed in every state. This is a stricter standard of solvency, the implications of which will be discussed later.

Finally, policies may be valued on either the *full net level premium basis* or according to *modified reserve plans,* methods that permit all or a portion of the normal first-year reserve to be used in meeting the excess of first-year expenses over first-year premium loading. (Modified reserve plans are described in chapter 18.)

Reserves may be classified as terminal, initial, and mean, according to the time of valuation. As its name implies, the *terminal* reserve is the reserve at the end of any given policy year. The *initial* reserve for any particular policy year is the reserve at the beginning of the policy year and it is equal to the terminal reserve for the preceding year increased by the net level annual premium for the current year. The *mean* reserve is the average of the initial reserve and terminal reserve for any year of valuation. For example, the initial reserve, computed on the basis of the 1980 CSO Male Table and 4.5 percent interest, for the 5th policy year of a $1,000 ordinary life contract issued at age 25 is $33.71. This sum is obtained by adding the net level annual premium of $7.49 to the terminal reserve for the 4th policy year, $26.22. The initial reserve of $33.71 will earn interest of $1.52 during the 5th year, producing a fund of $35.23 at the end of the year, from which the cost of insurance, $1.65, is deducted to yield the 5th-year terminal reserve of $33.58. The mean reserve for the 5th policy year then becomes

$$\frac{33.71 + 33.58}{2} = \$33.65$$

In the illustration for this particular policy year, the initial reserve is larger than the terminal reserve because the cost of insurance is greater than the interest on the initial reserve. This is not always true, however. Under many circumstances and policy durations, including policies issued at the younger ages and those with high interest assumptions, the terminal reserve is larger than the initial reserve. This relationship would obviously prevail at all ages of issue and at all durations for policies purchased with a single premium.

The initial reserve is used principally to determine dividends under participating policies. One of the major sources of surplus from which dividends can be paid, as will be shown later, is a rate of investment earnings in excess of that assumed in the calculation of premiums. In allocating excess interest earnings to individual policies, the initial reserve is generally selected as the base to which the excess interest factor is applied on the theory that it represents the amount of money invested throughout the year on behalf of a particular policy and hence is the measure of that policy's contribution to the pool of excess interest earnings.

The terminal reserve is also used in connection with dividend distributions. Insurers allocate mortality savings on the basis of the net amount at risk, and the terminal reserve must be computed to determine the net amount at risk. On policies issued prior to 1948 the terminal reserve also serves as a basis for surrender values (nonforfeiture values); the predeath benefits are equal to the terminal reserve less a surrender charge. (The surrender charge exists during the early years only.) For policies issued since 1948 surrender values are calculated in accordance with the terminal reserve concept but with a so-called adjusted premium rather than with the net annual level premium.

The chief significance of the mean reserve is its use in insurers' annual statements. One of the most important items that must be reported to regulators is the aggregate amount of reserves. Since policies are written throughout the year, on any given reporting date some policies will just be commencing a policy year, some will just be completing a policy year, and some—the overwhelming majority—will be somewhere between one policy anniversary and the next. To calculate the exact reserve on all outstanding policies would be a tremendous—and unnecessary—task. Therefore it is assumed for purposes of the annual statement that on the date of valuation all policies are at exactly the mid-point between two policy anniversaries. This assumes that policies are written at a uniform rate throughout the year, which is not precisely the case, but it is accurate enough for regulatory purposes. Since life insurance companies' annual statements are invariably prepared as of December 31, all policies are valued as if they were written on June 30 by reporting the mean reserve.

The remainder of this chapter is devoted to terminal reserves computed on the full net level premium basis.

METHODS OF DETERMINING THE RESERVE

As stated earlier, reserves may be ascertained prospectively or retrospectively. Since the retrospective method is easier to grasp, it will be discussed first.

Retrospective Method

The retrospective method of valuation can be explained in terms of either one policy or all policies in a given classification. The group or aggregate approach will be described first.

The retrospective reserve arises out of the level premium design. Under that arrangement premiums in the early policy years are more than adequate to cover the death claims, thereby creating a fund that can be drawn upon in the later years of coverage when death rates rise sharply and claims exceed current premium income. In that sense the reserve may be regarded as an accumulation of unearned premiums (a form of partial-prefunding somewhat similar to a layaway plan for merchandise purchases). The retrospective reserve is sometimes even described as the *unearned premium reserve*. The prefunding generates investment income that benefits the surviving policyowners, showing up on the company's financial statement as a liability item. As a matter of fact, reserves in the aggregate constitute the major liability item on the insurer's balance sheet, typically accounting for about 90 percent of all insurer liabilities. Most of an insurance company's assets (typically 80 percent) are held in offset to policy reserves and are for the benefit and protection of the policyowners. Premiums are lower than they would have to be if there were no investment earnings associated with reserves. The exact manner in which prefunding leads to the creation of reserves is demonstrated in table 16-1 (which is shown at the end of this chapter).

Progression of Reserve Funds

Table 16-1 shows the progression of reserve funds on a group of ordinary life contracts issued to males aged 35 and written in the amount of $1,000. According to the 1980 CSO Male Table, 9,491,711 persons would be alive at age 35 out of an original group of 10 million individuals alive at age zero. Therefore it is assumed in the illustration that the group of people taking out an ordinary life contract at age 35 is composed of the survivors of the original group of 10 million. The net level premium for an ordinary life contract issued at age 35, computed on the basis of the 1980 CSO Male Table and 4.5 percent interest, is $11.60 per $1,000 of face amount. Thus the group will contribute a total of $110,144,947 (9,491,711 x $11.60433) in premiums at the beginning of the first policy year. Since it is assumed that no death claims will be paid until the end of the year, the entire sum of $110,144,947 will earn interest throughout the year at the rate of 4.5 percent, producing earnings of $4,956,523. Therefore a sum of $115,101,469 will have accumulated by the end of the year, from which anticipated death claims in the amount of $20,028,000 will be deducted. This will leave a fund of $95,073,469 that, divided equally among the 9,471,683 survivors, will yield an individual reserve of $10.04.

The sum of $95,073,469 is carried over to the beginning of the 2d policy year and is augmented by the second annual premium of $109,912,535 (9,471,683 x $11.60433), producing a sum of $204,986,004, which will likewise be invested at 4.5 percent interest throughout the year. Interest earnings of $9,224,370 will bring the accumulated sum up to $214,210,375. According to the 1980 CSO Male Table, 21,217 persons will die during the year, and the payment of their claims at the end of the year will reduce the fund to $192,993,375, or $20.42 per surviving policyowner. The terminal reserve for the 2d policy year will be carried forward to the beginning of the 3d policy year, and the process of adding annual premiums, crediting interest on the combined sum, and subtracting death claims is repeated. The process continues until the last of the policyowners is assumed to have died.

Note that in the early years net premium income greatly exceeds the tabular death claims. During that period therefore both premium and investment income contribute to building up the reserve fund. For each year that goes by, however, premium income declines (because of the reduction in the number of policyowners); while for a long period the dollar value of death claims increases. By the 23d policy year, death claims catch up with premium income (death claims exceed premium income from then on until the end of the mortality table), but for a few years thereafter, interest on the accumulated fund (including current premiums) is more than adequate to absorb the deficiency in net premium income, and the aggregate fund continues to grow. Beginning in the 35th policy year, however, death claims exceed both premium income and interest earnings, and the total fund begins to decline. In other words, after the 35th policy year, a portion of the principal must be used to pay death claims. Death claims reach a maximum in the 44th policy year,[2] totaling $329,936,000 but, even after tapering off, continue to exceed current premiums and investment earnings. The reserve fund continues to shrink until, with the payment of the death claims of the last 10,757 survivors in the 65th policy year, it is completely exhausted.

Aggregate versus Pro Rata Reserves

A sharp distinction must be drawn between the aggregate reserve and the pro rata portion of that reserve allocable to an individual policyowner. As table 16-1 shows, the individual reserve increases each year, eventually equaling the face amount of the policy (before payment of the last set of death claims). It continues to increase after the aggregate reserve begins its decline because the number of survivors decreases at a faster rate than the aggregate fund. The individual reserve must accumulate to the face amount of the policy; if each group of policyowners is to be self-supporting, there is no other source of funds from which the final death claims can be paid.

In theory, of course, the aggregate reserve cannot be allocated to individual policyowners. Insurance is a group proposition, and the reserve is a group concept. To be sure, the fund is held to guarantee performance under individual contracts, but it is computed on a group basis. If an occasion should ever arise whereby the total reserve fund would have to be apportioned among the various policyowners, as in the event of liquidation, such apportionment should, strictly speaking, take into account the relative state of health of the various policyowners and their respective chances of survival. A policyowner in poor health would be entitled to a relatively greater share of the aggregate reserve than one who is in good health since the value of his or her contract, as measured by the relative chances of death, would be greater. Apportionment on the basis of the relative *value* of the policies would clearly be impossible. For all practical purposes therefore the reserve under a particular policy is considered to be its pro rata share of the aggregate reserve.

Cost of Insurance

The retrospective method of reserve valuation may also be illustrated with reference to an individual policy. Such an illustration, however, presupposes a familiarity with the cost-of-insurance concept, which was discussed briefly in chapter 2. There it was pointed out that under level premium insurance, the company is never at risk for the full face amount of the policy. This is attributable to the fact that a reserve is created under the contract with the payment of the first premium, and if the policy remains in force, it is available for the settlement of any death claim that may arise. In the event of a policyowner's death, the company returns the reserve under the contract and adds enough to it from sums contributed by all policyowners in the deceased's age and policy classification—including a contribution from the deceased—to make up the amount due under the contract. The sum that each policyowner must contribute as his or her pro rata share of death claims in any particular year is called the *cost of insurance*. It is the amount the policyowner must pay for protection.

The cost of insurance is determined by multiplying the net amount at risk (face amount of the policy less the reserve) by the tabular probability of death at the insured's attained age. Thus if at the end of 20 years the reserve under an ordinary life policy issued at age 30 is $264.27, the cost of insurance for the 20th year is $735.73 x 0.00956, or $7.03. The net amount at risk is $735.73, and the probability of death at age 49, according to the 1980 CSO Male Table, is 9.56 per 1,000. Therefore that policy's share of death claims during the 20th year of insurance is $7.03 per $1,000 of the policy's face amount.

The cost of insurance for a $1,000 ordinary life policy issued at age 35 is shown in table 16-2 (at the end of this chapter) for each policy year to the end of the mortality table. As might be expected, the figure increases each year through the 57th policy year, or age 91, at which point it amounts to $38.52. It then declines in each of the following 5 policy years since the net amount at risk is *decreasing* at a more rapid rate than the death rate is *increasing*. The mortality rate increases more rapidly than the amount at risk decreases for policy years 63 and 64, and the cost of insurance increases again in those years.

It is not until the 29th policy year, or age 63, that the cost of insurance exceeds the net level premium of $11.60 for an ordinary life policy of $1,000 issued to a male aged 35. This means that through the 28th policy year, each annual premium makes a net addition to the policy reserve.[3]

In applying the cost-of-insurance concept to the determination of a retrospective reserve, it is necessary to know the terminal reserve for the policy year in question—the very value that is being sought. This poses no problem if the computation is being performed algebraically, but it creates a mathematical impasse if the reserve is being computed arithmetically. To avoid the introduction of algebraic symbols, this arithmetic contradiction will be ignored in the following illustrations.

The net level premium for an ordinary life policy of $1,000 issued at age 35 is $11.60433. Invested at 4.5 percent interest, this sum will amount to $12.13 at the end of the first year. The policy's share of death claims during the first year is $2.09 ($989.96 x 0.00211), which, deducted from the accumulated sum of $12.13, leaves $10.04 as the terminal reserve for the first year. This sum will be supplemented at the beginning of the 2d policy year by the second net level premium of $11.60, producing a sum of $21.64 that will be invested at an assumed rate of 4.5 percent interest throughout the year and will earn $0.97. Thus a fund of $22.61 will have accumulated by the end of the 2d year, from which $2.19 will be deducted as the cost of insurance ($979.58 x 0.00224), producing a 2d-year terminal reserve of $20.42. This process continues until, by the end of the 10th policy year, the reserve is $115.41. The accumulation during the 11th year then takes the following form:

Terminal reserve for 10th year	$115.41
Add: net level annual premium	11.60
Initial reserve for 11th year	$127.01
Interest earnings at 4.5 percent	5.72
Fund at end of 11th year	$132.73
Deduct: cost of insurance	3.96
Terminal reserve for 11th year	$128.77

It may be said that the retrospective terminal reserve for any particular policy year is obtained by adding the net level annual premium for the year in question to the terminal reserve of the preceding year, increasing the combined sum by one year's interest at the assumed rate, and deducting the cost of insurance for the current year. If the policy is paid up or was purchased with a single premium, there will be no annual premiums to consider, and the cost of insurance must be met entirely from interest earnings on the reserve. The terminal reserve for the 11th year under a 10-payment life policy issued at age 35 in the amount of $1,000 would be obtained as follows:

Terminal reserve for 10th year	$303.19
Interest earnings at 4.5 percent	13.64
Fund at end of 11th year	$316.83
Deduct: cost of insurance	3.12
Terminal reserve for 11th year	$313.71

If an ordinary life policy issued at age 35 becomes a death claim during the 11th policy year, it contributes a total of $132.73 toward the payment of its own claim, leaving only $867.27 to be contributed by other policyowners. If the policy is still in force at the end of the year, it contributes $3.96 toward the payment of death claims under other policies in its classification, leaving $128.77 as the terminal reserve. Note that the policy makes a contribution toward the cost of insurance whether it becomes a claim or not, a fact that has been alluded to earlier but not statistically demonstrated. It is interesting to note the difference in the 11th-year cost of insurance between the ordinary life ($3.96) and 10-payment life ($3.12) policies, which is attributable solely to the difference in the reserves or, conversely, the amount at risk.

Prospective Method

Although the retrospective method of computation clearly demonstrates the origin and purpose of the reserve, its use is not preferred by actuaries. It is seldom used in actual reserve calculations for scheduled or fixed-premium policies. (As noted earlier, however, it is the method often used for flexible-premium policies.) State valuation laws invariably express reserve requirements in terms of the prospective method. This does not mean that a company must use the prospective approach since any method that will produce reserves equal to or in excess of those that would be derived by the statutory formula is acceptable. Nevertheless, insurers tend to prefer the prospective method because of its simplicity.

The prospective reserve, V, under a policy issued at age x, at the end of any given number of years, t, is equal to the net single premium for the policy in question at the age of valuation, A_{x+t}, minus the net level premium at age of issue, P_x, multiplied by the present value of a life annuity due of $1 for the balance of the premium-paying period calculated as of the age of valuation, represented by $\ddot{a}_{x+t}$.[4] The full net level reserve 10 years after issue for an ordinary life contract for $1,000 issued to a male at age 35 is therefore determined as follows:

$$_{10}V_{35} = A_{35 + 10} - (P_{35} \times \ddot{a}_{35 + 10}), \text{ or}$$

$$_{10}V_{35} = A_{45} - (P_{35} \times \ddot{a}_{45})$$

Substituting known values in the formula, the computation of the reserve becomes a mere arithmetic exercise:

$$_{10}V_{35} = \$303.19 - (\$11.60433 \times 16.18157) = \$115.41$$

Stated verbally, the 10th-year reserve for an ordinary life policy of $1,000 issued at age 35 is equal to the net single premium for a whole life policy issued at age 45, $303.19, minus the product of the net level premium for an ordinary life policy issued at age 35, $11.60433, and the present value of a whole life annuity due of $1 calculated at age 45, $16.18157. The present value of a *whole* life annuity due of $1 was used since premiums are to be paid throughout the insured's life.

This formula symbolizes the earlier definition of a reserve as the difference between the present value of future benefits and the present value of future premiums. A_{x+t} represents the present value of future benefits, and the product of the values within the parentheses represents the present value of future premiums. For any particular policy except term insurance, the present value of future benefits increases each year since the insured is one year older and the policy one year closer to maturity. This is the same as stating that the net single premium for a policy increases with the attained age of the insured. On the other hand, the present value of future premiums declines since each year, fewer premiums remain to be paid and they are nearer to collection. Under any particular fixed-premium policy, the net level premium the policyowner pays remains the same throughout the premium-paying period, but the present value of each dollar to be received by the company decreases with each passing year. At age 35, for example, the present value of a whole life annuity due of $1, computed on the basis of the 1980 CSO Male Table and 4.5 percent interest, is $18.29. By age 45, however, it has declined to $16.18; and by ages 55, 65, and 75, it has fallen to $13.46, $10.27, and $7.02, respectively. The manner in which the present value of future benefits and the present value of future premiums diverge to create the necessity for a reserve is illustrated in figure 16-1.

Line *AB* represents the present value of future benefits or the net single premium for a whole life policy at each of the attained ages from 35 to 100. Line *AC* represents the present value of future premiums, the values for which are derived by multiplying the net level premium for an ordinary life policy issued to a male at age 35—namely, $11.60—by the present value of a whole life annuity due of $1 at each of the attained ages from 35 to 100. At any point on the horizontal axis, the difference between lines *AB* and *AC* represents the reserve.

At age 35 the net single premium for an ordinary life policy is $212.27, and the present value of future net level premiums at the inception of the contract is likewise $212.27. There is no reserve at this point. The net single premium for an ordinary life policy issued to a male at age 36 is $220.18, while the present value of future net level premiums for a policy issued at age 35 is only $210.14. Therefore a terminal reserve of $10.04 comes into existence at the end of the first policy year. By the end of the 10th policy year, the present value of future net

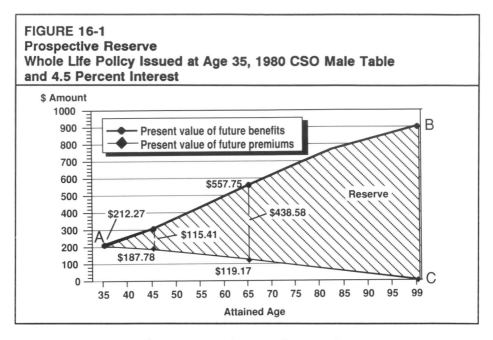

FIGURE 16-1
Prospective Reserve
Whole Life Policy Issued at Age 35, 1980 CSO Male Table
and 4.5 Percent Interest

level premiums will have declined to $187.78 ($11.60 x $16.18157), while the net single premium for an ordinary life policy at the beginning of the next year—that is, at the insured's age 45—will have risen to $303.19. The difference of $115.41 must be on hand in the form of a reserve. At age 65 the net single premium for an ordinary life policy is $557.75, while the present value of future premiums at the age-35 rate is only $119.17. The reserve at the end of the 30th policy year therefore is $438.58. The two sets of values continue to diverge until at age 100, when the present value of future premiums is zero because there are no more premiums to be paid, whereas the net single premium for an ordinary life policy at age 100—if one could be purchased at such an advanced age—would be $1,000 since the policy would immediately become a claim. Thus the reserve at age 100 would be equal to the face amount of the policy, a principle noted earlier.

The values for line *AB* remain the same for the attained ages shown for any whole life policy, irrespective of the age of issue, but the values for line *AC* depend on a specific age of issue since the net level premium remains constant. Hence the slope of the curves differs with different ages of issue and with different types of policies; nevertheless, for any permanent form of insurance, the disparity between the two sets of values will ultimately equal the policy's face amount.

Application to Other Types of Contracts

This method can be used to determine the reserve under any type of life insurance or annuity contract and for any duration. For example, the reserve at the end of 15 years under a 20-payment life policy issued at age 30 is $303.19 − ($13.26 x $4.544), or $242.93. The sum of $303.19 represents the net single premium for a *whole* life policy issued at age 45, A_{x+t}, while $13.26 represents the net level premium for a 20-payment life policy issued at age 30. In this case, however, the level annual premiums take the form of a *temporary* life annuity—namely, the present value of a temporary life annuity due for 5 years, computed as of age 45. This value is $4.55.

Under limited-payment whole life or endowment policies, the present value of the temporary life annuity due becomes zero after all premiums have been paid, and the reserve becomes the net single premium for the policy in question at the insured's attained age. Thus the reserve at the end of 30 years under a 20-payment life policy issued at age 35 is the net single premium for a whole life policy issued at 65. This means that at any particular attained age the reserves under all paid-up whole life policies are identical (if they are based on the same mortality table and interest rate assumption), regardless of age of issue.[5] The same is true of all paid-up endowment policies with the same maturity date. This principle is illustrated in figure 16-2, which shows the reserves under different forms of whole life policies issued at age 35.

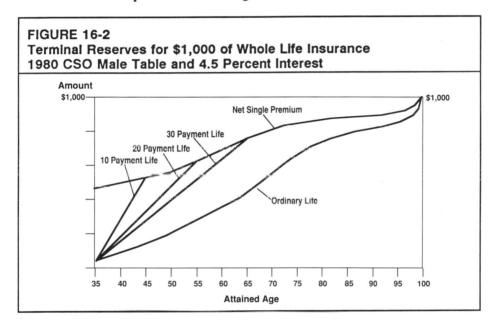

FIGURE 16-2
Terminal Reserves for $1,000 of Whole Life Insurance
1980 CSO Male Table and 4.5 Percent Interest

Significance of Actuarial Assumptions

In measuring its liabilities under outstanding contracts, whether accomplished retrospectively or prospectively, an insurance company must assume certain rates of mortality among its policyowners and a certain rate of earnings on the assets underlying the reserves. The assumptions as to mortality are reflected in the choice of the mortality table used in the valuation, while the appraisal of investment potential is reflected in the rate of interest selected for the computations. The reserve values heretofore cited are based on the 1980 CSO Male Table and 4.5 percent interest. However, other assumptions have been and are being used in reserve computations. It is important therefore to note the impact of the choice of basic actuarial assumptions on reserves.

Mortality

There is a widespread belief that the higher the rates of mortality assumed in a reserve computation, the greater the reserve will be. The fact is that the *level* of mortality, *per se,* does not determine the size of the reserves. A mortality table that shows a much higher death rate at every age than another table could produce a much lower reserve than that computed on the basis of the other table. The factor that governs the size of the reserve is the amount of bend of the mortality curve or the rapidity of increase in the rate of mortality from age to age. (Mathematically, the higher the second derivative of the mortality function, the higher the reserve required.) The sharper the bend in the slope of the mortality curve, the greater the reserve will be. This is true even though the steeper curve shows a lower rate of mortality at all ages up to the terminal age. This principle is illustrated in a crude fashion in figure 16-3.

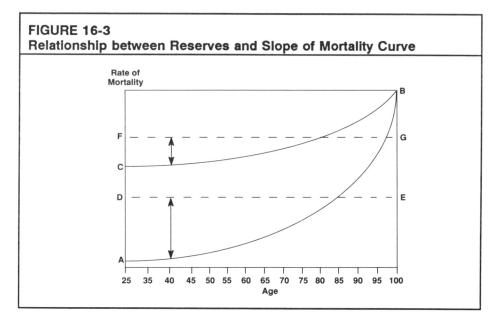

FIGURE 16-3
Relationship between Reserves and Slope of Mortality Curve

Curves *AB* and *CB* represent the death rates from ages 25 to 100 under two hypothetical mortality tables, one reflecting unrealistically high rates of mortality and the other showing more normal rates. Lines *DE* and *FG* represent level premiums and are placed at such distances above points *A* and *C* as to create triangles beneath the broken lines, in each case approximately equivalent in area to the triangles that can be formed above the dotted lines. This obviously ignores the influence of compound interest and grossly exaggerates the redundancy of the level premiums in the early years of the insured's life, but it graphically illustrates the effect of leveling out mortality curves of differing slopes. It is apparent that the mortality table represented by curve *AB* would produce the higher reserves.

In practice it is not always possible to predict visually the relative magnitude of reserves under different mortality tables at various ages and durations.[6] A particular mortality table may show higher death rates at some ages and lower death rates at other ages, compared to another table. In such event the reserves under the specified table may be higher at some ages and durations than those of another table and lower at other ages and durations. For example, a select mortality table, which shows a rapidly increasing death rate during the early years of coverage as the effect of selection wears off, produces larger reserves for short durations than a table that does not exhibit such a sharp increase in death rates.

Interest

Unlike a change in mortality assumptions, which may produce either an increase or a decrease in reserves depending on age of issue and duration, a change in the interest assumption will affect the magnitude of reserves in the same direction — but not necessarily to the same extent — at all ages of issue and durations.[7] Specifically, a decrease in the assumed rate of interest increases reserves, while an increase in the rate decreases reserves.

The impact of a change in interest assumption on reserves is not easily explained in terms of the conventional retrospective and prospective approaches. For example, it might be concluded, retrospectively, that a reduction in the assumed rate of interest would result in the accumulation of a smaller reserve at the end of any given period short of the maturity of the contract or the end of the mortality table. Such a conclusion, however, ignores the fact that the lower interest assumption implies a larger net premium, and the problem becomes one of measuring the effect of accumulating a series of larger net premiums at a lower rate of interest. Inasmuch as the augmentation of net premiums more than compensates for the loss of interest earnings involved in the lower interest rate, a larger reserve results. On the other hand, an increase in the assumed rate of interest would require a smaller net premium, offsetting for a time the influence of the higher rate of interest earnings and producing a reserve that is smaller at all durations up to the end of the mortality table or earlier maturity of the contract than that computed on the basis of a lower interest assumption.

Prospectively, the analysis is complicated by the fact that the present value of future benefits and the present value of future premiums are affected in the same direction by a change in the interest assumption. However, inasmuch as the present value of future benefits is always influenced to a greater degree than is the present value of future premiums, a decrease in the assumed rate of interest always produces a larger reserve, and an increase in interest produces a smaller reserve.

The simplest explanation revolves around the fact that the reserve must accumulate to the face amount of the policy by the end of the mortality table for a whole life contract or by the maturity date for an endowment policy. Therefore the lower the rate of interest at which the reserve is to be accumulated, the larger the fund to which the lower rate is to be applied must be at any given time. To take a very elementary example, if $1,000 must be accumulated by the end of any particular year and only 2.5 percent interest can be earned on invested funds, a sum of $976 must be on hand at the beginning of the year. If a yield of 3 percent can be realized, only $971 need be on hand at the beginning of the year.

During the decline in interest rates during the 1930s and 1940s, many life insurance companies reduced the interest assumption in computing reserves under old contracts, which, of course, meant that the reserves under such contracts were increased. This was accomplished by transferring funds from the surplus account to the reserve account (at one time or over a period of years) or by diverting to the reserve account a portion of current mortality, interest, and loading savings that would otherwise be distributed as dividends. Once the necessary funds were transferred to the reserve account, the policies thereafter were treated as if they had been written on the lower interest basis in the first place, except that surrender and loan values were usually not increased. Insurers were then in a position to meet their reserve requirements with lower earnings on their invested funds.

In some states, notably New York, a reserve-strengthening program of this sort can be undertaken only with the insurance commissioner's consent, and once it has been carried out, it can be reversed only with official consent. This requirement is in the interest of preserving equity among the various classes of policyowners.

It is clearly possible that similar reserve strengthening may again be required in the future if the economy ever sustains a long enough period of low investment returns. The investment returns available in the early 1990s were often alarmingly close to the guaranteed rates in the contracts. If investment returns remain at or below the level of contract guarantee rates long enough for the insurer's entire portfolio to be reinvested, there will be no investment returns to supplement the low rates on new portfolio investments. Such a scenario could force life insurers to strengthen their policy reserves.

STATUTORY REGULATION OF RESERVES

Because the basis on which a life insurance company's policy liabilities are computed is subject to regulation by the various states, such liabilities are called *legal reserves*. The states prescribe only the basis on which *minimum* reserves are to be calculated. Therefore as noted earlier companies are permitted to use any other basis that will yield reserves equal to or larger than those produced by the statutory method. The specifications are couched in terms of the mortality table to be used, the maximum rate of interest to be assumed, and the formula to be applied. The specifications differ between life insurance and annuities and among ordinary, group, and industrial life insurance. Special rules apply to proceeds left with the insurance company under supplementary agreements.

Prior to 1948 the universal legal basis for computing minimum net level premium reserves for ordinary insurance was the American Experience Table and 3.5 percent interest, applied under the prospective method of valuation. In most states some modification of the net level premium reserve was recognized and approved. Under the Standard Valuation Law, which became effective in all states in 1948 and with a few exceptions was applicable to all policies issued between December 31, 1947, and December 31, 1965, the minimum reserve basis for all ordinary policies was the 1941 CSO Table and 3.5 percent interest, likewise applied under the prospective formula. However, a modified reserve standard (described in chapter 18), was prescribed in lieu of the net level premium reserve basis. The use of the 1958 CSO Table for all new ordinary insurance became mandatory in 1966; the other features of the Standard Valuation Law remained unchanged. Twenty years later the 1980 CSO Table was mandated for valuation of individual life insurance policies. Other tables are prescribed for the valuation of group insurance, industrial insurance, and annuities.

Annual valuation of policy liabilities is required in every state.

SAFETY MARGINS IN THE LEGAL RESERVE

In practice insurance companies generally compute their legal reserves on a more conservative basis than required by law. Most companies use the same mortality and interest assumptions to compute reserves that they use to calculate premiums. Even though state valuation laws permit the use of a 6 percent interest assumption, the majority of life insurance companies are using a lower interest rate than permitted by law or regulation to value policy reserves for policies currently being issued; some have converted all outstanding policies to that basis, regardless of the assumptions used at the time of issue. Obviously, this provides a margin of safety beyond that contemplated in the valuation laws.

Another margin of safety is provided through the use of net premium valuation. This, however, is a matter of law. Under this method of valuation, it is assumed that only the net premium (whether calculated in accordance with the actuarial assumptions prescribed by law or in accordance with assumptions actually being used by the company) is available year by year, including the first year, for the payment of death claims and that the rates of mortality experienced and the rate of interest earned have been and will continue to be in exact accordance with the assumptions underlying the net premiums. Loading, whether in connection with past or future premiums, is not taken into account.

This has not always been the case. In the early years of insurance in this country, gross premium valuation was the rule. Furthermore, it was customary to ignore future expenses and to assume that the entire gross premium would be available for the payment of claims. The present practice, which is the outgrowth of legislation designed to eradicate the evils of the earlier system, assumes that the whole of the loading will be required for expenses. The truth lies somewhere between these two assumptions. The entire loading is normally not needed for expenses, and the excess portion might well be taken into account in evaluating a company's financial position. Certainly, that portion of loading in excess of future expense requirements constitutes a source of financial stability.

SUPPLEMENTAL RESERVES

If the gross premium charged by an insurance company for a particular class of policies should be less than the valuation net premium,[8] the company must establish and maintain a *supplemental reserve,* which often used to be called a deficiency reserve, for those policies. Such a requirement has long been a feature of state insurance laws. Recently the laws were changed to retain the required supplemental reserve but to eliminate use of the title "deficiency reserve." Emphasis on price competition had pushed many insurers' gross premiums to levels below valuation net premiums in recent decades. The *indeterminant premium policy* was introduced specifically as a way of reducing the burden of such deficiency-based supplemental reserves. The insurer can base reserves on the maximum possible premium and thus avoid the burden of additional reserves even if the actual gross premium being charged is lower than the net valuation premium.

Reserve laws are founded on the premise that the use, in the prospective reserve formula, of a net level premium larger than the gross premium that will actually be received overstates the present value of future premiums and consequently understates the amount of reserves required. The extent of the deficiency is assumed to be represented by the present value of the excess of the valuation net premium over the gross annual premium. This presumes that the entire gross premium is available for the payment of policy claims—which, of course, is contrary to the facts. Thus the formula for calculating supplemental reserves understates, by the present value of future expenses, the sum of money needed to supplement the conventional policy reserves.

The required supplemental reserve at any particular age is computed by multiplying the excess of the valuation net premium over the gross annual premium by the present value of a life annuity due of $1 for the remainder of the premium-paying period. If a company calculates its reserves on the basis of the 1980 CSO Male Table and 4.5 percent interest, the valuation net premium for an ordinary life policy issued at age 35 is $11.60 per $1,000, and the present value of a whole life annuity due of $1 at that age is $18.29. For each dollar by which the gross premium falls short of the valuation net premium at that age, a supplemental reserve of $11.60 must be created. If the gross premium is $10.00, for example, the required deficiency reserve will be $18.29 x $1.60 (the valuation net premium of $11.60 minus the gross premium of $10.00), or $29.26 per $1,000 of coverage.

In contrast to ordinary policy reserves that increase with duration, the required supplemental reserves based on a gross premium deficiency for a given class of policies decrease as the years go by. This is a natural consequence of the fact that the present value of a life annuity due of $1 declines with each premium payment or with each increase in attained age. From a retrospective point of view, it is assumed that the supplemental reserve is drawn upon with each premium payment to offset the deficiency in the gross premium. Hence it must decline with duration. Under either the prospective or the retrospective point of view, it is apparent that the supplemental reserve will disappear altogether at the end of the premium-paying period.

Inasmuch as deficiency-based supplemental reserves are computed on the basis of actual valuation net premiums rather than the smaller net premium that would be used to compute minimum reserves, an insurer may be penalized for adopting conservative assumptions.

VOLUNTARY RESERVES

In addition to the legal reserve, which is held to meet specific policy obligations, life insurance companies set aside various *voluntary reserves,* some of which may serve a special purpose and some of which may simply be another name for surplus. Special-purpose reserves may be set up to cover future declines in the market value of nonamortizable securities, to smooth out mortality fluctuations, to meet expenses under supplementary agreements, and the like. A general-purpose reserve is likely to be called a *contingency reserve.* In some companies the contingency reserve is the balancing item between assets and liabilities, and no surplus is shown. Since all of such special reserves are voluntary in nature, they can be used to meet any of an insurance company's obligations.

In some states the amount of voluntary reserves, including surplus, that can be accumulated by a mutual life insurance company is limited by law. The purpose of such a limitation is to insure that the major portion of surplus earnings will be currently distributed to policyowners in the form of dividends. The accumulation is usually limited to 10 percent of the legal reserve as computed by the insurer. Therefore the more conservative the basis on which an insurer computes its policy liabilities, the larger the surplus or special reserves it can accumulate.

NOTES

1. The first part of this statement is not applicable to term insurance.
2. The *number* of deaths begins to decline after the 44th policy year because of the shrinking number of survivors; the death *rate*, of course, continues to increase.
3. It might be argued just as validly that through the 28th policy year interest on the accumulated fund makes a net addition to the policy reserve, depending on whether the cost of insurance is assumed to have been charged to net premiums or interest.
4. The general formula for the calculation of prospective reserves is as follows:

$$_t^k V_{x:n} = A_{x+t:n-t} - {}_kP_{x:n}\ddot{a}_{x+t:k-t}$$

   V = full net level premium reserve
   x = age of issue
   k = number of years in premium-paying period
   t = number of years elapsed since date of issue
   n = number of years in policy period
   A = net single premium
   P = net level premium
   $\ddot{a}$ = present value of a life annuity due of $1

   The notation n is used only in connection with term and endowment insurance contracts and temporary life annuities. A whole life policy is known to run to the end of the mortality table, so it is not necessary to show n values for it. If it is the ordinary life form, the k values can likewise be omitted from the formula since it is known that the premium-paying period is coterminous with the policy period. Thus the prospective reserve formula for an ordinary life policy can be expressed as follows:

$$_t V_x = A_{x+t} - P_x\ddot{a}_{x+t}$$

5. The reserve for any block of policies is usually calculated on the same basis no matter how long the policy remains in force. Therefore it is common for life insurers to have blocks of policies based on different mortality tables and different interest rates. For example, an insurer may have 12 blocks of whole life policies issued at age 30 based on the 1941 CSO Table, 20 blocks of policies issued at age 30 based on the 1958 CSO Table, and 10 blocks of policies issued at age 30 based on the 1980 CSO Table.

(continued on page 382)

TABLE 16-1
Progression of Reserve Funds for Ordinary Life Contracts of $1,000 Issued to Males Aged 35; 1980 CSO Male Table and 4.5 Percent Interest; Net Level Premium of $11.60433

(1) Policy Year	(2) Attained Age at Beginning of Policy Year	(3) Number Living at Beginning of Policy Year (Equals Number Insured)	(4) Aggregate Re- serve at End of Previous Year See (10)	(5) Annual Premiums Paid at Beginning of Policy Year (3) x $11.60433	(6) Total Sum on Hand at Begin- ning of Policy Year (4) + (5)
1	35	9,491,711	$ 0	$110,144,947	$110,144,947
2	36	9,471,683	95,073,469	109,912,535	204,986,004
3	37	9,450,466	192,993,375	109,666,326	302,659,701
4	38	9,427,785	293,598,387	109,403,128	403,001,516
5	39	9,403,461	396,812,584	109,120,865	505,933,448
6	40	9,377,225	502,464,454	108,816,413	611,280,867
7	41	9,348,906	610,469,506	108,487,790	718,957,296
8	42	9,318,148	720,552,375	108,130,864	828,683,239
9	43	9,284,975	832,800,985	107,745,914	940,546,899
10	44	9,249,042	946,938,509	107,328,936	1,054,267,445
11	45	9,210,289	1,062,956,480	106,879,233	1,169,835,713
12	46	9,168,382	1,180,571,320	106,392,930	1,286,964,250
13	47	9,123,274	1,299,769,641	105,869,482	1,405,639,124
14	48	9,074,738	1,420,356,884	105,306,254	1,525,663,139
15	49	9,022,649	1,542,228,980	104,701,796	1,646,930,776
16	50	8,966,618	1,665,011,661	104,051,594	1,769,063,255
17	51	8,906,452	1,788,505,102	103,353,408	1,891,858,510
18	52	8,841,435	1,911,975,143	102,598,929	2,014,574,072
19	53	8,771,057	2,034,851,906	101,782,240	2,136,634,146
20	54	8,694,661	2,156,386,682	100,895,715	2,257,282,398
21	55	8,611,540	2,275,739,106	99,931,152	2,375,670,257
22	56	8,521,377	2,392,412,419	98,884,871	2,491,297,290
23	57	8,423,722	2,505,750,668	97,751,650	2,603,502,318
24	58	8,318,510	2,615,447,922	96,530,735	2,711,978,657
25	59	8,205,461	2,720,968,697	95,218,877	2,816,187,574
26	60	8,084,266	2,821,721,015	93,812,490	2,915,533,505
27	61	7,954,271	2,916,737,513	92,303,986	3,009,041,499
28	62	7,814,753	3,004,930,366	90,684,973	3,095,615,339
29	63	7,664,788	3,084,953,029	88,944,729	3,173,897,758
30	64	7,503,368	3,155,303,158	87,071,558	3,242,374,716
31	65	7,329,740	3,214,653,578	85,056,722	3,299,710,300
32	66	7,143,418	3,261,875,263	82,894,580	3,344,769,843
33	67	6,944,474	3,296,340,486	80,585,968	3,376,926,454
34	68	6,733,084	3,317,498,145	78,132,929	3,395,631,073
35	69	6,509,613	3,324,963,472	75,539,697	3,400,503,169

(7) 4.5 Percent Interest for One Year on Sum in Col- umn (6) 0.045 x (6)	(8) Sum at End of Policy Year before Deduct- ing Death Claims (6) + (7)	(9) Death Claims Due at End of Policy Year	(10) Aggregate Reserve at End of Policy Year after Deducting Death Claims (8) − (9)	(11) Number Living at End of Policy Year	(12) Individual Reserve at End of Policy Year per $1,000 of Insurance (10) ÷ (11)
$ 4,956,523	$ 115,101,469	$ 20,028,000	$ 95,073,469	9,471,683	$ 10.04
9,224,370	214,210,375	21,217,000	192,993,375	9,450,466	20.42
13,619,687	316,279,387	22,681,000	293,598,387	9,427,785	31.14
18,135,068	421,136,584	24,324,000	396,812,584	9,403,461	42.20
22,767,005	528,700,454	26,236,000	502,464,454	9,377,225	53.58
27,507,639	638,788,506	28,319,000	610,469,506	9,348,906	65.30
32,353,078	751,310,375	30,758,000	720,552,375	9,318,148	77.33
37,290,746	865,973,985	33,173,000	832,800,985	9,284,975	89.69
42,324,610	982,871,509	35,933,000	946,938,509	9,249,042	102.38
47,442,035	1,101,709,480	38,753,000	1,062,956,480	9,210,289	115.41
52,642,607	1,222,478,320	41,907,000	1,180,571,320	9,168,382	128.77
57,913,391	1,344,877,641	45,108,000	1,299,769,641	9,123,274	142.47
63,253,761	1,468,892,884	48,536,000	1,420,356,884	9,074,738	156.52
68,654,841	1,594,317,980	52,089,000	1,542,228,980	9,022,649	170.93
74,111,885	1,721,042,661	56,031,000	1,665,011,661	8,966,618	185.69
79,607,846	1,848,671,102	60,166,000	1,788,505,102	8,906,452	200.81
85,133,633	1,976,992,143	65,017,000	1,911,975,143	8,841,435	216.25
90,655,833	2,105,229,906	70,378,000	2,034,851,906	8,771,057	232.00
96,148,537	2,232,782,682	76,396,000	2,156,386,682	8,694,661	248.01
101,577,708	2,358,860,106	83,121,000	2,275,739,106	8,611,540	264.27
106,905,162	2,482,575,419	90,163,000	2,392,412,419	8,521,377	280.75
112,108,378	2,603,405,668	97,655,000	2,505,750,668	8,423,722	297.46
117,157,604	2,720,659,922	105,212,000	2,615,447,922	8,318,510	314.41
122,039,040	2,834,017,697	113,049,000	2,720,968,697	8,205,461	331.60
126,728,441	2,942,916,015	121,195,000	2,821,721,015	8,084,266	349.04
131,199,008	3,046,732,513	129,995,000	2,916,737,513	7,954,271	366.69
135,406,867	3,144,448,366	139,518,000	3,004,930,366	7,814,753	384.52
139,302,690	3,234,918,029	149,965,000	3,084,953,029	7,664,788	402.48
142,825,399	3,316,723,158	161,420,000	3,155,303,158	7,503,368	420.52
145,906,862	3,388,281,578	173,628,000	3,214,653,578	7,329,740	438.58
148,486,963	3,448,197,263	186,322,000	3,261,875,263	7,143,418	456.63
150,514,643	3,495,284,486	198,944,000	3,296,340,486	6,944,474	474.67
151,961,690	3,528,888,145	211,390,000	3,317,498,145	6,733,084	492.72
152,803,398	3,548,434,472	223,471,000	3,324,963,472	6,509,613	510.78
153,022,643	3,553,525,812	235,453,000	3,318,072,812	6,274,160	528.85

TABLE 16-1 (Continued)
Progression of Reserve Funds for Ordinary Life Contracts of $1,000 Issued to Males Aged 35; 1980 CSO Male Table and 4.5 Percent Interest; Net Level Premium of $11.60433

(1) Policy Year	(2) Attained Age at Beginning of Policy Year	(3) Number Living at Beginning of Policy Year (Equals Number Insured)	(4) Aggregate Re- serve at End of Previous Year See (10)	(5) Annual Premiums Paid at Beginning of Policy Year (3) x $11.60433	(6) Total Sum on Hand at Begin- ning of Policy Year (4) + (5)
36	70	6,274,160	$3,318,072,812	$72,807,423	$3,390,880,235
37	71	6,026,268	3,295,577,845	69,930,803	3,365,508,648
38	72	5,765,331	3,256,019,537	66,902,803	3,322,922,340
39	73	5,490,613	3,197,735,846	63,714,885	3,261,450,731
40	74	5,201,587	3,119,190,014	60,360,932	3,179,550,946
41	75	4,898,907	3,019,950,738	56,848,533	3,076,799,272
42	76	4,584,446	2,900,794,239	53,199,424	2,953,993,663
43	77	4,261,105	2,763,582,378	49,447,269	2,813,029,647
44	78	3,932,489	2,610,999,981	45,633,900	2,656,633,881
45	79	3,602,553	2,446,246,406	41,805,214	2,488,051,619
46	80	3,274,541	2,272,001,942	37,998,854	2,310,000,797
47	81	2,950,885	2,090,294,833	34,243,043	2,124,537,876
48	82	2,633,724	1,902,981,080	30,562,602	1,933,543,683
49	83	2,324,920	1,711,749,148	26,979,139	1,738,728,287
50	84	2,026,726	1,518,777,060	23,518,797	1,542,295,858
51	85	1,742,478	1,327,451,171	20,220,290	1,347,671,461
52	86	1,475,966	1,141,804,677	17,127,597	1,158,932,273
53	87	1,230,823	965,941,225	14,282,876	980,224,102
54	88	1,009,829	803,340,186	11,718,389	815,058,575
55	89	814,659	656,566,211	9,453,572	666,019,783
56	90	645,788	527,119,673	7,493,937	534,613,610
57	91	502,572	415,455,223	5,832,011	421,287,234
58	92	383,472	321,145,160	4,449,936	325,595,095
59	93	286,281	243,055,875	3,322,099	246,377,974
60	94	208,381	179,564,983	2,418,122	181,983,105
61	95	146,721	128,512,344	1,702,599	130,214,943
62	96	98,309	87,662,616	1,140,810	88,803,426
63	97	60,504	54,994,580	702,108	55,696,688
64	98	31,450	29,149,039	364,956	29,513,995
65	99	10,757	10,149,125	124,828	10,273,953

(7) 4.5 Percent Interest for One Year on Sum in Col- umn (6) 0.045 x (6)	(8) Sum at End of Policy Year before Deducting Death Claims (6) + (7)	(9) Death Claims Due at End of Policy Year	(10) Aggregate Reserve at End of Policy Year after Deducting Death Claims (8) − (9)	(11) Number Living at End of Policy Year	(12) Individual Reserve at End of Policy Year per $1,000 of Insurance (10) ÷ (11)
$152,589,611	$3,543,469,845	$ 247,892,000	$3,295,577,845	6,026,268	$ 546.87
151,447,889	3,516,956,537	260,937,000	3,256,019,537	5,765,331	564.76
149,531,505	3,472,453,846	274,718,000	3,197,735,846	5,490,613	582.40
146,765,283	3,408,216,014	289,026,000	3,119,190,014	5,201,587	599.66
143,079,793	3,322,630,738	302,680,000	3,019,950,738	4,898,907	616.45
138,455,967	3,215,255,239	314,461,000	2,900,794,239	4,584,446	632.75
132,929,715	3,086,923,378	323,341,000	2,763,582,378	4,261,105	648.56
126,586,334	2,939,615,981	328,616,000	2,610,999,981	3,932,489	663.96
119,548,525	2,776,182,406	329,936,000	2,446,246,406	3,602,553	679.03
111,962,323	2,600,013,942	328,012,000	2,272,001,942	3,274,541	693.84
103,950,036	2,413,950,833	323,656,000	2,090,294,833	2,950,885	708.36
95,604,204	2,220,142,080	317,161,000	1,902,981,080	2,633,724	722.54
87,009,466	2,020,553,148	308,804,000	1,711,749,148	2,324,920	736.26
78,242,773	1,816,971,060	298,194,000	1,518,777,060	2,026,726	749.37
69,403,314	1,611,699,171	284,248,000	1,327,451,171	1,742,478	761.82
60,645,216	1,408,316,677	266,512,000	1,141,804,677	1,475,966	773.60
52,151,952	1,211,084,225	245,143,000	965,941,225	1,230,823	784.79
44,110,085	1,024,334,186	220,994,000	803,340,186	1,009,829	795.52
36,677,636	851,736,211	195,170,000	656,566,211	814,659	805.94
29,970,890	695,990,673	168,871,000	527,119,673	645,788	816.24
24,057,612	558,671,223	143,216,000	415,455,223	502,572	826.66
18,957,926	440,245,160	119,100,000	321,145,160	383,472	837.47
14,651,779	340,246,875	97,191,000	243,055,875	286,281	849.01
11,087,009	257,464,983	77,900,000	179,564,983	208,381	861.71
8,189,240	190,172,344	61,660,000	128,512,344	146,721	875.90
5,859,672	136,074,616	48,412,000	87,662,616	98,309	891.70
3,996,154	92,799,580	37,805,000	54,994,580	60,504	908.94
2,506,351	58,203,039	29,054,000	29,149,039	31,450	926.84
1,328,130	30,842,125	20,693,000	10,149,125	10,757	943.49
462,328	10,736,281	10,757,000	−20,719	0	0.00

TABLE 16-2
Cost of Insurance for $1,000 Ordinary Life Policy Issued at Age 35;
1980 CSO Male Table and 4.5 Percent Interest
Net Level Premium Reserves

(1) Policy Year	(2) Attained Age at Beginning of Policy Year	(3) 1980 CSO Male Mortality Rate	(4) Amount at Risk during Year ($1,000 − Reserve)	(5) Cost of Insurance (3) x (4)
1	35	0.00211	$989.96	$ 2.09
2	36	0.00224	979.58	2.19
3	37	0.00240	968.86	2.33
4	38	0.00258	957.80	2.47
5	39	0.00279	946.42	2.64
6	40	0.00302	934.70	2.82
7	41	0.00329	922.67	3.04
8	42	0.00356	910.31	3.24
9	43	0.00387	897.62	3.47
10	44	0.00419	884.59	3.71
11	45	0.00455	871.23	3.96
12	46	0.00492	857.53	4.22
13	47	0.00532	843.48	4.49
14	48	0.00574	829.07	4.76
15	49	0.00621	814.31	5.06
16	50	0.00671	799.19	5.36
17	51	0.00730	783.75	5.72
18	52	0.00796	768.00	6.11
19	53	0.00871	751.99	6.55
20	54	0.00956	735.73	7.03
21	55	0.01047	719.25	7.53
22	56	0.01146	702.54	8.05
23	57	0.01249	685.59	8.56
24	58	0.01359	668.40	9.08
25	59	0.01477	650.96	9.61
26	60	0.01608	633.31	10.18
27	61	0.01754	615.48	10.80
28	62	0.01919	597.52	11.47
29	63	0.02106	579.48	12.20
30	64	0.02314	561.42	12.99
31	65	0.02542	543.37	13.81
32	66	0.02785	525.33	14.63
33	67	0.03044	507.28	15.44
34	68	0.03319	489.22	16.24
35	69	0.03617	471.15	17.04

TABLE 16-2 (Continued)
Cost of Insurance for $1,000 Ordinary Life Policy Issued at Age 35;
1980 CSO Male Table and 4.5 Percent Interest
Net Level Premium Reserves

(1) Policy Year	(2) Attained Age at Beginning of Policy Year	(3) 1980 CSO Male Mortality Rate	(4) Amount at Risk during Year ($1,000 − Reserve)	(5) Cost of Insurance (3) x (4)
36	70	0.03951	$453.13	$ 17.90
37	71	0.04330	435.24	18.85
38	72	0.04765	417.60	19.90
39	73	0.05264	400.34	21.07
40	74	0.05819	383.55	22.32
41	75	0.06419	367.25	23.57
42	76	0.07053	351.44	24.79
43	77	0.07712	336.04	25.92
44	78	0.08390	320.97	26.93
45	79	0.09105	306.16	27.88
46	80	0.09884	291.64	28.83
47	81	0.10748	277.46	29.82
48	82	0.11725	263.74	30.92
49	83	0.12826	250.63	32.15
50	84	0.14025	238.18	33.40
51	85	0.15295	226.40	34.63
52	86	0.16609	215.21	35.74
53	87	0.17955	204.48	36.71
54	88	0.19327	194.06	37.51
55	89	0.20729	183.76	38.09
56	90	0.22177	173.34	38.44
57	91	0.23698	162.53	38.52
58	92	0.25345	150.99	38.27
59	93	0.27211	138.29	37.63
60	94	0.29590	124.10	36.72
61	95	0.32996	108.30	35.73
62	96	0.38455	91.06	35.02
63	97	0.48020	73.16	35.13
64	98	0.65798	56.51	37.18
65	99	1.00000	0.00	0.00

6. The determination of the effect on reserves that would be brought about by a change in mortality assumptions poses a mathematical problem of extreme complexity. For a discussion of the problem and the mathematical techniques, see C. Wallace Jordan, Jr., *Life Contingencies* (Chicago: Society of Actuaries, 1952), pp. 114–20; and E. F.Spurgeon, *Life Contingencies* (London: Cambridge University Press, 1947), pp. 112–16 and 188–90.

7. This is not true of term and other types of insurance policies whose reserves do not increase continously to the date of expiration or maturity.

8. The *valuation* net premium is the net premium used in the calculation of the company's policy reserves, whether they are computed on the net level premium basis or in accordance with one of the modified systems.

17

Gross Premiums

Dan M. McGill
Revised by Norma Nielson and Donald Jones

The previous discussion of rate making explains the derivation of *net* premiums, which, when interest is added, are sufficient to pay the assumed benefits under the life insurance contract. Furthermore, the policy should contribute to profit or surplus. The gross premium for "traditional products" is the amount that, when interest is added, will be sufficient to pay both benefits *and* expenses. It is the gross premium that policyowners pay.

Gross premium may be regarded in either of two ways. The gross premium is the net premium plus an amount called *loading*. Alternatively, the gross premium is an amount, independent of the net premium, found using realistic factors for mortality, interest, expenses, contingency allowances, and profit. The former method is typically used to find gross premiums for participating policies; the latter is typically used for nonparticipating policy premiums. Loading in participating policies, usually greater than is likely to be needed, includes an amount the company expects to return to the policyowner later as a *dividend.*[1]

These three considerations guide the company in setting its loading:

- Total loading from all policies should cover the company's total operating expenses, provide a margin of safety, provide a margin for a minimum dividend for participating policies, and contribute to profits or surplus.
- Company expenses and safety margins should be apportioned equitably over the various plans and ages of issue. In other words, each class of policies should pay its own costs.
- Resulting gross premiums should enable the company to maintain or improve its competitive position.

This chapter describes the manner in which a company attempts to fulfill these objectives and to resolve the conflict that may exist among them.

GENERAL CONSIDERATIONS

Nature of Insurance Company Expenses

A life insurance company's operating expenses fall into the two broad categories of investment expenses and insurance expenses. Investment expenses include all costs to make, service, and safeguard the company's investments. Accountants recognize these expenses as a reduction of gross investment income. Since these expenses are not covered by an explicit loading of the net premium, they are not considered in the remainder of this chapter.

383

Insurance expenses include all items of costs not related to the investment function. Among the various expense classifications insurers use, the most meaningful for calculating gross premiums organizes insurance expenses into

- those that vary with the rate of *premium*
- those that vary with the amount of *insurance*
- those that are the same for all *policies*

Items that vary with the premium rate are commissions to agents, state premium taxes, acquisition expenses other than commissions, and agency expenses. The first two items are defined directly as percentages of the gross premium involved, while the last two items may be expressed as percentages of either the premiums collected or the commissions paid. Some agency expenses and acquisition expenses other than commissions may be charged on a per-policy basis. Agency renewal expenses may be assessed entirely per policy, as illustrated later in this chapter.

Several expenses relate to the amount of insurance. Selection costs are the most sensitive to the size of the policy. For example, companies issue policies for less than a certain size without a medical examination. If an application warrants, a paramedic exam for small and moderate-size policies will usually run from $50 to $100. When a larger amount of insurance is involved, the company requires an electrocardiogram, X-rays, blood tests, and other expensive diagnostic procedures. In this event the examiner's fee may be $200 or more. Occasionally, the company may require two or more independent medical examinations. Investigation of the applicant's other characteristics, such as lifestyle, financial status, and character, is also more thorough for larger policy sizes. Therefore a larger policy often incurs a larger inspection fee. Other expenses that may vary with the size of the policy include those associated with the issue, maintenance, and settlement of the policy.

Examples of expenses assessed per policy include the costs of issuing policies, establishing the necessary policy records, sending premium notices, accounting for premium remittances, settling routine claims, and general overhead. As indicated above, certain agency and acquisition expenses may also be assessed per policy.

Nature of the Loading Formula

Based on this classification scheme, the typical loading to a net premium has three parts:

- a percentage of the premium
- a constant amount for each $1,000 of insurance
- a constant amount for each policy

Using all three of these elements produces a premium rate per $1,000 that decreases with an increase in the face amount of the policy. This happens because per-policy expenses, by definition the same for each contract, are smaller for each $1,000 of the face amount. Called *grading* of premiums, such prices that decline with policy size are a general practice today. Grading can be accomplished by setting broad amount classifications called *bands* and setting a uniform rate of expense loading per $1,000 within each band. To assess per-policy expenses on a band basis, the actuary must assume an average size policy within each band.

A more commonly used method for dealing with per-policy expenses—and the one illustrated in this chapter—is the policy-fee approach. The policy fee is designed specifically to cover expenses that are roughly constant per policy. The resulting composite rate varies incrementally with each $1,000 of insurance.

A common modification of the policy-fee system is to charge a smaller fee on policies below a certain size, such as $50,000, in the interest of minimizing the expense charge on small policyowners.[2] Above the specified size, the per-policy charge is constant, ranging from about $25 to $50. A combination of the two methods uses bands for policies below some level, such as $1 million, and a policy fee for policies over that amount.

LOADING OF PARTICIPATING PREMIUMS

The theoretical basis for the loading formula is the same as that for computing net premiums. The present value of income must equal the present value of payments. Specifically, the present value of policy expenses, margins for contingencies, and anticipated dividends should be divided by the present value of an appropriate life annuity due.

A key difference lies in the certainty of the two sets of present values. The contract specifies benefits with certainty. Policy expenses, on the other hand, are estimates at best. They are found only after a painstaking analysis of operating costs and the probable future trend of such costs. Allocating costs to the various policies and ages of issue also presents one of the actuary's most difficult tasks— and one that cannot be accomplished with complete equity.

Computation of Present Values

Cost studies usually precede adoption of a loading formula. Expenses are reduced to a unit basis and allocated among the various policy plans and ages at issue. Each unit expense rate is expressed either as a percentage of the premium, an amount per $1,000 of face value, or an amount per policy. While the first of these types is straightforward, the latter two require sophisticated cost studies to achieve valid rates.

To calculate the present value of these expenses, the time of their occurrence must be known. One must know whether the expenses occur at the inception of the contract, at periodic intervals after that, or only upon the occurrence of some particular event in the future. A typical formula might contain values for the following elements:

- expenses expressed as a percentage of the premium
  - those incurred only at time of issue
  - those incurred only during a definite number of renewal years
  - those incurred every year, including the first
- expenses expressed as an amount per $1,000 of insurance
  - those incurred only at time of issue
  - those incurred each year

> — those incurred only in the year of death
- expenses expressed as an amount per policy
    - those incurred only at time of issue
    - those incurred only during a definite number of renewal years
    - those incurred each year
    - those incurred only in the year of death

Expenses Incurred Only at Time of Issue

Under the first bulleted item expenses incurred only at time of issue include first-year commissions, agency expense allowances, and other acquisition costs. First-year commissions to the soliciting agent vary widely among companies and, to a lesser extent, among policy plans of the same company. A typical first-year commission on an ordinary life policy issued at age 32 might be 55 percent or more of gross premium. Additional expenses, including inspection reports, medical exam, administration, reserve establishment, and the override commission to the general agent or agency might also amount to as much as 55 percent of gross premium. Thus the total of all the expenses incurred at the time of issue may be substantially more than 110 percent of the first year's premium.

These costs are paid by the company during the first policy year while the policyowner pays only a level gross premium plus perhaps a modest policy fee. Consequently these first-year expenses must be amortized over the entire premium-paying period of the policy. To do this the actuary finds the level percentage of the gross premium that amortizes this first-year expense. If premiums are payable throughout the insured's lifetime and first-year expenses equal 110 percent of the premium, the actuary divides 110 percent by the present value of a whole life annuity due of $1 as of age 32. Based on the previously determined value of $16.49, a level 6.67 percent ($1.10 \div 16.49$) of each premium payment is available to amortize the acquisition expenses.

Expenses Incurred Only during a Definite Number of Renewal Years

Items of expense here include renewal commissions to the soliciting agent and agency expense allowances. Recent compensation agreements show many patterns of renewal commissions. Some provide a minimum commission or service fee throughout the life of the policy. For a simple illustration, assume a renewal commission of 5 percent payable for 9 years. Since these commissions will be paid only if the policy's premiums are paid, the actuary discounts for the probability that the insured dies or the policyowner lapses or surrenders the policy. Discounts also could apply for termination of the agent without vested rights to the renewal commissions. In practice, however, companies do not discount these expenses for termination of the policy or the agent. With a discount for mortality only, based on the 1980 CSO Male Table and 5.5 percent interest, the present value at issue of the 5 percent renewal commissions is 33.97 percent of the annual gross premium. This must also be spread over the entire premium-paying period of the policy, here assumed to be the lifetime of the insured. The percentage of the annual premium necessary to amortize these commissions is obtained by dividing 33.97 percent by 16.49, which yields 2.06 percent.

Expenses Incurred Every Year

State premium taxes are the only significant item of expense that occurs every year, including the first. These taxes vary somewhat among states, but they average about 2 percent. No computation of present value is required since the tax applies equally to each year. It adds 2 percent to the loading formula.[3]

Table 17-1 summarizes the assumptions and calculations for our illustration. Beside the type of expense or loading factor are two major columns. The first column shows the expense rates assumed; the second shows what must be added to the annual net premiums to recover expenses. Each of these major columns is subdivided into three subcolumns, one for each type of expense: percent of gross premium, per policy, and per $1,000 of insurance.

The previous discussion explains how the actuary finds the amount that must be added to the premium to recover the assumed expenses—but just for the percent-of-gross-premium expenses. Similar calculations are made for per-policy and per-$1,000 expenses.

Expenses Incurred at Year of Death

We must introduce one more increment—premium additions—to handle settlement costs at the policy's maturity. Premium additions to pay expenses at death are calculated in the same way as finding the present value of the death benefit, as explained earlier. To find the amount to add to the annual premium, divide this present value by the appropriate annuity-due factor.

The lower right-hand corner of table 17-1 displays the results. The expenses expressed as a percentage of the gross premium total 10.76 percent. Those expressed as an amount per $1,000 are $0.31 per $1,000. Those expressed as an amount per policy are $36.25. If no other factors were considered, this would be the loading formula. Other factors must be considered, however.

Adding of Margins

Most life insurance policies are long-term contracts with premiums that cannot be changed after issue. Many unforeseen developments may occur, however, before the company discharges its contractual obligations. Possible developments unfavorable to the company include epidemics, heavy investment losses, lower-than-anticipated interest rates, adverse tax legislation, and unexpected increases in operating expenses. A specific increment to the loading enables the company to accumulate funds to meet such contingencies if and when they arise. Since overcharges in a participating policy can be returned through the dividend formula, the company usually allows a generous amount for contingencies. An addition of 3 percent of the gross premium would be reasonable.

Mutual companies also usually load the premium intentionally to create surplus from which dividends can be paid. To provide these anticipated dividends, the company adds safety margins to the mortality and interest assumptions. The extent to which the expense-loading formula is used to create dividends depends on managerial viewpoints. The company decides where it wants to be along the spectrum between high-premium, large-dividend companies and low-premium, small-dividend companies. If management leans in the former direction, the

TABLE 17-1
Hypothetical Expense and Loading Factors for $100,000 Ordinary Life Policy Issued to a Male Aged 32

Type of Expense or Loading Factor	When Incurred	Expense Rate at Time of Occurrence			Annual Amount That Amortizes the Exposure		
		Percent of Gross Premium	Per Policy	Per $1,000	Percent of Gross Premium	Per Policy	Amount per $1,000
First-year commission	At issue	55%	$ 60.00		3.33%	$ 3.64	
Agency expense allowance	At issue	44	10.00		2.67	.61	
Other acquisition expenses	At issue	11			0.67		
Renewal commissions	2d to 10th policy year	5			2.09		
Agency expense allowance	2d to 10th policy year		5.00			2.06	
State premium taxes	Annually	2			2.00		
Selection	At issue		100.00	$1.50		6.06	$0.09
Issue	At issue		50.00	0.20		3.03	0.01
Maintenance	Annually		20.00	0.20		20.00	0.20
Settlement costs	At maturity		100.00	1.00		.85	0.01
Total Expenses					10.76%	$36.25	$0.31
Allowance for contingencies					3.00	3.00	0.50
Allowance for dividends					2.40		1.25
Grand Total					16.16%	$39.25	$2.06

addition to the loading formula will be large; if it favors the latter approach, the increment will be at a minimum level. The example in table 17-1 includes a loading for contingencies of 3 percent of the premium plus $.50 per $1,000 of the policy's face amount and a loading for dividends that consists of 2.40 percent of gross premium plus $3 per policy plus $1.25 per $1,000 of face amount.

Testing the Loading Formula

Before a formula is adopted, the company tests it at various pivotal issue ages, such as 15, 25, 35, 45, and 55. These tests show whether realistic assumptions about mortality, interest earnings, expenses, and cancellations produce a workable set of gross premiums. The premiums "work" if the group of policies is anticipated to develop sufficient assets to provide the surrender values promised under the contract, to meet the reserve requirements imposed by law or adopted by the company, to support a reasonable dividend scale, and to provide the desired addition to the company's surplus. Gross premiums are also compared to those of competing companies to see whether they meet the competition. Of course these two objectives are often in conflict.

Asset Shares

Adequacy tests for loading, as well as other aspects of product pricing, use *asset share* calculations. To understand the asset share, first think of a block of identical policies all issued on the same day and on different lives. As time passes, the assets accumulated for these policies could be measured and the share belonging to each allocated. This stream of actual asset shares would be of interest only historically. For them to be of value at the time of pricing, the actuary projects (forecasts) asset shares based on a set of actuarial assumptions. These assumptions may range from simple to complex. In the extreme, if one assumes no expenses other than benefits and no terminations other than for death or maturity, asset shares would equal the net level premium reserves described in chapter 16. For pricing purposes, however, the assumptions also include expenses and rates of termination.

The asset share calculation traces the share from the end of one policy year to the end of the next. Assumptions reflect the timing of the payment of premiums, expenses, and benefits. For premiums and expenses paid at the beginning of the year and benefits at the end of the year, the actuary would perform the following steps:

- Start with the total asset share at the end of a year.
- Add the premiums and subtract the expenses at the beginning of the next year.
- Add the investment income and subtract the benefits paid at the end of this new year.
- Allocate this total to each surviving and persisting policy.

To test the adequacy of participating premiums, the actuary compares the asset shares year by year to the policy surrender values and reserve. In a policy's early years, the asset shares are less than the surrender values because of the insurer's high first-year expenses. Therefore a loss occurs any time a policy terminates in the early years. When the asset share is larger than the surrender value but less than the reserve, the insurance company experiences a gain if the policy lapses, but it experiences a loss if the policy matures then as a death claim. At later durations the asset shares usually exceed the reserve, and the policy contributes to surplus when it is surrendered or matures. If, in the opinion of management, too many years pass before these crossover points are reached, then the loading should be increased. The converse would be true if the crossovers are too early.

The percentages and factors in table 17-1 were set for a policy issued to a male aged 32. Similar elements would be developed for other issue ages. In the process of adjusting the loading to balance the various factors involved, such as competitive considerations, the percentage and constant factors will be modified and may lose all linkage to the cost studies on which they were initially based. Frequently the only logic supporting the percentage and constant factors that evolve is that they represent the only combination that will produce a satisfactory result at all ages of issue.

In that spirit, we simplify our example here by adopting the following loading factors:

Percent-of-gross-premium expenses	16%
Constant expenses per $1,000	$ 2.00
Per-policy expenses	$42.00

Let us apply these factors to find the gross premium for a $100,000 ordinary life policy issued to a 32-year-old male. Recall that the net premium for benefits for this policy is $8.51. Thus 84 percent of the gross premium (that is, 100 percent minus 16 percent for percent-of-gross-premium expenses) must provide 100 x $8.51 for benefits and (100 x $2.00) + $42.00 for expenses. That is, 84 percent of the gross premium must be $851 + $200 + $42, or $1,093. Therefore the gross premium is $1,093 ÷ .84, or $1,301 to the nearest dollar.

This procedure for gross premiums is not followed by all mutual companies. Some mutual companies calculate their gross premiums using a process similar to the one that follows for nonparticipating premiums.

GROSS NONPARTICIPATING PREMIUMS

The chief difference between deriving gross participating premiums and gross nonparticipating premiums is the set of actuarial assumptions used. Conservative assumptions produce higher margins. In participating premiums these margins can be returned as dividends when they emerge. In nonparticipating premiums the lack of dividends may make high premiums particularly noncompetitive. Asset share calculations test for this possibility.

Two Basic Approaches

Two basic approaches are available to derive a gross nonparticipating premium. Under the first the actuary computes the premium based on the most probable assumptions about mortality, interest, expenses, and terminations, plus a specific addition for profit. The principal advantage of this approach is the explicit provision for profits for each plan of insurance and each age of issue.

The second approach uses assumptions that are more conservative than the most probable, but it makes no specific allowance for profit. Profits must emerge from more favorable experience than was assumed. Profit that varies widely among the various plans and issue ages is regarded as an advantage by some on the grounds that profit depends on the risk assumed. This second method is sometimes used alongside the first to show how large a profit margin is needed to assure the company a minimum return if deviations from the most probable assumptions occur.

The premium computation shown in the following pages uses the first approach.

Selecting the Most Probable Assumptions

Of the four assumptions affecting asset shares — mortality, interest, expenses, and terminations — only the impact of interest increases with duration. The impact of interest increases with the size of reserves and thus has its biggest impact at later durations, where it is most difficult to predict.

The impact of mortality and terminations decreases over time because the amount at risk decreases as the duration increases. The impact of expenses decreases because they occur primarily in the early years. While current mortality rates are easy to find, favorable and unfavorable changes in the future due to medical advances, underwriting changes, and social changes are difficult to project. To ignore the impact of medical advances is conservative for insurance rates but careless for annuity rates.

Economic changes greatly affect policy termination. For example, changes in unemployment and alternative investment opportunities can influence termination. Termination rates also vary from company to company, from plan to plan, and with issue age.

Illustrative Premium Calculation

We illustrate the process of setting gross nonparticipating premiums by calculating and testing the gross premium for a 10-payment ordinary life policy issued to a woman aged 32. This illustration uses an asset share calculation to test a *tentative premium*. The principles involved apply equally to the testing of a tentative participating premium.

The tentative premium can be quite arbitrary. When calculations are part of a general rate revision, the tentative premium is usually the current premium. Alternatively, it may be the premium charged by a competing company. For our illustration, the tentative premium is the 10-pay net level premium based on 1980 CSO Female Table mortality and 5.5 percent interest. For $100,000 of insurance, this is $1,451.57.

Our illustration (see table 17-2) uses expense factors consistent with those in table 17-1.

TABLE 17-2			
Expense Factors Used in Illustration			
Policy Year	Percent of Premium	Per Policy	Per $1,000
1	54%	$220	$1.70
2–10	4	25	.20
At settlement		100	1.00

Mortality rates used to test a trial or tentative gross premium should be the most realistic available. This example uses death rates from the 1975–80 select table.[4] Those select rates per 1,000 lives at ages 32 through 41 are compared with the 1980 CSO Female Table (which are aggregate rates) in table 17-3.

TABLE 17-3		
Deaths per 1,000 Lives		
Select and Aggregate Mortality		
Age	1975–80 Select Table	1980 CSO Female Table
32	0.38	1.45
33	0.44	1.50
34	0.54	1.58
35	0.65	1.65
36	0.76	1.76
37	0.86	1.89
38	0.97	2.04
39	1.08	2.22
40	1.19	2.42
41	1.31	2.64

Withdrawals, expressed as a rate per 1,000 policyowners, are assumed to occur according to the pattern in table 17-4.

Applying the death and withdrawal rates in tables 17-3 and 17-4 to an arbitrary number of persons allows us to prepare a table showing the number of persons living and persisting at the beginning and end of each year after that. That table enables us to predict the premium revenue that will be received at the beginning of each policy year and the number of persons entitled to a share of the group's fund at the end of each policy year. Table 17-5 presents these values, based on 10,000 persons and the death and withdrawal rates given above.

TABLE 17-4 Withdrawals per 1,000 Policies			
First year	200	Sixth year	8
Second year	100	Seventh year	42
Third year	80	Eighth year	36
Fourth year	66	Ninth year	30
Fifth year	55	Tenth year	25

TABLE 17-5
Number Living and Persisting the First 10 Policy Years

Policy Year	Number Living and Persisting First of Year	Rate of Death	Number Dying during Year	Rate of Termination	Number Terminating End of Year	Number Living and Persisting End of Year
1	10,000	0.00038	3.8	0.200	1000.2	7,997
2	7,997	0.00044	3.5	0.100	799.3	7,194
3	7,194	0.00054	3.9	0.080	575.2	6,615
4	6,615	0.00065	4.3	0.066	436.3	6,174
5	6,174	0.00076	4.7	0.055	339.3	5,830
6	5,830	0.00086	5.0	0.048	279.6	5,546
7	5,546	0.00097	5.4	0.042	232.7	5,308
8	5,308	0.00108	5.7	0.036	190.9	5,111
9	5,111	0.00119	6.1	0.030	153.1	4,952
10	4,952	0.00131	6.5	0.025	123.6	4,822

Implicit in the calculation of this table is the assumption that withdrawals occur only at the ends of the policy years. This might be the case for annual-premium business but for more frequently paid premiums, the withdrawals occur at other times during the policy year.

One additional set of values is needed before we begin the asset share calculation — the surrender values available each year to terminating policyowners. These values for the first 10 policy years under a $100,000 10-payment life policy issued at age 32[5] are assumed to be as shown in table 17-6.

TABLE 17-6 Surrender Values Used in Illustration			
First year	$ 0	Sixth year	$ 8,175
Second year	483	Seventh year	10,349
Third year	2,262	Eighth year	12,632
Fourth year	4,136	Ninth year	15,028
Fifth year	6,105	Tenth year	17,544

Assumptions about the following provide the raw materials to calculate the asset share:

- the number and volume of premiums to be received each year
- the number of death claims of $100,000 each plus settlement expenses and interest to the end of the policy year that will be incurred each year (based on the same death rates as those used to learn the number of premiums to be received)
- the number and amount of surrender payments that will be disbursed each year
- the rate of interest that will be earned on accumulated funds (5.5 percent)

These assumptions combine as shown in table 17-7 to produce the asset share per $100,000 at each duration. (See pages 396–397.)

According to table 17-7, 10,000 policyowners will pay a total of $2,777,222 in effective premiums at the beginning of the first year. These funds earn interest throughout the year at 5.5 percent and grow to $2,929,969 at the end of the year. Death claims will diminish this amount by $391,091 — $380,000 in claim payments, $760 in settlement expenses, and $10,331 in loss of assumed interest. The loss of interest arises because we have assumed that the total effective premiums will accrue interest to the *end* of the policy year. On average, however, claims will be paid at mid-year, so the company loses interest earnings on these payments. It is also assumed that 1,999 policyowners surrender their policies at the end of the first year, receiving $0 individually and in total.

At the end of the year a fund of $2,538,878 is assumed to be on hand. Dividing this pro rata among the 7,997 surviving and persisting policyowners gives each $317. That is the asset share per $100,000 at the end of the first year. The terminal reserve at each duration is shown for comparison. Observe that at the end of the first year the reserve exceeds the asset share by $1,071 and the asset share exceeds the surrender value by $317.

At the beginning of the second year, 7,997 surviving and persisting policyowners pay a total of $10,783,958 in premiums. When added to the fund from the end of the first year, this produces a total fund at the beginning of the second year of $13,322,837. At 5.5 percent interest, this fund amounts to $14,055,593 at the end of the second year before deduction of death and surrender claims. Death claims and settlement expenses, adjusted for loss of interest, and surrender payments reduce the fund to a net balance of $13,307,374. Divided pro rata among the 7,194 surviving and persisting policyowners, this fund yields an asset share of $1,850. This falls short of the second-year terminal reserve by $1,001 per $100,000, and surpasses the surrender value by $1,367.

This process continues through the next 8 years. By the end of the 10th policy year, the fund is seen to have grown to $77,302,999, an amount sufficient to provide $16,032 to each of the 4,822 surviving and persisting policyowners. This is $1,512 less than the full net level premium reserve and the surrender value at that point.

Evaluating the Trial Premium

By comparing the asset share at each duration with the comparable surrender value and reserve, the company can evaluate the appropriateness of the trial gross premium. Until the asset share equals or exceeds the surrender value, each termination is a direct drain on the company's surplus. In other words, the company gives back to each withdrawing policyowner more money than that policyowner has contributed to the company. This situation may prevail for several years under many plans and ages at issue. The asset share is usually negative during the first few years of a continuous premium whole life policy, takes several years to exceed the cash value, and takes even more years to exceed the reserve. However, under a high-premium policy, such as the 10-payment life shown in table 17 7, the asset share normally should exceed the surrender value by at least a small amount even at the end of the first year.

A more fundamental test companies use is the period required for the asset share to equal or exceed the full net level premium reserve. Until that occurs, the company has not recovered its acquisition expenses and is still showing a *book* loss for the block of business represented in the asset share calculation. Once the asset share exceeds the reserve, acquisition expenses have been recovered in full and that block of policies is contributing to the company's surplus. Based on many considerations a company decides how long it can afford—and is willing—to wait before recovering its outlay. That period of time is called the policy's *validation period*. If the company can wait 10 years to recoup its acquisition expenses, it uses gross premiums that accumulate asset shares exactly equal to the reserves at the end of the 10th policy year.

It would be sheer accident if a trial gross premium produced an asset share precisely equal to the full net level premium reserve at the end of the validation period. Variation will exist in one direction or the other. To eliminate the variation the trial gross premium is adjusted either upward or downward. The amount of this adjustment is found by dividing the difference between the asset share and the reserve at the end of the validation period by the future value of a $1 premium increase, and adding (or subtracting) the result to the trial gross premium.

The technique is illustrated, continuing with the example of the 10-payment life policy, by assuming a validation period of 10 years. A 10-pay life policy will

TABLE 17-7
Asset Share, $100,000 10-Pay Life, Issue Age 32

Policy Year	(1) Surviving and Persisting	(2) Expenses Per Policy	(3) Effective Premium Per Policy	(4) Total Effective Premium (1) x (3)	(5) Initial Fund $(11)_{n-1} + (4)$	(6) Initial Fund + Interest (5) x (1.055)
1	10,000	$1,174	$ 278	$ 2,777,222	$ 2,777,222	$ 2,929,969
2	7,997	103	1,349	10,783,958	13,322,837	14,055,593
3	7,194	103	1,349	9,701,292	23,008,665	24,274,142
4	6,615	103	1,349	8,920,369	31,493,551	33,225,696
5	6,174	103	1,349	8,326,209	39,304,820	41,466,585
6	5,830	103	1,349	7,862,288	46,774,293	49,346,879
7	5,546	103	1,349	7,478,461	54,023,427	56,994,715
8	5,308	103	1,349	7,157,416	61,190,336	64,555,805
9	5,111	103	1,349	6,892,297	68,447,083	72,211,672
10	4,952	103	1,349	6,677,573	75,961,751	80,139,647

have settlement costs and maintenance expenses after premiums have ceased. The present value of these costs, $350, is added to the 10th year reserve when determining a gross premium. The fact that the asset share is $1,512 less than the reserve at the end of the validation period means that the trial gross premium is high enough to make the policy profitable by the end of the second year. To find the required correction, the effect of changing the trial gross premium by $1 upon the accumulation at the end of 10 years is measured. Then, by simple proportion, the exact change in the premium that would increase (or decrease) the accumulation by the desired amount can be found.

It is helpful at this stage to visualize the change in the trial gross premium as an *increase* of $1, whatever the direction of the adjustment needed. (See table 17-8.) Then it will be apparent that this additional annual $1 payment will not have to bear any share of the death and surrender claims, since these were met through the original premium payments. However, the additional $1 should bear its proportionate share of expenses that vary directly with the size of the premium. Since these expenses were earlier assumed to be 54 percent of the first-year premium and 4 percent of the renewal premium, the effective additional premium will be $0.46 the first year and $0.96 for each of the other 9 years. The number of surviving and persisting policyowners at each duration remains the same, and so does the assumed rate of interest earnings. Therefore the additional premium

(7)	(8)	(9)	(10)	(11)	(12)	(13)
Death Claims + Expenses and Interest	Minimum Cash Value	Number of Surrenders	Amount Paid on Surrender	Fund Balance $(6)-(7)-(10)$	Asset Share $(11) \div (1)_{n+1}$	1980 CSO 5.5% NLP Reserve
$391,091	$ 0	1,999	$ 0	$ 2,538,878	$ 317	$ 1,388
362,136	483	799	386,083	13,307,374	1,850	2,851
399,820	2,262	575	1,301,141	22,573,182	3,412	4,388
442,524	4,136	436	1,804,561	30,978,611	5,017	6,005
482,949	6,105	339	2,071,630	38,912,005	6,674	7,704
516,046	8,175	280	2,285,867	46,544,966	8,393	9,489
553,636	10,349	233	2,408,159	54,032,920	10,180	11,361
589,957	12,632	191	2,411,062	61,554,785	12,043	13,325
625,967	15,028	153	2,301,527	69,284,178	13,992	15,384
667,622	17,544	124	2,169,026	77,302,999	16,032	17,544

Net premiums based on 1980 CSO Table and 5.5 percent interest.

of $1 will bring in an additional sum of $4,600 the first year. At 5.5 percent interest, that additional amount accumulates to $4,853 by the end of the first year.

Because of lower renewal expenses, the additional effective premiums for the second year will aggregate $7,677, which, when supplemented by the fund at the end of the first year and interest at 5.5 percent on the composite fund, amounts to $13,219 at the end of the second year. By the end of the 10th year, the additional premium of $1 paid each year by the surviving and persisting policyowners will accumulate to $78,667. Divided pro rata among the 4,822 policyowners surviving and persisting at that point, this sum would provide an additional $16.32 increment to the asset share for each policy. In other words, increasing the trial gross premium by $1 increases the asset share at the end of 10 years by $16.32.

For the 10-pay life policy in our illustration, at the end of the 10th policy year we need an asset share equal to the net level premium reserve (which for this example is also the net single premium for policy year 10 and later) plus $350 to cover the future expenses for a total of $17,894. The trial premium of $1,451.57 provided an asset share of $16,032—$1,512 less than is needed. Since each $1 increase in premium increases the asset share by $16.32 at the end of the 10th year, the tentative premium needs to be increased by $92.65 ($1,512/16.32) to

$1,544.22. This premium will accumulate an asset share at the end of 10 years exactly equal to the net level premium reserve if actual results conform precisely to the assumptions.

Table 17-8 presents the calculations supporting this adjustment.

TABLE 17-8
Accumulation of Annual Premium of $1

Policy Year	(1) Surviving and Persisting	(2) Expenses	(3) Effective Premium	(4) Total Effective Premium (1) x (3)	(5) Initial Fund $(6)_{n-1}$ + (4)	(6) Fund at Year End (5) x 1.055	(7) Asset Share $(6)/(1)_{n+1}$
1	10,000.00	$0.54	$0.46	$4,600	$ 4,600	$ 4,853	$ 0.61
2	7,996.96	0.04	0.96	7,677	12,530	13,219	1.84
3	7,194.10	0.04	0.96	6,906	20,126	21,232	3.21
4	6,615.00	0.04	0.96	6,350	27,583	29,100	4.71
5	6,174.39	0.04	0.96	5,927	35,027	36,954	6.34
6	5,830.36	0.04	0.96	5,597	42,551	44,891	8.09
7	5,545.73	0.04	0.96	5,324	50,215	52,977	9.98
8	5,307.66	0.04	0.96	5,095	58,072	61,266	11.99
9	5,111.06	0.04	0.96	4,907	66,173	69,813	14.10
10	4,951.83	0.04	0.96	4,754	74,566	78,667	16.32
11	4,822.00						

When constructing a set of gross premium rates, the detailed study just outlined would not be done for each policy and issue age. This would be too much work and would probably produce inconsistent rates. Rather, the procedure would be used for rates at quinquennial or decennial ages. These rates would be tested for adequacy for a simplified portfolio using policies with only these ages. The simplified book of business is selected to represent the company's overall book of business and is called a *model office*.

The asset share calculation is concerned only with the *adequacy* of the proposed gross premiums. Once this has been established, the gross premiums at the representative ages are compared with those of other companies operating in the same territory to learn whether the rates are competitive. A company whose rates are clearly out of line will have trouble holding its agents and obtaining new business. If the survey of other companies' rates shows the test set to be competitive, the company proceeds to derive the complete set of rates by formula or interpolation. If rates appear to be too high relative to those of the competition, the company considers adjusting its rates.

Developing a Schedule of Competitive Premiums

If the "most probable" mortality, interest, expense, and termination rates have been used in calculating gross premiums, there is little possibility that the competitive situation can be improved by changing any of those assumptions. Even with the same basic assumptions, however, the premiums can be reduced by extending the period over which acquisition expenses are amortized. This increases the drain on surplus, but it may be the most practical solution. If a specific allowance for profit has been made in the calculations, shaving this margin may reduce premiums slightly. If extending the validation period and narrowing the profit margin do not produce competitive premiums, more fundamental adjustments may be needed. Such adjustments might include more stringent underwriting requirements, less conservative (and thus higher yielding) investments, greater operating economies, or elimination of less persistent policies.

The final step in deriving a set of gross premium rates is to review the results for consistency among the various plans and ages at issue. Identical premiums should always be charged for identical benefits. The premium scale should contain no "bargain rates" since such rates are likely to attract an undue volume of business for certain plans and ages of issue, which may indicate the presence of a high level of adverse selection.

Participating Gross Premiums Derived through
Tentative Gross Premiums

As mentioned earlier, the technique underlying the calculation of nonparticipating gross premiums in larger stock companies is used by some mutual companies. It is modified to reflect the payment of policyowner dividends. In using this technique, a mutual company

- computes a set of specimen gross premiums at quinquennial or decennial ages, based on the most probable assumptions about mortality, interest, and expenses
- tests such premiums for adequacy by means of asset-share calculations

At this stage the computation does not allow for dividend distributions. The margins in the basic assumptions are so narrow that no funds are presumed to be available for distribution to policyowners. Trial gross premiums, adjusted to reflect the redundancy or deficiency in the asset share, are compared with the gross premiums (after dividends, in the case of participating gross premiums) of competing companies. Once the premiums have been fitted to the best competitive advantage, the company considers its dividend policy.

A dividend scale of any desired level and pattern can be developed without relating the resulting dividends to any particular sources of surplus. Margins to support the proposed dividend scale are added directly to the gross premiums. Usually several sets of premium rates, based on various assumed margins, are constructed and compared before the final set of representative gross premiums—with the built-in dividend scale—is selected. Gross premiums for all ages of issue usually are computed by loading the valuation net premiums in accordance with a formula that experimentation has found to develop rates approximately equivalent to the desired gross premiums when applied to net premiums. As pointed out earlier, such a formula usually is the sum of a percentage of the gross or net premium, a constant amount per $1,000 of insurance, and a policy fee.

Some companies vary the procedure by calculating the trial gross premiums on a nonparticipating basis and then adding the margin for a predetermined dividend scale before running the various asset-share tests. Dividend distributions operate as a decrement in such a procedure, along with death claims and surrender payments. Each approach produces the same results.

Premiums Paid at Intervals of Less than One Year

So far the calculations have assumed premiums to be paid annually. Theoretically, premiums paid more frequently than once per year could be calculated in precisely the same manner by using probability and interest functions based on shorter time units. To derive true monthly premiums, a mortality table that shows the rate of mortality month by month, rather than annually, is needed. Similarly, claim payments could be discounted monthly instead of yearly. Such precise computations are not used in practice, however, since mortality studies produce annual rates. Instead, actuaries calculate monthly, quarterly, and semiannual net premiums in a way that distributes deaths uniformly between whole ages. That technical procedure, which must include loadings for the expense of additional premium processing, is not covered here.[6]

NOTES

1. The subject of dividends is discussed in chapter 20.
2. When a policy fee is smaller than the constant expense per policy, the excess per-policy cost must be allocated based on an assumed average size policy.
3. Some companies now ignore premium taxes on annuity considerations in computing the basic gross premium for individual annuity contracts. Then the rates for annuities in states that tax annuity considerations are increased by the amount of the tax.
4. See Claude Y. Paquin, "An Extension of the 1975–80 Basic Select and Ultimate Mortality Tables, Male and Female—Actuarial Note," *Transactions of the Society of Actuaries,* vol. 38, 1986, pp. 205–224.
5. These are the minimum values required under the Standard Nonforfeiture Law on a 5.5 percent interest basis. Chapter 19 discusses the Standard Nonforfeiture Law in greater detail.
6. For a detailed discussion see Newton L. Bowers, Hans S. Gerber, James C. Hickman, Donald A. Jones, and Cecil J. Nesbitt, *Actuarial Mathematics* (Chicago, IL: Society of Actuaries, 1986).

18

Modified Reserve Systems

Dan M. McGill
Revised by Norma Nielson and Donald Jones

An insurance policy reserve represents (in present-value terms) the excess of the benefits promised over the net premiums yet to be collected. The reserve is zero at policy issuance because the present value of the benefits equals the present value of premiums at that instant. However, as time passes the value of the benefits promised (outgo) increases (nearer to time of payment and higher probability of payment) while the present value of premiums to be collected (income) decreases (fewer premiums left to collect). This relationship requires that the reserve increase with the passage of time.

More precisely, the reserve is the present value of future benefit payments (surrender and death) minus the present value of future incoming premiums. This broad definition can be applied to both the asset shares described in the previous chapter and to the net level premium reserves discussed in chapter 16. Asset shares include expenses and surrender benefits in the outgo; they use gross premiums as the income. They are useful management tools in product design and in measuring company performance. Net level premium reserves include only death and maturity benefits in the outgo and use a net level premium in the income. Regulators require life insurers to maintain this net level or *benefits-only* reserve to safeguard the policyowners in their jurisdiction. They require that the company show the reserve found in this manner as the liability for the policy on the annual statement it files with regulators.

Subtracting a level net premium from a level gross premium leaves a level loading with which to pay expenses. Since actual expenses are very heavy in the first year, early expenses in excess of the loading must be paid out of a company's accumulated capital, known as surplus, and later recouped. A company that enjoys a strong surplus position can easily manage this "loan" from surplus. Over the years aggregate repayments from renewal loadings tend to offset the amounts needed to support newly issued policies. This lessens the *net* strain on surplus from new business. Eventually repayments might exceed withdrawals.

A small, recently organized or undercapitalized company, however, finds it much more difficult to meet the surplus demand from new business. Typically its new business is a significantly larger proportion of its total business in force. If such a company attempted to absorb its entire first-year deficit out of surplus, it might be forced to limit new business. In any case, it would probably have to reinsure more of its business than would a stronger company.

Theoretically a company could solve this problem by charging a higher premium in the first year than in subsequent years, but this approach is not practical. From a sales standpoint, the company would prefer to charge a *lower* premium for the first year, not a higher one.

MODIFIED RESERVES

An alternative to adjusting the first-year gross premium is to allocate a larger share of the first-year gross premium to expenses and a smaller share to creating the reserve. With a level loading the single largest portion of the premium goes to the policy's reserve to assure the payment of future benefits. But remember that the objective of the reserve is to measure the company's liability against a solvency standard. Regulators agree that a smaller portion (down to the net cost of the first year's insurance) of the first-year gross premium can be recognized as the first-year net premium. This leaves a larger share of the gross premium for expenses. Of course, net premiums in future years must increase to keep the present value of net premiums equal to the present value of benefits. A reserve that results from modifying the net premium pattern from the level one is called a *modified reserve*.

Full Preliminary Term Valuation

The full preliminary term method of reserve valuation assumes that the first-year net premium needs to cover only the first-year benefits. The remainder of the first-year gross premium is available to help pay first-year expenses. This method produces a zero reserve at the end of the first year. The reallocation does not change the fact that the reserve needed at the end of the premium-paying period is the full net level premium reserve for that policy's duration. The only way to accomplish this is to allocate a larger share of each renewal gross premium to the reserve. Also since the net amount at risk under the full preliminary term method is slightly higher throughout the premium-paying period, the cost of insurance is a little higher. Both factors mean that full preliminary term net premiums after the first year must be larger than net level premiums.

One way to view the full preliminary term method is to consider the first year of coverage as term insurance and the original contract of permanent insurance as taking effect at the beginning of the second policy year. For modified reserve calculations, policies are considered to be a combination of term insurance for the first year and permanent insurance issued at an age one year older and for a period one year shorter than the actual contract. For example, a 20-year endowment issued at age 30 becomes, for purposes of reserve computation, a combination of a one-year term policy issued at age 30 and a 19-year endowment issued at age 31. A 30-payment life policy issued at age 25 is considered to be a one-year term policy written at age 25 and a 29-payment life policy issued at age 26. The origin of the term *preliminary term* arises from this view.

The first year, in which the policy is regarded as term insurance, requires no reserve at the end of the year. Therefore a larger portion of the premium can be used for expenses. Similarly, if the permanent contract is viewed as one written at an age one year older and for a period one year shorter than the original contract, the full preliminary term renewal net premium must be larger than the net level one. The difference will be equivalent to the annual sum necessary to amortize the first-year net level premium reserve over the remaining premium-paying period.

As an example, consider again the ordinary life policy issued to a 32-year-old male. Earlier, using the 1980 CSO Male Table and an interest rate of 5.5 percent, we calculated the net level premium to be $8.51 and the first-year reserve to be $7.16. On a modified-reserve-valuation basis the full preliminary term first-year premium (death benefit only) would be $1.73 ($1000 x .00183/1.055), the first year reserve would be zero, and the renewal premiums would equal $8.94 ($8.51 + $0.-43), where $0.43 is the annual amount required to amortize the $7.16 difference in the first-year reserves. (This is determined by dividing the reserve reduction by the present value of a stream of $1.00 payments for the premium-paying period.) Table 18-1 compares the two valuation methods.

TABLE 18-1
Comparison of Valuation Methods

	Net Level Premium Valuation		Full Preliminary Term Valuation	
	Premium	Reserve	Premium	Reserve
First year	$8.51	$ 7.16	$1.73	$0.00
Second year	8.51	14.64	8.94	7.54
Thereafter	8.51	Increasing	8.94	Increasing

Note: The full preliminary reserve wil equal the net level reserve each year after the premium-paying period ends.

Table 18-2 compares the amount available to pay expenses in the first year for the $100,000 policy (on the same basis illustrated in previous chapters).

TABLE 18-2
Amount Available for Expenses

	Gross Premium	Net Premium	Available for Expenses	Expenses	Deficiency
Net level premium	$1301	$851	$ 450	$1899	(1499)
Full preliminary Term	1301	173	1126	1899	(771)

Note: The full preliminary reserve will equal the net level reserve each year after the premium-paying period ends.

All the amounts in table 18-2 are considered paid at the beginning of the year. The $678 difference in the deficiency ($1449 − $771) is exactly the $716 reserve difference ([$7.16/1,000] multiplied by 100,000) when one year's interest is added to the $678.

Figure 18-1 illustrates these relationships for the $100,000 policy graphically. In net level premium reserve valuation, the loading is $450 each year, including the first. In contrast, the loading under the full preliminary term method of reserve valuation is $1,128 in the first year and $407 after that.

The increase in loading for the first year under the modified plan exactly offsets the reduction in loading for subsequent years. In other words, the present value of the two loading patterns is the same. Our earlier example computed reserves using a level premium of $851 throughout the life of the $100,000 face amount policy. With the full preliminary term method, we use $173 for the first policy year premium and $894 for subsequent years' renewal premiums. Again, the present values are identical.[1]

FIGURE 18-1
Comparison of Net Premiums under Full Preliminary Term Method
$100,000 Ordinary Life Policy, Issue Age 32
1980 CSO Male Table and 5.5% Interest

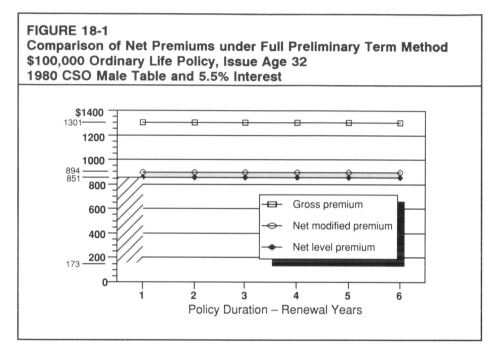

For most low-premium policies, making the additional loading available by computing reserves as if the first year of insurance were term insurance is still not sufficient to pay all first-year expenses. The difference, though smaller, must be drawn from surplus. Thus it is possible for a rapidly growing company to have a "capacity" problem, even if it uses modified reserves.

On the other hand, the reserves released under higher-premium forms of insurance by the full preliminary term method may provide more funds than are required to supplement the loading in the first-year premium. Consider, for instance, a $100,000 10-pay life contract issued to a woman aged 32, priced in the previous chapter at $1,560. The first-year expenses on this policy are $1,232. The one-year term insurance rate for a 32-year-old female is $137 ($100,000 x 0.00145/1.055) according to the 1980 CSO Female Table and 5.5 percent interest. Thus $1,423 is the available loading under the full preliminary term method ($1,560 − $137). (This could give the appearance that the loading exceeds the sum of actual first-year expenses, creating a surplus of $191.) The extent to which the first-year reserve can be reduced to make more funds available must be limited for extreme cases (discussed in the next section).

Modified Preliminary Term Valuation

While *full* preliminary term valuation is defined by a first-year net premium equal to the one-year term premium, *modified preliminary term* valuation refers to a broader family of reserve methods. Specifically modified preliminary term includes any valuation method in which the first-year net premium is at least as large as the one-year term premium but less than the net level premium.

Renewal net premiums are then set sufficiently high to accumulate the net level premium reserve by the end of the premium-paying period.

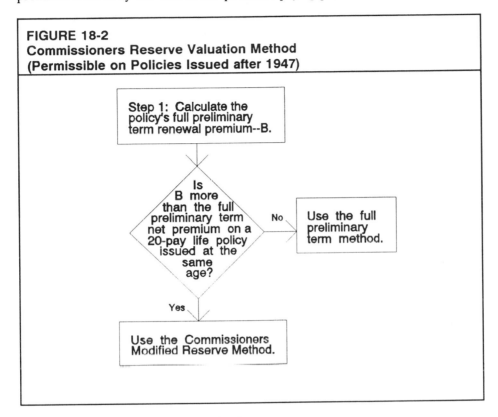

FIGURE 18-2
Commissioners Reserve Valuation Method
(Permissible on Policies Issued after 1947)

Step 1: Calculate the policy's full preliminary term renewal premium--B.

Is B more than the full preliminary term net premium on a 20-pay life policy issued at the same age?

No → Use the full preliminary term method.

Yes → Use the Commissioners Modified Reserve Method.

Commissioners Valuation Standard

Over the years, states developed and/or adopted a variety of modified preliminary term valuation methods. The lack of standard valuation methods, however, imposed a substantial administrative burden on many companies. Ultimately the Standard Valuation Law of the NAIC was developed as a reserve valuation method to deal with the first-year expense problem, and that method was acceptable to all states.

The Commissioners Reserve Valuation Method (CRVM), as the uniform system is known, is highly technical. The Standard Valuation Law states precisely the method to be used for policies with level gross premiums and level benefits. Other policies are to be handled in a "consistent manner." This general statement gives little guidance for such recently developed products as universal life. Figure 18-2 illustrates the CRVM for traditional products.

Table 18-3 compares the additional first-year expense allowances under the full preliminary term and the CRVM bases for various policies issued at age 32. Allowances under the full preliminary term basis for policies with net premiums greater than the 20-payment life net premium are largely hypothetical since few states ever permitted the unrestricted use of that method. Nevertheless, a comparison of the potential allowances under the two systems illustrates the restrictions intended by the CRVM.

TABLE 18-3 Additional First-Year Expense Allowance Full Preliminary Term and Commissioners Reserve Methods of Valuation, $1,000, Age 32, 1980 CSO Male Table and 5.5% Interest			
		Additional First-Year Expense Allowance	
Type of Contract	Net Level Premium	Full Preliminary Term Method	Commissioners Method
Ordinary life	$ 8.51	$ 6.77	$6.77
25-payment life	10.20	8.47	8.47
20-payment life	11.36	9.63	9.63
15-payment life	13.44	11.71	8.71
10-payment life	17.79	16.06	8.41

The Modified Premium

Reserves under the CRVM are computed in the same manner as net level premium reserves except that a modified annual level premium is substituted in the prospective reserve formula for the net level premium. The so-called modified premium spreads the present value of benefits and the additional expense allowance in the first year over the premium-paying period of the policy.

For an ordinary life policy issued at age 32 (based on the 1980 CSO Male Table and 5.5 percent interest) the modified premium is $8.94. The CRVM reserve at the end of the first policy year is zero (when enough decimal places are used): 1st CRVM reserve = $146.43 − ($8.94 x 16.37) = $0.

This shows that the entire first-year reserve is available for expenses, as is characteristic of full preliminary term valuation. This is confirmed by the modified premium, $8.94, which is the same as the net level premium at age 33. At the end of 10 years, the CRVM reserve is $80.18 (when carried to enough decimal places): $214.82 − ($8.94 x 15.06) = $80.18.

The Commissioners Reserve Valuation Method differs from the full preliminary term when the net renewal premium on the full preliminary term basis for a policy (such as a short-term endowment) exceeds the net level premium for a 19-payment life policy issued at an age one year older than the actual issue age. The modified premium for a 20-year endowment issued at age 32 is $29.70.

When this modified premium is inserted into the prospective reserve formula, it results in a positive value for the first-year reserve: 1st CRVM reserve = $374.722 − ($29.701 x $11.994) = $18.49. This means that some first-year premium, $18.49, applies to offset the reserve rather than to pay acquisition expenses allowance. The 10-year reserve is $360.81: $592.807 − ($29.701 x $7.811) = $360.81. For all policies issued at age 32 (based on the 1980 CSO Male Table and 5.5 percent interest) $10.47 is the maximum amount that can be added to the net single premium in calculating the modified premium ($12.209 − $1.735).[2]

Other values, of course, apply to other ages of issue. The maximum possible amount that can be added to the net single premium to derive the modified premium for any age of issue is the net level premium for a 19-payment life policy issued at an age one year older than the policy being valued, minus the net premium for one-year term insurance at the actual age of issue. By limiting the size of the modified premium that can be used in the reserve computation, the Standard Valuation Law in effect prescribes the minimum level of reserves—the primary objective of any valuation law.

Table 18-4 shows the reserve required for a 10-payment life policy issued to a woman aged 32 under each of the valuation methods we have described. The largest reserves occur with the net level premium method; the smallest occur using the full preliminary term method. Table 18-4 can assist students in understanding the relationship of reserves under the Commissioners Method to those required under other methods. Overall, an established company with normal distribution of insurance by age, duration, and plan is estimated to carry total reserves under the CRVM of about 95 percent of those computed on the net level premium basis. In any rapidly growing company, the aggregate difference between reserves on the two bases may be much larger.

TABLE 18-4			
Terminal Reserves under Various Methods of Valuation			
10-Payment Life Issued at Age 32			
1980 CSO Female Table and 5.5% Interest			
Years in Force	Net Level Premium	Full Preliminary Term	Commissioners Method
1	13.88	0.00	4.04
2	28.50	15.84	19.53
3	43.87	32.51	35.82
4	60.05	50.06	52.96
5	77.04	68.49	70.98
6	94.88	87.86	89.90
7	113.61	108.20	109.77
8	133.25	129.54	130.62
9	153.84	151.94	152.49
10	175.44	175.44	175.44
Renewal Net Premium	14.516	16.421	15.867

Although not an inherent feature of the CRVM, the Standard Valuation Law prescribes, as the minimum basis, the use of the 1980 CSO Tables and an interest rate no greater than a market-linked value that changes annually. Currently that interest rate is 5 percent for valuation of ordinary reserves.

STATUTORY REGULATION OF RESERVES

As emphasized in this chapter, reserves are an insurance company's principal liability. The company's financial statement is filed annually with regulators to report on the company's solvency. With solvency as the focus, the legal requirements for reserves provide a minimum below which the reserve cannot go. A company is free to incorporate safety margins (through more conservative assumptions or reserve methods, for example) and to provide higher reserve values.

Until now the discussion of modified reserves in this chapter has assumed that gross premiums always exceed net premiums. However, when net premiums are defined by a conservative reserve valuation basis and gross premiums by a competitive nonparticipating basis, net premiums for reserve valuation purposes may exceed gross premiums actually charged for the policy. In such a case the reserve needs to be based on the lower gross premium rates. This is accomplished indirectly by requiring the company to establish a *deficiency reserve* in addition to the net premium reserve. The deficiency reserve is the present value of the future excesses of net premium over gross premium. The sum of this deficiency reserve and the net premium reserve is the amount that would be obtained if the reserve were calculated on the basis of gross premium income.

NOTES

1. Actuaries can compute full preliminary term reserves on either a prospective or a retrospective basis; the calculation involves no new principles.
2. Note, however, that this is not the amount considered to have been "borrowed" from the first-year reserve. The extra amount made available for first-year expenses as a "loan" from the reserve is $26.50 less $1.71, the portion of $26.50 that must be repaid during the first year. In other words, a portion of the modified premium for the first year must be applied toward the amortization of the loan.

19

Surrender Values

Dan M. McGill
Revised by Norma Nielson and Donald Jones

Under their terms valid contracts of life insurance cannot be canceled by the insurer except for nonpayment of premiums. However, a policyowner may end the arrangement at any time. Depending on the amount of time the policy has been in force and the method by which premiums have been paid, a substantial value may have accumulated in the policy. This occurs when the life insurance is purchased with a premium that prepays some of the funds a company will need to pay future claims and expenses.

This chapter addresses the question of how value accumulated within a policy is divided if a policy ends before the death of the insured. The following terms used to describe a policy's discontinuation require some clarification:

- *Lapse* refers to termination of a life insurance policy through nonpayment of premiums *before* surrender values are available.
- *Surrender* refers to termination of a life insurance policy through nonpayment of premiums *after* surrender values are available.
- *Termination* refers to both lapses and surrenders. Typically, terminations during the first year or two are lapses and later ones are surrenders.

None of these terms applies to an action or inaction by the policyowner before the policy's grace period has expired.

GUIDING PRINCIPLES

Defining Equity

Experts offer three possible approaches to equitable treatment of a withdrawing policyowner. Each approach produces different costs for the insurance. At one extreme, the policyowner receives no refund of any amount. According to this view, the function of life insurance is viewed solely as providing benefits upon the death of the insured. Those who "drop out" of the venture forfeit all payments and all interest in the contract. This view generally has not been accepted since the early days of life insurance.

At the other extreme, it might be argued that terminating policyowners should receive a refund of all premiums paid, plus interest at the contractual rate, less a pro rata contribution toward death claims and the premium loading. A contract with such generous surrender values implicitly assumes that expenses occur evenly throughout the policy's premium-paying period and that the premium is sufficient to absorb expenses that arise each year. A separate process to find surrender values is not needed; withdrawing policyowners receive exactly the reserve under the policy. When higher expenses occur in early policy years, this approach leaves persisting policyowners to pay those costs that remain unpaid when a policy ends during its early years.

Supporters of this view argue that the healthy growth of a company benefits all policyowners and therefore the cost of acquiring new business should be charged to all policies. Strictly applied, this approach charges *all* acquisition expenses to the entire body of policyowners. A modified approach charges existing policyowners *some* acquisition costs of new policies.

The third and prevailing approach holds that a withdrawing policyowner should receive a surrender benefit—either cash or some form of paid-up insurance—approximately equal to the amount contributed to the company, minus the cost of the protection received, minus the expenses of establishing and maintaining the policy. Ideally, a policyowner's withdrawal should neither benefit nor harm continuing policyowners. The maximum benefit to a withdrawing policyowner would be a pro rata share of the assets accumulated by the company for the block of policies—that is, by definition, the policy's asset share. The actual surrender benefit should be reduced below the asset share, however, for several reasons.

Deductions from Asset Share

A company will usually reduce the surrender benefit to an amount less than the asset share of a surrendered policy. Five possible explanations for this include the following:

- adverse mortality selection
- adverse financial selection
- contribution to a contingency reserve
- contribution to profits
- cost of surrender

In addition, it could be argued that surrender benefits may need to be limited to prevent their payment from threatening the solvency of the insurance company.

Adverse Mortality Selection

Over the years actuaries have speculated about the effect of voluntary withdrawals on the mortality of those persisting in the insured group. Some actuaries maintain that most voluntary terminations result either from a reduced need for insurance protection or from a change in the insured's financial circumstances. They reason that termination occurs with little regard for the state of the insured's health, and they see little adverse mortality selection in withdrawals.

Other actuaries argue that persons in extremely poor health are not likely to surrender their policies and will instead borrow to maintain their protection. Many believe that those who do surrender are, on the average, in better health and can be expected to live longer than those who do not surrender. If surrender values are too high, the accumulated funds may not be sufficient to pay the death claims of the remaining policyowners. In view of a lack of conclusive data on the subject, some companies withhold a small portion of the asset shares from surrendering policyowners in order to offset any adverse selection that might occur.

Adverse Financial Selection

It has been observed that many terminations, particularly cash surrenders, tend to increase sharply during periods of economic crises and depressions. In addition, many cash surrenders occur when market interest rates are higher than those provided on life insurance cash values. Terminations reduce the inflow of cash to the company and, if cash is demanded, increase the outflow of cash. A company may be adversely affected (1) if it has fewer funds to invest at what might be an attractive rate of interest, and (2) if it is forced to liquidate assets at depressed prices. The policyowner's right to demand the cash value of a policy at any time forces the company to maintain a more liquid investment portfolio than would otherwise be necessary.[1] This reduces the yield on the portfolio. Most companies charge terminating policyowners with the resulting loss of investment earnings by reducing surrender values below what would be otherwise available.

Contribution to Contingency Reserve

Sound life insurance management demands that each group of policies ultimately pay its own way, including a provision for adverse contingencies like wars and epidemics. Newly issued policies depend on prior accumulations to provide these protective margins. Later those same policies leave the company with something less than the actual accumulations as a surrender value.

The difference between a policy's accumulation and its surrender value varies with the size of the company. The law of large numbers tells us that predictability increases with greater numbers. Applying the law of large numbers to contingency reserves means that a larger contingency reserve is needed *per policy* on a small block of business than would absorb the same financial variation in a larger block of business. The primary objective, as always, is safeguarding the security of the policies remaining in the group.

Contribution to Profits

Little needs to be said on this point, except that in a stock company, a deduction may be made from the asset share of the surrendering policyowner to compensate stockholders for the risk borne by capital funds. The size of the deduction varies depending on the level of profits already distributed to stockholders.

Cost of Surrender

All companies incur expenses to process the surrender of a policy. Some companies estimate aggregate expenses for surrenders and include them as part of the loading in the premium for all policies. Other companies charge the cost of the transaction to the particular policies involved by deducting it from the surrender value that would otherwise be available. Under the latter practice, the cost of surrender is a deduction from the asset share.

Assuring Company Solvency

In practice, surrender benefits must be limited if their payment might impair the security of remaining policyowners. When balancing the interests between terminating and continuing policyowners, conflicts are resolved in favor of continuing policyowners. Placing higher priority on the interests of continuing policyowners is consistent with general contract law. The party to a contract who is willing to continue under its original terms is not made to suffer through the inability or unwillingness of another party to honor the contract.

On the other hand, modern insurance contracts include surrender value as part of the policy's benefits. A policyowner who chooses to withdraw the surrender value arguably acts within the terms of the contract as much as the policyowner who keeps a policy in effect until it matures. Nonetheless the argument justifies favoring policyowners who wish to continue under the original terms of the contract.

NONFORFEITURE LEGISLATION

Early United States insurance policies made no provision for refunds upon termination before maturity. Forfeiture of all accumulated funds was still prevalent in the mid-1850s. Gradually companies recognized, with varying degrees of liberality, the withdrawing policyowner's right to such funds. Interest in the issue grew, and Massachusetts enacted the first nonforfeiture law in 1861. It evolved into the Standard Nonforfeiture Law, the first modern nonforfeiture legislation, which became effective in 1948 in most jurisdictions. Policies issued since that date have provided at least the minimum surrender values prescribed by law.

Laws to assure policyowners who voluntarily terminate their contracts a fair share of the value built up inside some policies are called nonforfeiture laws. Refunds required by such laws are called nonforfeiture values. Unless it refers to legislation, the adjective "surrender" is synonymous with "nonforfeiture" and is generally used in this text. Chapter 25 describes the nonforfeiture options (or surrender options) offered to a policyowner.

The Standard Nonforfeiture Law does not require specific surrender values. The only requirement is that surrender values are at least as large as those that would be produced by the method the law prescribes. In addition, each policy must contain a statement of the method used to find the surrender values and benefits provided under the policy at durations not specifically shown. This permits companies to use alternate formulas by describing them in their policies.

Rationale of the Standard Nonforfeiture Law

Minimum surrender values under the Standard Nonforfeiture Law reflect these two important principles:

- Surrender values should be derived independently of a policy's reserve.

- Such values should reflect approximate asset shares accumulated under the policies.

The technique used to accomplish these two objectives is called the "adjusted-premium" method.[2] This method reflects the philosophy that each group of policies issued on the same plan and at the same age should pay its own way, including the costs of acquisition. It recognizes that expenses are concentrated heavily in the first year and that first-year loading is not sufficient to absorb these expenses. The basic assumptions and techniques underlying the preliminary term method of reserve valuation described in chapter 18 are adopted. The difference between adjusted premiums used to derive reserves and surrender values is simple but subtle.

The adjusted-premium method derives its name from the manner in which surrender values reflect unamortized acquisition expenses. First-year expenses beyond normal recurring expenses are treated as an additional obligation under the policy. This amount is amortized over the premium-paying period in precisely the same manner as the present value of policy benefits is amortized. The amount that must be added to the net level premium to amortize this additional obligation is determined by dividing the excess first-year expenses by the present value of an appropriate life annuity due. The result, when added to the net level premium, produces the "adjusted premium." In short, the net level annual premium is adjusted to reflect the annual cost of liquidating the initial acquisition expenses. The actuary finds the surrender value at any duration by taking the difference between the present value of the benefits under the policy and the present value of future adjusted premiums.

The similarity between the adjusted-premium method and the prospective reserve should be apparent. The only difference is the use of adjusted premiums in one case and net level premiums in the other. With the same mortality and interest assumptions, the present value of future benefits is identical under either calculation. Therefore the present value of future adjusted premiums is larger than the present value of future net level premiums because the adjusted premium is larger than the net level premium. This means that the surrender value is smaller than the reserve. With identical mortality and interest assumptions, the difference between the reserve and the surrender value at any particular point in time is the unamortized first-year expenses. This difference decreases with each premium payment and disappears with the last payment.

It is important to note, however, that the mortality and interest assumptions employed by a company to calculate surrender values need not be the same as those used by the company to calculate premiums and reserves. The actual values promised may be computed on any basis that produces values at or above the statutory minimum values.

Illustration of the Adjusted Premium Method

There are three steps in deriving surrender values under the Standard Nonforfeiture Law. Step 1 is to find the special first-year expense allowance. The law safeguards terminating policyowners' interests by limiting the amount of first-year expenses that may be considered in computing the surrender values.[3]

The permitted values provide ample expense margins for a well-managed company.

Step 2 in the process is to calculate the adjusted premium. This may be either (1) the level annual premium required to amortize a principal sum equal to the present value of the benefits under the policy and the special first-year expense allowance or (2) the sum obtained by adding to the net level premium the annual increment needed to amortize the special acquisition expenses over the premium-paying period.

The former approach is illustrated here with an ordinary life policy issued at age 32. Assume that the maximum special first-year expense allowance for such a policy, calculated according to the prescribed formula, is $20.64 per $1,000. That amount is added to $140.28, the assumed net single premium for an ordinary life policy issued at age 32, to obtain the amount needed at the inception of the contract to meet the obligations under the contract—namely, $160.92. To obtain the equivalent annual sum, $160.92 is divided by $16.49, the present value of a whole life annuity due of $1 as of age 32, based on an interest rate of 5.5 percent. The result, $9.76, is the adjusted premium.

The second approach is equally simple. To find the amount that must be set aside out of each gross annual premium—including the first—to amortize the special costs of acquisition, divide $20.64 by $16.49. The answer, $1.25, is the amount that must be added to the net level premium for an ordinary life policy issued at 32—$8.51—to arrive at the same adjusted premium obtained above, $9.76.

Step 3 entails substituting the adjusted premium for the net level premium in the formula for prospective reserves. Recall from chapter 18 that the 10th-year terminal reserve for an ordinary life policy issued at age 32 is determined as follows: $214.82 − ($8.51 x $15.06) = $86.66.[4] The first element in the equation, $214.82, represents the net single premium for a whole life policy issued at age 42; the second element, $8.51, represents the net level premium for an ordinary life policy issued at age 32 (rounded to two digits after the decimal); the last element, $15.06, is the present value of a whole life annuity due of $1 calculated at age 42. All values are based on the 1980 CSO Table and 5.5 percent interest. To find the surrender value under this policy at the end of 10 years, substitute the adjusted premium, $9.76, for the net level premium, $8.51. The result, $214.82 − ($9.76 x $15.06) = $67.83, is the surrender value.

The difference between the reserve at the end of 10 years and the surrender value for the same period, $86.66 − $67.83, or $18.83, represents a form of surrender charge assessed to cover unamortized first-year expenses. The surrender value under the same policy at the end of 20 years is calculated as follows: $319.53 − ($9.76 x $13.05) = $192.16. Since the 20th-year terminal reserve for an ordinary life policy issued at 32 is $208.50, the unamortized acquisition expenses are reduced to $16.34. The disparity disappears completely when all premiums have been paid.

Summary of Steps

The detailed steps in the calculation of the 10th-year surrender value for an ordinary life policy issued at age 32, with all computed values based on the 1980 CSO Table and 5.5 percent interest, can be summarized as follows:

1) Find net single premium for ordinary life policy at age 32 ($140.28).
2) Find allowance for special first-year expenses ($20.64).
3) Add (1) and (2) ($160.92).
4) Find present value at age 32 of whole life annuity due of $1 ($16.49).
5) Divide (3) by (4) to find adjusted premium ($9.76).
6) Find net single premium for ordinary life policy at age 42 ($214.82).
7) Find present value at age 42 of whole life annuity due of $1 ($15.06).
8) Multiply (5) by (7) to find present value at age 42 of future adjusted premiums ($146.99).
9) Subtract (8) from (6) to find tenth-year surrender value ($67.83).

The surrender value under the adjusted-premium method also may be found retrospectively by accumulating the annual adjusted premiums (less the excess first-year expenses) at the assumed rate of interest and deducting death claims at the tabular rate. The process is identical to the calculation of retrospective reserves except that adjusted premium is used to reflect excess first-year expenses. The retrospective approach is particularly useful in considering modifications of the adjusted premium method.

Modifications of the Adjusted Premium Method

The illustration above computes *minimum* surrender values under a 5.5 percent interest assumption. Many companies offer surrender values greater than those required by law if such adjustments are supported by the company's expense rates, by competitive pressures, or by other considerations. Higher values are obtained by assuming lower first-year expenses than the maximum permitted by law or by assuming the maximum expenses and amortizing them over a shorter period than the number of years for which premiums are payable (or at an uneven rate over the entire period of premium payments).

Surrender Dividends

For a well-managed company, the asset share of a particular policy will, after a few years, exceed its surrender value and eventually will exceed the reserve. If the policy goes off the books, equity suggests that the withdrawing policyowner should be permitted to take some share of the surplus created. Such a final settlement with a withdrawing policyowner can be accomplished through a *surrender dividend*. The surrender dividend, because it is not guaranteed, provides more flexibility to the insurer than surrender values of the same amount.

RELATIONSHIP BETWEEN SURRENDER VALUES AND OTHER VALUES

Table 19-1 (at the end of this chapter) illustrates the relationship between surrender values, asset shares, and reserves, both level premium and modified. This table presents an asset share calculation for a participating ordinary life policy issued at age 32.

Death rates are based on varying percentages of the rates of tabular mortality. Specifically the rates assumed in table 19-1 for the first 6 policy years are 42, 52,

60, 66, 70, and 72.5 percent of the corresponding rates in the 1980 CSO Male Table. From age 38 the mortality rate is assumed to increase one-half percentage point for each year of attained age after that, reaching 79.5 percent of 1980 CSO male rates at the 20th policy year. After the first 5 years, these are the same mortality rates used in calculating dividends for this policy, the details of which are given in table 20-1. Mortality rates for the first 5 years below those in the dividend formula reflect the influence of selection. The rates used in calculating dividends usually do not reflect the savings from selection. Instead the savings are applied to amortize excess first-year expenses.

Withdrawals shown in table 19-1 approximate those in a study of ordinary insurance conducted by the Life Insurance Marketing Research Association (LIMRA) in the United States from 1983 to 1987. Combined with the assumed rates of mortality and applied to a radix of 10,000 insureds at age 32, these withdrawal rates determine the number of living and persisting policyowners shown in column (2).

A gross premium of $13.01 per $1,000 of coverage is assumed for $100,000 of insurance. This is the net premium, based on the 1980 CSO Male Table and 5.5 percent interest, loaded by 16 percent plus $2.50. Expenses are assumed to occur as shown in table 17-X. The effective first-year premium is −$566.12. The effective premium for the 2d through the 10th policy years is $1,164.93. Table 17-X reveals that the only expenses after the 10th year are the premium tax, maintenance expenses, and the cost of settlement. The first two types of expenses occur annually. The cost of settlement is incurred only once per policy and is included in the death claims. These reduced costs mean that for each year after the 10th, the effective premium is $1,234.98.

Effective premiums are assumed to accumulate at the rate of 6.25 percent, a rate that is higher than the rate of interest currently used in premium and reserve calculations, but one that realistically measures the interest being earned on long-term interest-bearing investments.

Cash values are assumed to be the minimum cash values computed on a 5.5 percent interest basis. Dividends are assumed to be paid according to the scale derived in table 20-1 with the full amount of the dividend for any particular year going to all persons who enter that year even if they fail to survive or persist to the end of the year. First-year dividends, however, are assumed to be paid only to those policyowners who either have survived and persisted or have died during the year. In other words, first-year dividends are not paid to those who withdraw during the year.

Column (14) of table 19-1 shows the asset share developed from these assumptions. Note that the asset share is negative the first and 2d years. This is normal for a policy of this type and premium. The asset share is also less than the net level premium reserve until the 8th year. This shows that the company does not recover its acquisition expenses for this group of policies until the 9th year. This is perhaps normal for mutual companies, but stock companies usually amortize their first-year expenses over a shorter period. As can be seen by comparing columns (14) and (15) of table 19-1, the excess of the asset share over the net level premium reserve—an amount that, by the end of the 20th year, amounts to $102.61 per $1,000—measures the contribution of each $1,000 policy to the surplus of the company. In later years, the asset share can be reduced through an increase in the dividend scale.

NONTRADITIONAL INSURANCE PRODUCTS

This chapter has discussed surrender values under ordinary life insurance products. Nontraditional products that were developed during the 1980s, such as universal life insurance, have an explicit *accumulated value* on which the contract's rate of interest is paid. The surrender value is the accumulated value minus an explicit surrender charge. Typically the surrender charge begins at 100 percent of the accumulated value for termination during the first year of the contract. Then it declines steadily until it disappears, usually at least 7 years after policy issue and sometimes as many as 20 years after policy issue.

The removal of the mysterious "black box" operation typical of surrender values in traditional life insurance is a defining characteristic of many modern nontraditional insurance contracts. The distinct surrender charge clearly displays the cost to consumers of purchasing permanent insurance only to cancel it after a short period.

NOTES

1. As pointed out elsewhere, all policies give the company the legal right to postpone payment of the cash surrender value for a period of 6 months. Enforcing this contractual provision has a serious effect on the company's position compared to the competition and on customer relations, however, and few companies choose to do so.

2. The term "adjusted premium" is usually used to represent only the premium defined in the Standard Nonforfeiture Law, which produces minimum values. Any other modified premium used to compute surrender values is usually called a "nonforfeiture factor." A nonforfeiture factor is employed to produce larger values than those required by law. In more complex methods of computing surrender values, several nonforfeiture factors may be used in the same policy.

3. The maximum special first-year expense allowance that may be used in finding the adjusted premium is the sum of 125 percent of the lesser of the policy's net level premium and $40 per $1,000 of insurance. For a policy with a nonlevel benefit amount and/or premiums, a more complex method is used. The percentage factors in the expense limitation formula consider expenses that depend on the amount of the premium and the plan of insurance. The constant factor of $20 per $1,000 reflects those expenses that depend on the number of policies or the amount of insurance.

4. The 5-cent discrepancy between this value and that in chapter 18 is eliminated by using the more exact net level premium amount of $8.5063.

TABLE 19-1
Asset Share Calculation
$100,000 Ordinary Life Policy Issued to a Male Aged 32
Gross Premium = $1,301

(1)	(2)	(2a)	(3)	(4)	(5)	(6)	(7)
Policy Year	Surviving and Persisting	Ex- penses	Effec- tive Prem- ium	Total Effective Premium (2) x (3)	Initial Fund $(13)_{n-1} + (4)$	Initial Fund + Interest (5) x (1.0625)	Death Claims + Expenses and Interest
1	10,000.00	$1,867	($566)	($5,661,200)	($5,661,200)	($6,015,025)	$793,839
2	7,993.85	136	1,165	9,312,277	1,847,287	1,962,742	820,021
3	6,708.17	136	1,165	7,814,544	6,830,900	7,257,832	831,414
4	5,762.10	136	1,165	6,712,443	11,260,574	11,964,360	828,780
5	5,006.05	136	1,165	5,831,693	15,095,556	16,039,028	810,724
6	4,348.43	136	1,165	5,065,617	18,051,288	19,179,494	781,473
7	3,819.96	136	1,165	4,449,987	20,420,055	21,696,308	743,077
8	3,355.23	136	1,165	3,908,613	22,251,261	23,641,964	710,635
9	2,946.55	136	1,165	3,432,526	23,634,176	25,111,312	680,119
10	2,616.57	136	1,165	3,048,121	24,823,217	26,374,668	662,395
11	2,349.14	66	1,235	2,901,142	26,064,036	27,693,038	647,817
12	2,132.01	66	1,235	2,632,991	27,258,309	28,961,954	643,398
13	1,955.72	66	1,235	2,415,274	28,441,867	30,219,483	643,230
14	1,813.03	66	1,235	2,239,052	29,660,266	31,514,033	651,792
15	1,698.31	66	1,235	2,097,383	30,949,211	32,883,537	664,516
16	1,590.37	66	1,235	1,964,071	32,132,636	34,140,925	677,240
17	1,488.78	66	1,235	1,838,614	33,222,028	35,298,405	688,445
18	1,393.19	66	1,235	1,720,560	34,228,367	36,367,640	701,461
19	1,303.21	66	1,235	1,609,442	35,160,381	37,357,905	713,505
20	1,218.53	66	1,235	1,504,856	36,027,832	38,279,572	730,394

(8)	(9)	(10)	(11)	(12)	(13)	(14)	(15)	(16)
Mini-mum Cash Value	Num-ber of Sur-ren-ders	Amount Paid on Sur-render	Divi-dend per $100,000	Total Dividend Paid (10) x (2)*	Fund Balance [(6) − (7) − (9) − −(11)]	Asset Share (12)/ (2)$_{n+1}$	1980 CSO 5.50% NLP Re-serve	1980 CSO 5.50% CRVM Re-serve
$0	1998	$0	$82	$656,126	($7,464,990)	($934)	$716	$0
0	1278	0	266	2,126,364	(983,643)	(147)	1,464	754
0	938	0	280	1,878,286	4,548,131	789	2,247	1,542
230	748	171,897	295	1,699,819	9,263,863	1,851	3,063	2,364
1,063	650	690,759	310	1,551,874	12,985,671	2,986	3,914	3,221
1,931	521	1,006,016	327	1,421,937	15,970,068	4,181	4,798	4,112
2,834	458	1,296,517	344	1,314,066	18,342,648	5,467	5,716	5,036
3,771	402	1,515,005	362	1,214,606	20,201,660	6,856	6,667	5,995
4,742	323	1,533,461	381	1,122,636	21,775,096	8,322	7,653	6,987
5,747	261	1,500,135	401	1,049,245	23,162,893	9,860	8,671	8,012
6,786	211	1,430,913	421	988,988	24,625,319	11,550	9,723	9,073
7,861	170	1,336,822	448	955,141	26,026,593	13,308	10,810	10,168
8,970	136	1,224,117	476	930,922	27,421,215	15,125	11,933	11,299
10,116	108	1,096,647	504	913,765	28,851,829	16,989	13,092	12,465
11,299	102	1,146,953	532	903,502	30,168,565	18,970	14,288	13,670
12,519	95	1,189,666	560	890,605	31,383,414	21,080	15,521	14,912
13,778	89	1,225,261	589	876,892	32,507,807	23,333	16,795	16,195
15,078	83	1,254,249	618	860,990	33,550,939	25,745	18,107	17,517
16,418	78	1,276,941	648	844,482	34,522,977	28,332	19,460	18,880
17,799	73	1,293,726	679	827,379	35,428,072	31,111	20,850	20,280

20

Surplus—An Insurance Company's Capital

Norma Nielson and Donald Jones

Preceding chapters stress the long-term obligations of life insurance companies. The premiums an insurer charges its customers cover the *expected* claims of those customers. The purpose of capital in any insurance company is to absorb *unexpected* upward fluctuations in claims. To meet long-term obligations, then, an insurance company needs capital that, in the terminology of insurance accounting, is called *surplus*.

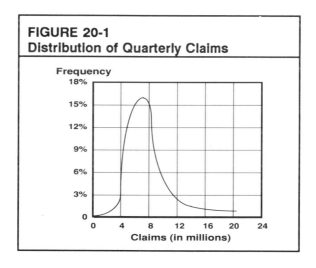

FIGURE 20-1
Distribution of Quarterly Claims

Suppose, for example, that a medium-sized life insurer expects claims to be $7.5 million during an upcoming period. Uncertainties are inherent in any such projection. This means that the situation is more accurately represented by a distribution than by a single number. Figure 20-1 illustrates one possible distribution, where aggregate claims for each quarter are plotted on the horizontal axis and the probability that each level of aggregate claims will occur is depicted on the vertical axis. The company expects claims of $7.5 million, but losses in excess of $16 million are possible theoretically, although highly improbable. Sophisticated statistical analysis that is beyond the scope of this book suggests that for this specific distribution the company should not expect aggregate claims to exceed $9 million in a bad year.

An epidemic or natural disaster that produces bad life insurance results in one quarter is also likely to affect subsequent quarters. Life insurers are particularly vulnerable to changes in claims caused by an epidemic or natural disaster because many of their contracts involved fixed premiums that cannot be adjusted upward.

One way to explain capital adequacy is by expressing how many quarters of bad experience a company's financial position can absorb. Based on the statistical analysis mentioned above, this insurer could have actual claims exceed expected claims by $1.5 million in a bad quarter. A firm with exposures illustrated by figure 20-1's distribution and capital of $3 million can remain solvent only through *two consecutive poor quarters*. An insurer with $6 million in capital can be confident of its ability to remain solvent through *four consecutive poor quarters*, and so forth.

MANAGING SURPLUS

The fundamental charge of top managers in insurance companies is to monitor the surplus accumulated within the company and deploy it in the best possible directions. This means

- assuring that the company meets the minimum statutory capital requirements in the states where it operates
- assessing the need for capital beyond those regulatory minimum requirements
- understanding the relationship between surplus and the investment function
- evaluating how much surplus is needed and available from various sources

Growing out of this surplus management process is the need for a system to distribute some surplus back to policyowners.

Minimum Statutory Capital Requirements

Because regulators understand the role of adequate capital in a company's solvency, each state has minimum capital requirements. In most states these requirements take the form of a law specifying a minimum amount of capital for a company to become licensed in that state. Most states specify amounts between $1 million and $2 million, but a few like Arizona are considerably lower. These fixed-dollar requirements may soon be relegated to history. The National Association of Insurance Commissioners (NAIC) is finalizing new capital standards that vary depending on the level of insurance and investment risk maintained by individual companies. Although the individual states still need to adopt risk-based capital standards, the NAIC is already implementing the new standard by mandating that the standardized annual statement contain the information and ratios needed for risk-based capital evaluation.

The Need for Capital Beyond Minimum Requirements

Companies have always needed capital beyond the statutory minimum amounts. The amount of capital required depends on the type of business a life insurer writes and the willingness of the company's owners and managers to take risks. The move by regulators toward risk-based capital requirements will, when fully implemented, impose a limit on how much risk the companies can choose to assume.

Traditionally most life insurance policies were issued for long terms and sold at fixed prices. These circumstances remove all possibility of future price adjustments and force an insurer to calculate its premiums conservatively. The degree of conservatism needed depends somewhat on the type of policies being sold. For example, a life insurance company writing participating insurance usually assigns its highest priority to the adequacy of gross premiums and can incorporate ample margins of safety into each basic assumption. The premiums of nonparticipating policies and policies paying market rates of interest must also meet the test of adequacy. However, contracts that include no provisions to adjust future costs in light of actual experience require careful consideration in order to develop premiums that will prove adequate over the long run *and* be competitive in the marketplace. The margins in such premiums will be narrower.

Relationship to Investment Function

An insurance company invests its capital in financial instruments whose values move with interest rates and equities markets. The straight line labeled *duration* in figure 20-2 illustrates an asset whose value declines 25 percent (from $80 to $60) when interest rates rise from 6 percent to 8 percent.

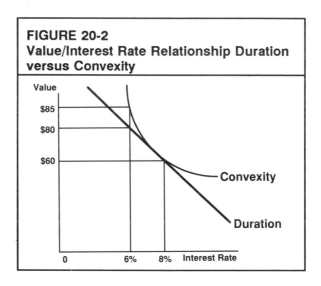

FIGURE 20-2
Value/Interest Rate Relationship Duration versus Convexity

When a life insurance company's assets and liabilities move in the same direction and at the same pace in response to interest rate changes, the company is said to have *immunized* its portfolio against interest rate risks. Immunization means that a financial risk has been effectively neutralized—that is, the losses expected in one part of the business are offset by gains somewhere else when market conditions and interest rates change. For example, an immunized portfolio will offset a decrease in income due to lower interest rates by increases in the market value of the bonds held in that portfolio. This requires a very precise combination of bonds, mortgages, and stock of the appropriate durations to accomplish this balance and maintain it over a wide range of interest rate environments.

Two somewhat more sophisticated concepts measure the sensitivity of the insurer's assets and liabilities to changes in interest rates. *Duration* is a representative time interval somewhat similar to the average holding period. Asset duration is the average time after requisition until assets (investments) mature; liability duration is the average period after policy issuance until a claim is paid. Optimal durations are affected by changes in interest rates. Liability durations also depend on events—like lapse, death rates, and policy loan demand—that are beyond the control of the insurer. Duration matching is an attempt to select asset durations that will closely match the cash flows from assets to the flows required by the insurer's liabilities. Surplus duration is related to asset duration, liability duration, and the firm's leverage. (These concepts are developed further in chapter 32.) *Convexity* measures the relative rate of change in the outside market and inside the company as interest rates change. As shown by the curved line in figure 20-2, price changes are much greater for lower interest rate changes than they are around high interest rates.

Understanding the confounding effects of interest rate changes permits management to protect a firm's surplus during unfavorable economic and underwriting cycles by implementing safeguards, such as constraints on asset duration compared to liability duration. Ideally, the effect of external events on a company's assets and liabilities will be matched in such a way that the company can remain solvent—preferably profitable—in a wide range of interest rate environments.

Sources of Surplus

To maintain its financial strength a growing insurance company needs regular additions to its capital. This is particularly true during periods of rapid growth because the costs of establishing a new policy exceed the premium collected in the first year. The primary source of capital is internal and comes from favorable deviations of actual experience from assumed experience on seasoned life insurance policies. External sources of surplus include traditional capital markets and reinsurance.

Insurance Operations

The immediate result of profitable operations is an increase in the company's surplus—that is, the company's assets grow more than its liabilities. The primary sources of insurance gains are *mortality savings, excess interest*, and *expense savings*. The word *savings*, while somewhat misleading, refers to the amount remaining from more efficient and economical operations than were assumed when setting the premiums. Often the savings reflect margins built intentionally into the premiums to produce surplus. Interest earnings greater than the assumed rate usually contribute the largest portion of insurer gains for policies that develop a cash value. This includes the realization of capital gains—that is, the sale of an asset for more than its book value. Any transaction that increases assets more than liabilities or decreases liabilities to a greater extent than assets—voluntary policy terminations at early durations,[1] for example—is a source of surplus. Supplementary features of the insurance contract, such as disability income and accidental death provisions, are examples of other sources of surplus.

Insurers also make assumptions about future expense levels (including anticipated inflation) when setting premium rates. If actual expenses remain lower than the assumed level this savings will contribute to surplus.

It is possible, of course, that a company will experience a loss with respect to one or more of the assumptions that enter the gross premium. For example, while AIDS deaths in the 1980s have not been sufficient in number to seriously affect the solvency of the life insurance industry, they have produced higher than expected mortality rates in some geographic regions and age categories, particularly for group insurance. These increased death rates, combined with generally declining interest rates during the early 1990s, make it much harder for life insurance companies to earn the profits anticipated.

Traditional Capital Markets

Financing sources for noninsurance companies usually include debt and equity (the corporation issues bonds or stock). Theoretically these same options are available for some insurance companies. Insurance companies usually buy bonds, however, rather than issue them. The issuance of new stock, a common approach to raising capital, is available only to stock insurance companies. Because mutual companies do not have stock, they cannot raise capital by issuing stock.

In recent years converting a mutual insurance company to stock form has become an option for mutual insurance companies wishing to expand their access to capital markets. This process is called *demutualization*. In 1986 Union Mutual Life Insurance Company completed the first demutualization by a healthy life insurance company. The company—now called UNUM Life Insurance Company—raised about $580 million in new capital, roughly doubling its surplus.

In 1988 a New York law permitting domestic mutual life insurance companies to convert to stock form took effect. This law addressed many formerly unanswered procedural and regulatory concerns. The Equitable Life Assurance Society of the United States became the first major company to use that law, announcing in the last days of 1990 its intent to pursue demutualization. Equitable obtained the required policyowner approvals for conversion during the first half of 1992. A French insurance company provided a large increase in surplus through the purchase of a large block of the Equitable stock.

Some new developments for insurers in the capital markets are (1) the issuance of unsecured corporate bonds by a mutual company and (2) the sale of part of real estate holdings to a newly formed real estate investment trust (REIT) sponsored by the insurer and financed by a public sale of the REIT.

Other Sources of Surplus

Reinsurance can serve as a major source of (it is perhaps more accurate to say substitute for) capital in the insurance business. Some studies show that the availability of reinsurance diminishes the importance of organizational form (stock or mutual) that a company uses, primarily because it equalizes access to capital.

Annual renegotiation of reinsurance treaties can be used to transfer more of a company's financial risk to outsiders when adequate internal capital is not available to support that risk. From a financial perspective, the company buying reinsurance is "borrowing" the use of the reinsurance company's capital. (See chapter 24 for a discussion of reinsurance arrangements.) While the analogy is imperfect, reinsurance serves a function similar to a line of credit. In the aggregate, the capacity of the insurance industry is enhanced by an amount up to the total capital available through the reinsurance market.

DISTRIBUTION OF SURPLUS

A profitable insurance operation produces a company with increasing surplus. The board of directors must determine how to allocate newly earned surplus among several competing needs. The most important of these are as follows:

- the need to finance company growth
- the need in some companies to provide investors with an acceptable return on their investment
- the need to remain competitive by returning a portion of premiums to policyowners whose policies generated those profits or retained surplus

Surplus to Meet a Company's Capital Needs

Unless the board of directors takes specific action, contributions to surplus remain in the company's surplus account. This increases the company's net worth (defined as the difference between the total assets and the total liabilities) and strengthens its financial position. From the surplus account, monies can be used to pay off debts or to pay the expenses associated with writing new business. Financing company growth undoubtedly presents the life insurer's largest internal demand for capital, regardless of whether it is a mutual or a stock company.

Return for Financial Investment

The shareholders in a stock company expect financial rewards for their investments. Rewards can take the form of dividends on the stock increases, increases in the market price per share, or some combination of the two. Only a portion of an insurance company's profits is normally distributed to stockholders in cash. The remainder stays in the company's capital account to finance the acquisition of new business and to provide a financial buffer against adverse contingencies. Such additions also tend to increase the share price of the company's stock.

Return of Premium Overcharge

A portion of the earnings from an insurance operation (stock and mutual companies) results from the company's deliberate overcharge for its participating products. The policy *dividend* refunds this amount to the customers who paid the higher price for participating insurance. It is important to differentiate between stockholder dividends and policyowner dividends.

No predetermined relationship exists between the surplus gains in a particular year and the dividends returned to policyowners. The gains enhance the appropriate surplus account as they accrue, and at the end of the calendar year the directors of the company, based on information then available and in light of a number of factors, decide what portion of the *total* increases in surplus should be distributed in dividends the following year and what portion should be retained as an increase in contingency reserves. The board of directors earmarks the amount as *divisible surplus,* and paying that sum becomes a formal obligation of the company. Once set aside by action of the directors, the divisible surplus becomes a liability and is no longer part of the company's surplus.

The decision to set aside funds for dividends requires an insurance company's managers to balance the need for a general contingency fund against the advantages of pursuing a liberal dividend policy. In any well-managed company the share of the total surplus to be distributed always involves careful consideration of the impact on the company's safety cushion. In some companies the importance attached to this component of financial operations is such that needed surplus is decided upon first, and the remainder becomes the divisible surplus.

Guiding Principles in the Distribution of Divisible Surplus

The apportionment of the divisible surplus among the various groups of policyowners is a complex matter and one that should measure up to a set of guiding principles established over many years. The system of distribution should be reasonably simple in operation, equitable, flexible, and understandable by policyowners and the agency force.

Simplicity. For practical reasons the method of distribution should be simple. A complicated formula is troublesome, expensive, and difficult to explain to policyowners and others. A small increase in accuracy may also be more apparent than real. Complicated refinements have only minor significance and are of questionable value.

Equity. The distribution of surplus should be equitable by allocating dividends to each policy on the basis of the proportion it has contributed to the insurer's surplus. Policies cannot be considered individually but must be dealt with on the basis of groups or classes, and the system of computing dividends or other distributions of surplus should be one that aims at approximate equity between classes and among individual policies within classes.

Flexibility. To say that the system of distribution must be adaptable to changing conditions is merely an extension of the statement that the method must be equitable. An insurer attains flexibility by separately recognizing as many sources of surplus as possible, using a formula that permits proper adjustments to the factors involved, and avoiding arbitrary expedients in annual adjustments to dividend scales.

Comprehensibility by Policyowners and Agents. This is a minor consideration, but policyowners occasionally ask about their dividends, particularly if a company has reduced its dividend scale. Such an inquiry may be addressed to the home office or to a field representative. In the interest of good public relations, the formula should afford policyowners an understandable explanation. Certainly the field force should have a general understanding of the sources of surplus and how they combine to produce a dividend scale.

The Desirability of a Nonreducing Dividend Scale

The minimum objective of most companies is to continue the current dividend scale. This usually implies a larger absolute distribution of surplus each year than that of the preceding year. Current additions to surplus historically have been sufficient to support the existing dividend scale. In years when adverse fluctuations in experience do not produce gains, the company may draw on funds accumulated in previous years to avoid reducing the scale. Similarly, in a year when additions to surplus are more than adequate to support the existing dividend scale, the excess often is added to existing surplus in order to avoid the expense and other complications of changing the scale. If, however, a significant disparity develops between the funds needed to maintain the existing scale and those currently available for distribution, and if the disparity is expected to continue over a long period, the board of directors must consider a change in the scale.

Determining whether a change in mortality or interest rates is permanent or temporary normally requires several years. The nature and magnitude of modifying the dividend scale will reflect the directors' judgment about the duration and future course of the relevant trends.

Special Forms of Surplus Distribution

In most states divisible surplus must be apportioned and distributed annually. However, sufficient theoretical and practical justifications exist for some degree of deferral that most states permit limited departures, under proper safeguards, from the general requirement of annual distributions. These departures take the form of either *extra* dividends or *terminal* dividends.

Extra Dividends. Extra dividends may follow one of two patterns. One is a single payment made after a policy has been in force a specified number of years, usually 5. Another is periodic additional dividends distributed at stated intervals. The single extra payment is usually a substitute for a first-year dividend. From a practical standpoint, this procedure has some distinct advantages and can be justified to some extent on equitable grounds. It reduces the strain of initial expenses and deters voluntary terminations during the early years. It also serves as a special system to assess a larger part of excess first-year expenses against policies that cancel during the first few years.

Periodic extra dividends, at every 5th year for example, have little justification in theory. Perhaps the only valid reason is that regular dividends are calculated on such a conservative basis that additional surplus remains even after annual dividends are paid. Extra dividends, while improving illustrative net-cost figures over a period of years, are paid only on those policies that remain in force. This is particularly true of a special dividend payable only at the end of 20 years. The 20-year extra dividend is further suspect when used to improve a company's showing in net-cost comparisons.

In Canada companies issue policies under which dividends are apportioned only every 5 years, but the amount of surplus set aside for deferred dividends during each 5-year period must be carried as a liability until paid. Under Canadian practices, it is customary for the company to pay an interim dividend when a policyowner dies during the period of deferral but not upon lapse or surrender.

Terminal Dividends. Terminal dividends refer to special dividends paid upon termination of a policy through maturity, death, or surrender. Such dividends are normally paid only after the policy has been in force for a specified period of years. Surrender dividends are usually a percentage of the surrender value, while mortality and maturity dividends may be a percentage of the face amount of the policy or of the reserve, the percentage varying by plan and duration.

Terminal dividends are available only from companies that subscribe to the philosophy that a withdrawing policyowner should receive back all or a portion of his or her contribution to surplus. Those companies that do not provide terminal dividends—and they are in the majority—either feel that each policyowner should make a permanent contribution to the company's surplus or they view any attempt to allocate the contingency fund to individual policies or classes of policies as impractical. However, the Standard Nonforfeiture Law requires the payment of *surrender* dividends whenever the rate of interest used in the calculation of reserves is more than .5 percent less than the rate used in the calculation of surrender values.

A terminal dividend payable at death should not be confused with a *postmortem* dividend. A postmortem dividend is payable at death and covers the period between the preceding policy anniversary and the date of death. It may be computed in various ways, but the most common practice is to provide a pro rata portion of the dividend that would have been payable for the full year. Most companies pay postmortem dividends and add the amount to the death proceeds under the policy. A few companies pay the full dividend for the year, thus giving effect to the arbitrary assumption that a company pays death claims at the end of the year. The loss of interest involved in this assumption is charged to surplus.

ILLUSTRATIVE DIVIDEND COMPUTATION

This section illustrates the principles explained earlier in this chapter through a hypothetical dividend calculation. Details of computing the 10th-year dividend of a $100,000 ordinary life policy issued to a male aged 32 are shown in table 20-1.

The steps in the calculation are as follows: The gross premium for the policy in this example is $12.51 per $1,000, plus a policy fee of $50. This premium is the net level premium ($8.51 per $1,000), computed using mortality from the 1980 CSO Male Table and 5.5 percent interest, plus loading. The loading developed in table 17-1 of chapter 17 and used in this example is 16 percent of the gross premium, plus $2 per $1,000, plus the policy fee of $50.

The mortality contribution to the 10th-year dividend is the tabular cost of insurance minus the actual mortality charge for the 10th year. The tabular charge in this example is the net amount at risk, multiplied by the 1980 CSO Male Table rate at age 41, 3.29 per 1,000, which yields $301. The actual mortality charge is

TABLE 20-1
Illustrative Dividend Calculation
$100,000 Ordinary Life Policy Issued to Male Aged 32
Reserve Basis: Full Net Level Premium Reserves, 1980 CSO Male Table, and 5.5% Interest

(1)	Gross premium: $12.51 x 100 + $50 policy fee	$1,301
(2)	Net level premium: 100 x 8.51	851
(3)	Loading: (1) − (2)	450
(4)	Mortality contribution to 10th-year dividend	
	(a) 9th-year terminal reserve	7,653
	(b) 10th-year terminal reserve	8,671
	(c) Tabular cost of insurance: {[100,000 − 4(b)]/1,000} x 3.29	301
	(d) Mortality charge: 0.695 x 4(c)	209
	(e) Return of tabular mortality: 4(c) − 4(d)	92
(5)	Interest contribution: (0.0625 − 0.055) x [(2) + 4(a)]	64
(6)	Loading contribution	
	(a) Expense charge: .115 x (1) + 35.00 + 20.00	205
	(b) Return of loading: (3) − 6(a)	245
(7)	Total dividend for the 10th year: 4(e) + (5) + 6(b)	401

the percentage of actual to expected mortality for age 41 multiplied by the tabular cost of insurance. The rate of mortality used in the calculation of an actual dividend varies by attained age and reflects the company's own mortality experience during recent years. In this illustration, the percentage was taken from the scale used in the construction of table 20-2. If we assume the actual rate of mortality at age 32 is 65 percent of the 1980 CSO Male Table rate and that the percentage increases by one-half point for each year of attained age, the assumed actual rate of mortality at age 41 would be 69.5 percent of the rate reflected in the table. The mortality saving at attained age 41 is 30.5 percent of the tabular rate. Therefore the mortality charge would be $209, which, deducted from $301, gives a mortality saving for the year of $92.

The interest contribution at all durations is calculated by multiplying the initial reserve for the year in question and the net level premium by the difference between the assumed rate of interest and the so-called dividend rate of interest. While the latter will bear a close relationship to the actual rate of interest the company earned in recent years, it might deviate in either direction in any particular year. In the illustration the dividend rate of 6.25 percent produces an excess interest factor of 0.75 percent when compared to the assumed rate of 5.5

percent. Applying this factor to the sum of the initial reserve of $7,653 produces an excess interest contribution of $64 for the year.

The loading in our example is 16 percent of the gross premium, $2.00 per $1,000 of insurance, and a per-policy expense of $42. Of this, 2.4 percent of the gross premium, $1.25 per $1,000 of insurance, and $3.00 per policy were included intentionally to provide future dividends. The difference between actual expenses and the policy's loading for our $100,000 example policy provides a savings of $245. This amount is available for dividend distribution, a portion of which may well have been included in the loading formula for that specific purpose. The assumptions described in this dividend illustration result in a total dividend of $401 — that is, $92 from mortality savings plus $64 from excess interest, plus $245 from expense savings.

Table 20-2 shows how dividends might be determined for the first 20 years of an ordinary life policy issued to a 32-year-old male. The following experience factors have been chosen arbitrarily:

- The mortality return is based on actual mortality being 65 percent of the table value at age 32 and increasing one-half point per year of attained age up to age 75. The mortality *savings* in table 20-2 then range from 35 percent at age 32 to 24.5 percent at age 51, the 20th year. These same assumptions were used in the example earlier in this chapter.
- The interest return reflects an excess interest factor of 0.75 percent times the initial reserve for each of the durations.
- The loading return is composed of the three factors, each graded by duration to illustrate the heavier expenses at early durations. For example, the 16 percent of gross premium loading is assumed to be released at the rate of .5 percent per year up to the 11th year and then increases by a full percent each year thereafter. These patterns have been chosen arbitrarily to illustrate the development of the dividend scale pattern. The pattern may vary by company, policy, or trends of the times.

Note that the rates used in the dividend computation represent *actual* experience of the company. They will *always* differ from the assumptions that were used to compute premiums, reserves, and surrender values.

GENERAL EQUITY OF THE DIVIDEND SCALE

Experts generally agree that a system of surplus distribution should, to the extent possible, be equitable. As explained earlier, equity is best served by a dividend formula that allocates to each policy its share of surplus in the proportion it has contributed to that surplus. To attain equity most companies in the United States and Canada employ a system of surplus distribution called the *contribution plan*. For reasons of simplicity noted above, consideration is usually limited to the three major sources of surplus: mortality savings, excess interest, and loading savings. A distribution plan that recognizes only these sources of surplus is called the *three-factor contribution plan*.[2]

The interest factor of the dividend formula seeks to credit each policy with its share of a company's investment earnings above the sum needed to meet its obligations. The evolution of computer technology has expanded the extent to which a particular policy's interest contribution can be traced. The strict equity of considering the different times of premium payments and different interest

TABLE 20-2
Dividends for First 20 Years of Ordinary Life Policy, Male Aged 32,
Net Premium Based on 1980 CSO Table and 5.5% Interest

Year	Initial Reserve	Amount at Risk	Mortality Return per $100,000 Amount at Risk	Loading Return Factors			Interest Return 0.0075x(2)	Mortality Return (3)x(4) +100,000	Loading Return (5)x1301 +(6)+(7)	Total Dividend (8)+(9) +(10)
				Percent of Gross Premium $1,301	Per Policy	Per $100,000 Face				
(1)	(2)	(3)	(4)	(5)	(6)	(7)	(8)	(9)	(10)	(11)
1	$ 851	$99284	$ 64	0.0%	$ 2.00	$ 10	$ 6.38	$ 63.70	$ 12.00	$ 82
2	1567	98536	66	0.5	2.50	180	11.75	64.86	189.01	266
3	2315	97753	68	1.0	3.00	180	17.36	66.64	196.01	280
4	3098	96937	71	1.5	3.50	180	23.24	68.68	203.02	295
5	3914	96086	74	2.0	4.00	180	29.36	70.95	210.02	310
6	4765	95202	78	2.5	4.50	180	35.74	74.10	217.03	327
7	5649	94284	83	3.0	5.00	180	42.37	77.76	224.03	344
8	6567	93333	88	3.5	5.50	180	49.25	81.90	231.04	362
9	7518	92347	94	4.0	6.00	180	56.39	86.49	238.04	381
10	8504	91329	100	4.5	7.00	180	63.78	91.50	245.55	401
11	9522	90277	107	5.0	8.00	180	71.42	96.30	253.05	421
12	10574	89190	114	6.0	9.00	180	79.31	101.78	267.06	448
13	11661	88067	122	7.0	10.00	180	87.46	107.01	281.07	476
14	12784	86908	130	8.0	11.00	180	95.88	112.58	295.08	504
15	13943	85712	138	9.0	12.00	180	104.57	118.16	309.09	532
16	15139	84479	146	10.0	13.00	180	113.54	123.48	323.10	560
17	16372	83205	155	11.0	14.00	180	122.79	129.06	337.11	589
18	17646	81893	165	12.0	15.00	180	132.35	134.89	351.12	618
19	18958	80540	174	13.0	16.00	180	142.19	140.40	365.13	648
20	20311	79150	186	14.0	17.00	180	152.33	147.39	379.14	679

rates apportioned to the cash value portion of premiums paid under universal life contracts is approximated in participating whole life contracts. For example, because policy loans can cost the insurance company much of the investment return it could otherwise earn, some companies vary the dividend on an individual policy depending on whether a policy loan was outstanding over the dividend year. Loans are very popular during periods of high interest rates, and they can be particularly costly at those times because they preclude the insurer from reinvesting the funds at the higher yields available. Thus if each policyowner receives dividends according to identical scales, those who do not borrow subsidize those who do borrow.

The growing use of *direct recognition* dividend scales since the late 1970s is an excellent example of attempts to increase the equity of dividend distributions. Direct recognition means that policy choices made by an individual policyowner are reflected in the policy dividends returned to that policyowner.

However, total equity cannot be attained in reality. Mortality experience, for example, varies widely with duration, occupation, amount of insurance, and plan of insurance. It is impractical to distinguish among these factors in computing the individual contributions to surplus from favorable mortality. Many factors affect the rate of expense, including the size of the policy and the variation in the premium tax rates among the different states. Recognizing all these factors would unduly complicate the dividend formula.

Also the divisible surplus will not, except by accident, equal the total "profits" or aggregate contributions to surplus. It is affected by considerations unconnected to the sources of surplus that cannot be related to individual policies or even to classes of policies. Therefore a method of distribution that calls for the computation of individual contributions to surplus would require modification to equal the sum available for distribution. Such modification is likely to disturb the relationship between the assumed contributions from different sources.

Thus under practical conditions it is not possible to refund the excess payments of individual policyowners exactly. In such matters policies must be dealt with as groups or classes. The system of computing refunds or dividends aims to approximate equity between classes and among individual policies within classes. As a minimum standard of equity, surplus distribution should consider the sources from which surplus arises and should not be oversimplified to cause injustice to any group of policyowners.

Testing the Dividend Side

Just as gross premiums and surrender values are tested by asset share calculations prior to adoption, so are proposed and existing dividend scales tested. Such a test combines a given set of gross premiums and surrender values with realistic assumptions about mortality, interest earnings, expenses, and voluntary policy terminations. The result shows whether the accumulated asset shares for the various plans, ages at issue, and durations meet the requirements of both adequacy and equity. An existing dividend scale should be tested periodically to assure that it meets the same objectives.

Over the life of any block of policies the aggregate dividends distributed will be somewhat less than the amount contributed to surplus. This is necessary if the company is to accumulate and maintain a contingency reserve sufficient to protect it from its liabilities. That is an objective of well-managed companies. As reserves increase, whether from the sale of new policies or the natural progression under old policies, the absolute size of the contingency reserve must also increase. Apart from interest earnings on the contingency reserve or "free surplus,"[3] the only source of such funds is the current earnings from policies. Therefore even over the long term, something less than the net additions to surplus from all blocks of policies will be returned to policyowners as dividends. Equity demands that each group of policies bear a share of this cost. This is just another way of saying that a policy's asset share should eventually exceed the reserve and that management expects each policy to make a permanent contribution to the company's surplus.

Other Issues

The dividend process described here is simplified to deal with only the major sources of surplus. Some elements of cost and price—such as policy size, smoking behavior, and gender—are commonly included today in premium computations. Should experience vary for these populations, some adjustment may be needed in the dividend scale. Furthermore, this discussion ignores several refinements that may be introduced in the interest of equity or under the pressures of competition.

Ordinary (immediate) annuities present unique problems in pricing and dividend policy. First, expense loading from any single premium contract can arise only in the first year. Second, as reserves under such policies decline with duration, excess earnings are likely to diminish each year. Finally, unless an actuary provides for future improvement in annuitant mortality, as with the use of projection factors, declining death rates among annuitants erode any margins in the mortality assumptions and may eventually produce mortality losses, offsetting the declining gain from excess interest.[4] Thus unless the margins in the actuarial assumptions are very conservative, which might produce noncompetitive rates, dividends are seldom used in annuity contracts. When they do appear, they are likely to be small and to become smaller over time.

NOTES

1. Surrender values are usually less than reserves during the early years of a policy. Under the Standard Nonforfeiture Law, they may be less until the end of the premium-paying period. A policy termination before the surrender value equals the reserve increases surplus since a liability item (reserves) is decreased more than an asset item (cash). The creation of surplus by the termination of policies does not mean that a termination is financially beneficial to the insurer. This is a mismatch of income and expense items of the statutory accounting system mandated by regulators. If the accounting rules required amortization of most acquisition expenses (rather than dealing with those expenses on a cash basis), the reverse might be true.

2. There are three other methods of apportioning surplus that are based on the contribution concept: experience premium method, asset share method, and the fund method. In common usage, the term *contribution method* is reserved for the method described herein as the three-factor contribution plan.

3. In many companies interest on these funds is taken into account in determining the excess interest factor.

4. The mortality element of an annuity dividend formula involves another complication, this one being philosophical in nature. Within a given class of life insurance policies,

mortality gains are created by the surviving members of the group, who are credited with the dividends. With a given group of annuitants, the mortality gains, if any, are created by those who die, while the dividends are payable to the surviving annuitants. This suggests that mortality gains should be discounted in advance and passed along to all members of the original group by means of a lower premium.

21

Selection and Classification of Risks (Part 1)

Dan M. McGill
Revised by Jeremy S. Holmes and James F. Winberg

The essence of the insurance principle is the sharing of losses by those exposed to a common hazard. This is made possible by contributions to a common fund by those exposed to loss from the common hazard. If the plan is to be scientific and equitable, however, each participant must pay into the fund a sum of money reasonably commensurate with the risk that the insured places on the fund. To accomplish this objective an insurance company prepares a schedule of premiums that represents its judgment as to the risk inherent in each category of applicants acceptable to the company. The function of the selection process is to determine whether an applicant's degree of risk for insurance is commensurate with the premium established for people in the same classification being considered. If within each broad risk category, various graduations of risk have been established, as would be true of a company that offers either preferred risk or substandard insurance, the evaluation of an application for insurance involves not only selection but also classification.

RISK CLASSIFICATION

It is neither possible nor desirable to establish risk categories in which each component risk represents a loss potential that is identical to that of all the other risks in the category. For practical reasons, the categories must be broad enough to include risks with substantial differences in loss potential. In life insurance the primary basis for the risk classification is the age of the applicant. Yet within each age group, the probability of death is greater for some than for others. These differences in risk stem from physical condition, occupation, sex, and other factors. Some persons in the group might be near death, while others might confidently look forward to a long lifetime comparatively free of bodily ailments. The relative frequencies of mortality expectation represented in any randomly selected group of people who are the same age approximates the curve shown in figure 21-1, with 100 percent representing average mortality for the group.

The graph reveals a wide range of mortality expectations for a group of persons falling within a risk category measured by age alone. Clearly, all should not be offered insurance on the same terms. Considerations of equity would suggest that those persons subject to the lowest degree of mortality should pay a lower premium than those who represent an average risk; those with greatly impaired longevity expectations should be charged more than the standard premium or even declined altogether.

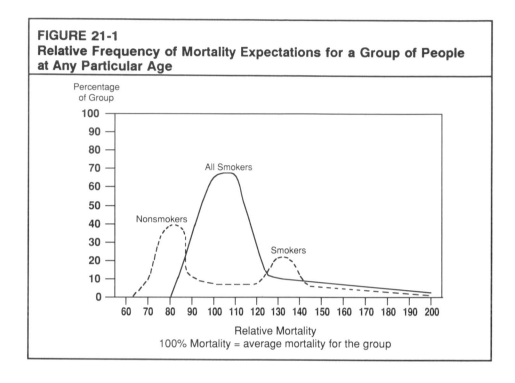

FIGURE 21-1
Relative Frequency of Mortality Expectations for a Group of People at Any Particular Age

The insurance company must establish a range of mortality expectations within which applicants will be regarded as average risks and hence entitled to insurance at standard rates or, conversely, the limits beyond which applicants will be considered either preferred or substandard and subject to a discount or surcharge. The insurance company should be guided by the principles set forth below.

After the limits for the various risk categories have been established, the company must adopt selection and classification procedures that will enable it to place applicants for insurance into the proper categories. This process is complicated by the fact that applicants for insurance may not fit the curve illustrated in figure 21-1. That curve depicts the mortality expectations of a randomly selected group, whereas applicants for insurance do not constitute such a group. The observation has frequently been made that a life insurance company could safely insure the life of everyone who passes by any designated location in a typical American city, so long as the practice does not become public knowledge. Unfortunately, the applications received by a life insurance company do not reflect such randomness. Instead, they are biased by antiselection (or adverse selection). Many who seek insurance have knowledge of an impairment that might be expected to shorten their life span or at least suspect that they have such an impairment that they may conceal. A company's underwriting procedures must either screen out such applicants or classify them into appropriate substandard groups. Thus it might be argued that the primary purpose of risk selection is to protect the company from antiselection. If there were no antiselection, there would be no need for the underwriting process except to separate and classify substandard risks.

GUIDING PRINCIPLES

There are certain fundamental principles that must govern the selection procedures of an insurance company if it is to operate on a sound basis. Some of these principles are mutually inconsistent, which means that a company must fashion its selection in such a manner as to balance these opposing principles.

Predominance of the Standard Group

The range of mortality expectations within which applicants will be regarded as average and hence entitled to insurance at standard rates should be broad enough to encompass the great percentage of applicants.[1] This is particularly important if the company does not offer substandard insurance. An excessive number of rejections undermines the morale of the agency force, increases the cost of doing business, and causes a loss of goodwill among the insurable public.[2] A disproportionate number of substandard policies may have similar effects. Apart from the practical considerations just mentioned, the broader the base of standard risks, the more stable the mortality experience of the group is likely to be. On the other hand, considerations of equity and competition prevent an unwarranted extension of the standard class.

Balance within Each Risk or Rate Classification

A company must obtain and maintain a proper balance among the risks in each rate classification. This is especially important within the classification of standard risks, which, in view of the principle stated above, is likely to have broad limits. If the overall mortality of the risks in the standard category is to approximate the theoretical average for the group—the goal of most companies—every risk that is worse than average must be offset by one that is better than average. If the range is broad, the margin by which the inferior risk fails to meet the norm for the group should be counterbalanced by the margin by which the offsetting superior risk exceeds the norm. Such precise offsetting or balancing of risks is more of an ideal than an attainable reality. A rough approximation is feasible, however, for a company using the numerical rating system, under which, as explained later, the mortality expectation of individual applications is expressed as a percentage of the average expectation, which is assumed to be 100 percent.

A recent development has constricted the standard range. Companies have developed varying degrees of preferred mortality classes based on such factors as smoking status, tobacco usage in any form, cholesterol level, family history, sports and avocation participation, and other factors. This further refinement of the traditional standard class serves to narrow the remaining standard range not only by removing the superior risks, but also, theoretically at least, by limiting the inferior higher risks allowed in the standard class.

Irrespective of the underwriting procedures used by a company, if each risk classification is overbalanced with risks whose longevity prospects are less favorable than the assumed average for the classification, the company will end up with excessive mortality costs and—unless it enjoys offsetting advantages in other areas of operations—will have difficulty in maintaining its competitive position. The force of this factor will not be diminished by further improving the overall mortality experience of the company unless the rate of improvement is greater than that of its competition—an unlikely situation.

Equity among Policyowners

The manner in which applicants are grouped for rating purposes should not unduly violate considerations of equity. Some discrimination among insureds is unavoidable since all risk classifications must be broad enough to include risks of varying quality. Nevertheless the spread between the best and worst risks within a classification should not be so great as to produce rank injustice.

There is also a practical side to this matter because if the spread is too great, the better risks may seek insurance with competing companies whose classification system is more equitable, leaving the first company with a disproportionate number of inferior risks. Consequently the first company will have to respond since its premium could be inadequate for the residual group of risks.

Compatibility with Underlying Mortality Assumptions

The foregoing considerations tend to be relative matters, concerned primarily with equity and competition. There is another factor, however, that operates as an absolute regulator of a company's underwriting standards—the mortality assumptions entering into the company's premiums. All mortality tables used by life insurance companies today reflect the experience of insured lives—lives that were subject to some degree of selection. A company's underwriting standards must be at least as effective as those utilized by the companies that supplied the data for the mortality table. Furthermore the companies that pool their mortality experience for the construction of modern mortality tables employ rather rigorous standards of selection. This is a factor of some importance to companies that, in a desire to capture a larger share of the life insurance market, might be tempted to lower their selection standards. The general improvement in mortality that has been such a prominent feature of the insurance scene during recent decades cannot be expected to nullify the long-run consequences of lax underwriting standards.

FACTORS AFFECTING RISK

In order to place an applicant for insurance into the proper risk classification, an insurance company needs reliable information about every factor that might significantly affect an applicant's longevity. As a matter of practice, companies seek applicant information about the following:

- age
- build
- physical condition
- personal history
- family history
- occupation
- residence
- habits

- morals
- sex
- plan of insurance
- economic status
- aviation activities
- avocation
- military service

Age

The applicant's age is the most important single factor on individual mortality expectations. Except for the first few years of life, resistance to disease and injury weakens with the passage of time, and the probability of death increases with age. Age is such a significant measure of the likelihood of death that it is the point of departure in classifying applicants for insurance. Each applicant is placed within the proper age classification and is then compared to the norm for that age to determine insurability.

One might assume that such a vital underwriting factor as age would be subject to verification at the time submitted. Ideally, verification of age is desirable in all cases, but practical considerations militate against it. To require proof of age at the time of application would inevitably delay the policy's issue and would be a source of irritation to the applicant. The agency force would object to the requirement, since many applicants would be unable or unwilling to submit documentary proof of their dates of birth. Therefore it is customary to accept the life insurance applicant's statement of age unless there is reason to believe that it is a misstatement.

Neither is it customary to require documentation of age at the time of a claim settlement unless the company has reason to question the accuracy of the stated date of birth. A typical circumstance in which a company would require verification of age would be if there are conflicting dates of birth on two or more documents. If a misstatement is discovered after the policy has become a claim, the amount of the proceeds is adjusted in accordance with the misstatement-of-age clause.

The situation is different with an immediate annuity. Under such a contract the relationship between the annuitant's age and the amount of the periodic payments is so direct and immediate that proof of age is required at the time the annuity is purchased.

The age of the applicant enters into a company's underwriting considerations in another respect. For reasons that will be explained later in this chapter, all companies have upper age limits beyond which they will not write insurance on any basis and somewhat lower limits for writing certain types of policies, such as term insurance. The absolute limit may be as low as 60 or as high as 75 or more. Under such circumstances, the age of the applicant may bar acceptability to the company on any basis. In other words, age alone—regardless of the other facts of the case—may render a person uninsurable. For that reason, a misstatement of age that induces a company to issue a policy it would not otherwise issue is grounds for rescission if discovered by the company during the contestable period (see chapter 40). Companies also have special underwriting rules for children and seniors, under which age may be an absolute determinant of insurability.

Build

The applicant's build — the relationship between height, weight, and girth — is one of the basic determinants of mortality expectation. This was one of the first discoveries in the area of medical selection. The earliest attempts to arrive at the ideal relationship between height and weight were rather crude, some drawing their inspiration from the physical proportions of certain ancient Greek athletes as revealed by statues dating back to the third century BC. Two statues in particular were considered to represent ideal proportions: The *Gladiator* and *Bronze Tumbler*.

The first comprehensive statistical study of the relationship between build and mortality covered the experience on policies issued by prominent life insurance companies from 1885 through 1908 and was published in 1913 as the *Medico-Actuarial Mortality Investigation*. The findings of this study, as refined and supplemented by subsequent investigations, served as the basis for the build tables used by life insurance companies in this country for the next several decades. These tables were eventually supplanted by the Build and Blood Pressure Study 1959, derived from findings of an investigation by the Society of Actuaries, which encompassed the ordinary policy issues of 26 leading companies from 1935 through 1953. These tables remained in use until 1980 when most companies adopted tables based on the Build Study 1979 (see table 21-1).

Compared to the 1959 tables, the 1980 tables raised the ranges of acceptable weight for shorter men and women. The lower portion of the table shows various combinations of height and weight, along with the average weight for each height. The upper portion of the table shows the mortality debits associated with each combination of height and weight in intervals of 25 points. As a group, people can be expected to experience mortality 25 percent higher than normal if they fall within the first overweight column. Thus an applicant in that classification would be assigned a debit of 25 points for purposes of the numerical rating system described in chapter 22. Build becomes a neutral factor when the weight is average or only slightly underweight or overweight. Beyond the average classification, debits are assessed, and the maximum debit for the age category in table 21-1 is 300 points. There is a special juvenile build table for people under 15. (There are also other build tables in common use that differ in both format and substance from the one presented here.)

With overweight male applicants, the company is also interested in the distribution of the excess weight. This involves a comparison of the chest (expanded) with the abdominal girth. Among well-built men of average height, the chest measurement (expanded) normally exceeds the abdominal measurement by two inches; this relationship is likely to be reversed among overweight persons. Insurance companies have prepared charts that assign debits for abdominal measurements in excess of chest measurements. The number of points depends on the person's age, the percentage he is overweight, and the number of inches by which the one measurement exceeds the other. Credits, derived the same way, are assigned when chest measurements are in excess of the abdominal girth. Under the numerical rating system, it is possible for an applicant to be credited with 20 points for a favorable relationship between his chest and girth or debited 70 points for an unfavorable one. Taking chest and abdominal measurements also enables a company to check on the accuracy of reported weights.

TABLE 21-1
Adult Build Table

Males and Females, aged 16 and over (feet and inches/pounds)

Ht.	Avg. Male Weight	Avg. Female Weight	+25	+50	+75	+100	+125	+150	+200	+250	+300
Ft. In.	Lbs.	Lbs.	Lbs.	Lbs.	Lbs.	Lbs.	Lbs.	Lbs.	Lbs.	Lbs.	Lbs.
4'8"	121	105	180	190	200	215	220	230	240	245	255
4'9"	124	108	185	195	205	215	225	235	245	255	260
4'10"	127	112	190	200	210	220	230	240	250	255	265
4'11"	130	116	195	205	215	225	235	245	255	260	270
5'0"	133	118	195	205	220	230	240	250	255	265	275
5'1"	136	122	205	210	225	235	245	250	260	270	280
5'2"	139	125	205	215	230	235	245	255	265	275	285
5'3"	143	129	210	220	230	245	255	265	275	280	290
5'4"	147	132	220	225	240	250	260	270	280	290	300
5'5"	151	135	225	235	245	255	265	275	285	295	305
5'6"	155	138	230	240	250	260	270	285	295	305	315
5'7"	159	143	235	245	255	270	280	290	300	310	320
5'8"	163	146	240	250	265	275	285	300	310	320	330
5'9"	167	151	250	260	270	285	295	305	320	330	340
5'10"	172	154	255	265	280	290	305	315	325	335	345
5'11"	176	158	260	275	285	300	310	325	335	345	355
6'0"	181	162	270	280	295	305	320	330	340	355	365
6'1"	185	166	275	290	300	315	325	340	350	360	370
6'2"	190	169	285	300	310	325	335	345	360	370	380
6'3"	195	173	290	305	320	330	345	355	365	380	390
6'4"	201	177	300	315	325	340	350	365	375	390	400
6'5"	207	180	305	320	335	345	360	370	385	400	410
6'6"	213	184	315	330	340	355	365	380	395	405	415
6'7"	219		320	335	350	365	375	390	405	415	425
6'8"	225		330	345	360	370	385	400	410	425	435
6'9"	231		335	350	365	380	395	410	425	435	450
6'10"	237		345	360	375	385	400	415	430	440	460
6'11"	243		355	370	385	390	410	420	435	450	465

Physical Condition

Next in general importance is the applicant's physical condition. In the short run, this factor may outweigh all others in importance. In evaluating an application for insurance, the company wishes to know whether there are any impairments of body or mind that would tend to shorten the life expectancy of the applicant. Questions designed to elicit information on the applicant's physical status are included in the application. If a sizable amount of insurance is involved, the information is also confirmed and supplemented by a medical examination and laboratory testing. The primary purpose of the medical examination is to detect any malfunctioning of vital organs. The heart and other parts of the circulatory system are subjected to special scrutiny.

Tests for Heart Disease or Impairment

Impairment of the heart may be evidenced by subjective symptoms—shortness of breath or pain in the chest—or by objective symptoms—changes in the quality of the heart sounds, murmurs, enlargement of the heart, persistently rapid or slow pulse, irregular pulse, poor reaction to exercise, abnormal blood pressure, or abnormalities revealed by X-ray and electrocardiogram.[3]

One of the most common manifestations of heart impairment is murmurs. A murmur is any sound other than those associated with the normal closing of the heart valves. Functional murmurs are considered harmless and are consequently of no significance to the underwriter; organic murmurs indicate damage to some part of the heart tissue. The problem is distinguishing between the two. Organic murmurs are regarded as serious and may cause the applicant to be rated highly or declined altogether. True functional murmurs are not rated, but if there is any doubt about their cause or origin, provision may be made for some extra mortality.

Enlargement of the heart (cardiomegaly) is a condition of underwriting significance, since it is nature's way of compensating for damage to the valves or other sections of the heart mechanism. Before 1979, extra mortality of 50 to 100 percent had been anticipated from an enlarged heart, without any other evidence of disease. The fallacy of that rule was demonstrated by the Blood Pressure Study 1979, which is the basis for blood pressure underwriting by most companies. This study covered about 4.35 million policies issued from 1950 through 1971 that were traced from 1954 policy anniversaries to 1972 policy anniversaries.

The findings of the study indicated lower extra mortality associated with hypertension than did the study published 20 years earlier. Specifically, among men with borderline blood pressures, regardless of treatment, the mortality ratios in the Blood Pressure Study 1979 were about 20 percentage points lower than in the Build and Blood Pressure Study 1959. The corresponding mortality ratios for high blood pressures were from 30 to 50 percentage points lower than in the earlier study. Among women with borderline hypertension, regardless of treatment, the mortality ratios were generally not much different from those in the 1959 study, but the corresponding mortality ratios for the upper range of high blood pressure were more than 50 percentage points lower than in the earlier study. This is believed to reflect the effects of antihypertensive treatment after issue of insurance.

High blood pressure may be a symptom of a condition that impairs longevity. It is particularly associated with kidney ailments. A combination of overweight and hypertension is always regarded seriously. Low blood pressure can usually be disregarded unless it is abnormally low or associated with some definite impairment, such as tuberculosis or congestive heart failure. High blood pressure that responds to treatment by returning to normal levels may receive favorable underwriting consideration, provided normal blood pressure levels are maintained for a reasonable period (one to two years).

The systolic pressure is more susceptible to emotion than the diastolic, so diastolic pressure is considered to be a better measure of the constant strain on the heart. (Systolic pressure is the higher pressure created by heart contractions, and the lower diastolic pressure is the residual reading created by blood in the body without the added pressure of a heart contraction.) Insurance experience indicates that both should be taken into consideration, and if both are higher than normal, the mortality rate will be greater than if only one of the two is out of line. For people at advanced ages, however, the systolic reading assumes more significance.

The condition of the circulatory system can also be evaluated by the pulse rate, normally 60 to 80 beats per minute. A rapid pulse is unfavorable, since it indicates that the heart has to work harder than usual to meet the body's needs. This may be a sign of an inefficient or impaired heart, an infection, or any other abnormal condition within the body that demands an extra supply of blood. An occasional rapid pulse can be overlooked for underwriting purposes, but a pulse rate that is persistently over 90 is regarded as significant. A rate persistently between 90 and 100 indicates mortality about 50 percent above normal, while a rate between 100 and 110 results in almost 200 percent above normal mortality. In general, a slow pulse is a sign of an efficient heart and is viewed as a favorable sign. An irregular pulse, or one that is slow to return to normal after exercise, is regarded unfavorably.

Blood Tests

Blood profile tests have gained added importance with the discovery of Acquired Immune Deficiency Syndrome (AIDS). The bleak outlook for those infected with the Human Immunosuppressive Virus (HIV) has mandated extensive random testing of insurance applicants. In turn this nearly universal blood testing has provided insurers with additional useful information regarding applicants' renal and liver function and blood lipids (fats, oils and waxes). The availability of this additional information has facilitated the proliferation of products offering preferred premium classifications.

Urinalysis

A standard feature of all medical examinations is the urinalysis. This important diagnostic procedure has a three-fold purpose: (1) to measure the functional capacity of the kidneys, (2) to detect infections or other abnormal conditions of the kidneys, and (3) to discover impairments of other vital organs of the body.[4] The ability of the kidneys to concentrate liquids is revealed by the amount of water in the urine, which is measured by the specific gravity test. Other tests, not a part of the standard urinalysis, measure the ability of the kidneys to excrete. The urine is examined chemically and microscopically for the presence of albumin, pus, casts, or red blood cells, which would indicate a diseased condition of the kidneys.

The presence of an undue amount of sugar in the urine suggests the possibility of diabetes, a condition characterized by an inability to metabolize carbohydrates and caused by a deficiency of insulin. The urinalysis may also reveal abnormalities of the bladder, prostate, and other sections of the urinary tract. A kidney condition revealed by an urinalysis may point to a circulatory ailment, such as heart disease or arteriosclerosis, since there is ample evidence that a close relationship exists between kidney and circulatory impairments. The urinalysis is also used to screen for the use of illicit drugs such as cocaine and marijuana. Urine testing for the presence of antibodies to HIV is also available.

In addition to the foregoing tests, the medical examiner carefully checks the other organs of the body for evidence of disease or functional disturbance, giving special attention to any factor or condition that might be related to any previous impairment disclosed by the applicant's medical history.

Personal History

The applicant's personal history sheds important light on his or her acceptability to the company. Consequently the person to be insured is asked to provide details about his or her health record, past habits, previous environment, and insurance status on the application for insurance.

The applicant's health record is usually the most important of the personal history factors. Complete information about previous illnesses, injuries, and operations may indicate the necessity for special additional tests or examinations. Particular emphasis is placed on recent illnesses and operations, and it is customary for the company to contact the attending physician or physicians for the medical details that normally would not be known to the applicant and might have a bearing upon insurability. The medical examination findings need to be supplemented by the subjective feelings and symptoms of the applicant. It is not the practice to consider an application from any person who is scheduled for diagnostic testing or surgery, currently under treatment for any condition, or not fully recovered from any illness.

The company also wants to know whether the applicant has ever been addicted to the use of drugs or alcohol, since there is always a possibility that the "cure" will prove to be only temporary. The past abuse may have caused irrevocable damage to one or more body systems. The personal history may reveal that the applicant has only recently left a hazardous or unhealthful occupation, raising the possibility that he or she may retain ill effects from the job or might return to the job in the future. It may also disclose that the applicant has changed residence to improve his or her health or has had intimate association with a person who has a contagious disease such as tuberculosis.

Finally, the company wants to know whether the applicant has ever been refused insurance by any other company or offered insurance on rated terms. An affirmative answer would indicate a prior impairment that might still be present. Information as to existing insurance also enables the company to judge whether the amount of insurance, existing and proposed, bears a reasonable relationship to the applicant's needs and financial resources.

Family History

Family history is considered significant because certain characteristics are hereditary. Build follows family lines, and to some extent, so do structural qualities of the heart and other organs. A greater than average susceptibility to infectious diseases may also be inherited. Hence the applicant is asked to provide information about the ages and state of health of parents and brothers and sisters if they are living, or if deceased, their ages at death and the causes of death.

Long-lived parents and siblings at one time were looked at as assuring a long life for an applicant, even though he or she was somewhat overweight or had some other impairment that would normally have been placed in the category of borderline risks. On the other hand, an applicant from a short-lived family, unless the deaths resulted from accidents, had to be better than average in other respects in order to be insured at standard rates. Except for cardiovascular-renal diseases and to a lesser (and declining) degree, tuberculosis, considerably less emphasis is now placed on family history with the exception of preferred-risk programs. This is because of the unreliability of family history details recited by the applicant and the difficulty of tracing the influence of heredity.

There is a tendency, which can be demonstrated statistically, for the applicant to exaggerate the ages of family members when they died. Unless his or her parents and siblings are dead or dying, the applicant generally reports them to be in good health; instances of hypertension, diabetes, and other impairments that would be regarded as significant by the home office underwriters are usually not disclosed. Furthermore it is not feasible to follow up on the applicant's family record. Even if the facts were accurately reported, there would still be insufficient evidence to measure the true impact of heredity on longevity. Only data concerning parents and siblings are usually required, whereas hereditary influences may extend back to grandparents and great-grandparents. Moreover, the influence of heredity may not have an impact until an individual is aged 60 or older, which is too late to be useful in evaluating the application of a younger person whose family record is relatively immature.

Despite the foregoing inadequacies, it has been determined that if a group of applicants — all free of any known personal qualities that would adversely affect their longevity — is divided into classes on the basis of their family histories as revealed in their applications, the lowest mortality will be found in the class with the most favorable record, and the highest mortality will be found in the class with the poorest record. The best group shows a mortality of about 85 percent of the average for all classes, while the poorest group reflects a mortality of about 115 percent. Therefore companies usually give a credit of 15 points for a very good family history and a debit of 15 points for a very poor history.

Occupation

There are many occupations that are known to have an adverse effect on mortality, and insurance companies must impose an extra charge on applicants engaged in such occupations. The higher mortality rate associated with these occupations may be attributable to a greater than normal accident hazard, unhealthful working conditions, or "socio-economic" hazards (see below).

Accident Hazards

Accidents, if not the most common hazard, are probably the most obvious. All people working with machinery are exposed to some accident hazard.

Construction workers are exposed to the hazard of falling. Underground miners—in addition to the hazard of machinery—run the risk of explosions, rock falls, fire, and lung disease. Some electrical workers are exposed to high voltages and some to the danger of falling from high places. Laborers handling heavy materials run the risk of having the materials fall on them. Railroad workers, particularly those around heavy rolling equipment, are subject to a high accident rate. Other groups subject to a higher than normal accident rate include fishermen, lumbermen, and farmers.

Dusts and Poisons

Many health hazards arise from the processes associated with a complex industrial civilization, but some of the more important were known to early civilizations. Dust is probably the most serious health hazard. It arises out of such industrial processes as grinding, drilling, and crushing, and is associated particularly with the mining industry. Organic dusts, which are largely derived from substances of animal and plant origin and are identified especially with the textile industry, produce irritation of the upper air passages and may lead to tuberculosis and other respiratory infections. Inorganic dusts, which are primarily metallic and mineral, will give rise to silicosis if they contain free silica and, in any event, increase the possibility of diseases of the respiratory organs. The lasting effects of exposure to dust make previous employment in the dusty trades an important underwriting factor. Asbestos exposure has also proven to be a serious health hazard.

The hazard from poisons exists in many industries, the number of which has been considerably increased by the expanding use of chemicals in industry. Lead poisoning—largely identified with the mining and smelting of lead but also found in printing, painting, file-cutting, and other processes—is one of the major hazards. Other health hazards include abnormalities of temperature, dampness, defective illumination, infections, radiant energy, and repeated motion, pressure, or electrical shock.

Socio-Economic Hazards

The socio-economic hazard is associated with occupations that employ unskilled and semi-skilled labor and pay commensurately low wages. The extra mortality that occurs among such people is attributable primarily to their unsatisfactory living and working conditions and to inadequate medical care. Their low economic status may reflect substandard physical or mental capacity.

There are some occupations that are thought to have a socio-economic hazard not because of low wages but because of the environment in which the people work. Bartenders, liquor salesmen, and entertainers, for example, are believed to represent a hazard purely because of environment.

All insurance companies have prepared and use occupational manuals in which they list the occupations that are deemed to have adverse effects on mortality. An applicant employed in one of the listed occupations will be required to pay an additional premium, even though all other factors are favorable. Previous employment in such an occupation may be the basis for an additional premium if there is reason to suspect that the applicant may return to the occupation. Because of greater emphasis on industrial safety and public health measures, the number of such occupations is declining steadily.

If an applicant is placed in a substandard classification because of an unfavorable current occupation, the rating is usually removed upon a subsequent change to an unrated occupation. The company cannot, of course, increase the premium if a policyowner changes from an unrated to a rated occupation after the policy has been issued, and it is not customary for such differences to be recognized for underwriting purposes.

Residence

The applicant's residence—present or prospective—is important, since mortality rates vary throughout different geographical regions of the United States and throughout the world. If the applicant is contemplating foreign travel or residence, the insurance company wants to know about it. It also wants to know whether the applicant has recently traveled or resided in a foreign country, particularly in the tropics. Differences among countries as to climate, living standards, sanitary conditions, medical care, political stability, and terrorist risk can be expected to have a decided effect on mortality.

Generally speaking, policies are not issued by United States companies to applicants whose permanent residence is in a foreign country, even though that country may have a climate and living conditions similar to those of the United States. Unless an insurance company has an organization and representatives in another country, it may not be able to get full information about applicants, and practical difficulties may arise in settling claims. Policies are freely issued to persons who plan to be abroad temporarily, provided they do not contemplate visiting crisis areas or making an extended stay in tropical countries. A small but growing number of American and Canadian companies do business in foreign countries and use special premium rates to account for the different mortality rates.

Habits

The term *habits*, for underwriting purposes, refers to the use of alcohol and drugs. The company is concerned about an applicant's habitual use of alcohol because of the impairment of judgment and reactions during intoxication; it is concerned about the use of drugs because of the effect on the applicant's health and behavior. Of course, prolonged immoderate use of alcohol may also be harmful to a person's health.

An insurance company is not concerned about a prospective insured who uses alcoholic beverages in moderate amounts on social occasions. It is concerned about the applicant who drinks to the point of intoxication. All investigations of the effect of drinking on longevity indicate that there is substantial mortality increase among heavy drinkers. Successful completion of an in-house alcohol treatment program, combined with several years of total abstinence, will render prior abusers insurable on some basis with most life insurers. There is still a substantial relapse rate among abusers, however.

A person who is known to be a drug addict cannot obtain insurance on any basis. Even after treatment, a former drug user may be considered uninsurable for as long a period as 5 years and at best will be rated heavily for a long period of years because of the possibility of resuming the habit. For example, a former drug addict may be rated up to 200 percent of standard mortality for the first 5 or 10 years after taking the cure; a rating of 150 percent thereafter is not unusual.

Morals

It is surprising to many people that an insurance company would concern itself with an applicant's morals. It seems like an unnecessary intrusion into the applicant's personal life. Actually, the company is interested in the moral fiber of the applicant, not because it wants to sit in judgment, but because it has been clearly established that departures from the commonly accepted standards of ethical and moral conduct involve extra mortality risks.

Marital infidelity and other kinds of behavior that are considered immoral are regarded seriously, partly because they are frequently found in combination with other types of risky behavior, such as overindulgence in alcoholic beverages, gambling, and the use of drugs. The hazards to longevity are the impairment of health and the possibility of violence.

Unethical business conduct is another form of moral hazard. Companies do not care to insure persons who have a record of numerous bankruptcies, operate businesses that are just within the law, or have a general reputation for dishonesty. The companies fear the applicant's misrepresentation and concealment of material underwriting facts on the part. A person who is dishonest in general business dealings is not likely to make an exception for insurance companies, which have always been prime targets for unscrupulous schemes.

Sex

The superior longevity of women is the basis for offering women life insurance coverage at lower premiums. It is also the basis for higher annuity premiums and lower benefits under life-income options for women. Under the 1980 CSO mortality table—sex distinct—males face a higher probability of dying during the late teens and early twenties than between ages 28 and 30. Females do not yet show elevated rates for the early adult years. Suicide, drug overdose, AIDS, and auto accidents are rising causes of death among young men and women.

Plan of Insurance

The plan of insurance is taken into account because policies differ not only as to the amount at risk but also as to mortality rates. All other things being equal, the smaller the amount at risk, the more liberal the underwriting standards of the company. Thus companies tend to be somewhat more liberal in underwriting single premium and limited payment policies, particularly when the extra mortality from a known impairment is not expected to be felt until middle or later life.

The higher initial premium discourages antiselection in connection with single premium and limited payment policies. The amount of antiselection is believed to be particularly great in connection with term insurance. The plan of insurance can be especially important in the consideration of substandard risks.

Economic Status

In the eyes of the law every person has an unlimited insurable interest in his or her own life. Thus the burden of preventing overinsurance is placed on the insurance company. The company carefully investigates the applicant's financial status in order to make sure that family and business circumstances justify the amount of insurance applied for and carried in all companies. This investigation also reveals whether the applicant's income bears a reasonable relationship to the amount of insurance applied for. The company is interested not only in preventing too much insurance on the life of the applicant but also in keeping the insurance in force once issued.

Aviation Activities

In the early days of aviation, any form of flying was considered to be so hazardous — and rare — that the risk was either excluded altogether (through an exclusion clause) or made subject to a substantial extra premium. As technical developments and improvements in pilot skills reduced the hazards of flying, underwriting restrictions were gradually relaxed. Today, the risk has been reduced to such a low level and air travel has become so common that companies do not consider it necessary to impose any underwriting restrictions on passenger travel on any type of nonmilitary aircraft, whether it is a commercial airliner, a company plane, or a personal aircraft. Furthermore, no occupational rating or restriction is applied to crew members on regularly scheduled commercial aircraft.

The treatment of private pilots depends on the person's age, experience, training, and amount of flying. For example, most companies will treat as a standard risk an applicant between the ages of 27 and 60 who has at least 100 hours of pilot experience and does not fly more than 200 hours per year. A person who flies between 200 and 400 hours annually might be charged an extra premium of $3 per $1,000; flying in excess of 1,400 hours per year might involve an extra premium of $5 per $1,000. An applicant under age 27 who is otherwise qualified as a standard risk might be charged an extra premium of $5 per $1,000. Credits are commonly allowed for advanced training, such as attaining the Instrument Flight Rated (IFR) designation. The underwriting treatment of a crew member of a military aircraft depends on the applicant's age and type of duty. Service with combat aircraft is regarded the least favorably, as one would naturally suppose. Accidental death benefit riders often exclude aviation deaths if the insured was the pilot or crew member of any type of aircraft.

When there is an indication that the applicant will be involved in any aeronautical activity that might present a special hazard, the applicant is usually required to complete a supplementary form that gives the company full details of past, present, and probable future aviation activities.

In recent years there has been a proliferation of flying in ultralight aircraft, for example, which are not nearly as regulated as regular aircraft. Based on mortality experience to date, this activity requires ratings in the range of $5 or more per $1,000.

In the absence of a specific restriction, all basic policies cover the aviation hazard in full. In other words, there is no presumption that the hazard is not covered or is subject to a limitation of liability. It is only when the company is put on notice, usually through the applicant's own disclosure, that an unusual aviation hazard exists that it takes any special underwriting action.

Avocation

Certain avocations are sufficiently hazardous to justify an extra premium, at least under given circumstances. Among the avocations that may entail an extra premium are automobile, motorcycle, scooter, and speedboat racing; sky diving, skin diving (to depths over 50 feet); and mountain climbing. Most of these avocations involve a flat extra premium of $3.50 to $10.00 per $1,000. An extra premium of $3.00 (or more) per $1,000 is required for hang gliding.

Military Service

For more than 100 years—at least as far back as the Civil War—American life insurance companies have taken special underwriting cognizance of the extra mortality risk associated with applicants engaged in or facing military service during a period of armed conflict. The underwriting action has taken three principal forms: outright rejection of the applicant, limitation on the face amount of insurance issued, or the attachment of a so-called war clause that limits the insurer's obligation to return of premiums, less dividends, with interest, if the insured dies under circumstances as defined in the war clause.

The use of a war clause has been the most common method of dealing with the extra hazard of military or naval service. Some companies have also used a "status" clause, which limits the insurer's obligation to return of premium if the insured should die while in military service outside the territorial boundaries of the United States, whether or not the cause of death can be attributed to military service. Other companies have used a rider, referred to as a "results" war clause, which limits the insurer's obligation only if the insured's death is the result of military service. While regarded as more liberal to the insured than the status clause, this provision limits liability even though the insured is no longer in a war zone at the time of death. Most companies have been willing to waive these clauses for an appropriate extra premium.

War clauses were widely if not universally used during both World Wars (especially World War II) in policies that were issued to persons of military age. After the cessation of hostilities, the clauses were generally revoked by the insurance companies without request from the insureds. During the Korean Conflict, war clauses were again inserted in policies that were issued to young men facing military service. With the termination of hostilities, use of the clauses was again discontinued, and such clauses in outstanding policies were voluntarily cancelled by the companies.

With the American involvement in Vietnam, life insurance companies were again confronted with the problem of assessing the risk in military service. There was no consensus among the companies as to the best approach to the problem, and a variety of practices were followed. One approach used by a number of companies was to refuse to write any coverage on military personnel at the lower ranks but to issue insurance in normal amounts to all other military persons, attaching a "results" type of war clause to policies written. Generally applications were not accepted on persons in combat units or on orders to combat zones.

The American-led action to expel the Iraqi military presence from Kuwait triggered the most recent challenge to the industry's risk classification practices. Once again, with the exception of the general demise of the war exclusion clause,[5] company practices were characterized by a lack of uniformity. During the military buildup, while some companies continued to issue unrestricted insurance, others sought to withdraw from the sale of insurance to military personnel in or under orders to report to the Persian Gulf. These companies cited their long-standing philosophies of not insuring *any* applicant (civilian or military) residing in or traveling to areas of political instability. Others simply defended their practice based on the extra risk of military duty in the Persian Gulf. However, what differentiated the Persian Gulf conflict in terms of its impact on insurer practices was the significant role of political pressure. Faced with the avowed threat by a number of state insurance department commissioners to label companies as unpatriotic in press conferences and to suspend their licenses for discriminatory practices (even companies described above who maintained nondiscriminatory restrictions on military or civilian applicants in areas of political instability), companies generally provided such coverage with normal restrictions on insurance face amounts.

NOTES

1. That this principle is being observed in practice is evidenced by the fact that approximately 90 percent of the applicants for ordinary insurance in the United States are currently being accepted at standard rates. Only 3 percent are declined, the remaining 6 to 7 percent being insured at substandard rates.
2. For the industry as a whole, an excessive number of rejections deprives the insurable public of a valuable economic service and could give rise to demands for governmental intervention.
3. Contrary to the general impression, a normal tracing on an electrocardiogram cannot be accepted as conclusive proof of the nonexistence of a heart irregularity since the valves, and even the muscles, of the heart may be defective without affecting the transmission of the electrical impulses recorded on the electrocardiogram.
4. The urinalysis is considered to be such a significant diagnostic procedure that the medical examiner is required to certify as to the authenticity of the specimen; for certain combinations of age and amount of insurance, the specimen may have to be forwarded to the home office for chemical analysis and microscopic examination.
5. A number of companies maintained war exclusion clauses on their accidental death benefit and premium-waiver-for-disability provisions.

22

Selection and Classification of Risks (Part 2)

Dan M. McGill
Revised by Jeremy S. Holmes and James F. Winberg

The preceding chapter reviewed the type of information an insurance company's underwriting department needs when considering an application for insurance. This chapter briefly describes the sources from which it obtains this information. Much of it comes from more than one source. This gives the company the means of verifying information that it considers critical to the underwriting decision and serves as a deterrent to collusion or fraud by any of the parties to the transaction.

SOURCES OF INFORMATION

The Agent

In a real sense, a company's field force is the foundation of the selection process. The other parts of the selection mechanism can go into operation only after the field force has acted. The home office can exercise its underwriting judgment only on the risks submitted by the agents and brokers. A company's overall selection process can be no stronger than its agency force. If agents submit consistently good business, the underwriting results will be favorable; if they submit consistently below-average risks, the underwriting results will be no better.

Most companies give their agents explicit instructions about the types of risks that will be acceptable and those that will be unacceptable, and they instruct the agents to solicit only those risks they believe to be eligible under the company's underwriting rules. Where eligibility for insurance is doubtful in any way, some companies, in order to save unnecessary expense and trouble, require the agent to submit a preliminary statement setting forth the facts of the case and the grounds upon which the doubt as to insurability is based. Some companies require a preliminary statement in all cases where an application for insurance in any company has been declined, postponed, or accepted at other than standard rates.

The agent is asked to supply a variety of information in the certificate, the details varying with the company. The information typically includes the following: how long and how well the agent has known the applicant; an estimate of the applicant's net worth and annual income; the applicant's existing and pending insurance, including any plans for the lapse or surrender of existing insurance; whether the applicant sought the insurance or whether the application was the result of solicitation by the agent; and whether the application came through another agent or broker.

The degree of selection exercised at the field level depends on the integrity and reliability of the agents and brokers. There is clearly some selection involved, since self-interest would cause the agent not to solicit insurance from persons who—because of obvious physical impairments, moral deficiencies, or unacceptable occupations—manifestly could not meet the underwriting standards of the company. Beyond that, the amount of selection practiced by the agent is rather limited. Since the agent's compensation depends on the amount of insurance he or she sells, the motive exists to submit any application, even though it is borderline, that stands a chance of being accepted. Hence the responsibility for applying the company's underwriting standards falls to the home office underwriters, who do not labor under the same conflicts of interest.

The agent is usually the only representative of the company who sees applicants face-to-face and can make any visual assessment. If there is anything unusual about the applicant that requires an explanation, it is up to the agent to convey that information to the home office. For example, a person whose weight is high for the given age and height could be very muscular rather than obese. The agent can include this information with the report that accompanies the application.

Experienced agents know what types of additional information the home office underwriters are likely to request when the application reveals specific health problems. These agents can expedite the process by asking for the supplemental reports at the same time the application is completed. Otherwise, the reports will not be generated until the home office staff has made a preliminary evaluation of the case and forwarded a request to the agent for the needed information. In some cases, the first supplemental report triggers a request for additional supplemental reports.

The home office evaluation is usually very expeditious if all the information needed to make the evaluation accompanies the application. The time needed to approve, reject, or rate the case can be extended by months if there is difficulty in obtaining reports, such as attending physician statements.

Another advantage that some experienced agents have is a reputation with the home office underwriters for thoroughness, accuracy, and attention to detail in furnishing applications and supporting documents. This reputation can benefit applicants who are on the borderline between classifications and can be rated either way. They may get the benefit of the lower premium class because of their agent's reputation. Borderline cases from agents who always argue with the home office evaluation and send applications with less than complete information are more likely to be classified under the higher premium category when it is strictly a judgment call.

The Applicant

Much of the information a company needs to underwrite a case is supplied by the applicant. This information is contained in the application, which constitutes an important part of the offer and acceptance process and will become part of the contract if the policy is issued. Application blanks vary in their content and design, but they usually consist of two parts—the first containing nonmedical questions and the second including questions to be asked by the medical examiner. (Many companies permit the agent to ask the medical questions subject to age and amount limitations under "nonmedical" programs, which are discussed later in this chapter.)

Statements made by the applicant in the first part of the application cover the particulars of identification, such as name, address, former and prospective places of residence, and place and date of birth. If the applicant has recently moved, including previous places of residence enables the company, through reporting services, to interview the applicant's former acquaintances. (The importance of obtaining the correct date of birth was explained in the previous chapter.)

Additional questions in the first part of the application relate to the applicant's occupation, including any changes within the last 5 years or any contemplated changes of occupation; aviation activities other than passenger travel on regularly scheduled airlines (if there is any unusual aviation hazard, details must be provided in a supplementary form); and the possibility of foreign residence. The application also elicits information about the applicant's insurance history including details of all insurance already in force, as well as declinations and other insurance company actions of underwriting significance.

The foregoing information—together with a statement of the amount of insurance applied for, the plan upon which it is to be issued, the names of the policy beneficiary and policyowner, and the respective rights of the insured, beneficiary, and policyowner as to control of the policy—completes the first part of the application. This section is usually filled out by the agent on behalf of the applicant, who must sign it and certify the correctness of the information. The applicant's signature is generally witnessed by the agent.

The answers to questions in the second part of the application normally must be recorded in the medical examiner's handwriting, and the applicant must sign the form to attest to the completeness and accuracy of its contents. This part of the application asks several groups of related questions. The first group seeks the details of the applicant's health record, including illnesses, injuries, and surgical operations, usually within the last 10 years. The applicant is also required to give the name of every physician or practitioner consulted within a specified period of time (usually the last 5 years) in connection with any ailment whatsoever. The second group of questions elicits information about the applicant's present physical condition. Another group of questions inquires about the applicant's use of alcohol and drugs, and there are questions about the applicant's family history.

The Medical Examiner

In addition to recording the answers to part 2 of the application, the medical examiner is required to file a separate report or certificate, which accompanies the application but is not seen by the applicant. The first portion of the report contains a description of the applicant's physical characteristics, which not only provides useful underwriting information but also guards against substituting a healthy person for an unhealthy applicant in the medical examination. Some companies ask the examiner to review the applicant's driver's license or other form of identification to establish conclusive identification. The examiner is also usually asked to indicate whether the applicant looks older than the age stated.

The basic purpose of the medical examiner's report is to transmit the findings of the physical examination. The medical examiner's comments are specifically required regarding any abnormalities of the applicant's arteries or veins, heart, respiratory system, nervous system, abdomen, genitourinary system, ears, eyes, and skin. The examiner also reports the urinalysis result, certifies that the urine examined is authentic, describes the applicant's build, and indicates the applicant's blood pressure.

In the final section of the report, the examiner may be requested to indicate any knowledge or suspicion that the applicant abuses alcohol or narcotics or has any moral deficiencies that would affect his or her insurability. The examiner is also asked about the prior patient/doctor relationship that has existed between the two of them, if any.

The medical examiner's report is considered to be the property of the insurance company and is carefully safeguarded at all times.

Attending Physicians

Attending physicians are a source of information on applicants who have undergone medical treatment prior to applying for insurance. When it appears that the information in the attending physician's files might influence the insurance company's underwriting decision, such information is sought as a matter of routine, only, however, after the application has been signed because it gives the insurer consent to seek medical and personal information.   Insurance companies have enjoyed a remarkable degree of cooperation from the medical profession regarding inquiries of this nature, with physicians normally providing all of the relevant information in their files.   However, their response is not always prompt, and their delay suspends the policy issuance process. To expedite the physician's response, insurers usually send a check along with the letter of inquiry to cover the physician's expenses incurred to supply the information.

Inspection Report

Insurance companies attempt to verify all information from the previously mentioned sources, generally in one of two ways. The first method is through telephone interviews conducted by insurance company staff. This method allows the insurer to structure the questions to best serve its purposes. The second alternative is to employ the services of an independent reporting agency. The unique advantage of these independent investigations is that they provide an evaluation of the applicant by a source having no interest in the outcome of the application.

The insurer's home office or its local agency may make the request for an inspection report. In either case, the report is filed directly with the insurance company's home office. Under provisions of the Fair Credit Reporting Act the applicant has the right to review the contents of the report at the offices of the agency that produced it.

The thoroughness of the inspection depends on the amount of insurance involved. When the amount of insurance is not large, the report is rather brief, commenting in a general way on the applicant's health, habits, finances, environment, and reputation. When a large amount has been applied for, the report tends to be comprehensive. It reflects the results of interviews with the applicant's neighbors, employer, banker, business associates, and others.   The inspection focuses particularly on the applicant's business and personal ethics.

The report calls attention to any bankruptcies and fire losses, and it comments on the applicant's use of alcohol, drugs, and other departures from "normal" social behavior. The inspection also occasionally uncovers physical impairments that were not revealed in the medical examiner's report.

The Medical Information Bureau

A final source of information is the Medical Information Bureau (MIB). This organization is a clearing house for confidential medical data on applicants for life insurance. The information is reported and maintained in code symbols to help preserve its confidentiality.

Companies that are members of the Bureau are expected to report any impairments designated on the official list. The designated impairments are related primarily to the applicant's physical condition but also include hereditary characteristics and addiction to alcohol and narcotics. If they have a bearing on insurability, any suspicious tendencies revealed in an examination are reported in order to bring the matter to the notice of all companies using the Bureau's records. All impairments must be reported whether the company accepts, postpones, or declines the risk, or offers a modified plan of insurance. In no event does the company report its underwriting decision to the Bureau.

A company normally screens all of its applicants against the MIB file of reported impairments. If the company finds an impairment and wants further details, it must submit its request through the MIB, but only after it first conducts its own complete investigation from all known sources. The company that reported the impairment is not obligated to supply further information, but if it agrees to do so, it provides the requested information through the MIB.

It should be emphasized that there is no basis for the widespread belief that a person who is recorded in the MIB files cannot obtain insurance at standard rates. The information contained therein is treated like underwriting data from any other source and, in the final analysis, may be outweighed by favorable factors. In many cases, it will enable a company to take favorable action, since favorable medical test results are reported as well as unfavorable ones. In any case, the rules of the MIB stipulate that a company cannot take unfavorable underwriting action *solely* on the basis of the information in the MIB files. In other words, the company must be in possession of other unfavorable underwriting facts or else determine through its own channels of investigation that the condition of impairment recorded in the MIB files is substantial enough to warrant an unfavorable decision.

CLASSIFICATION OF RISKS

Once all available underwriting information about an application for insurance has been assembled, the data must be evaluated and a decision reached as to whether the applicant is to be accepted at standard rates, placed in one of the various substandard classifications, or rejected entirely. This is clearly the focus of the vitally important selection process. Ideally the evaluation and classification system used by a company should (1) accurately measure the effect of each of the factors, favorable and unfavorable, that can be expected to influence an applicant's longevity; (2) assess the combined impact of multiple factors, including the situations in which the factors are conflicting; (3) produce consistently equitable results; and (4) be simple and relatively inexpensive to operate.

The Judgment Method of Rating

The earliest system used in the United States was the "judgment method" of rating. Under this method routine cases were processed with a minimum of consideration by clerks trained in the review of applications, and doubtful or borderline cases were resolved by supervisors relying on their experience and general impressions. The method is still used by many companies, particularly the smaller ones, and in all insurance companies, the element of judgment plays an important role.

The judgment method of rating functions very effectively when there is only one unfavorable factor to consider or when the decision is simply one of accepting the applicant at standard rates or rejecting the application altogether. It leaves something to be desired when there are multiple unfavorable factors (offset perhaps by some favorable factors) or when the risk, if it does not qualify for standard insurance, must be fitted into the proper substandard classification. To overcome the weaknesses of the judgment method of rating, the *numerical rating system,* devised over a half century ago, is used today by most insurers.[1]

The Numerical Rating System

The numerical rating system is based on the principle that a large number of factors enter into the composition of a risk and that the impact of each of these factors on the longevity of the risk can be determined by a statistical study of lives possessing that factor. It assumes that the average risk accepted by a company has a value of 100 percent and that each of the factors that enter into the risk can be expressed as a percentage of the whole. Favorable factors are assigned *negative* values, called *credits,* while unfavorable factors are assigned *positive* values, called *debits.* The summation of the debits and credits, added to or deducted from the par value of 100, represents the numerical value of the risk.

Assigning Weights to Risk Factors

Naturally, it would be impossible to assign weights to all the factors that might influence a risk. In practice values are generally assigned to the following 10 factors: (1) build, (2) physical condition, (3) medical history, (4) family history, (5) occupation, (6) aviation and avocation, (7) residence, (8) habits, (9) morals, and (10) plan of insurance.

The values assigned to the various factors are derived from mortality studies among groups of people possessing those characteristics or, in some cases, from estimates of what such mortality studies might be expected to show. For example, if the mortality experience of a group of insured lives with a particular medical history has been found to be 135 percent of that among all standard risks, a debit (addition) of 35 percentage points might be assigned to that medical history. The degrees of extra mortality cited in connection with many of the impairments discussed in the preceding chapter are the basis for the debits under the numerical rating system.

Hypothetical Case

The operation of the system can be illustrated with the following hypothetical case. The applicant is a married man, aged 32, living in Philadelphia, Pennsylvania, with two children. He is 6 feet 1 inch tall and weighs 290 pounds. He is in good physical condition except that, in addition to being overweight, his build is unfavorable—that is, his expanded chest measurement is one inch less than the girth of his abdomen (see chapter 21). His personal health record shows no operations, broken bones, ulcers, or other ailments that would have an adverse effect on longevity. His family is long-lived, and the family history reveals no tuberculosis, insanity, cardiac conditions, malignancies, or diabetes. He has been employed for several years as a warehouseman in an industrial plant. His habits and morals are good. The plan of insurance is 20-payment whole life insurance.

The company might evaluate the facts as follows: The applicant is overweight, which calls for a debit of 50 points according to table 21-1 (see chapter 21). The unfavorable build (girth greater than chest expanded) is the basis for an additional debit of 20 points. The favorable family history receives a credit of 15 points, and the plan of insurance, 20-payment whole life, calls for an additional credit of 10 points. The residence is a neutral factor (only debits are assigned to residence, and debits are usually assessed only for a foreign or tropical residence). Regarding habits and morals, there is no credit for good behavior, only debits for bad behavior. The occupation is also a neutral factor with no debits or credits. Thus the debits add up to 70 points and the credits add up to only 25. Hence the numerical value of the risk is 145.

The analysis is summarized below:

Base = 100

Factor	Debit	Credit
Weight: overweight	50	—
Physical condition: favorable	—	—
Build: unfavorable	20	—
Family history: superior	—	15
Occupation: favorable	—	—
Residence: normal	—	—
Habits and morals: favorable	—	—
Plan of insurance: 20-payment whole life	—	10
Total	70	25

Rating = 145

It should be noted that credits are generally not allowed when there are other ratable physical impairments or debits for blood pressure or other cardiovascular-renal impairments.

The ratings obtained by this method may go as low as 75 and as high as 500 or more. The ratings that fall between 75 and 125 are usually classified as standard, although some companies, especially those that do not write substandard insurance, may include risks that produce a rating of 130 (or if the applicant is below age 30, even 140) in the standard category. Risks that produce ratings beyond the standard limit are either assigned to appropriate substandard classifications or declined. The risk is rejected if the company does not write substandard insurance or if the rating is higher than that eligible for the highest substandard classification. Many companies are willing to accept risks that indicate a mortality rate up to 500 percent of normal.[2] Most companies feel that assessing mortality beyond 500 percent will yield results too erratic to price accurately.

Substandard Classifications

As will be explained in the following chapter, the broad category of substandard risks is subdivided into several classifications, each with its own scale of premiums. There may be as few as three or as many as 12 substandard classifications. The full significance of the earlier statements concerning the balancing of risks within each classification should now be apparent. With a spread of 50 percentage points in the standard classification, which comprises the great bulk of accepted risks, it is vitally important that each risk that falls within the 100 to 125 range be balanced (in percentage points) by one that falls in the 75 to 100 category. Otherwise, the average mortality for the entire group will exceed the norm of 100. With a rating of 145, the hypothetical case illustrated above would have fallen into a substandard classification.

The numerical rating system follows much the same procedure as systems that judge a risk without the benefit of numerical values. The same factors are considered, and the final decision is based on the relationship of the various favorable and unfavorable features of the risk. The numerical method, however, sets up objective standards that assist in the final valuation of the risk and allow for greater consistency of treatment. Lay underwriters can process all applications other than those requiring detailed medical analysis and the inevitable borderline cases. This not only expedites the handling of cases but also helps to hold down the expense of the selection process. Underwriters can consult with their home office medical directors on complex medical situations.

Criticisms against the System

Various criticisms, however, have been leveled against the numerical rating system. It has been alleged, for example, that (1) the system is too arbitrary, (2) there are many impairments concerning which knowledge is too limited to permit the assignment of numerical values, (3) the interrelated factors are non-additive in so many cases that it nullifies the value of the numerical process, and (4) too many minor debits and credits are taken into account in evaluating risk. Supporters of the system recognize its flaws but feel that it is still superior to any other method that has been devised. They stress that the procedure must be—and, in practice, is—applied with common sense. They admit that there are many impairments whose effect on longevity cannot be expressed numerically, but they point out that this constitutes a handicap under any method. They argue that under any system, the cases with interrelated impairments require the expert judgment of the insurer's medical staff and actuarial staff. Whether too many debits and credits are taken into account is a matter of opinion, of course; some companies have modified the numerical rating system to take only major impairments into account.

NONMEDICAL INSURANCE

In citing the medical examiner as a source of underwriting information, the preceding section implies that a medical examination is mandatory with any life insurance application. That is not the case.

A substantial portion of all new insurance is written without a medical examination. For example, neither group nor industrial life insurance ordinarily requires a medical examination. Furthermore, an increasing amount of ordinary life insurance is being sold without a medical examination. While any type of insurance sold without a medical examination might logically be called *nonmedical insurance*, the expression usually to refers to ordinary insurance sold in that manner.

History of Nonmedical Insurance

Nonmedical life insurance is not a recent innovation. The first life insurance was sold without medical examination. In the early days of life insurance in England, each applicant appeared before the directors of the company, who made their decision largely on the basis of personal appearance. Personal inspection by the company directors was later supplemented by recommendations of the applicant's friends and associates and eventually a medical examination was introduced. The medical examination quickly established its usefulness and was soon regarded as essential.

About 1886 companies in Great Britain began to experiment with nonmedical underwriting. To protect the companies against adverse selection, the policies, which were limited in amount, contained liens during the early years of the contract, or they were issued at advanced premium rates. Some companies offered only double endowments on a nonmedical basis.

Nonmedical underwriting as it is practiced today, however, began in 1921 in Canada. The immediate motivation for its development was the shortage of medical examiners, particularly in the rural areas. The desire to reduce expenses on the predominantly small policies issued in Canada at that time was also a strong influence.

Nonmedical underwriting spread to the United States around 1925 after the success of the Canadian experiment seemed assured. It gained increasing acceptance during the 1930s as American experiences proved favorable and enjoyed its greatest growth when a shortage of medical examiners developed during World War II. The practice of nonmedical underwriting is firmly entrenched today in both Canada and the United States.

Underwriting Safeguards

Because nonmedical insurance is subject to higher than normal mortality, at least for the first several policy years, insurance companies have adopted certain underwriting safeguards.

Limiting the Amount of Insurance

Perhaps the most important safeguard is a limit on the amount that will be made available to any one applicant. As explained more fully below, the limit is determined by the extra mortality that can be expected from eliminating the medical examination and the savings in selection expenses that will be available to absorb the extra mortality costs.

In the early days of nonmedical insurance, the limit was placed at $1,000. When the extra mortality turned out to be lower than expected, the limits were gradually raised. Today most companies will provide up to $100,000 on a nonmedical basis, subject to appropriate age restrictions, while many will issue up to $200,000 or $250,000 on that basis. The limit generally varies by age groups; the largest amounts are available to the younger age groups. A few companies are willing to write up to $500,000 at the younger ages.

The foregoing limits are for any one application for nonmedical insurance. Some companies will issue additional amounts, subject to an aggregate limit, after a specified period of time has elapsed. Most companies are willing to reinstate the original limits for any insured who, subsequent to obtaining one or more policies on a nonmedical basis, undergoes a medical examination satisfactory to the company. In other words, all nonmedical insurance issued to the person prior to the medical examination will be disregarded and additional amounts made available up to the applicable limits.

Limiting the Age of Issue

A second safeguard companies impose is a limit on the ages at which insurance will be issued. Studies have shown that the extra mortality resulting from waiving the medical examination increases with age and after a point will exceed any savings in selection expense. The point at which the extra mortality costs will exceed the expense savings is obviously a function of the underwriting age limit, but most companies place it around age 45 or 50. There is usually no lower age limit; most companies offer nonmedical insurance down to age zero.

Limiting Insurance to Standard Risks

A third safeguard is the general limitation of nonmedical insurance to standard risks. As a broad class, substandard risks must submit to medical examinations. Exceptions are commonly made, however, for risks that are substandard because of an occupational, aviation, or avocational hazard.

Relying on Other Sources of Information

A final safeguard, which is more general and pervasive in nature, is the intensive cultivation of the sources of underwriting information other than the medical examiner. Insurance companies place a heavier burden on the applicant, agent, and inspector to offset in some measure the absence of a medical examiner's findings. The application form used in connection with nonmedical insurance is elaborate, containing all the questions usually contained in an application blank as well as those normally asked by a medical examiner. A urine specimen and blood profile may be required for home office analysis. If the applicant has recently been under the care of a physician, a statement may be necessary from the attending physician (at the expense of the company). If any adverse medical information is revealed by the applicant's statement, the inspection report, or other source, the company may demand a complete medical examination.

A particularly heavy responsibility is placed on the agent, with great reliance on the agent's judgment and integrity. Agents may submit nonmedical applications only from applicants who appear to meet the company's underwriting requirements from a physical, medical, occupational, and moral standpoint. The agent must elicit from the applicant and accurately document most of the information that a medical examiner would seek. A detailed agent's certificate that records the agent's underwriting impressions of the applicant is also required. It is understandable that the privilege of submitting nonmedical business is not bestowed indiscriminately on the field force.

Inspection reports are sometimes ordered to supplement the larger nonmedical insurance applications, even though such information would not be requested for medically underwritten cases for the same or larger amounts of coverage.

Economics of Nonmedical Insurance

Several advantages are associated with nonmedical insurance. It lessens the demands on the time and talents of the medical profession, it eliminates the delays and inconvenience connected with medical examinations, and it removes one of the greatest psychological barriers to the sale of insurance. Important as these advantages are, insurers could not enjoy them if nonmedical insurance did not rest on a solid economic foundation. It must justify itself on a dollars-and-cents basis.

As mentioned earlier, nonmedical insurance is subject to a higher rate of mortality than medically examined business. This extra mortality is believed to stem from (1) impairments known to the applicant but deliberately concealed and (2) impairments not known to the applicant that could have been discovered by a medical examination. This extra mortality can be measured and expressed as a dollar amount per $1,000 of insurance.

The procedure customarily used to measure the extra mortality is to compare the mortality experience on nonmedical business with the mortality at the same ages, years of issue, and durations on business that was subject to a medical examination. This does not give a direct answer to the question of what the mortality on the nonmedical applicants would have been had they been selected by medical examination, since the two groups may not be comparable in all respects. For example, they might differ as to ratio of males to females, income level, and size of policies. Nevertheless, this method is the best available and is deemed satisfactory.

Studies reveal that most of the extra mortality occurs during the first 10 years after issue, although some extra mortality is observable up to 15 years after the policy is issued. The disparity between nonmedical and medical mortality increases with age of issue, both in absolute amount and as a percentage of the base mortality rate. This seems to indicate that up to a point at least, the importance and effectiveness of the medical examination grow greater with age.

Extra death claims are offset by the savings in medical examiners' fees and incidental home office expenses, less the increase in expenditures for inspection reports and attending physicians' statements. This net saving, it should be noted, is realized on *every* application that does not involve a medical examination, while the extra mortality is experienced only on those policies that remain in force until they become claims—a much smaller number because of lapses and surrenders. The savings in selection expenses are expressed as an amount per policy and range from $30 to $100.

Once the extra mortality per $1,000 and the expense savings per policy are known, it is a matter of simple arithmetic to determine the proper limits for nonmedical insurance. If at ages below 30, the extra mortality cost per $1,000 is $0.75 and the expense savings per policy is assumed to be $100, the company could safely offer about $133,000 of nonmedical insurance to applicants under 30 ($100 ÷ 0.75 = $133 rounded to nearest whole number). With the same expense savings and an extra mortality cost of $1.50 per $1,000 at ages 30 to 34, the proper limit for persons in that age group would be $67,000 ($100 ÷ 1.50 = $67 rounded). By the same logic, the limit for applicants aged 35 to 39 might be about $30,000. Thus the need for age limits and the equity of variable limits are apparent.

In practice, companies are inclined to offer larger amounts of nonmedical insurance than the above figures suggest. While the amount made available to any one applicant might seem excessive, all applicants do not request the maximum. Since the company's objective is to break even on its nonmedical business in the aggregate, it may safely set its limits higher than the precise relationship between the expected extra mortality and expense savings would support.

Furthermore, at ages under 30, the absolute rate of mortality is so low and the probability of finding impairments on examination so small that the nonmedical rules can be greatly relaxed. A particular company may also set its nonmedical limits on the basis of its own mortality experience and expense assumptions or in response to competitive factors. The increased use of blood and urine screening tests also allows for increased nonmedical limits.

Special Branches of Nonmedical Insurance

There are certain special situations in which policies may be issued on a nonmedical basis even when the company does not follow a general practice of issuing nonmedical policies. Three of the most common instances are discussed in this subsection.

Policyowner Nonmedical

Most companies are willing to issue insurance up to a stated limit on the basis of the applicant's declaration of good health if, within a short period prior to issuance—such as 3 to 6 months—standard insurance has been obtained from the company on the basis of a satisfactory medical examination. The reasoning behind this practice, of course, is that the policyowner's health is not likely to have deteriorated within such a short period of time, and any serious affliction would probably be apparent to the agent.

Some companies have extended this privilege to policyowners who apply for additional insurance within a much longer period, such as one to 5 years. Under such circumstances, however, the applicant is required to bring physical and medical histories up to date, and the case is underwritten on the basis of both the old and the new information. The general experience under this type of nonmedical insurance has not been very favorable and indicates some adverse selection among applicants.

This category of insurance without medical examination goes under the name of *policyowner nonmedical,* since it is limited to applicants who are already policyowners of the company.

Guaranteed Issue

One of the important contractual agreements under which retirement benefits are provided to superannuated employees is the individual contract pension trust. Under this arrangement, the benefits are provided through retirement annuity contracts or retirement income contracts that are purchased by the employer, through a trustee, for each of the employees who are eligible to participate in the pension plan.

Traditionally if retirement income contracts were used, each employee had to furnish evidence of insurability—a satisfactory medical examination. Current practice, however, includes underwriting such plans on a nonmedical basis. In fact, the arrangement frequently goes beyond the conventional concepts of nonmedical insurance. If the *group* is acceptable, the insurance company dispenses with individual underwriting and agrees in advance to accept all applications for insurance up to a formula- determined limit. This practice is known as *guaranteed issue.* There is no underwriting beyond a screening of the group.

A higher than normal mortality is anticipated on these products. The mortality rate is higher than that associated with ordinary nonmedical insurance, not only because of the absence of individual underwriting but also because the age distribution of the employees is likely to be higher than that of normal nonmedical groups.

In order to offset the anticipated extra mortality under guaranteed issue plans, most companies pay lower than normal commissions and separately classify the policies for dividend purposes.

Paramedical Examination

Somewhere between the medical examination and nonmedical evidence is another alternative—the paramedical examination. This examination is conducted by nurses or other medical technicians and consists of securing basic examination from measurements: height, weight, blood pressure, pulse rate and waist measurement.

The chief advantages of paramedical examinations are their reduced cost compared to a physician's fees and their convenience for the client since most services offer traveling examiners. The paramedical examinations, however, do not include the heart and other detailed reports typically provided by an insurance medical examiner.

INSURABILITY OPTION

With all new policies except those issued on a substandard basis and short-duration term policies, most insurance companies are now offering an option that permits the policyowner, at stated intervals and below a specified age, to purchase specified amounts of additional insurance *without evidence* of insurability. The additional insurance need not be on the same plan as the basic policy to which the option is attached; the option is exercisable in favor of any standard whole life or other cash value insurance policies offered by the company. Premiums for the new insurance are payable at standard rates on the basis of the insured's attained age on the option date. If the original policy contains a waiver-of-premium provision and accidental death benefits, the new policies will, at the insured's option, contain the same features. If premiums are being waived on the original policy at the time an option for additional insurance is exercised, premiums on the new policy will be waived from the beginning (and will continue to be waived if the insured is totally disabled).

The options vary as to details, but the first provision of this type,[3] which was introduced in the 1950s and has served as a pattern for most of those introduced later, permitted the insured to purchase up to $10,000 of additional insurance at 3-year intervals beginning with the policy anniversary nearest the insured's 25th birthday and terminating with the anniversary nearest the insured's 40th birthday. Under current policies the amount of insurance that can be obtained on each specified policy anniversary is usually limited to some percentage of the original face amount up to a specified maximum dollar amount, such as $60,000. Some policies also specify an aggregate limit (for example, two times the original face amount) on the amount of coverage that can be purchased under this option without evidence of insurability. Option amounts vary from company to company but may be as high as $100,000 per exercise option with some insurers.

Some contracts also permit the purchase of additional insurance upon the insured's marriage or following the birth of the insured's first child or subsequent children. Some contracts even provide coverage automatically for 60 to 90 days after each option date.

The option is available only for an extra premium that varies, not in proportion to the number of option dates remaining, as might be supposed, but with the age of issue. The schedule of annual premiums charged for the option by one company begins at $0.50 per $1,000 at age 0 and increases to approximately $2.00 per $1,000 at age 37. These premiums reflect the company's estimate of the average amount of extra mortality that it will experience on policies issued without evidence of insurability and, from the standpoint of the insured, may be regarded as the cost of "insuring" his or her insurability. Premiums for the option are payable to the last anniversary at which it can be exercised—usually age 40—or to the end of the premium-paying period of the basic policy, whichever is earlier.

Many insurers also offer guaranteed insurance under cost-of-living adjustments that increase policy amounts based on rises in economic inflation indicators, such as the Consumer Price Index. The insured typically can accept or refuse this offer, but if the insured refuses, the provisions may terminate. Guaranteed insurance under cost-of-living adjustments is typically offered at 3-year intervals from the issue date of the policy.

INSURANCE AT EXTREMES OF AGE

Applications for insurance at both extremes of age must be carefully underwritten. In both cases, the basic obstacle is limited insurable interest—which, if not recognized, may lead to speculation and excessive mortality.

In some families there is a demand for juvenile insurance, and most companies will write insurance on the lives of very young children, even down to 15 days old. These insurers attempt to cope with the lack of insurable interest in three ways: (1) by limiting the coverage to amounts much smaller than those available to adults, particularly at the early ages, (2) by seeing that the insurance on the child bears a reasonable relationship to the amounts in force on the other members of the family, especially the breadwinner, and (3) by seeking a large volume of juvenile insurance applications to minimize adverse selection.

From the standpoint of the basic mortality risk, juvenile risks are very attractive. With the exception of the first few weeks after birth, the death rate is very low and does not begin to climb until around age 10. The death rate is high immediately after birth because of the hazards of childbirth to the child, congenital defects, and the naturally delicate physique of a newborn infant. This period of heavy mortality can be avoided by limiting coverage to children who have attained the age of one, 3, or perhaps 6 months. Family economic circumstances seem to have greater influence on mortality at the younger ages than later in life, which makes it necessary to inquire about family finances. In general, juvenile insurance is sold without a medical examination.

At the other extreme—that is, at the older ages—the lack of insurable interest is only one of the complicating factors. In the first place, the volume of insurance issued at ages above 70 or 75 is not large enough to yield predictable mortality results. The restricted demand for insurance at those ages reflects the high cost of the insurance, the general inability to satisfy the medical requirements, and the limited need for new insurance. In the second place, a high degree of adverse selection is associated with applications received at those ages. Low volume in itself is suggestive of adverse selection, but when it is accompanied by burdensome premium payments, the environment is even more conducive to adverse selection. This antiselection may be exercised by the insureds themselves, aware of a serious impairment, or by a third party, perhaps a relative, who seeks insurance on the life of an elderly person for speculative reasons. A third factor, related to the others, is the relative ineffectiveness of the medical examination for elderly people. A routine medical examination does not reveal many conditions of a degenerative nature that can materially shorten the life of the elderly applicant.

Estate tax law changes of the 1980s have led to a dramatic expansion of marketing life insurance, particularly joint-life and survivorship products to applicants of advanced age. This has resulted in the extension of insurable ages to 80 or 85 by some insurers.

NOTES

1. The system was developed in 1919 by Arthur H. Hunter and Dr. Oscar H. Rogers, actuary and medical director, respectively, of the New York Life Insurance Company. It is described in a paper by Hunter and Rogers, titled "The Numerical Method of

Determining the Value of Risks for Insurance" and published in the *Transactions of the Actuarial Society of America,* vol. XX, part II (1919).

2. Some companies are willing to accept risks that appear to be subject to mortality up to 1,000 percent of normal.

3. This option was first introduced by the Bankers Life Insurance Company of Des Moines, Iowa, under the name of guaranteed purchase option.

23

Insurance of Substandard Risks

Dan M. McGill
Revised by Jeremy S. Holmes and James F. Winberg

Using the numerical rating system or some other method of rating, an insurance company classifies certain risks as substandard. A group or classification of risks rated substandard is expected to produce a higher mortality than a group of normal lives. The group concept must be emphasized, since—as with insuring standard risks—there is no certainty about any one individual's longevity expectations. All calculations therefore are based on the anticipated average experience of a large number of individuals, and the experience of any one individual is merged into that of the group.

This is an elementary concept, but it needs to be reiterated in any consideration of substandard insurance, involving, as it does, extra cost to or restricted benefits for policyowner or beneficiary. It is commonly supposed that if an individual is placed in a substandard classification and subsequently lives to a ripe old age, the company erred in its treatment of the case. However, if 1,000 persons, each of whom is suffering from a particular physical impairment, are granted insurance, it is certain that the death rate among them will be greater than the death rate among a group of people the same age who are free from of any discernible impairments. To allow for the higher death rates that will certainly occur within the substandard group, the company must collect an extra premium from—or impose special terms on—all who are subject to the extra risk since it is not known which of the members of the group will be responsible for the extra mortality. It is not expected that every member of the group will survive for a shorter period than the normal life expectancy. In fact, it is a certainty that this will not be the case; it is known merely that a larger proportion of people in a normal group will attain normal life expectancy.

The fact that certain members of the impaired group reach old age is, therefore, no indication that an error was made in their cases. If they had paid no extra premium, a still higher premium would have been required from the others. Generally speaking, nothing could—or should—be refunded to members of a substandard group who live beyond the normal life expectancy, provided that the extra premiums charged (or other special terms imposed) were a true measure of the degree of extra hazard represented by the group.

INCIDENCE OF EXTRA RISK

If a group of substandard risks is to be fairly treated, the degree of extra mortality represented by the group and the approximate period in life when the extra mortality is likely to occur must both be known within reasonable limits. It makes a great deal of difference financially whether the extra claims are expected to occur primarily in early life, middle age, old age, or at a level rate throughout the individuals' lifetimes. If the extra mortality occurs during the early years of the policies when the amount at risk is relatively large, the burden on the company will be greater than if it occurs later when the amount at risk is relatively small. Hence, between two substandard groups representing the same aggregate amount of extra mortality, the group whose extra mortality is concentrated later in life should pay a smaller extra premium than the group whose extra mortality occurs earlier.

There are innumerable variations in the distribution of the extra risk among different classes of substandard risks. It is impractical, however, for companies to recognize all the many patterns of risk distribution. The majority of companies therefore proceed on the assumption that each substandard risk falls into one of three broad groups. In the first group, the additional hazard increases with age; in the second group, it remains approximately constant at all ages; in the third, it decreases with age.

Examples of each type of hazard are easy to find. High blood pressure presents an increasing hazard. Occupational hazards represent a constant hazard, as do certain types of physical defects. (Even though most constant hazards tend to increase somewhat with age, they are treated as if they remain constant.) Impairments attributable to past illnesses and surgical operations are hazards that decrease with time, although not all illnesses and operations fall into this category.

TREATMENT OF SUBSTANDARD RISKS

Several methods have been devised to provide insurance protection to people with impaired health. With the exception of the lien, most United States life insurance companies utilize all the available methods. In general, companies make an effort to adapt the method to the type of hazard represented by the impaired risk, but departures from theoretically correct risk treatment are frequently made for practical reasons.

Increase in Age

One method of treatment, widely used in the past and still favored by many companies for joint-and-survivor products, is to "rate up" the age of the applicant. Under this method, the applicant is assumed to be a number of years older than his or her real age, and the policy is written accordingly. The number of years older is usually determined by adding the amount estimated as necessary to provide for the extra mortality to the net premium for the applicant's actual age, and then finding the premium in the standard table that most closely matches that total, and deriving the rate-up from the standard age in the table. For example, assume the net level premium for an ordinary life contract issued at age 25 is $12.55 per $1,000. If a male applicant for such a contract, aged 25, should be placed in a substandard classification that is expected to produce an extra mortality equivalent to $3.67, the correct net premium for the applicant would be $16.22 per $1,000. The net level premium in the standard table closest to this amount is $16.43, which is the premium for age 33. Therefore the applicant is rated up 8 years and is thereafter treated in all respects as if he were 33 years of age. His policy would contain the same surrender and loan values and would be entitled to the same dividends, if any, as any other ordinary life contract issued at age 33.

This method of dealing with substandard risks is suitable only when the extra risk is a decidedly increasing one and will continue to increase indefinitely at a greater rate. Although few impairments give rise to such a consistent and rapid increase in the rate of mortality as provided in the rated-up age method, the method is considered to be appropriate for all types of substandard risks where the extra mortality, in general, increases with age.

The chief appeal of the method for the insurance company is its simplicity. Policies can be dealt with for all purposes as standard policies issued at the assumed age. No separate set of records is required; no special calculations of premium rates, cash and other surrender values, reserves, and dividends are involved. For the applicant, the method is attractive because the higher premium is accompanied by correspondingly higher surrender values and dividends (if participating). Thus a portion of each extra premium is refunded as a dividend, and another portion is applied to the accumulation of larger surrender values than would be available under a policy issued at the applicant's true age. If the policy is surrendered for cash, the additional cash value is equivalent to a refund of a portion of the extra premium paid. To protect themselves against the use of the surrender privilege for this purpose, some companies add a slight loading to the original extra premium.

Extra Percentage Tables

The most common method of dealing with risks that present an increasing hazard is to classify them into groups based on the expected percentage of standard mortality and to charge premiums that reflect the appropriate increase in mortality. The number of substandard classifications may vary from three to 12, depending to some extent on the degree of extra mortality the company is willing to underwrite. Some companies are unwilling to underwrite substandard groups whose average mortality is expected to exceed 200 percent of standard, and they usually establish three substandard classifications with expected average mortalities of 150, 175, and 200 percent, respectively. Table 23-1 shows a scale

TABLE 23-1
Scale of Substandard Classifications

Class	Mortality (Percent)	Class	Mortality (Percent)
1	125	6	250
2	150	7	275
3	175	8	300
4	200	10	350
5	225	12	400
		16	500

of substandard classifications widely used by companies offering coverage up to 500 percent of standard mortality.

In effect, a special mortality table reflecting the appropriate degree of extra mortality is prepared for each substandard classification, and a complete set of gross premium rates is computed for each classification. The gross premium rates at quinquennial ages quoted by one company for an ordinary life contract under substandard tables A, B, C, and D, are set forth in table 23-2. For purposes of comparison the rate for a standard risk at each quinquennial age is also given.

TABLE 23-2
Illustrative Gross Annual Premium Rates at Quinquennial Ages for Ordinary Life Contract under Substandard Tables A, B, C, and D

Age	Rate For Standard Risks	Substandard Tables			
		A 125 Percent	B 150 Percent	C 175 Percent	D 200 Percent
15	$14.46	$15.74	$16.67	$17.53	$18.37
20	16.15	17.62	18.67	19.68	20.63
25	18.21	19.90	21.15	22.33	23.45
30	20.81	22.82	24.33	25.75	27.12
35	24.14	26.56	28.41	30.19	31.00
40	28.45	31.38	33.70	35.93	38.07
45	34.01	37.59	40.50	43.32	46.04
50	41.31	45.69	49.40	52.99	56.48
55	50.99	56.41	61.11	65.71	70.22
60	64.03	70.74	76.73	82.67	88.54
65	81.82	90.08	97.69	105.34	112.97

Perhaps the most notable feature of these premiums is that they do not increase in proportion to the degree of extra mortality involved. The rates under substandard table D, for example, are not double the rates at which insurance is made available to standard risks. Neither are the rates under table B one-and-one-half times the standard rates. There is a twofold explanation of this apparent inconsistency. In the first place, the rates illustrated in table 23-2 are gross premium rates, and the amount of loading does not increase from one rate classification to the other, except for commissions and premium taxes but remains constant (with minor exceptions). In the second place, the percentage of extra mortality is computed on the basis of actual—rather than tabular—mortality. The premiums for standard risks are calculated on the basis of the 1980 CSO Table, which contains a considerable overstatement of mortality at the young and middle ages, but additions to standard premiums to arrive at the substandard rates reflect only the excess mortality for the substandard classifications over the actual standard mortality. Hence the rates for the substandard classifications are not proportionally greater than even the net premiums for the standard risks.

The extra mortality under the extra percentage method is relatively small at the early ages, unless the percentage of extra mortality is high, since the normal (or base rate) mortality at such ages is small. As the base death rate increases, however, the margin for extra mortality increases very greatly. This explains why the method is appropriate for substandard risks whose impairments are expected to produce an increasing rate of extra mortality. Like the increase-in-age method, extra percentage substandard tables should, in theory, be used only when the hazard is expected to increase at a greater rate. In practice, however, they are used for all types of impairments that are expected to worsen as the years go by.

The reserves under policies issued in accordance with extra percentage tables must be calculated on the basis of the mortality assumptions underlying the premiums, which requires separate classification records and tabulations. Depending on company practice and state law, surrender values may be based on the special mortality table or may be the same as surrender values under policies issued to standard risks. Many companies do not make the extended term insurance nonforfeiture option (which is discussed in chapter 25) available under extra-percentage-table policies, especially at the higher percentages, and those that do compute the period on the basis of the higher mortality rate even when only the normal surrender value is allowed.

Extra percentage tables are sometimes used as a basis for determining the extra premiums needed under other methods of underwriting substandard risks. Thus the risk may first be assigned to an extra percentage table, after which the rating is translated into the equivalent age markup. This is a convenient way to determine the necessary step-up in age when statistics on the additional mortality expected from a particular impairment are available.

Flat Extra Premium

A third method of underwriting substandard risks is by assessing a flat extra premium. Under this method, the standard premium for the policy in question is increased by a specified number of dollars per $1,000 of insurance. Assessed as a measure of the extra mortality involved, the flat extra premium does not vary with the age of the applicant. It may be paid throughout the premium-paying period of the policy, or it may be terminated after a period of years when the extra hazard has presumably disappeared.

The flat extra premium method is normally used when the hazard is thought to be constant (deafness or partial blindness, for example) or decreasing (as with a family history of tuberculosis or the aftermath of a serious illness or surgical operation, in which case the flat extra is usually temporary in duration). The flat extra premium is widely used to cover the extra risk associated with certain occupations and avocations. When used for this purpose, the extra premium usually ranges from $2.50 to $10 per $1,000 of insurance. Unless a permanent impairment is involved, the extra premium is generally removed if the insured leaves the hazardous occupation or avocation.

At first glance, a flat extra premium for an extra hazard that adds an approximately constant amount to the rate of mortality at each age appears to be a fair arrangement. In practice, however, it works out equitably only if an allowance is made for the fact that the amount at risk is not a level sum under most policies. Except for term policies, the net amount at risk decreases with each year that elapses. Thus a flat extra premium becomes an increasing percentage of the amount at risk and, in effect, provides for an increasing extra risk.

When the extra risk is constant, the extra premium for a cash value contract should diminish each year in the proportion that the amount at risk decreases. To avoid the labor and expense that would be involved in such an annual adjustment, and in recognition of the fact that the flat extra premium is an approximation, most companies compute the flat extra addition on the basis of the average amount at risk. Some companies vary the extra premium with the plan of insurance, charging less for high cash value policies than for policies with lower reserve elements.

The flat extra premium is not reflected in policy values and dividends. It is assumed that the entire amount of the extra premium is needed each year to pay additional claims and expenses. The dividends and guaranteed values are identical to those of a comparable policy without the flat extra premium. Thus the policyowner must regard the flat extra premium as an irrecoverable outlay, a costly way to get even except through premature death.

Liens

When the extra mortality to be expected from an impairment is of a distinctly decreasing and temporary nature, such as that associated with convalescence from a serious illness, neither an increase in age, a percentage addition to the rate of mortality, nor a flat extra premium is an appropriate method of dealing with the risk. A more suitable method—from a theoretical standpoint, at least—is to create a lien against the policy for a number of years, the amount and term of the lien depending on the extent of the impairment. If adequate statistics are available, it is possible to calculate the term and amount of the lien that are equivalent to the extra risk undertaken. If such a method is utilized, the policy is issued at standard rates and is standard in all respects except that, should death occur before the end of the period specified, the amount of the lien is deducted from the proceeds otherwise payable. The method is frequently refined to provide for a yearly reduction in the amount of the lien on the theory that the hazard is decreasing.

The lien method has a psychological appeal, in that few persons who are refused insurance at standard rates believe themselves to be substandard risks and tend to resent the company's action in classifying them as such. If the only penalty involved is a temporary reduction in the amount of protection, most applicants are willing to go along with the company's decision, confident that they will survive the period of the lien and thus "prove" the company to have been wrong. The plan appeals to the applicant's sporting instinct.

A practical and serious disadvantage of the method is that a comparatively large lien is necessary to offset a relatively small degree of extra mortality. Furthermore the reduction occurs in the early years of the policy, when the need for protection is presumably the greatest. Frequently the beneficiary has no knowledge of the lien, and the company's failure to pay the face amount of the policy may be the source of great disappointment and resentment, to the detriment of the company's reputation in the community. There is also a possibility that the lien is in conflict with laws in certain states that prohibit any provision that permits the company to settle a death claim with a payment smaller than the face amount. These laws are known as "no-lesser-amounts" statutes.

Other Methods

A method of dealing with substandard risks when the degree of extra mortality is small or when its nature is not well known is to make no extra charge but to place all of the members of the group in a special class for dividend purposes, adjusting the dividends in accordance with the actual experience. This method can accommodate only those impairments that produce an extra mortality that does not exceed the normal dividend payments. Moreover a sufficiently large number of such risks must be underwritten to yield an average experience.

Some impairments can be dealt with by merely limiting the plan of insurance. The extra mortality associated with certain impairments is largely postponed to advanced middle age or old age. These impairments can be underwritten at no extra charge by issuing single premium or modified endowment contracts that have minimal amount at risk before the impact of the extra mortality. Being moderately overweight is a typical impairment that is adaptable to the endowment plan at standard rates.

REMOVAL OF SUBSTANDARD RATING

Frequently a person who is classified as a substandard risk and insured on that basis by one company subsequently applies for insurance with another company—or even the same company—and is found to be a standard risk in all respects. Under these circumstances the person's natural reaction is to request the removal of the substandard rating. The question is whether the company should remove the rating.

Theoretically the rating should not be removed unless the impairment on which it was based was known to be temporary or was due to occupation or residence. At the time the policy was originally issued, the insured was placed in a special classification of risks whose members were presumably impaired to approximately the same degree. It was known by the company that some of the members of the group would die within a short period, while others would survive far beyond their normal expectancy. It was likewise known that the health of some of the members would deteriorate with the passage of time, while some members would grow more robust. By the time the insured under consideration is in normal health, the health of many others in the original group has undoubtedly worsened. Many of them cannot now get insurance on any terms, while others are insurable only at a greater extra premium than that charged. If the company reduces the premiums for those whose health has improved, it should be permitted to increase the premiums of those whose health has deteriorated. Since the premiums of those in the latter category cannot be adjusted upward, the premiums of those in the former category should not be reduced.

As a practical matter, however, the company is virtually forced to remove the substandard rating of a person who can demonstrate current insurability at standard rates. If it does not do so, the policyowner will almost surely surrender the extra-rate insurance and replace it with insurance at standard rates in another company. Knowing this, most companies calculate their initial substandard premiums on the assumption that the extra premium will have to be removed for people who subsequently qualify for standard insurance. Thus the common practice is to remove the extra premium upon proof that the insured is no longer substandard.

Where an extra premium has been imposed on account of occupation, residence, or a temporary risk, it is proper to discontinue the extra premium upon termination of the condition that created the extra hazard without prior adjustment in the substandard premium. It is necessary to exercise care in these cases, however, particularly when the source of the rating was occupation or residence. There is always a possibility that the insured may subsequently return to the hazardous occupation or residence, or that his or her health has already been affected adversely. Hence it is customary in such cases to require that a specified period of time, such as one or 2 years, must elapse after cessation of the extra hazard before the rating will be removed. Occasionally, a medical examination is also required. At the end of the period, the adjustment is usually made retroactively to the change of occupation or residence.

VALUE OF SUBSTANDARD INSURANCE

The majority of life insurance companies in North America offer insurance to substandard risks. Several important companies that formerly confined their operations to standard risks are now willing to accept substandard risks. Some companies, however, refer to insurance on people who are substandard risks as classified insurance, rather than extra-rate or substandard insurance. There is a natural reluctance to call such business "substandard insurance" since the term suggests that the insurance is lacking in some of the essential qualities of standard insurance. This, of course, is not the case.

Substandard insurance is of great social importance since it makes insurance protection available to millions of American families that would otherwise be without it. Approximately 6 percent to 7 percent of all new policies are issued on a substandard basis. Extensive investigations into the rates of mortality prevailing among various types of substandard groups are continually being undertaken, resulting in further extensions of this class of business and in revisions of the terms upon which the insurance is offered. It is perhaps fair to conclude that life insurance is now available to all except those subject to such excessive rates of mortality as to entail premiums beyond their ability or willingness to pay.

24

Reinsurance

Dan M. McGill
Revised by Jeremy S. Holmes and James F. Winberg

Reinsurance is a device by which one insurance company or insurer transfers all or a portion of its risk under an insurance policy or a group of policies to another company or insurer. The company that issued the policy initially is called the direct-writing or primary company (also ceding company); the company or organization to which the risk is transferred is called the assuming company or reinsurer. The act of transferring the insurance from the direct-writing company to the reinsurer is called a cession.[1] If the reinsurer should, in turn, transfer to one or more companies all or a portion of the risk assumed from the primary company, the transaction is referred to as a retrocession. Thus the primary insurer cedes insurance to a reinsurer, which may then retrocede the coverage to still other companies.

PURPOSES OF REINSURANCE

In life insurance, reinsurance may be undertaken for one of two general reasons: (1) to transfer all or a specific portion of a company's liabilities or (2) to accomplish certain broad managerial objectives, including favorable underwriting results and the reduction of surplus drain from writing new business. Reinsurance undertaken for the purpose of transferring all or a substantial portion of a company's liabilities is called portfolio or assumption reinsurance. Reinsurance arranged for general business purposes is referred to as indemnity reinsurance.

Assumption Reinsurance

There are a number of reasons for assumption reinsurance. A traditional use has been to bail out insurance companies that find themselves in financial difficulties. Rather than liquidate the company, with almost certain losses to policyowners, two companies frequently work out a procedure whereby a solvent insurer assumes the policy liabilities of the company in distress in exchange for the assets underlying the liabilities and the right to receive future premiums under the policies. If the assets are not sufficient to offset the liabilities—a likely circumstance—the reinsurer may place a lien against the cash values of the ceded policies until the deficiency can be liquidated through earnings on the policies. A merger is another situation in which all the business of one company may be ceded to another.

In many instances assumption reinsurance involves only a segment of the ceding company's business. For example, a combination company[2] may decide to restrict its future operations to ordinary insurance and arrange to cede all of its outstanding industrial business to another company. Likewise, a company may decide to withdraw from one or more states and, in so doing, reinsure all policies outstanding in that geographical area. Assumption reinsurance is always tailored to the particular facts and requirements of the case under consideration and does not lend itself to generalization. Hence, it will not be further discussed in this book.

Indemnity Reinsurance

Indemnity reinsurance is characterized by a whole series of independent transactions whereby the primary insurer transfers its liability with respect to individual policies, in whole or in part, to the reinsurer. It is extremely widespread and may be used for any one of several reasons.

Limiting the Amount of Insurance on One Life

The most fundamental and prevalent use of indemnity reinsurance is to avoid too large a concentration of risk on one life. All companies, including the giants of the industry, have deemed it prudent to limit the amount of insurance that they will retain on any one life. These maxima, called retention limits, reflect the judgment of company management as to many factors, but they are strongly influenced by the volume of insurance in force, the amount of surplus funds,[3] and the proficiency of the underwriting personnel. The limits range from $1,000 in small, recently established companies to well over $20 million to $30 million in the largest companies.[4] There may be various limits within one company, depending upon the plan, age at issue, sex, and the substandard classification. Retention tends to be smaller at the lower and upper age groups and for plans under which the risk element is relatively large. It is clearly in a company's interest to retain as much of the risk as is consistent with safety, so the retention limit or limits are usually raised as the insurance in force and amount of surplus funds grow. To remain competitive and to retain the services of a qualified agency force, a company must be in a position to accept applications for any reasonable amount of insurance, regardless of its retention limit. Thus a company must have facilities for transferring amounts of insurance in excess of the amount that it is willing to retain at its own risk.

Stabilizing Mortality Experience

A closely related use of reinsurance, as yet limited in scope but receiving increasing attention, is to stabilize the primary company's overall mortality experience. This function is associated with so-called nonproportional reinsurance, one form of which transfers to the reinsurer all or a specified percentage of that portion of aggregate mortality claims for a given period in excess of a stipulated norm. Another form of nonproportional reinsurance provides protection against an undesirable concentration of risk on several lives, such as might be found among the passengers of a jet airliner or the employees of an industrial plant.

Reducing the Drain on Surplus

A third use of indemnity reinsurance is to reduce the drain on surplus caused by writing new business. As pointed out earlier, the expense of putting a new policy on the books greatly exceeds the first-year gross premium. This alone creates a strain on surplus, but when the insurer must also set aside funds to cover all or a portion of the first-year reserve, the strain is intensified. Under certain plans of reinsurance (to be discussed later), the burden of meeting first-year expenses and reserve requirements can be shifted to the reinsurer, thus permitting the primary company to write all the acceptable business produced by its agency forces.

Utilizing the Reinsurer's Expertise

A fourth use of indemnity reinsurance is to take advantage of the reinsurer's underwriting judgment. This is most likely to occur with applications from impaired lives. Some types of impairments are encountered so infrequently that even the largest companies do not have much opportunity to develop any experience with them. Those responsible for the selection of risks, upon encountering such an impairment, cannot evaluate the risk with the same degree of confidence that they feel in dealing with the more common varieties of impaired risks. For their own peace of mind, they are likely to seek the benefit of reinsurance, knowing that the selection of impaired risks is a special service of reinsurance companies. Even though the impairment is a common one and the underwriter has no hesitation about classifying the risk, the case may be submitted to one or more reinsurers to demonstrate to the soliciting agent that the most favorable terms were granted.

Transferring Substandard Insurance

A fifth application of indemnity insurance, closely related to the fourth, is to transfer all policies of substandard insurance. This use is brought into play when the primary insurer does not write substandard insurance on any basis. Yet in order to offer a full range of services to its agency force, the company may work out an arrangement whereby it can channel all applications from substandard risks to a reinsurer equipped to classify and underwrite such risks. A variation of this arrangement is to reinsure all substandard insurance policies that fall within a class above some stipulated percentage of anticipated mortality, such as 200 percent.

A company may also enter into a reinsurance agreement with another company to receive advice and counsel on underwriting matters, rates, and policy forms. This purpose is usually associated with small, newly organized companies that cannot afford a large enough staff to deal with all aspects of its operations. The relationship between the primary company and the reinsurer is that the latter becomes thoroughly conversant with the primary company's operations and is in a position to provide expert advice. While extremely valuable, this service of indemnity reinsurance is usually subsidiary to the fundamental function of spreading the risk.

Finally, with group insurance and pension plans, the company with which the master contract is placed may transfer portions of the coverage to several other insurers under instructions from the policyowner. Such an arrangement is specially fashioned and arises because the policyowner, for business reasons, wishes to divide the coverage among several insurers while looking to one for overall administration of the case.

PROPORTIONAL REINSURANCE

A number of plans have been developed for transacting indemnity reinsurance. The basic or traditional plans, designed for individual risks, are called proportional reinsurance, since under these plans a claim under a reinsured policy is shared by the primary company and the reinsurer in a proportion determined in advance. The precise manner in which a claim payment is shared by the primary company and the reinsurer depends on the type of plan employed.

Types of Plans

Proportional reinsurance is provided under two distinct plans: yearly renewable term insurance and coinsurance. A variation of the latter plan, called modified coinsurance, has also been developed.

Yearly Renewable Term Insurance

The yearly renewable term plan derives its name from the fact that the primary company, in effect, purchases term insurance on a yearly renewable basis from the reinsurer. The amount of term insurance purchased in any particular reinsurance transaction is the net amount at risk year by year under the face amount of insurance transferred to the reinsurer. This can be illustrated by a $1 million ordinary life policy issued on a male aged 35 by a company with a retention limit of $200,000. Under such circumstances $800,000 of insurance would ostensibly be transferred to the reinsurer. However, in the event of the insured's death, the reinsurer would pay not $800,000 but only the net amount of risk under an $800,000 policy. If the insured should die during the first policy year, the reinsurer would be liable for $800,000 less $8,820.96, the first-year terminal reserve[5] under the policy in question. If death occurred during the 8th policy year, the reinsurer would remit to the primary company $727,213.52, the face amount less the 8-year terminal reserve of $77,786.48. The reserves under the $800,000 of life insurance transferred to the reinsurer are held by the primary insurer and, in the event of the insured's death, would be added to the reinsurer's remittance to make up the full payment of $800,000 due under the reinsured portion of the original policy. The primary insurer would, of course, also be solely responsible for payment of the $200,000 of coverage it retained—which, in turn, would be composed of the net amount at risk and the accumulated reserves under $200,000 of coverage.

Whenever a policy is to be reinsured on a yearly renewable term basis, either the primary company or the reinsurer prepares a schedule of the amount at risk for each policy year under the face amount being reinsured. The reinsurer quotes a schedule of yearly renewable term premium rates that will be applied to the net amount at risk year by year. These rates are extremely competitive and usually reflect the lower mortality associated with the selection process.

The premiums are generally graded upward with duration under a wide variety of schedules. Some schedules grade the premium upward over as long a period as 15 years. There may be no charge other than a policy fee of nominal amount—for example, $5 or $10 for the first year of reinsurance coverage. The premium schedule may also reflect, through a policy fee or in some other manner, the amount of insurance involved. The expense loading is lower than in direct premiums since the primary company pays all commissions, medical fees, and other acquisition expenses connected with the policy. (Under most reinsurance agreements the premium tax is borne by the reinsurer in the form of a "refund" to the primary company.) As a further cost concession, some agreements of this type provide that the primary company share in any mortality savings on the reinsured business. Since it holds all the reserves, the primary company is responsible for surrender values, policy loans, and other prematurity benefits.

There are several advantages associated with the yearly renewable term basis of reinsurance. It permits the primary company to retain most of the premiums, giving rise to a more rapid growth in assets—a matter of special concern to small and medium-sized companies. For the same reason, it may be favored when the reinsurer is not licensed to transact business in the domiciliary state of the primary company, which would mean that the primary company would not be permitted to deduct the reserves on the reinsured policies from its overall reserve liability. (The same situation may lead to the use of a modified coinsurance arrangement.) This plan of reinsurance is also easier to administer than the more complicated coinsurance arrangements. Finally, it is thought to be more suitable for nonparticipating insurance where costs are fixed in advance.

Coinsurance

Under the coinsurance plan the primary company transfers (or cedes) the proportion of the face amount of insurance called for in the cession form, but the reinsurer is responsible not for just the net amount at risk but also for its pro rata share of the death claim. In the example cited under yearly renewable term insurance, the reinsurer is liable for the payment of $800,000, irrespective of the policy year in which the insured died. The reinsurer is also responsible for its pro rata share of the cash surrender value and other surrender benefits. In effect, the reinsurer is simply substituted for the primary company with respect to the amount of insurance reinsured. The primary or ceding company, however, remains liable to the policyowner for the full amount of any benefits if the reinsurer becomes insolvent or otherwise cannot pay its share of claims.

The primary or ceding company pays the reinsurer a pro rata share of the gross premiums collected from the policyowner,[6] and the reinsurer accumulates and holds the policy reserves for the amount of insurance ceded. Inasmuch as the ceding company incurs heavy expenses in putting the original policy on the books, it is customary for the reinsurer to reimburse the primary insurer for the expenses attributable to the amount of insurance reinsured. This reimbursement takes the form of a "ceding commission," which includes an allowance for commissions paid to the soliciting agent of the ceding company, premium taxes paid to the insured's state of domicile,[7] and a portion of the overhead expenses of the ceding company. Paying a portion of the primary company's overhead recognizes the fact that not only does a reinsurer incur relatively lower expenses on that portion of the face amount assumed by it, but the average amount of insurance per reinsurance certificate is also larger than the average size of the primary insurer's policy. Hence, the administrative expense per $1,000 of insurance is lower on that portion of the insurance reinsured than on the ceding company's normal business, and the reinsurer is willing to share the savings with the company that originated the business. There is normally no sharing of medical and other selection expenses, on the theory that such expenses are incurred on a per-policy basis and vary only slightly with the amount of insurance. The amount of the ceding commission is negotiated between the ceding insurer and the reinsurer.

If the original policy is participating, the reinsurer must pay dividends on the portion of insurance it assumes according to the primary company's dividend scale. This can prove burdensome if the net investment earnings of the reinsurer do not approximate those of the primary company or if the mortality under the ceded policies is not as favorable as that underlying the dividend scale. As a matter of fact, the mortality rates on reinsured policies as a whole tend to be higher than those on direct business, possibly because of the larger amounts of insurance involved and the less rigid underwriting standards of the many small and medium-sized companies that rely heavily on reinsurance. The anticipated higher mortality is taken into account in arriving at the ceding commission.

In the event that the original policy is terminated voluntarily, the reinsurer is liable for its pro rata share of the cash surrender value. If the policy is surrendered for reduced paid-up insurance, the reinsurer may remain liable for its proportionate share, or its share may be reduce paying the appropriate cash surrender value to the primary insurer. Should the policy be exchanged for extended term insurance, the reinsurer usually retains its proportionate share of liability, although its share may be reduced by any policy indebtedness. The reinsurer does not ordinarily participate in policy loans, settlement options, or installment settlements under family income or maintenance policies. The reinsurer's obligation in the event of the insured's death is discharged by a single-sum payment to the ceding company.

Modified Coinsurance

Many companies regard the reinsurer's accumulation of substantial sums of money as an unessential feature of a reinsurance arrangement and one that can be disadvantageous to the primary company. Apart from a company's natural desire to retain control of the funds arising out of its own policies, it may be apprehensive about entrusting another company to accumulate the funds necessary to discharge the primary company's obligations under a policy. This apprehension is heightened by the knowledge that the primary insurer's basic liability to the policyowner or beneficiary is not affected by the reinsurer's inability to make good on its obligation to the primary company. This problem is of more immediate concern when the reinsurer is not licensed to operate in the primary company's home state since in many states the primary company is not be permitted to include sums due from the reinsurer as assets in its balance sheet. These considerations have led to a modification of the coinsurance method, under which the primary company retains the entire reserve under the reinsured policy.

Under this arrangement the ceding company pays the reinsurer a proportionate part of the gross premium, as under the conventional coinsurance plan, less whatever allowances have been arranged for commissions, premium taxes, and overhead. At the end of each policy year, however, the reinsurer pays over to the ceding company a sum equal to the net increase in the reserve during the year, less one year's interest on the reserve at the beginning of the year. In more precise terms, the reinsurer pays over an amount equal to the excess of the terminal reserve for the policy year in question over the terminal reserve for the preceding policy year, less interest on the initial reserve for the current policy year. It is necessary to credit the reinsurer with interest on the initial reserve since a part of the increase in the reserve during the year is attributable to earnings on the funds underlying the reserve, which are held by the ceding company. The reserves are usually credited with interest at the rate used in the primary company's dividend formula or, in the case of nonparticipating insurance, a rate arrived at by negotiation.

Under this arrangement the reinsurer never holds more than the gross premium, as adjusted for allowances, for one year. Under one variation of this method, the anticipated increase is even deducted in advance from the gross premium. In many reinsurance transactions using the modified coinsurance plan, the foregoing adjustments are based on the aggregate mean reserves, rather than on the individual terminal reserves. Apart from the reserve adjustment, the modified coinsurance basis is identical to the straight coinsurance basis, and the description of the coinsurance arrangement in the preceding section is equally applicable to the modified form.[8]

The modified coinsurance plan bears such a strong resemblance in net effect to the yearly renewable term basis of coinsurance that one might question why modified coinsurance would ever be used. One answer is that the premium paid by the primary company is geared to the premium received from the policyowner, rather than being arrived at through negotiation. The second answer is more complex but rests on the fact that under a modified coinsurance plan, reinsurance costs reflect the incidence of expense and surplus drain incurred by the primary company. Under the yearly renewable term plan, the ceding company is responsible for maintaining the reserves at the proper level. Under the modified coinsurance arrangement, however, the reinsurer, out of the premium received from the primary company, must each year turn back a sum equal to the increase in reserves (less one year's interest on the reserve at the beginning of the year), as well as the ceding commission. Over the lifetime of the reinsured policy, the total cost of modified coinsurance and yearly renewable term should be approximately the same, but the net cost of reinsurance in the early years is normally less under modified coinsurance.

NONPROPORTIONAL REINSURANCE

The great bulk of life reinsurance is transacted on the basis of proportional reinsurance, as described above, but in recent years increasing interest has developed in an approach that relates the reinsurer's liability to the mortality experience on all or a specified portion of the primary company's business, rather than to individual or specific policies of insurance. Widely used in property-casualty insurance, this approach is referred to as nonproportional reinsurance, since the proportion in which the primary company and the reinsurer will share losses is not determinable in advance. This type of reinsurance coverage is available from both American and European reinsurers in three forms: stop-loss reinsurance, catastrophe reinsurance, and spread-loss reinsurance.

Stop-Loss Reinsurance

Stop-loss reinsurance is highly developed in casualty insurance but it is still in a growth stage in life insurance, serving primarily as a supplement to conventional reinsurance rather than as a substitute for it. Thus plans follow no fixed pattern. In essence, however, stop-loss reinsurance arrangements undertake to indemnify the primary company if its mortality losses in the aggregate, or on specified segments of its business, exceed by a stipulated percentage what might be regarded as the normal or expected mortality. The agreements commonly invoke liability on the reinsurer's part if the primary company's aggregate mortality exceeds by more than 10 percent the "normal" mortality, which, of course, must be defined explicitly or implicitly in the agreement. Normal mortality is usually defined as a specified percentage of the tabular mortality for the categories of business covered by the agreement. Thus if the mortality under the policies subject to a particular stop-loss reinsurance agreement is running around 50 percent of the 1980 CSO Table, the agreement might stipulate that the reinsurer will absorb all losses in excess of 110 percent of the normal level of mortality, defined as 50 percent of the 1980 CSO Table rates. Another way to express the reinsurer's obligation is to stipulate that the reinsurer will indemnify the primary company for all claims in excess of a specified percentage of tabular mortality, such as 60 percent of the 1980 CSO Table.

Under some agreements the reinsurer indemnifies the primary company for only a specified percentage (for example, 90 percent) of the excess mortality, an arrangement intended to encourage careful underwriting by the primary company. Under most agreements the reinsurer's liability during any contract period, generally a calendar year, is limited to a stipulated dollar amount. Under any of these arrangements, if the mortality for the contract period is below the level at which the reinsurer's obligation would attach, the reinsurer makes no payment to the primary company.

This approach to reinsurance lends itself to great flexibility, since the agreements can be written to cover only selected portions of the primary company's business, varying levels of mortality, and periods of varying durations. The premium for stop-loss reinsurance is arrived at by negotiation and involves the use of highly refined actuarial techniques, as well as a large element of judgment. The basic appeal of this coverage is that it provides protection against adverse mortality experience arising out of an unexpectedly large number of small claims or an unexpected increase in the average size of claims. It is a form of reinsurance on the amounts at risk retained under conventional reinsurance agreements. Since the unit cost of protection under this approach is less than under proportional reinsurance, a company can reduce its total outlay for reinsurance by increasing its retention limits under conventional agreements and reinsuring the retained amounts under stop-loss arrangements. Another advantage of this approach is its relative ease of administration, attributable to the absence of individual policy records.

Adherents to conventional (proportional) reinsurance arrangements see many practical disadvantages to stop-loss reinsurance. They point out that it is short-term, rate-adjustable, cancelable coverage available under conventional arrangements. They call attention to the limit on the reinsurer's liability, as well as exclusion of the war risk. They emphasize the restrictions on the primary company's underwriting practices necessarily imposed by the reinsurer. Finally, they question for a number of reasons whether any cost savings will, in fact, be realized in the long run.

At its present stage of development in the United States, stop-loss reinsurance serves primarily as a supplement to conventional reinsurance arrangements rather than as a substitute for them.

Catastrophe Reinsurance

Like stop-loss reinsurance, catastrophe reinsurance was first developed for property-casualty insurance lines. As its name implies, it usually provides for payment by the reinsurer of some fixed percentage, ranging from 90 to 100 percent, of the aggregate losses (net of conventional reinsurance) in excess of a stipulated limit in connection with a single accident or catastrophic event, such as an airplane crash, explosion, fire, or hurricane. Catastrophe reinsurance is clearly intended to serve only as a supplement to proportional reinsurance agreements. The level of losses at which the reinsurer's liability attaches may be expressed in terms of dollar amount or number of lives. The contract usually covers a period of one year and limits the reinsurer's liability for that period. The coverage is attractive to insurance companies that have a concentration of risks in one location, such as might arise under a group insurance policy. The risk involved is essentially accidental death attributable to a catastrophic occurrence.

While the reinsurer's liability under a catastrophe type of agreement is high, the probability of loss is low. Hence the premiums for this type of coverage are generally low. Moreover, being based on reasonably adequate data, they are more readily calculated than premiums for other forms of nonproportional reinsurance. The expense element of the premium is minimized through the use of aggregate reporting procedures.

Spread-Loss Reinsurance

A final type of nonproportional reinsurance is the spread-loss reinsurance. Under this type of agreement, the reinsurer collects an annual premium of a stipulated minimum amount, of which a certain portion (such as 20 percent) is allocated to expenses and profit, with the balance credited to a refund account until the account reaches a specified maximum figure, such as the sum of 3 years' premiums. During any calendar year when the primary company's aggregate death claims (net of conventional reinsurance payments) exceed a specified limit, the reinsurer pays the claims in excess of the limit but adjusts the premium to reflect the claims experience. The agreement provides that any amounts paid by the reinsurer for a given year, plus 20 percent, must be returned to the reinsurer by the primary company during the next 5 years.

The spread-loss agreement can be terminated by either party, with proper notice, at the end of any contract year, except that the primary company cannot terminate the arrangement under circumstances that would cause a loss to the reinsurer. In other words, the reinsurer must be permitted to recover all payments made to the primary company. It is apparent that the main purpose of this type of reinsurance is to spread the financial effects of an unfavorable mortality experience in any one year over a period of 5 years. About the only risk the reinsurer takes is the continued solvency of the primary company. Consequently the mathematical basis of the premium charge is completely different from the other two forms of nonproportional reinsurance.

REINSURANCE AGREEMENT

Arrangements between ceding insurers and reinsurers are generally formalized by a reinsurance agreement (also called a reinsurance treaty). Such agreements describe the classes of risk that will be subject to reinsurance, the extent of the reinsurer's liability, and the procedures by which the transactions are to be carried out. These agreements are broadly classified as facultative or automatic.

Types of Agreement

The facultative agreement establishes a procedure whereby the primary insurer may offer risks to the reinsurer on an individual case basis. The essence of the arrangement is that the primary company is under no obligation to offer—and the reinsurer is under no duty to accept—a particular risk. Each company reserves full freedom of action, and each risk is considered on its merits. The arrangement takes its name from the fact that each party retains the "faculty" to do as it pleases with respect to each specific risk.

The automatic agreement, on the other hand, binds the primary insurer to offer—and the reinsurer to accept—all risks that fall within the purview of the agreement. The agreement sets forth a schedule of the primary insurer's limits of retention and provides that whenever the primary company issues a policy for an amount in excess of the limit for each policy, the excess amount is to be reinsured automatically. The primary company does not submit the underwriting papers to the reinsurer, and the reinsurer does not have the option of accepting or rejecting the risk.[9]

Under a facultative arrangement the primary company submits a copy of the application from the insured, together with all supporting documents, to the prospective insurer. The primary insurer also submits a form that specifies the basis on which reinsurance is desired and the proportion of the face amount that the originating company proposes to retain. This form, which constitutes the offer for reinsurance, supplies all information about the risk in the possession of the primary company, including the amount of insurance already in force on the risk. The agreement normally provides that the reinsurer will phone, telegram, or facsimile its acceptance or rejection to the primary company.

Under an automatic arrangement the reinsurer is obligated to accept a specified amount of reinsurance, including amounts for supplemental coverage on the basis of the primary company's underwriting appraisal. The maximum amount that can be transferred automatically to the reinsurer depends on the quality of the ceding company's underwriting staff, as well as its limits of retention. It is fairly common for the reinsurer to obligate itself to accept automatically up to four or more times the primary company's retention. However, when the retention limits of the primary company are fairly high, the reinsurer may limit its obligation to an amount equal to the primary company's limit. The agreement specifies that the originating company will retain an amount of insurance equal to its retention limit and will not reinsure it elsewhere on a facultative basis.[10] In other words, if the primary company should decide to retain less than the full retention indicated for the particular classification in which the risk falls, the reinsurer is relieved of its obligation under the automatic agreement, and the entire transaction will have to be handled on a facultative basis. The agreement also usually includes a so-called "jumbo" clause, which stipulates that if the total amount of insurance in force on an applicant's life in all companies—including policies applied for—exceeds a specified amount, reinsurance is not automatically effected. The agreement normally makes provision for facultative reinsurance of those risks not eligible, for one reason or another, for automatic reinsurance.

Cession Form

The reinsurance agreement stipulates that the primary insurer, after delivering its policy to the insured and collecting the first premium, is to prepare a formal cession of reinsurance (in duplicate), which gives the details of the risk and schedule of reinsurance premiums, including the ceding commission, if any. One copy of the cession form goes to the reinsurer; the other is retained by the primary company. The form is identical for both facultative and automatic insurance. In effect, it is the individual contract of insurance; the entire reinsurance agreement is incorporated into it by reference.

The cession form describes the basis on which the reinsurance is being effected—that is, whether it is yearly renewable term insurance, coinsurance, modified coinsurance, or some other type. If one of the coinsurance arrangements is being used, provision is made for paying a ceding commission to the primary or ceding company.

Provision is also made for the manner in which premiums are to be paid. All premiums are generally payable on an annual basis subject to prorated refunds in the event of terminations other than on policy anniversaries. The reinsurer bills the primary insurer monthly for reinsurance premiums falling due during that month. The bill also includes first-year premiums arising from cessions of reinsurance received since the date of the previous billing and refunds of premiums due to policy cancellations, as well as other small adjustments that arise from time to time.

Claims Settlement

The policyowner is not a party to the reinsurance agreement and looks to the issuing company to fulfill the obligation of the contract.[11] Consequently the reinsurance agreement stipulates that any settlement made by the primary insurer with a claimant is binding on the reinsurer,[12] whether the reinsurance was originally automatic or was accepted facultatively by the reinsurer. Despite this contractual right to settle claims at its discretion, the primary insurer will invariably consult with the reinsurer in doubtful cases.

If the policy is to be settled on an installment basis, the reinsurer will nevertheless discharge its liability by paying a lump sum to the primary insurer. This is true not only of settlement option arrangements but also of contracts, such as the family income and retirement income policies, which provide for settlement on an installment basis. If a policy is settled for less than the face amount, such as might happen from a misstatement of age or the compromise of a claim of doubtful validity, the reinsurer shares in the savings. If the primary insurer contests a claim, the reinsurer bears its proportionate share of the expenses incurred.

Reduction in the Sums Reinsured

Once a sum of insurance has been reinsured, the reinsurer is at risk for that amount as long as the amount retained by the primary company remains in force, subject to two important exceptions. One exception is in instances where the total amount of insurance on a particular risk is reduced after a portion of the insurance has been reinsured. This can result from the maturity or expiration of policies in accordance with their terms or through the voluntary termination of policies by nonpayment of premiums. Some agreements provide that the full amount of the reduction will come out of the sum reinsured (up to the amount reinsured, of course), while other agreements call for proportionate reductions in the amounts held by the two insurers.

The other exception applies to increases in the primary insurer's limits of retention and is especially significant to young and growing insurance companies. The provision states that if the primary company increases its limits of retention, it may make corresponding reductions in all reinsurance previously transferred. In the case of a \$5 million policy written by a company with a \$1 million retention limit, \$4 million would originally have been reinsured. If the primary company later increases its retention limit for that particular class of policy to \$2 million, it would be permitted to recover \$1 million of the \$4 million that had been reinsured. This procedure is referred to as the recapture of insurance.

Recapture Provision

Recapture is usually permitted only after the policies involved have been in force for a specified period of time. This restriction is clearly designed to enable the reinsurer to recover its acquisition expenses. It is customary to restrict recapture of insurance arranged under a renewable term plan to policies in force for 5 or more years, while amounts ceded on a coinsurance basis must typically remain in force for 10 or more years before being subject to recapture. The recapture provision provides an effective method of recovering amounts of insurance previously reinsured when the primary company holds the reserves, as under the yearly renewable term and modified coinsurance arrangements, but it may be ineffective under the coinsurance plan, since the reinsurer is obligated to release only the cash values—not the reserves—for the amounts recaptured. If there is a differential between the surrender value and the reserve under a policy, as there is likely to be, the primary company may conclude that it is not worthwhile to recapture the insurance, at least until the differential between the surrender value and the reserve is insignificant.

Duration of the Agreement

Subject to the provisions described in the preceding section, a reinsurance agreement remains effective for reinsured policies as long as the original insurance continues in force. For new insurance, however, most agreements make provision for cancellation by either party with 90 days' notice. During that period, the agreement remains in full force and effect, and the reinsurer must accept all new insurance exceeding the retention limit with an automatic treaty. It is anticipated that the primary company can make other reinsurance arrangements within a period of 90 days.

Insolvency of the Primary Insurer

In general, reinsurance agreements are regarded as contracts of indemnity, and the reinsurer's liability is measured by the actual loss sustained by the primary insurer. An important exception is in the case of the primary insurer's insolvency. Virtually all agreements provide that the reinsurer must remit in full to the insolvent carrier that issued the original policy, even though the claim against the insolvent company will have to be scaled down. Many states, including New York, will not permit a primary company to treat amounts due from reinsurers as admitted assets or to deduct reserves held by reinsurers from its policy liabilities unless the reinsurance agreement requires the reinsurer to discharge its own obligation in full in the event the primary company becomes insolvent.

It is important to note that a claimant under a reinsured policy issued by a company that is insolvent at the time of the claim is not permitted to bring action directly against the reinsurer but must look to the insolvent carrier's general assets for the settlement of the claim. On the other hand, when the issuing company is insolvent, the reinsurer is given the specific right to contest claims against the primary insurer in which it has an interest, with all defenses available to the reinsurer that are available to primary insurer.

Experience Rating

It is becoming increasingly common for reinsurance agreements to contain a provision permitting a primary company to share in any mortality gains or losses arising under reinsured policies. This is a form of experience rating found in many lines of insurance, including the various group coverages written by life companies. In this case, the primary company is treated as the policyowner, and the mortality refund (or surcharge, as the case might be) is calculated on the combined experience under all reinsured amounts with a particular reinsurer. The practice originated in the 1920s but was generally discontinued in the 1930s because of the disastrous claims experience on "jumbo" risks. In recent years, there has been renewed interest in the arrangement, and there are many variations in practice. A common arrangement is to have the primary insurer participate in any gains or losses on reinsurance amounts below a specified limit and not participate in the experience on amounts in excess of such limit. The purpose of this variation is to permit the primary company to share in the favorable mortality experience of the bulk of reinsured risks but to avoid the undesirable fluctuations in its overall experience that might result from unpredictably heavy mortality among very large risks. (Note that arrangements that permit the primary insurer to share the gains from favorable mortality experience on reinsured risks lessen the importance of recapture provisions.)

These mortality refunds are a matter of accounting between insurance companies and should not be confused with dividends to policyholders, although under participating policies, all or a portion of the savings may be passed on indirectly to policyholders. Agreements that provide for sharing mortality savings on reinsured risks with the primary company are usually referred to as experience-rated agreements.

Supplementary Coverages

The reinsurance agreement covering life risks may or may not apply to supplementary coverages, such as accidental death benefits and total disability benefits. If the basic agreement is facultative, it is likely to cover supplementary benefits as well as the life risk; if it is automatic, a separate agreement may be used for the supplementary coverages, particularly the accidental death benefits.

Many companies have lower limits of retention for accidental death benefits than for basic life risks. For example, a company may be willing to retain $400,000 of coverage under a basic life policy but only $100,000 of accidental death coverage. Therefore a policy for $200,000 with accidental death provisions would require reinsurance for the supplementary coverage but not for the basic coverage. For this reason the reinsurance of accidental death benefits may be set up under a special agreement.

Reinsurance may be provided on either a coinsurance or yearly renewable term basis, depending on the plan used for basic life risks. If the coinsurance plan is used, the premium for the accidental death benefits is based on the premium charged the insured, less a first-year and renewal expense allowance. If the renewable term plan is used, the premium is usually a flat rate per $1,000, irrespective of age of issue or the type of contract issued to the policyowner. The benefits are reinsured on a level-amount basis, since only nominal reserves are accumulated in connection with such coverage.

Disability benefits may likewise be reinsured on either a coinsurance or a yearly renewable term basis. The premium is the same as that charged the insured, less a first-year and renewal-expense allowance. It is customary to limit the reinsurance of disability benefits to an amount not exceeding that attaching to the face amount of life coverage reinsured.

Substandard Reinsurance

The general principles governing reinsurance of standard risks are also applicable to substandard insurance. For substandard reinsurance on either the coinsurance or the modified coinsurance basis, the primary or ceding company pays the reinsurer appropriate portions of the additional premiums collected from the policyowner, subject to a ceding commission for reimbursement of the ceding company's acquisition expenses. If the reinsurance is accomplished on the yearly renewable term basis and the substandard risk is classified according to a multiple of standard mortality, the reinsurance premiums are usually calculated on the same multiple of the standard reinsurance rate. If the policyowner is charged a flat extra premium, the primary insurer pays the reinsurer the same premium as for a standard risk, plus an appropriate share of the flat extra premium. The flat extra premiums, however, are not reduced as the net amount at risk declines.

NOTES

1. The term "cession" also refers to a document executed by the primary company in accordance with the reinsurance agreement that describes the risk being transferred and provides a schedule of reinsurance premiums and allowances, if any.
2. A combination company writes both ordinary and industrial insurance.
3. A rule of thumb, subject to many exceptions, is that the retention limit should be equal to 1 percent of capital and surplus.
4. Some newly established companies reinsure all their business for a number of years, although the companies may be motivated by reasons other than (or in addition to) the avoidance of mortality risk.
5. The figure is the full net level premium reserve under the 1980 CSO aggregate table plus 4 percent interest. Small and medium-sized companies, which are an important segment of the reinsurance market, almost invariably use the Commissioners Reserve Valuation Method. On that reserve basis, there would be no reserve under an ordinary life policy at the end of the first year, so that the amount at risk would be the face of the policy.
6. There are exceptions to this practice. Sometimes when the ceding insurer offers both participating and nonparticipating policies, all reinsurance will be arranged on the basis of the ceding company's nonparticipating gross premium rates in order to avoid the complexity of dividend accounting.
7. In most—if not all—states, the ceding company is not permitted to deduct premium taxes on amounts of insurance transferred to reinsurers. By the same token, reinsurers are not required to pay premium taxes on insurance assumed under reinsurance agreements.
8. In the settlement of claims under the modified coinsurance plan, the reinsurer is charged with the face amount of insurance transferred to it but credited with the reserve on that sum.
9. In recent years, a modified type of automatic agreement has been developed under which the reinsurer's obligation becomes fixed only after the reinsurer has had an opportunity to screen its files for any unfavorable information relating to the risk. The primary company sends the reinsurer a notice of intention to bind, and unless the reinsurer notifies the primary company of unfavorable information on the risk within a specified time, the reinsurance automatically goes into effect. This method, without slowing down the primary company's underwriting and issuing procedures, makes the reinsurer's confidential files, built up over many years of operation, available to the issuing company. Moreover, there are some automatic agreements, under which the primary company submits the underwriting papers to the reinsurer which has the option of declining to reinsure the risk.
10. Such a provision is obviously not included in an agreement under which the ceding company is to transfer all amounts of substandard insurance written by it.
11. Under portfolio reinsurance, policyholders are usually given the right to proceed directly against the reinsurer in pressing a claim for settlement.
12. An exception is made when the entire risk is carried by the reinsurer. Under such circumstances, the agreement provides for consultation with the reinsurer before an admission or acknowledgement of a claim by the primary company.

25

Settlement Agreements

Dan M. McGill
Revised by Edward E. Graves

Most life insurance policies provide that upon maturity the proceeds shall be payable to the designated beneficiary in one sum, generally referred to as a *lump sum*. Many life insurers now make the lump-sum death benefit payable through an interest-bearing account against which the beneficiary can draw checks. The way these accounts work is similar to the way a money market fund works. The beneficiary can withdraw the total proceeds in one transaction or make partial withdrawals as funds are needed merely by writing checks. The balance in the account continues to earn interest until withdrawn. Even though the beneficiary can leave the benefits in the account and earn more investment income, over 90 percent of beneficiaries still choose a single lump-sum withdrawal and take possession of all the proceeds.

Life insurance companies have a wide range of periodic income options available to beneficiaries and policyowners. These alternatives are varied enough to fit nearly every set of circumstance that beneficiaries encounter. Collectively these contractual choices are known as settlement options. They constitute an important feature of a life insurance contract and can play a vital role in the protection of the insured's dependents. Knowledge of their characteristics and the manner in which they can be used is essential to successful life underwriting.

GENERAL CONCEPTS AND RULES

When the proceeds of a life insurance policy are payable in a lump sum, the company's liability under the policy is fully discharged with the payment of such sum. If, however, the company retains the proceeds under one of the optional methods of settlement, its liability continues beyond the maturity of the policy and must be evidenced by some sort of legal document. That document is the *settlement agreement.*[1]

The settlement agreement contains the designation of the various classes of beneficiaries and a detailed description of the manner in which the proceeds are to be distributed. During the early development of deferred-settlement arrangements, settlement agreements were tailored to fit the insured's exact specifications and were typewritten in their entirety. As the requests for deferred settlements multiplied, it became necessary, for reasons of economy and administration, to standardize the various arrangements and privileges that the company would make available. As a result, the modern settlement agreement is composed primarily of preprinted provisions, some of which are general in scope and apply to any option that might be elected, and some of which pertain to only one specific option. All of the rights, privileges, and restrictions that the company is willing to make available are included and become effective by appropriate action of the policyowner (usually by making a check mark in a box opposite the provision in question). The only portion of the agreement that must be filled in concerns beneficiary designations and any modifications of the printed provisions that are acceptable to both parties. A specimen settlement agreement of the type generally used today is shown at the end of this chapter.

The typical settlement agreement is one entered into between the insurance company and the insured, or policyowner, to control the distribution of the policy proceeds to third-party beneficiaries after the insured's death. Depending on company practice, the agreement may be a basic part of the insurance policy, or it may be separate and distinct from the policy. It can be drawn up at the time the policy goes into effect or at any time prior to the insured's death. Although the insured can revoke the agreement at any time and substitute a new agreement, he or she can revoke the beneficiary designation only if such right has been specifically reserved. The policyowner may or may not give the primary beneficiary the right to set aside the prior agreement after the insured dies. Upon the insured's death, the insurance company's obligation under the original contract terminates, and it assumes a new obligation, which is defined by the terms of the settlement agreement.

The insured may also enter into a settlement agreement with the insurer to provide payments to himself or herself from a surrendered policy's cash value. If the agreement relates to the proceeds of an endowment policy, it can be entered into at the policy's inception or at any time prior to the policy's maturity.

If the insured did not elect a deferred settlement or did elect one but gave the primary beneficiary the right to set it aside, under the rules of most companies the beneficiary may elect a settlement option and enter into an agreement with the company to govern the distribution of the proceeds. The beneficiary is usually given 6 months after the insured's death in which to elect a settlement option, provided the check proffered by the insurer in full settlement of the death claim has not been cashed. Insurers pay interest on the portion of proceeds still held by the insurer after the insured dies. The interest starts accruing from the date of death (even if the election of the specific option is made long after the insured dies) and continues accruing until the underlying proceeds are distributed to the beneficiary.

When a beneficiary elects the settlement option or when the policyowner elects a deferred settlement for his or her own benefit, a spendthrift clause cannot be included in the settlement agreement (if it is included, it will not be enforceable). A spendthrift clause states that the proceeds will be free from attachment or seizure by the beneficiary's creditors. This clause may properly be embodied in a life insurance policy or settlement agreement procured by one person for the benefit of another, but it cannot be incorporated into an agreement at the behest of the party for whose benefit the agreement is being drawn up.[2] This offers an argument for having the insured elect the settlement option on behalf of the beneficiary, especially if the beneficiary has credit problems (or may be expected to have them in the future).

Under the rules of many companies, a settlement agreement entered into between the company and the beneficiary must provide that any proceeds unpaid at the time of the beneficiary's death will be paid either to his or her estate in a lump sum or in a single sum or installments to irrevocably designated contingent beneficiaries. In other words, the beneficiary cannot designate *revocable* contingent beneficiaries.

Companies that impose this limitation fear that designating revocable contingent beneficiaries to receive proceeds that are already in existence at the time the designation is made might be construed as a disposition of property to take effect at the primary beneficiary's death. If the beneficiary's action should be so construed, the settlement agreement would be ineffectual as to the residual proceeds unless the agreement had been executed with all the formalities of a will—which, of course, is not the practice. Some insurance companies, however, feel that such a construction of the settlement agreement is a remote contingency and they therefore permit the beneficiary to designate contingent beneficiaries with the right of revocation.

Contract Rates versus Current Rates

As pointed out earlier, the liability of the insurer at the maturity of a life insurance policy is generally stated in terms of a single-sum payment. In making other modes of settlement available, the company promises a set of installment benefits, based on various patterns of distribution, that have a present value precisely equal to the lump-sum payment. The policy contains tables that show the amount of periodic income that will be payable under the different options for each $1,000 of proceeds left with the company. Under each option a specified *rate* of income per $1,000 of proceeds is guaranteed in the policy; these are referred to as *contract rates*. It is important to note that insurers can and often do credit investment earnings in excess of the guaranteed rate to the funds supporting settlement options.

From time to time, a company will modify the actuarial assumptions underlying the benefits provided under the optional modes of settlement, which means that the amount of periodic income per $1,000 of proceeds will change. Historically, because of declining interest yields and growing longevity, these modifications have produced lower benefits per $1,000 of principal. Such benefit modifications are, of course, reflected only in those policies and settlement agreements issued after the change. The benefits under existing agreements cannot be modified without the specific consent of the policyowner. (Consequently, insurers rarely take steps to modify existing settlement agreements.) In order to distinguish the rates of income available under existing policies and settlement agreements from rates that are applicable to contracts currently being issued, the latter are referred to as *current rates*. For policies and agreements issued since the latest rate changes there is, obviously, no difference between the contract and current rates. For all others, however, the distinction can be significant.

Contract rates are always available to the policyowner, except for options that can be "negotiated"—that is, options not contained in the original policy. If a policyowner wants the proceeds to be distributed in a manner not provided for in the original policy and his or her request is granted, the benefits will almost invariably be based on the rates in effect at the time the option was requested. Thus if a policy does not contain all the options that the applicant thinks he or she might want to utilize, the applicant should try to have them added to the policy by endorsement at the time the policy is issued or as soon thereafter as possible.

Under most companies' rules a beneficiary who is entitled to a lump-sum payment can choose to leave the proceeds with the company under the interest option or elect one of the liquidating options at contract rates. Contract rates are usually available to the beneficiary if a liquidating option (any option other than the interest option) is elected within a specified period after the insured's death—usually somewhere in the range of 6 months to 2 years. If within the 6-month period, the beneficiary elects the interest option, he or she can switch to a liquidating option at contract rates up to 2 years after the insured's death. Moreover, if—during the prescribed period of 6 months to 2 years—the beneficiary elects to have a liquidating option go into effect at some specified date beyond the 2-year period, contract rates will apply. On the other hand, if the beneficiary requests a change of option after the permissible period, the requested benefits will be made available only at current rates, if at all.

It is important to grasp the rationale of the restrictions on contract rates. They are *not* designed primarily to prevent an indefinite projection of contract rates into an uncertain future. Rather, they are intended to protect the insurance company from adverse mortality and financial selection. For example, if a beneficiary could elect a life income option at any time, his or her attitude toward that right would be influenced by the condition of his or her health. If, after the insured's death, the beneficiary's health deteriorated, he or she would not consider a life income option appropriate, unless it were the cash refund type. On the other hand, if the beneficiary's health over the years were excellent, he or she might elect a life income option. Since beneficiaries as a group could be expected to react in this manner, without a time limit or option selection the company would find itself with an undue proportion of healthy annuitants.

Likewise, if a beneficiary has the choice of withdrawing the proceeds and placing them in some other type of investment or leaving them with the company to be liquidated under one of the installment options, he or she would probably place the investment burden on the insurer if it provided a higher return than could be obtained in the open market. The reverse would be true if the market yield were higher than that provided by the insurer. While the behavior of one or a few beneficiaries has little impact on the insurance company, the adverse action of tens of thousands could be financially devastating to the insurer.

Right of Withdrawal

As stated earlier, the beneficiary may be given the right to withdraw all or a portion of the proceeds held by the insurer under a deferred-settlement arrangement. If the beneficiary can withdraw all of the proceeds at any one time, subject only to a delay clause, he or she is said to have an *unlimited* right of withdrawal. However, if the privilege is subject to restrictions, it is generally identified as a *limited* right of withdrawal.

The right of withdrawal may be limited as to the following:

- the frequency with which it can be invoked
- the minimum amount that can be withdrawn at any one time
- the maximum amount that can be withdrawn at any one time
- the maximum amount that can be withdrawn in any one year
- the maximum amount that can be withdrawn in the aggregate

The first two types of limitations are imposed by the insurers to control the cost of administration, while the last three are imposed by the policyowner (often a parent of the beneficiary) to prevent dissipation or too rapid exhaustion of the proceeds by the beneficiary. The right of withdrawal can usually be invoked only on dates when regular interest or liquidation payments are due. Most companies permit withdrawals on any such dates, but some restrict the privilege to a stated number of withdrawals per year, such as three, four, or six. Although some insurers have no minimum requirement, the minimum amount that can usually be withdrawn at any one time ranges from $10 to $1,000.

Most policies reserve the right to delay cash withdrawals under settlement options for a period of up to 6 months. This is a counterpart to the delay clause required by law in connection with loan and surrender requests.

The policyowner may provide that the right of withdrawal will be *cumulative*. This means that any withdrawable amounts that are not withdrawn during a particular year can be withdrawn in any subsequent year, in addition to any other sums that can be withdrawn pursuant to the terms of agreement. Thus if the settlement agreement permits the beneficiary to withdraw up to $1,000 per year in addition to the periodic contractual payments and provides that the right will be cumulative, the beneficiary's failure to withdraw any funds during the first year would automatically give him or her the right to withdraw $2,000 during the second year. No withdrawals during the first or second years would bestow the right to withdraw $3,000 during the third year, and so on. A *noncumulative* right of withdrawal, whether exercised or not, expires at the end of the period to which it pertains. Most limited rights of withdrawal are noncumulative.

A right of withdrawal is included in a settlement agreement in order to provide flexibility. It can be invoked to obtain funds for unexpected emergencies or to meet the problem of a rising price level. It is especially desirable during the period when the beneficiary has dependent children to care for. In most cases, however, the right should be hedged with reasonable restrictions in order to prevent premature exhaustion of the proceeds.

Right of Commutation

The right of *commutation* is related to the right of withdrawal. To commute, in this sense, is to withdraw the present value of remaining installment payments in a lump sum. The term is properly applied only to a right attaching to proceeds distributed under a liquidating option. Hence it does not apply to proceeds held under the interest option. For all practical purposes, however, the right of commutation is identical to an unlimited right of withdrawal.

The right of commutation is not implicit in an installment arrangement; in order to be available, it must be specifically authorized in the settlement agreement. Commutation is specifically and intentionally denied the beneficiary in the spendthrift clause that is sometimes made part of the settlement agreement.

Minimum-amount Requirements

To hold down the cost of administering proceeds under deferred-settlement arrangements for which there is no specific charge, life insurance companies will not accept a sum less than a specified amount (such as $2,000 or $10,000) under a settlement option and will not provide periodic installments in amounts less than $25 or $50. If the proceeds of a policy are split into two or more funds with different options, the foregoing requirements apply to each fund. The minimum-payment requirement also applies to each beneficiary. Thus a policy large enough to satisfy the requirements if payable to the widow(er) alone might have to be paid in a lump sum if several children become payees as contingent beneficiaries.

These requirements are usually referred to in the policy as rules subject to change. Because of the anticipated variation, the specific dollar amounts are rarely stated in the policy.

There is usually a special requirement for proceeds held under the installment amount option. Most companies will not make monthly payments of less than $5 or $6 per $1,000 under this option. The requirement is sometimes stated as a percentage; the minimum is usually 4, 5, or 6 percent liquidation per year. This special rule is designed to assure liquidation of all proceeds and interest within a reasonable period of time.

STRUCTURE AND FUNCTIONAL CHARACTERISTICS OF SETTLEMENT OPTIONS

Life insurance settlement options, as a group, embody these three basic concepts:

- retention of proceeds without liquidation of principal
- systematic liquidation of the proceeds without reference to life contingencies
- systematic liquidation of the proceeds with reference to one or more life contingencies

A number of options have evolved from this conceptual foundation, but they can be reduced to these four fundamental options:

- the interest option
- the installment time option or fixed-period option
- the installment amount option or fixed-amount option
- the life income option

These four options will be discussed under the conceptual classification mentioned above.

Retention of Proceeds at Interest

Structure of the Option

The simplest and most flexible of all settlement options is the interest option. The fundamental concept underlying this option is that the proceeds will be maintained intact until the expiration of a specified period or until the occurrence of some specific event. It is an interim option; it postpones the ultimate disposition of the proceeds and must be followed by a liquidating option or a lump-sum distribution.

The company guarantees a minimum rate of interest on the proceeds, which is payable at periodic intervals, usually monthly. If the policy was participating, the proceeds will be credited with the actual rate of interest earned by the company or, more likely, a rate approximately equal to the interest factor in the dividend formula. Excess interest is usually paid once a year on one of the normal interest payment dates.

The interest on proceeds left with the company may constitute a significant portion of the primary beneficiary's income. Indeed, it is sometimes adequate for all the beneficiary's income needs. Frequently a life income is provided to the primary beneficiary (usually, the insured's spouse) through the interest option, with the proceeds at the primary beneficiary's death applied to the needs of the contingent beneficiaries (often the insured's children). To determine how much principal must be left with the company to provide an interest income of a desired amount, see tables 25-1 and 25-2.

Tables 25-1 and 25-2 are based on the assumption that the proceeds will yield even percentages between 3 percent and 8 percent annual interest. Thus the annual income per $1,000 is assumed to be $30, $40, $50, $60, $70, or $80. However, if payments are to be made monthly rather than annually, the amount of each payment will be somewhat *less* than a proportionate share of the annual interest, owing to an adjustment made for loss of interest. If, instead of paying interest at the end of the year, the company pays at the end of the first and each subsequent month, it loses 11 months' interest on the first payment, 10 months' interest on the second, 9 on the third, and so on. Altogether it loses 11/24 of one year's interest. At 3 percent, the interest on $30 is $0.90, 11/24 of which is $0.41. Thus the effective amount of interest earned is $29.59, which divided by 12, yields $2.50 as the proper monthly payment, rather than $2.47 (30÷12). Such adjustments are preprogrammed into financial calculators' solutions.

Functional Characteristics

The primary beneficiary can be given varying degrees of control over proceeds held by the company under the interest option. If the policyowner wants the proceeds to go intact to the contingent beneficiaries eventually, he or she will give the primary beneficiary no rights in the proceeds other than the right to receive the interest for a lifetime or for some other specified period. If the policyowner wants to provide flexibility to meet unforeseen needs, he or she may grant the primary beneficiary a limited right of withdrawal. This creates no complications for the insurance company and is always permitted.

Further flexibility and control may be provided by giving the primary beneficiary the right to elect a liquidating option within a specified period or at any time. Most insurance companies permit this flexibility, but as explained earlier, unless the liquidating option is elected within a stipulated period after the insured's death, the benefits will be provided on the basis of current rather than contract rates. The settlement agreement itself may stipulate that after a specified period of time, or upon the occurrence of a stipulated contingency, the proceeds will be applied under a liquidating option for the benefit of either the primary beneficiary or the contingent beneficiaries, or both. In that event, contract rates will apply.

TABLE 25-1
Amount of Principal Needed to Provide a Specified Annual Interest Income at Various Rates of Interest

Annual Income Desired	Annual Interest Rate					
	3%	4%	5%	6%	7%	8%
$ 100	$ 3,350*	$ 2,500	$ 2,000	$ 1,700	$ 1,450	$ 1,250
250	8,350	6,250	5,000	4,200	3,600	3,150
500	16,700	12,500	10,000	8,350	7,150	6,250
750	25,000	18,750	15,000	12,500	10,750	9,400
1,000	33,350	25,000	20,000	16,700	14,300	12,500
2,000	66,700	50,000	40,000	33,350	28,600	25,000
10,000	333,350	250,000	200,000	166,700	142,900	125,000
20,000	666,700	500,000	400,000	333,350	285,750	250,000
100,000	$3,333,350	2,500,0000	2,000,000	1,666,700	1,428,600	1,250,000

The values above are interest-only payments; payments would continue without change and without liquidating the principal. Assumes end-of-year payments.
*All numbers have been rounded up to the nearest $50.

TABLE 25-2
Amount of Principal Needed to Provide a Specified Monthly Income at Various Rates of Interest

Monthly Income Desired	Equivalent Annual Interest Rate					
	3%	4%	5%	6%	7%	8%
$ 100	$ 40,000*	$ 30,000	$ 24,000	$ 20,000	$ 17,150	$ 15,000
250	100,000	75,000	60,000	50,000	42,900	37,500
500	200,000	150,000	120,000	100,000	85,750	75,000
750	300,000	225,000	180,000	150,000	128,600	112,500
1,000	400,000	300,000	240,000	200,000	171,450	150,000
2,000	800,000	600,000	480,000	400,000	342,900	300,000
3,000	1,200,000	900,000	720,000	600,000	514,300	450,000
4,000	1,600,000	1,200,000	960,000	800,000	685,750	600,000
5,000	2,000,000	1,500,000	1,200,000	1,000,000	857,150	750,000

The values above are interest-only payments; payments would continue without change and without liquidating the principal.

*All numbers have been rounded up to the nearest $50.

The beneficiary may be given complete control over the proceeds by receiving an unlimited right of withdrawal during his or her lifetime, as well as the right to dispose of the proceeds after his or her own death. One or the other of these rights must be present if the proceeds are to qualify for the marital deduction,[3] which can be very important if the insured has a large enough estate to create a federal estate tax liability. As pointed out earlier, the only forms of disposition by the beneficiary that many insurance companies will permit are payment to the beneficiary's estate or payment to irrevocably designated contingent beneficiaries. If the primary beneficiary is given an unlimited right of withdrawal, the guaranteed rate of interest may be lower than would otherwise be the case. Needless to say, if the beneficiary is entitled to a lump-sum settlement but chooses to leave the proceeds with the insurer under the interest option, she or he can retain any privileges the insurance company is willing to grant.

Most companies are willing to retain proceeds under the interest option throughout the remaining lifetime of the primary beneficiary or for 30 years, whichever is longer. Thus the interest option may be available to contingent beneficiaries. A few companies will hold the proceeds throughout the lifetime of the primary beneficiary and the first contingent beneficiary. From the company's standpoint, some limit is necessary to control the cost of administration and to avoid an indefinite projection of contract rates. (If the insured or the beneficiary elects a liquidating option for the contingent beneficiaries to commence upon termination of the interest option, contract rates will be applicable.)

As a general rule, a company will not accumulate the interest credited to proceeds retained under the interest option. In other words, it insists upon paying out the interest at least annually. This is to avoid any conflict with the laws in several states that forbid the accumulation of trust income except that payable to a minor beneficiary. By analogy, these laws can be applied to proceeds held by a life insurance company. Most—but not all—companies will therefore permit the accumulation of interest income payable to a minor beneficiary; otherwise, a guardian might have to be appointed to receive the interest distributions.

Insurance companies' unwillingness to accumulate interest has a profound impact on the technique of programming, as will be apparent later.

Systematic Liquidation without Reference to Life Contingencies

Proceeds left with a life insurance company to be liquidated at a uniform rate without reference to a life contingency must be paid out either over a specified period of time, with the amount of each payment being the variable, or at a specified rate, with the period of time over which the liquidation is to take place being the variable. If the period over which the liquidation is to occur is fixed, the amount of each payment depends on the size of the fund, the rate of interest assumed to be earned, the time when the first payment is to be made, and the interval between payments. If the amount of each payment is fixed in advance, the period over which the liquidation is to take place depends on these same factors. An option is available for each situation. The *fixed-period option* (also called an installment time option) provides payments over a stipulated period of time, while the *fixed-amount option* (also called an installment amount option) provides payments of a stipulated amount. The two options are based on the same mathematical principles and differ only as to whether emphasis is attached to the *duration* of the payments or to the *level* of payments. If the insured or the beneficiary wants the assurance of *some* income, however small, over a specified period, he or her should select the fixed-period option. If, however, the need is for temporary *adequacy* of income, irrespective of its duration, the insured or the beneficiary should choose the fixed-amount option. In some situations, the decision will turn on the flexibility under the two options.

Fixed-period Option

Structure of the Option. If a given principal sum is to be liquidated at a uniform rate over a specified period of years, the amount of each *annual* payment can be derived from a financial calculator or from compound discount tables. For example, if $1,000 is to be liquidated in annual installments over a 20-year period and the undistributed proceeds are assumed to earn interest at the rate of 3.5 percent, the amount of each payment *due at the beginning of the year* will be $1,000 ÷ $14.71 = $67.98. In other words, the present value of a series of annual payments of $1, at 3.5 percent interest, *due at the beginning of the year,* for a period of 20 years, is $14.71. If $14.71 will provide $1 per year for 20 years, then $1,000 will provide an annual payment equal to 67.98 times $1 since it takes $14.71 to support each series of $1 payments, and $1,000 will support 67.98. The monthly payment for 20 years at 3.5 percent interest from $1,000 is $5.78.

The amount of annual, semiannual, quarterly, or monthly payment for each $1,000 of proceeds for any period of years can be computed using a financial calculator. The $1,000 amount is entered as the present value using the PV key (clear the financial section of the calculator before starting to calculate). For annual payments enter the number of payments (20) using the n key and enter the annual interest rate (3.5 percent) using the i key. The calculation of payments on a monthly basis requires changing the number of payments (in our example 20 x 12 = 240 total payments) for the n key and changing the annual interest rate to a monthly rate equivalent to the annual rate (in our example 3.5÷12 = .29166) for the i key. Remember to set the calculator in a beginning of period mode (or due mode) before solving for the payment amount using the PMT key.

Table 25-3 shows the guaranteed installments for each $1,000 of proceeds at 3.5 percent interest. Obviously, the numbers in the table would change if a different interest rate were used.

Functional Characteristics. The essence of the fixed-period option is the certainty of the period over which the proceeds will be distributed. Hence any developments that increase or decrease the amount of proceeds available are reflected by variation in the size of the monthly payments and not in the duration of the payments. Additional proceeds payable by reason of the insured's accidental death increase the amount of the monthly payments. Dividend accumulations and paid-up additions have the same effect. If prepaid or discounted premiums are considered part of the proceeds, they can be applied under a settlement option and, in the case of the fixed-period option, raise the level of payments. (Under the provisions of some policies, however, such premium deposits are treated as belonging to the insured's estate and do not become part of the proceeds payable to third-party beneficiaries.) Policy loans, if still outstanding at the policy's maturity reduce the proceeds available and hence the size of the monthly benefits.

TABLE 25-3
Guaranteed Installments per $1,000 of Proceeds (3.5 Percent Interest), Beginning-of-period Payments

Number of Years Payable	Annually	Semiannually	Quarterly	Monthly
1	$1,000.00	$504.34	$253.30	$84.67
2	508.60	256.54	128.84	43.08
3	344.86	173.98	87.41	29.22
4	263.04	132.72	66.69	22.29
5	213.99	107.99	54.27	18.14
6	181.32	91.51	45.99	15.37
7	158.01	79.76	40.09	13.40
8	140.56	70.96	35.67	11.92
9	127.00	64.12	32.24	10.78
10	116.18	58.66	29.50	9.86
11	107.34	54.21	27.26	9.11
12	99.98	50.50	25.40	8.49
13	93.78	47.37	23.83	7.96
14	88.47	44.70	22.49	7.52
15	83.89	42.39	21.33	7.13
16	79.89	40.37	20.32	6.79
17	76.37	38.60	19.43	6.49
18	73.25	37.03	18.64	6.23
19	70.47	35.63	17.94	5.99
20	67.98	34.37	17.31	5.78
21	65.74	33.24	16.74	5.59
22	63.70	32.26	16.23	5.42
23	61.85	31.28	15.76	5.26
24	60.17	30.43	15.33	5.12
25	58.62	29.65	14.94	4.99
26	57.20	28.94	14.58	4.87
27	55.90	28.28	14.25	4.76
28	54.69	27.67	13.95	4.66
29	53.57	27.11	13.67	4.56
30	52.53	26.59	13.40	4.48

Some companies permit the beneficiary to repay a policy loan after the insured's death in order to have the full amount of proceeds payable under a settlement option. Excess interest, if any, may be paid in one sum at the end of each year or added in pro rata proportions to each of the regular benefit payments during the following year.

The fixed-period option is a very inflexible arrangement. The only flexibilities are to permit the beneficiary to choose the date on which the option becomes operative, rather than having it go into effect automatically at the policy's maturity, and to grant the beneficiary the right of commutation. If the option is designed not to go into operation automatically upon maturity of the policy, the proceeds are held under the interest option until such time as the beneficiary indicates that liquidation should commence. Limited withdrawals are not permitted, presumably because of the administrative expense involved in recomputing the benefits and recasting the agreement after each withdrawal. Insurers are willing, however, to permit the settlement agreement to be terminated by the beneficiary's withdrawal of all proceeds remaining with the company.

Fixed-amount Option

Structure of the Option. The fixed-amount option is based on the simple proposition of distributing a specified sum each month, or at some other periodic time interval, until the proceeds are exhausted. Mathematically, it is based on the same compound discount function that underlies the fixed-period option. The application is different, however.

The principle can be explained in terms of $1,000 to be distributed in equal annual payments of $100, the first payment being due immediately. It is obvious that the liquidation will extend over a minimum period of 9 years since the principal alone will provide payments for that period of time. The problem is to determine how much longer the payments can be continued because of crediting compound interest to the unliquidated portion of the principal.

The first step is to use a financial calculator and enter the known information; then solve for the number of periodic payments that will be made (find n).

In this example calculation, assume that $50,000 is available to be paid out in monthly installments of $3,000 each and the interest earned on the undistributed balance is 4 percent annually. After clearing the financial calculator and setting it in beginning-of-period (due) mode, the entries are as follows: $50,000 is the PV; −$3,000 (note: the sign of the PV must be the opposite of the sign of the payment for the calculator to work) is the PMT; 4÷12=0.3333% is the monthly interest rate. Then the duration of payments can be found by solving for n. In this example n=18, indicating that the payments will continue for 18 months. The aggregate amount of payments is $54,000, indicating that $4,000 of interest is earned on the $50,000 capital base before the last benefit payment is made.

Functional Characteristics. Since the amount of each payment is fixed under this option, any augmentation in the volume of proceeds or interest lengthens the period over which payments will be made; any diminution in the amount of proceeds shortens the period. Thus dividend accumulations, paid-up additions, accidental death benefits, and excess interest extend the period of liquidation, whereas loans outstanding at the insured's death and withdrawals of principal by the beneficiary shorten the period. This is true even though the payments are to terminate at a specified date or at the occurrence of some specified event, with the balance of the proceeds being distributed in some manner.

The fixed-amount option offers a great deal of flexibility. As with the fixed-period option, the beneficiary can be given the right to indicate when the liquidation payments are to begin. In the meantime, the proceeds will be held at interest, with the interest payments going to the primary beneficiary. Unlike the fixed-period option, the beneficiary can be given either a limited or an unlimited right of withdrawal. Under this option, withdrawals will merely shorten the period of installment payments and will not necessitate recomputing benefit payments.

The beneficiary can also be given the right to accelerate or retard the rate of liquidation. That is, he or she can be given the privilege of varying the amount of the monthly payments, subject to any limitations the insured might wish to impose. For example, the insured might direct the company to liquidate the proceeds at the rate of $3,000 per month, while giving the beneficiary the option of stepping up the payments to $5,000 per month or reducing them to any level acceptable to the company. Under such circumstances, the insured is not likely to prescribe any minimum rate of liquidation.

Furthermore, the beneficiary can be given the privilege of discontinuing payments during particular months of the year or from time to time. For example, when the proceeds of an educational endowment policy are being paid out to a beneficiary who is enrolled in a college or university, payments can be discontinued during the summer vacation months. Similarly, larger-than-usual payments can be provided for months in which tuition and other fees are payable. Such flexibility stems from the fact that the fixed-amount option basically creates a savings account from which withdrawals can be made to suit the beneficiary's convenience.

Finally, this option can include a provision for transferring the remaining proceeds to another liquidating option. If the transfer is to take place at a specified date or age, contract rates will be available. If the beneficiary has the right to transfer the proceeds at any time, the conversion will be subject to current rates.

Systematic Liquidation with Reference to Life Contingencies

The proceeds of a life insurance policy may be liquidated at a uniform rate over the lifetime of one or more beneficiaries. This type of arrangement, peculiar to life insurance companies, is of very great value. It protects a beneficiary against the economic hazard of excessive longevity—that is, it protects the beneficiary against the possibility of outliving his or her income.

Structure of the Life Income Options

Any settlement option based on a life contingency is called a *life income option.* The principle underlying a life income option is identical to that underlying an annuity. As a matter of fact, a life income option is nothing more than the annuity principle applied to the liquidation of insurance proceeds. Hence there are as many variations of the life income option as there are types of immediate annuities. Among the single-life annuities, there are the pure or straight life annuity, life annuity with guaranteed installments, the installment-refund annuity, and the cash-refund annuity. There are similar annuities based on two or more lives.[4]

While there is a counterpart among the life income options for every type of immediate annuity, it is not customary for a company to include the whole range of annuity forms in its life insurance policies. The typical policy provides for a life income with payments guaranteed for 10, 15, and 20 years and the installment-refund option. Some companies include the joint-and-last-survivor annuity, and a few show the straight life annuity. Virtually all will make additional options available upon request.

Mathematically, the straight life income option is equivalent to a pure immediate annuity. To be precisely accurate, it is the same as a life annuity due since the first payment is due immediately upon maturity of the policy or upon election of the option, whichever is later. The monthly income provided per $1,000 of proceeds depends on the age and sex of the beneficiary and the insurer's assumptions as to mortality and interest. Although the schedules of income guaranteed under various insurers' policies are similar, there is currently little uniformity among companies as to the combination of mortality and interest assumptions used to calculate the income payments. Benefits are provided at *net* rates, and there is no charge for the use of the life income settlement.

The life income option with a specified period of guaranteed payments is mathematically a combination of a fixed-period installment option of appropriate duration and a pure *deferred* life annuity.[5] For example, a life income option that promises to provide payments of a specified amount to a beneficiary aged 45 throughout his or her remaining lifetime and in any event for 20 years is a combination of a fixed-period installment option running for 20 years and a pure life annuity deferred to the beneficiary's age 65. If the beneficiary does not survive to age 65, the portion of the proceeds allocated to the deferred life annuity is retained by the insurance company without further obligation.

Since the life income settlement options are essentially annuity contracts available without any applicable sales commissions or other expense loadings, they often provide more benefits for the same contribution than do separate annuity contracts. The only way to be certain that the settlement option is less costly is to make price and benefit comparisons with the annuity contracts available from other insurers. If annuity contract is found to be more advantageous than the settlement option, that life insurer should be carefully scrutinized to determine its long-term financial strength.

The installment refund option—which, as indicated in chapter 6, promises to continue the monthly payments beyond the annuitant's death until the purchase price of the annuity or, in this case, the proceeds of the life insurance policy have been returned—is a combination of a pure immediate life annuity and decreasing term insurance in an amount sufficient to continue payments until the proceeds, without interest, have been paid out in full. At the inception, the term insurance is in an amount equal to the proceeds, less the first payment due immediately, but it decreases with each periodic payment and expires altogether when the cumulative benefit payments equal or exceed the life insurance proceeds committed to the installment-refund option.

The cash-refund option is likewise a combination of a pure immediate life annuity and decreasing term insurance. Since the refund is payable in cash rather than payable in installments, however, a slightly larger amount of term insurance is required.

To use a life income option in planning a client's estate, the life underwriter needs two types of tables. The first type enables the life underwriter to compute the amount of insurance required to meet the life income needs of the beneficiary or beneficiaries. It shows the amount of principal needed to provide $10 a month under the various life income options for a wide range of male and female ages.

The values for such a table, based on one set of actuarial assumptions, are presented in tables 25-4 and 25-5.

The second type of table shows the amount of monthly income that will be provided for each $1,000 of proceeds under the life income options and ranges of ages. After the life underwriter determines how much insurance in multiples of $1,000 is needed, he or she can demonstrate to the client, through the second type of table, exactly how much income can be provided with the actual and contemplated insurance. The values for this type of table, calculated on the same basis as the values for tables 25-4 and 25-5, are shown in tables 25-6 and 25-7.

Functional Characteristics

Since the life income option contemplates the complete liquidation of the proceeds during the beneficiary's lifetime, it follows that any circumstances that enlarge the volume of proceeds will increase the amount of each periodic payment, while shrinkages in the proceeds will decrease the size of the payments. In this connection, it is interesting to note that excess interest is usually payable only under the annuity form calling for a guaranteed number of payments and, even then, only during the period of guaranteed installments. This is another way of saying that excess interest is payable on the portion of the proceeds applied under the fixed-period installment option but is not payable on that portion of the proceeds allocated to the deferred life annuity. Some companies guarantee a lower rate of interest on the fixed-period option portion of the arrangement than under the deferred life annuity.

The life income option is extremely inflexible. Benefits are calculated on the basis of the age and sex of the primary beneficiary, and once the payments have begun, no other person can be substituted for the designated beneficiary, even with an adjustment in the benefits. No right of withdrawal is available and no commutation privilege exists for benefits payable under a deferred life annuity. Otherwise, persons in poor health would be inclined to withdraw the proceeds. When the benefits are guaranteed for a specified period of time, however, a few companies will permit the proceeds payable under the fixed-period installment option to be commuted. If the commutation privilege is exercised, the beneficiary is usually given a deferred life annuity certificate. This certificate provides for life income payments to the beneficiary if he or she survives the period during which the guaranteed payments were to have been made.

USE OF SETTLEMENT OPTIONS

Adaptation of Settlement Options to Basic Family Needs

The opening chapter of this book described the basic family needs that life insurance can meet. The manner in which settlement options can be adapted to a family's various needs is outlined below.

Nonrecurrent Needs

Cleanup or Estate Clearance Fund. The first need in point of time, as explained in chapter 1, is a fund to meet the expenses that arise from the

TABLE 25-4
Principal Amount Needed to Provide Life Income
of $10 per Month at Selected Male Ages

Age	Life Annuity	10-Year Certain + Life	20-Year Certain + Life
50	$2,074.72	$ 2,092.4386	$2,151.0323
51	2,043.45	2,062.7682	2,126.4265
52	2,011.56	2,032.5134	2,101.7083
53	1,979.00	2,001.6522	2,076.9307
54	1,945.73	1,970.1663	2,052.1523
55	1,911.70	1,938.0465	2,027.4383
56	1,876.88	1,905.2949	2,002.8620
57	1,841.21	1,871.9240	1,978.5044
58	1,804.65	1,837.9573	1,954.4541
59	1,767.18	1,803.4327	1,930.8080
60	1,728.77	1,768.4122	1,907.6737
61	1,689.46	1,732.9815	1,885.1662
62	1,649.31	1,697.2468	1,863.4048
63	1,608.41	1,661.3293	1,842.5077
64	1,566.86	1,625.3595	1,822.5883
65	1,524.77	1,589.4676	1,803.7493
66	1,482.26	1,553.7817	1,786.0778
67	1,439.45	1,518.4284	1,769.6418
68	1,396.43	1,483.5328	1,754.4876
69	1,353.31	1,449.2195	1,740.6001
70	1,310.18	1,415.6112	1,728.0929
71	1,267.12	1,382.8293	1,716.8311
72	1,224.21	1,350.9933	1,706.8147
73	1,181.51	1,320.2200	1,697.9912
74	1,139.07	1,290.6243	1,690.2966
75	1,096.96	1,262.3231	1,683.6587
76	1,055.28	1,235.4283	1,677.9980
77	1,014.12	1,210.0381	1,673.2300
78	973.61	1,186.2301	1,669.2662
79	933.85	1,164.0560	1,666.0169
80	894.98	1,143.5380	1,663.3935
81	857.11	1,124.6717	1,661.3114
82	820.36	1,107.4297	1,659.6907
83	784.85	1,091.7671	1,658.4572
84	750.68	1,077.6228	1,657.5428
85	717.92	1,064.9197	1,656.8857

Male 1983 Individual Annuity Table
(4 percent interest net rates)

TABLE 25-5
Principal Amount Needed to Provide Life Income
of $10 per Month at Selected Female Ages

Age	Life Annuity	10-Year Certain + Life	20-Year Certain + Life
50	$2,237.91	$2,244.7293	$2,272.6161
51	2,208.92	2,216.6597	2,247.8142
52	2,179.14	2,187.8547	2,222.5817
53	2,148.53	2,158.3038	2,196.9426
54	2,117.07	2,127.9981	2,170.9289
55	2,084.73	2,096.9326	2,144.5825
56	2,051.51	2,065.1151	2,117.9610
57	2,017.38	2032.5550	2,091.1317
58	1,982.33	1,999.2603	2,064.1720
59	1,946.35	1,965.2489	2,037.1739
60	1,909.45	1,930.5356	2,010.2380
61	1,871.65	1,895.1533	1,983.4812
62	1,832.98	1,859.1360	1,957.0284
63	1,793.45	1,822.5286	1,931.0152
64	1,753.15	1,785.3961	1,905.5879
65	1,712.08	1,747.7927	1,880.8914
66	1,670.28	1,709.7883	1,857.0756
67	1,627.71	1,671.4403	1,834.2843
68	1,584.36	1,632.8252	1,812.6609
69	1,540.18	1,594.0268	1,792.3413
70	1,495.16	1,555.1662	1,773.4541
71	1,449.38	1,516.4019	1,756.1091
72	1,402.92	1,477.9123	1,740.3840
73	1,355.91	1,439.8962	1,726.3185
74	1,308.52	1,402.5704	1,713.9114
75	1,260.89	1,366.1510	1,703.1193
76	1,213.21	1,330.8508	1,693.8614
77	1,165.59	1,296.8726	1,686.0267
78	1,118.20	1,264.4172	1,679.4831
79	1,071.14	1,233.6701	1,674.0847
80	1,024.57	1,204.8069	1,669.6856
81	978.63	1,177.9807	1,666.1476
82	933.48	1,153.3068	1,663.3430
83	889.29	1,130.8537	1,661.1568
84	846.23	1,110.6411	1,659.4863
85	804.47	1,092.6360	1,658.2403

Female 1983 Individual Annuity Table
(4 percent interest net rates)

TABLE 25-6
Monthly Lifetime Benefit for Male per $1,000 Annuity Purchase (Net Rates)

Age	Life Annuity	10-Year Certain + Life	20-Year Certain + Life
50	$ 4.82	$4.78	$4.65
51	4.89	4.85	4.70
52	4.97	4.92	4.76
53	5.05	5.00	4.81
54	5.14	5.08	4.87
55	5.23	5.16	4.93
56	5.33	5.25	4.99
57	5.43	5.34	5.05
58	5.54	5.44	5.12
59	5.66	5.54	5.18
60	5.78	5.65	5.24
61	5.92	5.77	5.30
62	6.06	5.89	5.37
63	6.22	6.02	5.43
64	6.38	6.15	5.49
65	6.56	6.29	5.54
66	6.75	6.44	5.60
67	6.95	6.59	5.65
68	7.16	6.74	5.70
69	7.39	6.90	5.75
70	7.63	7.06	5.79
71	7.89	7.23	5.82
72	8.17	7.40	5.86
73	8.46	7.57	5.89
74	8.78	7.75	5.92
75	9.12	7.92	5.94
76	9.48	8.09	5.96
77	9.86	8.26	5.98
78	10.27	8.43	5.99
79	10.71	8.59	6.00
80	11.17	8.74	6.01
81	11.67	8.89	6.02
82	12.19	9.03	6.03
83	12.74	9.16	6.03
84	13.32	9.28	6.03
85	13.93	9.39	6.04

Male 1983 Individual Annuity Table
(4 percent interest net rates)

TABLE 25-7
Monthly Lifetime Benefit for Female per $1,000 Annuity Purchase (Net Rates)

Age	Life Annuity	10-Year Certain + Life	20-Year Certain + Life
50	$ 4.47	$4.45	$4.40
51	4.53	4.51	4.45
52	4.59	4.57	4.50
53	4.65	4.63	4.55
54	4.72	4.70	4.61
55	4.80	4.77	4.66
56	4.87	4.84	4.72
57	4.96	4.92	4.78
58	5.04	5.00	4.84
59	5.14	5.09	4.91
60	5.24	5.18	4.97
61	5.34	5.28	5.04
62	5.46	5.38	5.11
63	5.58	5.49	5.18
64	5.70	5.60	5.25
65	5.84	5.72	5.32
66	5.99	5.85	5.38
67	6.14	5.98	5.45
68	6.31	6.12	5.52
69	6.49	6.27	5.58
70	6.69	6.43	5.64
71	6.90	6.59	5.69
72	7.13	6.77	5.75
73	7.38	6.94	5.79
74	7.64	7.13	5.83
75	7.93	7.32	5.87
76	8.24	7.51	5.90
77	8.58	7.71	5.93
78	8.39	7.91	5.95
79	9.34	8.11	5.97
80	9.76	8.30	5.99
81	10.22	8.49	6.00
82	10.71	8.67	6.01
83	11.24	8.84	6.02
84	11.82	9.00	6.03
85	12.43	9.15	6.03

Female 1983 Individual Annuity Table
(4 percent interest net rates)

insured's death and to liquidate the current outstanding obligations. These are claims against the insured's probate estate and must be satisfied before any property can be distributed to the heirs. The size of the fund varies, but for estates of less than $600,000, it averages 15 percent of the probate estate. For larger estates the percentage is higher because of the progressive nature of death tax rates.

The conventional method of handling proceeds intended for estate clearance is to have them paid to the insured's estate in a lump sum. This recognizes that payment of the claims against the estate is an obligation of the executor or administrator, and fulfilling this obligation requires cash within a relatively short time after the insured's death. In recent years, however, for estates of more than $600,000 there has been a shift toward having the policy owned by the spouse or a life insurance trust. By making the life insurance proceeds payable to the spouse or the trust, funds can be made available to the insured's estate either by purchasing noncash assets from the estate or by loaning money to the estate. Under the interest-only option the beneficiary may leave the proceeds with the insurer to earn interest until they are needed by the beneficiary or the executor. If the insurance is more than adequate for the needs of the estate, the excess can go to the insured's dependents without having to pass through the probate estate and the attendant delay and expense. These advantages are especially important when the potential estate liabilities are large but unpredictable and a substantial amount of insurance is involved. While some insurers do not permit executors or trustees to elect life income settlement options, most are willing to make the interest option available to a trustee or an executor during the period of estate administration.

If the probate estate is modest and the insured's spouse is the sole or major beneficiary of the estate, it may be advantageous to have the insurance intended for estate clearance payable to the widow(er) under the interest option with the unlimited right of withdrawal. He or she can use whatever portion of the proceeds is needed to pay the debts of the insured's estate and apply the remainder to his or her own needs, perhaps in the form of a deferred settlement. This procedure will reduce the cost of estate administration, particularly the executor's fee. It will also take advantage of the special inheritance tax exemption available in most states when insurance proceeds are payable to third-party beneficiaries, especially the insured's widow(er) and children. This advantage is offset to the extent that payment of the insured's debts out of the insurance proceeds enlarges the taxable distribution from the estate unless funds were made available through loans to or asset purchases from the estate. By using the interest option and a spendthrift clause, the insured can protect the proceeds from the beneficiary's creditors.

The obvious disadvantage of this arrangement is that the beneficiary, through poor judgment, may pay claims that were not valid or, through stupidity or greed, refuse to use the insurance proceeds for the purposes for which they were intended. This behavior is, of course, more likely when the beneficiary is not the sole legatee of the estate, and it may result in forced liquidation at great sacrifice of valuable estate assets. Another risk in this arrangement, unless properly safeguarded, is that the widow(er) might die before clearing the insured's estate, with the proceeds going to his or her estate or to minor contingent beneficiaries. Both situations would then make it impossible for the proceeds to be used to pay the insured's debts.   To guard against such an untoward development, it is possible to make the insured's estate the contingent beneficiary if the widow(er) should predecease the insured or die within 6 months after the insured's death. If the primary beneficiary survives the insured by six months, the children can become the contingent beneficiaries of any unused proceeds.

If the estate liabilities are large and a life insurance trust is going to be used for other purposes, the estate clearance fund can be made payable to the trustee in a lump sum or under the interest option (if permissible).   A provision in the trust agreement authorizes the trustee to lend money to the estate or to purchase estate assets. Thus the trust may come to hold assets formerly held by the estate.

Mortgage Cancellation Fund. If there is a mortgage on the insured's home, the insured usually attempts to provide enough insurance to liquidate the mortgage upon his or her death so that the family can continue to occupy the home.   In some cases, the insurance is provided through a special mortgage redemption policy, embodying the decreasing term insurance principle.

If the mortgage can be prepaid, there is usually a provision for a lump-sum payment either to the insured's surviving spouse or to his or her estate. This is predicated on the assumption that it takes less insurance to liquidate the mortgage with a single-sum payment than to provide a monthly income equal to the regular monthly payments. If the mortgage has no prepayment privilege or can be prepaid only with a heavy penalty, an income settlement can be arranged to provide funds in the required amount and frequency for the mortgage payments. Either the fixed-period option or the fixed-amount option is satisfactory, although the fixed-period option would be difficult to use if elected before the insured's death.

Emergency Fund.   If a life insurance trust is not created, perhaps the most satisfactory arrangement for emergency funds is by electing the interest option with a limited or an unlimited right of withdrawal. The widow(er) is normally the beneficiary. Another method of making emergency funds available is through the fixed-amount   option   with   appropriate   withdrawal   privileges.   Under   this arrangement a somewhat larger fund can be set aside than that needed for the regular installments.

Educational Fund.   As indicated earlier, the fixed-amount option is ideally suited   to   liquidating   proceeds   intended   to   finance   a   college   education   or professional training. However, the interest option, with appropriate withdrawal privileges, can also be used to cope with inflation. The payments can be made directly to the student, to the educational institution on his or her behalf, or to an adult relative or friend.

Income Needs of the Family

Readjustment Income.   The   readjustment   period   is   the   interval   of time—usually one to 3 years in duration—immediately following the insured's death, during which income is usually provided at or near the level enjoyed by the family during the insured's lifetime.   In the dependency period thereafter, the income drops to a more realistic and sustainable level.

Theoretically, the income for the readjustment period can be provided through the fixed-period option, the fixed-amount option, or the interest option with the right of withdrawal. If a step-down within the period is contemplated, which may be advisable if the dependency period income represents a drastic reduction, the fixed-amount option can be used because it allows adjustments to the amount. Some estate planners provide the same contractual income in the readjustment period as in the dependency period, with the thought that the widow(er) can use the withdrawal privilege to cushion the financial shock during the readjustment period.

Dependency Period Income. Broadly speaking, the dependency period extends from the date of the insured's death until the youngest child is self-sufficient or perhaps in college. In planning terminology, however, the dependency period is the interval between the end of the readjustment period and the youngest child's self-sufficiency, usually assumed to occur at age 18, unless a child is mentally or physically handicapped.

In practice a combination of social security survivorship benefits and the interest on life insurance proceeds being held for other purposes frequently meets a substantial portion of the family's income needs during this period. If not, additional income can be provided through the fixed-period or fixed-amount options. If, at the time the program is being set up, the youngest child is 6 years old and additional income of $600 per month is desired until the child is 18, it does not seem to matter whether proceeds in the amount of $68,530 are set aside under a fixed-period option providing $600 per month for 12 years or whether the same sum is set aside under a fixed-amount option providing $100 per month as long as the proceeds hold out, which would be exactly 12 years if there were no withdrawals from the fund and no excess interest over the assumed 4 percent rate were credited to it. Under most circumstances, however, the fixed-amount option will prove to be more satisfactory.

Perhaps most significant is that the right of withdrawal can be granted in connection with the fixed-amount option but not with the fixed-period option. In some cases, it may be unwise to give the beneficiary this privilege, but in general, it injects an element of flexibility into the settlement plan that may be urgently needed, particularly with the prospect of continued inflationary pressures. Moreover, moderate withdrawals will not necessarily shorten the period of income payments since the withdrawals may be offset in whole or in part by dividend accumulations and excess interest credits. Another argument in favor of the fixed-amount option is that provision can be made for increasing the size of the monthly payments to offset the loss of income from social security as each child reaches age 18.

Life Income for Surviving Spouse. In life insurance planning, it is necessary to break the widow(er)'s basic need for life income into two periods. One period runs from the youngest child's 18th birthday to the widow(er)'s age 62, and the other starts at the widow(er)'s age 62. This breakdown is necessary because the widow(er)'s income from social security terminates when the youngest child reaches age 18 (unless a child is totally disabled) and does not resume until the widow(er) reaches age 62. (A permanently reduced benefit is available at age 60.)

The period in between is usually called the social security gap or the blackout period.

Income during the blackout period can be provided by making the life income option operative upon the insured's death or upon termination of the social security survivorship benefits. Alternatively, the interest-only option can be left in place until the surviving spouse needs more income and then converted to a life income option.

In most cases, after the blackout period income to the surviving spouse will be provided by social security benefits and payments under a life income option, the only practical way of ensuring a definite income for the remainder of the widow(er)'s life. If a large sum of insurance is available and the beneficiary both is financially able and desires to preserve the principal for the benefit of contingent beneficiaries (such as children), the interest option can be used until the primary beneficiary's death.

The primary beneficiary's age and health should be considered before making a life income settlement option election. If the beneficiary is unlikely to survive very long because of poor health or very old age, choosing a life income option could result in a significant forfeiture. Selecting a period-certain guarantee would at least limit such forfeiture. The beneficiary is less likely to be concerned about a possible forfeiture if there are no children or grandchildren to receive such residual funds.

NOTES

1. Such a document may also be referred to as a *supplementary contract, supplementary agreement,* or *settlement statement.* Some companies do not use a special agreement; the beneficiary simply retains the policy, possibly with an endorsement, as evidence of the company's continuing obligation.
2. However, the beneficiary's election of a deferred settlement does not necessarily deprive him or her of the protection of this clause.
3. See chapter 11 for a discussion of federal estate taxes and the marital deduction.
4. See chapter 6 for a thorough discussion of the various types of annuities.
5. Such an option may also be viewed as a combination of a pure deferred life annuity and decreasing term insurance, the latter being represented by the guaranteed payments.

SAMPLE SETTLEMENT AGREEMENT
ABC-XYZ Life Insurance Company

How Benefits Are Paid

You can have insurance benefits and the net cash surrender value paid immediately in one sum, or you can choose another form of payment for all or part of them. If you do not arrange for a specific choice before the Insured dies, the beneficiary will have this right when the Insured dies. If you do make an arrangement, however, the Beneficiary cannot change it after the Insured dies.

The options are as follows:

A. Deposit: The sum will be left on deposit for a period mutually agreed upon. We will pay interest at the end of every month, every 3 months, every 6 months, or every 12 months, as chosen.

B. Installment Payments: There are two ways that we pay installments:
1. Fixed Period. We will pay the sum in equal installments for a specified number of years (but not more than 30). The installments will be at least those shown in the Table of Guaranteed Payments.
2. Fixed Amount. We will pay the sum in installments as mutually agreed upon until the original sum, together with interest on the unpaid balance, is used up.

C. Monthly Life Income: We will pay the sum as a monthly income for life. The amount of the monthly payment will be at least that shown in the Table of Guaranteed Payments. You may choose any one of three ways to receive the monthly life income. We will guarantee payments for at least 10 years (called 10-Year Certain), at least 20 years (called 20-year Certain, or until the payments we make equal the original sum (called Refund Certain). If at the payee's age the benefit would be the same for more than one period certain, we will deem that the longest period has been chosen.

D. Other: We will apply the sum under any other option requested that we make available at the time of the Insured's death or net cash surrender value withdrawal.

We guarantee interest under the Deposit option at the rate of 3 percent a year and under either Installment option at 3.5 percent a year. We may raise these guaranteed rates. We may also allow interest under the Deposit option and under either Installment option at a rate above the guaranteed rate. The payee may name and change a successor payee for any amount we would otherwise pay to the payee's estate.

The Deposit, Installment, and Monthly Life Income options do not participate in dividends.

SAMPLE SETTLEMENT AGREEMENT (Continued)
ABC-XYZ Life Insurance Company

Any arrangements involving more than one of the options or a payee who is not a natural person (for example, a corporation) or who is a fiduciary must have our approval. Details of all arrangements will be subject to our rules at the time the arrangement takes effect. These include rules on the minimum amount we will apply under an option and minimum amounts for installment payments, withdrawal or commutation rights, naming payees and successor payees, and proving age and survival.

Payment choices (or any later changes) will be made and will take effect in the same way as a change of Beneficiary. Amounts applied under these options will not be subject to the claims of creditors or to legal process, to the extent permitted by law.

SAMPLE SETTLEMENT AGREEMENT (Continued)
ABC-XYZ Life Insurance Company

TABLE OF GUARANTEED SETTLEMENT PAYMENTS (Minimum Amount for Each $1,000 of Policy Proceeds Applied)		
Option B1 Fixed-period Installments		
Number of Years' Installments	Monthly Installment	Annual Installment
1	$84.70	$1,000.00
2	43.08	508.60
3	29.21	344.86
4	22.28	263.04
5	18.12	213.99
6	15.36	181.32
7	13.38	158.01
8	11.91	140.56
9	10.76	127.00
10	9.84	116.18
11	9.09	107.34
12	8.47	99.98
13	7.94	93.78
14	7.49	88.47
15	7.11	83.89
16	6.77	79.89
17	6.47	76.37
18	6.20	73.25
19	5.97	70.47
20	5.76	67.98
21	5.57	65.74
22	5.40	63.70
23	5.24	61.85
24	5.10	60.17
25	4.97	58.62
26	4.84	57.20
27	4.73	55.90
28	4.63	54.69
29	4.54	53.57
30	4.45	52.53

SAMPLE SETTLEMENT AGREEMENT (Continued)
ABC-XYZ Life Insurance Company

TABLE OF GUARANTEED SETTLEMENT PAYMENTS (Minimum Amount for Each $1,000 of Policy Proceeds Applied)

Option C
Male Monthly Life Income per $1,000

Age	10-Year Certain	20-Year Certain	Refund Certain
50	$4.50	$4.27	$4.28
51	4.58	4.32	4.35
52	4.67	4.38	4.42
53	4.75	4.44	4.50
54	4.85	4.50	4.58
55	4.94	4.56	4.66
56	5.04	4.62	4.74
57	5.15	4.68	4.83
58	5.26	4.74	4.93
59	5.37	4.81	5.03
60	5.49	4.86	5.13
61	5.62	4.92	5.24
62	5.75	4.98	5.35
63	5.88	5.04	5.48
64	6.03	5.09	5.60
65	6.17	5.14	5.74
66	6.32	5.19	5.88
67	6.48	5.24	6.03
68	6.64	5.28	6.18
69	6.80	5.32	6.35
70	6.97	5.35	6.53
71	7.15	5.38	6.71
72	7.32	5.41	6.91
73	7.50	5.43	7.12
74	7.67	5.45	7.34
75	7.85	5.47	7.58
76	8.02	5.48	7.82
77	8.19	5.49	8.09
78	8.36	5.50	8.38
79	8.52	5.50	8.67
80	8.67	5.51	9.00
81	8.81	5.51	9.34
82	8.94	5.51	9.70
83	9.06	5.51	10.10
84	9.16	5.51	10.52
85 and over	9.26	5.51	10.96

SAMPLE SETTLEMENT AGREEMENT (Continued)
ABC-XYZ Life Insurance Company

TABLE OF GUARANTEED SETTLEMENT PAYMENTS
(Minimum Amount for Each $1,000 of Policy Proceeds Applied)

Option C
Female Monthly Life Income per $1,000

Age	10-Year Certain	20-Year Certain	Refund Certain
50	$3.96	$3.89	$3.87
51	4.02	3.94	3.93
52	4.09	4.00	3.99
53	4.16	4.06	4.05
54	4.24	4.12	4.11
55	4.32	4.18	4.18
56	4.40	4.24	4.25
57	4.49	4.31	4.33
58	4.58	4.38	4.41
59	4.68	4.45	4.49
60	4.78	4.52	4.58
61	4.89	4.59	5.67
62	5.00	4.66	4.77
63	5.12	4.73	4.00
64	5.25	4.80	4.99
65	5.39	4.88	5.10
66	5.53	4.95	5.22
67	5.68	5.01	5.35
68	5.83	5.08	5.49
69	6.00	5.14	5.64
70	6.17	5.20	5.79
71	6.34	5.26	5.96
72	6.53	5.30	6.13
73	6.72	5.35	6.32
74	6.92	5.38	6.52
75	7.12	5.42	6.73
76	7.32	5.44	6.96
77	7.53	5.46	7.21
78	7.75	5.48	7.47
79	7.96	5.49	7.75
80	8.16	5.50	8.05
81	8.36	5.51	8.39
82	8.55	5.51	8.73
83	8.73	5.51	9.12
84	8.90	5.51	9.53
85 and over	9.05	5.51	9.97

26

The Regulation of Life Insurance (Part 1)

Jon S. Hanson

In the United States, government has exercised perhaps as much if not more control over the business of insurance than any other private business activity. However, despite periodic federal interest, at least to date, the primary responsibility for regulation continues to rest with the states. This chapter will concentrate on life insurance regulation at the state level. The next chapter will discuss state insurance regulation within the environment of potential and/or actual federal controls.

DEVELOPMENT OF INSURANCE REGULATION AT THE STATE LEVEL

Evolution of Regulation

Although insurance existed in the United States before the American Revolution, the industry did not mushroom until the mid-1800s when the country experienced rapid expansion in its territory, population, and business activity. Unfortunately, not all early insurers were adequately capitalized or competently managed, and this resulted in numerous insolvencies that left policyowners without payments for their losses. In response, the initial regulatory devices were simply periodic reports on an insurer's financial condition, and those reports were the basis for legislative action, judicial relief, taxation, and the information by which the buyer could determine the safety of the enterprise. When they proved insufficient, beginning in the early 1850s, state legislatures created administrative agencies to supervise insurers. Today, all states have an insurance department.

As the new insurance industry spread across the continent, problems and abuses inevitably emerged. Because individual states were regulating a business conducted across state lines, there was conflicting and discriminatory legislation and administrative action. This generated a sentiment for reform. Failing to achieve congressional action, proponents of federal regulation financed a test case to challenge the constitutionality of state regulatory authority on the basis that insurance was commerce and when conducted across state lines, was beyond the power of the state to regulate. In the 1869 landmark decision *Paul v. Virginia*,[1] the United States Supreme Court determined that insurance was not interstate commerce and hence not subject to federal jurisdiction under the congressional power over interstate commerce. In a series of subsequent cases in which insurers sought to avoid features of state law to which they objected, the Court upheld the right of a state to regulate the business of insurance.[2] Thus the *Paul* decision was the foundation for the evolving body of state insurance regulation to the virtual exclusion of the federal government.

In the period from the 1840s to the early 1900s—the era of the robber barons—private enterprise enjoyed a broad range of freedom to act as it saw fit. Within this climate, life insurance companies grew rapidly. Excesses developed as life insurers pushed for market share and control over assets. Acquisition costs seemingly knew no limits, and excessive commissions encouraged misrepresentations in order to write more and more business. Adverse publicity led to the famous Armstrong Investigation (conducted by a committee of the New York state legislature named after its chairman, Senator William W. Armstrong). This investigation uncovered numerous insurer abuses resulting in substantial policyowner losses. The ensuing recommendations aimed at ensuring sound financial management of insurers and responsible treatment of policyowners were enacted by the New York legislature, and they set the pattern for other states.[3] The Armstrong Report therefore is the basis of much of modern life insurance regulation.

Although the first half of the twentieth century witnessed the continued development of insurance regulation at the state level, federal regulations loomed on the horizon. In the early 1940s, the Department of Justice brought a federal antitrust action against an association of 200 stock fire insurance companies, alleging a conspiracy to fix and maintain noncompetitive premium rates and to monopolize trade. In the 1944 landmark case of *U.S. v. South-Eastern Underwriters Association*,[4] the Supreme Court overturned 75 years of legal precedent that had commenced with *Paul* when it found that insurance can fall within the embrace of Congress's power over interstate commerce.

This decision sent shock waves through the insurance industry and the insurance regulatory communities for at least four reasons. First, various practices previously deemed immune from the federal antitrust laws were overnight subject to such laws. Regardless of the merits of ultimately applying antitrust laws to insurance, there was little doubt that the immediate application of such laws would have caused chaos and impeded the ability of the industry, especially property and casualty insurers, to provide personal and commercial coverage to the public. (For example, collecting cooperative data, making rates, and drafting policy forms, even though done under regulatory scrutiny, were perceived likely to be illegal.)

Second, the decision raised grave concern about the continued viability of state insurance regulation since its application could very well have been deemed to be a burden on interstate commerce and therefore invalid under the Supremacy Clause of the United States Constitution. This would have obviated the regulatory safeguards, and because no regulation had developed at the federal level at this time, a regulatory vacuum would have emerged.

Third, numerous federal statutes in an infinite number of areas had been enacted without thought as to their applicability to insurance. This raised the specter of duplicating and/or conflicting state and federal law as well as the applicability of legislation that had not been considered for and was inappropriate to insurance.

Fourth, the decision cast doubt on the validity of state laws taxing the insurance business. If the laws were invalid, the states would have been deprived of a significant source of revenue.

In response Congress enacted the McCarran-Ferguson Act (hereafter referred to as the McCarran Act)[5] in 1945, through which it opted to preserve the state regulatory system and invited the states to preempt the federal antitrust laws by regulating the business of insurance. The act retained the role as federal overseer for Congress. Since 1945, insurance regulation has evolved within this framework.

State Insurance Regulation Agencies

State regulation of insurance involves these four agencies:

- the legislature
- the regulator
- the courts
- the National Association of Insurance Commissioners (NAIC)

Legislature

Within the constraints imposed by the federal and state constitutions and the congressional permissive authority as set forth in the McCarran Act, the state legislatures have the ultimate power to enact and amend insurance law. Legislation establishes the broad legal framework governing the way the insurance system functions. General standards apply to the insurance mechanism and to the administrative agency responsible for the day-to-day regulation of insurance. The legislature also commonly issues detailed mandates or requirements in particular areas of concern.

Regulator

Since effecting legislative standards, prescriptions, and restraints needs more than legislative proclamation and sporadic judicial enforcement, state legislatures have created insurance departments that have broad administrative, quasi-legislative, and quasi-judicial powers over the insurance business. Typically, an insurance department is headed by a commissioner, superintendent, or director (hereafter the common term commissioner will be used). A few states vest ultimate responsibility in a commission or board, which selects an individual commissioner to carry out policy. Nearly one-fourth of the states elect the commissioner; in the remaining states commissioners are appointed, usually by the governor. In some states the insurance department is combined with another department (such as the department of banking or securities), and in some states the insurance commissioner has other duties (such as state auditor, comptroller, or securities commissioner).

Despite the differences in state insurance laws, their administrative enforcement has much in common. Enforcement techniques include the following powers: to grant, deny, or revoke licenses to do business; to compel disclosure and to conduct financial and market-conduct examinations; to conduct investigations and promulgate regulations; to approve or disapprove filings of rates and policy forms; to order an insurer's rehabilitation, liquidation, or conservation; to issue cease-and-desist orders and to levy penalties or fines; and to remove officers and directors. These powers (and the informal powers stemming from them) give the insurance commissioner substantial clout with which to regulate the insurance business.

Courts

The Courts also have a significant role in insurance regulation. Courts adjudicate conflicts between parties (a dispute between an insurer and policyowner over whether coverage applies or the amount of the claim, for example). They enforce criminal penalties against those violating the insurance laws. Occasionally insurers, agents, or others seek to overturn statutes, regulations promulgated by the insurance commissioner, or orders issued by the commissioner; courts rule on whether such regulations are arbitrary or unconstitutional. The courts have also become involved in many cases attempting to define the parameters of state and federal authority under the McCarran Act.

NAIC

By the 1870s regulators' ability to cope with numerous insurers doing business across state lines came under increasing strain. At the same time, insurers were subjected to uncoordinated, duplicative, sometimes conflicting, and sometimes discriminatory multiple state regulations. To alleviate these problems, in 1871 several states joined together to form what is now known as the National Association of Insurance Commissioners. The NAIC, an unincorporated voluntary association, consists of the principal regulatory authorities of each state. The organization's original objectives included the promotion of uniformity in insurance laws and regulations, the dissemination of information to the regulators, and the establishment of means to fully protect the interests of policyowners and preserve state insurance regulations.

In its early years the NAIC sought ways to cope with interstate insurers, especially with respect to their financial condition, through such mechanisms as accounting regulations, standard annual statements that an insurer must file in each state in which it does business, uniform valuation of insurer securities for financial reporting purposes, and a coordinated system for insurer financial examinations. In addition, the NAIC served as a common forum for the development of model laws and regulations. Furthermore, through the NAIC, regulators could exchange information and share expertise, and various industry and consumer groups, government agencies and individuals could be given an opportunity to be heard on and participate in solving regulatory issues. As will become evident in the following discussion, the NAIC now has a major role in the regulation of the business via its extensive committee system and permanent staff.

Each insurance commissioner is responsible for the insurance regulation in his or her state. As a voluntary organization, the NAIC has no authority over its individual members who may or may not adopt in whole or in part a particular NAIC work product for implementation in their own states. Thus the traditional role of the NAIC has been to offer its work products for the individual states' consideration and use. Over the years, a substantial number of NAIC recommendations have been adopted by all or a substantial number of states. Consequently, the NAIC has become a fundamental force in the development and preservation of state insurance regulation.

Despite traditional state sensitivity to being told what to do by the NAIC, there are arguments urging stronger efforts to encourage the use of NAIC work products. Individual states have a stake in the nature and quality of regulation provided by other states. There are interstate implications in insolvencies, underwriting results, market conduct, and financial disclosure. Furthermore, the quality of state regulation as a whole can substantially affect the regulatory authority between the states and the federal government. Thus to the extent a particular NAIC work product can promote effective and efficient regulation and consistent treatment between states, there is strong justification for its implementation in the various states.

Recently, the NAIC took a significant step to exert greater pressure for widespread adoption of programs it deems crucial to effective regulation of insurers' financial condition when it adopted and implemented an accreditation program. There has even been serious discussion of an interstate compact to give NAIC actions the force of law. Thus the question no longer appears to be if particularly important NAIC work products should have widespread state adoption, but how that can be accomplished in the most appropriate, effective, and acceptable manner. The future viability of state insurance regulation may depend on the answer.

GOALS OF INSURANCE REGULATION

Reflecting Americans' pragmatic rather than theoretical approach to regulatory problems, the insurance legislative and regulatory process tends to respond to specific abuses, perceptions of abuse, and crises. From various regulatory activities, objectives, and legislation, the overall goals of insurance regulation can be discerned.[6]

Internal Goals

The first of two broad categories of insurance regulatory goals relates to the internal workings of the insurance business. These internal goals can be further divided into two groups. First, a fundamental function of the insurance mechanism is to provide security. To do so, it must be reliable. The cornerstone of *reliability* is regulation to ensure not only that an insurer is technically solvent but also that it is sufficiently solid so that it can properly perform its function in the community. Regulations for *solidity* abound in insurance law. Nevertheless, the government has yet to develop a way to immunize an insurer totally from potential insolvency. Consequently, an additional insurance regulatory goal is to protect policyowners and third-party claimants against insolvency losses through the use of guaranty funds.

The second broad category of internal goals embraces a wide range of insurance regulatory objectives regarding an insurer's conduct in the marketplace. An insurer should treat its whole body of policyowners in a reasonable manner. The regulatory goal of *reasonableness* is therefore the basis for a variety of objectives, the most visible of which being reasonableness of price and product quality. (Reasonableness of price is determined by the cost of the product in relation to the value received.) The goal of *equity* refers to fair treatment between policyowners. For example, premiums cannot be unfairly discriminatory; each policyowner should bear only the cost of his or her own insurance so far as that cost can practicably be determined. The goal of *fairness* attempts to prevent mistreatment of individual policyowners in such areas as claims practices, agent misrepresentations, and service.

External Goals

Without internal objectives the insurance business would not function in an acceptable manner. In addition to internal goals, there are external goals of society at large, arising from the relationship between the insurance business and the broader political, economic, and social environment within which the business functions.

One set of external goals stems from attitudes on liberty, democracy, and federalism (dispersing decision-making power away from the national government). Public policies and political structures place an emphasis on *federalism*. The McCarran Act explicitly recognizes the concept of federalism as it relates to insurance regulation. Although there is a continuing ebb and flow in the debate over state versus federal regulation, to date, the consensus supports the primacy of state control.

The second set of external goals that have an impact on the insurance system are those derived from economic and social policy—socialization of risks, availability of coverage, and reasonableness of price. *Socialization of risk* extends security on a broad basis, at least in the areas of workers' compensation and national health insurance. A more limited goal is ready *availability of coverage*. That is, even when persons are not under legal compulsion to purchase insurance, to the extent that they desire to do so, coverage should be available to cover their basic needs. Recently, increasing emphasis has also been placed on the *affordability* of coverage; not only should coverage be readily available to all who desire it but the price charged for that coverage also should not exceed what the buyer can afford to pay. Implementing this concept necessitates subsidies from some source and may very well conflict with the goal of reasonable price in relation to costs for those policyowners paying the subsidy. Therefore the extent to which this objective will ultimately be realized is not yet determined.

LICENSING: FOUNDATION OF REGULATORY CONTROL

Formation and Licensing of Insurers

Originally, an insurer could be formed only by a special act of the legislature. When this proved to be a burdensome and unwieldy procedure, states passed general incorporation laws under which charters could be obtained directly from a state official. Although technically incorporation confers legal existence on the insurer, by itself it does not grant the company the authority to engage in the insurance business. Generally, all insurers doing business within the state must obtain a license (called a certificate of authority in some states), which is a formal document certifying that the company has complied with all applicable laws and is authorized to engage in the kinds of insurance specified. When issued to a domestic insurer, the license usually does not need to be renewed periodically. However, in some states, it can be revoked for cause.

In addition, an insurer must obtain a license from every other state in which it wants to do business. The requirements for licensing foreign (out of state) and alien (out of country) insurers are generally similar to the requirements for domestic insurers. However, a foreign or alien company is usually required to appoint a resident of the licensing state as its attorney, for service of legal process and to deposit a specified amount of securities with a designated state official to assure payment of claims to policyowners residing in that state. A license obtained from a nondomiciliary state usually must be renewed annually.

The insurance commissioner, for sufficient reason, can refuse to issue a license in the first instance, fail to renew a license that has expired, or revoke a license before its normal expiration date. The grounds for such actions may differ in statutory language between states, but they are quite similar in substance. The commissioner may be authorized to deprive a company of the privilege of doing insurance business in the state on such broad grounds as that it "is in the public interest" or "will best promote the interest of the people of the state."

Without the license it is illegal for an insurer to do business in the state. In order to obtain and retain the license, the insurer must comply with the regulatory conditions imposed. Thus the licensing power is the foundation of regulatory control.

Controls over Unauthorized Insurers

As the foundation of regulatory control, the power to license is not without problems. Insurers that only advertise, have a mail-order business, or conduct only sporadic activities in a state have maintained that they are not legally "doing business" in the state and are therefore beyond the scope of that state's control. By refusing to apply for a license, these unauthorized (unlicensed) insurers seek to avoid regulation in states other than their states of domicile. However, state regulators have not been without legislative response.

Following an effort to regulate misrepresentative advertising of unauthorized mail-order insurers,[7] the NAIC adopted the Unauthorized Insurers Model Act in 1968 to subject unauthorized insurers to the jurisdiction of the insurance commissioner and the courts of the enacting state. (Subsequently, 27 states enacted the model act [or something similar], and 10 other states adopted related legislation or regulation.) The act seeks to afford those in the state the benefits of the protection provided by regulatory safeguards, prevent unfair competitive advantage between unauthorized and authorized insurers (the latter being subject to regulatory constraints and mandates), and preserve premium tax revenue. The act states that it is illegal for any insurer (other than specified exceptions) to transact insurance business in the state without a license. Any specified act effected by mail or otherwise by or on behalf of an unauthorized insurer is deemed to constitute such transaction. These acts include proposing to make an insurance contract, taking an application for insurance, receiving or collecting premiums, issuing or delivering contracts of insurance to residents of the state or to persons authorized to do business in the state, soliciting insurance, and adjusting claims. Through the courts, the insurance commissioner may seek to enjoin such illegal activity.

Two basic constitutional questions arise when a state exerts its regulatory authority over unauthorized insurers. First, does a state exceed the constitutional bounds of due process when it attempts to assert jurisdiction over such insurers? Although the answer to this question depends on the circumstances of each situation, when the United States Supreme Court let a Wisconsin Supreme Court decision stand that upheld the insurance commissioner's authority to apply that state's unauthorized insurers law against mail-order insurers, it appears that as a general proposition, due process does not preclude the exercise of state regulatory authority against unauthorized insurers.[8] Second, can a state effectively enforce its decisions against out-of-state insurers? The Unauthorized Insurers Model Act contains a reciprocal enforcement provision. The courts of each state enacting this provision will enforce judicial determinations of the courts of the reciprocal states having a similar provision as if they were judicial decrees of the enacting state.

Unfettered activity by unauthorized insurers can seriously undermine a state's ability to regulate the insurance business. Although state regulatory response has not been fully effective, techniques have been implemented adequately enough, at least to date, to provide acceptable control.

Licensing of Agents

No element of the insurance business deals more closely with the insurance-consuming public than agents and brokers (the focus here is on agents). Consequently, no person may act as agent for an insurer within the state without first obtaining a license to do so. No insurer may issue a contract of insurance through or compensate any person (other than certain deferred compensations, such as renewal commissions) who acts as an agent unless that person has a currently valid license. A license once granted may be revoked for good cause. Since an agent's livelihood depends on being licensed and since obtaining and maintaining a license are conditioned on compliance with the insurance law and regulations, the state's licensing power is the foundation of regulatory control over agents.

Regulation of agents exists to protect the insurance-consuming public from harmful acts or omissions. Licensing requirements attempt to screen out incompetent or unscrupulous agents or subsequently remove those who slip through the initial screening from the marketplace.

Obtaining the License

In 1973 the NAIC adopted an Agents and Brokers Model Licensing Act (which has been frequently amended). Although all states have agent licensing laws, only a few states have enacted the model act *per se*. Nevertheless, the act pulls together licensing features commonly used throughout the country.[9]

Pursuant to the model act, an insurance agent (an individual, partnership or corporation appointed by an insurer) is one who solicits applications and/or negotiates for a policy of insurance on behalf of an insurer. Although a partnership or corporation may be licensed as an agent, the members of the partnership and the officers, directors, stockholders, and employees of the corporation licensed as an insurance agent must also qualify as individual licensees. Typically, the provisions of agent-licensing laws apply to all or virtually all lines of insurance and types of insurers. The review and approval of an applicant's qualifications are conducted within the context of the particular license for which the application is sought (that is, an examination for a life insurance license covers life insurance). To obtain a license the proposed licensee submits an application to the insurance department providing information about his or her character, experience, and general competence. The commissioner must deem the applicant to be competent, trustworthy, and financially responsible, and to have good personal and business reputations. Each insurer for which the applicant is to be licensed submits a notice of appointment along with some kind of statement or certification of trustworthiness and competence by a responsible officer of the insurer.

To assure a certain minimum level of competence in the line of insurance for which the applicant is seeking a license, the applicant must usually pass a written examination testing his or her knowledge of the lines of insurance to be handled under the license, the duties and responsibilities of the licensee, and the pertinent insurance laws of the state. As an alternative, in some states, the commissioner may be authorized to accept the applicant's successful completion of an approved course of learning (for example, completion of the Chartered Life Underwriter program).

Duration of License

Power to Refuse, Deny, or Revoke. The NAIC model act provides for annual renewal of agent and broker licenses. Commonly, however, a state will issue an agent's license that continues indefinitely (contingent on the payment of annual fees) until the licensee dies, the insurer's appointment is terminated, or the license is suspended or revoked by the insurance commissioner. The commissioner can refuse to issue a new license and revoke or suspend an existing license on various grounds, such as material untrue statements in the license application, violation of or noncompliance with the state's insurance laws or regulations, fraudulent or dishonest practices, and demonstration of untrustworthiness, incompetence, or financial irresponsibility.

Continuing Education Requirements. Consumer confidence in the insurance industry depends on the demonstrated knowledge, experience, and professionalism of the insurance agent with whom the customer chooses to do business. In response to the rapidly changing life insurance marketplace, continuing education for life insurance agents has been increasingly accepted as an important way to ensure that agents acquire, retain, improve, and update the knowledge and skills essential to advising and serving life insurance buyers.

In 1978 the NAIC adopted the Agents Continuing Education Model Regulation. Licensed agents must annually complete courses or programs of instruction (such as the Chartered Life Underwriters program of The American College) approved by the commissioner and provide the commissioner with written certification that he or she has done so. Failure to do so subjects the agent to license suspension. Although the required credit hours and the course content can vary significantly by state, by the end of 1992, approximately 80 percent of the states conditioned the retention of the agent's license to do business upon earning continuing education credits.

SUBSTANTIVE CONTENT OF STATE INSURANCE REGULATION

Having reviewed the development of state insurance regulation, its fundamental goals, and licensing as the foundation of regulation, here the focus shifts to the substantive content of such regulation, especially that applicable to life insurance.

Security: Reliability of the Insurance Institution to Perform Its Insurance Obligations

Financial Condition: Solidity of the Insurer

Since the purchase of a life insurance policy initiates a transaction whose duration may span the better part of a century, the insurance-consuming public needs (and demands) assurance that the insurer will survive and be financially able to make the payments required by its contract. This fundamental public need for security translates into the regulatory goal of insurer financial soundness (solidity). To achieve this goal, regulators try to ensure that an insurer maintains assets at least equal to its currently due and prospectively estimated liabilities (including minimum capital and surplus requirements). Thus a substantial body of regulation has evolved covering a life insurer's assets (the bulk of which consist of investments), liabilities (the bulk of which consist of reserves), and capital and surplus.

Regulation of Insurer Investments. Although an insurer has a wide variety of assets necessary to operating an insurance enterprise (building, furniture and equipment, computers, and so forth), the bulk of its assets are held in the form of investments. It is essential that an insurer investment portfolio be of good quality so that the needed funds are available in the amounts and at the times called upon by its promises. Therefore not surprisingly, regulatory attention has long focused on the conduct of insurer investment operations.

Limitations on the nature of the investments permitted. Insurance companies' investment activities are conducted within the limitations established by state insurance law and regulations. Although state laws vary, they have a degree of commonality because of the common nature of the problems, the role of the NAIC and a requirement that a foreign insurer licensed to do business in the state must comply substantially with that state's law.[10]

In general, state controls seek to preserve the safety of the assets standing behind policyowner reserves and to prevent a life insurer's undue control of other companies through proportionately heavy investments in any one firm. To achieve these objectives, investment regulation has specified the eligible types of investment (such as bonds, mortgages, preferred and common stocks, and real estate) and the minimum quality criteria for individual investments within the eligible categories. In addition, quantitative limitations are imposed on the amounts that can be placed in eligible investments. (For a detailed discussion of controls over life insurer investments, see chapter 32.)

Valuation of assets. A review of an insurer's balance sheet gives an idea of the capital and/or surplus margins available for contingencies *if* the assets have been properly valued and the liabilities correctly stated. Most state laws authorize the insurance commissioner to set the rules determining the value of the securities. As a practical matter, if each state imposed its own valuations, there would be duplication of expenses incurred by the states and individual insurers; more important, there would be conflicting valuations. An insurer doing business in several states would report different values for the same securities in different states. This would constitute a burden on the filing insurers, and submitting differing asset valuations in the different states would result in virtually incomparable financial statements. In turn, this would adversely affect financial analyses and greatly complicate coordinated regulatory actions by the states.

Avoiding such problems was a major reason for the formation of the NAIC in 1871. The NAIC has created an annual statement blank (with detailed accompanying instructions) that insurers file. It is accepted by all states. The accounting and other rules governing the annual statement are continually under review and subject to change by the NAIC. In addition, the NAIC created the Securities Valuation Office to value, on a uniform basis, the securities held in the portfolios of virtually every insurer in the United States. As a consequence, every insurer holding the same security reports the same value for that security in its annual statement submitted to all states.

Mandatory security valuation reserve and its successors. Life insurers must value common stocks at market value for annual statement purposes. To avoid giving an undue impression of instability in the insurer's operations, the NAIC introduced the mandatory security valuation reserve (MSVR) in 1951. On the insurer's balance sheet, the MSVR was shown as a liability even though its nature was essentially that of a contingency fund or earmarked surplus. The MSVR served to accumulate a reserve over a period of years to protect against adverse fluctuations in the value of securities (stocks and bonds). A maximum amount was established for the MSVR according to a formula. Until the maximum was reached, capital gains and losses were absorbed by the reserve to avoid affecting the level of reported surplus. However, if the MSVR balance became zero, capital losses would directly decrease surplus.

In December 1991 the NAIC adopted two reserves to replace the MSVR: the asset valuation reserve (AVR) and the interest maintenance reserve (IMR). The AVR/IMR approach improves the old system by focusing on all invested assets, rather than on just stocks and bonds. The AVR imposes reserve requirements on real estate and commercial mortgages, as well as on stocks and bonds. This compels life insurers with troubled real estate portfolios to come up with additional reserves to meet NAIC requirements. The IMR attempts to capture realized gains and losses that result from changes in interest rates and permits the insurer to amortize them over the life of the investment.

Regulation of Reserves. The majority of an insurer's liabilities consist of policy reserves, which are the estimated amounts of funds needed, in combination with estimated future net premiums to be received, to provide the benefits promised in the insurer's life and annuity contracts. If an insurer fails to maintain the proper amount of assets to match its liabilities, including adequate policy reserves, the insurer may become insolvent and unable to pay claims. Thus establishing adequate reserves and reporting reserves accurately are essential to ensure an insurer's solidity. State law, based on the Standard Valuation Law (initially adopted by the NAIC in the early 1940s and brought up-to-date by periodic amendments through 1991), prescribes the method by which minimum policy reserves are calculated.

Pursuant to the law, the commissioner annually values (or causes to be valued) an insurer's liabilities for all outstanding life insurance, annuity, and pure endowment contracts. The statutory method is set forth in terms of the mortality tables to be used, the maximum interest rates to be assumed, and the valuation methods to be applied. Over time as circumstances change, the NAIC adjusts the mandated assumptions, such as the mortality table used and the interest rates assumed.

The states prescribe only the basis upon which minimum reserves are to be computed. Insurers are permitted to use any other basis that results in reserves that are equal to or greater than those generated by the statutory method. However, the insurer must disclose the details of the basis for its policy reserves as part of the NAIC annual statement that it files.

Furthermore, along with its annual statement, every life insurer must annually submit the opinion of a qualified actuary, stating that the reserves are computed appropriately, are consistent with prior reported amounts, and comply with the laws of the state. The actuarial opinion must also state whether the reserves are adequate to meet the company's obligations. The opinion must be based on standards adopted by the Actuarial Standards Board of the American Academy of Actuaries.

Capital and Surplus Requirements. On an insurer's balance sheet, the excess of assets over liabilities is the insurer's capital and surplus for a stock company and the insurer's surplus for a mutual company.

Traditional requirements. Traditionally, all states have established minimum capital and surplus requirements that an insurer must meet to obtain a license to do business. Although the details and the amounts vary significantly by state, a state insurance code sets forth minimum fixed-dollar capital and surplus amounts that differ according to the line or combination of lines of business to be written and the type of insurer. By the early 1990s minimum fixed-dollar capital requirements ranged from less than $500,000 to $6 million, depending on the state of domicile.

Over the years the required levels have sometimes been criticized as being inadequate. However, in determining whether the traditional system has fallen short, it is appropriate to ask what purpose the requirements are intended to serve. One function is to screen certain insurers out of the marketplace. The higher the minimum capital and surplus levels, the fewer small, undercapitalized insurers with a strong potential for failure entering the business. High entry requirements also tend to discourage operators seeking to utilize an insurance company as a source of unethical or fraudulent aggrandizement of personal wealth.

If the basic purpose of imposing capital and surplus requirements were limited to the screening function, simply increasing the fixed-dollar levels for the minimum requirements would probably suffice. However, most view capital and surplus requirements not only as a screening device but also as protection against inadequate reserves, inadequate premiums, decreases in the value of assets, uncollectible reinsurance, catastrophic events, and shortfalls in investment income. That is, higher capital and surplus requirements (assuming the absence of a corresponding decrease in the level of established reserves) are a greater buffer to absorb at least some adverse operational experience or other financial setback.

Risk-based capital. With the failures of banks and other financial institutions (including the savings and loan debacle), the several property and liability insurer failures in the 1980s, and the financial impairment of some high-profile life insurers in the early 1990s, momentum built for strengthening the existing system of regulating the insurance enterprise's financial solidity. The traditional fixed-dollar minimum capital and surplus requirements—perceived as being too low and not effectively related to the riskiness of an insurer's current operations—were a prime target.

In December 1992, the NAIC adopted risk-based capital requirements for life insurers to better enable the regulators to ensure that insurers maintained an adequate financial cushion to protect against a wide range of risks to their financial condition. At the heart of the risk-based capital requirements is a formula to calculate the minimum amount of capital/surplus an insurer should have in view of that insurer's exposure to asset default risk, insurance risk, interest rate risk, and business risk. The riskier the individual insurer's operations, the greater the risk-based capital required to avoid regulatory action. The regulator can compare the insurer's actual capital/surplus with its risk-based capital to better assess whether there is need for regulatory action. The risk-based capital formula approach is incorporated into the NAIC annual statement blank effective in 1993.

The NAIC also adopted the Risk-Based Capital for Life and/or Health Insurers Model Act, which sets forth several regulatory action levels of increasing severity, each succeeding level triggered by a worsening relationship between the insurer's actual capital and its adjusted risk-based capital (or some other specified event). At the *company action* level the insurer must submit proposed corrective actions to the commissioner for review and approval. At the *regulatory action* level the commissioner performs an examination of the insurer and orders corrective actions. If the *authorized control* level is reached, the commissioner is authorized to place the insurer under rehabilitation or liquidation. Finally, at the *mandatory control* level the commissioner causes either rehabilitation or liquidation. Thus the act is designed to enhance the regulator's authority and willingness to intervene if an insurer experiences financial difficulty.

Monitoring Financial Condition of Life Insurers. Establishing minimum standards and imposing specific prohibitions or restrictions are of little use if the regulator lacks sufficient means to ascertain failure of an insurer's compliance with the requirements or has inadequate methods of enforcement in the event of violation. Over the years, in addition to personal contacts and street knowledge about insurers doing business in their states, the regulators have developed a series of formal monitoring mechanisms to detect problem companies. Those used on a widespread basis have evolved in the context of state collective efforts through the NAIC. Insurance departments have three basic mechanisms for detecting financially troubled insurers: financial statements, early warning systems, and examinations.

Financial statements. The NAIC annual statement blank filed by insurers in each state in which they do business is the foundation of financial regulation. Insurers must prepare these statements in accordance with regulatory accounting principles that have evolved in response to the overriding concern with solvency. Statements are designed to provide a conservative (liquidating) measure of statutory surplus using statutory accounting principles (as distinguished from focusing on the insurer as an ongoing concern, which would use generally accepted accounting principles, commonly referred to as GAAP). The NAIC's establishment of a standardized annual statement promotes the basic objective of uniformity in financial reporting, an area where comparability of data is extremely important.

The annual statement (including a balance sheet and operation statements) is a source of voluminous information on the insurer's financial condition and operations. Insurance department analysts review the annual statements, and data is extracted from them to be processed by individual states, the NAIC, and private analytical computer systems. The ensuing analysis can trigger more in-depth investigations, including a specifically targeted or a comprehensive examination of an insurer when there are suggestions of serious financial difficulty.

Failure to file an accurate annual statement, signed by a responsible officer of the insured, is a violation of law.[11] Knowingly making a false entry of a material fact in any book, report, or insurer statement, or omitting to make a true entry of any material fact is also illegal. Violators are subject to monetary fines, license revocation, or possible criminal sanctions for fraud. The individual states and the NAIC review the annual statements, using various cross-checks and tests to detect problems in the accuracy of reporting. Nevertheless, whether due to inadvertent error, sloppy accounting practices, or intentional misrepresentation, reporting erroneous information has not been uncommon. In response, several individual states and the NAIC have moved to require independent certified public accountant (CPA) audits of annual statements[12] and actuarial or qualified reserve specialist certification of the adequacy of policyowner reserves as a test of the validity of the information submitted in the annual statement.[13] However, the requirement of CPA audits does not limit the commissioner's authority (although, ideally, it reduces the need) to conduct insurance department examinations.

Early warning systems. In the early 1970s, the NAIC established a computer database consisting of information derived from individual insurance company annual statements. From this the early warning system known as the Insurance Regulatory Information System (IRIS) evolved. IRIS consists of two phases: (1) the statistical phase, during which the NAIC compiles information from insurer financial statements and computes a variety of financial ratios that are made available to the state insurance departments and (2) the analytical phase, during which a team of insurance department experts from different states conducts a financial analysis. The latter phase focuses on insurers that exhibit a number of ratios outside the specified acceptable ranges. IRIS and individual state early warning systems, either separately or in conjunction with each other, seek to detect insurers heading for financial trouble far enough in advance that timely remedial action can be taken or the insurer closed down as soon as possible.

Examinations. States have long had the authority to send experts into an insurance company to conduct an in-depth examination of its financial condition. However, since many insurers do business in several states—if not nation-wide—if each state were to exercise its power to examine each company, there would be an immense duplication of effort, unnecessary and considerable expense, and conflicting examination reports. To avoid these problems the NAIC has established a coordinated examination system under which examiners representing different states conduct a single examination of the company on behalf of all states in which the insurer does business. In addition, the NAIC has developed (and updates on an ongoing basis) the *Examiner Handbook* to maintain and improve the quality and uniformity of examinations conducted under the auspices of the NAIC.

The 1990 NAIC Model Law on Examinations (replacing its 1956 version) authorizes the commissioner to conduct examinations whenever he or she deems necessary and to determine the scope of the examination. Nearly half of the states have adopted the model law (or something similar), and all states have enacted some type of law or regulation governing examinations. The objective is to focus insurance department resources on companies having or likely to have financial difficulty.[14] However, all insurers still have to be examined at least once every 5 years. In lieu of examining a foreign insurer, the commissioner may accept the examination report of the insurer's state of domicile.

Supervision, Rehabilitation and/or Liquidation

When an insurer experiences substantial financial adversity, the commissioner has the responsibility and the authority to act. If the commissioner believes that with proper management the insurer can be made solvent again, he or she can supervise or rehabilitate the insurer. If the insurer is hopelessly insolvent at the outset or if after efforts to supervise or rehabilitate it, it is apparent that the insurer cannot be saved, the commissioner can move to place the insurer into liquidation. The commissioner's authority to conduct rehabilitation and liquidation proceedings applies only to domestic insurers. If an insurance commissioner is concerned about the financial condition of an out-of-state company, he or she may suspend or revoke that insurer's license to do business in the state.

In 1977 the NAIC adopted the Insurers Supervision, Rehabilitation and Liquidation Model Act. As of 1992, a substantial majority of the states had adopted the act or similar statutory provisions. The model establishes a comprehensive and modernized system for rehabilitation and liquidation.[15]

Protection against Loss: Guaranty Funds

Regardless of the efficacy of regulations to avoid it, insurer insolvency will occur. However, not until a 1960 congressional investigation highlighted numerous insolvencies, especially high-risk automobile insurers, did the insurance guaranty fund concept achieve widespread application as a way to improve insurer reliability. Responding to both the problem of insolvency and the threat of federal insolvency legislation, the NAIC adopted a Model Guaranty Fund Law in 1969 for property and liability insurance to assume the insolvent insurer's claim-paying function and absorb the insolvent insurer's funding deficiencies in the payment of claims. In 1970 it did likewise for life and health insurance. (The act was substantially revised in 1985 and again amended in 1987.) As of 1991, all states had enacted some type of guaranty fund law both for life and health insurance and for property and liability insurance, a few of which preceded—but most of which are patterned after—the NAIC models.

The NAIC Life and Health Insurance Guaranty Association Model Act is intended to protect policyowners, insureds, beneficiaries, annuitants, payees, and assignees against losses due to an insurer's impairment or insolvency. The protection extends not only to paying claims, such as cash values and already owing death benefits, but also to the continuation of coverage since an insured may be elderly or in impaired health, rendering him or her unable to obtain new and equivalent coverage from other insurers. This protection is through a statutorily created Guaranty Association whose membership consists of all insurers licensed to do business in the state in coverages under the act.

Protection is afforded primarily to persons residing in the state. The act covers life, health, and annuity contracts. Coverages for certain insurance products have been excluded (nonguaranteed aspects of variable contracts, for example). The association is liable for no amounts in excess of the obligations under the covered contract; nor will its liability exceed $100,000 in cash values or $300,000 for all benefits (including cash values) with respect to any one life, $100,000 for health insurance benefits, and a total of $5 million on unallocated annuity contract benefits.

Although the association is intended to act after the insurer has been deemed insolvent pursuant to an order of liquidation, if the commissioner finds an insurer to be potentially unable to fulfill its contractual obligations, the association may guarantee, assume, or reinsure any or all of the insurer's policies under certain conditions. This authority enables the association to provide early assistance that helps to avoid or minimize further deterioration and thereby save costs in the long run. If the insurer is found insolvent by a judicial order of liquidation, the association can either (1) guarantee, assume, or reinsure (or cause to be guaranteed, assumed, or reinsured) the insurer's policies and contracts or assume payment of the insolvent insurer's contractual obligations and provide money or pledges to discharge such duties or (2) with respect to life or health policies, provide benefits and coverages. Any new contracts can be offered without new underwriting.

Any person receiving benefits pursuant to the act is deemed to assign the rights under the covered policy to the association, thereby enabling the association to recoup, at least in part, the claims it pays and the costs it incurs from the insurer's assets. When an insurer is declared insolvent, the fund assumes the responsibility for the payment of policyowner claims; funds for such payments are derived from assessments against member insurers based on a percentage of the insurer's relevant premiums written in the state. If the assessments fail to provide sufficient funds in a given year, the association is empowered to borrow funds that can later be repaid out of future assessments.[16]

Although there is a high degree of similarity in the overall structure of life insurance guaranty funds from state to state, few if any state laws are identical, and many exhibit significant variations from one another. Variations arise in such areas as maximum claim amounts, insurance products covered, insurer assessment limits, and assessment recoupment provisions.

While the guaranty funds have functioned reasonably well, critics have raised concerns about whether the funds are structured to handle future much larger insolvencies. Suggestions for improvement range from dealing with specific administrative and coordination problems, reducing variances in the protection afforded between states, and utilizing interstate compacts to replace the current system with a single federal insolvency fund. But no matter how the guaranty system evolves in the years ahead, in addition to regulation to prevent or minimize the size of insolvencies, some type of guaranty fund system has become a vital element in achieving the fundamental insurance regulatory goal of ensuring a reliable insurance mechanism.

Insurer Operations: Reasonable, Equitable, and Fair Treatment of Policyowners

As noted earlier, in addition to the goal of reliability, state insurance regulation has a second body of fundamental goals aimed at the insurer's conduct in the marketplace: reasonableness (which seeks to bar mistreatment of the whole body of policyowners), equity (which seeks to avoid unfair discrimination between individual policyowners), and fairness (which seeks to prevent mistreatment of policyowners as individuals). The following regulatory areas foster one or more of these three goals.

Policy Forms

Policy forms used by insurers are subject to some degree of regulation to protect policyowners, insureds, and beneficiaries against unfair and deceptive provisions and practices.

Policy Form Content. Standard provisions. Although there is no statutory standard life insurance policy, states require life insurance contracts to contain certain specified standard provisions, either as set forth in the statute or whose effect is the same in substance to those in the statute. Provisions more favorable to the insured than those required by statute may also be used. Provisions that are unfairly prejudicial to those interests are excluded.

Generally, the standard provisions, as recommended by the NAIC and mandated by the states, include the following: an entire contract clause, an incontestable clause, a grace period, reinstatement, nonforfeiture values, policy loans, annual apportionment of dividends, a misstatement of age provision, and settlement options. Individual states impose other requirements on policy terms (for example, prohibiting any exclusion from liability for death other than specified limited exclusions, such as a war clause, a suicide clause limited to 2 years, an aviation exclusion, and a hazardous occupation and/or a residence exclusion for 2 years).

Nonforfeiture provisions. Level premium life insurance involves charging more premiums than necessary for protection in the policy's early years in order to accumulate monies, as reflected by insurer policy reserves, to fund the higher cost of protection as the insured grows older. The question arises as to what should be done with the accumulated funds if the insured fails to pay the premium or wishes to terminate the policy.

Starting with Massachusetts in 1861, states began to enact nonforfeiture laws defining the minimum amount that must be returned upon surrender of a policy to prevent forfeiting equities accumulated in level premium policies. Updating and standardization were achieved in the 1940s with NAIC adoption of the Standard Nonforfeiture Law for Life Insurance and its subsequent enactment in virtually all states. The model[17] law has been amended on several occasions through the 1980s. No life insurance policy may be issued in a state unless it contains, in substance, the provisions specified in the law or corresponding provisions that, in the opinion of the commissioner, are at least as favorable to the defaulting or surrendering policyowner.

The minimum nonforfeiture value at any policy duration is the present value of the guaranteed future benefits under the policy, minus the present value of future adjusted premiums and the amount of any policy indebtedness. The adjusted premiums reflect the high first-year expenses associated with putting the policy on the books. The law sets forth the method of calculating the adjusted premiums, including the mortality table and the maximum interest rate to be used, both of which have been updated over time.

The values that have to be returned to the policyowner are referred to as *nonforfeiture values,* and the alternative forms that the policyowner can select are referred to as *nonforfeiture options.* The Standard Nonforfeiture Law requires policies to contain three nonforfeiture options: cash surrender value, reduced paid-up insurance, and extended term insurance. (The nature of these options is discussed in chapter 19.)

Readability. To reduce the potential for deception of or misunderstanding by insureds, several states have adopted *readable contract* laws or regulations such as the NAIC Life and Health Insurance Policy Language Simplification Model Act, whose purpose is to establish minimum standards for policy readability. (As of 1992, a majority of the states had adopted the model or something similar to it.) In essence, these regulations require that insurance contracts be written in simplified language, using a minimum number of technical or legal phrases and employing a basic vocabulary readable by someone with a high school education. The laws must usually pass a test that predicts the difficulty that readers will experience with the policy's text, based on such measures as average sentence length and syllable density.

Unfair discrimination. Standard provisions and readability requirements regulate policy form and content by mandating what an insurer must include in its policies. Insurance regulation deals with what should *not* be contained in policies. As a prime example, the NAIC Model Unfair Trade Practices Act prohibits unfair discrimination between individuals of the same class and life expectancy in the benefits payable and in the terms and conditions of a life insurance policy or annuity contract. If a commissioner finds unfairly discriminatory provisions, he or she may disapprove the policy.

Substantive content of special types of policies. The policy form and content requirements noted above have general applicability to different types of life insurance policies. In addition, certain types of policies are subject to more comprehensive treatment by regulations designed for their particular nature (for example, variable annuities, variable life insurance, market-value adjustment contracts, index policies, and universal life insurance). (Regulation of these policies is considered in chapter 27.)

Filing Policy Forms. State law provides that a policy form may not be used in the state until it is filed with and approved (or not disapproved within a specified number of days) by the insurance commissioner. Typically, the commissioner is empowered to disapprove policies or provisions that do not contain statutorily prescribed provisions or are deemed to be unfair, deceptive, or objectionable in some other statutorily specified way.

Rates

It is beyond the scope here to trace the long, complex, and convoluted history of rate regulation of property and liability insurance. Suffice to say that the basic statutory standards have been that rates cannot be excessive, inadequate, or unfairly discriminatory. These standards have been administered through a variety of detailed rate regulatory laws involving filing and approving rates. Although life insurance and annuity rates cause the same basic regulatory concerns as property and liability insurance, the regulatory response has been significantly different because life and annuity rates are not generally subject to commissioner approval.[18]

The regulatory approach to excessive life insurance rates has been at least twofold. First, with several hundreds of life insurance companies competing for business, traditionally competition has been relied on as being sufficient to curb rate excessiveness. The promulgation of life insurance price disclosure regulations (discussed later in this chapter) to assist potential buyers in making an intelligent choice among competing products further enhances the competitiveness of the life insurance marketplace. Second, as a result of the Armstrong Investigation, New York enacted a complex expense limitation law to curb the amount of expenses that can be incurred in producing new business and continuing existing business. Although such provisions have not been enacted on a widespread basis, their impact extends beyond New York state since even out-of-state insurers doing business in New York must comply with the requirements.

The adequacy of premiums is indirectly regulated by the imposition of policyowner reserve liability requirements. Under the Standard Valuation Law, states mandate the establishment of minimum reserves. When an insurer is compelled to establish reserves at a higher level than it would have done in the absence of the minimum requirements, greater assets are needed to offset the higher reserves. This, in turn, should lead the insurer to charge adequate premium rates.

To deter unfairly discriminatory rates, state statutory provisions aimed at unfair trade practices, as mentioned earlier, include prohibitions against making or permitting any unfair discrimination between individuals of the same class and equal expectation of life in the rates charged for any life insurance policy or annuity.

Market Conduct

In addition to overseeing insurer operations as to the products sold (controls of policy forms and content) and the prices charged, state insurance regulation is also directed at insurer treatment of the insurance-consuming public in terms of market conduct.

Unfair Trade Practices Act. States have long exercised regulatory control over certain unfair trade practices, such as misrepresentation, rebating, and discrimination. In response to the McCarran Act's invitation (pursuant to the "regulated by the state law" proviso) to oust federal insurance regulation, the NAIC developed and virtually all states enacted the model Unfair Trade Practices Act, which is at the heart of regulatory efforts to ensure appropriate market conduct. Since then the act has been amended several times, most recently in 1992, and the amendments have been widely adopted to broaden the scope of prohibited conduct, to expand enforcement authority, and to establish commissioner rule-making authority.

The act's basic prohibition is that it is an unfair trade practice for an insurer or agent to commit a defined practice if such practice is committed flagrantly and in conscious disregard of the act or any rule promulgated thereunder, or such practice is committed with such frequency to indicate a general business practice. The act then defines prohibited conduct in the following areas: misrepresentation and false advertising of insurance policies; false information and advertising generally; defamation; boycott, coercion, and intimidation; false financial statements and entries; stock operations and advisory board contracts; unfair discrimination; rebates; prohibited group enrollments; failure to maintain marketing and performance records; failure to maintain complaint-handling procedures; misrepresentations in insurance applications; and unfair financial planning practices. In addition, the act contains a separate section directly aimed at prohibiting coercion in credit insurance. Moreover, after a notice and hearing, the commissioner may promulgate rules and regulations to identify specific methods of competition or practices that are generally prohibited in the above areas.

The commissioner is empowered to examine and investigate the affairs of an insurer or agent to determine whether such person(s) has been or is engaging in proscribed unfair practices. Whenever there is reason to believe that an unfair practice has occurred, after an appropriate hearing, the commissioner may issue a cease-and-desist order and may, at his or her discretion, order monetary penalties specified in the act or suspend or revoke the person's license if that person knew or should have known that such conduct was in violation of the act. Violations of cease-and-desist orders incur further monetary penalties. Furthermore, not only does failure to maintain marketing and performance records or complaint-handling procedures constitute an unfair trade practice, but, to aid enforcement, state insurance departments (both individually and collectively through the NAIC) can also perform market-conduct examinations separate from but similar to examinations for financial solidity.

Business-generating Activity.   Insurance regulators exercise a substantial measure of control over the methods by which insurers and their agents obtain business.

Misrepresentation in getting business: solicitation and advertising in general. Misrepresentation for the purpose of inducing the payment of an insurance premium was adjudged more than 100 years ago to be a crime in Massachusetts. During the present century, legislation has been enacted to penalize such conduct. The Unfair Trade Practice Act, which reflects the current widely adopted approach, contains provisions to combat the use of misrepresentations in efforts to acquire business. First, the act defines as an illegal unfair practice the making, issuing, or circulating (or causing to be made, issued, or circulated) of any estimate, illustration, statement, sales presentation, omission, or comparison that misrepresents the benefits, advantages, conditions or terms of any insurance policy or the dividends to be received. Second, the act also defines as an unfair practice the making, publishing, disseminating, circulating, or placing before the public in a newspaper or magazine or on radio or television an untrue, deceptive, or misleading advertisement about the business of insurance or about an insurer in the conduct of its insurance business.   Third, the model act contains an antidefamation provision defining as a prohibited unfair trade practice the making of or aiding in oral or written statements that are false or maliciously critical of the financial condition of any insurer and that are calculated to injure such person.

As insurers and agents solicit business through a variety of business-generating activities, they are subject to these general constraints.   Violation of these constraints can result in not only an order to stop but also monetary fines and possible license revocation.

Although the insurance regulator can exert control over advertising practices utilizing the general provisions contained in the Unfair Trade Practices Act, to gain more specificity and to better provide guidance to insurers and agents, the NAIC developed Model Rules Governing the Advertising of Life Insurance in 1975.   These rules regulate the form and content of advertisements, establish minimum disclosure requirements in advertising life and annuity contracts, and provide enforcement procedures.   As of 1992, 18 states had adopted either the NAIC model rules or comparable rules, and another 11 states had put their own independent set of related rules into place.

Policyowner dividends.   The model act explicitly proscribes statements, sales presentations, illustrations, comparisons, or omissions that misrepresent policyowner dividends or share of surplus to be received on an insurance policy or that make any false or misleading statements about dividends or share of surplus previously paid on any insurance policy. The advertising rules further specify that an advertisement (the word advertisement is used in the broad sense) must not state or imply that either the payment or the amount of dividends is guaranteed. Dividend illustrations must be based on the insurer's current dividend scale and must contain a statement that they are not guaranteed and not estimates of future dividends.

Unfair financial planning practices. Amendments to the Unfair Trade Practices Act in the 1980s defined certain of an insurance producer's financial-planning activities as unfair trade practices. It is unlawful for an agent to hold himself or herself out as a financial planner, investment adviser, or other specialist engaged in the business of giving financial planning or investment advice when that person is, in fact, engaged only in the sale of insurance policies. Even if the person is engaged in the business of financial planning, he or she must disclose that he or she is also an insurance salesperson and that a commission for the sale of an insurance product will be received in addition to any fee the prospect pays for the financial planning service. An insurance producer may not charge a fee for financial planning unless it is based on a written agreement.

Price disclosure. Several factors enter into rational decision making when purchasing a life insurance policy, including the suitability of the policy to what the buyer wants and needs, the quality of the policy, the solidity of the insurer, the service to be provided by the agent and/or insurer, and of course, the cost. Other things being equal, policyowner interest is better served by purchasing at lower rather than higher prices. If the other factors are unequal, the prospective purchaser needs to weigh price differentials against the differences in other factors that are important to him or her. Therefore meaningful information is an essential element in insurance consumer protection.

Furthermore, insurance regulation relies on competition as the primary means to prevent excessive rates. Effective price competition is predicated on buyer willingness and ability to purchase insurance from lower-cost companies. This, in turn, requires that buyers be able to compare prices of policies issued by different insurers. Adequate disclosure of life insurance pricing information is fundamental not only to serving the prospective policyowner in his or her individual purchase decision, but also to maintaining an effective competitive marketplace, which benefits life insurance consumers as a whole by tending to keep prices overall at reasonable levels.

Increased consumer education and price awareness in the early 1970s demanded improved cost-comparison methods. Consequently, the NAIC developed, adopted, and has frequently amended the NAIC Model Life Insurance Disclosure Regulation, which mandates general disclosure requirements and price comparison information. Over 30 states have adopted or closely followed some version of the NAIC model regulation, and additional states have implemented somewhat different cost disclosure requirements.

The 1992 version of the NAIC model regulation seeks to improve the quality of information offered to prospective life insurance buyers to better enable them to select the plan most suitable to their individual circumstances, to improve their understanding of the basic features of the policy to be purchased, and to enhance their ability to evaluate relative costs of similar types of policies. To achieve these purposes insurers are required to give the prospective purchaser a buyer's guide containing a clear explanation of products and how to shop for them and a policy summary containing essential information pertaining to the particular policy being considered.[19] In general, the insurer must give both of them to the prospective policyowner before accepting the applicant's initial premium unless either the policy or the policy summary contains a 10-day (or longer) unconditional refund provision. If so, the guide and summary may be delivered with or prior to the policy.

Among the elements the policy summary is required to disclose are two interest-adjusted cost indexes for the policy. These indexes reflect the time value of money by recognizing that money is paid and received at different times and that costs can be better compared by using a specified interest assumption. The *Net Payment Cost Comparison Index* is useful when the main concern is that benefits are to be paid at death. This index helps to compare costs at some future point in time, such as 10 or 20 years, if premiums continue to be paid and cash values are not withdrawn. The calculations reflect the time value of money, assuming a specified rate of 5 percent. The index is derived from an estimate of the average annual net premium outlay the policyowner incurs (premiums less dividends) adjusted by interest (5 percent) to reflect the point in time when the premiums are paid in and the dividends paid out during a 10- or 20-year period.

The *Surrender Cost Comparison Index* is useful when the main concern is the level of the cash values. This index compares the costs of surrendering the policy and withdrawing the cash value at some future point in time, such as 10 or 20 years. The surrender cost index is the payment index less the annualized equivalent of the cash value available to the policyowner at the end of the 10- or 20-year period, adjusted for interest. The result is the average amount of each annual premium that is not returned if the policy is surrendered for its cash value.

Although the use of these cost indexes is subject to caveats—including the fact that they do not reflect actual net costs to the individual policyowner[20]— the prospective cost estimates can be valuable in giving the applicant a relative sense of which similar policies are high or low in cost. Over time, as circumstances change and different products evolve, changes in the information provided and the comparative cost measures are to be expected. Nevertheless, despite the current limitations in the NAIC cost-disclosure approach, the mandate that insurers furnish buyer guides and policy summaries marks a major advancement in enhancing informed life insurance buyer decision making.

Replacement. Replacement is a transaction in which a new life insurance or annuity contract is to be purchased and it is known, or should be known, by the proposing agent that, because of such transaction, an existing life insurance or annuity has been or will be terminated, converted, or otherwise reduced in value. An existing insurance policy may be replaced by another policy from the same insurer or by a policy issued by a different insurer. When a policyowner is induced to discontinue and replace a policy through agent or insurer distortion or misrepresentation of the facts, it is referred to as "twisting." However, replacement is broader than twisting since it may occur in the absence of any misrepresentation.

The replacing agent's motives may be laudable or less so. If an agent accurately discloses the facts and the replacement works to the policyowner's benefit, regulatory concern is served. However, because of high first-year commissions on new policies, agents have financial incentives not only to take business away from another insurer but also to replace a policy in their own company and thereby generate another first-year commission. Furthermore, insurers seeking new business may not be adverse to taking it away from a competitor even though doing so may not benefit the policyowner.

Traditionally, most replacements were considered to be detrimental to the policyowner since he or she had already incurred the high first-year expenses, since the premiums under the new policy might be higher because of the policyowner's increased age, and since the suicide and incontestable provisions might expire sooner (if they have not already done so) under the existing policy. However, in more recent years, with changing conditions (including higher interest rates and improved mortality experience), a policyowner may substantially improve his or her situation by replacing an existing policy in either the same or a different company.

To protect policyowners' interests regulators must balance the need to preserve the opportunity to replace a policy when it benefits the policyowner and the need to reduce potential injury to policyowners from unprofessional agents and insurers. As a starting point, the Unfair Trade Practices Act contains prohibitions against misrepresentation, including misrepresentations to induce the lapse, forfeiture, exchange, conversion, or surrender of any insurance policy. In 1969—followed by significant revisions in 1978 and 1984—the NAIC adopted what is now called the Replacement of Life Insurance and Annuities Model Regulation. Whereas the original version established minimum standards of conduct, the 1978 version shifted the focus to providing the buyer with full disclosure of information in a fair and accurate manner, including ample time to review the information before making a final decision. Approximately 40 states have promulgated regulations governing life insurance replacement, most based on either the original or revised versions of the NAIC model.

When an agent submits an application for life insurance or an annuity to his or her insurer, it must include a statement about whether or not the policy is a replacement. If it is, the agent must give the applicant a prescribed notice alerting the applicant to the need to compare the existing and the proposed benefits carefully and to seek information from the agent or insurer from whom he or she purchased the original policy. The replacing insurer must advise the other insurer of the proposed replacement and provide information on the replacing policy or contract, as required in the Model Life Insurance Disclosure Regulation (or the Model Annuity and Deposit Fund Disclosure Regulation).[21] The replacing insurer must also give the applicant a 20-day free look at the replacement policy, during which he or she has an unconditional right to a full refund of all premiums paid if he or she decides not to retain the policy. The existing insurer or agent has 20 days to furnish the policyowner with policy information on the existing policy, prepared in accordance with the disclosure regulation, containing premium, cash values, death benefits, and dividends computed from the current policy year. Both insurers and agents are responsible for the accuracy of the information submitted to the existing policyowner.

Free look. Although the life insurance transaction is long term, a significant number of policies lapse within 2 years of purchase. Since early cash values tend to be very small in comparison to the premium paid because of heavy acquisition costs and other expenses), the failure to continue a life insurance policy can be quite costly to the policyowner. Thus the decision to do so reflects serious dissatisfaction with the original decision to buy.

To give policyowners enough time for sober, unpressured reflection on such a substantial long-term financial commitment, a majority of states have enacted a "free look" law, which gives the policyowner 10 or 20 days to reconsider the decision to replace a policy. If he or she determines that the purchase was unwise for any reason, the insurer is required to rescind the replacement policy and refund monies paid. Versions of the free look requirement are included in the life insurance disclosure and replacement regulations.

Rebates. Rebating is reducing the premium or giving some other valuable consideration not specified in the policy to the buyer as an inducement to purchase insurance. The classic rebate situation involves an agent who agrees to give a portion of his or her commission to the buyer as a reduction of the first premium to induce the prospect to insure.[22]

Between 1885 and 1905, as a part of a larger package of abusive practices to acquire business at any price, rebating became commonplace in the fierce competition between agents. Antirebate laws were enacted to prevent excessive and ruinous competition. Ultimately, prohibition against rebating was incorporated into the NAIC Unfair Trade Practices Act in 1947.

The proponents of maintaining the antirebate laws include the life insurance industry (which does not want legislative changes that would make it more expensive and difficult to attract and retain an agency force) and the national and local life insurance agent trade associations (viewing rebates as unwarranted pressure on their compensation). The arguments against rebating include the following: (1) Rebating results in varying first-year charges to similarly situated policyowners, which is inequitable discrimination against consumers who lack the economic leverage to demand rebates or the knowledge to do so. (2) Permitting rebates can lead to destructive rate cutting ("ruinous competition") that can adversely affect insurers' financial condition. First, replacements prevent insurers from recovering issue expenses normally amortized over several years. Second, insurers pressured to raise commission rates to enable agents to compete by rebating might be unable to raise premiums to recover the increased expenses. (3) Lured by a rebate, a policyowner can more easily be encouraged to replace his or her existing policy. (4) Many agents and agencies are not well positioned to offer significant rebates. (5) Permitting rebating encourages agent turnover and aggravates agent shortages. This lessens the number of agents available to service the public and to foster competition in the marketplace. Since life insurance tends to be sold rather than bought, the fewer the number of agents, the smaller the amount of life insurance sales, and the greater the underinsurance of the public. (6) Buyers may be more influenced by the size of the rebate—the deal they can make—than by the total long-range costs, the nature and suitability of the products, and the quality of agent counseling and service.

Despite these contentions, the 1980s witnessed increasing agitation to eliminate the ban against rebating. Antirebating critics argue as follows: (1) Antirebate laws needlessly shelter agents from competition, thereby contributing to excessive insurance rates. (2) Ruinous competition and the increased likelihood of insolvency are "sham arguments." The amount of an agent's rebate does not affect the amount of the premium received by the insurer to fund its obligations. How an agent spends his or her money is irrelevant to insurer solvency. (3) The antidiscrimination rationale lacks substance. The life insurance business is replete with examples of discrimination (economies of size garner better rates, insurers discriminate in underwriting, agents discriminate in selecting their prospects, and so on). (4) In stifling competition between agents, the ban on rebates permits the less competent or inefficient agents to be compensated on a basis equivalent to the most knowledgeable and efficient agents.

In recent years, lawsuits have been brought in several states challenging the constitutionality of the antirebate provision. In 1986 the Florida Supreme Court overturned that state's law prohibiting rebates as a violation of the Florida Constitution's due process clause.[23] For many persons, including courts in other states, the Florida Supreme Court's due process analysis has proven unpersuasive. In 1990 Florida enacted a law regulating rebates but also permitting insurers to prohibit their agents from rebating commissions. The constitutionality of such a law is being challenged. In California, when voters adopted a broad referendum (commonly referred to as Proposition 103) covering a wide gamut of insurance issues, they repealed the ban on rebates in that state.

Elsewhere, the influence of proponents of continuing the ban on rebates have prevailed. To date, no other state supreme court has found the antirebate provision to be unconstitutional. Unless change is compelled at the federal level, it appears that the antirebate provision will remain the law in the vast majority of states for at least the immediate future. In the meantime, Florida and California are a testing ground that may reveal whether the fears of proponents of the ban or the claims of proponents of change are realistic or exaggerated.

Privacy. When underwriting, a life insurer typically investigates factors bearing on the applicant's insurability, especially when the amount of insurance applied for is substantial. Several states require that the insurer obtain permission from the applicant to make this investigation. A central reporting agency, the Medical Information Bureau (MIB), receives and retains information about underwriting impairments of persons who have applied for insurance. Through this source, an insurer can often verify the accuracy of an applicant's statements if he or she has previously applied for insurance.

In recent years privacy has become a sensitive issue (even more so with the proliferation of AIDS). Several states have imposed restrictions on the underwriting information an insurer may obtain, in part due to the concern that the information may be disclosed to others. In 1979 the NAIC adopted the Insurance Information and Privacy Protection Model Act (amended in 1981) to establish standards for the collection, use, and disclosure of information gathered by insurers, agents, or insurance support organizations. The act tries to achieve a balance between the need for information necessary to conduct the insurance business and the public's interest in privacy. The commissioner is empowered under the act to examine insurers, agents, and support organizations to ascertain compliance with the Privacy Act, issue cease-and-desist orders, and issue reports. Violations are subject to monetary penalties and/or revocation of an insurer's or agent's license. Furthermore, any person whose rights are violated may seek damages through the judicial process. By mid-1992, approximately 15 states had adopted some form of privacy regulation, most of which is patterned after the NAIC model act.

Unfair Discrimination. All states have enacted laws or promulgated regulations, in substantial part based on NAIC models (especially the Unfair Trade Practices Act), proscribing unfair discrimination in a wide variety of contexts. Moreover, the commissioner has the authority to further define unfair trade practices and promulgate regulations.

The law prevents *unfair* discrimination, not simply discrimination. Some discrimination among policyowners is deemed appropriate since not all policyowners present the same degree of risk. In contrast, unfair discrimination refers to inequality of treatment among policyowners that is not justified by underwriting considerations or sound business practices or that is deemed unacceptable because of external public policy objectives. As an example of unacceptable discrimination, the model act defines refusing to insure, refusing to continue to insure, or limiting the amount of coverage available to an individual because of sex, marital status, race, religion, or national origin as an unfair trade practice. Here, no reference is made to unfair discrimination. Whether or not there are valid underwriting or actuarial reasons, these types of discrimination are banned as a matter of fundamental social policy.

As discussed earlier, among the specific prohibitions in the model act are making or permitting any unfair discrimination between individuals of the same class and life expectancy in the rates charged for life insurance or annuities, the dividends paid, other benefits paid, or in the contract's terms and conditions. Furthermore, it is illegal discrimination to refuse to insure solely because another insurer has rejected granting a new policy or has cancelled or failed to renew an existing policy. Insurers must base their decisions on sound underwriting, rather than on another insurer's action.

To further define unfair trade practices the NAIC adopted a model regulation in 1979 proscribing as unfair discrimination any life and health insurer's refusal to insure, refusal to continue to insure, or charging a different rate for the same coverage solely because of an applicant's physical or mental impairment unless the rate differential is based on sound actuarial principles or is related to actual or reasonably anticipated experience. A 1978 model regulation (as amended in 1984) does the same with respect to blindness, except that there is no exception for actuarial experience. Nearly half of the states have adopted legislation or regulations pertaining to mental and physical impairments (10 of which are based on the NAIC model), and most states have done so pertaining to blindness (approximately 35 of which are based on the NAIC model).

In 1975 the NAIC adopted the Model Regulation to Eliminate Unfair Sex Discrimination, which prohibits denying benefits or availability of coverage on the basis of sex or marital status. As of 1992, over 15 states had adopted the model regulation (or something similar), and another nine states had effected related legislation or regulations. The model regulation refrained, however, from mandating the same rates for men and women. Women's life expectancy is greater than men's, generally resulting in lower life insurance rates and higher annuity rates for women. Traditionally, such rate discrimination has been deemed equitable and appropriate, rather than unfair, since the rates reflect actual cost experience.

However, in the 1980s there were demands for nondiscriminatory unisex or gender-neutral insurance rates, regardless of the actuarial soundness of such classifications. Although group contracts now have unisex rates, life insurance companies have generally resisted unisex rates for individual policies. (Gender-neutral rating laws are a good example of an external goal's impact on the insurance industry, as discussed previously in this chapter.)

Policyowner Dividends. Nature and distribution. Because of the long-term nature of a life insurer's obligations and because of fixed premiums, charges for premiums need to be established on a conservative basis. Barring unusually adverse experience, conservative premiums should generate gains that increase the size of the insurer's surplus. How this gain is allocated to surplus depends on whether the insurer writes participating or nonparticipating policies. (Nonparticipating policies guarantee the amount insured but do not entitle the insured to receive any benefits other than those explicitly set forth in the contract.) Most participating life insurance is written by mutual insurers; nonparticipating insurance is written by stock insurers.

The increase in surplus for mutual (participating) companies is normally greater since premiums are intentionally established more conservatively. The higher premium cost to the policyowners is adjusted by dividends paid to them. The extra margins built into conservative premiums and better-than-assumed mortality, interest, and expense experience the source of these dividends.

Mandated annual distribution. Although a life insurer's management has considerable latitude in fashioning dividend policies, regulatory concerns have led to some limitations and mandates. An early source of regulatory concern arose out of the use of tontine and semitontine life insurance policies, which were very popular in the late 1800s. These policies enabled insurers to accumulate vast surpluses that were neither properly accounted for nor allocated to policyowners. Instead, management often squandered such funds in extravagance and corruption.

As a result of the Armstrong Investigation, New York enacted a statute requiring the annual apportionment and distribution of dividends to policyowners. Most states now require that an insurer make an annual apportionment of divisible surplus. Commissioners review insurer dividend formulas from time to time, often in conjunction with their examination of the insurance company. A few states limit the amount of aggregate surplus an insurer may accumulate to an amount not to exceed a specified percentage of the legal reserve.

Limits on stockholders' charge. The requirement for annual distribution of policyowner dividends is inapplicable to stock companies issuing nonparticipating policies. However, a potential conflict of interest arises in those stock companies issuing both participating and nonparticipating policies. In some states, as well as in Canada, there are laws or regulations limiting the amount of participating policies' unused margins that the company can allocate to the benefit of the stockholders (commonly referred to as the stockholders' charge). For example, in New York and Wisconsin, stockholders of insurers authorized to do business in the state are limited to 10 percent of the profits on participating business or $.50 per $1,000 of insurance in force, whichever is larger.

Unfair discrimination. Although annual policyowner dividends are mandated and the dividend formulas are subject to periodic review by the insurance departments, insurers still have wide latitude in establishing dividend policy, as noted above. However, they are constrained by the Unfair Trade Practices Act, which defines as an unfair trade practice making or permitting any unfair discrimination in the policyowner dividends payable between individuals of the same class and life expectancy. Commissioner review and enforcement are the same here as they are for other unfair trade practices.

Unfair Settlement Practices

An insurance company's basic function is to pay justified claims. Failure to administer the claims function to assure prompt and full payment of claims contravenes the basic regulatory goal of the insurance-consuming public's fair treatment. The Unfair Trade Practices Act originally included a full section defining certain patterns of settlement practice conduct as unfair and subject to the commissioner's full investigative and enforcement powers. However, in 1990, the NAIC opted to establish a free-standing act separate from the Unfair Trade Practices Act.[24] The Model Unfair Claims Settlement Procedures Act sets forth standards for the investigation and disposition of claims arising under insurance policies. To supplement the act and further elaborate on insurer and agent obligations, the NAIC adopted the Unfair Claims Settlement Practices Model Regulation. It establishes minimum standards that relate to specific forms of misrepresentation, failure to acknowledge communications, failure to promptly investigate claims, and failure to effect prompt, fair, and equitable settlements. In addition, an insurer is required to maintain complete claim files that are subject to the commissioner's examination. Several states have adopted the model regulation, and several others have similar or modified versions.

Illustrative Areas Giving Rise to Solidity and Marketplace Regulatory Concerns

Whereas some aspects of insurance regulation aim at achieving either reliability of the insurance mechanism or reasonable, equitable, and fair treatment in the marketplace, other portions are concerned with *both* sets of insurance regulatory goals. In this context the following discussion relates to AIDS, fraud, management quality, and insurers in hazardous financial condition.

The Special Problem of AIDS

Impairing Financial Condition. The Acquired Immune Deficiency Syndrome, commonly referred to as AIDS, was first diagnosed in the early 1980s. The spread and the magnitude of this lethal disease has staggered the nation. In addition to the victim's personal tragedies, there are the potential adverse effects on life and health insurers and their policyowners. The focus here is on life insurance.

The disease has reached near-epidemic proportions, promising a substantial increase in both the number of cases and the number of deaths in the years ahead. Life insurers anticipate significantly increased costs, with no compensating premiums, arising from AIDS-related deaths under existing policies that contain no exclusion for AIDS and were not underwritten for AIDS. Therefore to avert threats to their financial condition and widespread harm to their existing policyowners, life insurers try to underwrite prospective policyowners to avoid writing business on people who have or are likely to contract AIDS.

Traditionally, an insurer may ask an applicant various medical questions and require submission to a medical examination as a part of the underwriting process to determine whether or not to issue a policy and at what premium. Generally, medical underwriting and testing are lawful unless declared otherwise by statute or regulation. However, the emergence of AIDS as a social and political issue has complicated the insurer's task. Public compassion for AIDS victims and their dependents has exerted pressure to make life insurance available to them at an affordable cost. Consequently, conflicts have emerged between the needs of AIDS victims and the adverse economic consequences to insurers and their policyowners in providing coverage to people with AIDS. Questions have arisen regarding an insurer's right to ask (in the application for insurance or otherwise) whether the applicant has evidenced symptoms of AIDS or has been tested for the AIDS virus (and the results of the test), to test insurance applicants for exposure to the AIDS virus, and to deny insurance coverage based on test results. These questions, in turn, have led to issues pertaining to discrimination and privacy.

Discrimination. Clearly, people with AIDS (or the AIDS virus) present a much greater mortality risk than people who do not have the disease. As noted earlier, insurers are required by law to base premium rates on reasonable mortality assumptions and may not unfairly discriminate between applicants of equal life expectancy. Thus under general insurance unfair discrimination laws, insurers are permitted—perhaps even required—to treat AIDS victims differently from other classes of insureds.

However, discrimination can be viewed from another perspective. AIDS is concentrated more heavily within a few segments of the population—homosexuals, bisexuals, and intravenous drug users. While far from all persons in these segments contract AIDS, it is not unknown for insurers, in their efforts to reduce their exposure to insuring AIDS victims, to underwrite applicants on the basis of their sexual preference. This is argued to be unfair discrimination.

In 1986 the NAIC tried to deal with the issue by adopting underwriting guidelines. Although recognizing the fundamental importance of properly assigning risk classifications to determine coverage and establish a fair price, the guidelines prohibit as unfair discrimination determining insurability on the basis of sexual orientation. The guidelines prohibit questions intended to elicit an applicant's sexual orientation, but insurers can continue to seek medical information, including information that enables the underwriter to assess the risk of the applicant's having AIDS or the AIDS virus. The use of objective medical facts is not deemed to be a violation of the NAIC guidelines as long as the facts are not used to establish sexual preference that, in turn, becomes the basis for denying coverage. As of 1992, most states had adopted some requirement with respect to AIDS underwriting, with 17 states following the NAIC approach or something similar thereto.

Drafters of the NAIC guidelines were unable to achieve a consensus on the issue of AIDS testing. A few states have imposed restrictions on an insurer's ability to screen out likely AIDS candidates by limiting or prohibiting the use of certain tests to reveal AIDS or the virus that can cause AIDS. However, there has been no successful movement to mandate insurers to make coverage available to AIDS victims. In states that permit testing, the insurer must obtain the written consent of an applicant who is requested to take an AIDS-related test, and the use of the test must be revealed.

Privacy. Critics assert that the underwriting process to discover the AIDS virus violates the applicant's right to privacy—a major concern because of the possible economic, medical, and social consequences that could result from improper release of positive AIDS test results. Those against limitations on insurers' ability to underwrite stress that insurers have long maintained confidentiality of medical test results in such sensitive areas as chemical dependency, alcoholism, and syphilis. Furthermore, as discussed earlier, protections are afforded under state insurance privacy laws. The combination of state privacy laws and insurers' demonstrated ability to maintain confidentiality, they say, balances the applicant's need for privacy with the insurer's need for information.

Deterrence of and Sanctions against Fraud

As accumulators of substantial amounts of financial resources, insurance companies have sometimes been the scene of a variety of fraudulent or near fraudulent activities. An insurer can be victimized by fraud from at least three sources.

Insurance Claims against an Insurer. Policyowners, beneficiaries, or third-party claimants, either individually or as a part of a conspiracy, may seek to extract unwarranted funds from the insurer. Although this problem appears to be much more prevalent in other lines of insurance, life insurers have not been totally immune (for example, murder for life insurance claims). The primary deterrent is a state's general criminal and civil laws against fraud. In addition, approximately half of the states have enacted specific laws against insurance fraud, some of which are based on the 1980 NAIC Model Insurance Fraud Statute. This statute specifically defines as a felony presenting any written or oral statements or documents to support a claim knowing that they are false, misleading, or incomplete concerning any fact material to the claim. A few states have established antifraud units within their insurance departments to investigate insurance claim fraud.

Business Relationships. An insurer might be the victim of unethical or fraudulent conduct perpetrated by those with whom it has entered into business relationships by providing insurance and insurance services. Two prime candidates emerge. First, fraudulent activities by agents or brokers can victimize insurers. For example, agents or brokers can obtain multiple commissions through layering arrangements, skim portions of premiums off the top before remitting them to the insurer, or write unauthorized business to generate additional commissions. If an agent is given authority to arrange for reinsurance on blocks of business he or she writes, the agent can formulate such arrangements to maximize compensation, rather than to effect real and sound reinsurance protection. Fraudulent activity significantly contributed to the financial impairment—even insolvency—of several insurers, especially property and liability insurers, in the early and mid-1980s. In addition to state and federal general criminal and civil laws against fraud as the main legal or regulatory defense against agent or broker conduct, the commissioner has the power to revoke an agent's or broker's license to do business.

Second, an insurer may be the victim of reinsurance fraud. The purchase of adequate reinsurance and the reinsurer's willingness and ability to perform on its obligations are essential to an insurer's financial well-being. However, since an insurer's insolvency caused by its inability to collect on its reinsurance is much more of a factor in the property and liability industry, no further discussion of this problem is warranted here.

Internal Fraud. A third source of fraud or unethical conduct against an insurer is the insurer's own management or the management of its parent company or affiliates in a holding company system. In the several insolvencies or near insolvencies in the past decade, some managements (or members thereof) embarked on activities to extract funds from the insurer for their own personal gain. For example, undue or excessive funds were drawn out of insurers to pay management and service fees to a parent holding company or an affiliate in which the insurer's management had an economic interest. Insurers loaned funds to parents, affiliates, or individuals that were not repaid in whole or in part. Extravagant salaries and expense allowances, unearned bonuses, and questionable fringe benefits were authorized in several situations; questionable dividends were upstreamed to a parent holding company; unearned commissions were paid to agencies affiliated with management members.

The war against internal fraud is conducted in a variety of ways. First, to the extent that unethical individuals can be screened out of management or ownership positions beforehand, the likelihood of internal fraud is minimized at the outset. At the time of an insurance company's formation and/or licensing, the commissioner is authorized to investigate the character and competence of incorporators, stockholders, and management and to withhold approval if his or her findings are negative. Similarly, under the holding company laws, when there is a change in an insurer's control, a registration statement must be filed including biographical information about the persons controlling or managing the insurer. An acquisition can be disapproved if the commissioner is not satisfied with the competence, experience, and integrity of the people in control. In addition, establishing sufficiently high minimum capital and surplus requirements may indirectly screen out potential fraud.

A second approach to combat internal fraud is to regulate conduct to deter fraudulent activities. Along with general prohibitions against fraud that are applicable to all insurers, the insurance holding company laws establish standards for transactions between affiliates and require disclosure of material transactions. The ongoing evolvement of the model holding company law is, in part, a reflection of the concerted effort to strengthen the law as new abuses emerge.

Finally, industry sanctions deter fraud by removing unethical insurers from the scene. In general (and specifically with the insurance holding company laws), a commissioner has great power over an insurer. The commissioner may suspend or revoke an insurer's license to do business or institute rehabilitation or liquidation proceedings if he or she deems further transaction of business to be hazardous to policyowners. The commissioner may also cause criminal proceedings for willful violation of the law to be instituted. In addition to state laws implicitly directed at insurance fraud and general state and federal criminal laws prohibiting fraudulent activities, as discussed previously, actions brought under the federal mail fraud statutes or the federal Racketeer Influenced and Corrupt Organization Act (RICO)[25] have occasionally proven effective.

Regulation for Sound Insurance Management

Management quality, experience, and integrity (or lack thereof) determine the nature of an individual insurer, the insurance industry as a whole, and most of the ensuing regulatory problems. As noted earlier, regulators have specific legal authority to consider management quality when, for example, an insurer is being formed, seeks a license or license renewal, or engages in activities within a holding company system. Also as noted before, in addition to taking direct action against individual management members by causing their removal or instituting civil penalties or criminal actions, a commissioner has the ultimate authority to suspend or revoke an insurer's license to do business or even place the insurer in rehabilitation or liquidation.

Although broad, regulatory power over management quality is not without practical limitations. For example, in the absence of strong indications in a person's background—a criminal record or a pattern of involvement with financially troubled insurers—competency and integrity are difficult to assess in advance of performance. Thorough background investigations of the thousands of ever-changing senior managers may be beyond insurance departments' physical capability. Furthermore, courts are reluctant to deprive a person of his or her career or to deprive a company of its ability to do business. Often it is difficult to build a case that is strong enough to overcome this judicial reluctance. Consequently, regulatory efforts may be unsuccessful or may not even be brought at all.

Hazardous Financial Condition in General

In 1985, the NAIC adopted the Model Regulation to Define Standards and Commissioner's Authority for Companies Deemed to Be in Hazardous Financial Condition. As of 1992, this model act or something similar to it had been adopted in approximately half of the states; a few other states have adopted related legislation or regulations.

The purpose of the model regulation is to establish standards that a commissioner may use to find that an insurer is in a financial condition that renders its continued operation hazardous to the public or to its policyowners. It enumerates a litany of tests, inquiries, and events that might indicate that the insurer has serious problems. If the commissioner determines that transacting business is hazardous in light of these factors, he or she may order the insurer, subject to an appropriate hearing and judicial review, to take specific corrective actions. By specifically defining the standards of hazardous financial condition, both the regulators and the regulated have better guidelines, and the commissioner's position is bolstered should his or her actions be subject to judicial challenge.

See chapter 27, which deals with state insurance regulation within the framework of federal controls, for Part 2 of this discussion on the regulation of life insurance.

NOTES

1. 8 Wall 168, 183 (1869).
2. See, for example, *New York Life Ins. Co. v. Deer Lodge County,* 231 U.S. 495 (1913).
3. About the same time, a series of legislative investigations were conducted in New York and other states concerning property insurer ratemaking, which provided the impetus for several state laws regulating rates and prohibiting unfair rate discrimination and rebates.
4. 322 U.S. 533 (1944).
5. 15 U.S.C. Secs. 1011–1015.
6. Professor Spencer Kimball has done so in a comprehensive manner. The discussion in this chapter is a brief summary of parts of his classic work. Kimball, "The Purpose of Insurance Regulation; A Preliminary Inquiry into the Theory of Insurance Law," 45 *Minnesota Law Review* 471 (1961).
7. In 1961, the NAIC adopted and 17 states subsequently enacted the Model Unauthorized Insurers False Advertising Act (or something similar to it). Also all states adopted in some form the 1948 NAIC Unauthorized Insurers Process Act under which insurer performance of a specific act (such as issuing or delivering an insurance policy to a state resident or soliciting applications and/or collecting premiums for such insurance) constitutes an appointment of the insurance commissioner as the insurer's attorney for service of process purposes. An insured (or beneficiary) may bring legal action involving a claim against an unauthorized out-of-state insurer by serving legal process on the insurance commissioner of the insured's home state.
8. *Ministers Life and Casualty Union v. Haase,* 141 N.W.2d 287 (Wis. 1966), 385 U.S. 205 (1966) (*per curiam*) reh. denied 385 U.S. 1033 (1967).
9. The act also calls for licensing a person acting as a consultant or analyst. For more information on the controls over persons engaging in financial planning, see discussions of the Unfair Trade Practices Act in this chapter and the federal Investment Advisers Act of 1940 in chapter 27.
10. Although primary state concern focuses on domestic insurers, states also have a legitimate interest in the solvency of foreign insurers licensed to do business in the state (hence the substantial compliance requirement).
11. For example, the NAIC Model Unfair Trade Practice Act defines the knowing filing with the insurance commissioner of any false material statement of fact as to the insurer's financial condition as an illegal practice.
12. The NAIC annual statement instructions were modified, starting with the 1991 statement, to require a CPA audit as does the NAIC Model Rule (Regulation) Requiring Annual Audited Financial Reports.
13. See previous discussion of the Standard Valuation Law requirement for an actuarial opinion.
14. The traditional approach of examining every insurer at approximately the same intervals (for example, 3 to 5 years) resulted in expending too much time and resources on financially sound insurers with a corresponding insufficient amount of attention directed toward the more marginal insurers.
15. The grounds in the model act for petitioning for an order of rehabilitation are numerous. They include the following: insurer financial condition such that further transaction of business would be financially hazardous to its policyowners, creditors, or the public; embezzlement, diversion of insurer assets or fraud endangering the insurer's assets in an amount threatening the solvency of the insurer; insurer failure to remove an executive found, after a hearing, to be untrustworthy in handling the insurer's business; control of the insurer by one found, after a hearing, to be untrustworthy; insurer refusal to submit to examination; insurer transfer or attempted transfer of substantially its entire property

or business without commissioner approval; and insurer violation of the insurance law of the state and/or any valid order of the commissioner. Grounds for an order of liquidation include the preceding grounds plus insurer insolvency.

16. The model act authorizes a member insurer to reflect an amount reasonably necessary to meet its assessment obligations in its premium rates and dividend scales. This contemplates that the cost of the assessments to the insurer can be appropriately passed on to its policyowners, the persons afforded protection by the act. However, life insurance premiums cannot be changed for existing policyowners. Building assessment costs into premium rates for future and nonexisting policyowners can be argued to be both impractical and unfair. Thus the model act offers an optional section, for acceptance or rejection by the individual states as they see fit, providing for reducing an insurer's premium, franchise, or income tax liability by the amount of the assessments. Commonly referred to as the premium tax offset, this provision has the effect of spreading the cost of the assessments among the taxpayers of the state.

    Substantial concern has arisen as to whether the guaranty funds have the capacity to meet current and future liabilities. Between 1976 and 1991, life and health insurance claims have caused $680 million of guaranty fund assessments, with estimated future assessments up to $4.2 billion. (This includes a $1.9 billion estimate for Executive Life Insurance Company but does not include estimates for First Capital Life, Fidelity Bankers Life, and Mutual Benefit Life.) Although there is concern about the adequacy of the current maximum annual limits and the industry's capacity to meet future assessments, since guaranty fund claim payments are spread out over a period of time, not all liabilities need to be assessed against the solvent insurers in one year. Furthermore, in aggregate, the life and health industry's current annual capacity approximates $3 billion. Thus while the aggregate assessment costs are far from trivial, the National Organization of Life and Health Guaranty Association (NOLHGA) maintains that the overall capacity of the system is adequate. (NOLHGA is a national association of the state life and health guaranty funds. It helps coordinate the activities of the state funds, compiles statistics, conducts research, and deals with regulatory and legislative issues affecting the funds.)

17. The NAIC also adopted the Standard Nonforfeiture Law for Individual Deferred Annuities, which most states have enacted.

18. Although indirect regulation of rates for life insurance is the general rule, credit life insurance is a significant exception.

19. Since the original formulation of the regulation, product innovations necessitated special treatment in certain circumstances, such as universal life.

20. The actual cost of a life insurance policy to an individual depends on his or her own circumstances and the actual cash flows experienced under the policy. This cannot be ascertained until the contract expires by death, maturity, or surrender and then only with some assumption as to the time value of money to the individual.

21. If a state has not adopted the model regulation on disclosure, it is believed that the relevant provisions are incorporated in the state's replacement regulation.

22. Rebating can assume many other forms, such as providing interest-free promissory notes for premiums, discharging prior indebtedness, offering free counseling services, promising loans not specified in the policy, and extending credit.

23. *Department of Insurance v. Dade County Consumer Advocate's Office*, 492 So.2d 1032 (Fla. 1986).

24. States were left with the option of retaining these provisions in the Unfair Trade Practices Act.

25. 18 U.S.C. Secs. 1961 *et seq.*

27

The Regulation of Life Insurance (Part 2)

Jon S. Hanson

With early Supreme Court decisions barring federal control, followed by the McCarran Act invitation for the states to regulate, as discussed in chapter 26, the vast bulk of insurance regulation fell to the states. Nevertheless, the federal presence was felt, is increasing, and at some point may assume a dominant role. Thus understanding the regulation of insurance requires a sense of the interaction between the state and federal levels of government.

ALLOCATING REGULATORY AUTHORITY BETWEEN FEDERAL AND STATE GOVERNMENT

The allocation of authority (dual, exclusive, superior, or subordinate) over a challenged activity is often resolved by the courts. In the context of insurance regulation, this involves the constitutional issues relating to

- the applicability of the preemption doctrine
- the limitations posed by the Commerce Clause
- the impact of the McCarran Act

The Preemption Doctrine

The preemption doctrine is founded on the Supremacy Clause of the United States Constitution, which declares that the Constitution and federal law are "the supreme Law of the Land."[1] When federal legislation or regulation is applicable to conduct that is also subject to state law or regulation, whether the latter survives is determined in accordance with the preemption doctrine. The preemption doctrine reflects judicial efforts to delineate the spheres of federal and state government authority within the federal system.

The Supreme Court has established two criteria in evaluating whether a particular state law or regulation should be preempted.[2] First, state law or regulation must give way—is preempted—if this is the "clear and manifest purpose of Congress." Congressional preemptive intent may be found in explicit statutory command or inferred from the statute's structure and purpose. Second, the Court seeks to ascertain whether federal and state law are so inconsistent that the state law must be preempted. Under this conflict test, preemption clearly occurs when federal law mandates action prohibited by state law or *vice versa*. As the degree of state interference with the federal legislative scheme diminishes, the presence of preemptive conflict becomes much less certain.

The congressional intent and the conflict tests are quite general and therefore subject to a wide range of judicial interpretations. The Court's willingness to preempt state law has dramatically oscillated over time between a high degree of solicitude for federal interests (thereby favoring preemption) and greater respect for and tolerance of state concerns. In recent years the tendency has been toward state regulations. Nevertheless, there is little doubt that, in the absence of McCarran Act protection, both actual preemptions and uncertainty about whether future regulatory efforts would be preempted would circumscribe states' ability to respond to regulatory problems.

Commerce Clause Limitations

Congressional authority underlying legislation that affects the insurance business is typically predicated on its power to regulate interstate commerce under the Commerce Clause of the United States Constitution.[3] The Commerce Clause not only authorizes Congress to act, it also limits the states' power to erect barriers against or unduly burden interstate commerce even in the absence of congressional legislation. As the volume and complexity of commerce and its regulation have grown, the Supreme Court has developed several tests to distinguish between state actions that the Commerce Clause permits and those that are prohibited.

There are at least three questions that the criteria raise. First, the discrimination against interstate commerce test raises the question about whether the state treats domestic companies more favorably than out-of-state companies. Second, the impermissible risk of inconsistent regulation test asks whether the subject of regulation is national in nature or admits only one uniform system or plan of regulation. Third, the balancing test weighs legitimate state interests in relation to the degree of burden (excessive or incidental) on interstate commerce. Failure of any one of these tests presumably finds state regulation an undue burden on interstate commerce and therefore prohibited by the Commerce and Supremacy Clauses. If there were no McCarran Act protection, the validity of the broad range of state insurance laws and regulations would be open to challenge as an undue burden on interstate commerce. Although there is a general sense that a major portion of state regulation would survive the challenge, uncertainty would always be present.

McCarran Act and Its Impact on Constitutional Limitations

In the *South-Eastern Underwriters Association* case, the Supreme Court overturned 75 years of legal precedent and held that insurance can fall within the embrace of Congress's power over interstate commerce, thereby rendering the preemption doctrine and interstate commerce limitations to state insurance regulation applicable. In response, Congress enacted the McCarran Act in 1945, declaring that continued regulation of the "business of insurance" by the states is in the public interest and that the business of insurance and every person engaged in it are subject to state insurance regulation. In subsequent constitutional challenges to state authority, the Supreme Court has made it clear that when Congress carves out an area for state law, state law prevails in that area even if it is in direct conflict with a federal statute, regulation, or policy.[4] Consequently, to the extent the McCarran Act applies, it bars challenges premised on the Commerce Clause.

The McCarran Act also provides that no law of Congress impairs or supersedes state law regulating the business of insurance unless such federal law "specifically relates" to the business of insurance. Although not definitive, one lower court said that, in order to preempt state law, the federal law must expressly declare that the state insurance regulation is preempted before the McCarran Act is rendered inapplicable.[5] Generally, therefore, existing federal legislation does not appear to specifically relate to the business of insurance.

Even if a federal law or regulation does not specifically relate, it may still apply to a particular activity if the activity does not constitute the business of insurance. However, even if the challenged activity falls outside the scope of the McCarran Act, the particular state regulatory effort being challenged may still survive under the principles of the preemption doctrine or the criteria as to what constitutes an unconstitutional undue burden on interstate commerce.

EARLY FEDERAL-STATE INTERACTION

In its *South-Eastern Underwriters Association* decision, the Supreme Court made it clear that the federal government has the ultimate authority to regulate the interstate aspects of the insurance business. Although Congress decided initially to vest this authority with the states, it reserved the right to oversee state regulation of insurance and to change such authority in whatever areas, in whatever ways, and at whatever time it believed appropriate.

State authority and regulatory exclusivity did not remain unchallenged. Although private parties resorted to the judicial forum to avoid state controls, generally unsuccessfully,[6] the most serious and persistent early challenges to the applicability of the McCarran Act arose from two federal agencies, the Federal Trade Commission (FTC) and the Securities and Exchange Commission (SEC).

In the FTC Act, Congress declared "[u]nfair methods of competition in commerce, and unfair or deceptive acts or practices in commerce" illegal and created the FTC as the regulatory agency to enforce the law. This statutory proscription served as the model for the basic proscription in the NAIC Unfair Trade Practices Act. Thus if the FTC Act were applicable to insurance, federal and state law would cover the same ground.

Following the adoption of the McCarran Act, which contains a major proviso that the federal antitrust law (including the FTC Act) applies to the business of insurance to the extent such business is not "regulated by State law," the FTC tested the boundaries of its jurisdiction by seeking cease-and-desist orders against some insurers for alleged misleading advertising. In 1958 the Supreme Court found that the states into which health insurance advertising was mailed and then distributed locally by agents had enacted legislation prohibiting unfair advertising (the state Unfair Trade Practices Act) and had implemented a system to enforce it. Such conduct was regulated by state law; FTC jurisdiction was barred.[7]

Judicial blunting of its early intrusions in insurance regulation did not permanently dampen FTC enthusiasm to make its presence felt. Armed with broad authority to investigate, the FTC evinced an aggressive interest in a variety of insurance areas in the 1970s. However, by 1980 the FTC had accumulated enough political opposition that Congress prohibited FTC studies or investigations of the business of insurance unless specifically requested by a majority vote of either the House or Senate Commerce Committee. Although this action effectively ended most insurance-related FTC projects, Congress maintained the option of either lifting this ban in its entirety or directing a study of a particular area. Thus the FTC remains a potential major regulatory factor.

The FTC was not alone in asserting federal jurisdiction. In the late 1950s the SEC showed increasing interest in the variable annuity concept emphasizing investment results. In a series of cases over several years, the SEC successfully asserted substantial control over different investment-oriented insurance products. (SEC regulation is discussed more fully later in this chapter.)

INCREASING APPLICABILITY OF FEDERAL ANTITRUST LAW TO THE BUSINESS OF INSURANCE

Narrowing the Scope of McCarran Act Antitrust Exemption

Judicial Scope

With the enactment of the McCarran Act, Congress confirmed the principle of retaining state insurance regulation, and it declared that the federal antitrust laws should apply to the business of insurance only to the extent that the business is not regulated by state law. The actual scope of the McCarran antitrust exemption depends on judicial interpretation of three key elements in the Act: (1) the "business of insurance," (2) "regulated by State law," and (3) boycotts.

Business of Insurance. If the activities under consideration do not constitute the "business of insurance," even if performed by an insurer or an insurance agent, they are not protected by the McCarran Act. Not only are such activities subject to antitrust laws but they are also subject to any relevant federal law (even though not specifically relating to insurance). Thus the scope that the courts give to the business of insurance is crucial to the vitality of the McCarran Act.

Following the enactment of the McCarran Act, most people believed that the statutory language, "business of insurance," offered a broad umbrella. Despite a boycott provision in the McCarran Act and the fact that variable annuities had been found to wander off the insurance reservation, these situations were rare exceptions, rather than the rule. Early unsuccessful challenges vindicated this perception. Consequently, the McCarran Act comfort index was quite high.

However, in 1979 the Supreme Court dropped a bombshell in *Group Life & Health Co. v. Royal Drug*,[8] with an aftershock 3 years later in *Union Labor Life Insurance Co. v. Pireno*.[9] Both cases involved arrangements by a health insurer with health care providers in efforts to reduce the cost of health insurance. The availability of the McCarran Act defense against these antitrust actions turned upon whether the insurers' contracts with the health providers constituted the business of insurance. In finding that they did not, the Court asked three questions to determine whether a given activity or conduct is the business of insurance: (1) Does such activity or conduct have the effect of transferring or spreading policyowner risk? (2) Does the activity or conduct constitute an integral part of the relationship between the insurer and the insured? (3) Is the activity or conduct limited to entities within the insurance industry?

With these decisions, the Supreme Court cast a pall over those in the insurance industry and regulatory communities relying on the McCarran Act exemption. The first criterion — transferring and spreading policyowner risk, a concept that is subject to significant stretching or technical narrowing as the mood strikes the Court — is particularly troublesome. An affirmative finding of all three elements clearly establishes the conduct as a part of the business of insurance. However, an unresolved issue is whether every one of these three criteria must be met before the McCarran protection is available or whether each is a factor to weigh in arriving at a decision. If all three are required, the scope of the McCarran exception would appear to have been severely circumscribed.

Regulated by State Law. Even if the activities under consideration constitute the business of insurance, to the extent that they are not "regulated by state law," they lose their McCarran antitrust immunity. The Supreme Court standard is that insurance legislation that proscribes conduct and authorizes enforcement through a scheme of administrative supervision that is not a mere pretense satisfies the regulated-by-state-law requirement of the McCarran Act.[10] With subsequent lower court elaboration, the prevailing articulation of the standard became whether state law "proscribes, permits or authorizes" the challenged conduct. As long as there is a statute or regulation covering the general area under consideration that is capable of being enforced, or as long as the regulatory scheme is comprehensively and meaningfully administered, it need not address every detail of the business of insurance.[11]

However, to meet the McCarran standard, the state law must be an insurance regulation, as distinguished from general law that only incidentally applies to the insurance industry. That is, the regulation needs to be aimed directly or indirectly at protecting or regulating the policyowner-insurer relationship.[12] The law also needs to be the law of the state in which the challenged activity is practiced and has its impact.[13]

The argument has been advanced, both in a judicial context and by critics of state insurance regulation, that the regulated-by-state-law standard should be met only if state regulation is "effective." Adopting that test would place the courts in the role of overseer of the effectiveness of state law, heretofore the function of Congress. Whether over time the Supreme Court will continue to avoid giving the test its judicial approval is not certain.[14]

Boycott. To successfully raise the McCarran Act defense against an antitrust challenge, the activity cannot constitute a boycott. In general, a boycott can be defined as a group or concerted refusal to deal.[15] This refers to a method of pressuring a target party with whom one has a dispute by withholding and getting others to withhold patronage or services from the target. If the term boycott, as used in the McCarran Act, is defined broadly, it could very well emasculate the McCarran antitrust exemption.

Because of the history of the boycott provision's origin in the McCarran Act, one line of lower court cases found that the term boycott, as used in the act, was limited to protecting only insurers and agents from the type of activities that arose in the *South-Eastern Underwriters* case. However, the Supreme Court disagreed in *St. Paul Fire & Marine Insurance Co. v. Barry,*[16] when it held that the term boycott should be interpreted in the tradition of the antitrust laws, which includes concerted refusals to deal with customers who are the ultimate target of the boycotters.

Although *Barry* found that an absolute refusal to deal on any terms constituted a boycott within the meaning of the McCarran Act, there are also conditional refusals to deal (refusals to deal except on certain terms). Many practices condemned by the antitrust law can be seen as conditional refusals to deal. For example, an allegation of price fixing can be viewed as a refusal to deal except at the price agreed upon; assuming insurers develop and utilize an agreed-upon policy form, a plaintiff can simply allege a refusal to deal except on the insurers' terms as to the content of the policy. *Barry* neither decided nor gave clear signals as to whether a conditional refusal to deal gives rise to a boycott. If such conditional refusals to deal are deemed to be boycotts, the term has become so broad in the context of insurance company activities that the McCarran Act antitrust exemption could become a virtual nullity.

Potential Congressional Action

Over the past 30 years, insurance regulatory reform initiatives have been proposed by presidential commissions, various federal regulatory and administrative agencies, the Department of Justice, the General Accounting Office, and both houses of Congress. Most have recommended that the McCarran Act be either amended or repealed. In the 1980s and early 1990s numerous bills were introduced in Congress to alter the status of the McCarran Act. They ranged from a total repeal of the act to more limited versions that would repeal the proviso clause that gives rise to the antitrust exemption. Some would alter the proviso to apply the antitrust laws in general to the insurance business but at the same time provide "safe harbors" for specified collective activities of insurers. Another would affirm continued state insurance regulation by retaining the antitrust exemption but would redirect certain activities currently under state control to regulation under federal antitrust law. And more important, several bills would directly or indirectly vest authority in the FTC over unfair and deceptive trade practices. Although to date the McCarran Act has proven resistant to change or repeal, the persistency and intensity of efforts to do so may ultimately result in congressional changes that have far-reaching implications for insurers, agents, regulators, and insurance consumers.

In short, the scope of the McCarran Act antitrust exemption has been significantly eroded by judicial interpretation of the "business of insurance," "regulated by State law," and "boycott" standards in the act. Whether the judicial narrowing will continue, reverse, or stabilize is yet to be determined. Although even under the narrower exemption, many antitrust challenges have been rebuffed by the courts, several have not. Clearly, the door has been opened to applying antitrust law to the insurance business. Future judicial decisions and Congress may push the door open wider.[17]

Overview of the Nature of the Federal Antitrust Laws

Since the insurance industry, agents, and regulators may have to function within an antitrust environment even more in the future, a basic awareness of the antitrust laws is essential to a better understanding of the regulation of insurance.

Substantive Content of Antitrust Law

Federal antitrust law consists of four statutes: the Sherman,[18] Clayton,[19] Robinson-Patman,[20] and FTC[21] Acts. However, since the legal standards in these laws are couched in very broad language, judicial interpretation in the context of a multitude of fact situations gives antitrust law its real substance and content.

The Clayton Act prohibits certain types of conduct, such as tying, exclusive dealing arrangements, interlocking directorates, and mergers that may substantially lessen competition or tend to create a monopoly. The Robinson-Patman Act, an amendment to the Clayton Act, focuses on unfair price discrimination. Since these two acts, to a significant extent, relate to commodities, much of what they contain may not be directly applicable to insurance. However, the provisions relating to acquisitions and mergers and interlocking boards have been applied.

The FTC Act prohibits unfair trade methods of competition and unfair and deceptive practices. The Supreme Court has made it clear that the activities that violate the Sherman or Clayton Acts also violate the FTC Act. Consequently, this act is both an unfair trade practices and an antitrust law. It renders the FTC a major antitrust player.

The Sherman Act is the oldest and the heart of the antitrust law. Sec. 1 states that every contract, combination, or conspiracy, in restraint of trade is illegal. There are two major elements in a Sec. 1 offense. First, there must be either explicit or implicit action; unilateral action is not proscribed. Second, the challenged conduct must be a restraint of trade. However, the Supreme Court has ruled that only unreasonable restraints violate Sec. 1.[22]

In the context of the insurance business, less attention has been focused on Sec. 2 of the Sherman Act, which deals with various types of activity relating to monopolization. Monopoly power is "the power to control market prices or exclude competition."[23] Under antitrust law, the meaning of monopoly has not been confined to the pure monopoly (one firm seller) but also embraces firms that are dominant in the market—that is, firms that have a high degree of monopoly power. Monopoly is defined in terms of a given product and geographic market. If the court finds that the relevant market in a given insurance situation is a line of insurance in a given state—a not unlikely result—there may be several markets around the country that are highly concentrated (a few sellers writing a high percentage of the business). Such circumstances create potential antitrust offenses or at least allegations of monopolization. The combination of monopoly power and predatory pricing (prices set below costs to drive competitors out of the market) is a likely candidate for a Sec. 2 offense. Thus Sec. 2 assumes a greater role in the insurance arena than some might realize.

Enforcement of Antitrust Law

The Department of Justice and the FTC, as the antitrust enforcement agencies, may bring civil actions for injunctive relief to restrain or prevent violations of both the Sherman and the Clayton Acts. The FTC has exclusive authority to enforce Sec. 5 of the FTC Act. The FTC functions through administrative hearings, and if it finds a violation, it can issue cease-and-desist orders. Conduct violating the Sherman Act can be subject to criminal actions. Corporate defendant violations are punishable by fines; individuals, including corporate officers, can be fined and/or imprisoned. Private parties also can bring actions for treble damages under the Sherman and Clayton Acts.

State Action Doctrine

The state action doctrine might provide antitrust immunity in addition to that available under the McCarran Act. In *Parker v. Brown*,[24] the Supreme Court presumed that Congress did not intend the Sherman Act to nullify a state's control over its officials. That act prohibits private action, not state action.

The crucial issue is what constitutes state action, and more specifically, to what extent does action of private parties, such as insurers or agents, taken within the framework of state legislative policy and regulatory enforcement constitute state action? In 1980 the Court adopted a two-prong test to determine whether the challenged activity of a private party constitutes state action that makes it exempt from the federal antitrust laws.[25] First, the challenged conduct must be a restraint on competition that is "clearly articulated and affirmatively expressed as state policy." A state policy that permits, even though it does not compel, anticompetitive conduct can qualify as state action as long as the state clearly articulates its intent to adopt a permissive policy.[26] Second, the articulated state policy to displace competition must be actively supervised by the state. Passive acceptance of private action is not enough.[27]

Although the state action and the McCarran Act antitrust immunities overlap, they are not the same. The formulations of the basic principles governing the scope of the two exemptions (the state action's articulated policy and the McCarran Act's "business of insurance") and the regulation requirement (the state action's active supervision and the McCarran Act's "regulated by state law") are different. The application of different principles to the same fact situations often yields different results. Thus the availability of the McCarran Act exemption might afford antitrust immunity in situations where the state action doctrine would not and *vice versa*.

Impact of Applying Antitrust Law to the Insurance Business

Direct Impact on the Insurance Industry

General application of antitrust law to the insurance business could proscribe a wide variety of activities and practices heretofore deemed appropriate and beneficial. Furthermore, other activities, even though they may not ultimately be found to be a violation of antitrust law, might be deterred because of the threat of lengthy, time-consuming, and costly litigation that could result in very large treble-damage judgments.

Application of the Substantive Content of Antitrust Law. Although evaluating the seemingly infinite number of ways antitrust law could challenge industry conduct is beyond the scope of this chapter, a few illustrations will highlight the problem. While property and liability insurers appear most vulnerable to antitrust challenge, life insurers and their agents are not immune.

Pricing. Price fixing is one of the major focuses of antitrust law. Property and liability insurers, with their long history of collective ratemaking through rating bureaus, are particularly vulnerable to antitrust challenge. However, pricing activity problems can also emerge outside the rating bureau context on the life insurance side of the business.

For example, an insurer who has captured a significant share of a market (which might be defined as a particular type of insurance policy in a state or even smaller geographical area) and competes with low prices might be the subject of an antitrust suit by a disgruntled competitor alleging monopolization through predatory pricing. There is a very indistinct line between competitive prices and predatory prices, especially with respect to life insurance, where the actual cost of the product is not known until some time in the future. Furthermore, since life insurers differ from most other business organizations in that they do not know the true cost of their products until years after they are sold, gathering and sharing information collectively is essential to reasonably predict future costs. Nevertheless, sharing or exchanging current or projected prices or other ratemaking information could be highly susceptible to charges of price fixing.

Policy forms. There is a lot of room for uncertainty about the legality under antitrust laws of insurers' collective work on policy form development even though it is often encouraged by state regulatory practices and conducted within the framework of state regulatory policy approval standards and mechanisms. For example, competitors' joint efforts to exclude coverages on standardized policy forms can be viewed as concerted refusals to deal—that is, boycotts.

Selling practices. Selling practices by both insurers and agents could be subject to challenge. For example, tie-in sales—conditioning the sale of a health insurance policy on the purchase of a life insurance policy or tying the sale of a life insurance policy to a waiver-of-premium disability rider—might constitute *per se* violations. Antitrust actions have also been brought alleging illegal tying when the availability of group insurance is conditioned on being a member of a group, even though being a member of a group is a fundamental group underwriting concept. Furthermore, a widespread failure to engage in rebating might be susceptible to an antitrust challenge as a conspiracy that creates an unreasonable restraint of trade. Insurers also need to be aware that imposing certain restrictions on agents' rebating or other agent business practices or activities (such as territorial or customer restrictions) could result in vertical restraint issues.

Pooling. State policy includes maximizing the availability of insurance to those needing coverage. Among the techniques used are sanctioning various voluntary pooling arrangements and mandatory residual market mechanisms. The insurance industry is replete with voluntary pools to serve a wide variety of needs (providing markets for extraordinarily large coverages or particularly risky businesses, for example, or enabling small insurers to combine in a way that makes them better able to compete with their larger brethren). In order to function, participants in pools use common classifications, rates, and policy forms, and they engage in other joint activity. Because the activities are in concert, pooling could run afoul of antitrust laws. Although antitrust laws include a number of provisions defining permissible and impermissible joint ventures, most likely some insurance pools would be prohibited and the legality of others determined only after lengthy and complex litigation involving the application of the rule of reason.

Chilling Effect of Potential Litigation. The pervasive uncertainty about how antitrust principles will be applied in different insurance contexts chills not only the ardor of the more aggressive competitors but also the willingness of many insurers to participate in collective mechanisms to serve various public policy objectives. The threat of litigation is real. Antitrust law permits, even encourages, such actions by providing for treble damages. Private parties have not been reluctant to bring antitrust actions to deter an overly vigorous competitor or to obstruct efforts to control costs, such as those relating to automobile and health insurance. It is also not unknown for treble damage litigation to be used for commercial shakedowns. The possibility of treble damages, the creativity of plaintiff antitrust lawyers, the potential of large and hugely expensive class action litigation, the civil and criminal penalties available to the government, and the uncertain results when applying antitrust law to insurance all tend to stifle even activity that might ultimately pass antitrust muster. Thus the threat of litigation promises to render insurers less willing to act in a creative and flexible manner in conducting their insurance operations and competing in the insurance markets.

For the most part, insurers' activities are rooted in sound and legitimate insurance purposes, but the application of antitrust law might very well deter, if not actually prohibit, the achievement of those purposes. The application of antitrust law would impose a wholly new and not necessarily beneficial form of regulation on the insurance industry. The state action doctrine might provide some relief, but it does not promise to provide an adequate substitute for a viable McCarran Act exemption. Moreover, dependence on the state action doctrine would constrict the range of options available to the states in responding to regulatory problems if they feel compelled to opt for more stringent anticompetitive approaches to ensure successful invocation of the state action exemption.

Impact on Regulation: Dual Regulation

If and when the antitrust laws become generally applicable to the insurance business, either because of judicial or congressional narrowing of the McCarran Act antitrust exemption or the elimination of the exemption, it will not only have a direct impact on insurers, as illustrated above, but it will also change the insurance regulatory structure dramatically.

Judicial Preemption. To the extent the McCarran antitrust exemption becomes inapplicable, thereby resulting in a general application of antitrust law to the insurance business, the preemption doctrine comes into play. As discussed earlier, whether a state law or regulation survives is determined by the Supreme Court's two-test approach in evaluating whether a particular state law or regulation should be preempted: the congressional intent test and the conflict test. Although in specific instances under the preemption doctrine, antitrust law may override conduct carried out under state insurance regulation, based on recent cases and a generally more conservative Court, it does not appear that the Supreme Court would be inclined to apply antitrust law in a manner that would achieve a wholesale preemption of the state insurance regulation. Consequently, if the insurance antitrust exemption is narrowed or repealed, the application of the preemption doctrine promises to result in full-scale dual regulation that the courts will try to accommodate as best they can. Under this likely scenario, insurers, agents, and buyers will need to thread their way through two different sets of regulatory requirements (state insurance regulation and federal antitrust law) enforced by two very different sets of mechanisms, people, and philosophy.

FTC Involvement as a Regulator. The narrowing or repeal of the McCarran insurance antitrust exemption also gives rise to the specter of substantial regulatory, as distinguished from antitrust, control by the FTC.

DUAL FEDERAL-STATE REGULATION AND STATE RESPONSES

Since the late 1950s, state exclusivity in the regulation of insurance has significantly eroded. In addition to the increasing overlay of federal antitrust law, as discussed above, the following illustrates the emergence of dual regulation.

Trade Practices: Potential Role for the FTC

If the McCarran antitrust immunity is narrowed by judicial interpretation or congressional action, both the Department of Justice and the FTC would accrue additional authority to challenge insurer and agent conduct, resulting in preemption or dual regulation. Even more ominous from the perspective of state insurance regulation, however, would be congressional action that directly or indirectly removes the bar to FTC regulatory and antitrust jurisdiction over the insurance industry. Various bills introduced in Congress over the past few years would do just that.

The FTC is not only an antitrust enforcement agency but also a major regulatory agency with sweeping authority over both competitive and consumer practices pursuant to Sec. 5 of the FTC Act, which bans unfair methods of competition and unfair or deceptive acts or practices.[28] In addition, the FTC is responsible for enforcing the Clayton Act, which bans activities ranging from price discrimination to anticompetitive mergers.

To define and enforce the broad proscriptions of Sec. 5, the FTC has both adjudicatory and rulemaking authority. If it determines in an adjudicatory proceeding that a party is engaged in an unfair trade practice, it may issue a cease-and-desist order even if the conduct was undertaken pursuant to state law. Furthermore, the FTC has the authority to promulgate rules that preempt state law.[29] Thus the introduction of the FTC into the regulation of the insurance business promises not only extensive dual regulation but also very likely dominant federal regulation in those antitrust and trade practice areas embraced by Sec. 5.

Investment-oriented Products: SEC as Major Regulatory Participant

Application of Federal Securities Laws to Variable Insurance Products

By 1940, Congress had enacted a comprehensive statutory framework governing all facets of the securities industry and securities markets. Nevertheless, despite affirmation of Congressional authority over insurance as part of interstate commerce in the *South-Eastern Underwriters Association* case, since the federal securities laws did not specifically relate to insurance, the McCarran Act was deemed to render them inapplicable to insurance. Furthermore, the Securities Act of 1933 expressly exempted an insurance policy or annuity contract issued by an insurer, and the Investment Company Act of 1940 expressly exempted insurers. Consequently, until the late 1950s, federal securities regulation of life insurance products remained virtually nonexistent.

Judicial Application: Variable Annuity Cases. By the late 1950s, some insurers had developed variable annuity products under which premiums paid to the insurer were allocated to a separate account. Instead of fixed benefits, the amount of benefits varied in accordance with the investment experience of the separate account, which was not subject to the traditional statutory limitations on equity investments.[30] At the commencement of the payout period, benefits might be either fixed or variable. Although the insurer continued to assume the mortality and expense risks, the annuitant assumed the investment risk.

In *SEC v. Variable Annuity Life Insurance Company (VALIC)*,[31] the Supreme Court determined that the concept of insurance involves some assumption of investment risk by the insurer and a guarantee that at least some of the payments will be paid in fixed amounts. Since *VALIC*'s variable annuity failed to meet these criteria, the Court found the contract to be a security, subject to the registration and prospectus requirements of the Securities Act of 1933. Although other insurers sought to design variable annuity products to avoid the implications of the *VALIC* decision, the Supreme Court went to some length to sustain the SEC's assertion of jurisdiction.[32]

Following *VALIC*, the Prudential Insurance Company expressed willingness to register its variable annuity as a security under the 1933 Act but maintained that it was entitled to be exempt from the Investment Company Act of 1940. That act exempts an insurance company whose primary and predominant business is the writing of insurance. Prudential primarily issued fixed-dollar insurance products, presumably fitting the exemption. Although the SEC concurred that Prudential itself was exempt, it ruled that the separate account containing the assets funding the variable annuity was an investment company that had to be registered. In *Prudential Insurance Co. of America v. SEC*,[33] the lower court affirmed the SEC's position, and the Supreme Court refused to review.

As a result of these cases, a variable annuity contract constitutes a security under federal law and is subject to the registration, prospectus, and antifraud requirements of the Securities Act of 1933; the separate account funding the variable annuity is an investment company subject to the 1940 Act. Although a variable annuity may be a security for federal purposes, however, it can still be insurance for state insurance regulatory purposes. Consequently, variable annuities are subject to dual regulation by the SEC and the state insurance commissioners.

Regulatory Application of Federal Securities Laws to Variable Life Insurance. In the early 1970s some insurers introduced variable life insurance (VLI), which provides cash values and death benefits that vary based on the investment experience of the underlying separate account. Although policyowners assume some of the investment risk, the insurer typically guarantees a minimum below which the death benefit cannot fall. Consequently, with respect to the death benefit, the insurer assumes not only the mortality and expense risk but also investment risk. More recently, insurers introduced a flexible premium policy, commonly referred to as a variable universal life policy, under which the policyowner may vary the amount and/or frequency of policy premiums as well as the level of the death benefit protection.

In an effort to launch VLI, the life insurance industry petitioned the SEC to exempt VLI policies containing specified features, such as the substantial guaranteed minimum death benefit, from the federal securities laws on the bases that the main purpose of the product was to provide protection against death, that the investment element was incidental, and that the policies were pervasively regulated by the states. Initially, the SEC adopted blanket exemptive rules under both the Investment Company and the Investment Adviser Acts since reconciliation with state insurance regulation would be very difficult. At the same time, however, the SEC expressly expected state regulation to provide "material protections to purchasers substantially equivalent to the relevant protections that would be available under the Investment Company Act."

The National Association of Insurance Commissioners (NAIC) responded by developing its Variable Life Insurance Model Regulation, adopted in 1973, which contained significant restraints on product design to ensure that the product would primarily be insurance rather than an investment. Initially, the SEC accepted the model, but in 1975 it rescinded its exemption, concluding that a blanket exemption rule deferring to a state regulatory pattern administered by diverse regulatory authorities would not assure adequate investor protection. Consequently, VLI policies are treated as securities under the 1933 act, and the separate accounts that fund VLI are subject to direct SEC control as investment companies.

SEC Regulation of Variable Insurance Products

Four federal securities laws have become quite relevant to life insurance companies that issue variable annuities and variable life insurance (hereafter in combination referred to as variable insurance).

The Securities Act of 1933. A major function of the securities markets is to enable the distribution of large blocks of new securities to the public through which the issuer of the securities seeks to raise funds by their sale. The fundamental philosophy underlying the 1933 Securities Act is disclosure of accurate information needed by a prudent investor to make an intelligent decision as to whether to buy the security. (The SEC does not pass upon the merits, or lack thereof, of a security.) Disclosure is achieved through (1) filing a registration statement with the SEC containing detailed information on the security, the issuer, the underwriting arrangements, financial statements, the officers, and security holdings, (2) providing a prospectus to potential buyers (containing much of the information in the registration statement), and (3) antifraud provisions that ensure that such disclosure is full and accurate.

Since variable insurance products are deemed to be securities, prospectuses must be delivered in conjunction with their offer and sale. The prospectus must be kept current for as long as payments may be accepted from contract owners.

As part of the registration process, financial statements certified by independent public accountants must be filed for the separate account (as the issuer of the security) and the insurer (as the guarantor of the mortality and expense guarantees). In general, compliance with the registration and prospectus requirements of the 1933 act has posed no insurmountable difficulties in the sale of variable insurance contracts.

However, the elusive objective of a highly readable and easily understandable prospectus describing the variable insurance contract being offered has been a source of periodic SEC and industry concern and conflict. The prospectus must include the merits and disadvantages of the investment, and it must disclose the nature of the risk and expense charges incurred. Given the complexity of the products, the requirements of the Securities Act, and the advent of new products, fulfilling this objective promises to engage the SEC and the life insurance industry on an ongoing basis.

The Securities Exchange Act of 1934. A second basic function of the securities markets is to provide a way to trade outstanding securities. The 1934 Securities Exchange Act governs this activity through disclosure requirements, prevention of fraud and manipulation, regulation of the securities exchange markets, regulation of the over-the-counter (OTC) market (trading securities other than on a securities exchange, such as the New York Stock Exchange), and control of credit in securities markets. In the context of regulating life insurance company products, the most relevant provisions are those relating to the OTC market and broker/dealers. A broker is defined as any person engaged in the business of effecting transactions in securities for the account of others. A dealer is any person engaged in the buying and selling of securities for his or her own account as part of a regular business. The broker/dealer is the entity under the 1934 act responsible for supervising the activities of the salespersons. Insurance companies, or their affiliates, which distribute variable insurance contracts are required to register as broker/dealers. In most instances, affiliates have been formed for this purpose.

The 1934 act provides for the creation and registration of qualified associations of brokers and dealers, subject to SEC oversight and control, for self-regulation of their members. A broker/dealer who does not belong to a qualified association may not effect a transaction in the OTC market. Since currently the only such association is the National Association of Securities Dealers (NASD), the sale of variable insurance products necessitates membership in the NASD.[34]

Pursuant to the requirements of the 1934 Securities Exchange Act, no broker/dealer or associated person can become a member of NASD unless qualified under appropriate standards of training and experience. The NASD must promulgate rules designed to prevent fraudulent practices and promote equitable principles of trade; safeguard against unreasonable profits, commissions, or other charges; prevent unfair discrimination between customers, issuers, or broker/dealers; and provide appropriate discipline (censure, suspension, or expulsion) for the violation of its rules. Imposing the act's informational and examination requirements on a wide range of people spread throughout the insurer's operations and training, supervising, and licensing agents selling variable insurance products have both posed problems.

Insurer personnel. As noted above, a broker/dealer and its associated persons must meet standards as to training, experience, and other qualifications. Substantial information must be filed for each person engaged in securities activities, including information about sales, trading, research, investment advice, advertising, public relations, and recruiting and training salespersons. Furthermore, the broker/dealer must certify that on the basis of diligent inquiry and other information, it has reason to believe that the person is of good character and reputation and is qualified to act as an associated person. Associated persons must also successfully complete a securities examination.

Since the definition of an associated person is quite broad, including any partner, officer, director, branch manager, or employee (other than those whose functions are clerical or ministerial), this causes serious practical problems for insurers. Throughout an insurance company that sells variable contracts, there are several departments and people who have at least some contact with the business. Who must take the examinations and for whom must the information be filed? Obviously, agents selling variable contracts and their supervisors are subject to the requirements, but what about the insurer's board of directors and top executives whose primary activities are in other areas? The time and expense burdens of these informational and examination requirements were somewhat relieved when the SEC took the position that an insurer would not be required to register as a broker/dealer as long as a subsidiary so registers and complies with all requirements.

Agents selling variable insurance. A person selling securities, which includes a life insurance agent selling variable insurance products, must register individually as a broker/dealer unless he or she is an associated person of a broker/dealer. The definition of an associated person includes one who is controlled by the broker/dealer. Thus if an independent agent is under sufficient control of the broker/dealer, he or she need not register as a broker/dealer. If a broker/dealer establishes a relationship with an independent agent, the broker/dealer is responsible for either ensuring that the agent is registered as a broker/dealer or assuming the supervisory responsibilities attendant to the associated person relationship. Thus life insurance agents selling variable insurance (or mutual fund) products are subject to the training, examination, experience, and supervision requirements promulgated by the NASD. These requirements pose significant difficulties for the individual agents who are basically insurance salespersons and for the insurers bearing the expense of educating, training, and supervising those agents.

Consequently, agents entering the variable contracts market are confronted with a different selling environment. Prospectuses must be used, sales loads must be disclosed, and projections of investment results are prohibited. In addition to requirements pertaining to business conduct, agents must comply with NASD standards of commercial honor and equitable principles of trade, and they must recommend only suitable products fitting the customers' circumstances.

The Investment Company Act of 1940. As an issuer of securities, an investment company engages primarily in the business of investing, reinvesting, and trading securities. In essence, an investment company enables an investor to invest in a pool of securities (for example, a mutual fund or a separate account funding a variable annuity). An investment company's accumulation of liquid and readily negotiable securities has offered a tempting target for exploiters. To counteract actual and potential abuses, Congress enacted the Investment Company Act of 1940, which encompasses six main areas governing investment companies: (1) registration of investment companies, (2) provisions aimed at honest and unbiased management, (3) security owner participation and control through both general and special voting rights,[35] (4) adequate capital structure, (5) financial statements and accounting, and (6) selling activities. Securities issued by investment companies (such as mutual fund shares and variable insurance contracts) are subject to various selling limitations, including the prospectus requirements, rules on permissible commissions to avoid unconscionable or grossly excessive sales loads (maximum sales loads are prescribed in certain situations), and controls of standards for and filing of sales literature.

Some of the most difficult issues pertaining to the viability of variable contracts under federal securities laws have arisen in connection with the 1940 Investment Company Act. The SEC has accommodated the life insurance industry in some areas through exemptive relief or modifying some of its rules or interpretations.[36] In other areas, however, exemptive relief has been denied, leaving the industry to its own devices as to how to cope with the problem.[37]

Confronted with products that did not fit neatly within the act, the SEC in its early administrative decisions determined that variable insurance contracts should be regulated as periodic payment plans that were essentially a means of purchasing investment company securities by installment. Pre-1940 abuses in the marketing and sale of periodic payment plans had prompted enhanced regulation focusing on the types of sales and related charges allowed and the manner in which they may be deducted and, at times, refunded. Defining variable insurance contracts as periodic payment plans, however, has subjected them to controls that may not be suitable to variable insurance. Although the SEC has issued numerous exemptive orders and rules to handle insurer problems, the basic problem—that the provisions were not drafted with variable insurance in mind—remains.

The major area of difficulty in attempting to accommodate the provisions of the 1940 act with the nature of variable insurance products involves the regulation of various charges: sales loads, administrative expense charges, mortality and expense risk charges, investment-related charges such as advisory fees and with respect to VLI, the cost of death protection. The problems posed include the following: (1) The current securities law regulatory emphasis on limiting the individual charges inhibits product design and pricing. (2) Unlike periodic payment plans in which sponsors incur little capital expense, the administration of variable insurance contracts demands substantial administration and capital. SEC application of "at cost" and "reasonable expense" concepts under the 1940 act makes it difficult for an insurer to realize a satisfactory return on the use of its administrative and capital resources. This encourages insurers to emphasize fixed-dollar contracts (even to the exclusion of issuing variable contracts) that are not subject to such pricing limitations. (3) To be motivated to sell complex variable contracts, life insurance agents must be able to generate compensation comparable to that for selling fixed-dollar products. Because of SEC limitations, compensation tends not to be sufficiently comparable, thereby creating a marketing bias against the sale of VLI. (4) The SEC has concentrated its regulatory efforts on the securities elements of the variable insurance products and has avoided regulation of the insurance elements. Unfortunately, securities-related and insurance-related charges cannot be neatly divided for regulatory purposes. Some charges that insurers characterize as insurance charges may have components deemed appropriate for investment regulation under the 1940 act. Furthermore, as long as the SEC regulates only investment-related charges, the potential exists for insurers to evade such charge limits by adjusting insurance charges to the extent permitted by state law.[38] On the other hand, insurers have been strongly against the SEC's exercising control over insurance elements of the contracts.

For these reasons the SEC Division of Investment Management has concluded that the regulation of specific charges under the 1940 act is inappropriate for variable insurance and has recommended legislative changes that would grant the SEC authority to adopt rules to assure the reasonableness of aggregate contract charges and the manner in which they are deducted. (The SEC would no longer examine individual contract charges or the manner in which they are deducted or refunded.) However, granting such authority is viewed, at least by some in the insurance community, as giving the SEC control over insurance charges and prices, something that not even state insurance regulators have with respect to most types of life insurance products.

Investment Adviser Act of 1940. An investment adviser is any person who for compensation engages in the business of advising others, either directly or indirectly, about the value of securities or the advisability of acquiring or disposing of securities. An investment adviser must register under the Investment Adviser Act, pay a registration fee, maintain certain records, be subject to SEC oversight and examination, comply with antifraud provisions and certain requirements as to investment advisory contracts, and must not be compensated based on a share of the capital gains of the investment company funds.

Advising separate accounts. If an insurer wants to serve as an investment adviser to its separate account, the insurer has to register as an investment adviser. The SEC has taken a no-action position on several provisions in the act that would have been difficult, if not impossible, for the entire insurance company to comply with. To avoid these issues, many insurers choose to register a subsidiary, rather than the insurer itself, as the investment adviser.

Advising prospective buyers: financial planners. During the 1980s, there was a increasing demand for relatively low-cost financial planning services. The number of individuals and organizations offering financial planning services grew dramatically. A financial planner can be defined as a person who offers individualized advice on securities investments, nonsecurities investments such as life insurance, and the management of financial affairs. An insurance agent who offers and sells only insurance products and provides no other financial services is not considered to be a financial planner.

Outside of the Unfair Trade Practices Act provisions dealing with financial planners, states regulations vary. Generally, life insurance agents may act as financial planners but cannot use that or a similar designation to imply that the agent is generally engaged in an advisory business in which compensation is unrelated to sales unless that is actually the case. States differ as to whether a life insurance agent can collect a fee for financial planning services and, if the agent can, under what conditions.

In addition to state requirements, life insurance agents engaging in financial planning services may find themselves subject to the Investment Adviser Act of 1940. In dealing with the applicability of the act to financial planners, the SEC uses three elements to define who is an investment adviser under the act. An individual is an investment adviser if he or she (1) provides advice or issues reports or analyses regarding securities, (2) is in the business of providing such services, and (3) does so for compensation. The advice need not relate to specific securities but may relate to the advisability of investing in securities generally. The compensation element can be met by receiving compensation in any form from any source, even if it is not a separate fee. Whether a person is "in the business" is determined by an analysis of the facts and circumstances, including the frequency of the activity. Providing advice with some regularity, even when it is not the person's primary business activity, renders the person subject to the Investment Advisers Act. Furthermore, a person is deemed to be in the business if he or she holds himself or herself out as an investment adviser, receives separate or additional compensation that is a clearly definable charge for providing advice about securities, or offers specific investment advice on other than isolated instances.

A life insurance agent advising on variable insurance products (securities) would appear to fall within the definition of an investment adviser except for the exclusion for a broker/dealer whose performance of investment advisory services is solely incidental to the conduct of its business as a broker/dealer. As a general proposition, this exclusion relieves the broker/dealer and its associated persons (agents) from investment adviser status when they provide investment advice as an essential component of their brokerage business. However, the SEC considers how individuals represent themselves to prospective clients in determining the scope of the exclusion. Even if an insurance agent is a registered representative of a broker/dealer, if he or she holds himself or herself out as a financial planner, the likelihood of being deemed an investment adviser increases. In view of the increasing frequency of insurance agents who engage in financial planning, the SEC's sensitivity to supervising financial planning activities adequately, and the tendency of private litigants to sue those with the deepest pockets (insurers), both insurers and agents need to be alert to the registration and antifraud responsibilities of agents who engage or appear to engage in financial planning.

State Regulation of Variable Insurance Contracts

Despite the evolvement of SEC regulation, issuing variable insurance still constitutes doing insurance business that is subject to state regulation.

Regulation of Variable Annuities. In the 1970s the NAIC adopted its Model Variable Contract Law, authorizing separate accounts and imposing some limitations thereon, as did most states. The NAIC next adopted a model regulation geared to variable annuities. Approximately half of the states have adopted the model (or similar regulation); most other states have adopted somewhat different controls.

In determining whether an insurer may issue a variable annuity, a commissioner must be satisfied that issuing such contracts will not render the insurer's operations hazardous to the public or its policyowners. Variable annuity policies must be filed with and approved by the commissioner, as are other life insurance policy and annuity contract forms. The regulation mandates that the policy include a statement that the benefits will vary, a description of the means by which the insurer determines the amount of the variable benefits, the investment factors to be used, and the grace and reinstatement provisions. The reserve liability must be established pursuant to the Standard Valuation Law in accordance with actuarial procedures recognizing the nature of the benefits provided. Annually, an insurer must give its variable annuity contract owners both a statement of the investments held in the separate account and information on the values pertaining to the individual's policy.

A state's general proscriptions as to unfair trade practices apply to variable contract situations. States commonly, as does the NAIC model regulation, prohibit illustrations of benefits that include projections of past investment experience into the future or make predictions of future investment experience. However, in permitting the use of hypothetical, assumed rates of returns to illustrate possible benefit levels, the model regulation accepts the argument that illustrations based on certain specified investment return assumptions, as distinguished from projections of an individual company's experience, can contribute to a meaningful presentation to prospective purchasers.

To sell variable annuities an individual needs to be licensed as a life insurance agent. The examination for an agent's license includes questions that the commissioner deems appropriate on the history, purpose, regulation, and sale of variable annuities. An agent must also comply with the training, examination, and business conduct requirements of the federal securities laws. The commissioner may deny, suspend, or revoke an agent's license to sell variable annuity contracts on grounds akin to those applicable in nonvariable annuity situations.

Regulation of Variable Life Insurance. After the SEC decided to resume direct regulation of VLI under the 1940 Investment Adviser Act, the NAIC substantially amended its model regulation in 1982 to eliminate restrictions no longer relevant to avoiding SEC assertion of authority, to bring the model regulation into conformity with the 1980 changes in the Standard Valuation and Nonforfeiture Laws, and to enable the development and sale of flexible-premium variable life plans—that is, variable universal life insurance. Over 30 states have adopted the NAIC model VLI regulation or something similar thereto; more than 10 additional states have related legislation or regulations.

An insurer is authorized to write VLI only if the commissioner finds that the plan of operation to issue VLI is not unsound; the general character, reputation, and experience of management and other relevant persons reasonably ensure competent VLI operations; and the method of operations is not likely to render them hazardous to the public or policyowners.

Mandatory policy benefit and design requirements cover several areas. The insurer must bear the mortality and expense risks, whose charges are subject to maximums stated in the contract. For scheduled premium policies, the insurer must provide a minimum death benefit in an amount at least equal to the initial face amount of the policy. Changes in the variable death benefit must be made at least annually; the cash value must be determined at least monthly. Computation of values must be based on reasonable assumptions acceptable to the commissioner.

A VLI policy must contain statements about the variable and fixed nature of the death benefits, the variable nature of the cash values subject to specified minimum guarantees, and any required minimum death benefit. The policy must also provide for a grace period, reinstatement, and policy loans. VLI policies must be filed with and approved by the commissioner before use. Reserves for VLI must be established under the Standard Valuation Law in accordance with actuarial procedures that recognize the variable nature of the benefits. The insurer must maintain assets in the separate account that have a value at least equal to the valuation of reserves for the variable portion of the VLI policies.

The insurer has to deliver specified information to the applicant for a VLI policy before the execution of the application. Under the Securities Act of 1933, delivery of the prospectus meets this requirement since the prospectus contains the information the regulation requires. The application for a VLI policy must contain prominent statements that the death benefits may be variable or fixed under specified conditions and that cash values may increase or decrease according to the experience of the separate account (subject to minimum specified guarantees). It must also contain questions designed to elicit information about the suitability of VLI for the applicant. Each insurer must establish (and maintain) written standards of suitability and must not recommend VLI to an applicant in the absence of reasonable grounds to believe that the purchaser is not unsuitable after reasonable inquiry about the applicant's insurance and investment objectives, financial situation, and needs.

The insurer's sales materials, which are subject to the NAIC life insurance advertising rules, may not be false, misleading, deceptive, or inaccurate. The insurer must disclose in writing, prior, or contemporaneously with the delivery of the policy, all charges that might be made against the account, such as taxes, broker's fees, insurance costs, and mortality and expense guarantees.

The insurer must give its VLI policyowners annual reports on cash values, death benefits, partial withdrawals, or policy loans, and must also furnish a financial statement summary of the separate account, a list of investments in it and charges against it, the net investment return for the past year, and any changes in investment objectives. Before its use in the state, all information provided to applicants and the form of any reports to policyowners must be submitted to the commissioner. Material will not be approved if found to be false, misleading, deceptive, or inaccurate.

The VLI regulation and the Uniform Agent and Broker Licensing Act now contemplate examining all agents applying for a license on both traditional and variable contracts. The agent must comply with the federal securities law requirements on training, examinations, and business conduct. The commissioner may reject an application for, suspend, or revoke an agent's license to sell VLI on the same grounds used for other forms of life insurance.

Dual Regulation

Following the variable annuity cases discussed earlier in this chapter, insurers and agents selling variable insurance contracts have become subject to the broad gamut of regulatory, disclosure, and antifraud requirements of the Securities Act of 1933, the Securities Exchange Act of 1934, the Investment Company Act of 1940, and the Investment Advisers Act of 1940. Although in many situations the SEC has tried to accommodate the federal securities laws to the nature and structure of the life insurance industry, the unique attributes of the contracts, and the role of state insurance regulation, it has not backed away from enforcing the fundamental concerns embodied in these laws to defer to state regulation. Therefore, while SEC regulation of variable contracts is very real and very detailed, the SEC has not tried to achieve exclusive control by preempting state regulatory activity.

The states have continued to view variable contracts as insurance products subject to the full range of insurance regulation. State legislatures and regulators have developed a regulatory framework to deal with the unique nature of these products and to allow for the substantial federal presence. The design of variable insurance contracts, the sales and distribution process, and the administrative mechanisms must satisfy the requirements of both federal and state securities laws. Dual federal and state insurance regulation is a fundamental fact of life for insurers and their agents operating in the variable insurance contract arena.

Regulation of Hybrid/General Account Products

With respect to the federal securities laws, insurance products can be classified as falling into one of three categories. First, there are the traditional contracts, under which virtually all of the investment risk remains with the insurer, contract values do not vary, and the contracts are funded through an insurer's general account. Such contracts remain within the domain of state insurance regulation. Second, there are variable insurance contracts, under which the investment risk is transferred to the buyer, and contract values vary frequently with investment performance. These contracts must be registered as a security under the Securities Act of 1933, and their underlying separate account must be registered as investment companies under the Investment Adviser Act of 1940. Third, there are *hybrid* contracts, which are the focus of the next section of this chapter.

Securities Act of 1933: Applicability of Sec. 3(a)(8) to Hybrid Contracts. Responding to high interest rates, life insurers in the 1970s began to offer a variety of new annuity products, generally referred to as guaranteed investment contracts (GICs).[39] Although GICs had investment guarantees similar to those in a traditional annuity, they also involved the payment of interest in excess of what was guaranteed. Single-premium deferred annuities (SPDAs) particularly interested the SEC. SPDAs were excess interest contracts under which the purchaser typically made a substantial single payment. The insurer guaranteed to pay a minimum interest (typically 4 percent to 6 percent) for the life of the contract, with the possibility that it would periodically declare excess interest. These products were marketed primarily as an investment vehicle with little focus on the traditional annuity features. Similar to other securities, the ability of the contract owners to earn the high anticipated rates of interest depended on the investment portfolios and the investment acumen of the insurer. The products were sold as tax-deferred investment vehicles and as alternatives to certificates of deposit and municipal bonds.

Because marketing the products as investments and paying excess interest at the company's discretion shifted some of the investment risk to the purchaser, the SEC undertook to determine whether such contracts were securities that should be subject to the registration, prospectus, and antifraud provisions of the Federal Securities Act of 1933. In doing so, the SEC embarked on a road that significantly broadened the scope of its reach to life insurance products funded out of an insurer's general (as distinguished from its separate) account.

Ever since the *VALIC* decision in 1959, regulators, courts, and insurers have wrestled with the issue of just how much investment risk an insurer must assume under an annuity or life insurance contract to come within the Sec. 3(a)(8) exclusion, which expressly excludes an insurance policy or annuity contract issued by an insurer from the 1933 act. In reaching their determination, the courts have focused on the extent to which the insurer bears the investment risk, how the contract is marketed, and to a lesser extent, whether the insurer assumes the mortality risk.

After a period of several years, pressured to clarify the status of fixed annuity contracts under the federal securities laws and to effect more objective standards in applying Sec. 3(a)(8), in 1986, the SEC adopted Rule 151. This rule provides that if an insurer's contract meets the following three basic conditions, the insurer can rely on the Sec. 3(a)(8) exclusion:[40] (1) The insurer is subject to the state insurance commissioner's supervision, (2) the insurer assumes the investment risk under the contract, and (3) the contract is not marketed primarily as an investment. Investment risk will be deemed to be the insurer's if the insurer guarantees the principal amount of purchase payments and interest credited for the life of the contract, credits a minimum specified rate of interest, and guarantees that any excess interest above the required minimum will not be reduced within one year. Although Rule 151 applies specifically to annuities, the SEC has indicated that the same principles also apply to life insurance. Furthermore, courts have applied the standards of Rule 151 to a life insurance policy.

As of 1992, the courts and the SEC agreed that the investment risk assumption is the most crucial factor in determining whether a contract falls within the parameters of Sec. 3(a)(8). They concur that purchase payments and minimum interest rates must be guaranteed. However, there is considerable uncertainty as to what extent excess interest rates and credited excess interest must be guaranteed and whether a contract with less than a year-long guarantee of excess rates or a contract not guaranteeing credited excess interest can fall within Sec. 3(a)(8).

How the contract is marketed is also an important factor in determining the availability of the Sec. 3(a)(8) exclusion. For the most part, the courts have found that a contract meets Rule 151's marketing condition despite references to the "investment" aspects of the insurer's investment abilities, the excess interest rates, and the tax advantages. Since investment management is the lifeblood of life insurance companies, it is appropriate for the insurer to tout its investment experience in relation to the insurance product. However, although the SEC maintains that a contract will not qualify for the Sec. 3(a)(8) exclusion if it is marketed with primary emphasis on current discretionary interest rather than on the product's usefulness as a long-term device for retirement or income security purposes, there is some suggestion that this may not be the case for the courts.

Both the SEC and the courts agree that mortality risk assumption is less of a factor for falling within Sec. 3(a)(8) than investment risk assumption and the manner of marketing. However, to what extent mortality risk assumption is a factor and how its meaningfulness is to be evaluated remain uncertain.

Even though the life insurance industry has sought to avoid registering general account products under the 1933 Securities Act, doing so does have at least three advantages. First, there is increased flexibility in product design since the insurer no longer has to worry about designing a product to meet SEC exclusion standards. Second, registration eliminates legal uncertainty and potential liability under the 1933 act for illegally selling an unregistered product. Third, a registered product can be marketed as an investment. On the other hand, the disadvantages include registration and prospectus disclosure requirements and costs, periodic reporting requirements, restrictions on advertisements, and requirements that agents have a securities license.

Applicability of the Investment Company Act of 1940 to Life Insurer General Accounts. Sec. 3(c)(3) of the Investment Company Act of 1940 excludes an insurer whose "primary and predominant business activity is the writing of insurance." In the context of hybrid (GIC) contracts, this raises at least two fundamental issues as to the act's applicability.

First, the *Prudential* case held that a separate account funding a variable annuity is separable from the insurance company and constitutes an investment company not covered by the exclusion for insurance companies. In contrast, hybrid or GIC contracts are funded out of an insurer's general account. This poses the question about whether such general accounts are subject to the 1940 act as investment companies. To date the SEC has not sought to regulate general accounts underlying such contracts.

The second question is at what point an insurer loses its ability to rely on the Sec. 3(c)(3) exclusion. This is a problem when an insurer's registered general account products become a high enough percentage of its business that its primary and predominant business is no longer issuing unregistered products (for example, the situation in the *VALIC* case). The rapid growth of various types of excess interest and variable insurance contracts during periods of high interest rates (as occurred in the 1980s) demonstrated that such a possibility is not a remote one. If the 1940 Investment Company Act ever does become applicable to a life insurer's general account, the regulatory complexities and the potential for dual or preemptive regulation would be greatly magnified.

Federal Securities and State Insurance Regulation of Hybrid Contracts. The SEC and the courts have established general principles that determine whether an insurance product is excluded from the 1933 Securities Act. Although the governing principles are easy to understand, their application to a particular situation is often difficult.

SPDAs. In 1991 a lower federal court enjoined persons offering unregistered securities, including SPDAs, from further violations of the antifraud provisions of the 1933 Securities Act and 1934 Securities Exchange Act. The SEC charged that the defendants misrepresented the risks, the returns, and the purported guaranteed nature of the securities. The SEC successfully argued that these

SPDA contracts were securities subject to the 1933 act that did not fall within the Sec. 3(a)(8) exclusion because of the investment risk assumption and the marketing factors.

Market value adjustment contracts. A market value adjustment feature (MVA) is generally designed to avoid problems of disintermediation when the current or market interest rate is guaranteed for a specified period and a withdrawal occurs before the end of the guaranteed period. Upon early withdrawal or surrender before the end of the period of guaranteed excess or discretionary interest, the insurer adjusts the proceeds paid to reflect changes in the market value of portfolio securities supporting the contract. If the value of the securities has decreased, the amount payable on surrender decreases. (The opposite also applies.) On occasion, the adjustment could invade previously credited interest or principal. Even though the purchaser can avoid an MVA by holding on to the contract until the end of the term, the MVA feature does shift investment risk to the contract owner who decides to surrender the contract during the guaranteed period. Whether the shift is enough to require registration under the 1933 act depends on the terms of the MVA feature. However, MVA contracts probably cannot obtain the protection of Rule 151, which requires that the insurer guarantee the principal amount of purchase payments (premiums) and all interest credited to them.

Whether or not MVA contracts are subject to the 1933 act, they are subject to state insurance regulation. In the mid-1980s the NAIC adopted the Modified Guaranteed Annuity Model Regulation, defining an MVA contract as a deferred annuity contract whose underlying assets are held in a separate account and whose values are guaranteed for a specified period of time. The contract must contain nonforfeiture values based on a market-adjusted formula if the contract is held for less than the guaranteed period of time. The assets must be held in a separate account during the period in which the contract owner can surrender his or her contract. The regulation mandates contract benefit and design requirements and covers reserve liabilities, separate accounts, and annual reports to contract owners. An agent must hold a variable annuity license to sell such annuity contracts. By 1992, five states had adopted either the model or something similar to it, and two states had adopted related legislation. (In 1986 the NAIC also adopted the Modified Guaranteed Life Insurance (MGLI) Model Regulation.)

Index policies. Prior to Rule 151, the insurance industry thought that annuity contracts whose accumulation rates were tied to external indexes fell within the Sec. 3(a)(8) exemption. Although the buyer bears the investment risk of the external index's going up and down, the insurer bears the investment risk of its investments underlying the contract achieving a higher or lower rate than the external index. Nevertheless, the SEC apparently holds the view that Rule 151 does not protect indexed-interest-rate annuity contracts from application of the 1933 Securities Act on the theory that externalization shifts the investment risk to the contract owner. Thus the prospects are substantial that interest-indexed contracts are subject to the act.

In 1988 the NAIC adopted the Interest-Index Annuity Contracts Model Regulation, covering individual annuity contracts whose interest credits are linked to an external reference. However, as of 1992, no state had enacted this legislation, leaving the regulation of such contracts, for the most part, to existing rules and regulations.

Universal life insurance. The late 1970s and early 1980s witnessed soaring inflation, spiraling interest rates, growing demands for term (as opposed to permanent) insurance, a flood of policy loans and surrenders to take advantage of higher interest rates available elsewhere, and heightened consumer sophistication. An increasing number of life insurance companies concluded that new products were needed to respond to the changes in the marketplace. These factors contributed to the emergence of universal life insurance (as well as SPDAs, MVA contracts, and indexed annuities, as discussed earlier).

Universal life insurance generally refers to a whole life policy with flexible premiums, adjustable death protection, a cash value credited at current rates of interest, and funding through the insurer's general account. Through this vehicle insurers seek to satisfy the public's needs for both protection and savings within the framework of one product.

In essence, the premiums go into a side fund from which the insurer makes two deductions: a charge for insurance protection (in effect, term insurance) no greater than the maximum charge guaranteed in the policy and a charge for insurer expenses and profit. The money remaining in the side fund earns interest for the policyowner. The insurer guarantees that the annual rate of interest credited on the cash value will not be less than a stated percent. (It may not exceed the maximum rate permitted under the Standard Nonforfeiture Law.) In addition, excess interest is provided at a rate determined at either the company's discretion (the excess rate may be guaranteed for a specified period of time, such as one year) or according to a stipulated external financial index (for example, 90-day Treasury bill or long-term corporate bond indexes). Typically, to qualify for excess interest, the fund must be a minimum size. This fund is referred to as the policy's cash value, but unlike the traditional whole life policy cash value, its growth is based on a variable, rather than a fixed, rate of interest. Unlike variable contracts utilizing a separate account, the funding vehicle for universal life is the insurer's general account.

Commonly, a universal life insurance policy grants the policyowner a choice in the manner of determining the death benefit. One option is for the death benefit to equal the face amount of the policy or the cash value plus a pure risk amount (a specified amount or a specified percentage of the cash value), whichever is greater. The second option is for the death benefit to equal the face amount of the policy plus the cash value. Typically, policyowners can, from time to time, change the death benefit option chosen and increase (subject to evidence of insurability) or decrease the face amount of the policy, thereby affording considerable flexibility. Some policies also provide cost-of-living increases in the amount of the death benefit.

Within limits, policyowners can vary the amount of annual premium they pay upward or downward, depending on their personal circumstances and preferences. If they skip a premium payment, the charge will simply be taken out of accumulated cash value.

Under a traditional whole life policy, funds can be withdrawn by either a policy loan (on which interest must be paid) or by surrendering the entire policy for its cash value minus a surrender charge, if any. In contrast, a universal life policy permits partial withdrawals from the cash value investment fund. Thus a universal life policy functions much like a savings account or a money market investment fund.

By unbundling the savings and protection elements of a traditional whole life policy, universal life offers flexibility in the amount of premiums paid, the determination of death benefits, and the withdrawal of cash values. Cash values are accumulated on a variable basis, enabling the policyowner to benefit from high interest rates; disclosure of the company fee portion of the premium is improved. Universal life has been described as being essentially a package of term life insurance coupled with an investment fund with the added benefit that the returns on the investment fund are tax deferred.

SEC involvement with universal life insurance. SEC concern with a life insurance company's general account products has extended to universal life. In 1981 the SEC Division of Investment Management sent a letter to several life insurers that were marketing universal life insurance, requesting their views on the status of the product under the 1933 Securities Act. This inquiry suggested possible assertion of SEC jurisdiction even over general account products containing traditional insurance guarantees. Such an expansive application of the federal securities laws would constitute pervasive federal regulation of the core of the life insurance business. However, to date, the SEC has not concluded that universal life falls outside the Sec. 3(a)(8) exclusion from the 1933 act.

State regulation of universal life insurance. As insurers began to offer universal life insurance policies, various states started issuing guidelines that differed widely in their comprehensiveness and sometimes conflicted with one another. Consequently, the NAIC developed a model regulation to address several areas of regulatory concern, including compliance with the standard valuation and nonforfeiture laws, the matching of assets and liabilities, the need for mandatory or prohibited policy design features, and disclosure and periodic reporting. The purposes in drafting the model were to supplement existing life insurance policy regulations, provide guidance in areas where regulatory gaps existed, and treat universal life as another insurance product, rather than as a form of investment requiring a wholly new regulatory treatment. In 1983, the NAIC adopted the Universal Life Insurance Model Regulation (last amended in 1989). As of mid-1992, over 10 states had adopted the model regulation or similar regulation.

The regulation establishes the minimum valuation standard and minimum reserve requirement for universal life policies, and it governs nonforfeiture values for both flexible and fixed-premium policies. It imposes certain mandatory policy provisions: An insurer must provide periodic disclosure, at least annually, to policyowners. There must be guarantees of minimum interest credits and maximum mortality and expense charges. No figures based on nonguaranteed amounts can be included in the policy. The policy must describe the method of calculating the cash surrender value and must provide a 30-day grace period.

Specific disclosure requirements are imposed on the advertising, solicitation, or negotiation of a universal life insurance policy. At the time of application, the agent must give the applicant a summary statement of the policy substantially in accord with a prescribed form. Policy premiums, death benefits, and cash values must be illustrated for the current interest rate actually being paid on existing policies in force and for the interest rate guaranteed in the policy. The regulation is not intended to conflict with or supersede the Unfair Trade Practices Act or the Model Regulation on Advertising and Solicitation.

As with conventional whole life insurance, the insurer maintains life insurance reserves required by state law for the death benefit payable under the universal life policy. The cash value of a universal life policy is computed in a manner similar to the calculation of cash values for traditional whole life policies, albeit on a monthly rather than an annual basis. The cash value so computed must comply with the minimum requirements of the Standard Nonforfeiture Law.

In addition, the Universal Life Insurance Model Regulation sets forth information that must be furnished to the insurance department to better enable the commissioner to determine that the insurer is adequately matching assets and liabilities. A *statement of actuarial opinion,* including an assurance of sound investment practices is also required.

Acquisitions and Mergers: Interplay of Federal Antitrust Law, Federal Securities Laws, and State Insurance Regulation

Three major bodies of law (antitrust law, state insurance regulation, and securities law) at the state and federal levels, each with its own focus and sense of priorities, have regulatory authority over acquisition and merger activity involving insurance companies.[41] The Department of Justice, the FTC, and the state insurance commissioners seek to prevent changes in control that would adversely affect the competitiveness of the marketplace. In addition, state insurance commissioners approve or disapprove acquisitions and mergers in terms of their actual or potential impact on policyowner and public interest with respect to the insurer's continued ability to do business, its financial condition, fairness to policyowners, and the competence and integrity of the new owners and management. The same acquisitions and mergers pose different concerns for the SEC, whose focus centers on investor protection through full disclosure in the framework of a balanced treatment between the acquirer and the management of the target company.

With multiple exercise of regulatory authority involving both state and federal government, the prospect for constitutional challenge is quite real. Most likely, however, the Supreme Court will accommodate various regulatory and public policy interests in a way that leaves multiple regulation of acquisitions and mergers substantially intact.

Direct Federal Solvency Regulation

The early and mid-1980s witnessed a small increase in the number of insurance company insolvencies and near insolvencies, especially in (but not limited to) the property and casualty insurance industry. Concern continues over the financial condition of insurers, including some high-profile life insurance companies, as a result of three large life insurer insolvencies in 1991. With the specter of the savings and loan crisis, the pressure for a substantive and direct federal regulatory involvement, as distinguished from the traditional congressional role as overseer, has escalated. After an intensive investigation led by Congressman John Dingell, legislation has been introduced that, if passed, would create direct federal regulation for insurance company solvency. Although support for federal involvement (including support from some segments of the insurance industry) has significantly increased, at this writing the ultimate fate of such legislation is still uncertain.

Alternative State Responses to Nationwide Regulatory Problems

Since its inception, state insurance regulation has been confronted with the problem of regulating a business that crosses state lines. As discussed in chapter 26, to cope with a regional and national business, the states joined together in 1871 through the NAIC to coordinate their activities and achieve the necessary degree of uniformity to enable a nationwide industry to function as it addressed state regulatory concerns at the same time. For more than 120 years, the NAIC has proven to be resilient and flexible in dealing with insurance regulatory problems. While far from perfect, this voluntary collective state effort has proven to be a remarkable force in the industry.

Although the states continue as the prime regulator of the insurance business, there are competing demands of the other relevant regulatory disciplines, resulting in a considerable amount of dual state and federal regulation of the business. Furthermore, while not new in nature but perhaps new in intensity, there have been recent efforts to supplant large portions of state insurance regulation with direct federal insurance regulation—for example, the proposed legislation for direct federal solvency regulation, mentioned above.

To address defects in solvency regulation, as well as to avert federal intervention, the states have responded with increased activity at the individual state level and voluntary cooperative activity through the NAIC to develop appropriate model laws and regulations. But, unlike the past, when the states could voluntarily select which elements of an NAIC work product to adopt or reject, the NAIC is exerting pressure to gain widespread state compliance with its solvency program through the NAIC accreditation program.

NAIC Standards and Accreditation Program

Specific aspects of solvency regulation and guaranty fund legislation were discussed in chapter 26. In addition, in 1989 the NAIC established Financial Regulation Standards to serve as baseline standards to encourage states to upgrade the quality of insurance solvency regulation. Establishing national standards within the flexible framework of state insurance regulation was undertaken, in part, to demonstrate that direct federal solvency regulation is undesirable and unnecessary. It is anticipated that adopting the NAIC standards will achieve greater uniformity and consistency between the states.

The NAIC standards cover three elements of a state regulator's capability: (1) the laws enacted and the regulations adopted,[42] (2) regulatory practices and procedures with respect to effective financial analysis and financial examinations,[43] and (3) department organizational practices and procedures.[44] Periodically, the NAIC may add to, modify, or eliminate standards in response to new situations and improved regulatory techniques.

In 1990, recognizing that what one state does or does not do can have a dramatic impact on the fate of other states' regulation, the NAIC adopted an accreditation program to provide an incentive for states to improve their solvency regulatory programs to meet NAIC standards. Commencing in January 1994, accredited states will not accept examination reports from nonaccredited states, thereby impairing the ability of insurers from nonaccredited states to do business in the accredited states until they undergo a second examination acceptable to the accredited states. Furthermore, an accredited state may decide not to license an insurer domiciled in a nonaccredited state.

States seeking accreditation must undergo a multiphase accreditation review. Initially, the state conducts a self-examination of how its regulatory capabilities meet the NAIC standards on model laws and regulations in place, sufficient staffing in terms of numbers and expertise, and other technical capabilities. After a preliminary review by the NAIC and after the state has dealt with suggested changes, the insurance department is subjected to an on-site review by an independent audit team. Thereafter, the NAIC Accreditation Committee votes whether to accredit the state. To assure continued compliance, a state faces an annual desk audit and a complete review every 5 years. If the NAIC changes its standards, states are given a specified period of time, such as 3 years, to bring their laws, regulations, and practices into conformity to preserve their accreditation. At the end of 1992, 19 states had been accredited, accounting for at least 70 percent of the total United States premium.

Whatever the criticisms of particular aspects of the NAIC accreditation program for solvency regulation, the approach may herald a new era in state insurance regulation. Although directed at regulation for solvency, the basic approach—standards coupled with a strong incentive to gain individual state compliance—can be applied to other facets of regulation. The NAIC has again demonstrated its flexibility in combining the virtues of regulation at the state level with the necessity of adequately regulating a nationwide business.

Interstate Compacts

Although the NAIC accreditation program has commanded the most attention, the concept of interstate compacts has been advanced as an alternative state response to the need for coordinated and consistent regulation of a nationwide industry. Under the Contract Clause of the United States Constitution, the states may enter into an agreement with one another, subject to the approval of Congress, to institute uniform standards, rules, and enforcement mechanisms deemed necessary and appropriate to regulate certain aspects of the insurance business. As legislatively enacted statutes, compacts take precedence over previously enacted statutes. Since compacts are legally binding contracts with other states, they take also precedence over subsequently enacted conflicting statutes. State actions contrary to the compact impair the contract rights of the other states in violation of the Contract Clause of the United States Constitution.[45] A state may not unilaterally abrogate its compact responsibilities. Thus interstate compacts afford a constitutional, statutory, and contractual basis for uniform legislation.

As an agreement entered into by the states, the states can determine the precise nature and scope of an interstate compact's authority and mechanisms. An interstate compact could establish a primary compact agency to serve a subordinate agency in each state that is a party to the compact. This primary agency may have rulemaking and enforcement powers to establish uniform standards in those areas deemed to require uniform treatment, while leaving the majority of regulatory issues to be handled under the current system of regulation. In the context of insurance regulation, a natural candidate for the primary compact agency would be the NAIC, although other possibilities might also be considered.

Although the ultimate fate of the interstate compact concept for insurance regulation is unclear, it is a viable alternative to direct federal regulation of insurance, and it is a significant evolutionary step beyond the NAIC accreditation approach.[46]

Convergence of Financial Services and Internationalization of Trade

Convergence

In the 1980s there was a notable movement toward the convergence or closer integration of financial services. Commonly, financial services are defined as including deposit-taking and lending institutions (banks, savings and loans, and other thrifts), securities and investment services, insurance, and real estate services. The convergence (or integration) of financial services refers to a marketplace phenomenon characterized by the movement of various financial institutions across traditional boundaries (legal or otherwise), the development of products designed to compete across traditional boundaries, and the entry of nonfinancial companies into the financial services marketplace.[47]

It is beyond the scope of this chapter to predict the nature of insurance business regulation in the future. It appears safe to assume, however, that the extent to which the economic, technological, and political forces foster or deter further convergence of financial services, they will also have a substantial impact not only on the nature of regulation but also on the locus of regulation at the state and/or federal level. The ultimate locus of regulation, in significant part, will reflect the effectiveness of current regulatory structures in responding to changing circumstances and needs.

Internationalization

In addition to the move toward the convergence of financial services in the United States, financial services in general and insurance in particular are becoming increasingly internationalized. Although international trade in goods and services must confront a host of government-imposed trade barriers, the evolution of bilateral discourse and agreements between nations, regional trading blocks (the European Union, formerly the European Community, and the North American Free Trade Agreement), and worldwide trade negotiations (General Agreement on Tariffs and Trade) pushes for increased free trade.

Negotiating reciprocal agreements with other nations may have a significant impact on the nature and locus of insurance regulation. Even if such agreements only compel comparable treatment between domestic and foreign insurers, thereby leaving current regulatory institutions intact, the increased internationalization of the marketplace will give rise to problems that insurance regulation must confront.

NOTES

1. U.S. Const. Art. VI, sec. 8, clause 2.
2. *Jones v. Rath Packing Co.*, 430 U.S. 519 (1977).
3. U.S. Const. Art. I, sec. 8, clause 3.
4. *Western Southern Life Insurance Co. v. State Board of Equalization of California,* 451 U.S. 648, 652-53 (1981) (sustained constitutionality of state retaliatory tax); *Prudential Insurance Co. v. Benjamin* (1946) (upheld state tax discriminating against interstate commerce).
5. *John Alden Life Insurance Co. v. Woods,* [1982 Transfer Binder] Fed. Sec. L. Rep. (CHH) Para. 98,617 (D. Idaho, Dec. 19, 1981), p. 93,064.
6. See, for example, *Prudential Insurance Company v. Benjamin,* 328 U.S. 408 (1946); *Robertson v. California,* 328 U.S. 440 (1946).
7. *American Hospital and Life Insurance Co. v. FTC,* 243 F.2d 719 (1957), aff'd, 357 U.S. 560 (1958); *National Casualty Co. v. FTC,* 245 F.2d 883 (1957), aff'd, 357 U.S. 560 (1958) (per curiam).
8. 440 U.S. 205 (1979).
9. 458 U.S. 119 (1982).
10. *National Casualty,* 357 U.S. at 564-65.
11. See, for example, *California League of Independent Insurance Producers v. Aetna Casualty and Surety Co.,* 175 F. Supp. 857 (1959); *Ohio AFL-CIO v. Insurance Rating Board,* 451 F. 2d 1178 (6th Cir. 1971), cert. denied, 409 U.S. 917 (1971).
12. *SEC v. National Securities, Inc.,* 393 U.S. 453, 460 (1969).
13. *FTC v. Travelers Health Association,* 362 U.S. 293 (1960).
14. See endnote 27.
15. A unilateral refusal to deal, as distinguished from a group refusal, does not constitute a boycott. However, this does not prevent a plaintiff from alleging a group refusal to bring the case under the antitrust law.
16. 438 U.S. 531 (1978).
17. Furthermore, while beyond the scope of this chapter, note that state antitrust law may become more significant in insurance regulation.
18. 15 U.S.C. Secs. 1–7.
19. 15 U.S.C. Sec. 12 *et seq.*
20. 15 U.S.C. Secs. 13, 13a–c. and 21a.
21. 15 U.S.C. Sec. 41 *et seq.*
22. *Standard Oil Co. of New Jersey v. United States,* 221 U.S. 1, 60 (1911). The Supreme Court has adopted two alternative approaches in determining whether certain activity constitutes an unreasonable restraint of trade. Pursuant to the *rule of reason* approach, the Court looks closely at the impact of the challenged conduct to determine whether it promotes or suppresses competition. If it suppresses competition, the conduct constitutes an unreasonable restraint of trade violating Sec. 1. Alternatively, when confronted with certain types of restraints that are plainly anticompetitive and lack any redeeming virtues, the Court will find that such restraints are *per se* unreasonable. That is, the Court presumes such conduct to be an illegal, unreasonable restraint without undertaking the time-consuming and expensive rule-of-reason analysis. In the past, the types of conduct giving rise to *per se* treatment included price fixing, division of markets, some boycotts, and some tying arrangements.
23. *United States v. E.I. duPont de Nemours & Co.,* 351 U.S. 377, 391 (1956).
24. 317 U.S. 341 (1943).

25. *California Retail Liquor Dealers' Association v. Midcal Aluminum, Inc.,* 445 U.S. 97 (1980).
26. *Southern Motor Carriers Rate Conference, Inc. v. United States,* 471 U.S. 48 (1985).
27. In *Federal Trade Commission v. Ticor,* 112 S.Ct. 2169, 2177 (1992), the Supreme Court found that to qualify as state action, the state must exercise "sufficient independent judgment and control so that the details of the rates or prices have been established as a product of deliberate state intervention, not simply by agreement among private parties." (In this case the regulator failed to fully examine the filed rates and did not follow up in a timely way.) Whereas some lower courts had defined "active supervision" in terms of whether the state established, staffed, funded, and empowered a regulatory program, the Supreme Court now seems to be saying that it will evaluate the effectiveness of the state regulatory scheme in applying the state action doctrine.

   The question is also raised whether *Ticor* heralds a tightening of the "regulated by State law" standard under the McCarran Act.
28. 15 U.S.C. Sec. 45.
29. *Fidelity Federal Savings & Loan Association v. De La Cuesta,* 458 U.S. 141, 153 (1982).
30. As discussed in chapter 26, state investment law has traditionally confined life insurer investments primarily to those that are fixed dollar in nature, mostly bonds and mortgages. To enable insurers to issue products whose benefits vary according to the fluctuating investment performance of equity securities (such as variable annuities and subsequently variable life insurance), states enacted separate account legislation. Subject to certain safeguards, a domestic life insurer is authorized to establish one or more separate accounts, may allocate funds to the account(s) to provide for life insurance or annuities payable in fixed or variable amounts, and may invest such funds without regard to the statutory limitations generally imposed on common stock investments.
31. *SEC v. Variable Annuity Life Insurance Co.,* 359 U.S. 65 (1959).
32. See *SEC v. United Benefit Life Insurance Co.,* 387 U.S. 202 (1967).
33. 326 F.2d 383 (3d Cir.), cert. denied 377 U.S. 953 (1964).
34. Originally many insurers and their affiliates opted to be a broker/dealer directly under the supervision of the SEC rather than become members of the NASD. Recently, however, membership in the NASD has become mandatory.
35. See endnote 37.
36. Congress amended the 1933 and 1940 acts in 1970 to exempt variable contracts and their underlying separate accounts used solely to fund qualified pension or profit-sharing plans.
37. For example, the SEC was adamant that the provisions for security owner voting and control as to electing directors, reviewing principal underwriting and investment advisory contracts, approving changes in investment policy, and ratifying selection of independent auditors are fundamental to achieving the protections intended by the Investment Company Act. Insurers argued that these were impossible to comply with under those state insurance and corporate laws mandating that an insurance company's affairs (which includes separate account assets) be managed by the insurer's board of directors. The SEC refused to budge on the belief that these provisions ensure that the people who have an investment risk have the ultimate voice in policy. In response, the NAIC promulgated its model variable contract law, and many states enacted legislation permitting security owner (variable contract owner) control of separate accounts in compliance with the federal securities laws.
38. Beginning in 1980, the SEC interpreted the 1940 Investment Company Act to require insurers to obtain exemptions to deduct the risk charges from the assets of the separate account. The volume of these applications led to proposed Rule 26a–3 in 1984 and

reproposed in 1987 but never adopted. The debate found the insurance industry claiming that the SEC failed to adequately acknowledge the insurance nature of the charges while it sought to limit risk charges so that they could not be used as a hidden funding vehicle for distribution expenses. In the mid-1980s the SEC Division of Investment Management took the position that it would not support exemptions from the act for risk charges exceeding specified levels.

39. Guaranteed investment contracts are also known as guaranteed interest contracts, guaranteed income contracts, guaranteed insurance contracts, or guaranteed return contracts.

40. In adopting Rule 151, the SEC emphasized that the rule is designed to provide a safe harbor, rather than to delineate the outer limits of Sec. 3(a)(8). That is, if a contract meets the standards of the rule, the exemption is available. However, if a contract does not meet the standards, it still may be within the exemptive provision based on reference to the principles embodied in the rule and the relevant judicial interpretations of Sec. 3 (a)(8). However, there is some judicial authority suggesting that Rule 151 is not simply a safe harbor but constitutes the exclusive means of relying on Sec. 3(a)(8).

41. For a discussion of insurance company acquisitions and mergers and regulation thereof, see chapter 28.

42. The standards with which the states are to comply embrace such areas as examination authority, capital and surplus requirements, NAIC accounting practices and procedures, corrective actions with respect to insurers deemed to be in financially hazardous condition, valuation of investments, holding company legislation, risk limitation, investment regulations, admitted assets, minimum standards as to liabilities and reserves, reinsurance ceded, CPA audits, annual actuarial opinions on insurer reserves, receiverships, guaranty funds, participation in the NAIC IRIS system, risk retention, and business transacted with a producer-controlled property/casualty insurer. Typically, adopted standards tie directly to specific NAIC model laws or regulations.

43. For example, these standards deal with sufficient staff to perform financial analysis of domestic insurers and the requirements to perform the financial analysis function effectively, adequate resources to examine all domestic insurers on a periodic basis, access to qualified specialists in the examination process, examination procedures, scheduling of examinations, and preparation of examination reports.

44. These standards deal with such items as allocation of responsibility and accountability for financial surveillance and regulation, ongoing job performance evaluation, adequate pay structure, and adequate department funding.

45. "No State shall . . . pass any law impairing the obligation of contracts. . . ." U.S. Const., Art. I, sec. 10. However, compacts can be drafted with termination, modification, withdrawal, and other provisions to soften the rigidity of locking states into the provisions of the compact once adopted.

46. A group of state legislators has drafted an interstate compact to oversee state guaranty funds and coordinate insurer liquidations.

47. The ongoing saga of bank efforts to enter into the sale and/or underwriting of insurance and the insurers' and insurance agents' resistance thereto is a vivid portrayal of competing industries attempting to use (or circumvent) various regulatory agencies, the courts, and legislatures at both the state and federal levels to enhance their competitive positions.

28

Types of Life Insurance Carriers

Jon S. Hanson

In light of the different demands and circumstances in a vigorous and free society, it is only natural that various types of organizations have emerged as providers of life insurance. These organizations may be categorized into these three broad groups:

- commercial life insurers
- other private providers of life insurance
- government agencies[1]

COMMERCIAL LIFE INSURANCE COMPANIES

Most life insurance in force today is written by commercial life insurance companies. Although theoretically coverage could be issued by an individual or a partnership, to ensure the promise of security, it is essential that the insurance provider be permanent in order to be around when its long-term obligations come due. Since the corporate form of organization tends to be more permanent than other alternatives (a corporation's existence continues beyond the death of any or all of its owners), it is the only form of business organization sanctioned by state law to underwrite life insurance.

Generally speaking, there are two different types of life insurance corporations, stock and mutual insurers. Both types of insurer must meet the formation, licensing, capital and/or surplus, and other state law requirements to do business. (See chapters 26 and 27 on the regulation of insurance.)

Stock Life Insurance Companies

Profit Orientation

To obtain the initial operating capital necessary to enable a new company to begin to operate, the founders of a stock insurer sell shares of stock in the company that is being created. (In the future, if more funds are needed, additional shares may be offered for sale.) The people who purchase transferable ownership interests in the shares of stock own the insurer. If the company operates successfully, the value of the stockholders' investments will grow. Hence they may profit both by income from periodic payments (stockholder dividends) and gains arising from the sale of their stock. On the other hand, if the insurer is unsuccessful, the stockholders may lose some or all of their investment.

Whatever the ultimate result, a stock insurer is organized and operated primarily for the purpose of earning profits for its stockholders. In its quest for profits, a stock life insurer offers a wide range of products and services that benefit not only the insurance-consuming public (policyowners, insureds, and beneficiaries) but also the public at large (insurance protection, savings mechanisms, sources of investment funds for business and government, and employment opportunities).

Management Accountability

The stockholders elect the board of directors that in turn appoints and oversees the management and operation of the company.[2] Although it is not unknown for dissatisfied stockholders to vote to replace board members and thereby change control of the company, because of the number and dispersion of stockholders, direct replacement of the board is very difficult and therefore rare.[3]

Nevertheless, management is subject to other forms of accountability that restrict trading the insurer's stock in the open market. The investment community constantly monitors management performance. Changes in stock prices, among other things, reflect stockholder views on management performance. If stockholders believe that the performance is poor, they can sell their stock, which drives the share price down and leaves management vulnerable to a hostile takeover.[4] Thus a stock company's management is under real and constant pressure to generate an acceptable level of earnings that translate into stockholder dividends and increase the value of the stock.

At the same time, policyowner interests are neither irrelevant nor ignored. Although policyowners in most stock insurance companies lack legal control over management,[5] successful business operations in a competitive marketplace require a certain degree of customer satisfaction and a good business reputation. Furthermore, life insurers are subject to comprehensive state insurance regulations aimed at fostering policyowner interests.[6]

Distribution of Surplus to Shareholders

The surplus of a stock life insurer is the amount by which the insurer's assets exceed the sum of its liabilities and capital (capital is the amount of money the stockholders have invested in the company). Stockholders share in the insurer's surplus either through liquidation of the company or the payment of stockholder dividends.

Liquidation. Although an insurer may be liquidated in a situation that benefits stockholders, liquidation typically occurs when an insurer becomes financially impaired with little prospect for recovery. After the insurer closes down and the assets are gathered pursuant to a court order for liquidation, any assets remaining after satisfying the insurer's liabilities are distributed to the stockholders. Usually, however, few if any assets remain for such distribution.

Stockholder Dividends. Cash dividends are the usual means by which stockholders receive part of the insurer's surplus. A gain in the company's surplus may arise from a specific provision for profit in the gross premiums charged for its policies or from favorable interest, mortality, and expense experience compared to the assumptions in the establishment of premium rates. Management may elect to pay a portion of its surplus to stockholders in the form of dividends as compensation for the use of their capital funds, it may retain surplus to enhance policyowner security against future adverse contingencies, or it may utilize surplus to finance insurer operations, such as new business, acquisitions, and so forth. If shareholders are dissatisfied with their dividends or the growth in the value of their stock, as noted above, they may either sell their shares or seek to replace the existing board of directors.

Nonparticipating Policies

Traditionally stock life insurers issue nonparticipating policies for which they charge fixed premiums. These policies are sometimes referred to as guaranteed cost policies since they involve neither future increases in premiums nor refunds. (Stock companies cannot issue assessable policies that would permit an insurer to demand an increase in the premium to recapture losses.) Under a nonparticipating policy, policyowners do not share in the profits the insurer experiences (hence the term nonparticipating). In stock companies issuing only nonparticipating policies, the entire net worth of the insurer, while available for the protection of policyowners against adverse developments, represents assets held for the ultimate benefit of the shareholders.

Many stock life insurers currently issue (or have at one time issued) participating life insurance[7] either exclusively or in addition to nonparticipating policies. As explained earlier, under a participating policy the policyowner shares (participates) in the insurer's gains through policyowner dividends. Most states impose no special regulation on participating insurance sold by stock insurers. In the absence of any special charter provisions, statutory restrictions, or other legally binding agreements, the insurer's entire net worth, after payment of dividends to participating policyowners, is held for the ultimate benefit of the shareholders. However, the charters of some stock companies and a few states limit the extent to which stockholders of the company may benefit from profit on the participating business.

Mutual Life Insurance Companies

Policyowner Orientation

Like a new stock company, a mutual insurer needs funds to operate. However, it issues no stock and has no stockholders. Instead, the initial funds come from the first premiums paid by the original policyowners or monies the insurer borrows. However, it is difficult to attract a sufficiently large number of individuals who are willing to apply for insurance and pay the first premium to a company that is not yet in existence and unable to issue policies until it has the specified number of applications, premiums, and the minimum initial surplus required by statute. Although mutual insurers play a major historical role in the life insurance business, because of these reasons and the lack of a profit incentive in their formation, few (if any) new mutual insurers are being formed. A new mutual insurer may emerge, however, from the conversion of an existing stock company to a mutual company (a process called mutualization).

In theory, the policyowners own and control a mutual company, but the actual ownership continues to be a subject of debate.[8] Nevertheless, it is clear that a mutual company's policyholders possess certain rights, including the rights to vote and to share in the insurer's surplus. The company is obligated to operate in their interests, and its primary purpose is to provide reliable and low-cost insurance to its policyowners.

Management Accountability

The management of a mutual insurer is virtually immune to pressure from policyowners. With no publicly traded ownership interests, the threat of outside takeover is not a factor. Although policyowners have the right to vote for the board of directors, each policyowner is entitled to only one vote, regardless of the number or size of policies he or she owns. Moreover, a collective effort by a diffuse body of policyowners is most difficult; the cost to an individual of organizing a challenge to management will most likely far exceed any possible financial return. Consequently, the mutual insurers' directors and management wield control that is virtually unhindered by the exercise of the policyowner's right to vote. Nevertheless, they must be cognizant of policyowner interests to be successful.

Mutual insurers are subject to the protections afforded by state insurance regulation. However, they are not subject to the conflicting pressures of also having to satisfy stockholder interests.

Participating Policies/Sharing in Surplus

Mutual life insurers issue participating policies. Although they are theoretically owners of a mutual insurer, participating policyowners do not have individual access to the insurer's surplus. Rather, the assets represented by the surplus are held by the company for the benefit of the policyowners as a group. Except through the insurer's possible liquidation or demutualization, an individual policyowner participates in the surplus via distribution of a policyowner dividend declared by the company's board of directors. Management has broad latitude in declaring dividends, albeit subject to regulatory constraints and mandates. Since the participating policyowner typically pays a premium higher than that for a comparable nonparticipating policy, the policyowner dividend usually reflects this excess amount plus a share in the insurer's gain in operations.

Generally, mutual companies issue only participating policies, but some mutuals also issue nonparticipating policies. It is not uncommon for a mutual company to issue some of its nonforfeiture options and dividend options on a nonparticipating basis. Nonparticipating term insurance riders are sometimes attached to basic participating policies. A few mutual companies have even offered a regular line of nonparticipating life insurance, although some states have restricted or prohibited them from doing so.

A question often raised by prospective buyers is whether they should purchase life insurance from a stock or a mutual company. The relative desirability tends to focus on the comparative financial strength and the price of protection afforded by the two types of insurers. Although there are some theoretical differences, the debate generally has more academic than practical interest. The basic factors determining an individual insurer's financial solidity and price competitiveness are the quality of its management, management's philosophy toward allocating gains in a way that reduces policyowner costs, and the insurer's regulatory supervision, rather than inherent differences between the stock and mutual forms of organization.

At the end of 1991, there were an estimated 2,105 United States legal reserve life insurance companies. Approximately 95 percent were stock companies; the remaining 115 companies were mutuals. Mutual life insurers, which are usually older and larger, possessed nearly 44 percent of the assets and wrote nearly 40 percent of the life insurance in force.[9]

Conversion: Mutualization/Demutualization

Mutualization of Stock Companies

In times past, some stock insurance companies have converted to the mutual form of organization. The primary reasons for conversion have been management's desire to gain freedom from stockholder demands or to avoid being taken over by another company through a change in stock ownership. (Since a mutual has no stock, a potential purchaser has no stock to buy.) In essence, mutualization involves retiring the insurer's outstanding capital stock and transferring control of the insurer to the policyowners.

The laws in several states outline the procedure for mutualization. Generally, after the mutualization plan is developed by management and ratified by the board of directors, it must be approved by the insurance commissioner of the insurer's state of domicile, by the stockholders, and by the policyowners in accordance with the provisions of state law. The plan must include the price of the shares and the terms under which they will be purchased. (The price must be sufficiently high to induce the stockholders to sell but not so high that the insurer will lack adequate surplus to continue operations soundly.) The plan typically establishes a trust to receive the shares from the stockholders. Since the stockholders representing a majority of the stock must approve the plan initially, the bulk of the stock is usually turned over to the mutualization trustee promptly after the adoption of the plan. This places control of the insurer in the hands of the trustee until the last shares are received, at which time the stock may be cancelled and the insurer is fully mutualized.

Although in theory the process of mutualization is quite simple, in practice some stockholders may refuse to surrender their shares, perhaps because they feel that the price is too low. However, unless they are successful in court, the stockholders ultimately have little alternative but to turn in their stock since no other market for their shares usually exists after adoption of the mutualization plan. Nevertheless, the complete process may take a long time, and mutualization has not proven to be very popular in recent years.[10]

Demutualization of Mutual Companies

An estimated 105 mutual life insurance companies converted to the stock form of organization between 1930 and 1969.[11] Sixteen mutual life insurers did so over the 25-year period from mid-1966 to mid-1991.[12] Nevertheless, prior to the 1980s, demutualization generated relatively little regulatory concern, as evidenced by the lack of laws or regulations in many states governing the process. In recent years, however, an insurer's organizational form has been perceived as highly important in the increasingly competitive marketplace because of its impact on the insurer's ability to raise capital and adapt to changing marketplace conditions. Consequently, a growing number of mutual insurers have either undertaken or are considering demutualization.[13]

Reasons for Demutualization

The reasons underlying demutualization stem primarily from the perceived competitive disadvantages of the mutual form of organization.

Ability to Raise Capital. First, the mutual insurer's ability to raise capital is limited essentially to retained earnings from underwriting gains and investment income and to borrowing. In contrast, stock insurers not only can draw on retained earnings but they also can raise capital by offering common, preferred, and convertible stock for sale; by financing alternatives such as convertible debentures and warrants; and by utilizing the full range of debt instruments. The ability to raise investment capital more easily puts a stock insurer in a better position to grow rapidly in insurance writings, to finance development of new insurance products, and to avoid statutory or practical limitations inherent in debt financing. Furthermore, access to outside capital may better enable an insurer to strengthen a weak financial statement. The importance of full access to capital has increased with the integration of financial services.[14]

Expansion Flexibility. Second, because of its ability to buy, sell, or exchange its own stock, a stock insurer possesses greater flexibility to expand through acquisitions or diversification. Unlike mutual insurers, stock companies can create upstream holding companies that facilitate expansion into other businesses, perhaps even non-insurance-related businesses, beyond the confines of insurance regulations. Effective diversification in the financial services, in fact, depends on use of an upstream holding company. For example, in the absence of an upstream holding company, a life insurer's acquisition of a bank would be subject to the investment restrictions placed on life insurance companies. It could also render the insurer itself a bank holding company subject to federal banking as well as state insurance regulations. (See discussion of holding companies later in this chapter.)

Noncash Employee Incentives. Third, the stock form of organization offers additional noncash incentive compensation (for example, stock options and payroll-based stock ownership plans) to attract and retain key officers, directors, and employees.

Tax Advantage. Fourth, with the Deficit Reduction Act of 1984, the tax advantages insurers used to enjoy have eroded significantly. The Act limited the deductibility of dividends mutual insurers pay to policyowners. This (and other changes) shifted more of the industry's federal tax burden to the mutual companies. Many mutuals view the federal tax law as biased in favor of stock insurers. Conversion to a stock company might result in tax savings.

However, before a mutual company opts to demutualize, it should carefully consider alternative (and perhaps better) ways to achieve its objectives prior to embarking on the difficult process of conversion. The cost and the complexity of demutualization are monumental (valuation and allocation of surplus to policyowners, along with legal, regulatory, actuarial, accounting, and tax problems). The cost of demutualization and the required distributions to policyowners could significantly deplete the insurer's surplus, thus severely impairing its ability to function. In addition, following conversion, by virtue of its being a stock company, the insurer becomes accountable to stockholders and vulnerable to hostile takeovers.[15] Moreover, once a mutual insurer converts to a stock company, it is subject to the ongoing expense and problems of complying with federal and state securities laws from which mutuals are now largely exempt.

Abuses in and Regulation of Demutualization

The history of demutualization includes several cases of abuse in the distribution of a mutual company's surplus or the transfer of ownership or control flowing from the conversion. On several occasions, managers effected a conversion for the purpose of transferring control of the company to themselves with little infusion of capital on their part. The distribution of surplus redounded not to the benefit of the policyowners who traditionally are deemed to be the mutual insurer's owners but to the existing management.

The perceived inequitable results of such conversions generated legislative responses, including several state laws prohibiting demutualization. In 1923, the National Association of Insurance Commissioners (NAIC) reflected the then prevailing sentiment by proposing a model law prohibiting a mutual insurer from converting to a stock company. Other states enacted laws that, while permitting demutualization, were designed to prevent recurrence of past abuses.

More recently, some states have repealed the total prohibition of demutualization. These and other states have enacted new laws to strengthen protections and vest substantial authority in the insurance commissioner to monitor the conversion process and safeguard the interests of the mutual policyowners.[16] State willingness to shift from the earlier prohibitory approach stems from (1) the recognition that conversion to a stock company may be essential to some mutual insurers' viability and survival in today's competitive marketplace and (2) increased confidence in the state's ability to fashion a regulatory framework that balances legitimate business objectives and policyowner interests.

Alternative Modes of Demutualization

Currently, most states regulate insurer demutualization either directly or indirectly. Generally, the law of the insurer's domicile governs.[17]

Although there are basically three alternative approaches to demutualization —some form of direct or pure conversion, merger, or bulk reinsurance[18]—the basic steps in the process are similar. A specified number of the board of directors must prepare and adopt a plan and submit it to the insurance commissioner in the insurer's state of domicile. The insurer must demonstrate that the demutualization is fair and equitable to the policyowners, that there are sound reasons for the conversion, and that the reorganization is in the interest of the company and the policyowners and not detrimental to the public. The commissioner may order an examination of the insurer and obtain an independent appraisal value of the company. After review, public hearing, and approval by the commissioner, policyowners are given notice of the conversion and an explanation of what they will receive in exchange for giving up their membership rights in the insurer. If the requisite number of policyowners vote in favor of the plan, and the insurer obtains final approval from the commissioner, the company proceeds to implement the conversion. If the company will be issuing securities to the public, it may also be required to register them with the Securities and Exchange Commission and state securities commissioner(s) prior to their sale.

Pure Conversions. The pure conversion approach involves amending the mutual insurer's articles of incorporation to reorganize the company from a mutual to a stock form of organization. A majority of states now have statutes expressly authorizing a mutual insurer to directly convert to a stock company. Virtually all of these states condition the conversion on obtaining the approval of the commissioner, whose function is to ensure that the mutual insurance company's policyowners are treated equitably. Generally, such laws preclude plans vesting control in or distribution of surplus to management and mandate that surplus be distributed to the policyowners.

Determining the portion of surplus to which an individual policyowner is entitled, however, is difficult because (1) a mutual company does not record the amount that an individual policyowner has forgone when the company retained earnings in lieu of paying policyowner dividends, and (2) portions of surplus are attributable to former, rather than current, policyowners. In varying degrees of specificity, the pure conversion laws govern the procedures to accomplish the conversion. Although the requirements differ among states, some of the laws prescribe (1) the method of valuing the distributable surplus, (2) the proportionate amount of total surplus that must be distributed to policyowners, (3) which policyowners are entitled to receive the distributed surplus,[19] (4) the determination of each policyowner's share of the surplus, (5) the form of surplus distribution (cash and/or stock),[20] and (6) the percentage of policyowners necessary to approve the conversion.

If a state neither expressly prohibits nor expressly authorizes conversion, a second possible (albeit risky) pure conversion approach is a common law conversion—that is, a mutual insurer converts to a stock company simply by amending its articles of incorporation. However, many general laws and some insurance case laws pertaining to corporate mergers and consolidations hold that a corporation cannot effect such corporate structural changes in the absence of express statutory authority. Thus the validity of common law conversions is highly suspect whether challenged by the insurance commissioner or disgruntled policyowners.

In states where a mutual company is established under a special charter or enactment, it may be possible to achieve a pure conversion through a statutory amendment of the company's charter.

Conversion by Merger or Bulk Reinsurance. States that expressly prohibit a mutual insurer's pure conversion to a stock company and states that have no pure conversion authorization statute may afford mutual companies the option of a merger or bulk reinsurance. To effect demutualization through a statutory merger, the mutual insurer organizes or purchases a stock company, the two companies merge, and the stock company is the survivor. The mutual company therefore ceases to exist. Under the bulk reinsurance approach, the mutual insurer cedes all of its insurance business and transfers all of its assets and liabilities to a stock insurer the mutual company has organized or acquired. After the transaction, the mutual insurer is dissolved.

Both a statutory merger and bulk reinsurance conversions must be approved by the insurance commissioner and in some states by the mutual policyowners. Again, management has to demonstrate that the terms of the proposed transaction are fair to the policyowners. Pursuant to either statutory prescription or commissioner discretion, the commissioner is likely to evaluate many of the same factors codified in the pure conversion statutes in determining whether the mutual policyowners are treated fairly.

Licensing/Readmission Problems

If the conversion is by a merger or bulk reinsurance arrangement, some very difficult practical readmission problems could arise if the surviving stock company is not licensed to do insurance business in the states where the mutual insurer had been licensed. Many insurance departments have taken the position that the mutual company's certificate of authority is not transferred to the surviving stock corporation. Thus many states require the surviving stock company to file for admission to do business in that state, submit all of its policy forms, pay all fees, and make all statutory deposits required of new foreign insurers. This takes time, and unless it is done in advance of the actual demutualization, the new insurer might be unable to do business in many states for some time.

Furthermore, many states impose a "seasoning" requirement on insurers. An insurer applying for admission to do business in the state must have been actively engaged in the business of insurance for a specified period (typically 3 years). If the surviving stock company is newly created and lacks previous operating experience, it may be unable to obtain a license to do business until after the seasoning period. (Some states waive the seasoning requirement in the demutualization situation.) In some states, if the surviving corporation has been in existence for less than a year, in the absence of an annual statement, the insurance department will not even review the company's application for admission.

When the conversion from a mutual to a stock company is achieved by the pure conversion procedure, these readmission problems are more likely to be avoided because the new stock company is not a separate new entity. One court has held that the mere amendment of articles of incorporation does not create a new company.[21] However, this conclusion may not be accepted by a particular state.

Other Nongovernmental Providers

Although most life insurance in the United States is written by commercial companies, there are other nongovernmental providers of life insurance, including fraternal benefit societies, assessment societies, and savings banks. Since these other providers write only a small portion of the total amount of life insurance in the United States, their treatment here will be very brief.

Fraternal Benefit Societies

Fraternal life insurance is issued by fraternal benefit societies that were formed to provide social and insurance benefits to their members. They provide life insurance on a basis similar to that offered by commercial insurers. The modern fraternal life insurance certificate or contract is akin to a commercial company policy and contains most of the provisions found therein.

Assessment Associations

Although most assessment associations today utilize the level premium and do not operate solely on an assessment basis, these providers do not establish actuarially based premiums as do commercial and fraternal life insurers and can still levy assessments when needed. On occasion problems have arisen when policyowners have been unaware of the association's right to charge such assessment.

Savings Banks

In 1907 Massachusetts enacted a law authorizing savings banks in that state to establish life insurance departments to sell over-the-counter life insurance and annuity contracts to persons residing or working in the state. The Massachusetts law sought to provide a system of low-cost insurance by eliminating the sales costs of agents' commissions and home collection of industrial insurance premiums. In 1938 and 1941 respectively, New York and Connecticut enacted similar legislation. Efforts to establish savings bank life insurance in other states have proven unsuccessful. Savings banks have the authority to sell the normal types of ordinary policies, annuities, and group insurance. The terms of the contracts are similar to those of commercial life insurers. However, the maximum amount of insurance any one applicant can obtain is limited by law in each state.[22]

GOVERNMENT-PROVIDED LIFE INSURANCE

Governmental agencies offer various forms of life insurance protection. These agencies include the Department of Veterans Affairs, the Social Security Administration, and the State of Wisconsin. Because these governmental agencies are not the main thrust of this book, the treatment of these agencies and the forms of life insurance protection they offer will be necessarily brief.

Department of Veterans Affairs

Since World War I, the United States government has made life insurance available to current and former members of the armed services. More recently, Congress created Servicemen's Group Life Insurance (SEGLI) to provide members of the uniformed services on active duty with life insurance written on a group basis through private life insurance companies. SEGLI in the maximum amount of $100,000 (periodically increased from the original $10,000 maximum) is provided automatically to essentially all members of the armed forces unless such persons affirmatively elect no insurance or insurance in reduced amounts. No evidence of insurability is required. The coverage continues during active duty through 120 days after separation from the service. The individual is free to name any beneficiary he or she chooses.

Under the Veterans Insurance Act of 1974, Congress also created a program of postseparation insurance that will automatically convert SEGLI to a 5-year nonrenewable term policy known as Veterans Group Life Insurance (VGLI). At the end of the term period, the insured may convert VGLI to an individual commercial life insurance policy at standard rates with any of the participating insurers.

Social Security Administration

Governments, both state and federal, play an important role in providing economic security to individuals and families. Although this book focuses primarily on private life insurance, because social security is so pervasive that it affects the design and sale of life insurance products, a short discussion of the program is appropriate.

The Social Security Administration, an agency of the Department of Health and Human Services, administers the Social Security OASDI (Old Age, Survivors, and Disability Insurance) program. The availability of coverage under the OASDI program is tied to gainful employment. For the worker and members of his or her family to be entitled to benefits, the worker must have achieved insured status. There are three categories of insured status: (1) fully insured, (2) currently insured, and (3) disability insured. Which benefits are available depend on the individual worker's insured status. OASDI provides retirement, disability, and spouse's and child's benefits to retired and disabled workers and their families and widow(er)'s, mother's/father's, parent's, child's, and lump-sum death benefits to survivors of a deceased worker if he or she dies while insured under the program. After a worker's death, a modest separate $255 lump-sum burial allowance is paid to the surviving spouse or other designated person.[23]

State of Wisconsin

Wisconsin is the only state in which government is authorized to sell life insurance. In 1911 the Wisconsin legislature created the State Life Insurance Fund. The Fund may issue life insurance policies in amounts up to $10,000 on the lives of persons who are within the state at the time the insurance is issued. The policies written are the standard forms issued by commercial companies on a participating basis.

INTERNAL ORGANIZATION OF LIFE INSURANCE COMPANIES

Effective organization is fundamental to an insurer's ability to develop and manage a life insurance operation that serves the needs of its insurance-consuming public on a sound and profitable basis.[24] Successful organization includes these four elements:

- clear allocation of responsibility
- clear delegation of the authority to carry out the responsibilities allocated
- accountability for the good or poor performance of responsibilities
- coordination of activities to achieve company goals

However, there is no one best organizational structure suitable for all life insurers all the time. Companies differ substantially in size, objectives, range of products, geographical areas of operation, and so forth. Furthermore, the exact form of any organizational pattern depends on the circumstances of the company's formation and evolution and on the personalities involved. Since most life insurance in force today is written by commercial life insurance companies, the following material on the internal organization of life companies is focused primarily on commercial insurers.

Organizational Structure

Levels of Authority

Subject to constitutional, statutory, and regulatory constraints, and to the company charter or bylaw authorizations and limitations, the stockholders in a stock company and the policyowners in a mutual company are a commercial life insurance company's ultimate source of authority. However, they usually do not direct the actual operations of their company but elect a board of directors to whom they give the authority for the company's conduct.

Authority can be defined as the right to control, command, and decide or otherwise settle issues. Most organizations have various levels of authority. At each level those possessing authority delegate specific responsibilities to their subordinates to make decisions and take certain actions. There are typically four levels of authority: the board of directors, executive officers, managers, and supervisors.

Board of Directors. The stockholders, or the policyowners if the insurer is a mutual company, elect and when necessary may replace the insurer's board of directors. The minimum number of directors is usually specified in the company's charter and sometimes by state law. The board and its various committees are the highest level of authority in the company.

Board members represent the interests of those who elected them. The board establishes corporate policy, appoints the chief executive officer and other executives of the company, delegates to them whatever authority and responsibilities it deems appropriate, holds them accountable for the performance of their responsibilities, evaluates company results and finances, fosters long-range planning, authorizes major transactions such as acquisitions or mergers, and declares dividends. The board meets periodically, approves or disapproves recommendations of its committees and company officials, and considers important matters concerning the conduct of the business.

To facilitate the exercise of its responsibilities and maintain closer and more frequent contact with key company operations, the board is usually divided into a number of standing committees. Committees handle whatever actions need to be taken between board meetings. The committees report to the board.

To enable the committees to perform their functions efficiently, one or more executive officers are often assigned to each committee. These officers are responsible for bringing background information, proposed recommendations, and the matters requiring committee action to each committee's attention. Not uncommonly, an executive officer is empowered to act for a committee between meetings on any matters within the committee's authority and to report his or her action at the next committee meeting.

The number of board committees and the scope of their duties vary from company to company. However, they commonly include the executive committee (sometimes called the insurance committee), the investment committee (sometimes referred to as the finance committee), the audit committee, the tax committee, and sometimes a claims committee.

The *executive committee* focuses on matters bearing on the insurer's general business. It deals with overall company policy, lines of business sold, territories in which the company operates, policies affecting company employees, other matters not assigned to a different committee of the board, and long-range planning.

The *investment committee* establishes the insured's investment policy, including the types of investments in which company funds are to be placed and the allocation of assets among the different types of investments (bonds, stocks, mortgages, and real estate). Although day-to-day investment activities are conducted by the insurer's investment department, the committee oversees all investment practices; the investment department proposes major investment transactions, which are then subject to committee approval or disapproval. The committee may also select the banks into which company funds are to be deposited and determine the amount of funds to be maintained in each account.

The *audit committee* oversees the insurer's accounting operations, supervises internal and external audits, and reviews the company's periodic financial statements. One of its primary functions is to ensure the integrity of the financial information used by the board in its decision-making activities and made available to outsiders, including federal and state regulators. The committee is also responsible for retaining a professional, independent outside auditing firm to perform periodic audits. (Internal audits may be conducted by the company's own accounting personnel.) Since this committee serves as the guardian of the integrity of the insurer's financial reports, company officers do not normally serve as members. Some states bar them from doing so.

The *tax committee* analyzes and evaluates the tax implications of various company policies, programs, and practices. It also keeps abreast of any relevant tax legislation.

The *claims committee* exercises general control over the payment of claims. This includes determining policy as to questionable or contestable claims.

Although it usually places considerable reliance on management recommendations, the ultimate responsibility for the insurer's legal and ethical conduct rests with the board. Simply rubber stamping management recommendations and actions may therefore result in personal liability for board members. With several insolvencies and the questionable management conduct of several property, casualty, and life insurance companies over the past decade, the responsible exercise of the board's authority has become a sensitive and important issue that board members cannot afford to ignore.

Executive Officers. The second level of authority within a life insurance company is its executive officers. Although the board has the highest level of authority, it vests broad administrative authority over the company in a chief executive officer (CEO), typically the president or chairman of the board. The CEO is primarily responsible for the selection, termination, and supervision of his or her subordinate officers and department heads.

The executive officers, usually vice presidents or senior vice presidents, report to the CEO and are responsible for carrying out company policies and general company management. In addition to serving on board committees and being part of the executive management team, executive officers usually have authority over a major division of company operations.

Managers. The third level of authority in a typical life insurance company is the managerial level. Company managers at this level focus on a particular phase of the company's activities, rather than on the operations of the insurer as a whole or a broad division of the company. These officers are responsible for translating company policy into plans for day-to-day operations and making decisions on matters within the scope of authority delegated to them.

Supervisors. Supervisors occupy the fourth level of authority. They manage the daily activities of subdivisions in various departments, directly supervise nonmanagement employees, and implement their manager's plans.

Span of Control

The people a manager directly supervises represent the manager's span of control.[25] The number of subordinates one manager can effectively supervise depends on a variety of factors. The simpler and more repetitive the tasks, the more people a manager can supervise easily. The greater the skills and competence of the manager and his or her subordinates, the broader the span of control the manager can handle. The higher the rate of turnover among subordinates (and therefore the need for more training) and the more widely dispersed subordinates are, the narrower the span of the manager's control. Whether a manager's span of control is broad or narrow, however, every employee should know for whom he or she works and to whom he or she is accountable.

A company utilizing broad spans of control requires fewer levels of management. Communication tends to be better. Decisions can be made more quickly because several levels of management are not involved. However, a flat (fewer levels of management) structure may result in managers or supervisors being responsible for more activities or people than they can effectively manage. By contrast, if a company adopts a narrow span-of-control philosophy, each supervisor or manager oversees only a few subordinates. Although this can enhance supervision, it may also boost company expenses because of additional management layers and increase communication problems from the top of the company down to the lower levels and from the lower levels up to the top. Historically, insurance companies have leaned toward several, rather than few, levels of management and narrow, rather than broad, spans-of-control. Recently, however, many insurers have begun to organize (or reorganize) to reduce the number of levels between the company president and entry-level positions.

Bases of Organization

A life insurance company's successful operation depends on the performance of several basic functions. Products must be developed and made ready for sale. A system to sell products must be created and implemented. Customers must be serviced. Claims must be paid. Funds received must be invested in a way that ensures the availability of sufficient funds to meet the insurer's obligations when they become due. An insurer may be organized in a variety of ways to perform these functions.

Traditionally, life insurers have been organized on a functional, product, or geographical basis, or a combination of these organizational formats.

Function

The term *function* refers to a distinct type of work, an element or step in a process, or some aspect of operations or management requiring special technical knowledge. *Organization by function* involves allocating closely coordinated activities to a single unit or department. The major functional areas of a life insurance company are marketing, actuarial, underwriting, customer service, claim administration, accounting, investments, legal, human resources, and information systems. A company organized by function establishes a separate department to perform each of these functions.

Product

Organization by product involves allocating work according to the products sold. Each line is administered by a major division of the company (for example, ordinary, group, or industrial insurance). Consequently, each division assumes responsibility for various functional activities with respect to that product, although some functions, such as investments, might continue to be handled centrally.

Geography

Under *organization by territory*, responsibilities are allocated to divisions in the company based on geographical areas. A company may divide its operations by states or regions. If the insurer does business in Canada, there may be a United States division and a Canadian division. Within each territorial division, the insurer may further divide its operations by functions and/or by products.

Profit Center

In recent years, other forms of organization have emerged. Some insurers now organize their activities around *profit centers*—segments of the company that control their own revenues and expenses and make their own decisions about operations. (Segments that are not profit centers are service centers, which provide support to the profit centers.) The profit center approach focuses on improving efficiency by controlling costs and thereby becoming more competitive and profitable. Profit centers tend to be organized by product since the insurer's product lines are the prime generators of the company's revenues. Since each profit center is responsible for its own readily measurable performance, one benefit of this approach is that decisions can be made lower in the organizational chain. Possible disadvantages of the approach are a lack of coordination between different elements of the company, duplication of efforts, and lost economies of scale.[26]

Functional Areas of a Life Insurance Company

Since life insurers have traditionally been organized on a functional basis and since certain functions need to be performed regardless of the form of organization, this section will briefly describe a functionally organized insurer. Keep in mind, however, that the following discussion is not intended to depict an actual company. It is presented to illustrate the functional form of organization. In addition, numerous interdepartmental committees can be employed to better coordinate activities as between departments.

Functional Departments

The *marketing/agency department* is responsible for the sale of new business, the conservation of existing business, and providing field services to policyowners. The department supervises the activities of the insurer's field force; recruits, selects, and trains agents; and conducts market analysis, advertising, and sales promotions. It also works with the actuarial and legal departments to develop new products, policy forms, and agent-company contracts.

The primary responsibility of the *actuarial department* is to see that the company's insurance operations are conducted on a sound financial basis. This includes determining appropriate premium rates and establishing adequate policy reserves. The department generally handles the insurer's mathematical operations, develops new policies and forms (including nonforfeiture values), analyzes earnings, provides statistical data from which the annual dividend scale is established, and conducts mortality, lapse, and other studies. The chief actuary and other company officers are jointly responsible for the accuracy of the annual financial statements required by the various insurance departments, especially the portions relating to policy liabilities and other items determined by actuarial calculation. Actuaries also typically participate in corporate strategic planning.

The *underwriting department* establishes standards for the acceptance or rejection of applicants for insurance and for applying these standards to ensure that the actual mortality the company experiences does not exceed that assumed in calculating the premium rates. Underwriting relies on medical underwriting judgment as to good health and lay underwriting judgment as to other factors relevant to an applicant's insurability. The home office underwriting department collaborates with medical and actuarial personnel in establishing general underwriting standards, is responsible for communicating matters concerning the selection of risks to the field force, and may be responsible for negotiating and managing reinsurance agreements (agreements through which the company transfers some or all of an insurance risk or risks to another insurer).

The *customer* or *policyowner services department* furnishes home office services to the insurer's field force and to customers, including policyowners, beneficiaries, and employees. Customer service personnel fulfill requests for information, assist in interpreting policy language, answer questions about policy coverage, and make changes requested by policyowners (new addresses, beneficiary designations, or mode of premium payments, for example). The department also computes and processes policy loans, nonforfeiture options, and dividends. In some companies the department processes commission payments to the insurer's agents, sends premium notices, and collects premium payments.

The *claim administration department* processes the claims against the company. Claim examiners review the claims filed by policyowners or beneficiaries, verify their validity, and authorize payments to the proper persons. Claims denied may result in litigation.

The *accounting department* establishes, supervises, and maintains the insurer's accounting and control procedures. It maintains the company's general accounting records, controls receipts and disbursements, oversees the company's budgeting process, and administers the payroll. It performs audits both in the field and in the home office. In conjunction with the actuarial department, the department prepares the financial statements used both internally and submitted to the regulatory agencies. The comptroller is one of the officers who certify the accuracy of the annual financial statements required by state insurance departments. The accounting department is also responsible for matters concerning federal, state, and local taxes. It may, in addition, perform various expense analyses and other statistical operations not undertaken by the actuarial department.

The *investment department* implements the insurer's investment program under policies established by the board of directors and under the supervision of the investment committee. The department constantly evaluates existing and new investments, recommends whether to hold or sell, and may negotiate with brokers, investment bankers, or directly with borrowers. Authorized members of the department buy and sell stocks, bonds, mortgages, real estate, and other assets. The investment department also advises the president and the board about possible acquisitions and mergers.

The *legal department* is responsible for the insurer's legal matters, including compliance with federal and state laws and regulations. This encompasses not only traditional general corporate and insurance law but also antitrust, securities, labor, pension, and tax law. The legal department evaluates current and proposed legislation and regulations affecting the company. It advises on questionable claims, oversees litigation, performs a variety of legal activities relating to the insurer's investment transactions, works with the accounting and auditing department to determine the company's tax obligations, and participates in the development of policy forms, agents' contracts, investment transactions, and other contractual forms used by the company.

The *human resources department* handles matters concerning the insurer's employees. The department develops company policy on hiring, training, and dismissal of employees. It ascertains appropriate levels of compensation, assures compliance with federal and state employment laws, and administers employee benefit plans.

Over the last 30 years or so, the computer has become an indispensable tool in life insurance company operations. The *information systems department* develops and maintains the company's computer systems. It assists other departments in developing or buying the computer systems and software they need to furnish information, maintain records, and administer products. The department also maintains company records in computerized files, provides data for the preparation of financial statements, and conducts analyses of various systems and procedures used throughout the company.

Interdepartmental Committees

A company may appoint a number of interdepartmental committees to coordinate the activities of various departments or to conduct an activity that falls outside a particular department's domain or requires input from two or more departments. The following are examples of committees that various insurers might establish: a marketing committee to evaluate the need for product revisions or new products; a budget committee to prepare the annual budget (the ultimate budget is subject to approval by the board of directors); a corporate communications (often called public relations) committee to coordinate company activities on advertising, publicity, and public relations; a research committee; and a human resources committee to provide interdepartmental coordination with the human resources department in such areas as personnel policies and training.

AFFILIATIONS

For a variety of reasons, life insurers buy or are purchased by other companies, merge with other insurers, or enter into strategic alliances with other companies. The basic purpose of these affiliations is to strengthen company operations and activities to increase efficiency and profitability. The rapidly changing world of financial services has spurred insurers to undergo various corporate restructurings and to undertake transactions that enhance their competitive position by expanding into new product or geographical areas and that help them survive the challenges of new competitors entering into traditional insurance areas.

Acquisitions: Friendly and Hostile Takeovers

An acquisition occurs when a company, an individual, a group of individuals, or some other group buys a controlling interest in a company. Mutual insurers can acquire but cannot be acquired since there is no stock to be purchased. Stock insurers can both acquire and be acquired.

The reasons for an acquisition vary greatly. Sometimes the stock acquired is solely for investment purposes, and the acquired company's management continues to direct the company operations. In other situations, the benefits of merging with another company may be the motivation for the acquisition. In these cases, the new controlling stockholder(s) may either retain the existing management or install new management.

The acquisition of a company can be friendly or hostile. In a friendly takeover the acquiring company offers to purchase a company. The company to be purchased agrees to the acquisition and the price for the stock. The board of directors of the company to be acquired approves the offer and publicly recommends to its stockholders that the offer be accepted. The acquisition requires the approval of both the stockholders and the insurance commissioner in each state in which any insurers involved in the acquisition are domiciled. The Securities and Exchange Commission (SEC) and the antitrust authorities may also be involved.

A hostile takeover occurs when the acquirer proceeds with a takeover even though the board of directors of the company to be acquired (the target company) refuses the acquisition offer. To obtain a controlling interest the acquiring company makes a tender offer—a public offer to purchase the target company's securities directly from the shareholders at a specified price—thereby circumventing the board of directors. As further discussed below, under the federal securities laws, the company making the tender offer files information with the SEC about the reasons for the acquisition, any plans to liquidate the target company or sell a major portion of its assets, and the source of funds for the acquisition. The acquirer then publicly announces the offer to purchase the target's stock at a specified price, usually significantly in excess of the market value of the stock. Not uncommonly, the purchase is conditioned on the acquirer's ability to obtain a certain percentage of the target company's shares within a specified period of time (to assure the acquirer of at least practical controlling interest if and when the tender offer is successful). If the takeover succeeds, the acquiring company obtains control, can elect a new board of directors, and can decide on management policy.[27]

In the 1980s the leveraged buyout (LBO) came into vogue as a means of acquiring a company. In an LBO the acquiring company finances the acquisition primarily through borrowing. After a successful takeover, the acquirer repays the debt from money generated by the acquired company's operations or through the sale of some of the acquired company's assets.

Mergers

A merger occurs when two or more companies are legally joined together to become one. One company may be absorbed by another—the surviving—company, or two or more existing companies may be merged into an entirely new company.

The advantages of a merger depend on the circumstances. An insurer in weakened financial condition, for example, may seek a stronger partner to help the insurer overcome its financial difficulties or gain access to additional surplus to fund expansion and growth. An insurer that has decided to offer new products or services may determine that it would be more feasible to merge with an existing company that already offers those products and/or services than to expend the time and money to develop them itself. An insurer that wants to expand into new geographical areas may find that joining an insurer already licensed and marketing in those areas is a more rapid and economical mode of expansion. Since unit costs decrease as the size of operations increases, a merger is also attractive to a company that wants to reduce the price of its products and increase profits through economies of scale. Moreover, large and growing companies often attract both security-minded customers and high-quality management and other personnel.

Mergers may also have significant drawbacks. A merger often incurs enormous legal and accounting costs. It can cause great anxiety among managers and employees, resulting in either the loss of key people or the cost in time and money to retain them. When merging companies are in different locations, there can be substantial costs to move personnel, as well as the inevitable costs of employee turnover. Many business relationships will need to be reviewed and perhaps reestablished, including contracts with agents. Difficulties will undoubtedly arise in efforts to blend different managements, corporate philosophies, and company systems. Finally, there is the danger that the perceived benefits of the merger may not be realized, at least to the extent the companies had contemplated, and that this will create new difficulties.

A merger between two or more insurance companies involves several steps. First, potential merger partners must be found and evaluated; usually, an independent actuarial or investment banking firm examines each company's financial condition. Then the boards of directors must approve the plan of merger, typically by a two-thirds majority vote of the stockholders or, if a mutual company, by two-thirds of the policyowners. Stockholders who disapprove must be paid a fair market value for the forced surrender of their stock if the merger actually occurs. The state insurance regulatory authorities in the insurer(s)' domiciliary state(s) must also approve the merger. The final merger document must be filed in the new or surviving company's state of domicile and a new or amended certificate of incorporation must be obtained. The merging companies' assets and liabilities must be transferred to the new or surviving company. And, finally, the new or surviving company must obtain licenses in all states where it does business.

Holding Companies

When a company acquires one or more companies (purchases a sufficient amount of stock to possess controlling interest), the acquired companies become subsidiaries of the acquirer, the parent company. The group of companies has formed a holding company system, and the parent company is the holding company.

A holding company is any person or organization (firm) that directly or indirectly controls an authorized insurer. (Control commonly means the power to vote 10 percent or more of the insurer's voting securities.) An insurance holding company system consists of two or more affiliated persons or organizations (firms), one of which is an insurer (that is, a holding company system is an insurer, its parent, subsidiaries and/or other affiliated organizations).

Trend Toward Holding Companies

Traditionally, insurers operated as independent, free-standing entities or as a part of insurance company groups. Originally, the holding company concept was utilized to acquire a group of companies in related lines. By the late 1960s, however, this changed in the insurance industry as a result of two trends.

First, to improve earnings and long-term growth, many insurers sought to diversify by venturing into new lines of insurance (for example, a life company acquiring a property and liability insurer) or into noninsurance enterprises, commonly in the financial services area (acquiring securities/broker-dealer organizations, mutual fund management companies, consumer finance companies and other related institutions). Several life insurers found that forming a holding company system gave them greater ability to diversify their services and products, imposed fewer restrictions on their investments, and enhanced their capital-raising flexibility.

Second, several life insurers were taken over by other insurers or noninsurance company acquirers and thus became part of a conglomerate (a group of unrelated businesses under the control of a holding company). Sometimes being part of the conglomerate contributed to the insurer's strength. On occasion, however, the acquirer was less interested in the insurer's well-being than in gaining access to the insurer's accumulation of liquid assets and substantial cash flows.

Nature of Holding Companies

A holding company may be an insurer or a general business corporation. As noted before, a mutual insurer, by its very nature, is not subject to acquisition by another company purchasing shares of the insurer's stock since there are no shares. However, a mutual insurer (or a stock insurer if it so chooses) can become involved in a *downstream holding company* system by creating or acquiring subsidiaries, perhaps including a downstream holding company, which, in turn, can acquire other enterprises as subsidiaries. The mutual insurer sits atop the holding company structure. A downstream holding company has fewer insurance regulatory concerns since the parent insurer, which continues to control its own destiny as well as that of any subsidiaries acquired downstream, remains directly subject to insurance regulatory control.

By contrast, there are *upstream holding company* systems in which the holding company acquires the insurer's stock. Stock insurers tend to become involved in upstream holding company systems in one of two ways. First, a stock insurer can organize an upstream noninsurance holding company that sits atop the intercorporate structure. The insurer's board of directors and management, or appropriate portion thereof, becomes the board and management of the holding company; the insurer becomes its subsidiary. As a noninsurance company, generally speaking, the new parent is outside the scope of insurance regulation. It can engage in a host of activities through its different subsidiaries, including insurance business, other financially related businesses, and totally unrelated enterprises. Second, as noted earlier, a stock insurer can become involved, either voluntarily or involuntarily, in an upstream holding company system by being acquired by an outside company that becomes the insurer's upstream holding company.

Alliances

Although acquisitions, mergers, and holding companies are common, insurers have also formed strategic alliances—which involve less drastic structural changes—to accomplish some of the same objectives. A strategic alliance is an ongoing relationship in which two or more independent organizations share the risks and rewards. Through this alliance, a life insurer gains access to the resources of other firms but still retains its independence.

Insurers have a long tradition of entering into some form of strategic alliance with other business firms—foreign and domestic insurers, securities firms, third-party administrators, commercial banks, and so forth. Through cooperation with other firms, an insurer can improve its ability to handle the increased competition from traditional competitors, the integration of financial services, and the globalization of the financial service marketplace.

Regulation

As mentioned earlier, firms can diversify or grow through internal development, by acquisition, or by merger. Often, acquisitions or mergers prove to be the more attractive routes. Although they have corporate advantages, however, since acquisitions and mergers may involve changing management, company structure, and perhaps even the competitive nature of the marketplace, they can give rise to public policy issues that come to the attention of the state insurance regulators, federal antitrust enforcement authorities, and the SEC.

State Insurance Regulation

Regulatory Concerns. Although acquisitions and mergers have long been subject to state insurance department regulatory approval, the rash of insurance company takeovers—many of them hostile—in the late 1960s heightened regulatory concerns. These takeovers usually involved tender offers, which enabled the acquiring company to avoid dealing directly with the target company's resistant management. Unlike affiliations involving willing partners, such as two companies agreeing to merge, tender offers were essentially unregulated.

Regulators became concerned when affiliations of insurers with noninsurance companies pursuing different interests began to occur, which gave control of the insurers to noninsurance parents outside of insurance regulatory control. Their concern increased when noninsurance holding companies that lacked insurance experience, focus, and orientation toward safeguarding policyowner interests started to acquire and control stock insurers. During the ensuing years, regulators' concern proved to be justified. Actual and potential abuses in these affiliations included rapacious acquirers looting insurers' assets, raiding insurer surplus to finance either the holding company itself or the operations of other holding company subsidiaries, subtle threats to insurer solvency, and circumvention of various state requirements enacted to protect the insurance-buying public.

At the same time, however, regulators acknowledged that the interests of the public, policyowners, and shareholders might not be compromised by—perhaps even be benefited by—permitting insurers (1) to engage in activities that would enable them to better use their management skills and facilities, (2) to diversify into new lines of business, (3) to have free access to capital markets to fund diversification programs, (4) to implement sound tax planning, and (5) to serve the public's changing needs by being able to compete with a comprehensive range of financial services. Nevertheless, regulators recognized that public, policyowner, and shareholder interests could be adversely affected if (1) persons seeking control of an insurer utilized that control contrary to policyowner and public interests, (2) the acquisition of an insurer substantially lessened competition, (3) an insurer in a holding company system entered into transactions or relationships with affiliated companies on unreasonable or unfair terms to the insurer, or (4) an insurer paid dividends to the noninsurance parent or other shareholders that jeopardized the insurer's financial condition.[28]

Holding Company Act. As regulatory concerns mounted, both the regulators and the insurance industry moved to develop a legislative response. In 1969, following legislative enactments in New York and Connecticut, the NAIC adopted a model Insurance Holding Company Systems Regulatory Act (hereafter referred to as the Holding Company Act) and a model regulation setting forth rules and procedural requirements to assist in carrying out the provisions of the act.[29] All states regulate the acquisition of insurance companies in some way, whether as a part of the act or separately from it. Furthermore, all states have enacted some type of holding company law, most of which are patterned after the NAIC model act (although not necessarily adopting all of the amendments made to it throughout the 1980s).

To exercise control over holding company situations, the model act (1) facilitates insurer diversification, (2) requires disclosure of relevant information relating to changes in the insurer's control and commissioner approval of such changes, (3) requires insurer disclosure of material transactions and relationships between the insurer and its affiliates, including certain dividends distributed by the insurer, and (4) establishes standards governing material transactions between the insurer and its affiliates. To avoid unnecessary multiple and conflicting regulation of insurers, the model act applies only to domestic insurers, except where otherwise specifically stated.

Insurer diversification. From the insurance industry's perspective, the traditional investment law limitations precluded or severely constrained insurer's ability to diversify and grow. This contributed to the pressure for insurers to organize holding company systems with the insurer as a subsidiary of a noninsurer parent that had the flexibility to acquire or establish subsidiaries in diversified fields. In response, the Holding Company Act relaxed some of the investment restraints but did so within a somewhat controlled environment.

Approval of acquisitions and mergers. Under the Holding Company Act, any person or organization (firm) acquiring securities that would result in obtaining direct or indirect control of a domestic insurer or entering into an agreement to merge with a domestic insurer must file specific information with the commissioner and obtain his or her approval before the acquisition or merger can be effected.[30] The information, as required by supplementary regulation, must include the method of acquisition; the identity and background of the applicant and individuals associated with the applicant; the nature, source, and amount of funding used for the acquisition or merger; future plans for the insurer; and financial statements. The information that must be provided to the commissioner not only alerts the target insurer to the potential takeover but also gives the insurer's management a better opportunity to make its case to the shareholders about whether or not to accept the offer.

Registration of insurers. Every insurer that is a member of an insurance holding company system and licensed to do business in the state (except a foreign insurer already subject to substantially the same disclosure requirements and standards in its domiciliary state) must register with the commissioner. Each registered insurer must keep the required information current.

Standards governing transactions between the insurer and its affiliates. Transactions within a holding company system are subject to several standards, including the fairness and reasonableness of terms, charges and fees for service. Expenses must be allocated to the insurer according to customary insurance accounting practice, and accurate and clear records must be maintained as to the nature, details, and reasonableness of transactions between affiliates. The insurer's surplus for policyowners, following dividends or distributions to affiliates, must be reasonable in relation to the insurer's liabilities and financial needs.

Insurer management. As early as 1972, some commissioners urged the adoption of management standards giving the insurer's officers control over all facets of the insurance operation, rather than permitting a general corporation's board of directors to usurp this function. The 1985 amendments to the act include provisions to this effect, stating that the insurer's officers and directors continue to be responsible for the insurer's management and must manage the insurer in a manner that ensures the insurer's separate operating identity.

Enforcement. In addition to various ways to monitor compliance with provisions of the holding company law — reviewing the various information filings, examining insurers and sometimes insurers' affiliates, and compelling the submission of books, records and other information[31] — the commissioner has a host of sanctions with which to enforce the act, including monetary penalties and recoveries, cease-and-desist orders, and license revocation. Furthermore, if it appears that any insurer or any director, officer, employee, or agent willfully violated the act, the commissioner may cause criminal proceedings to be instituted. The insurer is subject to dollar penalties; individuals are subject to fines, and if fraud is involved, imprisonment.

If violations of the act threaten a domestic insurer's solvency or make further transaction of business hazardous to policyowners, the commissioner may proceed under the state's rehabilitation and liquidation law.[32] (See chapters 26 and 27.) If the commissioner believes a violation makes the continued operation of an out-of-state insurer contrary to policyowner interest, after a hearing, he or she may suspend or revoke the insurer's license to do business.

In the 1980s, numerous insurers became insolvent or nearly so. Although a majority of insolvencies involved property and liability insurers, the life insurance industry was not immune. The record of insolvent insurance companies is replete with self-dealing abuses in relationships between insurers, their parent holding companies, and their affiliates, involving intercompany loans, dividends, management contracts, and investments. Regulators and liquidators were concerned that they did not have adequate access to the interrelated corporate networks' books and records affecting insurer operations and were thereby deterred from effective regulatory action. A series of amendments to the Holding Company Act in the 1980s reflect regulatory responses to such abuses.

Federal Antitrust Treatment of Acquisitions and Mergers

In the United States the first wave of corporate mergers occurred around the turn of the century. The only federal antitrust statute at the time was the Sherman Act. However, the need to prove either a conspiracy in restraint of trade or some type of monopolization activity rendered the act a somewhat less-than-effective deterrent to anticompetitive mergers. Consequently, Congress enacted Section 7 of the Clayton Act, which was ultimately amended to prohibit a corporation from directly or indirectly acquiring the stock or assets of another corporation if, in any line of commerce in any section of the country, it substantially lessened competition or tended to create a monopoly.[33] Unlike the Sherman Act, which requires finding actual anticompetitive effects, the test under Section 7 is probable effect in order to combat incipient monopolistic tendencies.

Prior to the 1960s, the Department of Justice and the Federal Trade Commission (FTC) showed little interest in challenging insurance company acquisitions and mergers, perhaps because there were few of them or that it was difficult to overcome a McCarran Act defense (see chapters 26 and 27). In the early 1960s, however, a few lower court decisions sanctioned the application of federal antitrust law to insurance acquisitions. Although the Supreme Court has not definitively determined whether the McCarran Act bars federal antitrust jurisdiction in many situations and even though good legal arguments support such a bar, as a practical matter, the potential for applying the federal antitrust law to insurance company acquisitions and mergers has become a fact of life.

To the extent that federal antitrust jurisdiction is not barred by the McCarran Act, the issue becomes whether a state insurance regulator applying holding company law is preempted by federal antitrust law. Since the Sherman and Clayton Acts were enacted long before the antitrust laws were deemed applicable to insurance, it appears unlikely that the Supreme Court would find Congressional intent to preempt. As to the conflict test under the preemption doctrine, antitrust law seeks to prohibit anticompetitive acquisitions and mergers. If the insurance commissioner disapproves the transaction, there will be no conflict with antitrust law. However, if the commissioner approves what antitrust law prohibits and if the McCarran Act defense to antitrust actions is inapplicable, preemption of the holding company law is probable. In short, unless Congress acts in some way to change the existing balance, dual assertion of federal antitrust law and state insurance acquisition and merger regulatory authority promises to continue in the years ahead.

Federal Securities Law: The Williams Act

The emergence of the tender offer technique and the frequency of its use revealed a deficiency in the disclosure of information to investors. Therefore in 1968 Congress enacted the Williams Act as an amendment to the Securities Exchange Act of 1934. (In 1970, this act was made applicable to insurance securities.) The central philosophy of the Williams Act is disclosure. Among other things, the act requires that upon the commencement of a tender offer, the offeror must file pertinent information with the SEC and provide such information to the target company's shareholders and management. All shares tendered must be purchased at the same price. The offer commences at the time of the first public announcement, and it must remain open for at least 20 days.

Congress believes that the Williams Act strikes a fair balance between the party making the takeover bid and the management of the target company by enabling both to present their cases to the shareholders. More important, compelling timely, full, and fair disclosure puts the shareholders in a position to make informed decisions.

In the absence of McCarran Act protection, insurance commissioner authority to approve or disapprove an acquisition pursuant to a tender offer is questionable under the preemption doctrine. Even though the commissioner reviews a tender offer from the perspective of protecting the policyowners, a disapproval of a tender offer precludes the offer itself. This directly affects those shareholders who want to accept the offer. Thus insurance commissioner disapproval would appear to constitutionally prohibit what Congress authorizes and fosters — the shareholders' freedom to make informed decisions about accepting or rejecting a tender offer for their shares.[34]

Consequently, the states' ability to protect policyowners from adverse acquisitions by tender offers most likely depends on the scope of the McCarran Act in such situations. In *SEC v. National Securities, Inc.,*[35] the Supreme Court found that an insurance commissioner's approval of an acquisition under an insurance holding company law's standard of the transaction's fairness to the *shareholders* was the regulation of securities, not the regulation of the "business of insurance." Hence the application of the Securities Exchange Act proxy rules were not barred by the McCarran Act. This decision has been cited in the proposition that acquisitions and mergers are not part of the business of insurance as that term is used in the McCarran Act.

However, in most acquisition and merger situations, the application of the holding company law focuses on standards to ensure the protection of policyowners and the competitiveness of the insurance marketplace. Although the *National Securities* decision suggests that this application constitutes regulating the business of insurance, the more recent judicial narrowing of this language leaves the issue in some doubt. In the meantime, states continue to regulate acquisitions and mergers under their holding company laws.

NOTES

1. The description of these major categories of insurance providers in this chapter does not and cannot encompass all possible variations that now exist or may arise in the future.
2. Owners of common stock are entitled to one vote per share. In addition, there may be a class of stockholders known as preferred stockholders who normally possess no right to vote for the board of directors but who must be paid their dividends before the common stockholders receive dividends.
3. As is typical with noninsurance corporations, a moderate-to-large stock insurance company, with its numerous and widely scattered stockholders, is likely to be controlled by its management group through management's ability to obtain proxies.
4. A takeover attempt affords stockholders an opportunity to sell shares at a more favorable price than they would otherwise obtain and/or to wait out the takeover attempt and the possible institution of new management.
5. In some companies, limited policyowner control is permitted by granting participating policyowners the right to elect some, albeit a minority, of the board of directors. Such an insurer blends both stock and mutual attributes and sometimes has been termed a "mixed" company.

6. Unfortunately, on occasion, stock life insurance companies have been used in less laudable ways for personal aggrandizement with little concern for the insurance-consuming public the companies profess to serve. Deterring, screening out, and removing such insurers from the marketplace are ongoing functions of insurance regulation.

7. It is sometimes difficult to ascertain what constitutes a participating policy. Some insurers pay dividends on nonparticipating policies. Others have reduced the participating policy gross premium to virtually the competitive level of nonparticipating gross premiums, resulting in very small projected policyowner dividends.

8. In purchasing a policy, the policyowner does not acquire an ownership interest that is freely transferable on the open market. Furthermore, whatever status a policyowner has, whether as an owner or member of the company, such status continues only so long as his or her policies are in force. It has been said that technically the assets and income of a mutual insurance company are owned by the company and that policyowners are contractual creditors, rather than owners.

9. *1992 Life Insurance Fact Book,* American Council of Life Insurance, pp. 107–108.

10. During the 25-year period from mid-1966 to mid-1991, only two stock life insurers converted to the mutual form of organization. *Life Insurance Fact Book,* p. 108.

11. J. Binning, "Conversion of Mutual Insurance Company," 6 Forum 127 (1971), as cited in John C. Gurley and James R. Dwyer, *An Analysis of the Insurance Regulatory Aspects of Demutualization,* (Chicago: Lord, Bissell and Brook, 1984), p. 1.

12. *1992 Life Insurance Fact Book,* p. 108.

13. A 1984 survey indicated that 80 percent of mutual life insurers with assets exceeding $2 billion, as well as 43 percent of other mutual life insurers participating in the survey, were considering demutualization. Approximately 22 percent of property and liability insurers surveyed were also considering it. Ernst and Whinney, *Demutualization: A Survey of Mutual Insurers,* 1984, pp. 2–3, as cited in Gurley and Dwyer, *An Analysis of the Insurance Regulatory Aspects of Demutualization,* p. 1.

14. As financial integration continues, the demand for capital to fund more sophisticated computer systems, increase sales and distribution capabilities, and improve access to potential customers accelerates. In the absence of funds for such investments, mutual life insurers may suffer a decline in their competitive position.

15. Some maintain that market discipline and management accountability to stockholders foster greater efficiency in company operations and better treatment of policyowners.

16. As of 1991, 41 states had statutes permitting mutual life or property/casualty insurers (usually both) to directly convert to the stock form of organization. Two states prohibited direct conversion, and seven states had no conversion law.

17. When large numbers of policyowners reside in other states, commissioners of those states may attempt to exercise some influence over the terms of the conversion plan.

18. As an alternative to demutualization, a mutual insurer might organize or acquire a stock subsidiary or a downstream holding company that in turn owns one or more stock life insurance companies. If the operations of such subsidiary are substantial enough, it may be possible for a mutual insurance company group to raise a significant amount of capital by offering stock in the subsidiary to public investors. If this approach is viable, it avoids some of the problems associated with demutualization, including vulnerability to a hostile takeover.

19. Some authorities believe that since all of the policyowners, living and dead, contributed to the surplus, all policyowners or their heirs should share in the distribution. Others believe that only current policyowners should participate. Still others conclude that only policyowners who have had policies in force for a minimum specified period (3 or 5 years, for example) should participate in the distribution.

20. If the insurer distributes the surplus in cash, it may severely weaken its financial condition and its ability to raise additional capital. On the other hand, distributing shares of stock in the converted company might shrink the number of stockholders to an unmanageable or very costly proportion.

21. *Bergeson v. Life Insurance Corporation of America,* 265 F.2d 227, 234 (10th Cir. 1959).

22. The current maximum limit for individual life insurance coverage is $100,000 in Connecticut, $250,000 in Massachusetts, and $50,000 in New York. In all three states, the maximum limit is an aggregate limit on any one life whether there is one or more policies issued by one or more savings banks.

23. For more detailed treatment see CLU course HS 326 Planning for Retirement Needs, The American College, 1993.

24. Another important element in the organizational structure of a life insurance company is the nature of its sales operations. This is discussed in chapter 29.

25. Drawn from Kenneth Huggins and Robert Land, *Operations of Life and Health Insurance Companies,* 2nd ed. (LOMA Life Management Institute, Inc., 1992), pp. 71–74.

26. *Ibid.,* pp. 82–83. Sometimes support functions are incorporated into a profit center so that each center has its own actuarial, underwriting, and information systems. Such centers have been termed strategic business units (SBUs). An SBU operates as a separate profit center, deals with its own customers, has its own management and support functions, and plans its own activities.

27. Hostile takeovers often involve long and expensive legal and financial battles. The target company may make a counteroffer to buy enough of the stock to prevent the acquirer from obtaining controlling interest. The target company's board may attempt to convince its stockholders that the takeover would not enhance the long-term value of the stock. If the target believes that it cannot prevent a hostile takeover, it may seek a takeover by a purchaser more to its liking (often called a white knight).

28. Appendix to the NAIC Model Holding Company Act containing an alternate (optional) section setting forth findings.

29. This activity was triggered by the declaration of an extraordinarily large cash dividend by a fire and casualty insurance company shortly after it had been acquired. Regulators envisioned that this means of extracting funds from insurers, if left unchecked, would not only limit the capacity of insurers to write business, but would also jeopardize the adequacy of an insurer's surplus.

      At the same time, many insurer managements became increasingly interested in holding company structures for a variety of reasons. For example, the property and liability business had been unprofitable, giving rise to managements' desire to be able to employ the industry's capital more profitably elsewhere. From a defensive perspective, life insurance stocks were thought to be relatively cheap, thereby rendering such insurers vulnerable to takeovers. Some viewed holding company legislation as a defensive mechanism against hostile takeovers.

30. However, the model act avoids imposing commissioner approval requirements in situations involving the acquisition of a holding company that, even though controlling a domestic insurer, is not primarily engaged in the business of insurance either directly or through its subsidiaries.

31. In 1988 the NAIC annual statement was amended to require detailed information on the inflow and outflow of funds between affiliated companies in an insurance holding company system. The disclosure of this information is designed to enhance the regulators' ability to monitor self-dealing transactions.

32. If an order for rehabilitation or liquidation is entered, the receiver may recover from a parent, affiliated company or person who otherwise controlled the insurer the amount of distribution paid by the insurer or any payment of bonuses, extraordinary salary adjustments, and the like that the insurer made to a director, officer, or employee if the distribution or payment was made within a year of the petition for rehabilitation or liquidation (unless the recipient did not know that it might adversely affect the insurer's ability to meet its obligations).
33. 15 U.S.C.A. Sec. 18.
34. See *Edgar v. Mite,* 457 U.S. 624 (1982).
35. 393 U.S. 453 (1969).

29

Life Insurance Marketing

Michael B. Petersen, Walter H. Zultowski
Archer L. Edgar, and Ram S. Gopalan

The highly respected management consultant and writer Peter Drucker writes in his book *People and Performance*, "Because its purpose is to create a customer, the business enterprise has two—and only these two—basic functions: marketing and innovation. Marketing and innovation produce results; all the rest are 'costs.'"[1]

In a life insurance company all of the marketing function and much of the innovation function are the responsibilities of the marketing department. It is here that all activities designed to attract new customers and retain existing customers are performed. These activities include the eight specific functions listed below:

- research
- product development and pricing
- distribution
- communications, including advertising and sales promotion
- policyowner service
- distribution personnel training and development
- marketing management and administration
- distribution support services

STRUCTURE OF MARKETING DEPARTMENTS

The organization of these functions usually depends on the size of the company, but in just about every situation, distribution is a line function and all the other functions are staff functions. In the largest companies all functions are individual departments with all the staff functions often reporting to a marketing services officer or to individual department heads, who in turn report to a chief marketing officer who has overall responsibility for marketing.

The title "chief marketing officer" is a generic one describing the function of the job. The actual title of this individual differs from company to company and includes such titles as senior vice president/marketing, vice president/sales, or agency vice president. In a very small company all marketing functions might be under the direct control of the chief marketing officer. For companies of any size, however, a number of variations exist regarding how marketing functions are structured.

For example, many companies sell more than one product line, marketing all or several of the following: individual life and health, group life and health, individual and group pensions, property and casualty insurance, and equities. In such cases a company might have separate marketing departments for each product line, each with its own individual staff functions and chief marketing officer. On the other hand, it might choose to have just one marketing department for each product line, with each product line operating as an individual subdepartment.

These are the most common organizational arrangements in the life insurance business but other approaches do exist, including organizing the marketing department by the markets the company serves, by the geographic regions it operates in, or by the different distribution systems it employs. A combination of these organizational structures (or parts of each) results in many possible variations for each basic structure.

Regardless of how a company's marketing structure is organized, all the staff functions exist for a single purpose—to aid distribution. A life insurance company must have a continuing, incoming flow of new profitable revenue, and the most effective and efficient way of doing this is through the distribution of its products, or to use Drucker's terminology, by creating and keeping customers. Theoretically there are many ways of doing this since a life insurance company's products can be—and are in fact—sold the same ways that any product can be sold, from vending machines in airports to direct solicitations in the mail. But one way has proven to be far more successful than any other, and that is personal solicitation by a commissioned individual in a face-to-face sales situation.

Need for a Field Organization

The first companies to sell life insurance in the United States had no agents. They sold only a small number of life insurance policies each year, and it seemed as if the business would never achieve any notable success. But in 1842 the directors of the Mutual Life Insurance of New York made a decision to appoint soliciting agents to sell their product, and the business has never been the same. J. Owen Stalson in his classic, *Marketing Life Insurance,* write as follows:

> Just advertising, just sales promotion, would, I believe, have won but little for the companies; it was the agent, supported in his efforts by advertising and sales promotion, which put life insurance in the ascendancy after 1842.

Those words, written more than 50 years ago about an event that happened more than 150 years ago, are as true today as they were then. As measured by new life premiums, 99 percent of all individual life insurance is sold by an individual producer, and only one percent is sold without an individual producer's involvement. This is true despite all the money and effort that have been spent in recent years on the development and implementation of mass marketing approaches, such as marketing through credit cards, associations, lending firms, and direct mail.

Functions of the Field Organization

From the company's point of view, therefore, the need for a field organization of individual producers is obvious because of the volume and growth in business that is generated, bringing stability and economies of scale. However, the need for individual producers is not just a matter of securing the largest amount of new business. The need arises also from companies' social duty to provide adequate life insurance protection for all who need it and therefore to perform in the greatest possible degree the function for which they are organized.

The use of individual producers is often unfairly criticized because the commissions and other remuneration paid to producers are perceived as unnecessarily increasing the cost of life insurance to policyowners. Such criticisms generally assume that the cost is a direct expense to policyowners for which they receive no compensating benefit. This is an unwarranted assumption. Even if the producer did no more than call the prospect's attention to the need for insurance and explain its benefits, the producer would still be rendering a considerable service of material value. Today most producers do much more than that. They render many types of services that would not be available if there were no producers, not the least of which is advice and recommendations about what product is best. Any comparison of life insurance's relative costs that does not take into account the differences in the services rendered is misleading.

Since consumers in the general public rarely apply for life insurance, irrespective of the obvious need for it, until they are solicited, producers perform an important service merely by calling attention to the need for protection and by persuading prospects to apply for it. Good producers also analyze applicants' needs and advise them about the most suitable types of policies, the amounts of protection required, the cost and method of premium payment, the more important provisions of the contract, the optional ways benefits can be paid, and the appropriate choice of and rights regarding a beneficiary. If prospects own a number of policies, the good producer will make suggestions for coordinating these policies with governmental and employer-supplied benefits to create a total plan for financial protection against all risks.

Good agents, in their advisory role, will also explain how life insurance can be used in many, many creative ways to achieve desired aims in such diverse areas as funding education, relieving tax burdens, continuing businesses, supplementing social security, paying off obligations, dissolving partnerships equitably, enhancing credit, financing business buy-sell agreements, canceling mortgages, and funding pensions.

The work of good producers does not end with the sale and the delivery of the policy. Life insurance needs are not static but require frequent review and adjustment to meet changing conditions. This is particularly true of beneficiary provisions. Therefore the relationship established by a producer with a client is a long and mutually beneficial one.

Marketing Department's Distribution Function

The geographic area in which a life insurance company can sell varies from a single state to the entire world. Regardless of how big the area is, a company must be able to exert some control over its distribution system while at the same time providing support services to the system. In the smallest company, one operating in a limited geographic area, the chief marketing officer and a small staff in the home office marketing department can provide this control and support. However, it is much more common for a company to be active over a very large area and to have a very large marketing department that operates in a very hierarchial organizational structure.

Under the chief marketing officer there are a number of layers of subordinates—depending on the size and complexity of the company's operation—with decreasing amounts of authority. The lowest tier, usually located in a geographic region of the country, controls and supports a specified number of field outlets. If that sounds obscure, that's because it is; the different combinations of contractual and reporting relationships between the field and the home office can be counted in the hundreds.

VARIETY OF PRODUCERS

Understanding the basic differences among the variety of producers makes it simpler to describe the many different ways that field sales operations are organized:

- *Ordinary agents* are producers who devote at least 75 percent of their time selling primarily individual life products for one company that generally provides financing, training, supervision, sales support, and office facilities (also called housing). There are approximately 117,000 ordinary agents, and their share of new life premiums is 41 percent.
- *Home service agents* are producers who spend at least 75 percent of their time selling ordinary and industrial individual life for one company that provides financing, training, supervision, sales support and office facilities. These agents sell in an assigned territory called a debit and sometimes collect premiums at the insured's house or office. There are approximately 37,000 home service agents, and their share of new life premiums is 5 percent.
- *Multiple-line exclusive agents* are producers who sell individual life as well as property and casualty products for one company that provides financing, training, supervision, sales support, and office facilities. There are approximately 84,000 multiple-line exclusive agents and their share of new life premiums is 11 percent.
- *Personal-producing general agents* (PPGAs) are producers who receive both a producer's commission and the overriding commission that would usually go to a manager or general agent on personally produced business. Many are single-individual operations but some PPGAs hire and support subproducers. PPGAs typically have contracts with several companies but often have a primary company relationship. They sometimes have to maintain a minimum production level to keep these contracts. There are approximately 25,000 PPGAs and their share of new life premiums is 15 percent.
- *Brokers* are full-time insurance producers who work independently and have no primary relationship or minimum production requirements with any company. There are two important distinctions between brokers and PPGAs: Brokers do not receive overriding (general agent) commissions, and there is neither a tendency nor an intent for the company to achieve a primary-carrier status with brokers.

- *Independent agents* are primarily property and casualty producers who have no primary relationship with a company. Brokers and independent agents who sell life insurance total about 75,000, and their share of new life premiums is 27 percent, the bulk of that going to brokers.
- *Financial planners* are producers who can usually be placed in one of the categories above. Although there is no agreed-upon definition of financial planners, it is usually understood that they provide clients with a total financial plan that includes everything from investments to insurance. Financial planners were at one time described as the wave of the future, but the popularity of the idea waned in the late 1980s. They are now decreasing in number, and those remaining are more open to specializing in a particular area of planning—most often, life insurance. About 12,000 producers call themselves financial planners.
- *Stockbrokers* should be included among producers because there are about 25,000 of them who sell some annuities, single premium life, and variable products.
- *Super producers* are a special kind of producer—one with sophisticated product knowledge and technical support. They represent about 7 percent of the entire field force, and a major segment of this group are the "superagents" of the life insurance business—those with whom we associate producer groups and producer-owned reinsurance companies. Although all super producers would fall into one of the categories above, they really represent a distribution system within a distribution system simply because they are different, with their special compensation arrangements, joint case work, country-wide partnerships, equity ownerships, influence on product development, technical expertise, shared knowledge, and even proprietary software.

STRUCTURE OF FIELD ORGANIZATIONS

All companies create similar products in much the same way. It is when companies attempt to get these products into the hands of consumers that they really begin to differentiate themselves. As we have noted earlier, although direct methods of marketing products do exist, their success has been limited, and in reality, the overwhelmingly dominant distribution method is the individual producer who makes face-to-face sales. Because these producers operate in field offices (typically called agencies) in locales wherever a market for life insurance exists, this method of distribution is called the agency system.

The agency system has two main branches. In the first, a company builds its own agency distribution system by recruiting, financing, training, motivating, housing, and supervising new agents to represent it "exclusively." This branch of the agency system is identified with the descriptive adjective "building." In the second, a company taps into the existing pool of agents created by the building branch referred to above to create an "instant sales force." This branch is referred to as being "nonbuilding."

The driving force in either of these branches is an individual who represents the company on the local level, either as an employee or an independent contractor, and who is the company's local sales force manager.

In the first branch of the agency system—the building agencies—the individual in charge is typically called a manager or general agent, and it is he or she who does the recruiting of new, inexperienced recruits and develops them into a sales force. In the second branch of the agency system—the nonbuilding agencies—companies win an established producer's attention through the use of an intermediary who acts as a sort of "manufacturer's representative"—either as an employee or independent contractor—and convinces established producers to sell his or her company's products through one sort of arrangement or another.

The producers described earlier are arrayed in the field in an almost countless variety of organizational structures based on company policy in the building companies and on the arrangement between the manager, general agent, or manufacturer's representative in the nonbuilding companies. For the most part, however, just about all of the existing field structures fall into one of the following general broad categories (or one very much like them):

- *Agency building—managerial.* In this type of field organization, the manager (along with a staff of second-line managers) is a direct extension of the company, and his or her role is strictly to hire, train, and manage a sales staff. In some companies production by the manager is either discouraged or not allowed, while in other companies it is allowed but not usually expected. Expenses tend to be borne entirely by the company. This form of organization is usually for home-service agents, multiple-line exclusive agents, and to a lesser degree, ordinary agents. Managers are compensated by salary, overrides, and commissions on personal production—all of these or a combination of them, depending on what the company wants the manager to do.

- *Agency building—general agent.* The goal in this type of field organization is also to build a sales staff, but the person in charge, usually called a general agent, is an independent contractor and is compensated primarily for building the agency's staff, although personal production is common. Quite often, the general agent is given an expense allowance and is then expected to manage his or her own agency expenses. The ordinary agent is the dominant producer in this structure.

- *Regional director approach (RDA)—personal-producing general agent.* This type of structure is favored by companies that prefer to have primary-carrier relationships with their PPGAs. Inherent in the evolution of this strategy was the concept of exclusive representation. However, because of the pressure of competition for qualified PPGAs, exclusive representation or exclusive territorial rights rarely exist today. Companies that employ this approach hire only experienced producers and are not committed to new agent development in any way. They provide little, if any, continuing generic education or training, some product orientation, and no office facilities or supervision. As the name of this type of structure implies, PPGAs are hired and supervised by regional directors. Typically, a regional director appoints about 12 PPGAs per year and maintains a working relationship with about 40 PPGAs.

- *Managing general agent approach—personal producing general agent.* This type of structure originated with independent agents in the casualty insurance business. There, an independent general agent representing a company in a particular region was authorized to appoint other independents to represent the company. While wielding more "clout" with the carrier, the managing general agent (MGA) operated essentially as a regional agency for the company and usually had territorial rights as well as certain powers. The MGA also often specialized in a particular product. The MGA concept differs from the RDA approach because the MGA is an independent contractor authorized by the company to appoint PPGAs, and there is much less primary company orientation. Typically the MGA is a franchisee who represents one company for a particular product in a particular territory. Since their producers are already paid the override, MGAs are compensated on a percentage of commissions and assume such administrative expenses as recruiting and mailing costs.

- *Brokerage supervisor approach.* The brokerage supervisor is a company employee who solicits business from producers with whom that company has no primary relationships. Brokerage supervisors are most often associated with agency-building companies — providing them with an additional distribution option — and with life affiliates of property-casualty companies where they primarily target independent property-casualty agencies. Companies that use this approach tend to offer a full line of products and rely on their ability to provide technical help to producers whose main business is not life insurance, such as property-casualty agents and stockbrokers. Because brokerage supervisors are usually housed in the field, they are able to solve local producers' problems when and where they occur.

- *Independent brokerage general agent approach.* This approach provides companies access to a producer through an independent brokerage general agent (IBGA) who is authorized to solicit business for the company and to appoint producers on its behalf. IBGA companies tend to be ones that offer specialty products or that provide process-oriented service, including liberal underwriting and speedy policy issue and commission payment, to producers who typically are agents of other companies. IBGAs offer some administrative services, usually represent several carriers for the same product, and are paid by overrides on business generated through their efforts while their producers are compensated by basic commissions.

Before we leave the subject of the structure of field organizations, it should be noted that some companies have provided their field forces with a larger number of products to sell or have expanded their distribution capacities without having an impact on their existing field force. Companies have done so by entering into manufacturer-distributor agreements with nonaffiliated companies. Under these agreements one company distributes products manufactured by the other company. Such agreements offer companies product diversification and the ability to capture outside business. The manufacturing company gets additional distribution capacity and easier access to producers; the distributing company adds income sources for its producers, enhances its agents' service capabilities, and has a chance to test market products without the cost and effort required to development the product itself.

RELATIONSHIP BETWEEN AGENT AND COMPANY

At one time it was common for the agent to contract with the general agent or manager. Today, however, the common practice is that the agent contracts with the company. The contract describes the authority, scope, and limits of the agent's job, and it determines the agent's legal relationship with the company, the restrictions concerning representation of other companies, and the compensation arrangements.

The contract's compensation provision is frequently handled by attaching a commission schedule or agreement. This attachment facilitates modifications of the commission provisions for new types of policies, changes in rates and cash value structures, and other changes in marketing strategies, such as raising or lowering commissions on certain products to encourage or discourage their sale.

Commission scales of companies that do business in the state of New York are limited by Sec. 4228 of the New York State Insurance Law. Although the commission scales of companies vary, there is a greater degree of uniformity among companies doing business in New York than among the commission scales of companies that are not limited by expense limitation laws.

For companies licensed in New York, the typical agent's commission rate for ordinary life insurance is 55 percent of premium for the first year, followed by 5 percent of premium for the next 9 years, after which a small service fee is paid for a further specified period. The commission rate for agents selling for companies not licensed in New York is usually higher—up to twice as high in some cases. But the variety of commission rates that exist, which depend on the product, age of the insured, location of the sale, condition of the sale, and marketing strategy of the company, means that the figures above are quoted only to provide a very broad guideline as to how commissions are structured.

In states other than New York, some companies pay renewal commissions only during the first few policy years (3, 4, 5, 6), and the rate often decreases each year rather than staying at the same percentage. Newly licensed agents, of course, have no immediate commission income. They are paid a specified amount until they can earn enough to survive on commissions, reach a designated time limit, or are terminated. Usually the amount paid is on the condition that the recruit fulfill specific minimum requirements in regard to such things as hours worked, interviews held, and training sessions completed. A validation schedule outlines the sales requirements that an agent must meet in order to continue being subsidized.

Agents, in certain situations or for particular reasons, are paid noncommission compensation. For most agents, this noncommission compensation is in the form of such programs as group life and health insurance, pension funding, and similar fringe benefits. When home-service agents collect premiums at the policyowner's home or office, they are paid for performing this function.

MARKETING COSTS AND PROFITABILITY

While it is true that a company can survive—even prosper—for a short period of time from positive profitability in any of a dozen functions, only marketing profitability can sustain a company for long periods of time. Therefore it is vitally important that a company's marketing operation is, in fact, profitable.

If a company is in a market with a properly priced product, service level, or distribution advantage that cannot be duplicated by the competition or has a captive market, the company should be profitable, regardless of the circumstances. However, those kinds of situations are very rare. For most companies profitability can be achieved only through the use of superior financial fundamentals. This is simple to illustrate: In a broad sense, profit equals revenues less expenses. In other words, profit comes from high revenues and low expenses. Revenues are properly managed by controlling the fundamental factors associated with getting new business: field productivity, agent retention, and the persistency of policies.

Productivity refers to how much business agents write and how large the policies are. According to LIMRA surveys, the typical agent in a low-productivity company writes an average of 49 polices per year, generating approximately $50,000 of new premium. The typical agent in a high-productivity company writes an average of 69 policies per year and the average policy is larger; this agent generates about $90,000 of new premium.

Retention refers to how long an agent stays with a company. Typically, 4 years after contracting 100 new agents a company with average retention has kept 18 of them. However, in companies with good retention, the 4-year retention rate is about 30 percent. High retention rates have a direct bearing on company profitability in two ways: (1) The company avoids the expenses associated with recruiting and training additional new agents, and (2) established agents have higher productivity than less experienced agents.

Persistency refers to how long policies remain in force and the insured pay premiums on them. The industry average is 86.5 percent—that is, 86.5 percent of the industry's policies will still be in force 13 months after they are written. A typical company with high persistency has a rate of 92.7 percent.

Control of Marketing Expenses

The other factor in the profitability equation is expenses. It is impossible to market without expenses; therefore the key to profitability on this side of the ledger is to control marketing expenses. The principal trap companies fall into that keeps them from managing expenses as well as they could is marginal pricing—allocating less than full fixed costs or less than full overhead costs to a product. Marginal pricing can be used sometimes, but never over a long time period and never with core products. Too often companies use marginal pricing to gain entry into a market, planning to remedy the situation later. This rarely works, however, because the marginal pricing is aimed at capturing a target market share that never materializes, because cost improvement measures that will make a product profitable are never realized, or because competitive conditions force the price to remain low.

While the building branch of the agency system would tend to have higher costs because of its expenses for recruiting and developing agents, these expenses are often offset by the higher commissions and support service costs incurred by nonbuilding companies. LIMRA studies show that when all types of companies are analyzed, there are high-cost companies and low-cost companies in each distribution system, and there is a band of relatively profitable companies that cuts across all distribution systems. This tends to indicate that with good quality management, any distribution system can be profitable.

It is obvious just how important producers are to the achievement of profitability, especially in regard to retention and productivity. For the most part, and whether or not they now sell in a building or nonbuilding organization, how producers were recruited into the business and developed in the performance of their skills is a key to how well they succeed. Almost without exception, all producers share the same early recruitment and developmental experiences.

RECRUITING, SELECTING, AND DEVELOPING PRODUCERS

Field office heads and their second-line managers are responsible for bringing new people into the life insurance business. It begins by the recruiter's establishing a clear picture of the type of person he or she wants to recruit. It is usually based on the market the producer will be working in and the type of individual who has achieved success in similar circumstances.

It is not the recruiter's purpose initially to be very selective; that comes later. The object at this point is to accumulate as many names as possible. To do this, recruiters use all of the sources at their disposal—personal contacts; referrals from other producers, clients, and friends of the agency; college and personnel placement offices; and newspaper ads.

Selection-Rejection Process

After the recruiter gets an individual's name and that individual exhibits some interest in a life insurance career, the process becomes very selective. It usually contains these three stages: obtaining all the facts relating to the candidate's background, experience, and personal qualifications; using an organized system for verifying and evaluating the facts; and devoting an adequate amount of time and effort to judge the facts and make an intelligent decision. These stages are accomplished through the implementation of a detailed selection-rejection process that has the following specific steps:

- a quick preliminary interview to determine if there are any obvious reasons why the candidate should be rejected and to convince the candidate to take an aptitude test
- the administration of an objective aptitude test that accurately predicts the chances of an individual's likelihood of success in the job of producer (and conforms to all equal opportunity rules and regulations)
- completion of a legal application form
- an evaluation interview in which the company can gain further information about the candidate and the candidate can learn about the job
- interviews with other people, if appropriate, such as spouses, other producers, and references
- a follow-up interview to clear up any questions on the part of either the recruiter or candidate

In addition to these selection steps, there are two additional ones that a recruiter should take to make sure the candidate is right for the job. One is precontract training—having the candidate actually do certain parts of the job before making a commitment. The other is giving the candidate a complete, honest, and realistic description of the job, including both the good and the bad aspects of the position.

Training Recruits

Newly contracted agents enter the financing period referred to earlier in this chapter and follow a validation schedule that details what they must produce to remain under contract. They are also required to follow a training program that usually includes attending a school (often held in the home office) and completing specific learning assignments determined by the agency office. Of course, before actually going out and selling, recruits must also obtain the licenses required by the agency or company.

Generally speaking, a new agent's training will cover these five areas:

- life insurance basics
- sales techniques
- company and agency procedures
- product knowledge
- company history, goals, plans, and policies

Often a new agent will make sales calls with the head of the agency, a second-line manager, or an experienced agent. There are industry-supported educational and skill-building courses that are available to new producers (commercial programs are also available). As agents progress in their careers, there are additional programs that lead to professional designations. Since modern agents sell technically and financially complex products, training and development is an ongoing process. In addition, companies and agencies provide a wide range of programs to motivate their salespeople. These include regular meetings, production awards, print recognition, and the opportunity to qualify for sales conventions that are typically held in resorts or exotic locales.

The amount of supervision that producers require varies greatly. New agents generally require more supervision than veteran agents. Common to all agents, however, is the formulation of a sales quota, construction of plans to achieve that quota, and periodic reviews to measure the producer's progress toward reaching the quota. Such quotas, plans, and reviews are usually not limited to a single measure but can include all or some of the following: premiums written, commissions earned, face amount sold, average premium per sale, number of policies, persistency rate, and activity (which includes prospects contacted, interviews conducted, sales literature mailed, telephone calls placed, sales interviews held, service calls made, and closings attempted). A producer's continuing development is also part of periodic reviews.

Administrative, Technical, and Sales Support

Several levels of support are provided to help producers make sales. Often, the amount of administrative support—secretarial help, proposal generation, and mailings—given to a producer depends on his or her production level, with a high-producing agent earning his or her own private secretary or administrative assistant. Technical support is given to producers in the form of computer-generated policy illustrations, computer analysis of client finances, computer-controlled sales and performance measuring, and word-processed mailings. In more computer-literate operations, computers are also used for maintaining client information databases, prospecting among existing policyowners, and policy creation. Advanced sales support is provided to help producers sell a product or to a market with which they are not familiar or that requires special knowledge. This is common in group insurance, pension, and business situations.

Educational Support

Agency managers and directors usually support professional educational programs such as LUTC, CLU, and ChFC.[2] Some insurance companies have established incentive programs to encourage agents to pursue these designations and increase their knowledge. Studies have repeatedly confirmed that CLU holders are more successful than non-CLUs in terms of sales and compensation. The most recent study from LIMRA indicates that ChFC holders earn even more on average than do CLUs and other non-ChFCs.

Some agencies require their agents to complete one or more professional designations within a short time after joining the sales force. If the company and agency deal with variable life and equity products such as mutual funds, the new agents will be given educational support to prepare for the examinations they must pass in order to sell those products. The Securities and Exchange Commission (SEC) mandates the examinations that are developed and managed by the National Association of Securities Dealers (NASD).[3] There are also educational programs provided by the Million Dollar Round Table (MDRT) and the Association of Advanced Life Underwriting (AALU).[4]

OTHER DISTRIBUTION CHANNELS

Banks and Department Stores

Typically, producers sell either in their own office or in the prospect's home or office. However, some sales are made, or at least begun, because a prospect visits an insurance facility. In these cases an individual salesperson is usually involved, although he or she may be salaried rather than paid a commission. For example, an insurance company or agent may install a producer behind a desk in a department store, in the lobby of a bank, or in the bank itself. Bank or savings and loan employees may hold agent contracts with a company and sell the insurer's products, or an insurer may provide a bank with products, usually annuities, that the bank markets to its customers. Banks may also use independent marketing organizations to do their insurance marketing for them.

Direct Response Marketing

Although direct response marketing accounts for only one percent of new premium income, LIMRA estimates that 4 percent of households in the United States buy life insurance directly in a year's time. Since there are over 90 million households in the United States, this small proportion still translates into a sizable market.

Direct response marketing is making sales to consumers through the mail, media advertising, or telemarketing. Standardized sales messages are made to consumers, orders are taken, products are delivered, and payments are remitted without the use of a salesperson. Some insurance companies rely completely on direct response systems to distribute their products while other companies use direct response as just one of several distribution methods.

As time progresses, direct response marketing is becoming more and more advanced technologically. Direct response firms engage heavily in market research and testing, and they maintain extensive computer-driven information-retrieval and telemarketing operations. The emphasis in such operations is instant access to customers' records to make sales or provide service. Most products distributed through direct response methods are designed to serve large market segments, are very affordable, and are uncomplicated in design and administration.

FUTURE OF LIFE INSURANCE MARKETING

There have been major revolutions in life insurance marketing, most notably with the introduction of soliciting agents in the 1840s, the rise of the debit agent in the 1880s, the advent of group insurance in the 1930s, and the growth of nonexclusive producer companies since the end of World War II. Radical change, therefore, is not unknown in life insurance marketing, and it might happen again. However, evolution seems to be more likely than revolution, and that evolution will be triggered by forces already in place that are sure to have some impact on how life insurance will be marketed in the future.

Increased Competition

One of these forces is an increase in competition. Insurance products are no longer just marketed by purely insurance-related entities such as banks and stock-brokers. Government regulations now limit the activities of these noninsurance marketers, but these regulations could change. Any increase by noninsurance organizations, which have a totally different marketing orientation, could alter the ways insurance marketers operate.

Furthermore, the life insurance business is becoming a global business with foreign insurers invading the United States and vice versa. Many foreign insurers also have a different marketing orientation, and their approach, especially their relationship with banks, could force United States insurers to modify their distribution methods.

Demographic Shifts and a Move Toward Living Benefits

There is also a major demographic shift going on in the United States. The consequences are that the work force will grow more slowly than at any time since 1930, the average age of the work force will rise, meaning that the pool of younger workers entering the labor market will shrink; more women will continue to enter the work force; minorities will be a larger share of new entrants into the work force; and immigrants will represent the largest percentage increase in the work force since World War I. Such changes are bound to affect how producers are recruited and how they operate.

Another trend is that the focus of the life insurance business is turning more to living benefits than death benefits. The key result of this trend is that the business will be selling more annuities and other retirement and savings-oriented products than life insurance. Since these products have lower margins and pay lower commissions, there is some concern that, as core products, they will not be able to support the cost of existing distribution systems.

Changes in Distribution Systems

Finally, in the difficult financial environment in which the life insurance industry finds itself—a slow economy, the need to increase surplus, and the pressure of competing on the basis of price—companies might make a concerted effort to find the least expensive ways to distribute products. One suggested approach is to pay closer attention to the natural linkage between the market segment, the products serving that segment, and the distribution system serving that market. This approach recognizes that to be in any market that is not economically consistent with the company's distribution system or product, the company must meet or better the competition's performance standards in that market. Otherwise market share will decrease and acquisition costs will rise.

In the past companies could live with those inefficiencies because of the margins in place at the time. Those margins are gone and, most likely, will never return. Therefore companies must refine and exploit the market segment-product distribution system linkage. Over time, the distribution systems now in use gravitated to the markets they service without prior planning or direction. It is time, now say proponents of the approach, to attack these markets with planning and direction. This will lead to distribution system pluralism—that is, the many different distribution systems described earlier (and others yet to be developed) will be implemented across companies rather than across the industry.

NOTES

1. Peter Drucker, *People and Performance* (Tyler, TX: The Leadership Network, 1989).
2. LUTC stands for Life Underwriter Training Council (7625 Wisconsin Avenue, Bethesda, MD 20814). This organization has sales training courses and grants the designations LUTC and LUTCF. CLU stands for Chartered Life Underwriter, which is a designation granted by The American College (270 Bryn Mawr Avenue, Bryn Mawr, PA 19010). The program requires students to pass 10 examinations over courses dealing with taxes, finance, insurance, pensions, and related material and to have 3 years of experience. ChFC stands for Chartered Financial Consultant, which is a designation also granted by The American College. This 10-part program focuses more on the planning process.
3. The SEC regulates all securities publicly traded in the United States. It requires that these products be sold only by licensed persons and that a prospectus be supplied to potential purchasers before the sale transaction. The NASD has a series of tests, each geared to a specific product group or subgroup. These tests must be passed in order to obtain the NASD license needed to sell equity products.
4. Million Dollar Round Table (325 Touhy Avenue, Park Ridge, Il 60068) is an organization open only to the top 20 percent of agents, based on sales volume. The Association of Advanced Life Underwriting (AALU) is a membership organization affiliated with the National Association of Life Underwriters (NALU). (Both organizations are at 1922 F Street NW, Washington, DC 20006.)

30

Financial Statements and Ratings (Part 1)

Harry D. Garber

Life insurance company financial statements have evolved to meet the needs of its various audiences. To understand the structure and content of these statements, a good place to start is with the needs and goals of these audiences. They include investors, the Securities and Exchange Commission (SEC), state insurance regulators, creditors, security analysts, rating agencies, policyowners, company management, and agents and employees of the company. Each of these audiences has different interests, and the financial statements for each audience have different objectives. Not unexpectedly, the objectives overlap in many respects.

CONSIDERATIONS IN LIFE INSURANCE COMPANY ACCOUNTING

Let's consider the interests and objectives of each of these distinct audiences.

Users of Life Insurance Company Financial Statements

Investors are interested in the current level of and the prospective growth in the earnings of public companies in order to value these companies for investment purposes. Since investments may be made in debt instruments (for example, bonds) and in equity securities (for example, common or preferred stock), investors are also interested in an enterprise's current and prospective financial strength.

The SEC seeks to ensure that the financial statements and accounting rules used by publicly held companies, including stock life insurance companies, provide investors and other users with the required level of information. Fair and consistent presentation across industries is the norm; however, certain industries, such as insurance, have requirements tailored to their unique characteristics.

State insurance regulators are principally interested in the ability of the life insurance companies that operate in their jurisdictions to meet current and future obligations to policyowners and owners of other contracts with the insurer. This means that the regulators' focus is on the near-term and long-term financial safety and solvency of the company. To this end, they seek to assure that the financial statements filed by life insurance companies are based on conservative accounting principles and practices.

Creditors are interested in the likelihood that the amounts owed to them will be paid. Creditors include bondholders and suppliers of equipment and services to the life insurance company. Creditors whose obligations are due currently need information on the company's current liquidity position and/or its expected near-term cash flow from operations. This information, however, is rarely available in a timely fashion from the company's financial statements. Long-term bondholders are interested in assessing the ability of the life insurance company (or its parent company) to pay bond interest and principal due in the future. Although published financial statements can provide some of this information, these creditors usually require additional information not unlike that provided to the rating agencies described below.

Security analysts are an audience with similar but more expansive information requirements than investors. Although large corporate and mutual fund investment managers do their own research using financial statements and other public and private information available about a company, individual investors often rely heavily on the analyses and recommendations of the leading brokerage and investment banking firms' industry analysts.

Rating agencies are another audience for life insurance company financial statements. Their focus is the company's present financial position and how it may evolve in the future. It is important to these agencies that financial statements of companies in an industry be comparable and provide consistent results over the years. Because the principal agencies (A. M. Best, Standard and Poors, Duff and Phelps, and Moody's) depend mostly on their own in-depth data-gathering visits and interviews with the company's senior management, their needs for information do not impose additional requirements on the structure or content of the life insurance company's published financial statements. Other rating services, which depend almost entirely on published financial statements and other publicly available information, may find their analytical capability and the quality of their ratings limited by the information contained in these sources.

Policyowners and prospective policyowners are primarily concerned with two aspects of a company's position and performance. One is the company's ability to meet its benefit guarantees to policyowners; the second is the company's performance in those areas that will affect future charges to policyowners for insurance coverage. Key performance areas include investment income, mortality costs, expenses, and persistency. Policyowner interest is most acute at the time of purchasing an insurance contract (which often involves comparisons among several companies), but this interest may continue throughout the lifetime of a contract. A life insurance company's policyowners therefore are interested in financial statements that permit them to assess the company's safety and solvency and to compare the current levels and trends of the company's performance in the areas that affect policyowner costs (investment income, mortality, expenses, and persistency) with those of other companies. Businesses, particularly those acting in a fiduciary or quasi-fiduciary capacity as policyowners or sponsors of 401(k) or other benefit plans, have an obligation to deal only with insurance companies with unquestionable positions of safety and solvency.

Members of the insurance *company management,* as well as the company's board of directors are interested in having financial statements that fairly portray the company's financial position and progress, particularly as they relate to its principal life insurance competitors. The financial statement should not only fairly measure the results of an individual company's operations but should also ensure comparability among companies. In particular, measurements of current year earnings should neither favor nor disfavor companies that are making investments in capacity or growth for future profits versus companies that are profiting largely from past investments. If financial statements do not recognize the appropriate value of investments in capacity or growth, companies may focus too much on short-term actions to the detriment of long-term performance.

Agents and employees share the interests of company management, policy-owners, and in the case of stock companies, shareholders. As representatives of the company, their most immediate concern is that financial statements accurately inform policyowners about operational results and financial strength. Agents, in particular, must advise clients and respond to clients' questions on issues of company safety and solvency and on policy funding adequacy. Very often, the agent's advice and counsel must be given in competition with other agents and brokers, placing greater intensity and focus on these issues.

In addition to the different perspectives of the several audiences described above, the structure of life insurance company financial statements is shaped by the nature of the business the company conducts. Most contracts issued by life insurance companies involve long-term commitments. Policy accumulations are invested for long periods of time, and many contracts remain in force for decades. Because the company's actual financial results for each block of contracts can be determined only after it has run its full course, measuring financial results on in-force contracts often depends as much on the assumptions and accounting conventions used as it does on cash receipts and payments (premiums received, investment income received, death claims and surrender values paid, and expenses paid). This factor shapes life insurance company financial statements as much or more than the goals and objectives of the various audiences for these statements.

The remainder of this chapter describes the structure and content of life insurance companies' published financial statements. It will become clear that these statements largely, but not fully, satisfy the objectives of certain of these audiences and leave others largely unfulfilled. Despite the significant expansion in the amount of information provided in financial statements in recent years, no statement (or set of statements) can economically meet all needs. As indicated above, the shortfalls in the ability of financial statements to meet the objectives of a particular audience can sometimes be bridged by additional information or in-depth visits, but this is not always practical.

Form and Composition of Life Insurance Company Financial Statements

Financial statements are a primary means for a life insurance company, or for that matter any enterprise, to communicate information to the audiences described earlier. In one of its financial accounting concepts statements, the Financial Accounting Standards Board (FASB) identified three objectives of financial reporting. These are paraphrased below:

- to provide information that is both useful and comprehensible to audiences in making rational investment, credit, and similar decisions
- to provide information that is helpful in assessing the amounts, timing, and uncertainty of prospective cash receipts from sales of products or services and from investments (dividends, interest, and sales or redemption of securities)
- to provide information about a company's economic resources (assets), claims on those resources (liabilities), and the effects of transactions, events, and circumstances that change those resources and claims

Financial statements have evolved over time and now encompass many reports, schedules, exhibits, and explanations. The three most common and significant reports are as follows:

- statement of financial position
- income statement
- statement of cash flows

Statement of Financial Position

The statement of financial position, more commonly called the balance sheet, lists the company's assets, liabilities, and its equity position at the end of the fiscal period. Comparable numbers are also shown for one or 2 prior years. (For life insurance companies, the calendar year is the fiscal year; the statement date is December 31 of that year.)

Assets are economic resources that the company owns or controls. Assets include cash, investments (stocks, bonds, mortgages, and real estate), real property used in the business (buildings, parking lots, and so on), and premiums and other amounts receivable from customers. There are events or transactions that can cause a change in the value of an asset that a life insurance company holds. For example, the market price of a common stock can go up (or down) and can increase (or decrease) the value of the company's investment in that stock relative to its original cost. Similarly, in the case of the investment-income-receivable asset, experience has shown that the amount due and accrued will not always be collected, particularly if the business is behind in its payments. Therefore total investment income due and accrued will be reduced by an estimate of the amount that will not be received to determine the appropriate asset value.

Certain assets, such as buildings, furniture, computers, and equipment, are usually worth less as they age. For financial reporting purposes, a useful life is determined for each such asset or asset class and the cost of the asset is written off or depreciated over its productive years. Depreciation is an expense in the income statement and a reduction in the asset's carrying value. Over time, the cumulative amount of depreciation for an asset grows until, at the end of its useful life, the statement or book value of the asset is reduced to zero (or some residual or salvage value if resale is possible). When applied to intangible assets such as goodwill, the term *amortization* is used to describe a similar process.

Liabilities, on the other hand, are obligations to transfer assets or to provide services to others: policyowners and contractowners, creditors, employees, suppliers, or taxing authorities. Liabilities include such items as policyowners' account balances and future benefits payable, short- and long-term debt, dividends not yet paid to policyowners and/or shareholders, and taxes payable.

In the insurance industry, the terms *liability* and *reserve* are often used interchangeably. However, these terms have distinctly different meanings in other accounting contexts and for other industries. For example, policy reserves (discussed in detail in chapter 16) are liabilities. The allowances for uncollectible investment income mentioned above are often called reserves, but they are classified with and used to reduce assets.

Equity is, very simply, the difference between assets and liabilities. A company's equity is the book measurement of the ownership interest. The insurer's own common and nonredeemable preferred stock, the related paid-in capital, and its retained earnings/surplus are typical components of equity.

Equity is increased when the owners of a business make additional investments in the company or when a company's net earnings are retained in the business instead of being returned to the owners as dividends. Equity is decreased when a company has a net loss from operations, pays dividends to shareholders, or otherwise returns assets to its owners.

The distinction between liabilities and equity is not always clear. For example, redeemable preferred stock has characteristics of both debt and equity. The asset valuation reserve (AVR) is reported as a liability in the annual statements filed with state regulators, but it is often treated as equity. (The AVR will be discussed more fully later in this chapter.)

Income Statement

Unlike the statement of financial position, which presents the company's position on the date of the statement, the income statement (which is also referred to as the statement of operations, or statement of earnings) presents the company's revenues, expenses, and earnings (losses) for the accounting period specified (a fiscal year or a fraction thereof). Earnings serve to build the company's equity and, in the case of stock companies, to provide the funds for distribution as dividends to shareholders. Year-to-year trends in a company's earnings, which are usually expressed as earnings per share of stock outstanding, are a principal factor affecting the stock market's evaluation of the value (price) of the company's stock.

Revenues are inflows of cash or other assets that result from an enterprise's business operations. In the case of a life insurance company, major sources of revenue include premiums and other contract charges and income from its investments. Expenses, on the other hand, are outflows or other uses of assets (or incurred liabilities) required to provide products and services to a company's clients. Benefits paid to policyowners or contractowners, salaries, commissions, employee benefits, and taxes are a few of the more significant expenses life insurers report in the income statement.

In financial reports a distinction is drawn between revenues and expenses from the insurance company's normal ongoing business activities and its gains and losses. One distinguishing characteristic of gains and losses is that they are usually the direct result of specific management actions. For example, when an investment is sold, the difference between the amount the company receives and the current carrying value of the investment represents a gain or loss. Similarly, the discontinuance or sale of a business may produce a gain or loss. Security analysts tend to treat gains and losses differently from (and place less importance on) income from regular business operations in evaluating a company's economic performance.

Statement of Cash Flows

In addition to the balance sheet and income statement, a life insurance company's financial statement contains a cash flow statement and supplementary material that provides additional details regarding the balance sheet and income statements. The cash flow statement and the supplementary material will be discussed in greater detail in a later section of this chapter.

GAAP and Statutory Financial Statements: Approaches

Although the goals and objectives of the several audiences for life insurance company financial statements are now well understood, this was not always the case. Life insurance company statements have evolved in form and content as these audiences have grown in influence and their requirements have become more clearly defined and articulated.

Statutory Accounting and Reporting

Until the 1960s, state regulators were the only group with a substantial interest in life insurance companies' published financial statements . There were few major stock life insurance companies and limited investor interest in such companies. The Accounting Principles Board, the predecessor of today's Financial Accounting Standards Board, had just come into being in September 1959 and would not issue its first opinion until 1962. There had been no major life insurance company insolvencies since the Great Depression, and most individual life insurance was sold in situations in which there was little policy-owner concern about insurer safety and solvency and, given the relatively low level of price competition, whether the company's illustrations of future policy performance would be realized.

In this environment the state insurance departments defined the contents of the only published financial statements for life insurance companies. The statutory financial statements they prescribe, commonly called the NAIC blank or the "blue blank" (because of the color of its cover), must be filed by life insurance companies in each state in which they arc liccnscd to do business. The statutory statement places primary emphasis on solvency and stability. As a result, this statement focuses principally on the balance sheet. The statutory accounting practices (SAP) are a form of liquidation-basis accounting—that is, accounting as if the insurer is expected to cease operations in an orderly fashion in the near future. SAP tends to value both assets and liabilities conservatively. Some of the traditional statutory accounting practices include immediately charging furniture and equipment purchases directly against surplus, immediately expensing all costs (including policy and contract acquisition costs), and computing policy reserves on the basis of conservative (low) interest rates. The effect of this emphasis on the balance sheet is to lessen the value of the income statement as a source of information and dependable trends.

Statutory accounting and reporting requirements are established by each state's legislature, which enacts the insurance laws and authorizes the regulations that govern insurance companies in that state. The state insurance department, headed by an insurance commissioner, interprets and enforces the prescribed statutory requirements. A life insurance company must comply with the requirements in each state in which it does business. Even though *each* state independently enacts its individual body of law, much similarity exists because of the influence of the National Association of Insurance Commissioners (NAIC), an organization made up of state insurance department regulators.

The NAIC helps to promote uniformity among the states. Model laws and regulations are developed by the NAIC that each state is then encouraged to pass. The NAIC has also codified statutory accounting practices into policy manuals and produces an annual statement guide that covers the information to be included in every report, schedule, and exhibit that make up the NAIC blanks.

Until the advent of generally accepted accounting practices (GAAP), many life insurance companies also published a condensed version of the statutory financial statement to include in the company's annual report. Mutual life companies produce such statutory statements to this day. This condensed statement, while still compiled in accordance with statutory accounting practices, more closely resembled the traditional financial statement found in the annual reports of noninsurance enterprises. However, while the balance sheets and income statements of life insurance companies looked similar to those of noninsurance enterprises, the numbers were based on two separate and distinct accounting methodologies. Uniformity in the underlying accounting policies and procedures used by insurers was needed to achieve comparable financial statements.

GAAP Accounting and Reporting

During the 1960s, investors showed an increased interest in life insurance companies as potential investments. At the same time, analysts' frustration with the statutory financial statements was growing. The accounting practice that required acquisition costs to be written off immediately tended to tint the income statements of fast growing companies negatively. As a result, security analysts developed several different rule-of-thumb adjustments to the statutory operating statements and used the "adjusted" income to advise investors in purchases and sales of life insurance company stock.

It soon became clear to the SEC and the American Institute of Certified Public Accountants (AICPA) that an environment in which state insurance regulators established accounting rules for life insurance companies and analysts developed different techniques for adjusting the resulting income statements for investment recommendations was not healthy. Investors needed a more controlled, standardized information flow. The AICPA was asked to develop an accounting structure for life insurance companies that would be in accord with the set of GAAP developed for other types of enterprises. This effort was completed in the early 1970s.

The GAAP statement seeks the best possible measure of a company's past performance to provide users (investors, creditors, company managements, rating agencies, and so forth) with information to evaluate potential future performance. The focus of GAAP reporting is on the income statement and the statement of cash flows and on making the results of operations between periods easy to compare.

The underlying accounting principle influencing GAAP is to match income and expense so that profits emerge over the lifetime of a life insurance policy in a pattern that is more reasonably related to the policy margins than the profits would have been if all costs had been charged off in the year of sale, as they are under SAP. (Some FASB and SEC actions in the early 1990s diluted the focus on the income statement to some degree but did not disturb the essential nature of GAAP for life insurance companies.)

GAAP accounting standards usually apply to all United States business enterprises and to foreign operations that have United States filing requirements. In some instances, special guidance is developed on an industry-wide basis; the insurance industry is a case in point.

The authoritative accounting pronouncements that, taken as a whole, make up GAAP have been developed and enforced by three bodies. Like its predecessors, FASB has been the principal GAAP-standard-setting body since 1973. The AICPA, through its statements of position, accounting and auditing guides, and similar technical services, interprets existing GAAP. Finally, the SEC continues to affect GAAP through its direct and indirect influence on FASB, its own codified accounting and reporting policies, and case-by-case actions on the accounting practices used by companies seeking approval of registration statements.

During the development of the GAAP accounting structure for life insurers, there was a split between the mutual and stock segments of the industry. The mutual segment argued that GAAP accounting was not required for mutual companies, which were not investor-owned, and that the proposed GAAP treatment of policy dividends as a policy benefit was not in accord with mutual company dividend practices.

The mutual companies were successful in convincing the SEC and the other standard-setting organizations that the new GAAP structure should not be applied to them. As a result, stock companies have prepared both statutory and GAAP financial statements since 1973, while mutual companies have issued only statutory financial statements.

Over the years, mutual companies have been required to file more financial statements with the SEC, frequently because of an increasing amount of separate account activity and various kinds of asset-based financings and public debt offerings. The noncomparability of the mutual company's statutory financial statements and the stock company's GAAP financial statements is, in the view of the SEC, a growing concern.

Therefore the exemption for mutual insurers is being examined and FASB has been asked to develop and implement a GAAP structure for mutual life insurance companies by 1995.

LIFE INSURANCE COMPANY FINANCIAL STATEMENTS

Substantive GAAP/Statutory Differences

Some of the principal differences between statutory accounting practices and GAAP are described below.

Deferred Acquisition Costs

Under GAAP, acquisition costs are capitalized and amortized over the life of the book of policies or contracts. These costs can be amortized in proportion to anticipated premiums (in the case of traditional life insurance) or in proportion to estimated gross profits (in the case of deposit-type contracts, such as universal life and deferred annuities). As discussed previously, under statutory accounting practices, these costs are expensed in the year incurred.

Furniture and Equipment and Similar Assets

With GAAP, purchases of furniture, equipment and similar assets are treated as assets and are depreciated over their useful lives. Under statutory accounting practices, except for computer hardware and related operating systems, these purchases are charged directly against surplus in the year of purchase. The statutory accounting treatment of computer systems purchases is similar to the GAAP treatment.

Federal Taxes

Using statutory accounting practices, federal income taxes are charged as incurred (based on the net taxable income reported in the company's federal income tax returns). Under GAAP, in addition to the charge for federal income taxes incurred, a net deferred-tax liability (or asset) is established to recognize the estimated future tax effects of temporary differences between the measurements of revenue and expenses and of assets and liabilities required under the applicable tax laws and the measurements of these items required under GAAP. A deferred-tax liability (or the increase in such a liability during a year) increases the federal tax charge against income; the reverse is true for a deferred-tax asset.

The effect of the deferred-tax approach is to adjust the federal tax charge in the GAAP financial statement so that it is consistent with the pretax revenue and expense and the asset and liability measurements reflected in the GAAP statement, rather than the comparable measures in the federal income tax return. As an example, if a company uses accelerated real estate depreciation for tax purposes but straight-line depreciation for GAAP statement purposes, a deferred-tax liability would be recorded for the excess of accelerated tax depreciation over financial reporting depreciation.

Asset Valuation

Valuation allowances are established under GAAP accounting to adjust asset values for improvements in value deemed to be other than temporary. These valuation allowances reflect the losses that company management expects to realize on the sale or other disposition of the asset, on foreclosure (in the case of mortgage loans), on the borrower's failure to meet scheduled payments, or from shortfalls of cash flows (on investment real estate). The establishment of a valuation allowance or the increase in such an allowance is recorded as a charge to income.

Traditionally, valuation allowances that are part of specific categories of assets have not been established under statutory accounting practices. Instead, an asset valuation reserve is established as a liability. The purposes of the AVR are to absorb both realized and unrealized gains and losses on substantially all invested assets other than policy loans and to serve as a general reserve for possible asset losses. (Gains and losses that are due to changes in the level of interest rates since the date of the investment's acquisition are captured in the interest maintenance reserve [IMR], a companion reserve to the AVR.) Each year the AVR is increased by formula-based contributions and by the realized and unrealized net capital gains on securities, mortgages, and real estate, and it is decreased by the capital losses on these investments. The formula contributions vary depending on the relationship of the AVR balance to the defined maximum level. If the reserve balance is small compared to the defined maximum, a larger annual contribution is required than if greater than the defined maximum.

Although statutory accounting does not call for the establishment of valuation allowances for individual investments or investment categories, there is a growing trend among companies to establish such allowances and to reduce the carrying values for those assets in their statutory financial statements. Any such reduction in asset value, which would be treated as an unrealized capital loss in statutory accounting, would reduce the company's AVR and would have no current-year effect on the company's earnings or surplus.

One final note on asset valuation: Responding to the savings and loan and bank failures of the late 1980s, in 1993 the SEC and FASB adopted a requirement (FASB 115) that, except in rare circumstances, securities be carried at market value. This requirement will apply only to GAAP financial statements. Insurers and other financial institutions are unhappy about the new standard because it will force an insurer's surplus accounts, as the residual balancing account on the balance sheet, to become more volatile.

Policy Reserves

Policy reserves are computed differently under SAP and GAAP. Historically, statutory policy reserves were computed using interest rates, mortality tables, and valuation standards prescribed by state statutes and regulations, while GAAP policy reserves for insurance contracts were computed using interest, mortality, and persistency assumptions established by the company's actuary at policy issue (usually based on the company's own experience). More recent trends in statutory practices have expanded the range of acceptable interest and mortality assumptions, which in turn permit the application of somewhat more actuarial judgment. In addition, the statutory and GAAP approaches to accumulation-type products (for example, universal life and deferred annuities) tend to be similar.

Subsidiaries

Investment in a subsidiary is treated for statutory purposes as a common stock, but the value of the investment is usually based on cost adjustments for the life insurance company's share of income or losses after the date of acquisition. (If the subsidiary is also an insurance company, a statutory measure of income or loss is used.) GAAP requires consolidation (inclusion of the subsidiary on a line-by-line basis) of all majority-owned subsidiaries unless control is likely to be temporary or does not rest with the majority owner. This GAAP accounting practice has the effect of increasing each applicable asset, liability, revenue, and expense measure in the life insurance company's financial statements by the corresponding amounts from the operations of majority-owned subsidiaries.

Nonadmitted Assets

The concept of *nonadmitted assets* applies only to the statutory balance sheet. Under the insurance laws or some state regulations, certain assets or portions thereof are considered to have no value for statutory reporting purposes and are reflected as a direct reduction of surplus. Some examples of nonadmitted assets are equipment and furniture (discussed above), prepaid expenses, agent debit balances, and travel advances.

Special Reserves; Loss Recognition

Statutory accounting practices do not impose significant restraints on the establishment of reserves for specific concerns or contingencies, although sometimes such a reserve must be treated as a designated element of surplus, rather than as a liability. (This is consistent with the focus on achieving a conservative measurement of a company's financial position.) In general, any losses that arise from establishing a special reserve or provision are charged directly against surplus under statutory accounting practices.

Under GAAP, accounting for such a loss contingency can occur only if it is probable that both an asset has been impaired (or a liability has been incurred) and the amount of the loss can be estimated with reasonable accuracy. In contrast to statutory accounting practices, these losses are charged against income in the current year, rather than being charged directly to shareholder equity, and they are reported as a reduction of an asset or as a liability.

Differences in GAAP/Statutory Form

The previous section covered the principal differences between statutory accounting practices and GAAP accounting practices. These are the *substantive differences* between the two different approaches to life insurance financial reporting. In addition to these, there are also differences in the form of presentation of statutory and GAAP financial statements.

The basic statutory financial statement (the so-called "blue blank") has the three basic statement forms (a balance sheet, an income statement, and a cash flow statement) plus a large set of supplementary exhibits, schedules, and notes. The form of this package, which is prescribed in precise detail by the NAIC, tends to be specific to life insurance companies, quite detailed, and resistant to change. (This resistance to change is evident in the new lines, new pages, and new exhibits or schedules that are added instead of reformatting or eliminating existing material.) The GAAP financial statement is also composed of the three basic statement forms, plus a set of explanatory notes. Compared with the blue blank, however, the form of this package is much less oriented to the life insurance industry, has much less detail, and permits more tailoring of the notes to a company's specific circumstances.

Each stock company prepares a statutory financial statement and a GAAP financial statement. A mutual company must prepare a statutory financial statement, and some also prepare a hybrid type of statement using the GAAP format and statutory numbers. This hybrid statement permits clearer public communication, and it is used, for example, in annual corporate reports, and sales prospectuses.

To highlight the differences between SAP and GAAP, the illustrative balance sheets in table 30-1 and the income statements in table 30-2 compare the GAAP numbers for a hypothetical company with the statutory numbers in a hybrid format. Each table is presented after a discussion of the main entries on each statement.

Illustrative Balance Sheets

Table 30-1 presents illustrative GAAP and statutory (hybrid format) balance sheets for a hypothetical life insurance company. The text that follows describes each of the main entries on that balance sheet, along with the reasons for differences between the GAAP and statutory amounts.

The illustration in table 30-1 is for a large stock life insurance company without a downstream, majority-owned, noninsurance subsidiary. As explained earlier, under GAAP reporting, such a subsidiary would have to have been consolidated on a line-by-line basis, with a resulting distortion of the GAAP-statutory comparisons for the life insurance company being illustrated.

Balance Sheet Entries

Fixed-maturity investments consist of publicly traded debt securities, privately placed debt securities, and redeemable preferred stock. Fixed maturities that are intended to be held to maturity are generally carried at amortized cost under GAAP. The difference, if any, between the original cost and the face amount and maturity value of the investment is reduced ratably over the life of the security. When a fixed-maturity investment is purchased at an amount above its face value, that premium is amortized to reduce the value to its final redemption value. The annual amortization of premium is recorded as a reduction of interest income. If a fixed-maturity investment is purchased at an amount below its face value, the discount is accrued each year by increasing the value of the security and the interest income.

Fixed maturities are carried in the annual statutory statements at values determined primarily by the NAIC Valuation of Securities manual; in GAAP statements fixed maturities are generally carried at amortized cost or, if in or near default, at market value. The GAAP carrying values of publicly traded securities are adjusted for sustained impairments in value by actual writedowns; privately traded debt securities generally reflect such adjustments by means of a valuation allowance, although the use of writedowns is also acceptable. The GAAP and statutory amounts may differ because of differences between the NAIC values and the company's estimates of value, and either amount might be larger.

Equity securities consist primarily of common stocks and nonredeemable preferred stocks. Under statutory accounting, equity securities are reported at the values published in the NAIC Valuation of Securities manual, which is the NAIC market-value determination for each stock. For GAAP, common and nonredeemable preferred stocks are reported at market; temporary changes in those securities' market value are recognized as unrealized gains or losses in shareholder equity. Equity securities include investments in subsidiaries that, for statutory purposes, are usually reported on the equity basis (that is, cost adjusted for the company's share of income or losses after the date of acquisition). GAAP requires consolidation (including the subsidiary on a line-by-line basis) of majority-owned subsidiaries. This has the effect for GAAP of increasing the corresponding assets, liabilities, revenues, and expense line items and reducing the equity securities amount. In general, except for companies with consolidated subsidiaries, the GAAP and statutory amounts for this line should be very close.

Mortgage loans on real estate are generally reported under SAP at the unpaid principal balances, net of unamortized premiums or discounts. Premium amortization or discount accrual on mortgage loans is spread over the life of the loan in a manner similar to that for fixed maturities. Under GAAP, mortgage loans are similarly reported, less an allowance for amounts estimated to be uncollectible. The change in this valuation allowance is reported as a realized investment gain or loss. In general, therefore, the GAAP measure of this asset will be less than the statutory measure.

Real estate reported in the statutory financial statements includes three categories: real estate occupied by the company, investment real estate, and real estate acquired to satisfy debt. Under SAP, real estate occupied by the insurer and investment real estate are carried at cost, less accumulated depreciation and encumbrances (mortgage or other debt related to the property). Real estate acquired when a mortgage loan is foreclosed (not repaid) is valued at the estimated fair value of the property at the time of the acquisition, but it is not valued at more than the unpaid balance of the foreclosed loan.

On a GAAP basis, real estate is classified as either an investment or as real estate used in the insurer's operations (which is treated as property and equipment), depending on its primary use. Real estate investments are reported at cost, less accumulated depreciation and an allowance for impairment of value. Rent earned from real estate is recorded as investment income when earned and reported with related expenses on an accrual basis. Depreciation on real estate is recorded as part of the operating cost of the property. Real estate encumbrances are treated as liabilities.

If there are no encumbrances on owned real estate, the GAAP numbers will tend to be lower (because of the different treatment of real estate used in the company's operations), but this difference may be more than offset by the amount of encumbrances.

Policy loans are loans collateralized by the cash values of the underlying policies and are stated at unpaid principal balances. Policy loans receive the same treatment in statutory and GAAP accounting.

Short-term investments are investments maturing within one year such as commercial paper and money market instruments. They are carried at amortized cost. Short-term investments receive the same treatment in statutory and GAAP accounting.

Other invested assets are invested assets not included in the aforementioned investment categories. The principal investments are real estate joint ventures and partnerships. These assets are valued on an equity basis (cost adjusted for the company's share of income or losses after the date of acquisition). In the absence of real estate encumbrances, the GAAP and statutory amounts should be similar.

Cash and cash equivalents in statutory accounting are limited to monetary items, such as cash, demand deposits, and savings deposits. In GAAP, cash and cash equivalents include monetary items and Treasury bills, commercial paper, money market funds, and federal funds sold. (Federal funds are commercial bank deposits at Federal Reserve Banks. Any excess reserve that one bank maintains on deposit can be lent on an overnight basis to another member bank.) Cash and cash equivalents are valued similarly under statutory and GAAP accounting. The

GAAP amount will be larger than the statutory amount if the company holds any of the types of investments treated as cash and cash equivalents by GAAP but not by SAP.

Deferred policy acquisition costs are capitalized and amortized for GAAP reporting. Under statutory accounting, these expenses are charged against income in the year in which they are incurred.

Accrued investment income is income earned but not yet received on investments. It includes interest income on bonds, mortgage loans, policy loans, short-term investments, and dividends declared on common and preferred stock investments. Accrued investment income is treated similarly under statutory and GAAP accounting, and therefore there should be no material differences in this asset amount under the two accounting methods.

Premiums and other receivables are principally premiums due from policy-owners but not yet paid by the balance sheet date. In the case of statutory accounting, this entry also includes the net premiums (the premiums determined without provision for expenses) on traditional life insurance policies and annuity contracts that are due between the statement date and the next policy anniversary. This modification of due premium is necessary because the statutory reserves on these policies are determined on the assumption that the full net annual premium is paid on the policy anniversary. In addition, this line includes fees and policy charges due under universal life and annuity contracts. Because statutory accounting includes an expanded definition of due premiums (to balance the traditional statutory reserve calculation methodology), the statutory amount will be considerably greater than the GAAP amount. (For other types of businesses, statutory and GAAP financial treatment is similar.)

Property and equipment is property owned and occupied by the company, leasehold improvements, furniture and fixtures, and computer equipment. Under GAAP accounting, purchases of property and equipment are treated as assets and are depreciated over their useful lives. Under statutory accounting, except for computer systems, these expenditures are charged directly against surplus in the year of purchase. The statutory accounting treatment for computer systems is similar to the GAAP treatment. Typically, the GAAP amount for property and equipment is much larger than the statutory amount.

Other assets are miscellaneous assets that don't fall into the categories discussed above. These assets have generally comparable accounting treatments. Therefore the amounts shown in the statutory and GAAP financial reports should be similar if the same assets are used in both reports. There may be some differences, however, because of different definitions for some of the balance sheet entries discussed above. For example, assets under corporate-owned life insurance would be included in this item in statutory reporting but might be classified as investment assets in GAAP.

Separate account assets are segregated from those of the general account for the purpose of funding variable life insurance, variable annuities, pensions, and other benefits. The assets of separate accounts are similar to those of the insurer and may consist of fixed maturities, stocks, short-term investments, mortgages, and real estate. The investments of separate accounts are usually valued based on fair market value.

Except for real estate encumbrances, which are netted against the related real estate for statutory reporting and treated as a liability for GAAP reporting, separate account assets receive similar treatment in statutory and GAAP reporting. Therefore these amounts should be the same unless the company has a separate account with leveraged real estate. In that case the GAAP amount will be greater by the amount of the outstanding debt.

Policyowners' account balances and *future policy benefits* are an insurance company's principal liabilities and represent the reserves established to provide future benefits that will become payable under the provisions of the insurance policies and annuity contracts in force. The GAAP reserves and account balances will ordinarily exceed comparable statutory amounts.

Other policyowners' funds, for statutory reporting, include amounts deposited and accumulated for guaranteed interest contracts, dividends left on deposit (dividend accumulations), and other items of a similar nature. Certain policyowner obligations that are treated as other policyowner funds for statutory reporting are included in policyowner account balances for GAAP, and therefore the GAAP amount for this item will usually be less than the statutory amount. For example, the liability for supplementary contracts without life contingencies is included on this line for statutory reporting and in policyowners' account balances for GAAP reporting.

Policyowners' dividends payable are the company's liability for dividends due but not paid prior to the end of the accounting period, plus a provision for the accrued portion of dividends that will become payable in the following year. For statutory reporting on individual policies, the accrued portion is the full amount of dividends that will be payable in the following calendar year on policies in force at the end of the year. For GAAP reporting on individual policies, the accrued amount is the portion of the dividend that would have accrued since the last policy anniversary if the dividend had accrued evenly over the policy year. (The remainder of the liability is, in effect, a part of the GAAP reserve for future policy benefits.) In these circumstances, the GAAP amount for this item will be less than the statutory amount. For group insurance contracts, the accrued portion of the dividend under both GAAP and statutory reporting is determined for the elapsed portion of the year and is based on the experience of the period.

Short-term and long-term debt represent contractual obligations to pay money on demand or on a fixed or determinable date. For statutory reporting, long-term debt, such as mortgages and other debts on real property, is netted against the related asset. GAAP reports such debt as a liability. Accordingly, the GAAP amount will usually be larger than the statutory amount.

Federal income taxes payable have a current component and, for GAAP only, a deferred component. Current federal income taxes payable are accrued taxes as of the statement date. Deferred taxes, which apply only to GAAP reporting, were discussed in detail earlier in this chapter. Statutory and GAAP reporting methods for current taxes are similar; the only difference should be in reporting the deferred-tax item under GAAP.

Other liabilities represent liabilities that are not related to the policyowners, such as general expenses due and accrued, commissions due and accrued, and employee and agent postretirement benefit liabilities. GAAP and SAP treat amounts due and accrued and qualified pension plan liabilities the same way. With respect to other postretirement benefits (for example, pension benefits in excess of the federal qualified plan limits and postretirement life and health insurance benefits), there is a difference between GAAP and statutory reporting.

TABLE 30-1
Balance Sheet (Statement of Financial Position)
(Amounts in $ Millions)

	GAAP	Statutory (Hybrid Format)
Assets		
Investments		
Fixed maturities	17,470	18,000
Equity securities	400	400
Mortgage loans	12,390	12,690
Real estate	1,330	1,200
Policy loans	3,410	3,400
Short-term investments	150	150
Other invested assets	2,465	2,300
Total investments	37,605	38,140
Cash and cash equivalents	765	385
Deferred policy acquisition costs	3,100	
Accrued investment income	550	575
Premiums and other receivables	90	330
Property and equipment	140	20
Other assets	350	415
Separate account assets	17,600	17,300
Total assets	60,200	57,165
Liabilities		
Policyowners' account balances	24,400	
Future policy benefits	11,875	34,660
Other policyowners' funds	800	1,800
Policyowners' dividends payable	200	350
Short-term debt	5	5
Long-term debt	1,060	260
Federal income taxes payable		
Current	210	210
Deferred	350	
Other liabilities	900	500
Separate account liabilities	17,500	17,200
Total liabilities	57,300	54,985
Commitments and Contingencies		
Asset valuation reserve (AVR)		580
Shareholders' Equity (Surplus)		
Common stock	5	5
Capital in excess of par	445	445
Retained earnings	2,375	
Surplus		
Special surplus fund		80
Unassigned surplus		1,070
Net unrealized investment gains	75	
Total shareholders' equity	2,900	1,600
Total Liabilities and Shareholders' Equity	60,200	57,165

Moreover, in some cases, the statutory reporting is not well defined. The tendency in statutory reporting is to move toward the GAAP model of earlier recognition of these costs. Until this happens, however, the GAAP amount for this liability will usually exceed the statutory amount.

Separate account liabilities consist of the reserves established for the variable life insurance, variable annuities, pensions, and other benefits funded through separate accounts. The reserve amounts vary directly with the investment performance of the separate account assets. The separate account liabilities will generally be smaller than the separate account assets, usually an indication that a portion of the company's surplus is invested in these accounts. The measure of the separate account liabilities under GAAP reporting is larger than the measure under statutory reporting.

The *asset valuation reserve* is a general purpose investment reserve that is unique to statutory financial reporting. The purpose and basis of this reserve was described earlier.

Commitments and contingencies are items that are not recorded in the financial statements but that do have a risk of loss. A loss contingency may be recognized through a charge to income. Disclosure of the accrual of and sometimes the amount of the loss contingency is necessary. In cases where no amount has been charged to income or the exposure to loss exceeds the amount accrued, additional disclosure of the contingency may be necessary. Commitments and contingencies, including such items as future commitments to lend funds and financial guarantees, are disclosed in the footnotes of both GAAP and statutory financial statements.

Shareholders' equity is common stock, capital in excess of par, and retained earnings/surplus. Common stock represents the par value of the common stock issued; capital in excess of par is the amount in excess of the par value paid for the stock when the stock was first issued to owners or investors; retained earnings/surplus is the company's accumulated net income or loss, less any shareholder dividends paid. The net unrealized investment gains entry under GAAP represent the unrealized gains (or losses) on certain equity securities that have not been reflected in the financial statements. The difference between GAAP and statutory total shareholder equity amounts is the net effect of all of the differences between these two sets of accounting practices.

Illustrative Income Statements

Table 30-2 shows statutory and GAAP income statements for the same hypothetical company. The following are descriptions of the several lines of the illustrative income statements and the reasons for any differences between the GAAP and statutory amounts.

Income Statement Line Entries

Premiums are defined very differently in statutory and GAAP reporting. Under statutory reporting, both premiums received under traditional life and health insurance policies and deposits under universal life and annuity accumulation contracts are classified as premiums. Under GAAP reporting, only the premiums associated with traditional life and health policies are classified as premiums; the other premiums are treated like bank deposits—that is, there is no income amount recorded when the deposits are received or any charge for deposits withdrawn. Under both statutory and GAAP reporting, premium amounts include payments on both new and renewed business, and these amounts are reduced by premiums paid on reinsurance purchased (ceded). The statutory amount will be larger than the GAAP amount primarily because of this definitional difference and secondarily because the total premiums for traditional life insurance are somewhat greater. (See discussion above for balance sheet item "premiums and other receivables.")

Universal life and investment-type product policy fee income, a GAAP-only concept, represents the amount of fee income for the period related to these types of products. This fee income includes premium-based charges, mortality charges and withdrawal charges on surrender of policies or contracts. This item arises from the basic deposit-type treatment of these contracts under GAAP.

Investment income, net, is the largest component of revenues under GAAP and the next-to-the-largest component under statutory accounting. The sources of investment income are interest income, dividends, and other income earned on investments. Investment income is presented *net*—that is, expenses related to the investment are subtracted from the related income. On a statutory basis, real estate is reported net of encumbrances; therefore the interest expense on such debt reduces statutory investment income. Similarly, the effect of consolidating certain investments on a line-by-line basis for GAAP reporting versus the equity presentation for SAP will create additional differences between GAAP and statutory investment income.

Investment gains (losses), net, are measured differently under statutory and GAAP reporting. With respect to the gain (loss) on investments sold or otherwise disposed of during the year, the accounting treatment is similar under statutory and GAAP reporting, although the numbers may differ if the assets sold or disposed of have specific valuation allowances under GAAP. Realized and unrealized gains (losses) on investments held by the company are included in this item for statutory reporting. Under GAAP reporting, unrealized gains (losses) are not included in this item but instead are credited (charged) directly to capital. In addition, in GAAP reporting, provisions for or increases in valuation allowances and writedowns on invested assets are included in realized gains and losses.

Commissions, fees, and other income are miscellaneous sources of income not included in the above items. They can be created the same way under GAAP and SAP. When there are differences, GAAP tries to match them with the associated coverage period whereas SAP tries to match them with the associated premium-paying period.

Policyowner benefits paid or provided for represent the amounts paid or set aside for death benefits, annuity benefits, surrender benefits, and matured endowments. These benefits are reported on an incurred basis under both SAP and GAAP. They include benefit payments due but unpaid at the balance sheet date, reported claims for which payment has been delayed pending completion of processing, claims resisted, and an estimate of the claims incurred during the year that had not been reported to the company by the balance sheet date. This item also includes the increases in reserves for policyowner benefits (for statutory reporting) and the increases in reserves for traditional life insurance policies (for

GAAP reporting). Under GAAP, surrenders of accumulation-type products are treated as a return of a deposit and not included in this item. Accordingly, the GAAP amount should be less than the statutory amount.

Interest credited to policyowners' account balances is the amount of interest credited to policyowner account balances for accumulation-type products. It is recognized separately only for GAAP reporting.

Allocation to (from) AVR is the current period's charge (credit) for the net increase (decrease) during the accounting period in the asset valuation reserve for fixed maturities, common and preferred stock, mortgage loans, real estate, and joint ventures. (See earlier discussion of the AVR.) This applies only to statutory reporting.

Policyowner dividends are the charges for dividends to policyowners for the accounting period. This entry includes dividends paid in cash, as well as dividends applied to pay premiums or to increase policy values. Under statutory accounting, the charge is determined as the apportionment for dividends to be paid during the following year, adjusted for the difference between the dividends paid during the year and the apportionment at the end of the preceding year. Under GAAP accounting, the charge is the amount of dividends becoming due and payable during the current accounting period plus (less) the increase (decrease) in year-end dividend accruals. The statutory and GAAP amounts should not differ materially.

TABLE 30-2
Income Statement (Statement of Operations)
(Amounts In $ Millions)

	GAAP	Statutory (Hybrid Format)
Revenues		
Premiums	1,725	5,075
Universal life and investment-type product policy fee income	600	
Investment income, net	3,080	2,980
Investment gains (losses), net	(150)	(125)
Commissions, fees, and other income	25	25
Total revenues	5,280	7,955
Benefits and Other Deductions		
Policyowners' benefits paid or provided for	2,055	6,430
Interest credited to policyowners' account balances	1,440	
Allocation to (from) AVR		70
Policyowners' dividends	340	330
Other operating costs and expenses	875	825
Total benefits and other deductions	4,710	7,655
Income from continuing operations before federal income taxes	570	300
Federal income tax expense	195	100
Net income	375	200

Other operating costs and expenses include operating and other pretax costs that do not fall into the earlier categories. Under statutory reporting, this item is composed principally of operating expenses. Under GAAP it also includes the interest on encumbrances. Operating expenses can be influenced to some extent by either shortening or lengthening the period over which acquisition costs are recovered. By increasing the length of the acquisition cost deferral period, an insurer can lower the operating expenses and consequently increase the reported gain from operations. Similarly, shortening the deferral period for acquisition costs will usually increase the operating costs and reduce gains from operations.

Federal income tax expense is the charge against earnings for federal income taxes. In statutory reporting, this is basically the charge for taxes payable on the operations during the accounting period. In GAAP reporting, the amount of this item is essentially the federal tax charge that would have been incurred on the amount of GAAP pretax income.

Cash Flow Statements

Like the income statement, the cash flow statement presents the several elements of the company's cash flow for the fiscal year ending on the statement date. The GAAP (and hybrid statutory) cash flow statement divides the life insurance company's cash flow into three parts:

- cash flow from insurance operations including investment income earned on existing investments
- cash flow from investing operations including the proceeds from maturity or sale of investments, along with the reinvestment of these proceeds
- cash flow from financing, including the sale by the company of bonds or stocks for corporate finance purposes, the repurchase of outstanding bonds or stocks, and the payments of dividends to shareholders

The cash flow statement is very important for nonfinancial businesses because cash usually represents a scarce resource in business operations and investment. (Business growth usually entails growth of inventories and receivables with commensurate cash requirements.) For life insurance companies, the cash flow statement has traditionally not been of great importance because the normal operations of these companies typically produce strong, positive cash flows. In the early 1990s, interest in life insurance companies' liquidity and in cash flow statements was heightened by the failures of two major life companies that were attributed largely to policyowner "cash runs" that could not be satisfied by these companies' (relatively inflexible) portfolios of invested assets.

The cash flow statement in the blue blank statutory accounting form does not follow the three-part breakdown of the GAAP (and hybrid statutory) report. Rather, it resembles an income statement form but with each line item measured on a cash basis.

Schedules and Notes

In addition to the three standard statement forms, each audited GAAP statement (and each hybrid statement), contains a set of notes that enhance or explain the statements in general or that provide additional data or explanations for specific line items. The statutory blue blank has a more abbreviated set of notes but contains several exhibits and many supporting schedules. These notes, exhibits, and schedules support or expand on specific entries in the three basic blue blank financial report forms and provide additional operational information.

The supplementary information in both the GAAP (and hybrid) financial statements and the statutory blue blank includes the following:

- a description of the company's accounting policies and practices
- an analysis of invested assets
- an analysis of investment income and of capital gains and losses on investments
- an analysis of expenses
- analyses of revenue and earnings by line of business (statutory) and by business segment (GAAP)
- an analysis of the company's pension plan charge
- additional information on leases, litigation and contingent liabilities

Similarly, the exhibits and schedules that are part of the statutory blue blank include information about the following items that are not covered specifically in the GAAP financial statement:

- the amounts of life insurance sold and in force
- the income on annuity contracts sold and in force
- details on policyowner benefits, reserves, and liabilities
- a 5-year display of certain sales, coverage in force, and financial information

See chapter 31 for Part 2 of this discussion on financial statements and ratings. Chapter 31 focuses on rating agencies and ratings, regulatory measures, and comparative performance measures.

31

Financial Statements and Ratings (Part 2)

Harry D. Garber

From 1906 until the mid-1980s, A.M. Best, a rating service that specialized in the insurance industry, was the recognized rating service for life and property-liability insurance companies. Most large insurance companies had a top rating (then A+) from A.M. Best, and those that did not were at a disadvantage in marketing their products.

During the 1980s, the three multi-industry rating services (Standard and Poor's, Duff and Phelps, and Moody's) began for the first time to rate large numbers of life insurance companies. These ratings are known as claims-paying ability or financial strength ratings. They are an outgrowth of the ratings that had been assigned traditionally by these agencies to the long-term debt, commercial paper, and preferred stock issues of companies, including insurance companies. The major difference is that a claims-paying ability rating represents an assessment of a company's ability to meet its obligations to all of its policyowners, while the traditional rating related to a particular bond or stock issue. Coming at a time of concern about the solvency of the life insurance industry resulting from the failures of Executive Life and Mutual Benefit, the many bank failures, and the collapse of the commercial real estate market, the substantial growth in the number of life insurance companies rated by these widely respected, traditional rating agencies had a strong impact on the industry and its customers.

RATINGS

The three multi-industry rating services have substantially similar claims-paying rating definitions, although they often differ on the rating assigned to a particular life insurance company. The broad rating classes used and their definitions are as follows:

- Triple A (AAA)—the highest claims-paying rating; capacity to honor insurance contracts extremely strong and highly likely to remain so over a long period of time
- Double A (AA+, AA, AA−)—very strong capacity to honor insurance contracts; differs only in small degree from the highest rating category
- Single A (A+, A, A−)—strong capacity to honor insurance contracts, although such capacity may be susceptible to the adverse effects of changes in circumstances over a long time period
- Triple B (BBB+, BBB, BBB−)—ability to meet insurance contract obligations considered to be adequate under most circumstances but likely

to exhibit less stability in changing economic conditions over long time periods than the higher rating categories

● Double B (BB+, BB, BB−), Single B (B+, B, B−)—ability to honor insurance obligations under stressful circumstances regarded as speculative

● C ratings—ability to honor insurance obligations extremely speculative, and policyowners, in many cases, may not receive timely payment of their claims; company vulnerable to liquidation and may be under regulatory supervision

● D ratings—company has been placed under an order of liquidation

The above rating definitions are paraphrases of the definitions published by Standard and Poor's. Duff and Phelps uses virtually the same rating categories and definitions.

Moody's and A.M. Best use categories and definitions that are similar to those used by Standard and Poor's and Duff and Phelps. The principal differences are in category designations, as follows:

● Moody's uses 1, 2, and 3 to modify the ratings (for example, Moody's A 1 is equivalent to S&P's A+, Moody's A2 is equivalent to S&P's A, and so on).

● Instead of BBB, BB, and B, Moody's uses Baa, Ba, and B, respectively.

The rough equivalences of the A.M. Best and S&P categories are shown in table 31-1.

TABLE 31-1 Rating Equivalences	
A.M. Best	S&P
Superior (A++, A+)	AAA
Excellent (A, A−)	AA
Very good (B++, B+)	A
Good (B, B−)	BBB
Fair (C++, C+)	BB
Marginal (C, C−)	B

The distribution of A.M. Best's ratings and those of the three multi-industry rating services as of late 1991 are shown in table 31-2.

Although there are differences in the distribution of the four services' ratings, be careful in drawing conclusions from this comparison because the population of the companies rated by any two rating services differs, sometimes significantly. Given that the risk of failure to meet policyowner obligations differs very little between the top three broad rating classes (AAA, AA, and A), the industry as a whole is highly rated in its capacity to meet policyowner obligations.

When there has been a material change in the company's circumstances that the rating agency has not had the opportunity to evaluate fully or if there are expected future events that could have a significant effect on the company's position, the rating agency will often place the company on a *watch list*. The

TABLE 31-2
Distribution of Ratings of Life Insurance Companies

	Duff and Phelps	Moody's	Standard and Poor's	A.M. Best
AAA	25%	12%	30%	38%
AA	64	46	48	35
A	10	32	17	13
BBB	-	4	3	11
Below BBB	1	6	2	3
	100%	100%	100%	100%
Number of companies rated	77	79	201	765

published notice of this action will usually indicate whether there are positive, negative, or developing expectations. An expected capital contribution from a parent company is a positive future event; reported losses from a natural disaster that are materially higher than would have been expected for that company is an example of a negative event that will require additional evaluation.

RATING PROCESS

The rating process, as conducted by Standard and Poor's, Moody's, and Duff and Phelps, usually involves the following distinct steps:

- an advance review by rating agency analysts of statutory and GAAP financial statements for the last few years and related material (The statutory blue blank is the principal financial statement source used for rating purposes; the GAAP statements are used as supplementary information. See chapter 30 for a discussion of SAP and GAAP accounting.)
- a meeting of rating agency analysts with the company's senior officials and managers. The meeting will include a meeting with the company's chief executive officer and the company officials responsible for the business areas that are most likely to affect the final rating.
- a review by a committee of experienced insurance analysts of the material and observations gathered in the on-site visit to determine a tentative rating. The result will be communicated to the company, which can request an additional review if it believes that material information was not fully considered.
- publication of the final rating once it has been established by the rating agency, along with suitable explanations, particularly if the rating has been changed

There are slight variations in this general process among the three multi-industry rating services, and there can be other variations depending on the rated company's circumstances. For example, one rating agency invites company officials, at the beginning of the third step above, to meet with members of the committee that will make the rating decision.

Companies seeking ratings for the first time usually have the option of withdrawing the rating request if they do not agree with the agency's rating decision. For a company with an existing claims-paying ability rating, this is almost never an option because the public perception of a decision not to be rated would probably be worse than the rating itself.

The A.M. Best process includes the same elements as those of the other rating services, but the order of the steps differs because A.M. Best releases its annual ratings in the spring of the year. In addition, A.M. Best does not require visits with company officials each year.

Rating Criteria

The criteria used by the four principal rating services in reaching their rating decisions, not surprisingly, have a large degree of commonality. They involve elements that are quantitative and elements that are largely qualitative. The quantitative elements frequently involve comparisons to industry norms developed independently by each of the services. Since a claims-paying ability rating is an evaluation of the company's ability to meet obligations maturing in the future, even the quantitative elements (which are necessarily based on the company's past performance) must be tempered by qualitative judgments.

Because statutory blue blank reports are available for all life insurance companies, the quantitative analyses of the rating services are presently based on data drawn from these reports. GAAP financial statements are used to provide certain supplementary information for stock life insurance companies. When GAAP reporting becomes required for mutual companies, it is likely that GAAP financial information will take on more importance in the rating process.

Measurements of Present and Future Financial Strength

A claims-paying ability rating must measure the company's present financial strength (relative to its obligations for future policyowner claims) and whether the company's financial performance is likely to increase or decrease this financial strength in the future. In describing the elements that are taken into account by the rating services, it is useful to categorize them into elements that are used principally to measure the company's current financial strength and elements that are used principally to form an opinion about the company's future financial performance. (Of course, most of these elements will, at least to some extent, affect both a company's present position and its future performance.)

Elements to Measure Current Financial Strength

The elements that principally measure a company's current position are

- capital
- liquidity
- asset/liability values
- other insurance/investment risks

Capital is required to provide the safety margin (over and above the amount of reserves and other liabilities) to assure that the company will be able to invest (in its businesses), to grow, and to meet its commitments. The amount of capital depends on the size of the company and on the riskiness of the company's investment portfolio and insurance lines. For example, an investment strategy that emphasizes high-yield bonds requires more capital than a strategy that emphasizes government bonds. Similarly, Guaranteed Investment Contracts (GICs), which guarantee a return to contract owners, require more capital than variable contracts in which the investment earnings of a separate account are passed through to policyowners.

Liquidity is the company's ability to make large and unpredictable payouts to policyowners or to meet other obligations. To determine whether a company is in a good liquidity position, the rating service looks at the amount of the company's cash and short-term investments (usually those maturing in less than one year) and the likelihood of sudden cash calls. For example, a company with a large block of annuity contracts on which the cash surrender values are available without penalty presents a greater risk than a company whose book of business consists largely of life insurance policies sold to meet estate planning needs.

Asset/liability values are a key element. Because the company's asset and liability values are taken into account in measuring the amount of the company's capital, the degree of conservatism in their measurement is a very important factor to the rating services in reaching a decision. The key question on assets is the degree to which the asset values reflect appropriate reserves for likely or potential losses; in the case of liabilities, the question is whether the reserves have an adequate margin for future interest requirements and/or insurance losses. For example, if the company's investment earnings are currently insufficient to cover the interest requirements of its GIC contracts and are not expected to be sufficient in the future, a reserve equal to the contract funds would not, by itself, be adequate. (A judgment about reserve and liability adequacy should be made with respect to the aggregate of all reserves and liabilities because a shortage in one area may be covered by excesses in others.)

Other insurance/investment risks include the degree of asset or insurance concentration risk, the use of reinsurance to reduce risk, and the company's vulnerability to reinsurer default. A concentration of investments in a particular geographical area or business/industry or a concentration of life insurance in force on a relatively small number of insureds increases risk and is the subject of rating agency review. Reinsurance ceded can reduce large life and health insurance risks to the company but only to the extent that the reinsurer is financially strong.

Elements to Measure Future Financial Strength

The following are the key elements that the rating services focus on to form opinions about the company's future financial performance:

- management/strategy
- company's capabilities
- ability to finance

The *management/strategy* element involves a review of the experience and accomplishments of the company's senior management and a review of the company's future strategy in relation to the competitive dynamics of the industry, the company's ability to execute the strategy, and the availability of the financial and other resources needed to implement the strategy successfully. Many aspects of this evaluation are obviously qualitative in nature but supplemented by the available quantitative data. The key issue for the rating agency is whether the company has the leadership, the market positioning, the competitive advantages, and the resources to execute its strategy successfully, and if it does not appear to have the ingredients to be fully successful, what the consequences are of partial success or failure.

The *company's capabilities* element for a life insurance company is an analysis of the various elements of competitive advantage and sources of profit. This element is a critical factor in assessing the company's ability to increase revenue and profits and to maintain or improve its financial position. The key considerations include the company's (1) marketing and sales capability and positioning, (2) investing skills and the ability to achieve market-level spreads between investment income earned and interest credited on policyowner funds, (3) underwriting system and skills and the ability to achieve market-level spreads between mortality/morbidity charges to policyowners and the claims incurred, (4) efficiency in marketing company products and servicing the business in force, and whether these efficiency levels will enable the company to achieve and to maintain the unit expense levels incorporated in its pricing structure, and (5) ability to achieve competitive policy persistency levels with the accompanying beneficial effects on revenue growth and unit costs.

The *ability to finance* element is the company's ability to raise the capital it may need to finance its strategic plan and general growth or to strengthen a capital position that is presently sub-par or that may be eroded by future adverse events. In addition to the capital that could be generated within the company, the rating agency also considers the state of the capital markets, the ability and intent of a parent company (of the insurance company) to provide capital and the (limited) options a mutual life insurance company has to raise capital.

The four rating services examine each of these elements, although their approaches vary and their examinations may not entail all of the detail suggested by these descriptions. Nevertheless, it should be clear that a full analysis and understanding of a life insurance company's current and future financial position requires gathering and analyzing much more information than is available in the company's published financial statements.

REGULATORY MEASURES

A primary function of state regulators is to ensure that to the extent possible companies will be able to meet their current and future obligations to policyowners. Life insurance companies will have the financial capability to meet these obligations as long as they are solvent and operate with sufficient safety margins to ensure future solvency. In recent years the NAIC has concentrated on developing tools to identify companies that are currently solvent but have adverse operating trends or potentially insufficient capital to withstand a period of sustained losses. The purpose of these tools is to identify companies whose position and operations should be reviewed by state regulators. In many (or most) cases of the companies so identified, no regulatory action will be required because the regulatory review will have shown that the adverse operating trends that triggered the review are not material or that the company has already taken appropriate actions to remedy the problems. In other cases the regulators will find that the triggering conditions are material and that the company has not adequately addressed them. In these circumstances the regulators will oversee the development and implementation of a plan to remedy these conditions or trends.

The two types of tools state regulators currently use are the insurance regulatory information system (IRIS) ratios and, starting with 1993, Risk-Based Capital (RBC). Unlike the ratings of the rating services that are intended to be measures of company risk, these regulatory tools are not, and are not intended to be, such measures of risk. Additional investigation by regulators is required to determine if a company that "failed" the tests must take any actions and what these actions should be. Failure of these tests does not by itself indicate that a company has a significant risk of insolvency or impairment. This is true regardless of whether or not regulators make the company take remedial actions.

IRIS Ratios

The IRIS ratios are successors to the early warning system developed by the state insurance regulators about 20 years ago. They identify companies for whom regulatory review and perhaps regulatory oversight is appropriate.

IRIS involves 12 ratios for life and health insurance companies. Each ratio is computed as a percentage, and depending on the ratio, it may be positive or negative. The specific IRIS ratios are presented in table 31-3, along with the usual range for each ratio. To establish the usual ranges for the IRIS ratios, state regulators reviewed the ratios for companies that had become insolvent or had experienced financial difficulties in recent years. The NAIC expects that in any year 15 percent of the companies will fall outside the usual ranges on four or more ratios.

There are no specific rules that determine the degree of regulatory response for a company whose results fall outside the usual ranges in a number of the IRIS tests. The response depends on such factors as the number of outside-the-usual-range results, their severity, the trends in the number and severity of previous outside-the-usual-range results, and the effects of previous reviews and actions.

Risk-based Capital

The capital standards imbedded in state law for life insurance companies have traditionally been quite low, ranging from a few hundred thousand dollars in some states to $2 million in New York. Moreover, such standards have never adequately recognized company size or risk.

In the early 1990s the NAIC developed, in consultation with industry experts, a risk-based capital (RBC) measure. As indicated earlier, this measure is used to determine whether and to what degree regulatory intervention is required. The RBC measure first became a requirement with the 1993 financial statements.

Under the RBC approach, a company determines the RBC standard amount of capital and surplus (based on the RBC formulas) each year. It then compares

TABLE 31-3
IRIS Ratios for Life and Health Insurance Companies

Ratio	Title	Usual Range
1	Net Change in Capital and Surplus Ratio (percentage of growth in capital and surplus, excluding new paid-in capital and surplus)	−10% to 50%
1A	Gross Change in Capital in Surplus Ratio (percentage growth in capital and surplus)	−10% to 50%
2	Net Gain to Total Income Ratio (including capital gains and losses)	Greater than 0%
3	Not used	
4	Adequacy of Investment Income Ratio (ratio of investment income to interest required on reserves and credits on deposit funds)	125% to 900%
5	Nonadmitted to Admitted Assets Ratio	Less than 10%
6	Real Estate to Capital and Surplus Ratio	Less than 200% (a) Less than 100% (b)
7	Investment in Affiliates to Capital and Surplus Ratio	Less than 100%
8	Surplus Relief Ratio (ratio of net reinsurance allowances to capital and surplus)	−99% to 30% (a) −10% to 10% (b)
9	Change in Premium Ratio (growth in premiums)	−10% to 50%
10	Change in Product Mix (change in percentage of total premiums each product represents)	Less than 5%
11	Change in Asset Mix (similar to ratio #10 but for asset classes)	Less than 5%
12	Change in Reserving Ratio (reserving ratio in rates of increase in reserves to single and renewal premiums; computed for individual life only)	−20% to 20%

(a) companies with more than $5 million of capital and surplus
(b) companies with $5 million or less of capital and surplus

its actual capital and surplus, including the asset valuation reserve (AVR), to the computed RBC measure. The regulatory response, if any, depends on the results of this comparison. A company whose actual capital and surplus exceeds the computed RBC standard requires no regulatory action. If the company's actual capital and surplus falls between 75 percent and 100 percent of the computed RBC standard, the company is required to file a plan of the actions it intends to take to eliminate this gap with its state regulators. If the company's actual capital and surplus falls between 50 percent and 75 percent of the computed RBC standard, the home state regulator has an obligation to undertake a detailed review of the company's operations and to mandate corrective actions. If the company's actual capital and surplus is below 50 percent of the computed RBC standard, the company is considered to be a candidate for seizure by the state regulator.

Categories of Risk

During the 20 years leading up to the NAIC's formal adoption of the RBC standards, there was a steady evolution in the identification and evaluation of the risks facing life insurers. The actuarial profession classified risks into these four categories:

- C-1 risks (the risks of asset default)
- C-2 risks (insurance risks, principally mortality and morbidity)
- C-3 risks (interest rate deficiency risks)
- C-4 risks (other business risks)

In recent years Lincoln National Life Insurance Company and Moody's rating service developed and published capital and surplus standards by assigning weights to the amounts of assets and liabilities in specific categories and, in some cases, to the amounts of specific income and disbursement elements. There was considerable overlap in their approaches to evaluating capital requirements, and these approaches, along with formulas developed by the Minnesota and New York insurance departments, provided a useful starting point for the NAIC in developing the RBC methodology.

Assets. The RBC risk-assessment basis recognizes all of the four types of risk described earlier. The risk factor that is the most important in terms of the proportion of the company's RBC it represents is the C-1 (asset default) risk. Computations of the RBC objective for asset default risk take the following items into account:

- types of assets
- quality mix of assets, including the NAIC rating classes for bonds
- degree of diversification in an asset class
- mix of asset maturities

For example, the bond factors (before adjustment) range from 0.3 percent for AAA bonds to 30 percent for bonds in default. These basic rates are then multiplied by the applicable degree of diversification factor (based on the number of issuers whose bonds are held in the portfolio). For less than 50 issuers, this factor is 2.5; for 200 issuers the factor is 1.45; for 500 issuers, the factor is 1.16. For other key asset classes, the basic factors applied to the amounts of assets to determine the asset default risk are as follows: for mortgages, 0.1 percent to 20 percent, depending on quality level and company experience; for common stock, 30 percent; for owned real estate, 10 percent to 15 percent, but 20 percent if held in a partnership; and for cash and short-term investments, .3 percent. For large companies the asset default (C-1) risk constitutes almost 75 percent of the total calculated RBC standard. For smaller companies the percentage of the RBC standard attributable to C-1 risk factors is somewhat smaller.

Insurance. The C-2 (insurance risk) element is intended to provide additional protection (over and above the required reserves) for adverse trends and experience in life insurance mortality and/or health insurance morbidity or for premium inadequacies. The life insurance factors, which are applied to the net life insurance risk, decrease as the company's insurance risk amount increases; this element therefore is a relatively more important component of the RBC standard for smaller companies than it is for larger companies. The health insurance factors are applied to premiums and vary by both type of health insurance coverage (hospital and medical insurance, disability income, and so on) and premium volume, with lower ratios applying to premium amounts in excess of $25 or $50 million per year for a coverage. For both life and health insurance, smaller factors apply to group insurance than to individual coverages. The C-2 factors represent about 10 percent to 15 percent of the RBC standard for larger companies and, as noted above, a relatively greater percentage for smaller companies.

Interest. The interest risk (C-3) is determined by applying factors to the amounts of insurance reserves. These factors depend on the level of risk (low, medium, or high) and on whether the company has received an unqualified actuarial opinion. Low-risk reserves include individual life insurance reserves and individual annuity reserves that cannot be withdrawn or that have a low withdrawal risk because of a market value adjustment feature. Individual annuity reserves permitting surrenders at book value but with large surrender charges (5 percent or more) are considered to be medium risk. The interest-risk factors range from about 10 percent of the total RBC standard for larger companies down to less than 5 percent for smaller companies for whom the insurance risk is relatively more important.

Business. The business risk (C-4) factors are 2 percent of life insurance premiums and annuity considerations and 0.5 percent of health insurance premiums. This element generally constitutes 5 percent or less of the total RBC standard for companies of all sizes.

RBC Adjustment Formula

In recognition of the fact that there are interrelationships among the different types of risks and that the separate risk calculations may overstate the total risk requirement, the total of the four risk elements is adjusted using the following formula:

$$RBC = [(\text{asset risk} + \text{interest risk})^2 + (\text{insurance risk})^2]^{1/2} + \text{business risk}$$

The result is to reduce the RBC capital standard to about 80 percent to 90 percent of what it would have been without this adjustment. As an example, let's assume that a company has determined the following preadjustment RBC standards:

Asset risk	$750 million
Insurance risk	200 million
Interest risk	125 million
Business risk	50 million

After the adjustment, the RBC standard is $948 million, compared to $1.125 billion when the standard components are independently calculated.

Testing RBC Effectiveness

Because the RBC standard is so new, there has been no opportunity yet to test its effectiveness in helping companies and regulators prevent life insurance company failures and policyowner losses. Clearly, it is an improvement on the previous minimal capital standards. But whether a standard with such heavy emphasis on responding to the asset-risk lessons of the late 1980s and early 1990s will serve the industry and regulators well in the unknown (and certainly different) world of the late 1990s and into the next century without substantial modification is still to be determined. (For example, could the more conservative investment philosophy that will inevitably follow the emphasis on the asset-risk component of the RBC significantly increase the interest rate deficiency risk or substitute the asset-liability mismatching risk for the asset-default risk?) The other critical dimension will be state regulators' effectiveness in monitoring the progress or, in some cases, guiding the improvement efforts of companies whose capital and surplus fall below the computed RBC standard.

The purpose of the RBC calculations and comparisons is to identify companies where regulatory oversight and action may be beneficial in preventing future failures and policyowner losses. There is no compelling evidence, however, that a company whose capital and surplus approximates the computed RBC standard has significantly greater risk than a company with substantially more capital and surplus (say, 150 percent of the computed RBC minimum standard). Except for companies with very weak current capital positions, the risk of future failure usually depends more on future business actions and results than on current capital strength.

Beginning in 1993, a company's statutory financial statement must disclose its total adjusted capital (the amount of the company's capital and surplus for purposes of the RBC comparison) and its authorized control level of capital (the amount of capital below which the regulators are authorized to seize the company), which is 50 percent of the computed RBC standard. RBC results are intended to be kept confidential, and there are explicit prohibitions on the use of

RBC results in a company's sales promotions and advertising. Nevertheless, it will not be difficult for outside parties to prepare lists showing the ratio of each company's actual capital and surplus to the computed RBC standard and for these lists to become available to policyowners and prospective policyowners.

COMPARATIVE PERFORMANCE MEASURES

Most life insurance products are long term, and policy benefits and policy-owner costs are not fixed at issue but depend on postissue company actions. Such actions include changes in the dividend scale (for participating business) and changes in interest crediting rates, mortality charges, or expense charges on accumulation and variable-type products.

As the insurance market has become more and more competitive, many policyowners, agents, and advisers have evidenced an increased interest in measures of insurance companies' financial position and performance. Companies' interest in comparing their performance to their peer companies' performance in several key areas has also increased. In addition to the analyses made by individual companies, several organizations have begun to measure and promulgate such comparative information. For the most part, these comparisons are based on information drawn from the statutory blue blank financial statements, which are available for all companies—mutual and stock—and contain more information related to pricing decisions than do the GAAP or hybrid financial reports. However, these published analyses can rarely, if ever, be used to demonstrate or measure real differences between companies or to highlight a company's standings among its peers. At best, they can be used as general directional pointers.

Financial Position and Performance Measures

The published comparisons tend to focus on a company's financial strength, earnings growth, and sales and growth of the insurance lines.

With respect to financial strength, many measures have been developed and published over the years to compare the relative financial strength of the leading life insurance companies. These have, typically, been ratios of capital (usually defined as surplus plus the asset valuation reserve) to one or more measure of risk (assets, reserves, and so forth). As companies diversified their investment portfolios by type and quality and their liabilities became equally diverse, these broad general ratios have become virtually meaningless. This diversity must be brought into any competitive calculations, but even then the results must be used with great caution because the relative risk measures assigned to different types of assets and liabilities are themselves often arbitrary. The RBC standard, which is probably the most sophisticated approach to such a standard, is used by the regulators only to highlight companies for further investigation and, if necessary, action. The rating agencies never base ratings solely on current measures of financial strength (unless the company is bordering on insolvency) but look at the combination of current financial strength and current and future earnings power.

With respect to earnings growth, the standards used most frequently are the various earnings-per-share measures included in the GAAP financial statements. Statutory measures of income are less valuable because of SAP's emphasis on conservative measurement of assets and liabilities and the prevalence of certain types of reinsurance transactions.

Regarding sales and growth in business, the statutory statement contains information that can provide bases for reasonably good comparisons among companies. A better service is the Life Insurance Management and Research Agency (LIMRA), which surveys a large group of companies to obtain consistent measures of new business for different types of coverage.

Pricing Performance Comparisons

Information on companies' performance in the key areas (investment return, mortality and morbidity, expenses, and persistency) that affect prices and nonguaranteed benefits is of great interest to competitors, customers, agents, and advisers. Many firms develop and publish various types of comparative measures to provide insights to these interested parties. Most are of limited value.

The reason these comparisons are limited in value is that modern pricing techniques recognize the particular characteristics of the markets the companies serve and the unique costs of providing coverage in those markets. Often there are trade-offs among different cost factors. For example, much business insurance is written on a guaranteed-issue basis, with the additional mortality cost covered by reduced commissions and underwriting cost savings. Most analyses of a company's experience and intercompany comparisons drawn from data in financial reports, on the other hand, must necessarily aggregate results for all markets the company addresses and, in some cases, for all lines of business. If a company that has a sizable amount of the business insurance described above is compared on an aggregate basis with a company that sells all of its insurance with full underwriting and full commissions, the former will show higher average mortality and lower average expenses. Although this statement is true, it has no significance because the customer purchases a product designed for a particular market, and the information required to compare the past and anticipated experience of the two companies in that market is almost never available from the companies' financial statements.

Theoretically, therefore, much information can be determined from a company's financial reports, but as described above, the information is usually too aggregated to be relevant to the company's pricing decisions in the market(s) of interest to the agent or policyowner. For example, in the case of investment income, companies usually have several portfolios of investments, each backing one or more classes of business. In addition, if the company prices on a "new money" basis, the overall portfolio rate does not reflect the rates for different classes of business. It is impossible to determine from the financial statements what investment return a company is earning on the assets associated with a particular class of business or how this performance compares with the comparable business of other companies.

The problem is even more complex in the case of mortality experience. Mortality expectations vary by age, sex, type of underwriting (for example, medical, paramedical, nonmedical, or guaranteed issue), and number of years since issue. Although the blue blank statements do show the net mortality costs (death claims incurred less reserves held) for the financial period, the information is of little value without an understanding of the company's expected mortality costs (based on the distribution of business by risk class) and its pricing objectives, which are simply not available from the published financial statements. There is a similar problem with respect to morbidity under health insurance policies, although the smaller level of policy accumulations and the absence of cash values mean that there is a closer connection between the premiums charged and the expected morbidity.

With respect to expenses, the statutory blue blank discloses the amounts of a company's commissions, general insurance expenses, and taxes for each principal line of business. There are also exhibits that present additional details on the components of these three expense categories but without a full breakdown by line of business. It is possible therefore to determine many ratios of expenses to various measures for a life insurance company's book of business. While these expense ratios can give a general indication of a company's expense situation, they cannot mark the company's exact standing with any degree of precision. The problem is the same as that described for mortality. Expenses vary significantly by policy year (acquisition costs are vastly higher than renewal administration costs), size of policy, type of coverage (variable universal contracts involve more service and administrative costs than term insurance, for example), type of customer (individual versus business), and market served. The pricing used by the company ordinarily reflects these differences. Unless two life insurance companies have remarkably similar portfolios of business, it is impossible to determine from any general expense ratios gathered from information in their financial statements whether a company is meeting its pricing expense objectives or whether there is a significant difference in the expense levels of two companies that would affect future pricing actions.

Since there is no way of knowing how any two companies match up in terms of their business profiles and expense objectives, the published expense ratios developed from financial statements must be used with extreme caution. Even intercompany expense studies within the industry are often difficult to understand and interpret because of different organizational approaches and accounting classifications.

32

Life Insurance Company Investments

Francis H. Schott

Over the past 20 years the role of investment performance and policy has evolved from being a mere adjunct of product and sales management to becoming the lifeblood of a life insurance company. Instead of insurance driving investment, we encounter in the 1990s a dynamic interaction of the two sides of the business. Overall success depends on the profitable integration of the accumulation and disposition of funds.

HISTORICAL PERSPECTIVE

Effects of Inflation and Technology

This historic development was caused by the sharp acceleration of inflation in the late 1970s and early 1980s and the attendant near tripling of interest rates between 1975 and 1982. Long-term investments in bonds and mortgages had dominated insurance portfolios as the counterpart to whole life policies, the main accumulation product. These investments, with an average maturity of roughly 20 years, turned out to leave the industry behind in terms of yield on the savings element of life insurance as market rates of interest adjusted to inflation. Large parts of the industry became noncompetitive in attracting funds and subject to heavy outflows through surrenders and policy loans as policyowners took their savings elsewhere.

Initially in self-defense but later as an aggressive sales tool, the industry developed universal life and other products to compete with the then higher current yields by passing investment yields directly through to policyowners, encouraging in turn a scramble for high-yield investments and competition for funds based on interest rates. The nature of insurance contracts makes it nearly impossible for an insurer to make major and significant changes instantaneously. Two significant tactics were utilized to speed up such adjustments: (1) the start-up of brand new subsidiary insurance companies with the entire portfolio invested at current yields and (2) the exchange of old, in-force policies with new contracts containing lower premiums and variable interest rates for policy loans.

Interest-rate-based competition survived the relatively short period of historically high yields, which ended by the early 1990s. The investment field is now dealing with the consequences. One of these consequences is the broadening of buyers' choices for insurance products and investment vehicles for the life insurance savings dollar. Another is an increase in the number of life companies that failed as sharpening competition cut into product margins and encouraged heightened investment risk-taking. Still another result is that annuities, with their highly visible yield link, have become more important than insurance in generating investable funds. The average maturity of the typical insurer's portfolio has also been cut in half, to roughly 10 years, both to minimize the yield lag if accelerating inflation returns and to accommodate the escape clauses in their contracts that corporate and individual policyowners now demand in anticipation of resurgent high interest rates and high inflation rates.

On the more technical side of portfolio management, investment executives have had to learn and implement new technical and analytical skills. First and foremost, they have had to evaluate the liability characteristics of different insurance products with respect to a more detailed and complex set of risk classification categories to arrive at correct maturity and risk characteristics of the corresponding assets. One aspect of this process has been termed *segmentation of the general account* (grouping assets according to their risk characteristics and establishing criteria to maintain prescribed ratios of holdings in each of these risk categories). Second, the rising risk of policyowners' massive and instantaneous withdrawal of funds has required not only shorter asset maturities but also protective techniques (such as staggered maturities) and the increased use of liquid instruments (such as U.S. Treasury and agency securities). In addition, options, futures, and other partial offsets to a riskier environment have become routine among many companies. Finally, the search for inflation protection has led some companies into enlarged equity positions in the general account, mainly through the use of equity kickers,[1] warrants, or similar devices attached to debt instruments.

The "financialization"[2] of life insurance portfolios has created new problems for regulators, policyowners, and investors. Excess debt generated during the 1980s among corporations and commercial real estate interests was spurred to dangerous levels by the supercharged speculation by individual investors based on expectations of continued high levels of inflation. This was extensive among depository institutions such as savings and loan companies, but to a moderate degree also among competition-driven insurance companies. Consequently, insurance regulators backed off in the late 1980s and early 1990s from the liberalization in the early 1980s of the quantitative investment rules that had long been a characteristic of insurance laws. The trend in the early 1990s was in the opposite direction—toward detailed limitations on the insurer's portfolio composition. Lowering the allowable proportion of low grade (junk) bonds is but one example. Substantial discretion—a *prudent-man rule*—continues to prevail for much of portfolio management.

Interaction between Regulators and Rating Agencies

As financial pressures increased through narrowing spreads on traditional insurance products, fierce competition in new product yields, and the rising cost of outside capital, commercial rating agencies entered the life insurance field for the first time in a serious and sustained manner. After the failures at Baldwin United and Charter Securities in the mid-1980s, ratings became important in the markets and to the companies. The negative publicity generated by a few major insurance company failures in the early 1990s (Executive Life, Mutual Benefit Life) prompted both insurance agents and insurance consumers to increase their insistence on dealing only with insurers having the highest-quality ratings.

An interaction of regulators and rating agencies developed as each sought to generate early warnings for the public, policyowners, and investors. Much of the attention of both regulators and rating agencies was focused on the investment portfolio.

The overexuberance and debt overhang of the 1980s was especially apparent in rising mortgage delinquencies and a moderate rise in nonperforming bond holdings. The entire experience of failures and widespread writedowns led the insurance regulators toward broadened asset reserves effective in late 1992, careful calculation of investment factors within the risk-based capital standards expected to be effective in all states by the end of 1994, and development of a National Association of Insurance Commissioners (NAIC) Model Investment Law. The NAIC has tightened up its self-examination procedures to make sure that agreed-upon laws and regulations are actually enforced in each state.

Meanwhile, the search for new capital—simply to grow modestly or just to stay in business, quite apart from regulation—began to dominate industry thinking in the early 1990s. Traditional conservatism reasserted itself in all phases of insurance management. Nevertheless, two decades of rapid evolution have strengthened and broadened the investment function in many important ways. Investment officers have acquired a far greater knowledge of market instruments, are more flexible and adaptable in their use of instruments and techniques, participate more in insurance product development and marketing, and are wiser to the perils of the marketplace. Should the country's economic performance improve in the second half of 1990s, investment management is poised to take advantage of developing opportunities and, one hopes, will not forget the lessons of the 1980s.

LIFE INSURANCE PORTFOLIO MANAGEMENT

Role of the Industry in Investment Markets

Some of the changes generated by life insurance's increased investment orientation are revealed by changes in the industry's aggregate assets. (See table 32-1.)

The first—and a crucial—observation is that despite economic instability and rapid change, the growth rate of industry assets over the 16-year period from 1975 to 1991, at over 11 percent annually, has been ahead of the inflation rate and comfortably in line with the average of other financial institutions. The industry has avoided such disasters as have befallen the savings and loan and mutual savings bank industries. (The number of these industries has shrunk by more than one-third over the 16 years covered. Widespread failures occurred as a consequence of excessive risk-taking in real estate and frequent fraudulent practices, associated partly with inadequate supervision.)

The life insurance industry has also done better than commercial banks because the industry has successfully adapted its products to the public's greater financial orientation. On the other hand, insurance has not grown as rapidly as mutual funds and money market funds because liquidity and flexibility in response to changing consumer demand have only gradually become life insurance industry attributes.

TABLE 32-1
Distribution of Assets of U.S. Life Insurance Companies

	1975		1991	
	$ billions	% of total	$ billions	% of total
U.S. government (Treasury)	$ 4.8	1.7	$ 77.8	5.0
U.S. government (agencies)	1.4	0.5	164.2	10.6
Corporate bonds	105.8	36.6	623.5	40.2
Mortgages	89.2	30.8	265.3	17.1
Stocks	28.1	9.7	164.5	10.6
Real estate	9.6	3.3	46.7	3.0
State and local government	4.5	1.5	10.2	0.7
Foreign government	4.5	1.5	17.3	1.1
Policy loans	24.5	8.5	66.4	4.3
Miscellaneous assets	17.0	5.9	115.3	7.4
Total	$289.4	100.0	$1,551.2	100.0

Source: American Council of Life Insurance (ACLI) *Fact Book,* 1992.

Changes in Investment Characteristics

Investments generally considered long term (corporate bonds and mortgages combined) accounted for over two-third of total investments in 1975 but were down to about 57 percent in 1991. The industry continues to be a leading supplier of corporate debt and commercial mortgage funds, holding about one-third of corporate bonds and one-quarter of commercial mortgages outstanding at the end of 1991. Yet the shift toward annuities and guaranteed interest contracts (GICs)[3] as sources of funds, together with the need for liquidity in a volatile external environment, has led to major changes in the characteristics of these investments.

First, the average maturity of the "nonmarketable" part of long-term investments has been cut sharply. Crudely and imprecisely, as average maturity was halved, the annual turnover rate of the portfolio was doubled in the 16-year period covered in table 32-1 to roughly 10 percent. This permits a more frequent "fresh look at your money," including its use to pay off liabilities instead of reinvesting.

Second, both bonds and mortgage investments have been heavily redirected toward public securities rather than toward directly negotiated deals with debtors. Thus marketable bonds (including privately issued mortgage-backed bonds) have gained heavily at the expense of direct placements, and securitized mortgages (including especially pass-through securities and collateralized mortgage obligations (CMOs) of federal housing agencies) have virtually become the exclusive life insurance method of investing in residential mortgages. (Efforts to securitize commercial mortgages are hampered by the individualized characteristics of commercial structures and by high underwriting costs associated with parcel-by-parcel securitization.)

Third, the tripling of United States government securities in their share of life insurance investments over the period studied is confirmation of the liquidity drive of the industry. (The $242 billion figure for U.S. Treasury and agency securities at year-end 1991 includes over $130 billion of federally backed mortgage securities, where good yield or "portfolio fit" with liabilities may count as heavily as liquidity *per se*.)

Separate Accounts, Pooled Separate Accounts

Common stocks in insurance companies' general accounts are limited to 10 percent of assets under New York insurance law, which tends to dominate investment regulations throughout the country. The desirable liquidity characteristic of equities is deemed to be largely offset by the problem of substantial price and total-return fluctuations of common stocks. The industry's general account holdings have remained well below the legal limit, but total holdings have risen to above 10 percent because separate accounts have gained relative to the general account. In such accounts, the nonguaranteed return of best-effort stock market investing flows through directly to the client. Separate accounts originated with the competition for corporate pension funds. Common stocks account for as much as 50 percent of aggregate pension fund assets because it is hoped that long-term equity gains may reduce the cost of pensions to companies. Hence insurance companies had to be granted separate-account powers (in the 1960s) to compete effectively for pension fund management.

Since the mid-1980s, the growth of investment choices and client discretion in growing individual products, such as variable life and deferred annuities, has provided a new vehicle for life insurance investment in common stocks — pooled separate accounts of individual clients. Bond funds for such clients are also growing. In the mid-1980s separate accounts passed the 10 percent mark as a share of life insurance assets, and they are likely to gain further in the 1990s — a clear manifestation of the rising importance of investment management in attracting funds to insurance companies. Separate accounts are advantageous to the industry because the impending risk-based capital standards treat such accounts lightly; the client, not the company, bears the risk.

Enhanced Liquidity

The growth of policy loans during disintermediation[4] periods was the original reason for turning toward enhanced liquidity in life insurance portfolios. When market interest rates were above those that insurance companies were able to charge contractually, as occurred during tight-money episodes, it paid the insured to take out a policy loan. (The proceeds could be invested at a rate above that paid to the insurance company, or borrowing at rates in excess of the cost of a policy loan could be avoided.) Legal and regulatory changes, combined with redesigned contracts, have enabled companies to whittle down the policy loan share of assets. Loan rates are now indexed to a bond market rate, or if they are fixed, tend to be at 8 percent. Yet concerns about liquidity and policy loan earnings remain.

Investment Organization and Principles

Life insurance investment has always been a spread business in the sense that management seeks a yield on investments in excess of the implicit rate credited to policies as their cash value grows over the years. Until universal life became a factor in the mid-1980s, however, this spread was known to very few and understood by even fewer. Business judgments and accounting factors relating to mortality, commissions, and operating expenses often helped to mask the investment yield spread and related issues. Once interest rates and/or equity performance became explicit, competition forced an all-around sharpening of pencils, and margins in general shrank. Meanwhile, the product portfolio was constantly expanding during the 1980s, and differential characteristics among products forced product-by-product asset management.

One obvious way to manage assets on a product-by-product basis is the individualization of product accounts. Thus whole life, universal life, single-premium life, variable life, single-premium annuities, and GICs for corporate savings plans can each be considered a specialized asset/liability problem subject to individual solutions. This may involve establishing product-differentiated subsidiaries of a parent company, formal separate accounts, or internal segmentation of the general account. Creating product-differentiated subsidiaries or separate product accounts typically requires much legal work and regulatory approval. Segmentation, however, is almost entirely at management's discretion, provided that the company makes no attempt to avoid its *de facto* responsibility for all liabilities, regardless of its internal accounting.

Investment management's first task in segmentation is to develop criteria by which to distinguish investment policy by product. The scheme in table 32-2 helps to illustrate the criteria and possible outcomes of such deliberations.

This scheme is far from noncontroversial. Moreover, it is only a sample of products and criteria. Thus the intuitive results—such as life insurance requires less liquidity than annuities and GICs, and total yield requirements are highest in the most investment-oriented and interest-sensitive products—are subject to further evaluation. For example, the specific withdrawal provisions of the company's single-premium deferred annuities (SPDAs) and the term distribution of the portfolio make a difference. Stiff back-end withdrawal penalties, a long stretch-out phase for the expiration of such penalties, and a large percentage of annuities to which the penalties still apply all work toward making the portfolio less susceptible to withdrawal and therefore to liquidity requirements, and *vice versa*. Because product and asset characteristics interact, they must be determined by simultaneous equations.

The recency of product differentiation and asset segmentation suggests that much in the type of scheme outlined here remains subject to review on the basis of future experience, especially for investment-sensitive products. The average duration of the huge amount of SPDAs put on the books in the late 1980s and early 1990s is unknown, as is the percentage of outstanding SPDAs still subject to surrender charges. Nor have all of the new products yet undergone a full interest rate and economic cycle. Nevertheless, asset/liability management by product is a vital step forward in making (eventually profitable) business decisions, and enough time has passed to permit verification of the direct relevance of surrender terms to the likelihood of actual withdrawal.

TABLE 32-2
Sample Characteristics of "Appropriate" Investment Portfolios by Product

	Liquidity Need	Duration	Total Yield Needs
Whole life	−	+	−
Universal life	=	+	=
Single-premium deferred annuities (SPDAs)	+	−	+
Guaranteed interest contracts (GICs)	=	−	+

= (portfolio average)
+ (above portfolio average)
− (below portfolio average)

Source: Author's consultations with life insurance investment officers.

Practical Investment Decisions and Problems

A study of yield curves offers a crude, yet instructive, approximation of the practicalities of modern investment management. At any given moment, an almost infinite variety of interest rates of the market confronts the financial intermediary who seeks funds for investment. To protect against interest rate risk means matching assets and liabilities, at least approximately, along the yield curve (defined as an array of interest rates by maturity of the underlying debt).

The normal yield curve is sloped upward because price and credit risk—as well as uncertainty itself—tend to increase with maturity. The steepness of this upward slope, however, varies sharply with the business cycle phase. Generally the slope is steepest at or near the bottom of the cycle and flattens as full employment and inflation dangers approach. About one-fifth of the time from 1970 to 1990 the yield curve was inverted—that is, short rates exceeded long rates, typically under the influence of the extremely restrictive monetary policy during inflation and interest rate peaks.

Figure 32-1 offers a sampling of yield curves for United States government and selected corporate securities at a reasonably "normal" time. It shows a total spread of about 9 percentage points between very short and highest-grade securities (90-day U.S. Treasury bills) and the longest low-grade corporate bonds (B-rated high-yield, or junk bonds of 10 years' maturity). Figure 32-1 also shows the relatively small spread between U.S. Treasuries and investment-grade (A-rated) industrial bonds. Even a difference of one-quarter point in average yield on the portfolio, however, can be highly significant to an insurance company's bottom line.

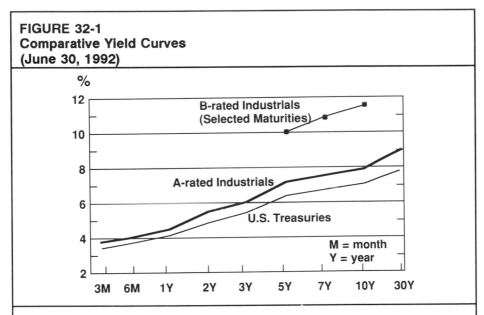

FIGURE 32-1
Comparative Yield Curves
(June 30, 1992)

U.S. Treasuries are Treasury bills (up to and including one year), Treasury notes (2-year to 10-year securities), and bonds (up to 30 years). A-rated Industrials are investment-grade industrial-company commerical paper (up to one year) and bonds beyond one year. B-rated Industrials are below-investment-grade (junk) bonds, with quotes available only in the 5-to-10-year maturity range.
Sources: Federal Reserve, Equitable Capital.

Investment Diversity

The first and most important point is that life insurance companies now operate throughout the maturity spectrum as they seek outlets for withdrawable funds generated by investment-sensitive insurance products. As late as the early 1970s, the industry operated almost exclusively at the long end of the yield curve (with only a marginal involvement at the shortest end).

A second key point is that the industry has also diversified by type of investment. As mentioned earlier, there has been a rise in public corporate bonds (compared to private placements) securitized mortgages, and directly negotiated deals. One may add junk bonds for general account or separate account investment, a greater variety of common stock and bond portfolios for pension or new-product investments (growth, income, or balanced accounts, for example), and the increased involvement of a few companies in equity real estate through such devices as joint ventures with developers (the insurance company receives a share of the equity in return for supplying a long-term mortgage). This diversity has added to the complexity of investment operations in a new-product environment for insurance. It has also created new wrinkles in investments that enhance the ability to ferret out additional niches of funds (with or without a major insurance component).

Attendant Risks

It stands to reason that increased complexity brings difficult problems. Among these, the actual process of matching maturities of assets and liabilities stands out. The first difficulty is that retail insurance sales cannot be matched with regularity and precision in an investment operation that has to be wholesale to be efficient. The very nature of an insurance company therefore creates a degree of mismatch. The second difficulty is that the actual maturity of liabilities may be misjudged or be in fact unpredictable. The disintermediation episodes of the 1970s and 1980s showed that even whole-life-based liabilities could suddenly "mature" by having contracts surrendered or cash reserves borrowed against if market rates exceeded inside rates by a large margin. The late 1980s and early 1990s may well prove that the prepayment risk on high-interest securities is a very real one when the general interest rate level turns down. A third (and fundamental) difficulty is that the cost of acquiring the liabilities may preclude precise maturity matching at orthodox credit risk levels.

Failure to resolve this last difficulty was at the bottom of most insurance company crash landings of the late 1980s and early 1990s. The "best" solution—foregoing the business—may be unacceptable to top management. Other noninvestment answers include reducing the expense margins necessary to acquire and administer the liabilities (possible but painful) and stiffening the backload penalties for withdrawals and thus reducing their probability (also possible but subject to the same competitive pressures that caused the problem in the first place).

The temptation therefore is to do one of the following: (1) risk a mismatch by taking in assets with longer maturities than the most probable maturity of liabilities, which improves the calculated financials in a normal yield-curve environment, or (2) take additional credit risk, thus obtaining higher returns at any given maturity of the yield curve. A third risk is diversifying investments insufficiently, which may or may not be directly related to the yield curve. Thus in the failure of Executive Life (California and New York, 1991), First Capital Life of California (1991), and Fidelity Bankers Life (Virginia, 1991) extra yield was obtained through excessive credit risk and concentration in junk bonds. (At Executive Life, maturity matching appeared to be very good until suspicions led to mass withdrawals, especially of SPDA funds, regardless of back-end penalties.) In the case of Mutual Benefit Life (New Jersey, 1991) an unusual concentration in one asset class and location—Florida mortgages—constituted a maturity mismatch, as well as an excessive credit risk, during a major commercial real estate recession.

Some Technical Aspects of Investment Management

The keen competition among asset managers has forced life insurance portfolio management to adopt highly technical and sophisticated evaluation and simulation models. The rapid evolution of academic finance and computer calculating capacity has also been a major factor in making the rigorous analysis feasible.

Duration Balancing

In practice, asset/liability matching is approximated through duration balancing of blocks of business (general account segments or their subsets). Duration, a traditional concept of bond finance, measures the weighted average maturity to term of a series of cash flows arising from an obligation. (For example, the less frequent interest and principal repayments are, the longer the duration of a bond. Thus duration can differ among two bonds of identical average and final maturity.) The duration of the corresponding liabilities tends to be even more difficult to estimate than that of assets, but even assets can deviate from initially calculated duration if restructuring or defaults occur, or if they have prepayment or call options. Thus the reinvestment risk for the large blocks of mortgage-backed securities acquired in recent years is considerable. The underlying mortgages can typically be prepaid when interest rates decline, and new securities can be substituted only at lower interest rate earnings while rates payable on the corresponding liabilities may not be equally adjustable.

In addition, duration itself changes with interest rate changes so that the value of any portfolio will tend to diverge from initial calculations. A concept known as *convexity* measures the variability of portfolio asset durations in response to interest rate changes. Convexity helps to define acceptable limits on the asset side to the almost inevitable mismatches of duration of liabilities.

Barbell Strategy

Barbell strategy is a concept applied in both liquidity and risk management. A portfolio may be forced into sufficient liquidity by having one concentration of assets at the shortest end of the yield curve while another concentration at the long end provides excess return over the yield requirements of the corresponding liabilities and thus offers a profit potential. Precisely the same strategy may be applied in concentrating on low-risk and high-risk assets rather than accepting middle-range risk throughout the portfolio. The measured weighted risk can therefore remain acceptable even while investment managers hope to exploit the potential extra return of, say, junk bonds or equity warrants. (Barbell strategy bears a family resemblance to traditional life insurance investment at only the shortest and longest maturity ends. Naturally, a barbell-weighted portfolio will not perform as hoped for when the yield curve steepens. The long securities may decline in value, while the short securities gain little, if any, in price.)

Hedging

Derivative securities transactions have multiplied immensely in financial markets and have gradually been practiced in life insurance investment management. New York insurance law restricts such transactions by characteristics and amounts; only hedging (and not speculating) is permitted, and amounts outstanding may not exceed 15 percent of admitted assets. Financial futures, options, and interest rate swaps have come into use, with hedging through Treasury bond futures contracts developing into a very broad and liquid market—possibly constituting the most frequent operation.

Suppose an insurance company has negotiated for a block of GIC money to be acquired 3 months hence at a rate guaranteed to the client for the next 5 years. Since the company does not yet have the cash to invest, it hedges by purchasing a 5-year U.S. Treasury bond futures contract at a yield known today to approximate (not necessarily match exactly) the guaranteed interest rate, with a forward delivery date roughly matching that of the expected funds delivery. The price change of the futures contract will then tend to inversely match the difference between the rate the company guaranteed at contract time and the rate actually available for investment when the cash is received. The insurance company has thus hedged the open position it assumed at the time of acquiring future funds and guaranteeing the rate it will pay.

The example above oversimplifies the process and the calculation and overstates the certainty of the result, but it accurately describes a practical method of reducing interest rate risk. One of the major possible refinements is the use of a combination of hedges—*synthetic hedges*—to closely approximate the terms of an interest rate guarantee that may have been extended but for which a direct public-market equivalent may not be available.

Covered Call Options

The sale of covered call options against a portfolio of marketable bonds illustrates permitted use of options. In broad markets, as exist for United States Treasuries, there will almost invariably be buyers of the right to purchase bonds at a predetermined "strike" price. This price may slightly or substantially exceed the actual cash price. Selling the option enhances current income on the bonds beyond their stated yield, but it gives up potential future price gains to the purchaser of the option. The operation is virtually riskless if the company holds the exact optioned bonds in its portfolio, and it is appropriate provided the client—whether the insurance operators or an outside investment client—understands the trade-off to obtain the extra yield.

Efficient Frontier Calculations

Modern portfolio theory can also be applied to common stock strategy. Offering investment management to pension clients through commingled or individual separate accounts requires insurance companies to handle "efficient frontier" calculations and to manage accordingly. It is assumed that risk and total return on equities will rise or fall jointly, and risk is typically measured by the price variability (the *beta*) of the stock relative to an average or index of stocks. (A beta larger than one means that the stock fluctuates more widely than the market; a beta smaller than one indicates that the stock fluctuates less widely.) Exposing the trade-off between risk and return determines the point on a constructed convex efficient frontier line that corresponds to the client's preference and thus attracts his or her business. If the preference turns out to be a simple averaging of stocks in the market the company can develop and offer an index fund with expected results similar to the market as a whole.

While analyses clarify risks and technical operations ameliorate these risks, neither analysis nor execution is cost free. Typically, the potential gain is reduced along with the risk, and although uncertainty is reduced, it is not eliminated. Thus investment management can avoid extremes, but the fact remains that obtaining satisfactory investment earnings involves risks. The risks increase sharply if a significant contribution to a company's bottom line is expected from the investment function. Such expectations may lead to untoward investment risk. Once bottom-line pressures are caused by insurance product terms and/or expenses that cannot be satisfied with conservative investments, investment management may be tempted to go out on a limb. When good investment judgment is overridden, technical expertise becomes largely irrelevant. Regulators and rating agencies have become increasingly alert to this problem since the recent investment-related failures.

REGULATION OF LIFE INSURANCE INVESTMENTS

Overview and Brief History

Life insurance investments are regulated in all 50 states, as are most aspects of insurance law and supervision. Until a few years ago, New York state law dominated investment regulation because of New York City's central role in financial markets and because for many years companies doing business in New York state accounted for about three-quarters of all United States insurance sales. In the early 1990s, however, a model insurance investment law was prepared under the aegis of the National Association of Insurance Commissioners (NAIC) with the goal of having it adopted by all 50 states.

Actual regulation has gone through three phases: reliance on traditional measures and methods prior to the 1980s (albeit with gradual refinements), substantial liberalization during most of the 1980s, and a search for modern and possibly tightened standards in recent years. These phases reflect the place of insurance in finance and its standing as a long-regulated industry. The market disruption by inflation and interest rate volatility beginning in the 1970s played a key role in confronting the industry and its regulators with serious new problems. Other important factors unhinging traditional regulatory measures were the cross-invasion of each other's territory by previously distinct types of financial institutions and the closely interrelated technological advances in back-office productivity through computerized data collection, record keeping, and client service.

A further and truly decisive factor contributing to the liberalization phase of the 1980s, however, was the nation's general turn toward deregulation. The movement was fostered initially in the 1970s by the hope that less regulation would mean more competition and therefore help to keep prices down in industries that had been closely regulated (trucking, air travel, commissions in securities transactions, and so on). By the early 1980s, the movement had gained impetus, and liberalization crept closer to the insurance industry via federal laws giving depository institutions interest-rate freedom and easing asset restrictions. This liberalization greatly influenced insurance regulators, although state-by-state regulation necessarily meant a much slower transition than in federally regulated industries.

By the late 1980s, the pendulum was beginning to swing back, and this trend accelerated in the early 1990s. Investment factors were a key to the latest change. Insolvencies, which had been few prior to 1987, accelerated. An ACLI study in 1990 found that 31 of 68 insolvency cases of 1985 to 1990 were related in part to investment problems, although other factors—fraud, underpricing—were even more frequent causes. (These various factors are of course not mutually exclusive.) By the early 1990s, however, investment problems had quite possibly become the leading cause of insolvencies. In addition, as will be noted later, insurance rating agencies' closer attention to insurance portfolios and their frequent downgradings based on investment problems implied that regulators might drop "behind the curve" and not be near the optimal mix of yield and risk unless they redoubled their investment analysis. Thus a push toward conservatism through regulation and supervision gained momentum in the early 1990s. Risk-based capital standards, another recently adopted regulatory item, were closely related to investment supervision since portfolio problems had given rise to capital deficiencies in the major insolvency cases of 1991. The risk-based capital model ties the minimum capital requirements to the risk characteristics of the investment portfolio. Many insurers have reacted by shifting more of their investments into higher-quality, lower-volatility assets.

Traditional Regulation

Pre-1970s regulation emphasized that policy reserves, conservatively valued, should fully cover insurance liabilities. (Since changes in law and regulation have been gradual—even marginal—many of the traditional requirements still apply.)

In the key New York state law therefore quality and diversification were enforced through investment prescriptions and proscriptions. Major latitude was granted for long-term, private-sector earning assets, such as corporate bonds and commercial and residential mortgages (total mortgages had a very generous quantitative limit of 50 percent of assets), as well as for United States government securities. Other investments, judged more risky and/or less reliable as to earnings, were—and remain—fairly strictly limited. Thus common stock can constitute only 10 percent of general account assets, as noted, even after several liberalizations over the decades; investment real estate is at 20 percent; foreign investment at 3 percent (although a separate 10 percent limit applies to Canadian holdings); and, very significantly, a leeway clause permits a liberalized 10 percent of assets to be held outside the otherwise applicable limits, thereby granting significant discretion to go into novel or generally more risky investments.

Qualitative Constraints

Within the quantitative freedom for corporate bonds and mortgages, qualitative standards still apply. Bonds must meet the issuer's earnings test, and lower-grade holdings are curbed. Commercial mortgages are subject to a 75 percent loan-to-value limit. Both bonds and mortgages are limited as to the percentage of assets for which any one debtor can account. (The leeway clause permits an out in specific cases, provided it is not yet fully used—for example, a mortgage loan can be 90 percent of appraised value if 15 percentage points are charged to the leeway, also known as the "basket clause.")

It is clear that an earnings test for bonds or a loan-to-value ratio for mortgages tends to emphasize the past or the present rather than to be an impossible-to-obtain reliable future forecast. The calculus of routine regulation does not encompass adverse general market developments. Thus judgment strongly influences management's investment decisions. While company capital and its adequacy are the bottom-line test for investment risk, regulators have sought to build intermediate barriers to cushion the effect of adverse portfolio developments.

Reserve Accounts

The first line of these defenses used to be the mandatory security valuation reserve (MSVR), which was a buffer (shock absorber) between the decline in value of market-traded securities and insurer surplus and capital. The MSVR has been supplanted by two reserve accounts (discussed more fully later in this chapter): (1) interest maintenance reserve (IMR) and (2) asset valuation reserve (AVR). Their combined function is essentially the same as the previous MSVR. The IMR and AVR recognize that there are multiple sources of asset value fluctuation risk, and they separate out the interest rate risk of fixed-interest securities. The NAIC, through a Securities Valuation Office, evaluates the quality rating of the bonds in insurance company portfolios.

Common stocks command MSVR holdings in a manner similar to the new AVR requirements. In fact, the stiff provisions of the rules applicable to equities have been a significant factor in curbing common stocks in the general account. The rules, reflecting the perceived wide fluctuations of equity prices, make it difficult to credit the gains from capital values to the policyowner, which make up a large proportion of the total return from equities over the long term. Curiously, however, equity real estate or mortgages have not been subject to the MSVR in traditional insurance regulation, perhaps on the theory that equity real estate was a minor holding and mortgages were not risky if they were restricted by loan-to-value rules. (Impending changes are discussed below.)

Writedowns

A second line of regulatory defense has been required writedowns of company assets as a consequence of adverse developments. Basically, bonds and mortgages are permitted to be held at cost and not at market value, thus stabilizing investment values. But a NAIC decision to recognize major problems and/or outright default of troubled investments points to any inadequacies in the remaining MSVR or company capital.

Liberalization and the Beginning of Retraction

By the early 1980s, although not abandoned, a great many quantitative rules had been liberalized. As discussed earlier, larger portions of total assets in equities in real estate, in foreign holdings, and in leeway investments had gradually been permitted. Liberalization reached a high point in 1983 when New York insurance law substituted a "prudent-man" rule for many of the inside prescriptions within each category of permitted assets (although the general quantitative limits by asset categories remained in effect). Actual and potential abuses soon forced reconsideration of liberalized regulation.

Below-investment-grade bonds (by the standards of bond rating agencies) had long constituted a substantial part of life insurance portfolios without creating any hazards. These bonds were companies' direct-placement issues that had not yet reached the financial ratios required for investment grade but could pass the earnings test(s) of insurance regulation. The lead insurance companies' close scrutiny of the borrower in such financings, combined with the earnings test(s), virtually assured very few credit problems in such a bond portfolio.

The merger and acquisition and leveraged buyout craze of the 1980s changed this situation materially. Coming at a time when new product needs drove insurance companies into the public market, high-yield, high-risk junk bonds infiltrated insurance portfolios. By 1987, perceiving impending danger, the New York Insurance Department issued an edict limiting such bonds to 20 percent of assets. This regulation was later broadened so that by 1992 the 20 percent limit had additional internal components further restricting holdings (including direct placements) by officially defining riskiness in progressive steps. These rules went beyond preliberalization regulations and, in effect, declared that similarly graded MSVR requirements were not sufficient.

Another important step in modifying liberalization also occurred during the mid-1980s. New York state adopted a rule—Regulation 126—requiring justification for the interest rate and cash-flow assumptions underlying the asset/liability match of interest-sensitive products. Aggressive companies had bid up the interest rates they offered on GICs, SPDAs and universal life during the high-rate environment of the early 1980s. Such guarantees on liabilities created surplus strain (weakening of capital ratios) because the earnings assumptions for the corresponding assets were held down by state regulation. High portfolio earnings of the blocks of funds involved were required in order to meet the guarantees and to eliminate the initial capital strain. In addition, the withdrawal privileges often extended for new products, qualified as they might be, generated potential cash-flow problems over questions of asset/liability matching with respect to maturities and values. The New York regulation asked company valuation actuaries to perform adequacy tests under a variety of interest rate scenarios over the life of defined blocks of business. The formulation and enforcement of this rule were key factors in helping regulatory and company actuaries reach an understanding with the investment side of the house about the dynamics of investment-sensitive products.

Model Investment Law, Expanded Asset/Interest Reserves, Risk-based Capital Standards

In addition to several substantial company failures directly related to investment problems, as noted before, the 1990s have witnessed a continuing severe commercial real estate recession. Nonperforming real estate loans rose to a post-Great Depression peak of about 7 percent in 1992. Furthermore, the weak economic growth in late 1991 and in 1992, following a general economic recession in 1990 to 1991, has prolonged the unusually large credit problems in the corporate sector, despite a solid recovery of general bond values associated with a major decline of interest rates. Thus investment regulation of insurance companies remains a challenge to state insurance departments—a challenge accentuated by the increasing role of rating agencies in evaluating company acceptability in the general insurance market. In particular, the regulators and the regulated alike have become aware that perceptions of a company's soundness, including its ratings, might be as important in avoiding runs (and ruin) as any objective standards applied by the regulators.

Reversion to Strict Rules

The repercussions from the crises among depository institutions are yet another factor in the insurance regulation of the 1990s, especially the emphasis on risk relative to capital in evaluating the need for and tightness of an institution's supervision. With the NAIC's Model Investment Law, anticipating potential company problems by appropriate regulation has therefore become the dominant theme.

The model law carefully defines allowed asset classes and establishes concentration limits within these classes, somewhat similar to previous regulations. Even prior to a final draft of the model law, the MSVR was transformed into an Asset Valuation Reserve, in which all classes of assets, including real estate, are exposed to reserving rules. In addition, the accumulation rules are stiffer.

Simultaneously, companies were subjected to a new reserve requirement, the Interest Maintenance Reserve. The IMR makes it mandatory to amortize security valuation gains from interest rate changes over the remaining life of a security, rather than having the gains contribute to the profits (or surplus) in the year in which they occur. This new provision will slow up the realization of profits originating in the interest rate declines of the early 1990s, but it will presumably also provide a cushion for interest-rate-caused losses in each sustained upturn of rates.

It appears likely that the eventual investment rules will vary with a company's capitalization, with strongly capitalized companies enjoying greater freedoms than weakly capitalized ones. As one example, weaker companies might be confined to publicly traded corporate bonds and negotiable private-placement bonds, whereas stronger companies could invest in private placements. Furthermore, for purposes of investment latitude, a company's capitalization might be measured not only by capital and surplus versus total assets but also by the ratio of capital to risk-weighted assets. The risk weighing might in turn be influenced by asset concentration ratios, such as an unusually large proportion of mortgages in one location or a large ratio of below-investment-grade bonds.

Unresolved Issues

Some very sticky issues might delay any final draft and implementation of the Model Investment Law. One such issue is the required integration of risk-based capital standards with the model law. (The risk-based capital standards, for which state-by-state adoption was being sought by the NAIC in the 1993–94 time frame, cover risks beyond those relating to investments alone. Other risks requiring capital include withdrawal potential on the insurance liability side and possible state guaranty fund calls.)

Another issue is the permissible extent of the use of derivative instruments and the disclosure requirements associated with their use. It seems clear that protection, rather than speculation, will remain the key to permissibility, but the distinction is more easily stated in theory than applied in practice. Advancing financial technology, from which insurance companies cannot be isolated, is in itself a problem since regulation is almost necessarily a step behind bright operators. (Gaps may also develop in understanding the latest techniques between these bright operators on the one hand, and top management and the directors on the other—a difficult internal company problem that occurs frequently.) Still another difficulty is the required length of any phase-in period for regulations more restrictive than the existing ones.

Reversion to strict rules appears desirable for many reasons. Reassuring the public of life insurance's soundness is the most important one; discovering and pursuing early warning supervision systems is a close corollary. Still, innovation in product design and investment policy should be encouraged, not suppressed. It is impossible to draw a Maginot line around the insurance industry when financial service institutions are characterized by increasing and highly competitive overlaps. The risk of failure—indeed, occasional actual failure—increases with the attraction of talented and spirited young people to the investment function and to the insurance industry in general. The problem is to confine greed, susceptibility to imprudence, and ambition itself to limits compatible with the productive function of investments within the conservative societal role of insurance. It is helpful that the competitors, especially the banking industry, are likewise experiencing more stringent tightening of capital adequacy and lending rules in the wake of the abuses of the 1980s.

LIFE INSURANCE INVESTMENTS AND COMMERCIAL RATING AGENCIES

Reasons for Rating Agencies' Important Role

Rating agencies' appraisal of life insurance investments seems destined to play an important role in the markets of the 1990s for three main reasons. First, the raters themselves have emerged from an industry-only interest to key players in the course of a single decade. The only traditional rating service, A.M. Best, even though it had a monopoly, languished in the shadows till the mid-1980s. The other three current leaders—Standard & Poor's, Moody's, and Duff and Phelps—all began their insurance-industry-specific services during the 1980s. (Weiss Research is a fourth and even more recent—and controversial—arrival.)

Second, the very fact of insurers' and raters' broadening interest in the ratings is directly related to the growing integration of insurers with the financial markets as both borrowers and lenders. The need for insurance companies to have the ability to issue commercial paper and to obtain bank credit lines was caused by periodic disintermediation problems, by the shortening of liability maturities, and perhaps most important for the future, by the need for access to capital through public equity and bond markets. Insurance companies suddenly needed ratings, a fact the raters correctly perceived as a profit opportunity.

Third, the vagaries of the business cycle—with special emphasis on the downside of commercial real estate and junk bonds in a recession—played a key role in the rise of life insurance defaults. Therefore investment portfolios immediately became a challenge to rating agencies. Once educated in facts and regulations, rating agencies soon began to produce elaborate tests, models and analyses on all the factors relevant to portfolio management—liquidity, asset/liability matching (including cash-flow testing), bond and real estate quality, and actual and possible delinquencies and defaults, as already discussed. The rating agencies had the ability and incentive to go beyond insurance supervisors' rules and regulations. In particular, the leading raters coming from the securities industry (Standard & Poor's and Moody's) brought criteria from outside institutional and market finance to bear upon the insurance industry, thereby educating their new clients in turn.

Impact of Ratings

Controversy began almost as soon as the number of raters and their published ratings began to rise in the mid-1980s. The element of judgment, common to most raters, opened the door to disagreements among equally qualified appraisers in much the same way in which investment portfolios differ even among managers with identical objectives. When the rating agencies used strictly quantitative tests to evaluate investments (and other factors) in their analysis, the very lack of supplementary qualitative judgment became a source of criticism. Ratings thus became publicity items at the exact time (1986–1991) when life insurance failures became significant.

The ratings services scrambled as junk bond and real estate problems multiplied. Downgradings typically followed a company's disclosure of extra reserving for investment problems, of outright writedowns, or of poor quarterly or annual results often associated with investment problems. Competition among insurance company field sales forces quickly spread the bad (or good) news, raising sharply the importance of high ratings in attracting new funds. The cause and effect of downgradings were sometimes indistinguishable since downgradings themselves, even if justified in the eyes of the rating agencies by mounting portfolio problems, could trigger runs on a company and force asset sales at distress prices.

By the early 1990s it was clear that the importance of ratings reinforced the return to conservatism in investment policy and supervision. But several questions have yet to be answered.

Liquidity Safety Net

The most important of these questions is whether the insurance industry needs a source of liquidity to tide a company over a temporary market and/or ratings-induced rough spot. Might Executive Life have survived had it been able to participate in the recovery of the junk-bond market after new supplies abruptly ceased in 1991? Would Mutual Benefit Life's real estate have come into its own in the mid-1990s? Might a conditional liquidity arrangement be preferable to impairment and liquidation proceedings or to forced mergers and/or the activation of guarantee funds? As an analogy, Federal Reserve credit is one of the options available to banking entities judged to be capable of recovering, and its quantity and terms have occasionally been stretched to help banks through crises.

The longer-term nature of nearly all life insurance portfolios leaves them vulnerable to a threatened run on an insurance company. Insurers have no safety net, no source of funds to help them through a crisis. The guarantee funds in each state kick in only after the regulators have taken control of a troubled insurer. Therefore the influence of published ratings and their changes will remain a major force in an insurer's survival. It has been proved that capital-strong companies can survive a downgrading, especially at or near the top of the rating grades. Weaker companies, however, may have to adopt new and possibly severe restraints on their investment portfolios in order to avoid potentially ruinous asset squeezes. Marketing considerations reinforced by regulatory developments and rating pressures will continue to move the industry in the direction of investment conservatism.

Glimpse into the Future

Few people would have dared predict the dramatic events of the late 1970s and the 1980s, especially the elevation of the investment function to its current importance, as a consequence of the product revolution. Clearly, caution is in order with respect to predictions for the rest of the 1990s. Nevertheless, several trends are clear enough that they will probably continue to be major factors until the close of the century.

Continued Conservatism

The most important of these trends is the swing toward investment conservatism in reaction to the swinging 1980s. Capital standards and the Model Investment Law will require such conservatism; continuous attention to ratings and their influence on marketing will reinforce it. There is a distinct possibility, however, that the combination of these factors will carry a trend that in itself is logical and desirable too far. As a result, the important role that life insurance investments has played in the long-term capital markets and in support of emerging companies may be diminished, to the detriment of national economic growth—especially if life insurers shift all of their assets to top-quality issues and abandon the intermediate-quality assets they have typically financed in recent decades.

In fact, the industry might have to raise so much outside capital to satisfy the new standards being imposed by insurance regulators that its historical net contribution to national investment might fall sharply in the 1990s, along with the change toward high-grade investments. The acceleration of the previously snail-like process of demutualization because of the need for outside capital was a sign of the times in 1992 when the Equitable, one of the largest companies, joined the demutualization parade, primarily to help cure a serious capital deficiency. Other mutuals were similarly deliberating the possibility of augmenting internal retained capital by going public. One mutual insurer (Prudential) was able to raise $300 million by issuing a new form of notes to institutional investors in mid-1993. This indicates that at least some of the strongest mutual insurers may raise capital on Wall Street without having to demutualize.

One consequence of the new conservatism was that the recovery of commercial real estate was delayed by insurer investment officers' reluctance or inability to renew their commitment to a sector subject to high capital requirements and asset reserves. The 20 percent average vacancy rate for office space in the early 1990s is unlikely to be cut before mid-decade to a more normal 8 percent to 10 percent. Other substantial real estate surpluses existed in hotel and shopping center space. Overbuilding of the 1980s, partly because of weakened underwriting standards, had come home to roost. Thus life insurers had to emphasize defensive management of the existing mortgage and equity real estate portfolio. While in the early 1990s supply and demand pressures to liberalize new financing were minimal, when construction again becomes a leading business investment, the new conservatism will be tested.

Similar considerations, although less extreme, could arise in the relation of corporate financing to life insurance investments. As leading life insurers curbed their appetite for risky loans in response to regulatory and marketing forces, the interest rate margins available on well-secured loans to stable businesses shrank sharply, regardless of whether these margins were measured against the cost of funds or against the alternative of government (or government-backed) securities. Conservatism itself thus increased the squeeze on life insurance earnings, and this conservatism will have to run its course to purge the excesses of the 1980s.

Money Management Diversification

A second important trend for the 1990s is further life insurance diversification into money management *per se*. The enormous progress of investment skills among insurance officers and of the investment selection aspects of life insurance products can be readily extended into the noninsurance field. A key incentive is the relatively low capital requirements in fee-for-service operations. A great number of leading insurers have acquired mutual fund affiliates and/or independent pension management firms to utilize the sophisticated investment skills of their employees more fully. The field forces of numerous insurers have also developed more refined financial planning knowledge and skills. In effect, many life insurance agents have become financial planners with full portfolio capability, including securities licenses.

The integration of this diversification and expansion into traditional life insurance marketing operations presents major problems in both home office and field force organization and management. The differences in marketing tactics and commission structure—indeed in corporate culture—cannot be bridged easily. One clearly emerging development in home office organization is to establish semi-independent investment subsidiaries; in effect, money market and securities portfolio management is declared another segment of investment operations, often more distinct organizationally than general account segments or separate accounts among themselves.

Investment Operation Overlap

A third likely trend for the 1990s is the increasing overlap of investment operations among different types of institutions. This trend is part of the larger issue of broadening franchises and direct competition among previously unassociated groups of institutions. But while it seems likely that the 1990s will see a full merger of commercial and thrift banking, the distinction between banking and insurance will probably persist. No doubt the removal of legal and regulatory barriers would bring a quick end to this separation, but significant public policy concerns and private turf considerations are likely to leave the basic barriers intact. On the other hand, the marriage of investment banking and brokerage with life insurance is proceeding apace in the 1990s—a logical development, given the trend toward broad-service financial management within the insurance industry. The legal obstacles appear somewhat more surmountable than for banks seeking to expand into the securities business; nevertheless, management skills to make the disciplines compatible are proving difficult to acquire.

Internationalization

A fourth important trend is the further internationalization of the investment business. Leeway provisions of existing laws or the new Model Investment Law are likely to be used increasingly to take advantage of investment opportunities in the European common market, the developing North American common market, and in dynamic Asian economies. Newly acquired portfolio management skills are also being marketed by several leading United States insurers to generate United States real estate and securities portfolios for foreign institutional investors. Last but not least, the imposition of more stringent United States capital standards for life insurers is certain to be followed by a search for new sources of capital. Leading foreign capital markets are a likely source, and foreign insurers might perceive new opportunities for combinations with United States firms. (Again, the demutualization experience of the Equitable in 1992 may point the way—more than two-thirds of the total additional capital raised in 1991–1992 came from a foreign source, the French AXA insurance group.)

In sum, new challenges and opportunities in life insurance investment management are readily apparent in the early 1990s, notwithstanding the conservative reaction to the 1980s. Consolidation and expansion alternate with the business cycle, more so on the investment side than on the product side of life insurance. Thus it appears that retrenchment in the early 1990s will be followed by further enhancement of the relative importance of the investment function of life insurance throughout the remainder of 1990s.

NOTES

1. An equity kicker involves lender participation in part of the change in value of an asset when sold, as an added inducement to loan the funds needed to purchase the asset.
2. Financialization is the creation of securities backed by an insurer's asset holdings, such as collateralized mortgage obligations, where the yield on the assets is paid to the security owner. They are often called pass-through securities.
3. GICs are frequently negotiated with employers as one of the employee options available in qualified plans. The contract specifies the investment earnings it will pay a year at a time (in advance). Usually these one-year guarantees are covered by existing asset holdings.
4. Disintermediation is the withdrawal of funds from financial institutions by the depositor/owners so they can invest directly in securities at high current yields. It usually occurs when interest rates go up very rapidly.

33

Group Life Insurance ⃰

Burton T. Beam, Jr.

The majority of this book is devoted to a detailed analysis of individual life insurance. However, a large portion of life insurance is written on a group basis. The significance of group life insurance is evident from the following statistics:[1]

- Coverage amounting to $3.8 trillion is in force under approximately 700,000 master contracts and 140 million certificates of insurance. This amount represents a doubling of the amount of insurance in force since 1980.
- Over 99 percent of the coverage in force is term insurance.
- Employer-employee groups account for approximately 90 percent of coverage in force.
- Group insurance amounts to almost 40 percent of total life insurance coverage, up from 20 percent in 1950.
- The amount of coverage under the average-size group life insurance certificate covering persons in employer-employee groups is approximately $25,000, compared to about $35,000 under the average-size ordinary life insurance policy in force.
- Over 700,000 beneficiaries each year receive a total of over $10 billion in benefits.

This chapter describes group life insurance by looking at its characteristics, the governmental environment within which it is written, and the types of coverage that are in force. The focus is on the use of group life insurance as an employee benefit. However, as is briefly mentioned later, some group insurance is written outside an employer-employee relationship.

GROUP INSURANCE CHARACTERISTICS

Group insurance is characterized by a group contract, experience rating of larger groups, and group underwriting. Perhaps the best way to define group insurance is to compare its characteristics with those of individual insurance, which is underwritten on an individual basis.

⃰Based on material in *Group Benefits: Basis Concepts and Alternatives*, 5th ed., The American College, Bryn Mawr, Pennsylvania, 1993.

The Group Contract

In contrast to most individual insurance contracts the group insurance contract provides coverage to a number of persons under a single contract issued to someone other than the persons insured. The contract, referred to as a *master* contract, provides benefits to a group of individuals who have a specific relationship to the policyowner. Group contracts usually cover individuals who are full-time employees, and the policyowner is either their employer or a trust established to provide benefits for the employees. Although the employees are not actual parties to the master contract, they can legally enforce their rights. Consequently employees are often referred to as third-party beneficiaries of the insurance contract.

Employees covered under the contract receive *certificates of insurance* as evidence of their coverage. A certificate is merely a description of the coverage provided and is not part of the master contract. In general, a certificate of insurance is not even considered to be a contract and usually contains a disclaimer to that effect. However, some courts have held the contrary to be true when the provisions of the certificate or even the explanatory booklet of a group insurance plan varies materially from the master contract.

In individual insurance the coverage of the insured normally begins with the inception of the insurance contract and ceases with its termination. However, in group insurance individual members of the group may become eligible for coverage long after the inception of the group contract, or they may lose their eligibility status long before the contract terminates.

Experience Rating

A second distinguishing characteristic of group insurance is the use of experience rating. If a group is sufficiently large, the actual experience of that particular group will be a factor in determining the premium the policyowner will be charged. It should be noted that the experience of an insurance company will also be reflected in the dividends and future premiums associated with individual insurance. However, such experience will be determined on a class basis and will apply to all insureds in that class. This is also true for group insurance contracts when the group's membership is small.

Group Underwriting

The applicant for individual insurance must generally show evidence of insurability. For group insurance, on the other hand, individual members of the group are usually not required to show any evidence of insurability when initially eligible for coverage. This is not to say that there is no underwriting, but rather that underwriting is focused on the characteristics of the group instead of on the insurability of individual members of the group. As with individual insurance, the underwriter must appraise the risk, decide on the conditions of the group's acceptability, and establish a rating basis.

The purpose of group insurance underwriting is twofold: (1) to minimize the problem of *adverse selection* (meaning that those who are likely to have claims are also those who are most likely to seek insurance) and (2) to minimize the administrative costs associated with group insurance. Because of group underwriting, coverage can be provided through group insurance at a lower cost than through individual insurance.

There are certain general underwriting considerations applicable to all or most types of group insurance that affect the contractual provisions contained in group insurance contracts as well as insurance company practices pertaining to group insurance. These general underwriting considerations include the

- reason for the group's existence
- stability of the group
- persistency of the group
- method of determining benefits
- provisions for determining eligibility
- source and method of premium payments
- administrative aspects of the group insurance plan
- prior experience of the plan
- size of the group
- composition of the group
- industry represented by the group

Reason for Existence

Probably the most fundamental group underwriting principle is that a group must have been formed for some purpose other than to obtain insurance for its members. Such a rule protects the group insurance company against the adverse selection that would likely exist if poor risks were to form a group just to obtain insurance. Groups based on an employer-employee relationship present little difficulty with respect to this rule.

Stability

Ideally an underwriter would like to see a reasonable but steady flow of persons through a group. A higher-than-average turnover rate will result in increased administrative costs for the insurance company as well as for the employer. If turnover exists among recently hired employees, the resulting costs can be minimized by requiring employees to wait a certain period of time before becoming eligible for coverage. However, such a *probationary period* does leave newly hired employees without protection if their previous group insurance coverage has terminated.

A lower-than-average turnover rate often results in an increasing average age for the members of a group. To the extent that a plan's premium is a function of the mortality (death rates) of the group, such an increase in average age will result in an increasing premium rate for that group insurance plan. This high premium rate may cause the better risks to drop out of a plan, if they are required to contribute to its cost, and may ultimately force the employer to terminate the plan because of its increasing cost.

Persistency

An underwriter is concerned with the length of time a group insurance contract will remain on the insurance company's books. Initial acquisition expenses, often including higher first-year commissions, frequently cause an insurance company to lose money during the first year the group insurance contract is in force. Only through the renewal of the contract for a period of time, often 3 or 4 years, can these acquisition expenses be recovered. For this reason firms with a history of frequently changing insurance companies or those with financial difficulty are often avoided.

Determination of Benefits

In most types of group insurance the underwriter will require that benefit levels for individual members of the group be determined in some manner that precludes individual selection by either the employees or the employer. If employees could choose their own benefit levels, there would be a tendency for the poorer risks to select greater amounts of coverage than the better risks would select. Similarly adverse selection could also exist if the employer could choose a separate benefit level for each individual member of the group. As a result this underwriting rule has led to benefit levels that are either identical for all employees or determined by a benefit formula that bases benefit levels on some specific criterion, such as salary or position.

Benefits based on salary or position may still lead to adverse selection because disproportionately larger benefits will be provided to the owner or top executives, who may have been involved in determining the benefit formula. Consequently most insurance companies have rules for determining the maximum benefit that may be provided for any individual employee without evidence of insurability. Additional amounts of coverage either will not be provided or will be subject to individual evidence of insurability.

Determination of Eligibility

The underwriter is also concerned with the eligibility provisions that will be contained in a group insurance plan. As mentioned, many group insurance plans contain probationary periods that must be satisfied before an employee is eligible for coverage. In addition to minimizing administrative costs, a probationary period will discourage persons in poor health from seeking employment primarily because of a firm's group insurance benefits.

Most group insurance plans normally limit eligibility to full-time employees since the coverage of part-time employees may not be desirable from an underwriting standpoint. In addition to having a high turnover rate, part-time employees are more likely to seek employment primarily to obtain the group insurance benefits that are available. Similar problems exist with seasonal and temporary employees, and consequently eligibility is often restricted to permanent employees.

Premium Payments

Group insurance plans may be contributory or noncontributory. Members of *contributory plans* pay a portion, or possibly all, of the cost of their own coverage. When the entire portion is paid by employees, these plans are often referred to as fully contributory or employee-pay-all plans. Under *noncontributory plans* the policyowner pays the entire cost. Since all eligible employees are usually covered, this is desirable from an underwriting standpoint because adverse selection is minimized. In fact, most insurance companies and the laws of many states require 100 percent participation of eligible employees under noncontributory plans. In addition, the absence of employee solicitation, payroll deductions, and underwriting of late entrants into the plan results in administrative savings to both the policyowner and the insurance company.

Most state laws prohibit an employer from requiring an employee to participate in a contributory plan. The insurance company is therefore faced with the possibility of adverse selection since those who elect coverage will tend to be the poorer risks. From a practical standpoint 100 percent participation in a contributory plan would be unrealistic since for many reasons some employees neither desire nor need the coverage provided under the plan. However, insurance companies will require that a minimum percentage of the eligible members of a group elect to participate before the contract will be issued. The common requirement is 75 percent, although a lower percentage is often acceptable for large groups and a higher percentage may be required for small groups. It should be noted that a 75 percent minimum requirement is also often a statutory requirement for group life insurance.

A key issue in contributory plans is how to treat employees who did not elect to participate when first eligible but who later desire coverage, or who dropped coverage and want it reinstated. Unfortunately this desire for coverage may arise when these employees or their dependents have medical conditions that will lead to a disproportionate number of claims once coverage is provided. To control this adverse selection, insurance companies commonly require individual evidence of insurability by these employees or their dependents before coverage will be made available. However, there is one exception. Some plans have recurring open enrollment periods during which the evidence-of-insurability requirement is lessened or waived for a short period of time.

Insurance companies frequently require that the employer pay a portion of the premium under a group insurance plan. This is also a statutory requirement for group life insurance in most states. Many group insurance plans set an average contribution rate for all employees, which in turn leads to the subsidizing of some employees by other employees, particularly in those types of insurance where the frequency of claims increases with age. Without a requirement for employer contributions younger employees might actually find coverage at a lower cost in the individual market, thereby leaving the group with only the older risks. Even when group insurance already has a cost advantage over individual insurance, its attractiveness to employees is enhanced by employer contributions. In addition, underwriters feel that the absence of employer contributions may lead to a lack of employer interest in the plan and consequently poor cooperation with the insurance company and poor plan administration.

Administration

To minimize the expenses associated with group insurance, the underwriter will often require that certain administrative functions be carried out by the employer. These commonly include communicating the plan to the employees, handling enrollment procedures, collecting employee contributions on a payroll-deduction basis, and keeping certain types of records. Underwriters are concerned not only with the employer's ability to carry out these functions but also with the employer's willingness to cooperate with the insurance company.

Prior Experience

For most insurance companies a large portion of newly written group insurance consists of business that was previously written by other insurance companies. Therefore it is important for the underwriter to ascertain the reason for the transfer. If the transferred business is a result of dissatisfaction with the service provided by the prior insurance company, the underwriter must determine whether his or her insurance company can provide the type and level of service desired. Since an employer is most likely to shop for new coverage when faced with a rate increase, the underwriter must evaluate whether the rate increase was due to excessive claims experience. Often, particularly with larger groups, poor claims experience in the past is an indication that there might be poor experience in the future. Occasionally, however, the prior experience may be due to circumstances that will not continue in the future, such as a catastrophe.

Excessive past claims experience may not result in coverage denial for a new applicant, but it will probably result in a higher rate. As an alternative, changes in the benefit or eligibility provisions of the plan might eliminate a previous source of adverse claims experience.

The underwriter must also be reasonably certain that the employer will not present a persistency problem by changing insurance companies again in the near future.

Size

The size of a group is a significant factor in the underwriting process. With large groups there is usually prior group insurance experience that can be used as a factor in determining the premium. In addition, adjustments for adverse claims experience can be made at future renewal dates under the experience-rating process.

The situation is different for small groups. In many cases coverage is being written for the first time. Administrative expenses tend to be high in relation to the premium. There is also an increased possibility that the owner or major stockholder might be interested in coverage primarily because he or she or a family member has a medical problem that makes individual life insurance coverage difficult or impossible to obtain. As a result contractual provisions and the benefits available tend to be quite standardized in order to control administrative costs. Furthermore, because past experience for small groups is not necessarily a realistic indicator of future experience, most insurance companies use pooled rates under which a uniform rate is applied to all groups that have a specific coverage. Since poor claims experience for a particular group is not charged to that group at renewal, more restrictive underwriting practices relating to adverse selection are used. These include less liberal contractual provisions and in some cases individual underwriting for group members.

Composition

The age and sex of employees in a group will affect the experience of the group. As employees age, the mortality rate increases. At all ages the death rate is lower for females than for males. Adjustments can be made for these factors when determining the proper rate to charge the policyowner. The major problem arises in contributory insurance plans. To the extent that higher costs for a group with a less-than-average mix of employees are passed on to these employees, a lower participation rate may result.

Industry

The nature of the industry represented by a group is also a significant factor in the underwriting process. In addition to different occupational hazards among industries, employees in some industries have higher-than-average death claims that cannot be directly attributed to their jobs. Therefore insurance companies commonly make adjustments in their life insurance rates based on the occupations of the employees covered as well as on the industries in which they work.

The underwriter must weigh factors other than occupational hazards as well. Certain industries are characterized by a lack of stability and persistency and thus may be considered undesirable risks.

THE GOVERNMENTAL ENVIRONMENT FOR GROUP LIFE INSURANCE

The character of group life insurance has been greatly influenced by the numerous laws and regulations that have been imposed by both the state and federal governments. The major impact of state regulation has been felt through the insurance laws governing insurance companies and the products they sell. Traditionally these laws have affected only those benefit plans funded with insurance contracts. The federal laws affecting group life insurance, on the other hand, have generally been directed toward any benefit plans that are established by employers for their employees, regardless of the funding method used.

State Regulation

Some of the more significant state laws and regulations affecting group insurance include those pertaining to the types of groups eligible for coverage, benefit limitations, and contractual provisions. Moreover, since many employers have employees in several states, the extent of the regulatory jurisdiction of each state is a question of some concern.

Eligible Groups

Most states do not allow group insurance contracts to be written unless a minimum number of persons are insured under the contract. This requirement, which may vary by type of coverage and type of group, is most common in group life insurance, where the minimum number required for plans established by individual employers is generally 10 persons. A few states have either a lower minimum or no such requirement. A higher minimum, often 100 persons, may be imposed on other plans, such as those established by trusts, labor unions, or creditors.

The majority of states also have insurance laws concerning the types of groups for which insurance companies may write group insurance. Most of these laws specify that a group insurance contract cannot be delivered to a policyowner in the state unless the group meets certain statutory eligibility requirements for its type of group. In some states these eligibility requirements even vary by type of coverage. While the categories of eligible groups may vary, at least five types of groups are acceptable in virtually all states: individual employer groups, negotiated trusteeships, trade associations, creditor-debtor groups, and labor union groups. Other types of groups, including multiple-employer welfare arrangements, are also acceptable in some states. Some states have no insurance laws regarding the types or sizes of groups for which insurance companies may write group insurance. Rather, eligibility is determined by the underwriting standards of insurance companies.

Individual Employer Groups. The most common type of eligible group is the individual employer group in which the employer may be a corporation, a partnership, or a sole proprietorship. Many state laws are very specific about what constitutes an employee for group insurance purposes. In addition to those usually considered to be employees of a firm, coverage can generally be written for retired employees and employees of subsidiary and affiliated firms. Furthermore, individual proprietors or partners are usually eligible for coverage as long as they are actively engaged in and devote a substantial part of their time to the conduct of the organization. Similarly directors of a corporation may also be eligible for coverage if they are also employees of the corporation.

Negotiated Trusteeships (Taft-Hartley Trusts). Negotiated trusteeships are formed as a result of collective bargaining over benefits between a union and the employers of the union members. Generally the union employees are in the same industry or a related one. For the most part these industries, such as trucking or construction, are characterized by frequent movement of union members among employers. The Taft-Hartley Act prohibits employers from paying funds directly to a labor union for the purpose of providing group insurance coverage to members. Payments may be made to a trust fund established for the purpose of purchasing insurance. The group insurance contract is then issued to the trustee. The trustees of the fund must be made up of equal numbers of representatives from the employers and the union. The trustees can elect either to self-fund benefits or to purchase insurance contracts with themselves as the policyowners. Since eligible employees include only members of the collective-bargaining unit, benefits for nonunion employees must be provided in some other manner.

Negotiated trusteeships differ from other types of groups in the way benefits are financed and the way eligibility for benefits is determined. Employers often make contributions based on the number of hours worked by the employees covered under the collective-bargaining agreement, regardless of whether these employees are eligible for benefits. Eligibility for benefits during a given period is usually based only on some minimum number of hours worked during a previous period. For example, a union member might receive coverage during a calendar quarter (even while unemployed) if he or she worked at least 300 hours in the previous calendar quarter.

Trade Associations. For eligibility purposes a trade association is an association of employers that has been formed for reasons other than obtaining insurance. In most cases these employers are in the same industry or type of business. In many such associations there is frequently a large number of employers who do not have the minimum number of employees necessary to qualify for an individual employer group insurance contract. While in some states the master contract is issued directly to the trade association, in most states it is necessary that a trust be established. Through payment of premiums to the association or the trust, individual employers may provide coverage for their employees.

Both adverse selection and administrative costs tend to be greater in trade association groups than in many other types of groups. Therefore most underwriters and state laws require that a minimum percentage of the employers belonging to the association, such as 50 percent, participate in the plan and that a minimum number of employees, possibly as high as 500, be covered. In addition, individual underwriting or strict provisions regarding preexisting conditions may be used, and employer contributions are usually required. To ensure adequate enrollment the underwriter must determine whether the association has the resources as well as the desire to promote the plan enthusiastically and to administer it properly.

Multiple-Employer Welfare Arrangements. The final type of eligible group designed to provide benefits for employees is the multiple-employer welfare arrangement (MEWA). MEWAs are a common but often controversial method of marketing group benefits to employers who have a small number of employees. MEWAs are legal entities (1) sponsored by an insurance company, an independent administrator, or some other person or organization and (2) organized for the purpose of providing group benefits to the employees of more than one employer. Each MEWA is either an insurance company or a professional administrator. MEWAs may be organized as trusts, in which case there must be a trustee that may be an individual but is usually a corporate trustee, such as a commercial bank.

MEWAs are generally established to provide group benefits to employers within a specific industry, such as construction, agriculture, or banking. However, employers are not required to belong to an association. MEWAs may provide either a single type of insurance (such as life insurance) or a wide range of coverages (for example, life, medical expense, and disability income insurance). In some cases alternative forms of the same coverage are available (such as comprehensive health insurance or basic health insurance).

An employer desiring to obtain insurance coverage for its employees from a MEWA must subscribe to and become a member of the MEWA. The employer is issued a joinder agreement, which spells out the relationship between the MEWA and the employer and specifies the coverages to which the employer has subscribed. It should be noted that it is not necessary for an employer to subscribe to all coverages offered by a MEWA.

A MEWA may either provide benefits on a self-funded basis or fund benefits with a contract purchased from an insurance company. In the latter case the MEWA, rather than the subscribing employers, is the master insurance contract holder. In either case the employees of subscribing employers are provided with benefit descriptions (certificates of insurance in insured MEWAs) in a manner similar to the usual group insurance arrangement.

In addition to alternative methods of funding benefits, MEWAs can also be categorized according to how they are administered, that is, whether by an insurance company or by a third-party administrator. It is generally agreed that there are three types of MEWAs. Unfortunately the terminology used to describe the three types is not uniform. In this chapter the following terminology and definitions will be used:

- fully insured multiple-employer trust (MET). Benefits are insured and the MET is administered by an insurance company. (Prior to 1982 all MEWAs were referred to as METs. At that time ERISA (Employee Retirement Income Security Act) was amended to clarify the regulation of such arrangements. The act used the term *multiple-employer welfare arrangement* rather than the term *multiple-employer trust*. Over time, MEWA has become the accepted overall terminology, but most insurance companies continue to use the term MET to describe fully insured MEWAs as a way to distinguish them from the more controversial self-funded MEWAs.)
- insured third-party-administered MEWA. Benefits are insured and the MEWA is administered by a third party.
- self-funded MEWA. Benefits are self-funded and the MEWA is administered by a third party. Self-funded MEWAs continue to be a source of controversy. To a large extent they have existed in a regulatory vacuum. There has been little oversight by the federal government, and states have been hampered in their attempts at regulation because insurance contracts are not used. As a result a large number of MEWAs have gone bankrupt as a result of mismanagement or fraud. It should be noted, however, that self-funded MEWAs have usually been used to provide medical expense benefits rather than life insurance benefits.

Creditor-Debtor Groups. Creditor-debtor relationships give rise to groups that are eligible for group term life insurance. While the types of creditors and debtors may vary, coverage is normally made available for organizations such as banks, finance companies, and retailers with respect to time-payment purchases, personal loans, or charge accounts. A unique feature of group credit life insurance is that the creditor must be the beneficiary of the coverage in addition to being the policyowner even though the debtors are the insured. Any payments to the creditor must be used to cancel the insured portion of the debt. Premiums for group creditor life insurance may be shared by the creditor and the debtor or may be totally paid by either party.

The following traditional restrictions imposed by eligibility statutes also reflect insurance company underwriting practices:

- maximum amount of coverage. Many states limit the maximum amount of coverage that may be written on a single debtor. In addition, since the amount of coverage can never exceed the amount of the indebtedness, coverage decreases as the debt is paid.
- maximum loan duration. It is common for states to limit the loan duration under contributory plans to maximum periods, such as 5 or 10 years. There is usually no maximum loan duration if the cost of the coverage is paid by the creditor.
- minimum participation percentage. Many states require that all eligible debtors be insured when the creditor pays the entire premium and that at least 75 percent of eligible debtors be insured under contributory plans.
- minimum number of entrants into the plan. In many cases this number is 100 for each policy year.

Because of the abuses associated with such factors as coercion, excessive premium rates, and lack of disclosure, many states have additional regulations pertaining to group credit insurance. Common provisions include

- proper disclosure to the debtor, including a description of the coverage and the charge for the coverage
- an option for the debtor to provide coverage through existing insurance or the purchase of a policy from another source
- a requirement that the charge by a creditor to a debtor for coverage may not exceed the premium charged by the insurance company
- a refund of any uncarned premium paid by the debtor if the indebtedness is paid prior to its scheduled maturity
- limitations on the maximum rates that may be charged by insurance companies

While this chapter concentrates on the use of group insurance as an employee benefit, it should be noted that group creditor insurance, particularly creditor life insurance, is a significant and growing form of group insurance. According to the American Council of Life Insurance, $250 billion of credit life insurance was in force at the end of 1990, under approximately 70 million individual policies or certificates of group insurance. Detailed statistics are not available, but it is estimated that between 80 and 90 percent of this amount is group insurance. While the amount of credit life insurance has increased within the past decade, the majority of the growth has been in the average size of the policy or certificate of insurance rather than in the number of policies or certificates of insurance.

Labor Union Groups. Labor unions may establish group insurance plans to provide benefits for their members, with the master contract issued to the union. In addition to the prohibition by the Taft-Hartley Act of employer payments to labor unions for insurance premiums, state laws generally prohibit plans in which union members pay the entire cost from their own pockets. Consequently the premiums come solely from union funds or partially from union funds and partially from members' contributions. Labor union groups account for a relatively small amount of group insurance, but most of it is life insurance.

Other Groups. Numerous other types of groups may be eligible for group insurance under the regulations of many states. These include alumni associations, professional associations, veterans' groups, savings account depositors, and credit card holders. Insurance company underwriting practices and state regulations may impose more stringent requirements on these types of groups than on those involving an employer-employee relationship. Individual evidence of insurability is frequently required for other than small amounts of coverage. In addition, a larger minimum size is generally imposed upon the group.

Contractual Provisions

Through its insurance laws every state provides for the regulation of contractual provisions. In many instances certain contractual provisions must be included in group insurance policies. These mandatory provisions may be altered only if they result in more favorable treatment of the policyowner. Such provisions tend to be most uniform from state to state in the area of group life insurance, primarily because of the widespread adoption of the NAIC model bill pertaining to group life insurance standard provisions. As a result of state regulation, coupled with industry practices, the provisions of most group life policies are relatively uniform from company to company. An insurance company's policy forms can usually be used in all states. However, riders may be necessary to bring certain provisions into compliance with the regulations of some states.

Benefit Limitations

Statutory limitations may be imposed on the level of benefits that can be provided under group insurance contracts issued to certain types of eligible groups. In the past most states limited the amount of group life insurance that could be provided by an employer to an employee, but only Texas still has such a restriction. However, several states limit the amount of coverage that can be provided under contracts issued to groups other than individual employer groups. In addition, some states limit the amount of life insurance coverage that may be provided for dependents.

Regulatory Jurisdiction

A group insurance contract will often insure individuals living in more than one state—a situation that raises the question of which state or states have regulatory jurisdiction over the contract. This issue is a crucial one since factors such as minimum enrollment percentages, maximum amounts of life insurance, and required contract provisions vary among the states.

Few problems arise if the insured group qualifies as an eligible group in all the states where insured individuals reside. Individual employer groups, negotiated trusteeships, labor union groups, and creditor-debtor groups fall into this category. Under the *doctrine of comity*, by which states recognize within their own territory the laws of other states, it is generally accepted that the state in which the group insurance contract is delivered to the policyowner has governing jurisdiction. Therefore the contract must conform only to the laws and regulations of this one state, even though certificates of insurance may be delivered in other states. However, a few states have statutes that prohibit insurance issued in other states from covering residents of their state unless the contract conforms with their laws and regulations. While these statutes are effective with respect to insurance companies licensed within the state (that is, admitted companies), their effectiveness with respect to nonadmitted companies is questionable, since states lack regulatory jurisdiction over these companies.

This does not mean that the policyowner may arbitrarily seek out a situs (place of delivery) that is most desirable from a regulatory standpoint. Unless the state of delivery has a significant relationship to the insurance transaction, other states may seek to exercise their regulatory authority. Therefore it has become common practice that an acceptable situs must be at least one of the following:

- the state where the policyowner is incorporated (or the trust is created if the policyowner is a trust)
- the state where the policyowner's principal office is located
- the state where the greatest number of insured individuals are employed
- any state where an employer or labor union that is a party to a trust is located

While a policyowner may have a choice of situs if these locations differ, most insurers are reluctant to issue a group contract in any state unless a corporate officer or trustee who can execute acceptance of the contract is located in that state and unless the principal functions related to the administration of the group contract will be performed there.

The issue of regulatory jurisdiction is more complex for those types of groups that are not considered to be eligible groups in all states. Multiple-employer welfare arrangements are a typical example. If a state has no regulation to the contrary and if the insured group would be eligible for group insurance in other states, the situation is the same as previously described. In addition, most other states will accept the doctrine of comity and will not interfere with the regulatory jurisdiction of the state where the contract is delivered. However, some states either prohibit coverage from being issued or require that it conform with the state's laws and regulations other than those pertaining to eligible groups.

Federal Regulation

Federal laws and regulations do not affect group life insurance contract provisions directly. Rather they affect the design of an employer's benefit plan. However, plan design often does influence the provisions of a group life insurance contract purchased by the employer. For example, the Age Discrimination in Employment Act prohibits an employer from eliminating benefits for older employees, but does allow some reduction in coverage. If an employer elects such reductions, they will be reflected in the benefits provided by the policy.

The two aspects of federal law that probably have had the greatest effect in the design of group life insurance plans are the Internal Revenue Code and ERISA.

The Internal Revenue Code determines the deductibility of employer contributions and the income taxation of employees who are provided coverage. Changes in the code have had a significant effect in the popularity of various types of group life insurance products.

ERISA requires employers to establish and maintain a group life insurance plan pursuant to a written plan document. This document specifies the plan fiduciary (or fiduciaries) who has the responsibility for selecting the insurance carrier. ERISA imposes duties on the fiduciary to protect plan participants. ERISA also requires the employer to disclose and report certain information to plan participants and the federal government.

GROUP TERM LIFE INSURANCE

The oldest and most common form of group life insurance is group term insurance. Coverage virtually always consists of yearly renewable term insurance that provides death benefits only, with no buildup of cash values. The group insurance marketplace with its widespread use of yearly renewable term contrasts with the individual marketplace, in which until recently such coverage has accounted for only a small percentage of the life insurance in force. This is primarily due to increasing annual premiums, which become prohibitive for many insureds at older ages. In group life insurance plans the overall premium, in addition to other factors, is a function of the age distribution of the group's members. While the premium for any individual employee will increase with age, the flow of younger workers into the plan and the retirement of older workers tend to result in a relatively stable age distribution and thus an average group insurance rate that remains constant or rises only slightly.

The following discussion of group term insurance focuses largely on common contract provisions, other coverages that are often added to the basic contract, and relevant federal tax laws.

Contract Provisions

The provisions contained in group term insurance contracts are more uniform than those found in other types of group insurance. Much of this uniformity is a result of the adoption by most states of the NAIC Group Life Insurance Standard Provisions Model Bill. This bill, coupled with the insurance industry's attempts at uniformity, has resulted in provisions that are virtually identical among insurance companies. While the following contract provisions represent the norm and are consistent with the practices of most insurance companies, some states may require slightly different provisions, and some companies may vary their contract provisions. In addition, negotiations between a policyowner and an insurance company may result in the modification of contract provisions.

Benefit Schedules

The purpose of the benefit schedule is twofold. It classifies the employees who are eligible for coverage and specifies the amount of life insurance that will be provided to the members of each class, thus minimizing adverse selection because the amount of coverage for individual employees is predetermined. A benefit schedule can be as simple as providing a single amount of life insurance for all employees or as complex as providing different amounts of insurance for different classes of employees. For individual employer groups the most common benefit schedules are those in which the amount of life insurance is based on either earnings or position.

Earnings Schedules. Most group term life insurance plans use an earnings schedule under which the amount of life insurance is determined as a multiple (or percentage) of each employee's earnings. For example, the amount of life insurance for each employee may be twice (200 percent of) the employee's annual earnings. Most plans use a multiple between one and two, but higher and lower multiples are occasionally used. The amount of insurance is often rounded to the next higher $1,000 and for underwriting purposes may be subject to a maximum benefit, such as $100,000. For purposes of the benefit schedule an employee's earnings usually consist of base salary only and do not include additional compensation like overtime pay or bonuses.

An alternative to using a flat percentage of earnings is to use an actual schedule of earnings such as the following:

Annual Earnings	Amount of Life Insurance
Less than $10,000	$ 10,000
$10,000 to $19,999	20,000
$20,000 to $29,999	40,000
$30,000 to $39,999	75,000
$40,000 to $49,999	100,000
$50,000 and over	150,000

This type of schedule may be designed so that all employees receive an amount of coverage that is approximately equal to the same multiple of annual earnings or, as in this example, larger multiples with higher earnings. Benefit schedules usually provide for a change in the amount of an employee's coverage when the employee moves into a different classification, even if this does not occur on the policy anniversary date. For example, the schedule above indicates that the amount of coverage for an employee earning $28,000 would increase from $40,000 to $75,000 if the employee received a $4,000 raise. Some schedules, however, specify that adjustments in amounts of coverage will only be made annually or on monthly premium due dates.

Position Schedules. Position schedules are similar to earnings schedules except that, as the example below shows, the amount of life insurance is based on an employee's position within the firm rather than on the employee's annual earnings.

Position	Amount of Life Insurance
President	$200,000
Vice presidents	100,000
Managers	60,000
Salespersons	40,000
Other employees	20,000

Because individuals in high positions are often involved in designing the benefit schedule, underwriters are concerned that the benefits for these individuals be reasonable in relation to the overall plan benefits. Position schedules may also pose problems in meeting nondiscrimination rules if excessively large amounts of coverage are provided to persons in high positions.

Even though position schedules are often used when annual earnings can be easily determined, they are particularly useful when it is difficult to determine an employee's annual income. This is the situation when income is materially affected by such factors as commissions earned, number of hours worked, or bonuses that are based on either the employee's performance or the firm's profits.

Flat-Benefit Schedules. Under flat-benefit schedules the same amount of life insurance is provided for all employees regardless of salary or position. This type of benefit schedule is commonly used in group insurance plans covering hourly paid employees, particularly when benefits are negotiated with a union. In most cases the amount of life insurance under a flat-benefit schedule is relatively small, such as $5,000 or $10,000. When an employer desires to provide only a minimum amount of life insurance for all employees, a flat-benefit schedule is often used.

Length-of-Service Schedules. In the early days of group life insurance, length-of-service schedules were relatively common and viewed as a method for rewarding longtime employees. However, because of the current view that the primary purpose of group life insurance is to replace income, such schedules are not extensively used. These schedules may also be considered discriminatory if a disproportionate number of the persons with longer service records are also the most highly paid employees. The table on the next page is an example of a length-of-service schedule.

Pension Schedules. Under pension schedules the amount of life insurance is a function of an employee's projected pension at retirement. For example, under an employer's plan the amount of life insurance for each employee might be 100 times the monthly pension that will be payable to the employee at normal

Length of Service	Amount of Life Insurance
Less than 2 years	$ 4,000
2 years but less than 5 years	8,000
5 years but less than 10 years	12,000
10 years but less than 15 years	16,000
15 years but less than 20 years	20,000
20 years or more	25,000

retirement age. However, the amount of life insurance may be subject to a maximum benefit.

Combination Benefit Schedules. It is not unusual for employers to have benefit schedules that incorporate elements from several of the various types previously discussed. While there are numerous possible combinations, a common benefit schedule of this type provides salaried employees with an amount of insurance that is determined by a multiple of their annual earnings and provides hourly employees with a flat amount of life insurance.

Reduction in Benefits. It is common for a group life insurance plan to provide for a reduction in benefits for active employees who reach a certain age, commonly 65 to 70. Such a reduction, which is due to the high cost of providing benefits for older employees, will be specified in the benefit schedule of a plan. Any reduction in the amount of life insurance for active employees is subject to the provisions of the Age Discrimination in Employment Act.

Benefit reductions fall into three categories: (1) a reduction to a flat amount of insurance, (2) a percentage reduction, such as to 65 percent of the amount of insurance that was previously provided, or (3) a gradual reduction over a period of years (for example, a 10 percent reduction in coverage each year until a minimum benefit amount is reached).

Eligibility

Group insurance contracts are very precise in their definition of what constitutes an eligible person for coverage purposes. In general, an employee must be in a covered classification, work full-time, and be actively at work. In addition, any requirements concerning probationary periods, insurability, or premium contributions must be satisfied.

Covered Classification. All group insurance contracts specify that an employee must fall into one of the classifications contained in the benefit schedule. While these classifications may be broad enough to include all employees of the organization, they may also be so limited as to exclude many employees from coverage. In some cases these excluded employees may have coverage through a negotiated trusteeship or under other group insurance contracts provided by the employer; in other cases they may have no coverage because the employer wishes to limit benefits to certain groups of employees. No employee may be in more than one classification, and the responsibility for determining the appropriate classification for each employee falls on the policyowner.

Full-time Employment. Most group insurance contracts limit eligibility to full-time employees. A full-time employee is generally defined as one who works no fewer than the number of hours in the normal work week established by the employer, which must be at least 30 hours. Subject to insurance company underwriting practices, an employer can provide coverage for part-time employees. When this is done, part-time is generally defined as less than full-time but more than some minimum number of hours per week. In addition, part-time employees may be subject to more stringent eligibility requirements. For example, full-time hourly paid employees may be provided with $20,000 of life insurance immediately upon employment, while part-time employees may be provided with only $10,000 of life insurance and may be subject to a probationary period.

Actively-at-Work Provision. Most group insurance contracts contain an actively-at-work provision, whereby an employee is not eligible for coverage if absent from work because of sickness, injury, or other reasons on the otherwise effective date of his or her coverage under the contract. Coverage will commence when the employee returns to work. The actively-at-work provision is often waived for employers with a large number of employees when coverage is transferred from one insurance company to another and the employees involved have been insured under the previous insurance company's contract.

Probationary Periods. Group insurance contracts may contain probationary periods that must be satisfied before an employee is eligible for coverage. When a probationary period exists, it rarely exceeds 6 months, and an employee will be eligible for coverage on either the first day after the probationary period has been satisfied or on the first day of the month following the end of the probationary period.

Insurability. While most group insurance contracts are issued without individual evidence of insurability, in some instances underwriting practices will require evidence of insurability. This commonly occurs when an employee fails to elect coverage under a contributory plan and later wants coverage or when an employee is eligible for a large amount of coverage. In these cases an employee will not be eligible for coverage until the employee has submitted the proper evidence of insurability and the insurance company has determined that the evidence is satisfactory.

Premium Contribution. If a group insurance plan is contributory, an employee will not be eligible for coverage until the policyowner has been provided with the proper authorization for payroll deductions. If this is done before the employee otherwise becomes eligible, coverage will commence on the eligibility date. During the next 31 days, coverage will commence when the policyowner receives the employee's authorization. If the authorization is not received within 31 days, the employee must furnish evidence of insurability at his or her own expense to obtain coverage. Evidence of insurability will also be required if an employee drops coverage under a contributory plan and wishes to regain coverage at a future date.

Beneficiary Designation

With few exceptions an insured person has the right to name the beneficiary under his or her group life insurance coverage. These exceptions include credit life insurance, where the creditor is the beneficiary, and dependent life insurance, where the employee is the beneficiary. In addition, the laws and regulations of some states prohibit naming the employer as beneficiary. Unless a beneficiary designation has been made irrevocable, an employee has the right to change the designated beneficiary at any time. While all insurance contracts require that the insurance company be notified of any beneficiary change in writing, the effective date of the change may vary depending on contract provisions. Some contracts specify that a change will be effective on the date it is received by the insurance company; others make it effective on the date the change was requested by the employee.

Under individual life insurance policies death benefits are paid to an insured person's estate if no beneficiary has been named or if all beneficiaries have died before the insured. Some group term insurance contracts contain an identical provision; others provide that the death benefits will be paid through a *successive beneficiary provision*. Under the latter provision the proceeds will be paid, at the option of the insurance company, to any one or more of the following survivors of the insured person: spouse, children, parents, brothers and sisters, or executor of the employee's estate. In most cases insurance companies will pay the proceeds to the person or persons in the first category that includes eligible survivors.

Two other provisions, each of which is often called a *facility-of-payment provision,* are sometimes found in group term insurance contracts. The first of these provisions provides that a specified amount, generally $500 or less, may be paid to any person who appears to be entitled to such a sum by reason of having incurred funeral or other expenses relating to the last illness or death of the person insured. The other provision applies to any beneficiary who is a minor or who is physically, mentally, or otherwise incapable of giving a valid release for any payment received. Under this provision the insurance company has the option, until a claim is made by the guardian for the beneficiary, of paying the proceeds to any person or institution that appears to have assumed responsibility for the care, custody, or support of the beneficiary. These payments will be made in installments in the amount specified under any optional method of settlement previously selected by the person insured, or, in the absence of such a selection, in installments not to exceed some specified amount, such as $100 per month.

Settlement Options

Group term insurance contracts covering employees provide that death benefits will be payable in a lump sum unless an optional mode of settlement has been selected. Each employee insured under the contract has the right to select and change any available mode of settlement during his or her lifetime. If no optional mode of settlement is in force at the death of the employee, the beneficiary generally has the right to elect any of the available options. The most common provision in group term insurance contracts is that the available modes of settlement are those customarily offered by the insurance company at the time the selection is made. The available options are not generally specified in the contract, but information about them is usually provided to the group policyowner. In addition, many insurance companies have brochures available for employees that describe either all or the most common options available. Any guarantees associated with these options will be those that are in effect when the option is selected.

In addition to a lump-sum option, most insurance companies offer all the following options: an interest option, an installment option for a fixed period, an installment option for a fixed amount, and a life income option.

Premiums

Group insurance contracts stipulate that it is the responsibility of the policyowner to pay all premiums to the insurance company, even if the group insurance plan is contributory. Any required contributions from employees will be incorporated into the employer's group insurance plan, but they are not part of the insurance contract and therefore do not constitute an obligation to the insurance company by the employees. Rather, these contributions represent an obligation to the employer by the employees and are commonly paid by payroll deduction. Subject to certain limitations, any employee contributions are determined by the employer or as a result of labor negotiations. Most states require the employer to pay at least a portion of the premium for group term insurance (but not for other group insurance coverage), and a few states impose limitations on the amounts that may be paid by any employee. The most common restriction limits the contribution of any employee to the greater of 60 cents per month per $1,000 of coverage or 75 percent of the premium rate for that employee. This limitation is adhered to by companies licensed to do business in the state of New York and is often incorporated into their contracts. However, for some hazardous industries a contribution higher than 60 cents per month per $1,000 is permitted.

Premiums are payable in advance to the insurance company or any authorized agent for the time period specified in the contract. In most cases premiums are payable monthly but may be paid less frequently. The rates used to determine the premium for any policyowner are guaranteed for a certain length of time, usually one year. The periodic premium is determined by applying these rates to the amount of life insurance in force. Consequently the premium actually payable will change each month as the total amount of life insurance in force under the group insurance plan varies.

Group insurance contracts state that any dividends or experience refunds are payable to the policyowner in cash or may be used at the policyowner's option to reduce any premium due. To the extent that these exceed the policyowner's share of the premium, they must be used for the benefit of the employees. This is usually accomplished by reducing employee contributions or by providing increased benefits.

Claims

The provision concerning death claims under group life insurance policies is very simple. It states that the amount of insurance under the contract is payable when the insurance company receives written proof of death. No time period is specified in which a claim must be filed. However, most companies require the completion of a brief form by the policyowner and the beneficiary before a claim is processed.

Assignment

For many years the owners of individual life insurance policies have been able to transfer any or all of their rights under the insurance contract to another party. Such assignments have been commonly used to avoid federal estate tax by removing the proceeds of an insurance contract from the insured's estate at death. Historically assignments have not been permitted under group life insurance contracts, often because of state laws and regulations prohibiting assignments. In recent years most states have eliminated such prohibitions, and many insurance companies have modified their contracts to permit assignments, or they will waive the prohibition upon request. Essentially an assignment will be valid as long as it is permitted by and conforms with state law and the group insurance contract. It should be noted that insurance companies will generally require any assignment to be in writing and to be filed with the company.

Grace Period

Group life insurance contracts provide for a grace period (almost always 31 days) during which a policyowner may pay any overdue premium without interest. If the premium is not paid, the contract will lapse at the end of the grace period unless the policyowner has notified the insurance company that an earlier termination should take place. Even if the policy is allowed to lapse or is terminated during the grace period, the policyowner is legally liable for the payment of any premium due during the portion of the grace period when the contract was still in force.

Entire Contract

The entire contract clause states that the insurance policy, the policyowner's application that is attached to the policy, and any individual (unattached) applications of any insured persons constitute the entire insurance contract. All statements made in these applications are considered to be representations rather than warranties, and no other statements made by the policyowner or by any insureds can be used by the insurance company as the basis for contesting coverage. When compared with the application for individual life insurance, the policyowner's application that is attached to a group insurance contract may be relatively short. Most of the information needed by the insurance company is often contained in a preliminary application that is not part of the insurance contract. On the delivery of many group insurance contracts the policyowner signs a final "acceptance application," which in effect states that the coverage as applied for has been delivered. Consequently a greater burden is placed on the insurance company to verify the statements made by the policyowner in the preliminary application.

The entire contract clause also stipulates that no agent has any authority to waive or amend any provisions of the insurance contract and that a waiver of or amendment to the contract will be valid only if it is signed by certain specified corporate officers of the insurance company.

Incontestability

Like individual life insurance contracts, group insurance contracts contain an incontestability provision. Except for the nonpayment of premiums the validity of the contract cannot be contested after it has been in force for a specified period, generally either one or two years. During this time the insurance company can contest the contract on the basis of statements by the policyowner in the application attached to the contract that are considered to be material misrepresentations. Statements by any insured person can be used as the basis for denying claims during this period only if such statements relate to the insurability of the individual. In addition, the statements must have been made in a written application signed by the individual, and a copy of the application must have been furnished to either the individual or his or her beneficiary. It should be pointed out that the incontestability clause will not be of concern to most covered persons, since evidence of insurability is not usually required and thus no statements concerning individual insurability will be made.

Misstatement of Age

If the age of any person covered under a group term insurance policy is misstated, the benefit payable will be the amount that is specified under the benefit schedule. However, the premium will be adjusted to reflect the true age of the individual. This is in contrast to individual life insurance contracts, where benefits are adjusted to the amount that the premium paid would have purchased at the true age of the individual. Under a group insurance contract the responsibility for paying any additional premium or the right to receive a refund belongs to the policyowner and not to the individual employee whose age is misstated, even if the plan is contributory. If the misstated age would have affected the employee's contribution, this is a matter to be resolved between the employer and the employee.

Termination

All group insurance contracts stipulate the conditions under which the contract may be terminated by either the insurance company or the policyowner. The circumstances under which the coverage for a particular insured person will terminate are also specified.

A group term insurance contract can be terminated for nonpayment of premium at the end of the grace period. Insurance companies may also terminate coverage for an individual employer group on any premium due date if certain conditions exist and notice of termination has been given to the policyowner at least 31 days in advance. These conditions include the failure to maintain a stated minimum number of participants in the plan and in contributory plans the failure to maintain a stated minimum percentage participation. The policyowner may also terminate the contract at any time by giving the insurance company 31 days' advance written notice. Moreover, the policyowner has the right to request the amendment of the contract at any time by notifying the insurance company.

The coverage for any insured person will terminate automatically (subject to any provisions for a continuation or conversion of coverage) when any of the following circumstances exist:

- The employee terminates employment.
- The employee ceases to be eligible (for example, if the employee no longer satisfies the full-time work requirement or no longer falls into a covered classification).
- The master contract is terminated by the policyowner or the insurance company.
- Any required contribution by the employee has not been made (generally because the employee has notified the policyowner to cease the required payroll deduction).

Temporary Interruption of Employment. Most group term insurance contracts provide that the employer may elect to continue coverage on employees during temporary interruptions of active full-time employment. These may arise from leaves of absence, layoffs, or the inability to work because of illness or injury. The employer must continue paying the premium, and the coverage may be continued only for a relatively short period of time, such as 3 months, unless the time period is extended by mutual agreement between the employer and the insurance company. Also in electing to continue coverage, the policyowner must act in such a way as to preclude individual selection.

Continuation of Coverage for Disabled Employees. Most group term insurance contracts make some provision for the continuation of coverage on employees whose active employment has terminated due to disability. By far the most common provision in use today is the *waiver-of-premium provision.* Under this provision life insurance coverage is continued without the payment of premium as long as the employee is totally disabled, even if the master contract is terminated. However, certain requirements must be met:

- The disability must commence while the employee is insured under the master contract.
- The disability must commence prior to a specified age, commonly age 60.
- The employee must be totally disabled. Total disability is normally defined as the complete inability of the employee to engage in any gainful occupation for which he or she is or becomes qualified by reason of education, training, or experience.
- The employee must file a claim within a prescribed period (normally 12 months) and must submit annual evidence of continuing disability.

If an employee no longer meets the definition of disability and returns to work, the employee may again be insured under the group insurance contract on a premium-paying basis as long as the employee meets the eligibility requirements of the contract. If for any reason the employee is not eligible for insurance under the group insurance contract, the conversion privilege can be exercised.

A few insurance companies refer to their waiver-of-premium provision as an extended death benefit. This terminology is somewhat confusing since historically an extended-death-benefit provision has allowed coverage to continue on a disabled employee for a maximum of only one year. After that time coverage ceases. This type of provision, once quite common, is still used occasionally but has generally been replaced by a waiver-of-premium provision.

Another provision relating to disabled employees is a maturity-value benefit. Under this type of provision the face amount of a totally disabled employee's group life insurance will be paid to the employee in a lump sum or in monthly installments. Like the extended-death-benefit provision, a maturity-value-benefit provision was once widely used but is no longer common.

A small but growing trend is for disabled employees to be continued as eligible employees under a group insurance contract, with the employer paying the periodic cost of their coverage just as if they were active employees. At the termination of the contract the insurance company has no responsibility to continue coverage unless a disabled employee is eligible and elects to convert coverage and pays any required premiums. However, depending on the provisions of the group insurance plan, the employer may have a legal responsibility to continue coverage on disabled employees in some manner.

Conversion. All group term insurance contracts covering employees contain a conversion privilege that gives any employee whose coverage ceases the right to convert to an individual insurance policy. The terms of the conversion privilege vary, depending upon the reason for the termination of coverage under the group contract. The most generous conversion rights are available to those employees who either have terminated employment or no longer fall into one of the eligible classifications still covered by the master contract. These employees have the right to purchase an individual life insurance policy from the insurance company without evidence of insurability, but it is usually one without disability or other supplementary benefits. However, this right is subject to the following conditions:

- The employee must apply for conversion within 31 days after the termination of employment or membership in an eligible classification. During this 31-day period the employee is provided with a death benefit equal to the amount of life insurance that is available under the conversion privilege, even if the employee does not apply for conversion. Disability and supplementary benefits are not extended during this period unless they are also subject to conversion. The premium for the individual policy must accompany the conversion application, and coverage will be effective at the end of the conversion period.
- The individual policy selected by the employee may generally be any form, except term insurance, customarily issued by the insurance company at the age and amount applied for. Some insurance companies also make term insurance coverage available, and a few states require that employees be

allowed to purchase term insurance coverage for a limited time (such as one year) after which an employee must convert to a cash value form of coverage.

- The face amount of the individual policy may not exceed the amount of life insurance that terminated under the group insurance contract.

- The premium for the individual policy will be determined using the insurance company's current rate applicable to the type and amount of the individual policy for the attained age of the employee on the date of conversion and for the class of risk to which the employee belongs. While no extra premium may be charged for reasons of health, an extra premium may be charged for any other hazards considered in an insurance company's rate structure, such as occupation or avocation.

It is estimated that only one or two percent of the employees eligible actually take advantage of the conversion privilege. Several reasons account for this. Many employees will obtain coverage with new employers; others are discouraged by the high cost of the permanent insurance to which they must convert. Still others, if they are insurable at standard rates, may find coverage at a lower cost with other insurers and be able to purchase supplementary coverage (such as disability benefits) that are not available under conversion policies. In addition, insurance companies have not actively encouraged group conversions because those who convert tend to be the poorer risks. Finally, since some employers are faced with conversion charges as a result of experience rating, they are also unlikely to encourage conversion.

A more restrictive conversion privilege exists if an employee's coverage is terminated because the master contract is terminated for all employees or is amended to eliminate eligible classifications. Under these circumstances the employee is given a conversion right only if he or she was insured under the contract for a period of time (generally 5 years) immediately preceding the date on which coverage was terminated. In addition, the amount of insurance that can be converted is limited to the lesser of (1) $2,000 or (2) the amount of the employee's life insurance under the contract at the date of termination reduced by any amount of life insurance for which the employee becomes eligible under any group life insurance policy issued or reinstated by the same or another insurance company within 31 days after such termination.

Accelerated and Living Benefits

Over the last several years many insurers have introduced an accelerated payout provision in their individual life insurance products. Under such a provision an insured is entitled to receive a portion of his or her death benefit while still living if one or more of the following events occur: (1) a terminal illness that is expected to result in death within 6 or 12 months, (2) a specified catastrophic illness, such as AIDS, a stroke, or Alzheimer's disease, and (3) the incurring of nursing home and possibly other long-term-care expenses. The categories of triggering events and the specific definitions of each vary among insurers.

Often what becomes popular in the individual marketplace starts to show up in the group insurance marketplace. Such is the case with accelerated benefits, but the number of insurers offering these benefits is still small.

Most group insurers allow accelerated benefits for terminal illnesses only. About half of these insurers use a life expectancy of 6 months or less; the other half use a life expectancy of 12 months or less. In either case the life expectancy must be certified by a doctor.

The amount of the accelerated benefit is expressed as a percentage of the basic life insurance coverage and may range from 25 percent to 100 percent. In addition, most insurers limit the maximum benefit to a specified dollar amount that may vary from $25,000 to $250,000. Any amount not accelerated is paid to the beneficiary upon the insured's death.

There are no limitations on how the accelerated benefit can be used. It might be used to pay medical expenses and nursing home care not covered by other insurance, or it could even be used to prepay funeral expenses.

Most insurers make a charge for an accelerated benefit, most commonly in the form of an additional premium that may be as high as 7 to 8 percent of the basic group life insurance premium. Instead of increasing the premium, a few insurers charge the insured by reducing the accelerated benefit by an amount equal to the interest that could have been earned on the money over the next 6 or 12 months.

Added Coverages

Group term insurance contracts often provide additional insurance benefits through the use of riders. These benefits are also forms of group term insurance and consist of (1) supplemental life insurance, (2) accidental death and dismemberment insurance, and (3) dependent life insurance. These added benefits may be provided for all employees insured under the basic group term contract or may be limited to certain classes of employees. With the exception of dependent life insurance these coverages may also be written as separate contracts.

Supplemental Life Insurance

The majority of group life insurance plans enable all or certain classes of employees to purchase additional amounts of life insurance. Generally the employer will provide a basic amount of life insurance to all eligible employees on a noncontributory basis. This is commonly a flat amount of coverage or a multiple of annual earnings. The supplemental coverage is contributory and may be either incorporated into the basic group life insurance contract or contained in a separate contract. The latter method tends to be more common when the supplemental coverage is available to only a select group of employees. Although the employee may pay the entire cost of the supplemental coverage, either state laws that require employer contributions or insurance company underwriting practices will often result in the employer's paying a portion of the cost.

The amount of supplemental coverage available will be specified in a benefit schedule. Under some plans an employee must purchase the full amount of coverage; under other plans an employee may purchase a portion of the coverage. The following are two examples of benefit schedules for a basic-plus-supplemental life insurance plan:

Type of Coverage	Amount of Life Insurance
Basic insurance	$10,000
Supplemental insurance	20,000

Type of Coverage	Amount of Life Insurance
Basic insurance	1 times salary
Supplemental insurance	1/2, 1, 1 1/2, or 2 times salary, subject to a maximum (including basic insurance) of $100,000

Giving employees the right to choose their benefit amounts leads to adverse selection. As a result, more stringent underwriting requirements are usually associated with supplemental coverage. These often include requiring individual evidence of insurability, except possibly when the additional amount of coverage is modest. Higher rates may also be charged for the supplemental insurance than for the basic coverage.

Accidental Death and Dismemberment Insurance

Many group life insurance contracts contain an accidental death and dismemberment provision that gives additional benefits if an employee dies accidentally or suffers certain types of injuries. Traditionally this group coverage was available only as a rider to a group life insurance contract. Now, however, it is common to find these benefits provided through separate group insurance contracts in which coverage is usually contributory on the part of employees. Such contracts are referred to as voluntary accidental death and dismemberment insurance.

Traditional Coverage. Under the traditional form of accidental death and dismemberment insurance an employee eligible for group life insurance coverage (and electing the life insurance coverage if it is contributory) will automatically have the accidental death and dismemberment coverage if it has been added by the employer. Under the typical accidental death and dismemberment rider the insurance company will pay an additional amount of insurance that is equal to the amount of coverage under the basic group life insurance contract (referred to as the principal sum) if an employee dies as a result of accidental bodily injuries while he or she is covered under the policy. It is specified that death must occur within 90 days following the date that injuries are sustained, but some courts have ruled this time period to be invalid and have required insurance companies to pay claims when longer periods have been involved. In addition to an accidental death benefit the following benefit schedule is provided for certain specific types of injuries:

Type of Injury	Benefit Amount
Loss of (including loss of use of):	
Both hands or both feet	The principal sum
The sight of both eyes	The principal sum
One hand and sight of one eye	The principal sum
One foot and sight of one eye	The principal sum
One foot and one hand	The principal sum
One hand	One-half the principal sum
One foot	One-half the principal sum
The sight of one eye	One-half the principal sum

In some cases the accidental death and dismemberment rider is written to provide the same benefits for any accident covered under the contract. However, it is not unusual to have a higher level of benefits for accidents that occur while the employee is traveling on business for the employer. These larger travel benefits may apply to death benefits only. They may also be limited to accidents that occur while the employee is occupying (or entering, alighting from, or struck by) a public conveyance and possibly a company-owned or personally owned vehicle. The following is an example of a benefit schedule reflecting some of these variations:

Type of Loss	Benefit Amount
Death while traveling on business when occupying, boarding, alighting from, or struck by any motor vehicle, airplane, or other conveyance, including company-owned or personally owned vehicles	3 times the principal sum
Death at all other times	2 times the principal sum
Dismemberment	Up to the principal sum (as shown in the previous schedule)

Death benefits are paid in accordance with the beneficiary provision of the group life insurance contract, and dismemberment benefits are paid to the employee. Coverage is usually written to cover both occupational and nonoccupational accidents. However, when employees are in hazardous occupations, coverage may apply only to nonoccupational accidents, in which case employees would still have workers' compensation coverage for any occupational accidents.

Coverage is generally not subject to a conversion privilege. When life insurance coverage continues after retirement, accidental death and dismemberment benefits normally cease. Like the life insurance coverage, however, it may be continued during temporary periods of unemployment. In contrast to the group term insurance policy to which it is attached, group accidental death and dismemberment insurance contains some exclusions. These include losses resulting from

- suicide at any time (It is interesting to note that, except for a few multiple-employer trusts, group term insurance does not contain a suicide provision.)
- disease or bodily or mental infirmity, or medical or surgical treatment thereof
- ptomaines or any infection other than one occurring simultaneously with and through an accidental cut or wound
- war
- travel or flight in any type of aircraft as a pilot, student pilot, or officer or member of the crew (There is a trend toward eliminating this exclusion, particularly when coverage is written on large groups.)

Voluntary Coverage. The provisions of voluntary group accidental death and dismemberment insurance are practically identical to those contained in a group life insurance contract with an accidental death and dismemberment insurance rider. However, there are a few differences. Voluntary plans usually require the employee to pay the entire cost of coverage, and they virtually always provide both occupational and nonoccupational coverage. Subject to limitations, the employee may select the amount of coverage desired, with the maximum amount of coverage available tending to be larger than when coverage is provided through a rider. Another difference is the frequent use in voluntary plans of a common accident provision, whereby the amount payable by the insurance company is limited to a stipulated maximum for all employees killed or injured in any single accident. If this exceeds the sum of the benefits otherwise payable for each employee, benefits are prorated.

Dependent Life Insurance

Some group life insurance contracts provide insurance coverage on the lives of employees' dependents. Dependent life insurance has been viewed as a method of providing the employee with resources to meet the funeral and burial expenses associated with the death of a dependent. Consequently the employee is automatically the beneficiary. The employee also elects and pays for this coverage if it is contributory. Coverage for dependents is almost always limited to employees who are themselves covered under the group contract. Thus if an employee's coverage is contributory, the employee must elect coverage for himself or herself in order to be eligible to elect dependent coverage.

For purposes of dependent life insurance coverage, dependents are usually defined as including an employee's spouse who is not legally separated from the employee and an employee's unmarried dependent children (including stepchildren and adopted children) who are over 14 days of age but under some specified age, commonly 19 or 21. To prevent adverse selection an employee cannot select coverage on individual dependents. Rather, if dependent coverage is selected, all dependents fitting the definition are insured. When dependent coverage is in effect for an employee, any new eligible dependents are automatically insured.

The amount of coverage for each dependent is usually quite modest. Some states limit the maximum amount of life insurance that can be written, and a few states actually prohibit writing any coverage on dependents. In addition, employer contributions used to purchase more than $2,000 of coverage on each dependent will result in income to the employee for purposes of federal taxation. However, amounts in excess of $2,000 may be purchased with employee contributions without adverse tax consequences. In some cases the same amount of coverage will be provided for all dependents; in other cases a larger amount will be provided for the spouse than for the children. It is also not unusual for the amount of coverage on children to be less until the children attain some specified age, such as 6 months. The following are examples of benefit schedules under dependent coverage:

Class	Amount of Insurance
Each dependent	$2,000

Class	Amount of Insurance
Spouse	50% of the employee's insured amount, subject to a maximum of $5,000
Dependent children: at least 14 days old but less than 6 months	$ 500
6 months or older	$1,000

A single premium applies to the dependent coverage for each employee and is independent of the number of dependents. In some cases the premium may vary, depending on the age of the employee (but not the dependents), but more commonly it is the same amount for all employees regardless of age. Dependent coverage usually contains a conversion privilege that applies only to the coverage on the spouse. However, some states require that the conversion privilege apply to the coverage on all dependents. Assignment is almost never permitted, and no waiver of premium is available if a dependent becomes disabled. However, if the basic life insurance contract contains a waiver-of-premium provision applicable to the employee, the employee's disability will sometimes result in a waiver of premium for the dependent coverage. A provision similar to the actively-at-work provision pertaining to employees is often included for dependents. It specifies that dependents will not be covered when otherwise eligible if they are confined in a hospital (except for newborn children, who are covered after 14 days). Coverage will commence when the dependent is discharged from the hospital.

Taxation

A discussion of group term insurance is incomplete without an explanation of the tax laws affecting its use. While discussions of these laws are often limited to federal income and estate taxation, federal gift taxation and taxation by the states should also be considered.

Federal Taxation

The growth of group term insurance has been greatly influenced by the favorable tax treatment afforded it under federal tax laws. This section will discuss the effects of these tax laws on basic group term insurance and on coverages that may be added to a basic group term insurance contract. A complete explanation of the federal tax laws pertaining to group term insurance and their interpretation by the Internal Revenue Service would be lengthy and is beyond the scope of this chapter. Consequently this discussion of federal tax laws will only highlight these laws.

Deductibility of Premiums. In general, employer contributions for an employee's group term insurance coverage are fully deductible to the employer as an ordinary and necessary business expense as long as the overall compensation of the employee is reasonable. The reasonableness of compensation (which includes wages, salary, and other fringe benefits) is usually only a potential issue for the owners of small businesses or the stockholder-employees of closely held corporations. Any compensation that is determined by the Internal Revenue Service to be unreasonable may not be deducted by a firm for income tax purposes. In addition, the Internal Revenue Code does not allow a firm to take an income tax deduction for contributions (1) that are made in behalf of sole proprietors or partners under any circumstances or (2) that are made in behalf of stockholders unless they are providing substantive services to the corporation. Finally, no deduction is allowed if the employer is named as beneficiary.

Contributions by any individual employee are considered payments for personal life insurance and are not deductible for income tax purposes by that employee. Thus the amount of any payroll deductions authorized by an employee for group term insurance purposes will be included in the employee's taxable income.

Income Tax Liability of Employees. In the absence of tax laws to the contrary, the amount of any compensation for which an employer receives an income tax deduction (including the payment of group insurance premiums) represents taxable income to the employee. However, Sec. 79 of the Internal Revenue Code provides favorable tax treatment to employer contributions for life insurance that qualifies as group term insurance.

Sec. 79 requirements. In order to qualify as group term insurance under Sec. 79, life insurance must meet the following conditions:

- It must provide a death benefit excludible from federal income tax.
- It must be provided to a group of employees, defined to include all employees of an employer. If all employees are not covered, membership must be determined on the basis of age, marital status, or factors relating to employment.

- It must be provided under a policy carried directly or indirectly by the employer. This includes (1) any policy for which the employer pays any part of the cost or (2) if the employer pays no part of the cost, any policy arranged by the employer if at least one employee is charged less than his or her cost (under Table I) and at least one other employee is charged more than his or her cost. If no employee is charged more than the Table I cost, a policy is not group term insurance for purposes of Sec. 79.

   A policy is defined to include a master contract or a group of individual policies. The term *carried indirectly* refers to those situations when the employer is not the policyowner but rather provides coverage to employees through master contracts issued to organizations such as negotiated trusteeships or multiple-employer welfare arrangements.

- The plan must be arranged in such a manner as to preclude individual selection of coverage amounts. However, it is acceptable to have alternative benefit schedules based on the amount an employee elects to contribute. Supplemental plans where an employee is given a choice, such as either 1, 1 1/2, or 2 times salary, are considered to fall within this category.

All life insurance that qualifies under Sec. 79 as group term insurance is considered to be a single plan of insurance, regardless of the number of insurance contracts used. For example, an employer might provide coverage for union employees under a negotiated trusteeship, coverage for other employees under an individual employer group insurance contract, and additional coverage for top executives under a group of individual life insurance policies. Under Sec. 79 these would all constitute a single plan. This plan must be provided for at least 10 full-time employees at some time during the calendar year. For purposes of meeting the 10-life requirement, employees who have not satisfied any required waiting periods may be counted as participants. In addition, employees who have elected not to participate are also counted as participants—but only if they would not have been required to contribute to the cost of other benefits besides group term insurance if they had participated. As will be described later, a plan with fewer than 10 full-time employees may still qualify for favorable tax treatment under Sec. 79 if more restrictive requirements are met.

Exceptions to Sec. 79. Even when all the previous requirements are met, there are some situations in which Sec. 79 does not apply. In some cases different sections of the Internal Revenue Code provide alternative tax treatment. For example, when group term insurance is issued to the trustees of a qualified pension plan and is used to provide a death benefit under the plan, the full amount of any life insurance paid for by employer contributions will result in taxable income to the employee.

There are three situations in which employer contributions for group term insurance will not result in taxable income to an employee, regardless of the amount of insurance: (1) if an employee has terminated employment because of disability, (2) if a qualified charity (as determined by the Internal Revenue Code) has been named as beneficiary for the entire year, or (3) if the employer has been named as beneficiary for the entire year.

Coverage on retired employees is subject to Sec. 79, and these persons are treated in the same manner as active employees. Thus they will have taxable income in any year in which the amount of coverage received exceeds $50,000. However, a grandfather clause to this new rule stipulates that it does not apply to group term life insurance plans (or to comparable successor plans or to plans of successor employers) in existence on January 1, 1984, for covered employees who (1) retired before 1984 or (2) were at least 55 years of age before 1984 and were employed by the employer any time during 1983. There is one exception to this grandfather clause; it does not apply to persons (either key or nonkey employees) retiring after 1986 if a plan is discriminatory. The factors that make a plan discriminatory are discussed later.

General tax rules. Under Sec. 79 the cost of the first $50,000 of coverage is not taxed to the employee. Since all group term insurance provided by an employee that qualifies under Sec. 79 is considered to be one plan, this exclusion applies only once to each employee. For example, an employee who has $10,000 of coverage that is provided to all employees under one policy and $75,000 of coverage provided to executives under a separate insurance policy would have a single $50,000 exclusion. The cost of coverage in excess of $50,000, less any employee contributions for the entire amount of coverage, represents taxable income to the employee. For purposes of Sec. 79 the cost of this excess coverage is determined by a government table called the Uniform Premium Table I. This table will often result in a lower cost than would be calculated using the actual premium paid by the employer for the coverage.

Uniform Premium Table I	
Age	Cost per Month per $1,000 of Coverage
29 and under	$ .08
30–34	.09
35–39	.11
40–44	.17
45–49	.29
50–54	.48
55–59	.75
60–64	1.17
65–69	2.10
70 and over	3.76

To calculate the cost of an employee's coverage for one month of protection under a group term insurance plan, the Uniform Premium Table I cost shown for the employee's age bracket (based on the employee's attained age at the end of the tax year) is multiplied by the number of thousands in excess of 50 of group term insurance on the employee. For example, if an employee aged 57 was provided with $150,000 of group term insurance, the employee's monthly cost (assuming no employee contributions) would be calculated as follows:

Coverage provided	$150,000
Less Sec. 79 exclusion	50,000
Amount subject to taxation	$100,000
Uniform Premium Table I monthly cost per $1,000 of coverage at age 57	$.75
Monthly cost ($.75 x 100)	$75

The monthly costs are then totaled to obtain an annual cost. Assuming no change in the amount of coverage during the year, the annual cost would be $900. Any employee contributions for the entire amount of coverage are deducted from the annual cost to determine the taxable income that must be reported by an employee. If an employee contributed $.30 per month ($3.60 per year) per $1,000 of coverage, the employee's total annual contribution for $150,000 of coverage would be $540. This reduces the amount reportable as taxable income from $900 to $360.

One final point is worthy of attention. When the Uniform Premium Table I was incorporated into the IRS regulations for Sec. 79, it resulted in favorable tax treatment for the cost of group term insurance, because the monthly costs in the table were always lower than the actual cost of coverage in the marketplace. Today group term insurance coverage can often be purchased at a lower cost than Table I rates. There are some who argue that in these instances the actual cost of coverage can be used in place of the Table I cost for determining an employee's taxable income. From the standpoint of logic and consistency with the tax laws this view makes sense. However, the regulations for Sec. 79 are very specific: only Table I costs are to be used.

Nondiscrimination Rules. Any plan that qualified as group term insurance under Sec. 79 is subject to nondiscrimination rules, and the $50,000 exclusion will not be available to key employees if a plan is discriminatory. Such a plan favors key employees in either eligibility or benefits. In addition, the value of the full amount of coverage for key employees, less their own contribution, will be considered taxable income, based on the greater of actual or Table I costs. A key employee of a firm is defined as any person who at any time during the current plan year or the preceding 4 plan years is any of the following:

- an officer of the firm who earns from the firm more than 50 percent of the Internal Revenue Code limit on the amount of benefits payable by a defined-benefit plan. This amount (50 percent of $115,641, or $57,820.50, for 1993) is indexed annually. For purposes of this rule the number of employees treated as officers is the greater of 3 or 10 percent of the firm's employees, subject to a maximum of 50. In applying the rule the following employees can be excluded: persons who are part-time, persons who are under 21, and persons with less than 6 months of service with the firm.

- one of the 10 employees owning the largest interests in the firm and having an annual compensation from the firm of more than $30,000
- a more-than-5-percent owner of the firm
- a more-than-one-percent owner of the firm who earns over $150,000 per year
- a retired employee who was a key employee when he or she retired or terminated service

Note that the definition of key employee includes not only active employees but also retired employees who were key employees at the time of retirement or separation from service.

Eligibility requirements are not discriminatory if (1) at least 70 percent of all employees are eligible, (2) at least 85 percent of all employees who are participants are not key employees, or (3) participants comprise a classification that the IRS determines is nondiscriminatory. For purposes of the 70 percent test, employees with less than 3 years' service, part-time employees, and seasonal employees may be excluded. Employees covered by collective-bargaining agreements may also be excluded if plan benefits were the subject of good-faith bargaining.

Benefits are not discriminatory if neither the type nor amount of benefits discriminates in favor of key employees. It is permissible to base benefits on a uniform percentage of salary.

One issue that arose after the passage of the nondiscrimination rules in 1984 was whether they applied separately to active and to retired employees. A technical correction in the Tax Reform Act of 1986 clarified the issue by stating that the rules do apply separately to the extent provided in IRS regulations. However, such regulations have yet to be issued.

Groups with fewer than 10 full-time employees. A group insurance plan that covers fewer than 10 employees must satisfy an additional set of requirements before it is eligible for favorable tax treatment under Sec. 79. These rules predated the general nondiscrimination rules previously described, and it was assumed that the under-10 rules would be abolished when the new rules were adopted. However, that was not done, so smaller groups are subject to two separate and somewhat overlapping sets of rules. It should again be noted that Sec. 79 applies to an employer's overall plan of group insurance, not to separate group insurance contracts. For example, an employer providing group insurance coverage for its 50 hourly employees under one group insurance contract and for its 6 executives under a separate contract is considered to have a single plan covering 56 employees and thus is exempt from the under-10 requirements. While the stated purpose of the under-10 requirements is to preclude individual selection, their effect is to prevent the group insurance plan from discriminating in favor of the owners or stockholder-employees of small businesses.

With some exceptions plans covering fewer than 10 employees must provide coverage for all full-time employees. For purposes of this requirement employees who are not customarily employed for more than 20 hours in any one week or 5 months in any calendar year are considered part-time employees. It is permissible to exclude a full-time employees from coverage under the following circumstances:

- The employee has reached 65.
- The employee has not satisfied the waiting period under the plan. However, the waiting period may not exceed 6 months.
- The employee has elected not to participate in the plan, but only if the employee would not have been required to contribute to the cost of other benefits besides group term life insurance if he or she had participated.
- The employee has not satisfied the evidence of insurability required under the plan. An employee's eligibility for insurance (or the amount of insurance on the employee's life) may be subject to evidence of insurability. However, this evidence of insurability must be determined solely on the basis of a medical questionnaire completed by the employee and not by a medical examination.

The amount of coverage must be a flat amount, a uniform percentage of salary, or an amount based on different employee classifications. These employee classifications, which are referred to as coverage brackets in Sec. 79, may be determined in the manner described earlier in this chapter in the section on benefit schedules. The amount of coverage provided to each employee in any classification may be no greater than 2 1/2 times the amount of coverage provided to each employee in the next lower classification. In addition, each employee in the lowest classification must be provided with an amount of coverage that is equal to at least 10 percent of the amount provided to each employee in the highest classification. There must also be a reasonable expectation that there will be at least one employee in each classification. The following benefit schedule would be unacceptable for two reasons. First, the amount of coverage provided for the hourly employees is only 5 percent of the amount of coverage provided for the president. Second, the amount of coverage on the supervisor is more than 2 1/2 times the amount of coverage provided for the hourly employees.

Classification	Amount of Coverage
President	$100,000
Supervisor	40,000
Hourly employees	5,000

The following benefit schedule, however, would be acceptable:

Classification	Amount of Coverage
President	$100,000
Supervisor	40,000
Hourly employees	20,000

If a group insurance plan that covers fewer than 10 employees does not qualify for favorable tax treatment under Sec. 79, any premiums paid by the employer for such coverage will represent taxable income to the employees. The employer, however, will still receive an income tax deduction for any premiums paid in behalf of the employees as long as overall compensation is reasonable.

Taxation of Proceeds. In most instances the death proceeds under a group term insurance contract do not result in any taxable income to the beneficiary if they are paid in a lump sum. If the proceeds are payable in installments over more than one taxable year, only the interest earnings attributable to the proceeds will be included in the beneficiary's income for tax purposes.

Under certain circumstances the proceeds are not exempt from income taxation if the coverage was transferred (either in whole or in part) for a valuable consideration. Such a situation will arise when the stockholder-employees of a corporation name each other as beneficiaries under their group term insurance coverage as a method of funding a buy-sell agreement. The mutual agreement to name each other as beneficiaries is the valuable consideration. Under these circumstances any proceeds paid to a beneficiary constitute ordinary income to the extent that the proceeds exceed the beneficiary's tax basis, as determined by the Internal Revenue Code.

In many cases benefits paid by an employer to employees or their beneficiaries from the firm's assets receive the same tax treatment as benefits provided under an insurance contract. This is not true for death benefits. If they are provided other than through an insurance contract, the amount of the proceeds in excess of $5,000 will represent taxable income to the beneficiary. For this reason employers are less likely to use alternative funding arrangements for death benefits than for disability and medical expense benefits.

Proceeds of a group term insurance contract, even if paid to a named beneficiary, are included in an employee's gross estate for federal estate tax purposes as long as the employee possessed incidents of ownership in the coverage at the time of death. However, no estate tax is levied on any amounts, including life insurance proceeds, left to a surviving spouse. In addition, taxable estates of $600,000 or less are generally free of estate taxation regardless of the beneficiary.

When an estate would otherwise be subject to estate taxation, an employee may remove the proceeds of group term insurance from his or her taxable estate by absolutely assigning all incidents of ownership to another person, usually the beneficiary of the coverage. Incidents of ownership include the right to change the beneficiary, to terminate coverage, to assign coverage, or to exercise the conversion privilege. For this favorable treatment, however, the Internal Revenue Code requires that such an assignment be permissible under both the group term insurance master contract and the laws of the state having jurisdiction. The absolute assignment is usually in the form of a gift, which is not without its own tax implications. The amount of insurance is considered a gift made each year by the employee to the person to whom the absolute assignment was granted. Consequently if the value of the gift is of sufficient size, federal gift taxes will be payable. Since the Internal Revenue Code and the Internal Revenue Service regulations are silent on the specific gift tax consequences of assigned group term insurance, there is disagreement about whether the gift should be valued at Table I costs or at the actual premium for the coverage.

The assignment of group term life insurance also results in the inclusion of some value in the employee's estate. If the employee dies within 3 years of making the assignment, the full amount of the proceeds will be included in the employee's estate. If death occurs more than 3 years after the assignment is made, only the premiums paid within the 3 years prior to death will be included in the employee's taxable estate. In the past a problem arose if the employer changed group insurance carriers, thus requiring the employee to make a new assignment and again be subject to the 3-year time limit. However, the Internal Revenue Service now considers this type of situation to be a continuation of the original assignment as long as the amount and provisions of the new coverage are essentially the same as those of the old coverage.

There has been some uncertainty about the taxation of accelerated benefits from a group term insurance policy. In the past such a benefit has not met the definition of a life insurance death benefit or any other income-tax-free benefit from a life insurance policy. However, at the time this book was being written, the IRS had just issued proposed regulations to clarify the situation. The regulations are subject to revision as a result of public comments, but it appears that accelerated benefits will be income tax free if made as the result of a terminal illness that is expected to result in death within 12 months of payment.

Treatment of Added Coverages. Supplemental life insurance can be written as either a separate contract or as part of the contract providing basic group term life insurance coverage. If it is a separate contract and if the supplemental group life insurance meets the conditions of qualifying as group term insurance under Sec. 79, the amount of coverage provided is added to all other group term insurance for purposes of calculating the Uniform Premium Table I cost. Any premiums paid by the employee for the supplemental coverage are included in the deduction used to determine the final taxable income. In all other ways supplemental life insurance is treated the same as group term insurance.

Many separate supplemental contracts are noncontributory, and the cost for each employee's coverage does not exceed Table I costs. In this case the supplemental contract does not qualify as group term life insurance under Sec. 79. As a result the value of the coverage is not included in an employee's income.

When supplemental life insurance coverage is written in conjunction with a basic group life insurance plan, employers have the option of treating the supplemental coverage as a separate policy of insurance as long as the premiums are properly allocated among the two portions of the coverage. There is no advantage in treating the supplemental coverage as a separate policy if it would still qualify by itself as group term insurance under Sec. 79. However, this election will minimize taxable income to employees if the cost of the supplemental coverage is paid totally by the employees and all employees are charged rates at or below Table I rates.

Premiums paid for accidental death and dismemberment insurance are considered to be health insurance premiums rather than group term insurance premiums. However, these are also deductible to the employer as an ordinary and necessary business expense, the same as for group term insurance. Benefits paid to an employee under the dismemberment portion of the coverage are treated as benefits received under a health insurance contract and are received income tax free. Death benefits received under the coverage are treated like death benefits received under group term life insurance.

Employer contributions for dependent life insurance coverage are fully deductible by the employer as an ordinary and necessary business expense if overall compensation of the employee is reasonable. Employer contributions do not result in taxable income to an employee as long as the value of the benefit is *de minimis*. This means that the value is so small that it is administratively impractical for the employer to account for the cost on a per-person basis. Dependent coverage of $2,000 or less on any person falls into this category. The Internal Revenue Service considers amounts of coverage in excess of $2,000 on any dependent to be more than *de minimis*. If more than $2,000 of coverage is provided for any dependent from employer contributions, the cost of the entire amount of coverage for that dependent (as determined by Uniform Premium Table I rates) will be considered taxable income to the employee.

Death benefits will be free of income taxation and will not be included in the taxable estate of the dependent for estate tax purposes.

State Taxation

In most instances state tax laws affecting group term insurance are similar to the federal laws. However, two major differences do exist. In most states the payment of group term insurance premiums by the employer will not result in any taxable income to the employee, even if the amount of coverage exceeds $50,000. In addition, death proceeds receive favorable tax treatment under the estate and inheritance tax laws of most states. Generally the proceeds are at least partially, if not totally, exempt from such taxation.

POSTRETIREMENT GROUP LIFE INSURANCE

Continuation of Group Term Insurance

The continuation of group term insurance on employees after retirement requires the employer to make two important decisions: the amount of coverage to be continued and the method to be used for paying the cost of the continued coverage. Although the full amount of coverage prior to retirement may be continued, the high cost of group term insurance coverage for employees at older ages frequently results in a reduction in the amount of coverage. In some cases employees are provided with a flat amount of coverage (such as $2,000 or $5,000); in other cases employees are provided with a percentage (such as 50 percent) of the amount of coverage they had on the date of retirement.

The cost of providing postretirement life insurance is usually paid from current revenue, with each periodic premium paid the insurance company based on the lives of all employees covered, both active and retired. Since retired employees have no salary or wages from which payroll deductions can be made, most postretirement life insurance coverage is noncontributory.

A few employers fund postretirement benefits through a retired lives reserve, which is a fund established during the working years of employees for the purpose of paying all or a part of the cost of group term life insurance for the employees after retirement. Once popular, retired lives reserves are used little today because of administrative costs and the limited amount of coverage that can now be prefunded on a tax-deductible basis.

Group Universal Life Insurance

Forms of group life insurance to provide protection both before and after retirement have been written for many years. The earliest form was group paid-up insurance. Under a group paid-up insurance plan the total amount of insurance coverage is determined the same way as it is for group term insurance plans (for example, a schedule related to earnings or a flat amount). The amount of insurance consists of accumulating units of single-premium whole life insurance and decreasing amounts of group term insurance, with a total amount of coverage remaining constant.

In the 1970s group ordinary insurance became popular. It can be viewed essentially as dividing a whole life insurance policy into two segments: a term portion and a permanent or cash-value portion. The total amount of coverage available to an employee is determined the same way it is in group term insurance. The cost of the term portion of the coverage is paid by the employer, and the permanent portion, which the employee may be able to decline, is generally paid by the employee.

As a result of changes in tax laws both forms of coverage lost much of their popularity, and few new plans are written today.

Beginning in the mid-1980s many of the large writers of group insurance started to sell group universal life insurance, a trend that has been greeted with much interest by insurers, employers, and even employees. This interest seems to stem primarily from five factors:

- the phenomenal success of universal life in the individual marketplace
- tax legislation that resulted in employer-provided term life insurance in excess of $50,000 becoming taxable after retirement
- the clarification of the tax treatment of universal life insurance. For the first few years after the introduction of universal life insurance, there was concern that the IRS would not grant it the same favorable tax treatment that was granted to traditional cash value life insurance policies. There was speculation that the interest paid on the cash value might become subject to taxation and also that the death benefit would be considered taxable income to the beneficiary. For the most part these fears have been laid to rest by tax legislation as long as a universal life insurance policy meets certain prescribed guidelines. Therefore the cash value of a universal life insurance policy accumulates tax free, and death benefits are free of income taxation.
- the interest of employers to contain employee benefit costs. Little needs to be said about the attempts of employers to minimize the costs of their employee benefit plans. Group universal life insurance plans can make life insurance available to employees with little cost to the employer.
- less favorable tax treatment for formerly popular products for prefunding postretirement life insurance—retired lives reserves and group ordinary life insurance

Group universal life insurance products are being marketed primarily as supplemental life insurance plans—either to replace existing supplemental group term life insurance plans or as additional supplemental plans. Some insurers are selling them as a way of providing the basic life insurance plan of the employee as well. Marketing efforts are touting group universal life insurance as having the following advantages to the employer:

- no direct cost other than those associated with payroll deductions and possibly enrollment, since the entire premium cost is borne by the employee. In this sense group universal life insurance plans are much like mass-marketed insurance plans
- no ERISA filing and reporting requirement as long as the master contract is issued to a trust and as long as there are no employer contributions for the cost of coverage. The current products are marketed through multiple-employer trusts, with the trust being the policyowner.
- the ability of employees to continue coverage into retirement, alleviating pressure for the employer to provide postretirement life insurance benefits

The following advantages are being claimed for employees:

- the availability of a popular life insurance product at group rates
- the opportunity to continue insurance coverage after retirement, possibly without any postretirement contributions
- flexibility in designing coverage to best meet the needs of the individual employee

The current plans being marketed are still evolving, and differences do exist among the plans being offered by competing insurance companies. Because of the flexibility given policyholders, the administrative aspects of a group universal plan are formidable, and most insurers originally designed their plans only for employers with a large number of employees, usually at least 1,000. However, most insurers that write the product now make it available for as few as 100 lives.

Skeptics, including employees of some insurance companies offering group universal life, wonder if the administrative aspects can be accomplished in such a manner that it can be offered at a cost that is significantly lower than coverage in the individual marketplace. In raising this question, they point out the administrative problems and costs that have arisen when universal life insurance has been included in mass-marketed individual insurance plans, as well as the highly competitive market for individual universal life insurance that has resulted in rates with extremely low margins for contributions to surplus. These drawbacks, coupled with the lack of employer contributions, make the potential for savings to employees through the group insurance approach less than for many other types of insurance. Other critics point out that the popularity of universal life insurance in general has decreased as interest rates have dropped over the last few years, and they wonder how successful universal life will be if interest rates drop further. However, plans that are installed are usually well received by employees, and participation generally meets or exceeds expectations.

General Nature

The general nature of group universal life insurance is essentially the same as individual universal life insurance. The following discussion focuses primarily on their differences.

Types of Group Universal Products

Two approaches have been used in designing group universal life insurance products. Under the first approach there is a single group universal life insurance plan. An employee who wants only term insurance can pay a premium equal to the mortality and expense charges so that there is no accumulation of cash values. Naturally an employee who wants to accumulate cash values must pay a larger premium.

Under the second approach there are actually two group insurance plans—a term insurance plan and a universal life insurance plan. An employee who wants only term insurance contributes to the term insurance plan, and an employee who wants only universal life insurance contributes to the universal life insurance plan. With this approach an employee purchasing universal life insurance must make premium payments that are sufficient to generate a cash value accumulation. Initially the employee may be required to make minimum premium payments, such as two or three times the cost of the pure insurance. If an employee who has only the term insurance coverage later wants to switch to universal life insurance coverage, the group term insurance certificate is cancelled, and the employee is issued a new certificate under the universal life insurance plan. An employee can also withdraw his or her cash accumulation under the universal life insurance plan and switch to the term insurance plan or can even have coverage under both plans. Typically an employee is eligible to purchase a maximum aggregate amount of coverage under the two plans. For example, if this amount is three times annual salary, the employee could purchase term insurance equal to two times salary and universal life insurance that has a pure insurance amount equal to one times salary.

Underwriting

Insurance companies that write group universal life insurance have underwriting standards concerning group size, the amounts of coverage available, and insurability.

Currently most group universal life insurance products are being limited primarily to employers who have at least 100 or 200 employees. However, a few insurers write coverage for even smaller groups. Some insurance companies also have an employee percentage-participation requirement, such as 20 or 25 percent, that must be satisfied before a group can be installed. Other insurance companies feel their marketing approach is designed so that adequate participation will result and therefore have no participation requirements.

Employees can generally elect amounts of pure insurance equal to varying multiples of their salaries, which typically start at one-half or one and range as high as three or five. There may be a minimum amount of coverage that must be purchased, such as $10,000. The maximum multiple an insurance company will offer is influenced by factors such as the size of the group, the amount of insurance provided under the employer's basic employer-pay-all group term insurance plan, and the percentage participation in the plan. In general the rules regarding the amounts of coverage are the same as those that have been traditionally applied to supplemental group term life insurance plans. The initial premium, which is a function of an employee's age and death benefit, is frequently designed to accumulate a cash value at age 65 equal to approximately 20 percent of the total death benefit.

Other approaches for determining the death benefit may be used, depending on insurance company practices and employer desires. Under some plans employees may elect specific amounts of insurance, such as $25,000, $50,000, or $100,000. Again an employee's age and the death benefit selected determine the premium. Some plans allow an employee to select the premium he or she wants to pay. The amount of the premium and the employee's age then automatically determine the amount of the death benefit.

The extent to which evidence of insurability is required of individual employees is also similar to that found under most supplemental group term life insurance plans. When an employee is initially eligible, coverage is usually issued on a guaranteed basis up to specified limits, which again are influenced by the size of the group, the amount of coverage provided under the employer's basic group term insurance plan, and the degree of participation in the plan. If an employee chooses a larger death benefit, simplified underwriting is used up to a second amount, after which regular underwriting is used. Guaranteed issue is often unavailable for small groups, in which case underwriting on the basis of a simplified questionnaire is used up to a specific amount of death benefit, after which regular underwriting is used.

With some exceptions future increases in the amount of pure insurance are subject to evidence of insurability. These exceptions include additional amounts resulting from salary increases as long as the total amount of coverage remains within the guaranteed issue limit. A few insurance companies also allow additional purchases without evidence of insurability when certain events occur, such as marriage or the birth of a child.

The Death Benefit

Under group universal life insurance products an employee usually has only one death benefit option available, and whether it is option A (level death benefit) or option B (increasing death benefit) depends on which one has been selected by the employer. In general there seems to be feeling that the availability of both options makes a plan more difficult to explain to employees and more costly to administer. Most employers have selected option B, which is generally more easily marketed to employees since the increasing total death benefit is a visible sign of any increase in their cash value or "investment." As a result several insurers now make only option B available with their group products.

Universal life insurance products give the insured the right to increase or decrease the death benefit from the level originally selected as circumstances change. For example, the policyowner might have initially selected a pure death benefit of $100,000 under option B. Because of the birth of a child, this might be increased to $150,000. Increases, but not decreases, generally require that the insured provide evidence of insurability.

Mortality Charges

Most products have a guaranteed mortality charge for 3 years, after which the mortality charge will be based on the experience of each particular group. As with experience rating in general, the credibility given to a group's actual experience will be greater for larger groups. Most insurance companies guarantee that any future increases in the mortality charge will not exceed a stated maximum.

The products designed for small groups typically use pooled rates that apply to all groups insured through a particular trust. Therefore the mortality charge for any employer will vary, not with the employer's overall experience but rather with the overall experience of the trust.

Expense Charges

Probably the greatest variations among group life insurance products occur in the expense charges that are levied. Typically a percentage of each premium, such as 2 percent, is deducted for expenses. In addition, there is a flat monthly charge, normally ranging from $1 to $3, to maintain the accumulation account. Some insurance companies levy this charge against all certificate holders, even those who are contributing only enough to have the pure insurance coverage. Other insurance companies levy the charge only against those accounts that have a positive cash value accumulation. A few insurance companies also load their mortality charges for expenses. Finally many companies levy a transaction charge, such as $25, that often applies to withdrawals in early policy years. A transaction charge may also apply to policy loans and additional lump-sum contributions. In evaluating the expense charges of different insurers, one should remember that an insurer with a lower-than-average charge may be subtly compensating for this charge by having a higher mortality charge or crediting a lower interest rate to cash value accumulations than would otherwise be paid.

Interest Rates

Most insurance companies guarantee that the initial interest rate credited to cash value accumulations will be in effect for one year. After that time the rate is typically adjusted quarterly or semiannually but cannot be below some contractual minimum such as 4.0 or 4.5 percent. The interest rate credited is usually determined on a discretionary basis but is influenced by the insurance company's investment income and competitive factors. However, some insurers stipulate that it will be linked to some money market instrument, such as 3-month Treasury bills. In general the same interest is credited to all groups that an insurance company has underwritten.

Several insurance companies are exploring the possibility of establishing separate accounts for group universal life insurance accumulations and allowing individual employees to direct the types of assets in which their accumulations are invested. Such a change will give employees much of the investment flexibility that is currently available under many 401(k) plans.

Premium Adjustments

Employees are allowed considerable flexibility in the amount and timing of premium payments. Premiums can be raised or lowered and even suspended. In the latter case the contract will terminate if an employee's cash value accumulation is inadequate to pay current mortality and expense charges. Of course premium payments could be reinstated to prevent this from happening. Additional lump-sum contributions may also be made to the accumulation account.

Two restrictions are placed on premium adjustments. First, the premium payment cannot be such that the size of the cash value accumulation becomes so large in relationship to the pure protection that an employee's coverage fails to qualify as a policy of insurance under IRS regulations. Second, since changes in premium payments through payroll deductions are costly to administer, many employers limit the frequency with which adjustments are allowed.

Loans and Withdrawals

Employees are allowed to make loans and withdrawals from their accumulated cash values, but for administrative reasons the frequency of loans and withdrawals may be limited. There are also minimum loan and withdrawal amounts, such as $250 or $500. In addition, an employee is usually required to leave a minimum balance in the cash value account sufficient to pay mortality and expense charges for some time period, possibly as long as one year. If an option A death benefit is in effect, the amount of the pure insurance is increased by the amount of the loan or withdrawal so that the total death benefit remains the same. With an option B death benefit the amount of the total death benefit is decreased.

The interest rate charged on policy loans is usually pegged to some index, such as Moody's composite bond yield. In addition, the interest rate credited to an amount of the cash value equal to the policy loan is reduced. This reduced interest rate may be the guaranteed policy minimum or may also be based on some index, such as 2 percent less than Moody's composite bond yield.

An employee can withdraw his or her entire cash value accumulation and terminate coverage. Total withdrawals are subject to a surrender charge during early policy years. The charge decreases with policy duration and is usually in addition to any transaction charge that might also be levied.

Dependent Coverage

Most products allow an employee to purchase a rider that provides term insurance coverage on his or her spouse and children. For example, one insurance company allows an employee to elect spousal coverage of $10,000 to $50,000 in $10,000 increments and coverage on children in the amount of either $5,000 or $10,000. Other insurers make varying amounts available.

Some insurance companies allow separate universal life insurance coverage to be elected, but usually only for the spouse. In such cases the coverage is provided under a separate group insurance certificate rather than a rider.

Accidental Death and Waiver of Premium

A group universal life insurance plan may provide accidental death benefits and a disability waiver of premium. These benefits are not optional for each employee; rather they are part of the coverage only if the employer has elected to include them in the plan. When a waiver of premium is included, all that is waived in case of disability is the portion of the premium necessary to pay the cost of the pure insurance protection for the employee and any dependents.

Employee Options at Retirement and Termination

Several situations may arise in which an employee is no longer actively working or a group universal plan might be terminated by the employer.

Several options are available to the retiring employee. First, the employee can continue the group insurance coverage like an active employee. However, if premium payments are continued, the employee will be billed by the insurance company, probably on a quarterly basis. Because of the direct billing, the employee may also be subject to a higher monthly expense charge. Second, the employee can terminate the coverage and completely withdraw his or her accumulated cash value. Third, the employee can elect one of the policy settlement options for the liquidation of the cash value in the form of annuity income. Finally, some insurers allow the retiring employee to decrease the amount of pure insurance so that the cash value will be adequate to keep the policy in force without any more premium payments. In effect the employee then has a paid-up policy.

The same options are generally available to an employee who terminates employment prior to retirement. In contrast to most other types of group insurance arrangements, the continuation of coverage does not involve a conversion and the accompanying conversion charge; rather the employee usually remains in the same group. This ability to continue group coverage after termination of employment is commonly referred to as portability. If former employees who continue coverage have higher mortality rates, this will be reflected in the mortality charge for the entire group. However, at least one insurer places terminated employees into a separate group consisting of terminated employees from all plans. These persons will be subject to a mortality charge based solely on the experience of this group. Thus any higher mortality due to adverse selection will not be shared by the actively working employees.

If the employer terminates the group insurance arrangement, some insurance companies keep the group in force on a direct-bill basis, even if the coverage has been replaced with another insurer. Other insurance companies continue the group coverage only if the employer has not replaced the plan. If replacement occurs, the insurance company terminates the pure insurance amount and either gives the cash value to participants or transfers it to the trustee of the new plan.

Enrollment and Administration

Variations exist in the method by which employees are enrolled in group universal life insurance plans. Some early plans used agents who were compensated in the form of commissions or fees, but several insurance companies have dropped this practice. The actual enrollment is typically done by the employer with materials provided by the insurance company. However, salaried or commissioned representatives of the insurer usually meet with the employees in group meetings to explain the plan.

The employer's main administrative function is to process the payroll deductions associated with a plan. As previously mentioned, employee flexibility may be somewhat limited to minimize the costs of numerous changes in payroll deductions.

Other administrative functions are performed by the insurance company or a third-party administrator. These functions include providing employees with annual statements about their transactions and cash value accumulation under the plan. Toll-free telephone lines are often maintained to provide information and advice to employees.

Taxation

Group universal life insurance products are not designed to be policies of insurance under Sec. 79. In addition, each employee pays the full cost of his or her coverage. Therefore the tax treatment is the same to employees as if they had purchased a universal life insurance policy in the individual insurance marketplace.

NOTE

1. Source: American Council of Life Insurance, *Life Insurance Fact Book*. This book is updated annually.

34

Fundamental Legal Concepts

Dan M. McGill
Revised by Burke A. Christensen

The following chapters are designed for the student of the principles of law that govern the creation and marketing of life and health insurance contracts. They are not intended to turn the student into an insurance lawyer. The goal is to enable the student to become sufficiently expert in the topics covered so that he or she may legitimately lay claim to the title of insurance professional.

It is not sufficient that a student or practitioner of life insurance understand only the economic and mathematical bases of the subject; he or she must also have a firm grasp of the basic legal relationships that have largely shaped its formal structure and influenced its content. The law of life insurance is derived predominantly from the general law of contracts; yet, contract law as applied to insurance contracts has been profoundly modified by the needs of the insurance business. On the one hand, insurance companies have sought to condition and limit the risks they assume; on the other hand, the insuring public has required and obtained protection against insurance companies' excessively legalistic interpretations of policy provisions. The resulting law is a compromise between these conflicting demands. The core of our study will be contract law, but one who knows only contract law will not fully grasp the law of insurance contracts.

This chapter is not concerned with legal abstractions and esoteric concepts. It deals with concrete legal principles and situations that field and home office representatives are certain to meet in the ordinary course of business. Most of the principles are encountered on a recurring—if not daily—basis. Recognition of situations and actions that have legal significance will enable life insurance company representatives to provide better service to the insuring public and more protection to their company against involuntary assumption of risk and unfavorable litigation.

Through a brief summary of the forms of law, the American judicial system, the general principles of contract interpretation, and the unique legal characteristics of a life insurance contract, this chapter will enhance the student's comprehension of the basic legal principles underlying life insurance.

FORMS OF LAW

> Law: The collection of rules of conduct recognized as binding on the members of a community for the violation of which a sanction is provided

American law, despite its varied and complex nature, can be classified into two broad, all-inclusive forms: (1) legislative law, which takes the form of legislation as enacted by parliamentary bodies and as promulgated by governmental agencies, and (2) case law, which is developed by courts and administrative agencies.

Legislative law, which we have defined to include regulations, consists of the general rules of conduct promulgated by a legally constituted body vested with the authority and power to issue such rules for all or a given portion of the population. For example, representatives of the people create constitutions; legislatures enact statutes; agencies issue regulations. All of these are forms of legislative law. Legislation is found chiefly in statute books and is generally identified as a "law" or an "act."

Case law consists of the narrow rules of conduct promulgated by the courts and administrative tribunals in the adjudication of particular controversies. Case law is located in the published and unpublished reports of judicial and administrative decisions.

The rule of law represented by legislation and regulation is stated in an official, explicated, textual form. Its future application to the acts of the public is generally quite clear.

This is not true of case law. Although case law settles controversy between the parties to that case, its application to other, future cases may by uncertain. In fact, a proposition of case law that may have an impact on the general public is not always directly stated but often must be inferred from the published opinions of a judicial or an administrative decision. Thus case law is flexible in form, while legislation is rigid.

Legislation[1]

The forms of legislative law presented here are in descending order of political authoritativeness as follows:

- the federal Constitution
- treaties
- federal statutes
- federal executive orders and administrative regulations
- state constitutions
- state statutes
- state administrative regulations
- local ordinances

The Federal Constitution

The primary functions of a constitution are to establish the framework of the government and to set forth the fundamental legal and political principles of a society. Thus the Constitution of the United States provides for a national government of three coordinate branches—the legislative, executive, and judicial—and sets down in some detail the powers and functions of each. At the same time it provides safeguards against infringement by the government of the basic human rights, such as freedom of speech, freedom of religious worship, and freedom of peaceful assemblage. In short the federal Constitution prescribes the powers of the various branches of the federal government and imposes limitations on those powers as they affect private individuals and the states.

The federal government of the United States came into being when the Constitution was ratified by the original 13 sovereign and individually independent states. Thus the federal government is a creation of the people of those states through a delegation of power by them to the federal government. As a result no powers can be exercised by the federal government unless they exist in the federal Constitution. This is not true of the states. The states retain all powers not granted to the federal government. This principle is recognized by the Tenth Amendment to the federal Constitution: "The powers not delegated to the United States by the Constitution, nor prohibited by it to the States, are reserved to the States respectively, or to the people."

Nevertheless, pursuant to Article VI, Section 2 of the federal Constitution, the supreme law of the land in the United States is the Constitution and the federal laws and treaties created under the authority of the federal Constitution. This is known as the Supremacy Clause. Only in those areas where the federal Constitution is silent are the states supreme.

Treaties

The treaties entered into between the government of the United States and foreign governments sometimes contain provisions as to aliens' rights that conflict with local law. In that event such treaties take precedence over state constitutions or statutes. For example, a treaty in 1850 between the United States and Switzerland provided that the heirs of a Swiss citizen who had died owning land in the United States should be entitled to inherit the land. This treaty was upheld by the Supreme Court of the United States in the face of a contrary legal doctrine of the state of Virginia, in which the land was located. In so holding, the court said, "It must always be borne in mind that the Constitution, laws and treaties of the United States are as much a part of the law of every state as its own local laws and Constitution. This is a fundamental principle in our system of complex national policy."[2]

Federal Statutes

The federal Constitution was, of necessity, couched in general terms. It was intended that Congress would address itself to matters requiring specialized rules and regulations. The statutes enacted by Congress within the scope of the powers given to the federal government by the Supremacy Clause therefore are of higher authority than any state constitution or statute.

Not all acts of Congress, however, create "law" in the sense in which the term is generally used. Some acts are directed at one individual by name or at a specifically identified group of individuals and are known as "private laws." They do not purport to lay down general rules of human conduct. Statutes of general application are labeled "public laws."

Federal Executive Orders and Administrative Regulations

Under Article II of the Constitution, the President of the United States has a power of rather indefinite scope to issue executive orders that, if they prescribe general rules of conduct, are laws, legislative in form. Within their proper scope executive orders are paramount to state law. In addition, many federal administrative bodies, such as the Internal Revenue Service, have power to make general rules, ordinarily identified as regulations. These are legislative in character and, when issued pursuant to a constitutional federal statute, are superior to all forms of state laws.

State Constitutions

A state constitution is, within the proper sphere of its operation, the "supreme law" of the state—subject, of course, to the priority of federal legislative law in its proper sphere. There is a significant theoretical difference between the state governments and the federal government. A federal governmental power exists only if it has been granted by the federal Constitution. The states, however, are the sovereign representatives of their people and possess all governmental powers that have not been delegated by the people to the federal government or limited by the state constitution. As a result a federal law is constitutional only if it is based on a delegation of power found within the federal Constitution. In contrast a state law is always presumed to be valid unless the state or federal constitutions specifically prohibit the state from exercising such a power.

In addition to outlining the framework of government and limiting the authority of state officials, state constitutions often prescribe general rules of conduct of the kind normally associated with acts of the state legislature. The purpose of such a provision is to place the rules contained therein beyond the power of alteration by the legislature.

State Statutes

This is a voluminous body of legislative law, since state legislatures have residuary powers to prescribe general rules of conduct. As explained above, state governments have all powers not specifically denied them by the federal Constitution, federal treaties, federal statutes, and the appropriate state constitution. The operations of life insurance companies and the contents of their policies are greatly affected by state statutes. In fact, all states have enacted so-called standard provisions that must be included, in substance, in all life insurance policies issued in the states.

To assist the states in preparing well-designed legislation that responds to the complexities of the life insurance business, the National Association of Insurance Commissioners (NAIC) has developed numerous model acts and regulations. These models may be considered by the state legislatures and insurance departments as they develop the laws that will be enacted in each state.

State Administrative Regulations

Administrative bodies or officials as a group are endowed with some of the characteristics of all three branches of government—judicial, executive, and legislative. They sometimes have authority, granted by statute, to adjudicate particular controversies and claims and in so doing perform judicial or quasijudicial functions. Their decisions, with their accompanying explanations, become precedents of administrative case law. In their capacity as prosecuting and law enforcement officials, they exercise executive powers. Finally, they are frequently empowered by statute to make general roles of conduct in their particular areas of responsibility; and these general rules, as "regulations," have the force and effect of law.

Regulations, orders, opinions, and rulings that are issued by the various state insurance departments constitute one of the most important sources of law for insurance companies. Similar regulations that are issued by state and federal securities regulatory authorities are also important to the business of insurance because many types of insurance products are subject to the state and federal securities laws.

Local Ordinances

The right to govern certain subordinate units of the state—for example, cities, towns, and counties—is delegated by the state to local governmental entities that have legislative powers limited to matters of purely local concern. The general rules enacted by these municipalities are usually called "municipal ordinances."

Case Law

Case law is a by-product of the settling of disputes. This has been the special province of the courts, and the great body of case law is composed of judicial decisions. However, as government has grown larger, administrative agencies have become an important source of case law. The decisions of administrative tribunals are referred to as *administrative case law* to distinguish them from the decisions handed down by the judiciary.

Precedent and the Principle of Stare Decisis

> **Precedent**: a previous decision by a court. If the precedent involves the same or closely similar law and facts as a new case, the second court can be expected to follow the precedent.

> **Stare decisis**: a Latin term that means that a court can be expected to follow a previous decision of that court or a higher appellate court in the same jurisdiction

JUDICIAL DECISIONS

When a court is called upon to decide a case involving a point on which there is no legislation or for which there is no clear legislative answers, it will look to the appropriate state or federal Constitution and to prior cases for precedents. If there is no clear statutory answer, the prior case law will control. If the court finds an applicable case law precedent, it will ordinarily decide the current dispute on the basis of the principles enunciated in the earlier case. If it finds no precedent squarely in point or applicable by analogy, it must originate a rule to resolve the dispute. Presumably the rule will reflect proper consideration of history, customs, morals, and sound social policy.

In creating new rules courts are making case law. The more situations coming before the courts for which there are no existing rules, the more new case law there will be. Moreover, each new rule becomes an integral part of the whole body of rules that the courts may use in the future.

American case law is rooted in the law of England as it existed at the time of the colonization of America. This is natural, since the early settlers brought with them the only law they knew. This law was composed of the rules followed by the English courts in the settlement of disputes and the existing statutory enactments of Parliament. Since the decisions of the English courts were assumed to reflect those principles, maxims, usages, and rules of action that had regulated people's affairs from time immemorial, they were designated as the "common law" of England. The influence of the common law of England on the development of American law continued well into the 19th century. Since the English common law was the fountainhead of American case law, the latter likewise came to be known as the "common law." In this sense the term common law distinguishes case law from statutory or constitutional law.

> **Common law**: originally the unwritten law as derived from the customs or ideas of justice in England and now the collection of judicial decisions, customs, and concepts of justice that define what is considered to be right and wrong. In contrasting them with legislative (or statutory) law, court decisions are often referred to as the common law. England, Canada, and the United States are common law countries.

> **Civil law**: the law derived from the law of Rome (in contrast with common law). Civil law is not based on court decisions (as is common law) but on the enactment of a comprehensive code. Italy and France are civil law countries. In contrast with criminal law, civil law refers to the obligations and rights created between private parties.

Common Law Compared to Civil Law

A broader use of the term common law distinguishes the entire system of English law from the legal systems developed in other parts of the world. It has acquired special significance in distinguishing between the English legal system—and systems based on it—and the code developed in the Old Roman Empire that today serves as the foundation of the legal systems in continental Europe and in the state of Louisiana.

The Roman civil law originated as the law of the city of Rome but was gradually extended to the entire Roman Empire. After the fall of the Roman Empire in the fifth century, this law was compiled into a code called "Corpus Juris Civilis." Since the compilation was carried out during the reign of Justinian, it is often referred to as the "Justinian Code."

The Justinian Code attempted to develop a rule to cover every possible type of legal conflict. One example is the rule to settle the question of survivorship when two people perished under circumstances that made it impossible to determine who died first. While there are many substantive differences between the

Roman civil law and the Anglo-American common law, the most significant difference lies in the impact on the entire legal system of the adjudication of a particular case. Under the civil law code, a case is brought within one of the general provisions and is settled by application of the rule contained therein to the facts of the case. The decision in a particular case is little influenced by previous litigation on the point involved and, in turn, will exert little—if any—influence on similar disputes arising in the future. Under the system of common law, however, a controversy not covered by legislation is decided only after a guiding rule has been sought in previously litigated cases; and—more important—once a decision has been made, it forms the basis for the settlement of future disputes. The more frequently a decision is used as a guide to action, the stronger it becomes as a precedent.

> **Equity**: a body of law developed to provide relief where legal remedies have failed

Law versus Equity

The term common law is also used to designate the rules applied by the courts of common law as contrasted with the rules applied by courts of equity. This is a third meaning of the expression.

The term "equity" is peculiar to Anglo-American law. It arose because of the failure of the common law to give adequate and proper remedy in some cases. In the early courts of England, the procedure for pursuing a legal remedy was very rigid. There were a fixed number of "forms of action," and every remedial right had to be enforced through one of these forms. The first step in any action was to apply to the king for a writ, which was a document addressed to the person responsible for the alleged wrong. This writ gave a brief summary of the facts upon which the right of action was based, and it contained certain technical formulas indicating the form of action being brought and the amount of money damages sought. The nature of these writs was fixed and could not be substantially altered. A writ had been developed not only for each form of action but also for the facts, circumstances, and events that would constitute the subject matter of the particular action. If no writ could be found that corresponded substantially to the facts constituting the basis for complaint, the injured party could obtain no relief in the courts. The only course of action available was a direct appeal to the conscience of the king.

Over a period of time the number of direct petitions became so great that the king had to delegate responsibility for dealing with them. Since the appeal was to the king's conscience, he began to refer such matters to his spiritual adviser, the chancellor, who, being an official of the Church, usually favored the ecclesiastical law or the civil law over common law. Once begun, the practice of delegating cases to the chancellor for his sole decision rapidly became the established method of dealing with such controversies. Eventually a separate court functioning under the chancellor and called the Chancery Court was created.

Following the English precedent, the American colonies (and later the states) established two sets of courts, one applying the rules of common law and called "courts of law," and the other applying rules of equity and good conscience and called "courts of equity." England still maintains separate courts of law and equity, but in this country, the two systems have been merged to the extent that the same court can hear both types of cases. Whether the case is heard in law or equity depends on the remedy sought. If there is a legal remedy the action must be brought in law; if there is no legal remedy or the legal remedy is inadequate, the suit can be brought in equity.

> **Legal remedies**: attempts to seek money damages for a failure to perform a contract as written

> **Equitable remedies**: attempts to enforce performance in a contract, to modify its terms, or to excuse performance for some reason

The distinction between law and equity is extremely important to life insurance companies. Equity gives them access to remedies that are otherwise unavailable and that are essential to their operation. Among the equitable remedies frequently invoked by life insurance companies are suits for rescission and restitution, suits for reformation of contracts, and bills of interpleader. (All of these terms will be explained later in this book.) Suits in equity are usually tried without a jury, which—in view of the traditionally hostile attitude of juries toward insurance companies—is considered to be a major procedural advantage.

Administrative Decisions

Administrative agencies are normally created by legislative enactment and are charged with the administration of laws that are general in character and that affect the rights and privileges of private citizens. When administrative agencies apply a law to a particular set of facts, they are making case law. Their decisions, when officially or unofficially reported and published, have the status of precedents. Precedents in this area, however, are regarded with less sanctity than are judicial decisions and are less likely to be applied to a different set of facts. An administrative tribunal, unlike the usual court of law, has jurisdiction over a limited class of cases.

RELATIONSHIP OF THE JUDICIARY TO LEGISLATIVE LAW

In our governmental system of check and balances, the courts have right to interpret or construe the law created by the legislative branch and enforced by the executive branch. The courts determine the meaning of the words used in the statute and decide whether a particular set of facts comes within the scope of the law created by the statute. The same function is exercised with respect to the federal and state constitutions. As a part of this function the courts determine whether or not a particular statute is in conflict with a constitutional provision.

In the process of determining the scope and meaning of statutory and constitutional provisions, the courts have developed a number of rules. These are known as rules of *statutory construction*. The fundamental purpose of all these rules is to ascertain and give effect to the intention of the legislature. One of the most basic rules is that if the language of the statute is plain and unambiguous and its meaning clear and definite, there is no room for judicial construction. The statute is said to have a "plain meaning," which the courts must enforce irrespective of their opinion of the wisdom or efficacy of the statute. Normally the meaning of a statute is sought from the words used by the legislature to express its intent. But if the language of the statute is ambiguous and may have more than one meaning, matters extraneous to the statute—such as its title, legislative history, conditions leading to its enactment, and so forth—can be taken into account in an attempt to arrive at its true meaning.

It stands to reason that all parts of a statute must be considered in any attempt to ascertain its meaning. Furthermore, the interpretation adopted by a court must be one that will give effect to the whole statute. Reflecting the traditional conflict between common and statutory law, the courts have decreed that statutes in derogation of the common law shall be strictly construed. This means that in order to change the common law a statute must do so clearly and explicitly or it will not be enforced. Finally, if there are two statutes dealing with the same subject matter, the latter one in time is to be given effect as the last expression of legislative intent.

> **Jurisdiction**: the power to interpret and apply the law. There are several types of jurisdiction.
>
> **Geographical jurisdiction**: the area governed by the legislative unit that created the court's jurisdiction. The courts of Pennsylvania, for example, have no jurisdiction in Utah.
>
> **Original jurisdiction**: the power to decide a case when it is first heard by a judge or jury
>
> **Appellate jurisdiction**: the power to review the decision of a lower court
>
> **Jurisdiction over the subject matter**: the power of a court to decide cases including certain subjects. For example, a state court has no subject matter jurisdiction to decide a case involving a treaty between the United States and France.
>
> **Jurisdiction over the person**: the power of a court to enforce its decision over a party to a lawsuit

CLASSIFICATION OF COURTS

Federal Courts

According to Article III of the federal Constitution, "The judicial power of the United States shall be vested in one Supreme Court and in such inferior courts as the Congress may, from time to time, ordain and establish." Pursuant to this constitutional power, the Congress has created numerous federal courts. At the head of the hierarchy stands the Supreme Court of the United States. The Supreme Court has original jurisdiction over all cases involving ambassadors, ministers, and consuls, and those in which a state is a party. In all other cases that can properly be brought before the Supreme Court, the court has appellate jurisdiction. Hence the principal jurisdiction of the court is appellate. It is the court of last resort for all cases involving federal law and for all cases coming to it from the inferior or lower federal courts involving questions of state law.

In 1891 Congress made provisions for intermediary courts of appeal in order to lessen the burden on the Supreme Court. These tribunals are known as the Courts of Appeals, of which there are now 13. Each Court of Appeals is assigned to a specified circuit that serves a certain number of states. Each of these courts has a minimum of three judges, who preside as a group. The jurisdiction of the Courts of Appeals is exclusively appellate. The decision of a Court of Appeals is subject to review only by the Supreme Court. For most cases, the decision of the Supreme Court to hear an appeal from a Court of Appeals, or any other court, is purely discretionary.

The federal courts of original jurisdiction for most matters are the District Courts. The country is presently divided into more than 90 judicial districts, with each state having at least one district and no district embracing territory in more than one state. There is one District Court for each judicial district, but most courts have more than one judge. The District Courts have jurisdiction over all cases arising under the federal Constitution or laws of Congress and over cases involving litigants with diversity of citizenship where the amount in dispute exceeds $10,000. For purposes of federal jurisdiction, diversity of citizenship is considered to exist whenever the litigating parties are citizens of different states in the United States or one is a citizen of the United States and the other is a citizen of a foreign country. For this purpose a corporation is considered to be a citizen of the state in which it is chartered. If the jurisdiction of the federal courts is based on diversity of citizenship, the subject matter of the dispute may be state law.

In addition to these courts of general jurisdiction, there are a number of federal courts that have jurisdiction—not always exclusive—over certain types of disputes. Among such courts are the Court of Claims, the Tax Court, the federal military courts, and the Court of Customs and Patent Appeals.

State Courts

In each state, there exists—by state constitutional provision and legislative enactment—a system of judicial tribunals, which embraces various courts of original jurisdiction and one or more of appellate jurisdiction. Usually there is one court of unlimited original jurisdiction that has the power to entertain any action, regardless of the amount involved or the nature of the relief requested, although it does not ordinarily have authority over the probate of wills or administration of deceased persons' estates. This state court of general original jurisdiction usually hears cases at the county seat of the various counties in the state and is known variously as the District, Circuit, Superior, or Common Pleas Court.

States usually have several inferior (in a hierarchical sense) courts, with jurisdiction limited as to certain subject matter (for example, probate), amounts in controversy (for example, $2,000), or relief sought (for example, divorce). The inferior courts are commonly named Municipal Courts, Police Courts, Magistrate's Courts, or Justice of the Peace Courts. There may be a separate court or a special division of a court to deal with problems of domestic relations or juvenile delinquency. In many states there is but one appellate tribunal, a court of last resort. In some, however, there is an intermediate tribunal with powers similar to those of the federal Courts of Appeals.

The name of the state court is not necessarily indicative of its place in the judicial hierarchy. In New York, for example, the general court of original jurisdiction (the trial court) is known as the Supreme Court, while the court of last resort is known as the Court of Appeals. In most states, however, the court of last resort is called the Supreme Court.

JURISDICTION OF COURTS

The jurisdiction of a court refers not only to its power to hear a case but also to its power to render an enforceable judgment. The constitutional or statutory provision creating a particular court defines its jurisdiction as to subject matter, parties, geographical area, and amounts involved. Jurisdiction over the person of the defendant is especially important. This jurisdiction is given effect by a summons from the court in which the case is to be tried. The summons, usually delivered to the sheriff to be served upon the individual or organization made defendant to the suit, must be served within the geographical area subject to the jurisdiction of the court issuing the summons. If a person comes into the state or county and is served with a summons while he or she is there, that person is then under the authority and jurisdiction of the court.

If the defendant is a nonresident of the place where the suit is brought, service of process may be accomplished by publication. This, however, does not normally give the court authority to render a personal judgment for damages. Accompanied by proper attachment proceedings, however, service by publication brings under the court's jurisdiction all attached property of a nonresident that lies within the territorial limits of the court; such attached property therefore is liable for the judgment debt and may be used to satisfy the judgment. Moreover, under the Unauthorized Insurers Service-of-Process Act, which is discussed in the following chapter, a policyowner residing in one state may obtain and enforce a judgment against an out-of-state insurance company by serving the summons on the insurance commissioner or other designated official of the state of the insured's domicile.

If a particular controversy falls within the jurisdiction of the federal courts, the plaintiff may bring his or her action in a federal court. If the plaintiff brings the action in a state court and the defendant acquiesces in the choice of jurisdiction, the case will be tried in the state court. If, however, the defendant does not wish the case to be heard in the state court, he or she can have it removed to the appropriate federal court. If a case involving a federal question is adjudicated in a state court, the decision of the state court on that question is subject to review by the Supreme Court of the United States, according to the conditions and limitations imposed by Congress.

CONFLICT OF LAWS

The jurisdiction of a court refers to its power to hear a controversy and to enforce its decision. Jurisdiction, however, is not determinative of the law that will be applied. A court of one state may have to apply the law, either statutory or common, of another state. The manner in which this could come about involves the *conflict of laws*—one of the most complex branches of the law.

The conflict of laws concept can be better understood if it is renamed "choice of laws." The latter is a more appropriate term because the issue is which law is to be applied when the laws of two or more jurisdictions seem relevant but are not in agreement.

The question of which law will govern the validity and interpretation of a life insurance contract is extremely important, since states have different attitudes toward various company practices and policy provisions and thus different laws on these issues. Broadly speaking, the matter is resolved on the basis of the *contacts* that a life insurance contract has with various territorial sovereigns that might be deemed to have an interest in determining the rights and duties of the parties to—and beneficiaries of—the contract. These contacts might arise out of the state's relationship to the home office, a branch office, the insured, or the beneficiary, to mention only the major possibilities. Theoretically, if a state has *any* relationship to—or contact with—an insurance contract, it has some (though perhaps only slight) claim to a voice in the determination of the rights and duties thereunder. In a typical case, there will be at least two states concerned with the policy—the state in which the home office is located and the state in which the insured is domiciled. But there can easily be more, so regardless of where the case may be heard, rules must be developed to determine which state has the paramount interest in interpreting and enforcing the contract.

The traditional rule followed by the majority of jurisdictions is that unless the parties agree otherwise, questions concerning the *validity* and *interpretation* of a life insurance contract will be resolved by the law of the state in which the contract was made and in which the last act necessary to bring the contract into existence took place. This is sometimes called the "place-of making rule." Since, under the usual circumstances, the contract becomes effective at the moment it is delivered by the agent to the insured and the first premium is collected, the place of making is typically the state in which the insured reside because that is where delivery was made. On the other hand, if the first premium is paid with the application and a conditional receipt is issued contingent on approval at the company's home office, the act that brings the policy contract into existence occurs at the home office of the company, producing a different result.

The traditional rule is that matters relating to *performance* of the contract are controlled by the law of state where the contract is to be performed. However, this rule seems inappropriate for insurance contracts and has not been adopted.

Disturbed by the fortuitous nature of the place-of-making rule and convinced that all policyowners should be protected by the laws of their states, some states have enacted statutes and some courts have adopted rules to the effect that all policies shall be governed by the laws of the state in which the insured is domiciled, regardless of where the contract came into existence. Other courts—feeling that the control of a state over a company incorporated under its laws assures equality of treatment of all policyowners, wherever they live—follow the rule that the laws of the insurer's state of incorporation will be applied in determining the validity and interpretation of a life insurance contract. In all these cases, the choice of the governing law is determined by the conflict-of-law rule of the state in which the case is being adjudicated.

A life insurance policy may contain a provision that its validity and interpretation will be governed by the law of a designated state, which may be neither the insured's state of domicile nor the state in which the home office is located. It appears that, while the insured or beneficiary can enforce this provision if the laws of the designated state are more favorable to him or her than the laws that would apply under the conflict-of-law rule, the insurance company is not permitted to invoke the provision.[3]

In more recent years there has been a tendency for the courts to follow a different doctrine, known as the "center of gravity," or "grouping of contracts" theory, to resolve conflicts of law problems, whether the matter in dispute involves the validity, interpretation, or performance of a contract. Under this theory, the courts, instead of regarding the parties' intention, place of making, or performance as conclusive, give emphasis to the law of the state that has the most significant contracts with the matter in dispute. The merit of this approach is that it gives the state with the most interest in the dispute paramount control over the legal issues. The principal disadvantage is the possibility that it will afford less certainty and predictability than the more rigid rules traditionally applied.

It should be noted that when the courts of one state apply the laws of another state, they apply *their* interpretation of what the law is in the other state. This may differ from the interpretation adopted by the courts of the other state.

In creating the federal judiciary[4] the Judiciary Act of 1789 provided that when trying cases based on diversity of citizenship, federal courts would be bound by the applicable laws of the state in which they were sitting (assuming no conflict of laws). In the famous case of *Swift v. Tyson*, decided by the United States Supreme Court in 1842, it was held that the word "laws" used in the act referred to statutory law and not to case law. Thus the federal courts were free to apply their own version of the common law in settling disputes not involving a federal or state statute. This ruling turned out to be highly significant for insurance companies, inasmuch as federal precedents were more favorable to the companies in many respects than the common law of the various states. This happy state of affairs was ended in 1938, when the United States Supreme Court in *Erie Railroad Company v. Tompkins,* overruled its earlier doctrine and held that the federal courts were obliged to apply the common law, as well as the statutory law, of the state in which the case is being heard. Three years later, the Supreme Court held that the federal courts would also have to follow the conflict-of-law rules of the state in which they sit. Thus for purposes of diversity jurisdiction, a federal court is in effect only another court of the state.

NOTES

1. The materials in this section were drawn largely from Noel T. Dowling, Edwin W. Patterson, and Richard R. Powell, *Materials for Legal Method* (University Casebook Series) (Chicago: Foundation Press, Inc., 1946), pp. 14−29. The classification of laws set forth in this section of the chapter was taken from that source.
2. *Havenstein v. Lynham,* 100 U.S. 483, 490 (1879).
3. See Edwin W. Patterson, *Essentials of Insurance Law,* 2d ed. (New York: McGraw-Hill Book Co., Inc., 1957), pp. 54 and 55, pp. 114 and 116, for citations.
4. Judiciary Act of 1789 SS 34, 1 Stat. 92 (1879) 28 U.S.C., SS 725 (1952).

35

Basic Principles of Contract Law

Dan M. McGill
Revised by Burke A. Christensen

Contract: an agreement enforceable at law

An insurance policy is a special kind of contract. To be extremely specific, it is an informal, aleatory, unilateral contract of adhesion to pay a stated sum subject to a condition precedent. This means, of course, that an insurance policy is not a formal, commutative, bilateral, negotiated, indemnitory, unconditional contract with right of subrogation. To understand what all these terms mean, a short course in contract law is necessary.

Many promises can be broken without penalty. But a contract creates a binding promise for which the law creates a duty of performance. This duty is imposed on the one who makes the promise, who is known as the promisor. The person to whom the promise is made is known as the promisee. Pursuant to a life insurance contract, the insurance company promises to pay a death benefit if the policyowner pays the premium. Since only the insurer makes a promise, it is the promisor. The policyowner is the promisee. To enforce that duty, the law provides a remedy to the promisee. If the promisor fails to perform as agreed in the contract, the promisee has two alternatives. He or she may sue for money damages on the contract. This is an action at law. Or if money damages are insufficient, the promisee may sue to require the promisor to fulfill its obligation under the contract. This is known as an equitable action.

In order for a contract to exist, the parties must fulfill certain requirements, which may change depending on the type of contract being created. For all contracts, however, three elements must exist: (1) a valid offer, (2) an acceptance of that specific offer, and (3) an exchange of consideration. There must also be a legal purpose for the contract, and the parties to the agreement must be legally competent.

> **Offer:** the manifestation of willingness to enter into a bargain, so made as to justify another person's understanding that his or her assent to that bargain is invited and will conclude it
>
> **Acceptance:** a manifestation of assent to the terms of an offer made in a manner invited or required by the offer
>
> **Consideration:** something of value bargained for and requested by the promisor and given by the promisee in exchange for the promise

For purposes of determining whether there has been an offer and an acceptance of that offer, it used to be said that for a contract to exist there must be evidence of a "meeting of the minds" between the parties involved. Since it is difficult for anyone (even judges) to read minds, this concept is no longer used. It is more precise to say that an agreement exists when there has been a "manifestation of mutual assent." This new standard merely requires an examination of the available evidence to determine whether each party had indicated an acceptance of the agreement.

GENERAL NATURE OF A LIFE INSURANCE CONTRACT

A valid agreement between a life insurance company and the applicant for insurance, represented by an instrument called the *policy* (from the Italian word polizza, meaning "a rolled document"), is a contract and as such, is subject to the general rules of contract law. However, in adapting these rules, which are familiar to all students of business law, to the life insurance contract, the courts have introduced substantial modifications because of certain peculiar characteristics of the life insurance contract. These characteristics—which, with one exception, are common to all types of insurance contracts—are briefly described in this chapter.

Aleatory Contract

> **Aleatory contract**: an agreement that conditions the performance by one party on the happening of an uncertain event

> **Commutative contract**: an agreement where each party expects to receive benefits of approximately equal value

The agreement contained in a life insurance policy is *aleatory* in nature, rather than *commutative*. In a commutative agreement, each party expects to receive from the other party, in one way or the other, the approximate equivalent of what he or she undertakes to give. Thus in an agreement to purchase real estate, the buyer agrees to pay a sum of money that represents the approximate value of the property to him or her, while the seller agrees to sell the property for a price that represents its approximate value to him or her. In other words, both parties contemplate a fairly even exchange of values. The courts generally will not consider whether the value exchanged would be equal to an objective observer unless there is such a huge discrepancy that it amounts to evidence of undue influence by one party or incompetence by the other. For most purposes, the worth of a thing is the price it will bring.

In an aleatory agreement, on the other hand, both parties realize that, depending on chance, one may receive a value out of all proportion to the value that he or she gives. The essence of an aleatory agreement is the element of chance or uncertainty. The prime example of such a contract is the wagering agreement. The term may also be applied to an endeavor where the potential gain or loss is governed largely by chance. Thus, the oil industry's exploration and drilling functions may be described as aleatory in nature. So is prospecting for gold, silver, or uranium.

In a life insurance transaction, the present value of the potential premium payments at the inception of the agreement is precisely equal, on the basis of the company's actuarial assumptions, to the present value of the anticipated benefits payable under the contract. In this sense the life insurance transaction is not aleatory. Moreover, the sum total of insurance transactions for a company, or for the entire life insurance industry, is not aleatory because of the predictability and stability provided by the theories of probability and the law of large numbers.

It remains true, however, that a particular policyowner may pay in to the insurance company a sum of money considerably smaller than the sum promised under the contract. Indeed, the face amount of the policy may become payable after the insured has paid only one installment of the first premium. This *chance* of obtaining a disproportionate return from an "investment" in a life insurance policy has motivated—and continues to motivate—many unscrupulous persons to seek life insurance through fraudulent means and for illegal purposes. The remedies for breach of warranty, misrepresentation, and concealment are invoked by the companies to protect themselves and society against fraudulent attempts to procure insurance. The requirement of an insurable interest is also designed to deal with the problems created by the fact that the life insurance policy is an aleatory contract. The aleatory nature of the insurance contract accounts in large measure for the modifications of general contract law as it is applied to the field of insurance contract law.

Unilateral Contract

Unilateral contract: an agreement in which only one party makes a promise

Bilateral contract: an agreement in which promises are made by both parties

Most contracts in the business world are *bilateral* in nature. This means that each party to the contract makes an enforceable promise to the other party. The consideration for such a contract is the exchange of mutual promises. Thus an order from a wholesaler to a manufacturer for a specified quantity of a particular item at a specified price, if accepted, is a bilateral contract. The manufacturer agrees (promises) to deliver the desired merchandise at an agreed-upon price, while the wholesaler agrees (promises) to accept and pay for the merchandise when it is delivered. Either party can sue if the other party fails to perform as promised.

Under a *unilateral* contract, on the other hand, only one party makes an enforceable promise. A contract is created because the nonpromising party to the contract performs his or her part of the bargain *before* the contract comes into existence. For instance, if the wholesaler in the example above had remitted cash with his or her order, the transactions would have become unilateral in nature, inasmuch as only the manufacturer (who made a promise to deliver) had anything to perform. In general, unilateral contracts are confined to situations in which one party is unwilling to extend credit to the other or to take the other's word for future performance.

As a general rule, a life insurance policy is a unilateral contract, in that only the insurance company makes an enforceable promise thereunder. The insurer's promise is given in exchange for performance by the policyowner of a certain act — payment of future premiums. As the consideration demanded by the company — namely, the application and the *first* premium or the *first* installment thereof — is given by the applicant, the contract goes into effect. Under the life insurance contract, the policyowner has made no promise to pay premiums subsequent to the first and is under no legal obligation to do so. If he or she does not pay additional premiums, the company will be released from its original promise to pay the face amount of the policy. Nevertheless, the policyowner incurs no legal penalties through failure to continue premium payments. On the other hand, the insurance company is obligated to accept the periodic premiums from the payer and to keep the contract in force in accordance with its original terms.

A life insurance contract may become a bilateral contract in some circumstances. For example, assume an agent of an insurer has authority to waive cash payment of the first premium. If an insurance policy is delivered by such agent in exchange for the applicant's promissory note or for the applicant's oral promise to pay premiums, a *bilateral* contract is created. In this situation the insurer's promise is exchanged for the applicant's promise.

Conditional Contract

> **Condition precedent**: an act or event that must occur before a duty is imposed or a right exists

> **Condition subsequent**: an act or event that will terminate an existing right

Closely related to the foregoing is the fact that the life insurance policy is a *conditional* contract. This means that the company's obligation under the contract is contingent on the performance of certain acts by the insured or the beneficiary. This does *not*, however, make the contract bilateral.

A condition is always inserted in a contract for the benefit of the promisor (the insurer) and hence is disadvantageous to the promisee (the policyowner). The following is a simple example of a conditional unilateral contract: Able promises to pay Baker $10 if she washes Able's car. The promised payment of the money is conditioned upon the performance of the act.

Conditions are not confined to unilateral contracts; a party to a bilateral contract can condition his promise in any manner acceptable to the other party. The following is an example of a conditional bilateral contract: Able promises to deliver 10 red rocking chairs, and Baker promises to accept them and pay Able $100 each if they are delivered prior to May 1st.

Conditions are classified as either precedent or subsequent. A *condition precedent* must be satisfied before legal rights and duties are created or continued, whereas a *condition subsequent* must be fulfilled in order to prevent the extinguishment of rights and duties already created in the contract. Whether a condition is precedent or subsequent depends on the intention of the parties to the contract. When the intention is not clear, the courts' tendency is to classify a condition as precedent in order to avoid a forfeiture.

The legal significance of a condition is quite different from and less burdensome than that of a promise. Failure to perform a contractual promise subjects the promisor to liability for damages to the promisee. Failure to perform or fulfill a condition does not subject the person involved (the promisee) to liability for damages but merely deprives him or her of a right or privilege that he or she otherwise would have had or might have acquired. It releases the promisor from his or her obligation to perform.

The promise of a life insurance company is conditioned on the timely payment of premiums. Payment of these premiums is considered to be a condition precedent to the continuance of the contract under its original terms. If this condition is not fulfilled, the company is relieved of its basic promise but remains obligated to honor various subsidiary promises contained in the surrender provisions and the reinstatement clause.

The company's promise to pay the face amount of the policy is always conditioned on the insured's forbearance from committing suicide during a specified period (usually one or two years) after the policy's issue and may be conditioned on the insured's death from causes not associated with war or aviation. Finally, the insurance company has no liability until satisfactory proof of death has been submitted by the beneficiary or the insured's personal representative.

Contract of Adhesion

> **Contract of adhesion**: a contract drafted by one part that must be accepted or rejected by the other party as it is written. There is no negotiation over the terms of the agreement.

A life insurance policy is also a contract of *adhesion*. This means that the terms of the contract are not arrived at by mutual negotiation between the parties, as would be the case with a *bargaining* contract. The policy, a complex and technical instrument, is prepared by the company and, with minor exceptions, must be accepted by the applicant in the form offered to him or her. The prospective insured may or may not contract with the company, but in no sense is the applicant in a position to bargain about the terms of the contract. The applicant must reject the contract entirely or "adhere" to it. Any bargaining that precedes the issuance of a life insurance contract has to do only with whether or not the contract is to be issued, the plan and amount of insurance, and to some degree the terms of the settlement agreement, although the settlement agreement itself is actually drafted by the insurance company.

The adhesive nature of the life insurance contract is highly significant from a legal standpoint. This importance derives from the basic rule of contract construction that a contract is to be construed or interpreted most strongly against the party who drafted the agreement. The avowed purpose of this rule is to neutralize any advantage that might have been gained by the party that prepared the contract. This means that if there is an ambiguity in a life insurance policy, the provision in question will be given the interpretation most favorable to the insured or his or her beneficiary. A rather prevalent view in insurance circles is that the courts, in their zeal to protect the insured, often find ambiguities in contracts where none exist.

Some who readily admit the soundness of this rule of construction in general and of its application to life insurance policies prior to the turn of the century question its continued application to policies currently being issued, considering the large number of provisions that are required by state statutes to be incorporated in such policies. Although these statutes do not prescribe the exact language to be used, many states require that the language of all policy provisions, including those voluntarily included, be approved by the state insurance department before sale of the policy form to the public. Such a requirement has the purpose, among others, of preventing the use of any deceptive or misleading language or of any provisions that would be unfair to policyowners. These factors have produced a relaxation of the strict rule of construction in some courts, but generally, all ambiguous provisions of the policy continue to be construed against the insurer.

Contract to Pay Stated Sum

> **Contract of indemnity:** an insurance contract that reimburses the insured only for actual losses incurred

> **Right of subrogation:** the right of an insurer to take the place of the injured insured and sue the party responsible for the damages incurred

Contracts issued by property and casualty insurance companies are usually contracts of *indemnity*. This means that the insured can collect only the amount of his or her loss, irrespective of the face of the policy—except, of course, that the recovery cannot exceed the face of the policy. Moreover, upon payment by an insurer of a loss caused by the negligence of a third party, as in the case of an automobile accident, the insurer acquires the insured's right of action against the negligent third party up to the amount of its loss payment and any expenses incurred in enforcing its rights. This is known as the doctrine of *subrogation*. While a provision giving effect to this doctrine is included in virtually every property and casualty insurance policy, the doctrine applies even in the absence of a policy provision.

A life insurance policy therefore is not a contract of indemnity, but one to pay a *stated sum*. This is presumably based on the assumption that because the value of a person's life to that person is without limit, no sum payable upon his or her death will be in excess of the loss suffered. Thus even though the insured has reached an age or a circumstance where he or she no longer has an economic value, upon his or her death the insurance company will still have to pay the sum agreed upon. The practical significance of this principle is that the insurance company, after paying the face amount of the policy, is not subrogated to the right of action of the decedent's estate when his or her death was caused by the negligence of a third party.

36

Formation of a Life Insurance Contract (Part 1)

Dan M. McGill
Revised by Burke A. Christensen

To be enforceable the agreement between a life insurance company and the person seeking insurance, represented by a written instrument called the policy, must meet all the requirements prescribed by law for the formation of a valid contract. In this and the following chapter, how each of the requirements is satisfied in the formation of a life insurance contract will be explained in specific terms.

LEGAL CAPACITY OF THE PARTIES

Parties to the Contract

There are two parties to the life insurance contract: the insurance company and the owner. The applicant is normally, but not necessarily, the owner and the person whose life is the subject matter of the contract. The person on whose life a policy is issued is the *insured.* A person or entity who takes out insurance on a person's life is referred to as the *applicant* or *owner.* The person whose life is insured is not a party to the contract unless he or she is also the owner. Two or more persons or entities may jointly apply for insurance on the life of another person, as is the case with some business continuation agreements. In the case of joint policies (either last-to-die or first-to-die) a person or entity may own a policy insuring more than one life.

The designation of a third party to receive the proceeds upon the policy's maturity does not make such a person a party to the contract. The third-party beneficiary need not know of the contract at its inception, may disclaim any benefits thereunder, and incurs no duties by virtue of his or her designation. The beneficiary may acquire certain rights that are enforceable against the company, but he or she acquires them only through the agreement between the company and the applicant or owner. Furthermore, the beneficiary's rights can be negated by any defenses available to the insurer against the owner. Even the rights of an irrevocable beneficiary may be defeated. This may be accomplished by policy loans (absent a policy provision requiring the beneficiary's consent) or by allowing the policy to lapse.

> **Assignee:** an entity to whom any right or interest is transferred (assigned)

An assignee, while possessing rights quite distinct from those of a beneficiary, occupies a position similar to that of the beneficiary in that he or she is an *interested* party but is not a party to the contract unless there has been an absolute assignment that has been consented to by the other party. It is worth noting that the voluntary payment of premiums by a person having no other relationship with the policy bestows no contractual rights or privileges on the premium payor.

The contractual relationship between the insurance company and the owner of the policy is that of conditional debtor and creditor. The insurance company incurs obligations only if certain conditions are fulfilled, and then its duty is only to carry out the terms of the contract. The insurance company is not a trustee in any sense of the word and is under no legal obligation to render an accounting of the premiums received or, in the absence of a showing of bad faith, of the apportionment of dividends.

Competency of the Insurer

> **Person:** a legal entity. In the law a natural person is a human being. Entities that exist only because the law creates them are artificial persons. Examples are trusts, corportions, and partnerships.

In the absence of specific legislation to the contrary, there is no reason why any person who has the legal capacity to enter into a contract cannot become the insurer under a life insurance contract. Freedom of contract is a constitutional and common-law privilege that must not be abridged unless the nature of the subject matter of the contract makes it a proper subject for the exercise of the police power of the state. Insurance—because of its magnitude, nature, and intimate bearing on the welfare of society—has been adjudged a proper subject for the exercise of such power.

The United States Supreme Court has ruled that a state may prohibit the making of insurance contracts by persons, either natural or artificial, who have not complied with the requirements of the law of the state. In many states, the statutes specifically prohibit natural persons (that is, human beings) from acting as life insurers. Even in those states that have not so legislated, the nature of the business—with its need for continuity and permanence of the insurer—has brought about the same result. Hence, while individual insurers were common in the early days of life insurance, today the legitimate insurance business is conducted exclusively by corporate insurers. If a corporation seeking to write life insurance in a particular state is legally organized, the only question that can arise regarding its capacity to contract is whether the corporation has complied with all the requirements for doing business in that state.

A contract issued by an unlicensed insurer is usually enforceable by the policyowner. This rule of law recognizes that a person who is solicited to buy insurance cannot be expected to inquire into the affairs of the insurance company to determine whether or not it has complied with all the statutory and regulatory requirements governing its operations and is fully qualified to enter into the proposed contract. On the contrary, the prospective insured is permitted to assume that the insurer is legally competent to enter into the proposed contract. In the event of a dispute, the insurer will not be permitted to use its own violation of statutory requirements as a defense against claims.

In order to assist the insured in enforcing claims against an unauthorized out-of-state insurer, all of the states (but not the District of Columbia) have enacted the Unauthorized Insurers Service-of-Process Act, which designates the insurance commissioner or some other state official as the agent of the unauthorized insurer for the purpose of accepting service of process. Designed to deal with companies that do business by mail, these statutes permit the insured to secure a judgment against the insurer in the courts of his or her own state. This judgment must be given "full faith and credit" by the courts of all other states in which the insurer has assets. Agents of unauthorized insurers are subject to both criminal and civil penalties and, in some states, are personally liable for claims under contracts they sold. It hardly seems necessary to add that an unlicensed insurer cannot maintain an action to enforce any claim arising out of an insurance contract made in violation of the laws of the state in which the suit is brought.

If the insurer is duly authorized to do business in a particular state but has failed to comply with some other requirement of the state law, the validity of its contracts will usually not be affected by the noncompliance. The contracts will be binding on both parties, but the insurer will be subject to whatever penalties are imposed for the violation of the law. If the statute requires certain provisions in such a contract, the contract will be deemed to contain such provisions.

Competency of the Applicant

All individuals are presumed to have legal capacity except those belonging to clearly defined groups that are held by law to have no capacity or only limited capacity to contract. For example, an alien enemy and a person judicially determined insane are wholly incompetent to enter into a contract. Others, such as minors and those who are mentally infirm but not adjudicated incompetent, have varying levels of contractual capacity.

Minors—or infants, as they are known to the law—do not lack capacity in the absolute sense and may enter into contracts that are binding on the other party. However, subject to certain restrictions, a minor can disaffirm a contract at any time during minority and demand a return of the monetary consideration that passed to the other party. Limitations on the right of a minor to void contracts are found in the general rules that an infant is bound to pay the reasonable value of necessities actually furnished to him or her. If the minor can make restitution for that which he or she received, it must be done.

American courts have held that a life insurance policy is not a necessity for a minor in the legal sense of the word. Hence, absent a statute to the contrary, a minor can disaffirm a life insurance contract at any time during minority and recover all premiums paid. A majority of the courts permit full recovery of premiums with no deduction for the cost of protection, while a few courts authorize the company to retain that portion of the aggregate premiums applied toward the cost of protection. In the latter case, recovery is limited to the policy's cash value or reserve. It is clear that only by permitting the insurer to deduct the cost of protection does the court compel the minor to make restitution to the insurer.

In recognition of the importance of life insurance and of the unfavorable position of a life insurance company in dealing with minors, most states have enacted statutes conferring the legal capacity to enter into valid and enforceable life insurance contracts covering their own lives on minors of a specified age and older. The age limit varies from 14 to 18, with age 15 predominating. A minor who satisfies the age requirement is permitted not only to purchase a life insurance policy but also to exercise all ownership rights in the contract. The statutes usually require that the beneficiary be a close relative; the eligible relationships are set forth in each state's law. Some of the statutes bestow legal capacity on a minor only for the purpose of negotiating insurance on his or her own life; the minor (in those states) still lacks legal capacity to become the owner of a policy on the life of another person.

A life insurance contract entered into between an American company and a resident of a foreign country is just as valid as one made with an American citizen unless a state of war exists between the two countries, in which case the contract is null. In the first instance, the resident of the foreign country would be described as an alien friend; in the second, as an alien enemy. A contract made with an alien friend is valid in all respects, while one with an alien enemy is void. No difficulties are likely to arise unless an alien friend with whom a contract has been made becomes an alien enemy through the outbreak of hostilities. In that event, it will generally be impossible, as well as contrary to public policy, for the parties to carry out the terms of the contract. In the case of life insurance, premium payments could not be made (unless the company had a branch office in the foreign country), and a question would arise as to the status of the policy.

The rulings of the courts in cases involving this problem have been diverse. In Connecticut and a few other states, it is held that all rights in such contracts are terminated and all equities forfeited. This is a harsh rule and permits the enrichment of the insurance company at the expense of one whose nonperformance was beyond his or her individual control.

A much larger number of states, including New York, hold that the contract is merely suspended during hostilities and can be revived by payment of all past-due premiums. Under this rule the policy of a deceased policyowner can be revived and the company forced to pay the face amount. This rule obviously exposes the company to a high degree of adverse selection.

A third rule, established in 1876 by the United States Supreme Court, holds that a contract is terminated for nonpayment of premiums caused by the outbreak of hostilities, but the policyowner is entitled to the reserve value computed as of the date of the first premium in default. The reserve is paid over to the governmental agency charged with the responsibility of assembling and holding property belonging to alien enemies. Under this rule, no action can be brought to recover the face amount of the policy; nor is the company under any obligation to revive the policy.

Although none of these solutions to the problem is completely satisfactory, the basis of settlement prescribed by the Supreme Court in 1876 seems to be the most equitable. However, that case was decided before nonforfeiture values were a common provision. It was also based on federal common law, which no longer exists. Today the practice would likely be to apply the automatic nonforfeiture provisions and perform the contract as written.

MUTUAL ASSENT

As in the case of other simple contracts, there must be a manifestation of mutual assent before a life insurance contract can be created. One party must make an offer to enter into an insurance transaction, and the other must accept the offer. One would naturally assume that the company, through one of its soliciting agents, makes the offer, which the prospective insured is free to accept or decline. That is not necessarily the case.

In many situations, the prospect is considered to have made the offer. As a general rule, and subject to the exceptions noted later, the prospect is considered to have made the offer whenever the application is accompanied by the first premium; the company is regarded as the offeror whenever the first premium is not paid (or at least not definitely promised) with the application. In the first situation, the prospect has indicated his or her unqualified willingness to enter into a contractual relationship with the company, even to the point of putting up the consideration. In the second situation, the prospect may refuse, without any legal penalties, to accept and pay for the contract issued by the company. The question of who is the offeror and who the offeree is important in determining the exact time at which the contract comes into existence, which may be of crucial significance. (This matter is dealt with later in this book.)

Many states now require that the policyowner be given a "10-day free look" after delivery of the policy. During that time the contract is in effect, but its continuation is subject to the policyowner's right to cancel the policy within the 10 days and receive a full refund of his or her premiums.

The Application

The chain of events that culminates in the formation of a life insurance contract begins with a conversation between the company's soliciting agent and a prospect for insurance, during the course of which the prospect is invited or — more accurately — urged to extend an offer to the company. Such invitations to deal have no legal consequences in the formation of the contract, although they may contain representations that will have consequences after the contract is made. If the invitation to deal comes from a broker, the representations will have no legal effect either before or after formation of the contract since a broker is considered to be the agent of the applicant for the purpose of procuring insurance.

The applicant's offer to the company, or an applicant's invitation to the company to make him or her an offer, as the case might be, is communicated in the form of an application. Unless there is a specific state statute requiring that the application be in writing, it is clear that the application and the contract can be either oral or written. Written applications for life insurance policies, however, are required as a matter of company practice.

The application for a life insurance contract serves the following purposes:

- It requests the insurer to issue a specific type of policy, providing a designated amount of insurance in exchange for a specified premium.
- It gives the name and address of the applicant (and person to be insured if different than the applicant), the name and relationship of the person or persons to whom the proceeds are to be paid, and the manner in which the company's obligation is to be discharged.
- It provides a detailed description of the risk that the insurer is asked to underwrite, including statements or representations as to the applicant's

(or person to be insured's) occupation, travel plans, family history, personal medical history, present physical condition, and habits.

- It puts the applicant on notice and requires an acknowledgment from him or her that the soliciting agent has no authority to modify any terms of the application or of the policy to be issued pursuant thereto (*the nonwaiver clause*).
- It authorizes the insurer to obtain information from other sources (including the Medical Information Bureau) about the health, lifestyle, and finances of the person to be insured.

The contents of the application relating to the first two functions constitute the offer in the technical sense since they fix the terms of the policy to be issued by the company as an acceptance of the offer. While the identification of the person whose life is to be insured is a necessary part of the offer, the detailed description of the risk is not actually a part of the offer. From a legal standpoint, the applicant's representations as to his or her medical history, present physical condition, and so on are merely inducements to the insurer; they are not promises or conditions of the contract. Neither does the nonwaiver clause relate to the offer. It is intended merely to prevent the applicant from successfully contending afterwards that he or she was misled as to the agent's apparent authority.

In the typical commercial transaction, the offer becomes a part of the contract ultimately consummated. This is not true of the offer leading to a life insurance contract unless the application is specifically made a part of the contract (a common insurance practice). It has long been established—first by court decisions and later by statutes—that once a life insurance policy is issued, the entire contract is contained in the policy. This rule, known historically as the *parol evidence rule,* has been stated as follows:

> All preliminary negotiations, conversations, and oral agreements are merged in and superseded by the subsequent written contract and unless fraud, accident, or mistake be averred, the writing constitutes the agreement between the parties, and its terms cannot be added to or subtracted from by parol evidence.[1]

A typical state statute provides that "every policy of life, accident or health insurance, or contract of annuity delivered or issued for delivery in this state shall contain the entire contract between the parties." In addition, most insurance policies contain a provision to this effect, as in this example: "This policy, the attached copy of the initial application, any application for reinstatement, all subsequent applications to change the policy and any endorsements or riders are the entire contract. No statement will be used in defense of a claim unless such statement is contained in the application(s)."

Since the company places great reliance on the information contained in the application and in the event of a contested claim would undoubtedly want to introduce evidence therefrom, it customarily incorporates the application into the contract, by reference as well as by physical attachment of a copy (usually a photostat) of the application to the policy. In most of the states there are statutes requiring that a copy of the application be physically attached to the policy if the statements in the application are to be treated as representations and are to be introduced into evidence in the event of litigation. Typical statutory language provides that "no application for issuance of any life, accident or health insurance policy, or contract of annuity shall be admissible in evidence unless a true copy of such application was attached to such policy when issued."

Effective Date of Coverage

The coverage under a life insurance policy becomes effective the instant the contract comes into existence. This, however, takes place only after certain conditions have been fulfilled, and those conditions can be fulfilled in more than one manner. The procedure by which a contract is brought into existence after the application's submission depends on whether the application is regarded as an offer or only as an invitation to the company to make an offer. That, in turn, depends on the time at which and the circumstances under which the first premium is paid. In that regard it is necessary to distinguish among three different sets of circumstances. The first set of circumstances is one under which the application is submitted without payment of the first premium.

Application without First Premium

Recall that when the applicant does not tender the first premium with the application, no application has been made. The application is regarded as only an invitation to deal. The approval of the application and the issuance of the policy constitute an offer from the company to the prospective insured, which is normally communicated by delivery of the policy. The applicant manifests his or her acceptance of the company's offer by accepting delivery of the policy and paying the first premium. This assumes that the soliciting agent does not have authority to extend credit. If the agent has authority to take a promissory note or even an oral promise of the insured in lieu of cash, an application accompanied by such a promise is an offer from the applicant to make a *bilateral* contract—an exchange of the applicant's promise for the insurer's promise.

Most companies specify in the application that the prospective insured must be in good health at the time of delivery of the policy, and some insurers condition the contract on the absence of any medical treatment during the interim between the application's submission and the policy's delivery. All these requirements—delivery of the policy, payment of the first premium, good health of the applicant, and absence of any interim medical treatment—are treated as conditions precedent that must be fulfilled before the contract comes into existence and the coverage becomes effective. Each of these requirements will be discussed below.

Delivery of the Policy. Delivery of the policy is a legal prerequisite to the validity of the life insurance contract only because many companies specifically make it so. Neither by statute nor by common law is the delivery of a formal policy requisite to the completion, validity, or enforceability of a contract of insurance. This is contrary to real estate law, for example, which holds that legal title to real estate is not transferred until the deed is delivered. The company could conceivably communicate its offer to the applicant in some other manner, and the applicant could manifest acceptance by notifying the company or the soliciting agent.

The controlling reason why many insurance companies make delivery of the policy a condition precedent to the formation of the contract is that it provides a way to establish the precise moment at which coverage under the contract becomes effective. Some carriers make no special provision in the application to set the date when coverage begins. Some provide that coverage begins when the policy is issued and the entire first year's premium has been paid. Several other actions of the company—such as approval of the application by the underwriting department, issuance of the policy, or mailing the policy to the soliciting agent for delivery—might be used to mark the inception of coverage. This could lead to much confusion and litigation unless the parties agree in advance that a definite determinable event, such as delivery of the policy, marks the beginning of coverage.

Despite this attempt to achieve certainty, litigation has developed over the meaning of the word "delivery." The issue is whether the condition can be satisfied only by a manual delivery or whether constructive delivery is sufficient. If it is clearly evident from the terms of the application and the policy that actual manual delivery is expected, the requirement will be strictly enforced. If, however, the requirement is couched in terms of a simple "delivery," the general rule is that the condition can be fulfilled by constructive delivery.

Constructive delivery has been held to take place whenever a policy, properly stamped and addressed to the company's agent, is deposited in the mail, provided no limitations are imposed on the manual delivery of the policy to the insured by the agent. There are a number of decisions, however, that hold that the requirement of delivery—and especially "actual delivery"—is itself a condition precedent that cannot be met by constructive delivery. (It should be noted that the issue of constructive delivery is not material if the other conditions—notably, payment of the first premium and the applicant's good health—are not met.)

To a large extent delivery is a matter of the parties' intention. It is a question of who has the *right* to possession of the policy, rather than who has actual possession. That being true, possession of the policy by the insured is at most only prima facie evidence of its delivery. The presumption of proper delivery can be rebutted by evidence that the insured obtained possession of the policy by fraud or for the purpose of inspecting it, or in any other manner manifesting a lack of intention on the company's part to effectuate a legal delivery of the policy. On the other hand, it has been held that if the first premium has been paid, the applicant is in good health, and the company has implicitly expressed its intention of being legally bound under the contract by delivering the policy to the agent to be unconditionally passed on to the applicant, the contract is in force. Even though the insured may die without actual possession of the policy, the company is liable for payment of the insured amount.

In view of the foregoing presumption, an agent must observe proper safeguards in relinquishing physical possession of a policy to an applicant before all conditions precedent have been fulfilled. The need for caution is greatly magnified if the policy, on its face, acknowledges receipt of the first premium, which is sometimes the case. The most common circumstance under which the agent may find it necessary to relinquish control over a policy without making a legal delivery is when the applicant expresses a desire to study the policy. In that event, the applicant is asked to sign a receipt acknowledging that the policy has been delivered only for examination and approval and that the first premium has not been paid. This acknowledgment is called an *inspection receipt*.

Payment of First Premium. It is customary for the application—and sometimes the policy itself—to stipulate that the first premium must be paid before coverage becomes effective. Payment of the full amount in cash is usually specified, and unless the company agrees to extend credit, any payment smaller than the full premium will fail to satisfy the requirement. The agent is usually not authorized to extend credit on behalf of the company, but he or she may pay the premium for the insured and seek reimbursement on a personal basis. If an agent is authorized to accept an applicant's promissory note in payment of the first premium, the applicant's tendering such a note will satisfy the condition precedent, but failure of the insured to pay the note at maturity may cause the policy to lapse.

Payment by check may be taken as absolute or conditional payment, depending on the parties' intention. If the check is accepted in absolute payment of the first premium, bank's failure to honor the check would not affect the validity of the policy but merely give the insurance company the right to sue the applicant for the amount of the check. On the other hand, if the check is accepted only as conditional payment, nonpayment of the check would cause the contract to fail. Most companies stipulate that checks are accepted subject to being honored by the bank, which is the common-law rule in the absence of evidence that the check was accepted as absolute payment.

Good Health of Applicant. The *delivery-in-good-health clause* is a by-product of the process by which risks are underwritten in life insurance. In most lines of property and casualty insurance, the local agent is given the authority to underwrite the risk and bind the coverage. There need be no lag between the inspection of the risk and the binding of the coverage. In life insurance, however, all underwriting information is forwarded to the home office, and the right to bind the risk rests solely with the executive officers of the company. Under such a system, which seems to be the only feasible one, there is an inevitable time lag between the submission of the application and the assumption of the risk by the insurer. In some cases, where the investigation of the applicant or the insured is very comprehensive and the collection of medical data involves correspondence with attending physicians and requests for supplemental diagnostic procedures, the lag might be as long as several weeks. Obviously the company would like to be protected against a deterioration of the applicant's health during the time it is considering the application. The way that insurance companies have chosen to accomplish this objective is the delivery-in-good-health clause.

While the exact wording of the good-health clause varies from company to company, the gist of the clause is that the policy will not take effect unless, upon the date of delivery, the applicant is alive and in good health. Some clauses provide that unless the first premium is paid with the application, the applicant must be alive and in good health upon payment of the first premium. This clause has the effect of making the applicant's good health a condition precedent to the effectiveness of the contract. Under the laws of some states, including Pennsylvania, if the applicant underwent a medical examination at the request of the insurer, the good-health requirement can be invoked only with respect to changes in the applicant's health occurring after the medical examination.

The fact that the good-health requirement is a condition precedent and has been enforced by the majority of courts has great significance in protecting life insurance companies against fraud. Even so, the protection of the good-health clause must be sought by the insurer during the policy's period of contestability. Once that period has expired, the good-health clause is void.

In attempting to rescind a contract on the grounds of misrepresentation or concealment, insurance companies are frequently required to prove that the applicant deliberately misrepresented the facts of the case. In fact, most states have enacted legislation that stipulates that no misrepresentation will void a policy unless the misrepresentation was made with an actual intent to deceive or unless it would increase the risk. To prove intent to defraud is always difficult and is frequently impossible. With the good-health clause, however, insurance companies can avoid that difficulty since intent is not involved. The clause is concerned with the existence of a condition and not with what may or may not have been known to the applicant. If the company can prove to the court's satisfaction that the applicant was not, in fact, in good health at the date of delivery of the policy, it can avoid liability under the contract. In practice, however, companies generally raise the issue only when they suspect that the applicant did not act in good faith or when there has been a material deterioration in the applicant's health in the interval between the date of the medical examination and the date of delivery of the policy.

As might be expected, the courts have frequently been called upon to define the meaning of the terms "good health" and "sound health." The courts have ruled that "good health," as used in the context of the clause under discussion, is a relative term, meaning not absolute freedom from physical infirmity but only such a condition of body and mind that one may discharge the ordinary duties of life without serious strain upon the vital powers. The term does not mean perfect health, but a state of health free from any disease or ailment that seriously affects a person's general physical soundness. Good health is not impaired by a mere temporary indisposition, which does not tend to weaken or undermine the constitution. One of the most comprehensive definitions was supplied by a Kansas court:

> [Good health] is not apparent good health, nor yet a belief of the applicant that he is in good health, but it is that he is in actual good health. Of course, slight troubles or temporary indisposition which will not usually result in serious consequences, and which do not seriously impair or weaken his constitution, do not establish the absence of good health, but, if the illness is of a serious nature, such as to weaken and impair the constitution and shorten life, the applicant cannot be held to be in good health.[2]

There has been a tendency on the part of some courts to narrow the application of the clause to cases where a change in the applicant's health occurs between the time of the medical examination and delivery of the policy to the applicant. This line of decisions is exemplified by a Pennsylvania case, in which the court stated that the good-health clause has no application to a disease the applicant may have had at the time of the medical examination unless fraud or misrepresentation can be proved, since presumably the applicant's physical condition was satisfactory to the company; otherwise, the policy would not have been issued. According to the court, "The legal scope of that provision is restricted to mean only that the applicant did not contract any new disease impairing his health, nor suffer any material change in his physical condition between the time of such examination and the date of the policy. . . ."[3]

This interpretation of the good-health clause is certainly at variance with the common understanding of the term good health and with the legal definition cited earlier, but it is consistent with the apparent purpose of the clause. As a matter of fact, companies have usually invoked the clause as a defense against a claim only where there has been a change in the applicant's health, or where there has been fraud or misrepresentation in the application. Moreover, the burden of proving that the applicant was not in good health at the time of delivery of the policy is usually on the insurance company, although a minority of courts have held that the insured or the beneficiary must prove compliance with the clause.

Medical Treatment after Submission of Application. Some policies issued today contain a clause that provides that the life insurance policy will not take effect if the applicant has received medical or hospital treatment between the time that the application was signed and the date of delivery of the policy.[4] Like the good-health clause, this clause is designed to deal with a change in the applicant's physical condition during the time the application is being processed. It is intended to be a condition precedent, and the courts generally treat it as such. In other words, if during the contestable period, the company can prove that the applicant received medical or hospital treatment between the date of the application and delivery of the policy and failed to disclose that fact to the company, the company can avoid liability under the contract. If the medical treatment is disclosed at the time the policy is delivered, the company, after consideration of the ailment, may conclude that the applicant's insurability is not impaired and waive the clause. The courts are very zealous in seeking a waiver of the clause manifested in the conduct of life insurance companies or their agents.[5]

Justification of Conditions Precedent. When the premium is not paid with the application, all conditions precedent must be fulfilled before the contract becomes effective. In general this means that the policy must be delivered by the agent while the applicant is alive and in good health, and the full amount of the first premium must be paid in cash or by a valid check at the moment of delivery. Delivery of the policy and payment of the first premium are supposed to be simultaneous transactions.

Recognizing the advantages to both the applicant and the company of having the coverage attach at the date of application, insurance companies have devised a procedure to accomplish this objective. This procedure, involving the use of a *conditional receipt,* is described in the following section.

Prepayment of First Premium

The applicant can avoid the legal consequences of conditions precedent by remitting the first premium with the application for insurance. Companies generally acknowledge receipt of the premium with a document called a *conditional receipt*, which binds the coverage without reference to delivery of the policy.

FIGURE 36-1
Insurability Premium Receipt

Face of the Receipt

RECEIVED FROM _____, Applicant,
Name of Proposed Insured
if other than Applicant _____
    Amount of cash
    settlement received $............................ in connection with the initial
premium for the proposed insurance for which an application is this day made to
the Ajax Life Insurance Company.

    Life Insurance and any additional benefits in the amount applied for (but not
exceeding a maximum liability of $50,000, including all additional benefits on all
pending applications to the company combined) shall be deemed to take effect
as of the date of this receipt, subject to the terms and conditions printed on the
reverse side hereof.

    The amount of settlement received shall be refunded if the application is
declined or if a policy is issued other than as applied for and is not accepted.
Any check, draft, or money order is received subject to collection.

_____   _____
  Date of Receipt   Signature of Agent

Back of the Receipt

    Subject to the limitations of this receipt and the terms and conditions of the
policy that may be issued by the company on the basis of the application, the life
insurance and any additional benefits applied for shall not be deemed to take
effect unless the company, after investigation and such medical examination, if
any, as it may require, shall be satisfied that on the date of this receipt each
person proposed for insurance was insurable for the *amount* of life insurance and
any additional benefits applied for according to the company's rules and practice
of selection; provided, however, that approval by the company of the insurability
of the Proposed Insured for a plan of insurance other than that applied for, or the
denial of any particular additional benefit applied for, shall not invalidate the terms
and conditions for this receipt relating to life insurance and any other additional
benefit applied for.

(Not to be detached unless issued under the requirements for using Conditional
Receipt)

Source: *Law and the Life Insurance Contract,* 6th ed., Irwin Professional Publishing, 1989, p. 148.

There are several forms of conditional receipt in general use today,[6] but the
two basic types are the *insurability* type and the *approval* type. The insurability

type is the most common by a large margin. The approval type is no longer widely used because it offers far less protection to the applicant than the insurability type.

Insurability Type. The insurability type of receipt (see figure 36-1) makes the coverage effective at the time of the application, provided the applicant is found to be insurable in accordance with the general underwriting rules of the company. Some receipts make coverage effective on the date of the application or the medical examination, whichever is later.

Coverage under such a clause, however, is not automatic. The applicant is considered to have made an offer to the insurer. The insurer, by issuing the conditional receipt, accepts the offer, subject to a condition—the condition that the applicant is found to be insurable. If the home office finds the applicant to have been insurable in accordance with its general underwriting rules on the date of the application or medical examination, the coverage attaches retroactively to the date cited. If the company finds that the applicant was not insurable at the time he or she submitted the application, the coverage never attaches under the policy applied for and the premium is refunded. For the coverage to be binding as of the date of application, the risk must be acceptable to the company under its underwriting rules on the plan and for the amount applied for and the premium rate on the application. If the risk is acceptable, but only on a plan or at a premium rate different from that on the application, the company is construed to have made a counteroffer that must be accepted by the applicant before the coverage can become effective.

If the applicant is found to have been insurable at the date of application, coverage attaches retroactively even though, in the meantime, the applicant may have died or suffered a deterioration in health. Companies are frequently called upon to consider the application of a person known to have died since applying for insurance, and they are careful not to permit knowledge of that fact to influence their underwriting decision. The same code of ethics is followed in reviewing the prepaid applications of persons who have subsequently suffered heart attacks or other physical impairments. If the applicant is to receive the fullest benefit of the conditional receipt, it is absolutely essential that the company apply general underwriting standards, rather than standards tailored to fit the individual case.

Approval Type. The approval type of receipt (see figure 36-2) states that the coverage is effective from the completion of the application, provided the company approves the application. The receipt usually makes no reference to the criteria that will be applied in the company's consideration of the application. Under the present state of the law, however, it is clear that the company must act reasonably and apply its customary underwriting standards.

Under the approval type of receipt, the company is not at risk if the applicant dies before the application is acted upon. Nevertheless judicial opinion is divided as to whether the insurer should be held liable for payment of the policy's face amount if the applicant dies before the company acts on the application.

There is a judicial trend, noticeable with respect to both the *insurability* and *approval* types of receipts, to find an ambiguity and to hold that there is coverage from the date of the receipt until approval or declination of the application. In recognition of this trend, a minority (but a growing minority) of insurers use a form of conditional receipt that places the company unconditionally at risk from the date of application, usually for a limited face amount and period of time, such as 60 days. The insurance remains in full effect unless and until the application is declined. Under this form of receipt, the applicant enjoys coverage for a brief period even when he or she is definitely an uninsurable risk.

FIGURE 36-2
Approval Premium Receipt

Face of the Receipt

RECEIVED FROM _____, Applicant,
Name of Proposed Insured
if other than Applicant _____
    Amount of cash
    settlement received $...................... in connection with the initial premium for the proposed insurance for which an application is this day made to the Ajax Life Insurance Company.

    Life Insurance and any additional benefits in the amount applied for shall be deemed to take effect as of the date of approval of this application at the home office of Ajax Life Insurance Company.

    The amount of consideration received shall be refunded if the application is declined or if a policy is issued other than as applied for and is not accepted. Any check, draft, or money order is received subject to collection.

_____   _____
    Date of Receipt   Signature of Agent

Back of the Receipt

    Subject to the limitations of this receipt and the terms and conditions of the policy that may be issued by the company on the basis of the application, the life insurance and any additional benefits applied for shall not be deemed to take effect unless the company, after investigation and such medical examination, if any, as it may require, shall be satisfied that on the date of this receipt each person proposed for insurance was insurable for the *amount* of life insurance and any additional benefits applied for according to the company's rules and practice of selection; provided, however, that approval by the company of the insurability of the Proposed Insured for a plan of insurance other than that applied for, or the denial of any particular additional benefit applied for, shall not invalidate the terms and conditions for this receipt relating to life insurance and any other additional benefit applied for.

(Not to be detached unless issued under the requirements for using Conditional Receipt)

Source: Adapted from *Law and the Life Insurance Contract,* 6th ed., Irwin Professional Publishing, 1989, p. 148.

Properly construed, the conditional receipt arrangement offers real benefits to both the insured and the insurer and is widely used. It protects the applicant against loss of insurability while the application is being processed, and it protects the company against a declination of the policy by the applicant after it has been issued—at considerable expense. The arrangement is feasible, since all applicants using the plan pay their premiums in advance, and the company is not exposed to adverse selection. Moreover, the arrangement does not involve any relaxation of underwriting standards.

The majority of courts interpret conditional receipts strictly in accordance with the language used by the insurer. Nevertheless, even these courts have a clear preference to find that coverage does exist, and to do so they are sometimes creative in discovering an ambiguity that can be construed in favor of the applicant. The minority of courts take a much more liberal view in favor of the applicant. They tend to ignore the language of the conditional receipt and find that coverage exists because the applicant, having paid the premium, would have reasonably expected it to exist. A decreasing number of courts seem to be willing to go so far as to rewrite the terms of the conditional receipt.

However, some insurers expect that some courts will find temporary coverage effective regardless of the conditions stipulated in the receipt. In order to eliminate the possibility of unintended temporary coverage, in some jurisdictions a few insurers have stopped accepting a premium payment with the application.

Advance Payment of First Premium without Conditional Receipt

The first premium is rarely remitted with the application without a conditional receipt being issued to the applicant. Under such circumstances, coverage does not attach until the application has been approved and the policy has been delivered.[7] The applicant is considered to have made an offer that can be withdrawn at any time before acceptance by the company. Acceptance is manifested by delivery of the policy.

As with policies whose premiums are not paid in advance, delivery can take the form of an actual physical transfer of the policy from the agent to the applicant or transmission through the mail in such manner as to constitute constructive delivery. However, if the application requires that the policy be delivered to the applicant while he or she is in good health, mailing the policy to the agent for delivery to the applicant is not likely to be regarded as constructive delivery since a condition has been imposed on its release. Mailing the policy directly to the applicant, regarded as a waiver of the delivery requirement, would be treated as a waiver of the good-health requirement only if the insurer had knowledge of a breach of the condition. The contract would become effective the instant the policy is placed in the mails, even if the insured never receives it.

Delay in Consideration of the Application

A life insurance company owes a moral duty (and in a minority of the states a legal duty) to the insuring public to consider all applications within a reasonable period and to render prompt decisions on the insurability of those seeking insurance. These two questions may arise in case of an unreasonable delay by the company in determining the insurability of an applicant:

- Does the unreasonable delay constitute an acceptance of the applicant's offer?
- Is the insurer liable for the damages caused by its delay if the applicant dies before the application is either accepted or rejected?

It seems clear that no presumption of acceptance should be allowed when the application is not accompanied by the first premium. In that event, no offer has been made to the company, and the company's silence could hardly be construed as acceptance of a nonexistent offer. A different situation exists, however, when the applicant remits the first premium with the application and thus makes a valid offer to the company.

As a general rule, silence is not construed as acceptance of an offer. To the contrary, after a reasonable time, the offeror can assume that the offer has been rejected and that he or she is free to deal with another party. If this were not the rule, people with goods to sell could flood the country with offers that the recipients would be obliged to reject so that they would not to become obligated to buy the goods. The writing of rejections could become an intolerable burden. A majority of courts have applied this general rule to the insurer's silence and have held that no matter how long the company delays, its silence will not bind it to a contract of insurance.

A few courts have made a distinction between *unsolicited* offers, the usual kind, and those made in response to the activities of agents who are paid to solicit offers, as is the case in life insurance. These courts have held that the insurer's unreasonable delay in rejecting an application constitutes an acceptance that completes the contract.

While in most states, delay in consideration of an application does not make an insurer liable under *contract,* some courts have recognized a liability of the company in *tort*—that is, a civil liability arising from other than a contract. Although they are distinctly in the minority (and it is believed that this is no longer an important trend in the law), these courts have held that since the company is operating under a franchise from the state, it is under duty to act promptly and with due care on all applications received by it. They argue that the state issues a charter or license in order that the public may have access to an important form of protection that, in the public interest, should be made available to all who can qualify for it. These courts believe that after the company solicits the application and obtains it along with the applicant's consideration, the company is bound to furnish the insurance that the state has authorized or to decline to do so within a reasonable time. An Iowa court ruled, "Otherwise the applicant is unduly delayed in obtaining insurance he desires and for which the law has afforded the opportunity, and which the insurer impliedly has promised if conditions are satisfactory."[8] Failure to live up to this obligation makes the insurer liable to the applicant for damages.

If an applicant who was insurable at the time of application dies before the insurance company—in disregard of its duty to act promptly—has approved the risk, many courts would hold that the applicant's estate could recover the amount of insurance applied for. It would seem that if the insurer is adjudged guilty of a tort, the beneficiary would be the logical person to receive damages. With a few exceptions, however, the courts hold that the beneficiary is not a party at interest until coverage becomes effective and thus cannot recover. (The question of tort liability is not likely to arise under a conditional receipt since the conditional receipt forms in general use provide for retroactive coverage.)

Operative Date of Policy

The foregoing discussion was concerned with determining the date on which coverage under a life insurance contract becomes effective. This date is usually referred to as the *effective date* of the policy. It may or may not be the same date as that on the face of the policy, which is significant for other reasons. The date on the policy governs the status of various policy provisions after the contract has gone into effect, and it is sometimes referred to as the *operative date* of the policy.

The policy may bear the date on which it was issued, the date on which the coverage becomes effective, or the date on which it was applied for. The most common practice is to date the policy as of the date of issue unless there is a conditional receipt. In this event the policy will bear the date of the application or the medical examination, whichever is later.

Backdating

Occasionally a policy carries a date earlier than the date of application. This is known as *backdating* (or antedating) the policy and is done only at the request of or with the consent of the applicant, usually to produce a lower insurance age and hence a lower premium.[9] The practice is not generally regarded to be in conflict with antirebating laws, but several states prohibit it when an age change is involved. Other states have attempted to control the practice by forbidding the issue of a policy that bears a date more than 6 months earlier than the date of the application, a limitation that many—if not most—companies have voluntarily adopted.

The practice of backdating policies—which, from a legal standpoint, refers to the use of any date earlier than the effective date of the policy—raises these three important questions:

- When does the next premium fall due?
- From what date does extended term insurance run?
- From what date do the incontestable and suicide clauses begin to run?

Premium Due Dates. When the antedating was done at the applicant's request and resulted in his or her lower contract age, the overwhelming majority of both state and federal courts hold that the due date of the next premium is established by the date of the policy. Even when the antedating does not benefit the applicant—that is, no age change is involved—the majority of the courts support the view that the policy date establishes the due date, on the grounds that certainty is preferable to uncertainty. In some jurisdictions, especially Missouri, it is held that the payment of an annual premium entitles the insured to a full year of protection and that the due date of the next premium is determined by reference to the effective date of coverage. For this reason, many companies do not refer to the first premium as an annual or quarterly premium but indicate instead the exact period covered by the first premium and the due date of the second premium.

Date of Extended Term Insurance. Fixing the period of extended term insurance in the event that there is a default in premium payments is closely related to the problem of determining the due date of the second and subsequent premiums. It would clearly be to the advantage of the insured and his or her beneficiaries to calculate the date of default from which the period of extended term insurance runs in reference to the effective date of the contract rather than from an earlier date of issue. If the insured dies, the choice of beginning date for the term insurance could make the difference between payment of the face amount of the policy and total avoidance of liability by the company. It is generally held, however, that the anniversary date fixed for premium payments also controls the inception date for extended term insurance.

Incontestable and Suicide Clauses. The general view regarding the incontestable and suicide clauses is that the date of issue establishes the point of departure. A few courts, however, arguing that the suicide clause is completely independent of the provisions dealing with premium payment, hold that the effective date of the policy controls. Some policies specify a certain date as being the "date of issue" for the purpose of these two clauses, and the courts usually recognize this date.

In summary, then, it may be said that backdating, if it is done without fraud or mistake and is not in violation of a state statute, is given effect whether it benefits the insured or the insurer.

NOTES

1. H. M. Horne and D. B. Mansfield, *The Life Insurance Contract,* 2d ed. (New York: Life Office Management Association, 1948), p. 46.
2. *Klein v. Farmers and Bankers Life Insurance Co.,* 132 Kan. 748, 753, 297 Pac. 730, 732 (1931).
3. *Davidson et al. v. John Hancock Mutual Life Insurance Co.,* 159 Pa. Super. 535, 49 A. 2d 186 (1946).
4. Industrial life insurance policies usually contain a provision that permits the company to void the contract (within the contestable period) if within 2 years prior to application for the policy the insured received hospital or medical treatment that he or she failed to disclose or to prove immaterial to the risk.
5. Some companies invoke the doctrine of continuing representations to deal with changes in insurability during the interim between submission of the application and delivery of the policy. The landmark case in this area of law is *Stipcich v. Metropolitan Life Ins. Co.,* 277 U.S. 311, 45 Sup. Ct. 512, 72 L.Ed. 895.
6. Muriel L. Crawford and William T. Beadles, *Law and the Life Insurance Contract,* 6th ed. (Homewood, IL: Irwin Professional Publishing, 1989), pp. 154–165.
7. A few courts have held to the contrary. Moreover, California has a statute that binds the insurer as of the moment of premium payment if the risk meets the underwriting requirements of the company.
8. *Duffie v. Bankers Life Assn.,* 160 Iowa 19, 27, 139 N.W. 1087, 1090 (1913).
9. A person's insurance age for ordinary insurance is his or her age at the nearest birthday. For insurance purposes, he or she becomes one year older 6 months and one day after his or her last birthday. It is possible to obtain a lower insurance age by dating a policy back only one day, but most cases involve a much longer period.

37

Formation of a Life Insurance Contract (Part 2)

Dan M. McGill
Revised by Burke A. Christensen

CONSIDERATION

Consideration: any benefit to the promisor or detriment to the promisee

Nature of the Consideration

The life insurance contract, like other contracts, must be supported by a valid consideration. In a unilateral contract, consideration is always given in exchange for a promise and, in the case of a bilateral contract, is itself a promise. Since only the company makes an enforceable promise, the life insurance contract is a unilateral contract. The consideration for the insurer's promise is the first premium or if premiums are to be paid more frequently than annually, the first installment of the first premium. Most policies state that the company's promise is given in consideration of the *application* and the first premium. This is apparently intended to give greater legal effect to the application, on which the company places great reliance. The following are two examples of this provision:

Your policy and the application make up the entire contract. We relied on the application in issuing this policy. A copy was attached to the policy when it was issued. Please examine it and let us know if there are any errors or omissions. The only statements that may be used to contest the policy are those in the application. In the absence of fraud, they will be representations, not warranties.

The consideration for this policy is the application and payment of the total initial premium on or before policy delivery.

Condition: a provision in a legal agreement that makes one event contingent upon the occurrence of another

Condition precedent: an event that must occur *before* another duty or right exists

Condition subsequent: an event that terminates an existing duty or right

Premiums after the first are not part of the legal consideration since otherwise the contract could not come into existence until they are all paid. Rather, payment of such premiums is a condition precedent to the continuance of the contract. This means that the insurer's promise is conditioned on the continued payment of periodic premiums. In other words, the contract contains a provision that makes the continued payment of premiums a condition that must occur before the insurer will have to perform on its promises. If the insured defaults in the payment of a premium after the contract is in force, the company is released (subject to the nonforfeiture laws) from its original promise to pay the face amount of the policy, but it remains obligated to honor various subsidiary promises contained in the surrender provisions and the reinstatement clause.

Form of the Consideration

The insurance company is entitled to receive the first premium, or the first installment thereof, in cash; it may, however, agree to accept any valuable property. The premium may be paid in cash, by check, by promissory note, or — in the absence of a prohibitive statute — by services, such as printing work or advertising. Some states forbid an insurance company to accept payment of any premium in services, presumably because the practice lends itself too readily to rebating. By placing an excessive value on the services rendered, a company or its agent could, in effect, refund a portion of the contractual premium charge. Today, payment of premiums by any method other than cash, policy loans, or financing programs (in the case of some college senior or graduate student plans) is generally prohibited.

Checks are readily accepted by insurance companies, but they are generally treated as conditional payments. That is, crediting the premium is usually conditioned on the bank upon which the check is drawn honoring the instrument. If the check is not honored when presented and the company holds that the premium has not been paid, its promise is no longer operative. This is true even if the check was tendered to the insurer in good faith by the insured. However, when the insured had sufficient funds in the bank to cover the check and the bank's failure to honor the check was based on a technical defect in the instrument, such as an improper signature or an incorrect date, or on a clerical error on the part of the bank, insurers are inclined to recognize a contractual obligation, provided the premium is subsequently paid in cash or by valid check.[1]

A company or its properly authorized agent may agree that the check constitutes an absolute payment of the premium. That is, the company accepts the liability of the parties to the instrument in satisfaction of the premium. Although this is not normal procedure, it may occur when the agent gives the applicant an unconditional premium receipt in exchange for his or her check. In this case, if the check is not paid when presented, the company may enforce its rights on the instrument, but it cannot validly claim that the premium has not been paid.

Promissory note: a written promise to pay a sum of money

While it is no longer a common practice, a company may also authorize some or all of its agents to accept the insured's promissory note in payment of the first premium (and subsequent premiums, for that matter). If the note is honored at maturity, there are no complications, but there is a real question about the status of the policy in the event that the note is not paid when due. In anticipation of this complication, a company may stipulate on the note, on any premium receipt, on the policy, or on all three that if the note is not paid at maturity, the policy will be forfeited. If such a provision is included, it will be enforced according to its terms. As soon as the maturity date of the note arrives, if the note remains unpaid, the company is entitled to repudiate the contract.

If the stipulation is included in the note or in the premium receipt *but not in the policy,* there is a conflict of opinion as to the rights of the company.[2] Some courts hold that the provision is invalid on the grounds that it violates the statute in most states that says that the policy and the application constitute the entire contract between the parties. Other courts uphold the provision on the grounds that the statute means simply that the policy contains the entire contract as of the time it was issued. The courts that entertain this view feel that the statute does not prevent the execution of subsequent agreements. They point out that if the policy is construed to contain all possible agreements relating to the contract, it would be contrary to the statute for the company to agree to an extension of time to pay a premium, whereas such agreements are generally recognized. Upholding the provision seems to be in accord with the evident intention of the parties.

If the forfeiture provision is contained in the policy but not in the note or the premium receipt, there is also a conflict of opinion. In states in which the entire-contract statute is strictly followed, the provision contained in the policy will be enforced according to its terms. In other states the decision turns on the interpretation of the note and the receipt. If the note and the receipt evidence an intention on the part of the insurer to accept the note as an unconditional payment, this subsequent agreement will override the provision contained in the policy. On the other hand, if there is no indication of an intention to accept the note as an unconditional payment, the provision in the policy will prevail.

If there is no forfeiture provision in the policy, the note, or the premium receipt, the note is considered to be an absolute payment of the premium, and the insurance company is limited to its rights on the note in the event that it is not paid at maturity. This is the usual case.

It should be observed that if the insurer or its authorized agent extends credit to the insured, the contract will be bilateral rather than unilateral. In this case, the consideration for the insurer's promise is the insured's promise to pay the amount of the first premium.

An agent who is not authorized to extend credit on behalf of the company may pay the premium for the applicant. In doing so, he or she is acting as the applicant's agent, and failure of the applicant to reimburse the agent will not invalidate the policy.

LEGALITY OF PURPOSE

General Considerations

To be enforceable a contract must be entered into for a legal purpose. All contracts are assumed to have a legal purpose, except those that contemplate a course of action that would contravene a statute or some other rule of law. It is not sufficient, however, that the agreement refrain from an act specifically prohibited by law; it must not tend to encourage illegality, immorality, or other conduct contrary to public policy. There is an exception to this rule. An insurance contract issued by an insurer unlicensed to do business in that state is an illegal contract. However, the law that makes such a contract illegal was enacted to protect the citizens of the state. Consequently, the law permits the insured, but not the insurer, the option to either avoid or enforce the contract.

Life insurance clearly does not require either party to perform an illegal act and, in that respect, qualifies as a perfectly valid contract. As a matter of fact, it is universally recognized as having a purpose highly beneficial to society and worthy of favorable legislative treatment. On the other hand, it has been acknowledged that without adequate safeguards, life insurance could lend itself to behavior that would be socially harmful and contrary to public policy. Specifically, it could provide the motivation for wagering, murder, and suicide.

Inducement to Wagering

Regarding the first of these dangers, remember that life insurance is an aleatory contract. This means that it offers the potential of a return out of all proportion to the investment in the contract. This characteristic quickly attracted elements of the population who hoped to enrich themselves through the operation of the laws of chance. In eighteenth-century England, life insurance became the means of satisfying a mania for gambling, which was discouraged but not prohibited. Speculative life insurance was likely to be taken out on anyone who was in the public eye. Persons accused of crimes punishable by death and those in disfavor with the royal court were favorite subjects for life insurance contracts. Prominent people became the object of speculative insurance as soon as press notices revealed them to be seriously ill, and the premium for new policies on such persons fluctuated from day to day in accordance with the reports or rumors of their condition. Newspapers of the day even carried premium quotations on the lives of persons known to be the object of speculative insurance, with the consequences described by a contemporary writer. "This inhuman sport affected the minds of men depressed by long sickness; for when such persons casting an eye over a newspaper for amusement, saw their lives had been insured in the Alley at 90 p.c., they despaired of all hopes, and thus their desolution *[sic]* was hastened.[3]

The situation became so intolerable that in 1774 Parliament enacted a law stating that a person contracting for insurance had to have an insurable interest in the life of the person to be insured. The statute added an indemnity element; upon the death of the insured, it was illegal to recover a sum in excess of the monetary interest that the policyowner had in the life of the insured.

In this country an insurable interest has always been required in all jurisdictions, but with the exceptions noted later, no attempt has been made to apply the indemnity concept that existed for a time in England. As late as 1960, the requirement of insurable interest was not based upon statute but resulted from a judicial application of the public policy against the enforcement of wagering contracts. All of the states require that an insurable interest between the applicant-owner and the prospective insured exist at the inception of the contract.

Murder of Insured by Beneficiary

The insurable interest requirement originated as a means of controlling wagering on human lives and still finds its greatest significance in that function, but it was also intended to reduce the threat of murder created by insuring one person's life for the benefit of another. The thought was that if the class of persons who can legally insure the life of another is restricted to those who are closely related to the proposed insured by blood, or possess such a financial relationship that they stand to gain more by his or her continued life than by his or her death, the temptation to murder the insured would be greatly curtailed. A further safeguard is that a person whose life is to be insured by another must give his consent to the transaction. Presumably, a prospective insured will not permit his or her life to be insured in favor of a person whose integrity or motives are questionable. The same reasoning underlies the rule, discussed later, that the beneficiary of a policy applied for or owned by the insured need not have an insurable interest in the insured. The law presumes that the insured, whose life is at stake, is capable of choosing beneficiaries who will not be motivated to commit murder to enjoy the insurance proceeds sooner.

The foregoing deterrents are supplemented not only by criminal penalties for murder but also by statutes and judicial rulings that prohibit the payment of insurance proceeds to a beneficiary who murders the insured. This restriction is based on a general rule of law that a wrongdoer is not permitted to profit by his or her wrongdoing. The insurance company is not relieved of its obligation to pay because the proceeds will be owed to contingent beneficiaries or to the insured's estate, depending on the policy language and the law in the particular jurisdiction involved.

> **Suicide:** the intentional killing of oneself. For insurance purposes it makes a difference whether the person was sane or insane at the time of the suicide.

Suicide

A final area in which there is the possibility of a conflict between life insurance and the public interest is the treatment of suicide. Suicide is contrary to many religious laws, and attempted suicide is ordinarily a penal offense. Thus suicide is contrary to public policy. Any contract that would encourage or act as an inducement to suicide would, by the same token, be contrary to public policy.

Some of the early court decisions in this country indicated that death by suicide should not be covered by a life insurance policy. In a leading case, the United States Supreme Court expressed the view that "death intentionally caused by the act of the insured when in sound mind—the policy being silent as to suicide—is not to be deemed to have been within the contemplation of the parties . . . [A] different view would attribute to them a purpose to make a contract that could not be enforced without injury to the public. A contract, the tendency of which is to endanger the public interests or injuriously affect the public good, or which is subversive of sound morality, ought never to receive the sanction of a court of justice or be made the foundation of its judgment."[4]

This view, which has since been rejected by the American courts but is still the law in England, was not universally entertained. To protect themselves against people who might apply for insurance with the deliberate intention of committing suicide, insurers adopted the precaution of inserting a clause in their policies that limited their liability to a return of premiums if the insured committed suicide within a specified period—usually, one or 2 years—after the date of issue. It was felt that such a clause would properly protect the insurers' interests and after a preliminary period during which any abnormal impulse toward self-destruction should have passed away, would provide coverage against a peril to which all people are subject. Such a clause was adjudged by the United States Supreme Court to conserve the public interest, and most of the states have enacted statutory restrictions on the insurer's right to avoid liability because of suicide during a limited period after the policy is issued. Although most states permit suicide exclusions for 2 years or less, a few states limit the maximum length of the suicide exclusion clause to one year.

Exception to Suicide Exclusion. An exception to this philosophy is the Missouri statute that precludes the defense of suicide at any time unless it can be proved that the insured was contemplating suicide at the time he or she applied for the insurance. The Missouri statute provides as follows: "In all suits upon policies of insurance on life hereafter issued by any company doing business in this state, to a citizen of this state, it shall be no defense that the insured committed suicide, unless it shall be shown to the satisfaction of the court or jury trying the case, that the insured contemplated suicide at the time he made his application for the policy, and any stipulation in the policy to the contrary shall be void." This statute has been upheld by the United States Supreme Court as not being in conflict with the state constitution or the federal Constitution, but the court intimated that the statute was inconsistent with public policy and sound morality.

The insured's state of mind at the time of the suicide can determine whether the death benefit is payable. New York, for example, prohibits exclusion of suicide while the insured is insane. Suppose the policy has a suicide clause, but the clause does not contain the phrase "while sane or insane." If the insured commits suicide while sane, the company will not be required to pay the death benefit. However, if the insured was insane at the time of the suicide, the insurer will be required to pay the death benefit. This rule is based on the theory that insanity is a disease that may infect all insureds, and the insurer has assumed that risk. Consequently, to avoid that risk suicide clauses usually specifically exclude liability for a suicide whether the insured was sane or insane. A sample suicide clause reads as follows:

> If the insured, while sane or insane, dies by suicide within two years after
> the date of issue, the death proceeds under this policy will be an amount
> equal to the premiums paid less any loan against this policy.

Note that if there is no suicide exclusion clause in the policy, the death benefit is payable even if the insured commits suicide and intended to do so when the policy was purchased. Note also that the insured's accidental death is not excluded even if it occurs as the result of insured's sane or insane act.

Insurable Interest

> **Insurable interest:** a relationship between the person applying for insurance and the person whose life is to be insured in which there is a reasonable expectation of benefit or advantage to the applicant from continuation of the life of the insured or an expectation of loss or detriment from the cessation of that life.

A typical insurable interest statute is the following Pennsylvania law: "The term 'insurable interest' is defined as meaning, in the case of persons related by blood or law, an interest engendered by love and affection, and in the case of other persons, a lawful economic interest in having the life of the insured continue, as distinguished from an interest which would arise only by the death of the insured." In its broadest sense, insurable interest is a "relation between the insured and the event insured against such that the occurrence of the event will cause substantial loss or harm of some kind to the insured."[5] Note that the life insurance definition does not require a *pecuniary* interest; it is broad enough to recognize a sentimental interest based on love and affection. Some cases support the opinion that a relationship by blood or marriage alone constitutes an insurable interest. Among blood relationships, only parent and child, grandparent and grandchild, and siblings have been recognized as sufficiently close to establish an insurable interest. Among relationships based upon marital ties, only the relationship between husband and wife is sufficient to establish an insurable interest. Beyond these four narrow categories, it is the majority role that sentimental attachment based upon relationship alone is insufficient to establish an insurable interest. Note further that a pecuniary interest need not be capable of exact measurement. Nor need it be based on a legal right. It is sufficient that there be a *reasonable expectation* of some financial gain or advantage.

Before a discussion of the various relationships that can give rise to an insurable interest, it is necessary to explain when the interest must be present.

Incidence of Insurable Interest

In property and casualty insurance, an insurable interest need not be present at the inception of the contract, but it must exist at the time of loss if there is to be any recovery under the contract. The requirements are reversed in the case of life insurance. In life insurance an insurable interest must exist at the inception of the contract but need not be present at the time of the insured's death. This striking difference in the application of the requirement results from the fact that property insurance is based on the principle of indemnity, while a life insurance contract is not. To use property insurance terminology, a life insurance policy is a *valued* policy. It is a contract to pay a stated sum upon the occurrence of the event insured against. The stated sum may be unrelated to the dollar value of the loss. Since the beneficiary has a legal claim to a fixed sum of money upon the insured's death, he or she need not prove that a loss was sustained by reason of the death.

One may concede that the insurable interest of one person in another person's life should not be the *measure* of recovery and still argue that if the former's interest has become *wholly* extinguished, his or her right to the face amount of the policy should likewise be extinguished. To permit a person whose interest in the life of the insured has been completely terminated to collect the proceeds at the insured's death gives the appearance of speculation and offends many people's sense of justice. However, the rule was adopted by the English courts at a time when surrender values were not available, and termination of a policy before maturity meant forfeiture of all accumulated values. For the courts to force a policyowner to lapse a policy and forfeit the entire investment element because an interest that was perfectly valid at the time the policy was issued had been extinguished would have been harsh. The courts were faced with the alternative of permitting the owner of the policy to collect the full face amount of the policy or nothing at all.

If the matter were being adjudicated today without regard to precedent, the courts would probably hold that extinguishment of insurable interest terminates a policy and the policyowner would be permitted to recover the cash value as of the date of extinguishment, together with premiums paid thereafter in mistaken reliance on the contract. As the matter now stands, an incipient insurable interest is all that is necessary to sustain the validity of a life insurance contract. Thus if a creditor procures insurance on the life of his or her debtor and the debt is subsequently extinguished, the creditor may keep the policy in force and collect the full amount of the policy when the insured dies. A policy procured by a partnership on the life of a partner is unaffected by the dissolution of the partnership and the transfer of the policy to a former member of the firm who no longer has an insurable interest. A corporation that procures a policy on the life of a valuable manager may collect the full amount of insurance, despite the fact that the manager had previously been discharged. A divorce does not deprive a spouse-beneficiary of the right to the proceeds of his or her former spouse's life insurance, even though he or she no longer has an insurable interest in the former spouse's life.

The foregoing rules are not followed in Texas. The Texas courts have traditionally required a continuing interest. That is, a person who takes out insurance on the life of another person must have an insurable interest in the insured at the maturity of the contract in order to receive the proceeds. Prior to 1953, Texas case law also required that any beneficiary or assignee in a policy procured by the insured have an insurable interest at all times. A later statute modified the requirement by stating that any beneficiary or assignee named by the insured will be *deemed* to have an insurable interest, but it left undisturbed the mandate of a continuing interest for the person who procures insurance on another's life.

This discussion has made no reference to policies procured by the person whose life is to be insured since in such cases there is no question of a continuing interest. If the view is accepted that a person has an insurable interest in his or her own life, then certainly the interest continues throughout life.

Relationships Evidencing Insurable Interest

In considering the relationships that give rise to an insurable interest, it is helpful to distinguish between the cases in which the applicant is applying for insurance on his or her own life and those where the applicant is seeking insurance on the life of another.

Policy Procured by the Insured

The question of insurable interest is not involved when a person, on his or her own initiative, applies for a policy on his or her own life. It is commonly said that a person has an unlimited insurable interest in his or her own life, but the expression is technically inaccurate since a person does not suffer a financial loss by his or her own death—or at least does not survive to claim indemnity for a loss. Hence it seems preferable to state that the issue of insurable interest is immaterial when a person applies for insurance on his or her own life. Regardless of how the status of the insured is characterized, the law considers the insurable interest requirement to have been met—for any amount of insurance.

For underwriting purposes, however, insurers do not accept the view that the applicant has an unlimited insurable interest or that the question is immaterial. An applicant's financial circumstances are carefully investigated, and the company limits the amount of insurance to that which can be justified by the applicant's financial status and earning capacity.

The law is well settled that when a person procures a policy on his or her own life, it is not necessary that the beneficiary have an insurable interest in the insured's life, either at the inception of the contract or at the time of the insured's death. United States law is unanimous on that point, the rationale being that insureds should be permitted to dispose of their human life value with the same freedom that they can exercise in disposing of their other property at death. The temptation to murder is considered minimized by the insured's judgment in choosing the objects of his or her bounty. As a matter of fact, the insured enjoys much greater latitude in disposing of his human life value, since insurance proceeds are not subject to restrictions on bequests to charitable organizations or claims of creditors (if properly set up). Some restrictions do exist in the community property and quasi-community property states, however.

Applications at Beneficiary's Instigation. The courts take a different view of the situation when the policy is applied for at the beneficiary's instigation. Such a transaction may arise out of a legitimate business relationship and have a useful purpose, or it may serve as a cloak for a wagering contract. When the application does not stem from a business or personal situation that would seem to justify the designation of the particular beneficiary as payee and the beneficiary agrees in advance to pay all premiums under the policy, the courts are inclined to regard the transaction as speculative in nature. For example, when a woman was induced to apply for insurance on her life in favor of the mortgagee of her husband's land, her employer, and her sister-in-law, and the beneficiary in each case was paying all premiums, the contract was declared to be a wager.

The payment of premiums by the beneficiary is not conclusive proof of wagering, but it gives rise to a strong inference. Since the question of insurable interest is important only at the policy's inception, it is immaterial whether later, because of a change of circumstances, the beneficiary assumes responsibility for premium payments in order to keep the policy in force.

In 1893 a North Carolina court ruled that a policy procured at a college's instigation covering the life of a wealthy man (a prospective donor) was invalid because the college had no insurable interest in his life. This changed during the 1900s, however, and it became an acceptable practice for donors to encourage charities and other nonprofit institutions to apply for life insurance on their lives, with the donors providing a means of paying the premiums, often using trusts. It was widely believed that the various state statutes regarding insurable interest included the relationship between a charity or nonprofit organization and its donors.

However, the IRS issued a private letter ruling in 1991 to a New York taxpayer disallowing income tax, gift tax, and estate tax deductions related to an intended gift of life insurance to a charity. The basis of the denial was an IRS interpretation that the charity lacked an insurable interest in the life of the donor under New York law. In swift reaction to the IRS's private letter ruling, New York and many other states amended their insurable interest statutes to acknowledge an insurable interest between charities and their prospective donors. Although there is disparity from one state to another, most of these revised statutes specifically recognize the relationship between donors and many classifications of nonprofit organizations as an insurable interest. As some tax authorities point out, a few of these statutes do not, however, explicitly express the donee organization's right to apply for the life insurance policy directly. Some tax advantages may be lost if an existing policy is donated to the organization, rather than purchased by the donee organization.

In practice an insurer makes no distinction between applications submitted at the prospective insured's initiative and those submitted at the prospective beneficiary's instigation. In all cases, the insurer requires that the original beneficiary have an insurable interest of some sort as a precaution against wagering, homicide, or other moral peril. If the prospective beneficiary does not appear to have a legitimate insurable interest, the company will request an explanation of the relationship; if the explanation is unsatisfactory, it will almost certainly reject the application.

Once the policy is issued, however, the company has no right to withhold approval of a change of beneficiary on the grounds that the proposed beneficiary lacks an insurable interest—or on any other grounds, for that matter, except failure to comply with the prescribed procedure for effecting such a change. Of course, if the circumstances surrounding the request for a change of beneficiary indicate an attempt to evade the underwriting requirements of the company or the legal requirement of insurable interest, the insurer may be permitted to rescind the policy on the grounds of fraud or on the grounds that the entire transaction was a subterfuge for procurement of insurance by a person lacking an insurable interest in the insured.

Policy Assignments. The insured may make the policy payable to a third party by means of an assignment, and as a general rule, it is not necessary for the assignee to have an insurable interest. The position of the courts is that it is immaterial whether the insured designates the payee of the policy within the contract itself, as with a conventional beneficiary designation, or with a separate instrument—an assignment.

A very few states, however, require the assignee to have an insurable interest, at least under certain circumstances. All states require an insurable interest if the insured was induced by the assignee to take out the policy since that would be tantamount to the assignee's applying for the insurance directly. If there is any indication at the time of application that an assignment is contemplated, the insurance company, as a matter of underwriting practice, will usually require evidence of the prospective assignee's insurable interest.

Under the doctrine adopted by the majority of American courts, there is nothing to invalidate successive assignments of a life insurance policy once it is validly issued. None of the assignees need have an insurable interest, and the insured need not give his or her consent to the assignments. This rule is based on the doctrine that a life insurance policy is a form of personal property and should be freely transferable. If a life insurance contract could be sold only to persons having an insurable interest in the insured's life, the market would be severely limited, and the owner of the policy would be handicapped in disposing of it.

Accelerated-Benefit Provisions. In recent years persons suffering from full-blown AIDS have sold their life insurance policies to viatical settlement companies (that keep the policies to collect the death benefit) in order to help finance needed health care during the terminal stage of their illness. Such policy sales prompted some life insurers to introduce accelerated-benefit provisions for life insurance policies. The IRS has even set forth requirements for tax-free treatment of life insurance proceeds paid during the last 12 months of life for terminally ill insured persons under these accelerated-benefit provisions.

Some states have imposed insurance regulations on viatical settlement companies to discourage unregulated commercial trading of life insurance policies covering terminally ill individuals. There is a concern that desperate people with few options may be taken advantage of by unregulated persons wagering on life insurance policies.

It seems repugnant and contrary to public policy for existing life insurance policies to be sold on the auction block to the highest bidder. (Such a market actually developed in England before the development of cash values in life insurance policies.) If the buyers of these policies had an insurable interest in the insured's life there would be less of a public policy concern.

A special set of rules is applicable when a policy is made payable to a creditor of the insured, whether the designation is as beneficiary or as assignee. Creditor situations will be discussed in the next section of this chapter.

Most policies are issued upon the application and at the initiative of the person to be insured. Hence the foregoing principles govern the typical situation. The rules applicable to the exceptional cases in which the applicant and the insured are not one and the same are set forth below.

Policy Procured by Person Other than Insured

In most jurisdictions consent of the person to be insured is usually essential to the validity of a life insurance contract taken out by a person other than the prospective insured. However, these jurisdictions usually make an exception for applications submitted by a spouse on the life of the other spouse or by a parent on the life of a child too young to apply for insurance in his or her own right. As a practical matter, the prospective insured's signature needed on the application to affirm the accuracy of the information in it. Hence insurers always require the signature of the person whose life is to be insured, except when that person is a minor.

In all jurisdictions, a third-party applicant must have an insurable interest in the life of the person to be insured. This statement presupposes that the applicant will be the owner of the policy and the person to receive the proceeds upon maturity of the contract. A more accurate statement of the requirement—as it is prescribed in some states, at least—is that the *person who procures the policy and is to receive the proceeds* must have an insurable interest in the insured. The New York Insurance Law, for example, states the requirement in such terms and provides that if the proceeds are paid to a person not having an insurable interest in the insured *at the time the contract was made,* the insured's personal representative may maintain an action to recover such proceeds from the person receiving them.

The insurable interest required may arise out of either a family or a business relationship. As explained earlier, if it arises out of a family relationship, it may be based on *love and affection* or on a legal or factual expectation of *financial* advantage from continuance of the life of the insured. Interests originating in business relationships are regarded as economic in nature.

Family Relationships. The doctrine that an emotional attachment constitutes a sufficient insurable interest, apart from financial considerations, has been expounded in various judicial opinions and incorporated into the statutes of some states. It appears that the doctrine serves both of the major objectives of the insurable interest requirement: the minimization of wagering and the prevention of murder.

In applying the doctrine, the closeness of relationship needed to satisfy the requirement is critical. The relationship of husband and wife is universally conceded to be close enough, although it is virtually always accompanied by an economic interest. The relationship of parent and child, based on both economic and familial ties, is generally regarded as sufficient to satisfy the law. A growing minority of courts have also recognized the relationships of sibling to sibling and grandparent and grandchild as sufficient.[6] Blood relationships more remote than the above such as uncle and niece, uncle and nephew, and cousin of any degree, have generally been rejected as insufficient. Aside from that of husband and wife, no tie growing out of affinity alone—such as an interest of an individual in his or her father-in-law, mother-in-law, brother-in-law, stepfather, or stepchild—has been recognized as a sufficient insurable interest.

The courts that do not subscribe to the belief that a sentimental value alone will satisfy the insurable interest requirement still find a valid insurable interest in close family relationships, apparently on the assumption that a legal or factual expectation of pecuniary value exists in such cases. Thus the legal obligation of spouses to support each other gives them insurable interests in each other's life. A parent is entitled to the services of a minor child and hence has an insurable interest in the child's life. A woman has an insurable interest in the life of her fiance, at least in states where the agreement to marry is a legal obligation.

An expectation of financial advantage from the continued life of a person which is not based on a legal obligation is referred to as a *factual expectation.* A factual expectation is generally not sufficient to support a contract of indemnity, such as those found in the property and casualty insurance branches, but it has long been regarded as sufficient in life insurance. In the earliest reported American decision involving life insurance, the Supreme Judicial Court of

Massachusetts upheld a policy in favor of the insured's sister on the grounds that the insured had been voluntarily supporting her and probably would have continued to do so had he lived. A foster child, though not legally adopted and hence without legal claim to support, has been held to have an insurable interest in the life of his foster father. A woman living with a man under the honest but mistaken belief that she was lawfully married to him was held to have had an insurable interest in his life because of her expectation (possibly misplaced) that he would have continued to support her. An illegitimate child is considered to have an insurable interest in the life of his or her putative father, who has contributed to the child's support.

When an insurable interest is based on a family relationship, there is no legal limit to the amount of insurance that may be validated by it. This is based on the concept that a life insurance policy is not a contract of indemnity and hence does not purport to reimburse a beneficiary for a specific pecuniary loss. Insurance companies, however, have their own strict guides limiting the amount of insurance they will underwrite. It would be extremely difficult, if not impossible, to place a precise valuation on an interest based on love and affection. Interests arising out of a legal entitlement to support could perhaps be valued, but those based on a factual expectation could be measured only in the roughest terms. Interests based on business relationships can usually be valued and, in general, can support only an amount of insurance that bears a reasonable relationship to the value of the interest.

Business Relationships. A variety of business relationships create an insurable interest. One of the most common is a contractual arrangement calling for unique or distinctive personal services. There are numerous examples of such arrangements in the entertainment world. A theatrical producer has an insurable interest in the life of an actor who has contracted to perform over a definite period and who would be extremely difficult to replace in the role. Likewise, a film producer has an insurable interest in the lives of the principal performers, which escalates as the film gets into production and the death of a star would disrupt operations and require refilming all scenes in which the deceased appeared. Professional sport teams have an insurable interest in the lives of their players.

The examples above are based on contractual or legal obligations, but factual expectations may also support an insurable interest. The importance of the business manager has led to the recognition that a corporation or other form of business enterprise has an insurable interest in the life of a manager or some other official whose services and skills are vital to the prosperity of the enterprise, even though the person has not assumed a legal obligation to work for the firm for any specified period of time. A firm's interest in its key officers and employees has been recognized by statute in many states and judicially sanctioned in the other states. Insurance taken out to protect such an interest is called *keyperson insurance* and is widely sold.

Another business relationship that gives rise to an insurable interest exists among partners in a partnership and stockholders in a closely held corporation. The consequences of the death of a general partner or active stockholder can be so detrimental that the parties involved frequently enter into an agreement for the disposition of the business interest of any individuals who might die while still active in the management of the firm. Specifically, the agreement binds the firm's surviving members to purchase the deceased member's interest at a specified price. It also obligates the deceased member's estate to sell his or her interest to the surviving members. The agreements are usually financed by insurance on the lives of the individuals involved, and either the other members of the firm or the firm itself applies for the insurance on any particular individual. In such cases, the courts have recognized an insurable interest, based on the factual expectation of a loss if the business has to be liquidated, upon a general partner's or stockholder's death..

Perhaps the most common business or commercial transaction that produces an insurable interest is by lending money.[7] Despite the fact that the obligation to repay a loan is not discharged by the death of a debtor—the obligation is enforceable against the deceased's estate—a creditor is universally conceded to have an insurable interest in the life of the debtor. This rule is based on the recognition that the creditor may not be able to collect the sum of money due from the debtor's estate because of insufficiency of assets. The creditor may protect his or her interest by taking out insurance on the debtor's life or by requiring the debtor to designate the creditor as payee under a policy taken out by the debtor.

If the creditor takes out insurance on the debtor's life *and pays the premiums,* he or she is permitted to retain the full amount of the proceeds, even though they exceed the amount of the debt, plus accumulated interest. In fact, the creditor can retain the full amount of the proceeds even if the debt has been completely extinguished. The only limitation imposed in most jurisdictions is that the amount of insurance must not be disproportionate to the amount of the debt as it existed at the time the policy was issued or as it was reasonably expected to be thereafter. The purpose of this requirement is to prevent using a debt as a cloak for a wagering transaction. In a leading case, for example, a policy for $3,000 taken out on the basis of a $70 debt was held to be a wager and hence invalid. Yet policies have been upheld when the amount of insurance was several times the debt. A Maryland court upheld a policy for $6,500 on a debt of $1,000, while a New York court validated a policy for $5,000 taken out to protect a debt of $2,823. These decisions are largely due to the notion that a creditor should be allowed to insure the debtor's life for a sum estimated to be sufficient to reimburse the creditor at the debtor's death for premiums paid on the policy, with interest thereon, plus the debt and accumulated interest. There is no clear rule on how much in excess of the debt can be taken out in life insurance on the debtor. The only guideline is that the amount of insurance must bear a reasonable relationship to the size of the debt.

If a debtor assigns an existing policy to the creditor as *security* for a loan, the creditor is permitted to retain only the amount of the creditor's interest and must pay the excess, if any, to the insured's estate or third-party beneficiary, as the case may be.[8] The creditor's interest is construed to comprise the unpaid portion of the loan, accumulated interest on the loan, and expenses connected with the loan, including any premiums paid on the policy. The same rule applies when the creditor is designated beneficiary if it is clear that the arrangement was intended to serve as security for the debt. In general, the creditor's rights are the same when the debtor procures new insurance and assigns it as collateral, provided the debtor pays the premium.

Occasionally a policy is assigned to the creditor *in satisfaction of the debt* and not as security for it. In those instances, the creditor is allowed to keep all the proceeds, even though they greatly exceed the amount of the debt canceled. The validity of such an arrangement has been upheld even when the creditor has induced the debtor to procure the policy.

Legal Effect of Lack of Insurable Interest

A life insurance contract not supported by an incipient insurable interest is a wagering contract and hence illegal. This does not mean, however, that the contract cannot be carried out according to its terms. The courts will not enforce an illegal contract, but they do not necessarily forbid the parties to observe the promises made under the illegal agreement.

If an insurance company feels that the applicant honestly believed that he or she had an insurable interest in the life of the person to be insured, it may honor its promise despite later evidence that there was no insurable interest. On the other hand, if the company feels that the applicant knew that no insurable interest existed and sought the insurance for speculative purposes, it may deny liability on the grounds of illegality. If the court sustains the company's contention, there will be no obligation under the contract. Not only will the company be relieved of paying the face amount of the policy (if the insured has died), but in some states it will also not be obligated to return the premiums paid under the contract.

Several states have relaxed the rule against nonenforcement of illegal contracts to allow the applicant or personal representative to recover all premiums paid if he or she applied for insurance in the honest belief that he or she had an insurable interest. In all jurisdictions recovery of premiums is permitted if the insurer's agent induced the applicant to apply for insurance by falsely leading the applicant to believe that he or she had a legitimate insurable interest.[9]

Moreover, in cases involving wagering policies, the courts have not strictly applied the doctrine that a partial illegality taints the *entire* transaction and makes it void for all purposes. The rule is frequently modified when a person applies for insurance on his or her own life at the instigation of a third party who lacks an insurable interest in the applicant but who pays the premiums and is designated beneficiary. From a strict legal standpoint, such a contract is illegal. Nevertheless, the courts may direct the insurance company to pay the proceeds to the insured's estate and nullify the interest of the offending beneficiary. Under such circumstances, however, the courts are practically unanimous in permitting the beneficiary to recover the premiums he or she paid on the policy out of the proceeds. The courts take the same attitude toward cases in which a policy is assigned to a third party who induced the insured to apply for the policy but has no insurable interest.

LEGALITY OF FORM

Some types of contracts have to be in a particular *form* in order to be legal. From a practical standpoint, this aspect of the formation of a contract refers to whether or not the contract has to be in writing or can be oral.

The Statute of Frauds, which was originally enacted in England in the seventeenth century and has become a part of the statutory law of nearly all the states of the United States, requires certain types of contracts to be in writing to be enforceable. The only section of the statute that might be construed to apply to a life insurance contract is that which requires written and signed proof of an agreement that by its terms cannot be performed within one year from its effective date. Since the insurer's promise may have to be fulfilled within one year or even one day from issuance of the policy, a life insurance contract falls outside the statute. Hence in the absence of specific legislation requiring a life insurance contract to be in writing, such a contract can be oral in form.

Some states specifically require life insurance contracts to be in writing, while others construe statutes prescribing standard provisions in the contract to mean that the contract itself must be in writing. All states have prescribed a set of standard provisions that must be included — in substance — in all contracts of life insurance. This requirement does not necessarily invalidate oral contracts; standard provisions are simply assumed to be a part of the oral agreement.

Statutes invalidating any terms in a policy that appear in a type face smaller than a designated size and statutes requiring a policy to be signed have been interpreted as not requiring a written contract. Charter provisions requiring all contracts to be in writing are usually disregarded by the courts if proof is furnished that an agent of the company led the "insured" to believe that he or she was covered under an oral agreement.

As a practical matter, oral contracts are rare; they usually occur only when an agent oversteps his or her authority and the company is estopped from denying responsibility for the agent's conduct. Because oral contracts are a potential source of misunderstanding and litigation, they are completely unsuitable for a transaction involving life insurance.

NOTES

1. See 50 ALR 2d, 630 (1956).
2. Muriel L. Crawford and William T. Beadles, *Law and the Life Insurance Contract,* 6th ed. (Homewood, IL: Irwin Professional Publishing, 1989), p. 315.
3. David Scott, *Every Man His Own Broker* (1761), quoted in C. Walford, *Insurance Cyclopaedia* (London: Charles and Edwin Layton, 1876), vol. IV, p. 187.
4. *Ritter v. Mutual Life Insurance Co.,* 169 U.S. 139, 154 (1898).
5. Edwin W. Patterson, Essentials of Insurance Law, 2d ed. (New York: McGraw-Hill Book Co., 1957), p. 154.
6. Buist M. Anderson, *Anderson On Life Insurance* (Boston: Little, Brown & Co., 1991, sec. 12.5, p. 364.
7. *Ibid.,* sec. 12.12.
8. *Ibid.,* sec. 12.11.
9. Crawford and Beadles, *Law and the Life Insurance Contract,* p. 48.

38

Avoidance of the Contract by the Insurer

Dan M. McGill
Revised by Burke A. Christensen

A warranty is a clause in an insurance contract that prescribes, as a condition of the insurer's liability, the existence of a fact affecting the risk assumed under the contract.

> **Warranty**: a statement which becomes part of the contract and is guaranteed by the maker to be true in all respects.[1]

> **Representation**: a statement [(made) at the time of the making of a contract] which induces a party to enter into a contract. It is not part of the contract.[2]

When a contract is created between two parties, it makes a great deal of difference whether the statements made by each side are warranties or representations. If a statement is a warranty and it later turns out to be untrue in any respect, the other party may rescind the contract. If the same statement is a representation that later turns out to be untrue, the other party may rescind the contract only if the representation was material to the formation or the contract.

The doctrine of warranties originated in marine insurance more than 200 years ago, and it still plays an important role in that branch of insurance. It was developed for the purpose of controlling the risk associated with a particular insurance venture. If a certain state of affairs was deemed to be a risk-reducing factor and insurance was arranged on the assumption that such a state of affairs would continue throughout the term of the policy, the policy would condition the coverage on the existence of the favorable state of affairs. The policy would *warrant* that the desired conditions would prevail. For example, the frequent wars during the 18th century made it highly desirable that British merchant vessels sail under the convoy of British warships, and it was customary for marine insurers to require an insured vessel to sail under convoy or pay a higher premium. If a shipowner warranted that his vessel would sail only under convoy and then permitted it to sail alone, his coverage would be nullified. It was not necessary for the insurer to prove that the breach—the failure to sail with a convoy—materially increased the risk; materiality was assumed. Neither was it necessary to establish bad faith or fraud on the part of the insured. The insurer had only to prove that the warranty was breached.

The use of warranties gradually spread to other branches of insurance where they were less suitable. They were no longer confined to contracts sold to businesses familiar with trade and insurance practices but were liberally interspersed in contracts sold to the general public, who had no concept of the significance of warranties. Abuses inevitably developed. The situation was particularly bad in fire insurance where there was no incontestable clause to ameliorate the effect of a breach of warranty.

Warranties are no longer of major importance in the law of life and health insurance. It used to be that statements made by the applicant for life insurance were warranties. But this is no longer the case. In the 1800s insurance companies developed a bad reputation because they strictly enforced their contractual right to rescind contracts if they discovered that any statement made by the applicant was inaccurate in the slightest respect. The courts strained the law in an effort to protect the insuring public, but most states found it necessary to provide statutory relief for those persons procuring life and health insurance and, less commonly, those seeking other types of insurance. The general effect of the statutory modifications is that no breach of warranty will void a contract unless it increases the risk, contributes to the loss, or occurs with fraudulent intent.

The special legislation directed at life insurance—and, in many states, at health insurance—was brought about by the fact that, for one reason or another, most companies had begun to incorporate the application into the policy, which, according to common-law doctrine, made all statements in the application warranties. To make doubly sure of this result, some companies, by express provision, made the applicant warrant the truth of all statements in the application. This meant that the company was in a position to void the contract if any one statement in the application was not literally true.

REPRESENTATIONS

Generally speaking, a representation is an oral or written statement made by a party to a contract prior to or contemporaneously with the formation of the contract.[3] It is not a part of the contract but rather is an inducement to the contract. A representation refers to facts or conditions existing at the time the statement is made.[4] It may be a fact within the knowledge of the person making the statement, or it may merely be an expression of opinion or belief. A representation does not bind the party making it to anything that may happen after the contract is made. If it did, it would be a promise or condition of the other party's promise and would have to be embodied in the contract. It would be the equivalent of a warranty. Finally, a representation need be only substantially true when made.

In life insurance representations are made by both the applicant and the soliciting agent, but for all practical purposes, only the applicant's statements have legal significance. Hence, the discussion in this chapter will be concerned only with the applicant's representations.

Since representations do not purport to change the *terms* of a contract, they are not subject to the parol evidence rule, discussed earlier, and in the absence of a prohibitory statute or policy provision, can be oral in form. However, most states have enacted statutes, directed at life insurance and referred to as *entire-contract statutes,* that state, in substance, that the policy and the attached application constitute the entire contract between the parties.[5] These statutes have been interpreted by the courts to exclude all of the insured's representations other than those contained in the application attached to the policy. In other words, the application or a copy thereof must be attached to the policy if the company is to treat the statements in the application as representations. In addition, most states require that every policy include a provision that excludes all of the applicant's statements other than those contained in the application from consideration. A typical provision reads as follows: No statement of the insured shall avoid this policy or be used in defense of a claim hereunder unless it is contained in the application and a copy of such application is attached to the policy when issued.

Technically, when the application is made a part of the contract, either by physical attachment to the policy or by reference to it in the policy, all the statements in the application pertaining to the risk become warranties. To avoid this untoward result, more than half of the states have enacted laws that convert statements in the application from warranties to representations. Other states have removed the sting from warranties by requiring that the matter misrepresented be material or, stricter still, have contributed to the loss, before a company can use the breach of warranty as a basis for voiding the contract.

Apart from statute or judicial ruling, most companies' policies provide that all statements in the application are deemed representations and not warranties. As a matter of fact, it is customary for insurance companies to incorporate into one omnibus clause provisions that state that the policy and the application attached thereto constitute the entire contract, that statements in the application are deemed representations, and that no statement of the insured will be used to void the policy or to contest a claim unless it is contained in the application attached to the policy. A typical provision is as follows:

> This policy is a contract between the owner and (name of insurer). This policy, the attached copy of the initial application, any applications for reinstatement, all subsequent applications to change the policy, and any endorsements or riders are the entire contract. No statement will be used in defense of a claim unless such statement is contained in the application. All statements contained in the application shall, in the absence of fraud, be deemed representations and not warranties.

Legal Consequences of a Misrepresentation

A representation has legal consequences only if a person, acting in reliance thereon, is induced to enter into a contract to which he or she would not otherwise have become a party. If the representation turns out to be false, the aggrieved party can sue to recover damages from the person who made the misstatement or to rescind the contract that he or she was induced to make. The first remedy is available against anyone who *fraudulently* or *deceitfully* makes a misrepresentation. The second remedy is available only if the person who makes the misrepresentation is a party to the contract. Thus if a life insurance company is induced to issue a policy because of the fraudulent misrepresentation of the medical examiner, it can recover damages, if any, from the medical examiner, but it cannot rescind the policy unless it can prove that the applicant conspired with the doctor to have the misrepresentation made or at least knew of the fraud before the policy was issued. Cases of this sort are occasionally unearthed, but the typical remedy for a misrepresentation in a life insurance application is rescission of the contract.

> **Rescission**: termination of a contract. The contract is declared void because of a material misrepresentation by one party. It is an equitable, not a legal, remedy.

> **Voidable and void contracts**: A contract is voidable if one party has the right to disaffirm it and thereby terminate the agreement. A "void contract" is unenforceable by either party. In fact, the term is an oxymoron. Since a contract is a legally enforceable agreement, it is either valid, voidable, or it does not exist.

Notice of Rescission

A misrepresentation does not of itself make a contract void; it only makes it voidable. The difference is that with a voidable contract the aggrieved party may elect to affirm the contract, in which event he or she is bound by its terms (but not precluded from suing for damages for any fraud involved), or he or she may elect to rescind the contract. The party is under an obligation to exercise this option within a reasonable time after discovering the falsity of the representation. In this respect, a misrepresentation differs from a breach of warranty, in that a breach of warranty can be offered in defense of a claim even when the company has delayed making its election between affirmation and rescission beyond a reasonable period. However, this distinction has lost some of its significance because of a number of court decisions that treat the insurer's retention of premiums after discovery of either a misrepresentation or a breach of warranty as a *waiver* or *estoppel* (see chapter 39). In any event, the insurer's delay bars its power to rescind on the ground of misrepresentation only if the insured was prejudiced by the delay.

An insurance company's notice of rescission must be accompanied by a tender of all premiums paid under the contract. This is necessary because the purpose of rescission is to wipe out the contract and restore the parties to the positions they occupied before the contract was made. If the insured owns the contract and is still alive, the tender of premiums is made to the insured, but if the insured is deceased it is usually made to the beneficiary, and in legal effect, is an offer of settlement. In those circumstances, a prudent insurer seeks a release from both the beneficiary and the insured's estate.

To make its rescission conclusive, the insurance company must obtain an adjudication of its power to rescind. It may do this by defending a judicial proceeding brought by the beneficiary to recover on the policy or by instituting a suit in equity to obtain a decree of rescission. In the former, the question of misrepresentation is usually left to a jury if there is any conflicting evidence, since the beneficiary's suit to recover the sum payable by the policy's terms is an *action at law*.[6] Suits in equity are usually tried by a judge who determines both the law and the facts. Insurance companies prefer suits in equity because of juries' tendency to favor the adversary of an insurance company.

Statements of Fact

To obtain a rescission of a life insurance policy on the grounds of a misrepresentation, the company must prove that one or more statements of *fact* in the application were both *false* and *material* to the company's decision to accept the risk or to set the premium. It is not necessary, unless required by statute, to prove that the statement was made with intent to deceive the insurer. While considerable authority can be found for the argument that only a *fraudulent* misrepresentation of a material fact will provide grounds for rescission, a majority of cases hold that an innocent misrepresentation of a material fact suffices to make a policy voidable. The doctrine is well established that the test of a misrepresentation is the *effect* on the insurer, not the *culpability* of the insured or the agent in making it. By the same token, it is held that a fraudulent misstatement of an immaterial fact will not make a policy voidable. The purpose of rescission is to protect the company—and, indirectly, its policyowners—against an increase in risk arising out of a misrepresentation, not to punish the insured whose dishonesty caused the company no harm.

Matters of Opinion

An important exception to the rule that a misrepresentation need not be fraudulent to obtain a recision exists when the misstatement is a matter of opinion, belief, or expectation. It is not sufficient that the applicant's belief about the status of a matter material to the risk turns out to be erroneous. If the applicant's statement accurately reflects his or her state of mind at the time of the assertion, no misrepresentation occurs. A statement of opinion is false only if the person making it does not have that opinion at the time the statement is made. Therefore, to void a policy on the ground of a false statement of opinion, the insurer must prove that the insured spoke fraudulently. This leads to the conclusion that a statement of opinion must be *false, material,* and *fraudulent* before it makes a policy voidable.

If the statement in the application is qualified by such words as "in my opinion" or "to the best of my knowledge and belief" or "the above is as near correct as I can recall," it is clearly one of opinion or belief. However, even unqualified statements will be construed by the courts to be statements of opinion if the fact to which they relate is deemed to be one not susceptible of the insured's accurate and conclusive determination. In other words, an unqualified assertion about a situation or an event for which there may obviously be differences of opinion may be construed as a statement of opinion.

A statement that the applicant "is in good health" has been held to be a statement of opinion[7] since it calls for an inference rather than a report on observed facts. Statements about the future are construed as expressions of intent or expectation and thus are also opinions, rather than representations of facts. The following are typical questions taken from the application form of a large life insurance company calling for a declaration of intentions:

- Do you intend to travel or reside outside the United States?
- Do you have any intention of becoming a pilot, student pilot, or crew member of any type of aircraft?

- Do you have any intention of becoming a member of a military organization?
- Do you contemplate any change in occupation?

Negative answers to such queries are of no avail in litigation unless the insurer can prove that at the time of application, the applicant had a definite intention of doing the thing that was the subject of the inquiry.

Rule of Continuing Representation

Moreover, a representation need be true only at the time it is made; it is not necessary that it continue to be true until the contract is consummated. At one time the federal courts and some state courts accepted the view that a representation had to be true at the moment the contract became effective, a doctrine referred to as the rule of *continuing representation*. With some exceptions, however, the view today is that the intervening falsity of a representation will provide grounds for rescission only if notice of the changed circumstances is fraudulently withheld from the insurer.[8] In other words, the applicant must be aware of the change, must realize that the change is material to the company's underwriting decision, and must deliberately withhold notice of the change to the company.

However, no such duty to disclose exists if the insurer has already accepted the risk. This would be the case if the applicant had paid some or all of the first premium and a conditional receipt had been issued. Legally, such subterfuge by the applicant is not construed to be a misrepresentation, but a concealment, which is discussed later in this chapter.

Concept of Materiality

A representation of the insured is significant only if it is communicated to the insurer and in some way influences the insurer's decision with respect to a contract. If a statement of the insured induces the insurer to enter into a contract that it would not have made had it known the true statement of the fact, or would have made only on different terms, the statement is *material*. More accurately, the *facts misrepresented* in the statement are material.

Extent of Falsity

A distinction must be made between the materiality of the subject matter of a question in the application and the materiality of a misrepresentation made in the answer to the question. Not all statements the insured makes in response to the insurer's questions about matters of consequence to the risk are material. To void a policy on the ground of a material misrepresentation, the company must prove not only that the insured made a misstatement about a matter of concern to the company, but also that the *extent* of the falsity was substantial enough to be significant. In other words, the *difference* between the actual facts relating to a matter material to the risk and the facts as falsely represented must be sufficient to induce the company's decision to accept the risk. This is simply another way of saying that knowledge of the true facts would have caused the company to reject the risk or to accept it only on different terms.

The distinction between a material matter and the materiality of a false response relative to the matter can be illustrated by any number of questions in the typical application form. For example, one large company's application form contains the following question: "Have you now or have you ever had or been treated for any disease or disorder of the nose, throat, lungs, or pleura?" Suppose that an applicant gives a negative answer to that question when, in fact, he or she had suffered an attack of tonsillitis 10 years earlier that was severe enough to require medical treatment. Obviously, the condition of the applicant's throat is material to the company's consideration of the risk, but is the undisclosed attack of tonsillitis 10 years ago of sufficient consequence to justify rescission of the policy?

Tests of Materiality

In adjudicating cases involving a misrepresentation, the courts may attempt to test the materiality of the misrepresented facts by referring to the underwriting practices of insurers generally or by referring to the practices of the particular company involved in the litigation. The first test has been characterized as the *prudent-insurer* standard, while the second has been designated the *individual-insurer* standard.

Prudent-Insurer Standard. The prudent-insurer standard has been adopted in the majority of jurisdictions, presumably because it is thought to provide objective standards for issues in which judgments are likely to be subjective or emotional. It is argued that the judgment of the litigating company's officers is likely to be warped by their assumption that anyone who dies within one or 2 years after issuance of the policy must have concealed some physical impairment. Under the prudent-insurer standard the judgment of objective experts on underwriting practices — usually officials of other companies — is substituted for the subjective opinions of the officers of the company that accepted the risk. A fundamental weakness of this standard is that it presupposes a uniformity of opinion and practice that does not exist. For example, medical directors of various insurance companies disagree about the significance of many types of impairments. Furthermore, relying exclusively on the testimony of outside experts may impose liability on an insurer, particularly a conservative one, for a risk that the company would unquestionably have rejected if it had had knowledge of the facts misrepresented.

Individual-Insurer Standard. The individual-insurer test, which is applied in many jurisdictions, has been adopted by statute in several important states. The New York Insurance Law, for example, states, "No misrepresentation shall be deemed material unless knowledge by the insurer of the facts misrepresented would have led to a refusal by the insurer to make such contract."[9] This test conforms to the basic principle of rescission for misrepresentation and has considerable support in judicial precedents involving transactions other than insurance contracts.

One would naturally assume that in applying this test, the courts would place great reliance on testimony of officials associated with the company involved in the litigation. Most states, by statute or court ruling, permit testimony as to the practices of the insurer involved in the litigation. The New York Insurance Law, for example, expressly permits the admissibility of the litigating insurer's underwriting practices as follows: "In determining the question of materiality, evidence of the practice of the insurer which made such contract with respect to the acceptance or rejection of similar risks shall be admissible."[10] Under this provision, the insurer's medical director (or some other qualified official) is permitted to testify in court that it is the company's practice to reject applications that reveal facts similar to those proved in the case under consideration. In fact, if qualified, the witness will be permitted to testify that had the insurer had knowledge of the facts misrepresented the company would have rejected the application in dispute. If the testimony is uncontroverted, the evidence (if not patently absurd) is ordinarily deemed conclusive, and the question of materiality will not go to the jury. In several other states, while the insurer is permitted to prove what it would have done had it known the facts later disclosed, such evidence is not deemed conclusive.

The individual-insurer test enables an insurer to apply its standards of insurability in all cases, including those in which the applicant did not disclose all the facts that the insurer requested. This, of course, assumes that the insurer is permitted to prove its standards of insurability, rather than leaving the matter to the conjecture of the jury or judge. Maintaining underwriting standards benefits not only the insurer but also the host of honest policyowners who have made no misrepresentations. Moreover, the test of what a particular insurance company would have done in a specific factual situation can be more accurately formulated and more reliably proved than the test of what insurance companies in general would have done.[11]

The principal disadvantage of the individual-insurer test is that the proof of materiality comes from the files of the insurance company and the testimony of its officials, and the counsel for the beneficiary has little chance of controverting it. His or her only hope is to prove that the company has not consistently followed its alleged practices.

Some recent decisions have ruled that misrepresented facts are material if knowledge of the facts *might* have caused the insurer to reject the application. This is a much stricter standard from the insured's standpoint and a much more difficult one to apply in practice. Facts that would have caused the company to further investigate the applicant even though, in the end, the company would have approved the application would be treated as material. A California statute even holds that misrepresented facts are material if knowledge of them would have led the company to make further inquiries or to delay acceptance of the application.[12]

Statutory Modification of the Common Law

The common-law effect of misstatements by an applicant for life insurance has been modified by statute in many states. The most significant modification is by statutes enacted in most states (and discussed earlier) that convert statements in the application from warranties into representations. The effect of these statutes is to eliminate the conclusive presumption of materiality of statements in the application, forcing the company to prove the statements' materiality.

Other statutes, which are far less prevalent, permit companies to void a contract only if the matter misrepresented increased the risk of loss. Such statutes usually apply only to representations. They were apparently intended to provide a more objective test of materiality than that furnished by the common-law definition. However, any fact that would be considered an inducement to contract under the common-law concept of materiality would, if so unfavorable as to be misrepresented by the applicant, tend to increase the risk. Hence, these statutes by judicial construction have been given the same effect as the prudent-insurer test of materiality.

A few states[13] have statutes that require the misrepresented fact to have contributed to the loss. The Missouri statute, which reads as follows, illustrates this type of legislation:

> No misrepresentation made in obtaining or securing a policy of insurance on the life or lives of any person or persons, citizens of this state, shall be deemed material or render the policy void, unless the matter misrepresented shall have actually contributed to the contingency or event on which the policy is to become due and payable, and whether it so contributed in any case shall be a question for the jury.[14]

Under this type of statute, an applicant can conceal or misrepresent a condition that, had it been known to the insurer, would have unquestionably caused it to decline the risk. Yet, the company will be held liable if the insured's death resulted from a cause not related to the misrepresented condition. For example, if an applicant concealed a serious heart impairment and later died in an automobile accident not caused by his or her heart condition, the company would have to pay the face amount of the policy, despite the fact that it would not have been at risk if the heart condition had been revealed at the time of application.

Sources of Litigation

Any statement in the application that is designed to elicit information directly relevant to the risk is a potential source of litigation. Yet some of the application's subject areas seldom serve as the basis for denial of a claim, while others are a frequent source of dispute. Whether the applicant's answer to a particular question is construed to be a statement of fact or a statement of opinion makes a significant difference.

Fact versus Opinion

Answers to questions concerning the amount of insurance the applicant carries and the disposition of applications he or she submitted to other companies are generally regarded to be statements of fact rather than of opinion. In recent years, however, insurance companies have rarely been successful in invoking a false answer to this group of questions as a material misrepresentation. Since the companies that do the bulk of the life insurance business are members of the Medical Information Bureau (MIB), they will ordinarily have access to information about impairments discovered by other companies. If a company were notified about detrimental information in the MIB files (see chapter 2) it would be permitted to void the contract only if there were other material information that the applicant should have disclosed.[15]

Unequivocal answers to questions about the applicant's past and present occupation are regarded as statements of fact. Yet there are few reported cases where the insurer attempted to void the contract on the basis of a misrepresentation as to occupation. The chief explanation for this is probably that the inspection report is likely to uncover any discrepancy in the applicant's statement as to occupation. Statements about a change of occupation are considered to be declarations of expectation and could serve as a basis for voiding the contract only if false and fraudulent.

Answers to questions about family history that call for information about events that occurred many years before or happened to relatives long separated from the applicant are deemed to be opinions. Rarely have answers to such questions been used as a basis for litigation. It would ordinarily be difficult for the insurer to prove the materiality of the facts misrepresented without also proving that the applicant suffered from a serious medical impairment traceable, in part, to family history. In that event, it would be simpler to void the contract on the grounds of the physical impairment. Answers to questions about exposure to contagious diseases, while significant for underwriting purposes, are of little value in litigation because of the difficulty of proving the materiality of the exposure.

The applicant's statements about his or her habits are usually treated as opinions. Questions directed at the applicant's use of intoxicating beverages or narcotics call for distinctions of degree, such as infrequent, moderate, or excessive use. Moreover, the applicant is asked for a self-evaluation, which he or she cannot be expected to do objectively. For these reasons, and because the inspection report reveals the most serious cases of addiction to alcohol or drugs, the applicant's statements as to habits seldom constitute the basis for litigation.

Medical Treatment

Answers to questions about specific ailments or diseases are in most — but not all — jurisdictions deemed to be statements of fact and not merely statements of opinion. An applicant is expected to know whether or not he or she has ever had or been treated for disorders of critical organs of the body. Some courts infer the applicant's knowledge of the falsity and materiality of the answer from the serious consequences to him or her of the disease and the treatment.[16] On the other hand, if the evidence indicates that the applicant's physician did not inform the applicant about the nature of his or her ailment — for instance, that it is an incurable disease — the applicant's statement as to that particular disease may be treated as an opinion and not be sufficient to permit the insurer's voiding the contract.

Answers to general questions about medical treatment, consultation, or hospitalization have been the ones most frequently invoked as defenses in litigation. The questions are usually regarding treatment that has taken place only during the last 5 years, and the applicant is expected to have a sufficiently keen awareness of the events to provide the insurer with accurate information. With some exceptions, the answers are treated as statements of fact and not of opinion. Except in states that have adopted the physician-patient privilege, the facts can be proved by the testimony or records of the physician or of the hospital.

Of course, the applicant's failure to disclose, or positive misrepresentation of, an instance of medical treatment is of itself neither material nor immaterial. The thing that is material is what the company would have learned, with the full cooperation of the physician or the hospital, if it had been put on notice as to the medical treatment and had made inquiry as to its nature. In order to avoid any disputes or disagreements about the materiality of an applicant's misrepresentation of his or her recent medical history, the New York Insurance Law states as follows:

> A misrepresentation that an applicant for life, accident, or health insurance has not had previous medical treatment, consultation or observation, or has not had previous treatment or care in a hospital or other like institution, shall be deemed, for the purpose of determining its materiality, a misrepresentation that the applicant has not had the disease, ailment or other medical impairment for which such treatment or care was given or which was discovered by any licensed medical practitioner as a result of such consultation or observation.[17]

It does not follow that in all cases the facts misrepresented by the applicant's failure to disclose a medical consultation will be sufficient to void the contract. If the consultation was for the purpose of obtaining treatment for a common cold or some other slight temporary ailment, the facts misrepresented would not, because of their immateriality, constitute grounds for avoidance of the contract.

Many states have enacted statutes that regard information about a patient's physical condition obtained by a physician through medical treatment or professional consultation as a *privileged communication,* which can be divulged only with the consent of the patient, or if deceased, his or her personal representative. In those states a physician is not permitted to give testimony about the medical treatment of an applicant for insurance unless the applicant or his or her personal representative agrees that the physician's findings be made public. If the physician is not permitted to testify, a suspicion arises that the ailment was one material to the defense of misrepresentation. The suspicion is so strong that since 1940, the New York Insurance Law has contained a provision that if the insurer proves that an applicant misrepresented the facts relating to a medical consultation and the applicant or any other person claiming a right under the insurance contract prevents full disclosure and proof of the nature of the medical impairment, such misrepresentation will be presumed to have been material.[18] The presumption can be rebutted by evidence from the claimant that the ailment was not material to the risk.

This provision, which followed a decision of the highest court of New York to the same effect, has been successfully invoked in New York courts and in federal cases governed by New York law. In other states having the physician-privilege statute, no such presumption of materiality arises.

CONCEALMENT

The doctrine of concealment is the final legal defense of the insurance company in its efforts to avoid liability under a contract that was obtained through the misrepresentation or concealment of material facts. Of the three basic grounds for avoidance (breach of warranty, misrepresentation, and concealment) concealment is the narrowest in scope and the most difficult to prove.

Nature and Legal Effect of a Concealment

In general law concealment connotes an affirmative act to hide the existence of a material fact. In insurance law, however, a concealment is essentially a nondisclosure; it is the failure of the applicant for insurance to communicate to the insurer his or her knowledge of a material fact that the insurer does not possess.

It is general law of long standing that one party to a contract is under no legal obligation during the period of negotiation to disclose to the other party information that the first party knows is not known to the second party and, if known, would be deemed material to the contract. The rationale of this rule is that prices in the marketplace should be set by the best-informed buyers and sellers, and as a reward for performing this economic function, they should be permitted to profit by their special knowledge of affairs. For some years, however, there has been a marked trend in the other direction. Among the numerous exceptions to the general rule are the requirements that one party not actively try to prevent the second party from discovering facts known only to the first party or give deliberately misleading answers to questions designed to elicit information material to the contract.

In insurance, the law of concealment, like the other two doctrines discussed earlier in this chapter, developed during the 18th century out of cases involving marine insurance. The relative inaccessibility of the property to be insured and the poor communication facilities, combined with the aleatory nature of the contract, caused Lord Mansfield, the father of English commercial and insurance law, to hold that the applicant for insurance was required by good faith to disclose to the insurer all known facts that would materially affect the insurer's decision about acceptance of the risk, the amount of the premium, or other essential terms of the contract, whether or not the applicant was aware of the materiality of the facts. Even though conditions affecting marine insurance have changed, the law has not. The person seeking marine insurance today, whether the shipowner or shipper, must disclose all known material facts in his or her possession to the insurer. Failure to do so, even though innocent, will permit the insurer to void the contract.

In English law, the doctrine of innocent concealment is strictly applied to all branches of insurance. In the United States, it is applied only to marine insurance. American courts have felt that the circumstances surrounding fire and life insurance are so different from those in marine insurance—particularly true in 1766 when the marine rule originated—that a different rule is justified. Under American law, except for marine insurance, a concealment will permit the insurer to void the contract only if the applicant, in refraining from disclosure, had a fraudulent intent.[19] In other words, *except for marine insurance, a concealment must be both material and fraudulent.* In marine insurance, it need only be material.

Test of Materiality

The doctrine of concealment may be regarded as a special manifestation of the doctrine of misrepresentation. The relationship between a misrepresentation and a concealment has been compared with that existing between the heads and tails of a coin. If a misrepresentation is the heads of a coin, a concealment is the tails. One is affirmative; the other is negative.

A concealment is misrepresentation by silence. It has legal consequences for the same reason that a misrepresentation does—namely, that the insurer was misled into making a contract that it would not have made had it known the facts. Hence, the general concept of materiality applied to a concealment is the same as that applicable to a misrepresentation: the effect on the underwriting decision of the insurer. "Fraudulent intent" is a subjective concept that is difficult to prove; many courts take the attitude that if the fact not disclosed by the applicant was *palpably* material, this is sufficient proof of fraud.[20]

The degree of relevance to a risk required of a fact to be palpably material has never been judicially defined. An illustration was provided in a famous 1896 decision by William Howard Taft,[21] then a judge of the 8th Circuit Court of Appeals, who indicated that an applicant for life insurance who failed to reveal to the insurer that he was on his way to fight a duel would be guilty of concealing a palpably material fact. This illustration was almost contradicted by a 1938 decision that an applicant's failure to disclose that he was carrying a revolver because of his fear of being killed by his former partner, whom he had accused of committing adultery with his wife, was not a palpably material concealment, even though the applicant was murdered a few months later by a person unknown.[22] Experts are occasionally called upon to testify as to the materiality of a concealed fact, but in cases settled in favor of the insurer, the judge has usually decided from his or her own knowledge that the fact concealed was palpably material.

The palpable materiality test is applied to the applicant's knowledge of materiality, while both the prudent-insurer and individual-insurer tests of materiality apply only to the *effect* on the insurer. In concealment cases, which are governed by statutes only in California and states that have adopted its laws, the prudent-insurer test seems to be the prevailing one.

Test of Fraud

The test of fraud is whether the applicant believed the fact that he or she did not disclose to be material to the risk. This test was approved long ago by the highest court of New York in a case involving the applicant's failure to disclose that he had once been insane.[23] The concealment was held not to be fraudulent. The insurer therefore must prove that an undisclosed fact is, *in the applicant's own mind,* material to the risk. As a general proposition, the insured's awareness of the materiality of the fact concealed can be proved by establishing that the fact was *palpably* material, a characteristic that would be apparent to any person of normal intelligence.

However, in concealment cases, as with warranties and representations, the law takes into account the powers of understanding and state of knowledge of the particular applicant involved. Thus the failure of an applicant who was the state agent for the company to notify the insurer of a cancerous condition of the spleen, discovered after submission of the application but before issue of the policy, was held to be fraudulent in view of the applicant's exceptional knowledge of the materiality of such a condition.[24] On the other hand, the failure of a less sophisticated applicant to disclose a toxic condition of the heart muscle, likewise discovered in the interim between submission of the application and issue of the policy, was held not to be fraudulent when evidence revealed that the applicant had refused to take additional insurance offered to him and had changed the basis of premium payments from monthly to semiannually.[25]

Scope of the Doctrine of Concealment in Life Insurance

The requirement that a concealment be proved by the insurer to have been fraudulent has narrowed the scope of the doctrine in all forms of nonmarine insurance. Its scope has been further narrowed in life insurance through the use of a detailed written application and, in larger cases, a medical examination. There is a presumption that the application elicits information about every matter that the insurer deems material to the risk, and if the applicant answers all questions asked in the application fully and truthfully, he or she is under no duty to volunteer additional information. This presumption can be overcome by evidence that the applicant willfully concealed other information that was material to the risk and that the applicant knew to be material. In practice, however, the doctrine is seldom invoked except for nondisclosure of a material fact discovered by the applicant between the time he or she signed the application and the time the contract was consummated.

The general (but not unanimous) view of the courts is that the applicant under the doctrine of continuing representations must communicate promptly to the insurer his or her discovery of such interim facts if they are so obviously material that the applicant could not fail to recognize their materiality. In one of the early cases on the subject, the insurance company was permitted to deny liability under a policy issued in ignorance of the fact that the applicant had undergone an operation for appendicitis during the period the application was being considered by the home office, even though the applicant was in the hospital at the time the disclosure should have been made.[26] In a later case involving the interim discovery of a duodenal ulcer, the Supreme Court of the United States had the following to say:

> Concededly, the modern practice of requiring the applicant for life insurance to answer questions prepared by the insurer has relaxed this rule (of disclosure) to some extent since information not asked for is presumably deemed immaterial.

But the reason for the rule still obtains, and with added force, as to changes materially affecting the risk that come to the insured's knowledge after the application and before delivery of the policy. Even the most unsophisticated person must know that, in answering the questionnaire and submitting it to the insurer, the applicant is furnishing the data on the basis of which the company will decide whether, by issuing a policy, it wishes to accept the risk. If, while the company deliberates, the applicant discovers facts that make portions of the application no longer true, *the most elementary spirit of fair dealing* would seem to require him or her to make a full disclosure.[27]

Since not all courts impose the duty of disclosure of interim changes and, in any event, violation of the duty must be proved fraudulent, many companies rely on the delivery-in-good-health and medical treatment clauses to protect themselves against interim changes in the applicant's physical condition. These clauses create conditions or warranties that must be fully satisfied before the company can be held liable under the contract.

The applicant is under no obligation to disclose interim developments, however material on their face, when the first premium is paid with the application and a binding receipt, conditioned on insurability at the date of application, is issued. Under such circumstances, the coverage becomes effective as of the date of application—or medical examination, if later—and changes in the applicant's insurability after that date are supposed to be immaterial to the insurer's deliberations. Of course, interim changes in the insured's physical condition can be used as evidence to support the company's contention that the insured concealed or misrepresented facts known to him or her when the application was made.

NOTES

1. Muriel L. Crawford and William T. Beadles, *Law and the Life Insurance Contract*, 6th ed. (Homewood, IL: Irwin Professional Publishing, 1989), p. 678.
2. *Ibid.*, p. 676.
3. *Ibid.*, p. 243.
4. Buist M. Anderson, *Anderson on Life Insurance* (Boston: Little, Brown & Company, 1991), pp. 243–44.
5. *Ibid.*, p. 245.
6. Sec. 4101 of the New York Civil Practice Law and Rules permits an insurer when sued by a beneficiary to have its equitable defense or counterclaim for rescission tried before a judge without a jury.
7. *Sommer v. Guardian Life Insurance Co.*, 281 N.Y. 508, 24 N.E. 2d 308 (1939). A *statement* that the applicant is in good health must be distinguished from the requirement that the applicant *be* in good health upon delivery of the policy, which requirement, as a condition precedent, is strictly enforced.
8. Anderson, *Anderson on Life Insurance*, pp. 243–44.
9. New York Insurance Law, Sec. 149 (2). For purposes of this statute, a contract issued on the basis of a higher premium is considered a different contract.
10. *Ibid.*, Sec. 149 (3).
11. *Crotty v. State Mutual Assur. Co. of Am.*, 80 A.D. 2d 801, 437 N.Y.S. 21 103 (1981).
12. California Insurance Code, Sec. 334.
13. Missouri, Kansas, Oklahoma, and Rhode Island require that the misrepresented fact must have contributed to the company's loss in order to be considered material. However, these statutes do not apply if the insurer can show that the answers in the application were made with intent to deceive.
14. Mo. Ann. Stat. Sec. 376.800 (reman 1968).

15. *Columbian National Life Insurance Co. of Boston, Mass. v. Rodgers,* 116 F. 2d 705 (10th Cir. 1941), certiorari denied, 313 U.S. 561 (1941).

16. See, for example, *Mutual Life Insurance Co. of New York v. Moriarity,* 178 F. 2d 470 (9th Cir., 1949).

17. New York Insurance Law, Sec. 149 (4).

18. *Ibid.*

19. This is not true in California. The insurance Code (Sec. 330) of that state provides that "concealment, whether intentional or unintentional," entitles the insurer to rescind the contract.

20. If the undisclosed fact is palpably material — that is, if its importance would be obvious to a person of ordinary understanding — it can be inferred that the applicant was aware of its materiality, an essential element in fraud.

21. *Penn Mutual Life Insurance Co. v. Mechanics Savings Bank & Trust Co.,* 72 Fed. 413 (6th Cir. 1896).

22. *New York Life Insurance Co. v. Bacalis,* 94 F. 2d 200 (5th Cir. 1938).

23. *Mallory v. Travelers Insurance Co.,* 47 N.Y. 52 (1871).

24. *McDaniel v. United Benefit Life Insurance Co.,* 177 F. 2d 339 (5th Cir. 1941).

25. *Wilkins v. Travelers Insurance Co.,* 117 F. (2d) 646 (5th Cir. 1941).

26. *Equitable Life Assurance Society of United States v. McElroy,* 83 Fed. 631 (8th Cir. 1897).

27. *Stipcicli v. Metropolitan Life Insurance Co.,* 277 U.S. 311, 316-17 (1928). Italics supplied.)

39

Waiver, Estoppel, and Election by the Insurer

Dan M. McGill
Revised by Burke A. Christensen

As discussed in the preceding chapter, a life insurance company may be able to avoid liability under a policy on the grounds of a breach of condition, a misrepresentation, or a concealment. Another possible insurer defense to a suit is lack of coverage under the terms of the policy. An insurer may not be permitted to assert any of these defenses, however, if additional facts show that it has waived the defense, has taken actions that amount to an estoppel, or has conclusively elected not to take advantage of it.

Various factual situations constitute the basis for a *waiver*, an *estoppel*, and an *election* (examples of each will be shown later in this chapter). Although they are legally distinct concepts, it is customary to refer to them all generically as a *waiver* and to describe any situation that could lead to the loss of an otherwise valid legal defense as a *waiver situation*. Simply and broadly stated, a waiver situation is one in which an insurance company's presumably valid defense to a policy claim has been—or may be found to have been—waived by the company.

If the foregoing definition of a waiver situation seems vague and general, it was intended to be. The boundaries of waiver law are indistinct, and the concepts employed tend to be amorphous.

This state of affairs is largely attributable to the underlying purpose of waiver law, which, in the case of life insurance, is to protect the policyowner and his or her beneficiaries against a harsh and overly legalistic interpretation of the life insurance policy and application. In perhaps no other branch of the law is there such a universal tendency to make the law fit the facts and if that is impractical, to create new law. A waiver has been described as "a kind of legal mercy, a way of tempering the wind to the shorn lamb."[1] In the process of providing mercy, the courts "have devised doctrines and asserted principles which are sometimes more creditable to the ingenuity and subtlety of the judges than easily harmonized with decisions rendered, under less violent bias, in other departments of the law."[2]

Edwin W. Patterson, Cardozo Professor Emeritus of Jurisprudence, Columbia University, and an eminent authority on the law of waiver, ascribed the state of confusion existing in this field to the use of "flexible concepts to analyze the significance of foggy facts."[3] Seeing hope for improvement, however, Patterson concluded that "the doctrines of waiver, once used as judicial whitewash to cover a multitude of minor defaults, are now used more sparingly and with more discrimination."[4] Nevertheless, in the years since these statements were made, the lack of clarity about the distinctions between waiver and estoppel has not improved.

Inasmuch as the *law of agency* is at the foundation of most waiver situations in life insurance, it is helpful to review the pertinent elements of that branch of the law before considering the more specific aspects of waiver.

LAW OF AGENCY

Principal: one for whom an agent acts

Agent: a person who acts for another

Agency can be defined as the relationship that results from the manifestation of consent by one person or entity (the principal) that another party (the agent) will act on the principal's behalf. The agent is subject to the principal's control. There must also by a manifestation of consent to the agency by the agent.

Almost any person can be an agent. A person is not required to have contractual capacity in order to act as an agent. For example, a minor who cannot sign a binding contract for himself or herself can still serve as an agent and may sign a binding contract for his or her principal. However, only a person or an entity with contractual capacity to perform a certain act may act as a principal and appoint an agent. Thus a corporation may be a principal but a partnership may not. One who appears to be an agent of a partnership is at best an agent of the partners themselves.

These general rules of agency law are modified when applied to the life insurance business. For example, life insurance agents must be of a certain minimum age, have contractual capacity, and be licensed by the state.

In the case of a life insurance company, the agents—in the legal sense—include the directors (acting as a body), the officers, home office supervisory personnel, agency supervisors, and soliciting agents. In the business sense, only agency field supervisors and soliciting agents are regarded as agents. In this chapter the term "agent" will be used in its broader, legal meaning, with the expression "soliciting agent" used to designate field sales personnel. Most waiver situations involve actions of soliciting agents.

General Rules

Power: the ability to say or do something. This ability may be inherent, given, implied or derived.

Authority: the power to act that is given to someone by another party

The following four general rules of the law of agency are particularly relevant to life insurance:

- presumption of agency
- apparent authority of agents
- responsibility for acts of agents
- limitations on powers of agents

Presumption of Agency

There is no presumption that one person acts for another. There must be some tangible evidence of an agency relationship. Thus if a person claims to represent a certain life insurance company and collects a premium with which he or she later absconds, the company is not responsible for that person's actions if it has done nothing to create the presumption that the person is its authorized agent. If, however, the company has by its conduct permitted the person to have the appearance of an agency relationship (such as leaving that person in possession of company property, application blanks, and receipt forms), a presumption can be raised that the person is in fact representing the company. (The presumption can be overcome by proof that the company materials were improperly acquired.)

Note that agency must be created by the principal. It cannot be created unilaterally by the purported agent.

The scope of authority for an agent's actions can be considerably broader than one might expect. There are three types of agency authority:

- *Express authority* is the power specifically given to the agent by the principal either orally or in writing.
- *Implied authority* refers to those powers not expressly given by the principal to the agent that are necessary to exercise the powers that are expressly given. This type of authority is sometimes also referred to as incidental authority.
- *Apparent authority* is the authority that the public reasonably believes the agent possesses based on the actions of the principal. Apparent authority may arise regardless of whether the agent has been given any express authority by the principal.

Apparent Authority of Agents

Most agency relationships are evidenced by a written instrument that expressly confers certain powers on the agent; it may also expressly withhold certain powers. A life insurance company's agency contract usually authorizes the field representative to solicit and take applications for new business, arrange medical examinations, and collect first-year premiums. It also sets forth a number of powers specifically denied the agent, including the right to make, alter, or discharge a contract; to extend the time for payment of premiums; to accept payment of premiums in other than current funds; to waive or extend any obligation or condition; and to deliver any policy unless the applicant is in good health and insurable condition at that time.

The agent's contract for one insurer, for example, provides that the company authorizes the agent to solicit applications for its insurance products. The contract then prescribes a substantial list of limitations on that authority as follows:

> The Agent shall have no authority for or on behalf of the Company to accept risks of any kind; to make, modify, or discharge contracts; to extend time for paying any premium; to bind the Company by any statement,

promise, or representation; to waive forfeitures or any of the Company's rights or requirements, or to place the company under any legal obligation by any act that is not within the authority granted by the Company in this contract or otherwise in writing.

Another insurer uses this coverage to limit the scope of authority granted by its agent's contract:

The Agent shall have no power or authority other than as herein expressly granted, and no other or greater powers shall be implied from the grant or denial of powers specifically mentioned herein.

An agent's power to bind his or her principal, however, may well exceed the scope of the principal's express authorization. This is because express authority is construed to convey authority to perform all incidental acts necessary to carry out the agency's purposes. Such acts fall under the heading of *implied* powers. For example, if an agent is expressly authorized to deliver a life insurance policy that can be properly delivered only upon the payment of the consideration, the agent has the implied power to collect the amount due and issue a receipt.

An agent's authority can also be expanded by conduct of the principal or agent that creates a justifiable belief by third parties dealing with the agent that he or she possesses powers that have not been vested in the agent and may—unknown to the third parties—have been expressly withheld by the principal. If third parties can prove that they were justified in relying on the presumption that the agent was acting within his or her authority, the principal will be *estopped* (precluded) from denying that the agent had such powers. In proving justifiable reliance, third parties need to demonstrate only that they exercised due diligence in ascertaining the agent's real authority. Authority created in this manner is referred to as *apparent authority*.

The doctrine of apparent authority can be illustrated by this example: An agent has habitually granted his or her policyowners extensions of time to remit premiums. Because the company has not taken action to deal with this infraction of its rules in the past, it would be precluded from denying that the agent had such authority until it notified the policyowners involved of the limitations on the agent's powers. The company's action with regard to one policyowner, however, would not create any presumption as to the agent's power to deal in a similar manner with other policyowners.

Responsibility for Acts of Agents

The principal is responsible for all acts of its agent when the agent is acting within the scope of express, implied, or apparent authority. This responsibility embraces wrongful or fraudulent acts, omissions, and misrepresentations, provided the agent is acting within the authority granted or implied by the principal. The principal is likewise responsible for any libel committed by an agent in the pursuit of his or her official duties. While there is no unanimity in the decisions, the weight of authority is that—in the absence of restrictions—a company is liable not only for the acts of its agents, but also for the acts of the subagents and employees to whom the agent has delegated responsibility. The liability of the company in such situations may depend on whether it has given the agent actual authority, or its actions have created an apparent authority, to delegate responsibility.

Secret limitations on the agent's authority are, under the doctrine of equitable estoppel, inoperative as to third persons. They are, of course, effective between the agent and the principal, and if the agent exceeds the actual authority given, he or she will be liable to the principal for any loss or damage. The agent, as might be expected, will also be liable to the principal for any loss or damage caused through the agent's fraud, misconduct, or mere negligence.

In the course of their daily business, insurance agents are frequently asked to express their opinion about the meaning of a particular provision. The general rule is that no legal effect is to be given to such opinions. This holding is based on the theory that an agent's opinion as to the meaning of any section does not create new obligations or modify old ones. This rule is followed particularly when the agent's authority is limited and the provision involved is clear and unambiguous. In certain jurisdictions, however, a company is bound by its agents' opinions, especially when the opinion is not inconsistent with the language of an ambiguous clause in the policy and the agent's opinion is relied on by the insured.[5]

The agent's knowledge about matters within the agency's scope is presumed to be knowledge of the principal. This rule is applied even though matters coming to the agent's attention are not, in fact, communicated to the principal. This rule is of critical importance, since in all their dealings with prospective and actual policyowners, soliciting agents and medical examiners are regarded to be the legal agents of the company. Hence loyalty to the company, as well as common decency, demands that field representatives communicate to the company all matters of underwriting or other significance that come to their attention.

Limitation on Powers of Agents

Limitations on an agent's powers are generally effective when the limitations have been properly communicated and do not conflict with existing law. All companies communicate to their policyowners through a clause in the application blank or in the policy (or both) the customary limitations on the powers of soliciting agents and other company representatives with whom the policyowner may come in contact. This provision, generally referred to as the *nonwaiver clause,* usually states that only certain specified representatives of the company (executive officers) have the power to extend the time for payment of a premium or to modify the terms of the contract in any other respect. The clause further requires that any modification of the contract must be evidenced by a written endorsement on the contract. For example, such a provision might read as follows: Only our President or one of our Vice Presidents can modify this contract or waive any of our rights or requirements under it. The person making these changes must put them in writing and sign them.

A nonwaiver clause will not be enforceable against acts or statements occurring prior to the policy's issue unless it is contained in the application and the application is attached to the policy. In other words, the applicant cannot be presumed to have knowledge of a limitation in an instrument that comes into his or her possession only after the transaction has been consummated. On the other hand, the assumption follows that limitations on the agent's authority contained in the application or the policy are effective with respect to acts occurring subsequent to delivery of the policy. Unfortunately for the insurance companies, experience has not always borne out this assumption.

Brokers as Agents

An insurance broker is a person (individual, partnership, or corporation) who acts as an agent of the insured in negotiating for insurance and in procuring the issuance of an insurance contract. In the eyes of the law, the broker is requested by the prospective insured to act for him or her, although in practice, the "request" is usually solicited by the broker. The broker usually receives all his or her compensation (in the form of commissions) from the insurance company, delivers the policy for the company, and collects the premium from the insured. As a consequence, the broker has come to be regarded as the agent of the company for the purpose of delivering the policy and collecting the premium. In fact, this status is recognized by statute in some states.

When the broker is regarded as the agent of the company only for these limited purposes, the broker's knowledge as to facts affecting the risk is not imputed to the company for the purpose of establishing a waiver or estoppel or for the purpose of obtaining reformation of the contract on the grounds of mistake.[6] In most states, however, there is legislation that provides that any person who solicits insurance for anyone other than himself or herself and procures a policy from the insurer will be deemed the agent of the insurer with respect to that policy.

MEANING OF WAIVER, ESTOPPEL, AND ELECTION

The legal concepts and rules employed in the adjudication of waiver situations have often lacked strong logic and consistency. The result is that the distinctions among waiver, estoppel, and election have become decidedly blurred, perhaps irretrievably so. Basically, however, the legal conceptions of waiver, estoppel, and election are derived from these two elemental principles:

- An individual should be bound by that to which he or she assents.
- An individual, whose conduct has led another to act or not to act in reliance upon a belief as to a fact or an expected future performance, ought not to be allowed to act in a way contrary to a belief or expectation he or she created.[7]

The first principle is at the foundation of waiver and election, while the second suggests the basis for several varieties of estoppel.

Waiver

Waiver: the voluntary and intentional giving up of a known right

The term "waiver" has been used with so many meanings that it almost defies analysis. Some courts try to distinguish it from estoppel, while other courts treat it as synonymous or interchangeable with estoppel. For example, one court might hold that the failure to demand an answer to an unanswered question in an application for life insurance constitutes a *waiver* of the right to make the demand, whereas another might hold that the company was *estopped* from demanding the answer. When a court does attempt to distinguish between waiver and estoppel, it ordinarily treats waiver as an act that indicates a manifestation of assent to something. For example, if a company elects to issue a policy even though the medical questions were not answered, it will be presumed to have waived the right to get the answers. On the other hand, an estoppel is treated as nonconsensual. This is because the purpose of the concept of estoppel is to redress a wrong and to prevent inequitable treatment of one party to a contract by the other. Thus if waiver is to be given a specific meaning, it would probably be appropriate to define it as a "manifestation of intent to relinquish a known right or advantage."[8] This meaning is similar to the following definition provided many years ago by the highest court of New York: "A waiver is the voluntary abandonment or relinquishment by a party of some right or advantage."[9]

While the foregoing definitions set waiver apart from estoppel, they do not distinguish it clearly from *election,* which, as noted in the discussion later in this chapter, likewise connotes a voluntary act.

Estoppel

> **Estoppel:** a loss of the ability to assert a defense because of prior actions that are now inconsistent with that defense

The doctrine of estoppel, developed centuries ago in the English courts, is a limitation on a person's right to change his or her mind. The law recognizes the right of individuals to change their minds, but it imposes certain restraints on that right when a contract has been created or when parties have acted reasonably in reliance on another person's representations or promises. The law of contracts attempts to distinguish the serious promise from the casual or jesting promise by means of a *consideration.* In the law of estoppel, a detrimental reliance or change of position by the other party is the test.

There are two broad types of estoppel: *(1) equitable estoppel* (also called *estoppel by representation* and *estoppel in pais*) and (2) *legal or promissory estoppel.*

Equitable Estoppel

Historically, equitable estoppel, so called because it originated in the equity courts, was the first to develop. It was confined to a representation of past or present fact; it did not apply to promises about future behavior. This original meaning has been preserved through the years and is reflected in the following comprehensive definition: "An [equitable] estoppel is a representation of fact made by one person to another which is reasonably relied upon by that other in changing his position to such an extent that it would be inequitable to allow the first person to deny the truth of his representation."[10]

The essence of the equitable estoppel is that if a party purports to make a true statement about a past or present fact to another party who relies on the truth of the statement to his or her substantial detriment, the first party will not be permitted to later deny the truth of the statement. The case is tried on an assumption contrary to fact. Thus equitable estoppel is a rule of evidence rather than one of substantive law.

Legal or Promissory Estoppel

The doctrine of legal or promissory estoppel has developed within the last century and is concerned with a statement of *future* conduct. It has been defined as "a statement as to his future conduct made by one person to another which is reasonably and foreseeably relied upon by that other in changing his position to such an extent that it would be inequitable to allow the first person to conduct himself differently from that which he stated."[11] In other words, if you make a promise in some circumstances you won't be allowed to change your mind.

The example that follows illustrates a promissory estoppel. Suppose P promises to give C $25,000 if C enters a particular college and receives a bachelor's degree. Suppose further that C matriculates at the designated college and completes all the requirements for the degree except passing the examinations for the final term when P notifies C of an intention to revoke the promise. Since C has made a substantial sacrifice in effort and money to attend college in reliance on P's promise, the courts would not permit P to revoke the promise. P's promise would be enforced, despite the fact that it was not supported by a consideration.[12] In other words, the law would recognize a valid contract. Some would even argue that C's actions in reliance on P's promise provide the consideration (or at least an equitable substitute) to support the contract.

The foregoing example illustrates the creation of a new obligation through a promissory estoppel. Some courts will not go that far in applying the doctrine, limiting its application to modifications of existing contracts, which is the typical application in life insurance situations. This application of promissory estoppel is of growing importance.

Election

In its original sense, election means a voluntary act of choosing between two alternative rights or privileges. Thus if a married man dies testate (with a will), his widow usually has the right to take under the will or under the appropriate intestate law. These are alternative rights, and the widow's act of choosing one is a voluntary relinquishment of the other. The similarity of an election to a waiver is readily apparent.

The concept of election has had only limited application in life insurance. Despite the fact that an election is an overt, manifested intent to be bound, the courts have occasionally found an election to exist in the inconsistent conduct of an insurer. For example, a company's acceptance of a premium after the discovery of a material misrepresentation has been viewed as an election by the company not to void the contract.

WAIVER SITUATIONS

In the remainder of this chapter, no attempt will be made to distinguish between waiver, estoppel, and election. The practical effect is the same, irrespective of the particular doctrine the court uses to justify its decision. The emphasis hereafter is on the types of factual situations in which the courts are likely to invoke one of the doctrines outlined above to deprive a life insurance company of a defense that would have enabled it to avoid paying a claim.

Breach of Condition Precedent

The validity of most life insurance policies is contingent on the fulfillment of three conditions precedent:

- the payment of the first premium
- the good health of the applicant at the time the policy is delivered
- the absence of new elements affecting insurability (for example, medical treatment) in the interim between the submission of the application and the delivery of the policy

Payment of First Premium

The existence of a life insurance policy is usually conditioned on payment of the first premium, or the first installment thereof, *in cash.* The cash-premium clause is typically coupled with the delivery-in-good-health clause.

The requirement that the first premium be paid in cash has been rather strictly enforced by the courts. Upon proof that the soliciting agent delivered the policy without payment of the premium, or any part thereof in any form, the courts in most jurisdictions hold that the policy is not in force, even though the agent orally assured the applicant that it would take effect at once. The view is that an agent having authority merely to solicit insurance and to collect premiums in cash has no actual or apparent authority to extend credit.

In reaching this conclusion, the courts seem to place great emphasis on the existence of a nonwaiver clause in the application, as opposed to the policy. In a leading New York case on the subject,[13] the court, holding that the cash payment requirement had not been satisfied through the payment of the premium by the soliciting agent on behalf of the applicant, stressed that the insured *agreed* in the application that the insurance would not take effect unless the premium was paid at the time the policy was delivered. In another case,[14] the taking of a promissory note payable to the soliciting agent was not deemed a waiver of the cash-premium clause since there was also a nonwaiver clause in the application.

The nonwaiver clause will not prevent a finding of waiver in all cases; it is merely notice to the applicant of the agent's limited authority. If it can be proved that the agent actually had authority to extend credit for all or a part of the premium, the agent's doing so will, in most courts, constitute an effective waiver of the cash-premium requirement. Thus an agent who had the power to employ subagents and had received detailed instructions from the home office as to how to deal with premium notes was held to have authority to issue a binding receipt in exchange for the applicant's note.[15]

In another case, it was proved that the insurer followed the practice of requiring its soliciting agents to remit only the difference between the gross premium and the agent's commission. It was held that the agent had authority to extend credit for the balance to an applicant who had paid the agent more than the amount remitted but less than the full amount due — despite the existence of cash-premium and nonwaiver clauses in the application.[16] In cases like this, the company's formal printed instructions to the agency force are not conclusive proof of an agent's actual authority. To avoid a waiver, the company's action must be consistent with its announced policy.

It is common practice, of course, for premiums to be paid by check. If the check is honored by the bank upon which it is drawn, the premium—for all intents and purposes—has been paid in cash. A check is considered to be a cash payment if an applicant has sufficient funds in his or her bank account to cover the check for a reasonable period of time.[17] If a check tendered in payment of the first premium is not honored upon presentation within a reasonable time, however, the status of the policy depends on the terms under which the check was accepted. If the premium receipt states that the check is accepted as payment only on the condition that it be honored (a common practice), the policy will not go into force if the check is not honored. If the premium receipt does not so state, however, some courts have construed the issuance of a premium receipt to be an *election* to treat the check as payment of the premium. In that event, the condition of the policy has been fulfilled, and nonpayment of the check merely entitles the insurer to sue the drawer of the check.

Delivery-in-Good-Health and Medical Treatment Clauses

Insurance contracts are normally issued subject to a good health clause, which is usually found in the application. This clause is made a part of the contract at the time the application is attached to the policy when it is issued and delivered to the policyowner. A typical good health clause reads as follows:

> The Company shall incur no liability under any policy issued on this application unless and until any policy is delivered to the Owner, and the first premium is paid prior to any change in the Proposed Isured's good health and insurability.

Some companies accomplish the same goal with language like the following:

> No insurance shall take effect on this application until a policy is delivered, the full initial premium is paid, and unless the statements in all parts of the application continue to be true, complete, and without material change.

The policy may be delivered to an insured who is not in good health when that fact is known by the agent, or when the agent does not inquire as to the state of the insured's health. In such a case, has the insurer waived its rights to contest the breach?

It is clear that either waiver or estoppel may prevent the insurer from asserting the good health clause as a defense. This may be avoided if the insurer has warned the policyowner about the good health clause and the limitations on the agent's power to alter the contract. Thus both of those clauses are usually prominently printed on the insurance application. Nevertheless, one court has held that the agent's failure to inquire about the insured's health resulted in a waiver of the carrier's right under the good health clause.

Misrepresentation in Application

The applicant for a life insurance policy must submit a written application that supplies various types of information, including information about the applicant's past and present health. The applicant may also have to undergo a medical examination, including an interrogation by the medical examiner. It is standard practice for the soliciting agent to fill out the application for the applicant and for the medical examiner to write in the answers to the questions which he or she asks the applicant.

There is always the possibility that the agent or medical examiner may incorrectly record information supplied by the applicant in the application. This may occur inadvertently or by design. Unless there is collusion, the medical examiner has little or no reason to falsify the medical records. The agent, however, because he or she is paid on a commission basis, does have an incentive to falsify information—either with or without the applicant's knowledge—that might adversely affect the application's acceptance.

If there is collusion between the applicant and any agent of the insurer to falsify the application, the insurer loses none of its defenses. If, on the other hand, the agent is acting alone and tells the applicant that an item of information is not being recorded correctly, the agent is likely to imply that the information is immaterial and should not be permitted to complicate home office underwriting officials' consideration of the application. In cases where the applicant's truthful answers have been falsely recorded in the application by the agent (or the medical examiner), it becomes important to determine the legal effect of these misstatements.

It is a well-settled rule that one who signs and accepts a written instrument with the intention of contracting is bound by its terms. However, if the instrument contains false statements, the aggrieved party has the right to avoid the contract. Hence in accordance with strict contract law, material misstatements in the application should give the insurance company power to avoid the contract, regardless of the circumstances surrounding the statements' falsification. However, the courts, recognizing that a life insurance policy is a contract of adhesion that the insured seldom reads, do not apply strict contract law in these cases. The rule supported by the weight of authority is that if the application is filled out by an agent of the company who—without fraud, collusion, or the applicant's knowledge—falsely records information that the applicant had provided truthfully, the company cannot rely on the falsity of such information in seeking to avoid liability under the contract.[18] According to one court, "To hold otherwise would be to place every simple or uneducated person seeking insurance at the mercy of the insurer who could, through its agent, insert in every application, unknown to the applicant, and over his signature, some false statement which would enable it to avoid all liability while retaining the price paid for supposed insurance."[19]

The key to the rule is that the agent, in filling out the application, is acting for the company, not for the insured. In other words, the soliciting agent is, in a legal sense, the agent of the company, the principal. This finding can support either of two legal theories, both of which have been used by the courts to justify their decisions. The first theory holds that there is no deception of the insurance company since it knew through its agent that the written statement or statements were not true.[20] The second theory, more widely used, recognizes that there is deception but holds that since the company through the knowledge of its agent knowingly issued a voidable policy, it is estopped from voiding it. In both theories, the insurer has a right of action against the agent for breach of his or her duty to the principal.

To find an estoppel against the insurer, the courts must permit testimony, usually from the beneficiary, as to the answers the applicant provided to the agent. This would seem to be in violation of the parol evidence rule, but the general holding is that the parol evidence rule does not exclude oral testimony to establish waiver or estoppel.

The courts are likewise inclined to find a waiver or an estoppel when the applicant knows an answer is false but the agent asserts that it is immaterial. The view is that the applicant is entitled to rely on the superior knowledge of the agent or medical examiner, as the case may be. Even a stipulation in the application that oral statements made to the agent will not be binding on the company has been held unenforceable. However, when the applicant knows that the agent or medical examiner is not truthfully reporting obviously material facts to the company, the applicant is guilty of fraud and cannot invoke the doctrine of estoppel, which requires honest reliance. The applicant's behavior in this situation is regarded as collusive.

Waiver Subsequent to Issuance of Policy

If a condition is breached after a policy has gone into effect, the breach can be waived by the insurer in either of two ways:

- by an express statement, usually in writing, from a representative of the insurer having the authority to waive the condition
- by the inconsistent conduct of the company and its representatives

With waiver by an express statement, attention must again be directed to the clause embodied in the application for a life insurance policy, stipulating that no provision of the contract can be waived except by a *written* endorsement on the contract signed by a designated officer of the company. This restriction is likely to be enforced with respect to *express* waivers, although the courts occasionally find that the company bestowed the waiver authority on representatives not designated in the nonwaiver clause, even local agents. Moreover, oral statements may be accepted as evidence of waiver. Note that this is not inconsistent with the parol evidence rule, which applies only to oral statements made prior to or contemporaneously with the formation of the contract. Most of the litigation concerning express waivers involves the authority of the person who allegedly approved the waiver. It is clear that if an important official of the company purports to waive a breach of condition, the waiver will be recognized and enforced by the courts. The validity of other alleged waivers will depend on the actual or apparent authority of the company representative making the statement.

A waiver after the policy is issued is more likely to be found in the inconsistent conduct of the company. When the company has knowledge of a breach or nonperformance of a condition and wishes to avoid the contract on that ground, it must pursue a course of conduct consistent with that intention. In their zeal to protect policyowners, the courts will seize upon inconsistent conduct on the part of the insurer as evidence of an intention not to exercise its power of avoidance. For example, if a company has followed a general practice of accepting and retaining premiums tendered after the expiration of the grace period, it will be estopped from denying the punctuality of any premiums so paid. Perhaps more important, it will be estopped from insisting on the timely payment of premiums in the future, unless it makes unmistakably clear to policyowners from whom overdue premiums have customarily been accepted that future payments must be made before expiration of the grace period. Any attempt by the company to collect a premium after the grace period has expired might be held to be a waiver unless accompanied by an invitation to the insured to submit an application for reinstatement.

The same rule applies when a company has established a practice of sending premium notices, although they are not required by statute or the policy. If, without adequate notice to policyholders, the company discontinued this practice, it would probably be held to have waived its right to insist on payment within the grace period, provided payment is tendered within a reasonable time. It used to be the practice of many companies to send out two premium notices—the second sometimes during the grace period. When those companies discontinued the second notice, they were careful to notify their policyowners of the change in practice in order to avoid the possibility of being charged with a waiver of the timely payment condition.

NOTES

1. Edwin W. Patterson, *Essentials of Insurance Law,* 2d ed. (New York: McGraw-Hill Book Co., Inc., 1957), p. 476.
2. John Skirving Ewart, *Waiver Distributed* (Cambridge, MA: Harvard University Press, 1917), p. 192.
3. Patterson, *Essentials of Insurance Law,* p. 494.
4. *Ibid.,* p. 483.
5. *Couch Cyclopedia of Insurance Law,* 2d ed. rev. (Rochester, NY: The Lawyers Cooperative Publishing Co., 1993), sec. 531.
6. *Mishiloff v. American Central Insurance Co.,* 102 Conn. 370, 128 Atl. 33 (1925); *Ritson v. Atlas Assurance Co.,* 279 Mass. 385, 181 N.E. 393 (1932).
7. *Couch Cyclopedia of Insurance Law,* secs. 71.1–71.3.
8. Patterson, *Essentials of Insurance Law,* p. 495.
9. *Draper v. Oswego County Fire Relief Assn.,* 190 N.Y. 12, 14, 82 N.E. 755, 756 (1907).
10. Patterson, *Essentials of Insurance Law,* p. 496.
11. *Ibid.*
12. H. M. Horne and D. B. Mansfield, *The Life Insurance Contract,* 2d ed. (New York: Life Office Management Association, 1948), p. 81.
13. *Drilling v. New York Life Insurance Co.,* 234 N.Y. 234, 137 N.E. 314 (1922).
14. *Bradley v. New York Life Insurance Co.,* 275 Fed. 657 (8th Cir. 1921).
15. *Schwartz v. Northern Life Insurance Co.,* 25 F. (2d) 555 (9th Cir. 1928).
16. *New York Life Insurance Co. v. Olliclh,* 42 F. (2d) 399 (6th Cir. 1930).
17. *State Life Insurance Co. v. Nolan,* 13 S.W. 2d 406 (Tex. Civ. App. 1929).

18. In New York, the insured is bound by false answers entered by the agent or medical examiner if the insured certifies as to the answers. *Bollard v. New York Life Insurance Co.,* 228 N.Y. 521, 126 N.E. 900 (1920).

19. *State Insurance Co. of Des Moines v. Taylor,* 14 Colo. 499, 508, 24 Pac. 333, 336 (1890).

20. *Heilig v. Home Security Life Insurance Co.,* 222 N.C. 21, 22 S.E. 2d 429 (1942).

40

The Incontestable Clause

Dan M. McGill
Revised by Burke A. Christensen

The preceding chapter discussed the impact of the doctrines of waiver, estoppel, and election on the right of a life insurance company to avoid liability under a policy because of fraud, misrepresentation, or breach of condition at the contract's inception. This chapter will consider an even more restrictive influence — the incontestable clause. This clause, without counterpart in any other type of contract, was once the source of considerable misunderstanding and litigation. A commonly held opinion is that no other provision of a typical life insurance contract has been the center of so much "controversy, misinterpretation, and legal abuse" as the incontestable clause.[1] While the incontestable clause is no longer the source of much litigation, the provision has a vital bearing on the protection afforded by a life insurance contract, and it is worthy of careful study.

NATURE AND PURPOSE OF THE CLAUSE

Incontestable clause: a provision in the insurance contract that waives most of the insurance company's rights to dispute the validity of the contract after a certain period of time

In its simplest form the incontestable clause states that a policy is incontestable from its date of issue, except for nonpayment of premium. The purpose of such a clause is to enhance a life insurance contract's value by providing assurances that its validity will not be questioned by the insurance company years after it was issued and has possibly given rise to a claim. It is important to understand that the incontestable clause applies to whether the contract is valid, not to whether the terms or conditions of the contract have been fulfilled. The clause was voluntarily adopted by insurance companies partly as a result of competitive pressures to overcome prejudices against the life insurance business created by contests based on technicalities and to give an assurance to "persons doubtful of the utility of insurance, that neither they nor their families, after the lapse of a given time, shall be harassed with lawsuits when the evidence of the original transaction shall have become dim, or difficult of retention, or when, perhaps, the lips of him who best knew the facts are sealed by death."[2]

A typical incontestable clause reads as follows: "We will not contest the validity of this policy, except for nonpayment of premiums, after it has been in force during the insured's lifetime for two years from the Policy Date. This provision does not apply to any rider providing accidental death or disability benefits."[3]

The incontestable clause is a manifestation of the belief that a life insurance policy's beneficiaries should not be made to suffer for mistakes innocently made in the application. As will be shown, therefore the beneficiary may be protected by the incontestable clause even if the error in the application is based on a fraudulent or material misrepresentation by the applicant or by a failure of a condition precedent to the existence of the contract. After the insured's death, it would be extremely difficult, if not impossible, for the beneficiary to disprove the allegations of the insurance company that irregularities were present in procuring the policy. If there were no time limit on the insurance company's right to question the accuracy of the information provided in the application, there would be no certainty during the life of the policy that the benefits promised by it would be payable at maturity. The honest policyowner needs assurance that at death the beneficiary will be the "recipient of a check and not of a lawsuit."[4] The incontestable clause provides that assurance. It is based on the theory that after the insurance company has had a reasonable opportunity to investigate the circumstances surrounding issuance of a life insurance policy, it should thereafter relinquish the right to question the validity of the contract.

Originally introduced in New York by voluntary action in 1864, the incontestable clause had become so firmly entrenched and was so obviously beneficial to all parties that the legislation that grew out of the Armstrong investigation in 1906 made the inclusion of the clause mandatory in life insurance policies. Other states followed New York's example so that, today, the clause is required by statute in all states. The laws of the various states differ as to the form of the clause prescribed, but no states permit a clause that would make the policy in general contestable for more than 2 years.

Effect of Fraud

It is generally agreed that the original purpose of the incontestable clause was to protect the beneficiary of a life insurance policy against the *innocent* misrepresentations or concealments of the insured. There was considerable doubt in the early years that the incontestable clause could operate to bar the denial of liability on the grounds of fraud. Basic tenets of contract law are that (1) fraud in the formation of a contract renders the contract voidable at the option of the innocent party, and (2) in general, parties to a contract are not permitted immunity from the consequences of their fraud. These two rules would seem to limit the applicability of the incontestable clause, therefore, to inadvertent misrepresentations or concealments. Nevertheless, over the years, judicial interpretation has firmly established the principle that the incontestable clause is also effective in cases involving fraud. Even more to the point, since no reputable life insurance company is likely to contest a policy under ordinary circumstances unless there is evidence of an intent to deceive, it may be concluded that the primary function, if not the purpose, of the incontestable clause is to protect the insured and the beneficiaries against the consequences of the insured's (or the policyowner's) fraudulent behavior or erroneous charges of fraud by the insurer.

Erroneous insurer charges of fraud are precluded by the clause for any policy in force beyond the contestable period. In holding that the expiration of the contestable period precludes a defense even on the grounds of fraud, the courts have been careful to emphasize that they are not condoning fraud. They justify their action on the grounds that the insurance company has a reasonable period of time in which to discover any fraud involved in procuring the policy and is obligated to seek redress within the permissible period of time. In line with this reasoning, one court stated as follows:

> This view does not exclude the consideration of fraud, but allows the parties to fix by stipulation the length of time which fraud of the insured can operate to deceive the insurer. It recognizes the right of the insurer, predicated upon a vast experience and profound knowledge in such matters, to agree that in a stipulated time, fixed by himself, he can unearth and drag to light any fraud committed by the insured, and protect himself from the consequences . . . The incontestable clause is upheld in law, not for the purpose of upholding fraud, but for the purpose of shutting off harassing defenses based upon alleged fraud; and, in so doing, the law merely adopts the certificate of the insurer that within a given time he can expose and render innocuous any fraud in the preliminary statement of the insured. . . .[5]

The incontestable clause has been described as a private contractual "statute of limitation" on fraud, prescribing a period shorter than that incorporated in the statutory enactment. This analogy with conventional statutes of limitations has been questioned by some critics,[6] but the basic purpose of the incontestable clause and statutes of limitation is the same: to bar the assertion of legal rights after the evidence concerning the cause of action has grown stale and key witnesses are no longer readily available.

The courts recognize that some unscrupulous persons are permitted to profit by their fraudulent action through the operation of the incontestable clause, but they proceed on the premise that the social advantages of the clause outweigh the undesirable consequences. "The view is that even though dishonest people are given advantages under incontestability clauses which any right-minded man is loath to see them get, still the sense of security given to the great mass of honest policyholders by the presence of the clause in their policies makes it worth the cost."[7]

Despite the courts' general adherence to the doctrine that the incontestable clause is a bar to a defense of fraud, there are some species of fraud so abhorrent that their nullification through the incontestable clause is regarded to be in contravention of public policy. For example, the incontestable clause has been held not to apply when a contract was negotiated with intent to murder the insured, even though the murderer was not the beneficiary.[8] In addition, in cases where the applicant lacks an insurable interest, it is the majority view that the courts will permit the insurer to deny liability beyond the contestable period.[9] Likewise, in cases where someone, presumably a healthier person and usually the beneficiary, has impersonated the applicant for purposes of undergoing the medical examination and answering the questions pertaining to the applicant's health, the courts have uniformly held the purported contract to be null and void on the grounds that there has been "no real meeting of minds."[10] While the term "no real meeting of minds" has been replaced by the better term "no manifestation of mutual assent," it is nevertheless quite correct to state that the purported contract never came into existence. Since the incontestable clause is a part of the contract, it cannot be enforceable if the contract is void. Finally, in a few cases, the courts have recognized execution for a crime as legitimate grounds for denial of liability,[11] although in other cases, the company has been held liable.[12]

Meaning of a Contest

A policy can be prevented from becoming incontestable only by appropriate legal action by the company during the contestable period or, under one type of incontestable clause (to be described later), by the death of the insured during the contestable period. The courts hold that there must be a "contest" during the contestable period, and it becomes a matter of interpretation as to what constitutes a contest within the meaning of the clause.

In some jurisdictions a notice of rescission accompanied by a return of the premium is deemed to constitute a contest. The majority of the courts, however, have held that there must be a court action that challenges the validity of the policy as a contract. Thus under the majority rule, the requirement of a contest can be satisfied only by a suit in equity for rescission before a court of competent jurisdiction or by a defense to a judicial (at law) proceeding seeking to enforce the contract. In the first instance, the company would be seeking rescission by a suit in equity; in the second case, it would be defending against an action at law instituted by the beneficiary in an attempt to collect the proceeds. A suit for rescission is permitted only when there is no adequate remedy at law, and in most jurisdictions, defense against a beneficiary's action is regarded as an adequate remedy. Equity proceedings, however, are always available to the company while the insured is alive during the contestable period and, as is pointed out below, are usually available after the death of the insured only under certain types of incontestable clause.

Detailed rules of legal procedure have evolved to establish the precise moment at which a contest has materialized. Once the contest has been joined, the contestable period stops running, and regardless of the outcome of the initial contest, the incontestable clause cannot be invoked to forestall any other proceeding. Thus if a contest is initiated with the insured during the contestable period, the beneficiary may be made a party to the proceedings after the expiration of the period specified in the incontestable clause.

The interpretation of the term contest is also important in another respect. Broadly interpreted, the incontestable clause could prohibit the denial of any type of claim after the contestable period has expired. It could force the company to pay a type of claim that was never envisioned under the contract. Fortunately, the majority of the courts do not interpret the clause in that manner. They make a distinction between contests that question the validity or existence of a contract and those that seek to clarify the terms of the contract or to enforce the contract's terms. In one widely cited case, the court stated as follows:

> It must be clear that every resistance by an insurer against the demands of the beneficiary is in one sense a contest, but it is not a contest of the policy; that is, not a contest against the terms of the policy but a contest for or in favor of the terms of the policy. In other words, there are two classes of contests; one to enforce the policy, the other to destroy it. Undoubtedly the term "incontestable" as used in a life insurance policy

means a contest, the purpose of which is to destroy the validity of the policy, and not a contest, the purpose of which is to demand its enforcement.[13]

The significance of this distinction will be brought out in the discussion of the incontestable clause's application to other contract provisions.

Inception of the Contestable Period

Where the *operative date* of a life insurance policy coincides with the *effective date,* there is little question about when the contestable period starts to run. It begins the day following the date on the policy.[14] When the effective date of protection is earlier than the date of the policy, however, some courts have made the beginning of the contestable period coincide with the commencement of insurance coverage, regardless of the date of the policy. This would be the normal case when conditional receipts are used. On the other hand, when the policy has been antedated so that the date of the policy is earlier than the effective date of coverage, the courts, applying the rule of construction most favorable to the insured, have usually held that the contestable period begins with the date of the policy. This would be applicable when a policy has been back-dated to obtain a younger insurable age. This is true whether the clause provides that the policy will be incontestable after a specified period from the "date of the policy" or the "date of issue." When the policy makes it clear that the contestable period starts to run only from the time the policy actually becomes effective, however, there is no reason to apply the rule of construction most favorable to the insured, and the courts will give effect to the contract as written.

TYPES OF INCONTESTABLE CLAUSES

As the incontestable clause went through a period of evolution, there were various changes in wording from time to time, usually to nullify the unfavorable interpretations developed out of litigation. The earliest forms of the clause were quite simple, and one that became involved in a precedent-making court decision read as follows: "After two years, this policy shall be noncontestable except for the nonpayment of premiums as stipulated. . . ." It was the insurers' expectation that if the insured died during the 2 years, the policy would never become incontestable. This clause served satisfactorily for many years until the celebrated *Monahan* decision impaired its usefulness to insurance companies.[15]

In that case the insured died within the 2-year period, and the company denied liability, alleging a breach of warranty. The beneficiary waited until the 2-year contestable period had expired and then brought suit against the company. The company defended on the grounds of breach of warranty. The beneficiary asserted that since the 2-year period for contesting the policy had expired, the insurance carrier was precluded from raising the breach of warranty as a defense. The Supreme Court of Illinois, agreeing with the beneficiary, held that the policy was incontestable and found for the beneficiary. This decision, which was accepted as a precedent in virtually all jurisdictions, established the far-reaching principle that the contestable period was not ended by the insured's death but continued to run until the specified time had elapsed.

The practical effect of the *Monahan* decision was that if a policyowner died within the contestable period, the company was forced to go into court during the contestable period to seek a rescission if it wanted to deny liability for any reason. If no action was brought before the period expired, the company was estopped from erecting any defense other than lapse from nonpayment of premiums. Much litigation was thus thrust upon insurance companies to avert claims that they regarded to be unwarranted—to their detriment in the public esteem.

In an effort to avoid the undesirable consequences of the *Monahan* case, many companies adopted a clause that provided that the policy would be incontestable after it had been *in force* for a specified period. It was believed that with such a clause, the death of the insured would stop the period from running since the policy would no longer be in force. When the clause was tested in the courts, however, the decisions (with some exceptions) held that a policy does not terminate with the death of the insured but continues "in force" for the benefit of the beneficiary. In other words, the contract still has to be performed. Thus this clause had the same weakness as the incontestable clause litigated in the *Monahan* case. Despite this disadvantage, some companies have continued to use the clause or to simply omit the words "during the lifetime of the insured," since this permits suits in equity, which are usually tried without a jury.[16]

Those companies that were willing to give up the advantage of suits in equity modified their incontestable clause to make the policy incontestable after it has been in force *during the lifetime of the insured* for a specified period. The courts have uniformly agreed that under this clause, the death of the insured during the contestable period suspends the operation of the clause and fixes the rights of the parties as of the date of death. Under such a clause, if the insured dies during the specified period, the policy never becomes incontestable, and the claimant cannot gain any advantage by postponing notification of claim until the specified period has expired. However, since a legal remedy is available—that is, a defense against a suit instituted by the beneficiary—the company cannot avoid a jury trial and obtain rescission of the policy by a suit in equity, except during the lifetime of the insured.

A final type of clause typically provides (with certain exceptions, to be noted), "This policy shall be incontestable after one year from its date of issue unless the insured dies in such year, in which event it shall be incontestable after 2 years from its date of issue." This clause does not solve the problem created by the *Monahan* decision since the death of the insured during the first year does not suspend the running of the period. However, should the insured die during the first year, the company will have a *minimum* of one year in which to investigate the circumstances of the case and, if desired, to institute a suit for rescission. Under all of the other types of clauses except the one requiring survivorship of the insured, it is possible for the company to have only a few days in which to investigate a suspicious death. In fact, it is quite likely that in many cases, the company would receive no notice of the of the insured's death until the contestable period had expired. The clause described in this paragraph is more favorable to the insured than the usual clauses since, if he or she survives the first year, the policy becomes incontestable at that time, and if he or she does not, the company's rights are no greater than they would have been under the typical clause. Note, however, that some companies limit the contestability of their policies to one year, whether or not the insured survives the period.

MATTERS EXCLUDED FROM INCONTESTABLE CLAUSE

Nonpayment of Premiums

The original incontestable clause excluded nonpayment of premiums from its operation, and the practice has continued to the present. This exception is not only superfluous today, but it has also created confusion as to the applicability of the clause to matters not specifically excluded. Payment of the first premium, or the first installment of the first premium, is a consideration of the life insurance contract and is usually made a condition precedent. Unless this requirement is satisfied, there is no contract and hence no incontestable clause. If subsequent premiums are not paid, the contract does not fail as of its inception and may, in fact, continue in force under the nonforfeiture provisions.

This has not always been the case, however, and there was probably some justification for the inclusion of the exception in the original clause. Early policies contained no surrender values, and default in premium, even years after policy's issue, resulted in avoidance of the contract from its inception. It is clear, though, that the termination or modification of a modern policy through nonpayment of premiums is not a contest of the policy. When an insurer denies a claim based on nonpayment of premiums it is, in fact, declaring the insurance contract valid and attempting to enforce one of the contract's terms—specifically the contract's requirement that the insurer's obligation to pay is conditioned on the policyowner's payment of premiums. Nevertheless, the historical precedent and the requirements of state statutes have made the exception a fixture.

The express exclusion of nonpayment of premium (and a few other conditions) from the operation of the incontestable clause has caused a minority of courts to apply the doctrine of *expressio unius est exclusio alterius*[17] to a company's attempts to avoid liability under other provisions of the policy. Under such a doctrine, if a particular hazard is not specifically excluded from the operation of the clause, a claim arising from that hazard cannot be avoided beyond the contestable period. This view arises from the idea that the incontestable clause precludes the insurer from disputing the *obligations* under the valid contract as well as disputing the validity of the contract.

For example, assume that the policy contains an incontestable clause that says, "This policy shall be incontestable after it has been in force during the lifetime of the insured, for a period of 2 years from the issue date, except for nonpayment of premiums." Assume that the policy also contains a war hazard exclusion clause. Since the incontestable clause refers to nonpayment of premiums as a permissible reason for contesting the policy but does not refer to the war hazard clause, a minority of courts prohibit the insurer from applying the war hazard exclusion if the insured dies after the time limit prescribed in the incontestable clause.

Disability and Accidental Death Benefits

Sometimes an insurer may wish to exclude policy provisions or policy riders relating to disability and accidental death benefits from the operation of the incontestable clause. A typical clause containing these exclusions might read as follows: "This policy shall be incontestable after it shall have been in force for 2 years from its date of issue except for nonpayment of premiums and except as to provisions relating to benefits payable in the event of total and permanent disability and provisions that grant additional insurance specifically against death by accident."

If the courts could be relied upon to interpret the incontestable clause in accordance with its basic objective of protecting third-party beneficiaries, it would be unnecessary to specifically exclude disability and accidental death benefits from its scope. Unfortunately, the courts have had some difficulty in distinguishing between a contest involving the validity of the policy and one relating to the coverage of an admittedly valid policy. The distinction is a critical one in connection with disability and accidental death provisions since it is frequently difficult to determine whether a claim filed under one of these provisions is valid. In order to avoid any possible conflict with the incontestable clause in adjudicating such claims, some companies keep the provisions entirely outside the operation of the clause. Under the type of clause cited above, the *validity* of the provisions relating to disability and double indemnity can be attacked at any time, even after the expiration of the contestable period.

The general rule is that unless there is a specific exception in the policy's incontestable clause, the disability and accidental death provisions are included within the incontestable clause. However, insurers may draft policy language that excludes those provisions from the scope of the incontestable clause. If such an exclusion exists, a majority of courts have upheld it, although many other courts have held otherwise.

The exclusion of disability benefits from the protection of the incontestable clause is not in conflict with the intent of the clause. The purpose of the clause is to forestall a contest over the contract's validity after the insured is dead and cannot defend the representations he or she made in the application for insurance. Disability claims are filed during the lifetime of the insured, who can defend his or her actions, both at the time the policy was applied for and at the time of the claim.

RELATIONSHIP TO OTHER POLICY PROVISIONS

Excepted Hazards

At one time it was the view of the courts and the state insurance departments that once the contestable period had expired, no denial of liability on the grounds of lack of coverage could be sustained unless the hazard involved in the litigation was specifically excluded in the incontestable clause itself. Moreover, no hazard could be excluded from the scope of the incontestable clause unless the exclusion was recognized in the statute governing the clause.[18]

This doctrine was attacked when the superintendent of insurance of the state of New York refused to approve a proposed aviation exclusion in a Metropolitan Life Insurance Company policy on the grounds that the exclusion was in conflict with the New York statute prescribing the substance of the incontestable clause. The superintendent's decision was appealed to the courts, and the issue was resolved in the *Conway* decision. The New York Court of Appeals ruled that there was nothing in the law that prohibited the issuance of such a restricted policy. The decision declared that the New York statute requiring an incontestable clause "is not a mandate as to coverage, a definition of hazards to be borne by the insurer. It means only this, that within the limits of the coverage, the policy shall stand, unaffected by any defense that it was invalid in its inception, or thereafter became invalid by reason of a condition broken . . . [Where] there has been no assumption of risk, there can be no liability . . ."[19]

Following the *Conway* decision, the various insurance commissioners reversed their rulings on the inclusion of aviation riders. Today it is the accepted view that a company may exclude any hazard that it does not wish to cover.

In general, the right to limit coverage has been invoked only with respect to aeronautical activities, military and naval service in time of war, and suicide. With advances in aeronautics, the aviation exclusion has lost most of its significance, and with few exceptions war clauses are not currently being added to policies. However, some insurers insert war clauses in new policies being sold to persons likely to be involved in a military action, such as the joint effort with the United Nations to get Iraqi troops out of Kuwait and the peace-keeping mission in Somalia. Once policies have been issued with such an exclusion, the clause remains part of the contract as long as it is kept in force. Limitations on the coverage of suicide, however, are contained in all policies.

Since the *Conway* decision, insurance companies could undoubtedly exclude death from suicide throughout the duration of the contract unless prohibited by statute. They feel, however, that it is a risk that they should properly assume, and their only concern is that they not be exposed to the risk of issuing policies to persons contemplating suicide. Consequently, they exclude death from suicide, whether the insured be sane or insane, for the first year or two after issue of the policy, with the risk thereafter being assumed in its entirety by the company. If the insured does commit suicide during the period of restricted coverage, the company's liability is limited to a refund of the premiums paid.

While the suicide exclusion is normally of the same duration as the contestable period, the suicide clause is independent of the incontestable clause. Since most suicide exclusions are of 2 years' duration and some policies are contestable for only one year, a conflict could develop if the insured commits suicide during the second year of the contract. With few exceptions, the courts have upheld the company's right to deny coverage of suicide beyond the contestable period.

Conditions Precedent

The incontestable clause is a part of the policy and cannot become effective until the policy has gone into force. There must be a contract before there can be an incontestable clause. Therefore the incontestable clause does not bar a defense that the policy was never approved by the insurance company.[20]

On principle, it would seem that if a policy provides that it will not become effective until certain conditions have been fulfilled, there would be no contract at all until those conditions had been satisfied. Hence the incontestable clause itself, as part of the contract, would not be operative. This would suggest that the incontestable clause should not prevent the insurer from denying liability on the grounds that the applicant was not in good health at the time the policy was delivered or that some other condition precedent was not fulfilled. However, most of the courts have reached the conclusion that the delivery-in-good-health requirement and other such conditions precedent should be accorded the same treatment as representations. Since the incontestable clause was designed to deal with misrepresentations, it follows therefore that the clause should bar suits based on nonfulfillment of conditions precedent if, at any time, both of the parties had treated the policy as having been operative.[21] This is the rule in most jurisdictions.

Misstatement of Age (or Sex)

Most life insurance policies contain a provision that stipulates that in the event of a misstatement of age (or sex), the amount payable under the policy will be such as would have been purchased at the correct age (or sex) by the premium actually paid. In most states a provision to this effect with respect to age misstatements is required by statute. In jurisdictions where the provision is mandatory, no conflict with the incontestable clause can arise. Even where the clause is not a matter of statute, the right of the company to reduce the amount of insurance (even after the contestable period has expired) has seldom been questioned. This is undoubtedly due to the fact that the misstatement-of-age (or sex) adjustment was firmly established before any controversy developed over the right of a company to limit the coverage of a policy beyond the contestable period. If it had been held that misstatement-of-age (or sex) adjustments were subject to the incontestable clause, insurance companies would probably have found it necessary to require proof of age (or sex) before issuing a policy.

A misstatement of age that contravenes a company's underwriting rules may, at the company's option, serve as a basis for rescission. It has been held, however, that such action has to be taken during the contestable period.[22] If the misstatement is discovered beyond the contestable period, it can still be dealt with in the conventional manner.

Reformation

It sometimes happens that a life insurance policy in the form issued by the company does not represent the actual agreement between the company and the applicant. This may be due to simple clerical errors, such as a misspelled name or an incorrect date, or to more substantial mistakes, such as an incorrect premium, wrong face amount, inappropriate set of surrender values, or incorrect set of settlement options. The mistake may favor either the insured or the company. The overwhelming majority of such mistakes are rectified without any controversy or litigation. From time to time, however, a policyowner will oppose the correction of a mistake in his or her favor. In one such case, the policy actually applied for and issued was an ordinary life contract, but through a printer's error, the surrender values shown in the contract were those for a 20-year endowment insurance policy.[23] The company discovered the error 2 months after the policy was issued but had to resort to legal action to rewrite the contract.

The appropriate legal action in such circumstances is a suit for reformation of the contract. This is an equitable remedy under which the written instrument is made to conform to the intention of the parties.[24] The party seeking relief must establish that there was either a mutual mistake in drafting the written instrument[25] or a mistake on one side and fraud on the other.

The remedy of reformation is clearly available to an insurance company during the contestable period. Moreover, it has long been the rule that reformation to correct a clerical error is not barred by the incontestable clause. A suit to rectify a mistake "is not a contest of the policy but a prayer to make a written instrument speak the real agreement of the parties."[26]

Reinstatement

All life insurance policies contain a provision permitting reinstatement in the event of lapse, subject to certain conditions. One of the conditions is usually evidence of insurability satisfactory to the company. Reinstatement will almost always necessitate a statement by the insured as to the current status of his or her health and will frequently involve a complete medical examination. It will also involve aspects of insurability other than health, just as at the time of original issue. A question arises about the legal effect of a misrepresentation or concealment in the reinstatement application not discovered until after the policy has been reinstated. Specifically, can a reinstated policy be rescinded after the original contestable period has expired?

If the incontestable clause specifically refers to a reinstatement of the policy, the language of the clause will control. For example, assume the clause provides that "this policy shall be incontestable after it has been in force during the lifetime of the insured, for a period of 2 years from the issue date or the date of its last reinstatement." In this event, the contract's reinstatement should begin a new 2-year contestable period. The insurer's renewed right to contest is applicable only to information provided in the reinstatement application.

When the incontestability clause does not refer to a reinstatement, there are conflicting views. One view, greatly in the minority, holds that the concept of incontestability does not apply to the reinstatement process.[27] Under this view, a suit for rescission or a defense against a claim is subject only to the conventional statute of limitations on fraud—which begins to run only *after the fraud has been discovered.*

At the other extreme, and also in the minority, is the view that the reinstatement clause is subject to the original incontestable clause.[28] If the original period of contestability has expired before the application for reinstatement is submitted, the reinstated policy is incontestable from the date of reinstatement. If a policy is reinstated during the original period of contestability, the reinstated policy can be contested during the remaining portion of the contestable period.

The majority opinion adopts a middle ground and holds that a reinstated policy is contestable for the same period of time as is prescribed in the original incontestable clause.[29] If the policy was originally contestable for a period of 2 years, the reinstated policy is again contestable for the same length of time. This is true even when the policy is lapsed and reinstated before the original period of contestability has expired. The reasoning is that the company needs the same period of time in which to detect any fraud in the application for reinstatement as it needed in connection with the original issue. It is hardly necessary to add that the policy becomes contestable again only with respect to the information supplied in the reinstatement process. In other words, the company does not have the right to question the validity of the contract on the grounds of irregularities in the original application.

NOTES

1. H. M. Horne and D. B. Mansfield, *The Life Insurance Contract*, 2d ed. (New York: Life Office Management Association, 1948), p. 181.
2. *Kansas Mutual Life Insurance Co. v. Whitehead*, 123 Ky. 21, 26, 93 S.W. 609, 610 (1906).
3. Muriel L. Crawford and William T. Beadles, *Law and the Life Insurance Contract*, 6th ed. (Homewood, IL: Irwin Professional Publishing, 1989), p. 419.
4. Horne and Mansfield, *The Life Insurance Contract*, p. 181.
5. *Kansas Mutual Life Insurance Co. v. Whitehead*, 123 Ky. 21, 26, 93 S.W. 609, 610 (1906).
6. Critics of this analogy point out that (1) the usual statute of limitations begins to run from the time the fraud is discovered, whereas under the incontestable clause, the period runs from the beginning of the contract, and (2) the typical statute of limitations applies to actions and not to defenses such as those invoked by life insurance companies during the period of contestability. See Benjamin L. Holland, "The Incontestable Clause," in Harry Krueger and Leland T. Waggoner (eds.), *The Life Insurance Policy Contract* (Boston: Little, Brown & Co., 1953), p. 58. These critics are content to identify the incontestable clause as a constituent part of the contract and peculiar to a life insurance policy.
7. *Maslin v. Columbian National Life Insurance Co.*, 3 F. Supp. 368, 369 (S.D.N.Y. 1932).
8. *Columbian Mutual Life Insurance Co. v. Martin*, 175 Tenn. 517, 136 S.W. 2d 52 (1940).
9. See Holland, "The Incontestable Clause," p. 68, n. 27, for citations.
10. *Ibid.*, p. 69 and citations in n. 31.
11. *Scarborough v. American National Insurance Co.*, 171 N.C. 353, 88 S.E. 482 (1916); *Murphy v. Metropolitan Life Insurance Co.*, 152 Ga. 393, 110 S.E. 178 (1921).
12. *Afro-American Life Insurance Co. v. Jones*, 113 Fla. 158, 151 So. 405 (1933).
13. *Stean v. Occidental Life Insurance Co.*, 24 N.M. 346, 350, 171 Pac. 786, 787 (1918).
14. There is some case law to the effect that the last day when a contest can be made is, in the case of a 2-year contestable provision, the second anniversary of the date of issue, rather than the day thereafter. These rulings were made with respect to policies that state that the policy is contestable for 2 years after the date of issue.
15. *Monahan v. Metropolitan Life Insurance Co.*, 283 Ill. 136, 119 N.E. 68 (1918).
16. *Massachusetts Mutual Life Insurance Co. v. Goodelman*, 160 F. Supp. 510 (E.D.N.Y. 1958).
17. "The enumeration of some is the exclusion of others," usually paraphrased as "enumeration implies exclusion."
18. This is still the case.
19. *Metropolitan Life Insurance Co. v. Conway*, 252 N.Y. 449, 452, 169 N.E. 642 (1930).
20. *McDonald v. Mutual Life Insurance Co. of New York*, 108 F. 2d 32 (6th Cir. 1939); *Harris v. Travelers Insurance Co.*, 80 F. (2d) 127 (5th Cir. 1935).
21. See Holland, "The Incontestable Clause", p. 64, n. 10, for citations.
22. *Kelly v. Prudential Insurance Co.*, 334 Pa. 143, 6 A. 2d 55 (1939).
23. *Columbian National Life Insurance Co. v. Black*, 35 F. 2d 571 (10th Cir. 1929).
24. The introduction of oral testimony is permitted in such cases, notwithstanding the fact that in so doing, the terms of the written instrument are changed. This is an exception to the parol evidence rule.
25. In this connection, it is held that knowledge by one party of the other's mistake is equivalent to a mutual mistake.

26. *Columbian National Life Insurance Co. v. Black,* 35 F. 2d 571, 577 (10th Cir. 1929). There are numerous later cases, 7 ALR 2d 504 (1949).

27. *Acacia Mutual Life Assn. v. Kaul,* 114 N.J. Eq. 491, 169 Atl. 36 (Ch. 1933); *Chuz v. Columbian National Life Insurance Co.,* 10 N.J. Misc. 1145, 162 Atl. 395 (Cir. Ct. 1932).

28. See Holland, "The Incontestable Clause," p. 78, n. 2, for citations. See also *Chavis v. Southern Ins. Co.,* 318 N.C. 259, 347 S.E. 2d 425 (1986).

29. *Ibid.,* p. 78, n. 3. *Sellwood v. Equitable Life Insurance Co. of Iowa,* 230 Minn. 529, 42 N.W. 2d 346 (1950).

41

The Beneficiary (Part 1)

Dan M. McGill
Revised by Burke A. Christensen

The beneficiary is the person, trust, or other entity named in the life insurance contract to receive all or a portion of the proceeds payable at maturity. The section of the contract dealing with the designation and rights of the beneficiary is in many respects the most significant one in the entire contract. It reflects the insured's decisions concerning the disposition of his or her human life value. It is the means by which the insured provides family financial security after he or she dies. In a well-planned estate, the beneficiary designations will be integrated with the election of a settlement option in the most effective way to carry out the insured's objectives.

There are many facets to a study of the beneficiary in life insurance, and the starting point is a description of the various categories of beneficiaries and beneficiary designations. Emphasis is placed on customary situations and policy provisions, and the student is cautioned that any particular case is decided on the basis of its own facts and the policy wording involved.

TYPES OF BENEFICIARIES

Beneficiaries can be classified from various points of view. For the purposes of this discussion, they will be classified as to

- nature of the interest
- manner of identification
- priority of entitlement
- revocability of the designation

Nature of the Interest

From the standpoint of the interest involved, beneficiaries fall into two broad categories:

- the estate of the *insured*
- a *third-party beneficiary*—an entity or person or persons other than the insured (the policyowner and the insurance company are the first and second parties to the contract)

The Estate of the Insured

The insured is normally designated as the person to receive the proceeds of an endowment insurance policy or a retirement income policy because those policies are designed primarily to provide benefits to the policyowner. The insured may designate someone else to receive the proceeds in the event of his or her death or may specify that the proceeds be payable to his or her estate. Proceeds are usually made payable to the estate only for a purpose associated with the settlement of the estate, such as the payment of last-illness and funeral expenses, debts, mortgages, and taxes. If any proceeds remain after the claims against the estate have been satisfied, they are distributed in accordance with the decedent's will or the appropriate intestate law.

Payment to the insured's estate is generally unwise because it exposes the proceeds to transfer costs and taxes that can otherwise be avoided. It is also considered highly undesirable to have the policy proceeds payable to the insured's estate when it is intended that they should go to certain specific individuals. The proceeds will be subject to estate administration and may be reduced through probate costs, taxes, and the claims of creditors. Moreover, distribution to the intended beneficiaries will be delayed until settlement of the estate has been completed.

When it is intended that the proceeds be paid to the insured's estate and be subject to the control of the executor or administrator, as the case may be, the proper designation is "the executors or administrators of the insured." If the policy involved is an endowment or a retirement income policy and the proceeds are to be paid to the insured if he or she survives to the date of maturity and to his or her estate if the insured does not survive, the proper designation is "insured, if living; otherwise to his or her executors or administrators." The simple designation "insured's estate" is effective, but such terms as "heirs," "legal heirs," or "family" are not because when those terms are used, the proceeds do not become part of the probate estate. The appropriate intestate law is followed in determining the legal heirs, who receive the proceeds directly, being treated as named beneficiaries, rather than heirs. In other words, the proceeds pass outside the probate estate.

When the insured is the applicant and designates himself or herself as beneficiary, the insured can exercise all rights under the policy without the consent of any other person. The policy is the insured's property and can be dealt with like any other property.

Third-party Beneficiary

There are three general types of third-party beneficiaries:

- the owner-applicant
- a donee or gratuitous beneficiary
- a creditor or a person who has furnished valuable consideration in exchange for the designation

When one person procures insurance on another person's life and becomes the owner of the policy, he or she is known as the owner-applicant. Ordinarily the owner will designate himself or herself as beneficiary, although it is not inconceivable that he or she would direct that the proceeds be paid to someone else, particularly in the event that he or she predeceases the insured. This type of arrangement is typically used with key-man insurance and business-continuation agreements, but it is by no means confined to such situations. It may be used by a creditor to protect his or her interest or by a family group to provide estate liquidity and minimize death taxes.

From the standpoint of ownership rights, the third-party owner occupies the same position as the insured who designates himself or herself as beneficiary. There is a difference, but it is of no legal significance: The insured owns his or her policy because he or she is the only party involved, while a third-party owner has his or her rights established by an express provision in the contract. The third-party applicant, like every other applicant, must have an insurable interest in the insured at the inception of the contract. There need be no insurable interest at the date of the insured's death; the third-party owner, or the beneficiary of his or her choice, is entitled to retain the full amount of the proceeds.

The second type of third-party beneficiary is the person who has furnished no consideration. Technically, this person is known as the *donee* or *gratuitous* beneficiary. In typical situations the insured designates a member of his or her family as beneficiary for no consideration other than "love and affection." It is not necessary for the donee beneficiary to have an insurable interest, although he or she usually does. Unless a specific notation is made to the contrary, the discussion in the succeeding pages is directed at the donee beneficiary.

The third type of third-party beneficiary is the person who has furnished a valuable consideration in exchange for the designation. A creditor may be designated as beneficiary under a policy on his or her debtor's life, although it is much more common for the policy to be collaterally assigned to the creditor. In either event, the creditor is permitted to retain only that portion of the proceeds equal to his or her interest at the time of the debtor's death. During the insured's lifetime, the creditor can exercise no rights in the policy without the insured's consent or joinder. Occasionally, a spouse is designated as beneficiary under a policy as part of a divorce settlement. The spouse's rights in the policy proceeds depend on the terms of the settlement if the insurer has notice of the settlement. The designation is usually irrevocable or, if revocable, can be changed only by an appropriate court order.

Manner of Identification

Classified by identification, beneficiaries may be termed *specific* or *class*. A specific beneficiary is an individual who is designated by name or in any other manner that clearly sets him or her apart from any other individual. A class beneficiary is a person not mentioned by name who belongs to a clearly identifiable *group* of persons designated as beneficiaries.

Specific Designation

In making specific designations, it is customary to identify the person both by *name* and *relationship* to the insured if there is a legal or blood relationship. For example, a son would be designated "Charles William Doe, son of the insured."

A wife would be designated "Mary Smith Doe, wife of the insured." Preferably the full name—first name, middle name, and surname—should be given. If the designated beneficiary is the insured's wife, her maiden name should also be included to prevent confusion and litigation in the event that there is be an antecedent or subsequent wife with the same first name. It invites litigation to designate the insured's spouse simply as "husband" or "wife." If the insured has married more than once, there is likely to be controversy as to whether the designation refers to the person who was married to the insured at the time the designation was made or the spouse who was married to him or her at the time of the insured's death.

The relationship accompanying the name in a beneficiary designation is regarded as descriptive only and not as a statement of entitlement. If a beneficiary is identifiable by name or otherwise, he or she is still entitled to the policy proceeds even though the stated relationship to the insured is no longer applicable—or never was. For example, if a man purchases a policy prior to his marriage and designates his fiancee by name as beneficiary, describing her as his wife, his death prior to their marriage does not deprive his fiancee of the policy proceeds. Nor does an invalid marriage have any effect on the beneficiary's entitlement.

Class Designation

A class designation is appropriate whenever the insured desires that the proceeds be divided equally among the members of a particular group, the composition of which may not be definitely fixed at the time of designation. Examples of such groups are children, grandchildren, brothers, sisters, or heirs. Perhaps the most common class designation is "children of the insured." This type of class designation is especially favored for the designation of secondary or contingent beneficiaries. It may also be used in combination with a specific designation—for example, when the insured designates living children by name and then adds "and any other surviving children born of the marriage of the insured and John Doe, husband of the insured."

From the standpoint of the law, class designations are entirely proper. Courts have repeatedly sustained the validity of such designations. From a practical standpoint, however, class designations present the problem of identifying the members of the class. No class designation is entirely free of possible complications. Even the simplest designations can cause difficulties. For example, the designation "children of the insured" seems to circumscribe the class precisely enough to permit ready identification. In discharging its responsibilities under such a designation, however, the insurance company has to determine whether the insured was also survived by any illegitimate children, children by a previous marriage or marriages, or adopted children. If the surviving children are adults, there is always the possibility that one of them has severed normal ties with the family. His or her whereabouts may be unknown to the other members of the family and perhaps even his or her existence denied or concealed by them.

Even the designation "children born of the marriage of the insured and Mary Smith Doe, wife of the insured," while quite precise, does not indicate whether adopted children of the marriage should be accorded the same status as natural children. For the sake of clarity and to avoid possible litigation, therefore, some designations include a statement that the word "children" will be construed to include adopted children.

Similarly, the use of the term "heirs" in a beneficiary designation makes it necessary for the insurance company to refer to previous court rulings as to the meaning of the term in the jurisdiction involved or, lacking these, to seek court interpretation. The company will then have to identify and locate the heirs. The perils to the company are so great that many companies will not even accept the designation "heirs."

When either the insured or the insured's spouse has children by a previous marriage, a class designation must be carefully worded to carry out the insured's intentions. The insured may wish to provide for all his or her children and those of his or her spouse by the spouse's former marriage, or the insured may want to confine his or her bounty to the children of the insured's current marriage. If the insured specifies that the proceeds are to be paid to "my children" or "children of the insured," the insured's children by any marriage would be included, but the children of the insured's spouse by a previous marriage would be excluded. On the other hand, by speaking, for example, of "my wife, Mary Smith Doe, and our children," the insured is not only excluding his wife's children by her former marriage but also any children he may have had by an earlier marriage and any he may have by a subsequent marriage.

Most companies today restrict the use of class designations. At best they lead to delays in settling death claims. At worst, they involve considerable trouble and expense for the company and possibly even multiple payment of some claims. Insurance companies, therefore, will not accept designations of a class whose relationship to the insured is remote or whose composition will be difficult of determination. Moreover, when the class is acceptable, it must be described as precisely as possible. All insurance companies, for example, permit the designation of children as a class. This protects the interests of unborn children. Otherwise, many children would be deprived of insurance protection through failure of the insured to revise his or her settlement plan after the birth of an additional child or children.

Priority of Entitlement

Primary and Contingent Beneficiaries

With respect to priority of entitlement, beneficiaries may be classified as *primary* and *contingent*. A primary beneficiary has the first claim to the insurance policy proceeds if the conditions on which they are payable are fulfilled. There may be two or more primary beneficiaries, in which event they will share the proceeds in the proportion specified by the insured. It is not implicit in such an arrangement that the beneficiaries share equally in the proceeds, except as to the members of a class. Class beneficiaries do share equally in the proceeds since, without mentioning names, it is impracticable to provide disproportionate shares. Any one of a group of primary beneficiaries, whether specifically named or designated as a class, therefore, enjoys rights in the policy equal to those of any other beneficiary.

The contingent beneficiary, frequently called the *secondary* beneficiary, has a claim to the proceeds that ripens only on the death or removal of the primary beneficiary. A contingent beneficiary is a person or organization that takes the place of the primary beneficiary if the primary beneficiary predeceases the insured or loses his or her entitlement in some other manner before receiving any proceeds. With the increased use of installment settlement plans, however, the contingent beneficiary has assumed importance in another role—namely, to receive the benefits under an installment option payable beyond the death of the primary beneficiary. In this role, the contingent beneficiary can become entitled to benefits even though the primary beneficiary survives the insured. This function is important in connection with the interest option, installment time option, installment amount option, and guaranteed installments under life income options.

The two functions of the contingent beneficiary are quite distinctive, and his or her rights thereunder are quite different. Under the original concept, the contingent beneficiary becomes the primary beneficiary on the death of the primary beneficiary during the insured's lifetime—subject, of course, to being divested of that position by the insured. The contingent beneficiary thus succeeds to all the rights of the original primary beneficiary, including those arising under the provisions for optional settlement. Upon the death of the insured, he or she is regarded as a "first taker" beneficiary, with all that this status implies under company settlement option practices. He or she might be given the right to take the proceeds in a lump sum, to elect a settlement option, or to designate contingent beneficiaries to receive any benefits unpaid at the time of his or her death.

At the death of the insured, proceeds payable in a lump sum vest immediately in the primary beneficiary (in the absence of a delay clause), and the interest of the contingent beneficiary or beneficiaries is terminated. If the primary beneficiary dies after the insured but before receiving a check from the insurance company, the proceeds go to the primary beneficiary's estate, not to the contingent beneficiary. If the proceeds are payable under an installment option, the contingent beneficiary becomes entitled to the benefits at the primary beneficiary's death. The contingent beneficiary is a "second taker" beneficiary, however, and under the practices of most companies has to take the proceeds under the distribution pattern prescribed for the primary beneficiary. In other words, a "second taker" contingent beneficiary is not usually permitted to commute the unpaid installments or to elect to have them paid out under a settlement arrangement different from that in effect for the primary beneficiary.

There may be, and usually are, two or more contingent beneficiaries. The typical insured designates his or her spouse as primary beneficiary and his or her children, by name or as a class, as contingent beneficiaries. For a lump-sum distribution, the designation might read, "Mary Smith Doe, wife of the insured, if she survives the insured; otherwise in equal shares to the surviving children of the insured." If the proceeds are to be distributed under an installment option, a more complex designation is necessary.

Levels of Contingent Beneficiaries

There may be various degrees of contingent beneficiaries, each successive level having a lower order of entitlement to the proceeds. Thus there may be first contingent, second contingent, and third contingent beneficiaries.[1] Two levels of contingent beneficiaries are provided for in the following designation: "Mary Smith Doe, wife of the insured, if she survives the insured; otherwise in equal shares to the surviving children, if any, of the insured; otherwise to Harry Doe, father of the insured, if he survives the insured." If the proceeds are to be paid out under an installment option, the agreement usually specifies that any installments remaining unpaid at the death of the last surviving contingent beneficiary will be paid in a lump sum to that beneficiary's estate. This obviates the necessity of reopening the insured's estate to receive the unpaid installments, which—if one or two levels of contingent beneficiaries have died—might precipitate a series of estate reopenings, with considerable expense and little benefit. Many persons designate an educational institution, hospital, or religious organization as the last contingent or ultimate contingent beneficiary.

Right of Revocation

Under modern practice, the identification of a beneficiary in the policy application may be unilaterally changed by the policyowner. If so, the designation is referred to as *revocable* and the designee as the *revocable beneficiary*. In some situations, the beneficiary designation may be changed, but only with the beneficiary's consent. If the insured does not have the unilateral right to change the beneficiary, the designation is properly described as *irrevocable* and the designee as the *irrevocable beneficiary*. This distinction is so significant that a word on the historical development of the concept of revocability seems warranted. Note, however, that the right to change the beneficiary must be included in the application or in the policy. Otherwise the initial designation is irrevocable.

Historical Development

Early life insurance contracts in the United States made no provision for a change of beneficiary. The insured simply entered into a contract with the insurance company that upon his or her death, the company would pay a specified sum of money to the person designated as beneficiary—usually the insured's spouse. Since there were no surrender values or other prematurity rights of significance to the insured, the person entitled to receive the death proceeds was regarded to be the owner of the policy. One of the early students of American insurance law had the following to say about the interest of the beneficiary:

> We apprehend the general rule to be that a policy, and the money to become due under it, belong the moment it is issued to the person or persons named in it as the beneficiary or beneficiaries, and that there is no power in the person procuring the insurance by any act of his or hers, by deed or by will, to transfer to any other person the interest of the person named.[2]

In 1888, the United States Supreme Court defined the interest of the beneficiary in substantially the same terms.[3]

In consonance with this concept of policy ownership by the beneficiary, the majority of the early court decisions held that the death of the beneficiary before the insured did not terminate his or her interest.[4] That is, the insured was not permitted to designate a substitute beneficiary; at his or her death, the proceeds were payable to the estate of the beneficiary originally named in the policy.

Around the turn of the century, some of the larger companies adopted the practice of including a provision in their policies that permitted the insured to substitute a new beneficiary even during the original beneficiary's lifetime, provided the policyowner had specifically reserved the right. Moreover, the change could be effected without the consent of the beneficiary. There was some doubt as to the validity of this practice until the standard forms that grew out of the Armstrong investigation of 1905 and 1906 and became statutory (or compulsory) in New York on January 1, 1907, included a change of beneficiary clause. This clause was supplemented shortly thereafter by another that stipulated that the beneficiary's interest, whether revocable or irrevocable, would terminate upon his or her death during the insured's lifetime, with such interest reverting to the insured. The designation of a contingent beneficiary to succeed to the interest of a deceased primary beneficiary was the next logical development.

Status of the Revocable Beneficiary

For some time after the validity of a reserved right to change the beneficiary had become well recognized, the revocable beneficiary was generally regarded to have a vested interest in the policy that could be defeated only by the exercise of the insured's right to revoke the designation. This view became known as the defeasible vested interest concept. Under that concept it was believed that the beneficiary's consent was necessary to the exercise of any policy rights by the insured other than the right to change the beneficiary. For example, the insured could not surrender or assign the policy, make a policy loan, or elect a settlement option without the consent of the beneficiary. Yet there was nothing to prevent the insured from revoking the beneficiary designation and then exercising the various policy rights and privileges.

During the last quarter century court after court has rejected the defeasible vested interest theory in favor of a more practical rule that considerably simplifies the administration of policy rights. The modern rule holds that a revocable beneficiary's interest is at most a mere expectancy that is subject to every other interest created by the insured and to every policy right or privilege exercisable by the policyowner alone. Under this concept the beneficiary's consent is not needed for the policyowner's exercise of any policy right or privilege.

The interest of a revocable beneficiary, such as it is, terminates upon his or her death during the insured's lifetime because of the reversionary clause referred to above. This is true even though there is no contingent beneficiary and the insured has failed to appoint a successor beneficiary. Thus the nature of the revocable beneficiary's interest comes into sharper focus. A revocable beneficiary has no enforceable rights in the policy prior to maturity and cannot interfere in any way with the exercise by the insured of his or her rights in the policy. The revocable beneficiary has an "expectancy" in the proceeds that will materialize only if *all* of the following conditions are fulfilled:

- The policy remains in force until the death of the insured.
- The beneficiary designation remains unchanged.

- The policy is not assigned.
- The beneficiary outlives the insured.

Despite the fulfillment of these conditions, the beneficiary's interest can be greatly impaired through policy loans negotiated by the insured.

On the positive side, the insured's right to revoke a beneficiary designation is extinguished at the insured's death, and the interest of the revocable beneficiary vests absolutely at that point. The beneficiary's interest in the proceeds is, of course, subject to any operative deferred settlement agreement.

There are circumstances under which an insured who has reserved the right to change the beneficiary will not be permitted to exercise that right. This would be the case, for example, if the policy were subject to a collateral assignment agreement. Similarly, when a spouse is designated beneficiary of a policy under an agreement made in contemplation of divorce, or when—by court order—an insured is directed to designate his or her divorced spouse as beneficiary of a policy intended to serve as security for alimony payments or in lieu of such payments, the right to change the beneficiary is relinquished.[5] In all such circumstances, the insurance company would permit a change of beneficiary if it had received no notice of the limitation on the insured's right.

Status of the Irrevocable Beneficiary

It is well settled that whenever the insured designates a particular person as the irrevocable beneficiary of a policy, the beneficiary acquires a vested interest in the contract. The exact nature of the interest depends on the terms of the contract.

At one time, an irrevocable beneficiary designation could equal co-ownership of the policy. If there were no conditions under which the beneficiary could be deprived of the right to receive the full amount of proceeds payable under the terms of the policy, that interest would be vested absolutely or unconditionally, and the beneficiary would be regarded as the sole owner of the policy. He or she could exercise all policy rights without the joinder of the insured and would even have the right to pay premiums to keep the policy in force. The insured would have no rights in the policy and, consequently, could do nothing with the contract without the beneficiary's consent that would in any way diminish or adversely affect the beneficiary's right to receive, at the insured's death, the full amount of insurance provided by the policy. If the beneficiary predeceased the insured, his or her interest in the policy would become a part of the beneficiary's estate, and his or her heirs would be entitled to the proceeds upon the policy's maturity.

Such absolute vesting is not common in modern policies. Most policies today provide that the interest of a beneficiary, even one irrevocably designated, terminates if the beneficiary's death occurs during the lifetime of the insured. In that event, all rights to the policy proceeds revert to the insured. This is sometimes called a *reversionary* irrevocable designation. Under this type of designation the interest of the irrevocable beneficiary is only conditionally vested. There is a condition—namely, the beneficiary's death before maturity of the policy—that can destroy his or her interest.

Since the insured can reacquire ownership rights in the contract's death benefit through the death of the beneficiary during his or her lifetime, the insured possesses a contingent interest in the policy's death benefit from the beginning. Thus in the usual circumstances, neither the insured nor the irrevocable beneficiary can exercise any policy rights or dispose of the policy without the consent of the other. For all intents and purposes, the insured and the beneficiary are regarded as joint owners of the policy when the beneficiary designation is irrevocable.

It is possible for an insured to procure a policy under which he or she does not reserve the right to change the beneficiary but does retain all other normal policy privileges.[6] In this case, even though the insured can diminish the beneficiary's interest in such a policy or destroy it completely by surrender, the insured cannot revoke the beneficiary's interest, such as it may be, and give it to another without the beneficiary's consent. As courts have pointed out, the terms and conditions of the policy are determinative of the rights of the insured and the interest of the beneficiary. In the majority of policies issued today, however, there are no specific conditions that would permit the insured to impair or destroy the interest of an irrevocably designated beneficiary.

Irrevocable beneficiary designations are not widely used. An irrevocable beneficiary designation does offer the advantage of protecting the beneficiary's interest in the proceeds during his or her lifetime and automatically vesting complete ownership rights in the insured in the event that he or she survives the beneficiary, but the same result can be achieved by an absolute assignment or an appropriately worded ownership clause.

SUCCESSION IN INTEREST

Whenever there is only one beneficiary in a beneficiary classification (primary, first contingent, and so forth), the interest of any beneficiary who predeceases the insured passes in the manner and according to the rules described in the preceding pages, unless the contract provides otherwise. Whenever there is more than one beneficiary in a beneficiary classification, however, a question arises as to the disposition of the interest of any beneficiary who dies before his or her interest materializes. The problem has frequently arisen with class designations, such as "my children," but it is equally relevant to multiple specific designations.

To pinpoint the problem, assume that A, the insured, names A's three children, B, C, and D, as primary beneficiaries of A's insurance, share and share alike, without designating any contingent beneficiaries and without specifying what the disposition should be of the share of any child who fails to survive him. Assume further that D predeceases A, leaving three children, E, F, and G. Who is entitled to D's share? (See figure 41-1.)

A policy provision on this point is controlling, but in the absence of a pertinent policy provision, D's interest might conceivably be disposed of in one of three ways. It might pass to A's estate, on the theory that where there are multiple designations, the interest of each beneficiary is severable and is contingent on the beneficiary's surviving the insured. The share might pass to B and C, on the theory that the designation of multiple beneficiaries creates a form of undivided interest, analogous to a joint tenancy, with right of survivorship. Finally, the share might pass to D's children, E, F, and G, on the theory that a primary beneficiary has a vested interest in the proceeds that cannot be defeated by his or her failure to survive the insured.

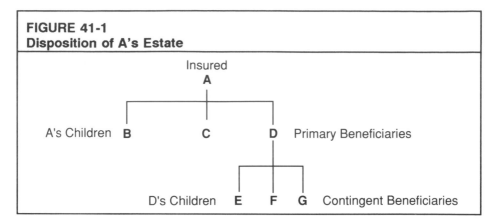

FIGURE 41-1
Disposition of A's Estate

The New York Rule and the Connecticut Rule

In the litigation that has developed around this question there has been no support for the view that a deceased beneficiary's interest should revert to the insured's estate, despite the fact that this would have been the outcome had the deceased beneficiary been the sole primary beneficiary. The majority of the decisions have followed the rule that the surviving beneficiaries of the classification to which the deceased beneficiary belonged are entitled to take the deceased beneficiary's share. In the example, therefore, B and C would be entitled to the full amount of proceeds. This doctrine is known as the New York Rule, since it was first espoused by the New York courts. From a practical standpoint, much can be said in favor of the rule. Most of the cases involve children, which means that if the deceased child's share were to revert to the insured's estate, it would ultimately be distributed to the surviving children—the other beneficiaries—reduced by its share of administration expenses and bequests to other persons, including the widow.

A substantial minority of the courts have followed the Connecticut Rule, which holds that the heirs of the deceased beneficiary are entitled to his or her share. In the above example, E, F, and G, therefore, would receive the proceeds to which D would have been entitled had D survived A. Each of D's children would receive one-ninth of the total proceeds; B and C would receive one-third each. This rule is in conflict with the prevailing view of a beneficiary's interest in a life insurance policy, but it reflects the desire of the jurists involved to carry out what they believe to be the insured's wishes.

Succession-in-Interest Clauses

In anticipation of this problem, many companies have incorporated a provision in their policies that—in the absence of contrary instructions from the insured—will control the disposition of the interest of any beneficiary who dies before becoming entitled to payment of his or her share of proceeds. This provision, commonly known as the succession-in-interest clause, is applicable to both primary and contingent beneficiaries and to beneficiaries designated irrevocably or revocably. A typical clause might appear as follows:

Succession in Interest of Beneficiaries

The proceeds of this policy whether payable in one sum or under a settlement option shall be payable in equal shares to such direct beneficiaries as survive to receive payment. The share of any direct beneficiary who dies before receiving payments due or to become due shall be payable in equal shares to such direct beneficiaries as survive to receive payment.

At the death of the last surviving direct beneficiary payments due or to become due shall be payable in equal shares to such contingent beneficiaries as survive to receive payment. The share of any contingent beneficiary who dies before receiving payments due or to become due shall be payable in equal shares to such contingent beneficiaries as survive to receive payment.

At the death of the last to survive of the direct and contingent beneficiaries:

(a) if no settlement option is in effect, any remaining proceeds shall be paid to the owner or to the executors, administrators, successors, or transferees of the owner; or

(b) if a settlement option is in effect, the withdrawal value of payments due or to become due shall be paid in one sum to the executors or administrators of the last to survive of the direct and contingent beneficiaries.

A direct or contingent beneficiary succeeding to an interest in a settlement option shall continue under such option, subject to its terms as stated in this policy, with the rights of transfer between options and of withdrawal under options as provided in this policy.

Note that this clause applies not only to the situations in which either a primary or a contingent beneficiary fails to survive the *insured,* but also to cases in which a contingent beneficiary fails to survive a *primary beneficiary.* The latter is important when proceeds are being paid out on an installment basis. If the proceeds are to be paid in a lump sum, specifying in the beneficiary designation that the proceeds will be paid only to those beneficiaries who survive the insured will solve the problem, provided this solution is in accord with the insured's wishes.

Per Stirpes

The disposition of deceased beneficiaries' interest envisioned by the succession-in-interest clause does not represent the desires of all policyowners. In designating their children as beneficiaries, many insureds want the share of a deceased beneficiary to go to the beneficiary's children, the insured's grandchildren. This can be accomplished by directing that the proceeds be distributed *per stirpes,* a Latin expression meaning "by the trunk." For example, in designating her husband as primary beneficiary and her children as contingent beneficiaries, an insured could use the following wording: "John Doe, husband of the insured, if he survives the insured; otherwise in equal shares to the surviving children of the insured, and to the surviving children of any deceased children of the insured, per stirpes." The expression "per stirpes" means that the deceased person's issue or lineal descendants take the share (of an estate or of the insurance proceeds) that the deceased would have taken had he or she survived. It is used in wills and trusts, as well as in insurance policies. The children represent the parents, and grandchildren represent the children, and so on down the "trunk." The words "by representation" are sometimes used in lieu of "per stirpes." The Connecticut Rule, referred to earlier, embodies the per stirpes concept.

Per Capita

Sometimes, however, an insured wants the children of a deceased beneficiary to share equally with the surviving members of the original beneficiary group. In the example used earlier, A might have wanted D's children to share equally with B and C, each taking one-fifth of the proceeds. A could have achieved this objective by specifying that the proceeds should go "in equal shares to such of B, C, and D, children of the insured, as may survive the insured, and to the surviving children of such said children as may be deceased, per capita."

In all these matters, the insurance company accedes to the wishes of the insured, requiring only that his or her desires be clearly expressed in the designation.

OWNERSHIP RIGHTS

Life insurance policies issued today offer many valuable rights and privileges in addition to the company's basic obligation to pay the face amount of the policy upon maturity. Most of these rights—such as surrender options, dividend options, policy loans, assignments, and change of beneficiaries—can be exercised during the insured's lifetime and are referred to as *prematurity rights.* It is essential, therefore, that the ownership of the various rights be clearly established and known to all parties concerned.

When a person applies for insurance on his or her own life and designates himself or herself or his or her estate as beneficiary, all ownership rights in the policy are vested in that person. The same is true if an insured designates another person as beneficiary but reserves the right to revoke the designation. The interest of such a third-party beneficiary is usually regarded as a "mere expectancy," so tenuous as not to interfere with the exercise of the insured's prematurity rights. In the rare case when a person applies for insurance on his own life and designates another person as beneficiary without reserving the right to revoke the designation (as is normal in most policies), the insured and the beneficiary are considered to be joint owners of the policy, and neither can exercise any prematurity rights without the consent of the other. Note that in none of these situations is the beneficiary considered to be the sole owner of the policy.

In today's complex world of business and finance, there are more and more situations in which it is desirable—or even essential—that the beneficiary (in the broadest sense) be the absolute owner of the policy. For example, if the insured wants to keep the proceeds out of his or her gross estate for federal estate tax purposes, the insured must divest himself or herself of all incidents of ownership. A creditor wants all ownership rights in a policy taken out on the debtor to secure a loan. Partners need to be absolute owners of policies on the lives of fellow partners used to finance business continuation agreements. Employers must be the owners of policies on the lives of key employees.

Sole and complete ownership of a policy can be vested in a person other than the insured in one of three ways, discussed briefly below. The first is through procurement of the policy by the prospective beneficiary. The beneficiary applies for the insurance with the consent of the insured and designates himself or herself as owner of the policy, as well as beneficiary.

The second method is the *transfer* of ownership rights in a policy originally issued to the insured by means of an endorsement on the policy. The insured directs the company to vest all his or her rights, privileges, and options in the beneficiary, and the policy is endorsed accordingly.

The third method is identical with the second, except that it involves the use of an absolute assignment form. This is the oldest procedure and one that is still preferred by many.

The owner of a policy, whether procured on his or her own application or by transfer from the insured, can designate a person other than himself or herself to receive the proceeds of the policy and can reserve the right to revoke the designation. He or she may also transfer ownership to another person, provided the transfer takes effect at the time it is made. Likewise, it is generally agreed that an insured—in transferring ownership of the policy to another person—may nominate a successor to take ownership in the event that the original transferee should die before the insured.

NOTES

1. In setting up successive classes of contingent beneficiaries, the insured must be careful not to violate the rule against perpetuities or statutory prohibitions against the unlawful accumulation of income.
2. George Bliss, *The Law of Life Insurance* (1871).
3. *Central National Bank v. Hume,* 128 U.S. 195 (1888).
4. *Couch Cyclopedia of Insurance Law,* 2d ed. rev. (Rochester, NY: The Lawyers Cooperative Publishing Co., 1993), vol. 4, secs. 27.130–27.136.
5. *Mutual Life Insurance Co. of New York v. Franck,* 9 Cal. App. 2d 528, 50 P. 2d 480 (1935).
6. *Morse v. Commissioner,* 100 F.2d 593 (7th Civ. 1938).

42

The Beneficiary (Part 2)

Dan M. McGill
Revised by Burke A. Christensen

It should now be clear that the rights of various parties can be vitally affected by the question of whether the primary beneficiary survives the insured, or *vice versa*. Under normal circumstances, this is a question of fact that can be easily and conclusively established. If, however, the insured and the beneficiary are killed in a common disaster, such as an automobile accident, an airplane crash, an explosion, or other untoward circumstance, it may well be impossible to determine who survived the other.

SIMULTANEOUS DEATH AND SHORT-TERM SURVIVORSHIP

In an attempt to avoid litigation to establish survivorship and provide an equitable basis for disposing of the property of the parties involved, 49 states and the District of Columbia have adopted the Uniform Simultaneous Death Act, which applies to all types of property and property rights. The underlying theory of the act is that in the absence of evidence to the contrary each person is presumed to be the survivor as to his or her own property. In the case of jointly held property, each party is presumed to be the survivor as to his or her share of the property. The act makes specific references to life insurance, stating that when the insured and the beneficiary have died and there is no sufficient evidence that they died otherwise than simultaneously, the policy proceeds will be distributed as if the insured had survived the beneficiary. This is a conclusive presumption, and it applies whether the beneficiary is designated revocably or irrevocably.

The objectives of the Uniform Simultaneous Death Act can be achieved through the inclusion of a *common disaster clause* in the policy. With language similar or even identical to that of the Act, this clause states that when the insured and beneficiary perish in a common accident, the insured will be presumed to have survived the beneficiary.

Short-Term Survivorship

The Uniform Simultaneous Death Act settles the question of survivorship when there is not sufficient evidence as to whether the insured or the beneficiary survived, but it does not eliminate the possibility of legal action by a personal representative of the beneficiary claiming that the beneficiary survived the insured. Moreover, it is not effective when it can be proved that the beneficiary, in fact, did survive the insured, even by a moment. In the absence of contrary instructions in the policy, the proceeds would, under such circumstances, go to the beneficiary's estate.

When there are contingent beneficiaries and the proceeds are held under the interest option or are payable in installments (other than a life income), the primary beneficiary's short-term survivorship creates no particular problems. The primary beneficiary's estate would be entitled to one monthly payment at most, and the remainder of the proceeds would go to the contingent beneficiaries. Under all other circumstances, however, the survival of the beneficiary for only a short period is generally considered to be an unfavorable event.

If the proceeds are payable to the primary beneficiary under a life income option, there is likely to be a substantial forfeiture of proceeds even though there are surviving contingent beneficiaries. If there are no refund features in the option, the company's obligation would be discharged completely by the payment of one monthly installment to the beneficiary's estate. If the payments are guaranteed for a specified number of years, some forfeiture would still be inevitable—the extent, of course, varying inversely with the length of the period. There would be no forfeiture, other than loss of interest, under the cash refund or installment refund form of life income option.

The problem of short-term survivorship is made clear if the proceeds are payable in a lump sum and the surviving spouse was the primary beneficiary. After probate the proceeds of both estates would pass under the surviving spouse's will or (if there was no will) to his or her heirs in intestacy. This may be a result the insured did not intend. Even if the results were acceptable, the proceeds would reach the beneficiaries only after going through estate administration and suffering some shrinkage. The cost consequences would be the same had the insured survived the beneficiary and died shortly thereafter unless contingent beneficiaries had been named to take the proceeds in that event.

Delayed Payment Clause

In an effort to avoid the undesirable consequences of short-term survivorship of the beneficiary (which is a far more common occurrence than simultaneous death), a few companies stipulate that the life insurance policy proceeds will be payable to the beneficiary only if he or she is alive at the time of payment. Other companies use a provision that states that the proceeds will be payable to a designated beneficiary only if the beneficiary survives the insured by a specified period of time, such as 10, 14, or 30 days. Insurers are understandably reluctant to delay payment for a protracted period, but some have been willing to defer payment up to 180 days. Such clauses solve the short-term survival problem very effectively, although no reasonable period would be long enough to cover every case that might arise.

The delayed payment clause has one disadvantage for the policyowner who anticipates a federal estate tax liability. The policyowner would normally want the proceeds of the life insurance policies to qualify for the marital deduction, which is a deduction allowed for all property passing outright to the decedent's spouse. (For a thorough discussion of the marital deduction, see chapter 11.) The vesting of insurance proceeds, or any property includable in the decedent's gross estate, can be delayed up to 6 months without jeopardizing their qualification for the marital deduction, provided the spouse survives the period and obtains complete dominion over the proceeds. But if the spouse does not survive the period, the proceeds do not qualify.

There are several solutions to this problem. One is the use of trusts. The insured could also elect payment of the proceeds under an interest option and then designate contingent beneficiaries. If the primary beneficiary is given the unlimited right of withdrawal, the proceeds will qualify for the marital deduction even though the surviving spouse never has an opportunity to exercise the right. If the beneficiary-spouse dies in a common disaster with the insured or dies from any cause shortly after the insured, the proceeds will pass to the contingent beneficiaries. In the event that the beneficiary survives the insured by an extended period, he or she will be permitted under the practices of most companies to elect a liquidation option at contract rates within a specified period, such as one or 2 years, after the insured's death. The portion of proceeds passing to others at the primary beneficiary's death will be includable in the primary beneficiary's gross estate for federal estate tax purposes, but if he or she dies within a specified period after the insured, the law allows a credit for any taxes paid on the same property in the insured's estate.

Reverse Common Disaster Clause

Another method of assuring the availability of the marital deduction when there is no evidence of survivorship is through the use of a reverse common disaster clause in the insurance policy. This clause makes the presumption that the *beneficiary* survives. Obviously, the clause should be used only when it is compatible with the insured's overall estate plan.

Installment Option

It should be emphasized that a perfectly satisfactory method of dealing with the short-term survivorship hazard is through the use of installment options (except life income options) with contingent beneficiaries. Neither the simultaneous deaths of the insured and the beneficiary nor the beneficiary's short-term survivorship presents any problems when the proceeds are to be distributed under the installment time or installment amount options or when they are to be held under the interest option with contingent beneficiaries to succeed to the primary beneficiary's interest. Again, an installment option should be used only if it meets the insured's distribution objectives.

EFFECTING A CHANGE OF BENEFICIARY

The owner of a life insurance policy normally retains the right to change the beneficiary. If so, he or she can remove not only the original beneficiary but also any successor beneficiaries that have been appointed. The policyowner may relinquish this right by a policy endorsement or by a collateral assignment of the policy. The right to change the beneficiary is a matter of contract, and the insurance company cannot refuse to assent to a change of beneficiary on the ground that the prospective beneficiary has no insurable interest or on any other ground. On the other hand, the company can—and does—prescribe the procedure the policyowner must follow to effect a change of beneficiary. Following the procedure is also a condition of the contract.

All insurers require written notice of a change of beneficiary, and a few specify that the change must be endorsed on the policy. Most insurers, however, merely require that the policyowner's written request be received and filed by the insurer.

Filing is preferred over the endorsement method because there are occasionally situations in which the insured is not able to produce the policy for endorsement. It may have been lost, or it may be in the possession of a person who refuses to release it—an estranged or divorced spouse, for example. In such cases, the company may recognize the change of beneficiary despite the lack of formal compliance with the procedural requirements, but it would probably do so only if the insurer were satisfied that there is no danger of the prior beneficiary's establishing a claim. The courts have consistently held that the policy provisions concerning change of beneficiary are for the protection of the company and can be waived under proper circumstances.

Divorce between the insured and the beneficiary deserves special mention. The general rule in all states except Michigan is that divorce in itself does not terminate the beneficiary's interest. This is based on the doctrine that the interest of a named beneficiary is a personal one, not dependent on the relationship to the insured that may have been stated in the designation. Thus a beneficiary designation that reads "to my wife, Emily" remains payable to Emily even after a divorce and the husband-insured's remarriage to another woman. In Michigan, a statute provides that a spouse's interest is automatically terminated by divorce, regardless of whether the spouse was revocably or irrevocably designated. Unless the court decree specifies otherwise, the insured's estate then becomes the beneficiary.

A MINOR AS BENEFICIARY

The designation of a minor as beneficiary creates problems that are not ordinarily encountered with an adult beneficiary. Perhaps the most obvious complication arises when an insured designates a minor as beneficiary without reserving the right to revoke the designation. This would now be a rare occurrence since most policies today routinely provide that the policyowner reserves the right to change a beneficiary designation. However, if the policy does not reserve the right and the insured wants to change the beneficiary, assign the policy as collateral for a loan, make a policy loan, or surrender the policy for its cash value, he or she could do so only with the minor's consent—which the minor does not have legal capacity to give. The insured might seek to have a guardian appointed for the minor, but it is highly unlikely that a court would permit the guardian to waive the minor's rights.

There will almost certainly be problems if the policy matures while the beneficiary is still a minor. The insurance company cannot safely make payments directly to the minor since he or she is not legally competent to receive payment and release the insurer. Upon the attainment of majority, the minor might repudiate the release in the receipt and demand payment of the proceeds once again. To protect itself the company would have to insist on the appointment of a guardian, which involves expense to the minor's estate. In some states insurance companies are authorized by special statutes to waive the guardianship requirement and make payment on behalf of the minor to an adult person, usually a parent or someone standing in place of a parent. However, the amounts that can be distributed under these statutes tend to be nominal; the usual limit is less than $500, although a few states permit amounts up to $1,500 to be paid in this manner.

Statutes in 44 states provide that persons who have attained the age of 18 years have reached the age of majority and thus are competent to receive and give full acquittance and discharge for any amount. Some of the remaining states give minors between the ages of 18 and 21 special capacity for limited amounts, ranging from $2,000 to $3,000, in any one year in the form of benefits payable upon the death of the insured, as long as the insurance policy or the policy settlement agreement specifically provides for direct payments to such minor. In some states the statute applies only to periodic payments that do not exceed the specified maximum in any one year.

Statutes in a few states also embrace benefits payable under annuity contracts. Some statutes permit either a lump-sum payment or periodic payments not exceeding the stipulated amount in any one year. For example, a New York statute permits the payment of $3,000 to a minor, either in a lump sum or in periodic payments not exceeding $3,000 per year. The New York statute also pertains to benefits payable upon the maturity of a policy as an endowment.

Difficulties also exist with respect to the election of settlement options by a minor or a guardian acting on the minor's behalf. The statutes above authorize installment payments directly to minors only when the settlement option was elected by the insured or other owner of the policy. They do not authorize the minor to elect a settlement option. Because it is quite clear that a minor lacks the legal capacity to elect a settlement option, most companies are not willing to run the risk of the minor's later repudiation of the contract unless the amounts involved are small. However, if the beneficiary is within one or 2 years of attaining his majority, an insurer may agree to a settlement involving the payment of interest only with a provision for payment of principal to the minor beneficiary at his or her majority or to his or her estate in the event of death.

THE TRUSTEE AS BENEFICIARY

There are circumstances under which it is advisable to have life insurance proceeds administered by a trustee. A trust can serve many useful purposes, but it is especially desirable when there is a need for great flexibility in the administration of the proceeds or when some of the beneficiaries are minors. It is a common practice for a parent to designate his or her spouse as primary beneficiary and to designate a trustee as contingent beneficiary to administer proceeds for the benefit of minor children. The trustee may be a natural person or a corporation, and the designation may be revocable or irrevocable.

It is essential that a trust agreement exists at the time the trustee is designated beneficiary. If the insured should die before instructions have been provided to the trustee, the trust would undoubtedly be dissolved as unenforceable. In such cases the courts have held that since there is nothing to guide the trustee as to the purpose or manner of distribution of the trust estate, the funds must be paid over to the person or persons presumably entitled to them. If the distributees were children, the proceeds would be paid to duly appointed guardians.

When a trustee is designated as beneficiary, it is usually intended that the trustee will collect the proceeds in one sum and administer them in accordance with the terms of the trust agreement. There are occasions, however, when the trustee deems it advantageous to make use of the insurance company's deferred-settlement options. Under these circumstances it becomes important to determine whether the trustee has the right to select such options.

Trustees as a class first developed a real interest in insurance policy settlement options in the 1930s, when the going interest rate on new investments dropped below the rate of return guaranteed in insurance company settlement options. Many companies, feeling that trustees were attempting to shift their investment responsibilities (for which they were compensated) to the life insurance industry, and having other reservations about the practice, refused to honor settlement option elections by trustees. When litigation in 1939[1] established the right of a trustee to elect a settlement option unless that right is denied in the insurance policy, many insurers inserted a prohibition in their policies against the use of settlement options by trustees. Today, however, few insurers continue that practice. Some policies stipulate that the power of all beneficiaries to select settlement options is subject to the insurer's consent. Others do not limit the rights of natural persons to select settlement options but reserve the right to deny the selection of settlement options to nonnatural persons (trusts and corporations).

In the absence of express permission in the trust instrument, there is a serious question whether a trustee has the legal right to use settlement options, even though the insurance company makes them available. It is standard practice therefore to include proper language in the trust agreement giving trustees the right to exercise ownership powers over life insurance policies. Absent such a clause, the issue hinges on whether or not a life insurance settlement option is a legal investment for a trustee. When the investment statute is the "prudent man" type, a strong argument can be made in favor of the legality of the practice. Many legal experts have concluded, however, that a trustee has an unquestioned right to elect a settlement option only when (1) the trust instrument expressly confers the right, and (2) the insurance policy does not deny the right.

NOTE

1. *First Trust Co. of St. Paul v. Northwestern Mutual Life Insurance Co.,* 204 Minn. 244, 283 N.W. 236 (1939).

43

Assignment of Life Insurance Contracts

Dan M. McGill
Revised by Burke A. Christensen

The life insurance contract, with its valuable prematurity rights and promise to pay a specified sum of money upon maturity, is an ideal form of collateral for credit transactions. Hence it is not surprising that the practice of assigning life insurance policies as collateral security has reached large proportions. Policies are, in addition, frequently assigned as a means of transferring ownership rights to another person or organization. It is important to note the circumstances under which a life insurance contract can be assigned and the manner in which the rights of the various parties involved are affected by the assignment.

RIGHT OF ASSIGNMENT

> **Assignment:** the transfer of some or all of a person's (the assignor's) ownership rights in property to another (the assignee). An *absolute assignment* is a transfer to the assignee by sale or gift of all the assignor's rights. A *partial assignment* transfers less than all the assignor's rights. A *collateral assignment* is a transfer of some or all of a property owner's interests to provide security for a loan. The collateral assignment terminates when the loan is repaid.

Assignment by the Insured or Owner of the Policy

It is a settled rule of law that anyone having an interest in a life insurance contract can transfer that interest, with or without consideration, to another person. Hence the contract need not (but frequently does) contain a provision expressly authorizing the owner to transfer his or her interest; it is an inherent right that can be restricted only by contract. Industrial life insurance policies contain limitations on the right of assignment, but ordinary insurance policies are generally free from restrictions other than requiring notice and making assignments subordinate to policy loans.

Consideration is a legal term that refers to something of value that is exchanged between two parties to a transaction. Anything that has value can serve as consideration. In a life insurance contract, the consideration exchanged is the policyowner's money and the insurer's promise to pay. A transfer without reciprocal consideration is a gift.

In the usual situation all ownership rights in a policy are vested in the policyowner (normally the insured). Among the incidents of ownership is the right to assign the policy. In addition to its contract law implications, the term *incidents of ownership* is extremely important for purposes of the federal tax law. According to IRC Sec. 2042, if the insured had any incidents of ownership in the policy during the 3 years prior to death, the policy's death proceeds are included in the insured's estate for federal income tax purposes. The right to assign the policy carries with it the power to transfer all rights and interests in the policy to another person. When someone other than the insured is the owner of the policy, it is customary for the policy to restrict the right of assignment to the owner. This is not a restriction on the assignability of the policy as such; it merely identifies the person who has the right to assign it.

The following are three sample assignment provisions:

> We will not be deemed to know of an assignment unless we receive it, or a copy of it, at our Home Office. We are not obligated to see that an assignment is valid or sufficient.

> • • •

> You may assign this policy as collateral security, subject to policy loans. Beneficiaries' interests and methods chosen for the payment of proceeds are subordinate to such an assignment.

> • • •

> Your interest in this policy may be assigned without the consent of any revocable Beneficiary. Your interest, any interest of the insured, and any interest of any revocable beneficiary shall be subject to the terms of the assignment. We will not be on notice of any assignment unless it is in writing; nor will we be on notice until a duplicate of the original assignment has been filed at our Home Office. We assume no responsibility for the validity or sufficiency of any assignment.

The person assigning the policy cannot transfer any interest greater than he or she possesses; nor can the obligation of the insurer be enlarged by an assignment. This means that the assignor of the contract cannot, by the unilateral action of assigning the contract, impair or defeat the *vested* interest of another party to the contract. In the typical case only one other party can be adversely affected by the assignment, and that is the beneficiary. But is the beneficiary's interest entitled to protection against infringement? The answer depends on whether the beneficiary designation is revocable or irrevocable.

Revocable or Irrevocable Beneficiary Designation

If the beneficiary designation is revocable, the majority rule is that the policyowner can assign the policy without the consent of the beneficiary and without complying with the formalities for changing the beneficiary designation. In some jurisdictions an absolute assignment is held to automatically extinguish a revocable beneficiary's interest to the extent of the assignee's interest. In other jurisdictions the revocable beneficiary's interest is unaffected unless changed by the assignee. As might be expected, the majority rule reflects the decision of those courts that the interest of the revocable beneficiary is not vested but is a mere expectancy. The minority view is that the beneficiary has a vested interest in the policy, but that the beneficiary's interest may be extinguished or terminated by the policyowner. This is known in the law as a *defeasible vested interest.* Courts that adhere to the defeasible vested interest theory hold that the policyowner cannot give the assignee an interest in the policy proceeds without obtaining the beneficiary's consent or revoking the beneficiary designation.

It is the rule in all states, however, that when the beneficiary designation is irrevocable, the policy cannot be assigned without the beneficiary's consent.

Assignment by the Beneficiary

In the absence of a provision to the contrary, the beneficiary can assign his or her interest, both before and after maturity of the policy. Prior to the policy's maturity, the beneficiary's interest is virtually worthless because the insured has the right to change the beneficiary. If the insured does not reserve that right or if the designation of a beneficiary is irrevocable, there is something of substance to be transferred. However, even that irrevocable interest is contingent upon the original beneficiary's survival of the insured, unless the beneficiary's estate is designated (as contingent beneficiary) to receive the proceeds if he or she predeceases the insured.

Upon maturity of the policy, proceeds payable in a lump sum vest in the beneficiary and can be assigned by him or her. When the proceeds are held by the insurer under a deferred-settlement agreement, the beneficiary's right of assignment is subject to the rights of the contingent beneficiaries, if any, and to restrictive provisions in the policy or settlement agreement. A common restriction for a policy or settlement agreement to contain is a *spendthrift clause,* which denies the beneficiary the right to commute, alienate, or assign his or her interest in the proceeds. Furthermore, in a few states the laws that protect insurance proceeds from the claims of the beneficiary's creditors prohibit an assignment of the beneficiary's interest.

EFFECT OF AN ASSIGNMENT ON A BENEFICIARY'S RIGHTS

The effect of an assignment on the rights of the beneficiary depends not only on the type of beneficiary designation but also on the type of assignment involved: an absolute assignment or a collateral assignment.

The absolute assignment divests the policyowner of all incidents of ownership and transfers all rights and interests in the policy absolutely and permanently to the assignee. It is designed for situations (such as a gift or a sale) in which the assignor's clear intent is to make the assignee the new owner of the policy. The collateral assignment, on the other hand, transfers to the assignee those rights — and only those rights — needed to protect a loan from the assignee to the assignor. It resembles a mortgage of land or a pledge of marketable securities. The arrangement is intended to be temporary; upon repayment of the loan, the assignment terminates, and all assigned rights revert to the previous owner. The assignee's interest in the policy is limited to the amount of the indebtedness and unpaid interest, plus any premiums paid by the assignee to keep the policy in force.

For reasons explained later in this chapter, absolute assignments have frequently been used when only a security arrangement was intended. In such cases the assignment is treated as a collateral one and is released upon satisfaction of the assignor's obligation to the assignee. In fact, the courts will enforce such a result if the assignor can prove that a collateral assignment between the assignor and assignee was intended.

If assignment of a policy is absolute in form, and the parties intended the assignment to be absolute in substance as well, the beneficiary's interest is completely extinguished, provided the designation was revocable, or if irrevocable, that the beneficiary joined in the assignment. If an assignment is collateral in substance, irrespective of its form, the beneficiary's interest will be extinguished to the extent of the assignee's interest, which is limited in the manner described above. If the policyowner attempts to assign the policy without the consent of the beneficiary when such consent is necessary, a valid transfer of the policyowner's interest takes place, but the beneficiary's interest is not affected. If the assignment affects a revocable beneficiary in a jurisdiction that sees a defeasible vested interest, the designation remains in effect until a change has been accomplished in the prescribed manner. If the assignment involves an irrevocable beneficiary, the designation is unaffected and no rights and privileges in the contract can be exercised by the assignee without the irrevocable beneficiary's consent.

With regard to whether the interest of a third-party beneficiary is subordinate to that of the assignee without a formal change of beneficiary, courts in general have based their rulings purely on the intent of the parties. Most of the litigation involved collateral assignments; in such cases, there is usually a clear intent to subordinate the beneficiary's interest to that of the creditor-assignee.

In absolute assignments the courts recognize this intent to subordinate the beneficiary's interest to that of the assignee in two ways. First, if the assignee can perfect his or her claim by observing the formalities of a change of beneficiary, the courts are willing to spare the assignee the trouble of doing so. Thus in cases involving absolute assignments that are not incidental to a credit transaction, some courts have concluded that a formal assignment with notice to the insurance company substantially conforms to the requirements for a change of beneficiary and operates as such. (This rationale is patently inappropriate for collateral assignments, however, since the beneficiary of record receives the proceeds in excess of the claims of the assignment.) Second, an absolute assignment of policy ownership does not operate to change the preexisting beneficiary designation. Consent of the beneficiary to the assignment is therefore regarded in all jurisdictions as conclusive evidence of intent to give a preferred status to the rights and claims of the assignee (the new owner), who must act in accordance with the policy provisions to name a new beneficiary.

In all states it is held that whenever the beneficiary of a policy is the insured or the insured's estate, the claims of the assignee will prevail over those of the executor or administrator of the insured's estate.[1] This is true whether the assignment is absolute or collateral in form. Accordingly, it is the current practice to use collateral assignment forms that require the beneficiary's signature. In the execution of assignments incidental to policy loans, insurers *require* this procedure unless the wording of the policy makes it unnecessary (as is the case with current policies). A sample provision reads as follows:

> The interest of any revocable beneficiary in this policy and any
> settlement option elected shall be subordinate to any assignment

made either before or after the beneficiary designation or
settlement option election.

The effectiveness of this type of provision has been upheld[2] even under the
laws of New Jersey, which historically has been one of the states requiring the
consent of a revocable beneficiary to an assignment of the policy. Nevertheless,
it would seem that an assignee who wants to avoid any possible legal complications upon the death of the insured would be well advised to designate himself
or herself as beneficiary. There could then be no doubt as to the assignee's right
to receive the proceeds.

EFFECT OF ASSIGNMENT ON OWNERSHIP RIGHTS

Concept of Ownership

There are two sets of rights in a life insurance policy: those that exist during
the insured's lifetime and those that arise after the insured's death. The first set
is known, quite logically, as prematurity rights, and the second set as maturity
rights. The most important of the prematurity rights are the rights to surrender
the policy for cash or paid-up insurance, to borrow against the policy, to designate
and change the beneficiary, and to assign the policy. Among the lesser—but still
significant—prematurity rights are the rights to elect settlement options, to elect
dividend options, to reinstate the policy, to convert or exchange the policy for
another, and to take advantage of the automatic premium loan feature. The
maturity rights include the rights to receive the proceeds, to elect settlement
options (unless usurped by the insured or owner), and to designate direct and
contingent beneficiaries (only under certain circumstances).

The concept of ownership of these rights has undergone dramatic development during the last century. The original concept was that all prematurity and
maturity rights were vested in the beneficiary and his or her estate. In other
words, the beneficiary was regarded as the absolute owner of the policy. Once the
insured's right to change the beneficiary was recognized, the insured and the
beneficiary were considered to be joint owners of the prematurity rights and the
beneficiary the sole owner of the maturity rights—subject, however, to the right
of the insured, if reserved, to divest the beneficiary of all interests in the policy
and the proceeds. Over the years this concept has been modified, and today, in
the absence of a contrary ownership arrangement, the insured is regarded to be
the absolute owner of the prematurity rights and the possessor of the power to
dispose of the maturity rights. If the insured has designated a third person as an
irrevocable beneficiary, such beneficiary is considered to be the sole owner of the
proceeds (when due at maturity), subject to the insured's reversionary interest,
and the insured and the beneficiary are looked upon as the joint owners of all
prematurity rights.

Ever since the concept of a beneficiary change was recognized around the turn
of the century, the insured has been identified with ownership rights, either as
sole or as joint owner. The most recent development is the insured's complete
dissociation or disattachment from ownership rights in the policy. This
development received its impetus from the growth of business insurance, juvenile
insurance, and insurance for estate-transfer purposes, where there is a distinct

need to have ownership of the policy in a person other than the insured, but it was also motivated by insurers' desire to clarify the ownership status of the various rights in the contract.

Dissociation is accomplished by specifying on the face of the policy that a particular person or firm is the owner of the policy and restricting the exercise of the various policy rights and privileges to the owner. In most cases the insured is designated as owner, but the insured, as such, has no rights in the policy. All prematurity rights are vested in the owner, including the right to control the disposition of the maturity rights. The owner is given express authority to designate and change primary and contingent beneficiaries. Furthermore, during the lifetime of the insured, the owner can exercise all the rights and privileges in the policy without the beneficiary's consent. The application for the policy makes no reference to the question of whether the applicant does or does not reserve the right to change the beneficiary. If the applicant wishes to create a joint ownership of the policy by the insured and the beneficiary, he or she can designate them as joint owners, with whatever survivorship provisions might be appropriate or desired.

The owner is given the sole right to assign the policy, and the interest of any beneficiary is made subject to the assignment. The assignee, however, does not necessarily become the owner of the policy. The policy may stipulate the manner in which a transfer of ownership is to be accomplished, and some policies state that ownership of the policy can be transferred only by a written instrument, satisfactory to the company, endorsed on the policy.

It can be seen therefore that a minimum of *five* parties other than the insurance company may be associated with a life insurance policy: the applicant, the insured, the owner, the beneficiary, and the assignee. In the great majority of cases, the applicant, insured, and owner are one and the same person. Nevertheless, the ownership of all rights and privileges is crystal clear, irrespective of the number of parties or interests involved. The next problem is to determine what happens to these rights and privileges when the policy is assigned.

Collateral Assignments

A collateral assignment is nothing more than a pledge, subject to the general rules of law governing such a transaction. A pledgor is entitled to get his or her property back upon paying the debt when due and after tendering the correct amount at the proper time, may recover the property in a legal proceeding. On the other hand, if the debt is not paid when due, the pledgee may, under authority of a court obtained in a suit for that purpose—or more commonly under the authority of the pledge agreement itself—have the property sold to satisfy the claim, including expenses of the sale. The sale can be private if the agreement gives the pledgee that alternative. The surplus remaining after the pledgee has been satisfied belongs to the pledgor.

Pledging a life insurance policy as collateral for a debt raises some additional issues. Since the pledgee is not the absolute owner of the policy, he or she cannot surrender the policy in the absence of a specific agreement to that effect. If the pledgor of an insurance policy dies before paying the debt for which the policy is security, the pledgee has a claim against the policy proceeds and may enforce that claim to the extent of the debt and other related charges. However, since the collection of the proceeds is not a sale, the pledgee does not have the power, in the absence of an express stipulation, to collect the full amount of the proceeds, holding the excess for the pledgor's representatives.

It was not customary before the development of the American Bankers Association (ABA) assignment form for collateral assignment forms to confer specific rights and powers in the policy on the assignee. When the assignee attempted to surrender a pledged policy or to take other action concerning it, most companies insisted that the owner of the policy join in the action. Furthermore, upon maturity of the policy, the assignee was permitted to collect only the amount of the outstanding indebtedness, unpaid interest, premiums paid on the policy, and other expenses incurred in connection with the loan. The remaining portion of the proceeds, if any, was paid to the beneficiary of record.

Many creditors resented having to prove the extent of their interest to the insurance company, preferring to receive the entire amount of proceeds and to account to the beneficiary for the excess over their claims, as they computed them. To make matters worse, the collateral notes (not the collateral assignment form) used by some banks proved to be defective, in that they failed to give the bank the unquestioned right to pay premiums on the policy in the event of the insured's default and to add the sums thus paid to the principal of the indebtedness. The bank's only recourse in some circumstances was to obtain title to the policy through foreclosure proceedings, thus establishing its right to pay premiums and to bring these payments under the protection of the collateral assignment. To obviate such difficulties, the ABA assignment form contains a provision that specifically authorizes the assignee to pay premiums and to add them to the amount of the indebtedness.

Whatever the impact of a collateral assignment on ownership rights, it is intended to be temporary in nature. As started earlier, once the loan is repaid by the assignor, the assignment is released and all ownership rights revert to their status before the assignment. An irrevocable beneficiary, for example, in joining in a collateral assignment, does not relinquish any vested rights in a policy; he or she merely agrees to subordinate his or her interest to that of the assignee during the time the assignment is in force. Once the assignment is terminated, the former status of all rights is restored. Repayment of the loan cancels the assignment, even though there may not be a formal release of the encumbrance.

Absolute Assignments

An absolute assignment conveys all the title, rights, and interests possessed by the assignor to the assignee. If the assignor owned all the rights in the policy, or if all persons having an interest in the policy joined in the assignment, the assignee becomes the new owner of the policy and can exercise all the rights therein without the consent of any other person. The transfer is intended to be permanent.

This was the conventional way of transferring ownership of a policy to another person. It was used, for example, when the insured wanted to make a gift of the policy or, on rare occasions, to sell the policy. It was the approved method of divesting the insured of all incidents of ownership in a policy, to the end that the proceeds would not be includable in his or her gross estate for federal estate tax purposes. Transferring ownership rights by means of an ownership endorsement is also used. Under this method and as specifically stated in the policy, ownership in the full legal sense can be transferred only by means of a written instrument, acceptable to the company, endorsed on the policy.

In the days when an absolute assignment was universally regarded as a full and complete transfer of ownership rights, many creditors—particularly banks—turned to it as a more effective method than collateral assignments of safeguarding their interests. They began to insist on an absolute assignment when a policy was being pledged as security for a loan. In this way, they hoped to avoid the restrictions that were frequently imposed on them in connection with collateral assignments. They wanted the right, without the consent of the insured, to surrender the policy for cash, to borrow the loan value, to elect paid-up insurance, and to exercise any of the other rights and privileges that might protect their interests. They also wanted the right to receive the full proceeds upon maturity of the policy, from which they would deduct amounts due them and pay over the excess to the insured or the beneficiary, as the case might be. In so doing, of course, they would deprive the beneficiary of the privilege of utilizing the policy's settlement options. In most cases, because of the smallness of the sums involved, this was not a serious disadvantage to the beneficiaries. When the sums involved were substantial and the options were favorable, however, this practice was a potential source of great loss to the beneficiaries.

In many cases, perhaps, the absolute assignment form worked out exactly as the banks and other creditors had hoped it would. In other cases, however, the insurance company, realizing that the intent was that the policy had been assigned only as collateral, refused to recognize the assignee as sole owner of the policy and insisted upon the insured's joinder in the exercise of the various policy rights. Insurers based their refusal on the failure of the assignment form to mention the specific rights conferred upon the assignee.

Dissatisfaction of both creditors and debtors with the absolute assignment form eventually led to the development of a form especially designed for the assignment of life insurance policies. It was developed by the Bank Management Commission of the American Bankers Association with the collaboration of the Association of Life Insurance Counsel. The official name of the form is "Assignment of Life Insurance Policy as Collateral," but it is popularly known as the ABA assignment form.

ABA Assignment Form

The essence of the ABA assignment form is that it sets forth clearly and specifically the rights that are transferred to the assignee and the rights that are not transferred and are presumably retained by the assignor. The assignment is absolute and unqualified in the sense that the rights vested in the assignee can be exercised without the consent of any other party. It is collateral in that the assignee's rights are limited to his or her interest, with all rights reverting to the assignor upon termination of the assignee's interest.

The form states that the following rights will pass to the assignee, to be exercised by him or her alone:

- the right to collect from the insurance company the net proceeds of the policy when it matures by death or as an endowment

- the right to surrender the policy for its cash value
- the right to assign or pledge the policy as security for loans or advances from the insurance company or other persons
- the right to collect and receive all distributions of surplus to which the policy may become entitled during the time the assignment is in force, as well as all dividend deposits and paid-up additions credited to the policy as of the date of the assignment, provided appropriate notice is given to the insurance company by the assignee
- the right to exercise all surrender options and to receive the benefits and advantages therefrom

The form stipulates that the following rights will not pass to the assignee, unless the policy has been surrendered:

- the right to collect from the insurance company any disability benefit payable in cash that does not reduce the amount of insurance (The so-called *maturity type* of permanent and total disability income provision found in some of the older policies provides for the deduction of each monthly payment from the face amount of the policy.)
- the right to designate and change the beneficiary, subject to the assignment
- the right to elect settlement options, likewise subject to the assignment

In consideration of the rights vested in him or her the assignee agrees as follows:

- to pay over "to the person entitled thereto under the terms of the Policy had this assignment not been executed" any sums remaining after the liabilities, matured or unmatured, to the assignee are satisfied
- not to surrender the policy or borrow upon it except for the purpose of premium payment, unless there has been a default in the obligations to the assignee or a failure to pay premiums when due, and in any event, not until 20 days after the assignee mails to the assignor notice of his or her intention to exercise such right
- upon request, and without unreasonable delay, to forward the policy to the insurance company for endorsement of any designation or change of beneficiary or any election of a settlement option

The insurance company is authorized to make payment to the assignee without investigating the reason for any action taken by the assignee, the validity or amount of the assignee's claims, or the existence of any default on the assignor's part. Upon surrender or maturity of the policy, the assignee is entitled to all the monies due but may, at his or her option, request a smaller sum. From the standpoint of the assignee, the right to receive the full proceeds eliminates one of the objections to the collateral assignment, but the assignee may also permit the proceeds in excess of his or her claims to be paid under the settlement plan selected by the insured. If the assignee requests the payment of a greater sum than the amount of the assignee's interest, he or she becomes what in law is known as a *resulting trustee* for the excess and must account under the principles of trusteeship to the insured or beneficiary, as the case may be, for such sum. In this connection, it is pertinent to observe that bank assignees tend to be reluctant to invoke their right under the ABA assignment form to collect more than their claim upon maturity of the policy. They prefer to avoid the responsibility of determining who under the policy language is entitled to the remainder of the proceeds.

The assignee is relieved of the obligations to pay premiums and policy loan principal or interest. If the assignee does pay any such items out of his or her own funds, the amounts so paid become part of the liabilities secured by the assignment, are due immediately, and draw interest at a rate not exceeding 6 percent annually until paid.

Other provisions of the form establish the superiority of the assignment instrument in case of conflict with any provisions of the note for which it is security, grant administrative discretion to the assignee in handling a claim, and certify that the assignor has no bankruptcy proceedings pending against him or her and has not made an assignment for creditors.

Until recently, the ABA form was the most widely used of all such forms. It no longer enjoys such popularity because differing requirements in various states make the ABA form inappropriate in some jurisdictions. In its place some insurers have prepared their own collateral assignment forms that are tailored to the varying state requirements. Policyowners should always seek the advice of competent local counsel when they intend to make a collateral assignment of a life insurance policy.

NOTICE TO THE COMPANY OF ASSIGNMENT

If the interest of an assignee is to be protected, the insurance company must be notified of the assignment, preferably as soon as the assignment has been executed. A life insurance policy is not a negotiable instrument; a transfer of rights in the policy, to be effective, must be recorded with the party who is under obligation to perform. If, without notice of an assignment, a life insurance company, upon maturity of a policy, pays the proceeds to the beneficiary of record, it will be absolved under the general rules of law from any further liability or obligation under the policy, even though a valid assignment of the policy was in effect at the date of the insured's death. To implement the law and to put all parties on notice, insurers incorporate a statement in their policies that no assignment will be binding on the company unless it is in writing and filed in the home office. This provision has no effect on the *validity* of an assignment, but it has a material bearing on the enforcement of the rights transferred to the assignee.

Multiple Assignees

The issue is broader than the rights of the beneficiary and the assignee. At the maturity of the policy, there may be more than one valid assignment of the policy in effect, and the relative rights of the assignees must be resolved. This can happen when one of the assignees failed to demand delivery of the policy with the assignment or when the insured obtained a duplicate copy or copies of the policy by alleging that the original had been lost. Although it is conceivable that an insured could innocently or inadvertently assign a policy while a valid assignment of the policy was still outstanding, in most such cases the insured is guilty of fraudulent behavior.

Definite rules of law have evolved to settle disputes arising over multiple assignments of the same interest. The English rule, adopted in a minority of American jurisdictions, holds that the assignee who first gives notice to the insurance company has prior claim to the proceeds, provided that such assignee, at the time the policy was assigned to him or her, had no notice of a prior assignment.[3] If the assignee did know of an earlier unrecorded assignment still in effect, he or she would, of course, have been guilty of fraud in accepting a second assignment of the same interest.

The American—or prevailing—rule is that the assignee who is first in point of time will be preferred, regardless of notice to the company.[4] This rule is subject to the important exception that if the prior assignee fails to require delivery of the policy and thus permits a subsequent assignee to obtain delivery of the policy with no notation of the prior assignment, the subsequent assignee's claim will be superior to that of the original assignee.

A third general rule, applicable under either the English or American rule, is that an assignee not guilty of fraud will be permitted to retain any proceeds that may have been paid to him or her. Thus an assignee with a preferred claim will lose his or her priority in any jurisdiction if that assignee fails to notify the insurer of the claim before the company has paid another assignee of record. In jurisdictions applying the American rule, the assignee first in point of time will have his or her interest protected even under the general rule as long as the assignee records the assignment with the insurance company at any time prior to payment by the company.

Policy loans or advances made by the insurer are subject to the foregoing rules. Since assignments involving policy loans or advances are automatically recorded with the company, no difficulties are likely to develop around them. The only time that an insurer would find its lien against the cash value and proceeds subordinate to that of another assignee would be if—with notice of another valid assignment and without the consent of the assignee—it went ahead and made a policy loan. Presumably, this would happen only through inadvertence. If a valid assignment of the policy had been executed prior to the policy loan but with no notice to the insurer, the company would be protected under the exception to the American rule.[5]

Bill of Interpleader

Whenever there are conflicting claims for insurance proceeds or other benefits, whether the claimants are assignees or beneficiaries, the insurance company generally seeks the assistance of the courts. To do otherwise would be to invite the possibility of having to pay the benefits more than once. In such circumstances, the insurer files a *bill of interpleader,* an equitable device, and pays the proceeds into court. In taking such action, it admits its obligation to pay and petitions the court to adjudicate the conflicting claims and determine who is entitled to receive the money. The insurer discharges its responsibility by paying the disputed sum over to the court. This is an extremely important legal remedy for insurance companies.[6]

OTHER MATTERS RELATING TO ASSIGNMENT

Company Not Responsible for Validity of Assignment

The policy provision pertaining to assignment almost invariably contains a statement that the company is not be responsible for the validity of any assignment of the policy. Some policies broaden the statement to include the word *effect* as well as *validity*. This provision is intended to protect the company against suits by a beneficiary or some other person alleging that the assignment was invalid because of the insured's incompetence or because the assignment was tainted with fraud or executed under duress. In the leading case,[7] an insured and his wife, who was the beneficiary of the policy, executed an assignment at a time when both were of advanced age and lacking in mental capacity. Upon the death of the insured, the company, having no knowledge of the incompetence of the insured and beneficiary, paid the proceeds to the assignee. Subsequently, the wife's guardian sued the company to recover the proceeds on the ground that the assignment was void. The court refused to hold the company liable for a second payment of the proceeds, giving as one of its reasons the exculpatory statement in the assignment provision. The court noted, however, that this clause protects the company only when it has no knowledge of a defect in the assignment instrument or of any irregularity in the circumstances surrounding the assignment.

Insurable Interest

The right of an owner to assign the policy to anyone of his or her choice, whether or not such person has an insurable interest in the life of the insured, is recognized in all jurisdictions when no financial consideration is involved. Such donee-assignees have been regarded to be in the same class as donee-beneficiaries as far as insurable interest is concerned. The position of the courts is that it is immaterial whether the insured designates the payee of the policy within the contract itself (a conventional beneficiary designation) or by means of a separate instrument (an assignment). If the applicant for insurance has an insurable interest in the life of the insured at the inception of the contract, an insurable interest on the part of the assignee is not required, either at the inception of the contract or at the time of the insured's death. Of course, if the insured were induced by the assignee to take out the policy, the assignee would have to have an insurable interest since in effect the assignee would be the applicant.

The situation is different when an assignment is made for a consideration. If the policy is assigned to a creditor as security for a debt, the assignee is permitted to retain only the amount of his or her interest, even though the assignment was absolute in form. Thus a creditor-assignee must have an insurable interest in the life of the insured at the maturity of the contract. If the creditor-assignee's interest is extinguished prior to maturity of the policy, the assignment terminates. While it is clear that a creditor has an insurable interest in the life of his or her debtor, the amount is not limited to the amount of the debt, and there is no clear rule as to how much more than the debt is acceptable public policy.

On the other hand, an assignment to a purchaser for value is valid in the federal courts and in all but four states, regardless of the question of insurable interest. In other words, in most jurisdictions a policy can be sold to a person who has no insurable interest in the life of the insured. In 1911 Mr. Justice Holmes explained the rationale of this doctrine: [8]

> Life insurance has become in our days one of the best recognized forms of investment and self-compelled saving. So far as reasonable safety permits, it is desirable to give to life policies the ordinary characteristics of property. . . . To deny the right to sell . . . is to diminish appreciably the value of the contract in the owner's hands.

Briefly, the argument is that there should be a free market for life insurance policies when a person in poor health can obtain the true value of his or her policy. The minimum price at which a policy should sell is the cash value, but the real value of a policy on the life of a person in poor health is somewhere between the cash value and the face amount of the policy, depending on the individual's chances of survival. If a person is ill and needs money for medical treatment, it is argued, he or she should be permitted to sell his or her policy to the highest bidder, without regard to insurable interest. The chances of murder are thought to be remote; in any case, the danger is probably not greater than when the insured designates a beneficiary who has no insurable interest.

Four states — Alabama, Kansas, Kentucky, and Pennsylvania — do not follow the majority rule. These states require the assignee to have an insurable interest when the policy is assigned for value. In these states such an assignment is permitted only up to an amount equal to the value paid by the assignee.

NOTES

1. See citations in Harry Krueger and Leland T. Waggoner (eds.), *The Life Insurance Policy Contract* (Boston: Little, Brown & Co., 1953), p. 89, n. 17.
2. *Phoenix Mutual Life Insurance Co. v. Connelly,* 188 F. 2d 462 (3d Cir. 1951), reversing, 92 F. Supp. 994 (D. N.J., 1950).
3. See Krueger and Waggoner, *The Life Insurance Policy Contract,* p. 69, n. 2, for a list of jurisdictions following the English rule. Such important insurance states as California, Connecticut, Ohio, and Pennsylvania follow this rule.
4. See *ibid.,* p. 70, n. 3, for a list of states following the American rule. New York is one.
5. *Patten v. Mutual Benefit Life Insurance Co.,* 192 S.C. 189, 6 S.E. (2d) 26 (1939).
6. Strictly speaking, a *bill of interpleader* requires that the insurance company be entirely disinterested in the outcome of the litigation. Under various state statutes and the Federal Interpleader Statute, the company can file a *bill in the nature of a bill of interpleader* when it does have an interest in the outcome — for example, when the representatives of the insured and the beneficiary killed in a common accident are claiming the proceeds, and the settlement agreement calls for the payment of the proceeds to the beneficiary under a life income option. If the beneficiary is held to have survived, the company may be able to discharge its obligations with one monthly payment. A more common example of the use of a bill in the nature of a bill of interpleader is when a company admits a death claim but denies liability for accidental death benefits.
7. *New York Life Insurance Co. v. Federal National Bank,* 151 F. 2d 537 (10th Cir. 1945), reversing 53 F. Supp. 924 (W.D. Okla. 1944), certiorari denied, 327 U.S. 778 (1946), rehearing denied, 327 U.S. 816 (1946).
8. *Grigsby v. Russell,* 222 U.S. 149, 156 (1911).

44

Protection against Creditors

Dan M. McGill
Revised by Burke A. Christensen

The protection enjoyed by life insurance against creditors' claims is a vast and complex subject, and it can be dealt with here in only the most cursory fashion. Emphasis will be on guiding principles with a minimum of substantiating detail. There are so many facets to the subject that a rather detailed outline is necessary. The most basic dichotomy distinguishes between protection available in the absence of special legislation and that available under statutes specifically designed to give life insurance a preferred status.

A life insurance policy is a valuable property right, and thus a policyowner's creditors may attempt to acquire an interest in the policy's value. A creditor may acquire an interest by operation of the contract in the following ways:

- The creditor can become the owner of the policy insuring the life of the debtor.
- The creditor can become the collateral assignee of the policy to the extent permitted to secure the debt.
- The creditor can be designated the beneficiary of the policy.

NONSTATUTORY PROTECTION

The topic of nonstatutory protection can itself be broken down into various subtopics, but the most important distinction is between creditors of the insured and creditors of the beneficiary.

Creditors of the Insured

Creditors of the insured may seek to satisfy their claims out of the cash value of a policy still in force or out of the proceeds of a matured policy. The legal principles involved in these two types of action are so different that they must be dealt with separately.

Before Maturity of the Contract

If the policy is payable to the insured or to a *revocable* third-party beneficiary, the insured is the owner of the policy and is entitled to the cash value upon surrender of the policy. The cash value is an asset of the insured and is reflected as such in his or her financial statements. It would seem therefore that in the absence of special statutory rules, the cash value of such an insurance policy would be available to the creditors of the insured on the same basis as any other personal property. Such is not the case, however.

In theory, the insured's creditor is entitled to the cash value of a policy owned by the insured; in practice, the creditor is generally unable to enforce his or her rights because of procedural difficulties. The normal collection processes are not effective against the cash value since the insurance company is under no obligation to pay the money to anyone until the insured exercises his or her privilege of surrendering the policy. Moreover, the courts are loath to force the insured to exercise the right to surrender. Direct action against the company, in the form of a garnishment or distraint proceeding, has uniformly been unsuccessful, while attempts by judgment creditors to force the insured to surrender the policy have been successful in only a few jurisdictions.

If the creditor has no contractual rights in the policy, he or she may seek to satisfy the debt by securing a judgment against the policyowner. The creditor may try to execute the judgment by seizing the debtor's property—including the insurance policy. The creditor might seek to obtain the cash value of an unmatured policy or the policy proceeds if the insured-debtor has died.

Bankruptcy Reform Act of 1978. Federal law and the laws of all 50 states permit creditors to protect themselves from defaulting debtors in this fashion. However, the states, as well as the federal government, create special protection from creditors for certain kinds of property. The applicable federal law is the Bankruptcy Reform Act of 1978. That law, like the state laws, exempts certain categories of property from creditors' claims. One category of property uniformly protected under these exemption laws is life insurance. This, like the tax advantages given to life insurance under the Internal Revenue Code, adds to the value of life insurance as the foundation of an individual's financial plan.

Under federal bankruptcy law, an individual filing bankruptcy may elect either the exemptions provided under the federal statute or those provided by the applicable state law. However, the federal Bankruptcy Reform Act of 1978 also permits states to "opt out" of the reach of the federal law. If a state passes such an opt-out statute, then its citizens are deprived of the federal alternative and may protect property from creditors only under that state's exemption statute. More than 75 percent of the states have enacted legislation to opt out of the federal bankruptcy system.

The situation is different when the insured is bankrupt and a trustee in bankruptcy has been appointed. The federal Bankruptcy Reform Act of 1978 provides that the trustee of the bankrupt's estate will be vested with the bankrupt's title, as of the date the petition in bankruptcy was filed, to all property that the bankrupt could have transferred by any means prior to filing the petition or that might have been levied upon and sold under any judicial process. Since a life insurance policy payable to the insured or to a revocable third-party beneficiary could have been transferred, title to it passes to the trustee in bankruptcy. The trustee, as owner of the policy, can then surrender it for its cash value. Policies without a cash value do not pass to the trustee in bankruptcy.

Note, however, that the interest of the trustee in bankruptcy is limited to the cash value of the insurance on the date the petition in bankruptcy was filed. Thus if the insured dies prior to adjudication of the bankruptcy and before the policy is surrendered, the excess of the proceeds over the cash value must be paid to the designated beneficiary, if any, or otherwise to the insured's estate. Under the federal law prior to the 1978 act, if the insured, within 30 days after the insurance company certified the amount of the cash value to the trustee, paid the trustee the sum of money so certified, the insured was entitled to recover his or her policy free from the claims of the creditors participating in the bankruptcy proceeding. (Funds borrowed for this purpose could have been repaid almost in full from the proceeds of a policy loan.) This provision was to prevent the hardship to the bankrupt's family if all his or her life insurance policies were to pass absolutely to the trustee in bankruptcy. Unfortunately, this provision, known as the *insurance proviso*, was not included in the Bankruptcy Reform Act of 1978.

Federal Tax Lien Act of 1966. There are special rules for federal tax liens against a person's property. Under the Federal Tax Lien Act of 1966, the government's lien overrides state exemption laws. The federal government may require the insurance company to withdraw the policyowner's policy loan values up to the amount of the tax and pay that amount to the government within 90 days after notice.

The government's right to the policy loan values extends to the policy proceeds if the federal tax lien was attached prior to the insured's death. In this case, the beneficiary will be paid only if the policy proceeds exceed the amount of the government's lien. However, if the insured dies prior to the attempted attachment of the federal tax lien, the state exemption laws apply and the proceeds will be protected to the extent of the state law.

After Maturity of the Contract

When proceeds are payable to the insured or the insured's estate, they become available to estate creditors on the same basis as any other unrestricted assets in the estate. When they are payable to a third-party beneficiary, however, they vest in the beneficiary immediately at the insured's death, whether the beneficiary designation was revocable or irrevocable. In this case, the proceeds are free from the claims of the policyowner's creditors.

Creditors of the Beneficiary

The cash value of a life insurance policy cannot be levied upon by a creditor of a third-party beneficiary, whether the designation is revocable or irrevocable. When the designation is revocable, the policyowner (whether or not he or she is also the insured) is the sole and absolute owner of the policy. When the designation is irrevocable, the policyowner has rights that cannot be defeated by a creditor of another person regardless of his or her status as beneficiary. Once the policy has matured, however, the proceeds are the property of the beneficiary and can be freely levied upon by his or her creditors.

STATUTORY PROTECTION

All states have seen fit to enact legislation providing special protection to life insurance against the claims of creditors. This legislation has a long history, the oldest law going back to 1840. The laws are a manifestation of a long-standing public policy that sets a higher priority on people's obligations to their spouses and children than on their obligations to their creditors. Today, these laws are based on the public policy that creditors should not be permitted to make someone destitute and a potential ward of the state. Since the creditor has the right to select his or her debtor, these state exemption laws caution a creditor to be careful in extending credit. They reflect a philosophy that has led to laws exempting workers' compensation awards, veterans' benefits, and other similar payments from attachment by creditors.

The state exemption statutes are diverse in nature. The broadest among them exempt all types of life insurance benefits from attachment by all types of creditors. At the other extreme are laws exempting modest amounts of policy *proceeds* payable to the insured's surviving spouse and children from claims of the insured's creditors. Some of the laws apply to all types of life insurance, while others protect only a particular form, such as group insurance, pensions, disability income, annuity income, or fraternal insurance. Some protect only insurance taken out by a married woman on the life of her husband. There are statutes that protect the insurance against the creditors of the insured only, creditors of the beneficiary only, or any unsecured creditors other than the federal government. Finally, some laws protect only policy proceeds, while others protect all types of benefits, especially cash values. To make matters more confusing, some states have more than one type of statute.

Whether the policyowner's creditors can obtain insurance policy funds depends on whether the creditor is trying to claim the death proceeds or the policy's cash value. In some circumstances, the result depends on the identity of the policyowner, the beneficiary, or the creditor.

The identity of the creditor changes the creditor's rights. The federal government can reach a policy's cash values via a tax lien, whereas a private citizen creditor cannot. The identity of the beneficiary is also important. As an example, see the New York exemption statute, which provides in part as follows:

> If any policy of insurance has been or shall be effected by any person on his own life *in favor of a third person beneficiary,* or made payable, by assignment, change of beneficiary or otherwise, to a third person, *such third person beneficiary,* assignee or payee *shall be entitled to the proceeds and avails* of such policy as against the creditors, personal representatives, trustees in bankruptcy and receivers in state and federal courts of the person effecting the insurance. (emphasis added)

Under this statute the policy's proceeds are not exempt from creditors' claims if the beneficiary is the insured, but they are exempt if a third person is the beneficiary.

The New York statute also provides special protection for certain policyowners as follows:

> . . . if the person effecting such insurance . . . shall be the wife of the insured, she shall be entitled to the proceeds and avails of such policy as against *her* own creditors . . . . (emphasis added)

A comparison of the New York and Oklahoma statutes points out that some statutes provide more protection for the policy values than others. The Oklahoma exemption statute protects the insurance policy *proceeds* from creditors. The New York statute extends the protection to the *proceeds and avails* of the policy, and it defines that term to include the death benefit, cash surrender and loan values, premiums waived, and dividends.

Types of Statutes

At first blush, it seems impossible to classify such a hodgepodge of legislation. Closer inspection, however, reveals patterns that can serve as the basis for classification. The most apparent breakdown is between statutes of general applicability and those that apply to specialized forms of life insurance, such as group insurance, annuities, and so forth. The general statutes may, in turn, be classified into six groups.

Married Women's Statute

The first group embraces those statutes that pertain only to policies taken out by or for the benefit of married women on the lives of their husbands. Appropriately known as *married women's statutes*, these were the earliest laws of this type enacted.[1] The early laws protected only a small amount of insurance per married woman, but the amount of insurance exempted under the modern statute is unlimited. As a rule, the protection is effective only against creditors of the insured.

Distributive Statute

In time, the married women's type of statute was followed by the so-called *distribution* type of statute. These laws provide, in essence, that proceeds payable to the insured's estate will pass to his or her spouse and children free of the claims against the estate. It would be assumed that the very language of these statutes would rule out any protection during the insured's lifetime, but in Tennessee, by a court decision, and in Florida, by statute, cash values were also protected. These laws have seldom protected the policy against claims of the beneficiary's creditors, however.

Procedural Statute

A somewhat later type of statute can be called the *procedural* type. The common characteristic of these laws is that they were enacted not as a part of the insurance law but as one of the general exemptions from execution that are frequently found in civil practice or procedure codes. Since they were general exemption statutes, they usually provided immunity from all types of creditors, including those of the beneficiary. The amount of insurance exempted is usually quite limited, and the cash values are typically not protected. This is perhaps the most heterogeneous group of statutes dealing with the protection of insurance from creditors' claims.

New York Statute

The type of statute that has wielded the greatest influence was first enacted in the state of New York in 1927. It has served as a model for the statutes of 15 other states and has affected the course of legislation in many other jurisdictions. A majority of states now have statutes similar to New York's. Hence it can be described as the typical state exemption statute. Unless the context suggests otherwise, the use hereafter of the term *New York statute* refers to that statute as a generic type, rather than to the specific law of New York state.

The New York statute applies to all policies of life insurance payable to a person or organization other than the insured or the person applying for insurance if he or she is not also the insured. It protects both the cash value and the proceeds against the creditors of the insured and the person procuring the insurance. The protection is available whether the beneficiary designation is revocable or irrevocable, and a reversionary interest in the insured is expressly declared to be immaterial.

The New York statute does not protect anyone against claims of the beneficiary's creditors. However, there are statutes that provide an exemption for proceeds even after they have been distributed to the beneficiary. These statutes bar the creditors of the insured as well as the beneficiary. Normally this protection would not be available to policy values after receipt; thus dividends payable in cash would usually be subject to seizure.

Comprehensive Statute

The broadest protection is available under the so-called *comprehensive statutes*. This type of statute exempts, without limitation, all types of benefits associated with life insurance from the claims of the creditors of the insured, beneficiary, third-party owner, or any other person or organization.

Spendthrift Statute

Finally, there are the laws, called *spendthrift statutes* and found in most states, that are concerned solely with the protection of proceeds held under a settlement agreement against the claims of creditors of the *beneficiary*. The statutes are designed to protect the proceeds only while they are in the hands of the insurer and not after they have been received by the beneficiary. Unlike the other exemption statutes, these laws do not provide automatic protection; they are, instead, permissive in nature. They permit the insurance company and the insured to agree that the proceeds will not be subject to encumbrance, assignment, or alienation by the beneficiary, or to attachment by the beneficiary's creditors. Such an agreement must be embodied in either the policy or the settlement agreement, and the beneficiary must not be a party to it.

Functional Analysis of the Statutes

The minimum objective of state exemption statutes is to provide protection against the claims of the insured's creditors for all or a portion of the proceeds payable to the insured's spouse and children upon the policy's maturity. The maximum objective, typified by the comprehensive statutes, is to provide unlimited protection against creditors of every description to all types of insurance benefits payable to anyone. An intermediate goal, representing the public policy of most jurisdictions, is to protect—both during the lifetime of the insured and upon his or her death—the benefits of an insurance policy payable to anyone other than the insured's estate from the insured's creditors. This objective involves protecting the cash value of the policy; otherwise, the policy may be destroyed by creditors' seizure before it has had an opportunity of serving its basic function—namely, the support of the insured's spouse and children after the insured's death.

Many of the early statutes spoke only of proceeds. Some courts adopted a narrow construction of the term, but most gave it a broad enough interpretation to include cash values. To indicate that prematurity values are to be protected, many statutes use the language "proceeds and avails." A few actually use the words "cash value." The result is that practically all statutes, other than the distributive and procedural types, exempt—by specific language or court interpretation—both the cash value and the maturity value.

The word "proceeds" has had to undergo interpretation in another direction. Does it include paid-up additions, accumulated dividends, and prepaid or discounted premiums, or are proceeds limited to the original face amount? The usual interpretation is that proceeds include all amounts payable upon maturity of the policy.

Exemption of the cash value is of singular importance in connection with the Federal Bankruptcy Reform Act of 1978. If a state does not opt out, the act recognizes all exemptions from creditors' claims granted under the law of the state in which the bankrupt resides. Thus to the extent that a state law exempts cash values, the trustee in bankruptcy cannot take title to the life insurance policies of a bankrupt policyowner. The revocability of the beneficiary designation does not affect the exemption. The bankrupt enjoys more protection under the typical state exemption statute than under case law.

As a matter of fact, the treatment of bankrupts under these laws has been the subject of severe criticism by creditor interests. These critics argue that all too often a person in financial difficulty places a substantial amount of assets in life insurance payable to his or her spouse and children, and then—after going through bankruptcy—uses the insurance to reestablish a business. Since most states permit a person who has become insolvent to maintain existing insurance or even acquire new insurance *for the protection of his or her family* without being in fraud of creditors, there is little that creditors can do to prevent abuse of an otherwise desirable relief provision. Admittedly, the law usually restricts the insurance that an insolvent debtor can acquire or maintain to a "reasonable" amount, but the courts tend to construe the limitation liberally.

The federal tax authorities, on the other hand, have not let state exemption statutes stand in the way of their collection of tax liens. This is true even under the broadest statutes. The government can obtain a policy's cash value through either forced surrender during the insured's lifetime or collection from the proceeds after death, provided a lien had been placed against the cash value before the taxpayer's death.

Among the general state exemption statutes, only those of the married women's and comprehensive types protect benefits payable to the insured or the third-party procurer of the insurance. Thus disability income and annuity payments are usually not exempt from attachment by creditors. In some states, however, these benefits are protected by special statutes.

Parties Entitled to Protection

Note that the intent of the exemption statutes is to protect third parties—not necessarily the policyowners—from the policyowner's creditors. Broadly speaking, state exemption statutes protect all third-party beneficiaries against the claims of the insured's creditors. The New York statute and those patterned after it also protect assignees and third-party owners. The comprehensive statutes protect all the above plus the insured. On the restrictive side, the married women's and distributive statutes protect only the insured's widow(er) and children. The clear trend therefore is toward increasing the number of parties who are given preference over the policyowner's creditors. A few statutes now permit exemption from the policyowner's creditors if the policy is paid to the insured's estate. Such statutes, however, are distinctly in the minority.

Consistent with the goal to subordinate the policyowner's creditors to those of third-party beneficiaries but not to the policyowner, the state exemption statutes do not protect the persons procuring the insurance from their own creditors. Thus with the exception of the comprehensive statutes, policyowners enjoy no protection under the exemption statutes against their own creditors. A policyowner cannot be compelled by his or her creditors to surrender a policy for cash and thus impair the rights of third parties, but if he or she voluntarily does so, the funds can be attached by creditors. Note that the cash value and death proceeds of an endowment policy are exempt in many jurisdictions, despite the fact that the insured is the beneficiary of the endowment proceeds. In a few states, proceeds of an endowment payable to the insured in the form of income are exempt up to the limits of monthly income stated in the law.

Nature of Limitations, if Any

As a rule, the statutes of broad application contain no limitations on the amount of insurance that will be protected thereunder. Several of the statutes, however, contain definite limitations, expressed in terms of either the face amount, a stated cash value, or the amount of annual premiums. For example, some states limit the exemption from creditors to $5,000 or $10,000 in proceeds payable only to a surviving spouse or minor child. The exemption in a few states is available against all creditors—the beneficiary's as well as the insured's. Several states exempt only such amounts of insurance as can be purchased with a maximum annual premium, such as $500, without specifying the plan of insurance. Some states exempt policy cash values only to certain limited amounts. When protection is afforded to disability and annuity payments, a limit such as $400 per month may be placed on the exempted amount of income.

Type of Creditors against Whom Protection Is Afforded

State exemption statutes as a class are concerned only with creditors of the insured. A sizable number of statutes also provide protection against the claims of *creditors of the beneficiary.* This is true of the comprehensive statutes, which tend to exempt all types of insurance benefits from all types of creditors. The procedural statutes, likewise, usually make no distinction between creditors of the insured and those of the beneficiary, but the exemption is typically available only for the amount of insurance that can be obtained with a specified premium, such as $500. The law in many states exempts the proceeds and avails of a policy purchased by a person on the life of his or her spouse against the claims of the purchaser's creditors. Several other states provide a limited amount of protection against the claims of a wife's creditors in connection with policies on her husband's life purchased by the wife with her own funds.

The most prevalent and significant form of statutory protection of insurance proceeds against the creditors of the beneficiary, however, is represented by those statutes that authorize the inclusion of spendthrift clauses in life insurance policies. This type of provision originated with personal trusts and had the dual purpose of protecting the trust income from the creditors of the trust beneficiary and preventing the beneficiary from alienating or disposing of his or her interest in the trust. The validity of such a restrictive provision was widely debated in this country during the latter half of the nineteenth century, but it was ultimately held to be valid in most jurisdictions, either by statute or by judicial decision.

Once the validity of a spendthrift clause in a trust agreement was well established, it was a logical development to introduce it into life insurance settlement agreements. At first its validity in this setting was very much in doubt, however, since life insurance companies did not segregate assets, accept discretionary powers, or otherwise conform to the trust pattern in the administration of proceeds under a deferred-settlement agreement. Now more than half of the states have enacted statutes stating that a spendthrift clause will be enforced if it is contained in either the life insurance policy or the settlement agreement, and the use of spendthrift clauses has become widespread. The following are two examples of spendthrift clauses:

> A beneficiary or contingent payee may not, at or after the insured's death, assign, transfer, or encumber any benefit payable. To the extent allowed by law, the benefits will not be subject to the claims of any creditor of any beneficiary or contingent payee.

> The proceeds and any income payments under the policy will be exempt from the claims of creditors to the extent permitted by law. These proceeds and payments may not be assigned or withdrawn before becoming payable without our agreement.

SCOPE OF EXEMPTION STATUTES

There is considerable diversity in state law as to the length of time proceeds payable under a life insurance policy are exempt from creditors' claims and the amount of physical change proceeds can undergo without losing their exempt status. With respect to claims of the insured's creditors, proceeds are generally regarded to be exempt as long as they can be identified as such. For example, the courts have almost universally extended the exemption to cover the bank account into which the exempt proceeds have been deposited. Furthermore, it has been held that real estate purchased with exempt insurance proceeds is not subject to creditors' actions.

The law is similarly diverse with respect to claims of the beneficiary's creditors. Some statutes that extend their cloak of protection to such claims state specifically that life insurance policy proceeds are exempt from claims of creditors, whether of the insured or the beneficiary, both before and after receipt by the beneficiary. Other statutes do not state that the proceeds are exempt while in the hands of the beneficiary, and the question may be raised as to whether under such statutes proceeds are protected against the beneficiary's creditors after the beneficiary receives the proceeds, particularly as to debts created after receipt. Finally, it seems clear that the protection afforded the beneficiary under a spendthrift clause, even though sanctioned by statute, does not extend beyond the instant of receipt of the proceeds.

NOTE

1. At the time these early laws were enacted, married women did not have legal capacity to own separate property.

How Much Life Insurance Is Enough?

Thomas J. Wolff

Editor's Note: Although an attempt can be made to measure the amount of life insurance required while a person is alive, the test of the accuracy of that measure will come after the person dies. Consequently the editor decided to ask a life insurance salesperson with broad experience both in planning estates and in working with families after death to author this appendix. While the balance of this text is written in the third person, the editor asked Mr. Wolff to write this section in the first person in order to fully reflect his experiences in both planning and settling estates.

WHO CAN DETERMINE NEEDS

Chapters 1 and 9 discussed the various needs that life insurance is designed to satisfy. The obvious question that these chapters raise is how much life insurance is enough. Since few lay people possess the necessary skills to evaluate their own requirements, the services of a qualified life insurance agent are normally required to help ascertain the amount and type of insurance best suited to a person's needs.

KEEPING IT SIMPLE

A legendary life insurance salesman, Grant Taggart, CLU, emphasized the importance of simplifying the need determination process. He stated it this way: "When someone dies money will be needed. The job of the agent is to determine who needs it and how much they will need. The agent must also possess the necessary skills to convince people to purchase the required insurance."

BUYER RESISTANCE

Why did Taggart feel it necessary to include the last sentence in his statement? One might think that once people know how much insurance is required, they will purchase it. Such, however, is not the case. Let's examine the reasons for this buyer resistance. Because death is an unpleasant subject for all of us, most people are reluctant to focus on making an appropriate determination of their life insurance needs. So the first step of Taggart's process, determining who will need money and how much, is in and of itself difficult for people to accomplish.

The second step, initiating the purchase of the appropriate amount of insurance, is even more difficult. Life insurance is an intangible product whose importance becomes evident at death. Since prospects don't believe they will die in the near future, they don't feel a sense of urgency. This problem is exacerbated by the fact that tangibles like cars, vacations, and a host of other inherently pleasing things compete with life insurance for the same dollars, so the purchase of insurance is often put off.

Life Insurance Has to Be Purchased before It's Needed

Prospects are right when they comment that they don't need life insurance "now." Where they are wrong is in postponing the purchase. The following anecdote, first shared with me by Alfred O. Grannum, CLU, will illustrate the point. In 1989 a United Airlines flight began losing power. The pilot, Captain Haynes, tried valiantly to control the vibrating aircraft, but it became evident that the plane would crash. If a Northwestern Mutual Life insurance agent who was on board had approached the passengers at that moment, no doubt all of them would have been willing to purchase life insurance. They finally knew they needed it.

Captain Haynes did a magnificent job of landing the plane in an Iowa cornfield. Nevertheless, half the passengers perished. The point is that like all other forms of insurance, life insurance must also be purchased before we need it so it will be there when we *do* need it.

The foregoing makes it abundantly clear that the professional life insurance salesperson performs the dual function of analyzing the need and motivating prospects to take action immediately. Retired insurance professor Joe Belth says one of the most important jobs of the agent is to get prospects to quit procrastinating. The planning process utilized by today's professional agent may review any number of needs, including death, disability, education, accumulation, and retirement. This section will address only the death need.

HOW TO DETERMINE DEATH NEEDS

A variety of analyses are employed to determine how much insurance is required. The client's situation will usually determine which analysis is used. For example, for a person of significant wealth (estates in excess of $600,000) an estate analysis may be warranted. In this type of analysis, assets and liabilities are carefully evaluated to determine the extent of estate taxes and other expenses. Recommendations usually include a plan for distributing assets and ideas for minimizing and paying estate expenses.

A business owner may have special needs that require an analysis of how best to plan for successor ownership. Yet another example might be a single person who has no financial family obligations. A very simple plan to pay final expenses and debts may suffice.

For the vast majority of prospects, such as married couples with or without children, and single parents, a typical needs analysis will address both cash needs at death and ongoing income needs of survivors. This section will address these situations.

Fact-Finding

To properly determine the type of analysis to use and subsequently to make recommendations, agents go through a process generally referred to as fact-finding. Dr. Tony Alessandra put it well when he said, "People don't buy life insurance when they are made to understand. They buy life insurance when they feel understood." Good fact-finding helps people to "feel understood." To put it another way, agents have to conduct their interviews in such a way that prospects feel they can trust the agents' motives for the recommendations being made. This is critical since agents do have a conflict of interest that is apparent to prospects. If a sale is consummated, agents earn a commission. If no sale is made, no commission is earned. Some "no commission" or "no load" life insurance is sold by financial planners and agents, who are typically compensated on a fee basis. However, these sales represent a tiny fraction of all life insurance sales.

Formula for Building Trust

My own formula for helping people "feel understood" and for building trusting relationships between prospects and agents is Q + 3L + 2R = TRUST. Let's examine each element of the formula.

Q = QUESTION

The first and most important element in the process is asking questions. It is impossible to understand people's needs and make appropriate recommendations in any other way.

There are two general categories about which questions are designed to elicit information: facts and feelings. Examples of factual information that is revealed are names, addresses, dates of birth, and assets and liabilities. While this information is important, even more significant are questions that indicate feelings, like What is your most important goal? How do you feel about your career? What is the most important thing to you in this world? How do you feel about your children's education?

The best fact-finding techniques will intersperse "feeling-finding" questions with fact-finding questions. Asking questions in a respectful manner helps build trust.

The First L = LOOK

A critical element in building trust is to look into a person's eyes. President Richard Nixon was often accused of having "shifty eyes." He was tragically also the only president in United States history to be forced to resign for lying to the American people. Even when a person doesn't initially look back at the agent, it is critical for the agent to continue to look directly into a prospect's eyes. As the interview progresses, eye contact will be made. Looking directly into someone's eyes helps build trust.

The Second L = LEAN

Les Giblin, an outstanding sales consultant, advocates that the questioner lean slightly forward as a prospect responds to questions. This implies, "I'm so interested in what you're saying that I'm hanging on every word." I adopted this technique many years ago and have found it to be an invaluable aid. Leaning helps build trust.

The Third L = LISTEN

All true professionals—doctors, lawyers, clergy, and life insurance salespersons—are good listeners. The famous sales motivator, Doug Edwards, put it more bluntly when he said, "After you ask a question, shut up."

Before its demise the investment firm of E.F. Hutton ran television commercials with the theme, "When E.F. Hutton talks, people listen." I always felt they had it backwards. In our office we have a different motto: "When people talk, we listen." Listening helps build trust.

The First R = RECORD

Picture yourself visiting a physician. You are one of many patients to be seen that day. The doctor asks you a number of questions, which you respond to after careful thought, but the doctor does not record the information. You probably wouldn't look favorably on this technique. The fact-finding process is designed to elicit information to use in designing a plan. Prospects will know that what they are sharing will be used to make recommendations if agents record the information provided. Recording helps build trust.

The Second R = REINFORCE

Many times people will share positive aspects of their lives. For example, they may indicate that they enjoy their work or that they have been successful in their career. When this happens, we have an opportunity to compliment people by reinforcing their achievements. In such a situation I might typically say, "You are really fortunate that you enjoy your work. So many people I talk to hate to go to work." Reinforcing is yet another way to build trust.

The Gift of Listening

The Q + 3L + 2R = TRUST formula is effective because it helps agents become good listeners. A good listener is a person who cares about other people. One might even say that listening is an act of love for another human being. Unfortunately good listeners are a rarity in today's society. We are all so involved with ourselves that we don't take the time to listen to others. To illustrate the point, ask yourself the following two questions: When is the last time someone sat down with you, one on one, and allowed you to talk about yourself (the most important person in the world) for 30 minutes?

And the second question: Wouldn't it feel good to have someone do that with you? I suspect the answer to the first question is "not in a long time." The answer to the second question is probably a resounding "yes." Agents doing thorough fact-finding, using Q + 3L + 2R, allow prospects to talk about themselves. A trusting relationship is the end result.

Needs Analysis

Once the fact-finding process is completed, an analysis of needs can commence. As indicated earlier, there are two types of needs this appendix will explore: cash needs and income needs. For illustrative purposes the explanation of the analysis that follows assumes a two-parent, two-income family with children. With slight modifications the analysis would be equally valid under a different family structure.

When an analysis is undertaken, it assumes death at the present time. The analysis is thus a snapshot of the current situation. Regular reviews occurring at least every other year are critical in order for the analysis to continue to be valid.

Although agents will usually provide suggested values for the needs being analyzed, it is vital that prospects either agree with those values or substitute values that more accurately represent their own desires. The completed analysis must, in all cases, represent clients' wishes. Agents should never force their recommendations on prospects.

Cash Needs

There are six cash needs:

- immediate money fund
- debt liquidation
- emergency fund
- mortgage/rent payment fund
- child/home care fund
- educational/vocational fund

See table 1 at the end of this appendix for a completed cash-needs analysis.

Immediate Money Fund. The first cash need is an immediate money fund for bills presented after death. They may include

- medical and hospital expenses
- burial/funeral expenses
- attorney's/executor's fees
- probate court costs
- state death taxes
- federal estate taxes

The amount required will vary widely from one situation to the next. Based on a study of estates completed by Dearborn Publishing, an amount equal to 50 percent of the higher wage earner's income may be sufficient in the typical case. This same amount is recommended for both spouses. The amount may be excessive for people with high incomes, and low for those with smaller incomes. A calculation of federal and state death taxes will be required for those with large estates in order to determine the amount needed for the immediate money fund.

Debt Liquidation. Most people will want to assure that their debts are liquidated at the time of death. In the case of married couples where both spouses are working, insurance should normally be provided on both lives since their combined incomes are helping to pay off the debt while they are alive.

Emergency Fund. This fund is for unexpected bills not readily payable from current income, such as major repairs to the home or car, or medical expenses. The benefit to be provided is arbitrary. I normally recommend an amount equal to 50 percent of the annual income of the higher-income spouse. I also recommend that both spouses be covered for this amount since either survivor faces the same potential emergency costs.

Mortgage/Rent Payment Fund. Most clients want to provide for full payment of the outstanding mortgage. Even if the mortgage has terms favorable to the borrower, I normally recommend providing enough funds to pay the mortgage. My experience with survivors indicates that they feel better about their future if they own a debt-free home. Thus even when it doesn't make economic sense to pay off the mortgage, it usually makes emotional sense because it provides peace of mind.

Many times an insurance policy can be arranged to provide a dual function. When permanent life insurance is utilized, the cash value can be used to pay off the mortgage before its maturity. The point at which cash values can accomplish the payoff is called the crossover point. This popular plan is known as a *mortgage vanish or mortgage acceleration plan.*

For those who don't own a house or condominium, a rent payment fund can be provided. While the amount selected is arbitrary, I normally recommend a fund equal to 120 percent rent payments (made over 10 years). The fund can be used to help insulate the survivor from future rent increases or as a down payment on a house or condominium.

No one would own a home and not insure it against loss by fire. Yet the chances of loss by fire are small, while the chances of loss due to death or disability are substantial (see table 2 at the end of this appendix). I use table 2 to reinforce the need to provide insurance to cover the mortgage.

Child/Home Care Fund. The child/home care fund is provided to pay for new expense created as a result of the death of a spouse formerly performing these duties without any cash outlay. Examples of this type of expense are baby-sitting, laundry, cleaning, and home and car repairs. Normally benefits are provided until the youngest child is 18.

Cornell University did a study (see table 3) to determine the amount of these costs. The study indicates that the cost of replacing the female spouse's services is usually substantially higher than replacing those of the male. A future study may well indicate that this gap has been overestimated since many male spouses in two-income homes perform tasks previously attended to by the female spouse. Under any circumstances the figures should be adjusted to reflect the unique aspects of a particular family's situation.

Once the child/home care amount is established, a timing discount can be applied because death benefits would be paid immediately while the funds would be used over a period of years (see table 3 for an example).

Educational/Vocational Fund. This fund is designed to provide for children's educational or vocational needs. The amount needed will vary depending on the types of schools being considered and the number of years of education planned for. In the typical situation where 4 years of college are planned, parents will want to provide as a minimum the average cost of 4 years in a publicly supported college. Currently that cost is about $45,000.

Although costs have been rising drastically, it is not necessary to consider future cost increases. Since the analysis assumes death at the present time, if in fact this occurs, the death proceeds can be invested until the children matriculate. The increasing value of the account should offset the increasing costs of education. As stated earlier, updating the plan on a regular basis is essential to assure that the amount provided continues to keep pace with inflation.

Capital Required. Once all the cash needs (of both spouses when applicable) are agreed upon, they are totaled. Next the existing life insurance (including group insurance but excluding accidental death benefits) and existing liquid assets are totaled, and the result is subtracted from the total cash need. Any deficiency is shown as additional capital required. Any surplus will be carried forward to the income-needs analysis.

Although social security does pay a maximum cash death benefit of $255, in the interest of simplicity I ignore this benefit in calculating the capital needs.

Income Needs. Once the cash needs are established, it is essential to analyze the family's ongoing income needs. See table 4 of this appendix for an example of a completed income-needs analysis.

Income Objective. The first step in analyzing income needs is to determine the income objective after death. Typically a percentage of the present gross total family income is selected. While the percentage selected will vary, I have found 70 percent to be the most generally accepted number. A government study by the Bureau of Labor Statistics confirms the 70 percent objective as reasonable for those earning over $60,000 and for all two-income families. The objective can be reduced somewhat at lower income levels (see table 4). The objective selected should permit a family to maintain their customary standard of living. One must never forget that a luxury once enjoyed becomes a necessity.

Tax Considerations. The question often asked is, Should the income objective be based on gross or net income? The key to successful planning is to keep the analysis as simple as possible. Therefore when doing an analysis, I utilize gross income to calculate the income objective. When calculating the income provided to a beneficiary after death, I also use gross income. This "gross" to "gross" calculation is simple, quite accurate, and keeps the discussions focused on needs rather than taxes.

Social Security Benefits. Once the income objective is established, the existing sources of income are analyzed. The first of these is social security benefits. Calculation of the precise amount of benefits in any given situation is quite complicated, especially because benefits change from year to year based on changes in the consumer price index. Calculation is further complicated by frequent social security legislative changes.

My experience indicates that prospects are not interested in all the nuances of this complicated benefit. Thus to maintain simplicity I use a table that provides approximate benefits (see table 5). Subtracting the social security benefit from the income objective yields the preliminary income shortage.

Benefits are payable to a spouse aged 60 and over or to a spouse of any age if he or she is caring for a child who is under 16 or disabled. Benefits are payable to children who are under age 18 (under age 19 if in high school) or any age if continuously disabled since before age 22.

Other Incomes. The next step is to identify any other sources of income. The most common item in this category is the income of a working spouse. There may also be income provided by a pension plan or other employer-sponsored programs. Another source of income could be nonliquid assets such as rental property. A note of clarification should be written to help survivors understand which assets are intended to fund which needs and whether or not liquid assets are intended to be retained by the survivors. Once all other income is identified, the total is subtracted from the preliminary income shortage. The balance (if any) is the total annual income shortage.

Method of Providing Capital. The only way to satisfy the income shortage is to provide capital to the heirs. Life insurance is the only source of instant capital at death. There are two methods used to calculate the amount of life insurance required—the capital-liquidation method and the capital-retention method.

Capital-liquidation method. In the capital-liquidation method, a pool of capital is created, and over the surviving spouse's lifetime this pool is liquidated. Normally at the spouse's death no assets remain. Another version of this method is to liquidate the capital over a defined number of years. This method works well when children, but no spouse, are being provided for.

The advantage of capital liquidation over capital retention is that less capital is required. However, there are several disadvantages:

- No capital remains when either the spouse dies or the selected period ends. Since most of us spend our lifetime building an estate, it is unnatural to plan for its total liquidation.

- If funds for the beneficiary are being provided under an annuity option for the lifetime of a beneficiary, it may be difficult or impossible to withdraw extra money that may be needed for a future contingency. For example, making a gift for a grandchild's education might not be possible.

- The third and most important reason I usually do not recommend the capital-liquidation plan is that it subjects beneficiaries to the ravages of inflation. The best way to illustrate the problem is to look at an example. Table 6 at the end of this appendix assumes a beneficiary is to receive $20,000 per year for life. Inflation is assumed to be 6 percent (the actual average rate of inflation over the past 20 years). Twenty years later the income required to maintain the same standard of living is over $64,000. The problem created is self-evident.

  There are annuities that can be invested in equity accounts and may offset the effect of inflation by increasing income over the years. While this strategy may help, it will not solve the inflation problem because the amount in the account is being reduced every year as the annuity is paid out. Thus the investment gains diminish as the capital shrinks.

- Generally planning of this type is done for relatively young clients—that is, those under 50. Table 7 shows the small amount of additional capital required to satisfy the capital need on a capital-retention basis rather than a capital-liquidation basis.

In spite of the foregoing data some advisers continue to recommend the capital-liquidation method. Typically the recommendation is to exhaust principal and interest over the person's life expectancy. In my opinion this is not a sound recommendation. By definition half of us will outlive our life expectancy. Furthermore, life expectancy has increased and is expected to continue increasing in the years ahead. What this means is that 50 percent of beneficiaries will run out of money before they run out of time. If the liquidation method is to be used at all, it must be designed to provide income to an age the beneficiary is not likely to outlive.

Capital-retention method. In the capital-retention method the amount of capital required is calculated assuming that only the income is utilized. To accomplish this, the income shortage is divided by the assumed interest rate and the result is the capital required. Any shortage of capital from the cash-needs analysis is added to this amount to arrive at the total new capital required. If there is a surplus of capital carried forward from cash needs, it is subtracted to arrive at the new capital required.

One of the critical factors in arriving at the amount of new capital required is the assumed interest rate. Although capital properly invested in a balanced portfolio may yield an annual return of as much as 10 percent, I usually recommend that the assumed interest rate be 4 percent.

If only 4 percent of the earnings is used, any excess can be added to the capital. This will cause the capital to grow each year. Table 8, which assumes earnings growth of 10 percent, shows how the growing fund will make the beneficiary's income inflation-proof. For example, at the end of 10 years usable income has gone from $4,000 to $6,800, precisely the amount required to keep pace with inflation.

The assumed interest rate can be calculated as follows:

Expected rate of return	10%
Rate of inflation	−6%
Usable family income	4%

The calculation is not foolproof. No one can accurately predict rates of return, inflation rates, and the effect of income taxes. I find, however, that prospects readily accept the validity of the concept.

The disadvantages of the capital-liquidation method were itemized earlier. The capital-retention method, used properly, overcomes those disadvantages to a significant degree. A personal experience will help illustrate the point. My father died at the age of 78 and left a substantial estate to my mother, who was then 72. My mother was able to live comfortably on the income provided, but she developed Parkinson's disease, making it necessary for her to go into a nursing home at the age of 85.

My mother was a very proud person. Her one request on entering the nursing home was that she have a private room, which cost $50,000 annually. As her Parkinson's progressed, she became depressed. It was concluded that she would benefit from help during the day. The cost of an aide for 6 hours a day was $50,000 annually, increasing the total cost per year to $100,000. Her capital was being drained rapidly.

The demeaning circumstances she found herself in were a heavy burden. The only thing she still had going was a sense of pride in paying for her care. Her great fear was that if she could no longer pay these expenses, she would lose her aide and her private room and become dependent on medicaid. Each time I went to visit her she had one question: "How is my money holding out?" I assured her that if she ran out, I would be able to assume her continuing care. "No!" she said emphatically, and then asked again, "How is my money holding out?"

At her death a small amount of capital remained. Had she lived much longer, she would have run out of money before she ran out of time. This personal story reinforces my belief that significant amounts of capital may be required well into our late 80s and 90s in order to satisfy the needs of life.

Complications of Income-Needs Analysis. An analysis of income needs requires an awareness of the possibility of several other adjustments.

Blackout period. In the analysis we have reviewed thus far, no adjustment has been made for the loss of social security benefits that normally occurs when the youngest children leaves home. This period is referred to as the *blackout period.* Moreover, the analysis does not demonstrate the resumption of a benefit for a surviving spouse after age 60. These omissions are covered in a footnote in table 4.

Keeping it simple is the reason for not including these calculations. The danger of providing so much information that prospects become confused and take no action is very real. Thus for most prospects I do not calculate the additional insurance required to cover the blackout period. However, in the total income analysis in table 9 the total need, including the capital required to replace social security during the blackout period, is considered.

Resumption of social security benefits. Yet another complication is that there is a resumption of social security benefits when the spouse of a deceased reaches age 60. Since this calculation is extremely complex, I never include it in the plan. The logic behind this is that even though the capital-retention method is used, it will be difficult to make the plan fully inflation-proof. The extra benefits social security provides at age 60 will be a welcome inflation-fighting addition for the beneficiary.

Purchase of Life Insurance. Establishing the amount of insurance needed is more important than selecting the type of policy. Once the need has been established, prospects will require help in selecting the type of life insurance.

There are three main factors that influence the selection of the appropriate policy or combination of policies:

- the amount of new insurance required
- the premium dollars available
- the objectives in addition to the death benefit to be satisfied

Unfortunately it will not always be easy to formulate a solution that provides for all the prospect's objectives. For example, clients may wish to utilize the cash values of permanent insurance to provide for retirement benefits. Yet the need for life insurance may be so great that the amount of premium available will only purchase term insurance. Unfortunately this type of situation is a rather common occurrence. The continuing evolvement of new policies and combinations of policies has helped to alleviate the problem to a significant degree, but the problem persists.

In my opinion, in most cases protection needs should be satisfied first because death can occur at any moment. On the other hand, there is usually time to satisfy accumulation and retirement objectives.

It is not always easy to convince prospects to proceed in this manner. Accumulating money for future use is a lot more pleasant than paying premiums that will only provide a benefit upon death. Nevertheless, a professional life insurance agent must make every effort to cover clients' cash and income needs fully.

Regular Reviews

I mentioned earlier that not only is it important for clients to purchase the required insurance, but it is equally critical to review and update the plan regularly.

Many developments, such as changes in assets and liabilities and composition of income and family, may require updating the program. Another major factor is inflation. One of the first questions I ask prospects, when reviewing their program, is, "When did you buy your last insurance?" Let's assume the answer is 5 years ago. I then ask, "I assume you felt your program was adequate at that time?" The response is usually positive. I then point out that based on inflation alone, they need to increase their insurance by a given percentage. Table 10 illustrates the problem. I then complete a new needs analysis to determine the actual new insurance required.

Settling the Death Claim

Settlement options and trusts are covered elsewhere in this book. However, in closing this section I want to add a few words based on my 40 years' experience in settling death claims.

When there are substantial amounts of capital (insurance and other assets) in an estate, the best results are achieved when clients utilize an inter vivos life insurance trust as the beneficiary of these assets. The trust provides an opportunity for flexibility and investment expertise while also safeguarding the assets from unwise dissipation by beneficiaries.

In view of relatively low guaranteed rates of return, settlement options in life insurance contracts have historically been perceived to be an unattractive choice for beneficiaries. As a result they have been utilized in a very small percentage of cases.

In recent years companies have responded with more attractive programs. In some cases these programs operate much as a money market fund in which checks can be drawn against balances left with the insurance company to earn interest.

Also if a company's settlement options are not competitive, agents should explore the possibility of having a beneficiary purchase an annuity at more competitive rates.

IN SUMMARY

A professional life insurance agent has the opportunity of providing substantial benefits to a prospective client. A thorough fact-finding interview will reveal prospects' needs. By completing both the cash-needs and income-needs analyses, the agent can determine the new capital required. While prospects will usually not be eager to purchase the required insurance, a skillful agent will be able to convince prospects of the importance of taking action immediately. Once a plan has been established, agents must offer to review and update the plan regularly.

Note: The 10 tables that follow are reprinted with the premission of Wolff-Zacklin & Associates, copyright © Vernon Publishing, Inc. 1992. All rights reserved.

TABLE 1

CASH NEEDS

	Joe	Donna
	Name	Name

Immediate Money Fund
This fund is for the bills presented after death, which will have to be paid. They may include:

- Medical and hospital expenses
- Burial expenses
- Attorney's/Executor's fees

- Federal Estate Taxes
- State death taxes
- Probate court costs

50% of the higher wage earner's annual income may be sufficient.[1]

$ __17,500__ $ __17,500__

Debt Liquidation ✓

- Total of installment credit
- Unpaid notes

- School and auto loans
- Outstanding bills

$ __3,000__ $ __3,000__ *

Emergency Fund
This fund is for unexpected bills not readily payable from current income. Such things as: major repairs to the home or automobile, medical emergencies, etc.

50% of the higher wage earner's annual income may be sufficient.

$ __17,500__ $ __17,500__ *

Mortgage/Rent Payment Fund ✓
What would it take to pay your mortgage off today?

or

What amount is sufficient for a ten-year rent fund?

Monthly rent $_____ x 120 mo.   = $_____

$ __60,000__ $ __60,000__ *

Child/Home Care Fund
To pay for new expenses created as a result of the death of a spouse formerly performing these duties without any cash outlay.

You:* Amount per year $ __3,100__ x __4.8__ = $ __14,880__
Factor

Spouse: Amount per year $ __12,100__ x __4.8__ = $ __58,080__
Factor

$ __14,880__ $ __58,080__

Number of years until youngest child is age 18[3]

Discount Factors[4]	1	2	3	4	5	6	7	8	9	10	11	12	13	14	15	16	17	18
	.93	1.8	2.6	3.4	4.1	4.8	5.4	6.0	6.5	7.0	7.5	7.9	8.4	8.8	9.1	9.5	9.8	10.1

Educational/Vocational Fund ✓
The cost of a four-year undergraduate education or comparable vocational training will vary by state and type of school.

$45,000 per child is usually the minimum that should be provided.

$ __45,000__ $ __45,000__ *

Subtotal

$ __157,880__ $ __201,080__

Total of current savings, other liquid assets and existing life insurance

- $ __65,000__   - $ __35,000__

New capital required

$ __92,880__ (A) $ __166,080__ (B)

[1]Estates in excess of $600,000 (the Unified Credit Equivalent) may have larger expenses.
[2]For appropriate annual amount on both spouses see table "What is the Economic Value of the Work We Do at Home?"
[3]Assuming a 7% rate of return.
[4]Discount factors used because funds available at death are used over a period of years.
* Applies only if spouse is employed.

TABLE 2

Our Home —
the largest investment
most of us make

We all insure it against the loss by fire, yet the chance of a total loss by fire is only 1 out of 100. However, the chance of loss due to death or disability before paying off a mortgage is much greater!

Age	Chance of Death Within 15 Years	Chance of Disability Within 15 Years	Chance of Death Within 30 Years	Chance of Disability Within 30 Years
20	1 in 37	1 in 14	1 in 12	1 in 8
25	1 in 34	1 in 12	1 in 9	1 in 7
30	1 in 26	1 in 10	1 in 6	1 in 6
35	1 in 18	1 in 8	1 in 4	1 in 4
40	1 in 12	1 in 6	1 in 3	1 in 3
45	1 in 8	1 in 5	1 in 2	1 in 2
50	1 in 5	1 in 5	1 in 2	Almost Certain

Doesn't it make sense to
insure these risks as well?

Source: 1980 Commissioners Standard Ordinary Mortality Table and 1985 Commissioners Disability Table
    Definition of disability: 90 days or more

TABLE 3

What Is The Economic Value Of The Work We Do At Home?

According to a recent Cornell University study[1], the following are the average **annual** dollar values of duties performed at home:

Number of Children	Both Spouses Working		One Spouse Working Outside the Home	
	Husband	**Wife**	**Working Spouse**	**Non-Working Spouse**
1	$3,100	$12,100	$2,750	$18,850
2	$4,150	$13,850	$3,800	$19,050
3 or more	$4,850	$15,600	$4,500	$20,800

To determine the amount of capital that may be required to offset the economic loss a death would create, multiply the applicable number in the table by the appropriate factor below.[2]

Number of years until youngest child is age 18

Discount Factors	1	2	3	4	5	6	7	8	9	10	11	12	13	14	15	16	17	18
	.93	1.8	2.6	3.4	4.1	4.8	5.4	6.0	6.5	7.0	7.5	7.9	8.4	8.8	9.1	9.5	9.8	10.1

[1]Source: Bulletin 60, New York State College of Human Ecology, Cornell University, Ithaca, N.Y., updated through August 1992
[2]Discount factors used because funds that become available at death are used over a period of years.

TABLE 4

INCOME NEEDS[1]

For Donna in the event of Joe's death

INCOME OBJECTIVE:

Based on a Government study by the Bureau of Labor Statistics[2], the following are typical income objectives in order to permit a family to "remain in their own world" after the death of a wage earner. Assumption is the mortgage on residence is paid, or a rent fund has been established, and educational expenses are provided for separately.

Annual Gross Income	Percentage of Gross Income Required
Up to $44,000	70%
$44,001 to $49,000	66%
$49,001 to $54,000	63%
$54,001 to $60,000	60%
Over $60,000	57%
Two Income Families[3] (At all income levels)	70%

Present Income (all income of both wage earners)	$ _____60,000_____
Income objective (__70__ % of above) $ ___42,000___	
Average annual Social Security[4] − $ ___9,500___	
Preliminary income shortage $ ___32,500___	
Other income (if any) − $ ___25,000___	
Total annual income shortage	$ _____7,500_____
Amount of capital required to provide this income ($ ___7,500___ + ___4___ %) Annual Income Shortage Assumed Interest Rate	$ ___187,500___
Cash needs requirement	$ ___92,880___
Total new capital required	$ ___280,380___

[1] Use a separate worksheet to calculate the Income Needs of each wage earner if desired.
[2] Source: Bureau of Labor Statistics Consumer Expenditures Survey; updated with Bureau of Labor Statistics Consumer Price Index through 5/91.
[3] The study found two-income households outspend their one-earner counterparts. Therefore, if both spouses are presently working, 70% of their Total Gross Income should be provided regardless of the Income Level.
[4] Only available until youngest child reaches age 18, unless beneficiary is over age 60. See Social Security Table. Use another worksheet to calculate the Income Needs during the blackout period if desired.

TABLE 5

Social Security Survivorship Benefits

Facts about deceased[1]		Average annual benefit if surviving spouse is not employed		Average annual benefit if surviving spouse is employed[2]		
Age	Approximate annual earnings	1 child	2 or more children	1 child	2 children	3 or more children
63 — 67	$58,000 or more	$20,300	$23,700	$10,200	$20,300	$23,700
	45,000	19,400	22,700	9,700	19,400	22,700
	35,000	18,400	21,500	9,200	18,400	21,500
	25,000	15,300	18,400	7,700	15,300	18,400
51 — 62	$58,000 or more	$20,700	$24,100	$10,300	$20,700	$24,100
	45,000	19,700	23,000	9,800	19,700	23,000
	35,000	18,600	21,600	9,300	18,600	21,600
	25,000	15,300	18,400	7,600	15,300	18,400
41 — 50	$58,000 or more	$22,200	$25,900	$11,100	$22,200	$25,900
	45,000	20,700	24,100	10,400	20,700	24,100
	35,000	18,900	22,000	9,500	18,900	22,000
	25,000	15,300	18,400	7,600	15,300	18,400
31 — 40	$58,000 or more	$23,500	$27,400	$11,700	$23,500	$27,400
	45,000	21,000	24,500	10,500	21,000	24,500
	35,000	18,900	22,100	9,500	18,900	22,100
	25,000	15,300	18,400	7,700	15,300	18,400
30 or under	$58,000 or more	$23,900	$27,900	$11,900	$23,900	$27,900
	45,000	21,100	24,700	10,600	21,100	24,700
	35,000	19,000	22,200	9,500	19,000	22,200
	25,000	15,500	18,600	7,700	15,500	18,600

[1] If earnings are not shown, use nearest amount illustrated. Actual benefits will depend upon wage history and actual age. Assumes death in January 1993.

[2] Assumes full-time employment. If surviving spouse is not employed full-time, somewhat larger benefits may be available for the one child and two children situations.

Benefits are payable to a spouse age 60 and over, or any age if caring for a child who is under 16 or disabled. Benefits are payable to children who are under age 18, or who are under age 19 if in high school, or who are any age if disabled before 22.

TABLE 6

Impact of Inflation —

The 20-year average annual inflation rate has been 6%[1]

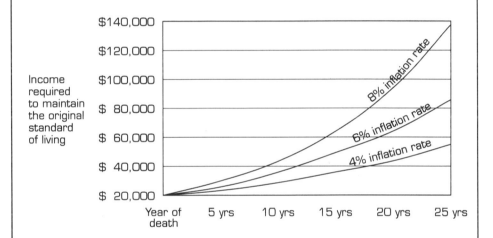

There are only two ways to guard against inflation:

1. People at work
2. Money at work

You can hedge against inflation by retaining capital (money at work).

[1]Source: U.S. Department of Labor, Bureau of Labor Statistics, Consumer Price Index 1971-1991.

TABLE 7

How much capital is needed to pay a survivor $7,000 per year?

Using principal and interest

Age of survivor	Approximate life expectancy	Using principal and interest @ 7%
30	50 Years	$96,600
35	45 Years	95,200
40	40 Years	93,300
45	35 Years	90,800
50	30 Years	86,900

If survivors live beyond life expectancy
they will have no further income.

Using interest only

1. **$100,000 @ 7% will provide $7,000 annually.**

2. **The $7,000 will be provided regardless of how long a survivor lives and the $100,000 will pass to the heirs.**

TABLE 8

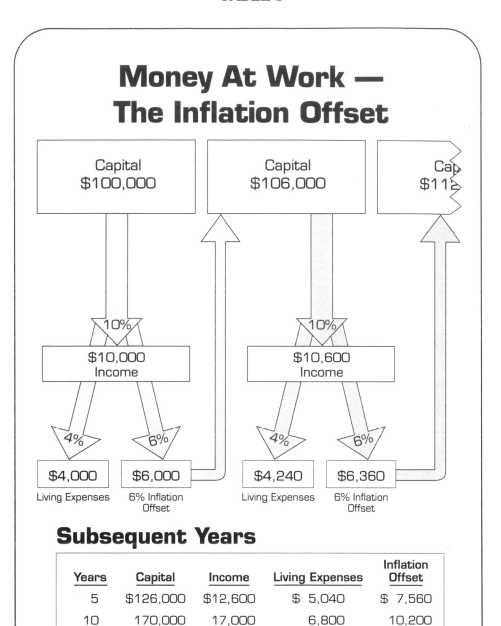

Money At Work —
The Inflation Offset

| Capital $100,000 | Capital $106,000 | Ca... $11... |

10%

| $10,000 Income | $10,600 Income |

4%   6%   4%   6%

| $4,000 | $6,000 | $4,240 | $6,360 |

Living Expenses | 6% Inflation Offset | Living Expenses | 6% Inflation Offset

Subsequent Years

Years	Capital	Income	Living Expenses	Inflation Offset
5	$126,000	$12,600	$ 5,040	$ 7,560
10	170,000	17,000	6,800	10,200
15	226,000	22,600	9,040	13,560
20	302,500	30,250	12,100	18,150

TABLE 9

TOTAL INCOME ANALYSIS

New Capital Required During Child Rearing Period $ _280,380_

Income Objective After Child Rearing Period (60 %) $ _36,000_
(See Below)

Social Security only available until youngest child reaches
  age 16, thus income will be reduced _4_
  years from now to Total of other income $ _32,500_
  and annual income shortage.

Income Shortage After Child Rearing Period $ _3,500_

New Capital Required ($ _3,500_ ÷ _4.0_ %) $ _87,500_
           Income Shortage   Assumed Interest Rate

Amount of Capital Required today to Equal $ _87,500_
  in _4_ years (_$87,500_ x _.855_) $ _74,810_
            New Capital Required Discount Factor

Total New Capital Required $ _355,190_

		Years Until Youngest Child Reaches 16	Discount Factors[1]		
			4%	5%	6%
Percentage of Gross Income Required		1	.962	.952	.943
Annual Gross Income	Children Gone	2	.925	.907	.890
		3	.889	.864	.840
Up to $44,000	60%	4	.855	.823	.792
$44,001 to $49,000	55%	5	.822	.784	.747
		6	.790	.746	.705
$49,001 to $54,000	51%	7	.760	.711	.665
$54,001 to $60,000	48%	8	.731	.677	.627
		9	.703	.645	.592
Over $60,000	45%	10	.676	.614	.558
		11	.650	.585	.527
		12	.625	.557	.497
Two Income Families[1]	60%	13	.601	.530	.469
(At all income levels)		14	.577	.505	.442
		15	.555	.481	.417
		16	.534	.458	.394

[1] A Bureau of Labor Statistics study found two-income households outspend their one-earner counterparts. Therefore, if both spouses are presently working, 60% of their Total Gross Income should be provided regardless of the Income Level.

TABLE 10

Is Your Life Insurance Adequate?

Year of Last Insurance Review	Assumed Amount of Life Insurance Owned	Amount of Life Insurance Required in 1993 to Provide the Same Benefits	Percentage Increase Required[1]
1983	$100,000	$145,000	45%
1984	100,000	140,000	40%
1985	100,000	135,000	35%
1986	100,000	130,000	30%
1987	100,000	128,000	28%
1988	100,000	123,000	23%
1989	100,000	118,000	18%
1990	100,000	112,000	12%
1991	100,000	106,000	6%
1992	100,000	103,000	3%

[1]Source: U.S. Department of Labor, Bureau of Labor Statistics – 1982-1992

About the Authors

Burton T. Beam, Jr., CLU, ChFC, CPCU, is director of continuing education at The American College and is responsible for the course material on group insurance and social insurance in the Chartered Life Underwriter (CLU) and Chartered Financial Consultant (ChFC) programs. The author of *Group Benefits: Basic Concepts and Alternatives* and *Employee Benefits,* he coauthors the employee benefit column in the *Journal of the American Society of CLU & ChFC.* Mr. Beam holds a BA from the University of Oregon and advanced degrees from the University of Oregon and the University of Pennsylvania.

Burke A. Christensen, JD, CLU, is vice president, educational services, and general counsel of the American Society of CLU & ChFC. He is the author of the column "Law and Life Insurance," published in *Trusts and Estate* magazine, and "Strictly Speaking," a column on professional and business ethics published in the *Journal of the American Society of CLU & ChFC.*

Archer L. Edgar is vice president, office of the president, of the Life Insurance Marketing and Research Association (LIMRA) and is directly accountable for the organization's human resources and financial functions. He joined LIMRA's research division in 1965, and as vice president, research information, he was responsible for the dissemination, interpretation, and accuracy of LIMRA research. A recognized industry expert on distribution systems and the agency system, Mr. Edgar holds an MS degree in economics from the University of Connecticut.

Harry D. Garber, FSA, MAAA, recently retired as vice chairman of the Equitable Life Assurance Society of the United States. During his career there, Mr. Garber served as chief financial officer and held a number of senior officer positions in which he was responsible for individual product development, pricing, underwriting, and administration; financial reporting; computer system development and operations; and government relations. He was instrumental in both the New York State demutualization law and the demutualization of the Equitable. He is past president of the American Academy of Actuaries and current vice president of the Society of Actuaries. He holds a BA in Mathematics from Yale University.

Ram S. Gopalan is program director, cost research, at the Life Insurance Marketing and Research Association (LIMRA). His work includes research on insurance company field costs and the application of cost studies to planning and management. Mr. Gopalan has published reports on cost evaluation techniques and comparative distribution costs in the insurance industry.

Jon S. Hanson, JD, served as executive director of the National Association of Insurance Commissioners (NAIC) from 1968 to 1982, when he established his own legal and consulting practice. He provides legal and related research on insurance and insurance regulatory problems to law firms, insurers, trade associations, and related organizations. Mr. Hanson has prepared briefs for submission to the United States Supreme Court and federal courts of appeal and has developed numerous model laws and regulations. He holds a law degree from the University of Michigan Law School.

Jeremy S. Holmes, CLU, FALU, FLMI, retired as chief underwriting officer and chief claim officer for The Travelers Insurance Company in July 1993 after 31 years of service. He is now national representative for Underwriting Services at GIB Laboratories. A graduate of the University of Hartford, Mr. Holmes is a member of the American Society of CLU & ChFC and past president and editor of the Executive Council of the Home Office Life Underwriters Association (HOLUA). While serving in that position, Mr. Holmes worked with Jon W. Webber, then president of the American Society of CLU & ChFC, to build stronger ties between The American College and HOLUA. HOLUA supported Mr. Holmes and contributor James F. Winberg's efforts toward this book.

Joseph W. Huver, CLU, ChFC, MSFS, worked for 14 years as an agent, manager, and broker specializing in pension and estate planning before founding Huver & Associates, Inc., the first independent structured settlement services firm in the eastern United States, in 1976. Mr. Huver was a founding member of the National Structured Settlement Trade Association (NSSTA) and currently serves on its board of directors. He is the author of *Structured Settlements: An Alternative Approach to the Settling of Claims,* published by the National Underwriter Company in 1992.

James F. Ivers III, JD, LLM, ChFC, is associate professor of taxation at The American College. His responsibilities include the development of the College's course in income taxation. Mr. Ivers is the coauthor of *Planning for Business Owners and Professionals,* published by The American College, and *Stanley and Kilcullen's Federal Income Tax Law,* published by Warren Gorham Lamont. A member of the bar in Pennsylvania, Florida, and Massachusetts, he is a consultant and frequent speaker on taxation and financial planning. Mr. Ivers is a graduate of Villanova University. He received his JD and his LLM from the Boston University School of Law.

Donald A. Jones, PhD, FSA, EA, MAAA, is director of the actuarial science program in the Mathematics Department at Oregon State University. For more than 30 years he was on the actuarial faculty of the University of Michigan. Dr. Jones has been an actuarial consultant to both private and public pension plans and to state regulators. Active in the Society of Actuaries, he is coauthor of *Actuarial Mathematics,* a textbook published by that society for its educational system. He holds a PhD in Mathematical Statistics from the University of Iowa.

Ted Kurlowicz, JD, LLM, CLU, ChFC, is professor of taxation at The American College. His responsibilities include preparation of courses in estate planning and planning for business owners and professionals. Mr. Kurlowicz has also participated in the development of examinations for the College. He received his bachelor's degree from the University of Connecticut, his law degrees from the University of Delaware and Villanova University, and a master's degree from the University of Pennsylvania.

John J. McFadden, JD, is professor of taxation at The American College. He is responsible for the College's graduate courses in advanced pension and retirement planning and executive compensation. Mr. McFadden is admitted to the Pennsylvania bar and is the author of books and articles related to pensions and executive benefits. He holds a law degree from Harvard Law School.

Norma L. Nielson, PhD, CLU, is a professor at the Oregon State University College of Business, where she teaches insurance, employee benefits, and risk management. She received her PhD in insurance in 1979 from the University of Pennsylvania. Dr. Nielson has published extensively and testified frequently on insurance matters. She is active in Oregon's health care reform efforts and is an officer and member of the board of directors of the American Risk and Insurance Association.

Michael B. Petersen is the director of editorial services for the Life Insurance Marketing and Research Association (LIMRA). He is frequent writer on industry topics, and his byline is a familiar one in industry publications. The author of more than 20 LIMRA publications, Petersen joined LIMRA in 1956. He was director of publications and public relations before being named to his current post in 1987.

Francis H. Schott, PhD, is a director and member of the Investment Committee at Mutual of America. He is also a director of the Federal Home Loan Bank of New York, the New Germany Fund, and the Foundation for Child Development. He retired in 1991 from the positions of Senior Vice President and Chief Economist at the Equitable Life Assurance Society and Chairman of the Investment Research Committee at the American Council of Life Insurance. He holds a bachelor's degree from Oberlin College and a PhD from Princeton University.

James F. Winberg, CLU, ChFC, FALU, FLMI, serves as underwriting consultant for Minnesota Mutual Life Insurance Company.   He joined Minnesota Mutual's Underwriting Department in 1973 after a 4-year tour of duty as a naval officer.   Mr. Winberg has held various positions in the department; currently he specializes in large life and disability cases.   Mr. Winberg serves on the Life Underwriting Education Committee of the Academy of Life Underwriting.   He holds a bachelor's degree from Luther College.

Thomas J. Wolff, CLU, ChFC, a well-known speaker throughout the insurance industry, is founder and principal of Wolff-Zackin & Associates, a multiple-line insurance agency in Vernon, Connecticut.   Past president of the National Association of Life Underwriters (NALU), he was a leader in the fight to restrain the Federal Trade Commission from further investigation of the industry.   A member of the Million Dollar Round Table (MDRT) for 35 consecutive years and an eight-time Top of the Table qualifier, Mr. Wolff is past president of the MDRT Foundation.   He holds a degree in economics from the University of Connecticut and is a recipient of the John Newton Russell Award, the industry's highest honor.

Walter H. Zultowski, PhD, is senior vice president of the Life Insurance Marketing and Research Association (LIMRA).   He joined LIMRA in 1978 as an associate scientist, moved through various managerial positions, and was named to his current post in 1990.   A highly regarded and widely known speaker in the field of life insurance and financial services marketing, Dr. Zultowski is a frequent participant in individual company strategic planning sessions and a frequent contributor to the industry's trade press.   He holds a PhD in psychology from the University of Tennessee.

Index

A.B.A. assignment form, 857–59
A.M. Best, 652
Accidental death benefits
    exception to incontestable clause,
        823–24
    reinsurance of, 489
    under group contracts, 17, 713–15
Accounting
    comparison of GAAP and SAP,
        642–51
    differences between GAAP and SAP,
        638–42
    generally accepted accounting
        practices (GAAP), 637–51
    statutory accounting practices (SAP),
        636–51
Accounting Principles Board, 636
Acquisition expenses
    under adjusted premium method,
        413
Acquisitions and mergers, 581
    federal antitrust treatment of,
        611–13
    state insurance regulation of, 609–11
Actuarial assumptions
    interest assumptions in general,
        338–39
    reserves of interest assumptions,
        effect on, 371–72
    reserves of mortality assumptions,
        effect on, 370–71
    for reserve valuation purposes,
        369–72
Adjustable life insurance
    definition, 55
    history of, 62
    table, 58
Adjusted-premium method, 413–15
Adult day care, 180
Adverse financial selection
    surrender values, effect on, 411
Adverse mortality selection
    under assessment insurance, 22

under group life insurance, 688
as justification for selection
        procedure, 436
for life insurance generally, 435–36
at older ages, 466
reinstatement of suspended policies,
        756
surrender value, impact on, 410–11
under term insurance generally,
        33–34
under term policy, 36
traceable to renewal privilege under
        term policy, 33
under yearly renewable term
        insurance, 24
Affiliations
    acquisitions and mergers, 605–7
    alliances, 608–9
    holding companies, 607–8
    regulation of, 609–13
Age of applicant
    as a selection factor, 439
    maximum age limitation, 439, 466
    misstatement of age clause, 439
    proof of, 439
Age setback, 126
Agency building
    general agent, 622
    managerial, 622
Agency, law of
    agent, definition of, 804
    apparent authority of agents, 805–6
    brokers as agents, 808
    falsification of application by agent,
        812–13
    limited powers of agents, 807–8
    nonwaiver clause, 758, 807
    presumption of, 805
    principal, definition of, 804
    responsibility of principal for acts of
        agents, 806–7
Agent
    apparent authority, 805–6

brokers as, 808
definition of, 804
falsification of application by, 812–13
limited powers of, 807–8
nonwaiver clause, 758, 807
presumption of agency, 805
relationship with company, 624
responsibility for acts of, 806–7
retention of, 625
secret limitations on authority, 807
as source of underwriting
      information, 453
use of inspection receipt, 761
Agents and Brokers Model Licensing
      Act, 527–28
Agents Continuing Education Model
      Regulation, 528
AIDS, impact on life insurance,
      548–550
discrimination, 549–50
privacy, 550
Aleatory contracts, 748–49, 774
Alternative minimum tax, 299
American Experience Table of Mortality
    reserves, effect on, 372
American Institute of Certified Public
      Accountants, 637–38
Amortization, 634
Amount of insurance to carry, 13–14
Annual exclusion, 246
Annuities
accumulation period, 117–18
actuarial considerations, 125–27
age setback, 126
calculating net single premium,
    348–54
cash-refund annuity, 115, 505
classification of, 111–12
deferred annuities, 111, 117–20
deferred whole life, 350–54
50 percent refund annuity, 115
immediate pure annuities, 112–13
immediate refund annuities, 113–17
income taxation of, 243–44
installment refund annuity, 114, 505
joint
    and last survivor annuity, 111,
        121–22
    life annuity, 120
    and one-half annuity, 121
    and two-thirds annuity, 121

life
    certain, 113–14
    deferred life, 348, 350–54
    life annuity due, 348
    life annuity immediate, 348–50
liquidation
    options, 119–20
    period, 118
modified cash refund annuity, 115–17
nature of, 109–10
principle, 110
proof of age, 439
pure deferred life annuity, 505
pure immediate annuities, 505
retirement annuity, 118
single-life, 112–20
in structured settlements, 129–30
types of, 109–137
uses of, 127–28
variable annuities, 122–25. *See also*
      Variable annuities
Annuity due, 330–31
Antedating of policies, 769–70
Application for life insurance
attachment to policy, 758–59
as consideration for contract, 771
entire contract statutes, 788
misrepresentation by agent, 813–14
mutual assent, 756–57
as offer to insurance company,
    756–57
parol evidence rule, 758
as source of underwriting information,
    453–54
submitted by broker, 757
Armstrong Committee, 521
Assessment associations, 597
Assessment insurance, 20–22
Asset share calculation
relationship between surrender and
      other values, 415–17,
      418–19
to test loading formula, 389–90
Asset valuation reserve (AVR), 530, 679,
    681
Assignment
    A.B.A. form, 857–59
    absolute form, 850, 852–53, 856–57
    bill of interpleader, 860
    by beneficiary, 852

as collateral for loans, 784, 850,
    852–53, 855–56
collateral form, 855–56
company not responsible for validity
    of, 861
insurable interest of assignee,
    782–83, 861–62
by insurer or owner of policy,
    850–51
multiple assignees, 859–60
need for beneficiary's consent,
    851–52
notice to insurer of, 859
of policy to third party, 780–81
rights of beneficiary, effect on,
    852–54
Automatic premium loans
    advantages, 214–15
    disadvantages, 215
    effect on whole life policies, 215–16
    nature of, 214
Aviation exclusion, 449–50, 825

Backdating of policies, 769–70
Balance sheet
    comparison of GAAP and SAP,
        642–47
    description of, 634
    entries, 634–35
Bankruptcy Reform Act, 864–65
Barbell strategy, 675
Bargaining contract, 751
Beneficiary
    assignment on rights of, effect of,
        852–54
    class, 833–34
    common disaster clause, 844
    contingent or secondary, 834–36
    contingent trust for minor
        beneficiary, 846
    creditor, 778
    defeasible vested interest concept,
        852
    designation, 705, 832–34
        of guardian as, 847–48
    divorce of, 847
    educational fund, 512
    effecting change of, 846–47
    emergency fund, 512
    of estate clearance fund, 511–12
    estate of insured, 831

"first taker," 835
heirs as, 834
insurable interest, 775
key person insurance, 14
manner of identification, 832–34
minor as, 847–48
mortgage cancellation fund, 512
per capita distribution, 842
per stirpes distribution, 841–42
primary, 834–35
priority of entitlement, 834–36
readjustment income, 512–13
remarriage clause, 847
reverse common disaster clause, 846
reversionary revocable designation,
    838–39
right
    to change, 836–37, 846–47
    of irrevocable, 838–39, 851–52
    of revocable, 837–38, 851–52
    of revocation, 836–39
    to select settlement options,
        492–93
simultaneous death of insured and,
    844–46
specific, 832–33
succession in interest, 839–42
third-party, 831–32
trustee as, 848–49
Uniform Simultaneous Death Act,
    844–45
Benefits
    death, 17
    disability, 17
    old-age, 17
    of survivorship, 347
Bernoulli's Law, 306
Beta, 676
Bilateral contracts, 749–50, 759, 773
Blood tests, 443
Blue blank, 636, 641–42
Board of directors, 599–600
Broker
    as agent, 620, 808
Broker/dealer
    and NASD regulations, 568–69
Build and Blood Pressure Study, 1959,
    440, 442
Business continuation insurance, 15–17
    insurable interest, 783–84
    need for, 16
    use of joint life policies, 50–51
Business overhead insurance, 166–67

Business uses of life insurance
  buy-sell agreements, 292–301
  employee benefit planning, 265–66
  executive bonus plans, 269–71
  nonqualified plans, 286–89
  qualified plans, 281–86
  split-dollar plans, 272–80
Buy-sell agreements
  for a closely held corporation, 16–17
  for a partnership, 16
  benefits, 292
  cross-purchase plans, 298, 298–99
  entity plans, 297, 298
  for partnerships, 295–97
  for S corporations, 299–301
  sole proprietorship continuation
     agreements, 293–95
  stock-redemption plans, 297, 298
  structure, 293
  types of, 297–99
Buy-sell funding, 168–70

Capital needs analysis, 203–6
Case law
  definition of, 735
  development of, 735
  forms of
    administrative decisions, 738
    judicial decisions, 738–39
  precedent, 738
  stare decisis, 738
Cash surrender value, 207
Cash values
  as basis for loans, 15
  under ordinary life insurance, 46–47
  use for retirement purposes, 47–48
Cash-flow statement
  comparison of GAAP and SAP, 650
  description of, 635–36
Certificates of insurance, 688
Charitable deduction, 246, 248
Charitable donations, 198–99
Check, payment of premium by, 761,
    811–12
Civil law
  common law, contrasted with,
    739–40
  development of, 739
Clayton Act, 561, 612
Cognitive impairment
  in long-term care insurance, 182

Collateral assignment, 272–73
Commerce Clause, 556
Commercial life insurance companies
  demutualization of, 592–96
  mutual life insurance companies
    management accountability, 591
    participating policies, 591
    policyholder orientation, 590–91
  mutualization of, 592
  stock life insurance companies
    distribution of surplus to
      shareholders, 589–90
    management accountability, 589
    nonparticipating policies, 590
    profit orientation, 588–89
Commissioners Reserve Valuation
    Method (CRVM), 405–7
  modified premium under, 406–7
Commissions
  ceding commission under reinsurance,
    480–81
Common disaster clause, 844
Common law
  civil law, contrasted with, 739–40
  "equity," contrasted with, 740–41
  source of, 739–40
  statutory modification of, 794–95
Commutation privilege
  definition of, 495
  under fixed-period option, 502–3
  under life income option, 506
Commutative contract, 748
Compound interest. *See also* Interest,
    compound
  discounted values, 327–30
Concealments
  distinguished from misrepresentation,
    798
  interim changes in health, 801
  in marine insurance, 798–99
  nature and legal effect of, 798–99
  palpable materiality, 799
  scope of doctrine of concealment,
    800–1
  test
    of fraud, 799–800
    of materiality, 799
Conditional contract, 750
Conditional receipt, 763–64
  approval type, 765–66
  insurability type, 765

Conditions
 precedent
  definition of, 750
  delivery of the policy, 759–60
  delivery-in-good-health clause,
   761–63
  exemplified by premium payments,
   750–51
  incontestable clause, relationship
   to, 825–26
  justification of, 763
  medical treatment clause, 763
  payment of first premium, 761
 subsequent
  conditions found in life insurance
   policy, 750–51
  definition of, 750
Consideration for contract
 extension of credit, 761
 form, 772–73
 nature of, 771–72
 payment by check, 761, 772
Constant ratio method, 65–66
*Consumer's Guide to Long-Term Care
  Insurance,* 186
Contingent trust for minor beneficiary,
  846
Continuing education requirements for
  agents, 528
Contract law
 principles of, 747–52
Contract of adhesion, 751–52
Contract rates, 493–94
Contributory plans, 691
Convexity, 675
Conway decision, 824–25
Corporate-owned life insurance, 299
Corridor test, 55, 57
Cost of insurance
 under joint life policies, 51
 level premium plan, relationship to,
  27–30
 retrospective reserves, with respect
  to, 364–66
Cost-of-living adjustments (COLAs), in
  disability insurance, 156–57
Courts
 American
  classification of
   federal courts, 742–43
   state courts, 743–44
  conflict of laws, 744–46
  jurisdiction of, 744

 Federal
  jurisdiction of, 742–43
  structure of, 742–43
  types of, 742–43
 state
  classes of, 743–44
  jurisdiction of, 743–44
Covered call options, 676
Credit insurance, 15
Creditor
 as assignee, 784
 as beneficiary, 784
 insurable interest of, 784, 861
Critical period income, 9–10
Cross-purchase plans, 169–70, 295–96,
  298
CSO 1941 Table
 general characteristics, 313
 safety margins, 309
Current assumption whole life insurance
 cash value illustrations, 81
 high premium design, 81–82
 indeterminate premium whole life
  policy, 80
 interest-sensitive whole life policy, 80
 low premium design, 81–82
 policyowner options, 82
 redetermination, 82
 uses of, 83
 as variation of whole life, 79–83
Custodial care, 179

Death of applicant prior to consideration
  of application, 765
Death proceeds
 income taxation of, 237–39
Death taxes, 196, 259
Decrements, 312–13
Defeasible vested interest of beneficiary,
  852
Deferred-compensation plans
 nonqualified, 286–89
 qualified, 281–86
Deficiency reserves
 nature of, 373
Definitions of insurance, 19
Delay in considering application, 767–69
Delivery of policy
 as condition precedent, 759–60
 constructive delivery, 760
 legal effect of, 759–61

Delivery-in-good-health clause
  as condition precedent, 761–63
  meaning of good health, 762–63
  as substitute for doctrine of
          concealment, 801
  waiver of, 812
Demutualization, 424
  of mutual life insurance companies
    alternative modes of, 594–96
    licensing/readmission problems,
        596
    reasons for, 593–94
    regulation of, 594
Department of Veteran Affairs, 597–98
Dependency period income, 9–10, 513
Dependent life insurance, 715–16
Direct federal solvency regulation,
        581–82
Direct-skip transfers, 257
Disability
  1985 Commissioners Disability Table,
        139–40
  definition, for social security
          purposes, 146
  probability of becoming disabled,
        139–42
  sources of funds for
    employer plans, 144
    no-fault auto insurance coverage,
        144
    nonoccupational disability funds,
        143–44
    salary continuation, 144
    social security, 141–44
    workers' compensation, 141–42
Disability income benefits, 17
  incontestable clause, exception to,
        823–24
  reinsurance of, 489
Disability income insurance
  business uses of, 166–70
    business overhead insurance,
        166–67
    buy-sell funding, 168–70
    key person coverage, 167–68
    salary continuation plans, 168
  concept of, 146–47
  cost-of-living adjustments (COLAs),
        156–57
  definition of disability for, 146–47
    any occupation, 146
    own occupation, 146
  dividends, 163

duration of benefit period, 152
elimination period, 150–51
exclusions, 165–66
flat-percentage amount, 157
future purchase options, 157
hospitalization, 162–63
incontestability, 160–61
increasing base benefit amount,
        157–58
inflation-protection provision,
        156–57
lapses in, 154–55
level of benefits payable, 155–58
limitations on coverage, 163–66
and long-term care insurance,
        149–50
long-term policies, 153–55
organ donations, 161
overinsurance, concern of, 145
partial disability benefits, 147
premium payments, 158–59
presumptive disability, 160
recurring disability provisions,
        151–52
rehabilitation benefits, 159–60
renewability, 148–49
residual disability benefits, 147–48,
        155
return-of-premium option, 159
short-term policicies, 152–53
situations warranting coverage,
        145–46
social security rider, 161–62
standard issue, modifying, 164–65
termination, 154–55
underwriting of, 164, 165
waiver-of-premium provision, 158
Discrimination, 537–38, 546–47,
        547–48
Distribution channels
  banks and department stores, 628
  direct response marketing, 628–29
Diversity of citizenship, 743
Dividends
  dividend scale, 430–33
    contribution plan, 430
    to convert policy to paid-up or
        endowment policy, 48
    direct recognition dividend scale,
        432
    in disability insurance, 163
    to distribute surplus, 589–90
    equity of, 430–33

testing dividend scale, 432–33
three-factor contribution plan, 430
excess interest factor, 362
extra dividends, 427–28
illustrative dividend computation,
428–30
interest factor, 362
policy, 540–41, 547–48
under substandard insurance policies,
470
surrender dividends, 415
terminal dividends, 428
Divisible surplus, 426–27
Doctrine of comity, 699
Duff and Phelps, 652

Educational fund, 11, 203, 512
Efficient frontier calculations, 676–77
Election
nature of, 810
Eligibility
in long-term care insurance, 181–82
Elimination period, in disability
insurance, 150–51
Emergency fund, 11, 203, 512
Employee benefit plans, 17
Endorsement method, 272
Endowment insurance, 32, 54–55,
344–47
benefit of survivorship, 347
calculation of prospective reserve,
369
net level premium, 358
net single premium, 344–47
Entity agreements, 169, 295–96, 297
Equity
as contrasted with law, 740
development of, 740–41
forms of action, 740
life insurance companies, significance
to, 741
Erie Railroad Company v. Tompkins,
746
Estate
beneficiary of, 831
clearance fund, 8–9, 506, 511–12
beneficiary of, 511–12
interest option, use of, 511
lump-sum settlement, use of, 511
trust, use of, 511–12

Estate planning
life insurance, uses of, 244–45,
258–64
equal shares to heirs, 262
estate enhancement, 258
estate liquidity/wealth
replacement, 258–59,
261–62
gifts to trusts, 260
outright gifts, 259–60
second-to-die policies, 262–63
Estate tax
of life insurance, 251–56
of transfers, 247–48
Estoppel
apparent authority of agents, 805–6
equitable, 809–10
legal or promissory, 810
misrepresentation in application,
813–14
nature of, 809
Evidence of insurability
waiver
under renewal provisions of term
insurance, 33
for term conversion, 34
Excess-benefit plans, 287
Exchange of policies
joint life policies, 51
ordinary life, 48–49
term insurance, 34–36
Exclusions
in long-term care insurance, 182
Executive bonus plans
carve-out bonus plan, 270
estate and gift tax planning, 271–72
reporting and disclosure requirements,
270–71
with group term plans, 269–70
Executive officers, 601
Expenses
incurred at time of issue, 386
incurred at year of death, 387
incurred during definite number of
renewal years, 386
incurred every year, 387
of an insurance company
insurance expenses, 383
investment expenses, 384
savings under nonmedical insurance,
462–63
Extended term insurance
under antedated policies, 770

as surrender benefit, 210–14
  advantages, 212
  disadvantages, 213–14
  policy loans, 211–12

Facility-of-payment provision, 705
Family insurance, 7–8
Family uses of life insurance
  charitable donations, 198–99
  confidential needs, 200–1
  daily living needs, 189
  death taxes, 196
  debts, 195–96
  dependents' education, 196–97
  emergencies, 192
  expenses associated with death,
    191–92
  funeral expenses, 191
  gifts to individuals, 199
  home health care, 199–200
  income to family survivors
    children, 193–94
    dependents, 193
    level of support, 195
    nondependents, 194–95
    parents, 194
  nursing home care, 199–200
  property damage, 192–93
  supplemental retirement income,
    199–200
  transfer of assets to younger
    generation, 200
  trusts, 197–98
Federal antitrust laws
  Clayton Act, 561
  enforcement of, 561–62
  Federal Trade Commission Act, 561,
    565
  impact on insurance business,
    562–64
    policy forms, 563
    pooling, 563–64
    potential legislation, 564
    pricing, 563
    selling practices, 563
  impact on regulation, 564–65
  McCarran Act, 556–57, 558–60,
    562
  overview, 560–62
  Robinson-Portman Act, 561

Sherman Act, 561
  state action doctrine, 562
Federal antitrust treatment
  of acquisitions and mergers, 611–12
Federal Constitution, 735–36
Federal securities law
  concerning acquisitions and mergers,
    612–13
Federal Tax Lien Act, 865
Federal taxation of life insurance
  estate taxes, 251–56
  generation-skipping transfer taxes,
    256–58
  gift taxes, 249–51
Federal Trade Commission Act, 561,
    565
Federal transfer tax system
  estate taxes, 251–56
  generation-skipping taxes, 256–58
  gift taxes, 249–51
Field organization
  functions of, 618–19
  need for, 618
  structure of, 621–24
Financial Accounting Standards Board
    (FASB), 633–34, 638
Financial needs analysis, 202–6
Financial statements, of life insurance
    companies
  comparison of GAAP and SAP,
    642–51
  differences between GAAP and SAP,
    638–42
  form and composition of, 633–36
  GAAP and SAP approaches, 636–38
  users of
    agents and employees, 633
    company management, 632–33
    creditors, 631–32
    investors, 631
    policyowners, 632
    rating agencies, 632
    SEC, 631
    security analysts, 632
    state insurance regulators, 631
Financial strength, measurement of
  current
    asset and liability values, 656
    capital, 656
    insurance and investment rules,
      656
    liquidity, 656

future
  ability to finance, 657
  capabilities, 657
  management strategy, 657
First-to-die joint life policy, 50–51
Fixed-amount option
  dependency period income, 513
  educational fund, 512
  emergency fund, 512
  excess interest, 503
  flexibility, elements of, 503–4
  mortgage cancellation fund, 512
  readjustment income, 513
  structure of, 503
  transfer proceeds, 504
  withdrawal privilege, 503–4
Fixed-period option
  commutation, right of, 502–3
  dependency period income, 513
  excess interest, 502
  mortgage cancellation fund, 512
  policy loans, 501–2
  present value of annual payments,
      501
  readjustment income, 513
  structure of, 501
Flat-percentage amount, 157
Forfeiture provision, 773
Fraternal benefit societies, 597
Fraud
  good-health clause as protection
      against, 762–63
  incontestable clause, effect of,
      818–20
  moral hazard, 448
Friendly takeover, 605–6
Full preliminary term valuation, 402–4
Fully insured pension plans, 284–85

Gender-distinct mortality, 359
Generally accepted accounting practices
      (GAAP)
  comparison with SAP
    balance sheets, 642–47
    cash-flow statements, 650
    income statements, 647–50
    supplementary information,
        650–51
  differences from SAP
    asset valuation, 639–40
    deferred acquisition costs, 638–39

  equipment, 639
    federal taxes, 639
    nonadmitted assets, 640–41
    policy reserves, 640
    subsidiaries, 640
  enforcement, 638
  hybrid statement, 641–42
  reporting requirements, 637–38
Generation-skipping tax
  of life insurance, 256–57
    direct-skip, 257
    taxable distribution and
        terminations, 257
  of transfers, 248–49
Gift taxes
  of life insurance
    annual exclusion, 246
    charitable deduction, 246, 248
    marital deduction, 246, 248,
        255–56
    unified credit, 246–47
Government-provided life insurance
  Department of Veteran Affairs,
      597–98
  Social Security Administration, 598
  State of Wisconsin, 598
Grace period, 815
Grading of premiums, 384–85
Gross nonparticipating premiums
  calculations for setting, 391–95
  deriving, 390–91
  developing schedule of competitive
      premiums, 399
  evaluating trial premium, 395–99
  selecting probable assumptions, 391
  using tentative gross premiums,
      399–400
Gross premiums
  contingencies, allowance for, 340
  definition of, 383
  loading formula, 384–88, 389
Group life insurance
  experience rating, 688
  federal regulation of
    benefit limitations, 698
    contractual provisions, 698
    eligible groups, 694–98
    jurisdiction, 698–99
  group contract, 688
  state regulation of, 693–99
  underwriting principles
    administrative functions, 692
    benefit levels, 690

composition of group, 693
eligibility, 690
length of contract, 690
nature of industry, 693
premium payments, 691
previously written policies, 692
size of group, 692–93
stability, 689
Group term life insurance
added coverage
accidental death, 713–15
dependent life insurance, 715–16
supplemental life insurance,
712–13
contract provisions
accelerated and living benefits,
711–12
assignment, 707
beneficiary designation, 705
benefit schedules, 701–3
claims, 707
eligibility, 703–5
entire contract clause, 707–8
grace period, 707
incontestability, 708
misstatement of age, 708
premiums, 706
settlement options, 705–6
termination, 708–11
taxation of
federal, 717–25
state, 725
Group term (Sec. 79) plans
nondiscrimination rules, 267–68
postretirement coverage, 268
requirements, 267
Table I rates, 266–67
Group term carve-out, 269–70
Group universal life insurance
accidental death and waiver of
premium, 732
death benefit, 729–30
dependent coverage, 731–32
enrollment, 732
expense charges, 730
interest rates, 730–31
loans and withdrawals, 731
mortality charges, 730
premium adjustments, 731
retirement and termination options,
732
taxation of, 733

types of, 728
underwriting, 728–29
Guaranteed cost policies, 590
Guaranteed investment contracts
(GICs), 575, 656
Guaranteed issue, 464
Guaranty funds, 534–36
Guardianship of minor beneficiary,
847–48

Holding Company Act, 610
Holding companies
nature of, 608
trend toward, 607–8
Home health care, 179, 199–200
Home service agent, 620
Hospitalization, in disability insurance,
162–63
Hostile takeover, 605–6
Human life value
diminishing nature of, 6–7
estimating economic value, 4–5
measurement of, 3–5
source of, 1–3
Hybrid products, 575–81

Illustration Questionnaire, 229–30
Immunized portfolio, 422–23
In lieu of plans, 286–87
Inadvertent gifts, 251
Incidental benefits, 281–82
Incidents of ownership, 252–54
Income statement
comparison of GAAP and SAP, 647
description of, 635
Income taxation
of annuities
amounts received as annuity,
243–44
payments before starting date, 243
of life insurance
annuity contracts, 243–44
death proceeds, 237–39
deductibility of premium payments,
242–43
estate planning, 244–45
living proceeds, 239–42
Incontestability, in disability insurance,
160–61

Incontestable clause
  accidental death benefits, 823−24
  under antedated policies, 770
  aviation clause, 825
  conditions precedent, 825−26
  contest, meaning of, 820−21
  contestable period, inception of, 821
  Conway decision, 824−25
  disability clause, 823−24
  excepted hazards, 824−25
  fraud, effect of, 818−20
  in government life insurance policies,
    825
  military or naval service, 825
  misstatement of age, 439, 826
  Monahan decision, 821−22
  nonpayment of premiums, 823
  purpose of, 817−18
  reformation, 826−27
  reinstatement, 827
  suicide clause, 825
  types of, 821−22
Indemnity, principle of, 752
Independent agents, 621
Independent brokerage general agent,
  623
Inflation protection
  in long-term care insurance, 181, 184
Inspection receipt, 761
Installment
  amount option, 846. *See also* Fixed-
    amount option
  time option, 846. *See also* Fixed-
    period option
Insurability option, 465
Insurable interest
  accelerated-benefit provisions, 781
  of assignee, 782−83, 861
  of beneficiary, 775, 779−80
  business relationship, 783
  of creditors, 778, 861
  as deterrent to murder of insured,
    775
  as deterrent to wagering, 774
  factual expectation, 782−83
  incidence of, 777−78
  lack of, 779−80
  legal obligation, 773−74
  love and affection, 782−83
  nature of, 777
  policy procured by insured, 779
  policy procured by person other than
    insured, 781−82

Insurance Information and Privacy
  Protection Model Act, 545
Insurance Regulatory Information
  System (IRIS), 533−34,
  658−59
Insurers Supervision, Rehabilitation and
  Liquidation Model Act, 534
Interest
  assumed earnings rate for actuarial
    computations, 371−72
  assumptions, 338−39
    reserves, effect on, 363−64,
      371−72
    under life insurance contracts, 339
  compound, 323−38
    future values, 324−26
      of annual payments, 330−34
      beginning-of-year payments,
        330−31
      calculator and spreadsheet
        functions, 334
      comparing, 333
      derivation of, 325
      end-of-year payments, 331−34
      of 1 at various rates of, 325
      relationship between interest
        rate and accumulation period,
        326
    present values, 327−30
      of annual payments, 335−37
      application of, 337−38
      calculator and spreadsheet
        functions, 338
      derivation of, 328−29, 335−37
      of 1 at various rates of, 329
      relationship between interest
        rate and discounting period,
        330
  definition of terms, 322−23
  simple interest, 323
Interest option
  blackout period, 514
  dependency period income, 513
  emergency fund, 512
  estate clearance fund, 511−12
  excess interest, 500
  flexibility, elements of, 497
  interest, accumulation of, 500
  permissible duration, 500
  readjustment income, 512−13
  structure of, 496
  withdrawal privilege, 500

Interest-Index Annuity Contracts Model Regulation, 578–79
Intermediate care, 179
Investment Adviser Act of 1940, 571–72
Investment Company Act of 1940, 566, 569–71, 577
Investment features of life insurance policies
  as a function of the level premium plan, 30
  liquidity, 42
  principal, safety of, 41
  yield, 42
Investment of life insurance companies
  changes in investment characteristics, 669–70
  effect of inflation, 666–67
  NAIC Model Investment Law, 668
  nature of, 41–42
  portfolio management, 667, 668–70
  and rating agencies, 667–68, 682–86
  regulation of, 529, 667–68, 682–86
  trends
    conservatism, 684–85
    internationalization, 686
    money management diversification, 685
    overlaps, 686
  valuation of, 529–30
Irrevocable trusts, 261

Joint life insurance, 50–51
Jurisdiction, forms of, 742
Justinian Code, 739–40
Juvenile insurance, 7
  underwriting of, 466

Key person insurance, 14, 167–68, 289–92, 783

Lapse, 409
Laws, conflict of, 744–46
  bases used to resolve conflicts, 744–46
  center of gravity rule, 746
  Erie v. Tompkins, 746

  grouping of contracts theory, 746
  place-of-making rule, 745
  Swift v. Tyson, 746
Legislation, 735–38
  definition of, 735
  forms of, 735–38
    federal
      constitution, 735–36
      executive orders and administrative regulations, 736–37
      statutes, 736
      treaties, 736
    local ordinances, 738
    state
      administrative regulations, 737–38
      constitutions, 737
      statutes, 737
  rules of statutory construction, 741–42
Level additions model, 65
Level premium plan, 24–30
  criticisms of, 40–41
  legal reserves, effect on, 25
  nature of, 24–25
  net amount at risk, effect on, 27–30
  ordinary life insurance, applied to, 26–27
  relationship to cost of insurance, 27–30
  term insurance, applied to, 25–26
  whole life insurance, applied to, 26–27
Leveraged buyout, 606
Licensing
  of agents, 527–28
  duration of license, 528
  of insurers, 525–26
  obtaining a license, 527–28
  requirements, 526–27
Life expectancy
  meaning of, 305
  under various mortality tables, 305–6
Life income
  for surviving dependent spouse, 10
  option, 504–6
    cash-refund annuity, 505
    commutation privilege, 506
    excess interest, 506
    inflexibility, elements of, 506
    installment-refund annuity, 505
    as pure immediate annuity, 505

structure of, 504–6
for surviving spouse, 513–4
for widow, 514
Life insurance carriers
commercial life insurance companies,
588–97
government-provided life insurance,
597–98
nongovernmental life insurance
providers, 596–97
Limited payment life insurance
joint life insurance, adaptability to,
50–51
nature of, 49–50
net level premium, 358
prospective reserve, calculation of,
369
single-premium policy, 50
Liquidation, 589
Living benefits
shift toward, 629–30
Living proceeds
income taxation of, 239–42
Loading, 340
of net premiums
loading formula, 384–85
setting, 383
of participating premiums
adding of margins, 387–89
asset-share calculations, 389–90
computing present values, 385–87
testing loading formula, 389
Long-term care insurance
benefits, 179–81
amounts, 180
duration, 180
inflation protection, 181
restoration, 181
types, 179
characteristics, 179–82
comparison of policies, 186–88
and disability insurance, 149–50
eligibility, 181–82
evolution of, 174–76
exclusions, 182
group coverage, 185
inadequacy of protection, 172–73
issue age, 179
NAIC model legislation, 176–78
need for, 171–73
preexisting conditions, 182
premiums, factors affecting, 183–85
renewability, 183

sources of
cash value life insurance, 174
life-care facilities, 173–74
personal savings, 173
welfare, 173
underwriting, 182–83
Long-term Care Insurance Model Act,
175
Long-term policies, 153–55
Loss sharing, 19
Lump-sum settlement
common disaster and short-term
survivorship problem, 845
estate clearance fund, 511
mortgage cancellation fund, 512

Managers, 601
Managing general agent (MGA), 623
Mandatory security valuation reserve
(MSVR), 530, 679
Margins, adding to premium, 387–89
Marital deduction, 246, 248, 255–56,
846
Market value adjustment contracts, 578
Marketing
costs and profitability
control of expenses, 625–26
productivity, 625–26
retention, 625–26
department in life insurance company
distribution function, 619–20
field organization, 618–19
structure of, 617–20
life insurance
changes in distribution systems,
630
demographic shifts, 629–30
future of, 629–30
increased competition, 629
Materiality
concept of, 792
falsity, extent of, 792–93
individual-insurers standard, 793–94
laws relating to, 795–97
prudent-insurers standard, 793
of representations, 792–94
tests of, 793–94
McCarran Act, 522, 556–57, 612–13
Medical consultation, 464, 797
Medical Information Bureau, 456, 796

Medical treatment clause, 763, 796−97, 812
Medico-Actuarial Mortality Investigation, 440
Military or naval service
  incontestable clause, 825
  underwriting for, 450−51
Minors
  as applicant for life insurance, 755−56
  contingent trust for minor beneficiary, 846
  guardianship, 847−48
  legal capacity of, 755−56, 847−48
  rights
    to receive proceeds, 847−48
    to select settlement options, 848
Misstatement of age, 439
Model office, 398
Model Investment Law, 681−82
Model Variable Contract Law, 572
Modified endowment contracts (MECs), 85−87, 241−42
Modified preliminary term valuation, 404−5
Modified premium, 406−7
Modified reserves
  Commissioners Reserve Valuation Method, 405−7
  full preliminary term valuation, 402−4
  limiting modified premium, 406−7
  modified preliminary term valuation, 404−5
  net level premium valuation, 402−4
  statutory regulation of, 407−8
  surrender values, impact on, 416
Monahan decision, 821−22
Money management diversification, 685
Moody's, 652
Moral hazard, 448
Mortality
  under assessment insurance, 22
  assumptions in company's underwriting standards, 438
  differences from published tables, 310
  distinction between male and female mortality, 126, 448
  nonstandard mortality, 311
  under yearly renewable term insurance, 24

Mortality tables
  additional decrements, 312−13
  adjustments to data, 308−9
  age setback, 126
  aggregate table, 311−12
  completing table, 310
  construction of, 306−8, 310
  extra percentage tables for substandard risks, 470−72
  GA 1951 Table, 309
  gender-distinct probabilities, 126
  multiple-decrement tables, 313
  1941 CSO table, 309, 313
  1958 CET table, 314
  1958 CSO table, 313
  1980 CET table, 314
  1980 CSO table, 315−17
  1983 Smoker-Nonsmoker table, 314
  probability of death, 303−4
  projections, 126−27, 309
  public tables, 313−14
  radix, 303
  reserves, effect on, 370−71
  safety margins, 127, 309
  select table, 311
  smoothing, 309
  statutory table, 313
  ultimate table, 311−12
  UP-1984 table, 314
  U.S. Life table, 304
  U.S. Mortality table, 318−21
Mortgage cancellation fund, 512
Mortgage redemption needs, 10−11
Multiple-employer welfare arrangement (MEWA), 695−96
Multiple-line exclusive agent, 620
Murder of insured by beneficiary, 775
Mutual life insurance companies, 590−92

National Association of Insurance Commissioners (NAIC)
  minimum standards for reserve and surrender values, 313
  model legislation, 176−78
  mortality tables, development of, 313
  NAIC Group Life Insurance Standard Provisions Model Bill, 700
  NAIC Model Investment Law, 668
  NAIC Model Laws on Examinations, 534

regulation of accounting practices, 636–37
uniform state laws, development of, 523–24, 530, 532
National Structured Settlement Trade Association, 135
Needs approach to life insurance, 8–11
  analysis, 202–6
  cleanup fund, 8–9
  dependency period income, 9–10
  educational needs, 11, 203
  emergency needs, 11, 203
  life income for surviving dependent spouse, 10
  lump-sum needs, 203–4
  monetary evaluation of, 12–13
  mortgage redemption, 10–11
  ongoing income needs, 204–6
  postdeath financial needs, 203–6
  readjustment income, 9, 204
  retirement, 11
  social security, 204–5
Negotiated trusteeships, 694–95
Net amount at risk, 27–30
Net premiums
  benefit of survivorship, 347
  net level premium, 354–59
    concept of, 354–55
    deferred annuity, 358–59
    endowment insurance, 358
    limited payment life, 358
    ordinary life, 356–58
    term insurance, 355–56
  net single premium, 341–54
    aggregate approach, 342–43
    concept of, 341
    deferred whole life annuity, 350
    endowment insurance, 344–47
    individual approach, 342
    life annuities, 348
    rate computations, 341–43
    term insurance, 343–44
    whole life insurance, 344
No-lesser-amount statutes, 473–74
Noncontributory plans, 691
Nonforfeiture legislation, 412–15
Nongovernmental providers of life insurance
  assessment associations, 597
  fraternal benefit societies, 597
  savings banks, 597
Nonmedical insurance
  economics of, 462–63

expense savings, 462–63
extra mortality, 462–63
guaranteed issue, 464
history of, 460
insurability option, 465
paramedical examination, 464
pension trusts, 464
policyowner, 463–64
underwriting safeguards, 460–62
Nonoccupational disability funds, 143–44
Nonparticipating policies, 590
Nonqualified deferred-compensation plans
  life insurance in,
    advantages, 286
    corporate-owned life insurance, 288–89
    death-benefit-only plans, 287
    income tax deferral, 288
    salary continuation plans, 287
    salary reduction plans, 286–87
Nonreducing dividend scale, 427
Nonwaiver clause, 758, 807
Numerical rating system
  as basis for substandard classifications, 459
  assigning weights to risk factors, 457
  criticisms of, 459–60
  description of, 457
  operation of, 458–59
Nursing home care, 199–200

OASDI, 8, 12–13
Operative date of policy, 759, 769–70
Oral contracts, 785–86
Ordinary agent, 620
Ordinary annuity, 332–33, 433
Ordinary life insurance
  distinctive features, 45–49
  endowment insurance, viewed as, 45
  joint life insurance, adaptability to, 50–51
  nature of, 44
  net level premium, 356–58
    derivation of, 365–66, 367–68
  prospective reserve, calculation of, 366–68
  reserve under full preliminary term valuation, 402–3

retrospective reserve, calculation of,
    364–66
surrender values, derivation of, 414
Organ donations, 161
Organization
    of life insurance companies, 598–605
Owner-applicant, 831–32
Ownership
    concept of, 854–55
    incidents of, 850–51
    of policy
        by beneficiary, 843, 854
        by insured, 842–43, 854
        by insured and beneficiary jointly,
            842, 854–55
        by person other than insured, 843
        prematurity rights, 842
        right by owner to assign policy,
            854–55
    rights, 842–43
        as alternative to irrevocable
            beneficiary designation,
            842–43
        as means of transferring
            ownership, 843
        prematurity, 842

Paid-up insurance
    under ordinary life policy, 47
Parol evidence rule, 758
Partial disability benefits, 147
Participating policies, 591
Parties to life insurance contract
    legal capacity
        alien enemies, 755
        applicant, 755–56
        insurer, 754–55
        minors, 755–56
        Unauthorized Insurers Service of
            Process Act, 755
        war, effect of on, 756
Partnerships
    using buy-sell agreements, 295–96
Paul v. Virginia, 520–21
Payment of premium
    by check, 761, 771–72, 812
    under antedated policies, 769
    as condition precedent, 761
    as consideration for contract, 771–73
    incontestable clause, relationship to,
        823

premium receipt, 773
prepayment of first premium,
    763–65
by promissory note, 772
Pension trusts
    in nonmedical insurance, 464
Per capita distribution of insurance
    proceeds, 842
Performance comparison of life
    insurance companies
    financial position, 663–64
    pricing, 664–65
Periodic Payments Settlement Act of
    1982, 131–32
Personal-producing general agents, 620,
    622–23
Per stirpes distribution of insurance
    proceeds, 841–42
Policy costs, methods of comparing
    Belth yearly price method of
        protection, 107
    Belth yearly rate of return method
        calculation, 104
        table, 106
    cash accumulation method
        calculations, 98
        definition, 91–92
        tables, 93–98
    comparative interest rate method,
        98–104
    equal outlay method
        calculation, 98
        tables, 99–103
    interest-adjusted indexes, 87–90
    Linton yield method, 98–104
    net cost method, 87
Policy illustrations
    combination coverage, 219–30
    factors and issues, 224–29
    Illustration Questionnaire (IQ),
        229–30
    participating policy premiums, 216–19
    Professional Practice Guideline
        (PPG), 224, 225–28
    split dollar, 221
    standardization of, 224, 229–30
    understanding use of, 255
    universal life, 221–24
Portfolio management
    changes in investment characteristics,
        669–70
    enhanced liquidity, 670–71

investment diversity
   barbell strategy, 675
   durations, 675
   hedging, 675–76
  organization of investments, 671–72
  pooled separate accounts, 670
  practical investment decisions,
     672–73
  role of industry, 668–69
  technical aspects, 667, 674–75
Postdeath financial needs
  lump sum, 203–4
  ongoing income, 204–6
Preemption doctrine, 555–56, 564–65
  in long-term care insurance, 182
Premium
  additions, 387
  computation of, 340
  definition of, 340
  in disability insurance, 158–59
  gross, 340
  net level. *See* Net premiums
  net single. *See* Net premiums
  payments, deductibility of, 242–43
Prepayment of premiums
  as alternative to retroactive
     conversion, 36
Present value
  calculating, 5
  in loading formula, 385–87
Presumptive disability, 160
Price performance comparison, 664–65
Privileged communications, 797
Postretirement group life insurance
  continuation of group term, 725–26
  group universal life insurance,
     726–33
Probate
  expenses, 258–59
  fund, 8–9
Producers, differences between
  administrative, technical, and sales
     support, 627–28
  educational support, 628
  recruiting, selecting, and developing,
     626–28
  selection-rejection process, 626–27
  training recruits, 627–28
Professional Practice Guideline (PPG),
    224, 225–28
Promissory note, use of, 772
  payment of premium by, 772

Protection of insurance benefits against
    creditors
  analysis of statutes, 868–870
  bankruptcy of insured, 864–65
  Bankruptcy Reform Act, 864–65
  of beneficiary, 865, 870–71
  comprehensive statute, 868
  distributive statute, 867
  Federal Tax Lien Act, 865
  of insured, 863–65
  limitations on, 870
  married women's statute, 867
  New York statute, 868
  nonstatutory protection, 863–65
  parties entitled to protection, 870
  procedural statutes, 867
  proceeds, 866–67, 869–70
  spendthrift clause, 868, 871
  state exemption statutes, 867–68
  statutory protection, 865–871
  tax claims of federal government, 865
  temporal scope of, 865–867
Pure conversions, 595

Qualified plans
  life insurance in
    death benefits, 285
    fully insured pension plans,
       284–85
    incidental death benefits, 286
    survivorship benefits, 285
    taxation of beneficiaries, 283–84
Qualified terminable interest property
    (QTIP), 256

Rating agencies
  impact on investments, 682–83
  liquidity safety net, 683–84
  listing, 652
Ratings of insurance companies
  categories, 652–53
  criteria, 655
  distribution of, 653–54
  measuring financial strength
    current, 655–56
    future, 656–57
    process, 654–55
    services, 652
Readjustment income, 9

Rebating, 544–45
Recruiting
    of producers, 626–27
Reduced paid-up insurance
    under ordinary life policy, 47
    as surrender benefit, 208–10
Reformation of contracts
    incontestable clause, relationship to,
        826–27
Regulation
    acquisitions and mergers, 581
    and AIDS, 548–50
    Agents and Brokers Model Licensing
        Act, 527–28
    Agents Continuing Education Model
        Regulation, 528
    capital and surplus, 531–32
    Commerce Clause, 556
    content of state regulation, 529–52
    by courts, 523
    direct federal solvency regulation,
        581–82
    dividend
        fraud, 550–52
        policy, 540–41, 547–48
    dual federal-state regulation, 564–84
        role of FTC, 565
        role of SEC, 565–81
        state response to regulatory
            problems, 582–84
    evolution of, 520–22
    federal antitrust laws
        impact on insurance business,
            562–64
        impact on regulation, 564–65
        overview, 560–62
    Federal Trade Commission, 557–58,
        565
    financial condition, 529–34
    goals of, 524–25
    of group life insurance
        federal, 699–700
        state, 693–99
    guaranty funds, 534–36
    hazardous financial condition, 552
    hybrid products, 575–81
    Insurance Regulatory Information
        System (IRIS), 533–34,
        658–59
    Insurers Supervision, Rehabilitation
        and Liquidation Model Act,
        534

    interaction between state and federal,
        555–58, 582–84
    interstate compacts, 583–84
    investments of insurance companies,
        529–30, 677–80
        history, 677–78
        liberalization of quantitative rules,
            679–80
        qualitative constraints, 678–79
        reserve accounts, 679
        writedowns, 679
    by legislatures, 522
    licensing
        of agents, 527–28
        Agents and Brokers Model
            Licensing Act, 527–28
        of insurers, 525–26
        obtaining, 527–28
        requirements, 526–27
    liquidation, 534
    market conduct, 539–48
    McCarran Act, 522, 556–57, 562
    NAIC standards, 523–24, 582–83,
        657–58
    nonforfeiture provisions, 537
    Paul v. Virginia, 520–21
    policy forms, 536–38
    preemption doctrine, 555–56,
        564–65
    price disclosure, 541–42
    privacy, 545
    rates, 538–39
    rebating, 544–45
    by regulators, 525–26
    replacement, 542–43
    of reserves, 530–31
    risk-based capital (RBC), 658–63
    *St. Paul Fire & Marine Insurance Co.
        v. Barry,* 559–60
    Securities and Exchange Commission
        (SEC), 557–58, 567–72
        Rule 151, 576–77
    for sound insurance management,
        552
    standard provisions, 536
    at state level, 520–24, 657–58
    twisting, 542–43
    *U.S. v. South-Eastern Underwriters
        Association,* 521, 556–58
    unfair discrimination, 537–38,
        546–47, 547–48
    unfair financial planning practices,
        541

unfair settlement practices, 548
unfair trade practices, 539–45
universal life insurance, 580–81
Regulation 126, 680
Rehabilitation benefits, under disability
 insurance, 159–60
Reinstatement, 826–27
Reinsurance
 accidental death benefits, 489
 assumption, 476–77
 automatic agreement, 485–86
 as source of capital, 424–25
 catastrophe, 484
 ceding commission, 480–81
 cession form, 486
 claims settlement, 486–87
 coinsurance, 480–81
 concept of, 476
 disability benefits, 489
 duration of agreement, 488
 experience rating, 488–89
 facultative agreement, 485–86
 indemnity, 477–79
 insolvency of the primary insurer, 488
 jumbo clause, 486
 modified coinsurance, 481–82
 nonproportional, 482–85
 proportional, 479–82
 purposes of, 476–79
 recapture provision, 487
 reduction in sums reinsured, 487
 spread-loss, 484–85
 stop-loss, 483–84
 of substandard risk, 489–90
 uses of, 477–79
 yearly renewable term insurance,
  479–80
Remarriage clause, 847
Renewability, 148–49, 183
Representation
 concept of materiality, 792–94
 continuing, 792
 legal consequences of
  misrepresentation, 789–90
 misrepresentation distinguished from
  concealment, 798
 nature and legal effect of, 787–80
 of opinion, belief, or expectation,
  791–92
 privileged communication, 797
 source of litigation, 795–97

Rescission and restitution, 826–27
 on grounds of misrepresentation or
  concealment, 790–92
Reserves
 aggregate versus pro rata, 364
 Commissioners Reserve Valuation
  Method, 405–7
 contingency, 374
 deficiency, 373, 408
 definition of, 401
 full net level premium valuation, 361
 full preliminary term, 402–4
 gross premium valuation, 373
 indeterminant premium policy, 373
 initial, 361–62
 interest assumption, effect of,
  363–64
 level premium plan, relationship to,
  25
 mean, 361–62
 methods of determining, 362–72
 modified plan, 361
 mortality assumptions, effect of, 313,
  370–71
 prospective, 360–61
 regulation of, 530–33
 retrospective, 360–61, 362
 safety margins, 373
 statutory regulation, 372–73, 407–8
 statutory standards for minimum, 313,
  372
 strengthening, 372
 supplementary, 373–74
 surrender values, relationship to,
  415–16
 terminal, 361–62
 types of, 360–62
 unearned premium, 362–63
 voluntary, 374–75
Residual disability benefits, 147–48, 155
Retention of agents, 625
Retired life reserves, 268
Retirement annuity, 118
Return-of-premium option, under
 disability insurance, 159
Reverse common disaster clause, 846
Reverse split-dollar plans, 277–79, 280
 estate tax considerations, 280
 as executive carve-out, 279
 PS 58 costs, 276–78
Revocable trusts, 260–61

Risk-Based Capital for Life and/or

Health Insurers Model Act,
532
Risk-based capital (RBC) measure
adjustment formula, 661–62
categories of risk
assets, 660–61
business, 661
insurance, 661
interest, 661
effectiveness of, 662–63
use of, 658
Risk pooling, 19
Robert Wood Johnson Foundation
grants, 173
Robinson-Portman Act, 561
Rule 151, 576–77
Rules of statutory construction, 741–42

S corporation
using buy-sell agreements, 299–301
*St. Paul Fire & Marine Insurance Co. v.
Barry,* 559–60
Salary continuation plans, 168
SEC v. National Securities, Inc., 613
Section 3(a)(8) exclusion, 575–77
Section 79
exceptions to, 717–18
plans, 266–68
requirements, 717–17
Section 162 plans, 268–72
Second-to-die policies, 262–63
Securities Act of 1933, 566, 567–68
Securities and Exchange Commission
(SEC)
Investment Company Act of 1940,
566, 569–71, 577
Investment Adviser Act of 1940,
571–72
regulation of variable insurance,
567–72
as regulatory participant, 565–81
Rule 151, 576–77
*SEC v. Variable Annuity Life
Insurance Company,* 566
Section 3(a)(8) applicability, 575–77
Securities Act of 1933, 566, 567–68
Securities Exchange Act of 1934,
568–69
universal life insurance, 580

Securities Exchange Act of 1934,

568–69
Securities Valuation Office, 530
Selection of risks
age of applicant, 439
alcohol or drug abuse, 444, 447
attending physician, 455
aviation activities, 449–50
avocation, 450
balance within risk classification,
437–38
blood pressure, 442–43
blood tests, 443
build, 440–41
Build and Blood Pressure Study,
1959, 440, 442
economic status, 449
family history, 444–45
guiding principles, 437–38
habits, 447–48
heart impairments, 442–43
inspection report, 455
insurability option, 465
insurance, limiting amount of, 461
judgment rating, 457
juvenile insurance, 466
maximum age restrictions, 466
medical examination, 454–55
medical examiner, 454
Medical Information Bureau, 456, 796
Medico-Actuarial Mortality
Investigation, 440
military service, 450–51
morals, 448
numerical rating system, 457–60
occupation, 445–46, 475
overweight and underweight, effect of,
440
personal history, 444
physical condition, 441–44
plan of insurance, 448
privileged communication, 797
purpose of, 435–36
rejections, effect of, 437
residence, 447, 475
role of field agent, 453
sex, 448
urinalysis, 443–44
Selection-rejection process, 626–27
Servicemen's Group Life Insurance,
597–98
Settlement
agreements, 491–519
options

commutation privilege, 495
contract versus current rates,
    493–94
dependency period income, 513
educational fund, 512
election by
    guardians, 848
    minors, 848
    trustees, 849
emergency fund, 512
estate clearance fund, 506–12
under group term life insurance,
    705–6
life income for surviving spouse,
    513–14
minimum-amount requirements,
    495–96
mortgage cancellation fund, 512
readjustment income, 512–13
withdrawal privilege, 494–95
7-pay test, 241–42
Sherman Act, 561, 612
Short-term policies, 152–53
Simultaneous death of insured and
    beneficiary, 844–46
    common disaster clause, 844
    delayed payment clause, 845–46
    marital deduction, 846
    reverse common disaster clause, 846
    short-term survivorship, 844–46
    Uniform Simultaneous Death Act,
        844–45
Single-premium deferred annuities
    (SPDAs), 575, 577–78
Skilled nursing care, 179
Social security rider, 161–62
Sole proprietorship continuation
    agreements, 293–94
Special or preferred-risk policies
    justification of, 51–52
    limitations on, 52
    nature of, 51–53
Spendthrift clause, 492, 852, 871
Split-dollar plans
    equity split-dollar plans, 276–77
    policy ownership, 272–73
    reporting and disclosure
        requirements, 274
    taxation of, 273–74
    traditional split-dollar plans, 274–76,
        280
Standard and Poor's, 652
Standard Nonforfeiture Law, 412–15

evolution of, 412
rationale of, 412–13
Standard Valuation Law, 405–7
State exemption statutes, 867–68
State premium taxes, 387
Statement of financial position, 634–35
Statement of operations, 635
Statute of Frauds, 785–86
Statutory accounting practices (SAP)
    blue blank, 636, 641–42
    comparison with GAAP
        balance sheets, 642–47
        cash-flow statements, 650
        income statements, 647–50
        supplementary information,
            650–51
    differences from GAAP
        asset valuation, 639–40
        deferred acquisition costs, 638–39
        equipment, 639
        federal taxes, 639
        nonadmitted assets, 640–41
        policy reserves, 640
        subsidiaries, 640
    reporting requirements, 636–37
Stock life insurance companies, 588–90
Stock redemption agreements, 295,
    296–98
Stockbrokers, 621
Structured settlements, 120–37
    advantages of, 130–32
    annuities, 129–30
    disadvantages of, 133
    National Structured Settlement Trade
        Association, 135
    nature of, 128–29
    Periodic Payments Settlement Act of
        1982, 131–32
    postsettlement opportunities, 136–37
    sample case, 133–34
    services, 134–35
    specialist, 135
    Uniform Periodic Payment of
        Judgments Act, 136
Subrogation, doctrine of, 752
Substandard risks
    aviation activities, effect of, 449–50
    classification of, 468
    dividend adjustments, 474
    extra percentage tables, 470–72
    flat extra premium, 473–73

    incidence of extra risk, 468–69

liens, 473—74
numerical rating system, use of, 459
occupation, effect of, 445—46
rated-up age, 469—70
reinsurance of, 489—90
restrictions on plan of insurance, 474
standard mortality, impact on,
        435—36
substandard rating, removal of,
        474—75
theory of, 468
treatment of, 469—74
value of substandard insurance, 475
Succession-in-interest of beneficiary,
        839—42
    Connecticut rule, 840
    New York rule, 840
    per capita distribution, 842
    per stirpes distribution, 841—42
    succession-in-interest clause, 840—41
Successive beneficiary provision, 705
Suicide clause, 770, 775—76, 825
Super producers, 621
Supervisors, 601
Supplemental executive retirement
        plans, 287
Surplus
    acquisition expenses, impact of, 401
    contribution plan, 430
    definition of, 420
    distribution of
        company's capital needs, 425
        return for financial investment,
            425
        return of premium overcharge,
            425—26
    divisible surplus, 426—27
    legal limitations on, 375, 531—32
    managing surplus
        minimum statutory capital
            requirements, 421
        need for capital beyond minimum
            requirements, 422—23
        relationship to investment
            function, 422—23
    sources of
        insurance operations, 423—24
        reinsurance, 424—25
        traditional capital markets, 424
    special forms of
        extra dividends, 427—28
        terminal dividends, 428
    three-factor contribution plan, 430

Surrender
    benefit, deduction from, 410—12
    charge, 411—12
    values, 46—49, 409—17
        accumulated value, 417
        adjusted premium method,
            413—15
        adverse mortality selection, effect
            of on, 410—11
        charge, 411—12
        contingency reserve, effect of on,
            411
        defects in old nonforfeiture
            legislation, 412
        definition of, 409
            lapse, 409
            surrender, 409
            termination, 409
        dividends, 415
        equitable treatment of
            withdrawing policyowners,
            409—410
        modification of adjusted premium
            method, 415
        nonforfeiture factor, 412—13
        options
            cash, 46—47, 207
            conversion, 48—49
            disposition of dividends, 48
            paid-up term, 47, 210—14
            reduced paid-up insurance, 47,
                208—10
            retirement income, 47—48
        profit allowance, effect of on, 411
        Standard Nonforfeiture Law, 206,
            412—15
        statutory standards for minimum
            values, 313
        under substandard insurance
            policies, 470
Swift v. Tyson, 746
Synthetic hedges, 676

Taft-Hartley trusts, 694—95
Tentative premium, 391, 399—400
Term insurance
    advantages of, 39—40
    adverse selection associated with,
        33—34, 36
    attained age conversion, 34
    automatic conversion, 36

convertibility, 34–36, 39
critique of, 38–42
decreasing term, 38
disadvantage of, 40–41
fallacious arguments in favor of,
    40–41
increasing term, 38
lack of finances for permanent
    insurance, 39–40
limit on renewability, 33–34
long-term contracts, 37–38
nature of, 32–33
net level premium, derivation of,
    355–56
net single premium, derivation of,
    343–44
nonlevel term, 38
prepayment of premiums as
    alternative to retroactive
    conversion, 36
re-entry insurance, 36–37
renewability, 33–34
retroactive conversion, 34–36
for temporary protection, 39
to 65, 38
use of, 39–40
yearly renewable term. *See* Yearly
    renewable term insurance
Theory of probability
life insurance, application to, 303–5
simple probability, 302–3
statement of, 302
Time value of money, 322–39
Top-hat plans, 287
Tort liability, 768
Transfer-for-value rule, 237–38
Transfers. *See also* Federal transfer tax
    system
direct-skip, 257
planning for, 245–49
within 3 years of death, 254–55
Trustee as beneficiary, 848–49
Trusts, 197–98
Twisting, 542–43

U.S. v. South-Eastern Underwriters
    Association, 521, 556
Unauthorized Insurance Model Act,
    526–27
Unauthorized Insurance Service-of-
    Process Act, 755

Underwriting
in disability insurance, 164, 165
in group life insurance, 688–93
in group universal life insurance,
    728–29
in long-term care insurance, 182–83
preferred risk policies, 52
Unified credit, 246–47
Uniform Periodic Payment of
    Judgments Act, 136
Uniform Simultaneous Death Act,
    844–45
Uniform state laws
Standard Valuation Law, 405–7
Unauthorized Insurers Model Act,
    526–27
Unauthorized Insurers Service-of-
    Process Act, 755
Unfair Trade Practices Act, 539–45
Uniform Simultaneous Death Act,
    844–45
Unilateral contracts, 749
Universal life insurance
death benefit options, 75–76
design, 77–79
development of, 70–71, 666
flexibility, 79
flexible premiums, 71–72
minimum premium approach, 72–73
policy loans, 76–77
prefunding, 72–74
SEC involvement with, 580
state regulation of, 580–81
tables, 59–61
target premium amount, 74–75
as variation of whole life, 70–79
withdrawals, 74
Unsolicited offers, 768

Validation period, 395
Valued policy, 777–78
Variable adjustable life insurance, 70
Variable annuities, 122–25
accumulation units, 122–23
annuity units, 123
surrender provisions, 124–25
theory of, 122

Variable life insurance
death benefits and investment

performance
    constant ratio method, 65–66
    level additions model, 65
federal securities law and, 566–67
investment options, 63–65, 66–67
National Association of Securities
        Dealers (NASD), 568–69
policy cash value, 67–68
prospectus
    expense information, 68
    investment portfolio information,
      69
    surrender charges, 69
qualified broker/dealers, 571–72,
      574–75
risks, 69–70
and securities laws, 567–72
as securities, 567
SEC objections to, 63
SEC regulation of, 567–72
state regulation of, 572–74
as variation of whole life, 62–70
Variable universal life insurance
    flexibility, 84–85
    income tax of early depletion, 85–87
    modified endowment contract
        provisions, 86–87
    nature of, 83–84
    as variation of whole life, 83–87
Veterans Group Life Insurance, 598
Viatical settlement companies, 781

Wagering
    in early years of life insurance, 774
    insurable interest requirement,
        relationship to, 774
Waiver
    acts of brokers, 808
    by express statement, 814–15
    by inconsistent conduct, 814–15
    nature of, 803, 808–9
    payment of first premium, 811–12
    of premium
      in long-term-care insurance, 184
      provisions, 158
    premium notices, 815
Warranties
    development of, 787–88
    in life insurance, 788
    in marine insurance, 787
    statutory modification of, 788

Watch list, 653–54
Whole life insurance, 26–27, 44–53
    functions of, 53
    net single premium, 344
      limited-payment, 49–50
      ordinary life, 44–49
    principal types of, 44–50
    variations of
      adjustable life, 55–62
      current assumption whole life,
        79–83
      endowment contracts, 54–55
      universal life, 70–79
      variable adjustable life, 70
      variable life, 62–70
      variable universal life, 83–87
Williams Act, 612–13
Withdrawal privilege
    dependency period income, 513
    emergency fund, 512
    estate clearance fund, 511–12
    under fixed-amount option, 503–4
    under interest option, 500
    readjustment income, 512–13
    types of, 494–95

Yearly renewable term insurance
    adverse selection, 24
    determining premium, 23–24
    limit on renewability, 24
    nature of, 22–23
    under reinsurance agreements,
        479–80
Yield on life insurance company
        investments, 42